October 21–25, 2013
Barcelona, Spain

Association for Computing Machinery

Advancing Computing as a Science & Profession

MM'13 Vol. 1 of 2

Proceedings of the 2013 ACM Multimedia Conference

Sponsored by:

ACM SIGMM

Supported by:

FXPAL, HUAWEI, technicolor, YAHOO! LABS, Google, Springer, Microsoft Research, facebook, Telefonica, IBM Research, NSF, University of Trento, Universitat Pompeu Fabra, Inria, and MEDIA MIXER

Association for
Computing Machinery

Advancing Computing as a Science & Profession

The Association for Computing Machinery
2 Penn Plaza, Suite 701
New York, New York 10121-0701

ISBN: 978-1-4503-2404-5 (Digital)

ISBN: 978-1-4503-2691-9 (Print)

Additional copies may be ordered prepaid from:

ACM Order Department
PO Box 30777
New York, NY 10087-0777, USA

Phone: 1-800-342-6626 (USA and Canada)
+1-212-626-0500 (Global)
Fax: +1-212-944-1318
E-mail: acmhelp@acm.org
Hours of Operation: 8:30 am – 4:30 pm ET

Printed in the USA

Message from the General Chairs

We are delighted to welcome you to the 21st ACM International Conference on Multimedia, ACM Multimedia 2013, which will be held from October 21th to October 25th, 2013 in Barcelona, Spain.

Barcelona was founded on the Mediterranean coast, between two rivers, over 2,000 years ago. Since then, it has been the traditional gateway to Spain. Through it entered Romans, Arabs and Christians, as well as the many diverse cultures, which came to enrich its heritage. The traces of this history and diversity can be followed as you walk through the city; through its Gothic Quarter, built on the Roman ruins; through its art-nouveau Eixample district, presided over by Gaudí's exuberant architecture, which at the same time reveals an ordered and rational urban layout. This diversity and harmony are also apparent in the character of the people of Barcelona, who are enterprising and hard-working, enjoy life and, in particular, have great civic pride and are lovers of culture.

These "multimedia" characteristics have made Barcelona into a first-class tourist destination and the ideal setting for meetings and congresses. This open, welcoming city, which shed its skin and opened up to the sea in order to host the 1992 Olympic Games, has since then focused its energies on another major global project: the 2004 Forum of Cultures. This event, the renewed expression of Barcelona's vocation to be an international benchmark for meetings and dialogue, has made it possible to complete the city's seafront, and improve significantly its range of services in the field of congresses, hotels and catering and culture. In a nutshell, Barcelona is the perfect venue for ACM Multimedia and we hope you will enjoy Barcelona as much as its inhabitants do it every single day!

ACM Multimedia is the premier conference and worldwide event bringing together multimedia experts and practitioners across academia and industry. The central feature of the conference, which continues this year as in every year since its inception, is the outstanding Technical Program. This year's conference features both oral and poster presentations covering all aspects of the multimedia field chosen through a highly selective review process.

In addition to the Technical Program, this year's conference features a diverse range of activities including Panels, Demonstrations, and Tutorials. Additionally, a wide array of Workshops brings focus on new topics for investigation. The conference features also special sessions on Brave New Ideas, a Grand Challenge contest and Open Source Software Competition and includes a Doctoral Symposium for mentoring graduate students. Finally, the conference provides a rich Multimedia Art Exhibition to stimulate artists and researchers alike to meet and discover the frontiers of multimedia artistic communication!

Innovations for this Year's Conference:

In attempt to continuously improve ACM Multimedia and ensure its vibrant role for the multimedia community, we have made a number of enhancements for this year's conference:

- The Technical Program Committee defined twelve Technical Areas for major focus for this year's conference, including introducing new Technical Areas for Music & Audio and Crowdsourcing to reflect their growing interest and promise. We have also changed the names of some traditional Technical Areas and provided extensive description of each area to help the authors choosing the most appropriate Technical Area for their manuscripts.

- We have introduced a new role in the organization of the conference: the author's advocate. His explicit role was to listen to the authors, and to help them if reviews are clearly below average quality. The authors could request the mediation of the author's advocate after the reviews have been sent to them and they had to clearly justify the reasons why such mediation is needed (the reviews or the meta-review were below average quality). The task of the advocate was to investigate carefully the matter and to request additional review or reexamination of the decision of the particular manuscript. This year, the author's advocate was Pablo Cesar, CWI, The Netherlands.
- We have decided to keep a couple of plenary sessions which will bring singular focus to conference activities: keynotes, Multimedia Grand Challenge competition, Best Paper session, Technical Achievement Award and Best PhD Award sessions. The other technical sessions are held in parallel to allow pursuit of more specialized interests at the conference. We have limited the number of parallel sessions to no more than 3 to minimize the risk of having overlapping interests.
- Workshops and Tutorials are held on separate days from the main conference in order to reduce conflict with the regular Technical Program.
- The Multimedia Art Exhibition features both invited and selected artists. It will be open for the duration of the conference in the satellite venue located in the center of the city.
- Following the last two years' precedent, Tutorials are made free for all participants.
- Recognizing that students are the lifeblood of our next generation of multimedia thinkers, this year's Student Travel Grant is greatly expanded.

We hope these innovations make for a special conference this year.

We greatly acknowledge those who have contributed to the success of ACM Multimedia 2013. We thank the many paper authors and proposal contributors for the various technical and program components. We thank the large number of volunteers, including the Organizing Committee members and Technical Program Committee members who worked very hard to create this year's outstanding conference. Every aspect of the conference was also aided by local committee members and by the hard work of Grupo Pacifico, to whom we are very grateful. We thank also ACM staff and Sheridan Communications for their constant support.

Finally, we thank our many supporters who generously supported ACM Multimedia 2013. They include FXPAL, HUAWEI, YAHOO! LABS, Technicolor, MediaMixer, Microsoft Research, Facebook, IBM Research, Telefonica, Google, and INRIA. Other generous support was kindly provided by SIGMM, Springer, and NSF.

ACM Multimedia 2013 General Chairs

Alejandro Jaimes
Yahoo Labs, Spain

Nicu Sebe
University of Trento, Italy

Nozha Boujemaa
INRIA, France

Message from the Technical Program Chairs

Benvinguts a Barcelona! We are excited to introduce the Technical Program of the *ACM International Conference on Multimedia 2013*. This year, we built upon the guidelines from previous editions of the conference and introduced several new procedures and policies with the goal of improving the quality of the review process, the feedback provided to the authors, and the overall diversity of the technical program.

As in the last couple of years, the conference review process was structured with a two-tier Technical Program Committee. Following a discussion process that involved the General Chairs and the Program Chairs, we revised and expanded the list of areas from last year's conference and defined 12 areas for 2013 to bring topic diversity and growth to the conference: Art, Entertainment and Culture; Authoring and Collaboration; Crowdsourcing; Media Transport and Delivery; Mobile and Multi-Device; Multimedia Analysis; Multimedia HCI; Music and Audio; Search, Browsing, and Discovery; Security and Forensics; Social Media and Presence; and Systems and Middleware.

The Technical Program Committee was first created by appointing Area Chairs (ACs). A total of 29 colleagues agreed to serve in this role. Each Area was represented by two ACs, with exception of two Areas (Multimedia Analysis and Search, Browsing, and Discovery) whose scope has traditionally attracted the largest proportion of papers and so required further coordination. The added topic diversity brought an increase in gender diversity to the ACs, which increased from approximately 12% in previous years to 22% for 2013. We also made a conscious effort to bring new talent and excellence into the community and to better represent emerging trends in the field. For this we appointed many young and well recognized ACs who served in this role for the first time. For each junior AC, we co-appointed a senior researcher as their co-AC to aid in their shepherding. In a second step, the Area Chairs were responsible for appointing the TPC members (reviewers) for their coordinated areas. This was a large effort to grow the TPC base for the conference as well as ensure proper expertise was represented in each area. We coupled this with a hard goal of limiting the number of submissions assigned to each TPC member for review. For example, two years ago, the average number of papers assigned to a reviewer was 9 with over 38% of the approximately 225 TPC members receiving 10 or more papers to review. With our design, we had a total of 398 reviewers receiving an average of 4.13 papers per reviewer. While we were unable to keep a hard ceiling limitation, only 2.51% of the TPC received 10 or more papers to review—all TPC members who had agreed to serve in more than one area. The Area Chairs were in charge of assigning all papers for review, and each submission was reviewed double-blind by three TPC members. Reviews and reviewer assignments of papers co-authored by Area Chairs, Program Chairs, and General Chairs were handled by Program Chairs who had no conflicts of interest for each specific case.

Another novelty introduced in the reviewing process was to set the paper submission deadline to a significantly earlier date than previous years, in order to allocate more time for reviews, rebuttals, discussions, and final decisions. Despite the reduced time given to authors, the response to the Call for Papers was enthusiastic with a total of 235 long papers and 278 short papers going through review.

The authors of long papers were asked to write a rebuttal after receiving the reviews. A new element in the reviewing process was the introduction of the Author's Advocate figure, created to provide authors with an independent channel to express concerns about the quality of the reviews for their papers, and to raise a flag about these reviews. All cases were brought to the attention to the corresponding Area Chair. After evaluating each case reported to him (16 reviews out of 761 long paper reviews), the Author's Advocate recommended in 5 cases that new reviews were generated and added to the discussion. The reviewers had a period for on-line discussion of reviews and rebuttals, after which the Area Chairs drafted a meta-review for each paper.

Decisions on long and short papers were made at the TPC meeting held at the University of Amsterdam on June 11, 2013. The meeting was physically attended by one of the General Chairs, three of the Program Chairs, the Author's Advocate, and 86% of the ACs. Many of the ACs who were unable to attend were tele-present online for discussions. On the first half day of the TPC meeting, the Area Chairs worked in breakout sessions to discuss the papers that were weak accepts and weak rejects, with the exception of conflict of interest papers which were handled out of band as previously mentioned. In the second half of the first day, the ACs met in a plenary session where they reviewed the clear accepts and defended the decisions on the borderline papers based on the papers themselves, reviews, meta-reviews, on-line discussions, and authors' rebuttal comments. In many cases, an emergency reviewer was added if there was clear intersection with a related submission area. If a paper had any conflict of interest during the plenary session with an Area, Program, or General Chair, they were excused from the room. On June 12, 2013, the Program Chairs finalized the process and conference program in a separate meeting—arranging the sessions by thematic narratives and not by submission area to promote cross-area conversations during the conference itself.

The review process resulted in an overall acceptance rate of 20.0% for long papers and 27.7% for short papers. All accepted long papers were shepherded by the Area Chairs themselves or by qualified TPC members who were in charge of verifying that the revised papers adequately addressed concerns raised by the reviewers and changes promised by authors in their rebuttals. This step ensured that all of the accepted papers are of the highest quality possible. In addition, four papers with high review scores were nominated at the TPC meeting as candidates for the Best Paper Award. Each nominated paper had to be successfully championed and defended by the ACs from that area. The winner will be announced at the Conference Banquet.

The Technical Program of ACM Multimedia would not have been possible without the research of the MM community of authors and the commitment of all the members of the TPC. It is now our turn to sincerely thank all of them for their participation, rigorous work, and engagement.

We hope you enjoy the program!

David A. Shamma
Program Co-Chair
Yahoo Labs, USA

Marcel Worring
Program Co-Chair
Univ. of Amsterdam
The Netherlands

Roger Zimmermann
Program Co-Chair
Nat. Univ. of Singapore
Singapore

Daniel Gatica-Perez
Program Co-Chair
Idiap and EPFL
Switzerland

Pablo Cesar
Author's Advocate
CWI
The Netherlands

Table of Contents

Session Order 7: Brave New Topics: Social and Cognitive Aspects

Session Chairs: Jiebo Luo *(University of Rochester)*
Shuicheng Yan *(National University of Singapore)*

Session Order 8: Action and Event Recognition

Session Chair: Winston Hsu *(University of Taiwan)*

Session Order 9: Streaming and Synchronization

Session Chair: Alan Smeaton *(Dublin City University)*

Session Order 10: Keynote Address

Session Chair: Nozha Boujemaa *(INRIA)*

Session Order 11: Multimedia Grand Challenge

Session Chairs: Yiannis Kompatsiaris *(CERTH)*
Neil O'Hare *(Yahoo!)*

Session Order 12: Demos

Session Chairs: Xavier Anguera *(Telefonica)*
Yi Yang *(CMU)*

Volume 2

Session Order 13: Posters 2

Session Order 16: Multimodal Analysis

Session Chair: Matt Cooper *(FX Pal)*

Session Order 17: Social Dynamics

Session Chairs: Lyndon Kennedy *(Yahoo! Research)*
Eric Gilbert *(Georgia Tech)*

Session Order 18: Annotation

Session Chair: Pablo Caesar *(CWI)*

Session Order 19: Scene Understanding

Session Chair: Dhiraj Joshi *(FX Pal)*

Session Order 20: Doctoral Symposium

Session Chairs: Hayley Hung *(TU Delft)*
Marco Cristani *(University of Verona)*

Session Order 21: Art Session Overview

Session Order 22: Workshops Overview

Session Order 23: Technical Session

MM 2013 Conference Organization

General Chairs: Alejandro (Alex) Jaimes *(Yahoo Labs, Spain)*
Nicu Sebe *(University of Trento, Italy)*
Nozha Boujemaa *(INRIA, France)*

Program Chairs: Daniel Gatica-Perez *(IDIAP & EPFL, Switzerland)*
David A. Shamma *(Yahoo Labs, USA)*
Marcel Worring *(University of Amsterdam, The Netherlands)*
Roger Zimmermann *(National University of Singapore, Singapore)*

Author's Advocate: Pablo Cesar *(CWI, The Netherlands)*

Multimedia Grand Challenge Chair: Yiannis Kompatsiaris *(CERTH, Greece)*
Neil O'Hare *(Yahoo Labs, Spain)*

Interactive Arts Chairs: Antonio Camurri *(University of Genova, Italy)*
Marc Cavazza *(University of Teesside, UK)*

Local Arrangements Chair: Mari-Carmen *Marcos (University Pompeu Fabra, Spain)*

Sponsorship Chairs: Ricardo Baeza-Yates *(Yahoo Labs, Spain)*
Bernard Merialdo *(Eurecom, France)*

Panel Chairs: Yong Rui *(Microsoft, China)*
Winston Hsu *(National Tawain University, Taiwan)*
Michael Lew *(University of Leiden, The Netherlands)*

Brave New Ideas Chairs: Jiebo Luo *(University of Rochester, USA)*
Shuicheng Yan *(National University of Singapore, Singapore)*

Doctorial Symposium Chairs: Hayley *Hung (Technical University of Delft, The Netherlands)*
Marco Cristani *(University of Verona, Italy)*

Open Source Software Competition Chairs: Ioannis (Yiannis) Patras *(Queen Mary, University of London, UK)*
Andrea Vedaldi *(Oxford University, UK)*

Tutorial Chairs: Kiyoharu Aizawa *(University of Tokyo, Japan)*
Lexing Xie *(Australian National University, Australia)*

Workshop Chairs: Maja Pantic *(Imperial College, UK)*
Vladimir Pavlovic *(Rutgers University, USA)*

Student Travel Grants Chairs: Ramanathan Subramanian *(ADSC, Singapore)*
Jasper Uijlings *(University of Trento, Italy)*

Publicity Chairs: Marco Bertini *(University of Florence, Italy)*
Ichiro Ide *(Nagoya University, Japan)*

Technical Demo Chairs: Yi Yang *(Carnegie Mellon University, USA)*
Xavier Anguera *(Telefonica Research, Spain)*

Proceedings Chairs: Bogdan Ionescu *(University Politehnica of Bucharest, Romania)*
Qi Tian *(University of Texas San Antonio, USA)*

Web & Social Media Chair: Michele Trevisol *(Yahoo Labs, Spain)*

History Preservation Chairs: Selcuk Candan *(Arizona State University, USA)*
Noboru Babaguchi *(Osaka University, Japan)*

MM 2013 Area Chairs

Frank Bentley *(Yahoo! Research, USA)*
Antonio Camurri *(University of Genova, Italy)*
Marc Cavazza *(University of Teesside, UK)*
Munmun De Choudhury *(Microsoft Research, USA)*
Matthew Cooper *(FXPAL, USA)*
Rita Cucchiara *(University of Modena, Italy)*
Pascal Frossard *(EPFL, Switzerland)*
Mohamed Hefeeda *(Simon Fraser University, Canada)*
Winston Hsu *(NTU, Taiwan)*
Jochen Huber *(MIT, USA)*
Dhiraj Joshi *(FXPAL, USA)*
Aisling Kelliher *(CMU, USA)*
Lyndon Kennedy *(Yahoo! Research, USA)*
Hyoung Joong Kim *(Korea University, Korea)*
Martha Larson *(TU Delft, The Netherlands)*
Cynthia Liem *(TU Delft, The Netherlands)*
Rainer Lienhart *(University of Augsburg, Germany)*
Tao Mei *(Microsoft Research Asia, China)*
Max Mühlhäuser *(TU Darmstadt, Germany)*
Wei Tsang Ooi *(NUS, Singapore)*
Bryan Pardo *(Northwestern Ubiversity, USA)*
Alan Smeaton *(Dublin City University, Ireland)*
Raphael Troncy *(EURECOM, France)*
Wanmin Wu *(Ricoh, USA)*
Shuicheng Yan *(NUS, Singapore)*
Zheng-Jun Zha *(NUS, Singapore)*
Lei Zhang *(Tsinghua University, China)*
Michael Zink *(University of Massachusetts, Amherst, USA)*
Roelof van Zwol *(Netflix, USA)*

MM 2013 Technical Program Committee

Maha Abdallah *(University of Paris 6, France)*
Dewan Ahmed *(University of Ottawa, Canada)*
Luca Maria Aiello *(Yahoo! Research, Spain)*
Kevin Almeroth *(University of California, Santa Barbara, USA)*
Maria Teresa Andrade *(University of Porto, Portugal)*
Oya Aran *(IDIAP, Switzerland)*
Grenville Armitage *(Swinburne University of Technology, Australia)*
Olivier Aubert *(University Claude Bernard Lyon, France)*
Yannis Avrithis *(National Technical University of Athens, Greece)*
Brian Bailey *(University of Illinois, USA)*
Santosh Basapur *(Motorola Mobility Inc., USA)*
Christian Bauckhage *(University of Bonn, Germany)*
Ali Begen *(Cisco Systems, Inc., USA)*
Frank Bentley *(Motorola Labs, USA)*
Nadia Berthouze *(University College London, UK)*
Vijay Bharadwaj
Giulia Boato *(University of Trento, Italy)*
Susanne Boll *(Universität Oldenburg, Germany)*
Jan Borchers *(RWTH Aachen, Informatik 10, Germany)*
Laszlo Böszörmenyi *(University Klagenfurt, Austria)*
Alessandro Bozzon *(Delft University of Technology, The Netherlands)*
Francois Bremond *(INRIA, France)*
Dick C.A. Bulterman *(CWI, The Netherlands)*
Christoph Busch *(CAST-Forum, Germany)*
Daragh Byrne *(Arizona State University, USA)*
Rui Cai *(Microsoft Research Asia, China)*
Simone Calderara *(University of Modena, Italy)*
Liangliang Cao *(IBM Watson Research Center, USA)*
Axel Carlier *(University of Toulouse, France)*
Mark Cartwright *(Northwestern University, USA)*
Federico Casalegno *(MIT, USA)*
Marc Cavazza *(University of Teesside, UK)*
Pablo Cesar *(CWI, The Netherlands)*
Teresa Chambel *(University of Lisbon, Portugal)*
Antoni Chan *(City University of Hong Kong, Hong Kong)*
Gary Chan *(The Hong Kong University of Science and Technology, Hong Kong)*
Surendar Chandra *(Backup Recovery Systems, EMC, USA)*
Edward Chang *(Google Research, USA)*
Shi-Fu Chang *(Columbia University, USA)*
Vincent Charvillat *(University of Toulouse, France)*
Berlin Chen *(National Taiwan Normal University, Taiwan)*
Chang Wen Chen *(State University of New York at Buffalo, USA)*
Francine Chen *(FXPAL, USA)*
Huizhong Chen *(Stanford University, USA)*
Kuan-Ta Chen *(Academia Sinica, Taiwan)*
Songqing Chen *(George Mason University, USA)*
Tim Cheng *(Univ. of California, USA)*
Elaine Chew *(Queen Mary, University of London, UK)*
Liang-Tien Chia *(Nanyang Technological University, Singapore)*
Konstantinos Chorianopoulos *(Ionian University, Greece)*
Wei-Ta Chu *(National Chung Cheng University, Taiwan)*
Ching-Hua Chuan *(University of North Florida, USA)*
Yung-Yu Chuang *(National Taiwan University, Taiwan)*
Mark Claypool *(WPI, USA)*
Karin Coninx *(Hasselt University - EDM, Belgium)*
Matthew Cooper *(FX Palo Alto Lab, Inc., USA)*
Marco Cristani *(Università degli Studi di Verona, Italy)*
Rita Cucchiara *(University of Modena and Reggio Emilia, Italy)*
Walid Dabbous *(INRIA, France)*
Elizabeth M. Daly *(IBM Research, Ireland)*
Madirakshi Das *(Eastman Kodak Company, USA)*

Ritendra Datta *(Google, USA)*
Sushovan De *(Arizona State University, USA)*
Munmun De Choudhury *(Microsoft Research, USA)*
Giorgio De Michelis *(Univrsity of Milano - Bicocca, Italy)*
Giovanni De Poli *(University of Padova, Italy)*
Arjen de Vries *(CWI, The Netherlands)*
Alberto Del Bimbo *(Universita degli Studi di Firenze, Italy)*
David Demirdjian *(Toyota Research Institute, USA)*
Luigi Di Stefano *(University of Bologna, Italy)*
Christian Dittmar *(Fraunhofer IDMT, Germany)*
Ming Dong *(Wayne State University, USA)*
Tiziana D'Orazio *(ISSIA CNR, Italy)*
Lingyu Duan *(Peking University, China)*
Zhiyao Duan *(University of Rochester, USA)*
Isao Echizen *(Tokyo Institute of Technology, Japan)*
Alexander Eichhorn *(Simula, Norway)*
Dan Ellis *(Columbia University, USA)*
Aiman Erbad *(Qatar University, Qatar)*
Slim Essid *(Telecom ParisTech, France)*
Georg Essl *(University of Michigan, USA)*
Sebastian Ewert *(Queen Mary University, London, UK)*
Jianping Fan *(UNCC, USA)*
Morwaread Farbood *(New York University, USA)*
Sidney Fels *(University of British Columbia, Canada)*
Jiashi Feng *(National University of Singapore, Singapore)*
Wu-Chang Feng *(Portland State University, USA)*
Wu-Chi Feng *(Portland State University, USA)*
Rogerio Feris *(IBM T.J. Watson Research Center, USA)*
Rebecca Fiebrink *(Princeton University, USA)*
Frederic Fol Leymarie *(University of London, UK)*
Federico Fontana *(Universita degli Studi di Udine, Italy)*
Piero Fraternali *(Politecnico di Milano, Italy)*
Jason Freeman *(Georgia Institute of Technology, USA)*
Gerald Friedland *(International Computer Science Institute, USA)*
Pascal Frossard *(EPFL, Switzerland)*
Yun Fu *(Northeastern University, USA)*
Takuya Fujishima *(Yamaha Corp., Japan)*
Andrew Gallagher *(Cornell University, USA)*
Huiji Gao *(Arizona State University, USA)*
Lluis Garcia Pueyo *(Google, USA)*
Ravi Garg *(UMD, USA)*
Daniel Gatica-Perez *(Idiap and EPFL, Switzerland)*
Weina Ge *(GE Global Research, USA)*
David Geerts *(IBBT / K.U.Leuven, Belgium)*
Bo Geng *(Peking University, China)*
Andreas Girgensohn *(FX Palo Alto Laboratory, USA)*
Jordi Gonzalez *(Universitat Autònoma de Barcelona, France)*
Masataka Goto *(National Institute of Advanced Industrial Science and Technology (AIST), Japan)*
Valerie Gouet-Brunet *(IGN - Laboratoire MATIS, France)*
Fabien Gouyon *(INESC Porto, Portugal)*
Costantino Grana *(University of Modena and Reggio Emilia, Italy)*
Guillaume Gravier *(CNRS, IRISA, France)*
Carsten Griwodz *(University of Oslo, Norway)*
Peter Grosche *(Huawei European Research Center, Germany)*
Yang Guo *(Bell Labs, Alcatel-Lucent, USA)*
Michael Gurevich *(University of Michigan, USA)*
Aristotelis Hadjakos *(TU Darmstadt, Germany)*
Thomas Haenselmann *(Saarland Univerity, Germany)*
Pål Halvorsen *(University of Oslo & Simula, Norway)*
Raouf Hamzaoui *(De Montfort University, UK)*
Jinyu Han *(Northwestern University, USA)*
Mei Han *(Google Inc, USA)*
Alan Hanjalic *(Delft University of Technology, The Netherlands)*
Tatsuya Harada *(The University of Tokyo, Japan)*
Gunnar Harboe *(Motorola, Switzerland)*
Melanie Hartmann *(AGT International, Germany)*
Alex Hauptmann *(Carnegie Mellon University, USA)*
Jiyin He *(CWI, The Netherlands)*
Junfeng He *(Columbia University, USA)*

Mohamed Hefeeda *(Simon Fraser University, Canada)*
Hermann Hellwagner *(University of Klagenfurt, Austria)*
Tristan Henderson *(University of St Andrews, UK)*
Niels Henze *(University of Stuttgart, Germany)*
Jason Hockman *(McGill University, Canada)*
Steven C. H. Hoi *(Nanyang Technological University, Singapore)*
Lars Erik Holmquist *(Yahoo! Labs, USA)*
Henry Holtzman *(MIT Media Lab, USA)*
Richang Hong *(Hefei University of Technology, China)*
Cheng-Hsin Hsu *(National Tsing Hua University, Taiwan)*
Winston Hsu *(University of Taiwan, Taiwan)*
Ke Hu *(Kuzer Co., USA)*
Yuheng Hu *(Arizona State University, USA)*
Gang Hua *(Nokia Research Center Hollywood, USA)*
Xian-Sheng Hua *(Microsoft Research Asia, USA)*
Polly Huang *(NTU, EE, Taiwan)*
Jochen Huber *(SUTD & MIT Media Lab, Singapore & USA)*
Wolfgang Huerst *(Utrecht University, The Netherlands)*
Benoit Huet *(Eurecom, France)*
Hayley Hung *(Delft University of Technology, The Netherlands)*
Ichiro Ide *(Nagoya University, Japan)*
Christian Jacquemin *(LIMSI-CNRS, France)*
Giulio Jacucci *(Helsinki Institute for Information Technology, Finland)*
Sina Jafarpour *(Yahoo! Research, USA)*
Vidit Jain *(Yahoo! Labs, USA)*
Frankie James *(General Motors Research, USA)*
S. Jamin *(University of Michigan, Ann Arbor, USA)*
Rongrong Ji *(Columbia University, USA)*
Shen Jialie *(Singapore Management University, Singapore)*
Wei Jiang
Yu-Gang Jiang *(Fudan University, China)*
Ajita John *(Avaya Labs, USA)*
Alexis Joly *(INRIA, France)*
Gareth Jones *(Dublin City University, Ireland)*
Dhiraj Joshi *(FX Palo Alto Lab, Inc., USA)*
Chris Joslin *(Carleton University, Canada)*
Oskar Juhlin *(Interactive Institute, Sweden)*
Yannis Kalantidis *(National Technical University of Athens, Greece)*
Ton Kalker *(DTS, inc, USA)*
Mohan Kankanhalli *(National University of Singapore, Singapore)*
Ian Kegel *(BT Innovate, UK)*
John Kender *(Columbia University, USA)*
Lyndon Kennedy *(Yahoo! Research, USA)*
Hyoung Joong Kim *(Korea University, Republic of Korea)*
Gudrun Klinker *(Technische Universität München, Germany)*
Ben Knapp *(Virginia Tech, USA)*
Stephan Kopf *(Mannheim University, Germany)*
Pavel Korshunov *(École Polytechnique Fédérale de Lausanne, Switzerland)*
Adarsh Kowdle *(Cornell University, USA)*
Wessel Kraaij *(Radboud University Nijmegen, The Netherlands)*
Mritunjay Kumar
Shang-Hong Lai *(National Tsing Hua University, Taiwan)*
Rodrigo Laiola Guimaraes *(CWI, The Netherlands)*
Paul Lamere *(The Echo Nest, USA)*
Oswald Lanz *(FBK-irst, Italy)*
Martha Larson *(Delft University of Technology, The Netherlands)*
Rynson Lau *(City University of Hong Kong, Hong Kong)*
Matt Lease *(University of Texas at Austin, USA)*
Hyowon Lee *(Singapore University of Technology and Design, Singapore)*
Jin Ha Lee *(University of Washington, USA)*
Marc Leman *(Universiteit Gent, Belgium)*
Mark Levy
Baochun Li *(University of Toronto, Canada)*
Congcong Li *(Google, USA)*
Jia Li *(Yahoo! Research, USA)*
Jia Li *(The Pennsylvania State University, USA)*

Kang Li *(UGA, USA)*
Xirong Li *(Renmin University of China, China)*
Xuelong Li *(University of London, China)*
Zhiwei Li *(Microsoft Research Asia, China)*
Zhu Li *(Hong Kong Polytechnic University, USA)*
Chunyuan Liao *(FXPAL Palo Alto, USA)*
Cynthia Liem *(Delft University of Technology, The Netherlands)*
Rainer Lienhart *(Universitt Augsburg, Germany)*
Yu-Ru Lin *(Harvard/Northeastern Universities, USA)*
Dong Liu *(Columbia University, USA)*
Jiangchuan Liu *(Simon Fraser University, Canada)*
Qiong Liu *(FX Palo Alto Laboratory, USA)*
Wei Liu
Yong Liu *(Polytechnic Institute of NYU, USA)*
Zhu Liu *(AT&T, USA)*
Antoine Liutkus *(Grenoble Institute of Technology, France)*
Alexander Loui *(Eastman Kodak Labs, USA)*
Lie Lu
Yijuan Lu *(Texas State University, USA)*
Jiebo Luo *(University of Rochester, USA)*
Mathias Lux *(University of Klagenfurt, Austria)*
Nazanin Magharei
Erik Mannens *(Ghent University, Belgium)*
Ketan Mayer-Patel *(UNC, USA)*
Stephen McKenna *(University of Dundee, UK)*
Andrew McPherson *(Queen Mary, University of London, UK)*
Tao Mei *(Microsoft Research Asia, China)*
Bernard Merialdo *(EURECOM, France)*
Florian Metze *(Carnegie Mellon University, USA)*
Vasileios Mezaris *(Centre for Research and Technology Hellas, Greece)*
Christian Micheloni *(University of Udine, Italy)*
Krystian Mikolajczyk *(University of Surrey, UK)*
David R. Millen
Max Muehlhaeuser *(Technische Universitaet Darmstadt, Germany)*
Meinard Mueller
Philippe Mulhem *(LIG-CNRS, France)*
Vittorio Murino *(University of Verona, Italy)*
Phivos Mylonas *(National Technical University of Athens, Greece)*
Frank Nack *(University of Amsterdam, The Netherlands)*
Klara Nahrstedt *(University of Illinois, Urbana-Champaign, USA)*
Alok Nandi *(Architempo, Belgium)*
Arun Narayanan
Paolo Nesi *(University of Florence, DSI, Italy)*
Shawn Newsam *(University of California, Merced, USA)*
Chong-Wah Ngo *(City University of Hong Kong, Hong Kong)*
Eric Nichols *(Indiana University, USA)*
Laurence Nigay *(LIG- University of Grenoble, France)*
Naoko Nitta *(Osaka University, Japan)*
Lyndon Nixon *(STI International, Austria)*
Jasminko Novak *(European Institute for Participatory Media, Germany)*
Noel E. O Connor *(Dublin City University, Ireland)*
Jauvane Oliveira *(LNCC/MCT, Brazil)*
Nuria Oliver *(Telefonica Research, Spain)*
Wei Tsang Ooi *(National University of Singapore, Singapore)*
Vincent Oria *(NJIT, USA)*
Nicola Orio *(University of Padova, Italy)*
Max Ott *(NICTA, Australia)*
Daniel Overholt *(University of California, Santa Barbara, Denmark)*
Wei Pan *(MIT, USA)*
Minwoo Park *(Eastman Kodak Company, USA)*
Geoffroy Peeters *(Ircam, France)*
Catherine Pelachaud *(CNRS Telecom ParisTech, France)*
Nils Peters *(University of California, Berkeley, USA)*
Julien Pettre
Dinh Phung *(Deakin University, Australia)*
Massimo Piccardi *(University of Technology, Sydney, Australia)*
Maria Da Graça Pimentel *(Universidade de Sao Paulo, Brazil)*
Hamed Pirsiavash

Stefan Podlipnig *(University of Innsbruck, Austria)*
Fatih Porikli *(MERL, USA)*
Balakrishnan Prabhakaran *(University of Texas at Dallas, USA)*
Yannick Prié *(LINA - University of Nantes, France)*
Mu Qiao
Nicholas Race *(Lancaster University, UK)*
Zafar Rafii
Nitendra Rajput *(IBM Research, India Research Lab, India)*
Sanjay Rao *(Purdue University, USA)*
Nikhil Rasiwasia *(University of California San Diego, USA)*
Carlo Regazzoni *(University of Genova, Italy)*
Paolo Remagnino *(Kingstone University, UK)*
Mikel Rodriguez *(INRIA, France)*
Michael Rohs *(University of Hannover, Germany)*
Enrico Rukzio *(Ulm University, Germany)*
Lloyd Rutledge *(Open Universiteit Nederland, The Netherlands)*
Harald Sack *(Hasso-Plattner-Institut, Universität Potsdam, Germany)*
Alireza Sahami *(University of Stuttgart, Germany)*
Jitao Sang *(Chinese Academy of Science, China)*
Maria Luisa Sapino *(Universita degli Studi di Torino, Italy)*
Nabil Sarhan *(Wayne State University, USA)*
Shin'Ichi Satoh *(National Institute of Informatics, Japan)*
Markus Schedl *(Johannes Kepler University, Austria)*
Ansgar Scherp *(University of Koblenz-Landau, Germany)*
Klaus Schoeffmann *(Klagenfurt University, Austria)*
Bjoern Schuller *(Technical University Munich, Germany)*
Nicu Sebe *(University of Trento, Italy)*
Doree Seligmann *(Avaya Labs Research, USA)*
Subhabrata Sen *(AT&T Research, USA)*
Joan Serrà *(Spanish National Research Council, Spain)*
Nikitas Sgouros *(University of Piraeus, Greece)*
David A. Shamma *(Yahoo! Research, USA)*
Caifeng Shan *(Philips Research, The Netherlands)*
Heng Tao Shen *(University of Queensland, Australia)*
Shu Shi
Shervin Shirmohammadi *(University of Ottawa, Canada)*
Börkur Sigurbjörnsson
Vivek Singh *(Massachusetts Institute of Technology, USA)*
Malcolm Slaney *(Yahoo! Research, USA)*
Paris Smaragdis *(University of Illinois, Urbana-Champaign, USA)*
Arnold W. M. Smeulders *(University of Amsterdam, The Netherlands)*
John Smith *(IBM T.J. Watson Research Center, USA)*
Cees Snoek *(University of Amsterdam, The Netherlands)*
Mohammad Soleymani *(Imperial College London, UK)*
Ryan Spicer *(Arizona State University, USA)*
Jürgen Steimle *(MIT Media Lab, USA)*
Eckehard Steinbach *(TU München, Germany)*
Ralf Steinmetz *(TU Darmstadt, Germany)*
Hari Sundaram *(Arizona State University, USA)*
Marco Tagliasacchi *(Politecnico di Milano, Italy)*
Kartik Talamadupula *(Arizona State University, USA)*
John Tang *(Microsoft Research, USA)*
David Temperley *(University of Rochester, USA)*
Jelena Tesic *(Mayachitra, USA)*
Qi Tian *(The University of Texas at San Antonio, USA)*
Christian Timmerer *(Klagenfurt University, Austria)*
Steve Tjoa
Dian Tjondronegoro *(Queensland University of Technology, Australia)*
Giorgos Tolias *(National Technical University of Athens, Greece)*
Naoko Tosa *(Kyoto University, Japan)*
Raphael Troncy *(EURECOM, France)*
Joe Tullio *(Google, USA)*
George Tzanetakis *(University of Victoria, Canada)*
Yoshitaka Ushiku *(the University of Tokyo, Japan)*
Leon Van Noorden *(IPEM, University of Ghent, Belgium)*
Roelof van Zwol *(Netflix, USA)*

Nuno Vasconcelos *(UCSD, USA)*

Nalini Venkatasubramanian *(University of California Irvine, USA)*

Ruben Verborgh *(Ghent University, Belgium)*

Roberto Vezzani *(Università degli Studi di Modena e Reggio Emilia, Italy)*

Marie-Luce Viaud *(Institut National de Audiovisuel, France)*

Changhu Wang *(Microsoft Research Asia, China)*

Feng Wang *(The University of Mississippi, USA)*

Hua Wang *(Colorado School of Mines, USA)*

James Wang *(The Pennsylvania State University, USA)*

Jingdong Wang *(Microsoft Research Asia, China)*

Ju-Chiang Wang *(National Taiwan University, Taiwan)*

Jun Wang *(Columbia University, USA)*

Meng Wang *(AKiiRA Media Systems Inc., Singapore)*

Xin-Jing Wang *(Microsoft Research Asia, China)*

Ye Wang *(National University of Singapore, Singapore)*

Andrew M. Webb *(Texas A&M University, USA)*

Michael Weber *(University of Ulm, Germany)*

Robert Wechsler *(MotionComposer, Germany)*

Joerg Widmer *(Institute IMDEA Networks, Spain)*

Lynn Wilcox *(FX Palo Alto Laboratory, USA)*

Marcel Worring *(University of Amsterdam, The Netherlands)*

Fei Wu *(Zhejiang University, China)*

Wanmin Wu *(Ricoh, USA)*

Xiao Wu

Jiangjian Xiao

Lexing Xie *(Australian National University, Australia)*

Lingxi Xie *(Tsinghua University, China)*

Xing Xie *(Microsoft Research Asia, China)*

Changsheng Xu *(Institute of Automation, Chinese Academy of Sciences, China)*

Shuicheng Yan *(National University of Singapore, Singapore)*

Jianchao Yang

Jie Yang *(Carnegie Mellon University, USA)*

Linjun Yang *(Microsoft Research Asia, China)*

Ming Yang *(NEC laboratories America, USA)*

Xin Yang *(University of California, Santa Barbara, USA)*

Yi Yang *(Carnegie Mellon University, USA)*

Yi-Hsuan Yang *(Academia Sinica, Taiwan)*

Woon Seung Yeo *(KAIST, Republic of Korea)*

Jude Yew *(National University of Singapore, Singapore)*

Jie Yu

Meng Yu *(University of California, Irvine, USA)*

Xinnan Yu

Junsong Yuan *(Nanyang Technological University, Singapore)*

Eric Zavesky *(AT&T Research, USA)*

Zheng-Jun Zha *(National University of Singapore, Singapore)*

Jian Zhang

Lei Zhang *(Microsoft Research Asia, China)*

Zhengyou Zhang *(Microsoft, USA)*

Yan-Tao Zheng *(National University of Singapore, Singapore)*

Zhigang Zhu

Roger Zimmermann *(National University of Singapore, Singapore)*

Michael Zink *(University of Massachusetts, USA)*

Goranka Zoric *(Mobile Life @ Interactive Institute, Sweden)*

MM 2013 Brave New Topics Program Committee

Kiyoharu Aizawa *(The University of Tokyo, Japan)*
Dick Bulterman *(CWI, Netherlands)*
K. Selcuk Candan *(Arizona State University, USA)*
Tat-Seng Chua *(National University of Singapore, Singapore)*
Jianping Fan *(UNCC, USA)*
Alan Hanjalic *(Delft University of Technology, The Netherlands)*
Qingmin Huang *(Chinese Academy of Sciences, China)*
Benoit Huet *(Eurecom, France)*
Jiebo Luo *(University of Rochester, USA)*
Tao Mei *(Microsoft Research Asia, China)*
Chong-Wah Ngo *(City University of Hong Kong, China)*
Mubarak Shah *(UCF, USA)*
Cees Snoek *(University of Amsterdam, The Netherlands)*
Hari Sundaram *(Arizona State University, USA)*
Qi Tian *(The University of Texas at San Antonio, USA)*
Shuicheng Yan *(National University of Singapore, Singapore)*
Zhenjun Zha *(Chinese Academy of Sciences, China)*

MM 2013 Doctoral Program Committee

Valerie G Brunet *(CNAM, France)*
Antonio Camurri *(University of Genoa, Italy)*
Surendar Chandra *(FXPAL Inc., USA)*
Elaine Chew *(Queen Mary University of London, UK)*
Isao Echizen *(National Institute of Informatics, Japan)*
Alexander Eichhorn *(Simula Research Laboratory, Norway)*
Federico Fontana *(University of Udine, Italy)*
Gerald Friedland *(ICSI Berkeley, USA)*
Thomas Haenselmann *(University of Mannheim, Germany)*
Benoit Huet *(EURECOM, France)*
Ichiro Ide *(Nagoya University, Japan)*
Christian Jacquemin *(LIMSI-CNRS, France)*
David R Millen *(IBM Research and the Center for Social Software, USA)*
Klara Nahrstedt *(University of Illinois at Urbana-Champaign, USA)*
Vincent Oria *(NJIT, USA)*
Maria L Sapino *(University of Turin, Italy)*
Shin'ichi Satoh *(National Institute of Informatics, Japan)*
Caifeng Shan *(Philips, The Netherlands)*
Arnold Smeulders *(CWI and University of Amsterdam, The Netherlands)*
George Tzanetakis *(University of Victoria, Canada)*
Ye Wang *(National University of Singapore, Singapore)*

MM 2013 Technical Demo Program Committee

Xavier Anguer Miro *(Telefonica Research Lab, Spain)*
Liangliang Cao *(IBM Research, USA)*
Lixin Duan *(SAP Research, Singapore)*
Yahong Han *(Tianjin University, China)*
Lu Jiang *(Carnegie Mellon University, USA)*
Florian Metze *(Carnegie Mellon University, USA)*
Zhigang Ma *(University of Trento, Italy)*
Chunhua Shen *(The University of Adelaide, Australia)*
Cees Snoek *(University of Amsterdam, The Netherlands)*
Wei Tong *(Carnegie Mellon University, USA)*
Jinhui Tang *(Nanjing University of Science and Technology, China)*
Jasper Uijlings *(University of Trento, Italy)*
Sen Wang *(The University of Queensland, Australia)*
Fei Wu *(Zhejiang University, China)*
Lexing Xie *(Australian National University, Australia)*
Yi Yang *(Carnegie Mellon University, USA)*
Shoou-I Yu *(Carnegie Mellon University, USA)*
Zheng-Jun Zha *(National University of Singapore, Singapore)*
Luming Zhang *(National University of Singapore, Singapore)*

MM 2013 Additional Reviewers

Marco Bertini
Niamh Caprani
Zhiyong Cheng
Patrick Chiu
Kevin Collins
Matthew Fong
Kenneth Funes
Stephen Gilroy
Siqiong He
Michiel Hildebrand
Yu Huang
Adarsh Kowdle
Sven Kratz
Martha Larson
Christoph Lassner
Bin Li
Liangyue Li
Wen Li
Yuncheng Li
Zhonghua Li
Taoran Lu
Xiguo Ma
Alvaro Marcos
Gregor Miller
Minwoo Park
Fabian Richter
Christian Ries
Stefan Romberg
Julian Seifert
Xianbiao Shu
Gaurav Srivastava
Jichao Sun
Yichen Tang
Emrah Tasli
Lam Tran
Nalini Venkatasubramanian
Dayong Wang
Jialei Wang
Jing Wang
Ju-Chiang Wang
Xinxi Wang
Zhaowen Wang
Julie Williamson
Christian Winkler
Pengcheng Wu
Meng Xu
Quanzeng You
Xiangqian Yu
Jianbo Yuan
Dian Zhang
Yu Zhang
Zhenxing Zhang
Peilin Zhao
Jinfeng Zhuang

ACM Multimedia 2013 Sponsors & Supporters

Sponsor

SIGMM

Corporate Supporters

FX PAL

HUAWEI

technicolor

YAHOO! LABS

Google™

Springer
science+business media

Microsoft®
Research

Corporate Supporters (continued)

facebook

Telefónica

Telefónica Investigación y Desarrollo

IBM Research

Institutional Supporters

NSF

UNIVERSITY OF TRENTO - Italy

Universitat Pompeu Fabra Barcelona

Inria

Project Supporter

MEDIA MIXER

Organizing Committee

General Chairs
Kien Hua (Univ. of Central Florida)
Yong Rui (Microsoft Research)
Ralf Steinmetz (Technische Univ. Darmstadt)

Program Chairs
Alan Hanjalic (Delft Univ. of Technology)
Apostol Natsev (Google)
Wenwu Zhu (Tsinghua Univ.)

High-Risk-High-Return Papers Chairs
Abdulmotaleb El Saddik (Univ. of Ottawa)
Rainer Lienhart (Univ. of Augsburg)
Balakrishnan Prabhakaran (Univ. of Texas at Dallas)

Panel Chairs
Wolfgang Klas (Univ. of Vienna)
Chang Wen Chen (Univ. of Buffalo)

Multimedia Grand Challenge Chairs
Changsheng Xu (Chinese Academy of Sciences)
Cha Zhang (Microsoft Research)

Technical Demo Chairs
Shu-Ching Chen (Florida Int. Univ.)
Stefan Göbel (Technische Univ. Darmstadt)
Carsten Griwodz (Univ. of Oslo)

Workshop Chairs
Andreas Mauthe (Univ. of Lancaster)
Max Mühlhäuser (Technische Univ. Darmstadt)
Hari Sundaram (Arizona State Univ.)

Tutorial Chairs
Hermann Hellwagner (Univ. of Klagenfurt)
Wei Tsang Ooi (National Univ. of Singapore)

Interactive Art Exhibit Chair
Andrea Cavallaro (Queen Mary Univ. of London)

Industrial Panel Chairs
Borko Furht (Florida Atlantic Univ.)
Ivica Rimac (Bell Labs/Alcatel Lucent)

Doctorial Symposium Chairs
Laszlo Böszörmenyi (Univ. of Klagenfurt)
Christian Breitender (Technical Univ. of Vienna)
Oge Marques (Florida Atlantic Univ.)

Focus Area Multimedia Security and Privacy Chair
Gerald Friedland (Int. Computer Science Inst., Berkeley)

Proceedings Chairs
Ying Cai (Iowa State Univ.)
Wallapak Tanavapong (Iowa State Univ.)

Local Arrangements Chairs
Mainak Chatterjee (Univ. of Central Florida)
Marshall Tappen (Univ. of Central Florida)
Cliff Zou (Univ. of Central Florida)

Travel Grant Chairs
Danzhou Liu (Symantec)
JungHwan Oh (Univ. of North Texas)

Sponsorship Chair
Mark Liao (Academia Sinica, Taipeh)

Finance and Registration Chairs
Tai Do (Microsoft)
Ning Jiang (Institute for Systems Biology)
Ming Li (California State Univ.)

Publicity and Social Media Chair
Grace Ngai (Hong Kong Polytechnic Univ.)

Web Chair
Alex Aved (U.S. Air Force)

History Preservation Chairs
Duc Tran (Univ. of Massachusetts in Boston)
Roy Villafane (Andrews Univ.)

SIGMM Chair
Shih-Fu Chang (Columbia Univ.)

SIGMM Records EiC
Carsten Griwodz (Univ. of Oslo)

SIGMM Director of Conferences
Nicu Sebe (Univ. of Trento)

About ACM Multimedia 2014

Since the founding of ACM SIGMM in 1993, ACM Multimedia has been the worldwide premier conference and a key world event to display scientific achievements and innovative industrial products in the multimedia field. At ACM Multimedia 2014, we will celebrate its twenty-second iteration with an extensive program consisting of technical sessions covering all aspects of the multimedia field in forms of oral and poster presentations, tutorials, panels, exhibits, demonstrations and workshops, bringing into focus the principal subjects of investigation, competitions of research teams on challenging problems, and also an interactive art program stimulating artists and computer scientists to meet and discover together the frontiers of artistic communication. Details and updates will be published on the conference's website: www.acmmm.org/2014

Call for Contributions

ACM Multimedia 2014 solicits submissions of contributions for the following programs (partial list, please visit the website for details):

- Full papers & Short papers
- High-risk-high-return papers
- Interactive art exhibition
- Open source software competition
- Multimedia grand challenge competition
- Tutorials
- Panels
- Doctoral symposium
- Technical demonstrations
- Workshops

Important Dates

The dates for submissions to the abovementioned contribution categories and other key dates will be provided on the conference's website. Please check the website frequently for the latest news and updates.

Conference Location – Orlando, Florida

Orlando, nicknamed "The City Beautiful," is also considered the theme park capital of the world. In addition to world-renowned tourist attractions and the most beautiful beaches in the U.S., Orlando is unique in its mix of academia and industry. It is nationally recognized for innovation in the areas of digital media, aerospace, microelectronics, nanotechnology, optics, photonics, and sustainable energy, and it also hosts the University of Central Florida, which is one of the largest and fastest growing universities in the country.

Association for Computing Machinery

SIGMM
Special Interest Group on Multimedia

Multimedia Framed

Elizabeth F. Churchill
eBay Research Labs,
2065 Hamilton Avenue
San Jose, CA 95125
churchill@acm.org

ABSTRACT

Multimedia is the combination of several media forms, More typically, the word implies sound and full-motion video. While multimedia technologists concern themselves with the production and distribution of the multimedia artifacts themselves, information designers, educationalists and artists are more concerned with the reception of the artifact, and consider multimedia to be another representational format for multimodal information presentation. Such a perspective leads to questions such as: Is text, or audio or video, or a combination of all three, the best format for the message? Should another modality (e.g., haptics/touch, olfaction) be invoked instead or in addition? How does the setting affect perception/reception? Is the artifact interactive? Is it changed by audience members? Understanding how an artifact is perceived, received and interacted with is central to understanding what multimedia *is,* opening up possibilities and issuing technical challenges as we imagine new forms and formats of multimedia experience. In this talk, I will illustrate how content understanding is modulated by context, by the "framing" of the content. I will discuss audience participatory production of multimedia and multimodal experiences. I will conclude with some technical excitements, design/development challenges and experiential possibilities that lie ahead.

Categories and Subject Descriptors

H.5.1 [Information Interfaces and Presentation]: Multimedia Information Systems

General Terms

Experimentation, Human Factors, Theory.

Keywords

Social Media; Design; Art; Multimedia; Multimodality; Installation; Performance; Wearables

1. A Summary

The beginnings of multimedia vary depending your perspective [2]. One could set the beginnings to be when humans first painted on cave walls in the Grotte de Lascaux, France. Or perhaps it was 1455 when the Gutenberg Press or in the 1800 with the birth of photography and the first 'movies'. Perhaps it was when the term was coined in the 1960's or more specifically with the Xanadu project in 1965 and the development of hypertext. Or maybe Pong heralded the beginning with its launch in 1972. Whatever your personal view, research developments in computer technologies (hardware and software), audio and telecommunications are the component pieces of the our everyday multimedia experience.

In this talk, I will focus on the experience of multimedia in general and more specifically on how the framing of multimedia artifacts affects how we experience them. Framing can be intentional–scripted creations produced with clear intent by technologists, film-makers, archivists, documentarians, designers, architects and media artists. Framing can also be unintentional. Everyday acts of interest and consumption make us, as viewers, co-producers in the experiences of multimedia artifacts as we view, download, annotate, comment and share multimedia artifacts online, we change how they are interpreted and understood by others. I will consider three research areas that have implications for our understanding of 'multimedia' now and in the future: (1) The psychology and psychophysiology of multimedia as multimodal experience, (2) I will discuss emerging practices with contemporary social media capture and sharing from personal devices and (3) Drawing on film theory/history, cultural studies and performance/theatre theory, I will discuss the ways in which multimedia artifacts are framed, and are experienced and transformed by consumers.

For illustration, I will draw on research into social media and online content sharing [4], multimedia art [1][3][5], and emplaced media installations [6] (Figures 1-4).

MM '13, Oct 21-25 2013, Barcelona, Spain
ACM 978-1-4503-2404-5/13/10.
http://dx.doi.org/10.1145/2502081.2512088

2. REFERENCES

[1] Crane, M. MacDonald, D. Minneman, S. and Winet, J. (1999). Endless beginnings: tales from the road to "now" where?. In *Art and innovation*, Craig Harris (Ed.). MIT Press, Cambridge, MA, USA.

[2] Dixon, S. (2007) Digital Performance: A history of new media in theatre, dance, performance art, and installation. Cambridge: MIT Press.

[3] Gonsalves , T. and Donaldson, T. Medulla Intimata, http://www.tinagonsalves.com/medulla.html.

[4] Liu, Y., Shafton, P., Shamma, D. and Yang, J. (2007). Zync: the design of synchronized video sharing. DUX '07. ACM, New York, NY, USA

[5] Minneman, S. (1997). Sunset Boulevard. In *ACM SIGGRAPH 97 Visual Proceedings: The art and interdisciplinary programs of SIGGRAPH '97* (SIGGRAPH '97), ACM, New York, NY, USA

[6] Yamada, T., Shingu, J., Churchill, E.F., Nelson, L., Helfman, J., and Murphy, P. 2004. Who cares?: reflecting who is reading what on distributed community bulletin boards. In UIST '04. ACM, New York, NY, USA, 109-118.

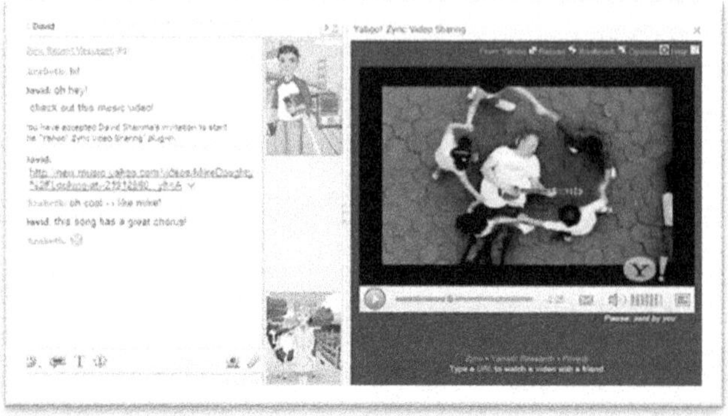

Figure 1: Zync video sharing in IM [4]

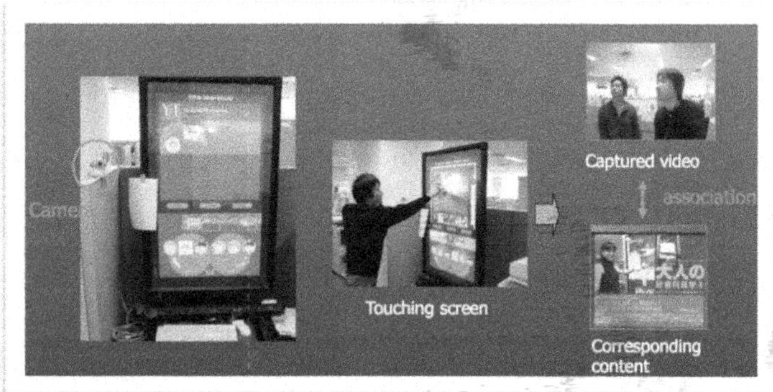

Figure 2: YeTI, a community bulletin board connecting offices in Japan and the US, with video annotation. When readers engage with material on the board, a short video is captured and associated with the content that is read. Content authors can see who engaged with the material posted along a timeline. Video annotations give a sense of who the readers are, their emotional reactions to what they are reading and the context in which they are reading the content [6]

Figure 3: Sunset, an installation on Sunset Boulevard[1][5]

Figure 4: MEDULLA INTIMATA–a hybrid new media work mixing public intervention with jewelry, fashion, performance, bio-metrics, technology and moving image, by Tina Gonsalves and Tom Donaldson [3]

"Wow! You Are So Beautiful Today!"

Luoqi Liu[1], Hui Xu[2], Junliang Xing[1], Si Liu[1], Xi Zhou[2], Shuicheng Yan[1]
[1]Department of Electrical and Computer Engineering, National University of Singapore
[2]Chongqing Institute of Green and Intelligent Technology, Chinese Academy of Sciences
{liuluoqi, elexing, dcslius, eleyans}@nus.edu.sg, {xuhui, zhouxi}@cigit.ac.cn

ABSTRACT

Beauty e-Experts, a fully automatic system for hairstyle and facial makeup recommendation and synthesis, is developed in this work. Given a user-provided frontal face image with short/bound hair and no/light makeup, the Beauty e-Experts system can not only recommend the most suitable hairdo and makeup, but also show the synthetic effects. To obtain enough knowledge for beauty modeling, we build the Beauty e-Experts Database, which contains 1,505 attractive female photos with a variety of beauty attributes and beauty-related attributes annotated. Based on this Beauty e-Experts Dataset, two problems are considered for the Beauty e-Experts system: what to recommend and how to wear, which describe a similar process of selecting hairstyle and cosmetics in our daily life. For the what-to-recommend problem, we propose a multiple tree-structured super-graphs model to explore the complex relationships among the high-level beauty attributes, mid-level beauty-related attributes and low-level image features, and then based on this model, the most compatible beauty attributes for a given facial image can be efficiently inferred. For the how-to-wear problem, an effective and efficient facial image synthesis module is designed to seamlessly synthesize the recommended hairstyle and makeup into the user facial image. Extensive experimental evaluations and analysis on testing images of various conditions well demonstrate the effectiveness of the proposed system.

Categories and Subject Descriptors

H.3.3 [**Information Search and Retrieval**]: Retrieval models; I.2.6 [**Learning**]: Knowledge acquisition

General Terms

Algorithms, Experimentation, Performance

Keywords

Beauty Recommendation, Beauty Synthesis, Multiple Tree-structured Super-graphs Model

http://dx.doi.org/10.1145/2502081.2502126.

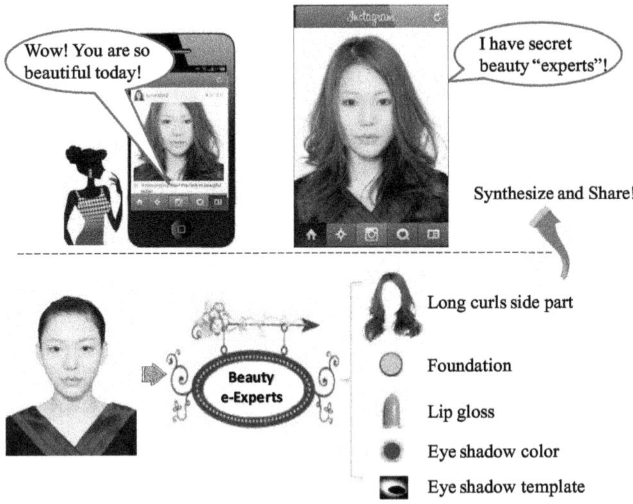

Figure 1: Overall illustration of the proposed Beauty e-Experts system. Based on the user's facial and clothing characteristics, our Beauty e-Experts system automatically recommends the suitable hairstyle and makeup products for the user, and then produces the synthesized visual effects. All the figures in this paper are best viewed in original color PDF file. Please resize ×2 for better visual effects.

1. INTRODUCTION

Beauty is a language, which enables people to express their personalities, gain self-confidence and open up to others. Everybody wants to be beautiful. Hairstyle and makeup are two main factors that influence one's judgment about whether someone looks beautiful or not, especially for female. By choosing proper hair and makeup style, one can enhance the whole temperament and thus look more attractive. However, people often encounter problems when they make choices. First of all, the effects of different makeup products and hairstyles vary for different individuals, and are highly correlated with one's facial traits, *e.g.* face shape, skin color, etc. It is quite difficult, or even unlikely, for people to analyze their own facial features and make proper choices of hair and makeup care & dressing products. Second, nowadays cosmetics have developed into a large industry and there exist an unimaginable variety of products. Making choices in such a great variety can cost people a lot of time and money. Therefore, how to choose the proper hairstyle & makeup rapidly becomes a challenge.

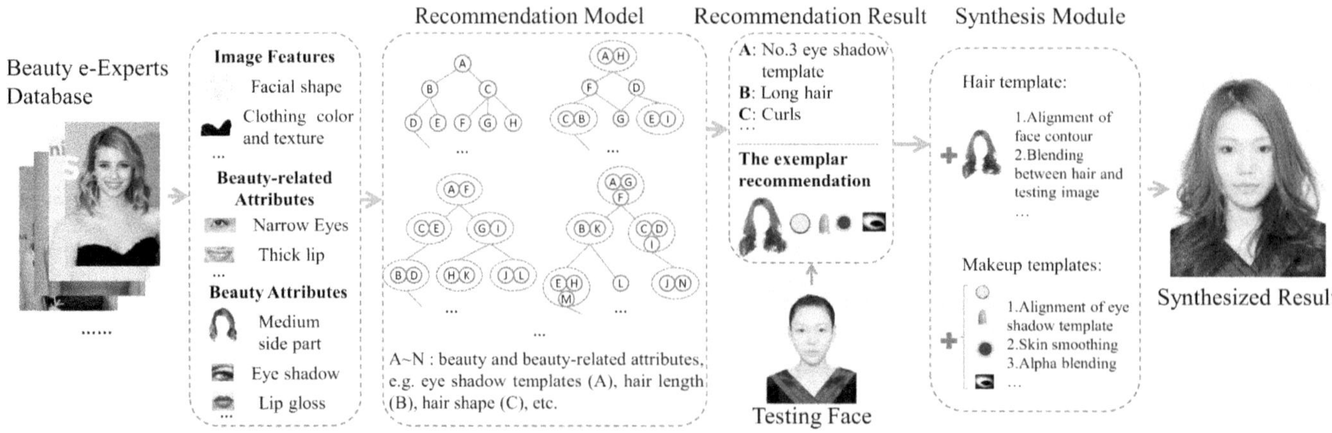

Figure 2: System processing flowchart. We firstly collect the Beauty e-Experts Database of 1,505 facial images with different hairstyles and makeup effects. With the extracted facial and clothing features, we propose a multiple tree-structured super-graphs model to express the complex relationships among beauty and beauty-related attributes. Here, the results from multiple individual super-graphs are fused based on voting strategy. In the testing stage, the recommended hair and makeup templates for the testing face are then applied to synthesize the final visual effects.

In order to solve this problem, people have made some attempts. Some virtual hairstyle & makeup techniques have been developed. Softwares like Virtual Haircut & Makeover[1], which allow people to change hairstyle and perform virtual makeup on their photos, have been put into use. With software of this kind, users can input a facial image, and then choose any hairstyle or makeup they prefer from the options provided by the system. Users can see the effects of applying the chosen hairstyles and also makeup products on their faces, and make decisions on whether to choose these hairstyles or makeup products in reality. But there exists a problem of too much manual work for these softwares. For example, users have to mark out special regions, such as corners of eyes, nose, mouth or even pupil, etc., on their photos manually. Besides, these softwares do not have recommendation function. Users have to make choices on their own, and adjust the synthetic effects of these choices manually. It is too complicated for unprofessional people to accomplish such a process.

The research is still quite limited in this field, although some researchers have tried some approaches. Tong *et al.* [28] extracted makeup from before-and-after training image pairs, and transferred the makeup effect defined as ratios to a new testing image. Guo and Sim [15] considered makeup effect existing in two layers of the three-layer facial decomposition result, and the makeup effect of a reference image was transferred to the target image. Some patents also try to address the hair suggesting problem, *e.g.* [25], which searches for hairstyles in a database from the plurality of the hairstyle parameters based on manually selected hair attributes by the user. These works all fail to provide a recommendation function, and the synthetic effects may not be suitable for every part of the face. Besides, to our best knowledge, most of these works need a lot of user interactions and the final results are highly dependent on the efforts of users.

The aim of this work is to develop a novel Beauty e-Experts system, which helps users to select hairstyle and makeups automatically and produces the synthesized visual effects as shown in Figure 1. The main challenge in this problem is how to model the complex relationships among different beauty and beauty-related attributes for reliable recommendation and natural synthesis. To address this challenge, we build a large dataset, Beauty e-Experts Dataset, which contains 1,505 images of beautiful female figures selected from professional fashion websites. Based on this Beauty e-Experts Dataset, we first annotate all the beauty attributes for each image in the whole dataset. These beauty attributes, including different hairstyles and makeup types, are all adjustable in the daily life. Their specific combination is considered as the recommendation objective of the Beauty e-Experts System. To narrow the gap between the high-level beauty attributes and the low-level image features, a set of mid-level beauty-related attributes, such as facial traits and clothing properties, are also annotated for the dataset.

Based on all these attributes, we propose to learn a multiple tree-structured super-graphs model to explore the complex relationships among these attributes. As a generalization of a graph, a super-graph can theoretically characterize any type of relationships among different attributes and thus provide powerful recommendation. We propose to use its multiple tree-structured approximations to reserve the most important relationships and make the inference procedure tractable. Based on the recommended results, an effective and efficient facial image synthesis module is designed to seamlessly synthesize the recommended results into the user facial image and show it back to the user. Experimental results on 100 testing images show that our system can obtain very reasonable recommendation results and appealing synthesis results. The whole system processing flowchart is illustrated in Figure 2.

The contributions of this work are summarized as follows:

- A comprehensive system considering both hairstyle and makeup recommendation and synthesis is explored for the first time.
- A large database called Beauty e-Experts Database is constructed, including 1,505 facial images with various hairstyles and makeup effects, and fully annotated with different types of attributes.
- A multiple tree-structured super-graphs model is proposed for hairstyle and makeup recommendation.

[1] http://www.goodhousekeeping.com/beauty

Figure 3: Some exemplar images from the Beauty e-Experts Dataset and the additional testing set. The left three images are from the Beauty e-Experts Dataset used for training, while the right two images are from the testing set.

2. DATASET, ATTRIBUTES AND FEATURES

Hairstyle & makeup products make a lucrative market among female customers, but no public datasets for academic research exist. Most previous research [27, 15, 28] only works for a few samples. Chen and Zhang [6] released a benchmark for facial beauty study, but their focus is geometric facial beauty, not facial makeup and hairstyle. Wang and Ai [29] sampled 1,021 images with regular hairstyles from Labeled Faces in the Wild (LFW) Database [18], which is not designed for hairstyle analysis. In addition, the sampled LFW database contains only a few hairstyles, since it is designed only for hair segmentation. In order to obtain enough knowledge to perform beauty modeling, we need a large dataset specifically designed for this task. In the following, we will describe the construction of the Beauty e-Experts Dataset, as well as its attribute annotation and feature extraction process.

2.1 The Beauty e-Experts Dataset

To build our Beauty e-Experts Dataset, we have downloaded $\sim 800K$ images of female figures from professional hairstyle and makeup websites (e.g. www.stylebistro.com). We search these photos with the key words like *makeup, cosmetics, hairstyle, haircut and celebrity.* The initial downloaded images are screened by a commercial face analyzer[2] to remove images with no face detected, and then 87 keypoints are located for each image. The images with high resolution and confident landmark detection results are retained. The retained images are further manually selected, and only those containing female figures who are considered as attractive and with complete hairstyle and obvious makeup effects are retained. The final 1,505 retained images contain female figures in distinct fashions and with clear frontal faces, and are thus very good representatives for beauty modeling. Besides, we also collect 100 face images with short/bound hair and no/light makeup, which better demonstrate the synthesized results, for experimental evaluation purpose. Figure 3 shows some exemplar images in the Dataset.

2.2 Attributes and Features

To obtain beauty knowledge from the built dataset, we comprehensively explore different beauty attributes on these images, including various kinds of hairstyles and facial makeups. All these beauty attributes can be easily adjusted and modified in the daily life and thus have practical meaning for our beauty recommendation and synthesis system. We carefully organize these beauty attributes and set their attribute values based on some basic observations or preprocessing on the whole dataset. Table 1 lists the names and values of all the beauty attributes considered in the work. For the first four beauty attributes in Table 1, their values are set intuitively, and for the last five ones, their values are obtained by running the k-means clustering algorithm on the training dataset for the corresponding features (the cluster number is determined empirically according to each specific attribute). The pixel values within the specific facial regions on each training image are clustered by Gaussian mixture models (GMM) in RGB color space. The centers of the largest GMM components are used as the representative colors. Then the colors are clustered by k-means to obtain the color attributes of hair and makeup templates. Hair templates and eye shadows are extracted by image matting [22]. For eye shadows, only the alpha channel is retained and further clustered to learn the eye shadow template attribute. The left eye shadows are sufficient for clustering. We show the visual examples of specific attribute values for some beauty attributes in Figure 4.

[2]OMRON OKAO Vision: `http://www.omron.com/r_d/coretech/vision/okao.html`

Table 1: A list of the high-level beauty attributes.

Name	Values
hair length	long, medium, short
hair shape	straight, curled, wavy
hair bangs	full, slanting, center part, side part
hair volume	dense, normal
hair color	20 classes
foundation	15 classes
lip gloss	15 classes
eye shadow color	15 classes
eye shadow template	20 classes

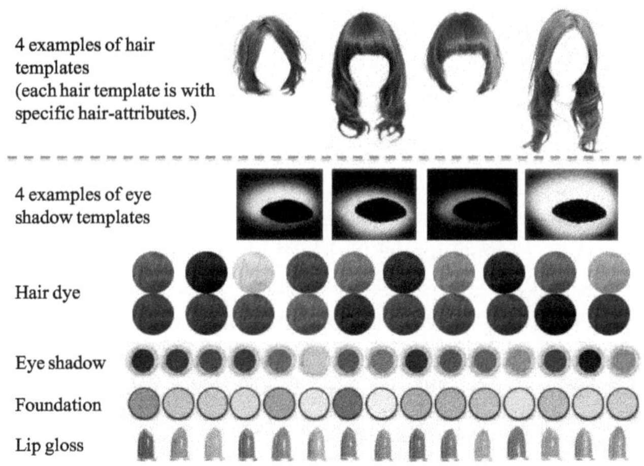

Figure 4: Visual examples of the specific values for some beauty attributes.

A straightforward way to predict the values of these high-level beauty attributes is using some low-level features to train some classifiers. However, since there is a relatively big gap between the high-level beauty attributes and the low-level image features, and the beauty attributes are intuitively related to some mid-level attributes like eye shape and mouth width, we further explore a set of mid-level beauty-related attributes to narrow the gap between the high-level beauty attributes and the low-level image features. Table 2 lists all the mid-level beauty-related attributes annotated for the dataset. These mid-level attributes mainly focus on the

Table 2: A list of mid-level beauty-related attributes considered in this work.

Names	Values
forehead	high, normal, low
eyebrow	thick, thin
eyebrow length	long, short
eye corner	upcurved, downcurved, normal
eye shape	narrow, normal
ocular distance	hypertelorism, normal, hypotelorism
cheek bone	high, normal
nose bridge	prominent, flat
nose tip	wide, narrow
mouth opened	yes, no
mouth width	wide, normal
smiling	smiling, neutral
lip thickness	thick, normal
fatness	fat, normal
jaw shape	round, flat, pointed
face shape	long, oval, round
collar shape	strapless, v-shape, one-shoulder, high-necked, round, shirt collar
clothing pattern	vertical, plaid, horizontal, drawing, plain, floral print
clothing material	cotton, chiffon, silk, woolen, denim, leather, lace
clothing color	red, orange, brown, purple, yellow, green, gray, black, blue, white, pink, multi-color
race	Asian, Western

facial shapes and clothing properties, which are kept fixed during the recommendation and the synthesis process.[3]

After the annotation of the high-level beauty attributes and mid-level beauty-related attributes, we further extract various types of the low-level image features on the clothing and facial regions for each image in the Beauty e-Experts Dataset to facilitate further beauty modeling. The clothing region of an image is automatically determined based on its geometrical relationship with the face region. Specifically, the following features are extracted for image representation:

- RGB color histogram and color moments on clothing region.
- Histograms of oriented gradients (HOG) [10] and local binary patterns (LBP) [1] features on clothing region.
- Active shape model [8] based shape parameters.
- Shape context [2] features extracted at facial points.

All the above features are concatenated to form a feature vector of 7,109 dimensions, and then Principal Component Analysis (PCA) [20] is performed to reserve 90% of the energy. The compacted feature vector with 173 dimensions and the annotated attribute values are then fed into an SVM classifier to train for each attribute a classifier.

3. THE RECOMMENDATION MODEL

A training beauty image is denoted as a tuple $(\langle \mathbf{x}, \mathbf{a}^r \rangle, \mathbf{a}^b)$. Here $\mathbf{x}$ is the image features extracted from the raw image data; $\mathbf{a}^r$ and $\mathbf{a}^b$ denote the set of the beauty-related attributes and beauty attributes respectively. Each attribute may have multiple different values, *i.e.* $a_i \in \{1, \dots, n_i\}$, where n_i is the number of attribute values for the i-th attribute. The beauty-related attributes $\mathbf{a}^r$ act as the mid-level cues to narrow the gap between the low-level image features $\mathbf{x}$ and the high-level beauty attributes $\mathbf{a}^b$. The recommendation model needs to uncover the complex relationships among the low-level image features, mid-level beauty-related attributes and high-level beauty attributes, and make the final recommendation for a given image.

3.1 Model Formulation

We model the relationships among the low-level image features, the mid-level beauty-related attributes, and the high-level beauty attributes from a probabilistic perspective. The aim of the recommendation system is to estimate the probability of beauty attributes, together with beauty-related attributes, given the image features, *i.e.* $p(\mathbf{a}^b, \mathbf{a}^r|\mathbf{x})$, which can be modeled using the Gibbs distribution,

$$p\left(\mathbf{a}^b, \mathbf{a}^r|\mathbf{x}\right) = \frac{1}{Z(\mathbf{x})} \exp\left(-E\left(\mathbf{a}^b, \mathbf{a}^r, \mathbf{x}\right)\right), \qquad (1)$$

where $Z(\mathbf{x}) = \sum_{\mathbf{a}^b, \mathbf{a}^r} \exp\left(-E\left(\mathbf{a}^b, \mathbf{a}^r, \mathbf{x}\right)\right)$, also known as the partition function, is a normalizing term dependent on the image features, and $E(\mathbf{a}^b, \mathbf{a}^r, \mathbf{x})$ is an energy function measuring the compatibility among the beauty attributes, beauty-related attributes and image features. The beauty recommendation results can be obtained by finding the most likely joint beauty attribute state $\hat{\mathbf{a}}^b = \arg\max_{\mathbf{a}^b} \max_{\mathbf{a}^r} p\left(\mathbf{a}^b, \mathbf{a}^r|\mathbf{x}\right)$.

The capacity of this probabilistic model fully depends on the structure of the energy function $E(\mathbf{a}^b, \mathbf{a}^r, \mathbf{x})$. Here we propose to learn a general super-graph structure to build the energy function which can theoretically be used to model any relationships among the low-level image features, mid-level beauty-related attributes, and high-level beauty attributes. To begin with, we give the definition of super-graph.

DEFINITION 1. *Super-graph: a super-graph $\mathcal{G}$ is a pair $\mathcal{G} = (\mathcal{V}, \mathcal{E})$ where $\mathcal{V}$ is called super-vertexes, consisting a set of non-empty subsets of a basic node set, and $\mathcal{E}$ is called super-edges, consisting of a set of two-tuples, each of which contains two different elements in $\mathcal{V}$.*

It can be seen that a super-graph is actually a generalization of a graph in which a vertex can have multiple basic nodes and an edge can connect any number of basic nodes. When all the super-vertexes only contain one basic node, and each super-edge is forced to connect to only two basic nodes, the super-graph then becomes a traditional graph. A super-graph can be naturally used to model the complex relationships among multiple factors, where the factors are denoted by the vertexes and the relationships are represented by the super-edges.

DEFINITION 2. *k-order super-graph: for a super-graph $\mathcal{G} = (\mathcal{V}, \mathcal{E})$, if the maximal number of vertexes involved by one super-edge in $\mathcal{E}$ is k, $\mathcal{G}$ is said to be a k-order super-graph.*

Based on the above definitions, we propose to use the super-graph to characterize the complex relationships among the low-level image features, mid-level beauty-related attributes, and high-level beauty attributes in our problem. For example, the aforementioned pairwise correlations can be sufficiently represented by a 2-order super-graph (traditional graph), while other more complex relationships, such as one-to-two and two-to-two relationships, can be represented by other higher order super-graphs. Denote the basic node set A as the union of the beauty attributes and beauty-related attributes, *i.e.* $A = \{a_i | a_i \in \mathbf{a}^r \cup \mathbf{a}^b\}$. Supposing the underlying relationships among all the attributes are repre-

[3]Although the clothes of a user can be changed to make one look more beautiful, they are kept fixed in our current Beauty e-Experts system.

sented by a super-graph $\mathcal{G}=(\mathcal{V},\mathcal{E})$, where $\mathcal{V}=\{\mathbf{a}_i|\mathbf{a}_i\subset A\}$[4] is a set of non-empty subsets of A, and $\mathcal{E}$ is the super-edge set that models their relationships, the energy function can then be defined as,

$$E\left(\mathbf{a}^b,\mathbf{a}^r,\mathbf{x}\right)=\sum_{\mathbf{a}_i\in\mathcal{V}}\phi_i\left(\mathbf{a}_i,\mathbf{x}\right)+\sum_{(\mathbf{a}_i,\mathbf{a}_j)\in\mathcal{E}}\phi_{ij}\left(\mathbf{a}_i,\mathbf{a}_j\right). \quad (2)$$

The first summation term is called FA (feature to attribute) potential which is used to model the relationships between the attributes and low-level image features, and the second one is called AA (attribute to attribute) potential and is used to model the complex relationships among different attributes represented by the super-edges. $\phi_i\left(\mathbf{a}_i,\mathbf{x}\right)$ and $\phi_{ij}\left(\mathbf{a}_i,\mathbf{a}_j\right)$ are the potential functions of the corresponding inputs, which can be learned in different ways. Generally, the FA potential $\phi_i\left(\mathbf{a}_i,\mathbf{x}\right)$ is usually modeled as a generalized linear function in the form like

$$\phi_i\left(\mathbf{a}_i=\mathbf{s}_i,\mathbf{x}\right)=\psi_{\mathbf{a}_i}\left(\mathbf{x}\right)^{\top}\mathbf{w}_i^{\mathbf{s}_i}, \quad (3)$$

where $\mathbf{s}_i$ is the values for attribute subset $\mathbf{a}_i$, $\psi_{\mathbf{a}_i}\left(\mathbf{x}\right)$ is a set of feature mapping functions for the attributes in $\mathbf{a}_i$ by using SVM on the extracted features (see Section 2.2), and $\mathbf{w}_i$ is the FA weight parameters to be learned for the model. And the AA potential function $\phi_i\left(\mathbf{a}_i,\mathbf{a}_j\right)$ is defined by a scalar parameter for each joint state of the corresponding super-edge,

$$\phi_{ij}\left(\mathbf{a}_i=\mathbf{s}_i,\mathbf{a}_j=\mathbf{s}_j\right)=w_{i,j}^{\mathbf{s}_i\mathbf{s}_j}, \quad (4)$$

where $w_{i,j}^{\mathbf{s}_i\mathbf{s}_j}$ is a scalar parameter for the corresponding joint state of $\mathbf{a}_i$ and $\mathbf{a}_j$ with the specific value $\mathbf{s}_i$ and $\mathbf{s}_j$.

3.2 Model Learning

The learning of the super-graph based energy function includes learning the structure of the underlying super-graph and the parameters in the potential functions.

3.2.1 Structure Learning

Learning a fully connected super-graph structure is generally an NP-complete problem, which makes finding the optimal solution technically intractable [21]. However, we can still find many good approximations which can model a very large proportion of all the possible relationships. Among all the possible approximations, tree structure provides a very good choice which can be learned efficiently using many algorithms [21]. Another merit of tree structure is that the inference on a tree can be efficiently performed using methods like dynamic programming. Based on these considerations, we therefore use the tree-structured super-graph to model the underlying relationships. To remedy the information loss during the approximation procedure, we further propose to simultaneously learn multiple different tree-structured super-graphs to collaboratively model the objective relationships. Learning multiple tree-structured super-graphs is also supposed to produce more useful recommendation results, since it is intuitively similar to daily recommendation scenario. These tree-structured super-graphs can be supposed to be different recommendation experts, each of which is good at modeling some kinds of relationships. The recommendation results generated by these experts are voted to form the final recommendation result.

For a 2-order super-graph, learning a tree-structured approximation can be efficiently solved using the maximum

[4]Note that in this paper we use $\mathbf{a}_i$ to denote a non-empty attribute set and a_i to denote a single attribute.

Algorithm 1 Candidate set of subsets generation for super-graph structure learning.

Input: basic node set $A=\{a_1,\ldots,a_M\}$, adjacency matrix $W=\{w_{ij}\}_{1\le i,j\le M}$, desired order of the super-graph k.
Output: candidate set of subsets $\mathcal{V}=\{\mathbf{a}_i|\mathbf{a}_i\in A\}$.

Initialization: set $\mathcal{V}$ with m unique subsets randomly collected from A, each of which has no more than $\lfloor(k+1)/2\rfloor$ elements. Set $w_{\max}=f(\mathcal{V},W)$.
while not converged **do**
  for $i=1\rightarrow M$ **do**
    for $j=1\rightarrow m$ **do**
      $w_j=f(\mathcal{V},W)$ if move a_i to $\mathbf{a}_j$.
    end for
    $w_l=\mathrm{argmax}_j(\{w_j\})$.
    if $l>w_{\max}$ **then**
      Move a_i to $\mathbf{a}_l$, $w_{\max}=w_l$.
      if $|\mathbf{a}_l|>\lfloor(k+1)/2\rfloor$ **then**
        Split $|\mathbf{a}_l|$ into two subsets.
        $m\leftarrow m+1$.
      end if
      if $m>\lceil 2\times M/(k-1)\rceil$ **then**
        Merge two smallest subsets.
        $m\leftarrow m-1$.
      end if
    end if
  end for
end while
Generate candidate vertex subsets.

spanning tree algorithm [7]. The edge weights in the graph are given by the mutual information between the attributes, which can be estimated from the empirical distribution from the annotations in the training data. For higher order super-graph, however, learning its tree-structured approximation will not be a trivial task, since the choices of vertex subsets for each super-edge are combinational.

Suppose for a super-graph built on basic node set $A=\{a_1,\ldots,a_M\}$ with M elements, we need to find a k-order tree-structured super-graph for these vertexes. We first calculate the mutual information between each pair of vertexes, and denote the results in the adjacency matrix form, i.e. $W=\{w_{ij}\}_{1\le i,j\le M}$. Then we propose a two-stage algorithm to find the k-order tree-structured super-graph.

In the first stage, we aim to find the candidate set of basic node subsets $\mathcal{V}=\{\mathbf{a}_i|\mathbf{a}_i\in\mathcal{V}\}$, which will be used to form the super-edges. The objective here is to find the set of subsets that has the largest amount of total mutual information in the result k-order super-graph. Here we first define a function that calculates the mutual information of a subset set with a specified mutual information matrix,

$$f(\mathcal{V},W)=\sum_{|\mathbf{a}_i|\ge 2}\sum_{a_j,a_k\in\mathbf{a}_i}w_{jk}. \quad (5)$$

Based on this definition, we formulate the candidate set generation problem as the following optimization problem

$$\begin{aligned}&\underset{\mathcal{V}}{\mathrm{argmax}}\quad f(\mathcal{V},W),\\ &\text{s.t. } |\mathbf{a}_i|\le\lfloor\frac{k+1}{2}\rfloor,\forall i,\\ &|\mathcal{V}|\le m,\end{aligned} \quad (6)$$

where the first inequation is from the k-order constraint from the result super-graph, $\lfloor\cdot\rfloor$ is the floor operator, and the

Algorithm 2 Learning multiple tree-structured super-graphs.

Input: basic node set $A = \{a_1, \ldots, a_M\}$, adjacency matrix $W = \{w_{ij}\}_{1 \le i,j \le M}$, number of desired super-graphs T.
Output: T tree-structured super-graphs $\mathbf{G} = \{\mathcal{G}_t\}_{t=1}^{T}$.
1: **Initialization**: set $\mathbf{G} = \emptyset$, $K = 5$.
2: **for** $t = 1 \to T$ **do**
3: Generate a random variable $k \in \{2, \ldots K\}$.
4: Obtain a candidate vertex subsets $\mathcal{V}$ using Alg. 1.
5: Calculate the mutual information between the elements pair with no more than k vertexes in $\mathcal{V}$.
6: Make a graph using the calculated mutual information as adjacency matrix.
7: Find its maximal spanning tree using the algorithm in [7].
8: Form the k-order tree-structured super-graph $\mathcal{G}_t$.
9: $\mathbf{G} \leftarrow \mathbf{G} \cup \{\mathcal{G}_t\}$.
10: **end for**
11: Generate tree-structured super-graph set $\mathbf{G}$.

parameter m in the second inequation is used to ensure that the generated subsets have a reasonable size to cover all the vertexes and make the inference on the result super-graph more efficient. Specifically, its value can be set as

$$m = \begin{cases} M, & k = 2, \\ 2\lceil M/(k-1) \rceil, & \text{otherwise}, \end{cases} \tag{7}$$

where $\lceil \cdot \rceil$ is the ceil operator. To solve this optimization problem, we design a k-means like iterative optimization algorithm to find the solution. The algorithm first initializes some random vertex subsets and then re-assigns each vertex to the subsets that result in maximal mutual information increment; if one vertex subset has more than $\lfloor (k+1)/2 \rfloor$ elements, it will be split into two subsets; if the total cardinality of the vertex subset set is larger than $2\lceil M/(k-1) \rceil$, two subsets with the smallest cardinalities will be merged into one subset. This procedure is repeated until converge. Alg. 1 gives the pseudo-code description of this procedure.

Based on the candidate vertex subsets, the second stage of the two-stage algorithm first calculates the mutual information between the element pair that satisfies the order restrictions in the each vertex subset. Then it builds a graph by using the calculated mutual information as adjacency matrix, and the maximum spanning tree algorithm [7] is adopted to find its tree-structured approximation.

The above two-stage algorithm is run many times by setting different k values and initializations of subsets, which then generates multiple tree-structured super-graphs with different orders and structures. In order to make the parameters learning in the following tractable, the maximal k-value K is set to be equal to 5. The detailed description of this process is summarized in Alg. 2.

3.2.2 Parameter Learning And Inference

For each particular tree-structured super-graph, its parameter set, including the parameters in the FA potentials and the AA potentials, can be denoted in a whole as $\mathbf{\Theta} = \{\mathbf{w}_i^{\mathbf{s}_i}, w_{ij}^{\mathbf{s}_i\mathbf{s}_j}\}$. We adopt the maximal likelihood criterion to learn these parameters. Given N i.i.d. training samples $\mathbf{X} = \{\langle \mathbf{x}_n, \mathbf{a}_n^r \rangle, \mathbf{a}_n^b\}$, we need to minimize the loss function

$$\begin{aligned} \mathcal{L} &= \frac{1}{N}\sum_{n=1}^{N} \mathcal{L}_n + \frac{1}{2}\lambda \sum_{i,\mathbf{s}_i} \|\mathbf{w}_i^{\mathbf{s}_i}\|_2^2 \\ &= \frac{1}{N}\sum_{n=1}^{N} \left\{ -\ln p\left(\mathbf{a}_n^b, \mathbf{a}_n^r | \mathbf{x}_n\right) \right\} + \frac{1}{2}\lambda \sum_{i,\mathbf{s}_i} \|\mathbf{w}_i^{\mathbf{s}_i}\|_2^2, \end{aligned} \tag{8}$$

where λ is the tradeoff parameter between the regularization term and log-likelihood and its value is chosen by k-fold validation on the training set. Since the energy function is linear with respect to the parameters, the log-likelihood function is concave and the parameters can be optimized using gradient based methods. The gradient of the parameters can be computed by calculating their marginal distributions [24]. Denoting the value of attribute $\mathbf{a}_i$ for training image n as $\hat{\mathbf{a}}_i$, we have

$$\frac{\partial \mathcal{L}_n}{\partial \mathbf{w}_i^{\mathbf{s}_i}} = \left([\hat{\mathbf{a}}_i = \mathbf{s}_i] - p\left(\mathbf{a}_i = \mathbf{s}_i | \mathbf{x}_n\right)\right) \psi_{\mathbf{a}_i}\left(\mathbf{x}_n\right), \tag{9}$$

$$\frac{\partial \mathcal{L}_n}{\partial w_{ij}^{\mathbf{s}_i\mathbf{s}_j}} = [\hat{\mathbf{a}}_i = \mathbf{s}_i, \hat{\mathbf{a}}_j = \mathbf{s}_j] - p\left(\mathbf{a}_i = \mathbf{s}_i, \mathbf{a}_j = \mathbf{s}_j | \mathbf{x}_n\right), \tag{10}$$

where $[\cdot]$ is the Iverson bracket notation, i.e., $[\cdot]$ equals 1 if the experssion is true, and 0 otherwise.

Based on the calculation of the gradients, the parameters can be learned from different gradient based optimization algorithms [21]. In the experiments, we use the implementation by Schmidt[5] to learn these parameters. The learned parameters, together with the corresponding super-graph structures, form the final recommendation model.

Here each learned tree-structured super-graph model can be seen as a beauty expert. Given an input testing image, the system first extracts the feature vector $\mathbf{x}$, and then each beauty expert makes its recommendation by performing inference on the tree structure to find the maximum posteriori probability of $p\left(\mathbf{a}^b, \mathbf{a}^r | \mathbf{x}\right)$. The recommendation results output by all the Beauty e-Experts are then fused by majority voting to make the final recommendation to the user.

3.3 Relations with Other Models

The proposed multiple tree-structured super-graphs model characterizes the complex relationships among different attributes from a probabilistic prospective. When the maximal order value K is set to 2, our model degenerates into the classical graphical model used by most previous works [4, 29, 24], where only the one-to-one pairwise correlations between two attributes are considered to model the complex relationships. Our model can generally model any order of the relationships. When the maximal order value K of the super-graph is set to 5, many other types of relationships, *e.g.*, one-to-two, two-to-two, and two-to-three, can be simultaneously modeled.

The pairwise correlations are also extensively modeled using the latent SVM model [30] from a deterministic perspective, which has been successfully applied into the problem like object detection [12], pose estimation [31], image classification [30], as well as clothing recommendation [23]. Compared with the latent SVM model, our tree-structured super-graph model not only can consider much more complex relationships among the attributes, but also is more efficient since tree structure makes both learning and inference process much faster. For a tree structured model with n nodes and k different values for each node, the time complexity of

[5] `http://www.di.ens.fr/~mschmidt/Software/UGM.html`

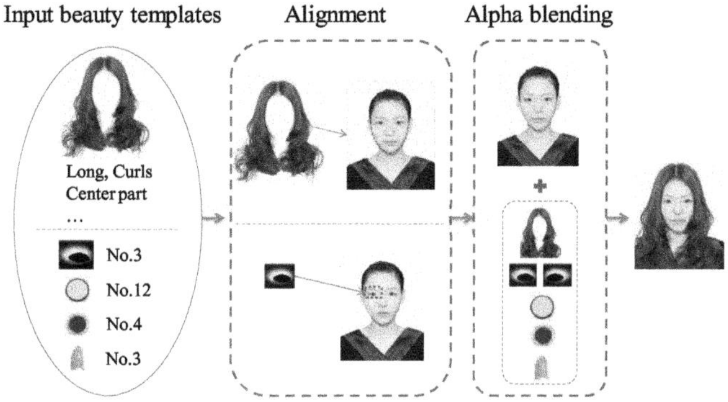

Figure 5: The flowchat of the synthesis module.

the inference process is only $O(k^2n)$, while a fully connected model (*e.g.* latent SVM) has the complexity of $O(k^n)$. Actually, during the training of the latent SVM model, some intuitively small correlations have to be removed manually to accelerate the training process. Our tree-structured super-graphs model, on the contrary, can automatically remove the small relationships during the structure learning process in a principled way. By extending to multiple tree-structured super-graphs, our model can produce much more reliable and useful recommendations as verified in experimental part, since it can well simulate the common recommendation scenario in our daily life, where one usually asks many people for recommendations and takes the majority or the most suitable one as the final choice.

4. THE SYNTHESIS MODULE

With the beauty attributes recommended by the multiple tree-structured super-graphs model, we further synthesize the final visual effect of hairstyle and makeup for the testing image. To this end, the system first uses beauty attributes to search for hair and makeup templates. A hair template is a combination of hairstyle attributes, such as long curls with bangs. We use the recommended hairstyle attributes to search the Beauty Expert Database for suitable hair templates. As mentioned in Section 2.2, each hair template is extracted from a training image. If more than one template is obtained, we randomly select one from them. If we cannot find the hair template with exactly the same hairstyle attribute values, we use the one which has the values most approximating to the recommended hairstyle attribute values. Each makeup attribute forms a template which can be directly obtained from the dataset. These obtained hair and makeup templates are then fed into the synthesis process, which mainly has two steps: alignment and alpha blending, as shown in Figure 5.

In the alignment step, both of the hairstyle and the makeup templates need to be aligned with the testing image. For hair template alignment, a dual linear transformation procedure is proposed to put the hair template on the target face in the testing image. The dual linear transformation process first uses a linear affine transformation to perform rough alignment and then adopts a piecewise-linear affine transformation [14] to perform precise alignment. Figure 6 gives an illustration of this process. In the linear affine transformation, the 21 face contour points generated by the face analyzer are adopted to calculate affine transformation matrix between the hair template and the testing face. The hair template then can be roughly aligned to the testing face using transformation matrix. In piecewise linear affine transformation, three subsets of keypoints, namely, the inner subset, the middle subset, and the outer subset, are sampled based on the result of rough alignment. In Figure 6, these keypoints in the three subsets are drawn in red, green and blue respectively. 11 points are sampled interlacedly from 21 face contour points to consist the inner subset. The points in the inner subset are extended on the horizontal direction with half of the distance between two eye centers. They form the middle subset of 8 points. 10 points in the outer subset are fixed on the edge of the image. Their coordinates are determined by the image corners or the horizontal lines of eye centers and mouth corners. Note that points of the middle and outer subsets are at the same position in both the hair template and the testing image, which aims to keep the overall shape of the hairstyle. The total 29 points in the three subsets are then used to construct a Delaunay triangulation [11] to obtain 46 triangles. Then affine transformations are applied within the corresponding triangles between the testing face and the hair template. After that, these points on the hair template are precisely aligned with the testing face.

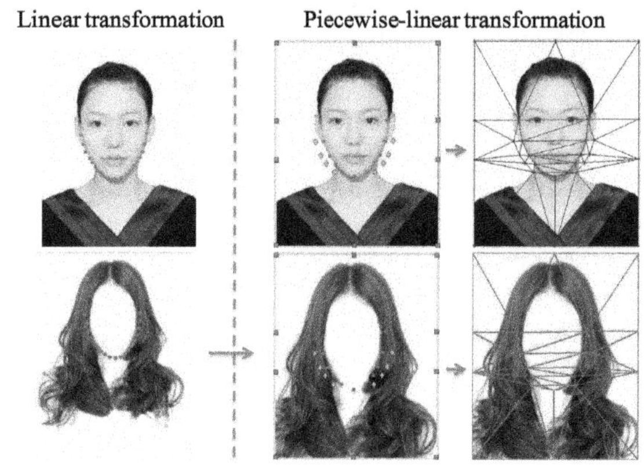

∘ Inner subset ▫ Outer subset ◇ Middle subset

Figure 6: Hair template alignment process.

For the makeup templates alignment, only the eye shadow template need to be aligned to the eye region in the testing image. Other makeup templates can be directly applied to the corresponding regions based on the face keypoint detection results. To align the eye shadow template to eye contour on the face, we use the thin plate spline method [3] to warp the eye shadow template by using the eye contour points. Because the eye shadow template attributes are learned by clustering from the left eye, the left template is mirrored to the right to obtain the right eye shadow template.

In the alpha blending step, the final result R is synthesized with hair template, makeup and the testing face I. The synthesis process is performed in CIELAB color space. L^* channel is considered as lightness because of its similarity to human visual perception. a^* and b^* are the color channels. We firstly use the edge-preserving operator on image lightness channel L^* to imitate the smoothing effect of foundation. We choose the guided filter [17], which is more efficient and has better performance near the edges among all the edge-preserving filters. It is applied to the L^* channel of facial region determined by facial contour points. Note that since we do not have contour points on the forehead, the forehead region is segmented out by GrabCut [26]. The final synthesis result is generated by alpha blending of the testing image I and hair and makeup template T in the L^*, a^* and b^* channels, respectively,

$$R = \alpha I + (1 - \alpha)T, \tag{11}$$

where α is a weight to balance I and T. For hair and eye shadow templates, the value of α is obtained from the templates themselves. For foundation and lip gloss, the α value is set to 0.5 for L^* channel, and 0.6 for a^* and b^* channels.

5. EXPERIMENTS

In this section, we design experiments to evaluate the performance of the proposed Beauty e-Experts System from different aspects. We first visualize and analyze the intermediate result of model learning processing. Then the recommendation result is evaluated by comparison with several baselines, such as latent SVM [30], multi-class SVM [5] and neural network [16]. The synthesis effects are finally presented and compared with some commercial systems related to hairstyle and makeup recommendation and synthesis.

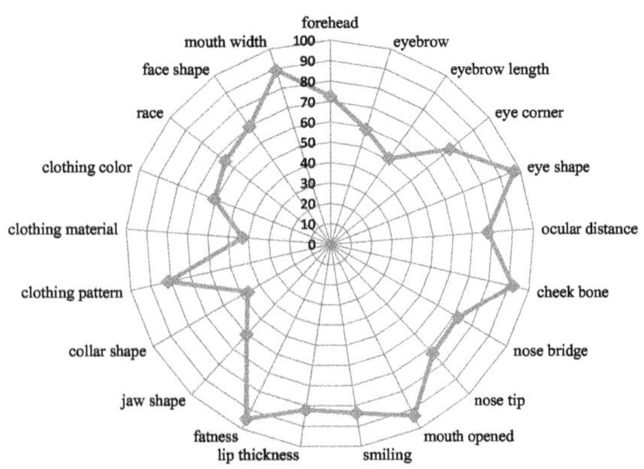

Figure 7: Accuracies of the predicted beauty attributes from the SVM classifier.

5.1 Model Learning and Analysis

We look into some intermediate aspects for a deep insight of the recommendation model structure and learning process. In Figure 7, we present the accuracy of predicted beauty-related attributes from the SVM classifier, which is used to build the FA potential function in the energy function to model the recommendation distribution (see Eqn. (2)). Note that we do not present the accuracy of beauty attributes, for we cannot obtain the ground truth label in this stage. It can be seen that most classifiers have the accuracies of more than 70%. It is sufficient to provide enough information to predict beauty attributes. Clothing-related attributes have the accuracy of 40% $\sim$ 50%, which is a little bit low. This is mainly caused by the large number of categories of clothing-related attributes.

We also visualize one example of the learned tree structure in the recommendation model in Figure 8. This tree structure is of order 4 and each super-vertex can only include two attributes at most (see Alg. 1). The weight of super-edge represents the mutual information between two related super-vertexes. From the results, we make some observation. Firstly, meaningful relationships are learned as shown in the tree structure. The super-edges between super-vertex "hair shape, hair length" and other 5 super-vertex are retained, while the super-vertex "eye corner" only remains one super-edge with other super-vertex. It means "hair shape, hair length" is more important and has broader relationship with other nodes than "eye corner" in this structure. Secondly, some highly correlated attributes are clustered into one super-vertex, such as "hair shape" with "hair length" and "eye shadow template" with "face shape". It well fit to the intuitive perception of humans. Long hair may match well with curled hair, and certain shape of eye shadow template may also fit to some face shapes. Thirdly, the correlation between super-vertexs is represented on the super-edges. The super-vertex "eye shadow template, eye shape" has the weight 0.5606 with 'eye shadow color, face shape", which is higher than the weight 0.0501 with "eye corner". It means "eye shadow template, eye shape" has stronger correlation with "eye shadow color, face shape".

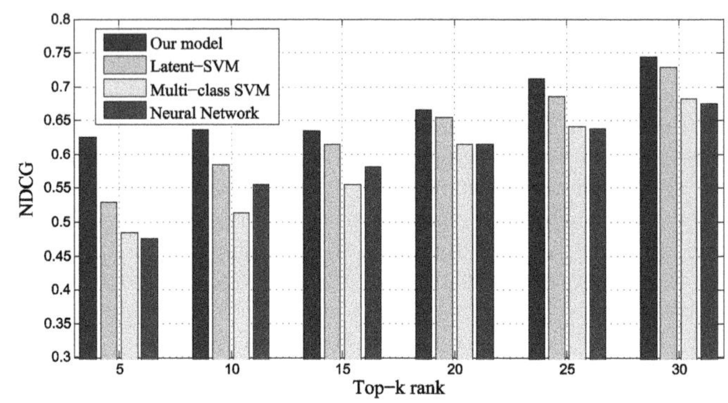

Figure 9: NDCG values of multiple tree-structured super-graphs model and three baselines. The horizontal axis is the rank of top-k results, while the vertical axis is the corresponding NDCG value. Our proposed method achieve better performance than the latent SVM model and other baselines.

5.2 Recommendation Results Evaluation

For the recommendation model in the Beauty e-Experts system, we also implement some alternatives using multi-class SVM, neutral network, and latent SVM. The first two baselines only use the low-level image features to train classifiers for high-level beauty attributes. The latent SVM baseline considers not only the low-level image features but also the pair-wise correlations between the beauty and the beauty-related attributes. We use the 100 testing images to evaluate the performance of the three baseline methods and our algorithm. To evaluate the recommendation result of the Beauty e-Experts system quantitatively, the human perception of suitable beauty makeups is considered as the ground truth measured on 50 random combinations of the attributes for all the 100 testing images. We asked 20 participants (staffs and students in our group) to label the ground truth of ranking results of the 50 types beauty makeup effects for each testing image. Instead of labeling absolute ranks from 1 to 50, we use a k-wise strategy similar to [23]: labelers are shown k images as a group each time, where k is set to 10. They only need to rank satisfying levels within each group. $C(k, 2)$ pairwise preferences can be obtained from the k ranks, and then the final rank is calculated across groups by ranking SVM [19].

In Figure 9, we plot the comparison results of our model and other baselines. The performance is measured by Normalized Discounted Cumulative Gain (NDCG) [13], which is widely used to evaluate ranking systems. From the results, we can observe that our model and latent SVM significantly

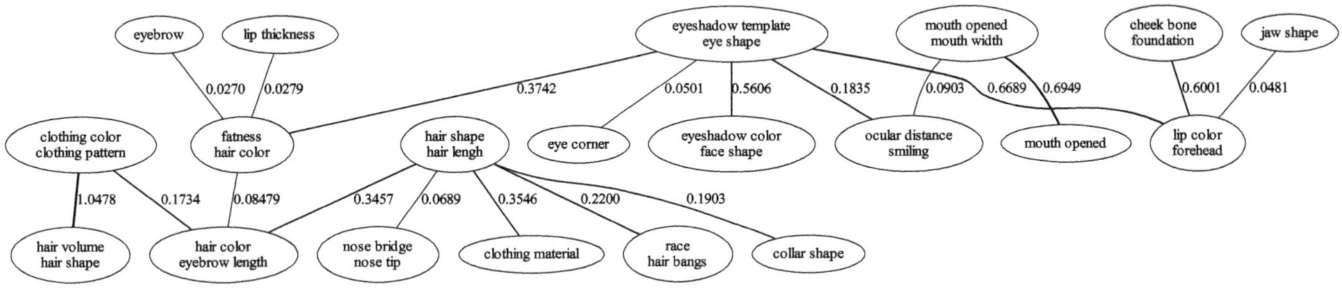

Figure 8: Visualization of one learned tree-structured super-graphs model.

outperform multi-class SVM and neural network. This is mainly because that our model and the latent SVM method are equipped with mid-level beauty-related attributes to narrow the semantic gap between low-level image features and the high-level beauty attributes. These two models are both able to characterize the co-occurrence information to mine the pairwise correlations between every two factors. From Figure 9 we can further find that our model has overall better performance than the latent SVM method, especially in the top 15 recommendations. With higher order relationships embedded, our model can express more complex relationship among different attributes. What is more, by employing multiple tree-structured super-graphs, our model tend to obtain more robust recommendation results.

5.3 Synthesis Results Evaluation

We compare our Beauty e-Experts system with some commercial virtual hairstyle and makeup systems, including Virtual Hairstyle (VH)[6], Instant Hair Makeover (IHM)[7], Daily Makeover (DM)[8], Virtual Makeup Tool (VMT)[9], and the virtual try-on website TAAZ[10]. They are all very popular in female customers on the Internet.

Table 3: Comparisons of several popular hairstyle and makeup synthesis systems.

	VH	IHM	DM	VMT	TAAZ	Ours
hairstyle	✓	✓	✓	×	✓	✓
makeup	×	✓	✓	✓	✓	✓
face detection	×	✓	✓	×	✓	✓
easy of use	×	×	✓	×	×	✓
500+ templates	×	×	×	×	✓	✓
composition freedom	×	✓	×	✓	✓	✓
recommendation	×	×	×	×	×	✓

We first compare these systems in an overview manner, which means that we focus on the comparison of the main functionalities among these systems. The comparison results are summarized in Table 3. It can be seen that IHM, DM and TAAZ systems can provide both hairstyle and makeup synthesis functions. They also provide face detection, which can largely reduce the manual workload. IHM, VMT and TAAZ ask users to choose makeup and hair products to perform composition, while VH and DM cannot support this, since their methods are mainly based on holistic transformation between the testing face and the example template. However, all these systems cannot support large data set with more than 500 templates and do not provide hairstyle and makeup recommendation functions. In the contrast, our Beauty e-Experts system can support all the functions mentioned above. What is more, it is fully automatic and can work in more general cases. The recommendation function of our system is really useful to help female users choose suitable hairstyle and makeup products.

Figure 10: Contrast results of synthesized effect among websites and our paper.

We then compare the hairstyle and makeup synthesis results with these commercial systems. As shown in Figure 10, the first column is the testing images, and other four columns are the results generated by DM, IHM, TAAZ, and our system, respectively. The reason why we select these three systems is that only these three can synthesize both the hairstyle and makeup effects. The makeup and hairstyle templates used in the synthesis process are selected with some user interactions to ensure that all the four methods share similar makeups and hairstyles. It can be seen that, even after some extra user interactions, the results generated from these three websites have obvious artifacts. The selected hair templates cannot cover the original hair area. IHM even cannot handle the mouth opened cases. We further present several testing faces with different hairstyle and makeup effects in Figure 11. These results still look natural with a variety of style changing, which demonstrates the robustness of our system.

6. CONCLUSIONS AND FUTURE WORK

In this work, we have developed the Beauty e-Experts system for automatic facial hairstyle and makeup recommendation and synthesis. To the best of our knowledge, it is the first study to investigate into a fully automatic hairstyle

[6]http://www.hairstyles.knowage.info
[7]http://www.realbeauty.com/hair/virtual/hairstyles
[8]http://www.dailymakeover.com/games-apps/games
[9]http://www.hairstyles.knowage.info
[10]http://www.taaz.com

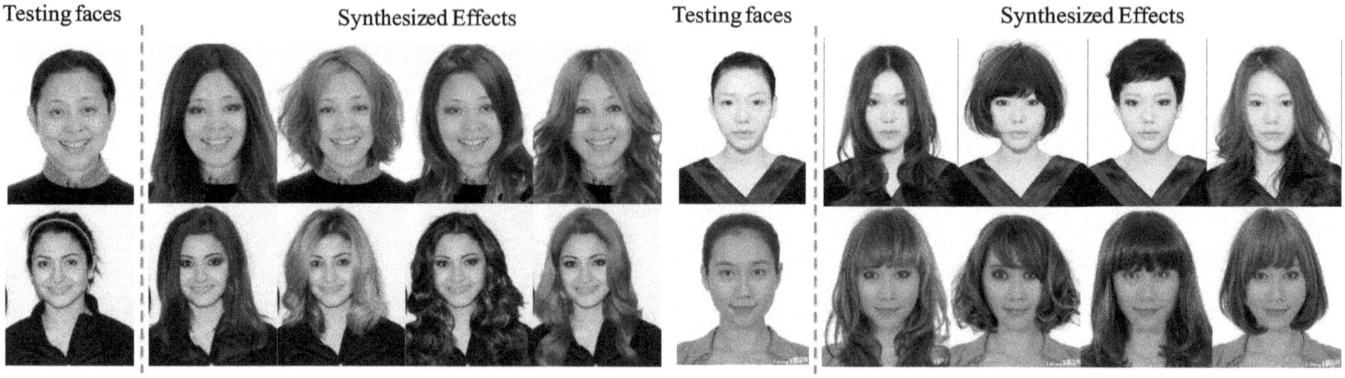

Figure 11: More synthesized results of the proposed Beauty e-Experts system.

and makeup system that simultaneously deals with hairstyle and makeup recommendation and synthesis. Based on the proposed multiple tree-structured super-graphs model, our system can capture the complex relationships among the different attributes, and produce reliable and explainable recommendations results. The synthesis model in our system also produces nature and appealing results. Extensive experiments on a newly built dataset have verified the effectiveness of our recommendation and synthesis models.

Current system is definitely not perfect yet. We are planning to further improve the system in the following directions. First of all, we may further consider to segment the hair region, and fill in the uncovered region with example-based inpainting techniques [9]. Secondly, we may extend current system for male users by constructing another male beauty dataset. At last, we also plan to extend current system to perform occasion-aware and personalized recommendation by introducing more occasion-related attributes [23] and employing information collected from personal photo album in a user's social network.

7. ACKNOWLEDGMENTS

This research is supported by the Singapore National Research Foundation under its International Research Centre @Singapore Funding Initiative and administered by the IDM Programme Office. Also it is partially supported by Singapore Ministry of Education under research Grant MOE2010-T2-1-087 and the "Extreme Facial Analysis" project from Ministry of Home Affairs, Singapore.

8. REFERENCES

[1] T. Ahonen, A. Hadid, and M. Pietikainen. Face description with local binary patterns: application to face recognition. *TPAMI*, 2006.

[2] S. Belongie, J. Malik, and J. Puzicha. Shape matching and object recognition using shape contexts. *TPAMI*, 2002.

[3] F. Bookstein. Principal warps: thin-plate splines and the decomposition of deformations. *TPAMI*, 1989.

[4] Y. Boykov and O. Veksler. Fast approximate energy minimization via graph cuts. *TPAMI*, 2001.

[5] C. Chang and C. Lin. Libsvm: A library for support vector machines. In *TIST*, 2011.

[6] F. Chen and D. Zhang. A benchmark for geometric facial beauty study. In *Int. Conf. Medical Biometrics*, 2010.

[7] C. Chow and C. Liu. Approximating discrete probability distributions with dependence trees. *TIT*, 1968.

[8] T. Cootes, C. Taylor, D. Cooper, and J. Graham. Active shape models-their training and application. *CVIU*, 1995.

[9] A. Criminisi, P. Perez, and K. Toyama. Region filling and object removal by exemplar-based image inpainting. *TIP*, 2004.

[10] N. Dalal and B. Triggs. Histograms of oriented gradients for human detection. In *CVPR*, 2005.

[11] M. de Berg, O. Cheong, M. van Kreveld, and M. Overmars. *Computational Geometry: Algorithms and Applications*. Springer-Verlag, third edition, 2008.

[12] P. Felzenszwalb, R. Girshick, D. McAllester, and D. Ramanan. Object detection with discriminatively trained part-based models. *TPAMI*, 2010.

[13] R. Feris and L. Davis. Image ranking and retrieval based on multi-attribute queries. In *CVPR*, 2011.

[14] A. Goshtasby. Piecewise linear mapping functions for image registration. *PR*, 1986.

[15] D. Guo and T. Sim. Digital face makeup by example. In *CVPR*, 2009.

[16] S. Haykin. *Neural Networks*. Prentice Hall, 1999.

[17] K. He, J. Sun, and X. Tang. Guided image filtering. In *ECCV*, 2010.

[18] G. Huang, M. Ramesh, T. Berg, and E. Learned. Labeled faces in the wild: A database for studying face recognition in unconstrained environments. Technical report, University of Massachusetts, 2007.

[19] T. Joachims. Optimizing search engines using clickthrough data. In *ACM KDD*, 2002.

[20] I. Jolliffe. Principal component analysis. *Encyclopedia of Statistics in Behavioral Science*, 2002.

[21] D. Koller and N. Friedman. *Probabilistic Graphical Models: Principles and Techniques*. MIT Press, 2009.

[22] A. Levin, D. Lischinski, and Y. Weiss. A closed-form solution to natural image matting. *TPAMI*, 2008.

[23] S. Liu, J. Feng, Z. Song, T. Zhang, H. Lu, C. Xu, and S. Yan. "Hi, magic closet, tell me what to wear". In *ACM MM*, 2012.

[24] T. Mensink, J. Verbeek, and G. Csurka. Tree-structured crf models for interactive image labeling. *TPAMI*, 2013.

[25] Y. Nagai, K. Ushiro, Y. Matsunami, T. Hashimoto, and Y. Kojima. Hairstyle suggesting system, hairstyle suggesting method, and computer program product. US Patent US20050251463 A1, 2005.

[26] C. Rother, V. Kolmogorov, and A. Blake. Grabcut: Interactive foreground extraction using iterated graph cuts. *TOG*, 2004.

[27] K. Scherbaum, T. Ritschel, M. Hullin, T. Thormählen, V. Blanz, and H. Seidel. Computer-suggested facial makeup. *CGF*, 2011.

[28] W. Tong, C. Tang, M. Brown, and Y. Xu. Example-based cosmetic transfer. In *FG*, 2007.

[29] N. Wang, H. Ai, and F. Tang. What are good parts for hair shape modeling? In *CVPR*, 2012.

[30] Y. Wang and G. Mori. A discriminative latent model of object classes and attributes. In *ECCV*, 2010.

[31] Y. Yang and D. Ramanan. Articulated pose estimation with flexible mixtures-of-parts. In *CVPR*, 2011.

GIANT: Geo-Informative Attributes for locatioN recogniTion and exploration

Quan Fang[1,2], Jitao Sang[1,2], Changsheng Xu[1,2]

[1]National Lab of Pattern Recognition, Institute of Automation, CAS, Beijing 100190, China

[2]China-Singapore Institute of Digital Media, Singapore, 139951, Singapore

{qfang, jtsang, csxu}@nlpr.ia.ac.cn

ABSTRACT

This paper considers the problem of automatically discovering geo-informative attributes for location recognition and exploration. The attribute is expected to be both discriminative and representative, which corresponds to a distinctive visual pattern and associates with semantic interpretation. For solution, we analyze the attribute at region level. Each segmented region in the training set is assigned a binary latent variable indicating its discriminative capability. A latent learning framework is proposed for discriminative region detection and geo-informative attribute discovery. Moreover, we use user-generated content to obtain the semantic interpretation for the discovered visual attribute. The proposed approach are evaluated on one challenging dataset including GoogleStreetView and Flickr photos. Experimental results show that: (1) geo-informative attributes are discriminative and useful for location recognition; (2) the discovered semantic interpretation is meaningful and can be exploited for further explorations.

Categories and Subject Descriptors

H.3.1 [**Information Storage and Retrieval**]: Content Analysis and Indexing; H.4.m [**Information Systems**]: Miscellaneous

General Terms

Algorithms, Experimentation, Performance

Keywords

Geo-informative Attributes, Location Recognition, Latent model

1. INTRODUCTION

The emergence of georeferenced media, e.g., geotagged photos, has opened up possibilities to extensive location related applications, including media organization [4], tourist assistant [14], location-based service [35], even law enforcement [12]. However, the fact that most media content has no available geographical information calls for the solution for location recognition.

MM'13, October 21–25, 2013, Barcelona, Spain.

Copyright 2013 ACM 978-1-4503-2404-5/13/10 ...$15.00.

http://dx.doi.org/10.1145/2502081.2502088.

Figure 1: Test question: Where were these photos taken and what's the informative cues that help you to judge?

Location recognition is different from general object recognition problems: while we can easily describe a class of car, scene or landmark, it is very difficult to exactly define a location due to its high diversity and large intra-class variance. The methods of existing work on location recognition fall into two categories: data-driven or instance-based methods [25, 15, 11, 18], and model-based methods [1, 17, 4, 18]. Data-driven methods turn to retrieve the most visually similar photos in the geo-tagged database. Although simple and effective, these methods suffer from huge storage cost and limited scalability as the available geo-tagged photos cannot provide a sufficient sampling of the location. Model-based methods build classifiers (e.g., SVM) or inference models (e.g., HMM) to learn the intrinsic geographical patterns for recognition. Compared with data-driven methods, model-based methods show better generalization capability. However, they suffer from two problems: First, they needs a well-built training dataset that contains comprehensive geographical information for each location. Second, we only get access to the final classification score and cannot recognize the geographical patterns that yields this score and interpret why these patterns are helpful for distinguishing this location. Therefore, it is desiring to discover and summarize the geographical patterns inside a location, which can largely alleviate the limitations of data-driven and model-based methods.

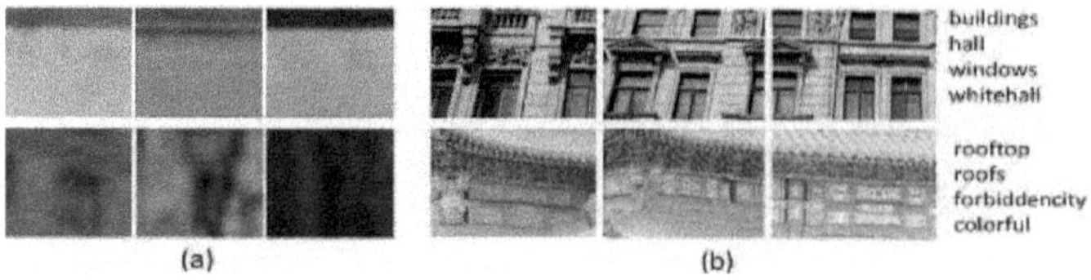

Figure 2: (a) visual words (clustered using SIFT). (b) geo-informative attributes with semantic interpretation.

It is well recognized that photos from one location share some distinctive patterns to contribute to location recognition. Look at the two groups of photos taken at London and Beijing in Figure 1, can you tell which is which? It is quite easy to make the right judgement. According to a survey recently released in [6], people are sensitive to a few localized, distinctive patterns for this location recognition task, e.g., windows with railing and the stylistic balcony are very indicative of London. In this work, we aim to discover these distinctive patterns at city scale, which we call **geo-informative attributes**, to serve as mid-level signatures for location recognition. Moreover, combined with user-generated annotations, we propose to attach semantic interpretations to the discovered visual attributes, which can significantly extend the application scope. Therefore, the geo-informative attributes we desire need to satisfy two properties: 1) *discriminative*, they occur much more frequently in this location than in others, and 2) *representative*, they are occur frequently in this location and semantically interpretable.

A common method for *discriminative* recognition problem is to conduct unsupervised learning over clustered visual words [26]. However, as shown on the left of Figure 2, the extracted visual words tend to be dominated by low-level features, e.g., small-scale textures like edge and corner, which capture little semantic meaning to satisfy the *representative* property. Inspired by recent region-based reconfigurable models utilized in scene and object recognition [29, 23], we consider discovering the discriminative and representative patterns at region level and define geo-informative attribute as a cluster of discovered regions. Shown on the right of Fig. 2, the discovered region cluster-based attributes show larger visual structures and capture interpretable semantics.

Specifically, the proposed framework includes two stages: geo-informative attribute discovery and geo-informative attribute interpretation. (1) For geo-informative attribute discovery, discriminative analysis is first conducted at photo level, where non-discriminative photos are filtered so that candidate region number can be significantly reduced. After that, we propose a region-based latent Support Vector Machine model (RLSVM) to detect the discriminative regions. Candidate regions are generated by hierarchically segmenting the remained photos and assigned with a binary latent variable that indicates whether the region contributes to recognizing this location. RLSVM scores photos considering all region latent variables and infers the configuration that best matches the location label. Regions activated in the derived configuration are considered discriminative. For each location, the geo-informative attributes are obtained by clustering the detected discriminative regions. (2) For geo-informative attribute interpretation, the associated user tags in Flickr are utilized and we present a novel learning algorithm in a discriminative manner. We first learn a bundle of discriminative SVM classifiers to measure the relatedness between tags and photo regions. Then these classifiers are used to score the attribute set and generate its corresponding interpretation by a compact set of semantic tags.

Location recognition can be performed directly using the proposed RLSVM model to simultaneously infer discriminative regions and estimate location label, or using the discovered attributes to constitute a geographical vocabulary, where any supervised methods can be combined. Moreover, the associated semantics enable interpretation of recognized results and provide potentials to high-level location exploration applications. Therefore, the contributions of this work is summarized as follows:

1. We propose to exploit geo-informative attributes for location recognition. The *representative* property is highlighted to make the discovered attribute interpretable and semantically meaningful.

2. We introduce a region-based latent SVM model to discover geo-informative attributes. For attribute interpretation, an iterative learning algorithm is introduced to exploit the region-tag correlation.

3. A real-world dataset from GoogleStreetView[1] and Flickr[2] is constructed for evaluation, where we validate that the discovered attributes are both discriminative and representative.

2. RELATED WORK

With the explosive growth of geo-referenced data, geographic referencing of photographs is an emerging research topic in computer vision [33, 20]. Related work includes data-driven geographical location estimation at city-scale or global scale [25, 15, 1, 4, 17], image-based localization [31, 19], landmark classification, recognition, and search [32, 2, 18, 28, 16, 3], geographical mining of photographs [6]. Estimating the geographical information directly from image visual content is a challenging problem. Generally, there are two types of methods for image based location recognition: data-driven method and model-based method. Data-driven method determines the geographical location of the input photo by retrieving the nearest neighbors from a pre-built database. This database can be constructed with tree-based structure [25] or a 3D model [28, 19] to preserve retrieval efficiency. Model-based method attempts to build models to extract the geographical patterns for location recognition, but such geographical patterns are not explicitly mined and explained. Our work aims to mine such geographical patterns through model learning. The mined patterns can be used for location recognition. On the one side, we propose a region based latent SVM model to mine the geographical patterns and estimate the geographical information simultaneously. This step is model-based. On the other side, a geo-informative attribute vocabulary can be constructed with the mined attributes. The constructed vocabulary can be further used to obtain the image representation of a

[1] http://www.google.com/streetview.
[2] http://www.flickr.com.

test sample. Combined with simply classifiers, we can estimate geographical location of the test sample. This step is instance-based. Therefore, the model framework in this paper can be treated as a combination of the data driven method and model-based method.

Our work is much inspired by the recent work [6], in that we are both devoted to exploring the discriminative visual attributes inside a city. However, we have significant differences in three-fold. (1) Motivation. We aim to discover the geographically informative visual elements directly towards location recognition, i.e., from geographical location estimation perspective; while [6] attempts to find a set of stylistic of visual elements to characterize a city such as windows, street signs, etc. (2) Methodology. [6] independently mines the visual elements starting with a number of seeds. The whole process is at patch-level, and the relations between patches inside a photo are ignored. We take into consideration the relations among the regions at the photo-level. To this end, we develop the Region based Latent SVM (RLSVM) model, where the geo-informative properties of regions are viewed as latent variables and the co-exist relations among patches inside a photo are considered. We examine the performance of the derived visual elements in [6] on location recognition and performance comparison in the experiments, where our proposed approach significantly outperforms the results in [6]. (3) Definition. We define the geo-informative attributes as both discriminative and representative. In addition to the mined geo-informative patches, we exploit the available associated text metadata to make the geo-informative attribute semantically meaningful, which satisfies the definition of attribute.

Our work also relates to the study of visual attributes. Visual attributes for classification and recognition have attracted extensive research interests in these years. Attribute-based representation for objects and scenes [9, 22, 24] can significantly enhance descriptive power and thus boost the task-dependent performance such as object recognition [7]. In our work, we focus on the geographical informative attributes, which are both machine-detectable and semantically meaningful.

3. GEO-INFORMATIVE ATTRIBUTE DISCOVERY

Our task is to discover discriminative and representative attributes that are characteristic of a location. Specifically, we aim to find region clusters that occur much more frequently within the given location than others. To this end, we divide the solution into three steps: (1) Non-discriminative photo filtering. We filter out the photos that frequently exist in all locations and reduce the candidate region number. (2) Discriminative region selection. This is the key step in the proposed framework. Each region is assigned a binary latent variable to indicate its discriminative capability, which is inferred by a specially designed latent model. (3) Geo-informative attribute generation. For each location, geo-informative attributes are obtained by visually clustering the detected discriminative regions. Location recognition can be easily performed by training a multi-class classifier over the attribute-constructed vocabulary.

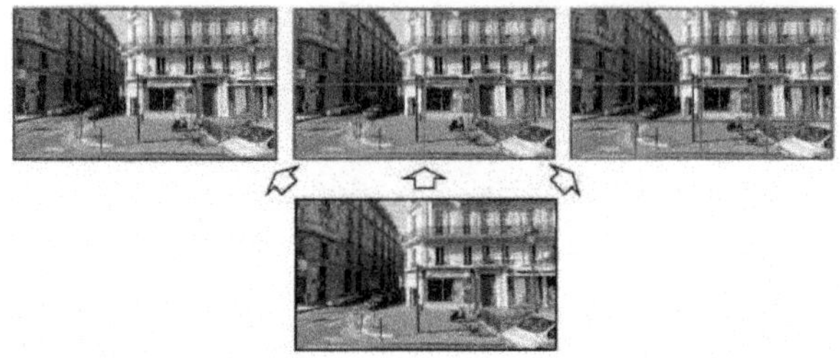

Figure 3: Region generation by hierarchically segmentation.

3.1 Non-discriminative Photo Filtering

Since we are interested in location recognition, the photos that occur in both the positive and negative sets, e.g., photos of trees, sky, cars, contain rare discriminative regions and can be removed before region-level analysis. Actually in later region selection step, one single photo can generate considerable number of regions via grid segmentation at multiple scales and the candidate region number is extremely large.

We take a simply yet effective method to filter the non-discriminative photos. For each location, its corresponding photos are treated as positive set, and the photos from other location form the negative set. Each image is extracted and represented as 809 dimensional feature vector including 81-dimensional color moment, 37-dimensional edge histogram, 120-dimensional wavelet texture feature, 59-dimensional LBP feature and 512-dimensional GIST feature. We compute the 50 nearest neighbors of each photo in a location, and reject samples with less than 15 neighbors in the positive set. By non-discriminative photo filtering, we succeed to reduce the candidate region set by 70.6% without sacrificing the recognition performance.

3.2 Discriminative Region Selection

After removing non-discriminative photos, the candidate regions are generated by segmenting the preserved photos using rectangular grids with 3-level spatial pyramids[3] (shown in Figure 3). As mentioned in the introduction, region-level patches can show larger visual structure and capture interpretable semantics. Assuming that each photo in the training set has been weakly labeled by its location, we encode training photo regions' discriminative capability as binary latent variables which are incorporated into the proposed RLSVM model for inference.

3.2.1 Region-based Latent SVM

Latent SVM [10] provides a framework where we can treat the desired state value as latent variables and consider different correlations into potential functions in a discriminative manner. In our work, the desired state is the discriminative capability of each region. Three types of potential functions are specially designed to encode the region-level latent variables into a unified learning framework. We propose the RLSVM model to search for the best configurations of laten-

[3] The reason we use this simple segmentation strategy is to reduce computational complexity for region selection. Validated from experimental evaluation, this strategy is both efficient and effective. Sophisticated segmentation algorithms can be considered to obtain better semantically meaningful regions.

t variables for each region, which is then used for attribute generation.

Formally, each training photo $\mathcal{I}$ is denoted as a tuple $(\mathbf{x}, l)$. Here $l \in \mathcal{K} \triangleq \{1, 2, \cdots, K\}$ is the location label. We focus on the city-scale location recognition in this paper. l refers to a city. Each photo consists of a set of overlapping multi-scale regions, which are denoted as $\{\mathcal{R}_i\}_{i=1}^N$. We use $\mathbf{x} = \{x_1, \cdots, x_N\}$ to indicate their corresponding visual feature vectors. For each region, the discriminative capability is encoded in a latent variable $z_i \in \mathcal{Z} \triangleq \{0, 1\}$, where $z_i = 1$ means the i-th region is discriminative and should be activated for location recognition, and $z_i = 0$ otherwise. Therefore, $\mathbf{z} = \{z_1, \cdots, z_N\}$ specify the discriminative regions within each training photo. In the following we will introduce how to incorporate $\mathbf{z}$ into the proposed RLSVM model and how to infer it along with model parameter learning.

We are interested in learning a discriminative function $f_{\mathbf{w}} : \mathcal{X} \times \mathcal{L} \rightarrow \mathbb{R}$ over a photo $\mathbf{x}$ and its location label l, where $\mathbf{w}$ are the model parameters. We use $f_w(\mathbf{x}, l)$ to measure the compatibility among the visual feature $\mathbf{x}$, the location label l, and the configurations of latent variables $\mathbf{z}$. $f_w(\mathbf{x}, l)$ takes the form of $f_w(\mathbf{x}, l) = \max_{\mathbf{a}} \mathbf{w}^T \mathbf{\Phi}(\mathbf{x}, \mathbf{z}, l)$ to score the confidence of photo $\mathbf{x}$ labeled as location l with the latent variable configuration $\mathbf{z}$, which is defined by combining different potential functions:

$$\begin{aligned} \mathbf{w}^T \mathbf{\Phi}(\mathbf{x}, \mathbf{z}, l) = & \sum_{i=1}^N \alpha^T \phi(x_i, z_i) + \sum_{i=1}^N \beta^T \varphi(z_i, l) \\ & + \sum_{(i,j)\in\mathcal{E}} \gamma^T \psi(z_i, z_j, x_i, x_j) \end{aligned} \tag{1}$$

In this model, parameter vector $\mathbf{w}$ is simply the concatenation of the parameters in all the factors. $\mathcal{E}$ is the edge set constructed between overlapping regions within each photo. The model presented in the above equation simultaneously considers the following relationships: the first term predicts the latent variable value from visual feature vector, i.e., how likely the region is discriminative; the second term models the compatibility between location label and latent variables; the third term describes the dependencies between latent variables of overlapping regions. Therefore, instead of predicting the location label from visual features directly, we encode discriminative region selection and mine the compatible relationships. The details of the three potential functions are described in the following.

Feature vs. Latent Variable Potential $\alpha^T \phi(x_i, z_i)$: This potential predicts region discriminative capability and contributes to the final confidence score by aggregating the discriminative ones. Here $\phi(x_i, z_i)$ represents a certain mapping of the visual feature x_i and the mapping result depends on the latent variable z_i. Model parameter α encodes the weight for different latent variable values. Specifically, it is parameterized as:

$$\alpha^T \phi(x_i, z_i) = \sum_{b\in\mathcal{Z}} \alpha_b^T \cdot \mathbb{1}(z_i = b) \cdot x_i \tag{2}$$

where $\mathbb{1}()$ is the indicator function.

Latent Variable vs. Label Potential $\beta^T \varphi(z_i, l)$: This potential function models the compatibility of location label l and the latent variable z_i. It is defined as

$$\beta^T \varphi(z_i, l) = \sum_{b\in\mathcal{K}} \sum_{c\in\mathcal{Z}} \beta_{b,c} \cdot \mathbb{1}(l = b) \cdot \mathbb{1}(z_i = c) \tag{3}$$

The parameter $\beta_{b,c}$ measures the compatibility between $l = b$ and $z_i = c$. In other words, how likely the latent variable $z_i = c$ relates to the location label $l = b$. After model learning, we select the latent variable z_l^* for location l as the latent discriminative label according to $\beta_{b,c}$, i.e., $z_l^* = \arg\max_{c\in\mathcal{Z}} \beta_c \cdot \mathbb{1}(z_i = c)$. Regions labeled with latent variable z_l^* are remained as discriminative regions.

Latent Variable vs. Latent Variable Potential $\gamma^T \psi(z_i, z_j, x_i, x_j)$: Since the regions sharing common spatial areas within the same photo should have similar discriminative capability, the latent variables for these regions are dependent. We construct a undirected graph $\mathcal{G} = (\mathcal{V}, \mathcal{E})$ for each photo, where vertex $v_i \in \mathcal{V}$ corresponds to a region $x_i \in \mathbf{x}$, and edge $(v_i, v_j) \in \mathcal{E}$ exists if region x_i and x_j overlap to each other or region x_i and x_j are neighborhoods. The pairwise similarity between overlapping regions is encoded in $p(x_i, x_j) = e^{-\|x_i - x_j\|}$ where $\|\cdot\|$ is the ℓ_2-norm.

This potential function models this pairwise dependence and penalizes similar latent variable values when the regions are dissimilar. Therefore, we define this potential as

$$\begin{aligned} \gamma^T \psi(z_i, z_j, x_i, x_j) = & \sum_{b\in\mathcal{Z}} \sum_{c\in\mathcal{Z}} \gamma_{b,c} \cdot p(x_i, x_j) \\ & \cdot \mathbb{1}(z_i = b) \cdot \mathbb{1}(z_j = c) \end{aligned} \tag{4}$$

where model parameter $\gamma_{b,c}$ captures the compatibility between latent variable configuration $z_i = b$ and $z_j = c$.

3.2.2 Model Learning and Inference

Given a set of M training photos $\langle \mathbf{x}^{(i)}, l^{(i)} \rangle (i = 1, 2, \ldots, M)$, we aim to learn the model parameter $\mathbf{w}$ that produces the correct location label l. Note that the discriminative latent variables are unobserved and will be automatically inferred along with model learning.

We adopt the latent SVM formulation [10, 30] to learn the model as follows:

$$\begin{aligned} & \min_{w,\xi\geq 0} \ \frac{1}{2}\|w\|^2 + C_1 \sum_{i=1}^M \xi_i \\ & \text{s.t.} \max_{\mathbf{z}} \mathbf{w}^T \mathbf{\Phi}(\mathbf{x}^{(i)}, \mathbf{z}, l^{(i)}) - \max_{\mathbf{z}} \mathbf{w}^T \mathbf{\Phi}(\mathbf{x}^{(i)}, \mathbf{z}, l) \\ & \geq \Delta(l, l^{(i)}) - \xi_i, \forall i, \forall l \in \mathcal{L} \end{aligned} \tag{5}$$

where C_1 is the trade-off parameter similar to that in SVMs, ξ_i is the slack variable for the i-th training example to handle soft-margin. Such an objective function requires that the score for ground-truth location label $l^{(i)}$ is much higher than that for other labels. The difference is recorded in a 0-1 loss function $\Delta(l, l^{(i)})$:

$$\Delta_{0/1}(l, l^{(i)}) = \begin{cases} 1 & \text{if } l \neq l^{(i)} \\ 0 & \text{otherwise} \end{cases} \tag{6}$$

The constrained optimization problem in Eq. (5) can be equivalently written as an unconstrained problem:

$$\begin{aligned} & \min_{\mathbf{w}} L(\mathbf{w}) = \frac{1}{2}\|w\|^2 + C_1 \sum_{i=1}^M R_i(\mathbf{w}) \\ & \text{where } R_i(\mathbf{w}) = \max_l \Big(\Delta_{0/1}(l, l^{(i)}) + \max_{\mathbf{z}} \mathbf{w}^T \mathbf{\Phi}(\mathbf{x}^{(i)}, \mathbf{z}, l) \Big) \\ & \quad - \max_{\mathbf{z}} \mathbf{w}^T \mathbf{\Phi}(\mathbf{x}^{(i)}, \mathbf{z}, l^{(i)}) \end{aligned} \tag{7}$$

We use the non-convex bundle optimization in [5] to solve Eq. (7). In a nutshell, the algorithm iteratively builds an increasingly accurate piecewise quadratic approximation of $L(\mathbf{w})$ based on its sub-gradient $\partial_{\mathbf{w}} L(\mathbf{w})$. The key issue is to compute the subgradients $\partial_{\mathbf{w}} L(\mathbf{w})$. We define:

$$\begin{aligned}
\mathbf{z}^{(i)^*} &= \arg\max_{\mathbf{z}} \mathbf{w}^T \mathbf{\Phi}(\mathbf{x}^{(i)}, \mathbf{z}, l), \forall i, \forall l \in \mathcal{L}, \\
\mathbf{z}^{(i)} &= \arg\max_{\mathbf{z}} \mathbf{w}^T \mathbf{\Phi}(\mathbf{x}^{(i)}, \mathbf{z}, l^{(i)}), \forall i \\
l^{(i)^*} &= \arg\max_{l} (\Delta_{0/1}(l, l^{(i)}) + \max_{\mathbf{z}} \mathbf{w}^T \mathbf{\Phi}(\mathbf{x}^{(i)}, \mathbf{z}, l))
\end{aligned} \tag{8}$$

where $\partial_{\mathbf{w}} L(\mathbf{w})$ can be further computed as:

$$\begin{aligned}
\partial_{\mathbf{w}} L(\mathbf{w}) =& \mathbf{w} + C_1 \sum_{i=1}^{M} \mathbf{\Phi}(\mathbf{x}^{(i)}, \mathbf{z}^{(i)^*}, l^{(i)^*}) \\
& - C_1 \sum_{i=1}^{M} \mathbf{\Phi}(\mathbf{x}^{(i)}, \mathbf{z}^{(i)}, l^{(i)})
\end{aligned} \tag{9}$$

Using the subgradients $\partial_{\mathbf{w}} L(\mathbf{w})$, we can optimize Eq. (5) using the algorithm in [5] and output the optimal model parameter $\mathbf{w}$.

At each optimization iteration, we also need to infer the latent attribute variables $\mathbf{z}$.

$$\mathbf{z}^* = \arg\max_{\mathbf{z}} \mathbf{w}^T \mathbf{\Phi}(\mathbf{x}^{(i)}, \mathbf{z}, l^{(i)}) \tag{10}$$

This is a standard max-inference problem and we use loopy belief propagation [21] to approximately solve it.

Given the learned parameters $\mathbf{w}$, we can directly apply RLSVM model to location recognition for a new photo $\mathbf{x}^t$. The location obtaining the highest score is the recognition result:

$$l^* = \arg\max_{l} \left\{ \max_{\mathbf{z}} \mathbf{w}^T \mathbf{\Phi}(\mathbf{x}^t, \mathbf{z}, l) \right\} \tag{11}$$

3.3 Geo-informative Attribute Generation

Through the RLSVM model learning, we can obtain the geo-discriminative regions for a location. For generating the geo-informative attribute, we apply the meanshift clustering algorithm on the detected regions. The clusters with large size are remained to construct the geo-informative attribute set.

We now describe our approach of *GIANT*: geo-informative attribute based location recognition. Denote the discovered geo-informative set as $\mathcal{A} = \{a_l\}_{l=1}^{K}, a_l = \{\mathbf{x}_i\}_{i=1}^{N_l}$, where $\mathbf{x}_i$ is the feature vector extracted from region i. We construct a geo-informative attribute dictionary $D = \{\mathbf{d}_m\}_{m=1}^{M}$ by sampling feature vectors $\mathbf{x}_i$ from $\mathcal{A}$. For a new photo y, it is hierarchically segmented with multiple regions $Y = \{\mathbf{y}_n\}_{n=1}^{N}$. We use a locality constrained coding method [27] to encode the feature $\mathbf{y}_n$ over the dictionary D. It is computed as:

$$\begin{aligned}
&\min_{S} \sum_{n=1}^{N} \|\mathbf{y}_n - D_n \mathbf{s}_n\|^2 \\
&s.t. \mathbf{1}^T \mathbf{s}_n = 1
\end{aligned} \tag{12}$$

where D_n is local bases formed by simply selecting the K nearest neighbors of $\mathbf{y}_n$ from D. $S = (\mathbf{s}_1, \cdots, \mathbf{s}_n)$ is the set of codes for Y. The final photo representation for y is obtained by performing the max pooling on the codes S. Then discriminative classifiers can be used to conduct the location recognition task.

Algorithm 1 Geo-informative Attribute Interpretation

Input: Image regions $\mathcal{X}$, tag vocabulary $\mathcal{V}_l = \{t_j\}_{j=1}^{T}$, attribute set $a = \{x_u\}_{u=1}^{U}$ in a location.
Output: Attribute set a with semantic tags $\mathcal{R}_T$.

Tag-region Relatedness Learning
for each tag t_j **do**
  $X \Leftarrow$ *region_select* $(\mathcal{X})$
  repeat
    $\{X_c\}_{c=1}^{C} \Leftarrow$ *cluster* (X),
    $\{N_c\}_{c=1}^{C} \Leftarrow$ *rand_sample* $\{\mathcal{X} - X\}$
    $\Psi_c \Leftarrow$ *svm_train* (X_c, N_c)
    $X_{new} \Leftarrow$ *filter* (Ψ_c, X)
    $X \Leftarrow X_{new}$
  until achieve convergence or maximum iteration
end for
Attribute Interpretation
score each x_u with all classifiers Ψ
compute tag scores by aggregating region responses
sort the tags according to scores in descending order
select the top n tags as $\mathcal{R}_T$
return $\mathcal{R}_T$

4. GEO-INFORMATIVE ATTRIBUTE INTERPRETATION

After obtaining the geo-informative attribute in a location, we aim to describe these attributes with semantic text for better human understanding. We develop a novel algorithm by exploiting the co-occurrence relationships between photos and the associated tags. We first learn a bundle of discriminative SVM classifiers for each tag to measure the relatedness between the tag and photo regions. These SVM classifiers are then used to score the geo-informative attribute set and obtain the semantic tags $\mathcal{R}_T$. The full approach is summarized in Algorithm 1.

Tag-region Relatedness Learning. Let $\mathcal{V}_l = \{t_j\}_{j=1}^{T}$ be the tag vocabulary constructed from the associated tags with photos in location l. For each tag t_j, we first find the photo regions $X = \{x_i\}_{i=1}^{N}$ which associate with tag t_j. Note that the photo regions inherit the text metadata of the source photo. Since the annotated photos reflect different aspects of tag t_j, there may exist significant visual variations. To address this, we perform meanshift on X to divide into several clusters $\{X_c\}_{c=1}^{C}$. A binary linear SVM classifier is then trained for each cluster X_c, using regions within the cluster as positive samples and the regions randomly sampled from the rest as negative samples. The trained discriminative classifiers are used to prune out the noise samples and outliers in X. The confidence scores indicate the relatedness between the tag t_j and a region x_i. Regions with low confidence scores are filtered out. The filtered set now becomes the new training set and the procedure is repeated until convergence. Finally, we can obtain a bundle of binary SVM classifiers for each tag.

Attribute Interpretation. Now we use the trained SVM classifiers to interpret the geo-informative attributes. For each region x_u in a geo-informative set $a = \{x_u\}_{u=1}^{U}$, we use all the classifiers to score x_u. Since a tag t_j has multiple classifiers, the region x_u can have multiple response scores. We select the maximum score as the relatedness score be-

Figure 4: Example photos in the collected dataset.

Table 1: Statistic of the collected dataset.

Dataset	GoogleStreetView	Flickr
# City	12	7
# Photo per city	nearly 10,000	2,000 ~ 3,000
# Total photo	139,840	13,503

tween x_u and t_j. We then aggregate all the response scores between tags and regions in a. For each tag t_j, the sum of all the corresponding response scores on each region x_u is calculated. We sort the tags and select the top n tags as the semantic interpretation set $\mathcal{R}_T$ for a.

5. EXPERIMENT

5.1 The Dataset

To evaluate the performance of geo-informative attribute discovery and interpretation, we construct a location recognition dataset crawled from GoogleStreetView and Flickr.

GoogleStreetView. Given a geographical location on the map, we collect a dense sampling of panoramas by using the Google Map API [13]. In this work, we select 12 well-known cities: *Barcelona, London, Paris, Chicago, Hongkong, Nyc, Sanfransisco, SaoPaulo, Singapore, Sydney, Taipei* and *Tokyo.* For each panorama, we extract two perspective photos with one on each side of the capturing vehicle. This results in approximately 10,000 photos per city. Shown on the top of Figure 4, the photos mostly relates to building facades and street scenes.

Flickr. We use Flickr API to retrieve photos taken in a city according to the geo-tag information. Textual metadata, e.g., the title, description and tags, associated with the photos are also crawled for attribute interpretation. We downloaded data for 7 cities: *Barcelona, London, Paris, Beijing, Berlin, Cairo* and *Istanbul.* The initially collected datatset is manually filtered to preserve only outdoor photos of buildings, street, etc. The number of photos in the final dataset for each city ranges from 2,000 to 3,000. Example photos from Flickr are shown at the bottom of Figure 4, which focus more on landmarks and show larger variance than the GoogleStreetView dataset.

Statistics for the collected dataset are summarized in Table 1. Since GoogleStreetView and Flickr have different coverage and focus, experiments conducted on both datasets will comprehensively evaluate the scope as well as performance of compared methods.

Figure 5: Discriminative region selection results.

5.2 Geo-informative Attribute Discovery

Implementation Issue. As shown in Figure 3, each photo is hierarchically segmented into 21 regions with different scales. We choose to represent each region by extracting a 809-dimensional feature vector [34], including 81-dimensional color moment, 37-dimensional edge histogram, 120-dimensional wavelet texture feature, 59-dimensional LBP feature and 512-dimensional GIST feature.

Since we conduct geo-informative attribute discovery with the proposed RLSVM model based framework on the whole GoogleStreetView and Flickr city dataset, the computation complexity is a big issue. Although non-discriminative photos are pre-filtered and we employ a simple segmentation strategy to reduce the candidate region number, computation complexity is still very high. Moreover, high intra-class variance makes the model difficult to converge. In our implementation for attribute discovery, divide and conquer strategy is used to deal with these issues. Specifically, we cluster the photos of each location into several subsets, where less intra variance is guaranteed within each subset. The number of clusters in each city dataset depends on the size of corresponding photo data. Each of the derived subset contains nearly 1000 photos. During model learning, each subset is treated as positive set and negative set is constructed by randomly sampling from photos in other locations. The detected discriminative regions in all subsets constitute the final discriminative region set and generate the geo-informative attributes for a location.

Experimental Results: The key step of attribute discovery is discriminative region selection. Each region is assigned a binary latent variable and contributes to attribute generation if its latent variable is inferred as positive. We show examples of discriminative regions in Figure 5. The non-grey-out regions are geo-discriminative regions. We can see that the regions dominated by sky, road and tree are detected as non-discriminative (shown as white masked), leaving the featured regions to construct geo-informative attributes.

In Figure 6, we visualize some of the discovered visual attributes for different cities (each row corresponds to one cluster, i.e., attribute). It is shown that the discovered attributes are geo-informative: (1) *discriminative*, they well distinguish the city from others, e.g., the Mediterranean coastview and Gaudi's modern building of *Barcelona* make it very different from the inland and classical counterparts of *London*; (2)

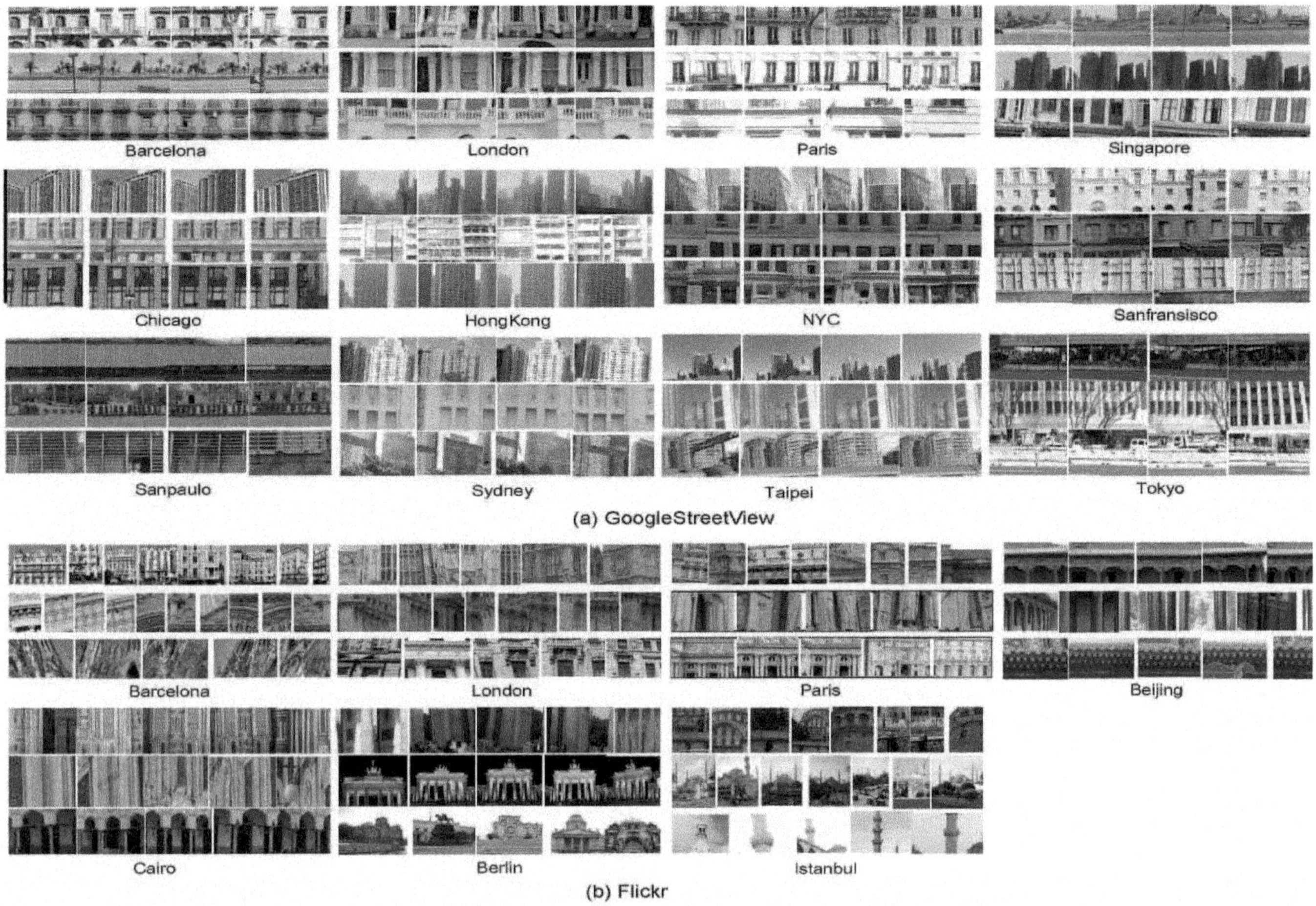

Figure 6: The discovered geo-informative attribute on GoogleStreetView and Flickr dataset.

Table 2: Location recognition mAP results for the examined approaches on GoogleStreetView dataset.

	kNN	LF+SVM	BoVW+SVM	DRLR	RLSVM	GIANT
Barcelona	23.83	10.05	55.31	49.30	53.97	**55.37**
Chicago	44.04	48.33	**52.20**	42.38	31.43	45.24
HongKong	73.05	73.54	39.72	72.57	57.04	**76.94**
London	61.82	50.0	36.19	64.29	78.33	**73.15**
NYC	23.54	34.47	**58.87**	38.11	26.94	44.41
Paris	31.77	61.08	33.98	57.88	59.11	**62.81**
Sanfransisco	34.39	14.99	52.22	42.26	**73.71**	51.1
SaoPaulo	65.61	60.98	47.17	66.10	**77.07**	70.0
Singapore	29.80	29.06	36.70	39.41	**67.49**	59.36
Sydney	50.99	30.45	30.94	**56.93**	56.88	50.74
Taipei	59.5	**71.25**	42.75	48.50	55.0	57.50
Tokyo	17.00	39.75	39.25	43.25	46.0	**49.5**
mean AP	42.95	43.66	43.86	51.75	56.89	**58.01**

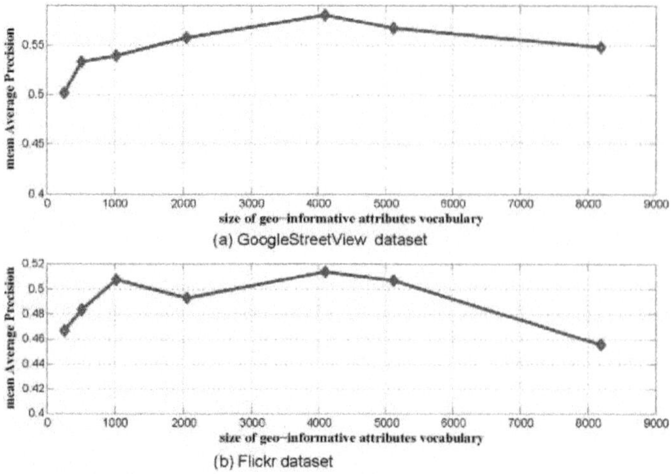

Figure 7: mAP under different sizes of geo-informative vocabulary on GoogleStreetView and Flickr dataset.

representative, they describe featured aspects of the city. We can see that the discovered attributes provide a more intuitive description for the city from GoogleStreetView dataset. Stylistic things such as windows, building facades, and street signs are very indicative of the cities, e.g., *Singapore* with its busy harbor, renowned business district and mixed East-West architectural style. In the Flickr dataset, the detected visual attributes focus on the distinctive features of the city buildings and famous landmarks. For the same city between the two datasets, we can also find some differences among the discovered attributes. For example, the mined attributes for London in GoogleStreetView exhibit streetview styles such as windows and roofs, while in Flickr more visual elements of scenic spots are shown. Similar results can be found in Barcelona and Paris. Different image content of the datasets contributes to this phenomenon. GoogleStreetView dataset contains more streetview scenes while Flickr dataset focuses on scenic spots.

5.3 Geo-informative Attribute for Location Recognition

In this subsection, we quantitatively evaluate the effectiveness of the proposed approach in task of location recognition. Two settings are considered: (1) *RLSVM*, directly using the proposed latent SVM model for location estimation (Eq. (11)); (2) *GIANT*, using the reconstruction coefficients over the discovered geo-informative attribute vocabulary as the feature representation, combining with SVM classifier for training and testing (Eq. (12)). In addition, four other approaches are implemented for comparison:

- *kNN* [15]: A pure data-driven photo matching method;
- *LF+SVM*: Low-level Features [34] combined with SVM;
- *BoVW+SVM*: Bag-of-Visual Word (we use SIFT and LLC [27] in the experiment) combined with SVM;
- *DRLR [6]*: Discriminative Region based Location Recognition, detecting discriminative regions at patch-level using a bottom-up iterative learning algorithm.

To evaluate the performance, we build the evaluation dataset by randomly sampling about 500 random photos for each city in GoogleStreetView and Flickr respectively. This results in 6,111 photos for GoogleStreetView and 3,501 photos for Flickr. In the evaluation, we random sample 100 photos per city for training and the rest for testing both for GoogleStreetView and Flickr.

We tune the parameters of each method to achieve the best performance: k for *kNN* is set to 20, the dictionary size for *BoVW* is set to 4,096, and C_1 in Eq. (5) is set to 100. For the choice of geo-informative attribute dictionary size, Figure 7 shows performance under different size of vocabulary on GoogleStreetView and Flickr dataset respectively. We can see that performance achieves the best on both datasets when the size is 4,096. Therefore, we set the number of discovered geo-informative attributes to 4,096. mAP (mean Average Precision) is ultilized as the evaluation metric, which is averaged over all test cities.

The compared location recognition results are shown in Table 2 and 3. Several observations can be made: (1) Due to the limited sampled data of a location, the performance of data-driven instance-based *kNN* method is inferior and unstable. There exists large variance between different cities and the performance is quite sensitive to the dataset. For example, on the Flickr dataset, kNN outperforms all other methods for Berlin and Istanbul while performs poorly for Barcelona, Beijing and Paris. (2) Large intra-class variance limits the performance of low-level feature based *LV+SVM* and *BoVW+SVM*, especially in the GoogleStreetView dataset. (3) *DRLR* uses similar idea of discovering discriminative region clusters and shows comparable recognition results. The superior performance of DRLR, RLSVM and GIANT validates the advantage of location recognition based on region-level attributes. However, *DRLR* detects discriminative regions independently and ignores relations between regions within the same photo. By explicitly considering pairwise region relations, our proposed *RLSVM* and *GIANT* achieves better results. (4) *GIANT* achieves the best performance among all the examined approaches. This demonstrates that the discovered attributes served as mid-level features are useful for location recognition and thus geo-informative. These results clearly validate the effectiveness of our proposed RLSVM model in discovering geo-informative attributes and location recognition.

5.4 Geo-informative Attribute Interpretation

In Figure 8 and 9, we visualize tag-based interpretation for the discovered attributes in Flickr dataset. Figure 8 illustrates one of the discovered geo-informative attribute with corresponding salient tags for each city. The font size of the tag is proportional to the tag importance. Figure 9 shows the detailed three attribute interpretation results in Berlin and Cairo. Tags are sorted by their importance scores. We can observe that the discovered attributes succeed to describe the visual attributes as well as capturing meaningful semantics. It provides a way for people to better understand the discovered attributes and conduct city exploration. For example, the extracted tags for Cairo describe the city from several aspects: "mosque, mohammed, religion, muslim, ali, tulun" illustrate the social and cultural feature of the attribute; and "architecture, citadelislam" describes its physical architecture property. The derived tags within each attribute interpretation are consistent with each other and well indicate the semantics of corresponding visual content. Moreover, combined with the interpretation, the discovered

Table 3: Location recognition mAP results for the examined approaches on Flickr dataset.

Method	Barcelona	Beijing	Berlin	Cairo	Istanbul	London	Paris	mean AP
kNN	35.5	54.1	**38.5**	44.0	**77.25**	46.75	31.5	46.8
LF+SVM	46.2	61.3	36.0	34.25	62.75	41.5	**53.25**	47.9
BoVW+SVM	42.25	**83.04**	23.5	32.25	71.5	55.5	36.75	49.26
DPLR	51.75	62.34	31.5	43.75	57.00	54.50	35.50	48.05
RBLSVM	42.0	64.59	36.75	43.5	68.75	52.5	37.5	49.37
GIANT	**57.5**	60.6	36.25	**48.25**	58.25	**55.75**	43.0	**51.37**

Figure 8: The discovered attributes with corresponding text interpretations on Flickr dataset.

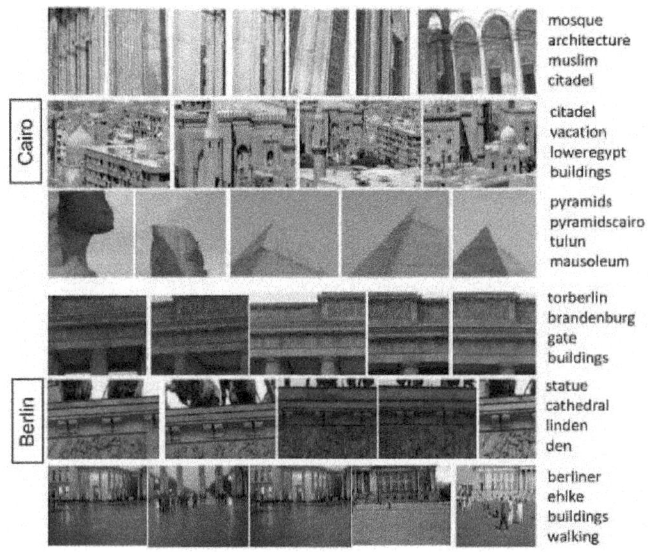

Figure 9: The discovered attributes with semantic interpretation in Berlin and Cairo.

attributes describe distinctive aspects and jointly serve as the semantic as well as visual summary of the location. By further investigation into the results, we can see that due to the inevitable noise in the user-generated tags, some tag descriptions are not very representative. For example, the tags for Beijing provide a rough description and do not precisely match the visual attributes.

Since in our work we focus on city-level geo-informative analysis, the derived interpretation will enable several attribute-based city culture or tourism exploration applications. For example, organizing and classifying cities by their semantic attributes can facilitate city introduction and tourism recommendation; analyzing the attribute distribution inside city provides possibilities to fine-grained city exploration and visualization at POI (Place-Of-Interest) level [8].

Figure 10: Example of failure photos.

5.5 Discussions

Focus and Limit To analyze the limits of our proposed approach, we investigate into the failure cases, which are shown in Figure 10. Can you tell the taken places of these photos? It is not an easy task to recognize the capturing city of the photos even for people who have been there. For the photos dominated by everywhere-seen trees, water, roads and sky, rare discriminative regions exist, which can not be handled by our approach. Actually, in real applications not all photos are expected to be located, e.g., indoor, fractional and non-feature ones. However, discussion about which kind of photo is geographically recognizable and whether it is valuable to estimate geographical information of such photos are beyond the scope of this paper.

In this work, we develop RLSVM-based model framework for geo-informative attributes discovery and location recognition. The RLSVM model can be enhanced by incorporating advanced region relations within or between photos and designing complex segmentation schemes and new potential functions. In the attribute interpretation, we use the user-contributed tags to interpret the discovered visual elements for better human understanding. Actually such sematic tags also contain geographical information and can be exploited for location recognition. For example, the presence of a location name associated with a photo is a good indicator of the belonging location for the test photo. One interesting extension is to combine the geo-informative attribute discovery and attribute interpretation in a unified principled model.

6. CONCLUSION

In this paper, we study the novel problem of discovering geo-informative attributes for location recognition and exploration. We propose the RLSVM model for discriminative attribute detection and the iterative learning algorithm for attribute interpretation. Extensive experiments conducted on the collected GoogleStreetView and Flickr datasets demonstrate that the discovered geo-informative attributes are both *discriminative* and *representative*, which validates the effectiveness of our proposed approach. In the future, we are interested in investigating into the following two directions: (1) Exploiting the mined geo-informative attributes for more location-based applications such as geographical search, visual summarization of a city, and travel recommendation; (2) Developing the nonlinear RLSVM model such as kernel RLSVM for integrating multi-modal information, towards more effective geo-informative attributes mining for location exploration.

7. ACKNOWLEDGEMENTS

This work was supported in part by National Basic Research Program of China (No. 2012CB316304), National Natural Science Foundation of China (No. 61225009), and Beijing Natural Science Foundation (No. 4131004). This work is also supported by the Singapore National Research Foundation under its International Research Centre @ Singapore Funding Initiative and administered by the IDM Programme Office.

8. REFERENCES

[1] C.-Y. Chen and K. Grauman. Clues from the beaten path: Location estimation with bursty sequences of tourist photos. In *CVPR*, pages 1569–1576, 2011.

[2] D. M. Chen, G. Baatz, K. Köser, S. S. Tsai, R. Vedantham, T. Pylvänäinen, K. Roimela, X. Chen, J. Bach, M. Pollefeys, B. Girod, and R. Grzeszczuk. City-scale landmark identification on mobile devices. In *CVPR*, pages 737–744, 2011.

[3] Z. Cheng, J. Ren, J. Shen, and H. Miao. Building a large scale test collection for effective benchmarking of mobile landmark search. In *MMM (2)*, pages 36–46, 2013.

[4] D. J. Crandall, L. Backstrom, D. P. Huttenlocher, and J. M. Kleinberg. Mapping the world's photos. In *WWW*, pages 761–770, 2009.

[5] T. M. T. Do and T. Artières. Large margin training for hidden markov models with partially observed states. In *ICML*, page 34, 2009.

[6] C. Doersch, S. Singh, A. Gupta, J. Sivic, and A. A. Efros. What makes paris look like paris? *ACM Trans. Graph.*, 31(4):101, 2012.

[7] K. Duan, D. Parikh, D. J. Crandall, and K. Grauman. Discovering localized attributes for fine-grained recognition. In *CVPR*, pages 3474–3481, 2012.

[8] Q. Fang, J. Sang, C. Xu, and K. Lu. Paint the city colorfully: Location visualization from multiple themes. In *MMM (1)*, pages 92–105, 2013.

[9] A. Farhadi, I. Endres, D. Hoiem, and D. A. Forsyth. Describing objects by their attributes. In *CVPR*, pages 1778–1785, 2009.

[10] P. F. Felzenszwalb, D. A. McAllester, and D. Ramanan. A discriminatively trained, multiscale, deformable part model. In *CVPR*, 2008.

[11] G. Friedland, J. Choi, and A. Janin. Video2gps: a demo of multimodal location estimation on flickr videos. In *ACM Multimedia*, pages 833–834, 2011.

[12] G. Friedland, O. Vinyals, and T. Darrell. Multimodal location estimation. In *ACM Multimedia*, pages 1245–1252, 2010.

[13] P. Gronat, M. Havlena, J. Sivic, and T. Pajdla. Building Streetview Datasets for Place Recognition and City Reconstruction . Tech. Rep. CTU-CMP-2011-16, Czech Tech Univ, 2011.

[14] Q. Hao, R. Cai, C. Wang, R. Xiao, J.-M. Yang, Y. Pang, and L. Zhang. Equip tourists with knowledge mined from travelogues. In *WWW*, pages 401–410, 2010.

[15] J. Hays and A. A. Efros. Im2gps: estimating geographic information from a single image. In *CVPR*, 2008.

[16] R. Ji, L.-Y. Duan, J. Chen, H. Yao, T. Huang, and W. Gao. Learning compact visual descriptor for low bit rate mobile landmark search. In *IJCAI*, pages 2456–2463, 2011.

[17] E. Kalogerakis, O. Vesselova, J. Hays, A. A. Efros, and A. Hertzmann. Image sequence geolocation with human travel priors. In *ICCV*, pages 253–260, 2009.

[18] Y. Li, D. J. Crandall, and D. P. Huttenlocher. Landmark classification in large-scale image collections. In *ICCV*, pages 1957–1964, 2009.

[19] H. Liu, T. Mei, J. Luo, H. Li, and S. Li. Finding perfect rendezvous on the go: accurate mobile visual localization and its applications to routing. In *ACM Multimedia*, pages 9–18, 2012.

[20] J. Luo, D. Joshi, J. Yu, and A. C. Gallagher. Geotagging in multimedia and computer vision - a survey. *Multimedia Tools Appl.*, 51(1):187–211, 2011.

[21] K. P. Murphy, Y. Weiss, and M. I. Jordan. Loopy belief propagation for approximate inference: An empirical study. In *UAI*, pages 467–475, 1999.

[22] D. Parikh and K. Grauman. Relative attributes. In *ICCV*, pages 503–510, 2011.

[23] S. N. Parizi, J. G. Oberlin, and P. F. Felzenszwalb. Reconfigurable models for scene recognition. In *CVPR*, pages 2775–2782, 2012.

[24] G. Patterson and J. Hays. Sun attribute database: Discovering, annotating, and recognizing scene attributes. In *CVPR*, pages 2751–2758, 2012.

[25] G. Schindler, M. Brown, and R. Szeliski. City-scale location recognition. In *CVPR*, 2007.

[26] J. van Gemert, C. J. Veenman, A. W. M. Smeulders, and J.-M. Geusebroek. Visual word ambiguity. *IEEE Trans. Pattern Anal. Mach. Intell.*, 32(7):1271–1283, 2010.

[27] J. Wang, J. Yang, K. Yu, F. Lv, T. S. Huang, and Y. Gong. Locality-constrained linear coding for image classification. In *CVPR*, pages 3360–3367, 2010.

[28] X. Xiao, C. Xu, J. Wang, and M. Xu. Enhanced 3-d modeling for landmark image classification. *IEEE Transactions on Multimedia*, 14(4):1246–1258, 2012.

[29] O. Yakhnenko, J. Verbeek, and C. Schmid. Region-Based Image Classification with a Latent SVM Model. Rapport de recherche RR-7665, INRIA, July 2011.

[30] C.-N. J. Yu and T. Joachims. Learning structural svms with latent variables. In *ICML*, page 147, 2009.

[31] F. X. Yu, R. Ji, and S.-F. Chang. Active query sensing for mobile location search. In *ACM Multimedia*, pages 3–12, 2011.

[32] Y. Zheng, M. Zhao, Y. Song, H. Adam, U. Buddemeier, A. Bissacco, F. Brucher, T.-S. Chua, and H. Neven. Tour the world: Building a web-scale landmark recognition engine. In *CVPR*, pages 1085–1092, 2009.

[33] Y.-T. Zheng, Z.-J. Zha, and T.-S. Chua. Research and applications on georeferenced multimedia: a survey. *Multimedia Tools Appl.*, 51(1):77–98, 2011.

[34] J. Zhu, S. C. H. Hoi, M. R. Lyu, and S. Yan. Near-duplicate keyframe retrieval by nonrigid image matching. In *ACM Multimedia*, pages 41–50, 2008.

[35] J. Zhuang, T. Mei, S. C. H. Hoi, Y.-Q. Xu, and S. Li. When recommendation meets mobile: contextual and personalized recommendation on the go. In *Ubicomp*, pages 153–162, 2011.

Online Human Gesture Recognition from Motion Data Streams

Xin Zhao
School of ITEE, The University of Queensland, Australia
x.zhao@uq.edu.au

Xue Li
School of ITEE, The University of Queensland, Australia
xueli@itee.uq.edu.au

Chaoyi Pang
AEHRC, CSIRO, Australia
Chaoyi.Pang@csiro.au

Xiaofeng Zhu
College of CSIT, Guangxi Normal University, China
zhux@itee.uq.edu.au

Quan Z. Sheng
School of CS, The University of Adelaide, Australia
qsheng@cs.adelaide.edu.au

ABSTRACT

Online human gesture recognition has a wide range of applications in computer vision, especially in human-computer interaction applications. Recent introduction of cost-effective depth cameras brings on a new trend of research on body-movement gesture recognition. However, there are two major challenges: i) how to continuously recognize gestures from unsegmented streams, and ii) how to differentiate different styles of a same gesture from other types of gestures. In this paper, we solve these two problems with a new effective and efficient feature extraction method that uses a dynamic matching approach to construct a feature vector for each frame and improves sensitivity to the features of different gestures and decreases sensitivity to the features of gestures within the same class. Our comprehensive experiments on MSRC-12 Kinect Gesture and MSR-Action3D datasets have demonstrated a superior performance than the stat-of-the-art approaches.

Categories and Subject Descriptors

I.4.8 [**Image Processing and Computer Vision**]: Scene Analysis - *Motion*; I.5.5 [**Pattern Recognition**]: Implementation - *Interactive systems*

Keywords

Gesture Recognition, Feature Extraction, Depth Camera

1. INTRODUCTION

Human body gesture recognition has many valuable applications in computer vision such as human-computer interaction, electronic entertainment, video surveillance, patient monitoring, nursing homes, smart homes etc. The early work done by Johansson [12] suggests that the movement

MM'13, October 21–25, 2013, Barcelona, Spain.
Copyright 2013 ACM 978-1-4503-2404-5/13/10 ...$15.00.
http://dx.doi.org/10.1145/2502081.2502103.

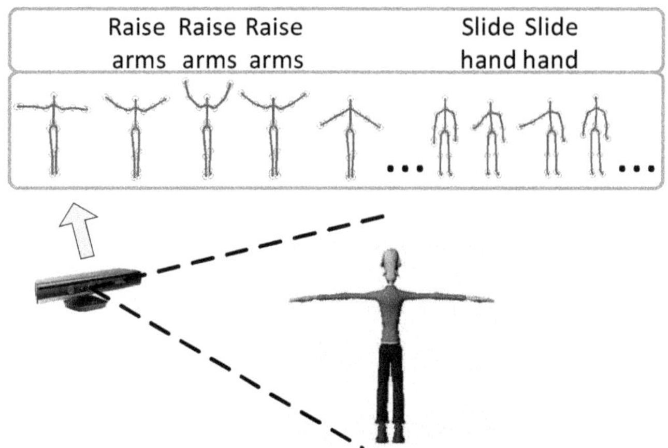

Figure 1: Scenario of online human gesture recognition from motion data stream. Depth camera is used to capture the human skeleton data stream. The gesture labels are assigned automatically to each frame by recognition. The frames without gesture label are considered as not belong to any pre-defined gesture.

of the human skeleton is sufficient to be used for distinguishing different human gestures. The recent introduction of cost-effective depth camera and the related motion capturing technique [27] enables the estimation of 3D joint positions of the human skeleton, which can further generate body motion data. This phenomenon has brought on a new trend of research on body-movement gesture recognition [6, 8, 16, 32].

Similarities exist among three concepts: *gesture*, *action*, and *activity*. The boundaries between them are not very clear. In this paper, we give our definitions based on [1].

- Gestures are elementary movements of human body parts, and are the atomic components used to describe meaningful motions of human body. One example of a gesture could be "stretching arms" or "raising legs".
- Actions are single-person activities that may be composed of multiple gestures organized temporally, such as "walking" and "waving".

- Activities refer to the interactions where two or more persons with/without objects involved.

As atomic components, gestures are less complex than actions. Research on gesture recognition lays foundation for action recognition. In this paper, we do not consider activity recognition, because objects that could be involved in activities may not be represented with the human skeleton. A scenario of online human gesture recognition from motion data stream is illustrated in Figure 1.

Gesture recognition needs to assign labels to gesture instances. Different gesture instances should be assigned with different labels, while the same gesture instances should be assigned with the same label. However, variations may occur to a gesture that has different appearances or different styles. We call this situation as *intra-class variations*. Recently, Veeraraghavan *et al.* [31] considered three sources of intra-class variations which may affect the performance of gesture recognition, namely *viewpoint*, *anthropometry*, and *execution rate*. Viewpoint variation describes the relationship between human body and the viewpoint of a camera. Anthropometry variation is related to the differences between human body sizes, and is about human physical attributes and does not change with human movements. Execution rate variation is related to temporal variability caused by the speed of human movement or by different camera frame-rates. Besides these three variations, we also advocate that the *personal style of gestures* is the fourth notable intra-class variation, which should also be considered, since different people may perform the same gesture differently.

There are two major challenges in dealing with intra-class variations. The first challenge is about how to continuously recognize gestures from unsegmented streams. Currently, most methods choose to segment gesture instances from streaming data before the recognition of gestures [8, 9]. Unfortunately, those methods suffer from the decision on the size of the segment when dealing with streaming data. By using either fixed-size or dynamic size of segments, the segmentation process itself on the streaming data introduces a new avenue of errors due to execution rate variation.

The second challenge is about the ability to differentiate intra-class variations from inter-class variations, because we need to decide whether those differences of gestures are within the same class or are between different classes. Misclassification errors may occur if we do not ignore the differences of intra-class variations or not discern the differences between classes. Online gesture recognition from motion data stream can be regarded as a problem of subsequence matching with multi-dimensional time series, where each dimension represents a specific human-body-part movement. Müller *et al.* and Sakurai *et al.* in [20, 25] proposed approaches to segment motion data stream and recognize gestures by comparing stream data with some pre-learned motion templates. A template in their approaches is at a gesture level. A template is a generic gesture instance used to match with the data stream for a class of gestures. The gesture-level motion template approaches have a major weakness on dealing with intra-class variations. Since the same gesture may have different instances because of intra-class variations, the problem of their approaches is in twofold: firstly, intra-class variations cannot be differentiated if one gesture class is represented by only one single motion template. Secondly, if every variation is to be represented by a different motion template, there must be a large number of motion templates for a single gesture class. In practice this is inefficient for dealing with real-time data streams.

A gesture may involve multiple human body parts. So a gesture is regarded as a combination of movements of human body parts. A movement is regarded as an elementary motion of one part of human body. So the granularity of motion template should be fine-tuned to be at a human-body-part movement level to reduce the redundant representation in the template modulation process. Once motion templates are represented at a human-body-part movement level, different gestures therefore, can be represented by different combinations of motion templates. So the motion templates with fine-tuned granularity can improve the efficiency of the gesture recognition.

Based on the above discussions, we consider to have a novel representation for extracting features of the human skeletons at a human-body-part movement level. This feature should also be able to represent inherent human motion characteristics such that the explicit prior segmentation process would be avoided. We call this new feature as *Structured Streaming Skeletons* (SSS). In this way, the structure of streaming skeletons is represented by a combination of human-body-part movements. So an SSS can be denoted by a vector of cardinal values of attributes that are used to describe the skeleton in a frame. Each attribute in SSS is defined as a similarity distance between the current skeleton stream and a pre-learned movement.

The two challenges involving the four intra-class variation problems mentioned above can then be dealt with by using the proposed new SSS feature as follows.

- **Viewpoint and anthropometry variations.** Motion data is generated as normalized pairwise distances of human body joints. Pairwise joints are regarded as one part of human body in this paper. Then the distances are normalized by the human body size. Therefore, SSS feature is *viewpoint* invariant and *anthropometry* invariant.

- **Execution rate variation.** The execution rate variation problem is solved by using SSS features because at each frame, each attribute is defined as the distance between the best subsequence ending at the current frame and a movement. The best subsequence is the one which is mostly similar to this movement among all subsequences ending at current frame. Different from prior segment approaches [8, 9], the size of segment can be optimized automatically during feature extraction. Therefore SSS feature is *execution rate* invariant.

- **Personal style variation.** To deal with this problem, we use *motion templates* at a granularity of human-body-part movements level. Each motion template is constructed by a human-body-part movement. Different from the approaches treating motion template at a gesture level [20, 25], we treat a template as a single dimension human-body-part movement. Therefore a gesture consists of multiple single-dimensional templates. One advantage is that different personal styles of gestures can be represented by different combinations of human-body-part movements. Therefore, SSS feature can be used to achieve *personal style* invariant.

The rest of this paper is organized as follows. Section 2 gives an overview of the related work. Section 3 describes our approach in details. Section 4 describes the experiments and the evaluations. Finally, the conclusion is given in Section 5.

2. RELATED WORK

Recognition of human gestures, actions, and activities has been extensively surveyed in recent publications [1, 5, 23, 30]. Most existing approaches [10, 14, 33, 35, 37] are about gesture and/or action recognition from color videos based on visual features, rather than the features of motion data that describe human-body-part movements. Because human-body-part movements can lead to better recognition of human gestures as well as actions, some researchers developed approaches to detect human-body-part locations first, then recognize human gestures and/or actions later. In most cases, their considerations are to recognize hand gestures online [2, 28] or recognize pre-segmented gesture instances off-line [29].

In research of online gesture and action recognition from motion data streams, Fothergill *et al.* in [8] adopted fixed-size sliding window and random forest classifiers to achieve online gesture recognition. Unfortunately, their approaches cannot handle execution rate variation and incorrect segmentation problems properly. In addition to fixed-size sliding window techniques, some researchers work on action segmentation from streaming data, then recognize the segmented action instances. Zhou *et al.* in [38] proposed a clustering algorithm to cut stream into action instances. Similarly, Gong *et al.* in [9] proposed an alignment algorithm for action segmentation. However, their approaches are all based on structure similarity between frames and are only suitable for segmenting cyclic actions. Since the structural similarity between frames of non-cyclic gestures are not always obvious, incorrect segmentation errors may occur. Incorrect segmentation will consequently introduce errors in classification process. Schwarz *et al.* in [26] generated the manifold embedding from joint positions of one frame into actions. However, the motion information is not fully considered, which may limit the approach to be scaled to more complex actions.

Template-based methods treat gesture and action recognition as a database query problem which matches data with templates in the database. Veeraraghavan *et al.* in [31] learned an average sequence and related function space of *Dynamic Time Warping* (DTW) [4] to represent each class of action. Müller *et al.* in [20] presented a procedure, where the unknown motion data is segmented and recognized by locally comparing it with available templates. The motion templates just keep the patterns of actions in the same class, with the variations ignored. Ellis *et al.* in [6] explored the trade-off between action recognition accuracy and latency. They determine key frames from motion data sequence to derive action templates. Sakurai *et al.* in [25] proposed an efficient approach to monitor streams, and to detect subsequences that are similar to a given template sequence. However, in these approaches, one action class is represented by only one template, which is insufficient to deal with intra-class variations.

Recently, Wang *et al.* in [32] proposed to learn one subset of human body joints for each action class. The subset joints are representative of one action compared to others. Additionally, they claimed that the relative positions of joints can result in more discriminative features. However, their approach is only applicable to the recognition of pre-segmented instances and cannot be used in online recognition of unsegmented data streams.

Li *et al.* in [7] proposed a *Bag of Visual Words* (BoVW) model, which is used by many researchers for action recognition from color videos, such as [24, 33]. In this paper our proposed SSS feature extraction method is different from (BoVW) model. Our SSS feature extraction method focuses on online gesture recognition from motion data stream. Each attribute of SSS feature vector has specifically defined similarity to a movement and is particularly well-suited for analyzing time-series. BoVW model uses histograms as the features for recognition of gestures. In order to count histograms, frames must be segmented first - this makes BoVW model cannot handle online gesture recognition well. More detailed discussions on the advantages of our SSS feature extraction method are given in next section.

3. PROPOSED APPROACH

Figure 2 shows the framework of our approach, which consists of two main stages: the *learning* and *prediction* stages. The goal of the learning stage is to construct a dictionary of templates and a gesture model. In prediction stage, motion data stream with unknown gestures are assigned with labels to each frame with the help of pre-learned template dictionary and the gesture model. Basically, the learning stage is off-line and prediction stage is online. We briefly describe these two stages as follows.

At learning stage, there are four steps:

1. **Motion data generation.** A training dataset captured by depth camera consists of 3D joint positions of the human skeletons. The training dataset has all gestures manually labelled on all frames. The training dataset is then scanned once. The output of this scanning is the motion data stream. The motion data stream is expressed as sequences of normalized numeric distance values of pairwise joints, which are viewpoint and anthropometry invariant. The motion data stream can be regarded as multi-dimensional time series. Each dimension represents a pair of specific human body joints. The dimensionality of motion data is determined by the number of joints that motion-capture software of depth camera can detect.

2. **Template dictionary learning.** This step is to create a dictionary of templates as a database of subsequences. We manually segment the training stream into gesture instances. Then we apply clustering algorithm to group gesture instances into a dictionary of motion templates represented as a set of subsequences. Here a template is defined as a one-dimensional time series representing distance values of two joints of human body during the time of a gesture instance. For example, in Figure 3, the motion data sequence is one instance of "slide hand" gesture. The normalized distance sequence between the joints of two hands can be a single template. As the consequence of clustering, all templates are elementary in the dictionary. We cluster each dimension of instances separately because they represent movements of different human body

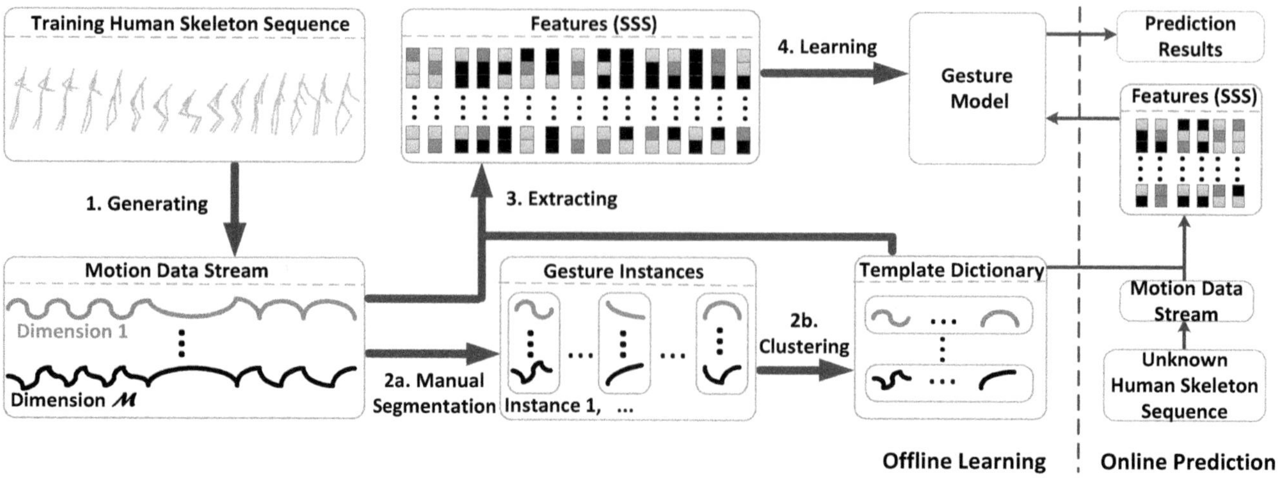

Figure 2: Framework of our approach in both learning stage and prediction stage.

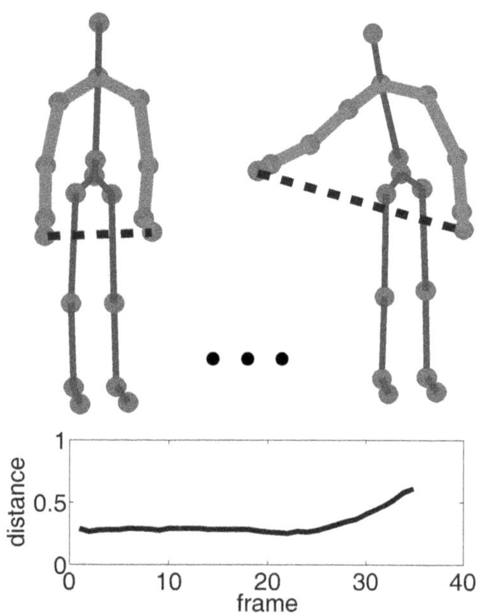

Figure 3: Example of normalized distances. The pairwise joints are "left hand" and "right hand". The upper part illustrates the skeleton sequence of one gesture instance. The lower part shows the normalized distances form a time series.

part. For ordinary human gestures, different human body parts have different movements. For example, the movement patterns of two feet may not be matched with the movements of two hands. So we cluster the movements of each human body part separately, the centroids of small number of clusters are enough to approximately represent all types of movements of this human body part. If we cluster movements of all human body parts together, like BoVW model, the required number of clusters will be very large, which decreases the efficiency of online gesture recognition. So our method has advantages over BoVM model. In our method, a gesture will be represented by a combination of a number of templates in the dictionary. This would increase the possibility to use these elementary templates to compose a large number of gestures and reduce redundancy for storage, therefore improve the efficiency of online processing.

3. **SSS feature extraction.** Based on the first two steps, a dictionary of templates is created. Now the training dataset will be scanned again for SSS feature extraction. The purpose of this step is to convert each frame into one SSS feature vector. Semantically, an SSS feature vector encodes the motion information in so-far scanned frames for the current frame. Here motion information is represented as pre-learned templates. Each SSS feature vector consists of a number of attributes represented as distance values. Each value is a minimum DTW distance between all the scanned subsequences (ending at the current frame) and a template in the dictionary for the given pair of joints. It should be pointed out that a template can only be applied to the dimension it belongs to. For example, if one template is about the joints of two hands, this template can be used to match frame sequences only on the dimension about the joints of two hands. Dimensionality of an SSS feature vector is determined by the number of templates in the dictionary. We use Figure 4 to illustrate details of SSS feature extraction that is also appeared in Figure 2.

   As indicated by Papapetrou *et al.* in [22]: if two sequences are similar to each other, their distances to template sequence are likely to be closer to each other. Similarly, if two sequences are not similar to each other, their distances to template sequence are likely to be farther from each other. Therefore, a distance value in our SSS feature is more meaningful and discriminative than histogram feature in BoVW model. SSS is specifically well-suited to the analysis of time series.

   At the end of this step the labels of gestures originally assigned to the training data frames by human become SSS feature vectors assigned to each frame and ready to be used to learn the gesture model.

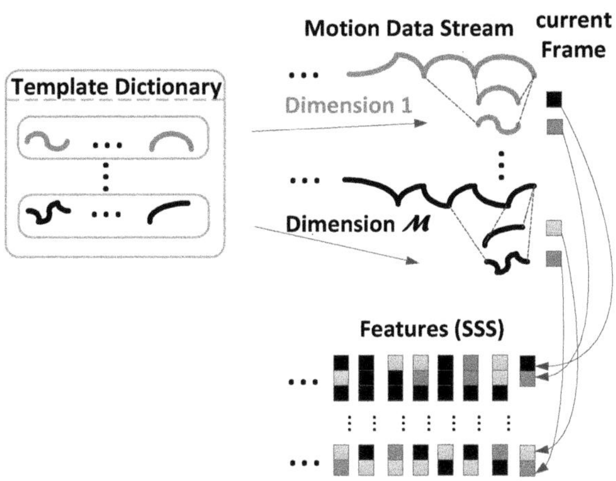

Figure 4: Example of SSS feature extraction.

4. **Gesture model training.** This step is to use a classifier to learn a gesture model from the extracted SSS feature vectors. In order to demonstrate the advantages of our proposed SSS feature extraction method, we use a basic classifier in the gesture model training. We choose a linear regression based classifier namely *Jointly Sparse Coding* [34] in this step. We will show that even using a simple classifier, the performance will be significantly improved compared with the state-of-the-art approaches.

   At the end of this step a gesture model is represented as a transformation matrix ready to be used for the prediction.

At prediction stage as illustrated in Figure 2, there are three steps performed in online prediction. Firstly, the input human skeletons captured from depth camera are translated into motion data stream using the method described in the learning stage. Then, each frame of motion data stream is mapped into an SSS feature vector also using the method described in the learning stage. Finally, at each frame, prediction is performed by a linear regression method that assigns each feature vector with a gesture label based on the learned gesture model.

3.1 Normalized Distances of Pairwise Joints

Certain amount $\mathcal{J}$ of joint positions are estimated by the motion capturing technique from depth videos. Each joint i has 3 coordinates $p_i(t) = (x_i(t), y_i(t), z_i(t))$ at frame t. For each pairwise joints i and j, $1 <= i < j <= \mathcal{J}$, we calculate their normalized distances: $s_{ij} = ||p_i - p_j||_2/path_{ij}$, where $path_{ij}$ is the path between joints i and j in the human skeleton. As shown in the upper part of Figure 3, $\mathcal{J} = 20$ joints are captured with Microsoft Kinect system [27], and $\mathcal{M} = \mathcal{J} \times (\mathcal{J} - 1)/2 = 190$ pairwise joints are generated. We take "left hand" and "right hand" for example. The dotted line is the Euclidean distance between them. The bold lines indicate the path of these two joints in the human skeleton. We can see that s_{ij} has no relationship with the body position, body orientation and body size. *i.e.*, viewpoint and anthropometry invariant.

We treat the normalized distance of one pairwise joints as one dimension of motion data. Along the time axis, the distances form a one-dimensional time series, as shown in the lower part of Figure 3. Therefore, motion data stream is a multiple dimensional time series: $\mathbf{S}(:, t) = \{s_{ij}(t)\}, 1 <= i < j <= \mathcal{J}$.

3.2 Template Dictionary

From training motion data stream $\mathbf{S} = [\mathbf{S}(:, 1), ..., \mathbf{S}(:, \mathcal{N})]$, where $\mathcal{N}$ is the number of frames in motion data stream $\mathbf{S}$, we manually segment all gesture instances and learn a template dictionary $\mathbf{D}$. One template is one dimension time series of one instance. For each dimension of motion data, we cluster these instances into $\mathcal{G}$ clusters. In each cluster, the gesture instance with minimum average distance to others on this dimension is chosen as one template. There are $\mathcal{G} \times \mathcal{M}$ templates in this dictionary. Therefore, template dictionary $\mathbf{D} = \{d_{ij}^g\}$, where i and j indicate the pairwise joints and g indicates the cluster index in this pairwise joints. Spectral clustering algorithm [21], which can be used in non-Euclidean space, is adopted for the clustering. K-means clustering algorithm [11] is not applicable to non-Euclidean space, so it is not suitable here. We also tested other clustering algorithms such as k-medoids clustering [13] and optics clustering [3]. Spectral clustering algorithm is the most robust one. DTW is adopted as the distance measure for time series to eliminate execution rate variation.

3.3 New SSS Feature

For recognition, each frame in $\mathbf{S}$ is required to be represented by an SSS feature vector. We compute the distances between the best fitting subsequences ending at this frame and template dictionary $\mathbf{D}$ as the SSS feature vector.

We use $\mathbf{S}(:, \tilde{t} : t)$ to represent all subsequences ending at frame t. From the dictionary $\mathbf{D}$, each template d_{ij}^g is used to find one best fitting subsequence $\mathbf{S}(:, \hat{t}_{ij}^g : t)$ among $\mathbf{S}(:, \tilde{t} : t)$. The distance between the template and the best fitting subsequence on related dimension is the minimum:

$$x_{ij}^g(t) = |s_{ij}(\hat{t}_{ij}^g : t) - d_{ij}^g| \quad (1)$$

$$\hat{t}_{ij}^g = \arg\min_{\tilde{t}} |s_{ij}(\tilde{t} : t) - d_{ij}^g| \quad (2)$$

Here, DTW is still used as the distance measure between two sequences to eliminate execution rate variation. The stream monitoring technique [25] can be used to detect the optimal starting point $\hat{t}_{ij}^g$.

We further use an SSS feature vector to represent one frame. Each minimum distance x_{ij}^g according to one template d_{ij}^g is one attribute of the SSS feature vector. In this paper, $\mathcal{G} \times \mathcal{M}$ templates in the dictionary $\mathbf{D}$ can generate a vector with $\mathcal{G} \times \mathcal{M}$ dimensions. We treat this vector $\mathbf{X}(:, t) = \{x_{ij}^g(t)\}$ as the SSS feature for frame t. $\mathbf{X} = [\mathbf{X}(:, 1), ..., \mathbf{X}(:, \mathcal{N})]$ is the SSS feature matrix for $\mathbf{S}$.

3.4 Classification

It is insufficient to use only one attribute of the feature to discriminate different gestures. How to learn a combination of these attributes, which is representative of identical gesture and discriminative compared with different gesture. This can be achieved by machine learning techniques. We adopt jointly sparse coding [34], which focus on feature selection and classification, to learn the combination.

Table 1: Notations.

Symbol	Description
$\mathcal{J}$	number of joints
$\mathcal{M}$	number of joint pairs
$\mathcal{N}$	number of frames
$\mathcal{G}$	number of clusters
$\mathbf{S}$	motion data stream
$\mathbf{D}$	template dictionary
$\mathbf{X}$	SSS feature matrix
$\mathbf{W}$	gesture model

Classic least square regression is used to learn a transformation matrix $\hat{\mathbf{W}}$ to transfer features into gesture labels. Furthermore, without reducing the effectiveness, the amount of involved attributes should be as small as possible to improve the efficiency. This can be achieved with $\ell_{2,1}$ norm regularization. In addition, the minimization of $\ell_{2,1}$ norm regularization will enable the algorithm to leverage the shared information across multiple gesture classes [18].

$$\hat{\mathbf{W}} = \underset{\mathbf{W}\in\mathbb{R}^{(\mathcal{G}\times\mathcal{M})\times\mathcal{C}}}{\arg\min} ||\mathbf{W}^{\top}\mathbf{X} - \mathbf{Y}||_F^2 + \lambda||\mathbf{W}||_{2,1} \quad (3)$$

where $\mathcal{C}$ is the number of gesture classes, matrix $\mathbf{Y} = [\mathbf{Y}(:,1), ..., \mathbf{Y}(:,\mathcal{N})]$, $\mathbf{Y}(:,t) \in \mathbb{R}^{\mathcal{C}}$ indicates the multiple labels for frame t in stream $\mathbf{S}$. If $\mathbf{S}(:,t)$ belongs to the cth gesture class, $\mathbf{Y}(c,t) = 1$, $\mathbf{Y}(e,t) = -1$, for $e \neq c$. If $\mathbf{Y}(:,t)$ does not belong to any $\mathcal{C}$ classes of gestures, $\mathbf{Y}(:,t) = -1$, matrix $\hat{\mathbf{W}}$ is the gesture model, with the help of $\ell_{2,1}$ norm regularization, many rows of $\hat{\mathbf{W}}$ are near to 0 [36]. We can prune invalid feature attributes. In this paper, the weight of the mth attribute in feature is measured with $||\hat{\mathbf{W}}(m,:)||_2$ We descendingly sort these weights. The first $\mathcal{K}$ attributes who's weight sum is up to 99% of the total are regarded as valid. Others are set to 0, and related template are noted as invalid templates. Here λ is the parameter to control regularization.

3.5 Prediction

In online prediction stage, given an unknown motion data steam, at frame t, we extract SSS feature $\mathbf{U}(:,t)$ only with the valid templates in dictionary $\mathbf{D}$. The attributes related with invalid templates are set to 0 without computation. If $max(\hat{\mathbf{W}}^{\top}\mathbf{U}(:,t)) \geq \beta$, the row index with maximum value indicates the gesture class, otherwise, this frame does not belong to any $\mathcal{C}$ classes of gestures. Here β is a parameter for leverage precision and recall.

In online prediction stage, at each frame, the time complexity of generating motion data is $O(\mathcal{M})$, the time complexity of extracting SSS feature is $O(\mathcal{M} \times \mathcal{K} \times \mathcal{A})$, where $\mathcal{A}$ is the average length of template sequence, and the time complexity of classification is $O(\mathcal{C} \times \mathcal{K})$.

The notations used in this paper are given in Table 1.

4. EXPERIMENTS

We chose MSRC-12 Kinect Gesture dataset [8] to evaluate our proposed SSS feature for online gesture recognition. To the best of our knowledge, this is the only one public dataset for the research of online human gesture recognition from motion data stream. However, this dataset is very large with more than 700,000 frames available for the ground truth testing. In addition, we also validated our approach in pre-segmented action recognition using MSR-Action3D dataset [15] which is a well-known action recognition dataset for bench-marking with relevant algorithms. However, the data has been pre-segmented for evaluating action instances already. So the advantages of our SSS feature on online prediction cannot be demonstrated. Moreover we can still use this dataset for the demonstration of the advantages of our SSS feature on the lower level granularity of recognition.

4.1 Results on MSRC-12 Kinect Gesture Dataset

MSRC-12 Gesture dataset comprises of 594 sequences, more than 700,000 frames (approximately 6 hours and 40 minutes) collected from 30 people performing 12 classes of gestures. In total, there are 6,244 gesture instances. The ending points of all gesture instances were manually labeled. Twenty human body joints ($\mathcal{J} = 20$) are captured with Microsoft Kinect system. The body poses are captured at a sample rate of 30Hz with an accuracy approximately two centimeters in joint positions. In this dataset, for research various methods of teaching human on how to perform different gestures, the participants were provided with three instruction modalities and their combinations to perform gestures. The three instruction modalities are i) text descriptions, ii) image sequences, and iii) video demos. There are also two combinations of the three modalities, *i.e.*, images with text, and video with text. When participants are given instructions, different modalities of instructions may cause different responses. For example, when instructions are given by videos, the gestures can be performed with an imitated pace from the images of video. This would cause the fixed-size sliding window approach can have less chances of segmentation errors.

For a comparison with the state-of-the-art work in [8], we use the same criteria (F-score) and latency-aware measure as that justified in [8]. Precision measures how often is the gesture actually present when the system predicts it is. Recall measures how many true gestures are recognized by the approach. Latency measures how much time is the delay between the true action starting point and the prediction. Following the experiment setting of [8] , we treat the previous 34 frames and ending point as one gesture instance. Thus, the average length of templates is $\mathcal{A} = 35$ frames. For a specified amount of tolerated latency $\triangle = 10$ frames, a fixed window of size $2\triangle$ is centered around each ending point. All the frames inside the window are given the same gesture label as the ending point, and other frames outside the window are regarded as negative samples. Therefore, the latency is 0.83s-1.5s ((35 ± 10)(frames)/30(Hz)). In this way, we obtain the ground truth label of each frame for evaluation. Each frame is treated as one sample for training and test. A balanced F-score between 0 and 1 combines precision and recall is chosen as the evaluation measure. We measure the intra-modality generalization performance: training and testing using the same instruction modality. For each modality, a "leave-person-out" protocol is used to split dataset into 10 disjoint sets. Here, disjoint is in terms of the person-gesture combination. In each set, we remove a set of persons from full dataset to obtain the minimum set that contains performances of all gestures. Nine sets are used for training, and one set is used for testing. We finally obtain five F-scores, one for each modality. Each F-score is an average over 10 repetitions and 12 gestures.

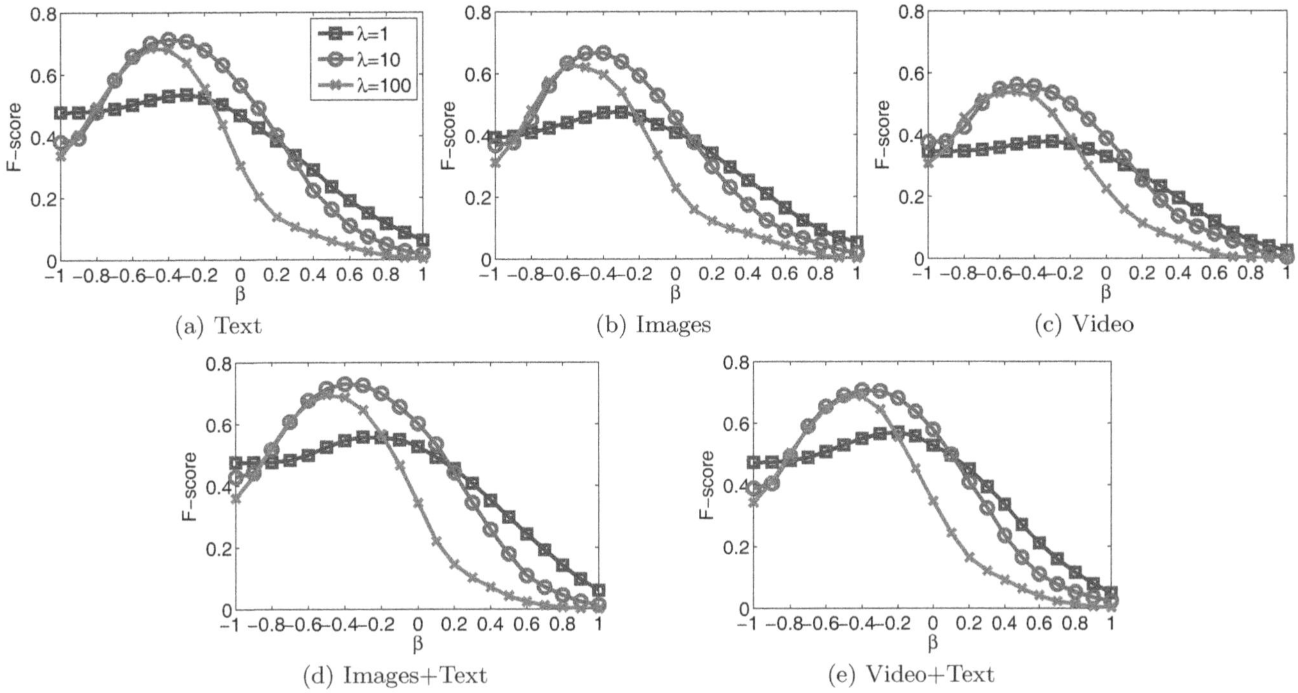

Figure 5: The relationship between recognition performance and parameters λ and β. The optimal parameters are stabilized at $\lambda = 100$ and $-0.5 \leq \beta \leq -0.3$.

Table 2: Comparison on MSRC-12 Gesture dataset on five modalities.

Method	Text	Images	Video	Images+Text	Video+Text
Ours	**0.713 ± 0.191**	**0.666 ± 0.194**	0.557 ± 0.291	**0.730 ± 0.148**	**0.707 ± 0.17**
Baseline [8]	0.479 ± 0.104	0.549 ± 0.102	**0.627 ± 0.053**	0.563 ± 0.045	0.679 ± 0.035

We compare our approach with the state-of-the-art method [8], which adopted fixed size sliding window and random forest classifiers for this dataset. In this dataset, we use fixed values $\lambda = 100$ and $\beta = -0.4$ for evaluation. These parameters are derived from an experiment that is designed to find the optimal parameters. In that experiment, parameter λ was firstly set as $\{10, 100, 1000\}$ and parameter β was set as $\{-1, -0.9, -0.8, ..., 0.8, 0.9, 1\}$. The dataset is also split into 10 disjoint sets (different from the 10 disjoint sets split for the evaluation) for finding the optimal parameters (λ and β). The reason we do not use conventional 10-fold cross validation is that it is very time consuming when dataset is large (with more than 700,000 samples in this dataset), so the parameters can be derived by an experiment. In fact, Fothergill *et al.* in [8] also chose the parameters in this way.

We show the effect caused by the parameter λ and parameter β when number of clusters $\mathcal{G}$ is fixed to 20 (the reason to choose parameter $\mathcal{G}$ as 20 will be discussed in following). The recognition F-scores of all modalities are illustrated in Figure 5. We can see that the optimal values of parameters stabilize at $\lambda = 100$ and $-0.5 \leq \beta \leq -0.3$.

Table 2 shows the comparison results for each modality. We can see that our approach obtains average improvement of F-scores by 10%. There are considerable improvements in "Text", "Images", and "Images+Text" modalities, which are more susceptible to execution rate variation. This demonstrates that our approach can handle incorrect segmentation problems. It worths to note that the instructions given by video modality is impractical in an experiment because the variations of different participants are mostly precluded by the behaviors of participants who are simply imitating the video instructions. In human-computer interaction applications, user should remember instructions by themselves, they have no chance to imitate the gestures by watching video instructions. In this case, the high F-score of video modality has little significance.

We notice that our approach presents more variance than that of the baseline. One explanation is that parameter β causes the variance. In our experiments, the F-score is the average over 10 repetitions and 12 gestures, with the same value of parameter β. The optimal value of parameter β is stable for the highest average F-score, but for different gestures in different repetitions, the optimal value of parameter β changes. In our current system, we adopt a linear regression classifier to demonstrate the advantages of our proposed SSS feature. It works well even with a simple classifier. In our future work, we will consider the model selection problem for our proposed SSS feature.

We also notice that "Text" exhibits better performance. As Fothergill *et al.* in [8] reported "the text provided a specific of what the sensor was going to pick up". So people can more clearly understand the key movements of differ-

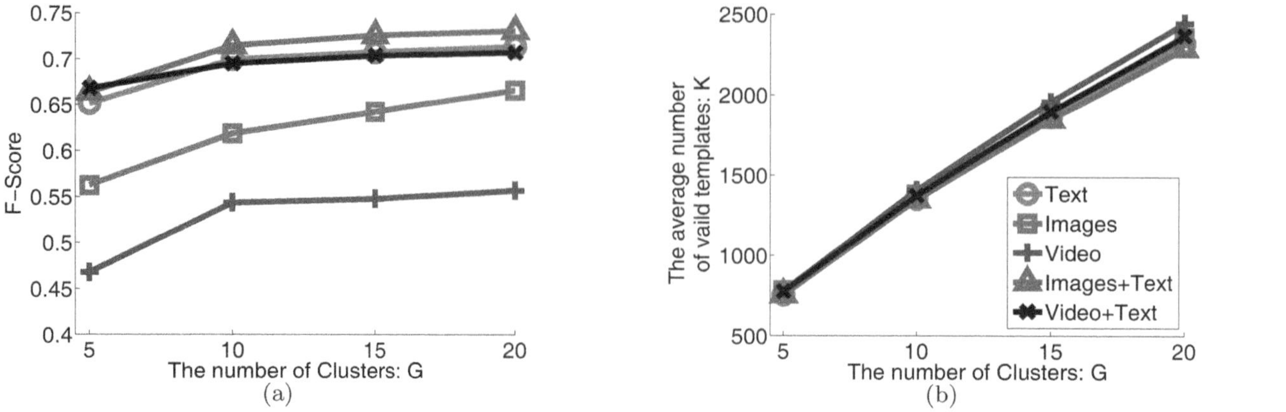

Figure 6: (a) The relationship between recognition performance and the number of clusters $\mathcal{G}$. (b) The relationship between the number of valid templates $\mathcal{K}$ and the number of clusters $\mathcal{G}$.

ent gestures. However, the research on the effect caused by modality of instruction is beyond the scope of this paper. For more details about MSRC-12 Gesture dataset, please refer to [8].

Furthermore, we research the effect caused by the number of clusters. We set $\mathcal{G} = [5, 10, 15, 20]$ respectively when $\lambda = 100$ and $\beta = -0.4$. The recognition F-scores and the number of valid templates $\mathcal{K}$ are illustrated in Figure 6. As the increasing number of clusters, F-scores increase slowly, and the number of valid templates increases linearly. Therefore, we choose $\mathcal{G} = 20$ to balance the effectiveness as well as the efficiency.

We preform our experiments with hardware of "i7 860 CPU" and "4G RAM", and software of Matlab hybrid with parts of C code. With our approach, In prediction stage, gesture recognition of one frame costs less than 2ms.

4.2 Results on MSR-Action3D Dataset

MSR-Action3D dataset [15] comprises of 557 pre-segmented action instances. There were 10 people performing 20 classes of gestures. Same as MSRC-12 Kinect Gesture Dataset, human body joints ($\mathcal{J} = 20$) were captured with Microsoft Kinect system.

Because the instances have been manually segmented, we simplify online extracting features as computing the distances between the pre-segmented instance and the template dictionary directly. Each instance is treated as one sample. We use fixed values $\lambda = 10$ and $\mathcal{G} = 20$ for experiments. In this dataset, the parameters are optimized on the test sets. In all comparing approaches, the parameters are optimized in the same way. The fairness of the comparison is evidenced by using the same experiment setting (the method of partition of training datasets and test datasets, and the method of parameter tuning) on the same standard dataset.

We compare our approach with the state-of-the-art methods on the cross-subject test setting [15, 32], where the samples of half number of persons are used as training data, and the rest are used as testing data. As Table 3 shows, our approach outperforms the other time series based methods [6, 17, 19, 20], which treat the motion data as an undivided whole set. The only approach [32] that outperforms ours uses a subset of joints for classification, which is similar to

Table 3: Comparison on MSR-Action3D dataset.

Method	Accuracy
Recurrent Neural Network [19]	0.425
Dynamic Temporal Warping [20]	0.54
Hidden Markov Model [17]	0.63
Multiple Instance Learning [6]	0.657
Our Approach	**0.817**
Actionlet Ensemble [32]	0.882

our approach, but it focuses on recognition at pre-segmented document level, and cannot be used in online recognition from unsegmented streams.

The confusion matrix is illustrated in Figure 7. We can see that for most actions, our approach works well, while for the similar actions such as "hand catch" and "high throw", "draw X" and "draw circle", there are some misclassifications. It can be seen that, for each action, there are about 10 instances performed by 5 people for training, which may be insufficient to distinguish these similar gestures.

5. CONCLUSIONS

Depth cameras are now widely used in applications of human-computer interaction. There is a growing need to apply depth cameras in human behaviors detections, such as gesture, action, and activity recognition. The effective and efficient recognition of human gestures in a real-time fashion has a significant impact on the recognition of human actions.

In a nutshell, our **contributions** are as follows:

- **New SSS feature.** We proposed a novel feature, namely, *Structured Streaming Skeletons* (SSS), for online gesture recognition from motion data streams to deal with four types of intra-class variations (*i.e.*, viewpoint, anthropometry, execution rate, and personal style), thereby effectively and efficiently solved the incorrect segmentation and inadequate template matching problems.

	highArmWave	horizontalArmWave	hammer	handCatch	forwardPunch	highThrow	drawX	drawTick	drawCircle	handClap	twoHandWave	sideBoxing	bend	forwardKick	sideKick	Jogging	tennisSwing	tennisServe	golfSwing	pickUpThrow
highArmWave	73.3	0.0	0.0	0.0	10.0	10.0	0.0	0.0	3.3	0.0	0.0	0.0	0.0	0.0	0.0	0.0	0.0	3.3	0.0	0.0
horizontalArmWave	0.0	96.7	0.0	0.0	0.0	0.0	0.0	0.0	0.0	0.0	0.0	0.0	0.0	0.0	0.0	0.0	3.3	0.0	0.0	0.0
hammer	0.0	0.0	77.5	0.0	4.2	4.2	0.0	4.2	0.0	0.0	0.0	3.3	0.0	0.0	0.0	0.0	6.7	0.0	0.0	0.0
handCatch	6.7	0.0	0.0	43.3	3.3	23.3	0.0	5.0	0.0	0.0	0.0	10.0	0.0	0.0	0.0	0.0	3.3	0.0	0.0	5.0
forwardPunch	0.0	0.0	0.0	0.0	72.6	16.7	0.0	0.0	0.0	0.0	0.0	10.7	0.0	0.0	0.0	0.0	0.0	0.0	0.0	0.0
highThrow	0.0	0.0	0.0	0.0	3.6	85.7	0.0	0.0	0.0	0.0	0.0	7.1	0.0	0.0	0.0	0.0	3.6	0.0	0.0	0.0
drawX	3.3	3.3	6.7	0.0	3.3	0.0	60.8	8.3	4.2	0.0	0.0	0.0	0.0	0.0	0.0	0.0	6.7	3.3	0.0	0.0
drawTick	0.0	0.0	6.7	0.0	3.3	0.0	0.0	80.0	6.7	0.0	0.0	0.0	0.0	0.0	0.0	0.0	0.0	3.3	0.0	0.0
drawCircle	0.0	3.3	3.3	0.0	3.3	0.0	13.3	10.0	63.3	0.0	0.0	0.0	0.0	0.0	0.0	0.0	0.0	3.3	0.0	0.0
handClap	0.0	0.0	0.0	0.0	0.0	0.0	0.0	0.0	0.0	76.7	13.3	0.0	0.0	0.0	0.0	10.0	0.0	0.0	0.0	0.0
twoHandWave	0.0	0.0	0.0	0.0	0.0	0.0	0.0	0.0	10.0	0.0	90.0	0.0	0.0	0.0	0.0	0.0	0.0	0.0	0.0	0.0
sideBoxing	0.0	0.0	0.0	3.3	0.0	0.0	0.0	0.0	0.0	0.0	0.0	96.7	0.0	0.0	0.0	0.0	0.0	0.0	0.0	0.0
bend	0.0	0.0	0.0	0.0	3.3	0.0	0.0	4.2	0.0	0.0	0.0	3.3	85.0	0.0	0.0	0.0	0.0	0.0	0.0	4.2
forwardKick	0.0	0.0	0.0	0.0	0.0	0.0	0.0	0.0	0.0	0.0	0.0	0.0	0.0	100.0	0.0	0.0	0.0	0.0	0.0	0.0
sideKick	0.0	0.0	0.0	0.0	0.0	0.0	0.0	0.0	0.0	0.0	0.0	0.0	0.0	0.0	100.0	0.0	0.0	0.0	0.0	0.0
Jogging	0.0	0.0	0.0	0.0	0.0	0.0	0.0	0.0	0.0	0.0	0.0	0.0	0.0	3.3	6.7	90.0	0.0	0.0	0.0	0.0
tennisSwing	0.0	0.0	3.3	0.0	0.0	0.0	0.0	0.0	3.3	0.0	0.0	0.0	3.3	0.0	0.0	0.0	90.0	0.0	0.0	0.0
tennisServe	6.7	0.0	0.0	0.0	0.0	0.0	0.0	0.0	0.0	0.0	0.0	6.7	3.3	0.0	0.0	0.0	0.0	83.3	0.0	0.0
golfSwing	3.3	0.0	0.0	0.0	3.3	0.0	3.3	0.0	0.0	0.0	0.0	0.0	0.0	0.0	0.0	0.0	0.0	3.3	83.3	3.3
pickUpThrow	0.0	0.0	0.0	0.0	0.0	0.0	0.0	0.0	0.0	0.0	0.0	0.0	14.3	0.0	0.0	0.0	0.0	0.0	0.0	85.7

Figure 7: The confusion matrix of our proposed approach for MSR-Action3D dataset.

- **None prior segmentation.** We detect the size of segment by dynamically matching with pre-learned templates. Execution variation is eliminated and there is no avenue for errors made by prior segmentations.
- **Fine-tuned granularity of motion templates.** We create a motion template dictionary at a granularity of elementary body-part-movement level. We consider human body as a combination of many small parts and perform body part analysis separately. One advantage is that personal styles of gestures can be represented by different combinations of human-body-part movements.
- **Superior online performance.** Because of the discriminative nature of SSS feature, the superior performance is achieved even with a simple classifier, with average improvement of F-scores by 10% (Table 2) compared with the stat-of-the-art approaches. Also our online prediction of gestures is extremely fast costing less than 2ms per frame. The latency is 0.83s-1.5s (in realtime response)[1].

Our further research will consider: i) the model selection based on our proposed SSS feature; ii) online gesture recognition with inaccurate skeleton data to reduce gesture recognition errors that are caused by incomplete skeleton tracking; iii) studies of real user experience.

6. ACKNOWLEDGEMENTS

This work was partially supported by the Australian Research Council (ARC) Discovery Project DP130104614.

7. REFERENCES

[1] J. K. Aggarwal and M. S. Ryoo. Human activity analysis: A review. *ACM Computing Surveys (CSUR)*, 43(3):16, 2011.

[2] J. Alon, V. Athitsos, Q. Yuan, and S. Sclaroff. A unified framework for gesture recognition and spatiotemporal gesture segmentation. *IEEE Transactions on Pattern Analysis and Machine Intelligence (TPAMI)*, 31(9):1685–1699, 2009.

[3] M. Ankerst, M. M. Breunig, H.-P. Kriegel, and J. Sander. Optics: ordering points to identify the clustering structure. *ACM SIGMOD International Conference on Management of Data (SIGMOD)*, 28(2):49–60, 1999.

[4] D. Berndt and J. Clifford. Using dynamic time warping to find patterns in time series. In *KDD workshop*, volume 10, pages 359–370, 1994.

[5] J. M. Chaquet, E. J. Carmona, and A. Fernández-Caballero. A survey of video datasets for human action and activity recognition. *Computer Vision and Image Understanding (CVIU)*, 117(6):633–659, 2013.

[6] C. Ellis, S. Masood, M. Tappen, J. LaViola, and R. Sukthankar. Exploring the trade-off between accuracy and observational latency in action recognition. *International Journal of Computer Vision (IJCV)*, 101(3):420–436, 2013.

[7] L. Fei-Fei and P. Perona. A bayesian hierarchical model for learning natural scene categories. In *IEEE International Conference on Computer Vision and Pattern Recognition (CVPR)*, volume 2, pages 524–531, 2005.

[8] S. Fothergill, H. M. Mentis, P. Kohli, and S. Nowozin. Instructing people for training gestural interactive systems. In *ACM annual conference on Human Factors in Computing Systems (CHI)*, pages 1737–1746, 2012.

[9] D. Gong, G. Medioni, S. Zhu, and X. Zhao. Kernelized temporal cut for online temporal segmentation and recognition. In *European Conference on Computer Vision (ECCV)*, pages 229–243, 2012.

[1]Our system demo video is attached as the supplementary material on YOUTUBE: http://youtu.be/l4zzmrXfdag

[10] T. Guha and R. K. Ward. Learning sparse representations for human action recognition. *IEEE Transactions on Pattern Analysis and Machine Intelligence (TPAMI)*, 34(8):1576–1588, 2012.

[11] J. Hartigan and M. Wong. A k-means clustering algorithm. *Journal of the Royal Statistical Society C*, 28:100–108, 1979.

[12] G. Johansson. Visual motion perception. *Scientific American*, 232(6):76–88, 1975.

[13] L. Kaufman and P. Rousseeuw. Clustering by means of medoids. *Statistical data analysis based on the L1-norm and related methods*, pages 405–416, 1987.

[14] H. Li and M. Greenspan. Model-based segmentation and recognition of dynamic gestures in continuous video streams. *Pattern Recognition*, 44(8):1614–1628, 2011.

[15] W. Li, Z. Zhang, and Z. Liu. Action recognition based on a bag of 3d points. In *CVPR Workshop*, pages 9–14, 2010.

[16] S.-Y. Lin, C.-K. Shie, S.-C. Chen, and Y.-P. Hung. Action recognition for human-marionette interaction. In *ACM international conference on Multimedia (MM)*, pages 39–48, 2012.

[17] F. Lv and R. Nevatia. Recognition and segmentation of 3-d human action using hmm and multi-class adaboost. In *European Conference on Computer Vision (ECCV)*, pages 359–372, 2006.

[18] Z. Ma, Y. Yang, Y. Cai, N. Sebe, and A. G. Hauptmann. Knowledge adaptation for ad hoc multimedia event detection with few exemplars. In *ACM international conference on Multimedia (MM)*, pages 469–478, 2012.

[19] J. Martens and I. Sutskever. Learning recurrent neural networks with hessian-free optimization. In *International Conference on Machine Learning (ICML)*, pages 1033–1040, 2011.

[20] M. Müller, A. Baak, and H.-P. Seidel. Efficient and robust annotation of motion capture data. In *ACM SIGGRAPH/Eurographics Symposium on Computer Animation (SCA)*, pages 17–26, 2009.

[21] A. Ng, M. Jordan, Y. Weiss, et al. On spectral clustering: Analysis and an algorithm. In *Advances in Neural Information Processing Systems (NIPS)*, pages 849–856, 2002.

[22] P. Papapetrou, V. Athitsos, M. Potamias, G. Kollios, and D. Gunopulos. Embedding-based subsequence matching in time-series databases. *ACM Transactions on Database Systems (TODS)*, 36(3):17, 2011.

[23] R. Poppe. A survey on vision-based human action recognition. *Image and Vision Computing*, 28(6):976–990, 2010.

[24] M. Ryoo. Human activity prediction: Early recognition of ongoing activities from streaming videos. In *IEEE International Conference on Computer Vision (ICCV)*, pages 1036–1043, 2011.

[25] Y. Sakurai, C. Faloutsos, and M. Yamamuro. Stream monitoring under the time warping distance. In *IEEE International Conference on Data Engineering (ICDE)*, pages 1046–1055, 2007.

[26] L. Schwarz, D. Mateus, V. Castañeda, and N. Navab. Manifold learning for tof-based human body tracking and activity recognition. In *British Machine Vision Conference (BMVC)*, pages 1–11, 2010.

[27] J. Shotton, A. Fitzgibbon, M. Cook, T. Sharp, M. Finocchio, R. Moore, A. Kipman, and A. Blake. Real-time human pose recognition in parts from single depth images. In *IEEE International Conference on Computer Vision and Pattern Recognition (CVPR)*, pages 1297–1304, 2011.

[28] Y. Song, D. Demirdjian, and R. Davis. Continuous body and hand gesture recognition for natural human-computer interaction. *ACM Transactions on Interactive Intelligent Systems (TiiS)*, 2(1):5, 2012.

[29] K. Tran, I. Kakadiaris, and S. Shah. Part-based motion descriptor image for human action recognition. *Pattern Recognition*, 45(7):2562–2572, 2012.

[30] P. Turaga, R. Chellappa, V. S. Subrahmanian, and O. Udrea. Machine recognition of human activities: A survey. *IEEE Transactions on Circuits and Systems for Video Technology (TCSVT)*, 18(11):1473–1488, 2008.

[31] A. Veeraraghavan, R. Chellappa, and A. K. Roy-Chowdhury. The function space of an activity. In *IEEE International Conference on Computer Vision and Pattern Recognition (CVPR)*, volume 1, pages 959–968, 2006.

[32] J. Wang, Z. Liu, Y. Wu, and J. Yuan. Mining actionlet ensemble for action recognition with depth cameras. In *IEEE International Conference on Computer Vision and Pattern Recognition (CVPR)*, pages 1290–1297, 2012.

[33] S. Wang, Y. Yang, Z. Ma, X. Li, C. Pang, and A. G. Hauptmann. Action recognition by exploring data distribution and feature correlation. In *IEEE International Conference on Computer Vision and Pattern Recognition (CVPR)*, pages 1370–1377, 2012.

[34] Y. Yang, Z. Ma, A. G. Hauptmann, and N. Sebe. Feature selection for multimedia analysis by sharing information among multiple tasks. *IEEE Transactions on Multimedia (TMM)*, 15(3):661–669, 2013.

[35] Y. Yang, I. Saleemi, and M. Shah. Discovering motion primitives for unsupervised grouping and one-shot learning of human actions, gestures, and expressions. *IEEE Transactions on Pattern Analysis and Machine Intelligence (TPAMI)*, 35(7):1635–1648, 2013.

[36] Y. Yang, Y. Yang, Z. Huang, H. Shen, and F. Nie. Tag localization with spatial correlations and joint group sparsity. In *IEEE International Conference on Computer Vision and Pattern Recognition (CVPR)*, pages 881–888, 2011.

[37] Z. Zhang and D. Tao. Slow feature analysis for human action recognition. *IEEE Transactions on Pattern Analysis and Machine Intelligence (TPAMI)*, 34(3):436–450, 2012.

[38] F. Zhou, F. Torre, and J. Hodgins. Aligned cluster analysis for temporal segmentation of human motion. In *IEEE Conference on Automatic Face and Gesture Recognition (FG)*, pages 1–7, 2008.

Attribute-augmented Semantic Hierarchy

Towards Bridging Semantic Gap and Intention Gap in Image Retrieval

Hanwang Zhang†, Zheng-Jun Zha†§, Yang Yang†, Shuicheng Yan‡, Yue Gao†, Tat-Seng Chua†

†School of Computing, National University of Singapore
§Institute of Intelligent Machines, Chinese Academy of Sciences
‡Department of Electrical Computer Engineering, National University of Singapore
{hanwangzhang,junzzustc}@gmail.com; {yang.yang,eleyans,dcsgaoy,dcscts}@nus.edu.sg

ABSTRACT

This paper presents a novel Attribute-augmented Semantic Hierarchy (A^2SH) and demonstrates its effectiveness in bridging both the semantic and intention gaps in Content-based Image Retrieval (CBIR). A^2SH organizes the semantic concepts into multiple semantic levels and augments each concept with a set of related attributes, which describe the multiple facets of the concept and act as the intermediate bridge connecting the concept and low-level visual content. A hierarchical semantic similarity function is learnt to characterize the semantic similarities among images for retrieval. To better capture user search intent, a hybrid feedback mechanism is developed, which collects hybrid feedbacks on attributes and images. These feedbacks are then used to refine the search results based on A^2SH. We develop a content-based image retrieval system based on the proposed A^2SH. We conduct extensive experiments on a large-scale data set of over one million Web images. Experimental results show that the proposed A^2SH can characterize the semantic affinities among images accurately and can shape user search intent precisely and quickly, leading to more accurate search results as compared to state-of-the-art CBIR solutions.

Categories and Subject Descriptors

H.3.3 [**Information Search and Retrieval**]: Retrieval Model

General Terms

Algorithms, Experimentation, Performance

Keywords

image retrieval, attribute, semantic hierarchy

MM'13, October 21–25, 2013, Barcelona, Spain.

http://dx.doi.org/10.1145/2502081.2502093.

Figure 1: Illustration of the semantic gap and intention gap in image retrieval.

1. INTRODUCTION

Content-based Image Retrieval (CBIR), a technique for retrieving images from a large database of digital images based on visual content, has been studied extensively since the early 1990s [29, 15, 27, 23]. It has gained increasing importance in both the academia and industry, in the current era of social media, because of the explosive growth of images shared in cyberspace and the compelling demands in various multimedia applications for Web and mobile clients. In spite of the remarkable progress made in the last two decades, CBIR remains challenging mainly due to two critical scientific problems for image retrieval as shown in Figure 1: (a) the Semantic Gap between the low-level visual features and high-level semantics [28, 2]; and (b) the Intention Gap between user's search intent and the query [38, 11], which hinders the understanding of user's intent behind a query.

Recent studies, especially those on TRECVID [21], have shown that a promising route to narrowing the semantic gap is to exploit a set of concepts to form the semantic description of visual content [31, 19]. As the amount and scope of semantic concepts increase, semantic hierarchy, such as ImageNet [4] and LSCOM [20], has been developed to organize the semantic concepts from general to specific and essentially partition the semantic space hierarchically, towards better addressing the semantic gap problem. The semantic hierarchy has been found to be encouraging in improving the understanding of visual content recently [7, 18]. However, there still lacks the correspondences between visual features and semantics, due to the intra-concept variations and inter-concept similarities on visual properties. On the other hand, to address the intention gap problem, Relevance Feedback (RF) has been introduced into image retrieval. RF collects user feedbacks on candidate images, indicating them as "relevant" or "irrelevant" and lets the system to infer users' search intent from the labeled images [24, 1]. Due to the discrepancy between user's intent and low-level visual cues, RF is often ineffective in narrowing search to target in practice.

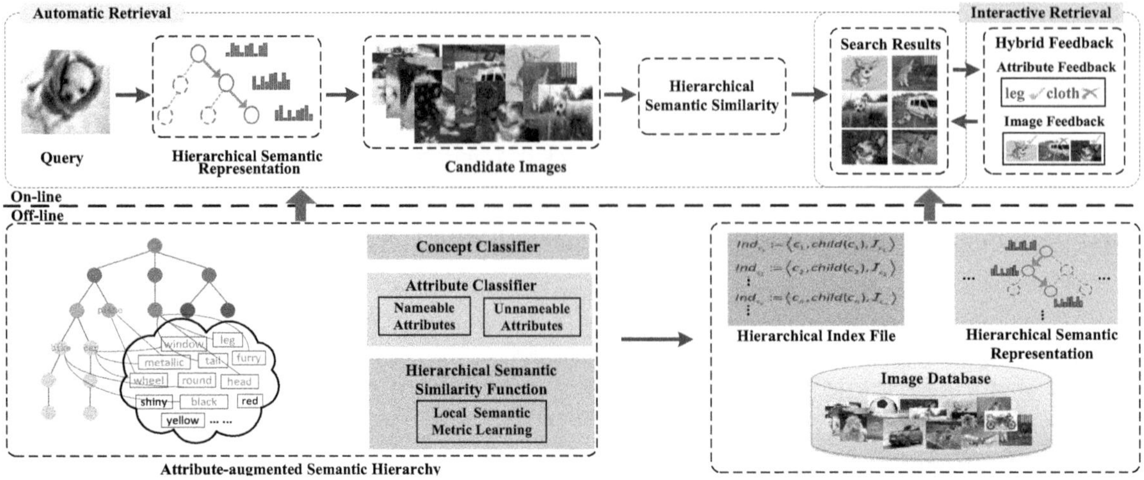

Figure 2: Illustration of the proposed Attribute-augmented Semantic Hierarchy (A^2SH) and the image retrieval system developed on A^2SH.

Motivated by the above observations, in this paper, we propose a novel Attribute-augmented Semantic Hierarchy (A^2SH), towards narrowing both the semantic and intention gaps, and demonstrate its effectiveness in both automatic and interactive Content-based Image Retrieval. Here, attributes refer to semantic descriptions of concepts such as the visual appearances (*e.g.*, "round" as shape, "metallic" as texture), sub-components (*e.g.*, "has wheel", "has leg"), and various discriminative properties (*e.g.*, "properties that dog has but cat do not"). Figure 2 shows an illustration of A^2SH. A semantic hierarchy consisting of semantic concepts is augmented by a pool of attributes. Each semantic concept is linked to a set of related attributes. For example, "car" is augmented by the attributes "window" and "metallic", *etc.* These attributes are specifications of the multiple facets of the corresponding concept and can act as an intermediate bridge connecting the concept and low-level visual cues. Moreover, they span a local semantic space in the context of the concept. On the other hand, the same attribute may have different semantics in the context of different concepts. For example, the attribute "*wing*" of concept "*bird*" refers to appendages that are feathered; while the same attribute refers to metallic appendages in the context of "*jet*". Hence, associating an attribute to concepts can reveal the heterogeneous meanings of the same attribute. We equip A^2SH with a set of concept classifiers and attribute classifiers. The concept classifier is used to predict the presence of a concept in images, while the attribute classifier aims to predict the presence of the attributes in the context of its associated concept. As a result, A^2SH is able to interpret the semantics of image content with a hierarchial semantic representation. In particular, an image can be represented as the responses from the concept classifiers as well as the linked attribute classifiers, leading to a hierarchical interpretation consisting of multiple levels of semantic granulations. Based on such interpretation, we develop a hierarchical semantic similarity function to precisely characterize the semantic similarities between images. The semantic similarity between any two images is computed as a hierarchical aggregation of their similarities in the local semantic spaces of their common semantic concepts at multiple levels. In the local semantic space of each concept, a local semantic metric is learnt to capture the semantic affinities between images in the context of the concept.

Based on the above A^2SH, we develop a content-based image retrieval system, which supports both automatic retrieval and interactive retrieval with user feedbacks. We expect A^2SH to both effectively narrow the semantic gap by structurlizing the semantics of image content with semantically meaningful hierarchical representations in terms of concepts and attributes, as well as the intention gap by shaping user search intent accurately from the feedbacks. The system flowchart is illustrated in Figure 2. In the offline part, we first learn the concept classifiers, attribute classifiers, and hierarchial semantic similarity function to equip A^2SH. We next use A^2SH to process the database images and obtain their hierarchical semantic representations. All the images are indexed hierarchically based on their semantic paths in the hierarchy to enable efficient large-scale retrieval. In the online part, a given query image is first processed by A^2SH, getting its hierarchical semantic representation, based on which a collection of candidate images are returned from the database according to the indexing. Similar images are then retrieved from the candidate set based on their hierarchical semantic similarities to the query. After the automatic retrieval, we present the results to solicit user feedbacks. We enable a broad channel of feedback to help user deliver search intent by providing hybrid feedbacks on attributes and images. While the image feedbacks collect positive and negative samples of user intent, the feedbacks on attributes compose a clearer semantic description of the intent [39], such as "*has head and leg, not furry.*" These hybrid feedbacks are analyzed by A^2SH, leading to a precise semantic interpretation of user intent, and are used to refine the search results. We expect the hybrid feedbacks leading to better search results with less interaction effort.

We evaluate the proposed system on a large-scale corpus of over one million Web images. The experimental results have demonstrated the superiority of the proposed system over state-of-the-arts CBIR approaches. The main contributions of this paper are summarized as follows:

- We propose a novel Attribute-augmented Semantic Hierarchy (A^2SH), in which each concept is augmented by a set of related attributes. A^2SH models the semantics of images in the form of a hierarchical semantic representation, which is semantically meaningful.

- We develop a CBIR system based on the proposed A^2SH and demonstrate the effectiveness of A^2SH in narrowing the semantic and intention gaps in image retrieval over a large-scale image data set.
- We learn a hierarchical semantic similarity function, which is able to accurately characterize the semantic affinities among images. Moreover, we develop a hybrid feedback mechanism to collect feedbacks on both attributes and images, which can help capture users' search intent more precisely based on A^2SH.

The rest of the paper is organized as follows. Section 2 reviews related work. Section 3 describes the elementary building blocks of the proposed A^2SH, including the concept classifiers, attribute classifiers, and hierarchical semantic similarity function. Section 4 elaborates the automatic and interactive image retrieval based on the proposed A^2SH. Experimental results and analysis are reported in Section 5, followed by conclusions and future work in Section 6.

2. RELATED WORK

2.1 Semantic Hierarchy

A semantic hierarchy is a formally defined taxonomy or ontology, where each node represents a semantic concept, such as WordNet [10], ImageNet [4], and LSCOM [20] etc. It organizes semantic concepts from general to specific and has been shown to be effective in boosting visual recognition [7, 18] and retrieval [30, 5, 3]. Most of the recent works of exploiting semantic hierarchy for image retrieval focus on designing a semantic similarity function that embeds hierarchical information. In the method proposed by Deselaers and Ferrari [5], given two images, their visual nearest neighbor images were first found, and their semantic distance was computed as a distance between the concepts of their neighbors. Deng *et al.* [3] developed a hierarchical bilinear similarity function for image retrieval. They first represented an image as a semantic vector $\mathbf{z}$ consisting of its relevances to a set of concepts, and defined the bilinear similarity between any two images as $\mathbf{z}_i^T \mathbf{S} \mathbf{z}_j$, where $\mathbf{S}$ is a matrix encoding the pairwise semantic affinities among the concepts. They have shown that this method achieves the state-of-the-art performance of image retrieval on ImageNet. Recently, Verma *et al.* [35] proposed to associate separated visual similarity metrics for every concept in a hierarchy and then learn the metrics jointly through an aggregated hierarchical metric. Different from existing works based on conventional semantic hierarchy, our work augments semantic hierarchy with a pool of attributes. The augmented hierarchy has better capacity in modeling the semantics of images. We characterize the semantic similarities among images by a hierarchical similarity function composed by a set of local semantic metrics learnt in the semantic spaces spanned by attributes in the context of various concepts.

2.2 Attributes

Attributes have attracted increasing attentions recently. Attributes refer to semantic descriptions of concepts such as sub-components (*e.g.*, "has wheel"), the visual appearances (*e.g.*, "round" as shape), and various discriminative properties (*e.g.*, "properties that dog has but cat do not"). Attributes are semantically meaningful as opposed to low-level visual features, and they are relatively easier to recognize automatically instead of the full concepts (*e.g.*, "dog", "car") [8]. Attributes can be exploited as intermediate-level descriptors of images to boost visual recognition [8, 17] and retrieval [12, 6, 9]. For example, Jaimes *et al.* [12] proposed a conceptual framework for indexing visual information based on semantic concepts and attributes. Douze *et al.* [6] proposed to represent an image by the concatenation of visual features and its response from attribute classifiers, and have shown that such representation can improve image retrieval significantly compared to pure visual features. Scheirer *et al.* [26] developed a probabilistic normalization method to normalize the responses from attribute classifiers, and have shown that the normalized representation is more effective. While most existing works represented images in the form of a flat semantic representations in terms of attributes, our work associate attributes to the concepts in a semantic hierarchy and represent images in the form of a hierarchical semantic representations, which are more semantically meaningful. Moreover, as aforementioned, associating an attribute to concepts can reveal the heterogeneous meanings of the same attribute.

2.3 Relevance Feedback

Relevance Feedback (RF) is a key technique to narrow down the intention gap in image retrieval [23, 1, 33, 2]. It attempts to capture users' search intent by iteratively collecting users' feedbacks on the retrieved images and refining the retrieval based on the feedbacks. A wealth of RF methods has been proposed to refine the original query or learn a relevance ranking function from the feedbacks, *i.e.*, the "relevant" and "irrelevant" images labeled by users. For example, the Query Point Movement (QPM) method [24] gradually refines the query point by moving it towards the "relevant" images and away from the "irrelevant" images. Tong *et al.* [34] proposed to learn a Support Vector Machine (SVM) from the "relevant" and "irrelevant" images, and then rank the images according to their responses from the SVM classifier. Tao *et al.* [33] proposed a asymmetric bagging and random subspace SVM method to learn a robust classifier from user feedbacks. Recently, Zhang *et al.* [39] developed an attribute feedback scheme, which collects user feedbacks on semantic attributes and ranks images according to the presence probabilities of the attributes in the images. Kovashka *et al.* [13] proposed to collect the user's relative judgments on attributes, such as "show me shoes that are more formal than these and shinier than those," to improve text-based image retrieval. Compared to these works, our work enables a broad channel of feedback to help user better delivery search intent by providing hybrid feedbacks on attributes and images. By modeling the feedbacks based on A^2SH, our work leads to a better understanding of user intent.

3. ATTRIBUTE-AUGMENTED SEMANTIC HIERARCHY

In this section, we first present a definition of the proposed Attribute-augmented Semantic Hierarchy (A^2SH) as follows:

Definition 1. *Attribute-augmented Semantic Hierarchy is a directed acyclic graph* $\mathcal{H} = (\mathcal{C}, \mathcal{A}, \mathcal{E}_C, \mathcal{E}_{CA})$*, consisting of a set of concepts* $\mathcal{C} = \{c\}$*, a pool of attributes* $\mathcal{A} = \{a\}$*, a* *set of concept-concept edges $\mathcal{E}_C$, where an edge is an* ordered *pair of concepts in $\mathcal{C} \times \mathcal{C}$, and a set of concept-attribute edges $\mathcal{E}_{CA}$, where an edge is an* unordered *pair of a concept and an attribute in $\mathcal{C} \times \mathcal{A}$. The set of attributes linked to concept c is $\mathcal{A}_c$.*

A^{2}SH organizes semantic concepts from general to specific, where each concept is augmented with a set of related attributes. These attributes comprehensively describe the multiple semantic facets of the concept, and span a local semantic space tailored to the concept. Next, we equip A^{2}SH with concept classifiers, attribute classifiers, and a hierarchical semantic similarity function. In particular, each of the concept classifiers predicts the presence of a semantic concept c in images. The attribute classifiers for the attributes $\mathcal{A}_c$ linked to concept c predict the presence of the attributes in the context of c. With such hierarchy, a given image can be represented as the responses from the concept classifiers as well as the linked attribute classifiers, leading to a hierarchical semantic interpretation consisting of semantics at multiple levels. The similarity between two images is computed by the hierarchical semantic similarity function, which aggregates their local similarities in the context of their common semantic concepts at multiple levels. A local semantic metric is learnt in the local semantic space of each concept.

3.1 Concept Learning

A concept classifier $f_c : \mathcal{X} \mapsto \{-1, +1\}$ predicts whether an image belongs to concept c, where $\mathcal{X}$ is an arbitrary feature space. Generally, given the concept classifiers in a hierarchy, the semantic path of an image can be efficiently predicted by the classifiers in a top-down fashion [32, 18]. Here, a semantic path $\mathcal{P}$ is a set of multi-level semantics $\mathcal{P} = (c_0 \rightarrow \ldots \rightarrow c_n)$ from the root c_0 and satisfies $\forall i > 0,\ f_{c_i}(x) = +1$. Next, we introduce the learning of the concept classifiers.

One way to learn each concept classifier is to use the conventional "one-vs-all" strategy, that is, learning the classifier by the images are from the concept as positive samples and images from others as negative samples. However, this strategy neglects the hierarchical relation among concepts, resulting in classifiers ineffective for hierarchical classification. Another way for concept classifier learning is to locally train the classifier for a concept by using the images from its siblings as negative samples [18]. However, this local training strategy results in classifiers that suffer from the "error progation" problem. To address the above problems, we here use the "hierarchical one-vs-all" strategy [32] to learn concept classifiers by exploiting the hierarchical relation among concepts and collecting training samples globally in the hierarchy. In particular, the positive training set $Pos(c)$ and the negative training set $Neg(c)$ are constructed as follows:

$$\begin{aligned} Pos(c) &= \{I_i,\ s.t.\ \mathcal{L}(I_i) \cap (c \cup descend(c))\}, \\ Neg(c) &= \{I_i,\ s.t.\ I_i \notin Pos(c)\}, \end{aligned} \tag{1}$$

where $\mathcal{L}(I_i) \subseteq \mathcal{C}$ is the set of concept labels for sample I_i. For each concept c, the positive training set $Pos(c)$ consists of images labeled as either the concept itself or one of its descendant concepts; while the negative training set $Neg(c)$ contains images which are not in $Pos(c)$. Based on $Pos(c)$ and $Neg(c)$, we train a binary linear Support Vector Machine (SVM) as the concept classifier f_c.

3.2 Attribute Learning

As aforementioned, we augment the concepts in a semantic hierarchy using a pool of attributes. Here, we exploit two types of attributes, including nameable attributes and unnameable attributes. **Nameable attributes** refer to the attributes that are human-nameable, such as the visual appearances and sub-components of a concept [39]. Moreover, a bunch of discriminative properties among concepts, such as "properties that dog has but cat do not" are automatically discovered. These discriminative properties are termed as **unnameable attributes**, since they are hard to be articulated explicitly by human. Such unnameable attributes are important in depicting a concept especially when the concept shares most of the nameable attributes with many others concepts. For example, "dog" and "cat" may share many nameable attributes, such as "furry", "tail", *etc.* while unnameable attributes need to be learned to differentiate the fur of cats from that of dogs using image examples. Together they offer a comprehensive description of the multiple facets of a concept.

3.2.1 Nameable Attribute Learning

A nameable attribute classifier $f_a^c : \mathcal{V} \mapsto \{-1, +1\}$ predicts the presence of a nameable attribute a of concept c in an image, where $\mathcal{V}$ is an arbitrary visual feature space. This classifier is learnt in the context of c, *i.e.*, using the positive samples of c with ground truth labelings of attribute a. Note that attributes normally correspond to partial visual cues of the whole image. For example, a component attribute may only appear at one or more regions in the image, and an appearance attribute may correspond to only partial channels of visual descriptors. Hence, the visual feature $\mathcal{V}$ describing the whole image may not characterize the attributes well. This motivates us to perform feature selection towards selecting the most informative feature $\mathcal{V}_a^c$ for learning the attribute classifier f_a^c.

We propose a hierarchical feature selection mechanism to select features in a bottom-up fashion [8, 39]. Without loss of generality, we start with selecting visual features $\mathcal{V}_a^c$ for attribute a in the context of concept c. Suppose we have already selected the most informative features $\mathcal{V}_a^{c'}$ for attribute a in the context of $c' \in child(c)$. We merge these features to form the following base features $\widetilde{\mathcal{V}}_a^c$:

$$\widetilde{\mathcal{V}}_a^c = \bigcup_{c' \in child(c)} \mathcal{V}_a^{c'}. \tag{2}$$

The base features serve as a set of candidate features, from which we perform feature selection to discover the most informative features for learning a in the context of c. Intuitively, selecting features from the base features $\widetilde{\mathcal{V}}_a^c$ instead of the raw feature $\mathcal{V}$ leads to more informative features for learning attribute a. For example, it is more effective to select features for the attribute "head" of "animal" from the union of the features for 'head" of "dog", "cat", *etc.* Given the positive samples $\mathcal{I}_c$ of c labeled with/without attribute a, we train an ℓ_1-norm linear regressor to select $\mathcal{V}_a^c$ from $\widetilde{\mathcal{V}}_a^c$. For attributes appearing in most of $\mathcal{I}_c$, there are insufficient negative samples of a left. In order to learn an effective linear regressor, we instead access the images of c's ancestors until sufficient negative samples of a are collected. The regression results in a sparse set of model parameters where the nonzero elements correspond to feature dimensions that are selective for a. By selecting the nonzero dimensions of

$\widetilde{\mathcal{V}}_a^c$, we finally get the most informative feature $\mathcal{V}_a^c$, based on which we train a linear SVM as the attribute classifier f_a^c.

3.2.2 Unnameable Attribute Discovery

Since unnameable attributes are usually hard to be articulated by human, we cannot manually label images being positive/negative to an unnameable attribute and thus cannot obtain unnameable attributes classifiers by supervised learning. Hence, we propose to automatically discover unnameable attributes in an unsupervised fashion. Inspired by [22], we define unnameable attributes as the hypotheses that help in distinguishing a concept and its siblings. Next, we detail an iterative approach for discovering unnameable attributes in the context of concept c.

At each iteration t, we maintain an attribute set $\mathcal{A}_t$ containing nameable attributes of the concepts $\mathcal{C}_c = c \cup sibling(c)$, and unnameable attributes discovered thus far. We are concerned with the classification among the images of the concepts in $\mathcal{C}_c$, denoted as $\mathcal{I}$, represented by the responses from the attribute classifiers of $\mathcal{A}_t$. We use a nearest neighbor classifier to classify $\mathcal{I}$ into $\mathcal{C}_c$. Based on the classification result, we construct a symmetric confusion matrix[2], which can be viewed as a fully connected graph whose nodes correspond to $\mathcal{C}_c$. A strong edge weight indicates high confusion between the concepts linked by the edge. Next, we perform a spectral clustering algorithm on this graph to obtain several clusters. Each cluster is a subset of concepts that are most confused with each other. For images in the i-th cluster, we employ an unsupervised max-margin clustering algorithm [40] to generate a hyperplane separating them into two classes. The hyperplane serves as a hypothesis that helps in distinguishing the most confused concepts in the i-th cluster. We regard the hypothesis as an unnameable attribute a_i. Then, we learn a linear SVM classifier $f_{a_i}^c$ for a_i using the images of the two classes split by a_i. Finally, suppose that we have discovered m unnameable attributes at iteration t, we add them to the attribute set $\mathcal{A}_{t+1} \leftarrow \{\mathcal{A}_t, a_1, ..., a_m\}$, which is in turn used for the next iteration. The discovery process ends if no more new hypotheses can be found.

3.3 Hierarchical Semantic Similarity Learning

From the concept and attribute classifiers learnt above, we can generate a hierarchical semantic representation of an image as $\{(c_0 \rightarrow ... \rightarrow c_n); (\mathbf{z}^{c_0}, ..., \mathbf{z}^{c_n})\}$, where $(c_0 \rightarrow ... \rightarrow c_n)$ is the semantic path predicted by concept classifiers, c_0 is the root of the hierarchy and $(\mathbf{z}^{c_0}, ..., \mathbf{z}^{c_n})$ is the local semantic representations in terms of attributes along the path. Specifically, $\mathbf{z}^c$ is composed by the responses from the attribute classifiers of concept c as follows:

$$\mathbf{z}^c = \left[f_{a_1}^c(\mathbf{x}), f_{a_2}^c(\mathbf{x}), ..., f_{a_{|\mathcal{A}_c|}}^c(\mathbf{x})\right]^T, \tag{3}$$

where f_a^c is the classifier for attribute $a \in \mathcal{A}_c$. We normalize f_a^c into the range of $[0, 1]$ by a probabilistic strategy [26].

With such hierarchical semantic representation of images, we formulate a hierarchical semantic similarity function to precisely characterize the semantic similarities between images by aggregating their local similarities along their common semantic paths. The hierarchical semantic similarity between any two images is defined as follows:

[2]It is constructed by the sum of the original confusion matrix and its transposition.

$$S(I_i, I_j) = \sum_{c \in \mathcal{P}_{ij}} s(I_i, I_j; c), \tag{4}$$

where $\mathcal{P}_{ij}$ is the common semantic path of image I_i and I_j, $s(I_i, I_j; c)$ is the local similarity between I_i and I_j in the context of c along the path $\mathcal{P}_{ij}$.

There are two conventional ways to define $s(I_i, I_j; c)$. The first is to set $s(I_i, I_j; c)$ to 1, such that $S(I_i, I_j)$ is reduced to the length of the common path of I_i and I_j. This lacks the fine characterization of the semantic affinities between the images along the path. The second is to calculate $s(I_i, I_j; c)$ as the visual similarity. This measurement suffers from the discrepancy between visual similarity and semantic similarity. Hence they are both unable to characterize the semantic affinities between images well. In order to precisely characterize the semantic similarities between images, we propose to learn a local semantic metric in the local semantic space of each concept.

3.3.1 Local Semantic Metric Learning

We define the local semantic distance between two images in the local semantic space of concept c as:

$$d\left(\mathbf{z}_i^c, \mathbf{z}_j^c; c\right) = \sqrt{(\mathbf{z}_i^c - \mathbf{z}_j^c)^T \mathbf{M}_c (\mathbf{z}_i^c - \mathbf{z}_j^c)}, \tag{5}$$

where $\mathbf{M}_c$ is a positive semi-definite symmetric matrix of size $|\mathcal{A}_c| \times |\mathcal{A}_c|$. $\mathbf{M}_c$ is the local semantic metric, which needs to be learnt to bring together the images of the same concept as close as possible and sperate the images of different concepts as far as possible. In particular, with $\mathbf{M}_c$, we expect the neighbor samples within the same semantic class c to be as close as possible, towards preserving the fine neighborhood relation within the class, and the samples from the siblings of c to be separated away with a large margin. To achieve this, for image $I_i \in Pos(c)$, we require the distance between I_i and its K-nearest neighbors $I_j \in Pos(c)$ as small as possible. $Pos(c)$ are the images belong to concept c. We denote $j \rightsquigarrow i$ as such neighborhood. Moreover, the distance between I_i and I_j should be smaller than that between I_i and any image I_k from sibling concepts. Let $\mathcal{S}(c)$ denote the set of images of sibling concepts, we can have a set of training triples as $\mathcal{T} = \{(i, j, k) : j \rightsquigarrow i, I_i \in Pos(c), I_k \in \mathcal{S}(c)\}$, based on which we formulate the metric learning objective as follows:

$$\begin{aligned} \min_{\mathbf{M}_c} & \sum_{j \rightsquigarrow i} d^2(\mathbf{z}_i^c, \mathbf{z}_j^c; c) + \lambda \sum_{(i,j,k) \in \mathcal{T}} \xi_{ijk} \\ s.t. \; & \forall (i, j, k) \in \mathcal{T}, \\ & d^2(\mathbf{z}_i^c, \mathbf{z}_k^c; c) - d^2(\mathbf{z}_i^c, \mathbf{z}_j^c; c) \geq 1 - \xi_{ijk}, \\ & \xi_{ijk} \geq 0, \;\; \mathbf{M}_c \succeq \mathbf{0}, \end{aligned} \tag{6}$$

where $\lambda > 0$ is the regularization constant. We employ the LMNN solver [37] modified with the above defined training triplets $\mathcal{T}$ to solve the metric learning problem. Note that solving the above problem is very efficient since the local semantic space is compact, *i.e.*, the dimension of $\mathbf{M}_c$ is low. With $\mathbf{M}_c$ we can compute the local semantic similarity between images as:

$$s(I_i, I_j; c) = exp(-d(\mathbf{z}_i^c, \mathbf{z}_j^c; c)), \tag{7}$$

which is in turn used to compose the hierarchical semantic similarities in Eq. (4).

4. IMAGE RETRIEVAL WITH A²SH

In this section, we develop a content-based image retrieval system based on A²SH. The system enables efficient and effective automatic retrieval and interactive retrieval with hybrid feedbacks.

4.1 Automatic Retrieval with Hierarchical Indexing

A^2SH provides a much more efficient similarity search due to the aforementioned compact hierarchical semantic representations. However, the cost of linear scan of the entire database can be very high even for such a compact representation especially for large-scale databases. In order to support efficient large-scale image retrieval, we develop a hierarchical indexing strategy. All the images are indexed hierarchically based on their semantic paths in the hierarchy. We define an index file as follows:

$$\text{Ind}_c := \quad < c, child(c), \mathcal{I}_c >, \tag{8}$$

where $child(c)$ is the children of the concept c, and $\mathcal{I}_c$ is the set of database images whose predicted semantic paths terminate at c.

Given a query image I_q, the retrieval with the hierarchical indexing is as follows. First, we generate the hierarchical semantic representation of I_q along its semantic path $c_0 \to ... \to c_n$ based on A^2SH. Next, we perform fast retrieval of candidate images by looking-up the index file Ind_{c_n}. The candidate images consist of the images indexed by c_n and its children $child(c_n)$. Note that the number of the candidate images is significantly reduced compared to the size of entire database. These candidate images are then ranked according to their hierarchical semantic similarities to the query as in Eq. (4). In practice, as the semantic path prediction may not be perfect, c_n may not be exactly the same as the ground truth semantic path terminal of the query image. To address this problem, we set a look-back level b (b=3 in the experiments) and retrieve more candidate images by the index file $\text{Ind}_{c_{n-b}}$. Note that when b=n, it retrieves all the database images as candidates, degenerating to linear scan.

Next, we analyze the time complexity of the retrieval, including three major steps: 1) semantic path prediction, 2) looking-up the index file to obtain candidate images and 3) generating Top K results according to the hierarchical semantic similarities of the candidate images. Denote the averaged fan-out (*i.e.*, averaged number of the children of a concept in the hierarchy) of A^2SH as F, the averaged leaf depth (*i.e.*, averaged depth over all the leaves) as D, and the concept classifier prediction cost as C. Therefore, we can estimate cost of the semantic path prediction at $\mathcal{O}(nFC)$, where $n \leq D$+b is the average depth of the predicted path, and the candidate images retrieval cost at $\mathcal{O}(F^{D-n+b})$, which is the cost for sub-hierarchy traversal. Note that C is a small constant, D and F are 6.3 and 3.8 in our ImageNet hierarchy, respectively. Hence, the prediction cost and the candidate retrieval cost are very small, and the time cost for for retrieval is mainly from the third step, *i.e.*, ranking candidate images, which has a time complexity of $\mathcal{O}(ndN_c$+$N_c \log N_c)$, where d is the average dimensions of local semantic spaces, and N_c is the number of the candidate images, which is much smaller than the size of the entire database.

4.2 Interactive Retrieval with Hybrid Feedback

Because of the presence of intention gap that hinders the understanding of user search intent by the system, the results from automatic retrieval often do not satisfy users' information needs. We therefore execute interactive retrieval by involving users' interaction with the system. We propose a Hybrid Feedback (HF) mechanism to help user deliver search intent by providing hybrid feedbacks on both the attributes and images. In particular, we allow a user to give "yes"/"no" feedbacks on attributes to state which attributes are in or not in his/her search intent, as well as relevance judgements on images to indicate which images are "relevant" or "irrelevant" to the intent. These hybrid feedbacks are then used to generate a precise semantic interpretation of user intent based on the proposed A^2SH. By iteratively collecting user feedbacks and refining the retrieval, the system can shape user intent more accurately and narrow the search to target gradually.

Suppose we are at the t-th feedback iteration. The system records the "relevant" images as $\mathcal{R}_t$ and the "irrelevant" images as $\overline{\mathcal{R}}_t$, as well as the "yes" attributes as $\mathcal{B}_t$ and the "no" attributes as $\overline{\mathcal{B}}_t$. Suppose the hierarchical semantic representation of a query image is $\{\mathcal{Q} = (c_0 \to ... \to c_n); \mathcal{Z} = (\mathbf{z}^{c_0}, ..., \mathbf{z}^{c_n})\}$, where $\mathcal{Q}$ is the semantic path and $\mathcal{Z}$ is the set of local semantic representations along the path. We refine the query representation at iteration t: $\mathcal{Z}_t$, tailoring it to user intent by incorporating semantic descriptions delivered by image feedbacks (*i.e.*, $\mathcal{R}_t$ and $\overline{\mathcal{R}}_t$), and attribute feedbacks (*i.e.*, $\mathcal{B}_t$ and $\overline{\mathcal{B}}_t$). More specifically, we refine the query $\mathcal{Z}_t$ to make it close to the semantic representation of relevant images while away from that of the irrelevant ones. This refinement is carried out along the semantic path for every local semantic representation of the query, leading to a hierarchical semantic interpretation of user intent. Formally, for $\forall c \in \mathcal{Q}$, we have

$$\begin{aligned}\mathbf{z}_{t+1}^c[a] =& \mathbf{z}_t^c[a] + \beta \sum_{i \in \mathcal{R}_t} (\mathbf{z}_i^c[a] - \mathbf{z}_t^c[a])/|\mathcal{R}_t| \\ &- \gamma \sum_{j \in \overline{\mathcal{R}}_t} (\mathbf{z}_j^c[a] - \mathbf{z}_t^c[a])/|\overline{\mathcal{R}}_t|,\end{aligned} \tag{9}$$

where β and γ are trade-off parameters. Through image feedbacks, the semantic representation of the query is shaped closer towards the semantic representations of relevant images as well as farther away from those of irrelevant ones.

User feedbacks on attributes $\mathcal{B}_t$ and $\overline{\mathcal{B}}_t$ state the desired and undesired attributes, respectively. That is to say, the attributes in $\mathcal{B}_t$ are expected be included in the query, while the attributes in $\overline{\mathcal{B}}_t$ are not. Hence, we refine the query $\mathcal{Z}_t$ by setting the values on the dimensions corresponding to $\mathcal{B}_t$ as 1 and the values on the dimensions for $\overline{\mathcal{B}}_t$ as 0. For $\forall c \in \mathcal{Q}$, we have

$$\forall a \in \mathcal{A}_c, \mathbf{z}_{t+1}^c[a] = \begin{cases} 1, & a \in \mathcal{B}_t, \\ 0, & a \in \overline{\mathcal{B}}_t, \\ \mathbf{z}_t^c[a], & otherwise. \end{cases} \tag{10}$$

The resultant query $\mathcal{Z}_{t+1}$ is then used to generate the new search results based on the aforementioned hierarchical semantic similarity function. Here, we emphasize the semantic dimensions corresponding to the attributes in $\mathcal{B}_t$ and $\overline{\mathcal{B}}_t$ to make them contribute more to the similarity, since they encapsulate users' clear intent on the attributes. Recall the distance function based on the local semantic metric in Eq. (5). We notice that emphasizing the dimensions is equivalent to giving large weights to the corresponding rows of the metric matrix $\mathbf{M}_c$ in similarity calculation. In our experiments, we set the weight to 0.7 for the rows corresponding to the attributes in $\mathcal{B}_t$ and $\overline{\mathcal{B}}_t$, and 0.3 for the rest.

5. EXPERIMENTS

In this section, we systematically evaluate the proposed Attribute-augmented Semantic Hierarchy (A^{2}SH) in content-based image retrieval. We first evaluate the elementary building blocks of A^{2}SH. Then, we investigate the effectiveness of A^{2}SH in automatic and interactive image retrieval.

5.1 Data and Methodology

5.1.1 Dataset Description

We conducted experiments on ImageNet [4], which is a large-scale corpus of images organized according to the WordNet hierarchy. Each concept in the hierarchy is depicted by hundreds to thousands of images collected from the Web. We used a subset of ImageNet with 1,860 concepts and 1.27 million images, which were used for ILSVRC 2012[4]. This data set contains a partial WordNet hierarchy and some isolated nodes outside WordNet. We used the WordNet hierarchy for evaluation. This hierarchy consists of 1.22 million images with 1,730 concepts, including 958 leaf concepts. Its maximum depth is 19. We merged the non-leaf nodes with no siblings into their parents since they are the sole heir to the semantics of their parents. This gives rise to a compressed hierarchy with maximum depth of 11, consisting of 1,322 concepts and the original amount of leaf concepts and images. We augmented this hierarchy with a pool of attributes, including nameable and unnameable attributes. We defined 33 nameable attributes[5] based on the attribute pool used in [8]. These attributes were linked to the concepts in a bottom-up manner. We first associated each leaf concept with its related attributes. Each non-leaf concept was then linked to the union of the attributes from its children. The unnameable attributes were automatically discovered for each concept as described in Section 3.2.2.

We randomly split the image set into a training subset with 50% of images for each concept, and a subset with the remaining images for testing. We generated ground truth on the images as follows. Based on the labeling of leaf concepts provided by ImageNet, we generated the labeling for each non-leaf concept in a bottom-up manner. A non-leaf concept was regarded as positive to an image if its any child is positive, otherwise, negative. For attributes, we conducted manual labeling. Since manual labeling is labor-intensive and time-consuming, we randomly selected 100 images of each leaf concept from the training subset for ground truth labeling. The attribute labeling in the context of non-leaf concepts was also generated in a bottom-up manner. We conducted image retrieval on the testing subset. We randomly selected 100 images from each of the 958 leaf concepts, giving rise to a total of 95,800 experimental queries.

[4]http://www.image-net.org/challenges/LSVRC/2012/index

[5]We removed the concept-specific attributes in [8, 39], such as *"jet-engine"*, since in our work, we have such concept-specific descriptions by linking the attributes (*e.g.*, *"wing"*) to concepts (*e.g.*, *"jet"*). We also added seven color attributes because of their effectiveness in image retrieval [25]. As a result, we have 33 attributes as follows: *black, blue, brown, cylinder, furry, glass, gray, green, handle, head, leg, metallic, plastic, rectangular, red, round, scale, screen, shiny, skin, smooth, spotted, stripped, tail, triangle, vegetation, wet, wheel, white, window, wing, wooden, and yellow.*

5.1.2 Visual Features

To represent image content, we extracted four types of visual features: edge, color, texture, and Scale Invariant Feature Transform (SIFT) descriptors [16]. While edge descriptor was extracted globally from the entire image, the other descriptors were extracted locally. In particular, edges were found using the standard canny detector and their orientations were quantized into 9 unsigned bins. This gives rise to a 9-D edge descriptor for each image. Color descriptors as the 3-channel LAB values were densely extracted from each pixel. Texture descriptors were computed for each pixel as the 48-D responses of texton filter banks [14]. SIFT descriptors were densely extracted from image patches at multiple scales of $\{8\times8, 12\times12, 16\times16\}$-pixel size, with 4-pixel step. For the color, texture, and SIFT descriptors, we adopted the state-of-the-art locality-constrained linear sparse coding (LLC) [36] method with max-pooling strategy to generate the global representations of images. We used a 512-D codebook for color and texture, 4,096-D for SIFT. As a result, we had 5,129-D global feature representation for each image. Since attributes usually correspond to image regions but not the entire image. To get features better characterizing attributes, we split each image into 2×3 grids, and extracted the above features from each grids. Finally, we obtained a 35,903-D (*i.e.*, $5{,}129 \times 7$) feature vector for each image.

5.1.3 Experimental Setting

We learnt linear SVM classifiers for concepts and attributes by employing LIBLINEAR toolbox[1]. We learnt ℓ_1 linear logistic regressors to select informative features for learning attributes. For local metric learning, we deployed the LMNN toolbox [37] with training triplets configuration as described in Section 3.3.1. The algorithmic parameters of the above models were tuned through five-fold cross validation. We applied the Weibull distribution [26] to normalize the responses from attribute classifiers.

To evaluate the effectiveness of the proposed **A^{2}SH** in automatic retrieval, we compared it against the following five representative retrieval solutions, including two flat methods and three hierarchical ones. a) **fVisual** retrieves images based on visual similarities with Eculidean metric; b) **fSemantic** represents each image into a flat semantic representation composed by the responses from the 1,322 concept classifiers and the 33 attribute classifiers of the root concept. It retrieves images based on such representation using the ℓ_1 distance; c) **hPath** performs retrieval based on the length of the common semantic path of an image and the query; d) **hVisual** computes the similarities between any two images by aggregating their visual similarities along their common semantic path, then conducts retrieval based on such similarity, and e) **hBilinear** [3] retrieves images by the recently proposed bilinear semantic metric which was reported achieving the state-of-the-art performance on ImageNet dataset.

To evaluate the effectiveness of **A^{2}SH** in interactive retrieval, we compared it to the following three interactive retrieval methods. a) **QPM** [24]: Query Point Movement method updates the query based on image feedbacks, and refines search results using the new query; b) **SVM** [34]: this approach learns a SVM classifier from the "relevant" and "irrelevant" images and ranks images according to their

[1]http://www.csie.ntu.edu.tw/ cjlin/liblinear/

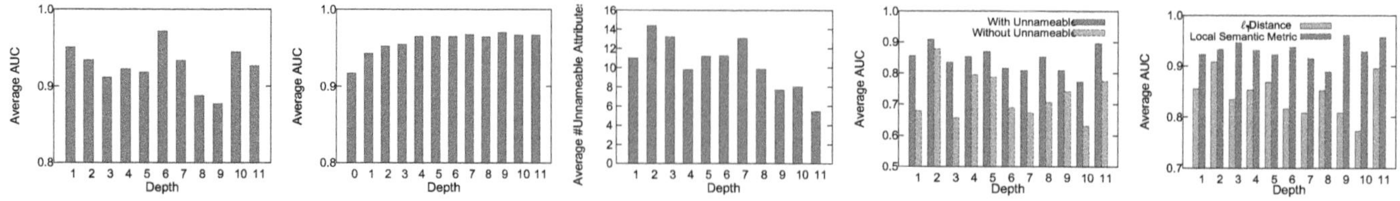

(a) (b) (c) (d) (e)

Figure 3: Performance at different depth levels measured by Average AUC: (a) concept classifers; (b) nameable attribute classifiers; (d) classification by exploiting unnameable attributes; (e) local semantic metrics. The average AUC at a depth level is obtained by averaging the AUC values of all the classifiers at that level. The average number of unnameable attribute discovered at different depth levels is shown in the subfigure (c). The depth of the root is 0.

responses from the classifiers; and c) **AF** [39]: the recently proposed Attribute Feedback approach collects user feedbacks on attributes and then ranks images according to the presence probabilities of the attributes in the images. Note that our approach enables hybrid feedbacks on attributes and images. For the sake of fair comparison, we incorporated image feedbacks into AF, such that it also uses hybrid feedbacks. Moreover, all the baseline methods were performed on the flat semantic representations of the images, rather than the low-level visual descriptors.

We conducted the evaluation in two settings with a fixed number of feedbacks and a fixed time limit, respectively. In the first setting, we conducted five feedback iterations with 20 feedbacks per iteration. For the QPM and SVM methods, 20 feedbacks on top 20 images were collected in each iteration. For the AF and our A^{2}SH methods, the same number of feedbacks were collected, including 5 attribute feedbacks and 15 image feedbacks. Five informative attributes were suggested in each iteration for soliciting attribute feedbacks. We here employed the suggestion strategy in [39]. Given a query, the feedback process was simulated by the computer according to the ground truth of the query category on the images and the association between the attributes and the category. In the setting of fixed time limit, we invited 25 novice users to interact with the system through the above four feedback methods, respectively. We did not constrain the numbers of feedbacks and iterations and allowed the users to interact with the system in a free way. Since it is time-consuming to and labor-intensive for users to evaluate a large number of queries. We randomly selected 10 images from each leaf concept as queries, giving rise to 9,580 queries in total, and assigned these queries to the users approximately evenly with no overlap between them. We set the time limit to 2 minutes in the experiments. For a given query in all the above evaluations, we used the search results from the best automatic retrieval method, *i.e.*, the proposed A^{2}SH, as the initial results for interactive retrieval.

All the experiments were conducted on a server with Intel(R) Xeon(R) CPU X5650 at 2.67 GHz on 24 cores, 48GB RAM and 64-bit Centos 5.4 operating system.

5.1.4 *Performance Metric*

We adopted the widely used metric AUC (area under ROC curve) value for classification performance evaluation. We adopted Average Precision at top K retrieved images (AP@K) for retrieval performance evaluation [21]. Denote R as the number of relevant images in the database. At any ranked position j ($1 \leq j \leq K$), let R_j be the number of relevant images in the top j results and let $I_j = 1$ if the j-th image is relevant and 0 otherwise, then AP@K is defined as $\frac{1}{min(R,K)} \sum_{j=1}^{K} \frac{R_j}{j} \times I_j$. Moreover, we also used the following hierarchical Average Precision at top K for retrieval performance evaluation. The hMAP@K is defined as $\frac{1}{min(R,K)} \sum_{j=1}^{K} \frac{D_{jq}^*/D_q^*}{j}$, where D_{jq}^* is the depth of the lowest common ground truth ancestor of ground-truth concept of the image ranked at position j and the query, D_q^* is the depth of the ground truth concept of the query. The intuition of hAP@K is that if a returned image does not exactly match the query, it is expected to be as semantically close to the query as possible, in order for a better user experience. We averaged the AP@K and hAP@K over all the queries to compute the MAP@K and hMAP@K, which are overall performance metrics.

5.2 Experimental Results

5.2.1 *Evaluations of Concept Classifiers, Attribute Classifiers, and Local Semantic Metrics*

Figure 3(a) shows the average AUC values of the concept classifiers at different depth levels in the hierarchy [4]. From these results, we can see that the concept classifiers at most levels achieve an average AUC above 0.9 except those at depth 8 and 9 with average AUC of 0.89 and 0.88, respectively. The performance of attribute classifiers is illustrated in Figure 3(b), from which we can see that the attribute classifiers at every level obtain an average AUC higher than 0.9. These results demonstrate the effectiveness of our concept and attribute classifiers in capturing the semantics of image content, leading to precise hierarchial semantic representations of images.

A bunch of unnameable attributes are discovered to complement the nameable attributes for better characterizing a concept. Figure 3(c) shows the average number of unnameable attributes discovered for the concepts at different depth levels. As aforementioned, we have no ground truth of the unnameable attributes on images and thus cannot evaluate the performance of their classifiers directly. Alternatively, we evaluated the effectiveness of unnameable attributes in improving the accuracy of distinguishing sibling concepts. In particular, for each set of sibling concepts in the hierarchy, we used the nearest neighbor classifier to classify their images based on the local semantic representations with or without unnameable attributes. The classification performance is illustrated in Figure 3(d). From the results, we can see that the discovered unnameable attributes can improve the classification performance significantly. This indicates that the unnameable attributes can help to provide a more comprehensive and discriminative description of the multiple facets of a concept.

We evaluated the effectiveness of the local semantic metrics as follows. We used the local semantic metric of each

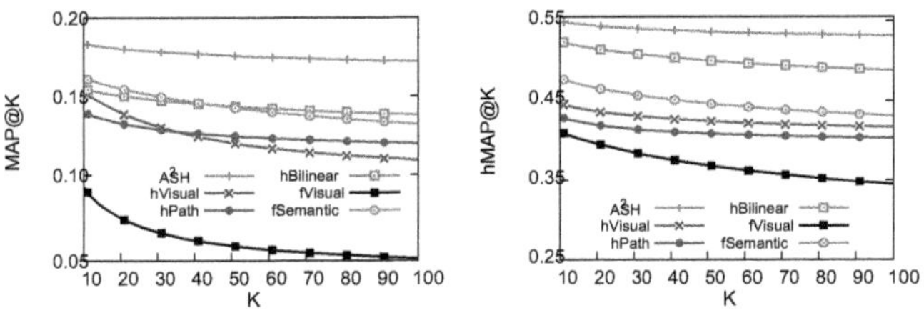

(a) (b)

Figure 4: Performance of automatic image retrieval over the 95,800 queries.

concept to help classifying the images of the concept from those of all its siblings by using the 5-nearest neighbor classifier [37]. We compared the local semantic metrics again the widely used ℓ_1 distance. The classification performance comparison is illustrated in Figure 3(e). We can see that the proposed local semantic metric outperforms the ℓ_1 distance significantly at every depth level. It achieves relative improvement 10.7% at various depth levels on average. This demonstrates the effectiveness of the local semantic metric and its capacity in composing an effective hierarchical semantic similarity to precisely characterize the semantic affinities among images.

5.2.2 *Evaluations of Automatic Retrieval*

Figure 4 illustrates the performance comparison between the proposed A^{2}SH and the other five automatic retrieval methods. We can see that A^{2}SH achieves the best retrieval performance in terms of both MAP and hMAP at all the top K results as compared to the other methods. The performance improvements of A^{2}SH over the other methods are significant. For example, A^{2}SH improves the performance by 22.4%, 23.1%, 41.5%, and 46.0% relatively in terms of MAP at the top 50 results as compared to the hBilinear, fSemantic, hPath, and hVisual methods, respectively. The corresponding performance improvements in terms of hMAP are 7.3%, 20.2%, 31.3%, and 26.5%, respectively. These results demonstrate the effectiveness of A^{2}SH in image retrieval. The superiority of A^{2}SH to the other methods arises from the following aspects: a) A^{2}SH models the semantics of images in the form of a hierarchical semantic representation consisting of multiple levels of concepts, each of which is associated with a local semantic representation in terms of related attributes. Such hierarchical semantic representation provides a more comprehensive and more precise interpretation of image semantics; and b) The hierarchical similarity function in A^{2}SH more accurately characterizes the semantic similarities among images by ensembling the local semantic metrics in the context of various concepts.

Table 1: Average retrieval time per query of automatic image retrieval over the 95,800 queries.

Method	fVisual	fSemantic	hVisual	hBilinear	A^{2}SH
Time (ms)	1.18×10^4	3.62×10^3	7.42×10^2	4.47×10^2	70.6

Table 1 lists the average retrieval time per query of the five automatic retrieval over the 95,800 queries by the five approaches. We can observe that A^{2}SH provides highly efficient retrieval. It significantly reduces the retrieval time by several orders of magnitude compared to the other methods. The reasons are two folds. First, A^{2}SH represents images in the form of a compact hierarchical semantic representation, enabling to fast similarity computation. Second, the hierarchical indexing in A^{2}SH significantly reduces the size of the search space. For the sake of fair comparison, we also accelerated the other four retrieval methods using indexing techniques. In particular, hVisual was carried out based on the hierarchical indexing in our A^{2}SH system. hBilinear was accelerated using the indexing technique in [3]. Here, we do not list the time cost of the hPath method, since it is a sub-procedure of A^{2}SH and hVisual, *i.e.*, retrieving candidate images from the hierarchical index files. The fSemantic method was accelerated by indexing the semantic concepts and attributes using inverted files. We also indexed the low-level visual features, which are high-dimensional and sparse as described in Section 5.1.2, by inverted files to accelerate the visual retrieval in fVisual and hVisual.

Table 2: Performance of interactive retrieval with 2-minute time limit over the 9,580 queries.

	MAP(%)			hMAP(%)		
RF Methods	@20	@50	@100	@20	@50	@100
A^{2}SH	**24.67**	**22.80**	**22.03**	**68.37**	**66.04**	**64.08**
AF	22.59	21.38	20.63	62.84	60.20	58.54
QPM	21.24	20.53	19.52	58.00	56.73	55.83
SVM	21.56	20.08	19.15	58.50	57.18	55.45

5.2.3 *Evaluations of Interactive Retrieval with Hybrid Feedbacks*

Figure 5 illustrates the performance of interactive retrieval with five feedback iterations in terms of MAP and hMAP at the top 20, 50, and 100 search results, respectively. From these results, the following observations can be obtained: a) The proposed A^{2}SH based interactive retrieval approach outperforms the other three methods at every iteration and all the top 20, 50, and 100 results; b) A^{2}SH significantly reduces the interaction efforts while it achieves comparable performance to the other three methods. For example, consider the MAP at top 20 results, A^{2}SH obtains a comparable performance at the 3rd, 2nd, and 2nd iteration as compared to AF, QPM and SVM at the last round, respectively. In other words, A^{2}SH can reduce labeling efforts by about 40%, 60%, and 60% as compared to the three methods, respectively; and c) The performance improvements of A^{2}SH and AF over QPM and SVM indicate the effectiveness of attribute feedbacks in delivering user search intent. The superiority of A^{2}SH to AF demonstrates that A^{2}SH can infer user intent more accurately from the feedbacks.

Table 2 lists the performance of the four interactive retrieval approaches with a fixed time limit of 2 minutes. From these results, we can see that the proposed A^{2}SH achieves the best performance in terms of both MAP and hMAP at all the top 20, 50, and 100 results. This demonstrates that A^{2}SH shapes user intent more precisely and quickly within the same interaction time and can generate more accurate search results as compared to the other methods.

6. CONCLUSIONS AND FUTURE WORK

In this paper, we proposed a novel Attribute-augmented Semantic Hierarchy (A^{2}SH) which organizes semantic concepts from general to specific, and augments each semantic concept with a set of related attributes, which are specifications of the multiple facets of the concept and act as an intermediate bridge connecting the concept and low-level visual features. We learned the concept classifiers, attribute classifiers, and hierarchical similarity function to equip A^{2}SH.

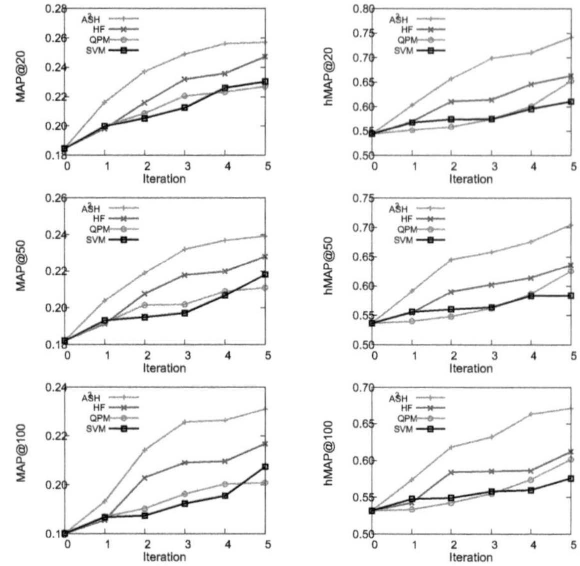

Figure 5: Performance of interactive retrieval with five feedback iterations over the 95,800 **queries.**

Based on the proposed A^2SH, we developed a content-based image retrieval system supporting both automatic retrieval and interactive retrieval with user feedbacks. A hybrid feedback mechanism was developed to collect broad array of feedbacks on attributes and images. These feedbacks were then utilized to improve the retrieval based on A^2SH. We systematically evaluated the A^2SH based image retrieval system on a large-scale corpus of over one million Web images. The experimental results demonstrated the effectiveness of A^2SH in bridging the semantic and intention gaps, leading to more accurate results compared to the state-of-the-arts CBIR approaches.

We will continue our future works in two directions. First, we will study how to build or refine the A^2SH automatically by mining concepts, attributes, and their intrinsic relations from online user-generated content. Second, we will apply the proposed A^2SH to other applications, such as the user-generated content organization and web video retrieval.

7. ACKNOWLEDGMENTS

This work was supported by NUS-Tsinghua Extreme Search (NExT) project under the grant No.: R-252-300-001-490.

8. REFERENCES

[1] M. Crucianu, M. Ferecatu, and N. Boujemaa. Relevance feedback for image retrieval: a short survey. *DELOS2 Report*, 2004.

[2] R. Datta, D. Joshi, J. Li, and J. Wang. Image retrieval: Ideas, influences, and trends of the new age. *ACM Computing Surveys*, 2008.

[3] J. Deng, A. C. Berg, and L. Fei-Fei. Hierarchical semantic indexing for large scale image retrieval. In *CVPR*, 2011.

[4] J. Deng, W. Dong, R. Socher, L.-J. Li, K. Li, and L. Fei-Fei. Imagenet: A large-scale hierarchical image database. In *CVPR*, 2009.

[5] T. Deselaers and V. Ferrari. Visual and semantic similarity in imagenet. In *CVPR*, 2011.

[6] M. Douze, A. Ramisa, and C. Schmid. Combining attributes and fisher vectors for efficient image retrieval. In *CVPR*, 2011.

[7] J. Fan, Y. Gao, and H. Luo. Integrating concept ontology and multitask learning to achieve more effective classifier training for multilevel image annotation. *TIP*, 2008.

[8] A. Farhadi, I. Endres, D. Hoiem, and D. Forsyth. Describing objects by their attributes. In *CVPR*, 2009.

[9] X. Felix, R. Ji, M. Tsai, G. Ye, and S. Chang. Weak attributes for large-scale image retrieval. In *CVPR*, 2012.

[10] C. Fellbaum. Wordnet. *Theory and Applications of Ontology: Computer Applications*, 2010.

[11] A. Hanjalic, C. Kofler, and M. Larson. Intent and its discontents: the user at the wheel of the online video search engine. In *MM*, 2012.

[12] A. Jaimes and S. fu Chang. A conceptual framework for indexing visual information at multiple levels. In *SPIE Internet Imaging*, 2000.

[13] A. Kovashka, D. Parikh, and K. Grauman. Whittlesearch: Image search with relative attribute feedback. In *CVPR*, 2012.

[14] T. Leung and J. Malik. Representing and recognizing the visual appearance of materials using three-dimensional textons. *IJCV*, 2001.

[15] M. Lew, N. Sebe, C. Djeraba, and R. Jain. Content-based multimedia information retrieval: State of the art and challenges. *TOMCCAP*, 2006.

[16] D. G. Lowe. Distinctive image features from scale-invariant keypoints. *IJCV*, 2004.

[17] Z. Ma, Y. Yang, Z. Xu, S. Yan, N. Sebe, and A. G. Hauptmann. Complex event detection via multi-source video attributes. In *CVPR*, 2012.

[18] M. Marszalek and C. Schmid. Semantic hierarchies for visual object recognition. In *CVPR*, 2007.

[19] F. Monay and D. Gatica-Perez. On image auto-annotation with latent space models. In *MM*, 2003.

[20] M. Naphade, J. R. Smith, J. Tesic, S.-F. Chang, W. Hsu, L. Kennedy, A. Hauptmann, and J. Curtis. Large-scale concept ontology for multimedia. *Multimedia, IEEE*, 2006.

[21] P. Over, G. Awad, M. Michel, J. Fiscus, G. Sanders, B. Shaw, W. Kraaij, A. F. Smeaton, and G. Quénot. Trecvid 2012 – an overview of the goals, tasks, data, evaluation mechanisms and metrics. In *TRECVID*, 2012.

[22] D. Parikh and K. Grauman. Interactively building a discriminative vocabulary of nameable attributes. In *CVPR*, 2011.

[23] Y. Rui, T. S. Huang, and S.-F. Chang. Image retrieval: Current techniques, promising directions, and open issues. *JVCIR*, 1999.

[24] Y. Rui, T. S. Huang, M. Ortega, and S. Mehrotra. Relevance feedback: a power tool for interactive content-based image retrieval. *TCSVT*, 1998.

[25] O. Russakovsky and L. Fei-Fei. Attribute learning in large-scale datasets. In *ECCV*, 2010.

[26] W. J. Scheirer, N. Kumar, P. N. Belhumeur, and T. E. Boult. Multi-attribute spaces: Calibration for attribute fusion and similarity search. In *CVPR*, 2012.

[27] N. Sebe, M. S. Lew, X. Zhou, T. S. Huang, and E. M. Bakker. The state of the art in image and video retrieval. In *Image and Video Retrieval*. 2003.

[28] A. Smeulders, M. Worring, S. Santini, A. Gupta, and R. Jain. Content-based image retrieval at the end of the early years. *TPAMI*, 2000.

[29] J. R. Smith and S.-F. Chang. Visualseek: a fully automated content-based image query system. In *MM*, 1997.

[30] C. G. Snoek, B. Huurnink, L. Hollink, M. De Rijke, G. Schreiber, and M. Worring. Adding semantics to detectors for video retrieval. *TMM*, 2007.

[31] C. G. Snoek and M. Worring. Concept-based video retrieval. *FTIR*, 2008.

[32] Y. Song, M. Zhao, J. Yagnik, and X. Wu. Taxonomic classification for web-based videos. In *CVPR*, 2010.

[33] D. Tao, X. Tang, X. Li, and X. Wu. Asymmetric bagging and random subspace for support vector machines-based relevance feedback in image retrieval. *TPAMI*, 2006.

[34] S. Tong and E. Chang. Support vector machine active learning for image retrieval. In *MM*, 2001.

[35] N. Verma, D. Mahajan, S. Sellamanickam, and V. Nair. Learning hierarchical similarity metrics. In *CVPR*, 2012.

[36] J. Wang, J. Yang, K. Yu, F. Lv, T. Huang, and Y. Gong. Locality-constrained linear coding for image classification. In *CVPR*, 2010.

[37] K. Q. Weinberger, J. Blitzer, and L. K. Saul. Distance metric learning for large margin nearest neighbor classification. In *NIPS*, 2006.

[38] Z.-J. Zha, L. Yang, T. Mei, M. Wang, and Z. Wang. Visual query suggestion. In *MM*, 2009.

[39] H. Zhang, Z.-J. Zha, S. Yan, J. Bian, and T.-S. Chua. Attribute feedback. In *MM*, 2012.

[40] K. Zhang, I. W. Tsang, and J. T. Kwok. Maximum margin clustering made practical. *TNN*, 2009.

Robust Evaluation for Quality of Experience in Crowdsourcing*

Qianqian Xu
BICMR, Peking University & University of Chinese Academy of Sciences, Beijing 100871, China
qqxu@jdl.ac.cn

Jiechao Xiong
School of Mathematical Sciences & BICMR, Peking University, Beijing 100871, China
xiongjiechao@pku.edu.cn

Qingming Huang⋆
University of Chinese Academy of Sciences & Institute of Computing Technology of Chinese Academy of Sciences, Beijing 100049, China
qmhuang@jdl.ac.cn

Yuan Yao⋆
School of Mathematical Sciences, LMAM-LMEQF-LMP, Peking University, Beijing 100871, China
yuany@math.pku.edu.cn

ABSTRACT

Strategies exploiting crowdsourcing are increasingly being applied in the area of Quality of Experience (QoE) for multimedia. They enable researchers to conduct experiments with a more diverse set of participants and at a lower economic cost than conventional laboratory studies. However, a major challenge for crowdsourcing tests is the detection and control of outliers, which may arise due to different test conditions, human errors or abnormal variations in context. For this purpose, it is desired to develop a robust evaluation methodology to deal with crowdsourceable data, which are possibly incomplete, imbalanced, and distributed on a graph. In this paper, we propose a robust rating scheme based on robust regression and Hodge Decomposition on graphs, to assess QoE using crowdsourcing. The scheme shows that the removal of outliers in crowdsourcing experiments would be helpful for purifying data and could provide us with more reliable results. The effectiveness of the proposed scheme is further confirmed by experimental studies on both simulated examples and real-world data.

Categories and Subject Descriptors

H.5.1 [**Information Interfaces and Presentation**]: Multimedia Information Systems—*Evaluation/methodology*; H.1.2 [**Models and Principles**]: User/Machine Systems—*Human factors*

*Area Chair: Martha Larson.
⋆Corresponding author.

MM'13, October 21–25, 2013, Barcelona, Spain.

http://dx.doi.org/10.1145/2502081.2502083 .

Keywords

Quality of Experience (QoE); Crowdsourcing; Paired Comparison; Robust Evaluation; Outlier Detection; LASSO; Hodge Decomposition; Random Graph

1. INTRODUCTION

Quality of Experience (QoE), which reflects the degree of a user's subjective satisfaction, has drawn increasing attention from multimedia researchers during recent years. The ultimate goal is to provide a satisfying end-user experience. Reaching this goal requires a technique that can measure the quality of multimedia content efficiently, reliably, and that is easy to implement in reality.

Among various subjective approaches for multimedia QoE evaluation, paired comparison is expected to yield more reliable results. This enables an easy and scalable implementation suitable for the purpose of calling on an Internet crowd [6] to participate in experiments using their personal computers (i.e., crowdsourcing [15]). Such a scheme uses mass collaboration and the wisdom of the crowd, and is more economical compared with conventional laboratory studies. A general framework for crowdsourcing scheme, called HodgeRank on Random Graphs (HRRG), is proposed in our previous work [33, 31]. The framework exploits various randomized paired comparison methods based on random graph theory to infer a global ranking from incomplete and imbalanced samples. It can be used to control inconsistency in paired comparison data, derive the constraints on sampling complexity to which the random selection must adhere, and allow an extension to online sampling settings [32].

Crowdsourcing subjective multimedia assessment, however, is not without pitfalls — The Crowd Is Not All Trustworthy [6]. In other words, since participants perform experiments without supervision, when the testing time for a single participant lasts too long, the participant may become impatient and may input random decisions. Such random decisions are useless and may deviate significantly from other raters' decisions. Such outliers have to be identified for QoE evaluation.

In [6], Transitivity Satisfaction Rate (TSR) is proposed for outlier detection, which checks all the intransitive triangles, e.g., $A \succ B \succ C \succ A$. In this way, we can identify and discard inconsistent (noisy) data provided by unreliable assessors. However, TSR can only be applied for complete and balanced paired comparison data. When the paired data are incomplete, i.e., have missing edges, the question remains open of how to detect the noisy pairs.

In this paper, we fill in this gap by presenting a robust outlier detection method for crowdsourcing QoE evaluation with incomplete and imbalanced data. Our algorithm is based on a linear model that has been exploited in HodgeRank [31]. Equipped with Hodge Decomposition theory, outlier detection can be solved via sparse approximation of cyclic rankings, which consists of both harmonic and triangular cyclic rankings. Such a scheme enables us to detect outliers by solving an L1-norm regularized least squares problem and recover the global ratings simultaneously.

We demonstrate the effectiveness and generality of the proposed method on both simulated examples and real-world data. Two real datasets are considered: PC-VQA (Paired Comparison based Video Quality Assessment, complete and balanced data) and PC-IQA (Paired Comparison based Image Quality Assessment, incomplete and imbalanced data), which include 38,400 and 23,097 paired comparisons, respectively. Experimental results show that the proposed outlier detection algorithm is a promising and robust assessment method suitable for crowdsourcing QoE evaluation.

Our contributions in this work are threefold:

1. A novel method for robust evaluation of QoE is proposed to deal with incomplete and imbalanced data in crowdsourcing experiments. As in robust regression, the framework provides the possibility of carrying out the assessment procedure with automatic detection of sparse outliers.

2. In the core of the framework lies the outlier detection, formulated as a LASSO problem based on sparse approximations of cyclic ranking projection of paired comparison data. Regularization paths of LASSO provide us an order on samples suspected to be outliers.

3. Global ranking after successful outlier removal provides us a robust evaluation score with more reliable results. Through experiments on both simulated and real-world data, we show that our algorithm works effectively in practice.

The remainder of this paper is organized as follows. Section 2 contains a review of related work. Then we describe the proposed framework in Section 3, which establishes the outlier detection model based on statistical linear model. Detailed experiments are presented in Section 4, followed by the conclusions in Section 5.

2. RELATED WORK

2.1 Crowdsourcing QoE

Existing methods of QoE evaluation can be divided into two categories: subjective assessment and objective assessment. *Objective* assessment builds objective quality measurement models (see [21], a survey paper, and its references) to predict perceived quality automatically and intelligently. It may or may not reflect humans' perceptual experiences. On the other hand, *subjective* assessment can provide ground-truth and verification for objective models. It is, however, labor-intensive and time-consuming.

In subjective viewing tests, stimuli are shown to a group of viewers, and then their opinions are recorded and averaged to evaluate the quality of the stimuli. Among various approaches to conducting subjective tests, Mean Opinion Score (MOS) [1] and paired comparison are the two most popular ones. In the MOS test, individuals are asked to specify a rating from Bad to Excellent (e.g., Bad-1, Poor-2, Fair-3, Good-4, and Excellent-5) to grade the quality of a stimulus. However, such a test may suffer from various problems such as ambiguity in definition of scales and dissimilar interpretations of the scale among users [6]. For this reason, the paired comparison method is currently gaining growing attention. In this approach, raters are asked to compare two stimuli simultaneously and vote on which one has the better quality based on their perceptions. The paired comparison method is an easier, less demanding task for raters, and yields more reliable data with less personal scale bias in practice. A shortcoming of paired comparison is its more expensive sampling complexity compared to the MOS test.

To tackle the cost problem, with the growth of crowdsourcing platforms, e.g., Amazon Mechanical Turk (MTurk) [20], more and more researchers tend to seek help from the Internet crowd to conduct user studies for QoE evaluation [6, 33, 31, 32, 11, 18]. However, a major challenge of crowdsourcing QoE evaluation is that not every Internet user is trustworthy. Therefore, it is necessary to detect unreliable input and remove them since they may cause inaccuracy in the estimation of QoE scores. For example, with complete and balanced data, the method in [6] proposes TSR to measure the consistency of participants' judgments. In contrast, the outlier detection method proposed in this paper provides a general framework for outlier detection when the paired comparison data are incomplete and imbalanced.

2.2 Statistical Ranking

QoE based on paired comparisons can be recast as a statistical ranking or rating problem with paired comparison data. This problem has been widely studied in various fields including decision science [24], machine learning [13], social choice [4], and statistics [19].

In particular, recent work in [17] takes a graph theoretic view, which maps paired comparison data to edge flows on a graph, possibly imbalanced (where different pairs may receive different number of comparisons) and incomplete (where each participant may only provide partial comparisons). It then applies the combinatorial Hodge Theory to achieve an orthogonal decomposition of such edge flows into three components: gradient flow for global rating (optimal in the L2-norm sense), triangular curl flow for local inconsistency, and harmonic flow for global inconsistency. Such a perspective provides us with a universal geometric description of the structure of paired comparison data, which may help understand various models, in particular the linear models with sparse outliers used in this paper.

2.3 Outlier Detection and Robust Statistics

Outliers, also called anomalies, are typically defined to be data samples that have an unusual deviation from the most common or expected pattern. Outliers are rare events, but once they have occurred, they may lead to a large instability of models estimated from the data. Outlier detection is a critical task in many fields and has been explored for a long time, especially in statistics [16]. In subjective quality evaluation in multimedia, outliers may arise due to different test conditions, human errors, or abnormal deviations in context factors such as those involving raters or systems. Various methods have been developed in literature for outlier detection and robust statistics. Among these studies, perhaps the most well-known one is robust regression with Huber's loss [16], which combines the least squares and the least absolute deviation problems. Recently, [10] discovered that robust regression with Huber's loss is equivalent to a LASSO problem, which leads to a new understanding of outlier detection based on modern variable selection techniques, e.g., [25]. There are also clustering-based, supervised learning-based, and semi-supervised learning-based procedures used in the artificial intelligence community [14]. However, there is no universal approach that is applicable in all settings. In this paper, we adopt a statistical linear model for the paired comparison data collected from an Internet-based crowd, namely HodgeRank model [31], and consider additive sparse outliers as they are defined in recent studies [30].

2.4 Random Graphs

Among various random graphs (i.e., Erdös-Rényi random graph [8], random regular graph [29], preferential attachment random graph [5], small world random graph [28], and geometric random graph [23]), Erdös-Rényi random graphs can be viewed as a random sampling process of pairs or edges independently and identically distributed (I.I.D.), hence they are well suited for the crowdsourcing scenario. In [33, 31], a random design principle based on Erdös-Rényi random graph theory is investigated to conduct crowdsourcing tests. Experimental results show that for a large Erdös-Rényi random graph $G(n, q)$ with n nodes and every edge sampled with probability q, it is necessary to have $q \gg n^{-1} \log n$ such that the graph is connected and global ranking is thus possible. To avoid global inconsistency from Hodge Decomposition, it suffices to have larger sampling rates at $q \gg n^{-1/2}$. In this paper, we also focus on this simple yet powerful random graph model particularly in the scenarios where outliers are present. We call it robust QoE evaluation in the setting of Erdös-Rényi random graph.

3. ROBUST HODGERANK

In this section, we propose a robust rating method based on Huber's robust regression and HodgeRank on graphs for multimedia quality assessment, thus is called robust HodgeRank here. Specifically, we first start from the linear model in HodgeRank and describe robust regression with Huber's loss. Then, we present how to detect outliers using Huber-LASSO, followed by an interpretation via Hodge Theory. Specific discussions are made with dichotomous choices. Finally, we discuss how to tune the regularization parameter in applications.

Let $\wedge = \{1, ..., m\}$ be a set of participants and $V = \{1, ..., n\}$ be the set of videos to be ranked. Paired comparison data is collected as a function on $\wedge \times V \times V$, which is *skew-symmetric* for each α, i.e., $Y_{ij}^{\alpha} = -Y_{ji}^{\alpha}$ representing the degree that α prefers i to j. Without loss of generality, one assumes that $Y_{ij}^{\alpha} > 0$ if α prefers i to j and $Y_{ij}^{\alpha} \leq 0$ otherwise. How to choose Y_{ij}^{α} can be seen in [33]. The strategy often used in QoE evaluation is dichotomous choice or a k-point Likert scale, $k = 3, 4, 5$. In this paper, we shall focus on the simplest case — dichotomous choice, in which Y_{ij}^{α} can be taken as $\{\pm 1\}$. However, the theory can be applied to more general case with multiple choices mentioned above.

In subjective multimedia assessment, it is natural to assume

$$Y_{ij}^{\alpha} = s_i^* - s_j^* + z_{ij}^{\alpha}, \qquad (1)$$

where $s^* \in \mathbb{R}^V$ is some true scaling score on V and z_{ij}^{α} are noise. Define the gradient operator (finite difference operator) [17, 33] by $\delta_0 : \mathbb{R}^V \to \mathbb{R}^E$ such that $(\delta_0 s)(i, j) = s_i - s_j$, then one can rewrite (1) as

$$Y = Xs^* + z, \qquad (2)$$

where the design matrix $X = \delta_0$.

If $z_{ij}^{\alpha} = \varepsilon_{ij}^{\alpha}$ represents independent noise with mean zero and fixed variance, the Gauss-Markov theorem tells us that the unbiased estimator with minimal variance is given by the following least squares problem (L2),

$$\min_{\sum_{i \in V} s_i = 0} \sum_{i,j,\alpha} (s_i - s_j - Y_{ij}^{\alpha})^2. \qquad (3)$$

Such an algorithm has been used in [33, 31, 32] to derive scaling scores in subjective multimedia assessment.

However, not all comparisons are trustworthy and there may be sparse outliers due to different test conditions, human errors, or abnormal variations in context. Putting in a mathematical way, here we consider

$$z_{ij}^{\alpha} = \gamma_{ij}^{\alpha} + \varepsilon_{ij}^{\alpha}, \qquad (4)$$

where outlier γ_{ij}^{α} has a much larger magnitude than $\varepsilon_{ij}^{\alpha}$ and is sparse as zero with probability $p \in (0, 1]$. When sparse outliers exist, (3) becomes unstable and may give bad estimation. How can one modify least squares problem to achieve a robust estimator against sparse outliers?

3.1 Robust Regression with Huber's Loss

Among various choices, Huber [16] proposes the following robust regression with Huber's loss function,

$$\min_{\sum_{i \in V} s_i = 0} \sum_{i,j,\alpha} \rho_\lambda (s_i - s_j - Y_{ij}^{\alpha}), \qquad (5)$$

where Huber's loss function $\rho_\lambda(x)$ is defined by

$$\rho_\lambda(x) = \begin{cases} x^2/2, & \text{if } |x| \leq \lambda \\ \lambda|x| - \lambda^2/2, & \text{if } |x| > \lambda. \end{cases}$$

When $|s_i - s_j - Y_{ij}^{\alpha}| < \lambda$, the comparison is regarded as a "good" one with Gaussian noise and L2-norm penalty can be used on the residual. Otherwise, it is regarded as a "bad" one contaminated by outliers and L1-norm penalty should be used which is less sensitive to the amount of deviation. So when $\lambda = 0$, it reduces to a least absolute deviation (LAD) problem or L1-norm ranking [22].

A crucial question here is how to choose λ, which is equivalent to estimating the variance of $\varepsilon_{ij}^{\alpha}$ properly. For this purpose, Huber [16] proposes concomitant scale estimation, which jointly estimates s and λ as follows:

$$\min_{\sum_{i \in V} s_i = 0, \sigma} \sum_{i,j,\alpha} \rho_{\lambda_0} \left(\frac{s_i - s_j - Y_{ij}^{\alpha}}{\sigma} \right) \sigma + m\sigma, \qquad (6)$$

where m is the total number of paired comparisons, $\sigma > 0$ is a scale parameter which estimates the standard deviation of $\varepsilon_{ij}^{\alpha}$, and λ_0 controls the shape of Huber's loss where the transition from quadratic to linear takes place. A larger λ_0 implies the Huber's loss becomes more similar to least squares regression, more efficient for normally distributed data but less robust; while smaller λ_0 makes it closer to least absolute deviation regression, more robust against outliers but less efficient for normally distributed data. [16] suggests to fix $\lambda_0 = 1.35$ in order to be robust as much as possible while retaining 95% statistical efficiency for normally distributed data. Note that for fixed σ, minimization problem (6) is equivalent to minimize (5) with $\lambda = \lambda_0\sigma$. Problem (6) becomes a convex optimization problem jointly in s and σ, which can be solved efficiently.

However, we find that in our applications the concomitant scale estimation (6) only works when outliers are sparse enough. To avoid this issue, we turn to a LASSO formulation of (5).

3.2 Huber-LASSO

It's not hard to see [10] the robust regression with Huber's loss (5) is equivalent to the following optimization problem:

$$\min_{\sum_{i\in V} s_i=0,\gamma} \frac{1}{2}\|Y - Xs - \gamma\|_2^2 + \lambda\|\gamma\|_1 \quad (7)$$
$$:= \sum_{i,j,\alpha}[\frac{1}{2}(s_i - s_j + \gamma_{ij}^{\alpha} - Y_{ij}^{\alpha})^2 + \lambda|\gamma_{ij}^{\alpha}|].$$

where $X = \delta_0$. Assume (7) has solution $(\hat{s}^{lasso}, \hat{\gamma}^{lasso})$. Here we introduce a new variable γ_{ij}^{α} for each comparison Y_{ij}^{α} such that $|\gamma_{ij}^{\alpha}| > 0$ is equivalent to $|\hat{s}_i^{lasso} - \hat{s}_j^{lasso} - Y_{ij}^{\alpha}| > \lambda$, i.e., an outlier. To be less sensitive to outliers, an L1-norm penalty of $\gamma_{ij}^{\alpha} = \hat{s}_i^{lasso} - \hat{s}_j^{lasso} - Y_{ij}^{\alpha}$ is added as in Huber's loss. Otherwise, an L2-norm is used to attenuate the Gaussian noise. This optimization problem is a partially penalized LASSO [26], and is called Huber-LASSO (or HLASSO) in this paper.

A precise equivalence between (7) and (5) is given in the following proposition.

Proposition. Assume (5) has solution $\hat{s}^{huber}$. Then

$$\hat{s}^{lasso} = \hat{s}^{huber}$$

and

$$\hat{\gamma}^{lasso} = \Theta_{\lambda}(Y_{ij}^{\alpha} - (\hat{s}_i^{lasso} - \hat{s}_j^{lasso})), \quad (8)$$

where $\Theta_{\lambda}(t) = \text{sign}(t)(|t| - \lambda)_+$ is the soft-thresholding function.

HLASSO shares the same piecewise-linear regularization paths $\lambda \mapsto \hat{s}_{\lambda}$ as classical LASSO, and thus can be solved efficiently, e.g., by the LARS algorithm [7].

However, HLASSO still suffers the following issues.

- HLASSO gives a biased estimation [9], $\hat{\gamma}$ and $\hat{s}$.
- Cross-validation to find optimal λ, turns out to be highly unstable here. Since every sample is associated with an outlier variable, leaving out samples thus loses all information about the associated outlier variables.

These issues can be alleviated using the following method.

3.3 Outlier Detection

There are two groups of variables in HLASSO (7), the score s and outlier γ, and the L1-norm penalty is only applied to γ. Therefore, via orthogonal projections of data Y onto the column space of X and its complement, one can split HLASSO into two subproblems with the two groups of variables decoupled. In particular, the outlier γ is involved in a standard LASSO problem, whose design matrix comes from random projections onto the complement of the column space of X. Thanks to the exploitation of Erdös-Rényi random graphs in crowdsoucring experiments [33, 31], positions of outliers can be consistently identified with cross-validation. After locating the outliers, one can drop those comparisons contaminated by outliers and use the least squares estimation to achieve an unbiased estimation.

To see this, let X has a full SVD decomposition $X = U\Sigma V^T$ and $U = [U_1, U_2]$ where U_1 is an orthonormal basis of the column space $\text{col}(X)$ and U_2 becomes an orthonormal basis for $\ker(X^T)$. Then the following result gives a precise statement of the split of HLASSO.

Proposition. The HLASSO solution $(\hat{s}, \hat{\gamma})$ can be obtained by the following two problems

$$\min_{\gamma} \frac{1}{2}\|U_2^T Y - U_2^T\gamma\|_2^2 + \lambda\|\gamma\|_1 \quad (9)$$

$$\min_{\sum_{i\in V} s_i=0} \frac{1}{2}\|U_1^T Xs - U_1^T(Y - \hat{\gamma})\|_2^2. \quad (10)$$

It can be seen that the original HLASSO is split into two separate optimization problems: the first is a standard LASSO problem and the second is a least squares problem. Equation (9) detects outliers and (10) modifies Y using the result of (9) and calculates scores. This score is the solution of robust regression with Huber's loss.

To solve the two issues in the last subsection, we make the following notes.

- Even though the estimator of (9) is biased [9] in the estimation of the magnitudes of γ, it can consistently identify locations of outliers under mild conditions. Such conditions, roughly speaking, require that the projection matrix U_2 satisfies an incoherence (irrepresentable) condition and the sparse outliers have large enough magnitudes, which can be found precisely as in [30], and have been widely used in sign consistency of LASSO [27]. Therefore, to avoid a biased score estimation (10), we suggest to discard the outliers picked out in (9) and run L2 on the rest of data (see Algorithm 1).
- For Erdös-Rényi random graph $G(n, q)$ in crowdsourcing experiments [31], the dimension of $\text{col}(X)$ equals to $n - 1$ and the dimension of $\ker(X^T)$ thus equals to $m - n + 1$ with $m \sim n^2 q$. To ensure connectivity of $G(n, q)$, one needs $nq \gg \log n$ which implies that asymptotically $(m-n+1)/m \to 1$. Therefore, for large n, U_2^T is arbitrarily close to a random projection matrix, which satisfies the incoherence condition for the consistency of outlier detection. Moreover, for cross-validation with sparse outliers, one can use a subset of random projections as the training set and the remaining orthogonal random projections as the validation set. This increases the stability of cross-validation in applications.

These observations suggest the following algorithm for outlier detection and robust ranking, denoted by LASSO+L2 for short.

Algorithm 1: Outlier Detection and Robust Ranking.

1 **Initialization:** Compute the SVD of X and obtain U_2;
2 **Solve the spilt problem** (9);
3 **Tuning parameter**. Determine an optimal λ^* by cross-validation with random projections;
4 **Rule out outliers and perform least squares (L2) to get an unbiased score estimation $\hat{s}$.**

3.4 Interpretation via Hodge Theory

The algorithm proposed above admits a neat interpretation from Hodge Decomposition for pairwise ranking on graphs [17]. Such a theory, referred to HodgeRank, was introduced by [33, 31] to multimedia QoE assessment. Roughly speaking, it says that all paired comparison data Y on graph G admits the following orthogonal decomposition:

aggregate paired comparisons =

global ranking $\oplus$ harmonic cyclic $\oplus$ triangular cyclic.

In particular, the latter two subspaces, harmonic and triangular cyclic rankings, are both called cyclic ranking here (i.e., subspace $\ker(X^T)$).

Note that in (9), the unitary matrix U_2^T is an orthogonal projection onto the subspace of cyclic ranking. Therefore, it enables the following interpretation of outlier detection LASSO via Hodge Decomposition. The outlier γ in (9) is a *sparse approximation of the projection of paired comparison data onto cyclic ranking subspace.* This leads us to an extension of outlier detection by TSR in complete case to incomplete settings.

3.5 Dichotomous Choice

In our crowdsourcing experiments on Internet, we often meet paired comparison data with dichotomous choices, i.e.,

$$Y_{ij}^{\alpha} = \begin{cases} 1 & \text{if } participant\ \alpha \text{ prefers } i \text{ to } j, \\ -1 & \text{otherwise.} \end{cases} \quad (11)$$

In [33], four general linear models are compared in terms of their total inconsistency in explaining the data, and we find that the uniform model in (1) is nearly the best. Below we present an equivalent form of (7), which groups outlier variables and solves the problem in a more efficient way.

Proposition. If $Y_{ij}^{\alpha} \in \{1, -1\}$, and let $w_{ij}^{\pm} = |\{\alpha : Y_{ij}^{\alpha} = \pm 1\}|$, then the solution of (7) is equivalent to:

$$\min_{\sum_{i \in V} s_i = 0, \gamma_{ij}^{\pm}} \sum_{i,j} [\tfrac{1}{2} w_{ij}^{+}(s_i - s_j + \gamma_{ij}^{+} - 1)^2 + \lambda w_{ij}^{+}|\gamma_{ij}^{+}| + \tfrac{1}{2} w_{ij}^{-}(s_i - s_j + \gamma_{ij}^{-} - 1)^2 + \lambda w_{ij}^{-}|\gamma_{ij}^{-}|]. \quad (12)$$

Here, we group all the outlier variables with the same preference on pair (i, j). This leads to a weighted LASSO with much smaller number of variables. Such a new formulation greatly improves the efficiency of the algorithm, which has been adopted in our experiments below. Similar tricks can be applied when paired comparisons have k discrete values.

PROOF. We are going to prove the property for the situation when paired comparisons have k discrete values.

Suppose $Y_{ij}^{\alpha} \in K$, $|K| = k$. Let $A_{i,j,u} = \{(i, j, \alpha) : Y_{ij}^{\alpha} = u\}, u \in K$, be the group of comparisons with same preference u on pair (i, j), $w_{ij}^{u} = |A_{i,j,u}|$ is the number of comparisons in this group and $\gamma_{ij}^{u} = \frac{1}{w_{ij}^{u}} \sum_{A_{i,j,u}} \gamma_{ij}^{\alpha}$ is the average of γ_{ij}^{α} in this group. Then for $(i, j, \alpha) \in A_{i,j,u}$, (7) becomes

$$\sum_{A_{i,j,u}} \left[\frac{1}{2}(s_i - s_j + \gamma_{ij}^{\alpha} - u)^2 + \lambda|\gamma_{ij}^{\alpha}|\right]$$

$$= \sum_{A_{i,j,u}} \Big\{\frac{1}{2}[(s_i - s_j + \gamma_{ij}^{u} - u)^2 + (\gamma_{ij}^{\alpha} - \gamma_{ij}^{u})^2 + 2(s_i - s_j + \gamma_{ij}^{u} - u)(\gamma_{ij}^{\alpha} - \gamma_{ij}^{u})] + \lambda|\gamma_{ij}^{\alpha}|\Big\}$$

$$= \frac{w_{ij}^{u}}{2}(s_i - s_j + \gamma_{ij}^{u} - u)^2 + \sum_{A_{i,j,u}} \Big\{\frac{1}{2}[(\gamma_{ij}^{\alpha} - \gamma_{ij}^{u})^2 + 2(s_i - s_j + \gamma_{ij}^{u} - u)(\gamma_{ij}^{\alpha} - \gamma_{ij}^{u})] + \lambda|\gamma_{ij}^{\alpha}|\Big\}$$

$$= \frac{w_{ij}^{u}}{2}(s_i - s_j + \gamma_{ij}^{u} - u)^2 + \sum_{A_{i,j,u}} \left[\frac{1}{2}(\gamma_{ij}^{\alpha} - \gamma_{ij}^{u})^2 + \lambda|\gamma_{ij}^{\alpha}|\right],$$

$$\text{since } \gamma_{ij}^{u} = \frac{1}{w_{ij}^{u}} \sum_{A_{i,j,u}} \gamma_{ij}^{\alpha},$$

$$\geq \frac{w_{ij}^{u}}{2}(s_i - s_j + \gamma_{ij}^{u} - u)^2 + \sum_{A_{i,j,u}} \lambda|\gamma_{ij}^{\alpha}|,$$

where equality holds iff $\gamma_{ij}^{\alpha} = \gamma_{ij}^{u}$, hence (7) becomes

$$\frac{w_{ij}^{u}}{2}(s_i - s_j + \gamma_{ij}^{u} - u)^2 + w_{ij}^{u}\lambda|\gamma_{ij}^{u}|.$$

The result follows from the sum over all the pair (i, j) and $u \in K$. □

Moreover, we would like to point out that the outlier detection LASSO above can be applied to the scenario of subject-based outlier detection. A simple way is to compute the percentage of outliers for an assessor, based on which one can evaluate the reliability of each assessor subject. For example, one can drop those unreliable assessors whose input data involve a large number of outliers beyond certain threshold. In other words, subject-based outlier detection can be a straightforward extension from our proposed framework on paired comparison judgment outliers.

3.6 Parameter Tuning

We have suggested cross-validation on (9) to tune parameter λ based on random projections, rather than traditional cross-validation on the origin problem (7) by leaving-out samples. This is because of a special feature in outlier detection LASSO. Since each variable is associated with a sample, sample leaving-out will lose all the information about the associated variable. Therefore, traditional cross-validation with leaving-out samples is expected to be highly unstable. To achieve a cross-validation based on random projections, one can randomly draw l-rows from projection matrix U_2^T, which can be regarded as l-random projections onto the $\ker(X^T)$, as the training set. The remaining rows of U_2^T are used for validation set. Cross-validation is then applied to such random projection based measurements using training and validation sets.

In practice, although cross-validation works for sparse and large enough outliers, we find it might fail when outliers become dense and small in magnitudes. However, when cross-validation fails, we still find it informative to look at the regularization paths of (9) directly. From the order that variables γ_{ij}^{α} become nonzero as regularization parameter λ

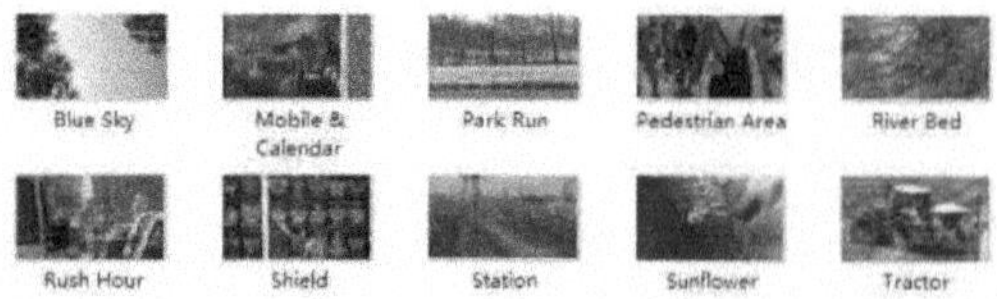

Figure 1: Reference videos in LIVE database.

changes from ∞ to small, one can faithfully identify the tendency that a measurement Y_{ij}^{α} is contaminated by outliers, even when cross-validation fails. Therefore, we suggest to use regularization paths to inspect the outliers in applications.

Prior knowledge can also be used to tune the regularization parameter. For example, if one would like to drop a certain percentage of outliers, say 5%, then the top 5% variables appeared on regularization paths can be regarded as outliers and dropped. Moreover, the deviation magnitudes sometimes can be used to determine outliers. For example in dichotomous choice, we can just set $\lambda = 1$. If $s_i - s_j > 0$, and $Y_{ij}^{\alpha} = -1$ so the residual $|\gamma_{ij}^{\alpha}| = |s_i - s_j - Y_{ij}^{\alpha}| > 1$, then this comparison is easy to pick out. On the other hand, if $Y_{ij}^{\alpha} = 1$, $|\gamma_{ij}^{\alpha}| > 1$ iff $s_i - s_j > 2$, the sample can reasonably be selected as an outlier.

4. EXPERIMENTS

In this section, we systematically evaluate the performance of the proposed outlier detection algorithm for QoE assessment. First, we describe the datasets used for the experiments, which include both simulated and real-world data. Then, Algorithm 1 is applied to both datasets. To avoid the situations in which the optimal choice of λ^* by cross-validation is too conservative to detect outliers when they are dense and of small magnitudes (as discussed in Section 3.6), we look at the whole regularization path $\hat{\gamma}_\lambda$ by varying λ from ∞ to 0. AUC for ROC curves is used in the experiments to measure if the true outliers are detected by early appearance on regularization paths. The higher the AUC, the better the performance. Finally, some further discussions are provided.

4.1 Datasets

Three datasets are used in this work. The datasets include simulated data, PC-VQA (Paired Comparison based Video Quality Assessment) data [33], and PC-IQA (Paired Comparison based Image Quality Assessment) data [32].

In simulated data, we first create a random total order on n candidates V as the ground-truth and add paired comparison edges $(i, j) \in E$ to graph $G = (V, E)$ randomly, with the preference direction following the ground-truth order. To create sparse outliers, a random subset of E is reversed in preference direction. In this way, we simulate a paired comparison graph, possibly incomplete and imbalanced, with outliers.

The second dataset, PC-VQA, collected by [33], contains 38400 paired comparisons for LIVE dataset [3] (Figure 1) from 209 observers. One of the advantageous properties of this dataset is that the paired comparison data is complete and balanced.

The third dataset, PC-IQA, contains 15 reference images and 15 distorted versions of each reference, for a total of 240 images which come from two publicly available datasets, LIVE [3] and IVC [2] (Figure 2). Totally, 186 observers, each of whom performs a varied number of comparisons via

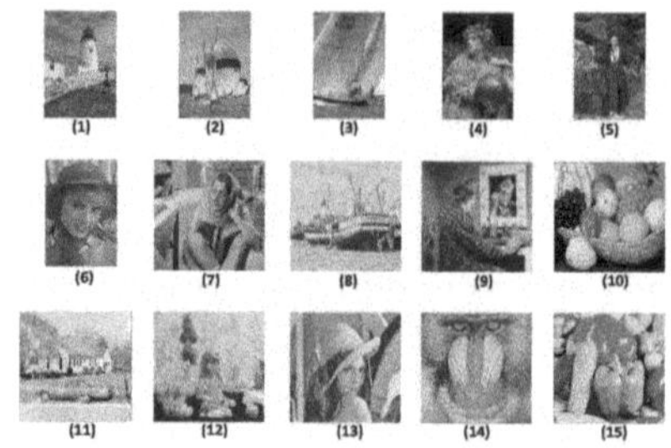

Figure 2: Reference images in LIVE and IVC databases. (The first six are from LIVE and the remaining nine are from IVC.)

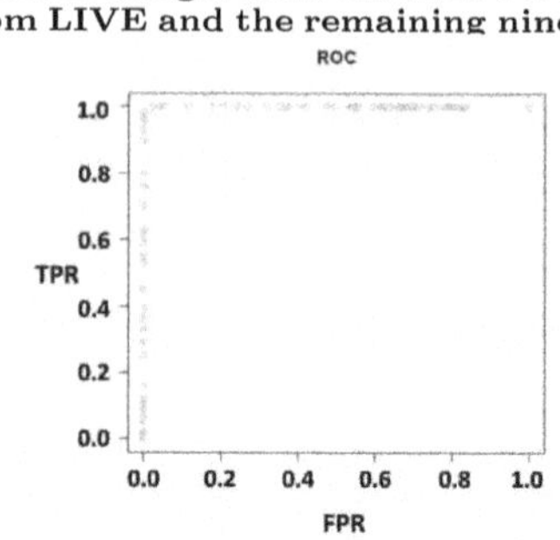

Figure 3: ROC curve of (2000,5%) for simulated data.

Internet, provide 23,097 paired comparisons (the resulting graph is incomplete and imbalanced) for subjective IQA.

These three datasets provide us both simulated and real-world paired data and hence can all be used for the experiments of QoE task. In the following, we first show the effectiveness of the proposed method on simulated data, then further confirm the effectiveness on real-world datasets.

4.2 Simulated Data

We choose $|V| = n = 16$ in the simulated graph $G = (V, E)$, which is consistent with the other real-world datasets. We make the following definitions of experimental parameters. The total number of paired comparisons occurred on this graph is SN (Sample Number), and the number of outliers is ON (Outlier Number). Finally, we define the outlier percentage OP = ON/SN.

In order to evaluate the performance of LASSO in outlier detection, for each pair of (SN,OP), we compute the regularization path $\hat{\gamma}^\lambda$ of LASSO by varying regularization parameter λ from ∞ to 0, which is solved by R-package `quadrupen` [12]. The order in which $\hat{\gamma}_{ij}^{\lambda}$ becomes nonzero gives a ranking of the edges according to their tendency to be outliers. Since we have the ground-truth outliers, the ROC curve can be plotted by thresholding the regularization parameter λ at different levels which creates different true positive rates (TPR) and false positive rates (FPR). For example, when SN = 2000 and OP = 5%, the ROC curve can be seen in Figure 3. With different choices of SN and OP, Area Under the Curve (AUC) are computed with standard deviations over 20 runs and shown in Table 1 to measure the performance of LASSO in outlier detection. It can be seen that when samples are large and outliers are sparse, AUC is close to 1. This implies that the regularization paths of LASSO give an accurate estimation of outliers (indicated by a small FPR with large TPR), where samples appearing early on LASSO paths are mostly contaminated by outliers. Figure 4 illustrates an example of such LASSO paths.

We note that when OP = 50%, i.e., half of the edges are reverted by outliers, Table 1 shows a rapid decrease of AUC to about 0.5, which is the performance of random guess.

Table 1: AUC over (SN,OP) for simulated data, 20 times repeat.

AUC (sd)	OP=5%	OP=10%	OP=15%	OP=20%	OP=25%	OP=30%	OP=35%	OP=40%	OP=45%	OP=50%
SN=1000	0.999(0)	0.999(0.001)	0.998(0.001)	0.996(0.003)	0.992(0.005)	0.983(0.010)	0.962(0.016)	0.903(0.038)	0.782(0.050)	0.503(0.065)
SN=2000	0.999(0)	0.999(0)	0.999(0)	0.998(0.001)	0.997(0.001)	0.992(0.004)	0.986(0.007)	0.956(0.019)	0.849(0.052)	0.493(0.086)
SN=3000	0.999(0)	0.999(0)	0.999(0)	0.999(0)	0.998(0)	0.996(0.002)	0.990(0.004)	0.971(0.013)	0.885(0.032)	0.479(0.058)
SN=4000	0.999(0)	0.999(0)	0.999(0)	0.999(0)	0.999(0)	0.997(0.001)	0.994(0.002)	0.980(0.008)	0.903(0.028)	0.519(0.055)
SN=5000	0.999(0)	0.999(0)	0.999(0)	0.999(0)	0.999(0)	0.998(0.001)	0.994(0.002)	0.984(0.009)	0.933(0.022)	0.501(0.066)

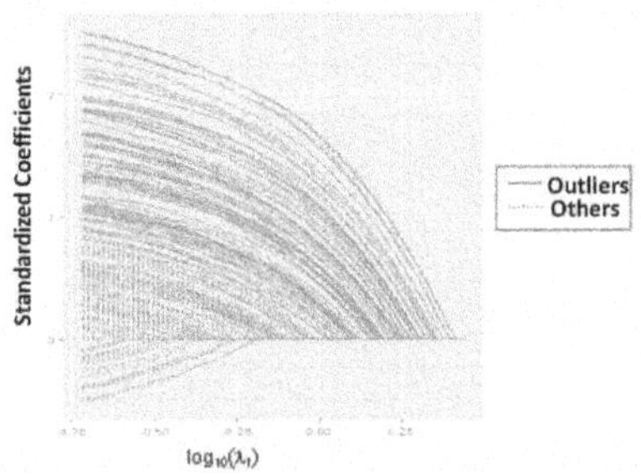

Figure 4: The regularization paths of (2000,5%) for simulated data. The true outliers (plotted in red color) mostly lie outside the majority of paths.

This is expected, since when more than half of the edges are perturbed, it is impossible to distinguish the signal from noise by any method. A phase transition can be observed in this table, that AUC rapidly approaches to 1 as long as OP drops below 50% and SN increases.

4.3 Real-world Data

As there is no ground-truth for outliers in real-world data, one can not exploit ROC and AUC as in simulated data to evaluate outlier detection LASSO here. In this subsection, we inspect the top p% pairs returned by LASSO regularization paths and compare them with the whole data to see if they are reasonably good outliers.

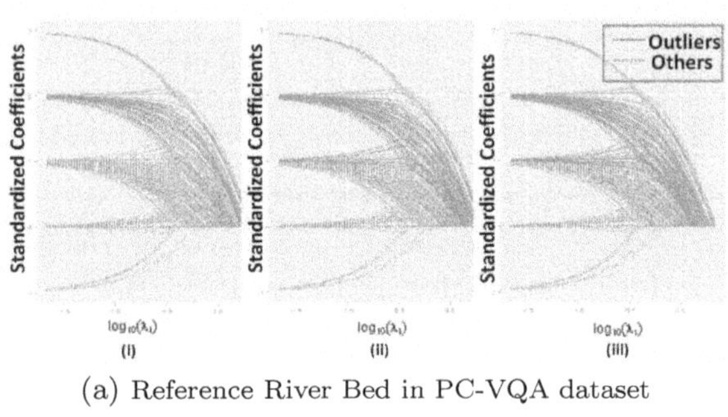

(a) Reference River Bed in PC-VQA dataset

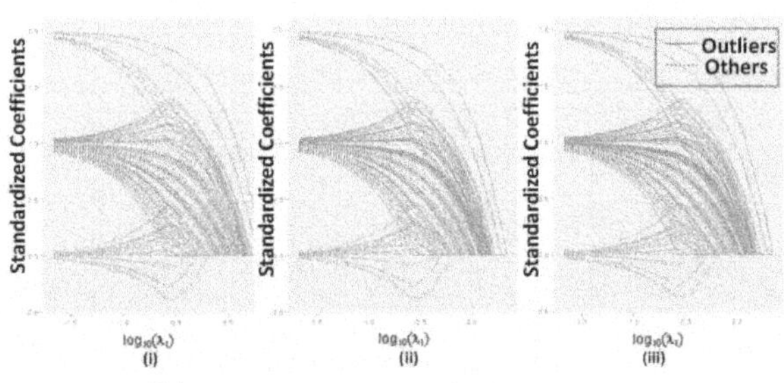

(b) Reference 10 in PC-IQA dataset

Figure 5: Regularization paths. (i) Top 2% outliers; (ii) Top 5% outliers; (iii) Top 8% outliers.

For simplicity, in the PC-VQA dataset, we randomly take River Bed as an illustrative example (other reference videos exhibit similar results). Figure 5(a) shows the top 2%, 5%, and 8% outliers picked by regularization paths in River Bed. In order to allow a closer inspection of these pairs, outliers are marked in three colors (red for top 2%, green for top 2%-5%, and blue for top 5%-8%) in the paired comparison matrix in Table 2(a). The paired comparison matrix is constructed as follows (Table 2(b) is constructed in the same way). For each video pair $\{i, j\}$, let n_{ij} be the number of comparisons, for which a_{ij} raters agree that the quality of i is better than j (a_{ji} carries the opposite meaning). So $a_{ij} + a_{ji} = n_{ij}$ if no tie occurs. In the PC-VQA dataset, $n_{ij} \equiv 32$ for all videos. The order of the video ID in Table 2(a) is arranged from high to low according to the global ranking score calculated by the least squares method (3). It is interesting to see that the outliers picked out are mainly distributed in the lower left corner of this matrix, which implies that the outliers are those preference orders with a large deviation from the global ranking scores by L2. In addition, the earlier a pair is detected by LASSO as an outlier, the closer it will be to the lower left corner and the larger such a deviation is. Moreover, Figure 6 further confirms this phenomenon. Here, all the top 5% outliers are reversed preference arrows pointing from lower quality to higher quality videos. Clearly one can see that video V6, V12, V2, V11, and V8 are the top 5 videos which brought in the largest number of outliers in data collection.

To see the effect of outliers on global ranking scores, Table 3(a) shows the outcomes of three ranking algorithms, namely L2, HLASSO, and LASSO+L2. We choose the λ which finds 5% outliers. As we noted earlier, the global ranking scores directly returned by HLASSO are possibly biased in the estimation of large outliers, hence LASSO+L2 is used toward less-biased solution. While video V3 is nearly the same quality as V7 in L2, both HLASSO and LASSO+L2 put V3 worse than V7. Removal of the top 5% outliers in LASSO+L2 further changes the orders of some competitive videos, such as V15 and V10, V2 and V11, which shows that the effect of outliers is mainly within the highly competitive groups.

The experiments above demonstrate the effectiveness of the proposed method on complete and balanced data. To illustrate the detection ability on incomplete and imbalanced data, the PC-IQA dataset is taken into consideration. Figure 5(b), Table 2(b), and Figure 7 show the experimental results on a randomly selected reference (image 10 in Figure 2). Similar observations as above can be made and we note that outliers distributed on this dataset are much sparser than PC-VQA, shown by many zeros in the lower left corner of Table 2(b). The outcomes of three ranking algorithms with the top 5% outliers are shown in Table 3(b) for PC-IQA. Based on 5% outliers detection, both HLASSO and LASSO+L2 differ with L2 in that image ID =

Table 2: Paired comparison matrixes, with red pairs for top 2% outliers, green for top 2%-5% outliers, and blue for top 5%-8% outliers.

(a) Reference River Bed in PC-VQA dataset

Video ID	**1**	**13**	**9**	**14**	**5**	**15**	**10**	**3**	**7**	**16**	**4**	**8**	**2**	**11**	**12**	**6**
1	0	29	28	31	32	30	32	31	30	27	27	31	25	31	32	32
13	3	0	23	22	24	24	14	22	25	29	28	27	25	27	28	31
9	4	9	0	25	5	20	26	25	15	26	23	27	26	27	30	31
14	1	10	7	0	14	29	19	22	14	23	23	23	27	23	26	25
5	0	8	27	18	0	14	11	12	22	13	22	18	25	30	31	30
15	2	8	12	3	18	0	20	24	13	23	18	17	28	22	30	29
10	0	18	6	13	21	12	0	18	11	13	18	27	26	26	28	29
3	1	10	7	10	20	8	14	0	14	17	19	19	18	28	28	32
7	2	7	17	18	10	19	21	18	0	18	8	23	9	15	30	30
16	5	3	6	9	19	9	19	15	14	0	18	24	23	20	30	30
4	5	4	9	9	10	14	14	13	24	14	0	17	15	23	30	30
8	1	5	5	9	14	15	5	13	9	8	15	0	25	13	19	24
2	7	7	6	5	7	4	6	14	23	9	17	7	0	18	17	29
11	1	5	5	9	2	10	6	4	17	12	9	19	14	0	24	26
12	0	4	2	6	1	2	4	4	2	2	2	13	15	8	0	19
6	0	1	1	7	2	3	3	0	2	2	2	8	3	6	13	0

(b) Reference 10 in PC-IQA dataset

Image ID	**1**	**6**	**9**	**12**	**10**	**2**	**16**	**7**	**15**	**11**	**8**	**13**	**14**	**3**	**4**	**5**
1	0	11	10	12	11	20	11	15	13	14	16	15	14	17	14	13
6	3	0	5	10	8	11	11	12	10	10	12	13	12	11	14	16
9	3	7	0	5	7	6	3	10	4	5	8	6	5	11	14	17
12	3	2	3	0	6	9	13	7	8	5	8	13	13	13	16	17
10	5	4	0	2	0	7	2	5	6	7	9	5	6	12	17	19
2	0	3	5	4	4	0	8	9	9	13	6	11	12	12	13	13
16	3	1	1	2	2	4	0	6	16	8	7	16	16	15	20	14
7	0	2	1	1	4	2	4	0	7	5	12	8	9	13	17	16
15	0	4	1	4	1	4	3	2	0	8	7	12	16	16	16	14
11	0	0	0	0	0	0	3	4	1	0	9	2	6	11	14	17
8	0	0	0	0	0	4	0	0	0	0	0	5	8	10	15	17
13	0	0	0	0	0	0	0	0	4	2	1	0	12	13	15	16
14	0	0	1	0	0	0	1	0	0	2	1	2	0	6	12	10
3	0	0	0	0	0	0	0	0	0	0	0	0	9	0	10	10
4	0	0	0	0	0	0	0	0	0	2	0	2	4	1	0	9
5	0	0	0	0	0	0	0	0	0	1	0	0	5	1	5	0

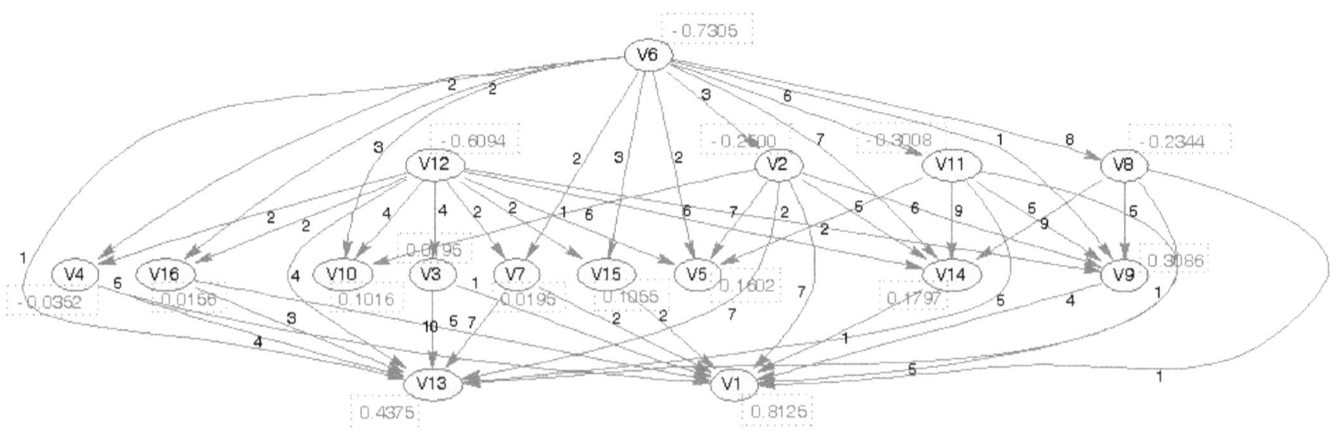

Figure 6: Top 5% outliers for reference River Bed in PC-VQA dataset. The integer on each curve represents a_{ij} defined in subsection 4.3 and the red decimal in dotted rectangle represents the global ranking score returned by L2 algorithm.

Table 3: Comparison of different rankings (5% outliers are considered). Three ranking methods are compared with the integer represents the ranking position and the number in parentheses represents the global ranking score returned by the corresponding algorithm.

(a) Reference River Bed in PC-VQA dataset

Video ID	L2	LASSO+L2	HLASSO
1	1 (0.8125)	1 (0.9245)	1 (0.8414)
13	2 (0.4375)	2 (0.6003)	2 (0.4615)
9	3 (0.3086)	3 (0.3620)	3 (0.3182)
14	4 (0.1797)	4 (0.3034)	4 (0.1978)
5	5 (0.1602)	5 (0.1996)	5 (0.1659)
15	6 (0.1055)	7 (0.1172)	6 (0.1098)
10	7 (0.1016)	6 (0.1458)	7 (0.1084)
3	8 (0.0195)	10 (-0.0021)	9 (0.0193)
7	8 (0.0195)	8 (0.0043)	8 (0.0194)
16	10 (0.0156)	9 (0.0015)	10 (0.0133)
4	11 (-0.0352)	11 (-0.0538)	11 (-0.0390)
8	12 (-0.2344)	12 (-0.2758)	12 (-0.2403)
2	13 (-0.2500)	14 (-0.3758)	13 (-0.2695)
11	14 (-0.3008)	13 (-0.3587)	14 (-0.3130)
12	15 (-0.6094)	15 (-0.7181)	15 (-0.6347)
6	16 (-0.7305)	16 (-0.8743)	16 (-0.7586)

(b) Reference 10 in PC-IQA dataset

Image ID	L2	LASSO+L2	HLASSO
1	1 (0.8001)	1 (0.8876)	1 (0.8144)
6	2 (0.6003)	2 (0.7034)	2 (0.6143)
9	3 (0.5362)	3 (0.6048)	3 (0.5484)
12	4 (0.4722)	4 (0.4886)	4 (0.4752)
10	5 (0.3472)	6 (0.2698)	5 (0.3368)
2	6 (0.3044)	5 (0.2859)	6 (0.3105)
16	7 (0.2756)	7 (0.2677)	7 (0.2757)
7	8 (0.1403)	8 (0.1398)	8 (0.1374)
15	8 (0.0965)	9 (0.0540)	9 (0.0865)
11	10 (-0.1609)	10 (-0.1815)	10 (-0.1563)
8	11 (-0.2541)	11 (-0.2813)	11 (-0.2620)
13	12 (-0.2964)	12 (-0.2927)	12 (-0.2958)
14	13 (-0.6215)	14 (-0.6478)	14 (-0.6361)
3	14 (-0.6315)	13 (-0.6246)	13 (-0.6315)
4	15 (-0.7822)	15 (-0.8098)	15 (-0.7889)
5	16 (-0.8262)	16 (-0.8639)	16 (-0.8287)

3 (`fruit_flou_f3.bmp` in IVC [2] database) is better than image ID = 14 (`fruit_lar_r1.bmp`). Such a preference is in agreement with the pairwise majority voting of 9:6 votes (Table 2(b)). Therefore, the example shows that under sparse outliers L2 ranking may be less accurate.

Moreover, LASSO+L2 further suggests that image ID = 2 should be better than image ID = 10, in contrast to the other two algorithms. A further inspection of the dataset confirms that such a suggestion by LASSO+L2 is reasonable. Figure 8 shows the two images (ID = 2 and ID = 10) from the IVC [2] database. There is a blurring effect in image ID = 2 and a blocking effect in the background of ID = 10. In the dataset, 4 raters agree that the quality of ID = 2 is better than ID = 10, while 7 raters have the opposite opinion. Clearly LASSO+L2 chooses the preference of the minority, based on aggregate behavior over population after removal of some outliers. Why does this happen? In fact, when a participant compares the quality between ID = 2 and ID = 10, his preference depends on his attention — on the foreground or on the whole image. A rater with foreground attention might be disturbed by the blurring effect, leading to $10 \succ 2$. On the other hand, a rater with holistic attention may notice the blocking effect in the background, leading to $2 \succ 10$. Which criterion might be dominant? To explore this question, we further collected more clean data (i.e., 20 more persons provide careful judgments in controlled lab conditions), among which a dominant percentage (80%) agrees with $2 \succ 10$, consistent with the LASSO+L2 prediction after removal of outliers. This suggests that most observers assess the quality of an image from a global point of view. Another less stable way is to select a subset of clean

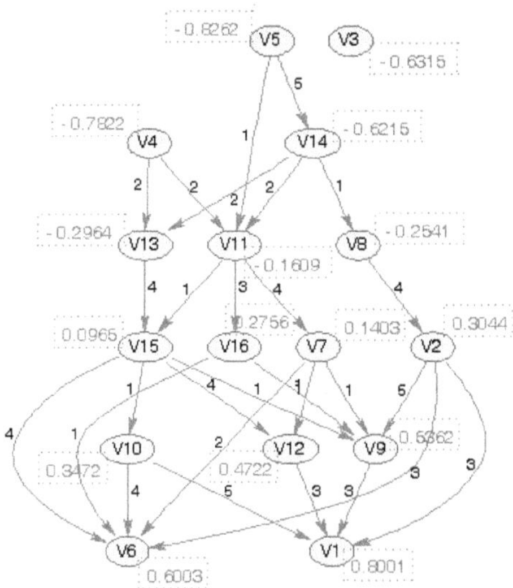

Figure 7: Top 5% outliers for reference 10 in PC-IQA dataset. The integer on each curve and the red decimal in dotted rectangle carry the same meanings with those in Figure 6.

data without outliers for validation, which points generally towards LASSO+L2<HLASSO<L2 in least squares error. Such a result suggests that for those highly competitive or confused alternative pairs, a large number of samples are expected to find a good ranking in majority voting; on the other hand, by exploiting intermediate comparisons of good confidence with other alternatives, it is possible to achieve a reliable global ranking with a much smaller number of samples, such as what LASSO+L2 does here.

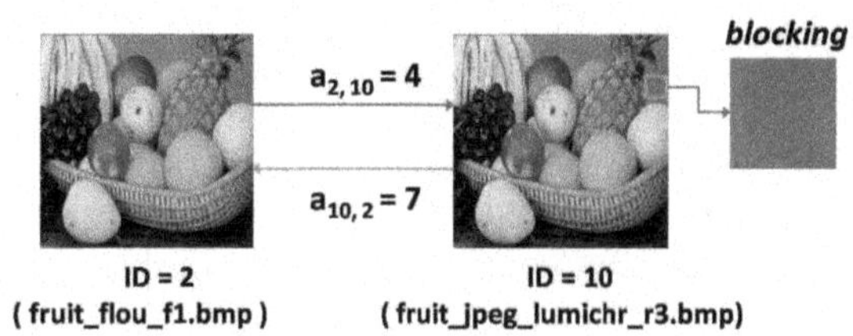

Figure 8: Dissimilar judgments due to multi-criteria in paired comparisons among users. The image is undistinguishable due to its small size, so image names in IVC [2] database are printed here.

4.4 Discussion

As we have seen, after dropping outliers, LASSO+L2 gives a different order on some images compared with L2, indicating that outliers may cause different rank aggregations. The differences mostly lie among the highly competitive alternatives. The order returned by HLASSO somewhere lies between the two orders returned by L2 and LASSO+L2, showing that the bias in HLASSO estimation makes it less sensitive to changes. From these results, we may conclude that outlier detection by our proposed framework is effective, and that using the framework, one can prune unreliable paired comparisons and achieve a good global ranking score with less data collected.

In our experiments, we observe that cross-validation may work when outliers with large magnitudes are sparse enough. When cross-validation works it helps to identify an optimal regularization parameter and sparsity pattern. However, in our QoE evaluation scenario, $|Y_t(i,j)|$ is bounded by 1. For this reason, it is hard for sparse outliers to satisfy the large magnitude assumption. In this case, cross-validation may exhibit conservative and unstable behavior, either picking out all the outliers or none of them. Therefore, as we suggested earlier, users applying our framework should compute regularization paths whenever possible to inspect outliers.

Additionally, we find that when raters are asked to consider different pairs of images, they implicitly take different salient features into account. Dissimilar judgments due to noise will vanish when the sample size goes to infinity while disagreements due to multi-criteria will persist with the increase of sample size. This phenomenon will require additional investigation in the future.

5. CONCLUSIONS

In this paper, we have proposed a framework for robustly assessing the QoE of multimedia content, in which outliers are automatically detected and robust global ranking scores are obtained after outlier removal. In such a framework, outliers are sparse approximations of cyclic ranking projections of paired comparison data and regularization paths of outlier detection LASSO provides us an informative procedure. In particular, outlier detection LASSO, provides benefits in crowdsourcing experiments with the Erdös-Rényi random graph designs. Experiments are presented with both simulations and two real-world datasets including both representative images and videos in QoE with crowdsourcing data. It is shown that a two-stage method (outlier detection LASSO followed by a least squares on cleaned data) can remove sparse outliers and achieve a global rating more consistent with the population than the least squares method applied to the whole data. The framework enables us to derive reliable global ratings after purifying data, and as such provides a helpful tool for the multimedia community, which exploits crowdsourceable paired comparison data for robust ranking. Finally, we would like to point out that with the rapid development of technologies for rich user interfaces, the proposed framework can be extended via stochastic optimization to assess users' experience in an online setting, which is a largely unexplored field and one of our future directions.

6. ACKNOWLEDGMENTS

This work was supported in part by National Basic Research Program of China (973 Program): 2012CB316400 and 2012CB825501, in part by National Natural Science Foundation of China: 61025011 and 61071157.

7. REFERENCES

[1] *ITU-R Recommendation P.800. Methods for subjective determination of transmission quality*, 1996.

[2] Subjective quality assessment irccyn/ivc database. `http://www2.irccyn.ec-nantes.fr/ivcdb/`, 2005.

[3] LIVE image & video quality assessment database. `http://live.ece.utexas.edu/research/quality/`, 2008.

[4] K. Arrow. A difficulty in the concept of social welfare. *Journal of Political Economy*, 58(4):328–346, 1950.

[5] A.-L. Barabasi and R. Albert. Emergence of scaling in random networks. *Science*, 286(5439):509–512, 1999.

[6] K.-T. Chen, C.-C. Wu, Y.-C. Chang, and C.-L. Lei. A crowdsourceable QoE evaluation framework for multimedia content. pages 491–500. ACM Multimedia, 2009.

[7] B. Efron, T. Hastie, I. Johnstone, and R. Tibshirani. Least angle regression. *Annals of Statistics*, 32(2):407–499, 2004.

[8] P. Erdös and A. Rényi On random graphs I. *Publicationes Mathematicae-Debrecen*, 6:290–297, 1959.

[9] J. Fan and R. Li. Variable selection via nonconcave penalized likelihood and its oracle properties. *Journal of American Statistical Association*, pages 1348–1360, 2001.

[10] I. Gannaz. Robust estimation and wavelet thresholding in partial linear models. *Statistics and Computing*, 17:293–310, 2007. arXiv:math/0612066v1.

[11] B. Gardlo, M. Ries, and T. Hoßfeld. Impact of screening technique on crowdsourcing QoE assessments. International Conference Radioelektronika 2012, Special Session on Quality in multimedia systems, 2012.

[12] Y. Grandvalet, C. Ambroise, and J. Chiquet. Sparsity by worst-case quadratic penalties. 2012. arXiv:1210.2077.

[13] R. Herbrich, T. Graepel, and K. Obermayer. *Large margin rank boundaries for ordinal regression*. MIT Press, 2000.

[14] V. Hodge and J. Austin. A survey of outlier detection methodologies. *Artificial Intelligence Review*, 22(2):85–126, 2004.

[15] J. Howe. The rise of crowdsourcing. *Wired Magazine*, 14(6):176–183, 2006.

[16] P. J. Huber. *Robust Statistics*. New York: Wiley, 1981.

[17] X. Jiang, L.-H. Lim, Y. Yao, and Y. Ye. Statistical ranking and combinatorial Hodge theory. *Mathematical Programming*, 2010.

[18] C. Keimel, J. Habigt, and K. Diepold. Challenges in crowd-based video quality assessment. In *Forth International Workshop on Quality of Multimedia Experience (QoMEX 2012)*, 2012.

[19] M. Kendall and B. Smith. On the method of paired comparisons. *Biometrika*, 31(3-4):324–345, 1940.

[20] A. Kittur, E. Chi, and B. Suh. Crowdsourcing user studies with Mechanical Turk. pages 453–456. SIGCHI conference on Human factors in computing systems, 2008.

[21] W. Lin and C.-C. J. Kuo. Perceptual visual quality metrics: A survey. *Journal of Visual Communication and Image Representation*, 22(4):297–312, 2011.

[22] B. Osting, J. Darbon, and S. Osher. Statistical ranking using the L_1-norm on graphs. *AIMS'*, 2012.

[23] M. Penrose. *Random Geometric Graphs (Oxford Studies in Probability)*. Oxford University Press, 2003.

[24] T. Saaty. A scaling method for priorities in hierarchical structures. *Journal of Mathematical Psychology*, 15(3):234–281, 1977.

[25] Y. She and A. B. Owen. Outlier detection using nonconvex penalized regression. *Journal of the American Statistical Association*, 106(494):626–639, 2011.

[26] R. Tibshirani. Regression shrinkage and selection via the LASSO. *J. of the Royal Statistical Society, Series B*, 58(1):267–288, 1996.

[27] M. J. Wainwright. Sharp thresholds for high-dimensional and noisy sparsity recovery using L_1-constrained quadratic programming (LASSO). *IEEE Transactions on Information Theory*, 55(5):2183–2202, 2009.

[28] D. Watts and S. Strogatz. Collective dynamics of 'small-world' networks. *Nature*, (393):440–442, 1998.

[29] N. Wormald. Models of random regular graphs. pages 239–298. In Surveys in Combinatorics, 1999.

[30] J. Xiong, X. Cheng, and Y. Yao. Robust ranking on graphs. *Journal of Machine Learning Research*, submitted, 2013.

[31] Q. Xu, Q. Huang, T. Jiang, B. Yan, W. Lin, and Y. Yao. HodgeRank on random graphs for subjective video quality assessment. *IEEE Transactions on Multimedia*, 14(3):844–857, 2012.

[32] Q. Xu, Q. Huang, and Y. Yao. Online crowdsourcing subjective image quality assessment. pages 359–368. ACM Multimedia, 2012.

[33] Q. Xu, T. Jiang, Y. Yao, Q. Huang, B. Yan, and W. Lin. Random partial paired comparison for subjective video quality assessment via HodgeRank. pages 393–402. ACM Multimedia, 2011.

Size Does Matter: How Image Size Affects Aesthetic Perception?

Wei-Ta Chu[†], Yu-Kuang Chen[†], and Kuan-Ta Chen[‡]

[†]Department of Computer Science and Information Engineering, National Chung Cheng University
[‡]Institute of Information Science, Academia Sinica

ABSTRACT

There is no doubt that an image's content determines how people assess the image aesthetically. Previous works have shown that image contrast, saliency features, and the composition of objects may jointly determine whether or not an image is perceived as aesthetically pleasing. In addition to an image's content, the way the image is presented may affect how much viewers appreciate it. For example, it may be assumed that a picture will always look better when it is displayed in a larger size. *Is this "the-bigger-the-better" rule always valid?* If not, *in what situations is it invalid?*

In this paper, we investigate how an image's resolution (pixels) and physical dimensions (inches) affect viewers' appreciation of it. Based on a large-scale aesthetic assessments of 100 images displayed in a variety of resolutions and physical dimensions, we show that an image's size significantly affects its aesthetic rating in a complicated way. Normally a picture looks better when it is bigger, but it may look worse depending on its content. We develop a set of regression models to predict a picture's absolute and relative aesthetic levels at a given display size based on its content and compositional features. In addition, we analyze the essential features that lead to *the size-dependent property* of image aesthetics. It is hoped that this work will motivate further research by showing that both content and presentation should be considered when evaluating an image's aesthetic appeals.

Categories and Subject Descriptors

I.2.10 [**Artificial Intelligence**]: Vision and Scene Understanding—*Perceptual reasoning*

Keywords

Crowdsourcing; Human perception; Image aesthetics; Quality assessment; Size-dependent aesthetics

1. INTRODUCTION

Image aesthetic quality assessment has generated a great deal of interest in recent years because it is a fundamental component of many multimedia applications, such as image summarization and automatic photo editing. Previous works have shown that the pixel-level features and compositional features of an image may jointly influence how humans evaluate the image aesthetically [3, 7, 13]. The content of a picture is certainly an important factor in determining whether the picture looks appealing; however, very little is known about whether and how a picture's aesthetic level is affected by *the way it is presented* to the viewer. In this work, we focus on the relationship between image aesthetics and display size, and consider the factors that determine the relationship.

Figure 1: Examples of how display size affects aesthetic ratings in a heterogeneous way.

When people surf online auction websites and browse the thumbnail images of products, those images and the full-size images of the products sometimes create very different impressions. The thumbnail version may look attractive, while the full-size version is unattractive, or vice versa[1]. In addition, on photo sharing websites such as Flickr, pictures shown in the default size (i.e., small or medium) are often more appealing than their full-size counterparts. Based on these observations, we posit that *some complicated mechanisms, psychological and/or physiological, cause the same picture to have very different levels of aesthetic appeal when it is shown in different sizes.* This phenomenon is the motivation for our study.

First, we conducted a pilot study to verify the effect of display size on image aesthetics. In the study, 117 subjects were shown 25 high-resolution images at random in two different display scales. The large images used 1200x1200 pixels, while the thumbnail versions used 120x120 pixels. The subjects were asked to give an aesthetic rating between 1 and 5 for each displayed image. Then, we averaged the score to obtain the representative rating. Figure 1 shows examples of pictures that were given *different aesthetic ratings for different display scales.* The small image of the girl in Figure 1(a) was ranked 5 (out of 25), while the large image was

[1]We observe that the first scenario occurs more frequently when the product pictures are taken by amateur photographers.

MM'13, October 21–25, 2013, Barcelona, Spain.

http://dx.doi.org/10.1145/2502081.2502102.

ranked 22; that is, viewers preferred the thumbnail version. By contrast, the thumbnail image and large image of the tree in Figure 1(b) were ranked 24 and 10 respectively. This is reasonable because the thumbnail of the tree is too complex and unclear, while the large image is much clearer. It is apparent that *the changes in display size may impact images' aesthetic appeals images in distinct ways*.

The findings of our pilot study seem intuitive and unsurprising; however, we should point out that existing works on aesthetics modeling *do not* consider the impact of display size. We used ACQUINE [4], a state-of-the-art image aesthetics assessment engine, to evaluate the thumbnail and large versions of the 25 images in the pilot study. ACQUINE ranked the large and small images in Figure 1(a) at 21 and 22 respectively, and the large and small images in Figure 1(b) at 24 and 23 respectively. The results provide strong evidence that *the effect of display size has long been overlooked* and the issue is worth further investigation. To the best of our knowledge, this is the first work that considers the effect of display size on image aesthetic assessment.

In this paper, we investigated the effect of display size on image aesthetic assessment systematically. First, we conducted an Internet crowdsourced experiment to collect the participants' assessments of 100 high-resolution images shown in a variety of resolutions (pixels) and physical dimensions (inches). Our data analysis reveals that image scaling influences a user's aesthetic assessment significantly, and the impact is *heterogeneous* across different image categories. Subsequently, we developed a set of partial least square regression (PLSR) models to describe the absolute and relative aesthetic ratings of any image based on the image's content and compositional features.

The contributions of this paper are three-fold:

1. Based on a large set of crowdsourced user ratings, we confirm that the display size significantly affects image aesthetics assessment. We also show that the effect is not consistent for all images; instead, it is highly dependent on image content.
2. Through our aesthetics prediction model, we show that the physical dimensions (in inches) of an image on a screen is more important than its resolution (in pixels) in terms of aesthetics perception. We demonstrate that assessment of an image's aesthetic quality should consider the image's content and how it is presented.
3. The prediction model provides promising performance compared with earlier size-agnostic approaches, as well as clues about features that tend to be more effective in aesthetics prediction.

The remainder of this paper is organized as follows. In Section 2, we review related works; in Section 3, we describe how image ratings are collected from Internet users; and in Section 4, we consider how display size impacts humans' aesthetic perceptions of pictures. We introduce a set of regression models to describe and predict the effect of display size on image aesthetics in Section 5, and evaluate the performance of the models in Section 6. In Section 7, we discuss applications of our models and the implications for future research. Section 8 contains our concluding remarks.

2. RELATED WORK

Earlier studies of image aesthetics focused on distinguishing professional photos from amateur photos [3,7,12–14]. Tong et al. [13] extracted blurriness, intensity contrast, colorfulness, and saliency values, and constructed discriminative models to classify images. Based on interviews with professional photographers, Ke et al. [7] concluded that simplicity, realism, and basic photographic techniques are important factors. To model image aesthetics, they extracted the spatial distribution of edges, color distribution, hue count, blur, contrast, and brightness. In addition to the visual appearance of images, Datta et al. [3] proposed using compositional features, such as the rule of thirds and aspect ratio, to model image aesthetics. Subsequently, Datta and Wang [4] extended the approach and developed ACQUINE, the first public online image aesthetics assessment platform. Recently, Dhar et al. [6] posited that image cues, such as compositional attributes, content attributes, and sky-illumination attributes, are good indicators of how humans evaluate aesthetic quality. Using prior knowledge of art and a survey, Li and Chen [8] extracted various global and local features from paintings and designed a data-driven machine learning scheme to classify high-quality and low-quality paintings.

Based on the relationship between saliency and aesthetics, Sun et al. [12] proposed using the rate of focused attention to evaluate aesthetic quality. The approach uses statistics derived from human observers' inputs to measure the degree to which salient objects are located in the subject's (i.e., the topic's) mask. In [14], as well as global image features, exposure, sharpness, and textural features are extracted from salient regions. The results reported in [12, 14] and a number of follow-up works show that the inclusion of salient regions is a promising way to quantify image aesthetics. Luo et al. [10] devised and compared various global and regional features to categorize photos, such as animals, plants, buildings, and portraits. As aesthetics assessment is highly subjective, Wu et al. [15] proposed that distribution vectors of human assessment, rather than scalar values, should be used to describe images. In their approach, constructing a prediction function to output a distribution label for a test image is formulated as a structural output learning problem, which is solved by the proposed support vector distribution regression algorithm.

Our study differs from previous works because it focuses on the impact of display size on aesthetic quality assessment. We analyze the issue and its effects systematically. Rather than developing further image analysis and aesthetics evaluation techniques, we investigate how a picture's display size affects viewers' aesthetic perception of it.

3. TRACE COLLECTION

In this section, we describe how we collected users' aesthetics ratings for images presented in different resolutions and physical dimensions. We first explain the experiment design and then summarize the collected trace.

3.1 Experiment Design

To recruit subjects from the Internet for the aesthetics ratings study, we developed a web-based platform in Adobe ActionScript and Flash. When a potential subject enters the system, the platform presents a welcome screen followed by an instruction page, which describes the goal of our study and the tasks the subject must perform during the experiment. If the subject agrees to participate, we present a user interface in the full-screen mode as shown in Figure 2(a) to inquire about the physical dimensions of the subject's computer monitor. The subjects may not know the exact size of their monitors, so we ask them to provide the viewable area of their monitors in centimeters. Because some participants may give erroneous information [2], either carelessly or intentionally, a rectangle is displayed on the screen and the participants are asked to measure the size of the rectangle on their monitors with a ruler. By comparing both inputs, i.e., the dimensions of the monitor and those of

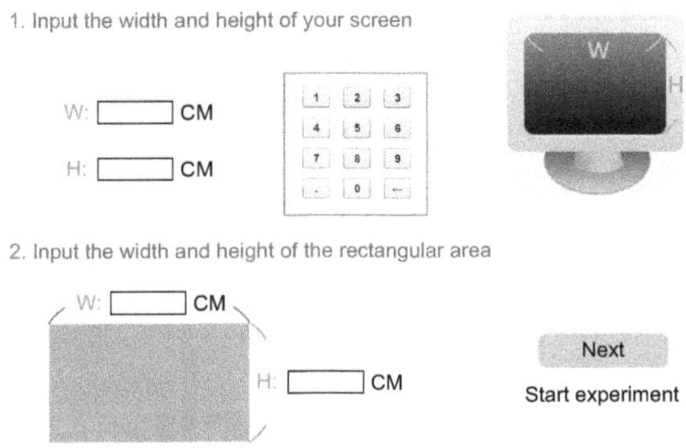

(a) The configuration interface where users are asked to input the physical dimensions of the viewable area of their computer monitors.

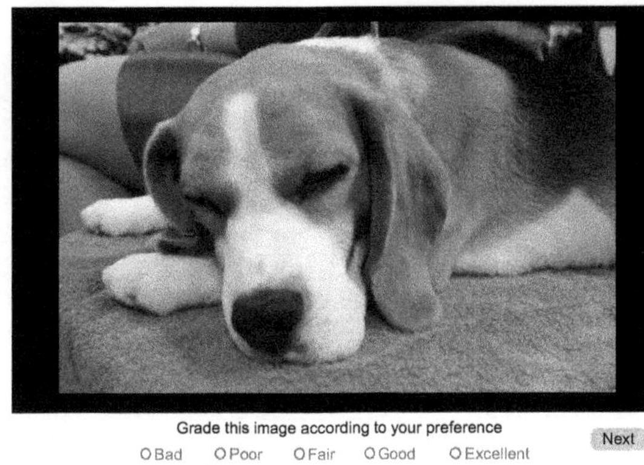

(b) The image rating interface where users are asked to rate each presented image on an MOS scale.

Figure 2: The user interfaces in our experiments

Table 1: Image Categories

Category	# Images	Category	# Images
Animal	15	Object	12
Architecture	16	Scenery	18
Art	9	Sport	10
Human	20		

the rectangle, we can detect and filter out erroneous inputs in the analysis stage.

Next, the system enters the image rating phase, which comprises 60 rounds. In each round, we randomly pick an image that has not been used in the experiment from an image pool and present it on the screen with a random scaling factor between 0.1 and 1.0. A scaling factor of 1.0 corresponds to a 1000x1000 display area; that is, an image is shrunk[2] so that it fits the display area. Similarly, an image presented with a scaling factor of 0.1 indicates that the image exactly fits a 100x100 display area. During the above scaling operations, we preserve the images' aspect ratios to ensure that the semantics of the images remain intact when they are presented in various scales.

When the experiment participants looked at a random image with a random display size, they were asked to grade their aesthetic perceptions of the picture on a five-point MOS (Mean Opinion Score) scale according to the options of Bad, Poor, Fair, Good, and Excellent. The participants were allowed unlimited time to rate each image. After the image had been rated, the round terminated and the system advanced to the next round until all 60 rounds in the experiment were completed. We consider that 60 rounds allows each subject to provide sufficient and consistent ratings without losing concentration.

We collected 100 high-resolution images from Flickr.com[3] to compile an image pool. The images were chosen arbitrarily based on the following criteria: 1) both the width and height of each image was at least 2000 pixels; 2) the images were released under a Creative Commons license[4]; and 3) the set of images covered a variety of subjects, such as humans, animals, scenery, and paintings.

[2]We use the bicubic interpolation function provided by the GD Graphics Library to perform image shrinking.
[3]`http://www.flickr.com/`
[4]`http://creativecommons.org/`

Table 2: Trace Summary

# Subjects	230
# Images	100
# Ratings	13,800 (60 ratings each subject)
Screen resolutions	1024x600 (min) to 1920x1200 (max)
Display resolutions	100x100 (min) to 1000x1000 (max)
Rating time per image	2.9 seconds (std. dev. 2.6 seconds)
Rating time per exp.	178.7 seconds (std. dev. 68.5 seconds)
Overall rating time	685 minutes

Figure 3 shows thumbnails of the collected images and Table 1 lists the categories of the images in the image pool.

3.2 Trace Summary

For the experiments, we recruited 230 subjects from the Internet community. Each subject was given a reward of virtual currency equivalent to 0.1 USD; and we collected $230 \times 60 = 13,800$ image ratings in 230 experiments. The screen resolutions used by a subject varied between 1200x600 and 1920x1200, depending on the subject's hardware and configurations. To accommodate the limits due to screen resolutions, our platform does not display images at a scale that does not fit the screen resolution. In other words, if a subject uses a screen resolution of 1280x800, we only show images at scales between 0.1 and 0.8, which correspond to 100x100 and 800x800 display areas respectively.

During the experiments, we also recorded the time taken to complete each image rating round. On average, the subjects spent 3 seconds in each round with a distribution spread over 1–8 seconds. As each experiment comprised 60 rounds, it took approximately 3 minutes for a subject to complete an experiment. This indicates that rating images aesthetically was not a difficult task and the experiments did not place a heavy workload on the subjects. Table 2 shows a summary of the collected trace.

The histogram in Figure 4(a) shows the distribution of all ratings given by the subjects. Most of the images were rated as Fair or Good, while smaller proportions were deemed Poor or Excellent. The findings imply that, generally, the quality of the images used in the experiments was high. The lower user ratings (Bad and Poor) may indicate that some pictures were regarded as unattractive or the display size was too small. We consider these issues in the next section.

Figure 3: The 100 images used in the experiments

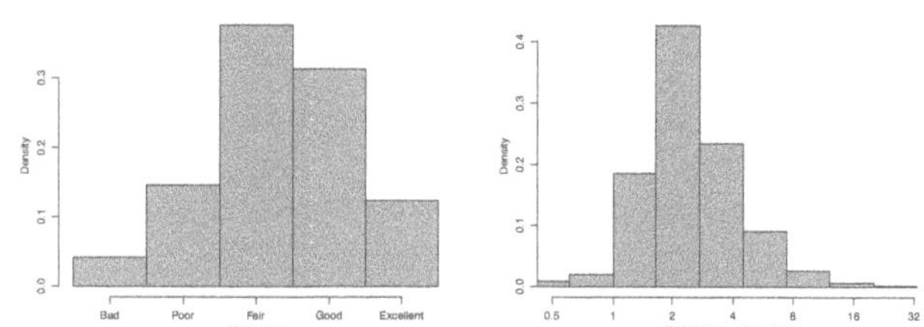

(a) User rating histogram (b) Rating time histogram

Figure 4: Histograms of the users' ratings and the time required to make rating decisions

4. DATA ANALYSIS

In this section, we investigate whether the display size of an image influences viewers' aesthetic perception of the image. If the size is important, in which way is the influence made? Does the display size affect viewers' perception of all images in the same way? In other words, is this effect content-dependent and a non-trivial matter to describe and predict?

For ease of discussion, we use the term "image scaling" to refer to shrinking an image with a specific scaling factor (or scale for short), which is between 0.1 (100x100 pixels) and 1.0 (1000x1000 pixels) in this study.

4.1 Image Size Does Matter

Our first question is *Does image scaling influence users' aesthetic perception of an image?* We analyze the collected traces to determine the relationship between image scaling factors and users' scores. The results are shown in Figure 5. In the scatter plot of

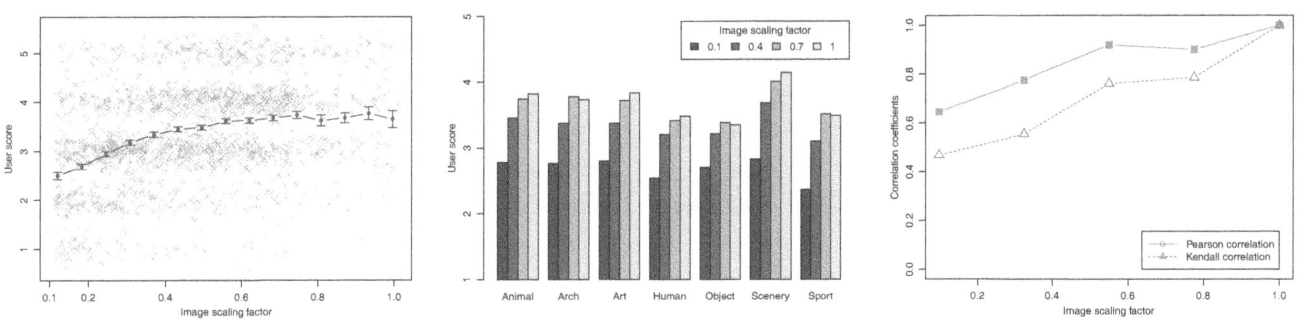

(a) The scatter plot of user scores vs. scaling factors. The blue circles denote the average user scores across different scales.
(b) The average user scores at different scales for images in the seven categories.
(c) The correlation coefficients between the average image ratings at 1.0 and those at other scales.

Figure 5: Evidence of the impact of image scaling on aesthetics ratings

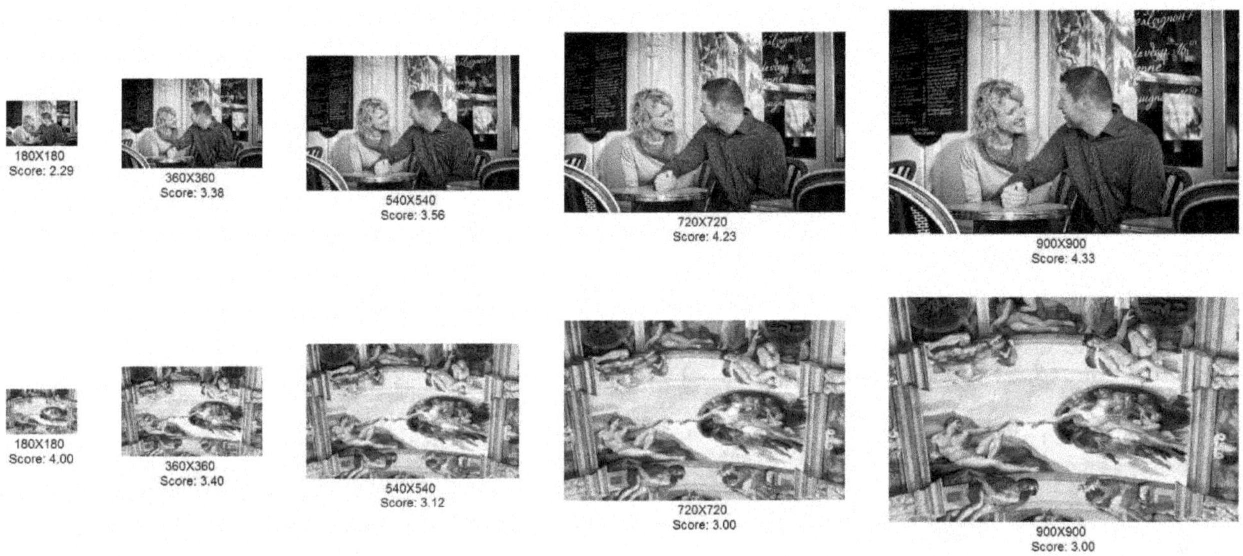

Figure 6: The impact of image scaling on users' scores can vary significantly. The top image (in the Human category) is given a higher rating when presented at a larger scale, while the bottom image (in the Art category) is rated higher when presented at a smaller scale.

the scaling factors and user scores (Figure 5(a)), each gray cross[5] corresponds to a user rating for an image presented at a particular scale; and the y-locations of the crosses (i.e., the user ratings) are randomly dispersed so that the crosses do not overlap. The blue circles indicate the average user scores across different image scale ranges, while the horizontal bars represent the 95% confidence intervals of the averaged scores. The trend of the blue circles indicates that, generally, the user rating increases with the image size; however, the effect diminishes when the scaling factor is larger than 0.7. The average user score at scale 0.1 is 2.5; while at scale 1.0, it is 3.5. Taken together with their narrow confidence intervals, the scores indicate that *the image size does influence users' aesthetic perception of the image.*

From a different perspective, in Figure 5(b), we plot the average user ratings at different scales for images in each of the seven categories listed in Table 1. The graph clearly shows that image scaling impacts the aesthetics ratings of images in all categories. Besides the two highest scales, in all the categories, the scores are significantly higher when the images are displayed at larger scales.

The above findings motivate the following question: *Is the impact of image scaling the same for all types of images*? To the answer the question, in Figure 5(c), we plot the correlation coefficients between the average user scores at scale 1.0 and those at a variety of other scales. Let s_j^i be the average user score of an image i displayed at scale j, and let $\mathbf{S}_\mathbf{j}$ denote the sequence $(s_j^1, s_j^2, \ldots, s_j^{100})$. Then, the lines in Figure 5(c) correspond to cor($\mathbf{S}_\mathbf{j}$,$\mathbf{S}_\mathbf{1.0}$), where $0.1 \leq j \leq 1.0$ and cor($\cdot$) denotes the Pearson and Kendall correlation coefficients respectively. Both lines in the graph indicate that image scaling has a heterogeneous effect on viewers' perceptions of different images in terms of their aesthetic quality. In other words, while some images are deemed slightly worse at smaller scales, others may be rated significantly worse or better at smaller scales, depending on the images' content.

4.2 Heterogeneous Effect of Image Scaling

The examples in Figure 6 illustrate how image scaling impacts user ratings in distinct ways. The top image, which is in the Human

[5]The gray crosses are less dense at scales larger than 0.8 because some participants used screen resolutions with less than 800 vertical scan lines, such as the widely used 1024x768 resolution.

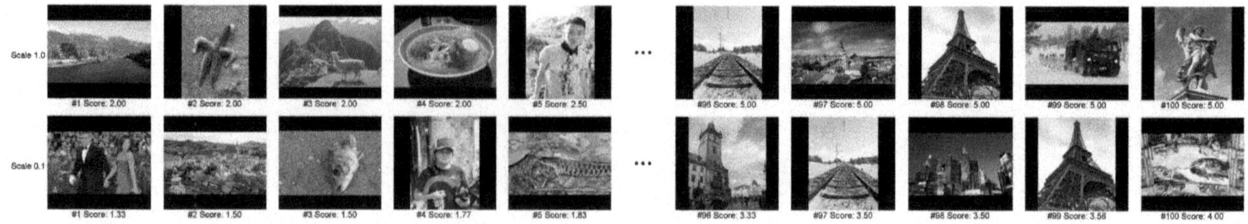

Figure 7: The top and bottom five images that receive the highest and lowest user ratings at scales of 1.0 and 0.1 respectively.

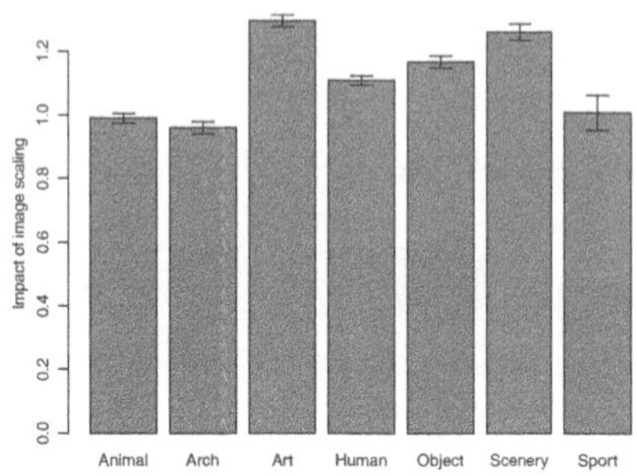

Figure 8: The differences in the average user scores between scale 0.1 and scale 1.0 for images in different categories.

category, receives a high score (4.33) at 900x900 resolution and a relatively low score (2.29) at 180x180 resolution. In contrast, the bottom image, which is in the Art category, receives a high score (4.00) at 180x180 resolution, but a relatively low score (3.00) at the 900x900 resolution. It seems that image scaling affects the aesthetics ratings of different images in a highly unpredictable and complicated way. Figure 7 shows the images that received the best and worst user ratings at the highest scale (1.0) and lowest scale (0.1). The sets of images are almost completely different; only the pictures of the Eiffel Tower and the Siberian Railway appear in both sets. The results further confirm that the aesthetics rankings of images are content-dependent and vary at different scales.

To determine whether the scaling effect is content-dependent and varies across the categories, we quantify the impact of scaling as the difference between the average score at the smallest scale (0.1) and that at the largest scale (1.0), as shown in Figure 8. The results indicate that the impact is content-dependent and varies across the categories. In general, the ratings of Art and Scenery pictures are more affected by image scaling than Animal, Architecture, and Sport pictures.

We also found that scaling affects perception of an image's aesthetic quality. Figure 9 shows the relationship between scaling and the ratings given to images at scale 0.1 and scale 1.0. Generally, images rated as good at a large scale tend to be regarded less favorably at small scales. On the other hand, images rated favorably at a small scale are generally less sensitive to image scaling in that they tend to receive a small "aesthetic bonus" when presented in a larger size.

5. AESTHETIC QUALITY PREDICTION

So far, we have shown that image scaling does impact the aesthetic ratings given to images; moreover, the impact is content-dependent and it is not homogeneous across all types of images. In this section, we investigate whether image content analysis can be exploited to model the impact of image scaling.

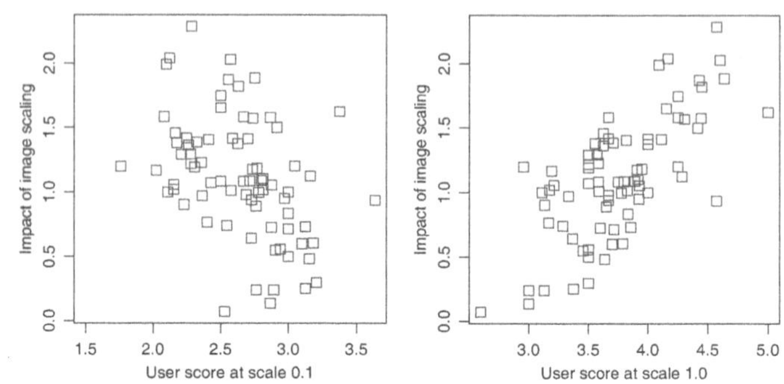

Figure 9: The impact of image scaling (quantified using the score difference between two extreme scales, 0.1 and 1.0) v.s. the user scores for the images presented at scale 0.1 and 1.0 respectively.

5.1 Model Construction

We utilize a data-driven approach to assess the influence of image scaling on aesthetic perception. The approach constructs a set of models to predict viewers' aesthetic perceptions based on features extracted from a set of images in various display sizes. We use the partial least square regression (PLSR) method to predict aesthetic perception. As an image's aesthetic quality can be described in terms of its *absolute* aesthetic value or in terms of its *relative* aesthetic ranking, we develop a *scoring model* and a *ranking model* respectively.

5.1.1 Scoring Model

Let $\boldsymbol{a}_1, ..., \boldsymbol{a}_n$ be m-dimensional feature vectors extracted from n training images to construct an $n \times m$ data matrix A. Each image is associated with an aesthetic score, denoted by b_i, and the combined scores of the images constitute a score column matrix $\boldsymbol{b} = (b_1, ..., b_n)^T$. The relationship between features and scores is then described as $A\boldsymbol{x} = \boldsymbol{b}$, where $\boldsymbol{x}$ is an $m \times 1$ column matrix that indicates how different columns are linearly combined to form the score matrix. Note that each column of A and $\boldsymbol{b}$ has a zero mean.

We treat different sizes of the same image separately. For example, an 800×600 image I_0 and its resized version 400×300 image I_1 are treated as different images. Feature vectors $\boldsymbol{f}_0$ and $\boldsymbol{f}_1$ are extracted from I_0 and I_1 and added into the data matrix A respectively.

The PLSR model uses latent variables to describe the relations between sets of observed variables. First, the data matrix A and the score matrix $\boldsymbol{b}$ are decomposed into $A = VP^T + E$ and $\boldsymbol{b} = U\boldsymbol{q}^T + \boldsymbol{f}$, respectively, where V and U are $n \times g$ matrices that contain g extracted latent vectors. The $m \times g$ matrix P and the $1 \times g$ vector $\boldsymbol{q}$ represent the loadings; and the $n \times m$ matrix E and the $n \times 1$ vector $\boldsymbol{f}$ are residuals. With the decomposed partial least components, the SIMPLS algorithm [5] is used to determine a set of weighting vectors $W = (\boldsymbol{w}_1, ..., \boldsymbol{w}_g)$ such that

$$[cov(\boldsymbol{v}_i, \boldsymbol{u}_i)]^2 = \max_{|\boldsymbol{w}_i|=1} [cov(A\boldsymbol{w}_i, \boldsymbol{b})]^2, \quad (1)$$

where $\boldsymbol{v}_i$ and $\boldsymbol{u}_i$ are the ith columns of matrix V and matrix U respectively, and $cov(\boldsymbol{v}_i, \boldsymbol{u}_i)$ is the covariance between $\boldsymbol{v}_i$ and $\boldsymbol{u}_i$. The matrices A and $\boldsymbol{b}$ are then deflated by subtracting their rank-one approximations based on $\boldsymbol{v}_i$ and $\boldsymbol{u}_i$. The process is repeated until the desired number of latent vectors is extracted.

The $m \times 1$ regression coefficient $\boldsymbol{\beta}$ is then estimated by $\boldsymbol{\beta} = W(P^TW)^{-1}V^T\boldsymbol{b}$. Given a test image represented by a vector $\boldsymbol{a}_q$, the corresponding aesthetic score can be estimated by $b_q = \bar{b} + \boldsymbol{a}_q^T\boldsymbol{\beta}$, where $\bar{b}$ represents the average of $\boldsymbol{b}$.

5.1.2 Ranking Model

In many applications, it is not necessary to determine an image's absolute aesthetic rating. For example, it may be sufficient to decide if a large picture is preferable to a scaled-down thumbnail version. Therefore, we also developed a ranking model that predicts the *relative ranking of a particular image among a set of images* at a given display size.

Assume an image I_0 has a scaling factor of 0.5. The feature vector that describes the scaling from I_0 to I_1 is derived by $\boldsymbol{a}^T_{I_0\to I_1} = (\boldsymbol{f}_1^T, \boldsymbol{f}_1^T - \boldsymbol{f}_0^T, d_s)$, where $\boldsymbol{f}_1^T - \boldsymbol{f}_0^T$ represents the dimension-wise feature difference. In this setting, d_s denotes the scaling factor difference. A positive d_s indicates that I_1 is a scaled-up version of I_0, while a negative d_s indicates that I_1 is a scaled-down version of I_0.

The matrix $\boldsymbol{b}$ represents the difference in rankings between multiple scales. Let there be n images with the same resolution as the image I_0, e.g., 800×800. The images are sorted in descending order according to their associated aesthetic scores. The rank of an image I_j is $r_j = 1/n$ if it has the largest score, and $r_j = n/n = 1$ if it has the lowest score. Thus, the rank difference in $\boldsymbol{b}$ that corresponds to $\boldsymbol{a}^T_{I_0\to I_1}$ is equal to $r_1 - r_0$.

The ranking model describes how an image is ranked aesthetically when it is shrunk to a particular scale. Given a test image I_q to be scaled down to $I_{q'}$ and that $\boldsymbol{a}^T_{I_q\to I_{q'}}$ is the feature vector, the predicted rank difference is $b_{I_q\to I_{q'}} = \bar{b} + \boldsymbol{a}^T_{I_q\to I_{q'}}\boldsymbol{\beta}$, where $\bar{b}$ is the mean value of $\boldsymbol{b}$. Therefore, the predicted aesthetic rank of $I_{q'}$ is equal to $r_q + b_{I_q\to I_{q'}}$, where r_q is the rank of I_q at the original resolution.

5.2 Display Size: Pixels or Inches?

Image scaling can be characterized by the changes of an image's resolution (in pixels) or by its physical dimensions (in inches) on a display device. To predict the aesthetic quality of images from the two perspectives, the scoring and ranking models are constructed and evaluated respectively in two modes: the *pixel mode* and the *physical dimension mode* (*dimension mode* for short). Note that the number of pixels cannot be converted to inches directly because the conversion depends on the characteristics of the display device and the current display mode. For example, an 1136x640 image can be shown on a 4" iPhone 5 screen as well as on a 27" computer monitor as a full-screen image. Although the number of pixels displayed is exactly the same, the pixels' physical dimensions are vastly different and may result in significantly different ratings of the aesthetic quality. This is the reason we provide two modes in the aesthetics prediction models.

In our dataset, the image resolutions range from 100×100 pixels to 1000×1000 pixels. Compared with the maximum display size of 1000×1000 pixels, a resized image $I_j^{(s)}$ comprised of $n \times n$ pixels is said to be scaled with a factor $s = n/1000$. Image variants and the associated aesthetic assessments are then categorized into 9 groups based on s, namely, [0.1, 0.2), [0.2, 0.3), ..., [0.9, 1]. For example, The *ground* aesthetic score for the image I_j with a scaling factor s between 0.1 and 0.2 is obtained by averaging all the scores given to $I_j^{(s)}$, $0.1 \le s < 0.2$. Let $g_j^{(1)}, g_j^{(2)}, ..., g_j^{(9)}$ denote, respectively, the average aesthetic scores for nine groups of variants derived from I_j. In the test phase, suppose a model running in the pixel mode predicts an aesthetic score for the image $I_j^{(0.13)}$, which is then compared with $g_j^{(1)}$ because images with scaling factors between 0.1 and 0.2 belong to the first group (out of 9).

Assume that the display size of images in the physical dimension mode ranges from $N_1 \times N_1$ inches to $N_2 \times N_2$ inches. Comparing with the maximum size $N_2 \times N_2$ inches, a resized variant $I_j^{(s)}$ of $n \times n$ inches is said to be scaled with a factor of $s = n/N_2$. The image variants and their aesthetic assessments are also categorized into 9 groups. Note that a 450×450-pixel image I_k, for example, would be categorized in the fourth group in the pixel model, but it is not necessarily categorized into the fourth group in the dimension mode.

In the experiments, we evaluate the performances of the models in the pixel mode and the dimension mode, and use a five-fold cross-validation scheme for model training and testing. We also calculate the Pearson correlation and Spearman correlation between the predicted results and the ground truth. The Pearson correlation indicates a model's prediction accuracy; while the Spearman correlation indicates the consistency between the rankings of the predicted results and the rankings of the ground truth.

5.3 Feature Selection and Fusion

We categorize the features proposed in the literature into compositional attributes and content attributes [6]. Table 3 shows the features and their corresponding dimensions, types, and references. Compositional attributes, content attributes, and a combination of them are denoted as **S**, **C**, and **B** respectively. The last feature (f_{27}) comprises the width and the height of an image, and is categorized with **O** (others). We consider that [1] and the Gabor wavelet texture [11] are important because details of textural details are clearly expected to change when images are scaled up/down. Hence, we include them in the feature vectors even though, to the best of our knowledge, they have not been used in image aesthetics modeling previously.

To determine how the features affect aesthetics prediction, we evaluate the performance of individual features based on the scoring model in the dimension mode. The results are presented as bar charts in Figure 10. We observe that f_5, f_9, f_{12}, f_{15}, f_{16}, f_{25}, and f_{27} are more effective for making predictions. Surprisingly, simple features like the intensity histogram (f_{15}), the hue histogram (f_{16}), and the physical dimensions of width and height (f_{27}) are effective predictive features.

The results in Figure 10 raise the following question: *Is there a guideline that we could use to estimate the effectiveness of feature vectors without conducting a large-scale test?* From f_9, f_{15}, and f_{16}, it seems that high-dimensional features play more important roles in making predictions. To verify the point, we calculate the ratio of the energy of an individual feature to that of all the features. Specifically, we divide the L2 norm of each feature by the total norm of all the features. The Pearson correlation between the prediction performance and the energy ratios is only 0.47, which means they are moderately correlated. It also appears that features that vary significantly as the image size changes are more effective for making predictions. To verify this conjecture, we calculate the L2 distance between an individual feature extracted from images

Table 3: The features used in this paper and their corresponding dimensions, types, and references

	Meaning	D	Tp	Rf
f_1	area of the centric region containing 70% of edge pixels	1	C	[8]
f_2	contrast, mean, and standard deviation of intensity, hue, and saturation	9	C	[8]
f_3	hue contrast, hue count, and hue frequency	3	C	[8]
f_4	mean values of hue, saturation, and intensity in the three largest regions	9	C	[8]
f_5	blurriness	1	C	[8]
f_6	mean and standard deviation of intensity, hue, saturation in the center region	6	C	[3]
f_7	mean Daubechies wavelet coefficients of hue image, saturation image, and value image, at three levels	9	C	[3]
f_8	average hue distance between the five largest regions	1	C	[3]
f_9	histogram of average RGB	256	C	[7]
f_{10}	dark mean	1	C	[10]
f_{11}	depth of field of hue image, saturation image, and value image	3	C	[6]
f_{12}	level 1 pyramid histogram of oriented gradients (PHOG)	40	C	[1]
f_{13}	Gabor wavelet texture	480	C	[11]
f_{14}	mean values of hue, saturation, and intensity in ROIs	3	C	
f_{15}	intensity histogram	256	C	
f_{16}	hue histogram	360	C	
f_{17}	ratios of areas of the three largest regions to the whole image	3	S	[8]
f_{18}	coordinate vector of the largest region	2	S	[8]
f_{19}	spatial variance of the three largest regions	3	S	[8]
f_{20}	number of regions whose areas are larger than 10% of the whole image	1	S	[3]
f_{21}	ratio of the total area of the five largest region to the whole image	1	S	[3]
f_{22}	ROI weighted by rule of thirds	1	S	[9]
f_{23}	diagonal edges	1	S	[9]
f_{24}	mean positions and slopes of horizontal lines and vertical lines	4	S	[10]
f_{25}	sum of edge magnitudes weighted by rule of thirds	1	B	[7]
f_{26}	visual symmetry evaluated by difference between PHOGs in the left and right halves of an image	1	B	
f_{27}	width and height of the image	2	O	

with a scale of 0.1 and that extracted from images with a scale of 1.0. The Pearson correlation between the prediction performance and the feature difference is only 0.34, which means they are also moderately correlated.

The above observations show that it is difficult to explicitly estimate the effectiveness of features merely based on the feature vectors. Fortunately, we found the feature weights discovered by the PLSR process implicitly indicate a feature's effectiveness. The process estimates a weight for each dimension of each feature vector. For example, f_{12} has 40 dimensions, so it has 40 corresponding weights after model fitting. First, we take the absolute values of all the weights, and use the maximum weight of all dimensions of a feature vector to construct a line graph, as shown in Figure 10. The reason for finding the maximum is that the PLSR process only uses the most important feature vectors to construct partial least square components. In Figure 10, the peaks of the line graph are consistent with effective features to some extent. Quantitatively, the Pearson correlation between the weights and performance is 0.61. The positive correlation coefficient shows that the weights learned by PLSR, though not perfect, are good indicators for estimating the features that are more effective. This characteristic strengthens the motivation for using PLSR rather than a nonlinear regression method like support vector regression (SVR). In fact, we did construct an SVR-based prediction model and found that its performance was similar

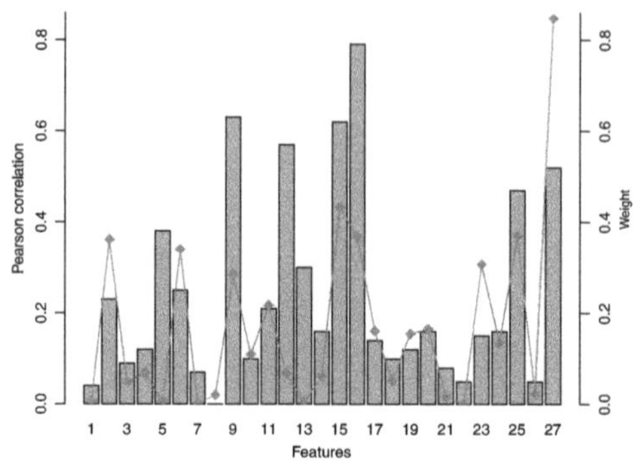

Figure 10: The prediction performance and feature weights obtained from the scoring model based on individual features

Table 4: The performance of the scoring model based on all the features and the selected features in the dimension mode

	All features	Selected features
Pearson	0.86	0.857
Spearman	0.87	0.867

to that of PLSR. We utilize the PLSR-based model in this study because it is more efficient, and the discovered feature weights can be used to estimate the features' effectiveness.

Based on the feature effectiveness analysis, we compare the performance achieved by fusing all the features described in Table 3 with that derived by only fusing features that have a Pearson correlation larger than 0.3. Table 4 shows the prediction performance of the scoring model in the dimension mode based on all the features and the selected features. We observe that the performance derived by fusing the selected features is almost the same as that achieved by fusing all the features. Many features proposed in the literature were designed for different datasets, but they embed similar information and redundant information would be discarded by the learning process. Adding more features only yields a marginal improvement unless they provide novel information. Nevertheless, in the following evaluation, all features are fused to construct models in order to faithfully capture the maximum attainable prediction performance.

6. EVALUATION

6.1 Score Prediction vs. Ranking Prediction

Given a test image, the scoring model predicts its absolute aesthetic score; therefore, we can see how the aesthetic rating changes when the image is displayed in different sizes. Meanwhile, the ranking model predicts the changes in the relative ranking when an image is scaled up/down. In this subsection, we evaluate the performance of both models in the dimension mode. Then, we compare the pixel and dimension modes in the next subsection (Section 6.2).

Table 5 shows the prediction performance of the scoring model based on three categories of features: content-based features, composition-based features, and a combination of them. We make two observations from the table. First, irrespective of the model, content-based features play an important role in predicting aesthetic perception. This may be because the dimensionality of content-based features is much higher than that of compositional features. The latter are usually based on photographic rules and conventions, and can be described by a few scalars. The second observation is that the scoring model is more accurate than the ranking model in predicting

Table 5: **The performance of the scoring and ranking models based on different feature categories in the dimension mode**

Scoring model	C	S	C+S	All
Pearson	0.83	0.33	0.83	0.86
Spearman	0.84	0.35	0.84	0.87
Ranking model	**C**	**S**	**C+S**	**All**
Pearson	0.65	0.23	0.65	0.65
Spearman	0.64	0.24	0.64	0.64

Table 6: The performance of the scoring models

Scoring model	Pixel mode	Dimension mode
Pearson	0.84	0.86
Spearman	0.84	0.87

Table 7: The Pearson correlations of the scoring and ranking models in both modes

	Pixel mode	Dimension mode
Scoring model	0.84	0.86
Ranking model	0.62	0.65

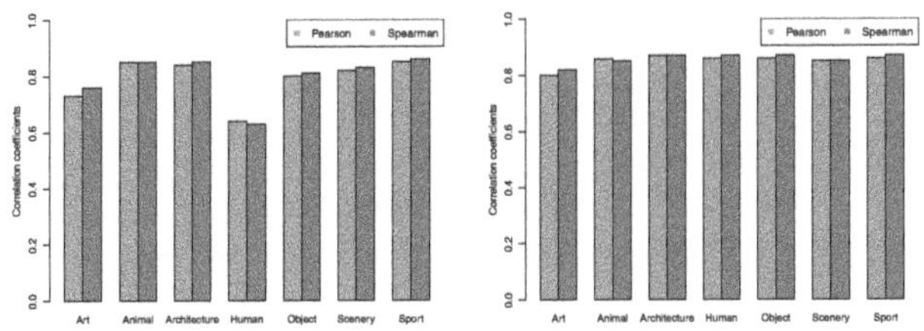

(a) (b)

Figure 11: Pearson correlations and Spearman correlations for different image categories. Left: the pixel mode; right: the dimension mode.

how aesthetic scores change in different scales. There is a trend in that *larger images tend to receive higher aesthetic ratings*, which is evident in Figure 5. On the other hand, the aesthetic ranking of an image in different scales seems to be more complicated, and it is harder to find a simple, general rule for rank prediction in a particular scale.

It may not be necessary to determine exactly how the ranking changes over multiple scales. In many situations, it is sufficient to assess whether an image is more aesthetically pleasing when it is scaled up (or down) to a certain size. Thus, we evaluate the ranking model from the perspectives of binary-decisions and ternary-decisions. From the binary-decision perspective, images in the ground truth dataset are categorized into two groups: *promoted images* and *demoted images*. An image is classified as promoted if gets a higher rank when it is scaled up (i.e, to a larger display size); otherwise, it is classified as demoted. From the ternary perspective, the ground truth dataset is divided into three classes: *promoted over 10%*, *demoted over 10%*, and *neither promoted or demoted over 10%*. The overall precision rates of evaluating the ranking model from the binary perspective and the ternary perspective are 0.79 and 0.58 respectively. Thus, the ranking model achieves a satisfactory performance in predicting promotion and demotion behavior.

6.2 Physical Dimensions Are More Important

We also investigate whether an image's resolution or its display size is more important in predicting perceptions of aesthetic quality. We compare the performance of both prediction models running in the pixel mode and the dimension mode. The Pearson correlation and Spearman correlation results in Table 6 show that both models achieve higher accuracy in the dimension mode than in the pixel mode. This is reasonable because the physical size of an image reflects how humans perceive it more directly, even though the number of pixels also matters.

7. DISCUSSION

7.1 Comparison with Human Assessors

To compare the prediction models with individual human assessors, we calculate the Pearson correlation and Spearman correlation between individual humans' assessments and the corresponding ground truths, which are obtained by averaging assessments over all the subjects. Surprisingly, the average Pearson correlation and the average Spearman correlation are 0.55 and 0.54 respectively. Comparing these results with those in Table 7 reveals two facts. First, image aesthetic assessment is more subjective than expected, such that the consistency between each individual's assessment and the ground truth is only moderate. Second, the proposed prediction model is slightly better than individual human assessors. One reason is that humans usually give one discrete value as the score, while the prediction models can output a real-valued score that more accurately reflects the general assessment of a group of people.

7.2 Content-dependent Prediction

The collected trace is categorized into seven types of images: art, animals, architecture, humans, objects, scenery, and sport. We investigate the prediction performance variations of the above categories. A five-fold cross validation scheme is used to construct and evaluate the scoring models for each image category. The performance variations are shown in Figure 11(a). The performances of the art and human categories are relatively worse than those of other categories. Figure 11(b) shows that the performance of art images in the dimension mode is also the worst among all the categories, but performance variations in this mode are smaller. These figures may indicate that humans are more likely have diverse individual interpretations for art and human images. Further investigations are required for more evidences of this observation.

7.3 Existence of "Best Display Size"?

We have verified that the aesthetic perception of an image is influenced by its display size and resolution. We now consider another question: *Is there a rule for finding the "best size" to display an image*?

Generally, higher resolution images are perceived as aesthetically better than lower resolution images. That is, the aesthetic score increases with an image's resolution; thus, the *the-bigger-the-better rule* is generally valid when displaying images. However, we should also consider the following question: When a set of images is displayed, are larger images always *ranked* higher than smaller images? We posit that, although an image's aesthetic score increases with the resolution, the degree of increase is not consistent for all images. In other words, some images may be ranked relatively higher when they are displayed in smaller sizes, while others may be ranked higher when they are displayed in larger sizes. To verify this point, we ranked the 100 images in each scale based on their user-rated aesthetic scores, and collected the rankings of specific images at different scales. Figure 12 shows the evolution of the normalized aesthetic rankings of three sample images. Note that a smaller normalized ranking score means the corresponding

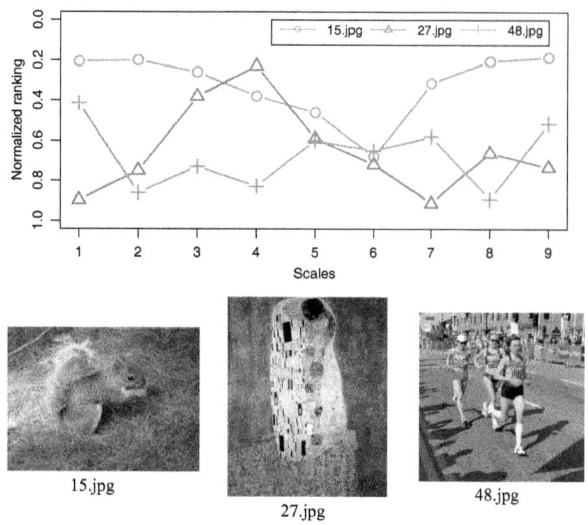

Figure 12: The evolution of the aesthetic rankings of three sample images in multiple scales

image is ranked higher (i.e., perceived more appealing), as defined in Section 5.2. Interestingly, the squirrel image (15.jpg) is ranked lower at scale 6, and higher at scales 1 and 9, i.e., the aesthetic quality of the medium-sized squirrel image is perceived as poorer than that of the smaller and larger images. By contrast, the medium-sized runner image (48.jpg) is ranked better than the smaller and larger scales. In most cases, aesthetic rankings are like the ranking of the painting image (27.jpg), which fluctuates across scales. Manual inspection of the image dataset revealed that 80% of the evaluation images did not follow a clear trend in terms of ranking evolution. This finding suggests that the mechanism humans use to compare the aesthetic quality of images is complex, and further study is needed to resolve this challenging issue.

7.4 Application of Findings

The proposed method predicts the aesthetic scores/rankings of images displayed in various sizes, and relevant information can be integrated into existing algorithms from various perspectives. First, the feature weights discovered by the PLSR process can be utilized by other algorithms to achieve better feature fusion. Second, the results of the scoring model can be used to decide the best way to present an image (i.e., the number of pixels or the physical dimension size) on different display peripherals, such as PC monitors and mobile phones, so that better aesthetic quality is guaranteed. Third, the results of the ranking model can be exploited in aesthetics-based image re-ranking as the display size of an image changes.

8. CONCLUSION

In this paper, we have demonstrated that an image's resolution and physical dimensions affect humans' aesthetic perception of it. Users' ratings were collected via a large-scale crowdsourced experiment, and a set of regression models was used to predict the aesthetic scores and aesthetic rankings of images. We show that the impact of image scaling is not consistent across images and is highly dependent on the image content. Through careful selection of features from a pool of content-based features and compositional features, the scoring model and the ranking model are constructed to predict the absolute aesthetic values and relative aesthetic rankings. The results of experiments conducted in the dimension mode demonstrate that estimating an image's aesthetic quality should consider its content as well as how it is displayed (i.e. its size).

We also discuss a number of potential future directions, including the fact that the *the-bigger-the-better* rule may not be valid in aesthetic ranking. To the best of our knowledge, this is the first work that investigates the impact of image resolution and display size on aesthetic quality assessment. Image features considering display size may be needed, and studies from various perspectives are highly encouraged in order to further the understanding of humans' visionary mechanisms for evaluating the aesthetic quality of images.

Acknowledgement

The work was partially supported by the National Science Council of Taiwan under the grants NSC101-2221-E-194-055-MY2 and NSC101-2221-E-001-012-MY3. The authors are in debt to Derec Wu and Ming-Hung Wang for their support on the design and implementation of crowdsourcing experiments.

9. REFERENCES

[1] A. Bosch, A. Zisserman, and X. Munoz. Representing shape with a spatial pyramid kernel. In *Proceedings of CIVR*, pages 401–408, 2007.

[2] K.-T. Chen, C.-C. Wu, Y.-C. Chang, and C.-L. Lei. A crowdsourceable QoE evaluation framework for multimedia content. In *Proceedings of ACM Multimedia 2009*, 2009.

[3] R. Datta, D. Joshi, J. Li, and J. Wang. Studying aesthetics in photographic images using a computational approach. In *Proceedings of ECCV*, pages 288–301, 2006.

[4] R. Datta and J. Wang. ACQUINE: Aesthetic quality inference engine — real-time automatic rating of photo aesthetics. In *Proceedings of MIR*, pages 421–424, 2010.

[5] S. de Jong. SIMPLS: an alternative approach to partial least squares regression. *Chemometrics and Intelligent Laboratory Systems*, 18:251–263, 1993.

[6] S. Dhar, V. Ordonez, and T. Berg. High level describable attributes for predicting aesthetics and interestingness. In *Proceedings of CVPR*, pages 1657–1664, 2011.

[7] Y. Ke, X. Tang, and F. Jing. The design of high-level features for photo quality assessment. In *Proceedings of CVPR*, pages 419–426, 2006.

[8] C. Li and T. Chen. Aesthetic visual quality assessment of paintings. *IEEE Journal of Selected Topics in Signal Processing*, 3(2):236–252, 2009.

[9] L. Liu, R. Chen, and D. Cohen-Or. Optimizing photo composition. *Eurographics*, 29(2):469–478, 2010.

[10] W. Luo, X. Wang, and X. Tang. Content-based photo quality assessment. In *Proceedings of ICCV*, pages 2206–2213, 2011.

[11] B. Manjunath and M.-Y. Ma. Texture features for browsing and retrieval of image data. *IEEE Transactions on Pattern Analysis and Machine Intelligence*, 18(8):837–842, 1996.

[12] X. Sun, H. Yao, R. Ji, and S. Liu. Photo assessment based on computational visual attention model. In *Proceedings of ACM Multimedia*, pages 541–544, 2009.

[13] H. Tong, M. Li, H. Zhang, J. He, and C. Zhang. Classification of digital photos taken by photographers or home users. In *Proceedings of PCM*, 2004.

[14] L.-K. Wong and K.-L. Low. Saliency-enhanced image aesthetics class prediction. In *Proceedings of ICIP*, pages 997–1000, 2009.

[15] O. Wu, W. Hu, and J. Gao. Learning to predict the perceived visual quality of photos. In *Proceedings of ICCV*, pages 225–232, 2011.

Non-Reference Audio Quality Assessment for Online Live Music Recordings

Zhonghua Li[1], Ju-Chiang Wang[1,2], Jingli Cai[1], Zhiyan Duan[1], Hsin-Min Wang[2], Ye Wang[1]
[1]School of Computing, National University of Singapore, Singapore
[2]Institute of Information Science, Academia Sinica, Taiwan
{lzhlynn,asriver.wang}@gmail.com; {jingli,zhiyan}@comp.nus.edu.sg;
whm@iis.sinica.edu.tw; wangye@comp.nus.edu.sg

ABSTRACT

Immensely popular video sharing websites such as YouTube have become the most important sources of music information for Internet users and the most prominent platform for sharing live music. The audio quality of this huge amount of live music recordings, however, varies significantly due to factors such as environmental noise, location, and recording device. However, most video search engines do not take audio quality into consideration when retrieving and ranking results. Given the fact that most users prefer live music videos with better audio quality, we propose the first automatic, non-reference audio quality assessment framework for live music video search online. We first construct two annotated datasets of live music recordings. The first dataset contains 500 human-annotated pieces, and the second contains 2,400 synthetic pieces systematically generated by adding noise effects to clean recordings. Then, we formulate the assessment task as a ranking problem and try to solve it using a learning-based scheme. To validate the effectiveness of our framework, we perform both objective and subjective evaluations. Results show that our framework significantly improves the ranking performance of live music recording retrieval and can prove useful for various real-world music applications.

Categories and Subject Descriptors

H.3.3 [**Information Search and Retrieval**]: Information filtering, Retrieval models; H.5.5 [**Sound and Music Computing**]: Systems

General Terms

Algorithms, Design, Experimentation

Keywords

Live music videos; audio quality assessment; learning-to-rank; and music information retrieval

MM'13, October 21–25, 2013, Barcelona, Spain.

http://dx.doi.org/10.1145/2502081.2502106.

Table 1: Different live video recordings and the corresponding audio quality ratings of the song "Hold it against me" by Britney Spears.

No	URL	AQ	Ord
1	http://www.youtube.com/watch?v=IkAI6MHtJCc	Good	1
2	http://www.youtube.com/watch?v=HtCkp40b5vA	Poor	4
3	http://www.youtube.com/watch?v=7P7JwaLRToM	Poor	5
4	http://www.youtube.com/watch?v=1CvxILczzgs	Good	3
5	http://www.youtube.com/watch?v=v0BWvX0xck8	Good	2
6	http://www.youtube.com/watch?v=kCI3It5YI_0	Poor	6

1. INTRODUCTION

The last decade has witnessed an explosion of musical data on video sharing websites. YouTube[1], Youku[2], and Nico Nico Douga[3] are now counted among the largest and most important sources of music information serving users, who can not only enjoy the official audio and video releases (both live and studio versions) of their favorite artists but also share their own recordings of live concerts with others who do not have the experience. The audio quality of the huge amount of live music recordings, however, varies significantly due to different recording factors, such as environmental noise, location, and recording device. In view of this, we try to improve live music video search by incorporating audio quality assessment.

When given a query, existing video search engines match it with the metadata of each video in the database and rank results according to their relevance. User feedback, such as view count and rating, may also be considered in the ranking or re-ranking process. To the best of our knowledge, however, most popular video search engines do not take the audio quality of the recordings into consideration. For example, the song "Hold it against me" by Britney Spears has several live recordings available on YouTube. We invited ten subjects to rank the order (Ord) of the top six videos retrieved using the query "Britney Spears Hold it against me live" after evaluating their overall audio quality (AQ). The result, summarized in Table 1, indicates that audio quality varies among different recordings. Not only could officially released versions (i.e., video No.2) have poor audio quality, videos with better audio quality could often be outranked by those with poorer quality. Because most users prefer live music videos with better audio quality, it is important to account for it when searching for live music. Although user

[1]http://www.youtube.com/
[2]http://www.youku.com/
[3]http://www.nicovideo.jp/

feedback may indirectly reflect audio quality (videos with better quality are preferred by users, leading to higher view counts and ratings), videos newly added to the database have little or no user feedback information and are thus given low rankings despite their superior audio quality. Therefore, a content-based audio quality assessment strategy is in great demand for long-tail retrieval of live music videos.

Previous research on perceptual assessment of sound quality started in the early 1990s. Most published regulations can be found in the ITU (International Telecommunications Union) Recommendations, which cover various assessment methods for both audio quality (e.g., perceptual evaluation of audio quality (PEAQ) [16,31–33]) and speech quality (e.g., perceptual evaluation of speech quality (PESQ) [18]). These approaches generally compare the quality of the sound signals processed/affected by a test system (e.g., a multimedia device, codec, and telecommunication network) with that of a reference signal in order to evaluate or improve the performance of the system. However, this so-called reference-based audio quality assessment may be inadequate for live music videos. Because recordings of the same performance can be taken under vastly different circumstances, it is seldom possible to find an appropriate reference video.

In this paper, we propose an automatic, non-reference audio quality assessment method for live music video search online. We define audio quality as a subjective metric that describes music audio content. As music is performed, recorded, and then perceived by users in a sequential manner, audio quality can also be assessed from different perspectives along this process. We thus summarize six aspects to assess audio quality, including "instrumental" and "vocal" aspects for the live performance, "environmental" and "equipment" aspects for the recording conditions during the concert, and "pleasantness" and "overall quality" aspects for the end-user perception of the recording.

Because the assessment procedure can be very subjective, we formulate the assessment task as a ranking problem and try to solve it using a learning-based scheme. There are two advantages for assessing audio quality in this way. First, a ranking mechanism (i.e., by saying that song A has better quality than song B) better controls the subjectivity than mere classification (i.e., by saying that song A has good quality while song B has poor quality). Second, the ranking-based assessment method can be directly applied to re-rank the "relevant" live music recordings for a query retrieved by video search engines.

To implement our framework, we first obtain human annotations on all the said six aspects for a set of live recordings downloaded from YouTube. Then, several learning-to-rank (LTR) models are trained using the annotated data to achieve effective online re-ranking of music video search results. The effectiveness of the proposed framework is demonstrated through objective cross-validation. We also create a large database of synthetic recordings to expand the scope of our experiments.

There are four main contributions in this paper:

- To the best of our knowledge, this work presents the first attempt to develop automatic audio quality assessment for online live music recording retrieval.
- We establish a collection of 500 live music recordings with human annotations obtained via a web-based interface and a database of 2,400 synthetically altered live music recordings in 8 different quality conditions.
- We formulate the audio quality assessment task as a ranking problem and tackle it using LTR approaches with various audio feature sets.
- We conduct both objective and subjective evaluations to demonstrate the effectiveness and the usability of the proposed framework.

Beyond the field of multimedia information retrieval, our work can make meaningful contribution to the following topics. First, audio quality assessment can function as an additional clip selection criterion for creating better live concert video mashups [28]. Second, as an auditory characteristic of a music piece, audio quality can be readily integrated into music similarity measures [35]. Consequently, our work can also facilitate the re-ranking stage in general music retrieval and recommendation services.

The rest of the paper is structured as follows. Section 2 reviews related literature on audio quality assessment. Section 3 outlines our proposed framework. Section 4 details our method from data collection, audio feature extraction, to model learning and testing. Objective and subjective evaluations are presented in Sections 5 and 6, respectively. Section 7 concludes our work and explores future directions.

2. RELATED WORK

Initially, the assessment of sound quality was carried out through subjective tests only [14,17], in which subjects rated the overall quality of a test sound (distorted signal) against the reference sound (original signal) using a five-point score based on the ITU-RBS.1284 standard [15]. For example, sounds with the quality ranging from very annoying to imperceptible are scored from 1 to 5. Although subjective test yielded reliable results, it was expensive and time-consuming. Therefore, methods were proposed to assess sound quality objectively and automatically.

At first, the objective methods compared the reference sound and the test sound using traditional measures developed purely from engineering principles (e.g., signal-to-noise ratio and total harmonic distortion). However, their performance was no match against that of methods incorporating the psychoacoustic characteristics of human auditory system. Moreover, as more non-linear and non-stationary distortions appear, the shortcomings of these algorithms become more evident.

To emulate the subjective assessment process, researchers constructed perceptual models by taking into account multiple psychoacoustic phenomena (e.g., absolute hearing threshold and masking) of human auditory system. For example, Karjalainen [22] was one of the first to use the auditory model, such as the noise loudness, for sound quality assessment. Brandenburg explored the level difference between the noise signal and the mask threshold and then proposed a noise-to-mask ratio for audio quality assessment [2,3]. Brandenburg's method was later extended to include the mean opinion scores [29, 30]. These efforts eventually led to the standardization of perceptual evaluation of audio quality (PEAQ) [16,31–33] and of speech quality (PESQ) [18].

PEAQ performs quite well on most of the test signals [32,33]. However, it mainly focuses on low-bit-rate coded signals with small impairments. Therefore, recent research

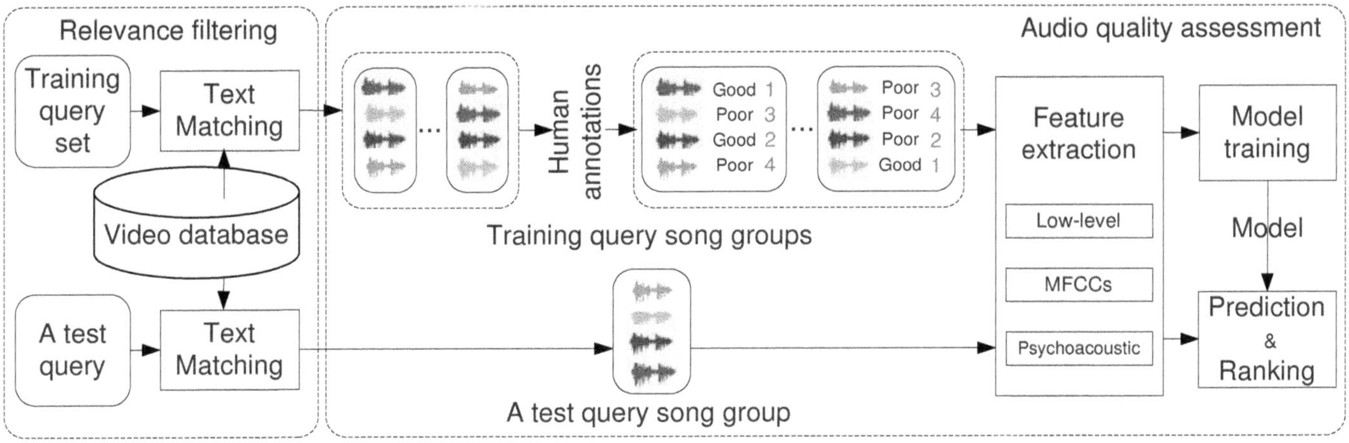

Figure 1: The system framework.

has honed PEAQ in several aspects. Barbedo and Lopes [1] developed a new cognitive model to map the output perceptual models to subjective ratings. Huber and Kollmeier [13] proposed a novel audio quality assessment method and extended the range of distortions on speech and music signals. More work is summarized in [4, 7, 32].

However, the ultimate goal of all the work mentioned above was to develop, test, or compare multimedia devices, codecs and networks for high-end audio or video services (e.g., VoIP and telepresence services) [4, 7, 32]. Moreover, both the reference signal and the distorted signal processed by the test system were available and generally well aligned. Doets and Lagendijk [8] studied the relationship between the parameters extracted from audio fingerprintings and the perceptual quality of compressed audio. However, the reference signals and the specific types of noises that may degrade the quality are required.

Recently, non-reference approaches have also been developed to assess the perceptual quality non-intrusively. Most work is related to quality assessment of speech, image or video signals. However, there is very little published work on non-reference audio quality assessment. For example, Malfait *et al.* [26] studied a non-reference quality assessment algorithm for speech, but it in fact relied on a semi-reference obtained from the reconstructed speech signal. Rix *et al.* [27] reviewed more work on non-reference quality assessment of speech. Hemami and Reibman [12] reviewed the background and related work in designing effective non-reference quality estimator for images and videos. Kennedy and Naaman [23] proposed a system that can manage and create a high quality concert video mashup by employing the audio fingerprintings of different video clips of the same event. They found that the most selected video clips tend to have higher audio quality. However, no systematic study was conducted for audio quality assessment in their work. Saini *et al.* [28] evaluated the quality of the visual information in live performance videos for creating a good quality mashup.

In the case of live music recordings created by common users, existing methods face two major difficulties. First, the audio quality of different recordings for the same live performance can be significantly different owing to various factors, such as the recording location/environment, starting point, duration, and recording device. Among the live music video recordings for a specific live concert, it is difficult to set up a reference due to the complex characteristics caused by the artist's performance, the environment of the concert venue, and the subjectivity of user perception. Second, unlike speech and studio versions of music, live music signals contain numerous and complex layers of information that may influence the assessment of audio quality (e.g., singing voice, various instrumental sounds, and unpredictable background noises). We hope that, by learning from annotated data, the learning-to-rank (LTR) algorithms can automatically assess the audio quality and predict the ranking of any live music recordings.

3. FRAMEWORK OVERVIEW

Our framework is based on how people assess the audio quality across multiple "relevant" recordings of the same song. We implement our framework in both the training and testing phases with a two-stage process (Figure 1), namely *relevance filtering* and *audio quality assessment*. Relevance filtering aims to identify the relevant songs, which should be live versions of the query song, regardless of audio quality. The second stage assesses the audio quality of each relevant song and produces a quality-based ranking.

3.1 Relevance Filtering

Searching music videos by metadata, such as artist name, song title and version type (e.g., official or live), is the most common and established method in general video retrieval systems, since most users tend to mark correct and sufficient metadata when they upload the music videos. In turn, the descriptive metadata can be used to accurately identify the live music videos relevant to a text-based query.

We use a text query with the format "artist_name song_name live" to search for live versions of a specific song on YouTube, assuming that this format can filter out most of the irrelevant as well as non-live videos. Given such a song query, the group of live versions returned is termed a *query song group*. At present, some manual efforts are also made to further check the returned recordings to ensure that they are relevant live versions to the given query. Our future work will make this filtering process fully automatic.

3.2 Audio Quality Assessment

In the training phase, we apply the learning-to-rank (LTR) algorithm to learn the model for audio quality assessment.

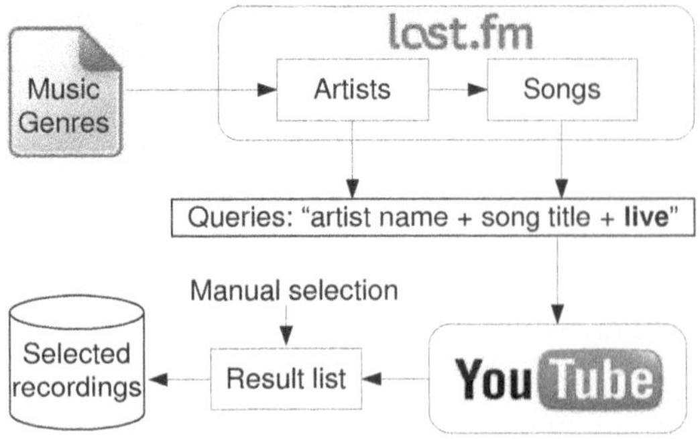

Figure 2: The diagram of collecting the live music videos.

We first create a set of training song queries and then generate the query song groups via relevance filtering. Next, subjects are invited to annotate each query song group (see Section 4.2) by rating the audio quality of each component version based on the six aspects of audio quality as well as ranking the order among all versions in a query song group. With the annotated data, the LTR algorithm learns a global model that considers the ranking relationship among the component versions of each training query song group. We will explain the rationale and realization of this learning scheme in Section 4.4.

In the testing phase (i.e., the proposed audio quality assessment system), relevant filtering first generates the query song group for a test query. Then, the learned LTR model predicts the ranking score for each component version in the query song group (see Section 4.4 for details). The system then outputs a ranked list based on these scores, with the versions in descending order in terms of audio quality. This way, the assessment stage can be seen as a re-ranking over the relevance filtering results.

Both training and testing data undergo the feature extraction procedure (see Section 4.3). Various audio features sets, such as low-level acoustic features, MFCCs, and psychoacoustic features, are extracted from all recordings. For efficient audio quality assessment online, feature extraction can be performed offline beforehand.

4. THE PROPOSED APPROACH

As there is no benchmark dataset available for the proposed application, our work starts with collecting the live music database and the associated annotations. Then, we discuss several audio feature sets and present the training and testing procedures of the employed LTR algorithms.

4.1 Data Collection

For objective performance study, we have constructed two annotated datasets, one human-annotated (ADB-H) and the other synthetically generated (ADB-S). For subjective evaluation, we have also created a non-annotated (NDB) dataset.

Figure 2 outlines the live music data collection process and also illustrates the relevance filtering stage in more detail. To create a diverse dataset, we choose four genres of music (i.e., rock, pop, electronic, and country) that tend to have more live recordings of concerts. For each genre, we select a number of popular artists with their signature songs by

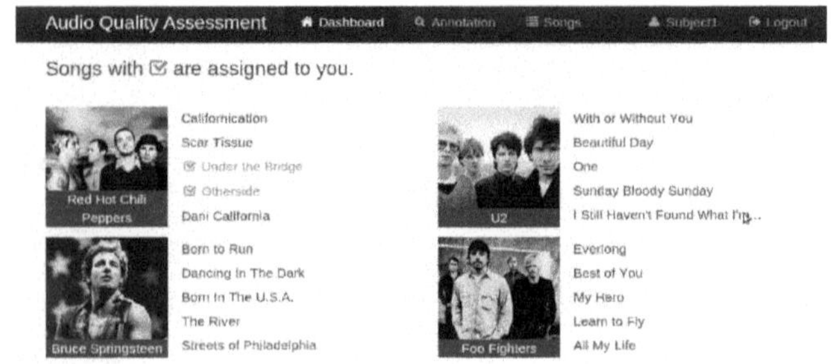

Figure 3: A snapshot of the song assignment for human annotation.

finding each artist's top tracks on Last.fm API.[4] We then search for live music recordings on YouTube using the query format "artist_name song_name live" and manually select the most relevant results.

For ADB-H, we generate 100 song queries (4 genres, 5 artists per genre, and 5 songs per artist) on YouTube and select 5 relevant versions of each song query from its top 20 results.[5] Efforts are also made to ensure that the 5 versions vary in their audio quality. ADB-H thus contains $100 \times 5 = 500$ live music recordings.

For ADB-S, we generate 200 song queries (4 genres, 5 artists per genre, and 10 songs per artist) in addition to the 100 queries used in ADB-H. The artists for these 200 song queries are different from those in ADB-H. Moreover, unlike ADB-H, we only select the relevant version with the best audio quality (denoted as the "clean version"). As will be detailed later, each of these $100 + 200 = 300$ clean versions are subsequently used to generate 7 additional noisy versions. ADB-S thus contains $300 \times (7 + 1) = 2,400$ items.

For NDB, we generate 100 queries (4 genres, 5 artists per genre, and 5 songs per artist) from a different group of artists. Then, ten versions among the top 20 search results are randomly selected for each query song, regardless of their relevance and live-ness. NDB thus contains 1,000 non-annotated music pieces.

4.2 Data Annotation

4.2.1 ADB-H

To obtain the ground truth for ADB-H, we build an audio quality assessment interface online (Figures 3, 4, and 5) and recruit 60 subjects with normal hearing for annotation. Each subject is assigned eight query song groups (see Figure 3) from two randomly chosen genres and performs two types of annotations within each group. For the first type, the visual channel of the recording is masked, and subjects rate the audio quality in the six perception aspects (Figure 4) – instrumental, vocal, environmental, equipment-related, pleasantness, and overall quality. The first five aspects are based on a scale of 1 to 5, and the overall rating is a binary choice. Only when the audio ratings are completed can subjects enable the visual channel (by clicking the "Toggle Visual" button) to rate the seventh aspect, visual quality (see Figure 4). Currently we only consider the audio-related quality aspects; the visual quality rating is intended for fu-

[4]http://www.last.fm/api

[5]It may happen that YouTube returns some non-live versions in the top 20 results.

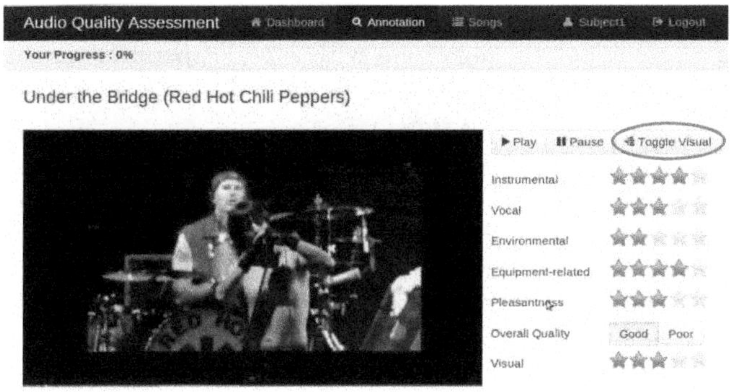

Figure 4: A snapshot of the interface for annotating the audio and visual quality.

Figure 5: The designed interface for labeling the ranking. The index of each live recording is dragged and dropped into a desired ranking position.

ture research. The second type of annotation takes place after all songs in the query song group have been rated. Subjects rank the overall audio quality of the five versions by a drag-and-drop mechanism (see Figure 5).

Since all live recordings used in our datasets are songs performed by their original artists, we assume that the subjects would not debate the merit of the performance itself. Therefore, subjects are reminded by the interface to neglect the intrinsic quality of the performance, e.g., whether the vocal is out-of-tune, cracked, off-beat, etc. In addition, we further clarify that, by "instrumental" and "vocal," we mean whether they sound clear, with the volume well-balanced, in the recording.

4.2.2 ADB-S

The significant time and manpower costs make it difficult to scale human-annotated datasets. We thus have created another annotated dataset by automatically generating various types of poor-quality recordings.

We applied the following noise effects, which are widely used in speech, TV, and movie productions [5], to the 300 clean versions.

- *Amplitude compression and then amplification*, where the compression uses the ratios of 4.47:1 for $|A| \geq -28.6$ dB, 0.86:1 for $-46.4 \text{ dB} < |A| < -28.6$ dB, and 1:1.61 for $|A| \leq -46.4$ dB ($|A|$ is the absolute amplitude value), and the amplification gains the volume of the entire song with a ratio of 1:4. This simulates clipped live music sound produced by non-professional recordings devices whose dynamic range may not be able to adapt to the extremely loud musical sounds in the concert.

- *Band-pass filtering* using a second order Butterworth filter with cut-off frequencies at 100Hz and 6000Hz. This can simulate a muffling effect.

Table 2: Applied noise effects and audio quality rankings (averaged across ten subjects) of the 8 synthetic versions in a query song group in ADB-S (AQ = 1: Good, 0: Poor; Ord = quality rank).

Version	1	2	3	4	5	6	7	8
Comp & Amp		√				√		
Band-pass			√				√	
White noise				√				√
Crowd noise					√	√	√	√
AQ	1	0	0	0	0	0	0	0
Ord	1	4	2	3	5	8	6	7

- *White noise addition* with a maximum magnitude of 512 quantization steps. White noise is a signal with an approximately uniform (constant) power spectral density. This effect simulates the noise generated by the recording devices.

- *Crowd noise addition* with real-life noises from the concert audience, such as clapping, cheering, singing, and screaming. We collect 30 crowd noise samples from Freesound,[6] a collaborative sound database online, using queries "concert noise," "cheering," and "screaming." A set of 30 audio clips of crowd noises are uniformly added into each clean version with the signal-to-noise ratio of 1:1.

Since live music recordings generally contain noise from multiple sources, we also experiment with certain combination of noise effects to simulate the poor-quality examples. Seven poor-quality versions (labeled "Poor") are generated for each clean version (labeled "Good"). Each query song group in ADB-S thus contains 8 component versions. To assess which noise effect degrades audio quality more, ten subjects were invited to rank the order of the 7 poor-quality versions for 20 randomly chosen query songs (see Table 2).

4.3 Audio Feature Sets

We consider three types of audio feature sets in this work. The feature extractor is implemented based on MIRToolbox [24] and the methods proposed in [9].

- **Low-level features** (13 dim): The feature set includes root-mean-square, brightness, zero-crossing rate, spectral flux, rolloff at 85%, rolloff at 95%, spectral centroid, spread, skewness, kurtosis, entropy, flatness, and irregularity.

- **Mel-frequency cepstral coefficients** (39 dim): This feature set contains static MFCCs, delta MFCCs, and delta-delta MFCCs.

- **Psychoacoustic features** (20 dim): This feature set covers loudness, sharpness, roughness, and tonality features (key clarity, mode, harmonic change, and the normalized chroma weights).

For each audio feature set, we extract all the features with the same frame decomposition of 50ms and 50% hop sizes to ensure easy alignment, thereby obtaining a set of frame-level feature vectors for a live recording. We summarize the song-level audio feature representation for a recording by taking the mean and standard deviation of its frame-level vectors.

[6] `http://www.freesound.org/`

4.4 LTR Model Training and Testing

4.4.1 Notations and Rationale

Suppose that the annotated dataset $\mathcal{S}$ contains M query song groups, $\mathcal{S} = \{\mathbf{s}^{(i)}\}_{i=1}^{M}$, where each group has N_i component versions $\mathbf{s}^{(i)} = \{\mathbf{v}_j^{(i)}\}_{j=1}^{N_i}$, and each component version contains its corresponding audio feature vector $\vec{x}_j^{(i)}$ and rank (or relevance) label $y_j^{(i)}$, i.e., $\{\vec{x}_j^{(i)}, y_j^{(i)}\} \in \mathbf{v}_j^{(i)}$. The rank label y can be binary, numerical, or ordinal score.

Our principle for leaning the ranking model is that we only consider the rank relationship (obtained by $\{y_j^{(i)}\}_{j=1}^{N_i}$) among different versions $\{\mathbf{v}_j^{(i)}\}_{j=1}^{N_i}$ within a query song group $\mathbf{s}^{(i)}$. In other words, we do not care about the audio quality comparison between $\mathbf{v}_p^{(a)}$ and $\mathbf{v}_q^{(b)}$, where $1 \leq p \leq N_a$, $1 \leq q \leq N_b$, and $a \neq b$, because subjects are not asked to compare them.

Within a query song group, versions do not differ from each other in their *musical content*, such as melody, harmony, rhythm, and instrumentation. Live concert recordings of Britney Spear's "Hold it against me," for example, will have similar, if not identical, melody, harmony, and rhythm regardless of where or how the music is recorded. Because audio features extracted from the waveform can be related to musical content as well as audio quality, comparing versions of different songs would disproportionately highlight the differences in musical content. As a result, music content will vastly overpower audio quality in the learning process. Therefore, we only compare different versions of the same song (i.e. within a query song group) to control for the differences in music content features and to ensure that the algorithm learns the most from features related to audio quality. Hypothetically, if the algorithm can exclude features related to musical content, the effect of the discrepancy in audio quality can be enhanced regardless of the data's live-ness and relevance. In the testing phase, we conduct subjective evaluation using the NDB database, which may contain non-live and irrelevant videos alongside live and relevant ones, to verify this hypothesis.

4.4.2 Formulation

The goal of model training is to learn a global ranking function $f(\cdot)$ for the audio feature vector $\vec{x}$ of a live music recording. Given a training dataset $\mathcal{S}$, the learning objective can be generalized to the minimization of the following loss function L with respect to f,

$$L(f;\mathcal{S}) = \sum_{i=1}^{M} p(\mathbf{s}^{(i)}) \cdot l(f;\mathbf{x}^{(i)},\mathbf{y}^{(i)}) + \lambda\|f\|, \quad (1)$$

where $p(\mathbf{s}^{(i)})$ is the prior model for $\mathbf{s}^{(i)}$, $l(\cdot)$ is the query-level loss function, $\mathbf{x}^{(i)} = \{\vec{x}_j^{(i)}\}_{j=1}^{N_i}$, $\mathbf{y}^{(i)} = \{y_j^{(i)}\}_{j=1}^{N_i}$, and $\|f\|$ represents the regularizer for f. Such a learning objective can be solved by many existing LTR algorithms.

In the testing phase, given an arbitrary query song group $\mathbf{s}^{(*)}$, the system ranks the component versions by sorting the scores $\{f(\vec{x}_j^{(*)})\}_{j=1}^{N_*}$.

4.4.3 Learning-to-Rank Algorithms

According to their input/output representations and loss functions, learning-to-rank algorithms can be categorized into three groups [25] – pointwise, pairwise, and listwise – all of which can be used in our framework. From each category, we adopt the algorithm with superior performance in our preliminary study.

- **Pointwise (MART):** For this approach, the annotations are converted to numerical scores. MART [11] uses a general gradient descent "boosting" paradigm with multiple additive regression trees to minimize the objective function.
- **Pairwise (SVM-Rank):** For this approach, the annotations in each query song group are converted into the pairwise orders among versions. Support vector machine (SVM) is generally regarded as one of the most powerful supervised learning methods. SVM-Rank [20, 21] minimizes the loss function with respect to a weight vector by considering all the pairwise orders as constraints.
- **Listwise (AdaRank):** For this approach, the annotations in each query song group are converted into a ranked list. Similar to AdaBoost [10], AdaRank learns a number of "weak rankers" and their associated weights and makes prediction by linearly combining them. We utilize AdaRank [36] to directly optimize the ranking evaluation measures with a boosting scheme.

We utilize RankLib [6] for implementing MART and AdaRank and the SVM^{rank} tool [21] for SVM-Rank.

5. OBJECTIVE EVALUATION

The goals of our objective evaluation are twofold. First, we compare the effectiveness of different LTR algorithms in terms of ranking performance based on the overall quality aspect, denoted by LTR method comparison (LTRC). Second, we study the performance with different audio feature sets based on the six perception aspects, denoted by audio features comparison (AFC). For each goal, we use both ADB-H and ADB-S, leading to four evaluation tasks in total, as summarized in Table 3.

5.1 Audio Quality Labels

We exploit three types of ground truth labels in ADB-H and ADB-S: binary, ranking, and numerical. Binary and ranking labels describe the overall quality aspect, while numerical labels rate the other five perception aspects, i.e. instrumental, vocal, environmental, equipment-related, and pleasantness. For the binary labels, "Good" is assigned a value of 1 and "Poor" 0. Recall that ADB-H consists of ranking order annotated by the subjects, with each query song group containing 5 versions, and that ADB-S uses ranking order as shown in Table 3, with each query song group containing 8 versions. Ranking labels are assigned as the reverse of the ranking order within the query song group so that the label of the best-quality version (rank 1) has the highest assigned value (5 for ADB-H or 8 for ADB-S) and vice versa. The numerical label, which is only applicable to ADB-H, takes the average rating of each component version.

5.2 Methods Compared

We implement three LTR algorithms (i.e., MART, SVM-Rank, and AdaRank) and a baseline method (i.e., *Random*) in the experiment. The Random method generates a permutation randomly for ranking the versions in each test

Table 3: Summary table for objective evaluation. The task names, LTRC and AFC, stand for "LTR method comparison" and "audio feature comparison," respectively.

Task	Dataset	Label Type	LTR Methods	Features	Aspect	Result
LTRC 1	ADB-H	Binary	Random, MART, SVM-Rank, AdaRank	All features	Overall	Fig. 6
		Ranking				
LTRC 2	ADB-S	Binary	Random, MART, SVM-Rank, AdaRank	All features	Synthetic	Fig. 7
		Ranking				
AFC 1	ADB-H	Numerical	SVM-Rank	Low-level, MFCCs, Psychoacoustic, All features	Instrument	Fig. 8
					Vocal	
					Environment	
					Equipment	
					Pleasantness	
		Binary			Overall	
		Ranking			Overall	
AFC 2	ADB-S	Binary	SVM-Rank	Low-level, MFCCs, Psycho., All features	Synthetic	Fig. 9
		Ranking				

query song group without accounting for their audio quality. We repeat the random permutation 10 times for each test query song group and calculate the average baseline performance. For each LTR algorithm, we perform a ten-fold cross-validation and calculate the average performance.

5.3 Performance Measure

The normalized discounted cumulative gain (NDCG) [19], a widely used metric in information retrieval, is adopted to measure the ranking performance. To calculate NDCG, the discounted cumulative gain (DCG) at a particular rank position p is first calculated in a way that penalizes the score gain near the bottom more than those near the top.

$$\text{DCG@}p = \sum_{i=1}^{p} \frac{2^{rel_i} - 1}{log_2(i+1)}, \quad (2)$$

where rel_i is the ground truth label of the recording at position i. It is then normalized so that the performance for each test query can be compared.

$$\text{NDCG@}p = \frac{\text{DCG@}p}{\text{IDCG@}p}, \quad (3)$$

where IDCG@p serves as the normalization term that guarantees the ideal NDCG@p to be 1. We summarize the performance by averaging the NDCGs over the test query set.

5.4 Result and Discussion

5.4.1 Comparison among LTR Algorithms

We first evaluate the effectiveness of each LTR algorithm holistically. All audio feature sets are concatenated into a single vector representation. The LTR models are trained with the binary or the ranking labels (both pertaining to overall quality) of either the ADB-H or the ADB-S dataset.

Figure 6 presents the average NDCG@5 on ADB-H. First, all LTR algorithms significantly ($p < 0.01$) outperform Random in all cases, demonstrating the effectiveness of our proposed approach. Trained with binary labels, MART, SVM-Rank, and AdaRank outdo Random by 11%, 17%, and 8%, respectively; with ranking labels, 16%, 17%, and 15%, respectively. Second, SVM-Rank achieves the best ranking performance of the three LTR algorithms. Interestingly, the performance difference between SVM-Rank and the other two are larger with binary labels than with ranking labels. This may be attributed to the difference of learning criteria

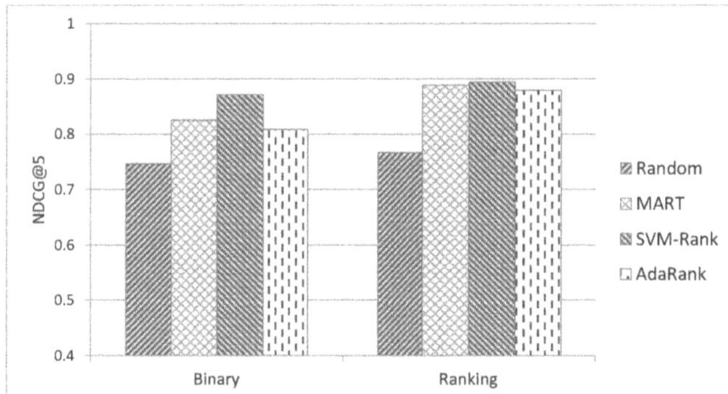

Figure 6: Performance based on overall quality using the binary and ranking labels on ADB-H.

among the three LTR approaches. For pairwise approach, the learning criteria do not compare training examples with the same binary labels, e.g., the approach does not need to discriminate the feature difference between two "Good" quality examples. While for the other two approaches, the feature difference between two "Good" quality examples are still taken into account, leading to certain randomness or contradiction during the learning process. For example, suppose a subject has the same binary labels in the case in Table 1, a listwise approach may convert the binary labels into #4>#5>#1>#6>#3>#2, which is much different from the ranking labels by human, #1>#5>#4>#2>#3>#6.

Figure 7 presents the the average NDCG@8 on ADB-S. MART, SVM-Rank, and AdaRank also significantly ($p < 0.01$) outperform Random with improvements of 31%, 93%, and 71% for binary labels and 31%, 51%, and 41% for ranking labels, respectively. Moreover, SVM-Rank achieves a remarkable performance of about 99% for both binary and ranking labels. This lends support to our hypothesis (Section 4.4.1) that minimizing the discrepancy in musical content features can magnify the learning potential with the audio quality features.

In sum, SVM-Rank achieves the best performance among the three LTR algorithms on both ADB-H and ADB-S. We thus adopt SVM-Rank in the following experiments.

5.4.2 Comparison among Different Audio Features

Using SVM-Rank, we compare the performance among different audio feature sets, namely low-level, MFCCs, psy-

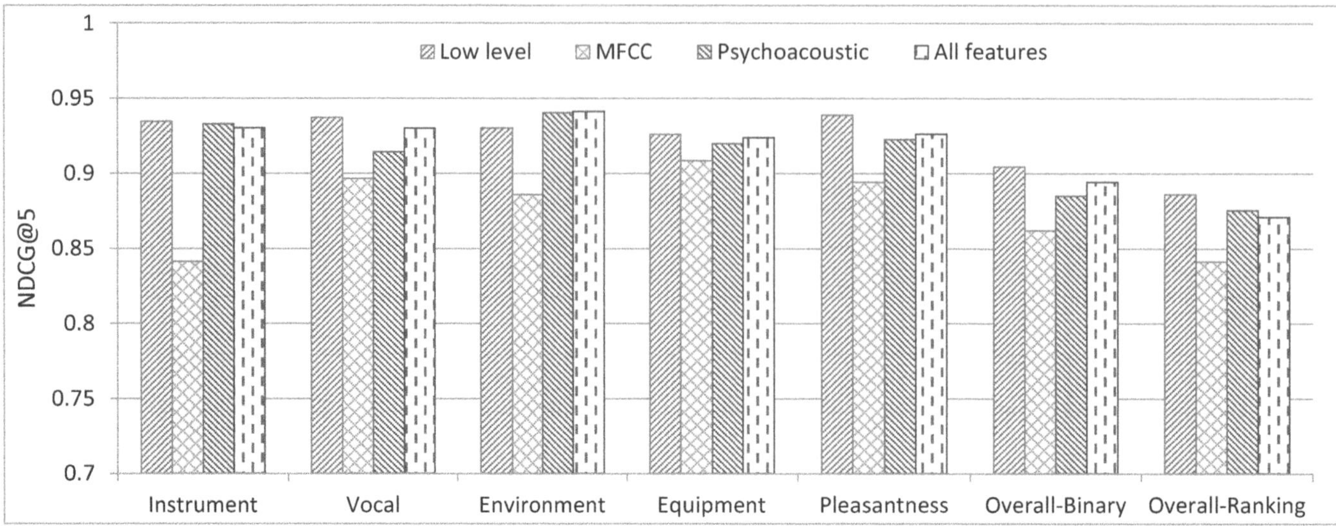

Figure 8: Performance on ADB-H using SVM-Rank with all types of labels and different audio feature sets. Except the overall quality aspect, the others are all numerical labels.

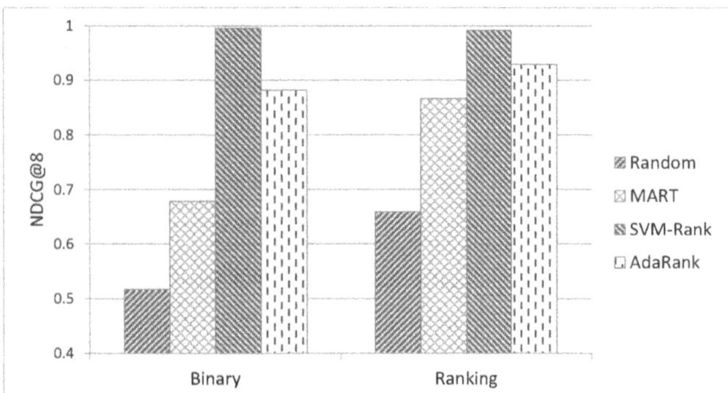

Figure 7: Performance based on overall quality using the binary and ranking labels of ADB-S.

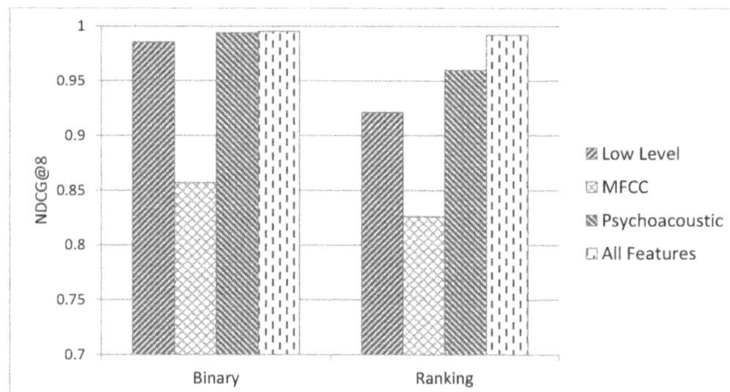

Figure 9: Performance of SVM-Rank on ADB-S using different audio feature sets.

choacoustic, and all three together. For ADB-H, we use all types of labels to train the SVM-Rank models, and Figure 8 shows the result. For ADB-S, we train SVM-Rank with the binary and ranking labels and show the result in Figure 9.

In almost all cases, we observe that both the low-level and psychoacoustic feature sets achieve better performance than MFCCs, as does the all-concatenated feature set. Recalling Section 4.4.1, we hope the learned model could neglect features related to musical content. Since MFCCs are developed to capture the spectral envelope based on human audition system, they tend to carry much more information about the musical content instead of the noise, and hence are less capable of identifying the difference in audio quality we are interested in. As shown in Figure 9, this phenomenon is more evident for ADB-S, in which all the noisy versions are generated directly from the clean one.

From Figure 8, we observe that the performance of the low-level and psychoacoustic feature sets with the numerical labels are very consistent with NDCG@5 $\approx$ 93%. Except in the case of environmental aspect, using low-level features always leads to superior performance, further demonstrating its effectiveness and robustness in this task.

6. SUBJECTIVE EVALUATION

To further evaluate the effectiveness and usability of the proposed approaches, a subjective study was carried out using NDB. Two SVM-Rank models trained with ADB-H and ADB-S (termed as SVM-Rank-H and SVM-Rank-S), respectively, are adopted to rank each query song group in NDB by audio quality. Their performance is evaluated in terms of (1) how users perceive the overall ranking quality of SVM-Rank compared to Random; and (2) how well SVM-Rank ranks the recordings with the best and the worst audio quality in a query song group.

6.1 Methodology

We recruit twenty subjects, all of whom are music lovers without auditory disorders. After a brief introduction to familiarize with the evaluation interface, each subject is asked to evaluate 10 test query song groups that are randomly chosen but represent all four music genres. For each of the first five groups (the first perspective), two ranked lists are presented in randomized order. One list is generated by Random, and the other is generated by SVM-Rank-H half the time and SVM-Rank-S half the time. Subjects listen through the two ranked lists and indicate the better one.

Table 4: **Supporting Rates of SVM-Rank-H and SVM-Rank-S when comparing with Random.**

	Rock	Country	Electronic	Pop	Avg
SVM-Rank-H	0.800	0.800	0.500	0.700	**0.720**
SVM-Rank-S	0.867	0.933	0.600	0.700	**0.800**

For each of the last five groups (the second perspective), they need to identify from a randomly permutated list the versions with the best and the worst audio quality. In summary, both SVM-Rank-H and SVM-Rank-S are evaluated with a total of 1,000 recordings (100 query song groups), half of which for overall ranking evaluation and the other half for best/worst audio quality ranking.

6.2 Performance Measure

The first perspective is measured by the *supporting rate* (SR) $SR_m = n_m/|S|$, where n_m is the number of test song groups on which method m outperforms Random, and $|S|$ is the total number of test song groups.

To measure the performance from the second perspective, we adopt both mean reciprocal rank (MRR) [34] and mean rank position (MRP).

$$MRR = 1/|S| \sum_{i=1}^{|S|} \frac{1}{rank_i}, \quad (4)$$

$$MRP = 1/|S| \sum_{i=1}^{|S|} rank_i, \quad (5)$$

where $rank_i$ denotes the rank of the best-quality version (or the worst-quality version) in the ranked list for the i-th query song group.

We denote the MRR for the best-quality and the worst-quality versions as MRR_b and MRR_w, respectively. A better ranking method would result in MRR_b closer to 1 and MRR_w closer to $1/N$, where $N = 10$ is the number of versions in a query song group. We calculate the MRR_b and MRR_w of Random, respectively, by using 100 random integers randomly generated between 1 and 10 as the ranking positions of all best-quality or worst-quality versions.

6.3 Results and Discussion

Table 4 presents the average SR of SVM-Rank-H and SVM-Rank-S when comparing with Random. The overall SR performance of SVM-Rank-H and SVM-Rank-S are significantly better than that of Random, clearly indicating that subjects are more pleased with the ranked lists generated by our approaches. The SRs in terms of different music genres show that both our approaches perform well for country and rock, but not for electronic. This is possibly due to the fact that electronic music tends to be intrinsically noisy and thus makes it more difficult for subjects to judge the differences in audio quality.

Table 5 presents the MRR performances of SVM-Rank-H and SVM-Rank-S. For Random, the calculated MRR_b and MRR_w are 0.301 and 0.299, respectively. Both SVM-Rank-H and SVM-Rank-S significantly ($p < 0.01$) outperform Random in the task of ranking the best/worst-quality versions. The MPRs of the best-quality and the worst-quality versions are 2.60 and 8.56, respectively, for SVM-Rank-H; and 2.70 and 7.78, respectively, for SVM-Rank-S. For Random, the MRPs are around 5.02 for both quality versions. These results indicate that our proposed approaches are able to rank the best-quality versions at higher positions and the worst-quality versions at lower positions. In terms of the four music genres, we observe that both SVM-Rank-H and SVM-Rank-S still perform very well for country music. Unlike the previous subjective evaluation perspective, however, identifying the best-quality and worst-quality versions of electronic music seems to have become relatively easier for subjects. Moreover, the performance variance among the four genres is also smaller.

Table 5: **The performance of SVM-Rank-H and SVM-Rank-S for ranking the best-quality (MRR_b) and the worst-quality (MRR_w) versions.**

	SVM-Rank-H		SVM-Rank-S	
	MRR_b	MRR_w	MRR_b	MRR_w
Rock	0.503	0.115	0.588	0.144
Country	0.698	0.116	0.703	0.188
Electronic	0.524	0.126	0.553	0.142
Pop	0.589	0.127	0.541	0.122
Avg	**0.574**	**0.122**	**0.586**	**0.146**

In summary, the results validate the effectiveness of our systems supported by evaluations using human perception and demonstrate the practical usability in ranking live music recordings according to audio quality. An interesting observation is that SVM-Rank-S generally performs slightly better than SVM-Rank-H. We have three plausible explanations for this. First, ADB-S (2,400 pieces) contains more training query song groups than ADB-H (500 pieces), which could benefit the model generalizability of SVM-Rank-H. Second, this result implies that our noise effects can reflect the real factors that degrade the audio quality of live music recordings. Third, the models learned from ADB-H may still involve the influence of musical content features. Since some query song groups in NDB may contain irrelevant recordings, the discrepancy in musical content may confuse their ranking prediction.

7. CONCLUSION AND FUTURE WORK

In this paper, we proposed a novel framework to assess audio quality for online live music search. Unlike previous reference-based audio quality assessment methods, our approach is non-referenced. We have established two music datasets of 500 annotated and 2,400 synthetic live music recordings for this study. We believe that the two constructed datasets can also serve as additional benchmark datasets for developing novel learning-to-rank algorithms in the machine learning research. Three LTR models with different audio feature sets were evaluated in terms of ranking performance based on different audio quality aspects. Our objective and subjective experimental results have shown that the proposed approaches can effectively rank live music recordings according to audio quality.

Our future work is fourfold. First, we will enlarge our datasets. Second, we will explore more audio features and learning algorithms to gain the effectiveness of audio quality assessment. Third, we will develop the segment-based approach, because the mean and standard deviation of the whole frame-level features may over-simplify the representation of the audio features of a recording. Fourth, we will integrate the proposed framework into general music retrieval and recommendation systems.

8. ACKNOWLEDGMENTS

This research is supported by the Singapore National Research Foundation under its International Research Centre @ Singapore Funding Initiative and administered by the IDM Programme Office.

9. REFERENCES

[1] J. Barbedo and A. Lopes. A new cognitive model for objective assessment of audio quality. *Journal of Audio Engineering Society*, 53(1/2):22–31, 2005.

[2] K. Brandenburg. A new coding algorithm for high quality sound signals. In *Proc. IEEE International Conference on Acoustics, Speech, and Signal Processing*, pages 141–144, 1987.

[3] K. Brandenburg and T. Sporer. NMR and masking flag: Evaluation of quality using perceptual criteria. In *Proc. International AES Conference on Audio Test and Measurement*, pages 169–179, 1992.

[4] D. Campbell, E. Jones, and M. Glavin. Audio quality assessment techniques – A review, and recent developments. *Signal Processing*, 89(8):1489–1500, 2009.

[5] C.-Y. Chiu, D. Bountouridis, J.-C. Wang, and H.-M. Wang. Background music identification through content filtering and min-hash matching. In *Proc. IEEE International Conference on Acoustics, Speech, and Signal Processing*, pages 2414–2417, 2010.

[6] V. Dang. Ranklib – A library of learning to rank algorithms. [Online] `http://www.cs.umass.edu/~vdang/ranklib.html`.

[7] A. A. de Lima, F. P. Freeland, R. A. de Jesus, B. C. Bispo, L. W. P. Biscainho, S. L. Netto, A. Said, A. Kalker, R. Schafer, B. Lee, and M. Jam. On the quality assessment of sound signals. In *Proc. IEEE International Symposium on Circuits and Systems*, pages 416–419, 2008.

[8] P. J. O. Doets and R. L. Lagendijk. Extracting quality parameters for compressed audio from fingerprints. In *Proc. International Conference on Music Information Retrieval*, pages 498–503, 2005.

[9] H. Fastl and E. Zwicker. *Psychoacoustics: Facts and models*, volume 22. Springer, 2006.

[10] Y. Freund and R. E. Schapire. A decision-theoretic generalization of on-line learning and an application to boosting. *Journal of Computer and System Sciences*, 55(1):119–139, 1997.

[11] J. Friedman. *Greedy function approximation: A gradient boosting machine*, 1999.

[12] S. S. Hemami and A. R. Reibman. No-reference image and video quality estimation: Applications and human-motivated design. *Image Communication*, 25(7):469–481, 2010.

[13] R. Huber and B. Kollmeier. PEMO-Q – A new method for objective audio quality assessment using a model of auditory perception. *IEEE Transactions Audio, Speech, and Language Processing*, 14(6):1902–1911, 2006.

[14] International Telecommunications Union Recommendation (ITU-R) BS.1116-1. *Methods for the subjective assessment of small impairments in audio system including multichannel sound systems*, 1997.

[15] International Telecommunications Union Recommendation (ITU-R) BS.1284-1. *General methods for the subjective assessment of sound quality*, 1997–2003.

[16] International Telecommunications Union Recommendation (ITU-R) BS.1387. *Method for objective measurements of perceived audio quality*, 1998.

[17] International Telecommunications Union Recommendation (ITU-R) BS.1534-1. *Methods for the subjective assessment of intermediate quality level of coding systems*, 2003.

[18] International Telecommunications Union Recommendation (ITU-R) P.862. *Peceptual Evaluation of Speech Quality (PESQ): An objective method for end-to-end speach quality assessment of narrow-band telephone networks and speech codecs*, 2001.

[19] K. Jarvelin and J. Kekalainen. Cumulated gain-based evaluation of IR techniques. *ACM Transactions on Information Systems*, 20(4):422–446, 2002.

[20] T. Joachims. Optimizing search engines using clickthrough data. In *Proc. the ACM International Conference on Knowledge Discovery and Data Mining*, pages 133–142, 2002.

[21] T. Joachims. Training linear SVMs in linear time. In *Proc. ACM International Conference on Knowledge Discovery and Data Mining*, pages 217–226, 2006.

[22] M. Karjalainen. A new auditory model for the evaluation of sound quality of audio systems. In *Proc. IEEE International Conference on Acoustics, Speech, and Signal Processing*, volume 10, pages 608–611, 1985.

[23] L. Kennedy and M. Naaman. Less talk, more rock: Automated organization of community-contributed collections of concert videos. In *Proc. International Conference on World Wide Web*, pages 311–320, 2009.

[24] O. Lartillot and P. Toiviainen. A Matlab toolbox for musical feature extraction from audio. In *Proc. International Conference on Digital Audio Effects*, 2007.

[25] T.-Y. Liu. Learning to rank for information retrieval. *Foundations and Trends in Information Retrieval*, 3(3):225–331, 2009.

[26] L. Malfait, J. Berger, and M. Kastner. P.563-8212, the ITU-T standard for single-ended speech quality assessment. *IEEE Transactions on Audio, Speech, and Language Processing*, 14(6):1924–1934, 2006.

[27] A. Rix, J. Beerends, D. Kim, P. Kroon, and O. Ghitza. Objective assessment of speech and audio quality – Technology and applications. *IEEE Transactions on Audio, Speech, and Language Processing*, 14(6):1890–1901, 2006.

[28] M. K. Saini, R. Gadde, S. Yan, and W. T. Ooi. Movimash: online mobile video mashup. In *Proc. ACM International Conference on Multimedia*, pages 139–148, 2012.

[29] T. Sporer. Objective audio signal evaluation–applied psychoacoustics for modeling the perceived quality of digital audio. In *Audio Engineering Society Convention 103*, page 4512, 1997.

[30] T. Sporer, U. Gbur, J. Herre, and R. Kapust. Evaluating a measurement system. In *Audio Engineering Society Convention 95*, page 3704, 1996.

[31] T. Thiede. Perceptual audio quality assessment using a non-linear filter bank. In *PhD thesis, Fachbereich Electrotechnik, Technical University of Berlin*, 1999.

[32] T. Thiede, W. C. Treurniet, R. Bitto, C. Schmidmer, T. Sporer, J. G. Beerends, and C. Colomes. PEAQ - the ITU standard for objective measurement of perceived audio quality. *Journal of Audio Engineering Society*, 48(1/2):3–29, 2000.

[33] W. Treurniet and G. Soulodre. Evaluation of the ITU-R objective audio quality measurement method. *Journal of Audio Engineering Society*, 48(3):164–173, 2000.

[34] E. M. Voorhees. The TREC-8 question answering track report. In *Proc. Text Retrieval Conference*, pages 77–82, 1999.

[35] J.-C. Wang, H.-S. Lee, H.-M. Wang, and S.-K. Jeng. Learning the similarity of audio music in bag-of-frames representation from tagged music data. In *Proc. International Society for Music Information Retrieval Conference*, pages 85–90, 2011.

[36] Q. Wu, C. J. Burges, K. M. Svore, and J. Gao. Adapting boosting for information retrieval measures. *Information Retrieval*, 13(3):254–270, 2010.

Enabling Low Bitrate Mobile Visual Recognition – A Performance versus Bandwidth Evaluation

Yu-Chuan Su, Tzu-Hsuan Chiu, Yan-Ying Chen
Chun-Yen Yeh, Winston H. Hsu
National Taiwan University, Taipei, Taiwan

ABSTRACT

The rapid development of technologies in both hardware and software have made content-based multimedia services feasible on mobile devices such as smartphones and tablets; and the strong needs for mobile visual search and recognition have been emerging. While many real applications of visual recognition require a large scale recognition systems, the same technologies that support server-based scalable visual recognition may not be feasible on mobile devices due to the resource constraints. Although the client-server framework ensures the scalability, the real-time response subjects to the limitation on network bandwidth. Therefore, the main challenge for mobile visual recognition system should be the recognition bitrate, which is the amount of data transmission under the same recognition performance. For this work, we exploit and compare various strategies such as compact features, feature compression, feature signatures by hashing, image scaling, etc., to enable low bitrate mobile visual recognition. We argue that thumbnail image is a competitive candidate for low bitrate visual recognition because it carries multiple features at once and multi-feature fusion is important as the size of semantic space increases. Our evaluations on two subsets of ImageNet, both contain more than 10,000 images with 19 and 137 categories, verify the efficacy of thumbnail images. We further suggest a new strategy that combines single (local) feature signature and the thumbnail image, which achieves significant bitrate reduction from (average) 102,570 to 4,661 bytes with merely (overall) 10% performance degradation.

Categories and Subject Descriptors

I.4.8 [**Image Processing and Computer Vision**]: Scene Analysis—*Object recognition*

Keywords

Mobile Image Recognition; Thumbnail Image; Bitrate; Multimodal Fusion

MM'13, October 21–25, 2013, Barcelona, Spain.
Copyright 2013 ACM 978-1-4503-2404-5/13/10 ...$15.00.
http://dx.doi.org/10.1145/2502081.2502110 .

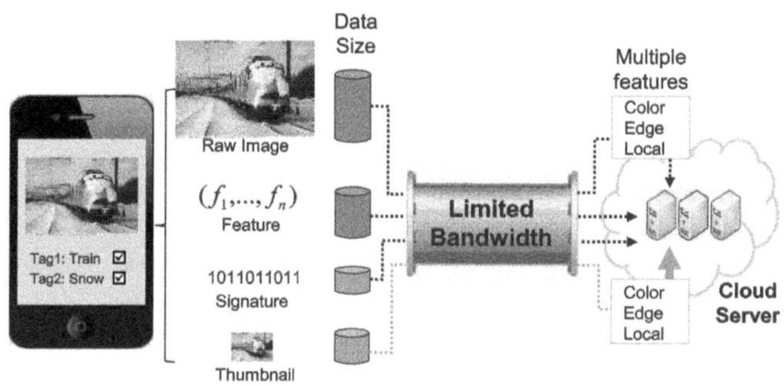

Figure 1: Low bitrate visual recognition. Images taken by a mobile device are classified on the server to ensure scalability over the large semantic space. The mobiles can send back information such as raw images, extracted features, compact signatures, or thumbnails, etc., for recognition in the server. Because the wireless connection between the server and mobile devices has limited bandwidth, the data transmission should be minimized to ensure prompt response, which is the main challenge for the mobile image recognition frameworks and also the key factor we would like to exploit in this work.

1. INTRODUCTION

Two ongoing trends are leading nowadays multimedia research and applications. The first is the increasing emphasis on the scale of data and the scalability of system. In visual recognition, the increase in scale does not only multiply the amount of data, but also the size of feature and semantic spaces [13, 28, 34]. The motivation for increasing the scale of visual recognition system is not only from research interests but also from real application needs. For example, since human can recognize tens of thousands of concepts and categorize them accordingly from images, an automatic photo annotation system would be limited if it can only recognize few concepts. Another example is event detection systems; since there exists an enormous amount of potential events, a general purpose event detection system would be applicable if more events can be detected in real-time response. Many new methods for scalable multimedia applications have been developed in the past few years [29, 34, 31], and the problem remains open with highly active research.

The second leading change is the paradigm shift from personal computer (PC) or workstations to mobile devices. While high quality camera becomes a basic component on current mobile devices, they are currently used as passive recorders. Combining with the growing computation capability and the rich contexts in mobile devices, the camera can enable more proactive and smart applications such as remote healthcare, lifelog, automatic photo annotation, etc. Among all potential applications, many of them depend on visual recognition technologies. For example, automatic tagging system can be easily combined with popular social network applications such as *Facebook* to enable more user friendly media sharing.

1.1 Physical Constraints on Mobiles

Although there exists many promising technologies for large scale visual recognition, most of them assume operating on PCs or even workstations, where the underlying assumption about available resources may not fit that of mobile devices.

Some of the most important limitations on mobile devices include: **Limited computing power**, where many visual recognition systems assume the computing power of server level CPU. This restricts the use of complicated recognition systems and multiple features, where it takes roughly 1 second for feature extraction of each feature on current mobile devices [8, 10, 20]. **Limited storage**, usually around 10 to 100 GB. The limited storage inevitably restricts the amount of models that can be stored on the devices. Meanwhile, it imposes a hard limit on the scalability of purely native system. **Limited network bandwidth**, which forbids the rapid communication with remote servers. It also degrades the user experience when real time response is required for the services. **Limited power/battery**, which limits both heavy computation and rapid network transmission on the device. These limitations indicate that methods which work fine on servers may not work on mobile devices, and further optimization for mobile devices is necessary.

1.2 Low Bitrate Mobile Visual Recognition

With the physical limitations on mobile devices, the objective of mobile visual recognition system is to maximize user satisfactory under given resource constraints. User satisfactory is influenced by different factors such as response time, accuracy, power consumption and the scale of the semantic space. One possible direction for the mobile system is to match the server-based systems in terms of accuracy and scalability, which are the focus of server based system, while minimizing the response time and power consumption, which are the new requirements of mobile system.

For visual recognition on mobile devices, any native systems will have limited scalability due to the storage constraint. To overcome the constraint, the client-server framework is an intuitive solution and is adopted in many mobile visual search systems [9, 18]. The framework, however, is subject to the limitation of network bandwidth, as illustrated in fig. 1. We proposed the comparison of **recognition bitrate**, which considers the recognition performance with respect to the amount of data transmission between mobile devices and the server as in fig. 2. Unlike traditional server based systems, which consider only the dimension of performance, we introduce the new dimension of data transmission. The new dimension is important in that we would like to minimize the data transmission while retaining a reasonable performance in real visual recognition applications. Low recognition bitrate leads not only to faster response time for applications, but also lowers network usage rate

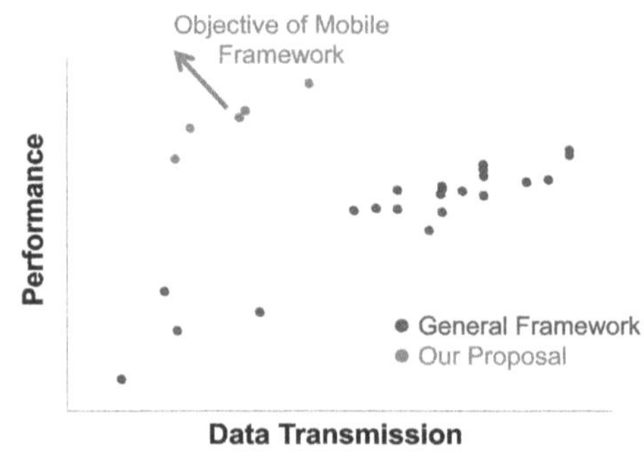

Figure 2: The goal for low bitrate mobile visual recognition. The objective of mobile visual recognition system is different from the general visual recognition systems, where the mobile system prefers the strategies that minimize the data transmission while ensuring the performance. For this work, we will exploit and compare various strategies such as state-of-the-art features, hashing learning methods, image scaling, etc., to enable low bitrate mobile visual recognition.

and battery consumption, which are important factors for real applications.

The limitation of wireless network on mobile devices has been widely acknowledged in mobile visual search [18]. For example, it takes 8 to 10 seconds on average to transmit a typical JPEG image over 3G network. Many efforts have been devoted to feature hashing or compression to enable visual search on mobile systems [33, 9], which provide some candidate strategies to achieve low bitrate mobile visual recognition including:

- *Transfer features with moderate dimension.* By using features with moderate data sizes and fair performance, the system can work with acceptable performance and data transmission.

- *Transfer compressed features.* The strategy exploits either feature with proper compression rate, such as compressed histogram of gradient, or compression schemes with small performance degrade, such as product quantization [29].

- *Transfer feature signature produced by hashing.* The strategy generates a compact signature that retains the performance. There exists a large family of hashing method, including random projection, spectral hashing, etc.

- *Transfer scaled-down images.* The images must be scaled down to be transfered over wireless network.

In most existing works on mobile visual search, transmitting images over the wireless network is considered infeasible for applications that require real-time response because of the image size. The claim, however, does not consider that it may not be necessary to transmit the original image to the server for visual recognition or retrieval. Research has shown that both human and computer system can recognize images with very small resolutions [31], which is much smaller in data size than general consumer photos. The fact that most existing visual recognition datasets are mainly consist of small images also indicates that very high resolution images may not be necessary for visual recognition. Besides, mobile applications based on sending thumbnail images over wireless network have been proposed [11]. Indeed, while sending original images over 3G network may be impossible, transmitting thumbnail images is well applicable yet the efficacy of thumbnail images for visual recognition has not been explored.

The dire needs for mobile visual recognition emerge but the applicable methods are still missing. To entail mobile visual recognition, we conduct a systematic study on the recognition performance with respect to transmission bitrate for mobile visual recognition. In particular, we compare different strategies such as compact features, feature compression, feature signature by hashing, image scaling, etc. Several state-of-the-art features are included for comparisons. The evaluation is conducted on two subsets of ImageNet, both with more than 10,000 images. By understanding the bandwidth requirements and performance ranges for these strategies, we can motivate new mobile-cloud-balanced learning methods and cost-effective features. Our key contributions include:

- We propose to use recognition bitrate as the comparison criteria for mobile recognition models, instead of focusing only on recognition rate.
- We conduct intensive comparisons among various strategies for low bitrate mobile visual recognition, including visual features, feature signatures and thumbnail images. In particular, we examine the performance of thumbnail images with respect to image scales, which is not well studied in previous works.
- We combine multiple features in the comparisons of visual recognition bitrate. In existing works on low bitrate descriptor, the effort is on decreasing the bitrate of a single feature. Our experimental result shows that multi-feature fusion can further reduce bitrate and becomes more important when the number and diversity of concepts increase.
- We propose to transfer thumbnail image along with single (local) feature signature, which is affordable in both network bandwidth and computation for current mobile devices and achieves near optimal recognition performance.

The remaining of this paper is organized as follows. In section 2, we describe related works. In section 3, we describe the datasets used for the evaluation, and the general setup for the evaluation is in section 4. In section 5, we discuss the importance of multi-feature fusion. In section 6, we discuss the effect of image scaling on visual recognition performance. In section 7, we compare the recognition bitrate of signatures. Finally, we conclude our discovery in section 8.

2. RELATED WORK

One of the ongoing change in visual recognition research is the enlargement of semantic space. The most popular dataset for large scale visual recognition is ImageNet [12]. It is a dataset with concept ontology and contains more than 20,000 synsets, or concepts, with an average of 650 images for each concept. The ImageNet dataset has enabled the study of scalable visual recognition. Based on the dataset, the ImageNet Large Scale Visual Recognition Challenge (ILSVRC) [4] is a contest that requires the recognition of 1,000 image categories. In ILSVRC 2010, there is a total of 1.2 million training images, which becomes one of the most popular image recognition dataset.

The development of visual feature has long been the center of visual recognition research. Among all visual features, local features have been proved effective in many domains. Many local features have been proposed since the advent of the difference of gaussian detector combined with SIFT descriptor introduced by Lowe [24, 25]; a large number of local features have adopted the SIFT descriptor with different detectors, such as Hessian affine detector and dense sampling [26]. For visual recognition systems, the local features from an image are usually pooled together to form a vector representation of the image for classification. There also exists many different pooling methods, such as Fisher vector or bag of visual word models [28, 30, 21]. Bag of word models can be further extended by multi-scaled spatial pyramid [22], which has been adopted in many state-of-the-art visual recognition systems.

While spatial pyramid method is superior in performance, it results in a high dimensional vector for each image and may even be larger than the original image in data size. The data size limits the scalability of systems and the transmission of features over wireless network in mobile devices. Feature compression methods such as product quantization have been introduced to increase the scalability of systems [29], where a compression rate of 64 to 128 can be achieved without significant loss of performance. Beside feature compression, various hashing methods that generate representative signatures from the original features are also studied, ranging from the data-independent random projection, data-dependent spectral hashing and semi-supervised sequential projection learning [5, 1, 33, 35].

With the explosive growth and prevalence of mobile devices, visual features that are more suitable for mobile devices have been developed. SURF is a local feature that reduce both computational cost and the dimension [3], and modification that makes the computation even more mobile friendly with moderate performance degrade is proposed [36]. Compressed histogram of gradient is a new local feature descriptor that aims to reduce the transmission bitrate [9], and residual enhanced visual vector is a new compact local feature pooling method that aims to reduce the data size and store the entire database for retrieval on the mobile devices [10].

Utilizing information in thumbnail images has been exploited before in different tasks. Torralba et. al. have conducted an object recognition study on a dataset of nearly 80 million tiny images with 32×32 pixel color images [31]. Their result shows that color images with 32×32 resolution are already recognizable by human. Thumbnail images are also used in new mobile services. In IMShare, a new mobile image sharing technique is built based on thumbnail images [11]. The thumbnail image of a photo taken by mobile devices and the detection results of local feature detector are sent to the server, where the server reconstructs the image by the thumbnail image and local feature descriptors extracted from the thumbnail image. These results show that thumbnail image do contain sufficient information for recognition, and that extracting meaningful features from thumbnail image is possible.

Figure 3: Example images from ImageNet137 dataset. The dataset consists of photos downloaded from internet. We also show the same images in different scales, as in the evaluation setting. Note the images are not shown in their original sizes but preserve their relative sizes and scales.

3. DATASETS

In this section, we describe the datasets used for the study. The goal of this paper is to study the recognition performance under different transmission bandwidths. In particular, we would like to study the performance of features extracted from different image sizes, which prohibit from directly using most of the popular datasets for visual recognition, because most of the datasets such as Scene [22] and Caltech256 [19] are mainly consist of images with low resolution compared with consumer photos. Besides, to evaluate the effect of increasing the scale of recognition system, the experiments require both large training set and semantic space.

To overcome the limit, we perform experiments on two subsets of ImageNet and screened out images with low resolution in the datasets. The choice of ImageNet is to ensure there exists enough images and classes for study. Specifically, we consider the following two dataset:

- **ImageNet19.** 19 categories from ImageNet 2011 Fall Release with the same categories of PASCAL Visual Object Classes (VOC) 2007 Challenge [15] were selected, following the protocol in [28]. We did not find the synset of "potted plant," and for the remaining 19 synsets, we downloaded only the synset itself without children synsets. In this dataset, images with length smaller than 500 pixels or width smaller than 300 pixels were discarded, which resulted in a total of 19886 images.

- **ImageNet137.** The training set of ILSVRC2010 was used to construct this dataset. In this dataset, images with length smaller than 800 pixels or width smaller than 600 pixels were discarded, and only categories with more than 60 images remaining were included, which resulted in 137 categories and a total of 12008 images. Some of the images are shown in fig. 3.

Note the two datasets have no overlapping categories. Following the convention of the PASCAL VOC Challenge [15, 16], each category was randomly and equally split into training and test sets, and we repeated the process 10 times. All results are averaged over the 10 runs of experiment with the statistical standard deviation also reported.

4. EXPERIMENTAL SETUP

In this section, we describe the features used in evaluation and the feature extraction procedures. Then we describe the classifier adopted for classification.

4.1 Features

To explore the optimal recognition performance given an image, we evaluate a variety of popular general-purpose features. Many of these features are adopted in the state-of-the-art visual recognition systems and are evaluated on both public datasets and recognition contests such as PASCAL VOC and ImageNet [16, 4, 28, 34]. The features can be categorized into the following two groups.

4.1.1 Global Features

Global features include all features that are non-local. While there exists a large number of global features ranging from color, texture to edge features, we choose some of the most widely used general-purpose feature as follow:

- **Color histogram.** We use 24 dimension color histogram in *HSV* color space where the histogram on each dimension is computed separately and then concated. For quantization, H is divided into 18 levels, S and V are divided into 3 levels.

- **Color Moment.** We use 225 dimension grid color moment; each image is divided into 5x5 grids and the first to third moments in *RGB* color space are extracted from each grid respectively.

- **Gabor.** We use 48 dimension log Gabor coefficients as features. 24 filters with 6 orientations and 4 scales are used to compute the response, and for each filter response, the first and second moment are extracted [23].

- **LBP.** We use local binary pattern with uniform patterns extension, which results in a 59 dimension histogram [2].

- **PHOG.** We use 3400 dimensional pyramid histogram of oriented gradient with 4 bin histogram and 3 level pyramid ($K = 4$, $L = 3$) [6].

We also examine the popular Gist [27, 14] feature, but the performance is only slightly better than color histogram on ImageNet19 despite of the high dimensionality (960), so we do not include it in further experiments.

4.1.2 Local Features

Local features have become the standard component of state-of-the-art visual recognition systems. Among the wide range of detectors as well as descriptors, we choose the following combinations in our evaluations:

- **DoG.** Difference of Gaussian detector + SIFT descriptor [24].

- **HA.** Hessian Affine detector + SIFT descriptor [26].

- **Dense.** Extract SIFT features with dense sampling, using 20×20 patches and overlapping windows shifted by 10 pixels. We use the Vlfeat library for Dense SIFT extraction [32].

- **SURF.** SURF detector + SURF descriptor [3].

We also examine Compressed Histogram of Gradient [9] (CHoG) descriptor which is especially designed for mobile visual search; we do not include it in the following discussions because its performance is similar to SURF in our preliminary test and is not especially representative.

4.2 Descriptors

To utilize local features in classification, local descriptors in an image are usually aggregated into a compact feature. Many descriptors were proposed in recent years, while Bag of Word (BoW) and Fisher Vector (FV) are the most popular ones among all descriptors. We choose the following two descriptors which are the variations of BoW and FV respectively in our evaluations:

- **LLC**. Locality constraint linear coding (LLC) is a variation of BoW and further combined with Spatial Pyramid (SPM). We choose LLC for its performance, and our preliminary tests also confirm that LLC significantly improves over BoW + SPM. In our experiments, we use codebook size $c = 200$ and 400 with pyramid level $l = 2$. Note that the codebook was constructed simply by K-means without optimization for LLC.

- **VLAD**. Vector of locally aggregated descriptors (VLAD) is a simplification of FV. The reasons for choosing VLAD over FV is twofold. The first is that in our preliminary tests, VLAD shows comparable performance with FV with smaller dimension (no covariance vector). The second is that computing VLAD requires less storage and computation resource, which is important on mobile devices. In our experiments, we use codebook size $c = 16, 64, 256$ respectively.

4.3 Feature Extraction

To evaluate the recognition performance with respect to varying image sizes, we extract the features from the same image at different scales. For ImageNet19 dataset, the images are scaled down to 1/2, 1/4, 1/8, and for ImageNet137 dataset, the images are scaled down to 1/2, 1/4, 1/8, 1/16, as shown in fig. 3. On feature extraction, every (scaled-down) image is scaled up to their original size using bilinear interpolation before feature extraction. Image up-scaling is performed for performance reasons; our evaluation shows that scaling up the images to the original size generally yields better performance. In particular, the image size directly corresponds to feature point number for Dense SIFT feature, which in turns affects performance. Therefore, we perform image up scaling for all features for the consistency of evaluation. No additional information other than the thumbnail image is used during feature extraction.

We also examined the performance of various feature extraction strategies. For example, we computed the SIFT descriptors on upscaled images using the salient points detected on the original images, which is the strategy adopted in *IMShare* [11]. The additional detector information in this strategy turns out to be unhelpful for recognition. We also examined the optimal scales up for thumbnail images on feature extraction, and the result is in favor of scaling up image to the original size.

4.4 Classifier

In this section, we describe the classifier adopted for classification and the method for multi-feature fusion. For all features, we use SVM with linear kernel for classification [17] with 1-vs-all framework for multi-class classification. Linear SVM is adopted because of its training and testing efficiency and its success in many state-of-the-art visual recognition system [16, 4, 28, 34]. The parameter of SVM is determined by 5-fold cross validation on the training set.

For multi-feature fusion, we apply late fusion strategy – averaging the normalized scores from different classifiers over varying features. We use late fusion instead of early fusion for its efficiency, which is important due to the large number of possible combinations. To perform late fusion, the decision values of each classifier are first normalized with sigmoid function, and the scores from the same modality over different categories of each image are then $L1$ normalized. The summation of normalized score over all features is used to determine the class label of the instance. We do not explore sophisticated fusion methods, because the focus of this study is on features rather than the sophisticated algorithms, which do not show significant performance gains.

4.5 Compression Factor of Images

For bitrate comparison, we have to estimate the image size (in storage). The average image size over the entire dataset is used as the estimator, and the images are all in JPEG format with the original image quality of ImageNet dataset. For thumbnail images, Image scaling is performed using OpenCV [7], and the thumbnail images are also in JPEG format with the default compression factor 95 in 100-scale of OpenCV.

Although changing the compression configuration may also reduce data size, we focus on image scaling because the efficacy of thumbnail image has been justified [31, 11]. Besides, image scaling is more straightforward for controlling image quality. Therefore, the compression configuration is kept the same throughout the evaluations.

5. MULTI-FEATURE FUSION IS IMPORTANT

We first evaluate the performance of different features and show that no single feature performs the best on all categories. The result implies the importance of multiple features, and we show that multi-feature fusion is more efficient than increasing feature and descriptor dimensions in improving image recognition performance. The overall classification performance of each feature for the two datasets are in fig. 4. The result shows that, on average, local features significantly outperform global features. Besides, Hessian affine SIFT performs better with VLAD, while Dense SIFT performs better with LLC and achieves the best performance when we consider only single feature.

Although the performance differences between different features seems significant, the situation is very different when we inspect closer about the classification results on category basis. The classification accuracy of 6 out of 19 categories in ImageNet19 are in fig. 5(A). We can see from the result that no single feature achieves the best performance in all categories, and in some categories, global features are comparable with local features. This implies the necessity of using multiple features to achieve robust overall classification performance.

The same observation can be made in ImageNet137 dataset, where the result of 12 out of 137 categories are in fig. 5(B). Note that nearly every feature, including global features, achieves the best in certain categories. The result leads to

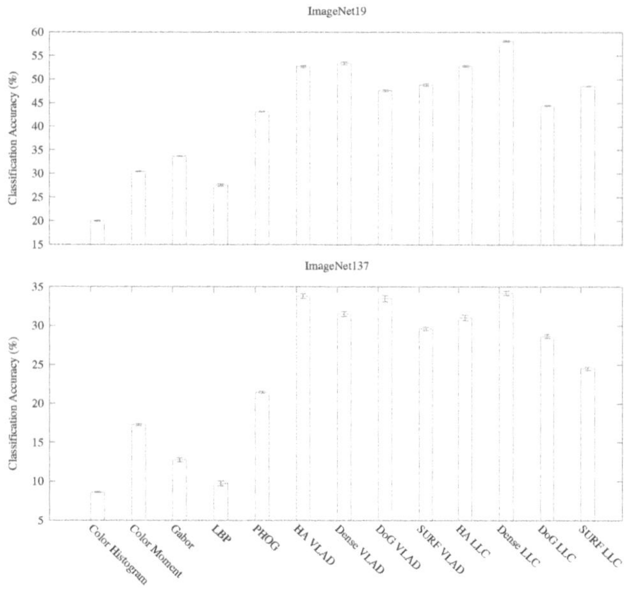

Figure 4: Average classification accuracies of different features on the original image. $c = 64$ for VLAD and $c = 400$ for LLC descriptor. On average, local features significantly outperform global features, and Dense SIFT + LLC achieves the optimal performance on both datasets. All results are reported with statistical standard deviation over 10 rounds of experiments.

the same conclusion that multi-feature fusion is important; it further indicates that multiple features are getting more important as the number and diversity of the categories to be recognized increases.

Based on the observation, we perform late fusion of multiple features for classification to verify the importance of multiple feature. We perform feature selection on late fusion by iteratively adding one feature at a time, where the feature that achieves the most performance improvement is selected. The process stops when no further features can improve the performance. The result is in fig. 6, where both absolute and relative improvements of each feature fused are reported. The relative improvement is defined by the absolute improvement divided by the optimal fusion performance. We can see that multi-feature fusion, even with a simple late fusion (i.e., averaging the normalized confidence scores from different modalities) strategy, can significantly increase the classification performance, and the relative improvement increases as the number of category increases. This result is consistent with the previous observation that the importance of multi-feature fusion increases as the diversity of categories increases.

A commonly used strategy to increase classification performance while using single feature, especially local features, is to increase the descriptor dimension. We next compare the effectiveness of increasing descriptor dimension and fusing multiple features. In particular, we compare the classification accuracy with respect to the total feature dimension,

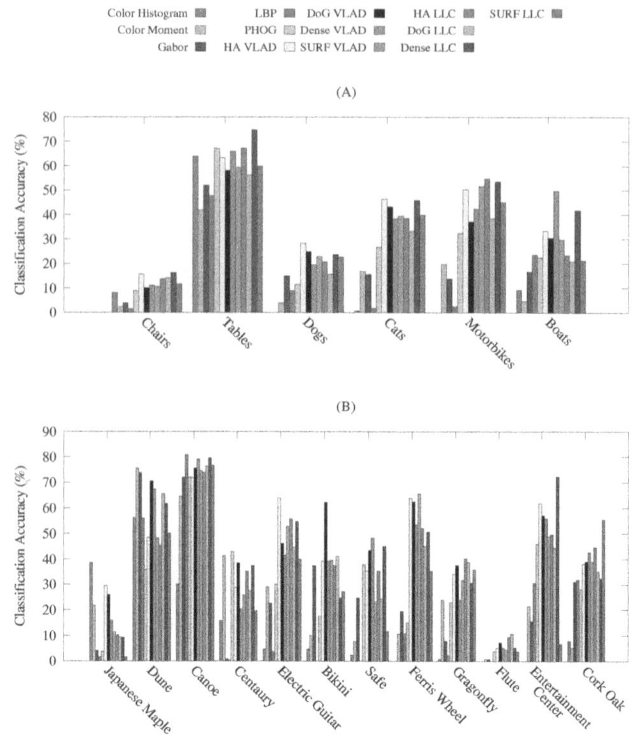

Figure 5: Results of 6 categories from ImageNet19 dataset are in (A), 12 categories from ImageNet137 dataset in (B). From ImageNet19, we can see that no single feature achieves the best performance in all categories. This indicates the necessity of multiple features to achieve optimal classification performance. In ImageNet137, which contains more categories and diverse concepts, every feature except Gabor achieves the best performances in different categories, and even the same local feature using different pooling methods show different performances. Compared with the results of ImageNet19 dataset, we can see the strong needs of multi-modal fusion across different features as the number of category increases[1].

because the dimension is proportional to the bitrate of the strategy. The dimension of multi-feature fusion is defined as the sum of the dimensions of all the features being fused. The result of ImageNet19 dataset is in fig. 7. It is obvious that multi-feature fusion achieves better performance than increasing the feature dimension under the same bitrate. The result indicates that when extracting multiple features is possible, using multiple features is more efficient for improving classification accuracy than using complicated models from a single feature.

6. IMAGE SCALING REDUCES BITRATE

In this section, we evaluate the recognition performance of features extracted from scaled down images and the recognition bitrate of the image. Our evaluation is based on the general claim that images taken by mobile devices are too large to be transfered over wireless network for prompt response time. In visual recognition, for example, transmitting images in the original high resolution may not be necessary,

[1]Since we have conducted intensive experiments of different configurations, all the figures are best seen in color.

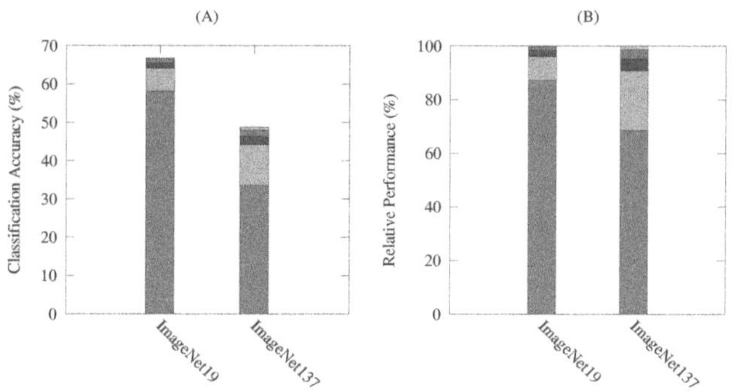

Figure 6: Results of multi-feature fusion. For (A), each section in the histogram indicates the absolute performance improvement of fusing one additional (best) feature. For (B), each section indicates the relative performance improvement over the optimal performance. The relative improvement increases in dataset with larger number and diversity of categories (ImageNet137), which confirms that multiple feature fusion is very important as the category (or concept) number increases.

because images with transferable size may achieve acceptable performance for applications.

Because the image size is dependent to the image content, we measure the average image size of the dataset for bitrate comparison. The result of ImageNet19 dataset is in table 1. Note that the average size difference between color image and gray scale image is small compared to the effect of image scaling; so we assume transmitting color image in the following discussions.

We first measure the performance degradation incurred by image down-scaling. The result of global features is in fig. 8, and that of local features is in fig. 9. We can see from the result that global features are more resistant to image down-scaling, while local features degrade more significantly. The performance of PHOG may even exceed DoG SIFT and SURF when the images are scaled down to 1/8 on ImageNet19 dataset. This indicates that multiple global features can be carried by a single scaled-down image without significant loss of information.

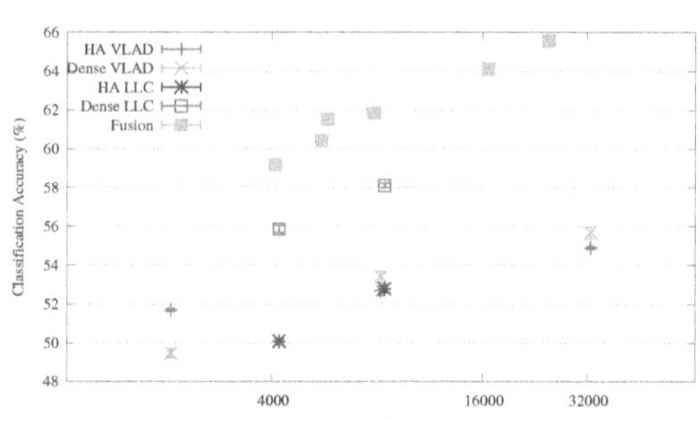

Figure 7: Recognition performance versus total dimensions of features on ImageNet19 dataset. Fusing multiple features, including global features, can significantly improve performance under the same feature dimension. Note that we only apply a simple late fusion strategy (i.e., average confident scores) to achieve the significant performance improvement.

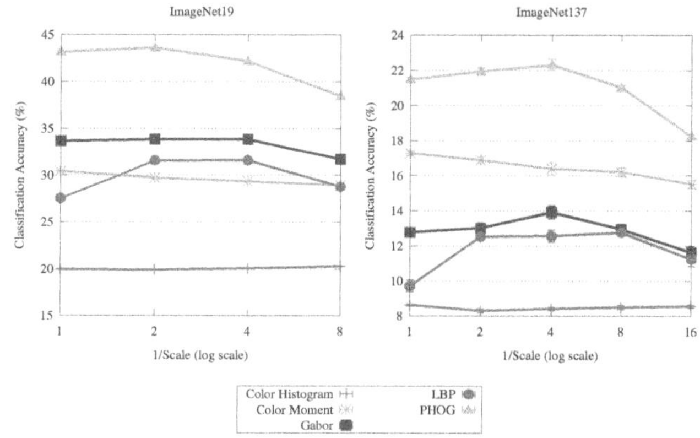

Figure 8: The performance changes of global features under different image scales on ImageNet19 dataset. The performance of global feature does not degrade significantly as the image being scaled down even to a tiny image. Therefore, we can compress and transmit all global features at once by sending a scaled down image without much loss of performance.

We next compare the performance of scaled-down image and image features under different bandwidth requirements. Based on the previous observation, we know that scaled down image contains information of multiple (global) features, therefore, the result of multi-feature fusion as well as that of the best single feature are reported. The result of ImageNet19 dataset is in fig. 10. The feature sizes are computed using feature dimension, where each dimension is stored in a double precision floating point number. We can see that performing multi-feature fusion with scaled down image achieves better performance under the same bandwidth, and the performance even does not degrade under moderate scaling. The result in ImageNet137 dataset is similar, as can be seen in fig. 11, with more significant improvements by multi-feature fusion.

The observation indicates that in mobile visual recognition, transmitting the high-resolution image over wireless

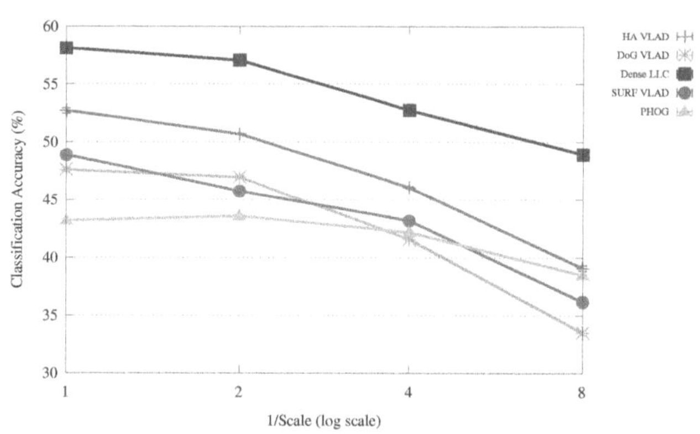

Figure 9: The performance change of local features under different image scales on ImageNet19 dataset. Local features degrade more significantly while image is scaled down. Note that the performance of PHOG even exceeds some local features when the image is scaled down to 1/8.

Table 1: **Average image size of ImageNet19 dataset. The average size of color images is slightly larger than that of gray images but contains color information which is important in some categories. The trade-off supports transmitting color images over gray images, and we assume transmitting color image in all following discussion.**

	SIFT LLC(400)	SIFT VLAD(64)	Original Color	1/2 size Color	1/2 size Gray	1/4 size Color	1/4 size Gray	1/8 size Color	1/8 size Gray
Bytes	67,200	65,536	102,570	31,581	27,094	10,352	8,711	3,637	2,912

network is impossible due to the original image size; meanwhile, it is not necessary to transmit the image in original size. Transmitting scaled down image may greatly reduce the bitrate without loss of performance; and by exploiting informations from multiple features, scaled down image may be more transmission efficient than image features.

Another benefit of transmitting scaled down image over transmitting features is the reduction of computation and storage overhead on mobile devices. Image features such as LLC require the storage of codebook and solving linear equations on the fly, and extracting multi-feature for real time application is computation intensive. Transmitting scaled-down image eliminates all the overhead, where the resource on server can handle these overhead without difficulty.

7. FEATURE SIGNATURE ACHIEVES LOWER BITRATE

In mobile visual search, much efforts have been devoted to generating a compact signature from the raw features to reduce the bitrate for retrieval. In this section, we compare the performance versus bitrate between scaled down image and image signature.

For signature generation, we use the data independent sparse random projection (RP) [1]. To verify the choice, we also compare the performance with two state-of-the-art hashing and compression methods such as the unsupervised product quantization (PQ) [29] and the supervised sequential projection learning hash (SPLH) [33], on ImageNet19 dataset. The result is in fig. 12. For PQ, the feature vector is first divided into subvector, with the dimension of subvector being $G = 8$ for VLAD and $G = 10$ for LLC. The average number of bits for representing each dimension is set to $b = 1$. For RP and SPLH, we set the projection matrix as a square matrix so the output bit number is the same as the input dimension; so the compression rate is 64 for all methods. Note the bit number of signatures are large (8k) to ensure recognition performance, because our goal is to build a mobile system with its performance comparable with server-based system. We can see from the result that SPLH does not perform as good as RP in high dimensional (8k) signatures; more importantly, it performs poorly with LLC. The performance of PQ and RP is comparable, and we choose RP for further experiments because of its computation efficiency and data independent property.

The result of signature is in fig. 13. We can see that the bandwidth requirement for signature is lower than that of the scaled-down image. This suggests that there exists redundant information in the scaled image which is not fully utilized by the recognition system yet. We also examine the performance of fusing multiple feature signatures. Under the two aspects of mobile visual recognition, that is, the recognition rate and bitrate, fusing multiple signatures turns out to be the best strategy with near optimal performance and roughly the same bitrate as thumbnail images. Note that the performance of fusing multiple feature signatures can not be further improve by including more signatures under our multi-modal fusion framework; it might indicate that there exists irreversible information lost in signature generation.

Although multiple (local) feature signatures achieve almost the best performance with low bandwidth, the strategy may turn out to be unfeasible when we consider the constraints in mobile computing. The most significant problem lies in the computing power on current mobile devices,

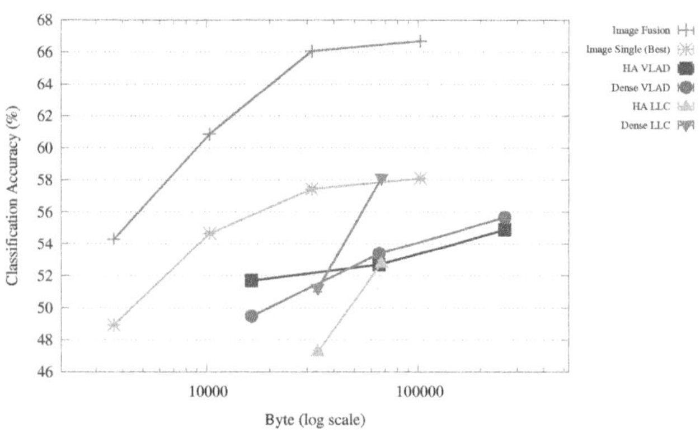

Figure 10: The recognition bitrate of scaled down image on ImageNet19 dataset. Because a scaled down image contains information of multiple features, the performance of both optimal single feature and multi-feature fusion is reported. With multi-feature fusion, scaled down image can significantly outperform the raw feature under given bitrate.

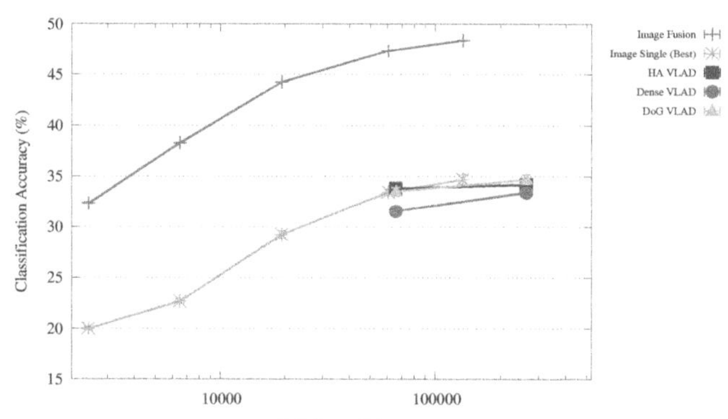

Figure 11: The recognition bitrate of scaled down image on ImageNet137 dataset. Although single feature performance degrades more significantly on ImageNet137 dataset, the fusion result of thumbnail image still outperforms raw features in recognition bitrate.

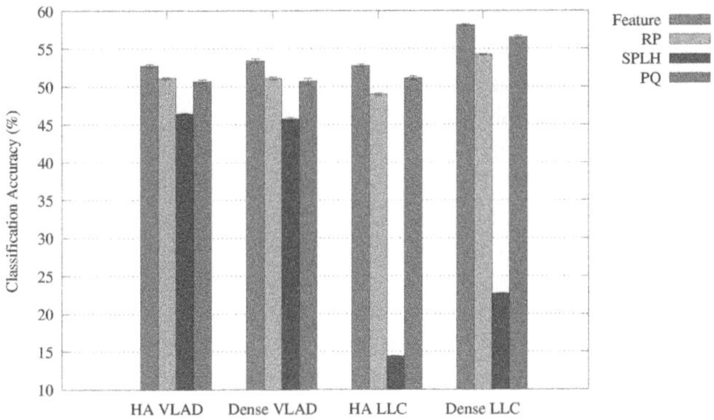

Figure 12: Performance comparison of different signature generation methods. Feature stands for the performance of the original feature. $c = 64$ is used for VLAD and $c = 400$ for LLC. For random projection (RP) and sequential projection learning hash (SPLH), the output bit number is the same as input dimension. For product quantization (PQ), the average bit number for each dimension is set to $b = 1$. Therefore, the compression rate is 64 for all methods. Note that we use high dimensional signatures (8k) to ensure that the recognition performance does not degrade significantly. Under the compression rate, RP outperforms SPLH, and SPLH performs poorly with LLC. The performance of RP and PQ is comparable; we use RP for its efficient computation in the following experiments.

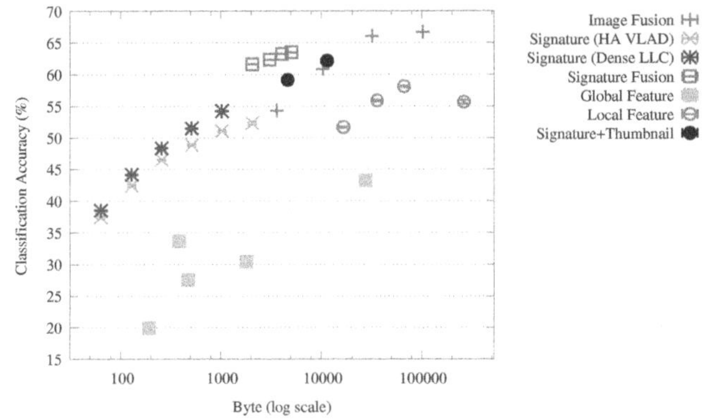

Figure 13: Bitrate comparison of all strategies, including feature signatures. Feature signature achieves lowest bitrate under similar accuracy. For the signature used to fuse with thumbnail image, we use HA+VLAD+RP because VLAD is more mobile friendly than LLC. Among all strategies, multiple feature signatures achieves lowest recognition bitrate, but is not feasible on current mobile devices due to the computation overhead of extracting multiple features on the devices. Combining single (local) feature signature and thumbnail image is the solution that best fits current mobile device constraints.

because it requires extraction of multiple features solely on the device which is computation intensive. Fortunately, it is feasible to compute at least single feature signature on mobile devices which is the basis of many mobile visual search system. Based on our own implementation, it takes less than a second on average to compute the signature of VLAD with SURF feature using codebook size $c = 64$ on iPhone 5. Therefore, a more realistic solution is to compute single feature signature on the device and send both the thumbnail image and feature signature to the remote server. The result of fusing thumbnail images and single feature signature is in fig. 13. We use Hessian affine local feature and VLAD descriptor with $c = 64$, with the 8,192 bits signature generated by sparse random projection. Note that we do not choose the signature with optimal performance (Dense+LLC+RP) because LLC is computation intensive and is formidable for mobile environments. The strategy balances among different constraints on the device, i.e., storage, network bandwidth and CPU, and it achieves almost the best performance with moderate bitrate. Under current physical constraints on mobile devices, this is probably the best strategy from our evaluations in terms of recognition bandwidth requirements.

8. CONCLUSIONS AND FUTURE WORKS

This paper presents a study on possible solutions for scalable mobile visual recognition system. We conduct a systematic evaluation on various strategies for mobile visual recognition under client-server framework in terms of recognition bitrate, and the experiments are conducted on two subsets of ImageNet; both datasets contain more than 10,000 images and one of them contains more than 100 categories. In particular, we compare the recognition bitrate of thumbnail images, various image features and feature signatures. The result shows that even a tiny image contains sufficient information for visual recognition, and by utilizing multiple features extracted from thumbnail images, the recognition bitrate of thumbnail image is much lower than raw image features. Although fusing multiple image signatures may achieve lower bitrate than thumbnail images, extracting multiple (local) features on mobile devices may not be feasible due to CPU and battery constraints. These experiments indicate that transmitting thumbnail images should be considered for mobile visual recognition systems.

We further recommend to combine single local feature signature and the scaled-down thumbnail image, which achieves near optimal performance under the constraint of current mobile environment. Using the strategy, we significantly reduce the average data transmission from 102,570 bytes to 4,661 bytes (i.e., thumbnail images scaled down to 1/8 of the original size and the 8,192 bits signature generated by random projection from Hessian affine feature with 64 centers VLAD descriptor), while the recognition accuracy only decreases from 0.67 to 0.59, which is still better than any single raw feature.

With the new aspects introduced in mobile visual recognition system, such as network bandwidth, power consumption, etc., there remains many to be explored. In this paper, we focus on the dimensions of feature and data transmission, and we will extend into other aspects in the future studies. In particular, we would like to extend the evaluation to real system and photos taken by mobile devices in the future, where the real world environment may bring new challenges. We would also like to evaluate the recognition bitrate of videos, because videos are generally larger in data size and consume a significant amount of mobile network bandwidth, and the evaluation on videos is expected

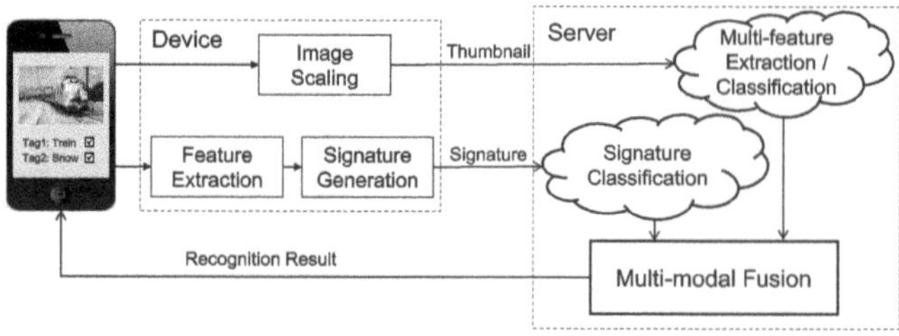

Figure 14: A recommended system design based on our evaluation results. Single (local) feature signature (e.g. HA+VLAD+RP) is computed on the mobile device, and is transmitted back to server along with the (down-scaled) thumbnail image. Server extracts multiple features from the thumbnail image and perform multi-modal fusion, then returns the results to the mobile device.

to have an even larger impact. Other exciting directions include better signature generations, where the side information from thumbnail images may be used to improve the compression rate and achieve lower bitrate. Similarly, a better compression technique for images may also lead to better recognition bitrate. Beside data compression on either thumbnail images or signatures, a better classification algorithm on the signature is also possible, where the signatures lie in Hamming space rather than Euclidean space in which general classification algorithms are developed.

9. REFERENCES

[1] D. Achlioptas. Database-friendly random projections: Johnson-lindenstrauss with binary coins. *J. Comput. Sys. Sci.*, 66, 2003.

[2] T. Ahonen et al. Face recognition with local binary patterns. In *ECCV*, 2004.

[3] H. Bay et al. Surf: Speeded up robust features. In *ECCV*, 2006.

[4] A. Berg et al. Large scale visual recognition challenge 2010, 2010.

[5] E. Bingham and H. Mannila. Random projection in dimensionality reduction: applications to image and text data. In *ACM SIGKDD*, 2001.

[6] A. Bosch et al. Representing shape with a spatial pyramid kernel. In *ACM CIVR*, 2007.

[7] G. Bradski. The OpenCV Library. *Dr. Dobb's Journal of Software Tools*, 2000.

[8] V. Chandrasekhar et al. Comparison of local feature descriptors for mobile visual search. In *ICIP*, 2010.

[9] V. Chandrasekhar et al. Compressed histogram of gradients: A low-bitrate descriptor. *Int. J. Comput. Vision*, 96(3):384–399, 2012.

[10] D. Chen et al. Residual enhanced visual vectors for on-device image matching. In *Asilomar Conference on Signals, Systems, and Computers*, 2011.

[11] L.-C. Dai et al. Imshare: instantly sharing your mobile landmark images by search-based reconstruction. In *ACM MM*, 2012.

[12] J. Deng et al. Imagenet: A large-scale hierarchical image database. In *CVPR*, 2009.

[13] J. Deng et al. What does classifying more than 10,000 image categories tell us? In *ECCV*, 2010.

[14] M. Douze et al. Evaluation of gist descriptors for web-scale image search. In *CIVR*, 2009.

[15] M. Everingham et al. The pascal visual object classes challenge 2007 results, 2007.

[16] M. Everingham et al. The pascal visual object classes challenge 2010 results, 2010.

[17] R.-E. Fan et al. LIBLINEAR: A library for large linear classification. *JMLR*, 9, 2008.

[18] B. Girod et al. Mobile visual search. *Signal Processing Magazine, IEEE*, 28(4):61–76, 2011.

[19] G. Griffin et al. Caltech-256 object category dataset. Technical Report 7694, California Institute of Technology, 2007.

[20] J.-F. He et al. Mobile product search with bag of hash bits and boundary reranking. In *CVPR*, 2012.

[21] H. Jégou et al. Aggregating local descriptors into a compact image representation. In *CVPR*, 2010.

[22] S. Lazebnik et al. Beyond bags of features: Spatial pyramid matching for recognizing natural scene categories. In *CVPR*, 2006.

[23] J.-G. Li et al. Face recognition using feature of integral gabor-haar transformation. In *ICIP*, 2007.

[24] D. G. Lowe. Distinctive image features from scale-invariant keypoints. *Int. J. Comput. Vision*, 60(2):91–110, 2004.

[25] K. Mikolajczyk et al. A comparison of affine region detectors. *Int. J. Comput. Vision*, 65(1-2):43–72, 2005.

[26] K. Mikolajczyk and C. Schmid. Scale and affine invariant interest point detectors. *Int. J. Comput. Vision*, 60(1):63–86, 2004.

[27] A. Oliva and A. Torralba. Modeling the shape of the scene: A holistic representation of the spatial envelope. *Int. J. Comput. Vision*, 42(3):145–175, 2001.

[28] F. Perronnin et al. Improving the fisher kernel for large-scale image classification. In *ECCV*, 2010.

[29] J. Sánchez and F. Perronnin. High-dimensional signature compression for large-scale image classification. In *CVPR*, 2011.

[30] J. Sivic and A. Zisserman. Video google: a text retrieval approach to object matching in videos. In *ICCV*, 2003.

[31] A. Torralba et al. 80 million tiny images: A large data set for nonparametric object and scene recognition. *PAMI*, 30(11):1958–1970, 2008.

[32] A. Vedaldi and B. Fulkerson. Vlfeat: An open and portable library of computer vision algorithms, 2008.

[33] J. Wang and S.-F. Chang. Sequential projection learning for hashing with compact codes. In *ICML*, 2010.

[34] J. Wang et al. Locality-constrained linear coding for image classification. In *CVPR*, 2010.

[35] Y. Weiss et al. Spectral hashing. In *NIPS*, 2008.

[36] X. Yang and K.-T. Cheng. Accelerating surf detector on mobile devices. In *ACM MM*, 2012.

Competitive Affective Gaming: Winning with a smile

André Mourão, João Magalhães
Departamento de Informática
Faculdade de Ciências e Tecnologia
Universidade Nova de Lisboa
Quinta da Torre, Caparica, Portugal
a.mourao@campus.fct.unl.pt, jm.magalhaes@fct.unl.pt

ABSTRACT
Human-computer interaction (HCI) is expanding towards natural modalities of human expression. Gestures, body movements and other affective interaction techniques can change the way computers interact with humans. In this paper, we propose to extend existing interaction paradigms by including facial expression as a controller in videogames. NovaEmötions is a multiplayer game where players score by acting an emotion through a facial expression. We designed an algorithm to offer an engaging interaction experience using the facial expression. Despite the novelty of the interaction method, our game scoring algorithm kept players engaged and competitive. A user study done with 46 users showed the success and potential for the usage of affective-based interaction in videogames, i.e., the facial expression as the sole controller in videogames. Moreover, we released a novel facial expression dataset with over 41,000 images. These face images were captured in a novel and realistic setting: users playing games where a player's facial expression has an impact on the game score.

Categories and Subject Descriptors
I.2.1 Applications and Expert Systems; **H.5.2** User Interfaces; **I.2.10** Vision and Scene Understanding.

General Terms
Human Factors, Design.

Keywords
Affective interaction, videogames, competitive games.

1 INTRODUCTION
Interaction between humans encompasses more than words, gestures or actions and the face is a fundamental part of communication. Facial expressions, for example, can help interaction by adding tone or intention to words. As Tian, Kanade and Cohn [28] put it, facial expressions are "the facial changes in response to a person's internal emotional states, intentions, or social communications". Facial expressions can represent a wide array of human behavior. Ekman et al. [7, 8] defined seven emotions that can be mapped into facial expressions. The face and the body can provide useful input in HCI. Steps towards this goal are gaining momentum and enabling users to control computers and game consoles with their bodies through facial expression [9, 20, 24, 25], gestures and other movements [21] (using depth-sensors, such as, Microsoft Kinect [12]) and to search information using their facial expressions [1]. This trend is also observed in recommendation systems that use text sentiment analysis [2].

In this paper, we propose to extend existing interaction paradigms by including facial expression based input in videogames. Affect-based interaction methods can greatly change the way videogames are designed and played. Thus, our objective is to research facial expressions as input in games. We argue that a game should be able to react to the player's facial expression as input. For example, in a fighting game, a punch thrown with an angry face could cause more damage; an adventure game could alter its outcome depending whether player acted surprised or not on a certain situation. To support our hypothesis, we researched affect-based interaction techniques in a computer. The proposed framework explores the player's facial expression as the sole controller of the game. Previous work has explored affective features in games [9, 21, 24, 25] or art exhibitions [11] but not at the level of interaction. The closest approaches, [7] and [13], are aimed at people with Autistic Spectrum Disorders (ASD). Their aim is to teach emotions by mimicking facial expressions.

NovaEmötions game is the central contribution of this article – it is an interactive game exploring affective features based on the face. Our scoring algorithm was designed to tackle the new challenges of affective interaction in videogames. We researched methods for measuring displays of affect, taking into account fair competitiveness and smoothed responses. Affect-based computer interaction still has many challenges to be researched and we believe the proposed game illustrates how such novel interaction paradigm can be embedded in computational systems. A game trial evaluation with 46 players showed that players got quickly engaged on the game and rapidly became competitive. We documented and captured the entire game sequences showing the player's affective responses during the game.

Other important contribution of this article is novel facial expression dataset made available to the scientific community for research purposes. We released more than 41,000 images of face images annotated with their facial expression. This dataset is unique in the following senses: captured in a realistic setting: user faces are not in fixed positions (about 50% of the face images are not front facing and are at different heights); users are playing a game where their facial expression play a role in the game, hence there is a true and direct interaction. We expect this dataset will help the development of new interaction technologies based on affective features.

This paper is organized as follows: Section 2 details the game dynamics and rules. The affect-based interaction implementation is detailed in Section 3. Section 4 reports the game evaluation and user trial. Section 5 we discuss work related to our approach.

MM '13, October 21 - 25 2013, Barcelona, Spain

http://dx.doi.org/10.1145/2502081.2502115

Figure 1. Top left: Player selection screen; top right: two players performing the *Surprise* expression; bottom left: winner screen; bottom right: high score screen.

2 GAME DESIGN

NovaEmötions is a game that explores players' facial expressions as the sole controller. Several challenges exist to accomplish such natural interaction [22]. The most critical one resides on designing smooth facial expressions recognition. The design of the game must not frustrate the user and must react homogeneously, independently of the expression being performed. With these requirements in mind, we identified the key design aspects of an affect-based interaction framework to be the following:

1. **Affective awareness** – users (i.e. players) must realize that the system (i.e. the game) is aware of them. This triggers a mindset that prepares them for the game interaction and the lack of a mechanical control;
2. **Affective challenge –** each game round must face a challenge to the player. This challenge assumes the form of an emotion that must be performed. The player displays the emotion through an intentional facial expression;
3. **Affect-based interaction** – the framework must limit the interaction to a well-defined set of affective user-responses. The reaction to players' displays of affection must be unambiguous and in real-time. Weakly specified interactions will frustrate users with unrelated actions-reactions.

We have found these design principles to be fundamental to achieve an effective interaction based on facial expression.

2.1 Gameplay

NovaEmötions is a two-players game where the objective is to perform a set of facial expressions. Players play simultaneously and facial expressions are competitively scored. The player that performs an expression closer to the one asked, wins a round – the player who wins more rounds wins the game. Each round consists of the following sequence (Figure 2):

1. A reaction image is displayed, along with the label of the expected expression;
2. When a face is detected, the facial expression is recognized, player's label is updated with the recognized expression and the scores are updated. The process is repeated through the round, until the timer ends;
3. At the end of the round, the player with the highest score wins a point. If the player's best score is the same, they both get one point;
4. The game will continue until a set number of images are displayed. In the end, a screen with the winner is displayed.

The main screen (displayed in Figure 1: Top right) is composed by three components: the player's information component (A) that contains the currently detected expression (A1), the last obtained score (A2) and the best round score (A3); the current round challenge expression label and stimulus image (B); and the game total round score and the current round timer (C). Players were asked to perform the expression of the expected label.

2.2 Affective awareness and challenge

Players must realize that the game is aware of their affective behavior. In the first step, everybody is detected by the game (square around the faces), Figure 1: Top left, and the two players are manually selected (blue square). This creates an affective setting where players quickly realize that the game is aware of them and of their facial expressions. This state of mind is reinforced by the fact that there is no mechanical control – the game tracks player's faces and monitors their facial expressions without interaction (other than the initial player selection).

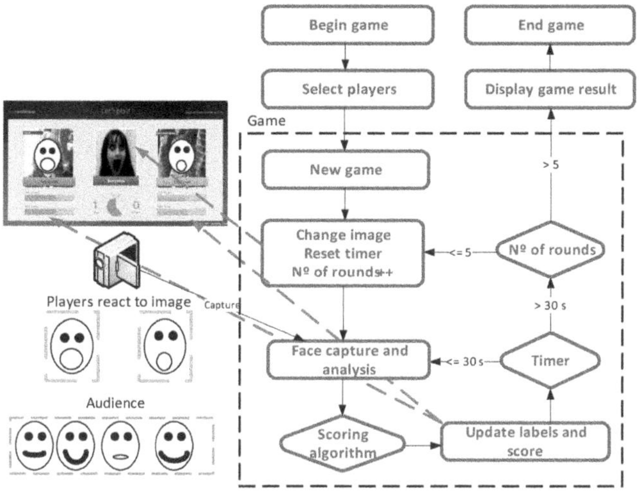

Figure 2. Game overview.

2.3 Assessing facial expressions

The previous section described the design aspects guiding our affect-based interaction game. In this section, we detail the researched framework at the core of the game: a computational representation of facial expressions and a facial expressions similarity computation. These elements will feed the most important element of the framework: the NovaEmötions scoring algorithm (section 2.4). The scoring algorithm is critical in the sense that it computes the game reaction to the player's affective expressions. Thus, it must offer a consistent response to all affective interactions, without favoring any particular facial expression due to algorithm accuracy issues.

2.3.1 Face detection and alignment.

The affective component of the proposed game runs in real-time and is unsupervised requiring no calibration (no need for user intervention to tune algorithms). Therefore, we use a face detection algorithm based on the Viola and Jones' algorithm [30]. To improve the alignment of the detected faces and reduce the false positives in face detection, the Viola and Jones' algorithm is also applied to eye detection. The alignment algorithm detects the eye pair and rotates the image with the assumption that the eyes have the same y-axis value. The variations in pitch and yaw are not corrected, due to a lack of reference points. Face detection is reliable with a $\pm 10^o$ roll and $\pm 5^o$ pitch and yaw. Faces rotated outside this range are ignored.

2.3.2 Facial expression detection

To represent facial expressions, we have chosen the expressions from the Emotional Facial Action Coding System (EMFACS) [8]. EMFACS is built on the assumption that there are seven facial expressions: *Happiness*, *Sadness*, *Surprise*, *Fear*, *Anger*, *Disgust* and *Contempt* and a state of no expression: *Neutral*. These facial expressions are decomposed into a set of Action Units (AU). An AU corresponds to visible muscle movements that we can approximate with Gabor wavelets and face regions determined by Gabor energy clustering (e.g. mouth or eyebrows).

Using ideas already deployed in visual analysis of facial expressions [32] [15], we implemented a dictionary of Gabor filters to extract face contours. Combinations of Gabor filters are widely applied in facial expression recognition because of their ability to detect the contours of the facial features (i.e., eyes, nose, mouth, brows and wrinkles) and filter out most of the noise present in the image [3]. To extract information concerning the face contours and expression traces, twenty-four Gabor filters with six orientations and four scales capture the different details of a facial expression. Dictionaries with this configuration have been found to work well on a number of domains, namely, facial expressions analysis [3] and image retrieval [18].

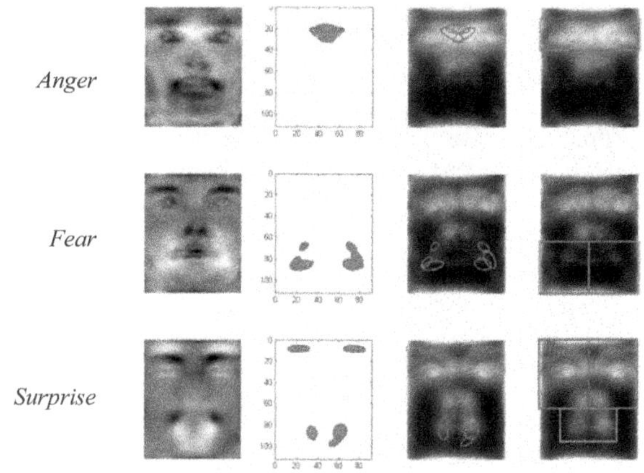

Figure 3. Creation of the expression regions.

In addition to the Gabor representation, our objective was to identify the face regions where the dominant facial expression changes are modelled by a *k*-means clustering [17]. We considered a sequence of images per expression/user, starting at neutral expression and ending at peak expression. To calculate the region with greater variation from the neutral expression, we took the frame with the maximal facial expression from each sequence and convolved it with the Gabor filters (Figure 3, column 1). To identify the regions with the dominant changes for the specific facial expression image, we subtracted the Gabor filters output of the neutral image of that sequence, and run the k-means clustering algorithm to detect the high-energy regions (Figure 3, column 2). Figure 3, column 3 exemplifies the clusters over original face images. For efficiency and robustness purposes, the resulting *k*-means clusters were approximated by rectangular regions (Figure 3, column 4). These regions are robust to small changes in the alignment of the facial features and simplify feature extraction, improving the algorithm's robustness.

Finally, we extract the average value and standard deviation of each rectangular region for each filter scale and orientation. To classify a facial expression and extract the expression label, we combine our representation with a multiclass SVM. The algorithm is described and evaluated in detail in [19]. Thus, the SVM classifier will classify each facial expression with a given expression label, i.e., the *playerEmoLabel* variable of the scoring algorithm.

2.3.3 Dissimilarity between facial expressions

To deploy affect-based interaction, we need to measure the intensity of a player's facial expression. We need to compare the player's facial expression to a set of reference facial expressions. This is done through a dissimilarity measure based on the L_0 norm. We use the L_0 norm since it measures the number of dimensions in a vector that are different from zero – thus, it is more robust. Using the representation described in the previous section, we compute the difference between the player's expression feature vector pf, and the average feature vector af_j of an expression j,

$$\Delta_j = (pf - af_j) = (\Delta_{j,1}, \dots, \Delta_{j,i}, \dots, \Delta_{j,n})$$

and remove the noisy dimensions that have a magnitude smaller than a threshold ε_0 ($\Delta_{j,i} = 0$ if $-\varepsilon_0 < \Delta_{j,i} < \varepsilon_0$). Computing the L_0 norm of this vector, produces a measure of the intensity of the facial expression – this will be the *playerEmoDissim* variable of the scoring algorithm.

2.4 Scoring algorithm

The game scoring algorithm must provide a realistic and balanced reaction to the players' expression. This is critical to keep the user responsive and immersed in the game. A significant challenge was to obtain a meaningful score that would answer players' expectations. In this section, we argue that although both expression dissimilarities and SVM are incomplete, a smoothed and temporally limited combination of these techniques can deliver a competitive scoring algorithm for affect-based games.

A baseline scoring algorithm would take the label from the SVM and the expression dissimilarity score to directly update the game interface. This approach has several properties and drawbacks inherited from the previously presented techniques:

1. Some players are detected more often than other players, giving them more chance to score;
2. The SVM classifier is highly accurate for the on-screen label of the player's face but it is not adequate for computing an expression score;
3. The expression dissimilarity is a good indicator of how close the player's expression is to average expression, but it is not adequate for providing the on-screen label;
4. A player's expression labeled as *Anger* could still achieve the highest score for a *Disgust* label.

To overcome these challenges, our approach was to devise a novel game scoring strategy to increase the competitiveness of the game and overcome algorithmic limitations. At the core of our approach is the prior knowledge that we know what the expected expression is. We explore this information, along with the score and the label, to create improved labels and scores to design the game's scoring algorithm.

2.4.1 Fair competitiveness

The first goal towards a fair game scoring scheme, is to reward the best facial expressions and not a large number of average facial expressions. This decision was made to avoid frustrating players that are not detected as often as others. Thus, the game encourages the most acute facial expressions.

The emotion label, output variable *Label,* to be shown to the player (Figure 1: Top right A1), is an indicator of how the player is being interpreted by the game. This label is determined by one of two ways (Algorithm 1, steps 1 to 3):

1. If the dissimilarity between the player's expression and the current round expression (*playerEmoDissim*) is above the HIGH_CONFIDENCE threshold, the label corresponds to this round's expression. This ensures players receive the correct label if they achieve a high dissimilarity value and the SVM output is ignored.
2. If the dissimilarity value (*playerEmoDissim*) is not high enough, the Label is assigned by the SVM classifier (step 3).

The HIGH_CONFIDENCE threshold was determined experimentally to an accuracy level of 95% on the CK+ dataset.

Once the label has been determined, the score of the current facial expression, we calculate the *ScoreMeter.* The score meter is displayed in the game screen at position A2, see Figure 1, top right.

If the current label is correct (Algorithm 1, step 4), but the dissimilarity is too low we assume there's too much noise in the image (Algorithm 1, step 5), and adjust the value by adding a uniformly random value between 0 and BONUS (Algorithm 1, step 6). This solves two issues: (i) the disagreement between the dissimilarity and the SVM, and (ii) provides a meaningful response to the user to keep him responsive.

Algorithm 1. Calculating the player's score and label.

Input:

playerEmoLabel	*label predicted by SVM classifier*
playerEmoDissim	*L_0 dissimilarity for the captured face image*
roundExpression	*label displayed to the user*
time	*current round time*

Output:

Label	*emotion label to display to the user*
ScoreMeter	*score for the last image to be displayed the user*
BestScore	*score of the player's best facial expression*

Algorithm:

```
1.  if playerEmoDissim > HIGH_CONFIDENCE
2.      Label = stimuliEmotion                    assumes SVM label
    else
3.      Label = playerEmoLabel assumes dissimilarity
                                                  label
    endif
4.  if Label == stimuliEmotion
5.      if playerEmoDissim < NOISY_EXPRESSION
6.          ScoreMeter = playerEmoDissim +
                              rand_uniform(0, BONUS)
        else
7.          ScoreMeter = playerEmoDissim
        endif
8.      ScoreMeter = temporalSmoothing(Score, time)
    else
9.      ScoreMeter = playerEmoDissim - rand_uniform(0, REACT)
    endif
10. if BestScore < ScoreMeter
11.         BestScore = ScoreMeter
    endif
```

If the player's facial expression is not recognized as the stimuli emotion (Algorithm 1, step 9), the score will be penalized by an uniform random value. This happens when the expression performed is not close to the expected one (both the classifiers and the dissimilarity gave results different from the expected label), so it's fair to penalize the score and show the incorrect *playerEmoLabel* (different from *roundExpression*).

Since in some cases the detected faces are too noisy and the visual analysis is too slow (search for faces on the image) we add a jitter to the player's last score to inform the player that the game is responding to their expressions. This is done in Algorithm 1, steps 6 and 9 where small random values are added to the score. These random values are small and don't have an influence on the game.

Finally, the best score (output variable *BestScore*) is displayed in the game screen at position A3, see Figure 1, top right. This corresponds to the best scored obtained until a given moment. The score of the round (*BestScore*) is the value that will determine which player wins the round. To avoid rewarding players that are detected more often than others and to reward the best peak expression, the *BestScore* is the best score of the round, instead of a sum of individual images scores (Algorithm 1, steps 10 and 11).

Figure 4. User study room conditions: two players are playing the game surround by an audience.

2.4.2 *Progressive competitiveness*

To maintain the competitiveness throughout the entire round duration we imposed a limit on players' score. This will allow players to adjust themselves to the camera and to train their facial expressions. The limit is progressively removed until the score is no longer limited. This is implemented on Algorithm 1: step 8. The score is capped to 30% on the first 10 seconds of the round, by multiplying the score value from by 0.5. Between 10 and 20 seconds, the multiplier increases linearly from 0.5 to 1. On the last 10 seconds, the score is fully unlimited (multiplier equal to 1).

3 EVALUATION

The real setting evaluation assesses the scoring algorithm's performance with 46 players who played the game for at least five rounds. A user study was conducted with these players to assess the different aspects of the game. An initial trial was conducted with more than 100 players.

3.1 Methodology

The purpose of the game evaluation is to assess the effectiveness of the addressed hypothesis: using affect-based interaction in competitive games. This evaluation was conducted on a real gaming environment, where the 46 volunteers were asked to play the game and to answer a questionnaire about their experience. In this section we discuss the performance of the game algorithms in this setting. Section 3.5 presents the questionnaire results.

Table 1. General game statistics.

Number of players	46
Total number of games played	29
Average nº of games played per player	1.26
Nº of images player per game (fixed)	5
Time per image (fixed)	30 seconds

Initially, players were briefed about the objective of the game and the interface was explained. Then, they played the game by themselves. The trial was conducted like a regular game session on a social environment (i.e. multiple friends watching), contrasting with the strictly controlled conditions when capturing images for most face datasets (e.g. the CK+ dataset). Figure 4 illustrates the experiment conditions. In our trial, players moved their faces a lot (sometimes even stopped looking at the camera) and performed unexpected actions (mainly laughter). At the end of the interaction, they were asked to answer the questionnaire. Table 1 summarizes the captured data statistics.

The camera processed 9 images per second. Each player's face was processed and its score updated, over than 4 times per second.. Note that the facial expression and the game UI are running in parallel on the same computer.

The SVM classifier was trained on the CK+ dataset, see [16] for details. A round expression corresponds to the average of all images of that given expression on the CK+ dataset.

3.2 A Novel Facial Expressions Dataset

The captured face data is available to the scientific community. We captured and classified 42,911 facial expressions, with an average of 295 facial expressions per round. These face images were captured in a novel and realistic setting: humans competing in games where players' facial expression have an impact on the game These images offer a novel view of facial expression datasets: players were competing using their own facial expressions as an interaction mechanism, instead of performing well defined prototype expression.

Figure 5. Example of captured faces.

Part of the data is available for research purposes[1]. It is composed of over 41,000 images annotated with a facial expression. Each image contains the information regarding the expected expression, the expression detected by the scoring algorithm and human judgments obtained by crowdsourcing. Evaluators were asked to choose one expression from the set *Happiness*, S*adness*, *Surprise*, *Fear*, *Anger*, *Disgust, Contempt, Neutral* (state of no expression), and *Ambiguous* (does not fit any of the categories). The crowdsource labeling job is described in [26].

3.3 Affective interaction assessment

The importance of the facial expression recognition in this game is twofold: first, it must recognize the presence of the expected facial expression; second, it ought to provide players with adequate feedback about how the game is assessing their facial expression. Table 2 contains the confusion matrix for the label (expected) expression versus the detected expression. This value is determined by taking the displayed image label (*roundExpression*) and comparing it to the label computed by Algorithm 1.

Table 2. Scoring algorithm confusion matrix.

	Ang.	*Con.*	*Dis.*	*Fear*	*Hap.*	*Sad.*	*Sur.*
Ang.	**54.91**	1.13	0.00	5.00	19.01	1.63	18.32
Con.	16.52	**62.50**	0.52	1.72	8.16	0.16	10.42
Dis.	9.09	4.53	**60.54**	3.61	11.39	0.52	10.32
Fear	4.41	4.63	0.82	**64.61**	8.72	2.68	14.13
Hap.	2.37	2.90	0.24	4.39	**84.89**	0.86	4.35
Sad.	7.92	3.42	1.40	3.54	10.91	**63.94**	8.87
Sur.	10.42	2.67	2.57	5.56	20.52	0.96	**57.30**

The global facial expression recognition rate of Algorithm 1 was 68.23%. This value corresponds to the rate where the player's detected expression (Figure 1: Top right A2) corresponds to the label (Figure 1: Top right B). We consider this value to be the percentage of successful interactions. The value is consistent across all expressions, except for *Happiness,* where it is visibly higher. We consider that it is because the *Happiness* expression is easier expressions to express and detected because we had more training data for this facial expression

Although we expected players to be always performing the expected expression, this was not true. The competitive setting put players the under pressure of wanting to win. This pressed players who performed a wrong or ambiguous expression, or were not able of acting the expression naturally. Although these situations reduced the classification performance, we observed that it is a consequence of the player's engagement on the game. In the Scoring algorithm assessment and the User study we will return to this issue.

3.4 Scoring algorithm assessment

To evaluate the scoring algorithm, we selected the best rounds and the worst rounds, and compared their performances. All game rounds were divided into these two categories: the best rounds are the ones that finished with more than 80% of the highest possible score, the worst rounds are the ones with less than 80% of the highest possible score. This allows us to observe the different gaming strategies. The three curves on the above graphs represent the score values from Algorithm 1: (a) *Score* is the current score meter displayed to the player; (b) *BestScore* is the best score of the round and (c) the *PlayerEmoDissim* is the dissimilarity returned by the L_0 metric.

In the "best rounds" graph, Figure 6, the scores evolved as expected: the *BestScore* is very similar to the time penalty, except for the unlimited zone, where players where still able to increase the *BestScore* slowly. Other very interesting fact is that the *playerEmoDissim*) is very consistent across the entire round with a value range between 74 and 80%. As this value is only dependent on the captured face image (not affected by the scoring algorithm, this means players were able to maintain consistent expressions across the round. Thus, they were consistently competitive during the entire round.

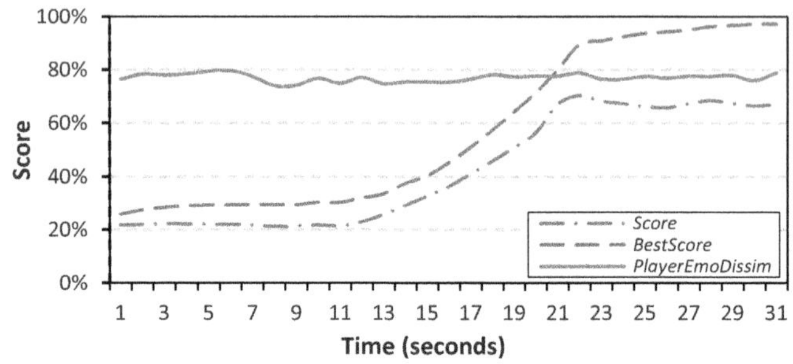

Figure 6. "Best rounds" score evolution.

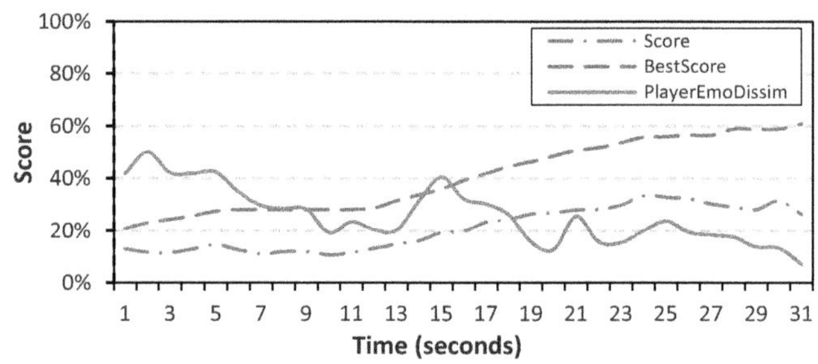

Figure 7. "Worst rounds" score evolution.

In the "worst round" graph, Figure 7, the most obvious difference is the scores range and the lack of consistency of the *PlayerEmoDissim.* It varied between 7% and 50% and it decreased as the round passed. The time penalty imposed on the score is also visible in both the *Score* and *BestScore*, but their values are much lower than the ones from the "best players". The *Score* value is much smoother than the *PlayerEmoDissim* value, showing that the Scoring algorithm was capable of smoothing out the dissimilarity inconsistencies and deliver a better gaming experience (players could be performing very poorly but their score would always correspond to their "*best*" facial expression).

Looking at both graphs, one can observe specific trends and differences across both categories. Best players had a high dissimilarity score throughout the round duration, meaning that they were highly competitive until the very last moment of the round. The worst players, showed a different trend: either they would stop performing the expected expression in the first moments or their attempts to perform the correct expressions got worse as the round went by.

[1] http://novasearch.org/datasets/

3.5 User Study

At the end of each game, players answered a questionnaire about their gaming experience. We took into account the heuristics from [5] that could be applied to NovaEmötions when preparing the questionnaire. Besides standard questions regarding player information (gender, age) and general gameplay (e.g. game objective, difficulties felt, enjoyment level), we also addressed NovaEmötions specific aspects such as interaction novelty, enjoyment and perceived accuracy (label accuracy and score accuracy). There were also open answer questions, where players could contribute with suggestions and critics.

Players were mostly undergraduate students, aged between 18 and 25 years old. The gender distribution was balanced (24 male and 22 female).

3.5.1 Game design assessment

Players found the game easy to understand (91% of the answers were "High" or "Very High") and enjoyed playing (91% of the answers were "High" or "Very High"), Figure 8. We consider that the difficulty level is adequate (not too high nor too low), as the majority of the answers regarding the difficulties felt during the game were "Medium". We consider this difficulty level adequate, as 91% of players enjoyed the game competitiveness.

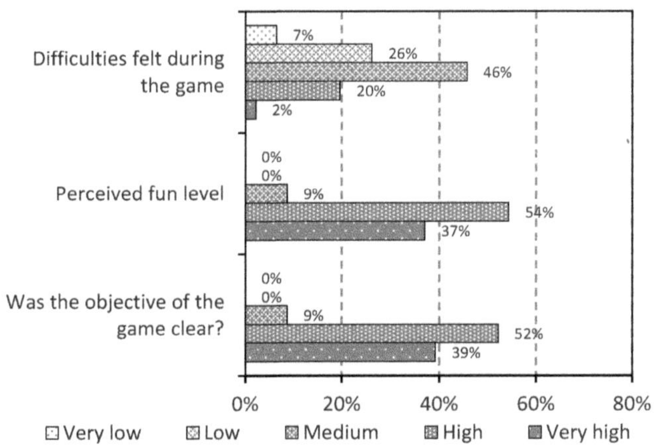

Figure 8. Game play assessment.

Regarding the image exhibition time (round duration) and number of rounds per game, Figure 9, 46% of the players wanted more images per game and 30% wanted less exhibition time per image. This is in line with what we observed: if one of the players got a very high score at the middle of the round, the competition on that round could end sooner. Thus, players expected affective stimuli to be shorter and more frequent.

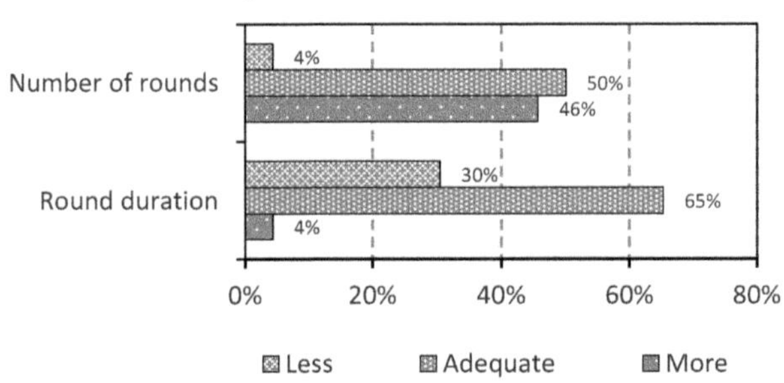

Figure 9. Rounds' duration and images.

When asked what would be the adequate number of players, 69% of the players chose "Two players", while the remaining 31% chose "More than Two players" (no one chose the option "One player"). One of the possible reasons for the relatively low number of "More than Two players" answers is that the users were presented with a two player version of the game, which could lead to a bias towards that answer.

3.5.2 Affect-based interaction

This group of questions concerns how players assess the various aspects of the game design (Figure 10). The large majority of players liked or loved the usage of facial expression as a controller (89%), and novelty of the controller type (98%). This is a highly positive result supporting the initial hypothesis of using the face as a game controller, and supports the effectiveness of the proposed solution.

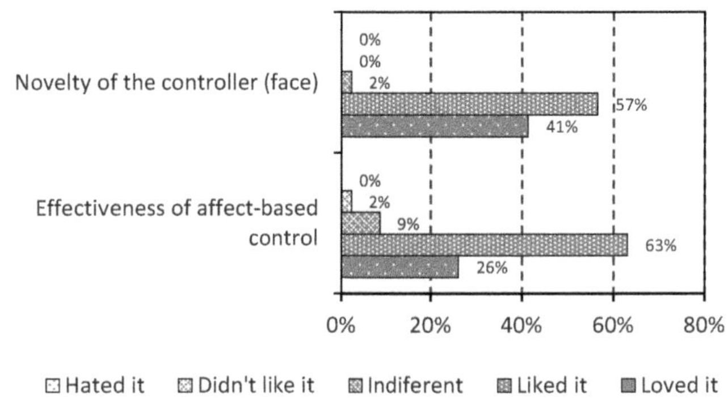

Figure 10. Affect-based interaction effectiveness.

Other critical aspect was the perceived accuracy of the score and the label by the players, Figure 11. Most of the players considered that the score was accurate most of the times (66%: 4 or over, average: 3.6), with a small reduction of when the question was about the label (43%: 4 or over, average: 3.3). This result is positive, as it shows that more than half of the players were satisfied with the label accuracy. It is important to compare these results to the algorithm's performance presented on Table 2. The perceived accuracy (3.3 in 5: 66% for label) is in line with the measured accuracy (68.23%) in our formal evaluation (the confusion matrix diagonal).

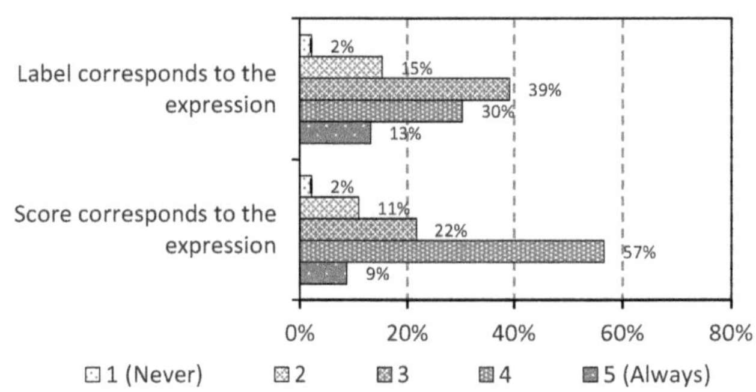

Figure 11. Perceived accuracy by the players.

We also investigated the accuracy of specific expressions and measured how players felt about the different expressions and expression-specific difficulties they encountered (Figure 12). There are three main important conclusions that can be drawn from these answers. Regarding the "Hardest expression to perform", the answers were quite distributed across expressions, except for contempt. In this specific question, 35% of the players reported that they did not know how to perform a *Contempt* expression. This result is backed up by our observations. Some players said that they did not knew how to make a *Contempt* expression, situation that did not happened with other expressions. All other expressions appealed for a player's reaction. Thus, we believe that *Contempt* is not a good expression for affect-based interaction gamming.

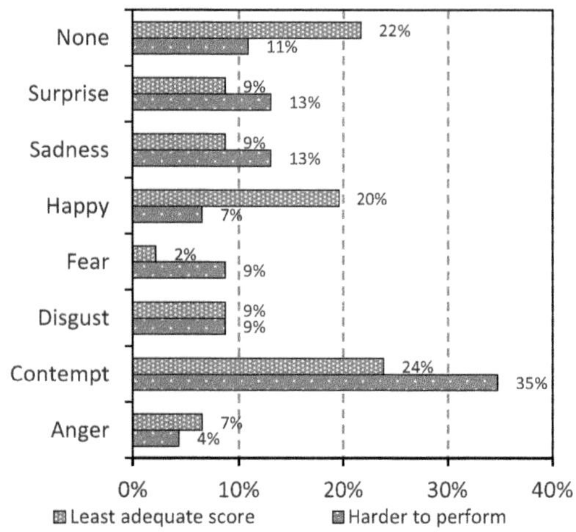

Figure 12. Expression specific assessment.

Regarding the expression whose score was least adequate, the two top results were *Contempt* (24%) and *Happiness* (20%), although the reason for the high percentage is different. In *Contempt*, there is possibly a relation with the previous question. Most players found this expression hard to perform and thought that the score was not accurate was a result. According to our study, volunteers found the *Happy* expression to be one of the easiest to perform and with the least adequate score. The cause for these answers is related to the classifier's good performance in detecting happy faces. Thus, the least adequate in this case, means players would get a higher score with less effort.

4 RELATED WORK

The Mimic Game [25] proposes an interesting application of facial expression recognition techniques: a synthetic agent mimics the facial expression and head pose of a person from a real-time video feed. The system detects the facial components and head pose using a calibrated Active Appearance Models (AAMs) [6] and maps the detected mesh into a two-dimensional emotion space. A point in this space corresponds to an emotion (from EMFACS) and intensity (from neutral face to full scale expression) pair. There are several games based on facial expressions aimed mainly at children with Autism Spectrum Disorders (ASD). What a Feeling [20] is another game based on the recognition of facial expressions by the player. The main idea is to make the player recognize the facial expression of the avatar in multiple situations (e.g. normal face, face with top omitted, micro-expressions). The therapist can control the exercises displayed to the patients. The Emotion Mirror [4] is a game designed to teach children with ASD about facial expressions. The main focus of the game is to mimic the facial expression of an avatar and to have the avatar mimic the player. The game's didactic approach cycles the direction of the interaction ("it mimics you" and "you mimic it") and rewards the player with a virtual ice cream that grows when the expression is correct. Both games use cartoonish avatars to produce the expressions, instead of the face of the player. Most of the studied facial expression based games are didactic and focused on helping people with ASD; their main objective is to reward well performed expressions and help players understand the different expressions. In contrast, our approach is based on competitiveness: it does not matter if your expression is completely correct, as long as it is better than the expression of your opponent. Thus, we argue that a facial expression can be used in non-didactic games.

Other types of affect based interaction are also being applied in games. Paiva et al. developed SenToy [21] a doll that recognizes emotion using motion sensors when manipulated by a user. Different gestures lead to the following emotions: *Anger*, *Fear*, *Surprise*, *Sadness*, *Gloating* and *Happiness*. The doll was evaluated in two trials: in the first trial (similar to a training stage), volunteers were asked to control the emotions of a virtual character by interacting with SenToy. In the second trial, the researchers tested the detected gestures from the first trial in a game. The users' response towards SenToy was very positive.

Novel techniques are being developed to evoke emotions on people using innovative media. Wang and Marsella [31] developed a video game called Emotion Evoking Game (EEG), designed to provoke emotions on the player. The game was created to aid the development of systems that analyze emotion and facial expression. They made a small study that consisted on having a small pool of volunteers that played a version of the game design to provoke four different emotions (boredom, surprise, joy and anger) at specific stages throughout the duration of the gamming session. The player's face was being captured with a webcam and they were asked to fill a form at the beginning and end of the game regarding their emotional state at the key moments of the game. The video from the camera was analyzed by the researchers and compared with the answers to the forms. The results were not consistent amongst emotions, producing some unexpected reactions to the programmed events in the game.

SOEmote [24] is the facial expression detection component for Everquest 2 that enables the game character to mimic the player's facial expression. The game detects the position of several facial features using a webcam and maps them into the face of the character. SOEmote also features a voice modulator integrated in the game's voice chat, allowing the player to alter its voice tone to better match the virtual character. Everquest 2 is a fantasy massively multiplayer online role playing game where players are encouraged to cooperate to defeat their enemies. SOEmotion allows players to extend immersion even further. Reception by the players was mixed [10, 27]: some players praised it for the innovation while others argued that it did not add anything to the game experience.

A key component of the proposed game is the facial expression analysis technique. Humans are able to recognize different facial expressions and infer what emotion an expression conveys. *Happiness*, *Anger* and *Surprise* are some of these emotion specific expressions [7]. One of most used systems to define facial expressions and the one we use is the Facial Action Coding System (FACS) [28]. FACS primary goal was "to develop a comprehensive system which could distinguish all possible visually distinguishable facial movements" [8]. FACS can be seen as an index of Action Units (AUs). An AU is an individual action that humans are able to distinguish, that can be performed by one or more muscles of the face. FACS is widely used as a standard since its introduction. It combines sets of different positions in face muscles and features to determine an underlying facial expression.

The EMFACS (Emotion FACS) system [8] was created by the developers of FACS to map AU combinations into emotions. EMFACS was built under the assumption that a facial expression conveys how the person is feeling. However, mapping facial expressions into emotions is challenging. Some facial expressions can be represented by various combinations of AU, e.g. Sadness can be represented as "AU1+4+15 or AU1+4+16" [16]. Some AU are only used for one particular expression (for example, AU20 is only present in the expression *Fear* [16]).

We deal with facial expression captured on an entertainment environment. For that reason, the player expression and crowdsourced expressions might differ from the expected prototype expressions. Nevertheless, we relied on the prototypes to give us a baseline expectation of the facial components actions. The physiological discussion of emotion versus facial expression is outside the scope of this paper.

After choosing a representation, it is necessary to turn an image into a set of features for facial expression recognition. Gabor wavelets were a popular choice at the First Facial Expression Recognition Challenge [29]. Littlewort et al. [15] used Gabor wavelets based features in automatic facial expression recognition in real-time video. They detected faces using an algorithm based on Viola and Jones' [30] face detection algorithm, extracted the facial features using Gabor filters and then used two approaches for recognition: multiclass decisions using SVMs and AdaBoost. They achieved good results with 91.5% recognition rate with SVMs. Gabor wavelets allow for automatic facial expression recognition; they eliminate manual selection of facial features.

Psychologists use images [14] to study facial expressions and emotional response on people. The international affective picture system (IAPS) [13] is a database of pictures used in the medical community to study emotional responses in people. It was built by showing various images to people and measuring their emotional response. Given the usage restrictions of this dataset, we could not use it in our gaming scenario with multiple persons being exposed to the images simultaneously. Savva et al. [23] studied body expression for emotion analysis using videogames to elicit movement. They tracked the positions of body parts across time to detect a series of abstract emotion categories (e.g. High-intensity negative emotions). They achieved an overall accuracy of 61.1%, comparable to the human observers' body expression agreement (61.49%).

Iacobini et al. [11] studied the contagion of emotions using interactive art. The art exhibition used facial expression recognition to measure the emotional state of the visitors and respond with a video from a database of emotional video portraits. At the end of the exhibition, interviews showed that the interaction with the exhibition was able to invoke emotional response and that the presence of more people added richness to interaction, as multiple people tried to collaborate influence the system. Some visitors also tried to control the responses of the exhibition through posed facial expressions.

5 CONCLUSION

In this paper, we proposed an emotion-based game exploring facial expressions as the sole interaction mechanism. The main conclusions to be drawn from our contributions concern three main points:

Gamification. Game trials illustrated how affective interaction can be successfully used as a computer game controlling mechanism. Despite the limitations of current state-of-the-art image-processing techniques, the proposed game design was able to deliver an emotion-based game. In particular, the NovaEmötions scoring algorithm is the key component implementing the game competitiveness: the affective interaction.

Affective-interaction and competitiveness. The images related to some expressions required a more difficult reaction. In line with the previous point, players reported that some of the expressions were hard to perform (in particular *Contempt*). The competitiveness factor of the game distorted the link between emotion and facial expression. *Contempt* did not work as well as other expressions in our game and we have considered removing it entirely. Thus, game designers must take into account if the expressions are recognizable and easy to perform by players when integrating facial expression recognition in a game.

From a **facial expression analysis** point of view, we observed that the game response time to players' facial expressions and round time was quite critical. A smoothed combination of a facial expression detector and similarity computation (Algorithm 1), provides an appropriate scoring of players' facial expressions. We believe more games will explore facial expressions to measure rage, strength or tiredness and let it play an active role on the game's outcome.

Social component is key. We observed that when players came in larger groups (5 or more people), they had more fun. The higher the number of people watching, the higher would be the enjoyment of the players (bursting into laugher would be more common). Thus, the social environment allowed people to explore the affective interaction more freely.

From the user study (Figure 10), we believe that affective interaction can be quite effective in social/party games, promoting interaction instead of isolation. Having the face on the screen (no "avatars") was critical. We observed that players started laughing when the face appears on the screen before the start of the game (in the "Player Selection screen").

The final contribution of this article is a **dataset of facial-expression images** of users controlling a game with their facial expression. As far as we are aware of, this is the first publicly available dataset captured in such affective gaming scenario.

Acknowledgements. We would like to thank the volunteers who tested the game and answered the questionnaires for the game evaluation and user study. We also would like to thank Bruno Cardoso for the insightful comments and useful discussions. This work has been partially funded by the Portuguese National Foundation under the projects UTA-Est/MAI/0010/2009 and PEst-OE/EEI/UI0527/2011.

6 REFERENCES

[1] Arapakis, I., Jose, J.M. and Gray, P.D. 2008. Affective feedback. *ACM SIGIR* (2008), 395–402.

[2] Arapakis, I., Moshfeghi, Y., Joho, H., Ren, R., Hannah, D. and Jose, J.M. 2009. Integrating facial expressions into user profiling for the improvement of a multimodal recommender system. *IEEE International Conference on Multimedia and Expo (ICME)* (2009), 1440–1443.

[3] Dahmane, M. and Meunier, J. 2011. Continuous emotion recognition using Gabor energy filters. *Affective Computing and Intelligent Interaction* (2011), 351–358.

[4] Deriso, D., Susskind, J., Krieger, L. and Bartlett, M. 2012. Emotion Mirror: A Novel Intervention for Autism Based on Real-Time Expression Recognition. *Computer Vision – ECCV Workshops and Demonstrations*. A. Fusiello, V. Murino, and R. Cucchiara, eds. Springer. 671–674.

[5] Desurvire, H., Caplan, M. and Toth, J. 2004. Using heuristics to evaluate the playability of games. *Human factors and computing systems (CHI)* (Apr. 2004), 1509–1512.

[6] Edwards, G.J., Taylor, C.J. and Cootes, T.F. 1998. Interpreting face images using active appearance models. *IEEE International Conference on Automatic Face and Gesture Recognition* (1998), 300–305.

[7] Ekman, P. 1999. Basic Emotions. *Handbook of Cognition and Emotion*. John Wiley & Sons.

[8] Ekman, P., Friesen, W. V. and Hager, J.C. 1978. *Facial Action Coding System: A Technique for the Measurement of Facial Movement*. Consulting Psychologists Press.

[9] EverQuest 2 Receives Facial Tracking Upgrade: 2012. *http://www.tomshardware.com/news/SOEmote-EverQuest-SOE-MMORPG-Live-Driver,16701.html*. Accessed: 2013-07-31.

[10] EverQuest II: SOEmote Released: *http://www.mmorpg.com/discussion2.cfm/thread/359738/*. Accessed: 2013-07-31.

[11] Iacobini, M., Gonsalves, T., Bianchi-Berthouze, N. and Frith, C. 2010. Emotional contagion in interactive art. *Kansei Engineering and Emotion Research* (2010), 1975–1984.

[12] Kinect for Xbox 360: *http://www.xbox.com/Kinect*. Accessed: 2013-07-31.

[13] Lang, P.J. 2008. International affective picture system (IAPS): Affective ratings of pictures and instruction manual. *Technical Report A-8, University of Florida, Gainesville* (2008).

[14] Lang, P.J. 1995. The emotion probe: Studies of motivation and attention. *American psychologist*. 50, 5 (1995), 372–385.

[15] Littlewort, G. and Fasel, I. 2002. Fully automatic coding of basic expressions from video. *INC MPLab Technical Report*. (2002), 6.

[16] Lucey, P., Cohn, J.F., Kanade, T., Saragih, J., Ambadar, Z. and Matthews, I. 2010. The Extended Cohn-Kanade Dataset (CK+): A complete dataset for action unit and emotion-specified expression. *IEEE Computer Vision and Pattern Recognition - Workshops* (2010), 94–101.

[17] MacQueen, J.B. 1967. Some Methods for Classification and Analysis of MultiVariate Observations. *Berkeley Symposium on Mathematical Statistics and Probability* (1967), 281–297.

[18] Manjunath, B.S. and Ma, W.Y. 1996. Texture features for browsing and retrieval of image data. *IEEE Trans on Pattern Analysis and Machine Intelligence*. 18, 8 (1996), 837–842.

[19] Mourão, A., Borges, P., Correia, N. and Magalhães, J. 2013. Facial Expression Recognition by Sparse Reconstruction with Robust Features. *Image Analysis and Recognition* (2013), 107–115.

[20] Orvalho, V., Miranda, J. and Sousa, A. 2009. What a Feeling: Learning Facial Expressions and Emotions. *Videojogos Conference* (2009), 1–11.

[21] Paiva, A., Costa, M., Chaves, R., Piedade, M., Mourão, D., Sobral, D., Höök, K., Andersson, G. and Bullock, A. 2003. SenToy: an affective sympathetic interface. *International Journal of Human-Computer Studies*. 59, 1-2 (2003), 227–235.

[22] Pantic, M., Sebe, N., Cohn, J.F. and Huang, T. 2005. Affective multimodal human-computer interaction. *ACM Multimedia* (2005), 669–676.

[23] Savva, N., Scarinzi, A. and Bianchi-Berthouze, N. 2012. Continuous Recognition of Player's Affective Body Expression as Dynamic Quality of Aesthetic Experience. *IEEE Trans on Computational Intelligence and AI in Games*. 4, 3 (2012), 199–212.

[24] SOEmote Guide: 2012. *http://soemote.com/guide/index.vm*. Accessed: 2013-07-31.

[25] Stoiber, N., Aubault, O., Seguier, R. and Breton, G. 2010. The mimic game: real-time recognition and imitation of emotional facial expressions. *ACM SIGGRAPH Talks*. ACM.

[26] Tavares, G., Mourão, A. and Magalhães, J. 2013. Crowdsourcing for affective-interaction in computer games. *Workshop on Crowdsourcing for Multimedia at ACM MM* (2013).

[27] The Daily Grind: Do you really want MMO innovation?: *http://massively.joystiq.com/2012/08/16/the-daily-grind-do-you-really-want-mmo-innovation/*. Accessed: 2013-07-31.

[28] Tian, Y.L., Kanade, T. and Cohn, J.F. 2005. Facial expression analysis. *Handbook of face recognition*. S.Z. Li and A.K. Jain, eds. Springer. 247–275.

[29] Valstar, M.F., Mehu, M., Jiang, B., Pantic, M. and Scherer, K. 2012. Meta-Analysis of the First Facial Expression Recognition Challenge. *IEEE Trans on Systems, Man, and Cybernetics, Part B: Cybernetics*. 42, 4 (2012), 966 – 979.

[30] Viola, P. and Jones, M.J. 2004. Robust Real-Time Face Detection. *International Journal of Computer Vision*. 57, 2 (2004), 137–154.

[31] Wang, N. and Marsella, S. 2006. Introducing EVG: An emotion evoking game. *Intelligent Virtual Agents*. 4133, (2006), 282–291.

[32] Yeasin, M., Bullot, B. and Sharma, R. 2006. Recognition of facial expressions and measurement of levels of interest from video. *IEEE Trans on Multimedia*. 8, 3 (2006), 500–508.

Tracking-based Interaction for Object Creation in Mobile Augmented Reality

Wolfgang Hürst
Information and Computing Sciences
Utrecht University
Princetonplein 5, 3584 CC Utrecht
The Netherlands
huerst@uu.nl

Joris Dekker
Information and Computing Sciences
Utrecht University
Princetonplein 5, 3584 CC Utrecht
The Netherlands
jorisdekker@gmail.com

ABSTRACT
In this work, we evaluate the feasibility of tracking-based interaction using a mobile phone's or tablet's camera in order to create and edit 3D objects in augmented reality applications. We present a feasibility study investigating if and how gestures made with your finger can be used to create such objects. A revised interface design is evaluated in a user study with 24 subjects that reveals a high usability and entertainment value, but also identifies issues such as ergonomic discomfort and imprecise input for complex tasks. Hence, our results suggest huge potential for this type of interaction in the entertainment, edutainment, and leisure domain, but limited usefulness for serious applications.

Categories and Subject Descriptors
H.5.2 [**Information Interfaces and Presentation (e.g., HCI)**]: User Interfaces – *Interaction styles*

Keywords
Augmented reality, hand gesture interaction, mobile interaction, user evaluation.

1. INTRODUCTION
Due to the success of devices such as Microsoft's Kinect, gesture-based input using motions of your body or parts thereof is currently one of the hottest trends in human computer interaction. For example, waving your hand in front of the screen is considered an intuitive motion for browsing through a sequence of documents or images (Fig. 1). Not surprisingly, researchers have also started exploring this kind of interaction on mobile devices such as smartphones and tablets using the integrated cameras to track gestures of hand motions [9, 23, 24]. This approach seems natural, because gestures are already the predominant interaction method on such devices using the integrated touch screen (Fig. 2A). Extending this to, for example, input via hand tracking could enable us to incorporate gestures in 3D (Fig. 2B). We can assume that this will be particularly useful in augmented reality (AR) scenarios where the video camera's live stream is enriched with virtual 3D objects [5]. Tracking your hand in such setups would enable us to directly interact with these virtual objects instead of

MM'13, October 21–25, 2013, Barcelona, Spain.
Copyright © 2013 ACM 978-1-4503-2404-5/13/10...$15.00.
http://dx.doi.org/10.1145/2502081.2502120

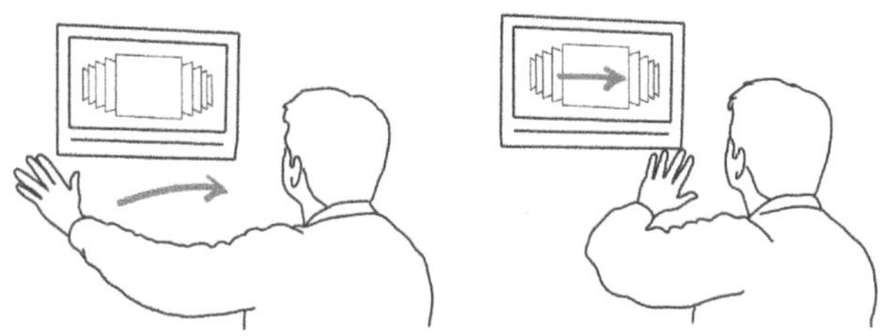

Figure 1. Gesture-based interaction via tracking of hand motions.

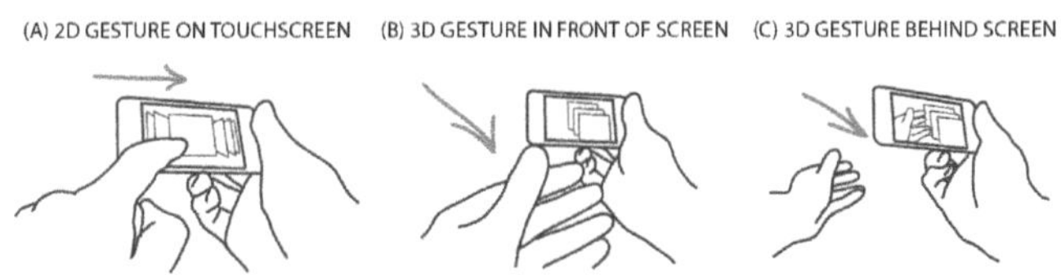

Figure 2. Gesture-based interaction on mobiles via touch or hand tracking.

just remotely controlling them (Fig. 2C). However, there are also many pitfalls and potential issues with such an approach. First, a mobile's camera range is rather limited and human ergonomics do not allow for much space to perform gestures in this setup (Fig. 3). Second, mobile devices just have one camera, which often also gives a rather low quality image. The latter issue makes it questionable that accurate hand tracking in 3D is even possible with sufficient accuracy. Nevertheless, despite these limitations, initial research suggests potential of this kind of interaction in certain domains (e.g., AR board games [12]).

While these interactions seem intuitive to interact with objects and manipulate them, there are also many situations in which people would actually like to create an object. For example, think about an educational AR game where students have to place objects on top of each other in a way that follows physical constraints, a leisure game that allows you to design your own game pieces, and so on. A common way for designers to create objects is by free-hand drawing or using drawing tools with functions to draw, for example, lines and simple shapes to create more complex objects. While the latter can also be done with a device such as a mouse, professional designers often prefer pen-based input. Naturally, much research has been done investigating gesture-based freehand 3D drawing or variations thereof [13, 14, 20, 25, 26]. But which of those, if any, are applicable in a mobile context as well? And can they be used to create objects in AR on a mobile device?

These are the questions that we will address in this paper. In particular, our research investigates the feasibility of object

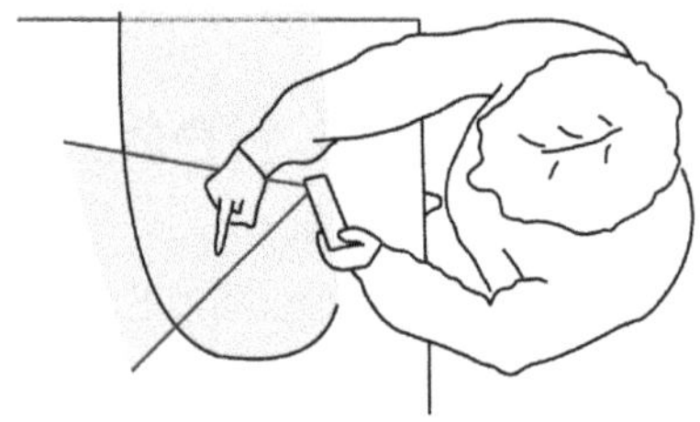

Figure 3. Looking at the intersection between the range that can be comfortably reached with ones arm and the range covered by the mobile's camera reveals a rather limited area in which gestures could be performed.

creation in mobile AR via finger- or pen-based freehand drawing. As said earlier, potential issues with this interaction concept are of technical nature (e.g., how well can we track gestures in 3D with the camera of a mobile?), as well as conceptual (e.g., how well can people draw in such a setup?). Here, we want to focus on the second issue, i.e. study the related human-computer interaction (HCI) issues. As such, our work contributes to the area of multimedia HCI in two ways. First, it illustrates how multimedia serves HCI by investigating new, multimedia-based interaction concepts for human-computer interaction. Second, by studying issues related to interaction, operability, and usability, we also address how HCI serves multimedia. In particular, we investigate human aspects with respect to object creation and manipulation in a multimedia system, i.e. a video-based AR implementation on mobile devices such as tablets and smartphones. We start by discussing related work in section 2. Based on this literature study and initial tests, we introduce a new concept for finger- or pen-based drawing and object creation in mobile AR and present a related feasibility study in section 3. The problems identified in this experiment are addressed by a revised interface design, which is evaluated by a formal user study in section 4. In section 5, we summarize our major contributions and discuss future work.

2. RELATED WORK

2.1 3D object creation via drawing

Reconstructional or sketch-based modeling [6, 19] enables users to create 3D objects by drawing 2D sketches which in turn are projected onto the image of a 3D model. However, determining the symmetry of elements, simplifying the geometry, and estimating the depth are non-trivial problems when constructing the 3D object based on 2D images making this approach less useful in our context. Likewise, contour sketching [13, 14] extracts 3D shapes from 2D contour sketches. Although the results of this approach can be quite impressive, they are highly influenced by the used algorithms. Free form sketching [20, 26] allows actual 3D drawing in an AR context by using hand tracking in 3D. A simple, yet powerful technique to create 3D models is used by Google SketchUp [10], where complex models are created by drawing simple 2D shapes and modifying them via extruding, scaling, cutting, etc. An interesting related approach is napkin sketch [25] where 2D drawing planes are placed in the 3D space and used to draw faces of related 3D objects.

2.2 Interaction via finger tracking

While research on tracking-based drawing is still limited, plenty of work has been done on finger tracking for object manipulation and interaction. MIT's Sixth Sense project [17, 18] uses camera-based gesture tracking of marked fingertips for interaction in a mobile scenario featuring a mini projector. [16] presents a detailed study on the usability of finger tracking for AR environments using head mounted displays. [8] is one of the first approaches using finger tracking in AR with a camera and projector mounted on the ceiling. A comparable setup is used by [15]. [7] uses markers attached to the index finger to realize interaction in an AR board game. All of these projects illustrate the power of hand- and finger-based interaction, especially in an AR context. However, due to problems such as the one illustrated in Figure 3, we cannot be sure if the related interaction techniques are fully applicable when AR objects are created on mobiles such as smartphones and tablets.

2.3 Tracking-based interaction on mobiles

For mobile phones and handhelds, [23, 24] track fingers to realize "in-air typing". [9] is a commercial example of a mobile tracking-based interface relying on hand motions. In relation to mobile AR, [22] uses automatic hand detection and tracking to create pre-specified AR objects. [11] uses hand drawn shapes to create AR objects. [2] presents an interesting system where 2D sketches are used to create 3D objects for a mechanical engineering education context. However, these systems work with sets of predefined shapes and do not allow the creation of random 3D objects. [1, 27] realize marker-less hand tracking on mobiles, but focus on technical aspects rather than usability, which is the major focus of our work. [3] presents a design study featuring various showcases for finger-based interaction in a mobile AR setting. Their proposal includes gesture based object creation, but a related prototype was neither implemented nor evaluated. As part of our own related work, we studied finger-based object interaction in mobile AR including basic operations such as translating, rotating, and scaling of 3D objects [12]. The related evaluations revealed significant issues when interacting with objects that are floating in midair, but verified usability of the interaction concept in situations where people were sitting on a table and interacting with virtual objects right in front of them. Based on this experience, we decided to follow a similar setup for the studies in this paper.

While in [12], we solely investigated the manipulation of objects (via translation, scaling, and rotation), the research presented in this paper focuses on authoring, i.e. the creation of new objects – a problem that is far more complex than the pure manipulation of existing ones. In the next subsection, we will discuss potential issues and limitations of using finger tracking-based interaction for object generation. The main contributions of this paper are the following two case studies investigating if and how we can deal with these issues and verifying the overall feasibility of this interaction concept.

3. THE VIRTUAL GRID CONCEPT

3.1 Identification of major potential problems

Based on above literature study and informal tests by ourselves and some of our colleagues, we identified the following potential problems when applying finger tracking to draw and interactively create 3D objects in a mobile AR setting where users are sitting on a table holding the device (smartphone or tablet) in one of their hands:

First, the possible workspace is rather limited (cf. Fig. 3), what also results in a rather low granularity of positions that can be tracked when a finger is moved in front of the mobile's camera.

Second, when making typical drawing gestures, we can expect a large amount of self-occlusions of your fingers, making accurate tracking very hard, if not impossible. This is particularly true for depth estimation – which in turn seems to be one of the major advantages of finger tracking compared to two-dimensional drawing on the device's touchscreen.

Third, another problem is obviously that many people are not really good at drawing. This can already be the case for 2D drawings but is certainly true for doing freehand drawings in 3D. Providing tools such as drawing of straight lines or geometric shapes could help lots of people, but might make the drawing process more complicated and harder to manage.

Finally, a general problem with all kind of tracking approaches that rely on gestures is that you cannot distinguish between different states. For example, when using a mouse, we can differentiate between moving a mouse pointer to a target position versus dragging an object to that position by pressing the mouse button in the latter case. When drawing on a touch screen, you can hover your finger over the screen to go to a target position, and draw by touching it. But how does one distinguish between, for example drawing with your finger in midair versus just moving it? Common approaches such as holding your finger at the start and end point of a drawing for a while in order to switch between states might be too complex and hard to handle in the given scenario.

3.2 First prototype: the virtual grid idea

Because the purpose of this research is to study the human aspects of finger tracking-based object creation, we decided to eliminate the computer vision and tracking related issues mentioned in the first problem above in order to fully concentrate on interaction related aspects. Therefore, we adopted [17, 18]'s approach and used markers that are attached to the user's fingers. Because such markers are relatively easy to track, this enables us to focus purely on the interaction, eliminating problems that are not due to erroneous tracking. In addition, we expect more insight into the question of what kind of tracking is actually required to implement a related system. For example, if most drawing options are done in a particular way, it might not be necessary to track the whole hand, but tracking just the index finger could be sufficient.

From our initial testing we could conclude that freehand drawings with no restrictions will not result in a reasonable, visually appealing result – even when we apply some smoothing to the jaggy finger movements. We also saw that interactions simulating operations from common modeling tools on the desktop will be too complex to handle. Therefore, we came up with the idea of an "intermediate" version that we call *virtual grid-based drawing*. It is a unique combination of the Google SketchUp approach [10] with the drawing planes approach [25] that provides relatively powerful object creation possibilities while yet promises to be still manageable and controllable. Grid-based drawing is also often used in CAD and common drawing programs. It is however unclear if such a grid-based approach works for freehand, tracking-based drawing in a mobile context as well, and how it should best be implemented.

For object creation in our implementation, users start with drawing a 2D shape on a flat, horizontally oriented grid, which is considered the ground face of the 3D object a user wants to create (Fig. 4A). Then, the user selects this face and creates an initial 3D object by extruding it (Fig. 4B). Finally, this shape can be modified by grabbing and shifting individual vertices (Fig. 4C). Iteratively repeating the last steps, i.e. selecting a face of the 3D object, extruding it, and shifting individual vertices, enables users to create more complex objects, including ones without a flat ground plane (Fig. 5A). Selecting a face also creates a related grid in the orientation of the face, allowing users to draw objects "floating" above the ground plane (Fig. 5B). Notice that this kind of construction does not allow you to create any random 3D object and that decomposing more complex interactions into the three basic operations "draw 2D shape", "extrude face", "move vertices" might lead to a large number of interactions. However, we do consider it a good compromise between providing reasonable flexibility and power in object generation with yet controllable and manageable operations.

In order to distinguish between different states, in particular "drawing on the ground plane", "face selection mode", "extruding mode", and "vertices shifting mode", we experimented with various approaches and decided to use one that relies on gesture recognition. For this, we placed two markers on the users' index finger as illustrated in Fig. 6, left. "Hiding" the second marker on top of the finger switches to a different state depending on the context (Fig. 6, right). For example, users can select "vertex editing", "drawing", and "extruding" mode as well as undo and delete operations via "virtual" buttons on the side of the screen (cf. Fig. 7). The intuition behind this two-marker approach is that the related hand shapes resemble holding a pen (when the marker is covered) versus simple pointing (when the marker is uncovered); cf. Fig 6.

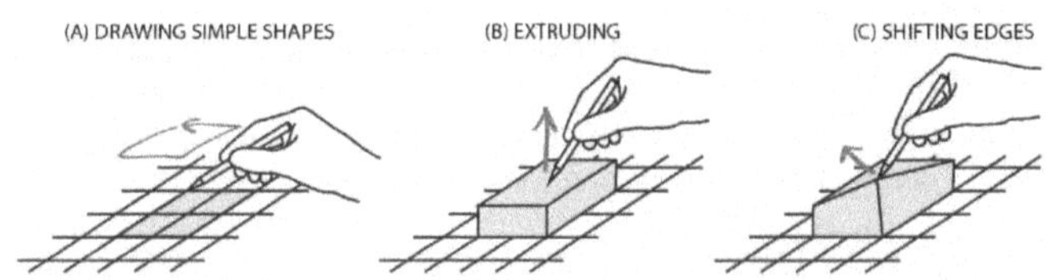

Figure 4. Basic virtual grid operations.

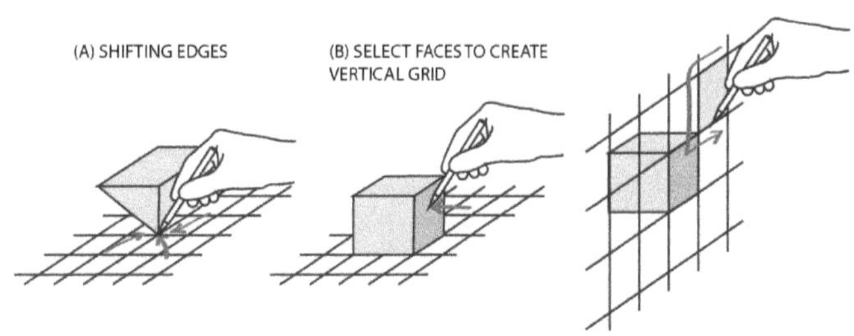

Figure 5. Iterative usage of the basic operations to create more complex objects.

Figure 6. Status selection via hand gestures recognized by two markers.

Figure 7. Tasks used in the feasibility study: creating a simple 3D box (left), creating two cubes on of which is floating over the other one (center), and crating a 3D object resembling a house (right).

3.3 Feasibility study

In order to verify the feasibility of the virtual grid concept, we set up an informal participant-based cooperative evaluation of our implemented prototype. Twelve subjects (ages 18-25, average 20.8 years) participated in this study. None of them have been involved in this project before this test nor did they have any relevant knowledge or experience considering the focus of the experiment. The global aim was to investigate if untrained users can handle the tracking-based input, to verify the usability of the virtual grid concept, and to identify potential issues and problems. Most of the subjects were students from our computer science programs, and thus tech-savvy and open to new and innovative technology. Although they therefore represent a somehow biased sample set, they are representative for the typical group of early adopters we expect for such software.

The implementation was done on a Motorola Droid/Milestone phone (3.7 inch display, 854x480 pixels resolution, 265 ppi). Markers were placed on the subjects' hand as illustrated in Figure 6. Tests were done in a common room with no significant distraction. Users were sitting comfortably on a chair in front of a table where fiducial markers were placed to create the relation between the augmented reality on the phone and the real world.

After a five minute introduction and demonstration of the system, each subject had to perform three tasks: first, drawing of a simple 3D object, second, drawing of two objects of which one was floating in midair, and third, drawing of a house-shaped object (Fig. 7). Tasks have been chosen to cover all basic operations, i.e. drawing (task 1), advanced extruding with a vertically oriented grid (task 2), and modification of object vertices (task 3). The total experiment took about 30 minutes, including a final interview and filling out a questionnaire. Participants were encouraged to follow a "think aloud" approach. A neutral observer made notes of their comments. Although the major focus of this study was on qualitative results, interactions on the phone were logged as well.

3.4 Results

All participants were able to successfully perform the first task. One did not succeed in the second one. Another one did not finish the second and third one correctly. While this result seems encouraging, we observed a major problem with the hand gestures used to switch between different states, since most users did not cover the second marker completely the whole time, but only when they started an action, resulting in lots of erroneous input requiring an undo or delete action. In addition, frequent occlusions of the upper marker confirmed our initial assumption that a full tracking of the hand, especially in all three dimensions, is unrealistic, even if advanced computer vision techniques will be used.

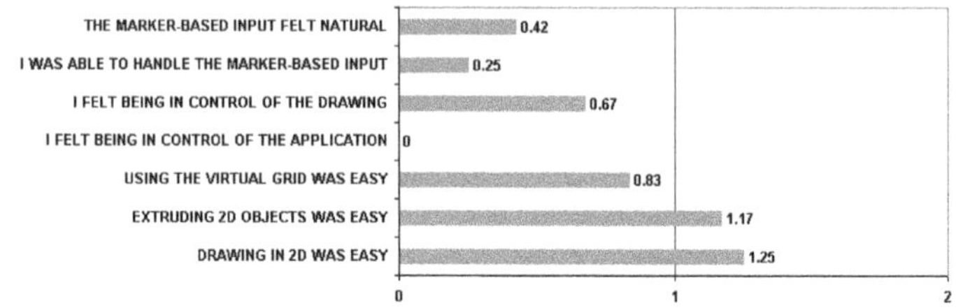

Figure 8. Questionnaire results from the feasibility study.

Figure 8 illustrates the subjects' answers from the final questionnaire, where they could rate different statements from -2 (totally disagree) to 2 (totally agree). Both the questionnaire results as well as the users' comments in the subsequent open discussion confirmed the impression that subjects felt very positive about drawing in 2D, with most people characterizing it as a natural and intuitive process. Although most subjects liked interaction during the more complex tasks as well, comments and ratings were generally a little less positive. However, this was only partly due to the more complex tasks, but to a large degree also because of the problems with the tracking mentioned above, and the lack of granularity and precision already identified in our informal pre-tests (cf. section 3.1).

In general, most participants saw the proposed approach as an entertaining, interesting, and innovative concept with a high potential for leisure applications such as gaming. Major negative comments – asides from the aforementioned tracking-related issues – included complaints about ergonomics from a few people who considered it too tiresome to hold the device and interact with it like this for a longer period of time. Others complained that the virtual elements were all placed on top of the video, resulting in the strange impression that the horizontal grid was floating on top of the hand, although the drawing suggested otherwise. Suggestions for improvement included adjustable grid sizes for better control and more flexibility, as well as a different placement of the buttons – although negative comments about the latter might also have been influenced by the low tracking performance as indicated above.

4. REVISED INTERFACE AND INTERACTION DESIGN

4.1 Revised design

Our feasibility study proved the potential of the virtual grid idea for drawing and 3D object creation in mobile AR applications, but it also revealed many issues and open problems. Therefore, we used the participants' feedback and observations from this first experiment to create a revised version that we evaluated in a more formal user study.

Figure 9. Pie menu appearing via a tap-and-hold gesture.

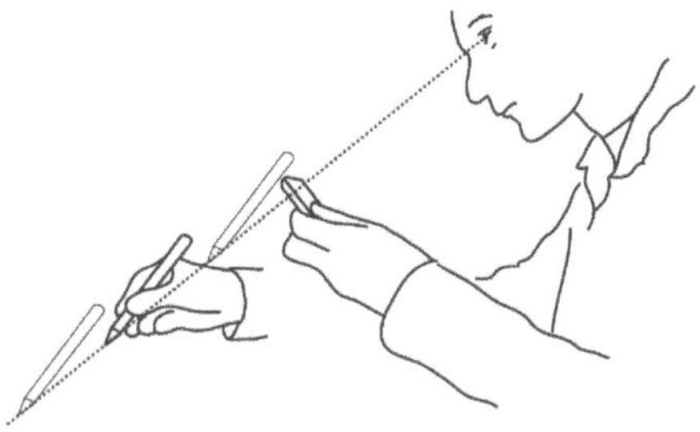

Figure 10. Depth-perception problem: different positions of the pen in 3D are mapped to the same position on the 2D screen.

Some of the participants mentioned potential ergonomic problems. While other researchers could not verify such ergonomic discomfort in their studies [3], our own related work suggests indeed potential issues if used over a long time, especially with heavier smartphones or tablets [12]. Therefore, we included tests with a 7-inch tablet into the second experiments and focused also on ergonomic issues.

Although participants often characterized the approach as natural and intuitive, the aforementioned problems with the tracking suggest that they did not see the hand movements and related shapes as natural as we were hoping. Therefore, we concluded that it might be better to use a real pen that can be tracked and used as a special kind of tangible interface [21]. Notice that a pen might also be easier for natural feature tracking with computer vision algorithms than a real hand. In our tests, we again relied on two markers that were attached to the top and tip of the pen, respectively.

Because using explicit hand gestures or shapes to switch states seems to be too complex to handle (or to remember), we tested two alternative versions. One was just regular buttons on the screen similar to the ones used in the prototype, but now made operable via the touchscreen. While this requires users to often switch between operations in front of the phone and behind it, we expect it to create less cognitive load because operations for creation are clearly separated from meta operations related to, for example, switching states or selecting functions.

The second option realized a tap-and-hold gesture that is also commonly used on touchscreens to evoke context menus. When holding the pen vertical on the table for a short time, a pie menu [4] appeared that enabled users to select from the respective options (Fig. 9). Although this worked very well, informal tests with some of our colleagues who were not otherwise involved in this project confirmed our concern that the cognitive load for this

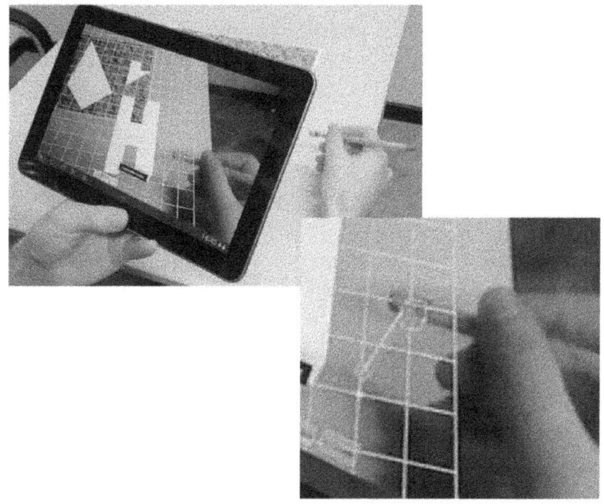

Figure 11. Visual feedback added to deal with the depth perception problem (enlargement on the right side).

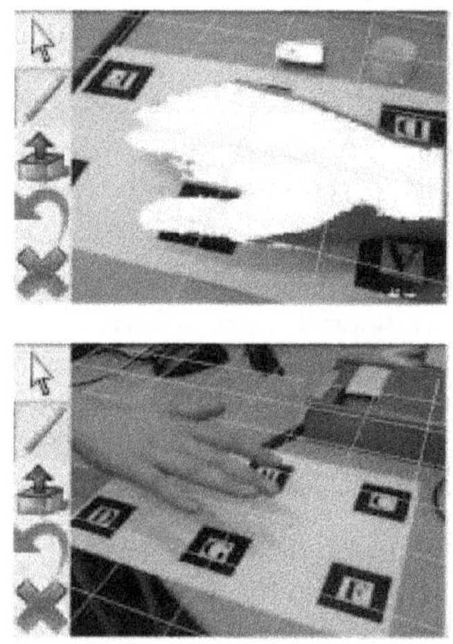

Figure 12. Image processing to improve visual feedback.

kind of interaction might be higher than for the first option. Hence, we decided to include the touchscreen and button-based approach into the prototype tested in our second evaluation. Notice that for light and relatively small smartphones these buttons could also be operated by the thumb of the hand holding the device.

Despite the good drawing performance in the tests, we had the impression that people were not always able to estimate the correct position of their own hand in 3D, due to the problem illustrated in Figure 10. Hence, we included visual feedback in form of a horizontal projection of the current pen position, in order to improve depth perception (Fig. 11). To further improve the visual feedback, we implemented a skin detection algorithm combined with a Stencil buffer, as illustrated in Figure 12. In addition, acoustic feedback was added for selecting and deselecting.

4.2 Formal evaluation

In order to verify the usability of the virtual grid concept with the revised interface, we set up a formal user study with 24 participants.

Our major objectives for this experiment include first, to verify the usability of the revised interface design, i.e. if it can cope with the identified problems in a way that confirms that such tracking-based interaction is a valid and promising approach for object creation in mobile AR.

Second, we want to further investigate the virtual grid by comparing different setups, in particular drawing with a grid versus drawing without a grid. Additionally, we want to verify the usefulness of the actual visualization to see if it is really necessary or if it is sufficient to just internally process the grid points.

Finally, we want to further study ergonomic discomfort, especially when using larger and heavier devices such as tablets. The latter will also provide us further insight in terms of usability of this approach for different devices.

24 subjects participated in the experiment (ages 19-28, average 20.6 years). They shared the same demographics and background as the ones participating in the preceding feasibility study. Yet, neither of them had participated in it, nor any knowledge about this project, nor any related relevant experience. Twelve used the Motorola phone that we also used in the feasibility study. The other group did the tests on a Samsung Galaxy Tab (7 inch display, 1024x600 pixels resolution, 170 ppi). Tests were done in a similar room and setup as the previous experiment with, again, the participants sitting comfortably on a chair in front of a table that provided fiducial markers to create the augmented reality on the phone and tablet.

To make sure all participants have the same preconditions, the test started with a short tutorial video shown on the devices that introduced the application and how to create objects using pen movements in front of the camera. After that, each subject had to perform three simple tasks: first, drawing shapes in 2D (Fig. 13, top), second, extruding objects in different directions (Fig. 13, center), and third, modifying objects by shifting some of their corners (Fig. 13, bottom). Between each task, subjects had to answer a short questionnaire. To evaluate the influence of the virtual grid, each task had to be done with no grid, with a virtual grid visualized but not active, with a virtual grid active but not visualized, and with it visualized and active. The session closed with an informal interview and discussions in which the participants provided further feedback. Relevant interaction data was logged on the devices, and a neutral observer made notes about important observations and unexpected events. The overall experiment took about 30 minutes per participant.

4.3 Results: usability

Usability of the proposed prototype was verified with respect to effectiveness, user satisfaction, and learnability. Considering the latter, users described the concept of using a pen as intuitive and were immediately able to handle it without any need for practice or training. However, we realized that most people started by holding the pen close to the table like in a "real" drawing situation, but after a while changed their behavior and used the pen in a more hovering mode with a larger distance to the actual drawing area. Hence, usage behavior changed from a typical drawing-like interaction to using the pen like a pointing device. Despite this unexpected usage, participants still rated the approach as intuitive and when asked if they found the usage natural, the smartphone users gave a rating on 0.25 and the tablet users rated it as 0.33 on a scale from -2 (absolutely not natural) to 2 (very natural). Significance of the slightly higher results for the tablet could not be proven (t-test with $p>0.05$). Situations where the pen was brought too close to the camera still happened, but generally subjects quickly identified the resulting problems and automatically moved the pen further away from the camera again.

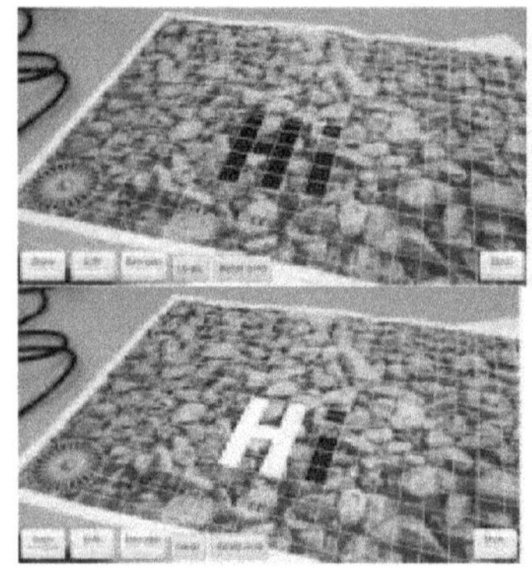

(Task 1: drawing 2D shapes on the ground grid)

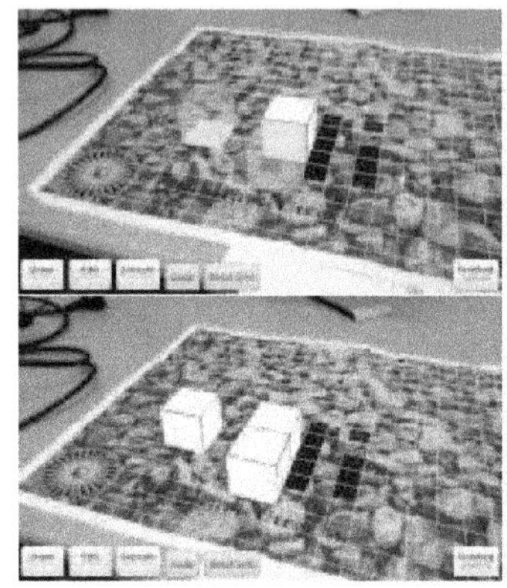

(Task 2: extruding to the top and to the front)

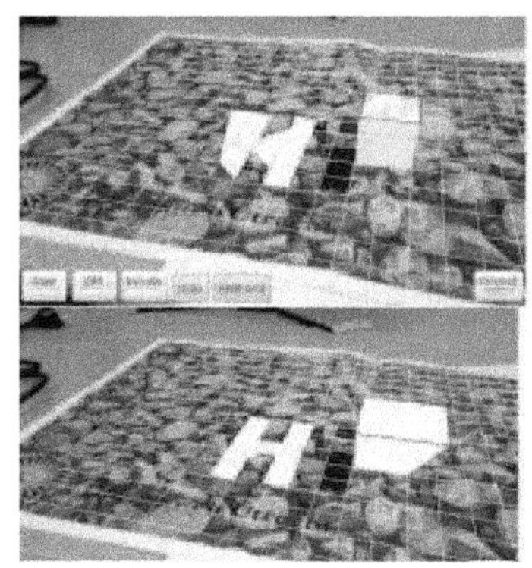

(Task 3: shifting vertices of two objects)

Figure 13.Tasks users had to perform in the evaluation (starting scene at the top, correct solution below it).

Negative comments were mostly related to a lack of depth perception, which might be reduced with the additional visual feedback but was obviously not completely eliminated. The importance of a good visualization was also illustrated by comments of some participants saying that editing by moving corners above the table surface was much harder (cf. right shape in Fig. 13, task 3). Some mentioned a lack of depth perception as the major reason, while others also noted the lack of a visualization of a grid at these positions. Surprisingly, some people also mentioned the lack of haptic feedback in such situations although there was no such feedback when, for example, extruding a face as well. A reason for this could be that editing required more input than extruding which required only a single "confirm/release" action.

Despite the negative comments, overall feedback was however quite positive. Asked if they enjoyed the test and using the pen as input device for mobile AR, the phone users gave an average rating of 0.5 and the tablet users one of 0.9 on a scale from -2 (absolutely not) to 2 (very much). Again, significance of the slightly better rating for the tablet could not be proven (t-test, $p>0.05$). Overall, the majority of subjects agreed that this kind of interaction would be very good for applications such as gaming or in other leisure contexts, but less suitable for serious applications requiring a high performance and detailed construction.

4.4 Results: virtual grid options

To evaluate the effectiveness of the different grid options, users were asked about how difficult it was to complete the task in each of the four setups (Fig. 14) and how well they felt in control of the application (Fig. 15). For both questions, a pairwise comparison of the "grid not functional" versus "grid functional" option showed a significant difference in user preference for both cases visible and invisible grids. Some users mentioned that a functional grid is particularly helpful for situations when drawing or editing does not take place in a horizontal plane. While according to Figure 14 and 15 there only seems to be a minor difference between the two options where the grid is functional, in the closing discussion, users expressed a rather strong preference for the case where it is also visualized.

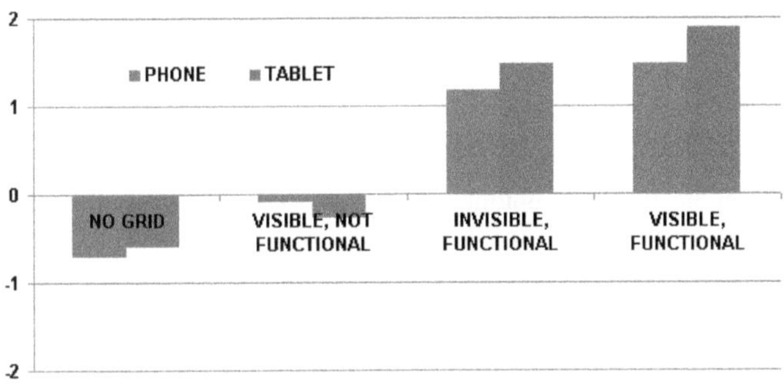

Figure 14. "Difficulty" ratings for the different grid options from -2 (very hard) to 2 (very easy).

Obviously, a non-active virtual grid results in a freehand drawing that will not exactly resemble the given target shape, as illustrated by one typical example in Figure 16. However, when asked about their subjective opinion of the quality of the results on a scale of -2 (very bad) to 2 (very good), users gave rather neutral ratings slightly above 0 for the two cases where the grid was not active, and about 1.8 for the two cases with a functional grid. This might seem surprisingly high, but is based on comments such as "it still looks like an 'H'". The high ratings for the cases in which the virtual grid was visible are expected since there were only very few mistakes in the final results (a look into the recorded data showed a correct result in 91.6% of the cases). To get an objective measure, we also calculated the Hamming distance between the drawings and the template, which is a measure for the area of symmetric difference between the two polygons. The result confirmed a difference between the two patterns: 16.1% (smartphone) and 16.6% (tablet) for the case with no grid visualized, versus 13.7% (smartphone) and 16% (tablet) for the visualized grid. Given the difficulty of the task, this still seems surprisingly reasonable compared to the "perfect fit" of 0%.

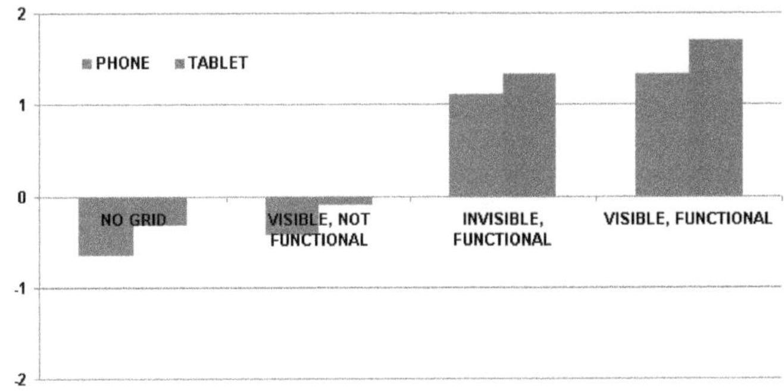

Figure 15. "Level of control" ratings for the different grid options from -2 (very bad) to 2 (very good).

Figure 16.Typical example for a result from the first task if the grid was not active.

4.5 Results: ergonomics and different devices

When asked at the end of the experiment if they felt any ergonomic-related discomfort, users gave an average rating of 0.0 for the smartphone and 0.75 for the tablet on a scale from -2 (absolutely not) to 2 (yes, very). Although these ratings reflect the assumption that the heavier and larger tablet might cause such problems, a significance of this difference could not be proven (t-test, $p>0.05$). Users who gave a more negative rating mostly mentioned "getting tired" as a reason but not actual physical pain or discomfort. Interestingly, while some did as expected mention the need to constantly hold the device as major reason, two subjects said that their arm holding the pen got tired after a while. While this effect is well known from touchscreen interaction – where it is often referred to as the Gorilla Arm effect – we did not expect it to be a problem in our setup because the tasks forced users to keep their arm in constant motion and also rested partly on the table's surface. Another interesting effect was that in order to make more precise input, users tried to move slower, which in turn resulted in a more shaky hand, achieving exactly the opposite effect of a more steady input.

Comparing user opinions about the phone versus the tablet that are reflected in the user ratings in the previous subsections, we generally see a slight preference for the tablet. However, as said, a significant difference for most of these cases could not be proven, and based on the related comments from the discussion we assume that they are mostly due to a newness and "coolness" factor. Some subjects using the mobile phone did however mention the small screen as a disadvantage for such drawing and object creation tasks, where one of the tablet users did.

4.6 Discussion and further observations

In general, the results of this second experiment confirmed that the changes made in order to deal with the problems identified in the feasibility study did indeed improve the system. However, the tests also confirmed our negative concerns insofar as they show that this is not an approach that can be used under all circumstances and especially not suitable for situations where longer interactions take place (which will most likely result in ergonomic discomfort and tiredness), where precise interactions are required (which are hard to do in midair even with perfect tracking), and when rather complex objects have to be created (because a further extension of the rather simple virtual grid concept would most likely result in a higher cognitive overload). But in situations where these characteristics do not apply, which is for example the case in many gaming and leisure applications, our results and the positive user feedback indicate that this can be a valuable, engaging, and useful interaction approach for creating 3D objects.

In contrast to using their index finger in the feasibility study, working with an actual pen proved to be very successful. Subjects were able to handle and use it intuitively without any training (even if they used it more like a pointing device rather than like a drawing pen), and the tracking of the pen worked flawlessly. The latter observation indicates that we will be able to also realize a robust marker-less tracking on the mobile device – something that is not a matter of cause for finger-based interaction due to problems identified in the feasibility study such as frequent self-occlusion. Tracking not only the pen's position but also its orientation, which according to our data analysis should be feasible in a robust way, would open further options for interesting interaction scenarios. The feasibility of an accurate depth tracking seems however doubtful, even if we rely on markers as done in our study. But it is important to notice that people can still move and interact in all three dimensions by not only moving their finger further away but also the device that is held in the other hand as illustrated in Figure 17. In this context, it is noteworthy that we did indeed observe that people were often "moving around" when performing the tasks in the second study to get a better view of the objects they were creating – a behavior that we did not observe in the initial feasibility study.

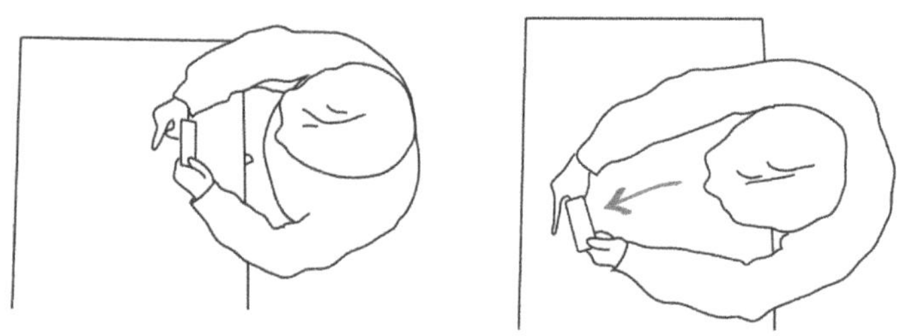

Figure 17. Depth movement of the pen and the device observed in the tests – a behavior that avoids potential problems with depth tracking and perception.

5. CONCLUSION AND FUTURE WORK

Our research presented in this paper investigates if and how the current trend of natural interaction by gestures via movements of parts of your body can be applied to mobiles such as smartphones and tablets. We particularly focused on more complex tasks that do not only allow you to just, for example, move an object by a hand motion, but to interactively create one and manipulate 3D shapes. By introducing the concept of a virtual grid, we showed that such interactions are indeed possible, but we also identified many limitations and open issues. Despite the initial character of our work, we can already draw certain conclusions that are helpful for designers who are thinking of incorporating similar interactions into their programs. First, there is a clear indication that such kind of input can be imprecise and tiresome, so it should only be applied to short tasks that are not too complex. Second, tracking your fingers in 3D is hard if not impossible to do on mobile phones – even with improved processor performance and better computer vision algorithms – due to the character of the source images. But using a pen and providing good visual feedback, such as visualization of the hand above the virtual objects (cf. Fig. 12), clearly improves the situation and offers many opportunities to map gestures made in front of the device to actual interactions. Third, freehand drawing is too difficult for most users, but approaches such as our proposed virtual grid design enable them to reliably draw at least simple geometric shapes.

Despite these conclusions, the case study presented in this paper can obviously only be considered a first step in the direction of tracking-based interaction on mobile devices. After our verification of the basic feasibility and identification of basic limitations of this interaction approach, further tests to gain more objective data should be done. In addition, it feels safe to say that people will most likely not suffer from significant ergonomic discomfort if we restrict ourselves to short, rather simple interactions. Yet, further studies are needed before we can apply this approach in order clearly evaluate the borderline upon which serious discomfort will appear. Also, the iterative application of the basic operations offered by our approach enable us to already create relatively complex objects, but how far can we go? Where is the tradeoff between how complex the operations can get and what is still manageable? How about adding textures to objects and more advanced graphics such as shading and light effects? There are also many options for this approach worth investigating, such as: What are optimum grid sizes? Can other visualizations improve usability? Finally, it is not clear yet, how such tracking-based interaction compares to other approaches such as the standard touchscreen interaction. Given our results from this paper, it seems obvious that touchscreen operation will outperform freehand movements considering performance and accuracy. But how about the entertainment value? All the limitations identified above forbid serious and everyday interactions, but do not necessarily pose a restriction in gaming and leisure applications where fun and engagement are often more important than preciseness and easy control. Other domains where they could be useful and that are worthwhile exploring include edutainment and education.

6. ACKNOWLEDGMENTS

This work was partially supported by a Yahoo! Faculty Research Grant.

7. REFERENCES

[1] M. Baldauf, S. Zambanini, P. Fröhlich, and P. Reichl. 2011. Markerless visual fingertip detection for natural mobile device interaction. In *Proceedings of the 13th International Conference on Human Computer Interaction with Mobile Devices and Services* (MobileHCI '11). ACM, New York, NY, USA, 539-544.

[2] O. Bergig, N. Hagbi, J. El-Sana, and M. Billinghurst. 2009. In-place 3D sketching for authoring and augmenting

mechanical systems. In Proceedings of the 2009 8th IEEE International Symposium on Mixed and Augmented Reality (ISMAR '09). IEEE Computer Society, Washington, DC, USA, 87-94.

[3] M. Luz Caballero, T.-R. Chang, M. Menéndez, and V. Occhialini. 2010. Behand: augmented virtuality gestural interaction for mobile phones. In *Proceedings of the 12th international conference on Human computer interaction with mobile devices and services* (MobileHCI '10). ACM, New York, NY, USA, 451-454

[4] J. Callahan, D. Hopkins, M. Weiser, and B. Shneiderman. 1988. An empirical comparison of pie vs. linear menus. In *Proceedings of the SIGCHI Conference on Human Factors in Computing Systems* (CHI '88). ACM, New York, NY, USA, 95-100.

[5] J. Carmigniani, B. Furht, M. Anisetti, P. Ceravolo, E. Damiani, and M. Ivkovic. 2011. Augmented reality technologies, systems and applications. *Multimedia Tools and Applications*, 51(1), January 2011, 341-377.

[6] S.-U. Cheon and S. Han. 2008. A template-based reconstruction of plane-symmetric 3d models from freehand sketches. *Comput. Aided Des.* 40(9), September 2008, 975-986.

[7] K. Dorfmüller-Ulhaas and D. Schmalstieg. 2001. Finger tracking for interaction in augmented environments. In *Proceedings of IEEE and ACM International Symposium on Augmented Reality, 2001*, 55-64.

[8] J. L. Crowley, F. Bérard, and J. Coutaz. 1995. Finger Tracking as an Input Device for Augmented Reality. In *Proceedings of the International Workshop on Face and Gesture Recognition*, Zurich, Switzerland, 195-200.

[9] EyeSight's Touch Free Interface Technology Software: http://www.eyesight-tech.com/technology/

[10] Google SketchUp: http://sketchup.google.com/

[11] N. Hagbi, O. Bergig, J. El-Sana, and M. Billinghurst. 2009. Shape recognition and pose estimation for mobile augmented reality. In Proceedings of the 2009 8th IEEE International Symposium on Mixed and Augmented Reality (ISMAR '09). IEEE Computer Society, Washington, DC, USA, 65-71

[12] W. Hürst and C. van Wezel. 2013. Gesture-based interaction via finger tracking for mobile augmented reality. *Multimedia Tools and Applications*, Vol. 62(1), January 2013, 233-258.

[13] T. Igarashi, S. Matsuoka, and H. Tanaka. 1999. Teddy: A sketching interface for 3d freeform design. SIGGRAPH '99, 409-416.

[14] O. A. Karpenko and J. F. Hughes. 2006. Smoothsketch: 3d free-form shapes from complex sketches. In *ACM SIGGRAPH 2006 Papers*, SIGGRAPH '06, 589-598.

[15] H. Koike, Y. Sato, and Y. Kobayashi. 2001. Integrating paper and digital information on EnhancedDesk: a method for realtime finger tracking on an augmented desk system. *ACM Trans. Comput.-Hum. Interact.* 8(4), December 2001, 307-322

[16] M. Lee, R. Green, M. Billinghurst. 2008. 3D Natural Hand Interaction for AR Applications. *Image and Vision Computing New Zealand* (IVCNZ 2008). 23rd International Conference.

[17] P. Mistry, P. Maes, and L. Chang. 2009. WUW - wear ur world: a wearable gestural interface. In *Proceedings of the 27th international conference extended abstracts on Human factors in computing systems* (CHI EA '09). ACM, New York, NY, USA, 4111-4116.

[18] P. Mistry and P. Maes. 2009. SixthSense: a wearable gestural interface. In ACM SIGGRAPH ASIA 2009 Sketches (SIGGRAPH ASIA '09). ACM, New York, NY, USA, Article 11, 1 page.

[19] L. Olsen, F. F. Samavati, M. C. Sousa, and J. A. Jorge. 2009. Sketch-based modeling: A survey. *Computers & Graphics*, 33(1), 85-103.

[20] S. Schkolne. 2002. Drawing with the hand in free space: Creating 3d shapes with gesture in a semi-immersive environment. *Leonardo*, Vol. 35(4), August 2002, 371-375.

[21] O. Shaer and E. Hornecker. 2010. Tangible User Interfaces: Past, Present, and Future Directions. Found. Trends Human-Computer Interaction 3, 1-2 (January 2010), 1-137.

[22] B.-K. Seo, J. Choi, J.-H. Han, H. Park, and J.-I. Park. 2008. One-handed interaction with augmented virtual objects on mobile devices. In *Proceedings of The 7th ACM SIGGRAPH International Conference on Virtual-Reality Continuum and Its Applications in Industry* (VRCAI '08). ACM, New York, NY, USA, Article 8, 6 pages

[23] T. Niikura, Y. Hirobe, A. Cassinelli, Y. Watanabe, T. Komuro, and M. Ishikawa. 2010. In-air typing interface for mobile devices with vibration feedback. In *ACM SIGGRAPH 2010 Emerging Technologies* (SIGGRAPH '10). ACM, New York, NY, USA, Article 15, 1 page.

[24] K. Terajima, T. Komuro, and M. Ishikawa. 2009. Fast finger tracking system for in-air typing interface. In *Proceedings of the 27th international conference extended abstracts on Human factors in computing systems* (CHI EA '09). ACM, New York, NY, USA, 3739-3744.

[25] M. Xin, E. Sharlin, and M. C. Sousa. 2008. Napkin sketch: handheld mixed reality 3d sketching. In *Proceedings of the 2008 ACM symposium on Virtual reality software and technology*, VRST '08, pages 223-226.

[26] B. Yee and Y. Ning. 2009. Augmented reality in-situ 3d sketching of physical objects. In *Proceedings of Intelligent User Interfaces* (IUI'09), Workshop on Sketch Recognition.

[27] S. Yousefi, F. A. Kondori, and H. Li. 2011. 3D gestural interaction for stereoscopic visualization on mobile devices. In *Proceedings of the 14th international conference on Computer analysis of images and patterns - Volume Part II* (CAIP'11), Ainhoa Berciano, Daniel Diaz-Pernil, Helena Molina-Abril, Pedro Real, and Walter Kropatsch (Eds.), Vol. Part II. Springer-Verlag, Berlin, Heidelberg, 555-562

Physical Modelling and Supervised Training of a Virtual String Quartet

Graham Percival
School of Engineering
University of Glasgow, UK
graham@percival-music.ca

Nicholas Bailey
School of Engineering
University of Glasgow, UK
nick@n-ism.org

George Tzanetakis
Dept. of Computer Science
University of Victoria, Canada
gtzan@cs.uvic.ca

ABSTRACT

This work improves the realism of synthesis and performance of string quartet music by generating audio through physical modelling of the violins, viola, and cello. To perform music with the physical models, virtual musicians interpret the musical score and generate actions which control the physical models. The resulting audio and haptic signals are examined with support vector machines, which adjust the bowing parameters in order to establish and maintain a desirable timbre. This intelligent feedback control is trained with human input, but after the initial training is completed, the virtual musicians perform autonomously. The system can synthesize and control different instruments of the same type (e.g., multiple distinct violins) and has been tested on two distinct string quartets (total of 8 violins, 2 violas, 2 cellos). In addition to audio, the system creates a video animation of the instruments performing the sheet music.

Categories and Subject Descriptors

H.5.5 [**Information Interfaces and Presentation**]: Sound and Music Computing; I.2.1 [**Artificial Intelligence**]: Application and Expert Systems

General Terms

Algorithms, Design, Human Factors

Keywords

Violin synthesis, physical modelling, intelligent feedback control, machine learning, autonomous music performance

1. INTRODUCTION

Computer synthesis of music performed by bowed string instruments is a challenging problem. Unlike instruments whose notes originate with a single discrete excitation (e.g., piano, guitar, drum), bowed string instruments are controlled with a continuous stream of excitations (i.e. the bow scraping against the string). Most existing synthesis methods utilize recorded audio samples. Although sampling performs reasonably well for single-excitation instruments, the results are not as good for continuous-excitation instruments.

MM'13, October 21–25, 2013, Barcelona, Spain.

ACM 978-1-4503-2404-5/13/10 ...$15.00.
http://dx.doi.org/10.1145/2502081.2502101.

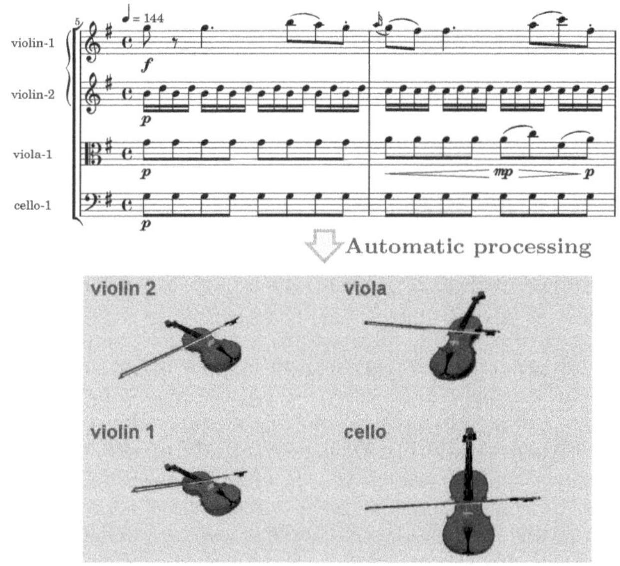

Figure 1: Video produced automatically from the sheet music, performed by two distinct string quartets: `http://percival-music.ca/mm2013.html`

There are a number of applications of computer synthesis of music. The main three are: interactive performance with novel interfaces, preparing an audio track with manual adjustments to the synthesis, and autonomous performance of music with no human input. It is the latter goal that this work focuses on; a typical example would be to allow a composer to quickly hear a rough performance of her work in progress, illustrated in Figure 1. Other applications could be to create audio and video as part of a digital violin tutor [37], or to allow users of a digital music library [10] to hear what the sheet music sounds like without requiring an audio recording; this could greatly mitigate copyright concerns.

Autonomous performance of music is tested in the Musical Performance Rendering Contest for Computer Systems [16], in which researchers write programs to perform piano music (generally Mozart or Chopin) which are then performed on a disklavier (a computer-controlled acoustic piano). In contrast, our work focuses on string quartets instead of piano.

1.1 Related Work

The usual method of synthesizing music in music notation programs is sample-based synthesis: a selection of samples from a library of recorded audio are concatenated. This process can be enhanced in various ways, such as Reconstructive Phrase Modeling [18] or Spectral Modelling Synthesis (SMS) [31], in which instead of concatenating the time-domain data directly, the samples are first analyzed in some manner and then reconstructed. For example, in SMS, a spectral analysis of the samples results in a set of partials plus a residual signal which is treated as filtered noise. A re-synthesis of these partials plus noise captures the transients at the beginning of notes much better than a technique relying on partial-based synthesis alone. SMS has been used to great effect in the Vocaloid singing synthesis program [17].

Analysis and resynthesis of recorded audio can also be used to create a virtual instrument which is then controlled with a virtual performer which creates a stream of control data, such as trumpet performances [7]. A similar approach was used to create violin performances: a neural network was used to predict spectral data based on (potentially) simulated physical actions [24]; the resulting virtual violin was then performed by recording physical actions of real violinists and re-synthesizing those recorded actions [19].

Another method of generating audio is by modelling the physics of the instrument in response to various actions (e.g., bow force for violin, air pressure for clarinet, strike position for drums). The mechanics of musical instruments is a well studied topic in acoustics and physical modeling synthesis uses computational techniques to simulate the physics of sound generation in instruments. A good overview of physical modeling is presented in [33] while the standard library is the Synthesis ToolKit in C++ [26, 32]. There are two main problems with physical models: they are more computationally intensive than most sample-based synthesis methods, and they are difficult to control. One early method of performing music with a physical model used a hierarchical set of expert systems which played a simulated trumpet [6]. Violin music has been created by recording physical actions from real violinists and re-synthesizing the actions with a physical model [9].

Assuming that the physical model acts similar to a real instrument, important clues to its performance can be gained by studying the actions of skilled musicians. Various systems have been created to record actions of real violinists (notably bow force, velocity and distance from bridge, although some projects recorded other factors) [9, 19, 38, ?], for either the analysis of musical performances or resynthesis of audio. Performing music by concatenating segments of these recordings is limited by three factors: it assumes that the behaviour of the physical simulation is sufficiently similar to the real instrument used to record the actions, it requires skilled musicians and specialized equipment to record the musicians' actions, and it assumes that the musicians will always use the same actions to produce the desired sound rather than adjusting their actions on the fly.

In this work on performing with multiple distinct string quartets, we used physical modelling to create the audio. Sampling synthesis and even SMS are limited to the instruments available in the sample library. Recording a new instrument — such as adding a second distinct-sounding violin to a library with one existing recorded violin — is an expensive undertaking, requiring a recording studio, audio engineer, a skilled violinist, etc. One might consider altering the original instrument's audio to create a "new" instrument, such as slightly altering the pitch or filtering the upper partials, but these techniques are not perfect. By contrast, creating a new instrument with physical modelling is much simpler: measuring physical constants from a new instrument can be done quickly. One important factor of sample-based synthesis is that it does not reproduce the sound of a particular instrument; rather, it produces the the sound a particular instrument, being played by a particular musician, performing a particular set of pitches and timbres. When recording a single note on a piano, the musician has minimal effect, as the only interaction is the speed and force of depressing the piano key. But for continuous-excitation instruments such as the violin, clarinet, or human voice, the musician's control of the instrument plays a huge role in the resulting sound. Recording the sound of a skilled musician is a benefit when seeking a quick reproduction of decent sound, but it limits the flexibility of the music.

Physical modelling allows us to consider the instrument separately from the musician and performance style. To address the problem of controlling the physical models, we turned to machine learning to train the system to perform virtual instruments. Previous uses of machine learning in performance focused on recognizing performer gestures [12], while machine learning has been used off-line to evaluate beginning violinists [2], recognize cellists from their timbre [3], rank violins (rather than violinists) [36], and estimate physical actions from violin audio [25]. Active learning [4] is a technique in machine learning in which the computer generates examples for the user to evaluate; it has been used to generate personalized audio equalizers [21]. In contrast, we use a supervised learning approach to "teach" the virtual performer/listener to characterize the quality of the sound generated by the physical model and adjust the controls dynamically to achieve correct intonation and good timbre.

1.2 Our System: Vivi, the Virtual Violinist

Our goal is to allow a string player (not necessarily a professional) to train the system to perform any simulated violin, viola, or cello in a few hours with no specialized equipment. Once the system (Figure 2) is trained to recognize good or bad timbre, it automatically calibrates various parameters for each specific instrument. Given an electronic version of sheet music, the system extracts musical events to create a list of notes with extra parameters such as "note begins a slur" or "*glissando* from A4 to C♯5". These notes are fed into an intelligent feedback loop which adjusts low-level physical actions in response to the audio and haptic output of the physical model.

Our work bridges the gap between physical modelling of instruments, machine learning on acoustic signals, and musical performance. The main contributions of this paper are: 1) an intelligent feedback control system for violins trained with supervised and adaptive learning with no additional hardware required, 2) a flexible method of calibrating the system to perform a new bowed string instrument (violin, viola, cello), 3) a complete platform for the performance of string quartets, allowing researchers to work on one individual aspect of the process without requiring them to be experts in other areas. To enable and encourage future research, the entire system and all training data is available under a permissive copyleft license (the GNU GPLv3).

This paper is structured as follows: Section 2 gives a summary of the physical modelling library we used, while Section 3 details the machine learning and feedback loops involved in performing notes. Section 4 discusses the calibration of initial values used for the feedback control, and Section 5 describes the interpretation of a musical score into notes. Section 6 gives an overview of the video output, and Section 7 discusses the system and future work. Section 8 gives concluding remarks.

2. PHYSICAL MODELLING

We used the Artifastring library [22, 23], a highly optimized C++ library performing physical modelling of violin, viola, and cello. The model's string vibrations and bowing algorithm was based on Demoucron's work [9]: given the constants in Table 1, the string displacement $y(x,t)$ at position x and time t, subject to external forces $F_i(x,t)$, is:

$$\begin{aligned}\rho_{\mathrm{L}}\frac{\partial^2 y(x,t)}{\partial t^2} - T\frac{\partial^2 y(x,t)}{\partial x^2} \\ + E\frac{\pi d^4}{64}\frac{\partial^4 y(x,t)}{\partial x^4} + R_{\mathrm{L}}(\omega)\frac{\partial y(x,t)}{\partial t}\end{aligned} = \sum_i F_i(x,t) \quad (1)$$

The wave equation (1) is decomposed into the sum of modes with eigenvectors $\phi_n(x) = \sqrt{\frac{2}{L}}\sin\left(\frac{n\pi x}{L}\right)$. The bow friction is modelled with the classical hyperbolic friction curve (Equation 2) [20], with the addition of the stochastic term $\mu_e = \mu_c u(t)$, where $u(t)$ is a uniform random value $0.95 \leq u(t) \leq 1.0$. $\Delta v = v_0^h - v_{\mathrm{b}}$, with v_0^h being the velocity the string would move under the bow if there were no external forces.

$$F_{\text{friction}} = \begin{cases} F_{\mathrm{b}}\left(\mu_d + \frac{(\mu_s - \mu_d)\mu_e}{\mu_e - \Delta v}\right) & \text{if } \Delta v < 0 \\ -F_{\mathrm{b}}\left(\mu_d + \frac{(\mu_s - \mu_d)\mu_e}{\mu_e + \Delta v}\right) & \text{if } \Delta v > 0 \end{cases} \quad (2)$$

For efficiency, Artifastring models the bow as a single point force. Modelling the bow as two point forces would require solving a pair of non-linear equations with two variables or a single quartic (polynomial of degree 4). As may be expected from a modal simulation, the resulting sound changes considerably if the bow position is a simply-rational position, meaning a proportion of the string away from the bridge with a small denominator, such as $\frac{1}{6}$ or $\frac{1}{7}$.

Symbol	Explanation
ρ_{L}	Linear density [kg/m]
T	Tension [N]
L	Length [m]
d	Diameter [m]
E	Young's Elastic Modulus
$R_{\mathrm{L}}(\omega)$	Frequency-specific damping
μ_s, μ_d, μ_c	Friction coefficients
s	String number [0,1,2,3]
x_b	Bow-bridge distance [normalized]
F_b	Bow force [N]
v_b	Bow velocity [m/s]
x_f	Left-hand finger position [normalized]

Table 1: Physical constants and control variables used. A body impulse from each instrument was also recorded.

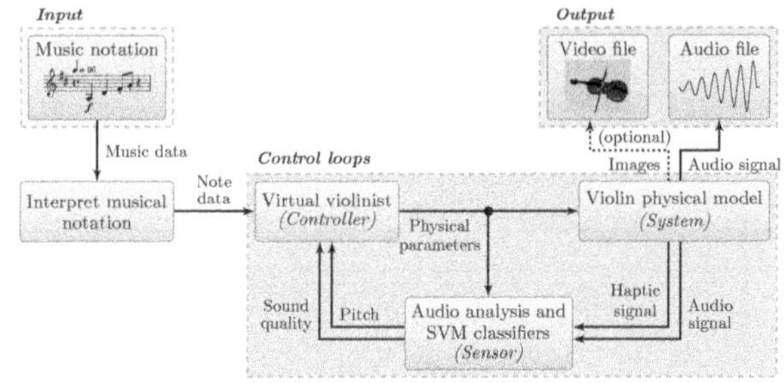

Figure 2: Overview of *Vivi, the Virtual Violinist.*

Finger forces were implemented as damped springs. The instrument body was modelled as a linear time-invariant system by convolving the sum of string outputs with 35 ms of a recorded impulse response. The library includes measurements of 5 violins, 2 violas, and 3 cellos. In addition to the audio output of the instrument body, the model also provides two signals for each string s: the audio output $A_s[t]$, and the right-hand haptic output arising from the force of the bow on the string $H_s[t]$. For further details, see [22].

3. INTELLIGENT FEEDBACK CONTROL

The mixed strength and curse of physical modelling is that it reproduces the real-world physics of instruments. When played by an expert musician, the results are very pleasing; however, as any parent or neighbour of a young child learning violin knows, when played by a novice the sounds can be rather harsh sounding. A violin is a complex system with many pitfalls which may not be apparent at first glance. For example, the pitch is not controlled exclusively from the left-hand finger placement: all actions of the bow (x_b, v_b, F_b) affect the pitch and can alter it by -70 to +20 cents[1] [28, 9]. Due to the non-linear friction equation, the string can react in a very different manner depending on those existing vibrations; furthermore, due to the stochastic $u(t)$ value, the string does not always react in the same manner. This is illustrated in Figure 3, and prompted us to use adaptive feedback control rather than preset control values.

[1]Cents are a logarithmic measurement system for musical pitch; given two pitches a and b, the cent $x = 1200 \cdot \log_2\left(\frac{b}{a}\right)$.

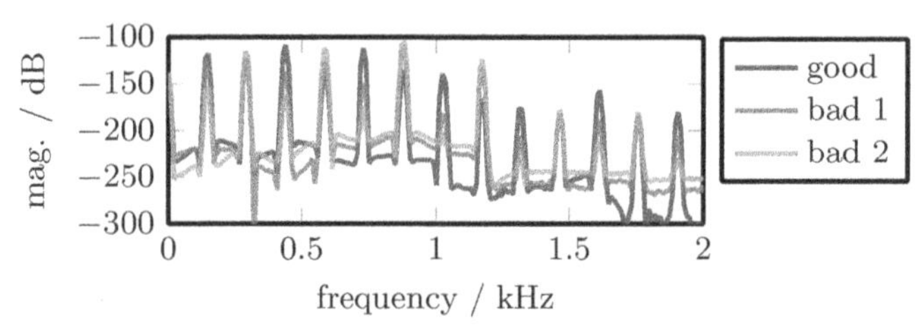

Figure 3: Different output with identical bowing parameters. Cello D string, bowed for 1 second with $x_b = 0.104$, $v_b = 0.5$ m/s, $F_b = 0.5$. The third example was created by bowing the string for 1 second with $v_b = -0.5$ m/s, then 1 more second after setting $v_b = 0.5$ m/s. There is a large different in the odd partials. Audio examples: `http://percival-music.ca/mm2013.html`

Note beginning	
p_s	Physical control variables as per Table 1
m_s	Target pitch (in MIDI)
k_b	Keep bow force (for slurs and ties)
k_e	Keep ears: do not reset pitch history (for ties)
y_b	Bow position along bow (for video output)
Note ending	
p_e	Physical control variables as per Table 1
m_e	Target pitch (in MIDI)
l_b	Lighten bow force (to change string cleanly)
k_v	Keep bow velocity (for slurs or "ring")

Table 2: Note modifiers: the musical score is separated into a series of notes, each of which is performed with the feedback control.

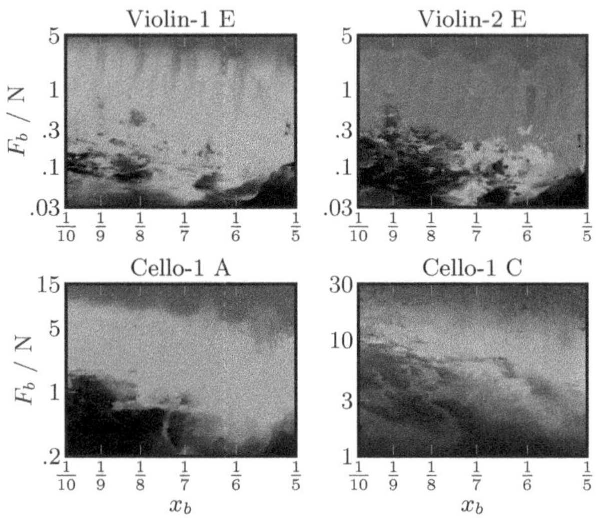

Figure 4: Schelleng diagrams of selected strings, the colour of each point indicating Red: standard deviation of spectral flatness measure (SFM); Green: mean of relative strength of f_0; Blue: mean of SFM. We desire a low standard deviation, strong f_0, and low SFM; so the best colour is light green.

To accommodate the variability of our instruments, we used feedback control (Figure 2). There are two feedback loops: bow control (timbre, from the right hand) and finger control (pitch, from the left hand). The precise behaviour of the control loops receives minor modifications based on the type of note (shown in Table 2), but those modifiers only apply to the beginning and ending of each note.

Past work [27, 30, 14, 9] simulated string behaviour with constant input parameters (or in the case of [14], constant bow acceleration) mapping the region of parameters which results in the desirable Helmholtz motion in which the bow slips once per cycle of the fundamental frequency of the sound [15]. These plots can provide valuable insights into the behaviour of the model. Schelleng famously predicted the range of bow forces which could establish Helmholtz motion for a given bow velocity and bow-bridge distance [27]. Schelleng's predictions were later tested with an automated machine [29], where it was found that the predicted maximum bow force was quite accurate, while the minimum bow

Dynamic	Bow position x_b (fraction of L)	Bow velocity v_b (m/s)
ff	0.104	0.50
f	0.118	0.42
mf	0.134	0.34
mp	0.154	0.26
p	0.176	0.18
pp	0.192	0.10

Table 3: Physical parameters determined by dynamic. The velocity will be negative for an upbow.

force differed from the predictions. Figure 4 shows "Schelleng diagrams" from empirical simulation. Each diagram was generated from one million simulations: 200 positions of x_b, 200 forces F_b, with each pair repeated 25 times to evaluate the stochastic behaviour. This exposes one problem of the modal simulation: on thin strings (e.g., violin E, cello A) the upper limit of F_b for good sound varies depending on whether x_b is close to a simply-rational position such as $\frac{1}{6}$.

To avoid the problematic bow positions x_b, we turned to real-world violin pedagogy [5], in which violinists are instructed to play in a specific bow position (termed "lanes on the Kreisler highway") for different dynamics. We take inspiration from another aspect of violin teaching, wherein the amount of bow for each note is often specified by the teacher (such as "half" or "quarter bow"), and the tempo is given by the piano accompaniment. Teachers sometimes direct students to imitate the teacher by playing music with the student (sometimes called the "mirror game"), in order to emphasize the amount of bow length to use. Students must therefore adjust their bow force to produce a good tone regardless of the teacher-imposed bow velocity. Acoustics research [28] showed that the overall loudness of a note is correlated with $\frac{v_b}{x_b}$. We set the bow velocity according to dynamic as well; the preset values for x_b and v_b are shown in Table 3.

3.1 Machine Learning and Active Learning

To train the computer to adjust the bow force F_b, we drew inspiration from human pedagogy: A human "teacher" will give judgements about simulated audio from the physical model. Those judgements are used to train a set of "virtual ears" which can then adjust the bow force in the absence of the teacher. This is analogous to young students practicing with the Suzuki violin method [34], in which a parent of the child is encouraged to aid in the home practice. Some poetic license is used here in calling the machine learning feedback "virtual ears". In addition to using the generated audio signal as input the supervise learning we also utilize a haptic signal from the bow's contact with the string. This "virtual finger" provides additional information that can help

Class c	Human judgement of sound	F_b in example
1	not audible	0.002 N
2	"wispy" or "whistling"	0.11 N
3	acceptable	0.83 N
4	"harsh" or "detuned"	5.32 N
5	not recognizable as violin sound	10.9 N

Table 4: Human judgements of bowing. Audio examples: `http://percival-music.ca/mm2013.html`

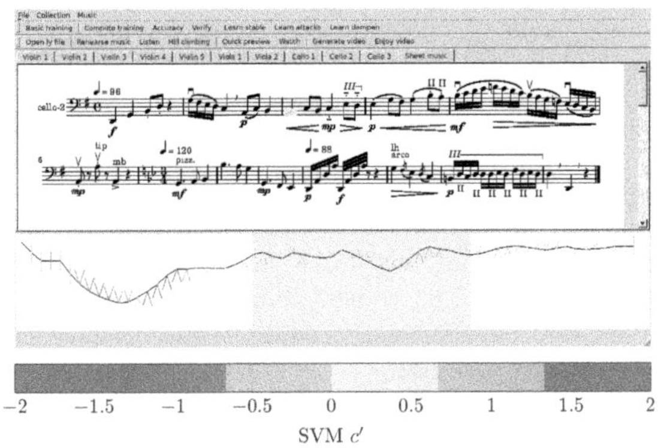

Figure 5: Screenshot of interactive training with our system. Middle portion of screen: the musical score with the first note in bar 3 highlighted. Bottom portion of the screen: shows the F_b used throughout the note (in black) and the SVM output c' (coloured arrows up or down); a portion of the SVM output has been selected (in yellow) for labelling and retraining.

String	Num.	String	Num.	String	Num.
Violin G	97	Viola C	59	Cello C	71
Violin D	67	Viola G	62	Cello G	68
Violin A	73	Viola D	54	Cello D	55
Violin E	56	Viola A	61	Cello A	99

Table 5: Number of examples in the datasets.

produce and maintain a good tone, intended to mimic a real musician's sensations in her bow hand.

There are five possible judgements about the sound, presented in Table 4. The initial training of the system takes place within an interactive python script, where the user freely adjusts F_b in order to create audio examples for each class. Once the initial training is complete, the user listens to music while watching the sheet music, and indicates any incorrect judgements by clicking on the note(s) in the score and labelling the questionable audio as shown in Figure 5.

Internally, features are extracted from the audio $A_s[t]$ from the currently-bowed string s, and haptic $H_s[t]$ output from the bow (Section 2). A standard set of features are extracted from each signal using Marsyas [35]. Time-domain features used were RMS, peak to average ratio, and zero crossings. Spectral-domain features used were the rolloff, centroid, relative energy in the f_0 peak, flatness measure, and power to average ratio. These features were computed on both the $A_s[t]$ and $H_s[t]$ signals and concatenated together. Finally, x_f and x_b were appended to the feature vectors. The resulting vectors were used to train one Support Vector Machine (SVM) classifier for each string. The "virtual ears" operate at 100 Hz, with a sampling rate of 44100 Hz, hop size of 441 samples, and window size of 2048 samples. There are a total of 12 SVMs, one for each string of each instrument. Once fully trained with the musical exercises in Section 4.3, the SVMs are very accurate (99.5%–100% accuracy in 10-fold cross-validation). Each training example in the databases (Table 5) consist of three files: audio data, haptic data, and musician actions.

3.2 Bow Control: Timbre

While performing a note, the "virtual ears" are used to dynamically adjust the bow force F_b in the simulation in order to fix any unpleasant sound. Concretely, the $A_s[t]$ and $H_s[t]$ signals from the currently bowed string s are fed into relevant SVM, which outputs a probability $p_c[h]$ that the input vector belongs to class c for hop h. We define the weighted mean of these probabilities $c'[h] = 3 - \frac{1}{5}\sum_{c=1}^{5} cp_c[h]$ to be used to adjust the bow force:

$$F_b[h+1] = \begin{cases} F_b^i & \text{if } h < W \\ e^{\ln(F_b[h]) - c'[h]K} & \text{else} \end{cases} \quad (3)$$

To avoid the initial transients which have little relation to the labelled audio from the sustained portion of the sound, we omit the first 30 ms (3 frames) from the control loop. We then begin filling the window, but avoid machine learning judgements until the window does not contain any uninitialized data (wait another 4 frames). We thus set $W = 7$. F_b^i and K are calibrated for each string, dynamic, and three pitches in Section 4. If the desired note parameters are not one of the calibrated values (e.g., a note in the middle of a *cresc.* or a different pitch), F_b^i and K are linearly interpolated from the nearest two calibrated values.

By default, notes are assumed to be détaché "on the string"; this is the first bow-stroke taught in the Suzuki method of violin playing [34]. In terms of the control loop, the bow force is non-zero before beginning to move the bow. The bow velocity v_b and position x_b are set based on the dynamics in Table 3. We experimented with setting v_b to 0 and accelerating to the target v_b, but this produced greater variability in the note attacks as the string would sometimes stabilize in undesirable states such as those shown in Figure 3. v_b is set to zero 50 ms before the ending of the note. For this final portion of the note, F_b is gradually reduced ($F_b(t+1) = 0.5 \cdot F_b(t)$) to avoid a sudden "pluck-like" sound which occurs if the bow force is suddenly set to zero.

The bow control loop is modified according to the following variables from Table 2. If k_b is enabled, then F_b^i is not used and $F_b(0)$ is retained from the final F_b in the previous note. If k_v is enabled, then then v_b is not set to zero at the ending of the note, and F_b is not reduced at the end of a note. In addition, F_b is not reduced if l_b is enabled.

3.3 Finger Control: Pitch

String players must adjust the finger position x_f to achieve correct intonation. Pitch detection was performed with the YINFFT algorithm, an extension [1] of the YIN algorithm [8]. The difference between the reference pitch and the output of YINFFT was taken modulo 12 to avoid octave errors; this value was median filtered with a filter of length 3, becoming the error term $e[h]$, which is used in

$$x_f[h+1] = \begin{cases} x_f[t] + K_M e[h] & \text{if } |e(t)| \geq 0.01 \\ x_f[t] & \text{else} \end{cases} \quad (4)$$

$K_M = 0.01$ and the cutoff of 0.01 MIDI pitch units were set experimentally.

The finger control loop is modified according to the following variables from Table 2. The reference pitch is always set according to m_s. If k_e is enabled, then the pitch filter buffer is not reset at the beginning of a new note.

3.4 Validating the Bow Controller

To verify that the feedback controller is useful, we performed a few tests comparing it with a naive set of actions (i.e. constant F_b). Past analysis of audio from violinists and cellists (i.e. focus on the performers) [2, 3] and violins (i.e. focus on the instrument) [36] used machine learning and statistical methods to distinguish good timbre from bad timbre, so we will do the same thing and rely on our "virtual ears" to provide judgements. Concretely, for each simulated note, we define the cost as the RMS of SVM judgements $c'[h]$ for all H frames. A cost of 0 indicates that the "virtual ears" found the note to be pleasing, while a cost of 2 indicates that the note had very bad timbre (either not audible or not recognizable as violin sound, as per Table 4).

$$\text{cost} = \sqrt{\frac{1}{H}\sum_{h=0}^{H}(c'[h])^2} \tag{5}$$

Three cases will be tested: the feedback loop as described, the feedback loop without haptic output, and disabling the feedback (i.e. using a constant F_b). Although F_b^i and K are normally calibrated (Section 4.2), for these evaluations we will vary F_b^i and fix K. While the feedback is active, we set $K = 0.05$; to disable the feedback, we set $K = 0$. In all cases, the "virtual ears" will provide SVM judgements $c'[h]$, but when $K = 0$, (Equation 3) will have no effect on F_b which will effectively disable the feedback control. Without the haptic signal, the lowest 10-fold cross-validation accuracy falls from 99.5% to 98.4%.

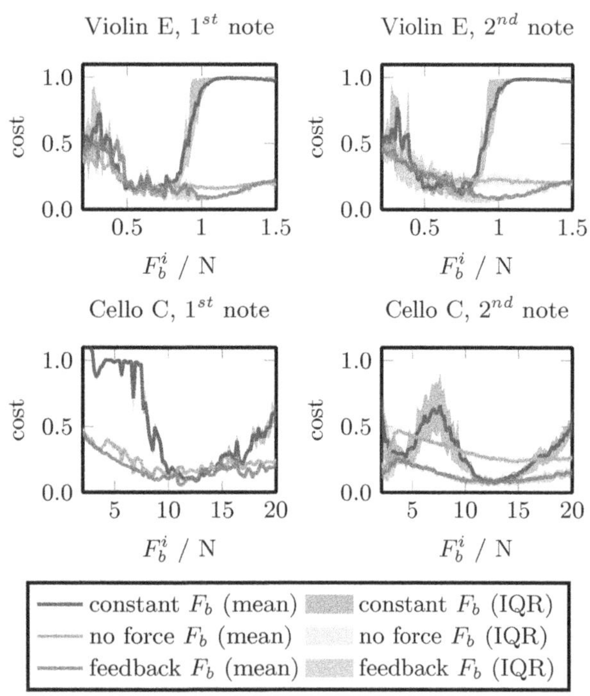

Figure 6: Comparison of naive vs. controlled performance of open strings *ff*, with the string initially at rest and then bowed for two notes. The range of costs arising from 50 simulations is shown by the inter-quartile range (IQR).

Figure 6 shows the system performing two notes (without resetting the string in between) on the two "extreme" open strings in the string quartet (violin E is the highest-pitch string, cello C is the lowest-pitch string). The feedback control is quite flexible, showing a lower cost if a poor F_b^i is used. However, if a good F_b^i is used (the middle of the F_b^i range shown), then there is only a small difference between the cost of a constant bow force and the feedback control. This is no surprise; the control loop exists to correct poor F_b values, and an optimal F_b requires no modification. In many cases of an optimal F_b, the string will either fall into Helmholtz motion during the initial attack (as discussed in Section 3.2, we omit the first 30 ms from the "virtual ears"), or else will reach Helmholtz motion soon thereafter as the string's vibrations evolve naturally under even a constant F_b. The effect of removing the haptic signal from the machine learning is not noticeable for the first note bowed, but the cost increases for the second note bowed. In some cases, the cost is higher than the optimal F_b^i values. This occurs if the "virtual ears" mistakenly directs the controller to change F_b when there is a good tone, or to move F_b in the wrong direction, then the timbre will suffer.

Although the pair of simulated notes failed to show a compelling advantage of feedback control over a finely-tuned constant F_b^i, the true strength of feedback control is revealed in the longer musical examples in Figure 7. Our system is trained interactively with users, so we wish to minimize the calibration time after each set of retraining. As a result, we rarely (if ever) have an optimal F_b^i. This is particularly relevant for notes requiring an F_b^i interpolated from two calibrated values. As shown in Figure 8, the system only calibrates three pitches for each string. A scale — especially a chromatic scale – requires a great deal of F_b^i values estimated from interpolating between calibrated values. The feedback controller with no haptic signals performed quite well with the regular scale but poorly on the C string. Closer examination of the data from the scale revealed that the cello D and A strings were "easier to play", in the sense that they easily produced good timbre. The distinction in playing difficulty was suggested by the Schelleng diagrams in Figure 4.

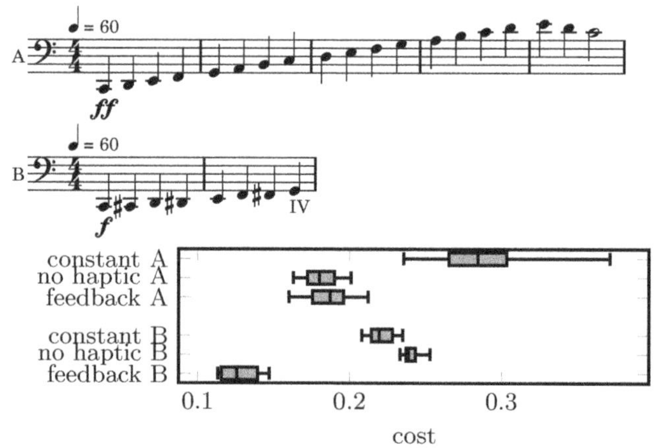

Figure 7: Comparison of naive vs. controlled performance of exercises, box plot of 10 simulations. Each box indicates the 25%, 50% (median), and 75% percentiles, while the whiskers indicate the minimum and maximum values.

Figure 8: "Basic fingers" evaluated for training and calibration. Only one string for each instrument is shown; other strings used the same positions (i.e. 0, 1, and 6 semitones above the open string).

4. CALIBRATION

The feedback control requires two values: the initial bow force F_b^i and rate of change K. These are calibrated with the trained machine learning and by performing simulations. This calibration is performed during the training sessions (at a time chosen by the user), so we were required to balance the quality of the calibrated values against the time users spend waiting. Values were calibrated for three finger positions for each string-dynamic pair, shown in Figure 8, On a modern desktop computer with four simultaneous threads operating, calibrating one string takes approximately five minutes.

4.1 Checking the SVM Behaviour

The 10-fold cross-correlation accuracy is computed for each SVM, but this does not guarantee that the SVM is adequate for controlling the bow force. If the training set does not cover the entire range of signals produced by the physical model, the SVM could be 100% accurate on a proper subset but not useful for controlling the model.

To check the behaviour, a series of simulations are performed. Checking the validity requires human attention, but this can be done visually instead of listening to each audio sample. A display similar to Figure 9 is shown, except that K is fixed at 0.05 and all three "basic fingers" are included in the same screen. A success "sanity test" is achieved if the extreme values of F_b^i on the left and right sides are red/dark and there exist some inner values in green/blue.

This process is also used to estimate the range of F_b to investigate in greater detail. It begins by using the maximum and minimum F_b values as F_b^i. After those two instances, it performs a binary search to find the boundary between the "too low", "too high", and "potentially good" F_b^i values. In particular, any simulation whose mean of c' is less than -0.1 is saved to a set of V_l; above 0.1 is V_h, while the remainder is V_m. At each step, two ratios are computed: $\frac{\min(V_m)}{\max(V_l)}$ and $\frac{\min(V_h)}{\max(V_m)}$, indicating the range between the low, middle, and high sets. The next exercise is computed with F_b^i being in the middle of the largest ratio. This is repeated until there are 9 examples.

4.2 Calibrating F_b^i and K

Once the SVM behaviour has been verified, we perform a grid search to find F_b^i and K (Figure 9. K is evaluated with 5 values linearly spaced from 0.0 to 0.2, while F_b^i is evaluated with 15 values linearly spaced from $\max(V_l)$ to $\min(V_h)$. Each (F_b^i, K) pair is evaluated by simulating 4 notes, all beginning from rest. As was done in Section 3.4, the cost of each pair is defined as the RMS of the c' judgements. An extremely high value of K can result in the system oscillating between F_b being too low and F_b being too high, particularly since the analysis window is slightly longer than 4 frames.

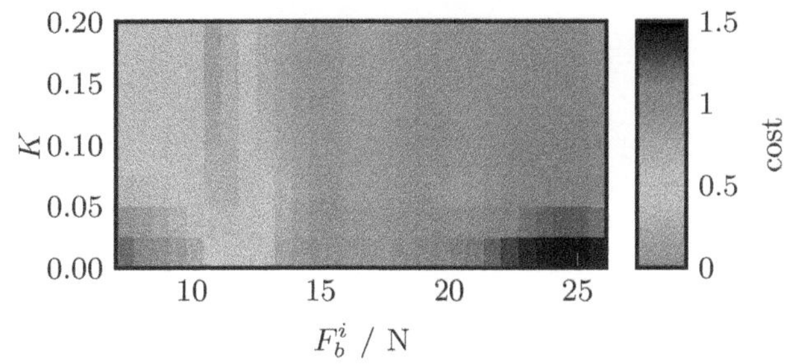

Figure 9: Calibrating Cello C, *ff*, open string

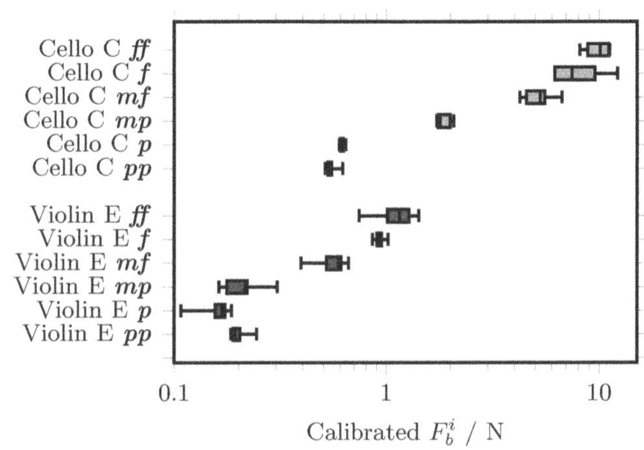

Figure 10: 10 calibrations of two open strings. Each box indicates the 25%, 50% (median), and 75% percentiles, while the whiskers indicate the minimum and maximum values.

Figure 10 shows multiple calibrations of two strings to demonstrate the reproducibility and usefulness of this step. There are clear differences in F_b^i for each string and dynamic.

4.3 Musical Exercises

After completing the initial calibration, the user is encouraged to listen to a number of musical exercises shown in Figure 11. This additional interactive training could be performed using any sheet music, but we prefer to use musical scales and exercises as they are traditionally a fundamental step in instrumental practice; as a musician, it "feels natural" to hear (and correct) mistakes in timbre by practicing scales. However, there are also solid technical reasons to practice scales before attempting more complicated music: it allows us to pinpoint and fix problems in isolation. Correcting mistakes in musical exercises involves a certain amount of repetition – identify a few mistakes, label them, retrain the SVM, then perform the exercise again. Retraining the SVM takes approximately five seconds provided that we skip the F_b^i stage, and simulating any of the exercises shown in Figure 11 takes less than one second. Longer music (naturally) takes more time to simulate, and longer to listen to. The musical exercises cover most of the potential problems which would be found in real music, so it is appropriate to ensure that the performance of these exercises is satisfactory before attempting more complicated sheet music.

Figure 11: Musical exercises; the first two scales are performed with all six dynamics, while the *cresc.* / *decresc.* is performed as notated.

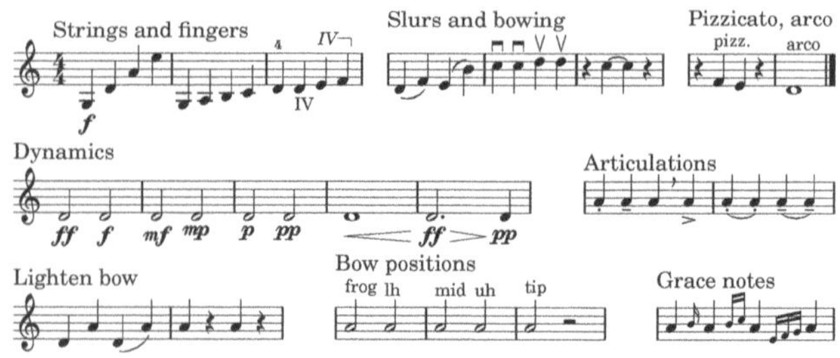

Figure 12: Musical notation understood

5. INTERPRETATION OF NOTATION

Our system interprets sheet music written for the LilyPond[2] music engraver. Music in MusicXML format can be converted to LilyPond using the `musicxml2ly` tool. Musical events (e.g., notes, slurs, dynamics) are extracted from LilyPond using scheme (a lisp variant). Figure 12 shows the musical notation which is supported. Once a list of music events has been obtained, they must be mapped onto the mid-level note modifiers described in Table 2.

Some musical notation has a clear meaning, but many elements of notation have no fixed meaning. The latter category is known amongst musicians as "interpretation", and is a matter of research and debate about historical performance practices, the composer's intentions, and/or the performer's desires. Since this paper focuses on the feedback control and interactive training of a string quartet, we avoided the question of interpretation by simply hard-coding values for ambiguous notation. Since the system was initially trained with the music in Suzuki violin books 1 and 2 [34], we chose constants which sounded best for Baroque and Classical music.

Unless otherwise specified, the system assumes that each note is played on the highest string s which can produce the desired pitch; in more musical terms, it assumes that all notes are in first position, other than higher-position notes on the E string. The finger position x_f and reference pitch m_s are set according to equal temperament. As discussed in Section 3, dynamics set x_b and v_b to the somewhat-arbitrary values specified in Table 3. Gradual changes of dynamics (*cresc.* or *decresc.*) are assumed to be a linear interpolation of x_b and v_b between the starting and ending dynamic. If the pitch is one of the "basic finger" positions, then F_b^i and K are set according to the parameters determined in Section 4. If the pitch is between 1 and 6 semitones above an open string, the parameters are linearly interpolated between those calibrated values. Finger positions higher than 6 semitones will have F_b^i and K set as the value calibrated for 6 semitones. When two or more notes are connected with a slur, the bow direction does not change between notes. In particular, v_b does not alternate, and the interior notes have k_b and k_v enabled. Two notes connected with a tie receive the same treatment, with the addition that the second note of the enables k_e. The bow direction can be specified with downbow and upbow signs. These set v_b as indicated, but do not enable k_b or k_v. In other words, the bow velocity returns to 0 at the end of each note, and each note begins with a new F_b^i.

[2]`http://lilypond.org`

Staccato and *portato* articulations indicate that the note should be shorter, but their exact musical meaning varies based on historical period, composer, and even the musician's personal style. We arbitrarily set a *staccato* note's duration to be 0.7 times the original duration (followed by a rest which is 0.3 times the original duration); a *portato* note is 0.9 times the original duration (again followed by a rest). When these articulations occur within a slur, they behave similar to two downbows in a row — the bow direction does not change but the bow velocity decelerates to 0 at the end of each note. A breath mark sets the previous note to 0.5 times the original duration (followed by a rest). In addition, the note has the additional modifier k_v. An accent indicates that the note should be "stronger". In our system, this is interpreted as doubling that note's F_b^i.

On a real violin, playing closer to the frog results in a heavier bow (increased F_b), while playing closer to the tip results in a lighter bow. However, this aspect of violin mechanics is not included in the physical model, so these indications are purely cosmetic for the video generation. The notation "frog" sets the bow-contact point along the bow hair to 0.0; "lh" (lower half) is arbitrarily 0.2, "mid" is 0.5, "uh" (upper half) is 0.8, and "tip" is 1.0.

Grace notes are implemented by "stealing" duration from the previous note. The duration of grace notes is fixed to be half of the notated duration; this is a reasonable approximation of the usual interpretation musicians use for grace notes.

6. VIDEO OUTPUT

In order to allow users to easily visualize the musical performances, we added computer animation using Blender[3], an open-source computer graphics suite which provides python bindings, allowing us to automatically convert any set of physical actions into computer animations. Using a physical model for the sound synthesis and animation allows the final product to blend seamlessly, in contrast to sampling approaches in which the animations are an entirely separate process from the sound generation. We only have one model (the violin in Figure 13); to create animations for other instruments, we use alternate camera angles as shown in Figure 1.

The bowing action places the bow on the string at position x_b, finding the location by linearly interpolating between the two ends of the relevant string. The contact point along the bow hair is found by linearly interpolating between the two ends of the bow hair according to the position along the bow hair given by the bow velocity.

[3]`http://www.blender.org`

Figure 13: Close-up of violin animation. The orange cones on the fingerboard indicate finger positions; this violin is playing a rolled A major chord. Video examples: `http://percival-music.ca/mm2013.html`

The four strings are not oriented on a single plane; the two inner strings are farther away from the instrument body than the two outer strings. This displacement is necessary to allow the bow to play each string without touching the other strings. The bow hair must therefore be placed at a different angle for each string. For each inner strings, the angle is set to be parallel to the adjacent strings (e.g., when the bow is on the A string, the bow hair is parallel to a vector from the E to D string). For the two outer strings, those angles are increased.

The video for each instrument in a string quartet is generated independently, then the images are concatenated to copy the normal seating arrangement of a string quartet, with violin 1 being in the bottom-left position and cello in the bottom-right. The audio for each instrument is generated as a monophonic audio file, but are mixed together with the instruments being panned linearly from -0.5 to 0.5.

7. DISCUSSION AND FUTURE WORK

The music created by our system is not suitable for most commercial applications. While physical modelling has the potential to allow more expressive music than than sampling-based approaches, this comes at the cost of increased difficulty of control, requiring highly skilled (virtual) musicians to achieve high-quality musical performances. Professional musicians require thousands of hours of deliberate practice to learn their craft [11]. The feedback control in our system does not completely replicate those years of training; the final audio contains occasional harsh attacks and squeaks, in a manner similar to the sounds produced by human students with a few years of training. This may be a boon for composers writing for student musicians, but most practical applications of synthesis would benefit from alternate methods rather than our system at the present time.

We plan to quantify the perceived quality of our music. We will perform a double-blind listening test, where participants will judge two or more performances of the same musical work. Participants will be asked to rank each performance on two axes: the quality of the performance, and the degree to which the performance is "human-like". One performance will be from our system, another from a commercial notation software package, and additional copies from any research projects which can create string quartet music. If the latter is not possible, then we will compare music from solo instruments rather than quartets. We will use established metrics such as the Friedman test and the Wilcoxon signed-rank test for evaluating the significance of our findings. In case the listener's musical background is a factor, we will conduct the survey with two groups: string players, and the general public.

There are a number of ways that we hope to improve the control loops. The present system relies on users with some amount of musical skill ($\approx$ 1 year of violin lessons) to judge whether the bow force F_b should be increased or decreased. We would like to remove even this small amount of background knowledge. Ideally, users would simply judge whether the audio was good or bad, and the system would determine the corrections required via more sophisticated machine learning which track time or state such as Hidden Markov Models and/or further calibration routines.

An alternate approach would be to deliberately imitate specific performances; this follows real-life violin pedagogy. Suzuki violin students are explicitly given audio recordings so that they can learn from them by attempting to imitate the recordings' sound. In addition to audio timbre distance metrics, such a system could involve video to estimate bow velocity or even bow-bridge distance. This type of approach was used by VocaListener and VocaWatcher [13] to create performances with Vocaloid singing synthesis [17] and a humanoid robot which matched a recording of a human singer.

The present system focuses on the low-level control, and used hard-coded values for many expressive musical decisions such as the length of *staccato* notes. Future work will provide a GUI to allow users to easily modify such stylistic decisions, allowing them to personalize the audio performances. There is an active research community focused on expressive computer music performances for piano music [16], but in the immediate future our goal is to give humans better/easier control over such decisions in a manner similar to Vocaloid.

Finally, we will add vibrato (an oscillation of the left-hand finger). This is a skill taught to musicians with 3–4 years of experience, and will likely require some musical analysis to suggest which note(s) should receive vibrato and which notes should be played "straight".

8. CONCLUSION

We have developed a method of synthesizing audio and animated video from musical notation. Unlike most existing music synthesizers, our method uses no recorded samples from musicians, instead using physical modelling and supervised machine learning to generate audio. This allows new instruments (e.g., a second distinct-sounding violin) to be added to the system with minimal effort. The machine learning and calibration routines are sufficiently flexible to apply to 4 violins, 2 violas, and 2 cellos with no manual tuning of constants.

To foster future research in this area, all code and data is available[4] under permissive copyleft licenses.

9. ACKNOWLEDGEMENTS

Many thanks to Marcos Press for creating the violin and bow models in Blender, and releasing it under the GPLv3.

[4]`http://percival-music.ca/vivi.html`

10. REFERENCES

[1] P. Brossier. *Automatic Annotation of Musical Audio for Interactive Applications.* PhD thesis, Queen Mary University, London, 2006.

[2] J. Charles, D. Fitzgerald, and E. Coyle. Violin sound quality detection. In *Irish Signals and Systems Conference*, 2008.

[3] M. Chudy and S. Dixon. Recognizing Cello Performers Using Timbre Models. Technical Report EECSRR-12-01, Queen Mary Uni., London, 2012.

[4] D. Cohn, L. Atlas, and R. Ladner. Improving generalization with active learning. *Machine Learning*, 15(2), 1994.

[5] C. D. Collins. *Connecting Science and the Musical Arts in Teaching Tone Quality: Integrating Helmholtz Motion and Master Violin Teachers' Pedagogies.* PhD thesis, George Mason University, 2009.

[6] P. R. Cook. A Hierarchical System for Controlling Synthesis by Physical Modeling. In *International Computer Music Conference*, Banff, Canada, 1995.

[7] R. B. Dannenberg and I. Derenyi. Combining instrument and performance models for high-quality music synthesis. *J. of New Music Res.*, 27(3), 1998.

[8] A. de Cheveigné and H. Kawahara. YIN, a fundamental frequency estimator for speech and music. *J. of the Acoustical Society of America*, 111(4), 2002.

[9] M. Demoucron. *On the control of virtual violins: Physical modelling and control of bowed string instruments.* PhD thesis, IRCAM, Paris, 2008.

[10] J. W. Dunn, D. Byrd, M. Notess, J. Riley, and R. Scherle. Variations2: retrieving and using music in an academic setting. *Comm. ACM*, 49(8), 2006.

[11] K. A. Ericsson, R. T. Krampe, and C. Tesch-Römer. The role of deliberate practice in the acquisition of expert performance. *Psychological Rev.*, 100(3), 1993.

[12] R. Fiebrink, P. R. Cook, and D. Trueman. Human model evaluation in interactive supervised learning. In *CHI '11*, 2011.

[13] M. Goto, T. Nakano, S. Kajita, Y. Matsusaka, S. Nakaoka, and K. Yokoi. VocaListener and VocaWatcher: Imitating a human singer by using signal processing. In *ICASSP*, 2012.

[14] K. Guettler. On the creation of the helmholtz motion in bowed strings. *Acta Acustica united with Acustica*, 88(6):970–985, 2002.

[15] H. L. F. Helmholtz. *On the sensations of tone as a physiological basis for the theory of music.* Longmans, Green, London, 3rd edition, 1895. A. J. Ellis (transl.).

[16] H. Katayose, M. Hashida, G. De Poli, and K. Hirata. On Evaluating Systems for Generating Expressive Music Performance: the Rencon Experience. *J. of New Music Research*, 41(4), 2012.

[17] H. Kenmochi and H. Ohshita. VOCALOID – Commercial singing synthesizer based on sample concatenation. In *Interspeech*, 2007.

[18] E. Lindemann. Music Synthesis with Reconstructive Phrase Modeling. *Signal Processing Magazine, IEEE*, 24(2), 2007.

[19] E. Maestre. *Modeling instrumental gestures: an analysis/synthesis framework for violin bowing.* PhD thesis, Universitat Pompeu Fabra, 2009.

[20] M. E. McIntyre, R. Schumacher, and J. Woodhouse. On the oscillations of musical instruments. *J. of the Acoustical Society of America*, 74(5), 1983.

[21] B. Pardo, D. Little, and D. Gergle. Building a personalized audio equalizer interface with transfer learning and active learning. In *ACM MIRUM*, 2012.

[22] G. Percival. *Physical Modelling meets Machine Learning: Performing Music with a Virtual String Ensemble.* PhD thesis, University of Glasgow, 2013.

[23] G. Percival, N. Bailey, and G. Tzanetakis. Physical Modeling meets Machine Learning: Teaching Bow Control to a Virtual Violinist. In *Sound and Music Conference*, 2011.

[24] A. Pérez. *Enhancing Spectral Synthesis Techniques with Performance Gestures using the Violin as a Case Study.* PhD thesis, Universitat Pompeu Fabra, 2009.

[25] A. Perez Carrillo and M. M. Wanderley. Learning and extraction of violin instrumental controls from audio signal. In *ACM MIRUM*, 2012.

[26] G. P. Scavone and P. R. Cook. RtMidi, RtAudio, and a synthesis toolkit (STK) update. *ICMC*, 2005.

[27] J. C. Schelleng. The bowed string and the player. *J. of the Acoustical Society of America*, 53(1), 1973.

[28] E. Schoonderwaldt. The violinist's sound palette: spectral centroid, pitch flattening and anomalous low frequencies. *Acta Acustica united with Acustica*, 95(5), 2009.

[29] E. Schoonderwaldt, K. Guettler, and A. Askenfelt. Schelleng in retrospect – a systematic study of bow force limits for bowed violin strings. In *ISMA*, 2007.

[30] S. Serafin, J. O. Smith III, and J. Woodhouse. An investigation of the impact of torsion waves and friction characteristics on the playability of virtual bowed strings. In *Applications of Signal Processing to Audio and Acoustics, 1999 IEEE Workshop on*, 1999.

[31] X. Serra and J. Smith. Spectral modeling synthesis: A sound analysis/synthesis system based on a deterministic plus stochastic decomposition. *Computer Music Journal*, 14(4):12–24, 1990.

[32] J. O. Smith. Physical Modeling Using Digital Waveguides. *Computer Music Journal*, 16(4), 1992.

[33] J. O. Smith. *Physical Audio Signal Processing.* online book, accessed 2012-Jan, 2010.

[34] S. Suzuki. *Violin Part Volume 1.* Summy-Birchard Music, 1978.

[35] G. Tzanetakis. Marsyas: a case study in implementing Music Information Retrieval Systems. In S. Shen and L. Cui, editors, *Intelligent Music Information Systems: Tools and Methodologies.* Information Science Reference, 2007.

[36] P. Wrzeciono and K. Marasek. Violin Sound Quality: Expert Judgements and Objective Measurements. In Z. Ras and A. Wieczorkowska, editors, *Advances in Music Information Retrieval*, volume 274. Springer Berlin / Heidelberg, 2010.

[37] J. Yin, Y. Wang, and D. Hsu. Digital violin tutor: an integrated system for beginning violin learners. In *ACM Multimedia*, 2005.

[38] D. Young. Wireless sensor system for measurement of violin bowing parameters. In *Stockholm Music Acoustics Conference*, 2003.

Using Quadratic Programming to Estimate Feature Relevance in Structural Analyses of Music

Jordan B. L. Smith
Centre for Digital Music
Queen Mary University of London
Mile End Road, London, UK
jordan.smith@eecs.qmul.ac.uk

Elaine Chew
Centre for Digital Music
Queen Mary University of London
Mile End Road, London, UK
elaine.chew@eecs.qmul.ac.uk

ABSTRACT

To identify repeated patterns and contrasting sections in music, it is common to use self-similarity matrices (SSMs) to visualize and estimate structure. We introduce a novel application for SSMs derived from audio recordings: using them to learn about the potential reasoning behind a listener's annotation. We use SSMs generated by musically-motivated audio features at various timescales to represent contributions to a structural annotation. Since a listener's attention can shift among musical features (e.g., rhythm, timbre, and harmony) throughout a piece, we further break down the SSMs into section-wise components and use quadratic programming (QP) to minimize the distance between a linear sum of these components and the annotated description. We posit that the optimal section-wise weights on the feature components may indicate the features to which a listener attended when annotating a piece, and thus may help us to understand why two listeners disagreed about a piece's structure. We discuss some examples that substantiate the claim that feature relevance varies throughout a piece, using our method to investigate differences between listeners' interpretations, and lastly propose some variations on our method.

Categories and Subject Descriptors

H.5.5 [Sound and Music Computing]: Methodologies and Techniques.

General Terms

Algorithms, Measurement, Experimentation, Human Factors, Theory.

Keywords

Music structure analysis, music perception, music cognition, repetition, quadratic programming.

1. INTRODUCTION

One of the most important aspects of music is that it is repetitive: individual sounds, notes and chords, dynamic gestures, rhythmic patterns, instrumentations, and so forth are all elements liable to repeat, whether identically or with some variation. The structure of repeating elements, while an abstract concept, is itself one of the most salient aspects of music to a listener. In a formal analysis, a listener can indicate which sections they believe are repetitions, and many of those studying music theory and music perception are interested in discovering how listeners make the analysis decisions they do. The task of discovering repetitions is also important in music information retrieval (MIR), since many MIR tasks can be performed or improved upon using information about music structure: for example, cover song detection [12] and chord transcription [19].

Recurrence plots, proposed by [4] for analyzing the motion of dynamical systems, can reveal repetitions in sequential data. A self-similarity matrix (SSM), originally proposed by [7], is a variation on such plots that moves beyond the usual feature-based methods of visualizing music, such as pitch rolls and other time-frequency representations. Unlike these, SSMs do not represent the musical content itself, but only the pattern of repetitions and recurrences that it contains. The features themselves are of course still important in any given application: an SSM based on pitch content may be effective for tracking melodic repetitions but not repetitions of percussive sounds. In MIR, SSMs have proven highly useful for estimating the large-scale structure that listeners find salient (for a review, see [27]).

In this article, we argue that SSMs could also be used for the inverse problem: studying the annotations of listeners to discover what aspects of the music they found salient. In particular, we show how the multiple SSMs generated from different features, as well as the segmentation of the listener, can be exploited to model which features were more important at which point in the piece. The approach is premised on the assumption that the structure of a piece of music can be represented as the weighted sum of feature matrix components, and that by finding the weights of these feature components, we in essence can model the potential reasons a listener might give to justify the analysis.

Accounting for listener attention is a key aspect of user modelling, for example, in music recommendation systems and user-centered music interfaces. The emphasis in this article is on motivating and defining a novel methodology, supported by several real-world examples. The approach has the potential for extensions to other multimedia domains—for example, to relate video annotations with time series data.

1.1 Previous methods in SSM calculation

Whereas earlier experiments with extracting structure based on SSMs focused on one feature at a time (e.g., [7] made SSMs de-

MM '13, October 21 - 25 2013, Barcelona, Spain

ACM 978-1-4503-2404-5/13/10...$15.00.
http://dx.doi.org/10.1145/2502081.2502124

rived only from Mel-frequency cepstral coefficients (MFCCs), and [1] used only chroma for chorus detection), it was soon realized that using multiple features could improve results. Eronen [6] calculated SSMs from MFCCs and chroma and summed the result, while [18] obtained three SSMs from chroma vectors, each calculated to reflect repetitions at different time scales, and took the element-wise product of the trio to reduce noise. Paulus & Klapuri's [26] optimization-based approach used information from separate SSMs reflecting timbral, harmonic and rhythmic similarity. In order to find transposed repetitions, [11] searched for maxima across multiple chroma-based SSMs. Rather than generate separate SSMs for separate features, [13] concatenated the features vectors for each frame and calculated a single SSM from the result.

However, simple combinations of SSMs rarely result in the exact structure that the experimenter hopes to extract. While SSMs provide an intuitive visualization of a piece, successful methods of automatic music analysis based on SSMs invariably employ complex post-processing steps to obtain the answer: this has taken the form of low- and high-pass filtering [11], erosion/dilation operations [21], dynamic programming [30], non-negative matrix factorization (NMF) [16], re-emphasis of transitive relationships [29], and so on. We may conclude that a simple sum of SSMs does not reflect the similarity judgements that a listener may make across an entire piece.

What information could the sum of SSMs be missing? One straightforward suggestion is a weight for each feature. Perceptual evidence supports this strategy: for example, in investigating the relative importance of different laws in a Generative Theory of Tonal Music, [10] found that laws relating to some features are more important than others. The idea to tune feature weights before analyzing structure has appeared before: to improve a structural segmentation algorithm, [25] chose feature weights to maximize the separability of vectors according to the Fisher criterion. In [15], the size of the window for calculating features was adapted to the estimated rate of change, improving the clarity of block patterns in SSMs. A hierarchical SSM proposed by [14] used different features and techniques at each time scale in a musicologically-informed manner.

Another aspect of listening that may be missed when SSMs are combined is that the focus of a listener's attention may shift at various points throughout a piece. For example, the self-similarity of a chorus of a given song may be very well accounted for by an SSM based on harmony, whereas the self-similarity of the guitar solo that follows may not be. Again, listener studies such as [2] and [3] demonstrate that the justifications listeners give for perceiving section boundaries can vary throughout a piece.

In the next section, we present a method of combining SSMs to exploit these facts of music perception—namely, that musical features vary in their relative salience, and that the attention of the listener is drawn to different features throughout a piece. Unlike previous work on adaptive parameter setting in music structure analysis [14, 15, 25], our aim is not to predict structure, but to discover connections between an audio recording and an accompanying analysis. Briefly put, our approach breaks a set of SSMs derived from various features into submatrix components, and then finds the optimal set of components to reconstruct the description of a piece given by a listener. The method may help those studying the cognition of musical form by illustrating what features best explain each part of the analysis. It may also be used to suggest reasons that two listeners disagree about the structure of a piece, an application discussed in Section 3.

2. PROPOSED METHOD

We first review how to calculate an SSM from acoustic data or from an annotation. In Section 2.2 we motivate our approach and explain the mathematics using a simple example, and in Section 2.3 demonstrate its use on the song "Yellow Submarine" by The Beatles.

2.1 Self-similarity matrix calculation

A self-similarity matrix (SSM), proposed by [7], can be thought of as a real-valued recurrence plot where element e_{ij} indicates the similarity between frame i and frame j of a sequence of frames. It is typical to use Euclidean or cosine distance [27] as a distance metric; here, we use cosine distance for its natural scaling between -1 and 1. Repeated sequences in recurrence plots are revealed as diagonal lines. In SSMs based on music, it is also common to see off-diagonal blocks, revealing the repetition of sections that are homogenous with respect to a given feature.

2.1.1 SSMs from annotations

Binary SSMs are commonly generated from structural annotations as diagrams (e.g., [27]) or to illustrate examples of song structure. Using cosine similarity, we set $e_{ij} = 1$ if frames i and j belong to sections with the same label, and -1 otherwise (see example in Figure 1). This section describes some variations on the usual approach that is relevant for our data.

The annotation in Figure 1, like all the examples in this article, are drawn from the Structural Analysis of Large Amounts of Music Information (SALAMI) dataset [31]. In the SALAMI annotation format, information about repeating sections is given at large and a small time scale, and sections may be distinguished with prime symbols (e.g., A vs. A'), which fuzzily indicates similarity with variation.

We include some of the richness of this description in the SSM by generating a separate SSM for each timescale and summing the

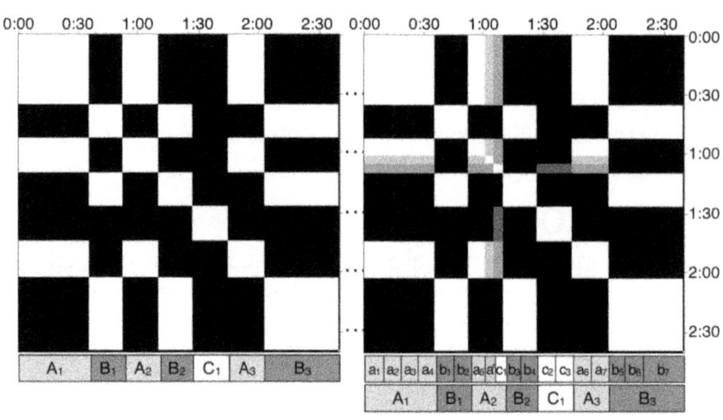

Figure 1. Left: SSM derived from annotation of "Yellow Submarine." Time progresses from left to right and from top to bottom. The large-scale annotation below it is from the SALAMI database (salami_id: 1634). Right: An alternative SSM derived using an additional layer of the annotation, where α, the relative weight of the large-scale labels, is set at 0.625 and β, the fractional similarity implied by primes, is 0.35.

results (see Figure 1). To emphasize one time scale over another, we can choose a weighting parameter $0 < \alpha < 1$, and multiply the large- and small-scale SSMs by α and $1 - \alpha$, respectively, before summing. A similar approach can act on prime symbols: when two frames have the same label but differ by a prime, instead of setting $e_{ij} = 1$, we can set it to some other value $-1 < \beta < 1$. Setting $\beta = 1$ would imply that A and A' are identical; $\beta = -1$ would imply they are completely distinct; and $\beta = 0$ would ignore the symbol.

2.1.2 SSMs from audio

The five different SSMs in Figure 2 were all calculated from a recording of "Yellow Submarine". Each one represents a different musical parameter: timbre, pitch, rhythm, tempo, and loudness.

MFCCs derive from the shape of a rescaled spectrum and hence can characterize a sound's timbre; chroma vectors estimate the power of each pitch class and hence characterize the harmonic content of the audio; fluctuation patterns (FPs) estimate the strength of low-frequency periodicities within Bark-scale frequency bands over windows that are several seconds long and hence characterize the rhythmic content [24]; periodicity histograms reflect the relative strength of different tempi by looking at sharp attacks in the audio and measuring the strength of periodicities in the tempo range of 40 to 240 bpm (0.6 to 4 Hz) [23]; and finally, the root mean square (RMS) of the waveform and the derivative of RMS estimate loudness and dynamic variations.

MFCCs and chroma were calculated using 0.19- and 0.10-second windows, respectively, with 50% overlap, using Queen Mary's Vamp Plugin set [17]. The twelve lowest MFCCs were kept, aside from the first, which correlates with loudness. FPs and periodicity histograms were calculated using 3-second windows and 0.37-second hops with the MA Toolbox [22]. FP vectors have 1200 elements, measuring 60 modulation frequencies in 20 Bark-scale frequency bands, while periodicity histograms have 2000 elements, indicating whenever any of 40 tempo ranges is activated beyond 50 fixed thresholds. While it is common to use dimensional reduction techniques to reduce the large size of the feature vectors, the relative differences between the raw vectors are still

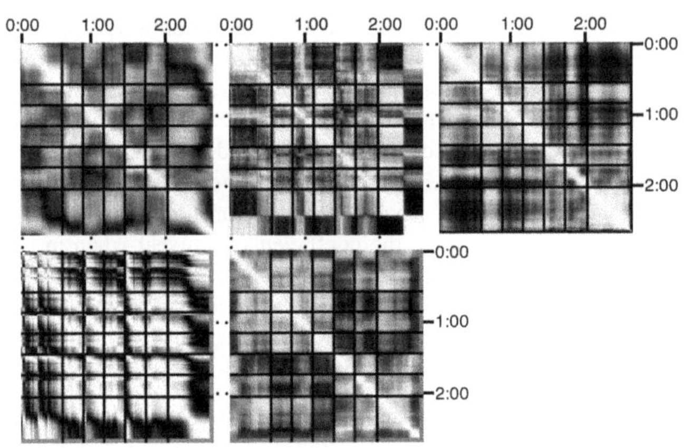

Figure 2. Five SSMs calculated from a recording of "Yellow Submarine." Highly similar frames produce white pixels, dissimilar frames produce black, and independent frames gray. From left to right, the SSMs represent (top row) MFCCs, chroma, FPs, and (bottom row) RMS, and periodicity histograms. The black lines indicate the boundaries of the structural annotation seen in Figure 1.

well captured in the SSMs in Figure 2. Lastly, RMS was calculated using 0.1-second windows and 50% overlap.

Each of the above features gives, for every frame, a vector of some length. We transformed the values in two ways: first, each vector dimension was standardized over the length of the piece to have zero mean and unit variance. Since no frame-wise normalization was used for any feature, this ensures the variance in each dimension is weighed equally, ensuring that repetitions in low-magnitude signals are detected albeit at the cost of some additional noise. The features were then smoothed in time; for the SSMs in Figure 2, a 10-second moving-average filter was used. Finally, the SSMs were calculated using cosine similarity.

2.2 Combining SSMs

Suppose we have an annotation for a song's structure, expressed as an SSM like in Figure 1, and want to find how best to explain it in terms of SSMs generated from the song's acoustic features, like those in Figure 2. We know that summing the feature matrices is a useful technique, and since we have the annotation we could try to calculate the optimal linear combination of feature matrices to reconstruct the annotation. This would provide a relative weight to each feature corresponding to its salience with respect to the entire song. However, knowing that the salience of different features can vary throughout the piece, we may wish to explain the annotation section by section.

Previous approaches to decomposing SSMs focused on discovering the structure of recordings, and hence used estimation techniques such as singular value decomposition [9] or NMF [16]. However, since our goal is to learn about the relationship between the known structure and the recording, we can use straightforward optimization techniques. We propose to use a quadratic program (QP), a generic formulation of an optimization problem, to find the optimal combination of feature-derived SSMs to derive the annotation-derived SSM in a piecewise fashion.

To illustrate the approach, we use a very simple example: suppose we have a piece with structure ABC, where the last section is twice as long as the previous sections (in general we may have s sections). The annotation matrix N could be:

$$N = \begin{bmatrix} 1 & -1 & -1 & -1 \\ -1 & 1 & -1 & -1 \\ -1 & -1 & 1 & 1 \\ -1 & -1 & 1 & 1 \end{bmatrix}$$

Recall that -1 indicates a contrasting pair and $+1$ indicates an identical pair. We would like to explain the reason behind each section using two features: a harmony-based feature and a timbre-based feature. (Again, in general we may have f features.) Suppose the pitch content of the song is identical for sections A and B, and the timbre is identical for sections B and C. For example, A, B and C could be the introduction, verse and chorus of a pop song, where the instrumentation changes after the introduction but stays constant thereafter, and where the pattern of chords only changes at the chorus. The two matrices F_1 and F_2, derived from the harmonic and timbral audio features, respectively, would be:

$$F_1 = \begin{bmatrix} 1 & 1 & -1 & -1 \\ 1 & 1 & -1 & -1 \\ -1 & -1 & 1 & 1 \\ -1 & -1 & 1 & 1 \end{bmatrix} \qquad F_2 = \begin{bmatrix} 1 & -1 & -1 & -1 \\ -1 & 1 & 1 & 1 \\ -1 & 1 & 1 & 1 \\ -1 & 1 & 1 & 1 \end{bmatrix}$$

Neither matrix equals the true underlying structure N, but we would like to reconstruct the annotation matrix using subsets of the feature matrices that correspond to the annotated sections. Since there are three sections and two feature matrices, there are six available components, shown below. We can generate these by applying three "masks," one for each section, to each feature. $M_{i,j}$, the element-wise product of the jth mask with F_i, will show how the jth section relates to the other sections with respect to the ith feature.

$$M_{1,1} = \begin{bmatrix} 1 & .5 & -.5 & -.5 \\ .5 & 0 & 0 & 0 \\ -.5 & 0 & 0 & 0 \\ -.5 & 0 & 0 & 0 \end{bmatrix} \qquad M_{2,1} = \begin{bmatrix} 1 & -.5 & -.5 & -.5 \\ -.5 & 0 & 0 & 0 \\ -.5 & 0 & 0 & 0 \\ -.5 & 0 & 0 & 0 \end{bmatrix}$$

$$M_{1,2} = \begin{bmatrix} 0 & .5 & 0 & 0 \\ .5 & 1 & -.5 & -.5 \\ 0 & -.5 & 0 & 0 \\ 0 & -.5 & 0 & 0 \end{bmatrix} \qquad M_{2,2} = \begin{bmatrix} 0 & -.5 & 0 & 0 \\ -.5 & 1 & .5 & .5 \\ 0 & .5 & 0 & 0 \\ 0 & .5 & 0 & 0 \end{bmatrix}$$

$$M_{1,3} = \begin{bmatrix} 0 & 0 & -.5 & -.5 \\ 0 & 0 & -.5 & -.5 \\ -.5 & -.5 & 1 & 1 \\ -.5 & -.5 & 1 & 1 \end{bmatrix} \qquad M_{3,2} = \begin{bmatrix} 0 & 0 & -.5 & -.5 \\ 0 & 0 & .5 & .5 \\ -.5 & .5 & 1 & 1 \\ -.5 & .5 & 1 & 1 \end{bmatrix}$$

The $M_{1,i}$ matrices correspond to how the sections interrelate with respect to harmony, and the $M_{2,i}$ matrices show the same with respect to timbre. The masks halve all of the elements in the off-diagonal sections so that the feature matrices can be reconstructed by summing the components (i.e., $\Sigma_{j=1..s} M_{i,j} = F_i$). We would like to find a linear combination of the component matrices $M_{i,j}$ that will approximate the annotation N as closely as possible. That is, we want the vector of coefficients $x = \{x_{1,1}, x_{1,2}, ..., x_{f,s}\}$ that minimizes the squared distance between the annotation and the reconstruction:

$$\Big(\Big(\sum_{j=1}^{s} \sum_{i=1}^{f} x_{i,j} M_{i,j} \Big) - N \Big)^2$$

This problem is solvable as a quadratic program (QP) if we imagine each component matrix $M_{i,j}$ to be a single row in a larger array $\mathbf{M}$. If each $M_{i,j}$ is an $n \times n$ matrix, then letting $k = (i-1) \cdot f + j$ we can let $\mathbf{M_k}$, the kth row of $\mathbf{M}$, be the horizontal concatenation of the n rows of $M_{i,j}$:

$$\mathbf{M} = \begin{bmatrix} M_{1,1_{(1,1)}} & M_{1,1_{(2,1)}} & \cdots & M_{1,1_{(1,2)}} & \cdots & M_{1,1_{(n,n)}} \\ M_{1,2_{(1,1)}} & M_{1,2_{(2,1)}} & \cdots & M_{1,2_{(1,2)}} & \cdots & M_{1,2_{(n,n)}} \\ \vdots & \vdots & \ddots & \vdots & \ddots & \vdots \\ M_{f,s_{(1,1)}} & M_{f,s_{(2,1)}} & \cdots & M_{f,s_{(1,2)}} & \cdots & M_{f,s_{(n,n)}} \end{bmatrix}$$

(In our example, $\mathbf{M}$ would have 6 rows and 16 columns, since there are 16 values in each of the 6 components $M_{i,j}$.)

If we similarly reshape N into a single row vector, and treat x as a column vector, then we may rewrite expression (1) as $(x^T\mathbf{M} - N)^2$. Expanding, we obtain the following expression for c, the reconstruction cost:

$$c(x) = x^T\mathbf{M}\mathbf{M}^T x - 2N\mathbf{M}^T x + NN^T \quad (2)$$

Here, $\mathbf{MM}^T$ is a square matrix with f rows and columns, and NN^T is a constant term which can be ignored in the QP. Our goal is to minimize $c(x)$ subject to any constraints we may place on x. We set $x \geq 0$ and interpret each coefficient $x_{i,j}$ as the relevance of feature i in explaining the similarity of section j to the entire piece. The final QP formulation is:

$$\min_x \; x^T\mathbf{M}^2 x - N\mathbf{M}^T x \quad (3)$$

$$\text{such that: } x_{i,j} \geq 0, \forall\, i = 1,..,f,\; j = 1,..,s$$

This is the standard form for QPs, and is quickly solvable on commercial software. All the QPs in this article were solved using the `quadprog` function in MATLAB's optimization package. The inequality is the only constraint placed on the solution; we do not enforce the typical constraint $\Sigma\, x_{i,j} = 1$ as its interpretation is unclear and we never encountered any problems with degenerate solutions.

Solving this quadratic program for our example gives $x = \{0, 0.6875, 1.0625, 1.25, 0.3125, 0\}$. The reconstruction of the annotation using these coefficients is:

$$\mathbf{M}^T x = \begin{bmatrix} 1.25 & -.44 & -1.16 & -1.16 \\ -.44 & 1.00 & -.72 & -.72 \\ -1.16 & -.72 & 1.06 & 1.06 \\ -1.16 & -.72 & 1.06 & 1.06 \end{bmatrix}$$

($\mathbf{M}^T x$ is actually a column vector, but here we have reshaped the result into the reconstructed matrix it represents.) The largest components are $x_{1,3}$ and $x_{2,1}$; indeed, the most explanatory components are $M_{1,3}$, which perfectly shows how section C is distinguished from A and B on the basis of its harmony, and $M_{2,1}$, which shows how A differs from the others on the basis of its timbre. The coefficient $x_{1,1}$ is 0, which properly reflects that the harmony of section A is meaningless for distinguishing it from the rest of the piece, and vice versa for $x_{3,2}$. The intermediate values of $x_{1,2}$ and $x_{2,2}$ reflect that it is relatively difficult to explain the middle section with these features. Component $M_{1,2}$ distinguishes section C at the expense of conflating A and B, while $M_{2,2}$ distinguishes A and conflates B and C. Since there is a greater cost for mischaracterizing the longer section, $x_{1,2}$ is larger than $x_{2,2}$.

The reconstruction cost $c(x)$ for the above solution is 1.125, compared to the maximum cost of 16.0 which is reached when every $x_{i,j} = 0$. If instead of this section-wise approach we had used a matrix-wise approach with two components, F_1 and F_2, we would have found the optimal coefficients 0.67 and 0.33, which gives a reconstruction cost of 5.33. Hence the section-wise approach gets over four times closer to the annotation than the matrix-wise approach. More importantly, the coefficients $x_{i,j}$ reveal when in the piece the different features are most relevant for determining its structure: in this case, harmony is an unimportant feature near the beginning of the piece, but becomes important later on, and vice versa for timbre.

The section-wise QP contains all solutions to the matrix-wise QP as a subset. The solution to the section-wise QP is thus guaranteed to be at least as good, and the reduction in reconstruction cost is no surprise. While this prevents us from quantitatively evaluating the effectiveness of the section-wise QP, we may use the matrix-wise QP as a performance ceiling and evaluate the result qualitatively.

2.3 Reconstructing an annotation SSM from audio SSMs

Using the features explained in Section 2.1.1 and the annotated information described in Section 2.1.2, we can formulate a QP using the method in Section 2.2. We demonstrate this procedure for the song "Yellow Submarine." Figure 3 illustrates how the five feature-derived SSMs and seven section masks produce 35 components. Labeling the component matrices $M_{1,1}$ through $M_{5,7}$, our goal is to find the coefficients $x = \{x_{1,1}, \ldots, x_{5,7}\}$ that minimize $c(x)$. We solve the QP and illustrate the weights x in Figure 4.

The results suggest that the first verse, A_1, is best explained by a combination of its chroma and fluctuation pattern vectors, that the first chorus, B_1, is explained almost wholly by its chroma vectors, and so forth. The prominence of FPs in the first and last sections reflects the fact that the FPs were very robust to the changes that occur partway through each section: midway through A_1, a number of nautical sound effects intrude and affect the MFCCs and chroma, and the fadeout in B_3 affects the similarity of other features. Referring to the top and bottom rows of components in Figure 3, it is clear that FPs best represent the homogeneity of the first and last sections.

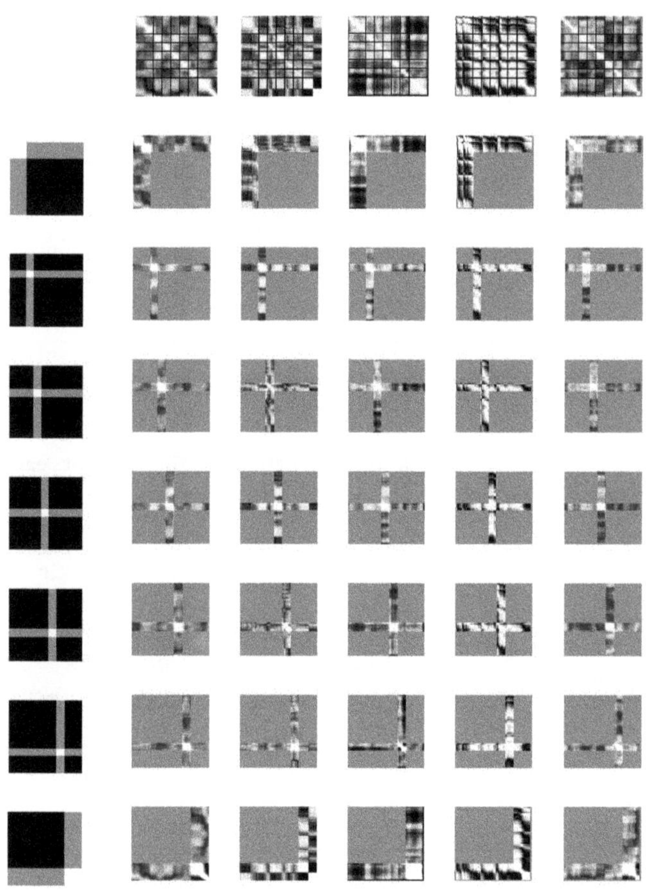

Figure 3. Illustration of matrix components. The feature matrices are given in the top row (left to right: MFCCs, chroma, FPs, RMS, and periodicity histograms); the masks in the left column represent each section in the annotation. Each component matrix is the element-wise product of a feature matrix and a mask. The feature matrices and the products are scaled from -1 (black) to +1 (white), while the masks are scaled from 0 (black) to +1 (white).

Section C_1 stands out from the piece as being best explained with a combination of timbre and tempo features. Indeed the most distinguishing feature of this section is its timbre, since it is an instrumental portion that contains many unusual sound effects like splashes and bells. Perhaps the arrhythmic nature of these sounds led the periodicity histograms to detect a strong dissimilarity with the rest of the piece.

Our method estimates connections between an analysis and the features, and our analysis of this example suggests that the connection plausibly relates to the listener's experience. However, whether the feature weights obtained by the QP actually correlate to the listener's justifications for their analysis remains a matter of conjecture. Settling this question would require paired data—annotations coupled with listener's self-reported justifications—that is not presently available, though we do plan to collect such data in the future.

2.3.1 Reconstruction cost

Subjectively, the x-values found by the QP are reasonable, but we would like to obtain some quantitative estimate of how well this method works compared to others. One measure of the quality of the output is the reconstruction cost c, which is the average squared deviation between the reconstructed matrix and the target annotation. (This is also the value of the objective function (2) at the solution found by the QP.) The maximum allowable reconstruction cost cannot exceed N^2, since this can be obtained trivially by setting $x = 0$. We can thus express the fractional reconstruction cost c/c_0, where c_0 is the cost at $x = 0$.

With this metric, we can compare the quality of different quadratic programs. To fairly estimate how much analyzing the song section by section instead of all at once improves the reconstruction, we need to run a second quadratic program: this one simply finds the coefficients $x = \{x_1, x_2, \ldots, x_f\}$ that makes the sum of the feature

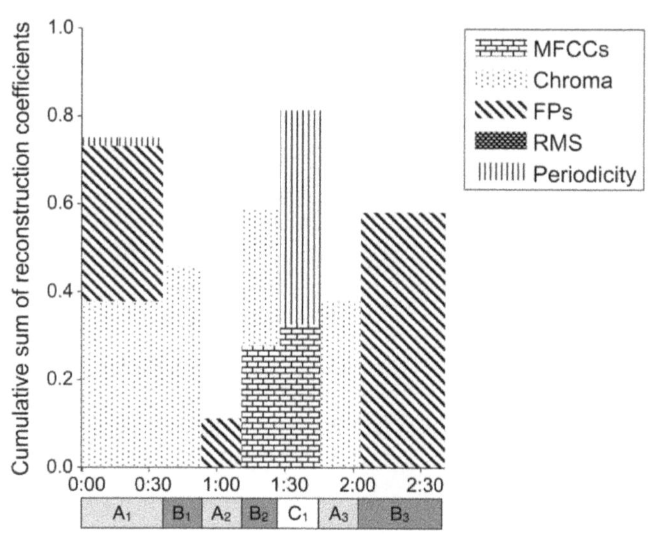

Figure 4. The optimal reconstruction coefficients for five different features for all sections of the song "Yellow Submarine." The height of each block is the value of the reconstruction coefficient for the section indicated on the *x*-axis. The annotation is given below the graph.

matrices as close to the annotation as possible. This method gives a fractional reconstruction cost of 0.81, whereas the section-wise method garnered a fractional cost of 0.68. This result is expected, since (as noted in Section 2.2) the coarse matrix-wise solution can never be better than the finer-grained solution. Still, by examining how this improvement tapers off with finer-grained formulations of the QP, as done in the next section, we can assess the limit of this method's effectiveness.

The matrices reconstructed using these two methods are pictured in Figure 5, along with a plot of the mean squared deviation from the annotation, which highlights those regions that are poorly reconstructed. The latter plots make evident that both approaches have trouble reconstruction the edges of the SSM, which describe how the very beginning and end of the song relate to the rest. The matrix-wise approach also has particular trouble reconstructing the third verse (section A_3)

2.3.2 Reconstruction using smaller sections

The section-wise approach was mathematically guaranteed to result in at least as good an approximate of the annotation as a linear combination of full matrices. We may expect even better approximations if we divide the matrix into smaller sections. However, if further segmentation is structurally irrelevant, the reductions in reconstruction cost will taper off. We repeated the previous QP using the finer segmentation of the small-scale sections as well as a "finest-scale" segmentation with segments every 2.5 seconds—shorter than the longest feature windows.

Looking at finer time scales reveals new insights: for example, it is very noticeable that section c_1 is poorly explained by all the features (Figure 6). Indeed, this small section contains a novel tune played on a brass instrument and sounds nothing like the rest of the piece. It doesn't even sound like the later sections c_2 and c_3, although their relatedness could be argued by their both containing sound effects and by their being some kind of variation of the usual A section. Also, whereas in the previous analysis (Figure 4) we saw that section C_1 was explained both by its distinct timbre and potentially confusing tempo, we can see now that each half of the section is better explained by one of these features. The first half, c_2, has less percussion than the second half and is arguably the more confusing.

Drilling down further to 2.5-second segments (Figure 7), the result is more detailed but not necessarily more informative: the sum of the coefficients leaves a similar "skyline", indicating that approximately the same amount of information is explained in each. However, a few parts are better explained at this smaller scale: the best explanation for a_5 and a' switches from FPs to

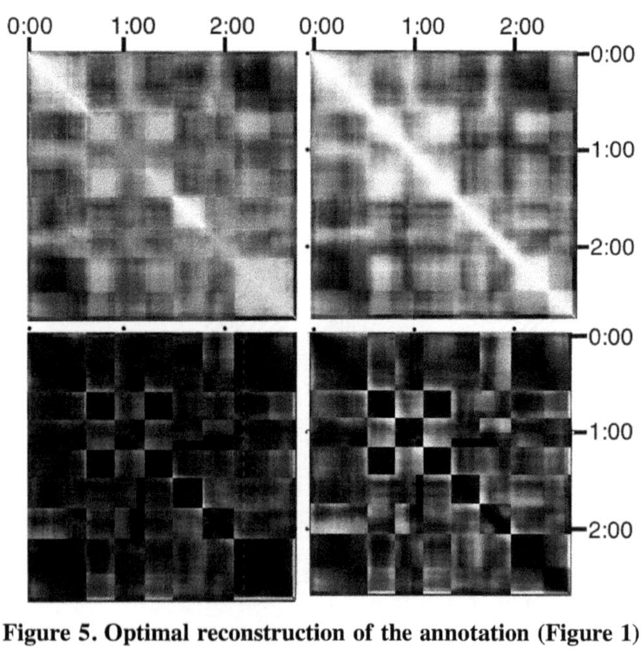

Figure 5. Optimal reconstruction of the annotation (Figure 1) using the section-wise approach (top left) and the matrix-wise approach (top-right). The mean squared deviation between each reconstructed matrix and the annotation is shown below the reconstruction. (Black pixels indicate where the reconstruction is most accurate.)

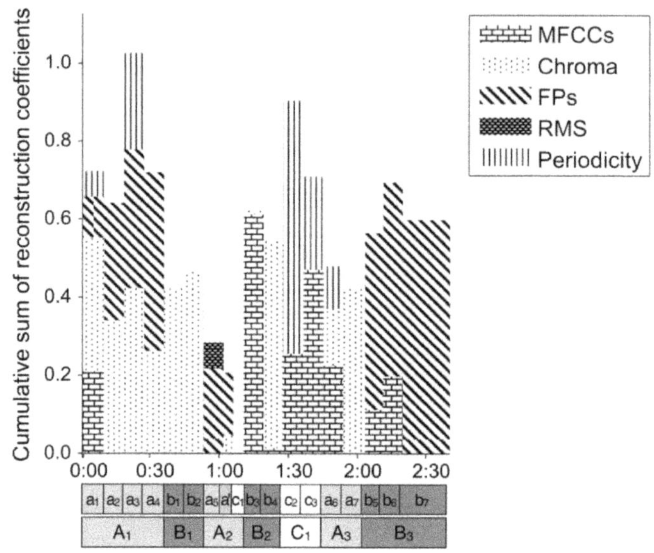

Figure 6: The optimal reconstruction coefficients for each small-scale section.

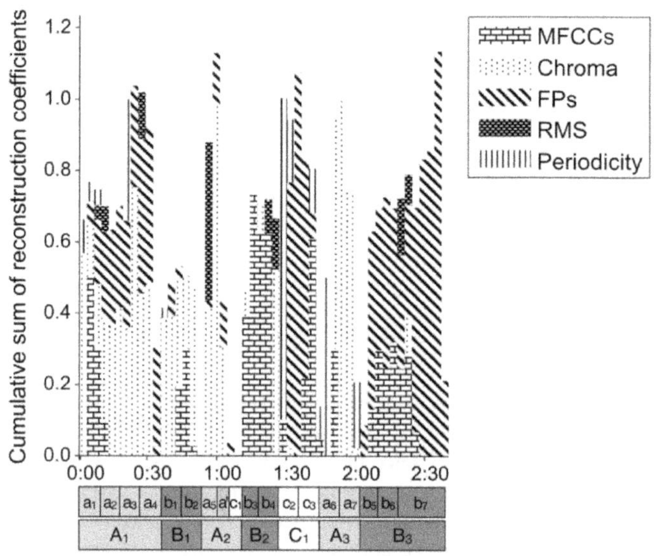

Figure 7: The optimal reconstruction coefficients for each 2.5-second frame in the piece.

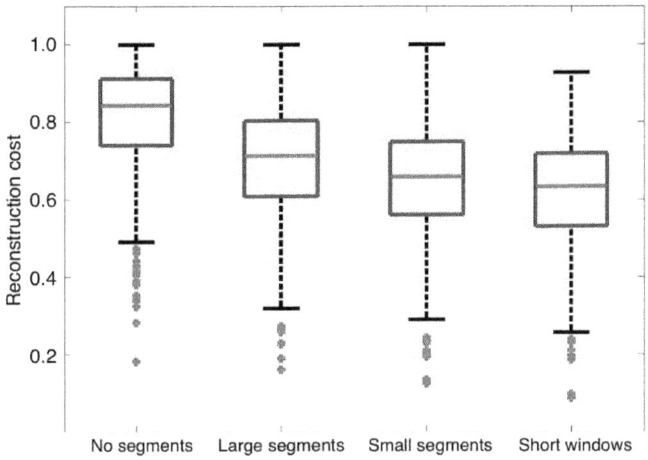

Figure 8. Boxplot of QP reconstruction costs obtained for QPs using no segmentation (matrix-wise sum) and the piece-wise decomposition at three time scales. Data include 704 recordings from the SALAMI corpus.

chroma, bringing A_2 in line with the other A sections. Also, the coefficients in b_7 are higher at this scale.

As stated earlier, finer-grained segmentations are guaranteed to lead to better reconstructions. In the above example, the fractional cost for the small-scale segmentation was 0.67 (compared to 0.68 for the large-scale segmentation), and for the short-window analysis it was 0.61. An analysis of reconstruction costs over a larger corpus reveals that this example is typical. The QP algorithm was executed on annotations for 704 recordings in the SALAMI dataset at the four levels of granularity: matrix-wise, large-scale, small-scale, and finest-scale. The reconstruction costs were computed for each and are plotted in Figure 8. We see that while large reductions in reconstruction cost are typical when moving from matrix-wise to large-scale QP formulations, there is less improvement moving from small-scale to short window, indicating diminishing returns when the segmentation proceeds beyond what the annotation contains.

3. VISUALIZING STRUCTURAL DIFFERENCES

The previous examples show that the relationship between the structure of a piece of music and its feature-derived SSMs can vary over time: repetitions in a feature that are irrelevant at one point in a piece may be foregrounded at another. Just as [15] and [25] argued that dynamic feature weighting could improve structural analysis, our examples show that dynamic feature interpretation could aid in applications based on structural information. Here, we focus on its use as a visualization tool.

For example, the data obtained by our approach may provide interesting visualizations for projects like SALAMI, which plans to execute several algorithms to annotate the musical structure for a large library [31]. To facilitate browsing in it they have developed a system to visualize each structural description with a diagram, like the annotation in the lower part of Figure 7 [5]. Providing the section-wise estimates of which features are estimated to be most salient could enrich these diagrams.

Our method of decomposing annotations is also suited to comparing annotations prepared by different listeners. We illustrate this with two examples. The first shows how a single large difference between two annotations is reflected in the reconstruction coefficients, and the second demonstrates the power of the approach to reconstruct greatly divergent analyses from the same set of components.

3.1 Investigating a single difference

As noted in the introduction, it is common for two listeners to analyze the same piece of music differently, and this may be because they are paying attention to different acoustic features. Our analysis method allows one to investigate the differences between two analyses, showing how each may have arisen by emphasizing certain features over others at certain times.

We illustrate this potential by reconstructing two different annotations of the piece "Garrotin", a solo flamenco guitar piece recorded by Chago Rodrigo. Two SALAMI annotators gave analyses that were similar overall (Figure 9): the piece begins and ends with many repetitions of the same main melodic gesture, and the middle of the song (roughly 0:40 to 1:00) consists of a number of different melodic episodes separated by short calls back to the main theme.

The analyses differ mainly in their treatment of the middle section: the first listener interprets it as a single episode, while the second listener analyzes it as two distinct episodes. The feature SSMs (Figure 10) show that this portion of the piece is quite self-similar with respect to pitch and timbre, but an internal contrast to the section is revealed in the FP-derived SSM at the shorter time scale (5 seconds). This difference is reflected in the solutions to the QP (Figure 11): the middle section of the piece is reconstructed best by chroma features when kept as one section, but reconstructed better by FPs when divided in two.

3.2 Reconstructing dissimilar analyses

In the previous example, a small disagreement was investigated. What if listeners have vastly different interpretations—is it still possible to find QP solutions that justify each interpretation equally well? We look at such an example now: "As the Bell Rings the Maypole Spins", by the World music band Dead Can Dance. In the song, a singer and bagpipes play a series of reels, and the pattern of reels repeats a few times before a long repetitive coda section ends the piece. The stark difference between the two annotations is apparent from the SSMs (Figure 12, top row). The first listener has identified a sequence of three reels as a self-contained repeating group, leading to large off-diagonal blocks in the middle of the SSM. The second listener has not identified these larger groupings, but does indicate that many of the reels are identical or similar to the coda section (from 3:40 onward), resulting in a series of thin bars in the SSM.

Despite the differences in the annotations, a QP using five features and three time scales has reconstructed the annotations qualitatively well (Figure 12, middle row). The fractional reconstruction costs for the first and second annotations, when using the large-scale segmentation, are .63 and .57, compared to .74 and .76 when using no segmentation.

Examining the reconstruction coefficients (Figure 13), we can observe that the two solutions depend on fairly distinct sets of

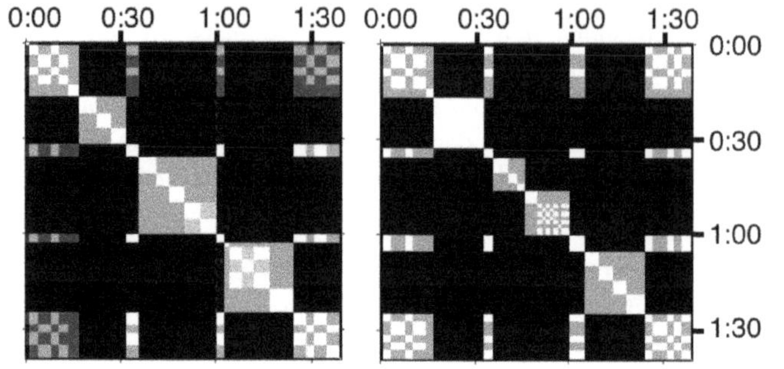

Figure 9. Annotations by two listeners for "Garrotin" (salami_id: 842).

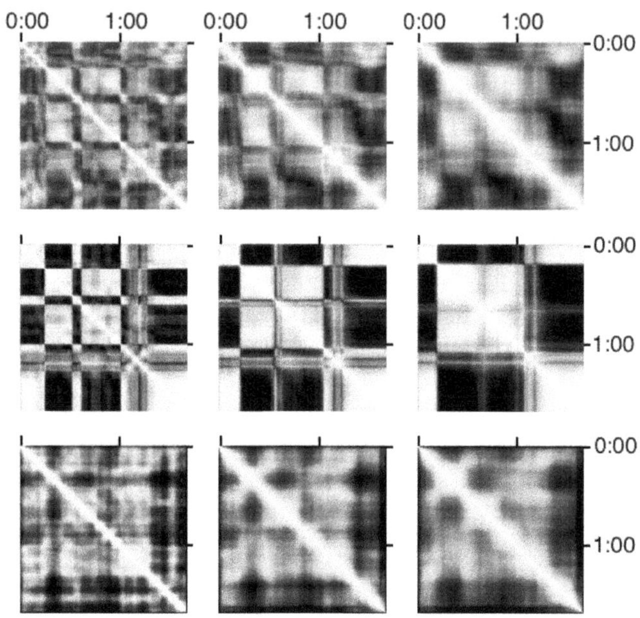

Figure 10. Feature matrices for the reconstruction of "Garrotin." In this example, three features are used: MFCCs (top row), chroma (middle row), and FPs (bottom row), as well as three smoothing window sizes: 5, 10 and 15 seconds (left, middle and right columns, respectively).

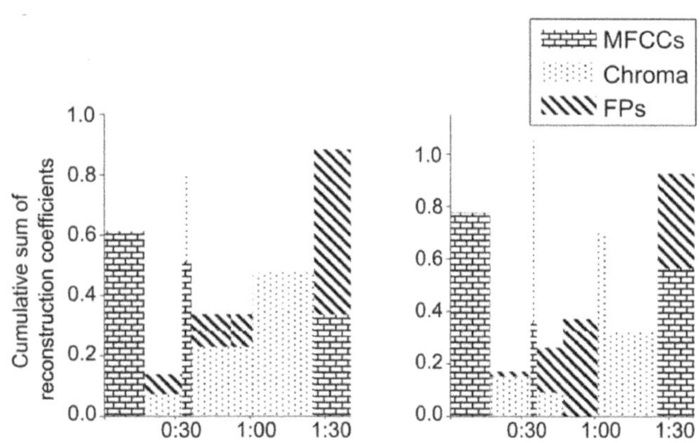

Figure 11. The optimal reconstruction coefficients for three different features for large sections of the song "Garrotin." The *x*-axis represents time. The coefficients shown here are the average of the coefficients for the three different time scales.

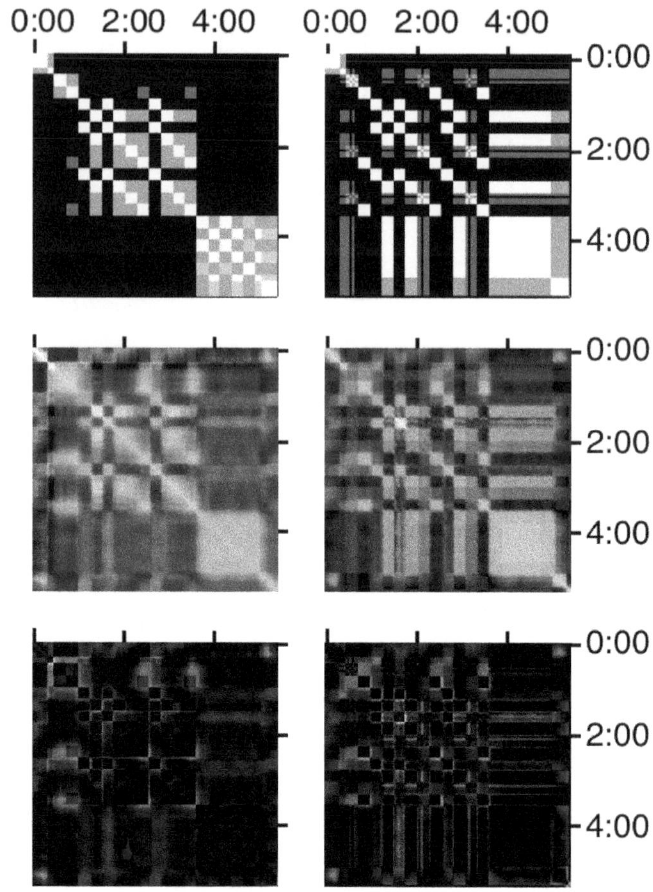

Figure 12. Top row: SSMs from two annotations for "As the Bell Rings the Maypole Spins", by Dead Can Dance (salami_id: 860). Middle row: reconstructed matrices. Bottom row: mean squared reconstruction error.

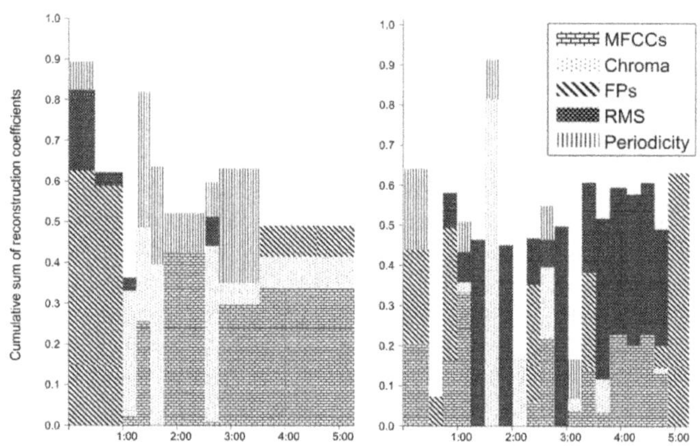

Figure 13. The optimal reconstruction coefficients for five features for large sections of the song "As the Bell Rings the Maypole Spins." The coefficients shown here are the average of the coefficients for the three different time scales.

features. The first annotation is explained best by FPs in the first section (up to 1:00), and thereafter mainly by MFCCs. By contrast, much of the second annotation is explained best by RMS. Both solutions involve a mixture of features between 1:00 and 2:30, but the mixtures are distinct.

4. CONCLUSION & FUTURE WORK

We have introduced the problem of estimating the relevance of different acoustic features to different sections of a structural analysis, and proposed a method of solving the problem based on quadratic programming. The approach is founded on the intuition that while acoustically-derived SSMs may not always reflect the true structure of a piece, components of SSMs for specific features may explain parts of the true structure. The data explored here relate to listeners' analyses, and it is possible that our method reveals insights into how listeners analyzed the pieces. However, to establish a correlation between the SSMs and the listeners' procedure for analyzing the piece would require new experimental data, the collection of which remains future work

The method presented is a general one and the parameters of the QP, such as the mask shape, could be modified in interesting ways to suit different problems. For example, if the masks (as in Figure 4) were altered to only include the upper left portion of the SSM, a future-agnostic analysis would result. The annotations considered here were all produced after the music had been fully heard, but response data that reflected one's real-time perception of structure would perhaps best be analyzed with such a future-agnostic framework.

Similarly, a QP using masks that emphasized the main diagonal might model a listening experience with less long-term memory. Such an analysis would provide a solution that explained local similarities and contrasts at the expense of more distant sections. This version would be useful if, for instance, once considered the acoustic similarity between the very beginning and end of a piece to be unimportant. (The more narrowly one focuses on the diagonal axis, the more this method resembles the novelty function calculation proposed by [8]. Except, instead of correlating the diagonal axis with a checkerboard kernel, we would be correlating it with the ground truth annotation.)

One important caveat with our approach is that it is crucial that the annotation used properly reflect the information that one seeks to explain. In this article we have taken for granted the "states" hypothesis of the annotations, to use the terminology of [28]. That is, we have assumed that a section with a single label is homogenous, and uniformly distinct from any differently-labeled section. It would be useful to extend our work to account for "sequence" interpretations of annotations, in which a section B is presumed to be a heterogeneous sequence of events that recurs exactly whenever B repeats. The use of structural information at multiple timescales, described in Section 2.1, is intended to mitigate this shortcoming, since in practice the short-time scale annotation often charts a "sequence"-like path through the blocks of the large-scale annotation. Implementing a sequential similarity metric is not straightforward since two annotated sections can have the same label but very different lengths, and an automatic alignment algorithm such as [20] would have to be incorporated..

5. ACKNOWLEDGMENTS

This research was supported in part by the Social Sciences and Humanities Research Council of Canada and by a QMUL EPSRC Doctoral Training Account studentship. We would like to thank the anonymous reviewers for their generous help in improving this submission.

6. REFERENCES

[1] Bartsch, M. and Wakefield, G. 2001. To catch a chorus: using chroma-based representations for audio thumbnailing. *IEEE Workshop on the Applications of Signal Processing to Audio and Acoustics* (New Paltz, NY, USA). 15–18.

[2] Bruderer, M., McKinney, M., and Kohlrausch, A. 2009. The perception of structural boundaries in melody lines of Western popular music. *Musicae Scientae*. 13, 2, 273–313.

[3] Clarke, E. F. and Krumhansl, C. L. 1990. Perceiving musical time. *Music Perception*. 7, 3, 213–251.

[4] Eckmann, J. P., Kamphorst, S. O., and Ruelle, D. 1987. Recurrence plots of dynamical systems. *Europhysics Letters*, 5, 9, 973–977.

[5] Ehmann, A. F., Bay, M., Downie, J. S., Fujinaga, I., and De Roure, D. 2011. Exploiting music structures for digital libraries. In *Proceeding of the International ACM/IEEE Joint Conference on Digital Libraries* (Ottawa, Canada). 479–480.

[6] Eronen, A. 2007. Chorus detection with combined use of MFCC and chroma features and image processing filters. In *Proceedings of the International Conference on Digital Audio Effects* (Bordeaux, France). 229–236.

[7] Foote, J. 1999. Visualizing music and audio using self-similarity. In *Proceedings of the ACM International Conference on Multimedia* (New York, NY, USA). 77–80.

[8] Foote, J. 2000. Automatic Audio Segmentation using a Measure of Audio Novelty. In *Proceedings of the IEEE International Conference on Multimedia and Expo*. 452–455.

[9] Foote, J. and Cooper, M. 2003. Media segmentation using self-similarity decomposition. In *Proceedings of the SPIE: Storage and Retrieval for Media Databases* (Santa Clara, CA, USA). 167–175.

[10] Frankland, B. and Cohen, A. 2004. Parsing of melody: Quantification and testing of the local grouping rules of Lerdahl and Jackendoff's *A Generative Theory of Tonal Music*. *Music Perception*. 21, 4, 499–543.

[11] Goto, M. 2006. A chorus section detection method for musical audio signals and its application to a music listening station. *IEEE Transactions on Audio, Speech and Language Processing*. 14, 5, 1783–1794.

[12] Grosche, P., Serrà, J., Müller, M., and Arcos, J. L. 2012. Structure-based audio fingerprinting for music retrieval. In *Proceedings of the International Conference on Music Information Retrieval* (Porto, Portugal). 55–60.

[13] Hargreaves, S., Klapuri, A., and Sandler, M. 2012. Structural segmentation of multitrack audio. *IEEE Transactions on Audio, Speech, and Language Processing*. 20, 10, 2637–2647.

[14] Jehan, T. 2005. Hierarchical multi-class self similarities. In *Proceedings of the IEEE Workshop on Applications of Signal Processing to Audio and Acoustics* (New Paltz, NY, USA). 311–314.

[15] Kaiser, F. and Peeters, G. 2012. Adaptive temporal modeling of audio features in the context of music structure segmentation. In *International Workshop on Adaptive Multimedia Retrieval* (Copenhagen, Denmark).

[16] Kaiser, F. and Sikora, T. 2010. Music structure discovery in popular music using non-negative matrix factorization. In *Proceedings of the International Society for Music Information Retrieval Conference* (Utrecht, The Netherlands). 429–434.

[17] Landone, C. Gasser, M., Cannam, C., Harte, C., Davies, M., Noland, K., Wilmering, T., Xue, W., and Zhou, R. 2011. QM Vamp Plugins. Available: <http://isophonics.net/QMVampPlugins>, accessed 1 October 2012.

[18] Marolt, M. 2006. A mid-level melody-based representation for calculating audio similarity. In *Proceedings of the International Conference on Music Information Retrieval* (Victoria, Canada). 280–285.

[19] Mauch, M., Noland, K., and Dixon, S. 2009. Using musical structure to enhance automatic chord transcription. In *Proceedings of the International Society for Music Information Retrieval Conference* (Kobe, Japan). 231–236.

[20] Müller, M. & Appelt, D. 2008. Path-constrained partial music synchronization. In *Proceedings of the IEEE International Conference on Acoustics, Speech and Signal Processing* (Las Vegas, NV, USA). 65–68.

[21] Ong, B. 2007. Structural Analysis and Segmentation of Music Signals. Ph.D. dissertation, University Pompeu Fabra.

[22] Pampalk, E. 2004. A Matlab toolbox to compute similarity from audio. In *Proceedings of the International Conference on Music Information Retrieval* (Barcelona, Spain). 254–257.

[23] Pampalk, E., Dixon, S., and Widmer, G. 2004. Exploring music collections by browsing different views. *Computer Music Journal*, 28, 2, 49–62.

[24] Pampalk, E., Rauber, A., and Merkl, D. 2002. Content-based organization and visualization of music archives. In *Proceedings of the ACM International Conference on Multimedia* (Juan les Pins, France). 570–579.

[25] Parry, R., and Essa, I. 2004. Feature weighting for segmentation. In Proceedings of the International Conference for Music Information Retrieval (Barcelona, Spain).

[26] Paulus, J. & Klapuri, A. 2006. Music structure analysis by finding repeated parts. In *Proceedings of the ACM Workshop on Audio and Music Computing Multimedia* (New York, NY, USA). 59–68.

[27] Paulus, J., Müller, M., and Klapuri, A. 2010. Audio-based music structure analysis. In *Proceedings of the International Society for Music Information Retrieval Conference* (Utrecht, The Netherlands). 625–636.

[28] Peeters, G. 2004. Deriving musical structures from signal analysis for music audio summary generation: "Sequence" and "State" approach. In *Computer Music Modeling and Retrieval 2771*. Springer Berlin / Heidelberg, 169–185.

[29] Peeters, G. 2007. Sequence representation of music structure using higher-order similarity matrix and maximum-likelihood approach. In *Proceedings of the International Conference on Music Information Retrieval* (Vienna, Austria). 35–40.

[30] Shiu, Y., Jeong, H., and Kuo, C.-C. J. 2006. Similarity matrix processing for music structure analysis. In *Proceedings of the ACM Workshop on Audio and Music Computing Multimedia* (New York, NY, USA). 69–76.

[31] Smith, J. B. L., Burgoyne, J. A., Fujinaga, I., De Roure, D., and Downie, J. S. 2011. Design and creation of a large-scale database of structural annotations. In *Proceedings of the International Society for Music Information Retrieval Conference* (Miami, FL, USA). 555–560.

Topology Preserving Hashing for Similarity Search

Lei Zhang[1,2], Yongdong Zhang[2], Jinhui Tang[3], Xiaoguang Gu[2], Jintao Li[2], Qi Tian[4]
[1]University of Chinese Academy of Sciences
[2]Institute of Computing Technology,Chinese Academy Of Sciences
[3]Nanjing University of Science and Technology
[4]University of Texas at San Antonio
{zhanglei09,zhyd,xggu,jtli}@ict.ac.cn, jinhuitang@mail.njust.edu.cn, qitian@cs.utsa.edu

ABSTRACT

Binary hashing has been widely used for efficient similarity search. Learning efficient codes has become a research focus and it is still a challenge. In many cases, the real-world data often lies on a low-dimensional manifold, which should be taken into account to capture meaningful neighbors with hashing. The importance of a manifold is its topology, which represents the neighborhood relationships between its subregions and the relative proximities between the neighbors of each subregion, e.g. the relative ranking of neighbors of each subregion. Most existing hashing methods try to preserve the neighborhood relationships by mapping similar points to close codes, while ignoring the neighborhood rankings. Moreover, most hashing methods lack in providing a good ranking for query results since they use Hamming distance as the similarity metric, and in practice, there are often a lot of results sharing the same distance to a query. In this paper, we propose a novel hashing method to solve these two issues jointly. The proposed method is referred to as *Topology Preserving Hashing* (TPH). TPH is distinct from prior works by preserving the neighborhood rankings of data points in Hamming space. The learning stage of TPH is formulated as a generalized eigendecomposition problem with closed form solutions. Experimental comparisons with other state-of-the-art methods on three noted image benchmarks demonstrate the efficacy of the proposed method.

Categories and Subject Descriptors

H.3 [**Information Storage and Retrieval**]: Content Analysis and Indexing, Information Search and Retrieval

General Terms

Algorithms, Performance

Keywords

Similarity Search, Approximate Nearest Neighbor Search, Binary Hashing, Topology Preserving Hashing.

MM'13, October 21–25, 2013, Barcelona, Spain.

ACM 978-1-4503-2404-5/13/10 ...$15.00.
http://dx.doi.org/10.1145/2502081.2502091.

1. INTRODUCTION

High-dimensional similarity search is a fundamental problem in many content-based search systems and also widely exists in many related application areas, such as machine learning, computer vision, information retrieval and data mining. Due to the linear time complexity, traditional linear nearest neighbor (NN) search is computationally prohibitive, especially when dataset contains millions or even billions of data points. To solve this problem efficiently, a number of methods have been proposed, such as KD-Tree [2] and Locality Sensitive Hashing (LSH) [1]. Recently, binary hashing [22, 29, 14, 4, 23, 13, 12, 10, 3] is becoming increasingly popular for efficient approximate nearest neighbor (ANN) search due to its good query and storage efficiency.

Given a dataset, binary hashing methods map each data point $\boldsymbol{x}$ to a binary code $H(\boldsymbol{x})$ and perform bit-wise operations to search neighbors. To capture meaningful neighbors, the neighborhood structure should be preserved after Hamming embedding. In many cases, the real-world dataset often lies on a low-dimensional manifold embedded in a high-dimensional space [14]. To characterize a manifold, its topology, which represents the neighborhood relationships between subregions and the relative proximities between the neighbors of subregions, is essential [11]. A lot of hashing methods [8, 29, 3, 14, 13, 12] have been developed to preserve the neighborhood relationships (we call neighborhood-preserving) by mapping similar points to close binary codes. In these methods, the neighborhood relationships are taken into account in hash function learning, however, the relative proximities between the neighbors, e.g. the rankings, are not. As a result, these methods cannot preserve the data topology well. More precisely, as shown in Fig. 1(b), for a data point $\boldsymbol{p}$ and its neighbors $\boldsymbol{q}_1$, $\boldsymbol{q}_2$, $H(\boldsymbol{q}_1)$ and $H(\boldsymbol{q}_2)$ are still neighbors of $H(\boldsymbol{p})$, however, the ranking between $H(\boldsymbol{q}_1)$ and $H(\boldsymbol{q}_2)$ is not preserved.

To preserve the local topology of a dataset, a straightforward way is to preserve the original distance after Hamming embedding. Many hashing methods [1, 9, 20, 10] have been developed (we call distance-preserving) and in these methods, the Hamming distance between binary codes are used as a reconstruction of the distance between data points in the original data space or a kernel space. Since the Hamming distance is bounded by the code length, the original distance to Hamming distance mapping is many-to-one, which indicates the reconstruction is far from optimal. On the other hand, characterizing a manifold with distances turns out to support and bolt it with rigid steel beam [11]. In many cases, the optimal embedding of a manifold needs some flexibili-

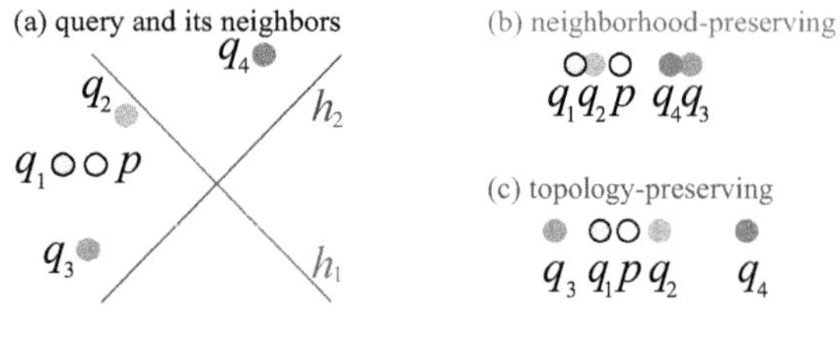

Figure 1: The essence of our proposed TPH. (a) A data point p and its neighbors. (b) In neighborhood-preserving hashing (h_1), the neighborhood relationship is preserved, but the ranking of neighbors is not. (c) In topology-preserving hashing (h_2), besides the neighborhood relationship, the ranking is also preserved. The hash functions are depicted as linear projections for the sake of illustration.

ty: some subregions should be locally stretched or shrunk to embed them in a low-dimensional space within which the topology can be well preserved. Moreover, most distance functions make no distinction between the manifold and its surrounding empty space, to some extent, the exact measure of distance depends not only on the manifold itself, but also, for a large part, on a given embedding of the manifold. As a result, although designed for distance-preserving, these methods [9, 10] still cannot preserve the local topology well.

Another limitation of most hashing methods is that these methods simply adopt the Hamming distance as distance metric. Since Hamming distance is bounded by the code length, there can be a lot of results sharing the same distance to a query in practice, posing a critical issue for similarity search, e.g. k nearest neighbor search, where ranking is important. Weighted Hamming distance [7, 30] have been developed to alleviate this limitation, however, they are all post-processing algorithms while the ranking information is already lost too much after embedding. Apparently, if the ranking information can be encoded in binary codes, this limitation would be better alleviated.

In this paper, we propose a Topology Preserving Hashing (TPH) method to solve the above two issues jointly. As stated in [11], a manifold can be entirely characterized by giving the relative proximities between its subregions. Actually, comparative information between distance, like inequalities or rankings, suffices to characterize a manifold for any embeddings. In this work, the relative proximities are revealed by the distances, i.e. the ranking of neighbors of each subregion. Therefore, the essence of our Topology Preserving Hashing is to not only preserve the neighborhood relationships, but also preserve the neighborhood rankings. As shown in Fig. 1(c), TPH ensures that $H(\boldsymbol{q}_1)$ and $H(\boldsymbol{q}_2)$ are neighbors of $H(\boldsymbol{p})$, and $H(\boldsymbol{q}_1)$ is still a nearer neighbor of $H(\boldsymbol{p})$ in Hamming space. Our method can be considered as a tight version of neighborhood-preserving and a loose version of distance-preserving. The main contributions of this paper are briefly outlined as follows:

(1) We propose a novel hashing method to learn the Hamming embeddings for a dataset, such that not only the neighborhood relationships between data points, but also the neighborhood ranking of each data point, is preserved after embedding. To the best of our knowledge, this is one of the first work that tries to incorporate neighborhood ranking information with hashing.

(2) Experimental results demonstrate the superiority of our method as compared with other state-of-the-art methods. Moreover, the limitation of most hashing methods, which is lacking in providing a good ranking for query results, is also well alleviated.

(3) The label information of a dataset can be easily leveraged in the learning stage of our method, extending it to a semi-supervised method to capture semantic neighbors in a simple manner.

The rest of this paper is organized as follows. The related work is discussed in Section 2. The Topology Preserving Hashing method is proposed in Section 3. Section 4 describes our experiments and Section 5 concludes this paper.

2. RELATED WORK

With the proliferation of various kinds of data, e.g. music, image and video, in content-based search systems, fast similarity search has attracted a significant attention. One classical kind of methods to address this problem is the tree-based index, e.g. KD-Tree [2]. However, this kind of methods cannot work well for high-dimensional data. Their performances degrade significantly to linear scan as the dimensionality increases. Moreover, most of visual descriptors, like SIFT [15] and GIST [18], are high-dimensional vectors. Therefore, tree-based indexes are not preferable in high-dimensional similarity search problems. Another kind of ANN search algorithm is based on vector quantization, such as kmeans LSH [19] and Product Quantization (PQ) [5]. The key of these methods is the compositionality. In PQ, by dividing each data into several subspaces and expressing data in terms of recurring parts, the representational capacity of PQ grows exponentially in the number of subspaces. In these methods [19, 5], each data point is represented by a reconstructed cluster center and the search process is performed in the original data space. As a result, the search process is time-consuming even with a inverted file indexing [5]. Recently, hashing based methods have been widely used for efficient similarity search [31, 23, 32] since it allows constant-time search. A lot of hashing methods have been proposed, and these methods can be roughly divided into two main categories [3, 14]: data-independent methods and data-dependent methods.

One representative kind of data-independent methods is hashing with random projections, such as Hamming Embedding [4] and Locality Sensitive Hashing (LSH) [1, 8, 6]. In these methods, the hash functions are random projections which are independent of dataset. Theoretically, it is guaranteed that the original distance or similarity are asymptotically preserved in Hamming space with increasing code length, hence LSH-related methods usually require long codes to achieve good precision. However, long codes result in low recall since the collision probability of similar points mapped to close binary codes decreases exponentially as the code length increases. As a result, LSH-related methods usually construct multi-tables to ensure a reasonable probability that a query will collide with its near neighbors in at least one table, which leads to a long query time and a high memory occupation. Another representative method is Shift Invariant Kernel Hashing (SIKH) [20]. It is a distribution-free method based on random features mapping for shift-invariant kernels, and the expected Hamming distance between the binary codes is related to the distance between data points in a kernel space. Similar to LSH, SIKH also needs relatively long codes to ensure good performance [3]. As a result, in practice, data-independent methods are often less effective than data-dependent methods.

To generate more compact codes, many data-dependent methods have been developed to learn hash functions from dataset. Semantic Hashing [22] adopts a deep generative model based on restricted Boltzmann machine to learn hash functions. In PCA-Hashing [28], the eigenvectors corresponding to the largest eigenvalues of the data covariance matrix are used to form a projection matrix for hashing. The spectral graph partitioning strategy is employed to develop new kinds of hashing methods, e.g. Spectral Hashing (SPH) [29, 12]. SPH uses the simple analytical eigenfunction solution of 1-D Laplacians as the hash function. In SPH [29], two important constraints on binary codes learning are introduced: (1) each hash bit balanced partitions the dataset; (2) different hash bits should be uncorrelated. These two constraints are widely accepted in many research works [26, 14, 3]. In [3], Iterative Quantization (ITQ) is proposed to learn an orthogonal rotation matrix to refine the initial PCA projection matrix [28] to minimize the quantization error of mapping the data from original data space to Hamming space. To minimize the reconstruction error between the original distance of data points and the Hamming distances of the corresponding codes, Binary Reconstruction Embedding (BRE) is proposed in [9]. In BRE, the Hamming distance is used as an reconstruction of the distance between data points in the original data space. In [10], the original LSH is generalized to a kernel space, called Kernelized Locality Sensitive Hashing (KLSH). KLSH is proposed to address the limitation that the original LSH methods cannot apply for high-dimensional kernelized data when the underlying feature embedding for the kernel is unknown. In KLSH, the Hamming distance is an approximation of the distance between data points in a kernel space. To exploit the spectral properties of the data affinity to generate better binary codes, many other algorithms, such as Semi-Supervised Hashing (SSH) [25, 26], Anchor Graph Hashing (AGH) [14], LDAHash [24] and Kernel-Based Supervised Hashing (KSH) [13], have been developed. Both labeled and unlabeled data are used in SSH [26] to learn hash functions to minimize the empirical error on the labeled data and maximize the information entropy regularization on all data. AGH [14] applies the similar formulation of SPH [29] for hash codes generation, while its neighborhood graph is constructed in a novel way such that it can be applied to large-scale dataset. Provided a set of positive and negative data pairs, LDAHash [24] learns the hash functions in a supervised manner by making the Hamming distance minimized between positive pairs and maximized between negative pairs. In [13], by leveraging label information and using the equivalence between optimizing the code inner products and the Hamming distances, KSH could map a dataset to compact codes whose Hamming distances are minimized on similar pairs and simultaneously maximized on dissimilar pairs.

In most existing binary hashing methods, including those methods discussed above, to capture meaningful neighbors, the neighborhood structure (i.e. local topology) of a dataset should be preserved after Hamming embedding. Mostly, the real-world data often lies on a low-dimensional manifold and to characterize a manifold, the neighborhood relationships between data points and the relative proximities between the neighbors of data points are both essential [11]. However, in most hashing methods [28, 29, 14, 3, 24], the neighborhood relationships are preserved, while the relative proximities are not guaranteed to be preserved. Even in the hashing methods [1, 20, 9, 10] developed for distance preserving, the topology is still not well preserved due to the fact that the original distance reconstruction using Hamming distance is far from optimal. Therefore, the learned codes of these methods are not the most optimal embedding for a dataset. In this paper, we propose a novel hashing method to solve the above problems. Besides the neighborhood relationships, the relative proximities between the neighbors of data points are also taken into account in the hash function learning process.

3. TOPOLOGY PRESERVING HASHING

This section describes our Topology Preserving Hashing (TPH) method. First, we introduce the motivation of topology preserving. Then, we give the deduction of TPH and formulate its learning stage as an optimization problem with closed form solutions. After that, we discuss some aspects of TPH which can be further developed and leave them for our future work. Some notations are given below to facilitate our discussion.

Given a dataset consists of n data points $\mathcal{X} = \{\boldsymbol{x}_i\}_{i=1}^n \in \mathbb{R}^d$ that form the columns of the data matrix $X \in \mathbb{R}^{d\times n}$, the paradigm of binary hashing is to first use a set of linear or non-linear hash functions $F = \{f_k : \mathbb{R}^d \to \mathbb{R}\}_{k=1}^m$ to map each $\boldsymbol{x}_i$ to $F(\boldsymbol{x}_i) \in \mathbb{R}^m$, and then binarize $F(\boldsymbol{x}_i)$ to embed $\boldsymbol{x}_i$ into the m-dimensional Hamming space[1] $\mathbb{H}^m \in \{-1,1\}^m$. The binary code of $\boldsymbol{x}_i$ is denoted as $\boldsymbol{y}_i = H(\boldsymbol{x}_i)$ and forms the i-th column of the code matrix $Y \in \{-1,1\}^{m\times n}$. In this paper, we restrict our attention to affine embedding:

$$H(\boldsymbol{x}) = \mathrm{sgn}(W^T\boldsymbol{x} + \boldsymbol{t}) \tag{1}$$

where W is a $d \times m$ projection matrix with each column the projection vector $\boldsymbol{\omega}_k$, and $\boldsymbol{t}$ is a $m \times 1$ vector. Without loss of generality, we could assume the data are zero-centered, i.e. $\sum_{i=1}^n \boldsymbol{x}_i = \mathbf{0}$, thus $\boldsymbol{t}$ is simply set to $\mathbf{0}$ and each hash function is given by $h_k(\boldsymbol{x}) = \mathrm{sgn}(\boldsymbol{\omega}_k^T\boldsymbol{x})$. Therefore, we can write the entire encoding process as $Y = \mathrm{sgn}(W^TX)$, where $\mathrm{sgn}(W^TX)$ is the matrix of signs of individual elements.

3.1 Motivation

As the real-world data often lies on a low-dimensional manifold [14], to capture meaningful neighbors with hashing, the neighborhood structure of the manifold should be preserved. To characterize a manifold, its topology, which represents the neighborhood relationships between subregions and the relative proximities between neighbors of each subregion, is essential [11]. As a manifold can be entirely characterized by giving the relative or comparative proximities: a first region is close to a second one but far from a third one, comparative information between distances, e.g. rankings, suffices to characterize a manifold. Therefore, more effective Hamming embeddings can be learned by taking account of the data topology in the learning stage. In this work, the relative proximities between neighbors of a data point are revealed by distances, i.e. the ranking of neighbors. Apparently, if the local topology is well preserved in Hamming

[1]We treat '0' bit as '-1' in our deduction and use '0' back in data embedding and query hashing. The conversion form -1/1 code to 0/1 code is trivial.

space, the ambiguity caused by ranking with Hamming distance can be well alleviated. As a result, topology preserving hashing is promising and our goal is to learn binary codes such that the local topology of a dataset is well preserved after the dataset has been embedded into Hamming space.

3.2 Topology Preserving Projection Learning

We begin with the definition of *local topology preserving* [16]: For data points $\boldsymbol{x}_i, \boldsymbol{x}_j, \boldsymbol{x}_s, \boldsymbol{x}_t$ in a metric space $(\mathcal{M}, d_\mathcal{M})$, where $d_\mathcal{M}(\cdot,\cdot)$ parametrizes the dissimilarity or distance in $\mathcal{M}$, and their Hamming embeddings $\boldsymbol{y}_i, \boldsymbol{y}_j, \boldsymbol{y}_s, \boldsymbol{y}_t$ generated by hash function $H(\boldsymbol{x})$. $H(\boldsymbol{x})$ is called topology preserving if the following condition holds:

$$\text{if } d_\mathcal{M}(\boldsymbol{x}_i, \boldsymbol{x}_j) \le d_\mathcal{M}(\boldsymbol{x}_s, \boldsymbol{x}_t), \text{ then } d_H(\boldsymbol{y}_i, \boldsymbol{y}_j) \le d_H(\boldsymbol{y}_s, \boldsymbol{y}_t) \tag{2}$$

where $d_H(\boldsymbol{y}_1, \boldsymbol{y}_2) = \|\boldsymbol{y}_1 - \boldsymbol{y}_2\|_2^2$ is the Hamming distance[2] between binary codes $\boldsymbol{y}_1$ and $\boldsymbol{y}_2$. This definition says that for a data point $\boldsymbol{p}$ and its neighbors $\boldsymbol{q}_1, \boldsymbol{q}_2$, if $\boldsymbol{q}_1$ is a nearer neighbor of $\boldsymbol{p}$, then $H(\boldsymbol{q}_1)$ is also a nearer neighbor of $H(\boldsymbol{p})$, which means the local topology of the neighborhood of a data point in the original data space is well preserved in Hamming space by hashing with $H(\boldsymbol{x})$.

Given $\mathcal{X} = \{\boldsymbol{x}_i\}_{i=1}^n \in \mathbb{R}^d$ in a metric space $(\mathcal{M}, d_\mathcal{M})$, our goal is to learn a set of m-bit Hamming embeddings $\{\boldsymbol{y}_i\}_{i=1}^n \in \{-1,1\}^m$ in a topology-preserving manner. We define the following objective function measuring the empirical accuracy of topology preserving:

$$\mathcal{O}(Y) = \frac{1}{2}\sum_{i,j,s,t} \operatorname{sgn}\left(d_\mathcal{M}(\boldsymbol{x}_i, \boldsymbol{x}_j) - d_\mathcal{M}(\boldsymbol{x}_s, \boldsymbol{x}_t)\right) \operatorname{sgn}\left(d_H(\boldsymbol{y}_i, \boldsymbol{y}_j) - d_H(\boldsymbol{y}_s, \boldsymbol{y}_t)\right) \tag{3}$$

Clearly, for two pairs $(\boldsymbol{x}_i, \boldsymbol{x}_j)$ and $(\boldsymbol{x}_s, \boldsymbol{x}_t)$, the summed term in Eq. (3) would be 1 if the relative proximity between $(\boldsymbol{y}_i, \boldsymbol{y}_j)$ and $(\boldsymbol{y}_s, \boldsymbol{y}_t)$ is consistent with that between $(\boldsymbol{x}_i, \boldsymbol{x}_j)$ and $(\boldsymbol{x}_s, \boldsymbol{x}_t)$, or -1 otherwise. Hence, $\mathcal{O}(Y)$ is a reasonable measure function. We replace the signs of summed terms with their signed magnitudes. This relaxation is quite intuitive in the sense that for a data point $\boldsymbol{p}$ and its neighbors $\boldsymbol{q}_1, \boldsymbol{q}_2$, it not only desires $d_\mathcal{M}(\boldsymbol{p}, \boldsymbol{q}_1) - d_\mathcal{M}(\boldsymbol{p}, \boldsymbol{q}_2)$ and $d_H(\boldsymbol{p}, \boldsymbol{q}_1) - d_H(\boldsymbol{p}, \boldsymbol{q}_2)$ to have the same signs in order to preserve the local topology, but also the larger $d_\mathcal{M}(\boldsymbol{p}, \boldsymbol{q}_1)$ than $d_\mathcal{M}(\boldsymbol{p}, \boldsymbol{q}_2)$, the larger $d_H(\boldsymbol{p}, \boldsymbol{q}_1)$ than $d_H(\boldsymbol{p}, \boldsymbol{q}_2)$. Meanwhile, if $d_\mathcal{M}(\boldsymbol{p}, \boldsymbol{q}_1) - d_\mathcal{M}(\boldsymbol{p}, \boldsymbol{q}_2)$ and $d_H(\boldsymbol{p}, \boldsymbol{q}_1) - d_H(\boldsymbol{p}, \boldsymbol{q}_2)$ have different signs, it also desires $|d_H(\boldsymbol{p}, \boldsymbol{q}_1) - d_H(\boldsymbol{p}, \boldsymbol{q}_2)|$ small in order to alleviate the local topology deviation. For brevity, we denote $d_\mathcal{M}(\boldsymbol{x}_i, \boldsymbol{x}_j)$ as d_{ij} and $d_H(\boldsymbol{y}_i, \boldsymbol{y}_j)$ as h_{ij} in the following. With this relaxation, $\mathcal{O}(Y)$ (3) becomes:

$$\mathcal{O}(Y) = \frac{1}{2}\sum (d_{ij} - d_{st})(h_{ij} - h_{st}) \tag{4}$$

Apparently, since d_{ij} is predefined, the most optimal solution Y is that makes the ranking of h_{ij} in $\{h_{ij}\}_{i,j=1}^n$ identical with that of d_{ij} in $\{d_{ij}\}_{i,j=1}^n$. As a result, based on the Rearrangement Inequality, the optimal Y will also maximize the following function:

$$\mathcal{T}(Y) = \frac{1}{2}\sum_{ij} d_{ij} h_{ij} = \frac{1}{2}\sum_{i,j} d_{ij}\|\boldsymbol{y}_i - \boldsymbol{y}_j\|_2^2 \tag{5}$$

[2]The actual Hamming distance is $\|\boldsymbol{y}_1 - \boldsymbol{y}_2\|_2^2/4$ when $\boldsymbol{y} \in \{-1,1\}^m$. For brevity, we simply use $\|\boldsymbol{y}_1 - \boldsymbol{y}_2\|_2^2$ to measure the Hamming distance.

Moreover, since $\mathcal{O}(Y)$ can be rewritten into the difference of two parts:

$$\mathcal{O}(Y) = \frac{1}{2}\sum (d_{ij}h_{ij} + d_{st}h_{st}) - \frac{1}{2}\sum (d_{ij}h_{st} + d_{st}h_{ij}) \tag{6}$$

Maximize $\mathcal{T}(Y)$ leads to maximizing the first part of $\mathcal{O}(Y)$, and based on the Rearrangement Inequality, the second part of $\mathcal{O}(Y)$ will not be maximized when $\mathcal{T}(Y)$ is maximized. Moreover, in view of the fact that the number of summed terms in $\mathcal{T}(Y)$ is $O(n^2)$, much less than that of $\mathcal{O}(Y)$, $O(n^4)$, instead of maximizing $\mathcal{O}(Y)$ directly, we try to maximize $\mathcal{T}(Y)$ alternatively. As a result, the optimization problem for solving Y is formulated as:

$$Y = \arg\max_{Y \in \{-1,1\}^{m \times n}} \mathcal{T}(Y) \tag{7}$$

In $\mathcal{T}(Y)$, d_{ij} weights each summed term $\|\boldsymbol{y}_i - \boldsymbol{y}_j\|_2^2$, thus we call it the **topo-weight** and denote it as τ_{ij}, as not only the original distance d_{ij} can be used as a topo-weight. More details about topo-weight is given in Section 3.3. By defining a **Topo-Weight Matrix** $S_t \in \mathbb{R}^{n \times n}$, $S_t(i,j) = \tau_{ij}$, problem (7) can be rewritten as:

$$Y = \arg\max_{Y \in \{-1,1\}^{m \times n}} \mathrm{Tr}\{Y \Gamma_t Y^T\} \tag{8}$$

where $\Gamma_t = D_t - S_t$, $D_t = \mathrm{diag}(S_t \mathbf{1}_{n \times 1})$. In the following, we call Γ_t the **Topo-Training Matrix**.

However, maximizing $\mathcal{T}(Y) = \mathrm{Tr}\{Y \Gamma_t Y^T\}$ is not easy to achieve because it is neither convex nor smooth. Motivated by the spectral methods for hashing [29, 14], we adopt the **Spectral Relaxation** [13] scheme to approximately maximize $\mathcal{T}(Y)$. After substituting Y with $\mathrm{sgn}(W^T X)$ and applying the spectral relaxation trick to drop the sign functions involved in $\mathcal{T}(Y)$, (8) becomes a quadratic optimization problem for solving W:

$$W = \arg\max_{W \in \mathbb{R}^{d \times m}} \mathcal{T}(W) \tag{9}$$

where $\mathcal{T}(W) = \mathrm{Tr}\{W^T X \Gamma_t X^T W\}$.

Maximizing $\mathcal{T}(W)$ is to preserve the neighborhood ranking of each data point. To preserve the data topology, we also have to preserve the neighborhood relationships as done in [29, 14, 23]. Suppose w_{ij} is the similarity between $\boldsymbol{x}_i$, $\boldsymbol{x}_j$ in the original data space. We call w_{ij} a **simi-weight** and define a **Simi-Weight Matrix** $S_s \in \mathbb{R}^{n \times n}$, $S_s(i,j) = w_{ij}$. The problem of solving W for neighborhood preserving is formulated as [29, 14]:

$$W = \arg\min_{W \in \mathbb{R}^{d \times m}} \frac{1}{2}\sum_{ij} w_{ij}\|\boldsymbol{y}_i - \boldsymbol{y}_j\|_2^2 \tag{10}$$

Applying the same spectral relaxation trick to problem (10), we have another quadratic optimization problem:

$$W = \arg\min_{W \in \mathbb{R}^{d \times m}} \mathcal{D}(W) \tag{11}$$

where $\mathcal{D}(W) = \mathrm{Tr}\{W^T X \Gamma_s X^T W\}$, $\Gamma_s = D_s - S_s$, $D_s = \mathrm{diag}(S_s \mathbf{1}_{n \times 1})$. We call Γ_s the **Simi-Training Matrix**.

In summary, the optimal projection matrix W should not only maximize $\mathcal{T}(W)$ (9), but also minimize $\mathcal{D}(W)$ (11). Hence, given a dataset X, we have two approaches to learn the optimal projection matrix W. It can be learned by maximizing the following two objective functions:

$$\mathcal{O}_1(W) = \mathcal{T}(W) - \beta\mathcal{D}(W) \quad (12)$$

$$\mathcal{O}_2(W) = \frac{\mathcal{T}(W)}{\mathcal{D}(W)} \quad (13)$$

In $\mathcal{O}_1(W)$, β is a positive scalar, which relatively weights the neighborhood-preserving term $\mathcal{D}(W)$. In this work, $\mathcal{O}_2(W)$ is used as the objective function as it somewhat resembles the spirit of linear discriminant analysis (LDA) [24] and has no regularization weight.

However, the current learning stage cannot scale well with the size of training set, as the Topo-Training Matrix Γ_t and Simi-Training Matrix Γ_s are both $n \times n$. Therefore, in practice, only a subset of X, X_t, is used as the training set to construct Γ_t and Γ_s. As a result, the objective function $\mathcal{O}_2(W)$ (13) measures only the empirical accuracy on X_t and is prone to overfitting especially when the size of X_t is small compared to the entire dataset X. To get better generalization ability, we add a regularization by incorporating conditions that lead to desirable properties of hash codes, independent of the performance on the training set. Here, the variances of hash bits are used as the regularization [26]. The overall learning stage of topology preserving hashing is formulated as the following optimization problem:

$$W = \arg\max_{W \in \mathbb{R}^{d \times m}} \mathcal{O}(W) \quad (14)$$

where

$$\mathcal{O}(W) = \frac{\mathrm{Tr}\{W^T A W\}}{\mathrm{Tr}\{W^T B W\}}$$
$$A = X_t \Gamma_t X_t^T + \alpha X X^T \quad (15)$$
$$B = X_t \Gamma_s X_t^T$$

α is a positive scalar relatively weights the regularization $\mathrm{Tr}\{W^T X X^T W\}$. In $\mathcal{O}(W)$, a column $\boldsymbol{\omega}_k$ of W with large norm makes its associated $\boldsymbol{\omega}_k^T A \boldsymbol{\omega}_k$ and $\boldsymbol{\omega}_k^T B \boldsymbol{\omega}_k$ the dominant factors in the numerator and denominator of $\mathcal{O}(W)$, thus affecting the actual maximum of $\mathcal{O}(W)$. Furthermore, in our hashing method, the direction of $\boldsymbol{\omega}_k$ is more important than its norm. As a result, we impose a "generalized normalization constraint" on W, which is $\boldsymbol{\omega}_k^T B \boldsymbol{\omega}_k = 1$. By adding this constraint, problem (14) is equivalent to:

$$W = \arg\max_{W=[\boldsymbol{\omega}_1, \boldsymbol{\omega}_2, \cdots, \boldsymbol{\omega}_m]} \mathrm{Tr}(W^T A W) \quad (16)$$
$$\text{s.t.} \quad \boldsymbol{\omega}_k^T B \boldsymbol{\omega}_k = 1, \ \forall k \in [1, m]$$

Note that, in most hashing methods [29, 26, 14], two important constraints are often imposed on hash function learning. One is all hash bits are independent (this constraint is often relaxed to hash bit decorrelation, i.e. $YY^T = nI_m$), and the other one is each bit maximizes its information entropy by balanced partitioning the dataset, i.e. $Y\mathbf{1}_{n\times 1} = \mathbf{0}$. However, these two constraints are not imposed on (16). In the following, we will show that, by using the solutions of (16) as hash functions, the learned binary codes Y somewhat satisfy these two constraints implicitly.

Problem (16) can be easily solved and the optimal solution W is given by the m generalized eigenvectors corresponding to the top m largest generalized eigenvalues of the following generalized eigendecomposition problem:

$$AW = BW\Lambda \quad (17)$$

In most cases, A and B are both positive definite Hermitian matrices. Therefore, eigenvectors $\boldsymbol{\omega}_k$ corresponding to different eigenvalues are linearly independent. Moreover, we also have $\boldsymbol{\omega}_i^T B \boldsymbol{\omega}_j = 0$, $\forall i \neq j$, which means W is weighted orthogonal with B, i.e. $W^T B W = I_m$. This can be viewed as a generalized orthogonality constraint on W. Since the orthogonality on projection matrix W is a relaxation of hash bit decorrelation [26], the learned binary codes of our method somewhat satisfies the decorrelation constraint. Meanwhile, by adding the regularization $\mathrm{Tr}(W^T X X^T W)$ with all data points to $\mathcal{O}(W)$, the balanced partition constraint is also intrinsically satisfied when X is zero-centered as proved in [26]. As a result, the decorrelation and balanced partition constraints are not imposed on problem (16).

After learning m projection vectors, one straightforward hashing method is using $h_k(\boldsymbol{x}) = \mathrm{sgn}(\boldsymbol{\omega}_k^T \boldsymbol{x})$ as the hash function to first project X on W and then binarize $Z = W^T X$ to embed X into Hamming space. This method is denoted as **TPH** in our experiments. However, the latter quantization step may distort the learned local topology, hence we have to find another way to binarize Z. It is easy to see that $\mathrm{sgn}(\boldsymbol{v})$ is the vertex of the hypercube $\{-1, 1\}^m$ closest to $\boldsymbol{v}$ in terms of Euclidean distance. To preserve the learned local topology well in Hamming space, a small quantization loss $\|\mathrm{sgn}(\boldsymbol{v}) - \boldsymbol{v}\|^2$ is desirable. One way to achieve this is to rotate $\boldsymbol{v}$ and map it to the nearest vertex [3]. Note that, for any orthogonal matrix $R \in \mathbb{R}^{m\times m}$, $\mathrm{Tr}\{RW^T AWR^T\} = \mathrm{Tr}\{W^T AW\}$ and $\mathrm{Tr}\{RW^T BWR^T\} = \mathrm{Tr}\{W^T BW\}$. Therefore, we are free to orthogonal transformation to rotate the projected data Z to minimize the following quantization loss [3]:

$$\mathcal{Q}(Y, R) = \|Y - RZ\|_F^2 = \|Y^T - Z^T R^T\|_F \quad (18)$$

where $\|\cdot\|_F$ denotes the Frobenius norm. Here, we use the iterative quantization procedure proposed in [3] to find a local minimum of $\mathcal{Q}(Y, R)$. It consists of two steps in each iteration: **fix** R and **update** Y; **fix** Y and **update** R. In the first step, Y is simply set to $\mathrm{sgn}(RZ)$. In the second step, minimization of $\mathcal{Q}(Y, R)$ is the classical Orthogonal Procrustes problem, the optimal R can be easily solved by computing the singular value decomposition of $ZY^T = U\Sigma V^T$ and setting $R^T = UV^T$, i.e. $R = VU^T$. For more details of this procedure, please refer to [3]. The final projection matrix is set to WR^T and the embedding of X is given by $\mathrm{sgn}(RW^T X)$. Hashing with the rotated projection matrix is denoted as **TPH-R** in our experiment, the whole procedure of TPH-R is outlined in Algorithm 1. Note that, TPH uses the projection matrix W learned in Step 2 of Algorithm 1 for hashing, thus its algorithm is not outlined.

3.3 Discussion

In the deduction of TPH, we call d_{ij} in $\mathcal{T}(Y)$ (5) topo-weight as it indicates the relative proximities between the neighbors of a data point, i.e. the data point is closer to one neighbor than another. Based on the Rearrangement Inequality, when maximizing $\mathcal{T}(Y)$, small d_{ij} yields small $\|\boldsymbol{y}_i - \boldsymbol{y}_j\|_2^2$ while large d_{ij} yields large $\|\boldsymbol{y}_i - \boldsymbol{y}_j\|_2^2$. Therefore, to preserve the local topology, the more similar a data pair, the smaller its topo-weight. Any $\tau_{ij} = f(d_{ij})$ can be used as the topo-weight when $f(\cdot)$ is monotonically non-decreasing w.r.t. d_{ij}. As a result, with metric learning method [27], TPH can be applied to practical applications where the similarity metrics beyond Euclidean distance used. In our ex-

Algorithm 1: Topology Preserving Hashing (TPH-R)

Input: Dataset X (zero-centered), Training set $X_t \subset X$, α the regularization weight and m the number of hash bits.

Output: Topology-preserving binary codes Y and hash function $H(\cdot)$.

1. Construct the Topo-Training Matrix Γ_t and Simi-Training Matrix Γ_s;
2. Solve the generalized eigenvalue decomposition
$$\left[X_t\Gamma_tX_t^T + \alpha XX^T\right]W = \left[X_t\Gamma_sX_t^T\right]W\Lambda$$
to determine m eigenvectors corresponding to the top-m largest generalized eigenvalue. Set the projection matrix $W = [\boldsymbol{\omega}_1, \boldsymbol{\omega}_2, \cdots, \boldsymbol{\omega}_m] \in \mathbb{R}^{d\times m}$;
3. Use the iterative quantization procedure proposed in [3] to get an optimal rotation matrix R such that the quantization loss $\mathcal{Q}(Y, R)$ (18) converges to a local minimum;
4. The rotated projection matrix is given by $P = WR^T$. The hash function of TPH-R is
$$H(\boldsymbol{x}) = \operatorname{sgn}(P^T\boldsymbol{x})$$
and the hamming embedding of X is $Y = \operatorname{sgn}(P^TX)$.

periments, we introduce two weighting schemes based on the similarity metric of original data space.

Although our TPH in this work is unsupervised, it can be extended to a semi-supervised method by adopting the following label-based weighting scheme. In the construction of Topo-Training Matrix Γ_t, if the label of each data point (e.g. semantic/class label) or pairwise relationship (similar or dissimilar) of each data pair is provided, then for a neighbor pair $(\boldsymbol{x}_i, \boldsymbol{x}_j)$, the associated topo-weight τ_{ij} is set to a small value, while for a non-neighbor pair, τ_{ij} is set to a relatively large value. By the same token, the label information can also be leveraged in the construction of Simi-Training Matrix Γ_s. By adopting this label-based weighting scheme, TPH is allowed to learn the projection matrix W in a semi-supervised manner. Experimental results in Section 4.4 demonstrate the effectiveness of adopting this label-based weighting scheme for semantic neighbor search.

In this paper, the simple linear projection is used as the hash function (1) and it still gives good similarity search performance in our experiments. Intuitively, different kinds of hash functions give rise to various hashing algorithms. In [9, 13], hash function with kernel κ plugged is given by

$$h_k(\boldsymbol{x}) = \operatorname{sgn}\left(\sum_{j=1}^{s} w_{kj}\kappa(\boldsymbol{a}_{kj}, \boldsymbol{x}) - b_k\right) \tag{19}$$

where $\boldsymbol{a}_{k1}, \cdots, \boldsymbol{a}_{ks}$ randomly selected from dataset are s kernel points of hash function $h_k(\cdot)$, $\boldsymbol{\omega}_k = (w_{k1}, \cdots, w_{ks})^T$ is the coefficient vector and $b_k = \sum_{i=1}^{n}\sum_{j=1}^{m}\kappa(\boldsymbol{a}_{kj}, \boldsymbol{x}_i)/n$ is the bias. If the set of kernel points of each hash function is identical, this embedding can be written more compactly in a matrix form:

$$Y = \operatorname{sgn}\left(W^T\left[K(\boldsymbol{x}_1), \cdots, K(\boldsymbol{x}_n)\right]\right) \tag{20}$$

where $K(\boldsymbol{x}_i) = (\kappa(\boldsymbol{a}_1, \boldsymbol{x}_i) - \mu_1, \cdots, \kappa(\boldsymbol{a}_s, \boldsymbol{x}_i) - \mu_s)^T$, $\mu_j = \sum_{i=1}^{n}\kappa(\boldsymbol{a}_j, \boldsymbol{x}_i)/n$ and $W = [\boldsymbol{\omega}_1, \cdots, \boldsymbol{\omega}_m] \in \mathbb{R}^{s\times m}$. It is interesting to find out that this embedding can be interpreted as first nonlinearly transforming each $\boldsymbol{x}_i \in \mathbb{R}^d$ to $K(\boldsymbol{x}_i) \in \mathbb{R}^s$ and then linearly projecting $K(\boldsymbol{x}_i)$ on W. Therefore, after transforming each $\boldsymbol{x}_i$ to $K(\boldsymbol{x}_i)$, the learning method of TPH can be used to learn W. As a result, more effective embeddings can be obtained in a relatively straightforward manner by introducing kernels. We leave this for our future work.

Another aspect of TPH that can be improved is the relative proximities between neighbors of data points preserved. In this paper, the relative proximities are revealed by distances, which are neighborhood rankings. In some nonlinear dimensionality reduction methods, such as locally linear embedding (LLE) [21], the relative proximities are revealed by local angles between neighbors and data points. To some extent, the preservations of local angle and distance are related and can be interpreted as two different ways to preserve local products [11]. In the next step, we would like to investigate whether the preservation of local angle can be incorporated to develop more effective hashing method.

4. EXPERIMENTAL RESULTS

4.1 Experimental Setup

Our experiments are carried out on three noted datasets: MINST70K[3], CIFAR10[4] and ANN-SIFT1M. The MNIST70K consists of 70K 784-dimensional images, each of which is associated with a digit label from '0' to '9', and is split into a baseset (training set, 60K) and a query set (10K). The CIFAR10 consists of 60K 32×32 images (baseset 50K, query set 10K) which are manually labeled into 10 classes. In our experiments, the images are represented with 512-dimensional GIST descriptors [18]. The ANN-SIFT1M [5] consists of almost 1M 128-dimensional SIFT descriptors [15], and contains three subsets: learning set (100K), baseset (1M) and query set (10K). We randomly select 1,000 points from the query set as queries in our experiments on ANN-SIFT1M.

There are many hashing methods, and some of them are either supervised [24, 13] or semi-supervised [25, 26]. Since our TPH in this work is essentially unsupervised, for fair comparison, we select some representative unsupervised methods for comparison. The selected baseline methods are LSH [1], PCAH [28], ITQ [3], SPH [29], AGH [14], BRE [9] (we use the unsupervised version), KLSH [10] and SIKH [20]. Among these methods, PCAH, ITQ, SPH and AGH are designed to preserve the original neighborhood relationships in Hamming space, while LSH, BRE, KLSH and SIKH are designed to approximate the distance between data points in the original data space or kernel space with Hamming distance. The source codes generously provided by the authors are used in our experiments. As for the parameters of each algorithm, we use the recommended settings in their papers.

In BRE, KLSH and TPH, a subset of dataset for training is essential. We randomly sample 2,000 points from the basesets of MINST70K and CIFAR10 (200 for each class), and 3,000 points from the baseset of ANN-SIFT1M as the training sets, respectively. For fair comparison, we use the same training set for these three methods. The regularization weight, α, is not fully tuned and is simply set to 0.1 for MINST70K, 0.2 for CIFAR10, and 1.0 for ANN-SIFT1M.

[3]http://yann.lecun.com/exdb/mnist/
[4]http://www.cs.toronto.edu/~kriz/cifar.html

To better validate our method, we also compare TPH with Semi-supervised Hashing (SSH) [26] and Product Quantization (PQ) [5]. As the quantization error of PQ is much smaller than most hashing methods [29, 3], the Euclidean neighbor search performance of PQ is often better than hashing based methods [5, 17]. However, as the search process of PQ is performed in the original data space, it often has a higher query time. Moreover, as PQ ignores the manifold structure of dataset, it is not effective for semantic neighbor search. By contrast, many hashing methods, e.g. AGH, SSH and our TPH, are more effective to capture semantic neighbor.

4.2 Evaluations for Similarity Search

We first evaluate TPH and TPH-R for similarity search. Since MINST70K is fully annotated, the neighbors of each query image are defined as those images with the same digit labels. For CIFAR10, the ground truth of each query is its top 5,000 Euclidean neighbors in the original data space [3, 20]. And for ANN-SIFT1M, a returned point is considered as a true neighbor if it lies in the top 1% points closest to the query, measured by the Euclidean distance [25]. In the learning stage, the topo-weight of data pair $(\boldsymbol{x}_i, \boldsymbol{x}_j)$ is simply set to the Euclidean distance, i.e. $\tau_{ij} = \|\boldsymbol{x}_i - \boldsymbol{x}_j\|_2$, and the simi-weight is $w_{ij} = \exp\{-\|\boldsymbol{x}_i - \boldsymbol{x}_j\|_2^2/\sigma^2\}$ [29], where σ is the kernel width and is set to the average pairwise distance of a sampled subset of each dataset.

Figure 2 gives the precision-recall curve on MINST70K using 32 bits binary codes. For clarity, the results are shown in two parts. From Fig. 2 it is clear that our TPH and its extension TPH-R perform best for similarity search on this dataset. More specifically, TPH outperforms most baseline methods except for ITQ (and AGH in low-recall case), and TPH-R gives the best search performance under most settings. Moreover, as shown on Fig. 2 and Fig. 3(c), even with a relatively short binary code (32 bits), the search performance of TPH-R is still better than all baseline methods with longer binary codes (96 bits). These comparisons indicate that, TPH preserves the neighborhood relationships better by learning from the topology of the intrinsic manifold structure of MINST70K. It is interesting to note that, in these experiments, the ground truth is defined based on semantic label. Although all the evaluated methods are unsupervised, they give reasonable good performance for semantic neighbor search, especially the TPH-R. This is because that, in MINST70K, mostly, the Euclidean distances between data points with same labels are smaller than the distances between data points with different labels. By using the Euclidean distance as topo-weight, neighbor pairs are given smaller weights than non-neighbor pairs, which is similar with adopting the label-based weighting scheme in Section 3.3. Therefore, the experimental results also indicate that TPH is capable of capturing semantic neighbors with the label-based weighting scheme.

Figure 3-5 give the precision-recall curves on MINST70K, CIFAR10 and ANN-SIFT1M under different code lengths, respectively. Once again, we can easily find out that our TPH and TPH-R outperform other state-of-the-art methods under most settings. These comparisons demonstrate the effectiveness of incorporating the neighborhood ranking information with binary codes learning. Note that, the performance improvement of TPH-R on ANN-SIFT1M is not as remarkable as those on MINST70K and CIFAR10. This result is reasonable, since the training samples is only 3‰ of the entire ANN-SIFT1M dataset. This sampling sparsity makes the data topology of the training set non-representative, thus the learned W are not optimal. To verify this, we retrain our model with 30K training samples and report the mAP (21) of TPH-R: The mAP values of TPH-R with 32, 48, 64 and 96 bits codes are 0.3327, 0.4015, 0.5022 and 0.5301, respectively. In this case, TPH-R outperforms ITQ under all settings (mAPs of ITQ are given in Table 1), which also indicates our method become more effective with more training samples.

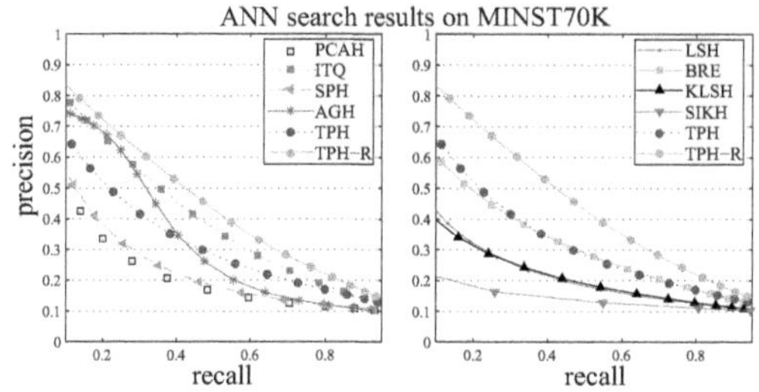

Figure 2: Precision-recall curve on MINST70K. All methods use 32 bits code.

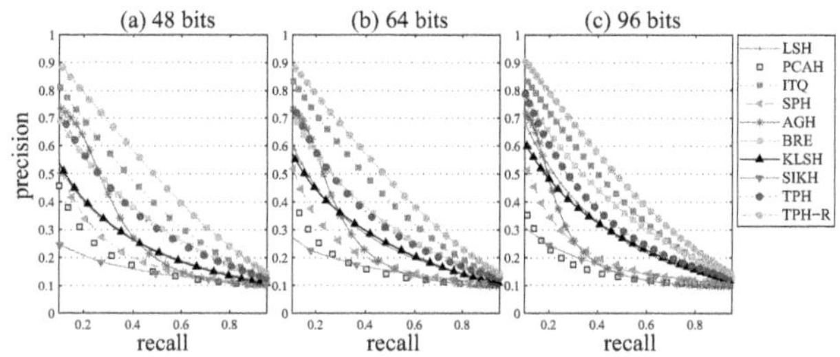

Figure 3: Precision-recall curves on MINST70K using different code lengths: (a) 48; (b) 64; (c) 96.

4.3 Evaluations for Topology Preserving

The above experiments demonstrate the superiority of TPH for similarity search. In this section, we conduct a series of experiments to evaluate the efficacy of TPH for the preservation of relative proximities, which is the ranking of neighbors in this work. In these experiments, the mAP is used as the performance metric. It is defined as:

$$\begin{aligned} \text{Precision} &= \frac{\text{number of retrieved neighbors}}{\text{number of all retrieved points}} \\ \text{mAP} &= \frac{1}{|Q|}\sum_{i=1}^{|Q|}\frac{1}{n_i}\sum_{k=1}^{n_i}\text{Precision}(R_{ik}) \end{aligned} \tag{21}$$

where Q is query set, $|Q|$ is its cardinality and n_i is the number of neighbors of query $\boldsymbol{q}_i \in Q$ in dataset. The neighbors are ordered as $\boldsymbol{x}_1, \boldsymbol{x}_2, \cdots, \boldsymbol{x}_{n_i}$ and R_{ik} is the set of ranked retrieval results from the top result to $\boldsymbol{x}_k$. This definition says that, for two hashing methods returning the same number of neighbors for a query, if one gives a better ranking for the neighbors, it would have a higher mAP, which indicates it preserves the local data topology better.

The mAP values of different methods with different code lengths on MINST70K, CIFAR10, and ANN-SIFT1M are given in Table 1. It is obvious that our TPH outperforms almost all baseline methods except for ITQ, and its exten-

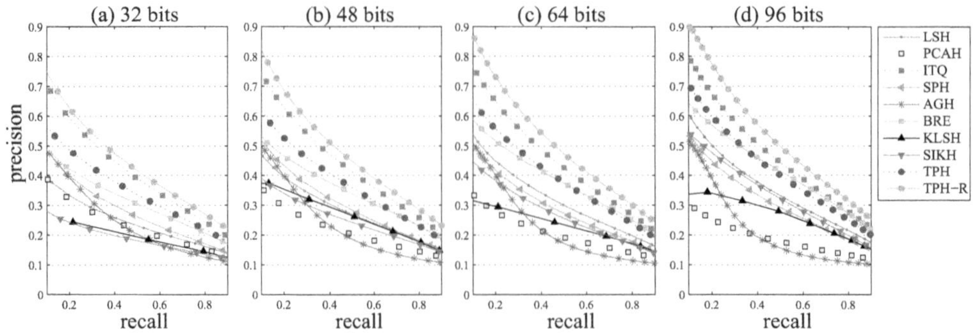

Figure 4: Precision-recall curves on CIFAR10 dataset. Code lengths: (a) 32; (b) 48; (c) 64; (d) 96.

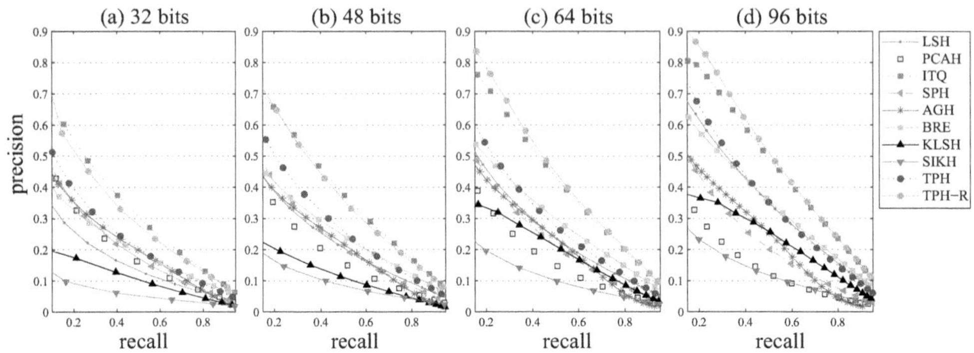

Figure 5: Precision-recall curves on ANN-SIFT1M dataset. Code lengths: (a) 32; (b) 48; (c) 64; (d) 96.

sion TPH-R again gives the best performance under most settings. These experimental results demonstrate that TPH and TPH-R preserve the local topology of a dataset better.

4.4 Leveraging Label Information

In this section, we show the performance of semantic neighbor search of TPH by leveraging label information. With label information, Topo-Training Matrix Γ_t and Simi-Training Matrix Γ_s can be constructed to better capture the semantic structure of a dataset, extending TPH semi-supervised.

Our experiments are carried out on MINST70K and CIFAR10. Each image in MINST70K is labeled with a digital number from '0' to '9' and each image in CIFAR10 is labeled into one of the following ten classes: *airplane*, *automobile*, *bird*, *cat*, *deer*, *dog*, *frog*, *horse*, *ship*, and *truck*. The neighborhood relationships are defined based on semantic labels. We adopt the label-based weighting scheme in Section 3.3 such that for a neighbor pair, its topo-weight is set to a small value, while for a non-neighbor pair, its topo-weight is set to a relatively large value. In the construction of Γ_t, for a neighbor pair, we set $\tau_{ij} = 1.0$, and for a non-neighbor pair, we set $\tau_{ij} = 10.0$ to ensure that the corresponding binary codes can be well separated in Hamming space. In the construction of Γ_s, the simi-weight is $w_{ij} = 1.0$ for a neighbor pair and $w_{ij} = \exp\{-\|\boldsymbol{x}_i - \boldsymbol{x}_j\|_2^2/\sigma^2\}$ for a non-neighbor pair. For comparison, we select some methods which give good performances in our previous experiments. In addition, we also compare our method with PQ [5] and SSH [26] for better validation. For PQ, the original data is decomposed into 8 subspaces and the asymmetric distance calculation (ADC) is used for neighbor search. For SSH, we use the same training set as that of TPH.

Table 2 reports the mAP values of different methods for semantic neighbor search on MINST70K and CIFAR10, and Fig. 6 gives the qualitative retrieval results of TPH leveraging label information applied on CIFAR10 using 32 bits codes. Our TPH with label information is denoted as **TPH-L**. We can easily see that, when label information is incorporated, the retrieval results are much more semantically consistent. Moreover, TPH-L gives a better ranking for the neighbors of each query. Since most of the compared baselines are unsupervised, the comparison results given here are not to show that TPH outperforms these methods for semantic neighbor search, but to demonstrate that, by leveraging label information, our TPH can be easily extended to a semi-supervised method to capture semantic neighbor effectively.

4.5 Summary

In summary, the experimental results demonstrate the efficacy of TPH for fast similarity search. From the results we can conclude that, by learning from the local topology of the intrinsic manifold structure of a dataset, TPH can generate more optimal Hamming embeddings, which not only preserve the neighborhood relationships between data points, but also preserve the neighborhood ranking of each data point. This finding has important implications for learning to hashing: the neighborhood ranking information is also valuable for effective hashing. Moreover, by leveraging label information, the learning stage of TPH can be easily extended to a semi-supervised manner, which gives TPH the capability of capturing semantic neighbors. In the future, we will refine the formulation of TPH, making the label information be better incorporated with the learning stage.

Table 1: **mAP values on MINST70K, CIFAR10 and ANN-SIFT1M under different settings. The best mAP among TPH, TPH-R and other methods is shown in bold face.**

dataset	MINST70K				CIFAR10				ANN-SIFT1M			
method \ #bits	32	48	64	96	32	48	64	96	32	48	64	96
PCAH	0.2456	0.2272	0.2159	0.2009	0.2409	0.2261	0.2155	0.2000	0.2136	0.2286	0.2167	0.1931
ITQ	0.4480	0.4620	0.4752	0.4815	0.4362	0.4591	0.4724	0.4893	**0.3173**	**0.3820**	0.4665	0.5083
SPH	0.2699	0.2544	0.2569	0.2604	0.2770	0.3023	0.2950	0.3131	0.2345	0.2750	0.3231	0.3103
AGH	0.3674	0.3311	0.3074	0.2777	0.2540	0.2515	0.2467	0.2390	0.2373	0.2835	0.3312	0.3390
LSH	0.2561	0.3064	0.3328	0.3702	0.2667	0.3111	0.3462	0.3807	0.1696	0.2543	0.3231	0.3603
BRE	0.3604	0.4006	0.4014	0.4470	0.3143	0.3484	0.3824	0.4219	0.2432	0.2998	0.3430	0.3553
KLSH	0.2227	0.2848	0.2956	0.3207	0.1996	0.2670	0.2100	0.2392	0.1045	0.1364	0.2367	0.3243
SIKH	0.1454	0.1562	0.1717	0.1867	0.1922	0.2481	0.2709	0.3309	0.0610	0.0960	0.1171	0.1302
TPH	0.3648	0.3878	0.3864	0.3934	0.3878	0.4144	0.4346	0.4625	0.2766	0.3312	0.3648	0.3687
TPH-R	**0.5027**	**0.5194**	**0.5213**	**0.5283**	**0.4558**	**0.4707**	**0.4936**	**0.5160**	0.3056	0.3810	**0.4803**	**0.5210**

Table 2: mAP values of semantic neighbor search on MINST70K and CIFAR10.

MINST70K

#bits	PQ	SSH	TPH-R	TPH-L
32	0.4454	0.4670	0.5027	**0.5161**
64	0.4521	0.4861	0.5213	**0.5333**

CIFAR10

#bits	ITQ	SPH	AGH	BRE
32	0.1634	0.1307	0.1340	0.1493
64	0.1740	0.1313	0.1345	0.1578
	PQ	SSH	TPH-R	TPH-L
32	0.1766	0.1982	0.1658	**0.2126**
64	0.1820	0.2144	0.1772	**0.2223**

5. CONCLUSIONS

To capture meaningful neighbors, most hashing methods are developed to preserve the neighbor relationships while ignoring the neighborhood rankings. In this paper, we show that the neighborhood rankings are as important as the neighborhood relationships for learning to hashing, and propose a novel hashing method, Topology Preserving Hashing (TPH), by incorporating the neighborhood ranking information with hash function learning. Our approach is distinct from prior works by not only preserving the neighborhood relationships between data points, but also preserving the neighborhood rankings. Since the ranking information is encoded in the codes, the ranking ambiguity of most hashing methods is also well alleviated. Experimental results on three large-scale image datasets containing up to one million high-dimensional data points show the efficacy of TPH. Moreover, although our method is entirely unsupervised in this work, it can be easily extended to a semi-supervised method for semantic neighbor search as demonstrated. In the future, we will evaluate more sophisticated techniques to solve the problem of topology preserving and apply our method to a large spectrum of information retrieval problems such as image retrieve and near-duplicate detection.

6. ACKNOWLEDGMENTS

This work is supported by National Nature Science Foundation of China (61273247, 61271428), National Key Technology Research and Development Program of China (2012-BAH39B02). This work was supported in part to Dr. Qi Tian by ARO grant W911BF-12-1-0057, NSF IIS 1052851, Faculty Research Awards by Google, FXPAL, and NEC Laboratories of America, and 2012 UTSA START-R Research Award respectively. This work was supported in part by NSFC 61128007.

7. REFERENCES

[1] A. Andoni and P. Indyk. Near-optimal hashing algorithms for approximate nearest neighbor in high dimensions. In *FOCS*, pages 459–468, 2006.

[2] J. L. Bentley and B. Labo. K-d trees for semidynamic point sets. In *SOCG*, pages 187–197, 1990.

[3] Y. Gong, S. Lazebnik, A. Gordo, and F. Perronnin. Iterative quantization: A procrustean approach to learning binary codes for large-scale image retrieval. *IEEE Trans. Pattern Anal. Mach. Intell.*, 2012.

[4] M. Jain, H. Jégou, P. Gros, et al. Asymmetric hamming embedding: taking the best of our bits for large scale image search. In *ACM Multimedia*, 2011.

[5] H. Jégou, M. Douze, and C. Schmid. Product quantization for nearest neighbor search. *IEEE Trans. Pattern Anal. Mach. Intell.*, 33:117–128, 2011.

[6] J. Ji, J. Li, S. Yan, B. Zhang, and Q. Tian. Super-bit locality-sensitive hashing. In *NIPS*, pages 108–116, 2012.

[7] Y.-G. Jiang, J. Wang, X. Xue, and S.-F. Chang. Query-adaptive image search with hash codes. *IEEE Trans. Multimedia*, 15(2):442–453, 2013.

[8] A. Joly and O. Buisson. A posteriori multi-probe locality sensitive hashing. In *ACM Multimedia*, 2008.

[9] B. Kulis and T. Darrell. Learning to hash with binary reconstructive embeddings. In *NIPS*, pages 1042–1050, 2009.

[10] B. Kulis and K. Grauman. Kernelized locality-sensitive hashing. *IEEE Trans. Pattern Anal. Mach. Intell.*, 34:1092–1104, 2012.

[11] J. Lee and M. Verleysen. *Nonlinear dimensionality reduction*. Springer, 2007.

[12] P. Li, M. Wang, J. Cheng, C. Xu, and H. Lu. Spectral hashing with semantically consistent graph for image

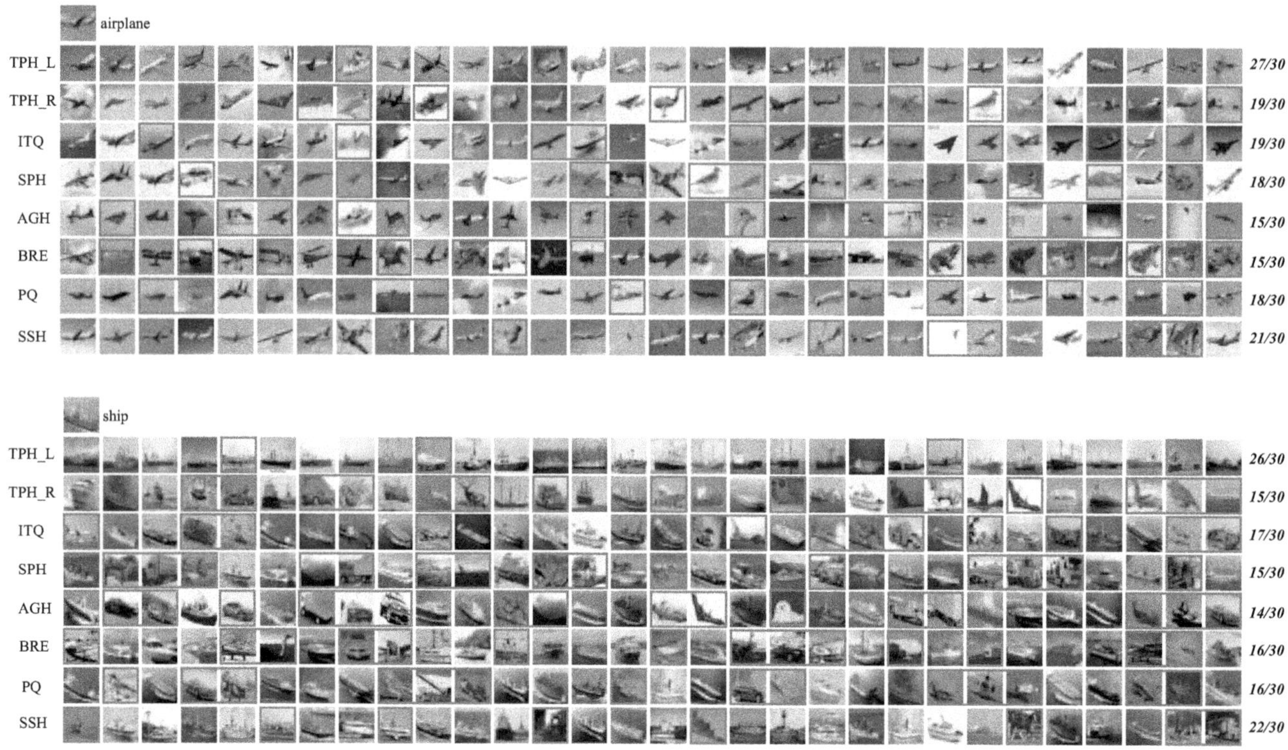

Figure 6: Qualitative retrieval results on CIFAR10 for two queries. Apparently, the retrieval quality of TPH with label information (the first row) is much better. The semantical consistency and ranking of the retrieval results are both significantly improved. Red rectangle denotes false positive. Best viewed in color.

indexing. *IEEE Trans. Multimedia*, 15(1):141–152, 2013.

[13] W. Liu, J. Wang, R. Ji, Y. Jiang, and S.-F. Chang. Supervised hashing with kernels. In *CVPR*, pages 2074–2081, 2012.

[14] W. Liu, J. Wang, S. Kumar, and S.-F. Chang. Hashing with graphs. In *ICML*, pages 1–8, 2011.

[15] D. G. Lowe. Distinctive image features from scale-invariant keypoints. *IJCV*, 60:91–110, 2004.

[16] D. Luo, C. Ding, F. Nie, and H. Huang. Cauchy graph embedding. In *ICML*, pages 553–560, 2011.

[17] M. Norouzi and D. Fleet. Cartesian k-means. In *CVPR*, pages 3017–3024, 2013.

[18] A. Oliva and A. B. Torralba. Modeling the shape of the scene: a holistic representation of the spatial envelope. *IJCV*, 42:145–175, 2001.

[19] L. Paulevé, H. Jégou, and L. Amsaleg. Locality sensitive hashing: A comparison of hash function types and querying mechanisms. *Pattern Recognition Letters*, 31(11):1348–1358, 2010.

[20] M. Raginsky and S. Lazebnik. Locality-sensitive binary codes from shift-invariant kernels. In *NIPS*, pages 1509–1517, 2009.

[21] S. Roweis and L. Saul. Nonlinear dimensionality reduction by locally linear embedding. *Science*, 290(5500):2323–2326, 2000.

[22] R. Salakhutdinov and G. E. Hinton. Semantic hashing. *Int. J. Approx. Reason*, 50:969–978, 2009.

[23] J. Song, Y. Yang, Z. Huang, H. T. Shen, and R. Hong. Multiple feature hashing for real-time large scale near-duplicate video retrieval. In *ACM Multimedia*, pages 423–432, 2011.

[24] C. Strecha, A. M. Bronstein, M. M. Bronstein, and P. Fua. LDAHash: Improved matching with smaller descriptors. *IEEE Trans. Pattern Anal. Mach. Intell.*, 34(1):66–78, 2012.

[25] J. Wang, S. Kumar, and S.-F. Chang. Sequential projection learning for hashing with compact codes. In *ICML*, pages 1127–1134, 2010.

[26] J. Wang, S. Kumar, and S.-F. Chang. Semi-supervised hashing for large-scale search. *IEEE Trans. Pattern Anal. Mach. Intell.*, 34(12):2393–2406, 2012.

[27] M. Wang, X.-S. Hua, J. Tang, and R. Hong. Beyond distance measurement: constructing neighborhood similarity for video annotation. *IEEE Trans. Multimedia*, 11(3):465–476, 2009.

[28] X. Wang, L. Zhang, F. Jing, and W. Ma. AnnoSearch: image auto-annotation by search. In *CVPR*, pages 1483–1490, 2006.

[29] Y. Weiss, A. B. Torralba, and R. Fergus. Spectral hashing. In *NIPS*, pages 1753–1760, 2008.

[30] L. Zhang, Y. Zhang, J. Tang, K. Lu, and Q. Tian. Binary code ranking with weighted hamming distance. In *CVPR*, pages 1586–1593, 2013.

[31] W. Zhou, Y. Lu, H. Li, Y. Song, and Q. Tian. Spatial coding for large scale partial-duplicate web image search. In *ACM Multimedia*, pages 511–520, 2010.

[32] W. Zhou, Y. Lu, H. Li, and Q. Tian. Scalar quantization for large scale image search. In *ACM Multimedia*, pages 169–178, 2012.

Order Preserving Hashing for Approximate Nearest Neighbor Search

Jianfeng Wang[†*] Jingdong Wang[‡] Nenghai Yu[†] Shipeng Li[‡]
[†]University of Science and Technology of China, P. R. China
[‡]Microsoft Research Asia, P. R. China
wjf2006@mail.ustc.edu.cn, {jingdw, spli}@microsoft.com, ynh@ustc.edu.cn

ABSTRACT

In this paper, we propose a novel method to learn similarity-preserving hash functions for approximate nearest neighbor (NN) search. The key idea is to learn hash functions by maximizing the alignment between the similarity orders computed from the original space and the ones in the hamming space. The problem of mapping the NN points into different hash codes is taken as a classification problem in which the points are categorized into several groups according to the hamming distances to the query. The hash functions are optimized from the classifiers pooled over the training points. Experimental results demonstrate the superiority of our approach over existing state-of-the-art hashing techniques.

Categories and Subject Descriptors

H.3.3 [**Information Storage and Retrieval**]: Information Search and Retrieval

Keywords

Order preserving hashing; approximate nearest neighbor search; learning to hash

1. INTRODUCTION

Nearest neighbor search (or similarity search) in large data sets has wide applications in machine learning and computer vision. However, exact nearest neighbor search is often intractable because of the large scale of the database and the curse of the high dimensionality. Instead, approximate nearest neighbor (ANN) search is more practical and has been attracting a lot of attention [32].

As one of the commonly-used approaches, hashing uses multiple integer-valued hash functions to map similar inputs to nearby hash buckets. The pioneering work, locality sensitive hashing (LSH) [8], adopts random projections to compute hash codes. It is probabilistically guaranteed that nearer points have a larger probability to share the same binary codes and farther points have a larger probability to be mapped to the farther binary codes. However, LSH is data independent and has been shown in practice to be weaker than data-dependent hashing methods. To improve the performance, LSH usually needs long code length or multiple hash tables resulting in a large space and time cost.

Recently many learning-to-hashing algorithms have been developed, such as [3, 4, 6, 7, 10, 14, 15, 16, 17, 20, 21, 22, 23, 24, 25, 27, 28, 29, 31, 34, 37, 38, 39, 40, 41]. Most algorithms aim to learn hash functions so that the similarities in the input space are kept in the hamming space, in various manners. Binary reconstructive embedding [16] aims to minimize the differences between the distances in the input (kernel) space and those in the hamming space. In real data sets that are usually not uniformly distributed, preserving absolute similarities/distances does not guarantee to produce good nearest neighbor search that concerns more the relative similarity than the absolute similarity. Instead, some other algorithms, e.g., [27, 34, 38], divide the point pairs into similar and dissimilar pairs, i.e., binary similarities, and find hash functions by preserving the binary similarities. Such approaches are more suitable to preserve semantic similarity and have little capability of differentiating multiple level similarities that are essential for nearest neighbor search.

In this paper, we propose a novel ANN search approach, order preserving hashing (OPH). The key idea is to learn hash functions based on a so-called order alignment criterion, which is some notion of similarity preserving. Order alignment means that the similarity order computed in the input space should be well preserved in the hamming space. and is essentially the goal of ANN search. Hashing with preserving orders is more general than binary similarity preserving, and advantageous over direct distance preserving in dealing with real skewed data.

Our formulation is also inspired by a widely-used bucket balance criterion, i.e., points are uniformly distributed in hash buckets. The joint consideration of such two criteria, if viewing each point as a query, results in a list of categories, where each category is composed of the points having the same hamming distance to the query. Then we formulate the category order alignment as a multi-class classification problem with each category viewed as a class. We present an easily-implemented optimization algorithm that incorporates Sigmoid relaxation, mini-batch stochastic gradient descent, and active set. Experimental results over standard

*The work was done during Jianfeng Wang was an intern at Microsoft Research Asia.

MM'13, October 21–25, 2013, Barcelona, Spain.

http://dx.doi.org/10.1145/2502081.2502100 .

sets demonstrate the superiority of our approach over existing state-of-the-art ANN search algorithm.

2. RELATED WORK

Hashing is a category of algorithms that map high-dimensional vectors into binary codes. Recently many hashing algorithms have been developed for approximate nearest neighbor search and have achieved a lot of success in multimedia applications, e.g., image search [5, 18, 36, 43], video retrieval [1, 33], duplicate discovery in video sequence [42] and document retrieval [31]. The common principle of different hashing algorithms is to align the similarities between the hamming space and the input space. Existing algorithms can be roughly divided into two categories, probabilistic similarity preserving and determinative similarity preserving.

Probabilistic similarity preserving. Locality sensitive hashing (LSH) [8], one of the typical representatives, is a method of performing ANN search in high dimensions, dependent on probabilistic dimension reduction of high-dimensional data (random projection is a widely-used way to dimension reduction). The key idea is to hash the points using several hash functions to ensure a probabilistic guarantee of similarities, i.e., for each function the probability of collision is much higher for objects (points) that are close to each other than those far apart.

There are various algorithms extending LSH, such as [11, 17, 25, 29]. Kernelized LSH [17] studies the hash functions by extending the idea of random projection to the kernel space. Shift-invariant kernel hashing [29] adopts a random cosine function to generate the hash codes and shows that the hamming distance is closely related to the shift-invariant kernel value. Super-bit LSH [11] orthogonalizes the random projections in batches and an unbiased estimate of the angle similarity is theoretically supported with a smaller variance under certain conditions. These approaches do not explore the data distribution for hash function construction and usually need longer hash codes or more hash tables to achieve a satisfactory performance, thus resulting in a large space and time cost.

Deterministic similarity preserving. In contrast to probabilistic similarity preserving, deterministic similarity preserving hashing algorithms formulate a problem that minimizes the misalignment rate between the similarities/distaces computed from the hamming and input space.

Binary reconstructive embedding [16] aims to align the hamming distance over the hash codes and the distance in the input Euclidean (and kernel) spaces. Iterative quantization hashing [3] constructs hash functions by rotating the axes so that the difference between the binary codes and the projected data is minimized [3], while the goal of isotropic hashing [14] is to make the variances along the rotated linear projections are as same as possible. Both iterative quantization hashing and isotropic hashing are related to multidimensional scaling and in some sense aim to keep the Euclidean distance.

Entropy-based coding [20] regards the similarities as a distribution and learns hash functions by preserving the normalized similarity distribution and minimizes the Kullback-Leibler divergence between the distributions computed from the input space and the hamming space. Spectral hashing (SH) [40] exploits the similarities in a different way and aims to minimize the summation of the hamming distance weighted by the similarities computed in the input space. The following works [6, 23] extend spectral hashing by generalizing to kernel hash functions.

Rather than preserving absolute similarities that are shown to have limited capabilities in dealing with real skewed data, algorithms on preserving binary similarities (point pairs are divided into similar and dissimilar pairs.) have been studied. The sequential projection learning scheme [38] aims to minimize (maximize) the hamming distance of similar (dissimilar) pairs. LDAHash [34] learns hash functions by minimizing (maximizing) the expectation of the hamming distances over positive(negative) pairs. The weakly-supervised approach [24] exploits the extra property, large margin to help learn hash functions. Minimal loss hashing [27] adopts a hinge-like loss function to penalize the case that the hamming distances of the similar points are larger than a threshold and the hamming distances of the dissimilar pairs are smaller than another threshold. The triplet similarity preserving hashing approach [28] is a framework of learning a broad class of hash functions, using a triplet ranking loss, is shown to be more flexible and very well suited to the preservation of semantic similarity.

Besides, there are hashing algorithms that exploit other information to improve the performance. Complementary hashing [41] learns multiple complementary hash tables instead of randomized hash tables. Multi-modality hashing [13, 23, 33] aims to learn hash functions by exploring multiple features. Various distance measures in the binary-code space, such as spherical hamming distance [7], Manhattan distance [15], weighted hamming distance [12, 39] and non-parametric distance [10], are considered to learn hash functions. Query-adaptive hashing [9] performs an selection of the most appropriate hash functions from a pool of functions.

3. FORMULATION

The reference data set is denoted by $\mathcal{X} = \{\mathbf{x}_1, \cdots, \mathbf{x}_N\}$ with $\mathbf{x} \in \mathbb{R}^d$. The hashing scheme for ANN search maps each point $\mathbf{x}$ to a m-dimensional binary vector $\mathbf{c}$ through a hash function $\mathbf{h} : \mathbb{R}^d \mapsto \mathbb{H}^m$, where $\mathbb{H}^m$ denotes the Hamming space of dimension m. We use $d_H(\mathbf{c}, \tilde{\mathbf{c}})$ to denote the hamming distance, i.e., the number of bits on which $\mathbf{c}$ and $\tilde{\mathbf{c}}$ differ.

An ideal hash function expects that the ordered lists computed from the hamming space and the original space are well matched, which we call *order alignment*. For a query point $\mathbf{x}$, denote the similarity order computed in the hamming space as $L^h = (i_1, \cdots, i_N)$ and the order computed from the original space, as $L^e = (j_1, \cdots, j_N)$. Order alignment between the two lists of points, called *point order alignment*, means $i_n = j_n$, $\forall n$.

In the hamming space, there are a limited number of $(m + 1)$ distance values. Therefore, searching in the hamming distance results in a set of ordered $m + 1$ categories, $(\mathcal{C}_0^h, \mathcal{C}_1^h, \cdots, \mathcal{C}_m^h)$, where $\mathcal{C}_k^h = \{i_1^k, \cdots, i_{M_k}^k\}$. Accordingly, the ordered list L^e is divided into $m + 1$ categories, $(\mathcal{C}_0^e, \mathcal{C}_1^e, \cdots, \mathcal{C}_m^e)$, which we call target categories, such that $|\mathcal{C}_k^h| = |\mathcal{C}_k^e|$. Order alignment between the two lists of categories, which we call *category order alignment*, means $\mathcal{C}_k^h = \mathcal{C}_k^e$.

However, category order alignment does not guarantee a good hashing. Considering the extreme case that all points are mapped to a same hash code, we can see category order alignment is satisfied, $|\mathcal{C}_0^h| = |\mathcal{C}_0^e|$ and $|\mathcal{C}_1^h| = \cdots = |\mathcal{C}_m^h| = 0$.

But this case does not lead to a good hashing. To handle such an issue, we propose to exploit another condition, *bucket balance*, which means that the points are uniformly distributed in all hash buckets and is helpful to guarantee search efficiency.

We aim to learn hash functions based on the above two properties, category order alignment and bucket balance. Given the target categories that are constructed according to the bucket balance property, category order alignment is regarded as a multi-class classification problem. That's for a query all the reference data points are assigned to one of $m+1$ target categories. To penalize the misalignment rate, we transform the multi-class classification problem to m binary-class classification problems. Specifically, we partition the target categories into m sets of binary super-categories, $\{(\mathcal{N}_0^e,\overline{\mathcal{N}_0^e}),(\mathcal{N}_1^e,\overline{\mathcal{N}_1^e}),\cdots,(\mathcal{N}_{m-1}^e,\overline{\mathcal{N}_{m-1}^e})\}$, where each pair of super-categories $(\mathcal{N}_i^e,\mathcal{N}_i^h)$ forms a binary-class classification problem. Here, $\mathcal{N}_i^e=\cup_{j=0}^{i}\mathcal{C}_j^e$ and $\overline{\mathcal{N}_i^e}=\mathcal{X}-\mathcal{N}_i^e$, and the super-categories in the hamming space, $\{(\mathcal{N}_i^h,\overline{\mathcal{N}_i^h})\}_{i=0}^{m-1}$, is similarly built. The objective function of penalizing misalignment rate is formulated as follows,

$$
\begin{aligned}
& L(\mathbf{h}(\cdot);\mathcal{X}) && (1)\\
=& \sum\nolimits_{n=1}^{N} L(\mathbf{h}(\cdot);\mathbf{x}_n) && (2)\\
=& \sum\nolimits_{n=1}^{N}\sum\nolimits_{i=0}^{m-1} L(\mathbf{h}(\cdot);\mathbf{x}_n,i) && (3)\\
=& \sum\nolimits_{n=1}^{N}\sum\nolimits_{i=0}^{m-1}(|\mathcal{N}_{ni}^e-\mathcal{N}_{ni}^h|+\lambda|\mathcal{N}_{ni}^h-\mathcal{N}_{ni}^e|), && (4)
\end{aligned}
$$

where $|\mathcal{N}_{ni}^e-\mathcal{N}_{ni}^h|$ and $|\mathcal{N}_{ni}^h-\mathcal{N}_{ni}^e|$ are the errors for the target binary super-categories, $(\mathcal{N}_{ni}^e,\overline{\mathcal{N}_{ni}^e})$, and $|\mathcal{N}_{ni}^h-\mathcal{N}_{ni}^e|=|\overline{\mathcal{N}_{ni}^e}-\overline{\mathcal{N}_{ni}^h}|$. λ is a trade-off parameter to balance the penalties for the two categories.

4. OPTIMIZATION

In this paper, we use the widely-used hash function, the linear projection, as an example implementation of order preserving hashing. The linear hash functions are formulated as follows,

$$
\begin{aligned}
\mathbf{h}(\mathbf{x}) &= \operatorname{sign}(\mathbf{W}^T\mathbf{x}+\mathbf{b}) \qquad (5)\\
&= [\operatorname{sign}(\mathbf{w}_1^T\mathbf{x}+b_1)\ \cdots\ \operatorname{sign}(\mathbf{w}_m^T\mathbf{x}+b_m)]^T,
\end{aligned}
$$

where $\mathbf{W}$ is a projection matrix of size $d\times m$, each column $\mathbf{w}_k\in\mathbb{R}^d$ is a projection vector and $\mathbf{w}_k^T\mathbf{w}_k=1$, $\mathbf{b}\in\mathbb{R}^m$ being the threshold for the hash function. $\operatorname{sign}(\cdot)$ is a sign function, where $\operatorname{sign}(z)=1$ when $z>0$ and $\operatorname{sign}(z)=0$ otherwise. For convenience, we formulate an augmented matrix $\overline{\mathbf{W}}\in\mathbb{R}^{(d+1)\times m}$, $\overline{\mathbf{W}}=[\mathbf{W}^T|\mathbf{b}]^T$, and then the normalization constraint can be equivalently written as $\overline{\mathbf{w}}_k^T\overline{\mathbf{w}}_k=1$. Accordingly, a point $\mathbf{x}$ is augmented as $\overline{\mathbf{x}}=[\mathbf{x}^T|1]^T$. As a result, $\mathbf{h}(\overline{\mathbf{x}})=\operatorname{sign}(\overline{\mathbf{W}}^T\overline{\mathbf{x}})$. The following description might drop the upper bar if not affecting the understanding.

Recalling that $\mathcal{N}_{ni}^h$ is formed by the points whose hamming distances to the point $\mathbf{x}_n$ are not larger than i, we have the following equations,

$$
\begin{aligned}
|\mathcal{N}_{ni}^e-\mathcal{N}_{ni}^h| &= \sum_{\mathbf{x}'\in\mathcal{N}_{ni}^e}\operatorname{sign}(d_H(\mathbf{h}(\mathbf{x}_n),\mathbf{h}(\mathbf{x}'))-i),\\
|\mathcal{N}_{ni}^h-\mathcal{N}_{ni}^e| &= \sum_{\mathbf{x}'\notin\mathcal{N}_{ni}^e}\operatorname{sign}(i+1-d_H(\mathbf{h}(\mathbf{x}_n),\mathbf{h}(\mathbf{x}'))).
\end{aligned}
$$

Here, the function $\operatorname{sign}(\cdot)$ is used to check if the point is correctly classified. Replacing $d_H(\mathbf{h}(\mathbf{x}_n),\mathbf{h}(\mathbf{x}'))$ by the equivalent form in the hamming space, $\|\mathbf{h}(\mathbf{x}_n)-\mathbf{h}(\mathbf{x}')\|_2^2$, we have

$$
\begin{aligned}
& L(\mathbf{W};\mathbf{x}_n,i)\\
=& \sum\nolimits_{\mathbf{x}'\in\mathcal{N}_{ni}^e}\operatorname{sign}(\|\mathbf{h}(\mathbf{x}_n)-\mathbf{h}(\mathbf{x}')\|_2^2-i)\\
&+\lambda\sum\nolimits_{\mathbf{x}'\notin\mathcal{N}_{ni}^e}\operatorname{sign}(i+1-\|\mathbf{h}(\mathbf{x}_n)-\mathbf{h}(\mathbf{x}')\|_2^2). \qquad (6)
\end{aligned}
$$

4.1 Relaxation

It can be observed that the function $\operatorname{sign}(\cdot)$ in Eqn. (5) and (6) is non-smooth, which makes the optimization uneasy. To address this issue, we propose to relax the $\operatorname{sign}(\cdot)$ to a Sigmoid function $\phi_\alpha(z)=\frac{1}{1+e^{-\alpha z}}$. Its first-order derivative is $\phi'_\alpha(z)=\alpha\phi_\alpha(z)(1-\phi_\alpha(z))$. Here α is used to balance the quality approximating $\operatorname{sign}(\cdot)$ and the smoothness degree. A larger α leads to a better approximation, but a more difficult optimization.

The hash function $\mathbf{h}(\mathbf{x})=\operatorname{sign}(\mathbf{W}^T\mathbf{x})$ is relaxed as

$$
\mathbf{h}(\mathbf{x})=\phi_\beta(\mathbf{W}^T\mathbf{x})=[\phi_\beta(\mathbf{w}_1^T\mathbf{x})\ \cdots\ \phi_\beta(\mathbf{w}_m^T\mathbf{x})]^T. \qquad (7)
$$

Besides, the function in Eqn. (6) is written by furthermore relaxing other two sign functions as follows,

$$
\begin{aligned}
L_{ni}(\mathbf{W}) &= L(\mathbf{W};\mathbf{x}_n,i)\\
&\triangleq \sum\nolimits_{\mathbf{x}'\in\mathcal{N}_{ni}^e}\phi_{\gamma_{i_1}}(d_{RH}(\mathbf{x}_n,\mathbf{x}')-i)\\
&\quad+\lambda\sum\nolimits_{\mathbf{x}'\notin\mathcal{N}_{ni}^e}\phi_{\gamma_{i_2}}(i+1-d_{RH}(\mathbf{x}_n,\mathbf{x}')), \qquad (8)
\end{aligned}
$$

where $d_{RH}(\mathbf{x},\mathbf{x}')=\|\phi_\beta(\mathbf{W}^T\mathbf{x})-\phi_\beta(\mathbf{W}^T\mathbf{x}')\|_2^2$ and γ_{i_1} and γ_{i_2} are the parameters.

The overall objective function is then written as,

$$
\begin{aligned}
\min_{\mathbf{W}}\ & L(\mathbf{W})=\frac{1}{N}\sum\nolimits_{n=1}^{N}\sum\nolimits_{i=0}^{m-1}L_{ni}(\mathbf{W})\\
\text{s.t.}\ & \mathbf{w}_k^T\mathbf{w}_k=1,\forall k=1,\cdots,m.
\end{aligned} \qquad (9)
$$

4.2 Quadratic penalty

We propose to use the quadratic penalty method [26] to solve this nonlinear constrained optimization problem in Eqn. (9).

$$
Q(\mathbf{W};\mu)\triangleq L(\mathbf{W})+\frac{\mu}{4}\sum\nolimits_{k=1}^{m}(\mathbf{w}_k^T\mathbf{w}_k-1)^2, \qquad (10)
$$

where $\mu>0$ is the penalty parameter. By driving μ to ∞, we penalize the constraint violations with increasing severity. We consider a sequence of values μ_t with $\mu_t\to\infty$ as $t\to\infty$, and seek the approximate minimizer $\mathbf{W}_t$ of $Q(\mathbf{W};\mu_t)$. Practically, $\mu_{t+1}=\kappa\mu_t$ with $\kappa>1$. In searching for $\mathbf{W}_t$, we use the minimizer $\mathbf{W}_{t-1}$ of $Q(\mathbf{W};\mu_{t-1})$ to construct an initial guess.

A gradient descent algorithm is adopted to minimize $Q(\mathbf{W};\mu_t)$. The gradient of $Q(\mathbf{W};\mu_t)$ is computed as follows,

$$
\begin{aligned}
\nabla_k Q_t &\triangleq \frac{\partial Q(\mathbf{W};\mu_t)}{\partial\mathbf{w}_k}\\
&= \frac{1}{N}\sum\nolimits_{n=1}^{N}\sum\nolimits_{i=0}^{m-1}\frac{\partial L_{ni}(\mathbf{W})}{\partial\mathbf{w}_k}+\mu_t(\mathbf{w}_k^T\mathbf{w}_k-1)\mathbf{w}_k\\
&\triangleq \frac{1}{N}\sum\nolimits_{n=1}^{N}\nabla_k L_n+\mu_t\nabla_k G.
\end{aligned}
$$

Here, $\partial L_{ni}(\mathbf{W})/\partial \mathbf{w}_k = \sum_{\mathbf{x}' \in \mathcal{N}_{ni}^e} \partial \phi_{\gamma_{i_1}}(d_{RH}(\mathbf{x}_n, \mathbf{x}') - i)/\partial \mathbf{w}_k + \lambda \sum_{\mathbf{x}' \notin \mathcal{N}_{ni}^e} \partial \phi_{\gamma_{i_2}}(i + 1 - d_{RH}(\mathbf{x}_n, \mathbf{x}'))/\partial \mathbf{w}_k$.

Each iteration of the gradient descent algorithm of minimizing $Q(\mathbf{W}; \mu_t)$ requires to (1) compute $\nabla_k L_n$ for each point $\mathbf{x}_n$ and (2) go through all the N points to compute a single $\nabla_k L_n$. The cost is $O(N^2)$ (neglecting m as $m \ll N$). Given the scale N of the reference dataset $\mathcal{X}$ is very large, the direct solution might not be feasible. We propose to use two speedup schemes: stochastic gradient descent and active set, to address the above two issues, respectively.

4.2.1 Stochastic gradient descent

The standard (batch) gradient descent algorithm would perform the iterations,

$$\begin{aligned}\mathbf{w}_k \leftarrow & \mathbf{w}_k - \eta \nabla_k Q_t \\ = & \mathbf{w}_k - \eta\Big(\frac{1}{N}\sum_{n=1}^{N} \nabla_k L_n + \mu_t \nabla_k G\Big).\end{aligned}$$

We propose to take mini-batches to update each iteration, where the true gradient is approximated by a sum over a small number of randomly sampled training examples. The iteration is updated as the following,

$$\mathbf{w}_k \leftarrow \mathbf{w}_k - \eta\Big(\frac{1}{|\mathcal{I}'|}\sum_{n \in \mathcal{I}'} \nabla_k L_n + \mu_t \nabla_k G\Big), \quad (11)$$

where $\mathcal{I}'$ is a subset, randomly sampled from $\mathcal{I} = \{1, 2, \cdots, n\}$ at this iteration, and $|\mathcal{I}'| \ll |\mathcal{I}|$. This mini-batches manner reduces the complexity of each iteration to $O(N|\mathcal{I}'|) = O(N)$.

4.2.2 Active set

Considering the derivative of the Sigmoid function, $f(\alpha, z) \triangleq \phi'_\alpha(z) = \alpha\phi_\alpha(z)(1 - \phi_\alpha(z))$, we can see that $\phi'_\alpha(z) \approx 0$ if $\phi_\alpha(z) \approx 0$. We can also easily show that the absolute value of each entry in the derivative of $d_{RH}(\mathbf{x}, \mathbf{x}')$, $\partial d_{RH}(\mathbf{x}, \mathbf{x}')/\partial \mathbf{w}_k = 2(\phi_\beta(\mathbf{w}_k^T\mathbf{x}) - \phi_\beta(\mathbf{w}_k^T\mathbf{x}'))(f(\beta, \mathbf{w}_k^T\mathbf{x})\mathbf{x} - f(\beta, \mathbf{w}_k^T\mathbf{x}')\mathbf{x}')$, is up-bounded. Consequently,

$$\nabla_k \phi_{\gamma_{i_1}} = \frac{\partial \phi_{\gamma_{i_1}}(d_{RH}(\mathbf{x}_n, \mathbf{x}') - i)}{\partial \mathbf{w}_k} \approx 0$$

if $\phi_{\gamma_{i_1}}(d_{RH}(\mathbf{x}_n, \mathbf{x}') - i) \approx 0$, and

$$\nabla_k \phi_{\gamma_{i_2}} = \frac{\partial \phi_{\gamma_{i_2}}(i + 1 - d_{RH}(\mathbf{x}_n, \mathbf{x}'))}{\partial \mathbf{w}_k} \approx 0$$

if $\phi_{\gamma_{i_2}}(i + 1 - d_{RH}(\mathbf{x}_n, \mathbf{x}')) \approx 0$. This suggests that it is unnecessary to go through all the N points when evaluating $\frac{\partial L_{ni}(\mathbf{W})}{\partial \mathbf{w}_k}$.

The approximation is obtained as follows,

$$\frac{\partial L_{ni}(\mathbf{W})}{\partial \mathbf{w}_k} \approx \sum_{\mathbf{x}' \in \mathcal{A}} \nabla_k \phi_{\gamma_{i_1}} + \lambda \sum_{\mathbf{x}' \in \mathcal{B}} \nabla_k \phi_{\gamma_{i_2}}. \quad (12)$$

Here, $\mathcal{A} = \mathcal{N}_{ni}^e - \mathcal{N}_{n(i-\Delta_{i_1})}^h$ and $\mathcal{B} = \mathcal{N}_{n(i+\Delta_{i_2})}^h - \mathcal{N}_{ni}^e$. $\mathcal{N}_{n(i-\Delta_{i_1})}^h$ consists of the points whose hamming distances to $\mathbf{x}_n$ are not larger than $i - \Delta_{i_1}$ and $\mathcal{N}_{n(i+\Delta_{i_2})}^h$ consists of the points whose hamming distances to $\mathbf{x}_n$ are not larger than $i + \Delta_{i_2}$. It means that $\frac{\partial L_{ni}(\mathbf{W})}{\partial \mathbf{w}_k}$ can be evaluated over the points in $(\mathcal{N}_{ni}^e - \mathcal{N}_{n(i-\Delta_{i_1})}^h)$ and $(\mathcal{N}_{n(i+\Delta_{i_2})}^h - \mathcal{N}_{ni}^e)$, which are related to false negative and false positive. In our implementation, $\Delta_{i_1} = \Delta_{i_2} = 1$. The set, $\mathcal{A}_{ni} = (\mathcal{N}_{ni}^e - \mathcal{N}_{n(i-\Delta_{i_1})}^h) \cup (\mathcal{N}_{n(i+\Delta_{i_2})}^h - \mathcal{N}_{ni}^e)$ are called active set, and hence its size is much smaller than the number of the reference data points, $|\mathcal{A}_{ni}| \ll N$. Thus, the cost of the gradient computation is greatly reduced, from $O(N)$ to $O(|\mathcal{A}_{ni}|)$.

$\mathcal{N}_{ni}^e$ is already available from the ground truth over the reference data points. To identify the active set $\mathcal{A}_{ni}$, we need additionally to obtain the points in $\mathcal{N}_{n(i-\Delta_{i_1})}^h$ and $\mathcal{N}_{n(i+\Delta_{i_2})}^h$, which is equivalent to retrieving the points whose hamming distances to $\mathbf{h}(\mathbf{x}_n)$ lie in $[0, i - \Delta_{i_1}]$ and $[0, i + \Delta_{i_2}]$. To make it, it needs to go through all the points to compute their hash codes. This step needs one pass of all the points, taking $O(N)$ time, However, in practice it is quite fast and only takes 5% of the time of the gradient computation over the active set because the hamming distance evaluation is very efficient. Thus, the active set scheme reduces a lot of time cost.

The overall algorithm is described in Algorithm 1.

Algorithm 1 Order Preserving Hashing

Input: Code length m and reference data $\mathcal{X}$
Output: Hash functions $\mathbf{w}_k, k = 1, ..., m$

```
initialize w_k, μ, max_outer_iter, max_inner_iter
Construct N^e_{ni}, n = 1,...,N; i = 1,...,m according to the
    bucket balance property
for outer_iter = 1 : max_outer_iter do
    for inner_iter = 1 : max_inner_iter do
        Generate randomly sampled examples I'
        Calculate N^h_{ni} on I'
        Construct active sets A_{ni} on I' according to
            Sec. 4.2.2
        Calculate ∂L_{ni}(W)/∂w_k according to Eqn. (12)
        ∇_k L_n ← Σ_i ∂L_{ni}(W)/∂w_k
        Update w_k according to Eqn. (11)
    end for
    μ ← κμ
end for
```

5. CONNECTIONS

The similarity order preserved in the proposed order preserving hashing approach is essentially some notion of similarity. This section discusses the connections with several representative similarity-preserving hashing approaches.

Relation to absolute similarity/distance preserving. Binary reconstructive embedding (BRE) [16] computes hash functions by preserving absolute distances, and entropy-based coding [20] aims to preserve the normalized similarity distribution. In contrast, our approach aims to preserve similarity orders (relative similarities), which is essentially the goal of nearest neighbor search. Experiments show that all the approaches achieve satisfactory performance when the data points are uniformly distributed and almost not skewed. However, in most real data sets that are usually not uniformly distributed and skewed, preserving relative similarities is more flexible than preserving absolute similarities (distances).

Relation to binary similarity preserving. Rather than preserving absolute similarities, hashing algorithms have been developed with the goal of preserving binary similarities, such as [19, 27, 38]. The former one [19] is different from our approach in that it is for learning a boosted search forest. The latter two [27, 38] are more related to our approach, and the idea is to learn hash functions, expecting that positive pairs in the hamming space are nearer or not larger than a threshold and negative pairs are farther or not smaller than another threshold. Positive pairs are defined as neighboring points for ANN search or points with the same semantic label for classification, and negative pairs are farther points or points with different labels. These approaches are more suitable for classification, but do not discriminate multiple similarities and hence cannot guarantee good ANN search performance. Instead, our approach takes into consideration order alignment, and is advantageous in discriminating multiple similarities.

Relation to ranking loss. The very recent work [28] presents a triplet ranking loss based hashing approach and demonstrates its application to classification. Such a loss is formed from a triplet, where one is more similar to a second one than the third one, or two with the same label and another sample with a different label. This ranking loss, if used for ANN search, is close to the order alignment property of our approach. The joint consideration of all the possible $O(N^3)$ triplets is equivalent to order alignment that is formed with $O(N^2)$ constraints. [28] samples a subset of triplets for the efficiency issue. Differently, our approach exploits it in an example-based manner, constructing the data satisfying the order alignment as the training data. Besides, we transform the problem to an equivalent problem, a set of multi-class classification problems, optimized with an easily-implemented algorithm.

6. EXPERIMENT

6.1 Setup

Approaches. We present the performance comparison of our approach, order preserving hashing (OPH), against several state-of-the-art hashing methods, including minimal loss hashing (MLH) [27], binary reconstructive embedding (BRE) [16], iterative quantization hashing (ITQ) [3], isotropic hashing (IsoHash) [14], kernelized supervised hashing (KSH) [21], anchor graph hashing (AGH) [22], spectral hashing (SH) [40], and unsupervised sequential projection locality hashing (USPLH) [38]. All the results were obtained with the implementations generously provided by their respective authors and by following their instructions to tune the algorithm parameters.

Data set. We report the search performance over five widely-used data sets: LabelMe [30], Peekaboom [35], GIST $1M$ [10], SIFT100K, and SIFT1M [10]. The first two data sets include 22,019 and 57,637 images, respectively. Each image is represented by a 512-dimensional GIST descriptor. $2K$ images are randomly sampled as the query set and the remaining as the reference set. The GIST1M data set contains $1M$ 960-dimensional GIST features as the reference set $1K$ features as the query set, and extra $500K$ features as the training set that is used to learn the hash functions. The SIFT100K data set contains $100K$ 128-dimensional SIFT features as the reference data set and extra $10K$ features as the query set, which are collected from the Caltech 101 data set [2]. The SIFT1M data set contains $1M$ SIFT features as the reference set, $10K$ features as the query set, and extra $100K$ as the training set. The ground-truth neighbors, exact K-nearest neighbors, for each query, are computed by linear scan, i.e., comparing each query with all the points in the reference data set using the raw feature.

6.2 Implementation

In the implementation of our approach as illustrated in Algorithm. 1, we initialize linear projections $\mathbf{W}$ of the hash functions by assigning each entry with a random variable sampled from a standard Gaussian distribution $\mathcal{N}(0, 1)$ and normalizing the augmented projection vector to have unit length. Both *max_outer_iter* and *max_inner_iter* are set 10 with μ initialized by 1 and $\kappa = 1.5$. The variable α, which is used to relax sign(z) to the Sigmoid function $\phi_\alpha(z)$, is selected according to the range of z. In particular, if $\max|z| = \zeta$, $\alpha = 2\log(\epsilon^{-1})/\zeta$ to guarantee that the approximation error is not larger than a small constant ϵ ($\epsilon = 10^{-6}$ in our implementation) if $\zeta/2 \leq |z| \leq \zeta$. This empirical rule is applied to determining β in Eqn. (7) and γ_{i_1}, γ_{i_2} in Eqn. (8). Specifically, $\beta = 2\log(10^6)/\sqrt{\max\|\mathbf{x}\|_2^2 + 1}$; $\gamma_{i_1} = 2\log(10^6)/(m-i)$ as $\max(d_{RH}(\mathbf{x}, \mathbf{x}') - i) = m - i$; $\gamma_{i_2} = 2\log(10^6)/(1+i)$ as $\max(i + 1 - d_{RH}(\mathbf{x}, \mathbf{x}')) = i + 1$. In each iteration of the mini-batch stochastic gradient algorithm, we randomly sample 200 training samples.

Rather than partitioning target categories into $m+1$ binary super-categories, which is impractical for larger m and takes much time cost in optimization, we sample a small number (S, set as 10 in our implementation) of binary super-categories, $\{(\mathcal{N}^e_{k_1}, \overline{\mathcal{N}^e_{k_1}}), (\mathcal{N}^e_{k_2}, \overline{\mathcal{N}^e_{k_2}}), \cdots, (\mathcal{N}^e_{k_S}, \overline{\mathcal{N}^e_{k_S}})\}$ with $|\mathcal{N}^e_{k_{s+1}} - \mathcal{N}^e_{k_s}|$ being almost the same. Besides, it is not guaranteed that strict bucket balance always leads to the best performance. Thus, we relax the bucket balance property by fixing the point membership in the super-category but perturbing k_s to $\{k_s - 1, k_s, k_s + 1\}$ (in other words, the hamming distance of the points in $\mathcal{N}^e_{k_s}$ from the query can be constrained to be no larger than $k_s - 1$ or $k_s + 1$). We determine those choices and the selection of λ, by validation with a randomly-sampled set, 5% of the training set, as the validation set. There are many possible combinations of the choices, which leads to huge time cost during validation. To eliminate the time cost, we validate the choice for each variable by fixing other variables and perform the validation several times such that on average each variable is checked at least 3 times.

All experiments are conducted on a workstation with an Intel Xeon CPU of 3.33GHz and 24GB memory. The training time of our Matlab implementation is no more than 6 hours through all the datasets, except that the training time for the 960-dimensional GIST1M data set for code length 256 is about 8 hours.

6.3 Results

We report the performance comparison in terms of widely-used quantitative schemes, recall vs. #(retrieved items), recall vs. code length, mean average precision, and the qualitative results.

Recall vs. #(retrieved items). This scheme is often used to evaluate the performance of the ANN search strategy based on hamming ranking: a certain number of top ranked points according to hamming distances are returned and followed by a possible reranking step, where a more costly ranking function over more accurate features is evaluated. The number of returned images clearly reflects the computational cost of the reranking stage, while recall, the fraction of retrieved images that are among the K-NNs of the query, gives the upper-bound performance.

Fig. 1 shows the performance comparison under various code lengths (from 32 bits to 256 bits) over the five data

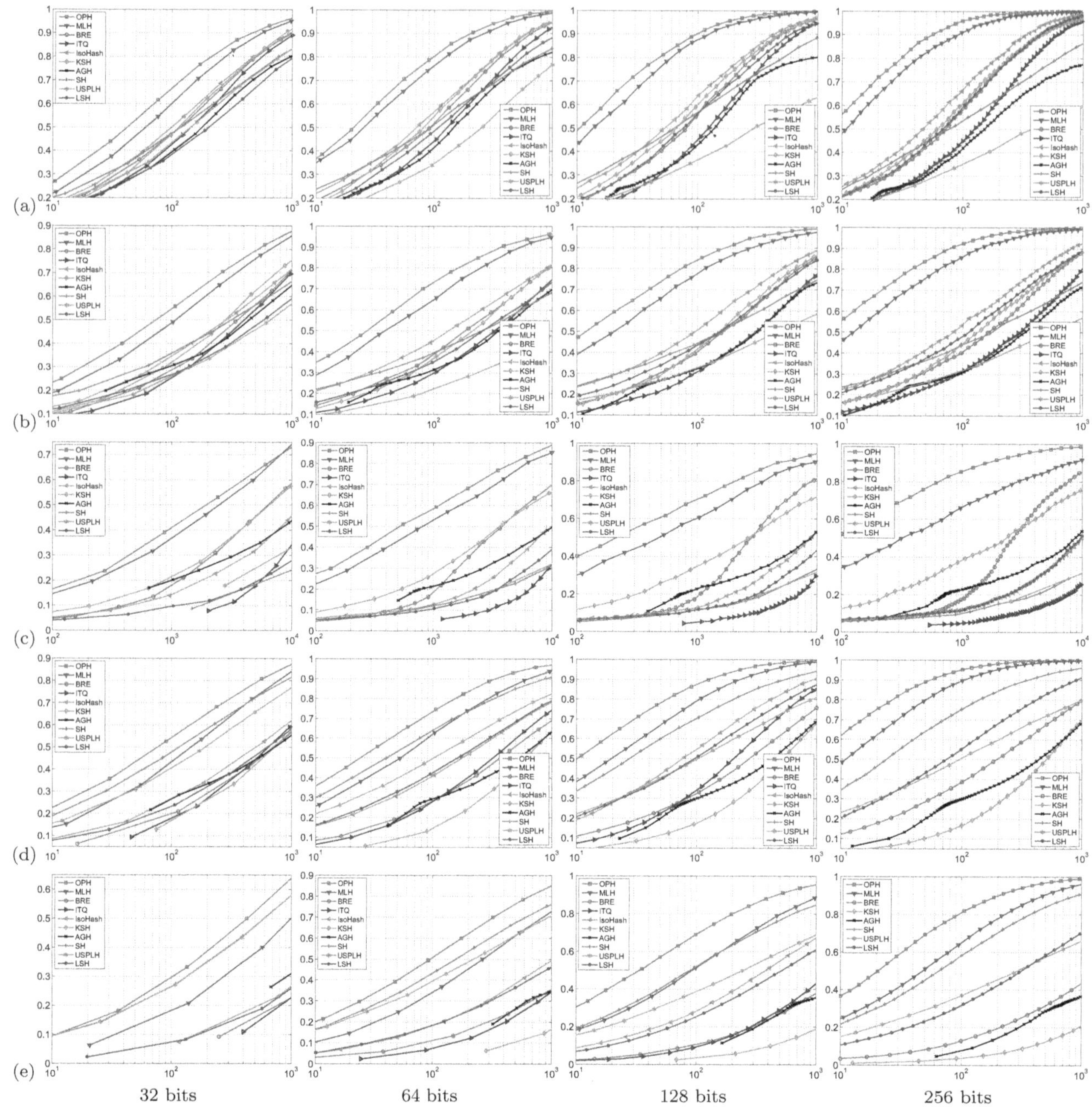

Figure 1: Performance comparison in terms of recall vs. #retrieved items under various code lengths. x-axis: #retrieved items. y-axis: recall. (a)-(e) correspond to Labelme, Peekaboom, GIST$1M$, SIFT$100K$, and SIFT$1M$, respectively.

sets for finding the nearest neighbor. The results for ITQ and IsoHash with code length 256 for 128-dimensional SIFT features are not available since the two algorithms can not generate hash codes with the length larger than 128 without using kernel hash functions. From these figures, we can see several observations. First, our approach (OPH) outperforms all the other approaches over all the five data sets and under all the code lengths. Second, the superiority of our approach gets more signification with longer binary codes. This is a desired property as longer hash codes are often used for real problems. Last but not least, by comparing (a)(22K GIST), (b) (57K GIST) with (c) (1M GIST), and (d) (100K SIFT) with (e) (1M SIFT), we find that the improvement of our approach over the second best approach (MLH) tend to be more significant in the larger reference set.

We present the performance in terms of recall vs. #(retrieved items) when finding different numbers (from 5 to 200) of nearest neighbors, which is shown in Fig. 2. The results of $K = 1$ have been shown in Fig. 1. Results with 128 bits are reported, and comparisons with other code lengths are similar. Overall speaking, our approach gets the better

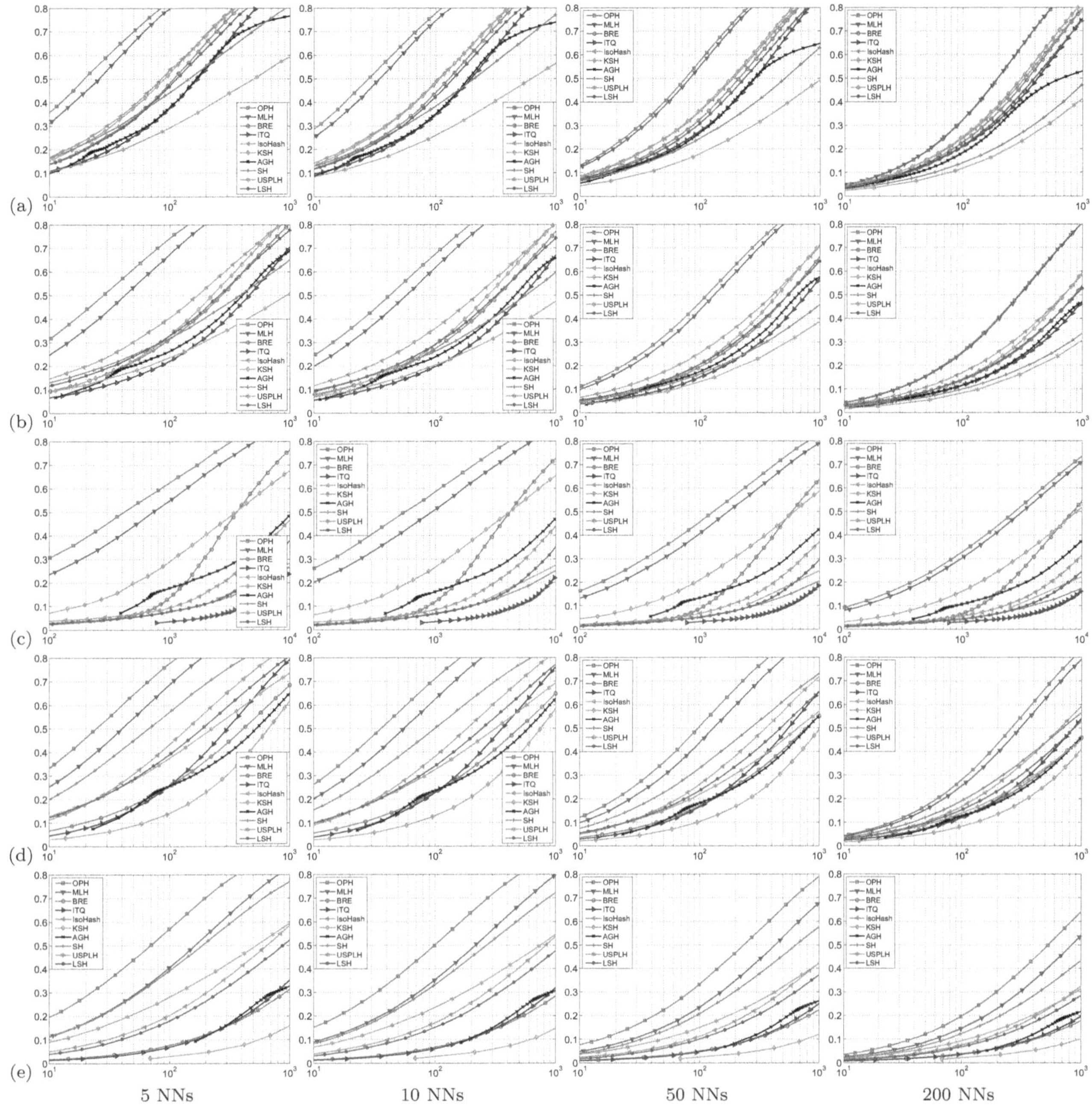

Figure 2: Performance comparison in terms of recall vs. #retrieved items when finding different numbers of nearest neighbors. x-axis: #retrieved items. y-axis: recall. (a)-(e) correspond to Labelme, Peekaboom, GIST1M, SIFT100K, and SIFT1M, respectively.

performance than all the other approaches. For the small data sets, (a) Labelme and (b) Peekaboom, our approach gets much improvement for 5, 10 and 50 NNs, and similar performance with the second best for 200 NNs. This is understandable as the points in small data sets are relatively easily discriminated. For the large data sets, (c) GIST1M, (d) SIFT100K and (e) SIFT1M, the improvement is much more significant, which indicates that our approach is more powerful in dealing with larger data sets. Furthermore, we find that the superiority of our approach is more significant for smaller K. This implies that our approach is much more useful in many applications, for examples, feature correspondence in the structure-from-motion problem and bag-of-visual-words for object retrieval only require to retrieve a few number of nearest neighbors.

Recall vs. code length. Fig. 3 shows the comparison. The results are obtained for finding the nearest neighbor when retrieving top-100 and top-200 ranked points corresponding to the first and second row of Fig. 3, respectively. We can see that our approach benefits a lot with a larger code length. It can also be observed the improvement of OPH is more significant on larger data sets. More impor-

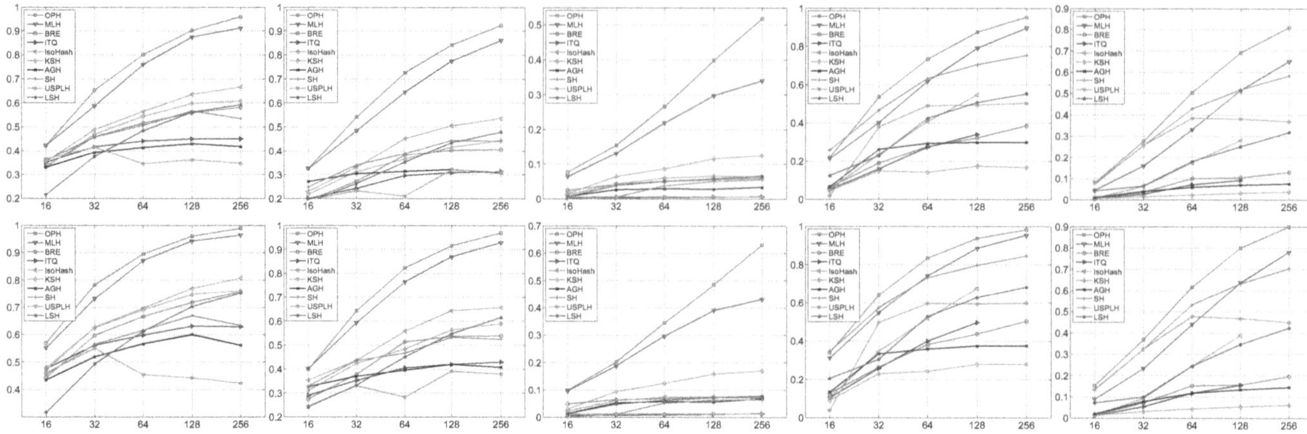

(a) Labelme (b) Peekaboom (c) GIST1M (d) SIFT100K (e) SIFT1M

Figure 3: Performance comparison in terms of recall vs. code length. x-axis: code length. y-axis: recall. The first row: recall@top-100. The second row: recall@top-200.

tantly, we find that our approach with 128 bits achieves similar and even better performance than other approaches with 256 bits, which indicates that our approach reduces the storage cost of saving binary codes when meeting the same recall target.

Mean average precision. Average precision (AP) of each query is the area of the precision-recall curve. Mean average precision is the mean of AP over all the queries and is useful to get an overview of search performance. The precision and recall scores are recorded by considering all possible numbers of candidates ranked by the hamming distance. The comparisons are shown in Table 1 with the ground truth being 50 nearest neighbors. On smaller data sets Labelme and Peekaboom, OPH is comparable, if not superior, to the state-of-the-art methods. One reason is data sets are small and relatively less challenged to differentiate. On larger data sets GIST1M, SIFT100K, and SIFT1M, the improvement is significant and impressive, which infers on average the rank list obtained from our approach is much better.

Qualitative results. Fig. 4 and 5 shows some qualitative results on Labelme (left of the figures) and Peekaboom (right of the figures) with code length 128. From Fig. 4, OPH offers a better performance than the others, and good qualitative results can also be observed in Fig. 5.

7. CONCLUSIONS

In this paper, we propose a new hashing approach, order preserving hashing, to approximate nearest neighbor search. The key idea is to maximize the alignment of category orders computed between the original and hamming space. Together with the bucket balance criteria, the problem of learning the hash function is cast to a multi-class classification problem. To penalize the misalignment rate, we transform the multi-class classification problem to multiple binary-class classification problems, for which Sigmoid relaxation, stochastic gradient descent and active set are employed to efficiently solve the problem. Extensive experimental results demonstrate the superiority of our approach.

Possible extensions. Our approach uses linear hash functions as an example, but is not limited and can be generalized to other hash functions, such as kernel hash functions or multi-layers neural nets. On the other hand, the target order can be defined as any metric in the input space and even a non-metric measure without being limited in the Euclidean distance.

8. REFERENCES

[1] L. Cao, Z. Li, Y. Mu, and S.-F. Chang. Submodular video hashing: a unified framework towards video pooling and indexing. In *ACM Multimedia*, pages 299–308, 2012.

[2] L. Fei-Fei, R. Fergus, and P. Perona. Learning generative visual models from few training examples: an incremental bayesian approach tested on 101 object categories. In *CVPR 2004 Workshop on Generative-Model Based Vision*, 2004.

[3] Y. Gong and S. Lazebnik. Iterative quantization: A procrustean approach to learning binary codes. In *CVPR*, pages 817–824, 2011.

[4] J. He, S. Chang, R. Radhakrishnan, and C. Bauer. Compact hashing with joint optimization of search accuracy and time. In *CVPR*, pages 753–760, 2011.

[5] J. He, J. Feng, X. Liu, T. Cheng, T.-H. Lin, H. Chung, and S.-F. Chang. Mobile product search with bag of hash bits and boundary reranking. In *CVPR*, pages 3005–3012, 2012.

[6] J. He, W. Liu, and S. Chang. Scalable similarity search with optimized kernel hashing. In *KDD*, pages 1129–1138, 2010.

[7] J. Heo, Y. Lee, J. He, S. Chang, and S. Yoon. Spherical hashing. In *CVPR*, pages 2957–2964, 2012.

[8] P. Indyk and R. Motwani. Approximate nearest neighbors: Towards removing the curse of dimensionality. In *STOC*, pages 604–613, 1998.

[9] H. Jégou, L. Amsaleg, C. Schmid, and P. Gros. Query-adaptative locality sensitive hashing. In *ICASSP*. IEEE, apr 2008.

[10] H. Jégou, M. Douze, and C. Schmid. Product quantization for nearest neighbor search. *IEEE Trans. Pattern Anal. Mach. Intell.*, 33(1):117–128, 2011.

[11] J. Ji, J. Li, S. Yan, B. Zhang, and Q. Tian. Super-bit locality-sensitive hashing. In *NIPS*, pages 108–116, 2012.

Table 1: Comparison in terms of mean average precision (%). The best scores are in bold font. Our approach OPH obtains a significant gain on larger data sets (SIFT100K, SIFT1M, GIST1M) and comparable performance or superior on smaller data sets (Labelme, Peekaboom).

Data Set	Code Length	Approaches									
		OPH	MLH	BRE	ITQ	IsoHash	KSH	AGH	SH	USPLH	LSH
Labelme	32	**21.11**	19.91	16.45	20.36	18.51	16.72	10.90	9.28	9.62	8.87
	64	**33.94**	32.48	27.59	32.09	28.35	24.57	12.04	11.18	17.66	17.57
	128	44.36	**45.22**	40.59	44.66	42.34	31.45	12.35	13.73	9.67	32.52
	256	56.85	55.89	53.31	**58.40**	57.35	36.32	13.10	14.54	9.61	49.64
Peekaboom	32	**13.00**	12.59	9.42	12.10	10.63	9.40	6.01	5.25	6.22	4.47
	64	**23.00**	21.65	18.70	21.20	19.67	14.64	6.74	6.25	8.73	10.62
	128	**34.14**	33.08	30.42	32.75	32.31	21.33	7.05	9.28	5.94	23.74
	256	45.42	44.42	42.08	46.60	**47.41**	24.86	7.45	10.21	5.99	39.54
GIST1M	32	**2.00**	1.74	1.14	1.68	1.39	1.15	0.94	0.68	0.26	0.56
	64	**4.12**	3.51	2.67	3.27	3.25	2.21	1.05	1.08	0.32	1.50
	128	**6.97**	5.96	5.24	5.14	5.21	3.83	1.09	1.45	0.31	3.12
	256	**10.43**	7.20	8.18	6.95	7.70	5.26	1.08	2.19	0.33	6.04
SIFT100K	32	**12.40**	9.97	5.14	8.14	7.06	4.75	4.97	10.09	8.01	5.02
	64	**25.17**	18.63	11.31	18.37	15.47	8.87	5.98	17.36	12.67	12.52
	128	**37.41**	32.13	20.76	32.44	28.27	12.69	6.46	22.51	16.19	24.50
	256	**51.57**	46.42	32.78	-	-	15.97	6.67	32.42	18.56	40.69
SIFT1M	32	**5.07**	3.07	1.51	2.69	2.31	1.26	1.11	4.23	3.92	1.49
	64	**13.58**	8.11	4.46	8.16	7.24	2.94	1.50	9.81	8.19	5.68
	128	**26.00**	18.01	10.58	17.87	16.53	5.04	1.68	15.56	10.52	14.05
	256	**39.88**	31.69	20.16	-	-	7.38	1.77	26.10	12.05	28.59

[12] Y.-G. Jiang, J. Wang, X. Xue, and S.-F. Chang. Query-adaptive image search with hash codes. *IEEE Transactions on Multimedia*, 15(2):442–453, 2013.

[13] S. Kim, Y. Kang, and S. Choi. Sequential spectral learning to hash with multiple representations. In *ECCV (5)*, pages 538–551, 2012.

[14] W. Kong and W.-J. Li. Isotropic hashing. In *NIPS*, pages 1655–1663, 2012.

[15] W. Kong, W.-J. Li, and M. Guo. Manhattan hashing for large-scale image retrieval. In *SIGIR*, pages 45–54, 2012.

[16] B. Kulis and T. Darrell. Learning to hash with binary reconstructive embeddings. In *NIPS*, pages 1042–1050, 2009.

[17] B. Kulis and K. Grauman. Kernelized locality-sensitive hashing. *IEEE Trans. Pattern Anal. Mach. Intell.*, 34(6):1092–1104, 2012.

[18] Y.-H. Kuo, K.-T. Chen, C.-H. Chiang, and W. H. Hsu. Query expansion for hash-based image object retrieval. In *ACM Multimedia*, pages 65–74, 2009.

[19] Z. Li, H. Ning, L. Cao, T. Zhang, Y. Gong, and T. Huang. Learning to search efficiently in high dimensions. In *NIPS*, pages 1710–1718, 2011.

[20] R. Lin, D. Ross, and J. Yagnik. Spec hashing: Similarity preserving algorithm for entropy-based coding. In *CVPR*, pages 848–854, 2010.

[21] W. Liu, J. Wang, R. Ji, Y. Jiang, and S. Chang. Supervised hashing with kernels. In *CVPR*, pages 2074–2081, 2012.

[22] W. Liu, J. Wang, S. Kumar, and S. Chang. Hashing with graphs. In *ICML*, pages 1–8, 2011.

[23] X. Liu, J. He, D. Liu, and B. Lang. Compact kernel hashing with multiple features. In *ACM Multimedia*, pages 881–884, 2012.

[24] Y. Mu, J. Shen, and S. Yan. Weakly-supervised hashing in kernel space. In *CVPR*, pages 3344–3351, 2010.

[25] Y. Mu and S. Yan. Non-metric locality-sensitive hashing. In *AAAI*, 2010.

[26] J. Nocedal and S. Wright. *Numerical Optimization*, volume 104 of *Springer Serials in Operations Research*. Springer-Verlag, London, 2006.

[27] M. Norouzi and D. Fleet. Minimal loss hashing for compact binary codes. In *ICML*, pages 353–360, 2011.

[28] M. Norouzi, D. J. Fleet, and R. Salakhutdinov. Hamming distance metric learning. In *NIPS*, pages 1070–1078, 2012.

[29] M. Raginsky and S. Lazebnik. Locality-sensitive binary codes from shift-invariant kernels. In *NIPS*, pages 1509–1517, 2009.

[30] B. Russell, A. Torralba, K. Murphy, and W. Freeman. Labelme: A database and web-based tool for image annotation. *International Journal of Computer Vision*, 77(1-3):157–173, 2008.

[31] R. Salakhutdinov and G. Hinton. Semantic hashing. *Int. J. Approx. Reasoning*, 50(7):969–978, 2009.

[32] G. Shakhnarovich, T. Darrell, and P. Indyk. *Nearest-Neighbor Methods in Learning and Vision: Theory and Practice.* The MIT press, 2006.

[33] J. Song, Y. Yang, Z. Huang, H. Shen, and R. Hong. Multiple feature hashing for real-time large scale near-duplicate video retrieval. In *ACM Multimedia*, pages 423–432, 2011.

[34] C. Strecha, A. Bronstein, M. Bronstein, and P. Fua. Ldahash: Improved matching with smaller descriptors. *IEEE Trans. Pattern Anal. Mach. Intell.*, 34(1):66–78, 2012.

Figure 4: Qualitative results of various approaches. For each row, the first image is a query image and the remaining are the ranking results by the learned hash codes. (a)-(j): OPH, MLH [27], BRE [16], ITQ [3], IsoHash [14], KSH [21], AGH [22], SH [40], USPLH [13], LSH [8].

Figure 5: Qualitative results of OPH. For each row, the first image is a query image and the remaining are the ranking results by the learned hash codes.

[35] A. Torralba, R. Fergus, and Y. Weiss. Small codes and large image databases for recognition. In *CVPR*, 2008.

[36] K.-Y. Tseng, Y.-L. Lin, Y.-H. Chen, and W. H. Hsu. Sketch-based image retrieval on mobile devices using compact hash bits. In *ACM Multimedia*, pages 913–916, 2012.

[37] J. Wang, O. Kumar, and S. Chang. Semi-supervised hashing for scalable image retrieval. In *CVPR*, pages 3424–3431, 2010.

[38] J. Wang, S. Kumar, and S. Chang. Sequential projection learning for hashing with compact codes. In *ICML*, pages 1127–1134, 2010.

[39] Y. Weiss, R. Fergus, and A. Torralba. Multidimensional spectral hashing. In *ECCV (5)*, pages 340–353, 2012.

[40] Y. Weiss, A. Torralba, and R. Fergus. Spectral hashing. In *NIPS*, pages 1753–1760, 2008.

[41] H. Xu, J. Wang, Z. Li, G. Zeng, S. Li, and N. Yu. Complementary hashing for approximate nearest neighbor search. In *ICCV*, pages 1631–1638, 2011.

[42] J. Yuan, G. Gravier, S. Campion, X. Liu, and H. Jégou. Efficient mining of repetitions in large-scale tv streams with product quantization hashing. In *ECCV Workshops (1)*, pages 271–280, 2012.

[43] Y. Zhuang, Y. Liu, F. Wu, Y. Zhang, and J. Shao. Hypergraph spectral hashing for similarity search of social image. In *ACM Multimedia*, pages 1457–1460, 2011.

Linear Cross-Modal Hashing for Efficient Multimedia Search

Xiaofeng Zhu† Zi Huang‡ Heng Tao Shen‡ Xin Zhao‡

†College of CSIT, Guangxi Normal University, Guangxi, 541004,P.R.China

‡School of ITEE, The University of Queensland, QLD 4072, Australia

{zhux,huang,shenht}@itee.uq.edu.au, x.zhao@uq.edu.au

ABSTRACT

Most existing cross-modal hashing methods suffer from the scalability issue in the training phase. In this paper, we propose a novel cross-modal hashing approach with a linear time complexity to the training data size, to enable scalable indexing for multimedia search across multiple modals. Taking both the intra-similarity in each modal and the inter-similarity across different modals into consideration, the proposed approach aims at effectively learning hash functions from large-scale training datasets. More specifically, for each modal, we first partition the training data into k clusters and then represent each training data point with its distances to k centroids of the clusters. Interestingly, such a k-dimensional data representation can reduce the time complexity of the training phase from traditional $O(n^2)$ or higher to $O(n)$, where n is the training data size, leading to practical learning on large-scale datasets. We further prove that this new representation preserves the intra-similarity in each modal. To preserve the inter-similarity among data points across different modals, we transform the derived data representations into a common binary subspace in which binary codes from all the modals are "consistent" and comparable. The transformation simultaneously outputs the hash functions for all modals, which are used to convert unseen data into binary codes. Given a query of one modal, it is first mapped into the binary codes using the modal's hash functions, followed by matching the database binary codes of any other modals. Experimental results on two benchmark datasets confirm the scalability and the effectiveness of the proposed approach in comparison with the state of the art.

Categories and Subject Descriptors

H.3.1 [**Content Analysis and Indexing**]: Indexing Methods; H.3.3 [**Information Search and Retrieval**]: Search Process

MM'13, October 21–25, 2013, Barcelona, Spain.

http://dx.doi.org/10.1145/2502081.2502107.

Keywords

Cross-modal, hashing, index, multimedia search

1. INTRODUCTION

Hashing is increasingly popular to support approximate nearest neighbor (ANN) search from multimedia data. The idea of hashing for ANN search is to learn the hash functions for converting high-dimensional data into short binary codes while preserving the neighborhood relationships of original data as much as possible [13, 15, 21, 31]. It has been shown that hash function learning (HFL) is the key process for effective hashing [3, 12]. Exiting hashing methods on single modal data (referred to *uni-modal hashing* methods in this paper) can be categorized into LSH-like hashing (e.g., locality sensitive hashing (LSH) [7, 8], KLSH [15], and SKLSH [21]) which randomly selects linear functions as hash functions, PCA-like hashing (e.g., SH [33], PCAH [30], and ITQ [10]) which uses the principal components of training data to learn hash functions, and manifold-like hashing (e.g., MFH [26] and [34]) which employs manifold learning techniques to learn hash functions.

More recently, some hashing methods have been proposed to index data represented by multiple modals[1] (referred to *multi-modal hashing* in this paper) [26, 36], which can be used to facilitate the retrieval for data described by multiple modals in many real-life applications, such as near-duplicate image retrieval. Considering an image database where each image is described by multiple modals, such as SIFT descriptor, color histogram, bag-of-word, etc, multi-modal hashing learns hash functions from all the modals to support effective image retrieval, where the similarities from all the modals are considered in ranking the final results with respect to a multi-modal query. *Cross-modal hashing* also constructs hash functions from all the modals by analyzing their correlations. However, it serves for a different purpose, i.e., supporting cross-modal retrieval where a query of one modal can search for the relevant results of another modal [2, 16, 22, 37, 38]. For example, given a query described by SIFT descriptor, relevant results described by other modals such as color histogram and bag-of-word can also be found and returned[2].

[1]Modal, feature and view are often used with subtle differences in multimedia research. In this paper, we consistently use the term modal.

[2]In this sense, cross-modal retrieval is defined more generally than traditional cross-media retrieval [35] where queries and results can be of different media types, such as text document, image, video, and audio.

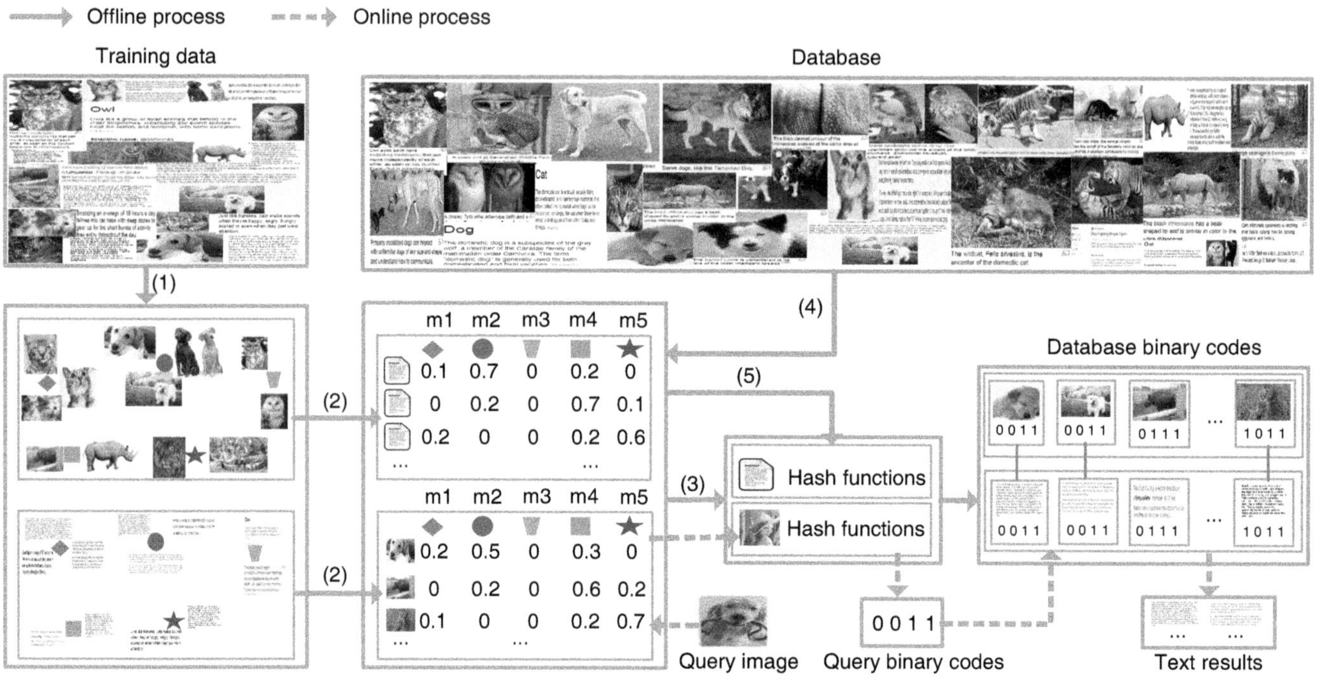

Figure 1: Flowchart of the proposed linear cross-modal hashing (LCMH).

While few attempts have been made towards effective cross-modal hashing, most existing cross-modal hashing methods [16, 22, 27, 37, 38] suffer from high time complexity in the training phase (i.e., $O(n^2)$ or higher, where n is the training data size) and thus fail to learn from large-scale training datasets in practical amount of time. Such a high complexity constrains the above methods from applications dealing with large-scale datasets. For example, multi-modal latent binary embedding (MLBE) [38] is a generative model such that only a small-sized training dataset (e.g., 300 out of 180,000 data points) can be used in the training phase. Although cross-modal similarity sensitive hashing (CMSSH) [2] is able to learn from large-scale training datasets, it requires prior knowledge (i.e., positive pairs and negative pairs among training data points) to be predefined and known, which is not practical in most real-life applications. To enable cross-modal retrieval, inter-media hashing (IMH) [27] explores the correlations among multiple modals from different data sources and achieves better hashing performance, but the train process of IMH with the time complexity $O(n^3)$ is expensive for large-scale cross-modal hashing.

In this paper, we propose a novel hashing method, named *linear cross-modal hashing* (LCMH), to address the scalability issues without using any prior knowledge. LCMH achieves a linear time complexity to the training data size in the training phase, enabling effective learning from large-scale datasets. The key idea is to first partition the training data of each modal into k clusters by applying a linear time clustering method, and then represent each training data point using its distances to the k clusters' centroids. That is, we approximate each data point with a k-dimensional representation. Interestingly, such a representation leads to the time complexity of $O(kn)$ for the training phase. Given a really large-scale training dataset, it is expected that $k \ll n$. Since k is a constant, the overall time complexity of the training phase becomes linear to the training data size, i.e., $O(n)$. To achieve high quality hash functions, LCMH also preserves both the intra-similarity among data points in each modal and the inter-similarity among data points across different modals. The learnt hash functions ensure that all the data points described by different modals in the common binary subspace are "consistent" (i.e., relevant data of different modals should have similar binary codes) and comparable (i.e., binary codes of different modals can be directly compared).

Fig.1 illustrates the whole flowchart of the proposed LCMH. The training phase of LCMH is an offline process and includes five key steps. In the first step, for each modal we partition its data into k clusters. In the second step, we represent each training data point with its distances to the k clusters' centroids. In the third step, hash functions are learnt efficiently with a linear time complexity and effectively with the intra- and inter-similarity preservations. In the fourth step, all the data points in the database are approximated with k-dimensional representations, which are then mapped into the binary codes with the learn hash functions in the fifth step. In the online search process, a query of one modal is first approximated with its k-dimensional representation in this modal which is then mapped into the query binary codes with the hash functions for this modal, followed by matching the database binary codes to find relevant results of any other modal. Extensive experimental results on two benchmark datasets confirm the scalability and the effectiveness of the proposed approach in comparison with the state of the art.

The rest of the paper is organized as follows. Related work is reviewed in Section 2. The proposed LCMH and its analysis are presented in Section 3. Section 4 reports the results and the paper is concluded in Section 5.

2. RELATED WORK

In this section we review existing hashing methods in three major categories, including uni-modal hashing, multi-modal hashing and cross-modal hashing.

In uni-modal hashing, early work such as LSH-like hashing methods [7, 8, 15, 21] construct hash functions based on random projections and are typically unsupervised. Although they have some asymptotic theoretical properties, LSH-like hashing methods often require long binary codes and multiple hash tables to achieve reasonable retrieval accuracy [20]. This leads to long query time and high storage cost. Recently machine learning techniques have been applied to improve hashing performance. For example, PCA-like hashing [10, 30, 33] learns hash functions via preserving the maximal covariance of original data and has been shown to outperform LSH-like hashing in [14, 17, 29]. Manifold-like hashing [18, 26] employs manifold learning techniques to learn hash functions. Besides, some hashing methods conduct hash function learning by making the best use of priori knowledge of data. For example, supervised hashing methods [14, 17, 19, 24, 28] improve the hashing performance using the pre-provided pairs of data with the assumption that there is "similar" or "dissimilar" pairs in datasets. There are also some semi-supervised hashing methods [30, 34] in which a supervised term is used to minimize the empirical error on the labeled data while an unsupervised term is used to maximize desirable properties, such as variance and independence of individual bits in the binary codes.

Multi-modal hashing is designed to conduct hash function learning for encoding multi-modal data. To this end, the method in [36] first uses an iterative method to preserve the semantic similarities among training examples, and then keeps the consistency between the hash codes and the corresponding hashing functions designed for multiple modals. The method multiple feature hashing (MFH) [26] preserves the local structure information of each modal and also globally considers the alignments for all the modals to learn a group of hash functions for real-time large scale near-duplicate web video retrieval.

Cross-modal hashing also encodes multi-modal data. However, it focuses more on discovering the correlations among different modals to enable cross-modal retrieval. Cross-modal similarity sensitive hashing (CMSSH) [2] is the first cross-modal hashing method for cross-modal retrieval. However, CMSSH only considers the inter-similarity and ignores the intra-similarity. Cross-view hashing (CVH) [16] extends spectral hashing [33] to the multi-modal case, aiming at minimizing the Hamming distances for similar points and maximizing those for dissimilar points. However, it needs to construct the similarity matrix for all the data points, which leads to a quadratic time complexity to the training data size. Rasiwasia et al., [22] employs canonical correlation analysis (CCA) to conduct hash function learning, which is a special case of CVH. Recently, multi-modal latent binary embedding (MLBE) [38] uses a probabilistic latent factor model to learn hash functions. Similar to CVH, it also has a quadratic time complexity for constructing the similarity matrix. Moreover, it uses a sampling method to solve the issue of out-of-sample extension. Co-regularized hashing (CRH) [37] is a boosted co-regularization framework which learns a group of hash functions for each bit of binary codes in every modal. However, its objective function is non-convex. Inter-media hashing (IMH) [27] aims to discover a common Hamming space for learning hash functions. IMH preserves the intra-similarity of each individual modal via enforcing that the data with similar semantic should have similar hash codes, and preserves the inter-similarity among different modals via preserving local structural information embedded in each modal.

3. LINEAR CROSS-MODAL HASHING

In this section we describe the details of the proposed LCMH method. For the purpose of interpreting our basic idea, we first focus on hash function learning for bimodal data from Section 3.1 to Section 3.5, and then extend it to the general setting of multi-modal data in Section 3.6.

In this paper, we use boldface uppercases, boldface lowercase and letter to denote matrices, vectors and scales, respectively. Besides, the transpose of $\mathbf{X}$ is denoted as $\mathbf{X}^T$, the inverse of $\mathbf{X}$ is denoted as $\mathbf{X}^{-1}$, and the trace operator of a matrix $\mathbf{X}$ is denoted as the symbol "tr($\mathbf{X}$)".

3.1 Problem formulation

Assume we have two modals, $\mathbf{X}^{(i)} = \{\mathbf{x}_1^{(i)}, ..., \mathbf{x}_n^{(i)}\}; i = 1, 2$, describing the same data points where n is the number of data points. For example, $\mathbf{X}^{(1)}$ is the SIFT visual feature extracted from the content of images, and $\mathbf{X}^{(2)}$ is the bag-of-words feature extracted from the text surrounding the images. In general the feature dimensionalities of different modals are different.

With the same assumption in [4, 11] that there is an invariant common space among multiple modals, the objective of LCMH is to effectively and efficiently learn hash functions for different modals to support cross-modal retrieval. To this end, LCMH needs to generate the hash functions: $f^{(i)} : \mathbf{x}^{(i)} \mapsto \mathbf{b}^{(i)} = \{-1, 1\}^c, i = 1, 2$, where c is the code length. Note that all the modals have the same code length. Moreover, LCMH needs to ensure that the neighborhood relationships within each individual modal and across different modals are preserved in the produced common Hamming space. To do this, LCMH is devised to preserve both the intra-similarity and the inter-similarity of the original feature spaces in the Hamming space.

The main idea of learning the hash functions goes as follows. Data of each individual modal are firstly converted into their new representations, denoted as $\mathbf{Z}^{(i)}$, for preserving the intra-similarity (see Section 3.2). Data of all modals represented by $\mathbf{Z}$ are then mapped into a common space where the inter-similarity is preserved to generate hash functions (see Section 3.3). Finally, values generated from hash functions are binarized into the Hamming space (see Section 3.4). With the learnt hash functions, queries and database data can be mapped into the Hamming space to facilitate fast search by efficient binary code matching.

3.2 Intra-similarity preservation

Intra-similarity preservation is designed to maintain the neighborhood relationships among training data points in each individual modal after they are mapped into the new space spanned by their new representations. To achieve this, manifold-like hashing [26, 27, 36, 39] constructs a similarity matrix, where each entry represents the distance between two data points. In such a matrix, each data point can be regarded as a n-dimensional representation indicating its distance to n data points. Typically, a neighborhood for a data point is described by its few nearest neighbors. To preserve the neighborhood of each data point, only few dimensions corresponding to its nearest neighbors in the n-dimensional representation are non-zero. In other words, the n-dimensional representation is highly sparse. However, to build such a sparse matrix needs quadratic time complexity, i.e., $O(n^2)$, which is impractical for large-scale datasets.

Observed from the sparse n-dimensional representation, only few data points are used to describe the neighborhood for a data point. This motivates us to derive a smaller k-dimensional representation (i.e., $k \ll n$) to approximate each training data point, aiming at reducing the time complexity for building the neighborhood structures. The idea is to *select k most representative data points from the training dataset and approximate each training data point using its distances to these k representative data points.* To do this, in this paper we use a scalable k-means clustering method [5] to generate k centroids which are taken as k most representative data points points in the training dataset. It has been shown that k centroids have a strong representation power to adequately cover large-scale datasets [5].

More specifically, given a training dataset in the first modal $\mathbf{X}^{(1)}$, instead of mapping each training data point $\mathbf{x}_i^{(1)}$ into the n-dimensional representation leading to quadratic time complexity, we convert it into the k-dimensional representation $\mathbf{z}_i^{(1)}$, using the obtained k centroids which are denoted by $\mathbf{m}_i^{(1)}$, $i = 1, 2, ..., k$.

For a $\mathbf{z}_i^{(1)}$, its j-th dimension carries the distance from $\mathbf{x}_i^{(1)}$ to the j-th centroid $\mathbf{m}_j^{(1)}$, denoted as $z_{ij}^{(1)}$.

To obtain the value of $z_{ij}^{(1)}$, we first calculate the Euclidean distance between $\mathbf{x}_i^{(1)}$ and $\mathbf{m}_j^{(1)}$, i.e.,

$$z_{ij}^{(1)} = \|\mathbf{x}_i^{(1)} - \mathbf{m}_j^{(1)}\|^2, \tag{1}$$

where $\|.\|$ stands for the Euclidean norm.

As in [9], the value of $z_{ij}^{(1)}$ can be further defined as a function of the Euclidean to better fit the Gaussian distribution in real applications. Denote the redefined value of $z_{ij}^{(1)}$ as $p_{ij}^{(1)}$, we have:

$$p_{ij}^{(1)} = \frac{exp(-z_{ij}^{(1)}/\sigma)}{\sum_{l=1}^{k} exp(-z_{il}^{(1)}/\sigma)}, \tag{2}$$

where σ is a tuning parameter for controlling the decay rate of $z_{ij}^{(1)}$. For simplicity, we set $\sigma = 1$ in this paper, while an adaptive setting of σ can lead to better results.

Let $\mathbf{p}_i^{(1)} = [p_{i1}^{(1)}; ...; p_{ij}^{(1)}; ...; p_{ik}^{(1)}]$, $\mathbf{p}_i^{(1)}$ forms the new representation of $\mathbf{x}_i^{(1)}$. It can be seen that the rationale of defining $\mathbf{p}_i^{(1)}$ is similar to that of kernel density estimation with a Gaussian kernel, i.e., if $\mathbf{x}_i^{(1)}$ is near to the j-th centroid, $p_{ij}^{(1)}$ will be relatively high; otherwise, $p_{ij}^{(1)}$ will decay.

To preserve the neighborhood of each training data point in the new k-dimensional space, here we also represent each training data point using several (say s and $s \ll k$) nearest centroids so that the new representation $\mathbf{p}_i^{(1)}$ of $\mathbf{x}_i^{(1)}$ is sparse. Therefore, in the implementation, for each training data point we only keep the values to its s nearest centroids in $\mathbf{p}_i^{(1)}$ and set the rest as 0. After this, we normalize the derived value to generate the final value of $z_{ij}^{(1)}$. According to the perspective of geometric reconstruction in the literatures [23, 25, 32], we can easily show that the intra-similarity can be well preserved in the derived k-dimensional representation, i.e., the invariance to rotations, rescalings, and translations.

According to Eqs.1-2, we convert the training data $\mathbf{X}^{(i)}$ into their k-dimensional representations $\mathbf{Z}^{(i)}, i = 1, 2$. That is, we can use a $k \times n$ matrix to approximate the original $n \times n$ similarity matrix with intra-similarity preservation. The advantage is to reduce the complexity from $O(n^2)$ to $O(kn)$. Note that one can select different numbers of centroids for each modal. For simplicity, in this paper we select the same numbers of centroids in our experiments. The next problem is to preserve the inter-similarity between $\mathbf{Z}^{(1)}$ and $\mathbf{Z}^{(2)}$ via seeking a common latent space between them.

3.3 Inter-similarity preservation

It is well known that multimedia data with same semantics can exist in different types of modals. For example, a text document and an image can describe exactly the same topic. Research has shown that if data described in different modal spaces are related to the same event or topic, they are expected to have some common latent space [16, 38]. This suggests that multi-modal data with the same semantic should share some common space in which relevant data are close to each other. Such a property is understood as inter-similarity preservation when modal-modal data are mapped into the common space. In our problem setting, multi-modal data are eventually represented by binary codes in the common Hamming space.

To this end, we first learn a "semantic bridge" for each modal $\mathbf{Z}^{(i)}$ in its k-dimensional space to map $\mathbf{Z}^{(i)}$ into the common Hamming space. To ensure inter-similarity preservation, in the Hamming space, data describing the same object from different modals should have same or similar binary codes. For example, in Fig.2, we map both the images' visual modal and textual modal via learnt "semantic bridges" (i.e., the arrows in Fig.2) into the Hamming space (i.e., the circle in Fig.2), in which two modals of an image are represented with same or similar binary codes in the Hamming space. That is, consistency across different modals is achieved.

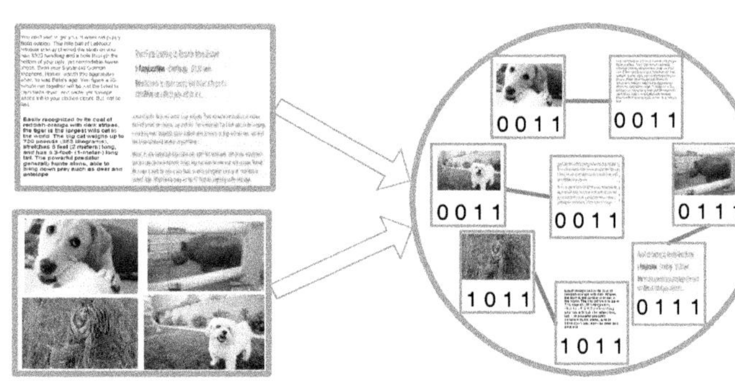

Figure 2: An illustration on inter-similarity preservation.

More formally, given $\mathbf{Z}^{(1)} \in \mathbb{R}^{n \times k}$ and $\mathbf{Z}^{(2)} \in \mathbb{R}^{n \times k}$ where n is sample size and k is the number of centroids, we learn the transformation matrix (i.e., "semantic bridge") $\mathbf{W}^{(1)} \in \mathbb{R}^{k \times c}$ and $\mathbf{W}^{(2)} \in \mathbb{R}^{k \times c}$ for converting $\mathbf{Z}^{(1)}$ and $\mathbf{Z}^{(2)}$ into the new representation $\mathbf{B}^{(1)} \in \{\mathbf{0}, \mathbf{1}\}^{n \times c}$ and $\mathbf{B}^{(2)} \in \{\mathbf{0}, \mathbf{1}\}^{n \times c}$

in a common Hamming space, in which each sample pair (describing the same object, i.e., $\mathbf{B}_i^{(1)}$ and $\mathbf{B}_i^{(2)}$ describing the i-th object with different modals) has the minimal Hamming distance, i.e., the maximal consistency. This leads to the following objective function:

$$\begin{aligned} \min_{\mathbf{B}^{(1)},\mathbf{B}^{(2)}} \quad & \|\mathbf{B}^{(1)} - \mathbf{B}^{(2)}\|_F^2 \\ s.t., \quad & \mathbf{B}^{(i)^T}\mathbf{e} = 0, \\ & \mathbf{b}^{(i)} \in \{-1, 1\}, \\ & \mathbf{B}^{(i)^T}\mathbf{B}^{(i)} = \mathbf{I}_c,\ i = 1, 2, \end{aligned} \tag{3}$$

where $\|.\|_F$ means a Frobenius norm, $\mathbf{e}$ is a $n \times 1$ vector whose each entry is 1 and $\mathbf{I}_c$ is a $c \times c$ identity matrix, the constraint $\mathbf{B}^{(i)^T}\mathbf{e} = 0$ requires each bit has equal chance to be 1 or -1, the constraint $\mathbf{B}^{(i)^T}\mathbf{B}^{(i)} = \mathbf{I}_c$ requires the bits to be obtained independently, and the loss function term $\|\mathbf{B}^{(1)} - \mathbf{B}^{(2)}\|_F^2$ achieves the minimal difference (or the maximal consistency) on two representations of an object.

The optimization problem in Eq.3 equals to the issue of balanced graph partitioning and is NP-hard. Following the literatures [16, 33], we first denote $\mathbf{Y}^{(i)}$ as the real-valued representation of $\mathbf{B}^{(i)}$ and solve the derived objective function on $\mathbf{Y}^{(i)}$ in this subsection, and then binarize $\mathbf{Y}^{(i)}$ into binary codes based on the median threshold method in Section 3.4.

To map $\mathbf{Z}^{(i)}$ into $\mathbf{Y}^{(i)} \in \mathbb{R}^{n\times c}$ via the transformation matrix $\mathbf{W}^{(i)}$, we let $\mathbf{Y}^{(i)} = \mathbf{Z}^{(i)}\mathbf{W}^{(i)}$. According to Eq.3, we have the objective function as

$$\begin{aligned} \min_{\mathbf{W}^{(1)},\mathbf{W}^{(2)}} \quad & \left\|\mathbf{Z}^{(1)}\mathbf{W}^{(1)} - \mathbf{Z}^{(2)}\mathbf{W}^{(2)}\right\|_F^2 \\ s.t., \quad & \mathbf{W}^{(1)^T}\mathbf{W}^{(1)} = \mathbf{I},\quad \mathbf{W}^{(2)^T}\mathbf{W}^{(2)} = \mathbf{I}, \end{aligned} \tag{4}$$

where orthogonal constraints are set to avoid trivial solutions.

To optimize the objective function in Eq.4, we first convert its loss function term into

$$\begin{aligned} & \|\mathbf{Z}^{(1)}\mathbf{W}^{(1)} - \mathbf{Z}^{(2)}\mathbf{W}^{(2)}\|_F^2 \\ & = tr(\mathbf{W}^{(1)^T}\mathbf{Z}^{(1)^T}\mathbf{Z}^{(1)}\mathbf{W}^{(1)} + \mathbf{W}^{(2)^T}\mathbf{Z}^{(2)^T}\mathbf{Z}^{(2)}\mathbf{W}^{(2)} \\ & \quad - \mathbf{W}^{(1)^T}\mathbf{Z}^{(1)^T}\mathbf{Z}^{(2)}\mathbf{W}^{(2)} - \mathbf{W}^{(2)^T}\mathbf{Z}^{(2)^T}\mathbf{Z}^{(1)}\mathbf{W}^{(1)}) \\ & = -tr(\mathbf{W}^T\mathbf{Z}\mathbf{W}), \end{aligned} \tag{5}$$

where $\mathbf{W} = [\mathbf{W}^{(1)^T}; \mathbf{W}^{(2)^T}]^T \in \mathbb{R}^{2k\times c}$ and

$$\mathbf{Z} = \begin{pmatrix} -\mathbf{Z}^{(1)^T}\mathbf{Z}^{(1)} & \mathbf{Z}^{(1)^T}\mathbf{Z}^{(2)} \\ \mathbf{Z}^{(2)^T}\mathbf{Z}^{(1)} & -\mathbf{Z}^{(2)^T}\mathbf{Z}^{(2)} \end{pmatrix} \in \mathbb{R}^{2k\times 2k}.$$

Then the objective function in Eq.4 becomes:

$$\max_{\mathbf{W}} \quad tr(\mathbf{W}^T\mathbf{Z}\mathbf{W}) \quad s.t., \mathbf{W}^T\mathbf{W} = \mathbf{I}. \tag{6}$$

Eq.6 is an eigenvalue problem. We can obtain the optimal $\mathbf{W}$ via solving the eigenvalue problem on $\mathbf{Z}$. $\mathbf{W}$ represents the hash functions to generate $\mathbf{Y}$ as follows:

$$\mathbf{Y}^{(i)} = tr(\mathbf{Z}^{(i)}\mathbf{W}^{(i)}) \tag{7}$$

where $\mathbf{W}^{(1)} = \mathbf{W}(1 : k, :)$ and $\mathbf{W}^{(2)} = \mathbf{W}(k + 1 : \text{end}, :)$.

3.4 Binarization

After obtaining all $\mathbf{Y}^{(i)}$, we get the median vector of $\mathbf{Y}^{(i)}$

$$\mathbf{u}^{(i)} = \text{median}(\mathbf{Y}^{(i)}) \in \mathbb{R}^c, \tag{8}$$

we then binarize $\mathbf{Y}^{(i)}$ as follows:

$$\begin{cases} b_{jl}^{(i)} = 1 & if\ \ y_{jl}^{(i)} \geq u_l^{(i)} \\ b_{jl}^{(i)} = -1 & if\ \ y_{jl}^{(i)} < u_l^{(i)} \end{cases} \tag{9}$$

where $\mathbf{Y}^{(i)} = [\mathbf{y}_1^{(i)}, ..., \mathbf{y}_n^{(i)}]^T$, $i = 1, 2; j = 1, ..., n$ and $l = 1, ..., c$.

Eq.9 generates the final binary codes $\mathbf{B}$ for the training data $\mathbf{X}$, in which the median value of each dimension is used as the threshold for binarization.

The learnt hash functions and binarization step are used to map unseen data (e.g., database and query) into the Hamming space. In the online search phase, given a query $\mathbf{x}_q^{(i)}$ from the i-th modal, we first approximate it with its distances to k centroids, i.e., $\mathbf{z}_q^{(i)}$ using Eqs.(1-2), and then compute its $\mathbf{y}_q^{(i)}$ using Eq.7, followed by the binarization on $\mathbf{y}_q^{(i)}$ to generate its binary codes $\mathbf{b}_q^{(i)}$. Finally the Hamming distances between $\mathbf{b}_q^{(i)}$ and database binary codes are computed to find the neighbors of $\mathbf{x}_q^{(i)}$ in any other modal.

3.5 Summary and analysis

We summarize the proposed LCMH approach in Algorithm 1 (training phase) and Algorithm 2 (search phase).

Algorithm 1: Pseudo code of training phase

Input: $\mathbf{X}$, c, k
Output: $\mathbf{u}^{(i)} \in \mathbb{R}^c$; $\mathbf{W}^{(i)} \in \mathbb{R}^{k\times c}$, i=1,2

1. Perform scalable k-means on $\mathbf{X}^{(i)}$ to obtain $\mathbf{m}^{(i)}$;
2. Compute $\mathbf{Z}^{(i)}$ by Eq.1-2;
3. Generate $\mathbf{W}^{(i)}$ by Eq.6;
4. Generate $\mathbf{u}^{(i)}$ by Eq.8;

Algorithm 2: Pseudo code of search phase

Input: $\mathbf{x}_q^{(1)}$, $\mathbf{u}^{(1)}$, $\mathbf{W}^{(1)}$
Output: Nearest neighbors of $\mathbf{x}_q^{(1)}$ in another modal

1. Compute $\mathbf{z}_q^{(1)}$ by Eq.1-2;
2. Compute $\mathbf{y}_q^{(1)}$ by Eq.7;
3. Generate $\mathbf{b}_t^{(1)}$ by Eq.9;
4. Match $\mathbf{b}_q^{(1)}$ with database binary codes in another modal;

In the training phase of LCMH, time cost mainly comes from the clustering process, new representation generation, and eigenvalue decomposition in generating hash functions. Applying a scalable clustering method, such as [5], clusters can be generated in linear time complexity to the training data size n. Generating the k-dimensional representations $\mathbf{Z}$ takes the complexity of $O(kn)$. The time complexity to generate $\mathbf{W}$ is $O(min\{nk^2, k^3\})$. Since $k \ll n$ for large-scale training datasets, $O(k^3)$ is the complexity to generate hash functions. Therefore, the overall time complexity is $O(max\{kn, k^3\})$. Given that $k \ll n$, we expect that $k^2 < n$ or both have similar scale. This leads to the approximation of $O(kn)$ time complexity for the training phase. Having k as a constant, the final time complexity becomes linear to the training data size. In the search phase, the time complexity is constant.

3.6 Extension

We present an extension of Algorithm 1 and Algorithm 2 to the case of more than two modals, which makes us to use the information available in all the possible modals to achieve better learning results. To do this, we first generate new representations of each modal according to Section 3.1 for preserving intra-similarity, and then transform new representations of all the modals into a common latent space for preserving inter-similarity across any pair of modals. The objective function for preserving inter-similarity is defined as:

$$\begin{aligned} \min_{\mathbf{B}^{(i)}, i=1,\dots,p} \quad & \sum_{i=1}^{p}\sum_{i<j}^{p} \|\mathbf{B}^{(i)} - \mathbf{B}^{(j)}\|_F^2 \\ s.t., \quad & \mathbf{B}^{(i)^T}\mathbf{e} = 0, \\ & \mathbf{b}^{(i)} \in \{-1, 1\}, \\ & \mathbf{B}^{(i)^T}\mathbf{B}^{(i)} = \mathbf{I}_c,\ i = 1, ..., p, \end{aligned} \tag{10}$$

where $\mathbf{e}$ is a $n \times 1$ vector, p is the number of different modals, $\mathbf{I}_c$ is a $c \times c$ identity matrix, the constraint $\mathbf{B}^{(i)^T}\mathbf{e} = 0$ requires each bit has equal chance to be 1 or -1, and the constraint $\mathbf{B}^{(i)^T}\mathbf{B}^{(i)} = \mathbf{I}_d$ requires the bits of each modal to be obtained independently.

To solve Eq.10, we first relax it to:

$$\begin{aligned} \min_{\mathbf{W}^{(i)}, i=1,\dots,p} \quad & \sum_{i=1}^{p}\sum_{i<j}^{p} \left\|\mathbf{Z}^{(i)}\mathbf{W}^{(i)} - \mathbf{Z}^{(j)}\mathbf{W}^{(j)}\right\|_F^2 \\ & s.t., \mathbf{W}^{(i)^T}\mathbf{W}^{(i)} = \mathbf{I}, i = 1, ..., p. \end{aligned} \tag{11}$$

We then obtain

$$\max_{\mathbf{W}} \ tr(\mathbf{W}^T\ \mathbf{Z}\mathbf{W}) \quad s.t., \mathbf{W}^T\mathbf{W} = \mathbf{I}, \tag{12}$$

where $\mathbf{W} = [\mathbf{W}^{(1)^T}; ...; \mathbf{W}^{(p)^T}]^T, \mathbf{W} \in \mathbb{R}^{pk \times c}$ and

$$\mathbf{Z} = \begin{pmatrix} -\mathbf{Z}^{(1)^T}\mathbf{Z}^{(1)} & \mathbf{Z}^{(1)^T}\mathbf{Z}^{(2)} & \dots & \mathbf{Z}^{(1)^T}\mathbf{Z}^{(p)} \\ \mathbf{Z}^{(2)^T}\mathbf{Z}^{(1)} & -\mathbf{Z}^{(2)^T}\mathbf{Z}^{(2)} & \dots & \mathbf{Z}^{(2)^T}\mathbf{Z}^{(p)} \\ \dots & \dots & \dots & \dots \\ \mathbf{Z}^{(p)^T}\mathbf{Z}^{(1)} & \mathbf{Z}^{(p)^T}\mathbf{Z}^{(2)} & \dots & -\mathbf{Z}^{(p)^T}\mathbf{Z}^{(p)} \end{pmatrix},$$

where $\mathbf{Z} \in \mathbb{R}^{pk \times pk}$.

After solving the eigenvalue problem in Eq.12, we obtain the hash functions of multiple modals (similar to Eq.7 to Eq.9 in Section 3.4). With hash functions and median thresholds, we can transform database data and queries into the Hamming space, to support cross-modal retrieval via efficient binary code comparisons.

4. EXPERIMENTAL ANALYSIS

We conduct our experiments on two benchmark datasets, i.e., **Wiki** [22] and **NUS-WIDE** [6], so far the largest publicly available multi-modal datasets that are fully paired and labeled [38]. The two datasets are bimodal with both visual and textual modals in different representations. In our experiments, each dataset is partitioned into a query set and a database set which is used for training.

4.1 Comparison algorithms

The comparison algorithms include a baseline algorithm BLCMH and state-of-the-art algorithms, including CVH [16], CMSSH [2] and MLBE [38]. BLCMH is our LCMH without preserving intra-similarity, with the purpose to test the effect of intra-similarity preservation in our method.

We compare LCMH with the comparison algorithms on two cross-modal retrieval tasks. Specifically, one task is to use a text query in the textual modal to search relevant images in the visual modal (shorted for "Text query *vs.* Image data") and the other is to use an image query in the visual modal to search relevant texts from the textual modal (shorted for "Image query *vs.* Text data").

4.2 Evaluation Metrics

We use mean Average Precision (mAP) [38] as one of performance measures. Given a query and a list of R retrieved results, the value of its Average Precision is defined as

$$\text{AP} = \{\frac{1}{l}\sum\nolimits_{r=1}^{R} P(r)\delta(r)\}, \tag{13}$$

where l is the number of true neighbors in ground truth, $P(r)$ denotes the precision of the top r retrieved results, and $\delta(r) = 1$ if the r-th retrieved result is a true neighbor of the query, otherwise $\delta(r) = 0$. mAP is the mean of all the queries' average precision. Clearly, the larger the mAP, the better the performance is. In our experiments, we set R as the number of training data points whose Hamming distances to the query are not larger than 2.

We also report the results on two other types of measures, including recall curves with different retrieved results and time cost for generating hash functions and searching database binary codes. Both mAP and recall curves are used to reflect the retrieval effectiveness and time cost is used to evaluate the efficiency.

4.3 Parameters' setting

By default, we set the parameter $k = 300$ for dataset **Wiki** and $k = 600$ for dataset **NUS-WIDE**. Among k centroids, we set $s = 3$ for representing each training data point with s nearest centroids. In our experiments, we vary the length of hash codes (i.e., the number of hash bits) in the range of [8, 16, 24] for dataset **Wiki** and [8, 16, 32] for dataset **NUS-WIDE**. Moreover, for calculating the value of recall curves, we set the number of retrieved results in the range of [250, 500, 750, 1000, 1250, 1500, 1700, 2000] for **Wiki** and [10000, 20000, 50000, 80000, 100000, 120000, 150000] on **NUS-WIDE**.

For all the comparison algorithms, the codes are provided by the authors. We tune the parameters according to the corresponding literatures. All the experiments are conducted on a computer which has Intel Xeon(R) 2.90GHz 2 processors, 192 GB RAM and the 64-bit Windows 7 operating system.

4.4 Results on Wiki dataset

The dataset **Wiki** [22] is generated from a group of 2,866 Wikipedia documents. In **Wiki**, each object is an image-text pair and is labeled with exactly one of 10 semantic classes. The images are represented by 128-dimensional SIFT feature vectors. The text articles are represented by the probability distributions over 10 topics, which are derived from a latent Dirichlet allocation (LDA) model [1]. Following the setting in the literature [22], 2173 data points form the database set and the remaining 693 data points form the query set. Due to that the dataset is fully annotated, semantic neighbors for a query is regarded as the ground truth, based on the associated labels.

The mAP results of all the algorithms on different code lengths are reported in Fig.3.(a-b). The recall curves for two query tasks on different code lengths are plotted in Fig.4. According to the experimental results, we can see that LCMH consistently performs best. For example, the maximal difference between LCMH and the second best one (i.e., MLBE) is about 4% in Fig.3.(a) and about 8% in Fig.3.(b) while the code length is 24. Moreover, both MLBE and CVH are better than CMSSH, which is with the same conclusion as in [38]. Besides, we also have three observations based on our experimental results. First, LCMH, MLBE and CVH outperform BLCMH and CMSSH which only consider the inter-similarity across modals and ignore the intra-similarity within a modal. Therefore, we can make an conclusion that it is useful for considering both the intra-similarity and the inter-similarity together to build cross-modal hashing. Second, although both CMSSH and BLCMH consider the inter-similarity, CMSSH improves BLCMH slightly since CMSSH employs prior knowledge, such as the predefined similar pairs and dissimilar pairs [2]. Third, according to the experimental results on mAP and recall curves, we see that all algorithms achieve their best performance when the number of hash bits is 16 for dataset **Wiki**. After achieving their peak, the performance of all algorithms degrades. A possible reason is that a longer binary code representation may lead to less retrieved results given the fixed Hamming distance threshold, which affects its precision and recall. Such a phenomenon has also been discussed in [18, 38].

Table 1: Running time for all algorithms while fixing code length as 16 for dataset Wiki and dataset NUS-WIDE. Both training time and search time are recorded in second.

Task	Methods	Wiki		NUS-WIDE	
		train	search	train	search
Image query vs. Text data	BLCMH	1.750	0.002	122.3	0.131
	CMSSH	1.453	0.001	10.75	0.127
	CVH	4.674	0.002	601.2	0.153
	MLBE	218.1	23.85	2562	37.51
	LCMH	2.018	0.003	186.3	0.171
Text query vs. Image data	BLCMH	4.890	0.001	139.9	0.156
	CMSSH	1.596	0.002	15.38	0.157
	CVH	10.19	0.006	635.8	0.195
	MLBE	342.7	29.87	2796	51.56
	LCMH	5.389	0.002	192.6	0.187

Table 1 shows the time cost of the training phase and the search phase of all the algorithms. We can see that MLBE is most time consuming since it is a generative model, followed by CVH, LCMH and CMSSH. Since CMSSH does not consider the intra-similarity, it is faster than LCMH. However, CMSSH has unsatisfactory performance in search quality as shown in Fig.3.

4.5 Results on NUS-WIDE dataset

The dataset **NUS-WIDE** originally contains 269,648 images associated with 81 ground truth concept tags. Following the literature [18, 30], we prune original **NUS-WIDE** to form a new dataset **NUS-WIDE** consisting of 195,969 image-tag pairs by keeping the pairs that belong to one of the 21 most frequent tags, such as "animal", "buildings", "person", etc. In our **NUS-WIDE**, each pair is annotated by at least one of 21 labels. The images are represented by 500-dimensional SIFT feature vectors and the texts are represented by 1000-dimensional feature vectors obtained by performing PCA on the original tag occurrence features. Following the setting in the literatures [18, 31], we uniformly sample 100 images from each of the selected 21 tags to form a query set of 2,100 images and the left 193,869 image-tag pairs serving as the database set. The ground truth is defined based on whether two images share at least one common tag in our experiments.

As shown in in Fig.3.(c-d), Fig.5, and Table 1, one can see that the ranking of all the algorithms on dataset **NUS-WIDE** is largely consistent with that on dataset **Wiki**. The maximal difference between LCMH and the second best one (i.e., MLBE) is about 6% in Fig.3.(c) and about 5% in Fig.3.(d) while the code length is 16.

Table 2: Running time with different number of centroids while fixing code length as 16 for dataset Wiki and dataset NUS-WIDE. Both training time and search time are recorded in second.

Task	Centroids	Wiki		NUS-WIDE	
		train	search	train	search
Image query vs. Text data	k = 300	2.018	0.003	62.53	0.168
	k = 600	8.439	0.003	186.3	0.171
	k = 1000	26.98	0.004	562.1	0.173
Text query vs. Image data	k = 300	5.389	0.002	65.18	0.185
	k = 600	11.89	0.003	192.6	0.187
	k = 1000	38.53	0.004	581.2	0.191

4.6 Parameters' sensitivity

In this section, we test the sensitivity of different parameters. First, we look at the effect of k. We set the different values on k (i.e., the number of clusters in the training phase) and report parts of results in Fig.6. From Fig.6, we can see that a larger k value leads to better results, since the k-dimensional representation can be more accurate in capturing the original data distribution in the training dataset. Nonetheless, more training cost occurs for a larger k value, as shown in Table 2. Our results show that a relatively small k value (e.g., k=300 and 600 for **Wiki** and **NUS-WIDE**) can achieve reasonably good results. Due to the space limit, we do not report the results on different s values. Generally, a good choice of s is between 3 to 5.

5. CONCLUSION

In this paper we have proposed a novel and effective cross-modal hashing approach, namely linear cross-modal hashing (LCMH). The main idea is to represent each training data point with a smaller k-dimensional approximation which can preserve the intra-similarity and reduce the time and space complexity in learning hash functions. We then map the

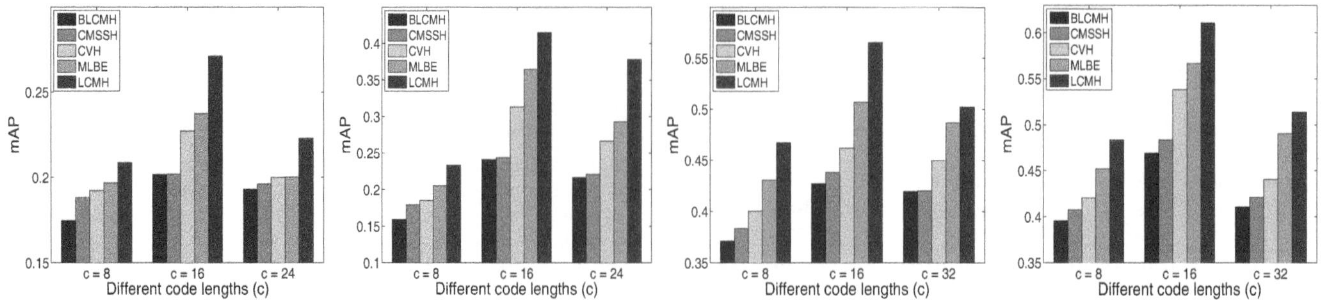

(a) Image query *vs.* Text data (b) Text query *vs.* Image data (c) Image query *vs.* Text data (d) Text query *vs.* Image data

Figure 3: mAP comparison with different code lengths for dateset Wiki (a-b) and for dataset NUS – WIDE (c-d).

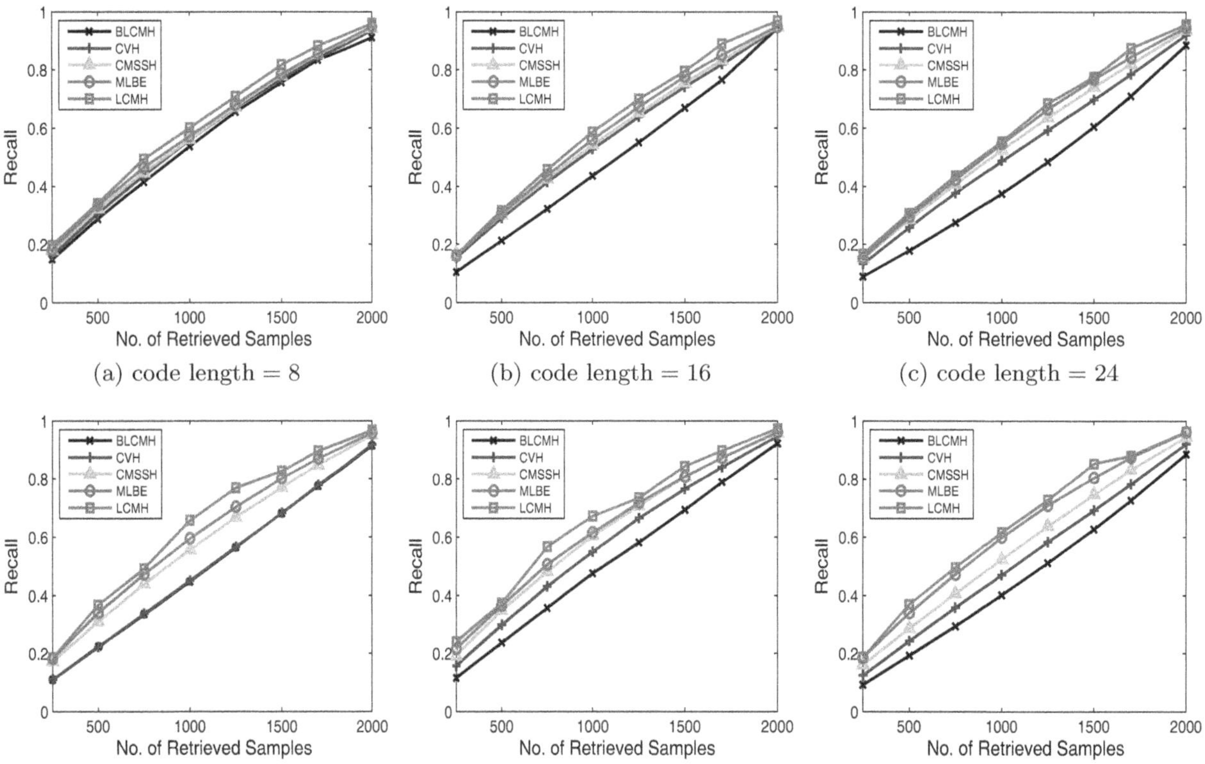

(a) code length = 8 (b) code length = 16 (c) code length = 24

(d) code length = 8 (e) code length = 16 (f) code length = 24

Figure 4: Recall curves with different code lengths for dataset Wiki. The upper row (a-c) is the task of image query *vs.* text data, the bottom row (d-f) is the task of text query *vs.* image data.

new representations of the training data from all modals to a common latent space in which the inter-similarity is preserved and hash functions of each modal are obtained. Given a query, it is first transformed into its k-dimensional representation which is then mapped into the Hamming space with the learnt hash functions, to match with database binary codes. Since binary codes from different modals are comparable in the Hamming space, cross-modal retrieval can be effectively and effectively supported by LCMH. The experimental results on two benchmark datasets demonstrate that LCMH outperforms the state of the art significantly with practical time cost.

6. ACKNOWLEDGEMENTS

This work was supported by the Australia Research Council (ARC) under research Grant DP1094678 and the Nature Science Foundation (NSF) of China under grants 61263035.

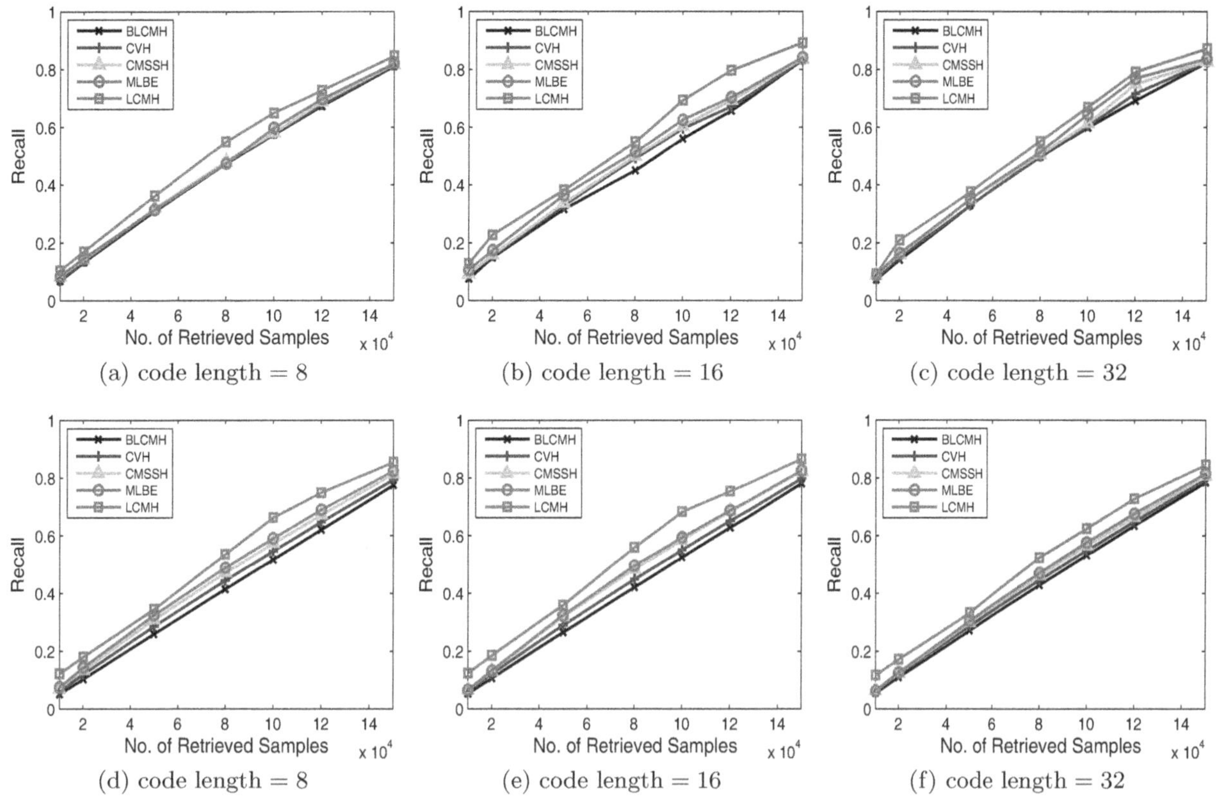

Figure 5: Recall curves with different code lengths for dataset NUS – WIDE. The upper row (a-c) is the task of image query *vs.* text data, the bottom row (d-f) is the task of text query *vs.* image data.

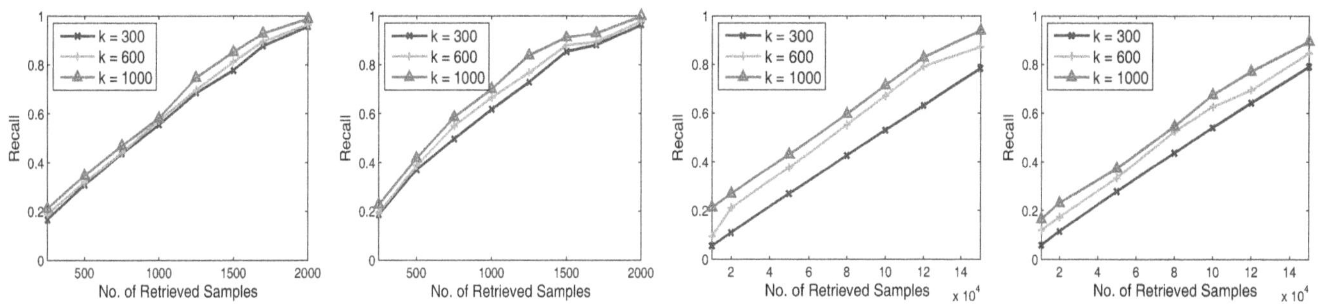

(a) Image query *vs.* Text data (b) Text query *vs.* Image data (c) Image query *vs.* Text data (d) Text query *vs.* Image data

Figure 6: Recall curves with different number of centroids while fixing the code length as 16 for dateset Wiki (a-b) and NUS – WIDE (c-d).

7. REFERENCES

[1] D. M. Blei, A. Y. Ng, and M. I. Jordan. Latent dirichlet allocation. *J. Mach. Learn. Res.*, 3:993–1022, 2003.

[2] M. M. Bronstein, A. M. Bronstein, F. Michel, and N. Paragios. Data fusion through cross-modality metric learning using similarity-sensitive hashing. In *CVPR*, pages 3594–3601, 2010.

[3] R. Chaudhry and Y. Ivanov. Fast approximate nearest neighbor methods for non-euclidean manifolds with applications to human activity analysis in videos. In *ECCV*, pages 735–748, 2010.

[4] M. Chen, K. Q. Weinberger, and J. C. Blitzer. Co-training for domain adaptation. In *NIPS*, pages 1–9, 2011.

[5] X. Chen and D. Cai. Large scale spectral clustering with landmark-based representation. In *AAAI*, pages 313–318, 2011.

[6] T.-S. Chua, J. Tang, R. Hong, H. Li, Z. Luo, and Y. Zheng. Nus-wide: a real-world web image database

from national university of singapore. In *CIVR*, pages 48–56, 2009.

[7] M. Datar, N. Immorlica, P. Indyk, and V. S. Mirrokni. Locality-sensitive hashing scheme based on p-stable distributions. In *SOCG*, pages 253–262, 2004.

[8] A. Gionis, P. Indyk, and R. Motwani. Similarity search in high dimensions via hashing. In *VLDB*, pages 518–529, 1999.

[9] J. Goldberger, S. T. Roweis, G. E. Hinton, and R. Salakhutdinov. Neighbourhood components analysis. In *NIPS*, pages 1–9, 2004.

[10] Y. Gong, S. Lazebnik, A. Gordo, and F. Perronnin. Iterative quantization: A procrustean approach to learning binary codes for large-scale image retrieval. *IEEE Trans. Pattern Anal. Mach. Intell.*, page accepted, 2012.

[11] R. Gopalan, R. Li, and R. Chellappa. Domain adaptation for object recognition: An unsupervised approach. In *ICCV*, pages 999–1006, 2011.

[12] P. Jain, B. Kulis, and K. Grauman. Fast image search for learned metrics. In *CVPR*, pages 1–8, 2008.

[13] H. Jégou, M. Douze, and C. Schmid. Product quantization for nearest neighbor search. In *CVPR*, pages 117–128, 2011.

[14] B. Kulis and T. Darrell. Learning to hash with binary reconstructive embeddings. In *NIPS*, pages 1042–1050, 2009.

[15] B. Kulis and K. Grauman. Kernelized locality-sensitive hashing for scalable image search. In *ICCV*, pages 2130–2137, 2009.

[16] S. Kumar and R. Udupa. Learning hash functions for cross-view similarity search. In *IJCAI*, pages 1360–1365, 2011.

[17] W. Liu, J. Wang, R. Ji, Y.-G. Jiang, and S.-F. Chang. Supervised hashing with kernels. In *CVPR*, pages 2074–2081, 2012.

[18] W. Liu, J. Wang, S. Kumar, and S.-F. Chang. Hashing with graphs. In *ICML*, pages 1–8, 2011.

[19] M. Norouzi and D. J. Fleet. Minimal loss hashing for compact binary codes. In *ICML*, pages 353–360, 2011.

[20] M. Norouzi, A. Punjani, and D. J. Fleet. Fast search in hamming space with multi-index hashing. In *CVPR*, pages 3108–3115, 2012.

[21] M. Raginsky and S. Lazebnik. Locality-sensitive binary codes from shift-invariant kernels. In *NIPS*, pages 1509–1517, 2009.

[22] N. Rasiwasia, J. C. Pereira, E. Coviello, and G. Doyle. A new approach to cross-modal multimedia retrieval. In *ACM MM*, pages 251–260, 2010.

[23] S. Roweis and L. Saul. Nonlinear dimensionality reduction by locally linear embedding. *Science*, 290(5500):2323–2326, 2000.

[24] R. Salakhutdinov and G. E. Hinton. Semantic hashing. *Int. J. Approx. Reasoning*, 50(7):969–978, 2009.

[25] L. K. Saul and S. T. Roweis. Think globally, fit locally: Unsupervised learning of low dimensional manifold. *J. Mach. Learn. Res.*, 4:119–155, 2003.

[26] J. Song, Y. Yang, Z. Huang, H. T. Shen, and R. Hong. Multiple feature hashing for real-time large scale near-duplicate video retrieval. In *ACM MM*, pages 423–432, 2011.

[27] J. Song, Y. Yang, Y. Yang, Z. Huang, and H. T. Shen. Inter-media hashing for large-scale retrieval from heterogenous data sources. In *SIGMOD*, pages 785–796, 2013.

[28] C. Strecha, A. A. Bronstein, M. M. Bronstein, and P. Fua. Ldahash: Improved matching with smaller descriptors. *IEEE Trans. Pattern Anal. Mach. Intell.*, 34(1):66–78, 2012.

[29] A. Torralba, R. Fergus, and Y. Weiss. Small codes and large image databases for recognition. In *CVPR*, pages 1–8, 2008.

[30] J. Wang, O. Kumar, and S.-F. Chang. Semi-supervised hashing for scalable image retrieval. In *CVPR*, pages 3424–3431, 2010.

[31] J. Wang, S. Kumar, and S.-F. Chang. Sequential projection learning for hashing with compact codes. In *ICML*, pages 1127–1134, 2010.

[32] K. Q. Weinberger, B. D. Packer, and L. K. Saul. Nonlinear dimensionality reduction by semidefinite programming and kernel matrix factorization. In *AISTATS*, pages 381–388, 2005.

[33] Y. Weiss, A. Torralba, and R. Fergus. Spectral hashing. In *NIPS*, pages 1753–1760, 2008.

[34] C. Wu, J. Zhu, D. Cai, C. Chen, and J. Bu. Semi-supervised nonlinear hashing using bootstrap sequential projection learning. *IEEE Trans. Knowl. Data Eng.*, 99:1, 2012.

[35] Y. Yang, D. Xu, F. Nie, J. Luo, and Y. Zhuang. Ranking with local regression and global alignment for cross media retrieval. In *ACM MM*, pages 175–184, 2009.

[36] D. Zhang, F. Wang, and L. Si. Composite hashing with multiple information sources. In *SIGIR*, pages 225–234, 2011.

[37] Y. Zhen and D.-Y. Yeung. Co-regularized hashing for multimodal data. In *NIPS*, pages 2559–2567, 2012.

[38] Y. Zhen and D.-Y. Yeung. A probabilistic model for multimodal hash function learning. In *SIGKDD*, pages 940–948, 2012.

[39] X. Zhu, Z. Huang, H. Cheng, J. Cui, and H. T. Shen. Sparse hashing for fast multimedia search. *ACM Trans. Inf. Syst.*, 31(2):509–517, 2013.

Online Multimodal Deep Similarity Learning with Application to Image Retrieval

Pengcheng Wu, Steven C.H. Hoi, Hao Xia, Peilin Zhao, Dayong Wang, Chunyan Miao
School of Computer Engineering, Nanyang Technological University, Singapore 639798
{wupe0003,chhoi,xiah0002,zhao0106,s090023,ascymiao}@ntu.edu.sg

ABSTRACT

Recent years have witnessed extensive studies on distance metric learning (DML) for improving similarity search in multimedia information retrieval tasks. Despite their successes, most existing DML methods suffer from two critical limitations: (i) they typically attempt to learn a linear distance function on the input feature space, in which the assumption of linearity limits their capacity of measuring the similarity on complex patterns in real-world applications; (ii) they are often designed for learning distance metrics on uni-modal data, which may not effectively handle the similarity measures for multimedia objects with multimodal representations. To address these limitations, in this paper, we propose a novel framework of online multimodal deep similarity learning (OMDSL), which aims to optimally integrate multiple deep neural networks pretrained with stacked denoising autoencoder. In particular, the proposed framework explores a unified two-stage online learning scheme that consists of (i) learning a flexible nonlinear transformation function for each individual modality, and (ii) learning to find the optimal combination of multiple diverse modalities simultaneously in a coherent process. We conduct an extensive set of experiments to evaluate the performance of the proposed algorithms for multimodal image retrieval tasks, in which the encouraging results validate the effectiveness of the proposed technique.

Categories and Subject Descriptors

H.3.3 [**Information Storage and Retrieval**]: Information Search and Retrieval; I.2.6 [**Artificial Intelligence**]: Learning; I.4.7 [**Image Processing and Computer Vision**]: Feature Measurement

General Terms

Algorithms, Experimentation

Keywords

deep learning; similarity learning; distance metric learning; online learning; image retrieval

1. INTRODUCTION

Similarity search is a fundamental issue of multimedia information retrieval research, which has been actively studied for years across several communities, including multimedia, signal processing, computer vision, and machine learning [28, 22]. The crux of similarity search lies in two key components: (i) effective feature representation and (ii) proper similarity functions over the feature space. On one hand, researchers in multimedia signal processing and computer vision have spent a few decades in searching and designing effective feature representations for content-based image retrieval (CBIR) [41, 36], ranging from early global features [31] (e.g., color, shape, and texture) to recent local features (e.g., SIFT and SURF features [30, 3] and their bag of visual words representations [49, 48]). On the other hand, various similarity/distance functions have been proposed for multimedia retrieval, such as typical Euclidean distance or cosine similarity. The key limitation of these early studies is that they often assume a fixed rigid similarity/distance function (e.g., Euclidean) for all applications, which may not be always optimal. Recent years have witnessed a surge of research efforts in Distance Metric Learning (DML) [50, 16, 15], which applies machine learning techniques to optimize distance metrics from training data or side information (e.g., logs of user relevance feedback in CBIR [16]) for multimedia applications.

Although a variety of DML algorithms have been proposed [50], most existing DML methods suffer from two critical limitations: (i) They usually learn a linear distance metric in the forms of Mahalanobis distances, which can be viewed as learning a linear projection to map feature vectors into another feature space; their linearity assumption however limits their capacity of measuring similarity for complex patterns; (ii) They are often designed for learning metrics on uni-modal data, i.e., either a single type of features or a combined feature space by a simple concatenation of multiple types of features, which could be sub-optimal for measuring similarity of multimedia objects with multimodal representations (e.g., it may fail to fully exploit the potential of all modalities whenever some modality significantly dominates the rest).

To tackle the above challenges, we propose a novel framework of Online Multimodal Deep Similarity Learning (OMDSL), which applies deep learning techniques [13] to learn a flexible nonlinear similarity function from images of multimodal feature representation via an efficient and scalable online learning scheme. Unlike conventional methods, OMDSL applies machine learning to address three key concerns in multimedia: (i) multimodal learning — a unique and key challenge for learning with multimodal contents in multimedia applications; (ii) deep learning — a powerful technique for learning a nonlinear similarity function, going beyond conventional linear/shallow machine learning approaches in multimedia retrieval studies; (iii) online learning — a family of efficient and scalable machine learning algorithms that are promising for mining large-scale multimedia data. Thus, OMDSL is partic-

MM'13, October 21–25, 2013, Barcelona, Spain.
Copyright 2013 ACM 978-1-4503-2404-5/13/10 ...$15.00.
http://dx.doi.org/10.1145/2502081.2502112.

ularly suitable for multimedia applications where data are multi-modal, complex, large in size, and growing rapidly.

To the best of our knowledge, this is the first work that attempts to explore deep neural networks together with online learning for learning a nonlinear similarity function for multimodal image retrieval. As a summary, the main contributions of this paper include:

- a novel framework of Online Multimodal Deep Similarity Learning (OMDSL), which learns both the optimal metrics for each modality and the optimal combination of multiple modalities from training data streams;
- an online learning algorithm to solve the multimodal deep similarity learning task for multimodal image retrieval;
- theoretical bound analysis on the proposed algorithm;
- extensive empirical performance evaluation of the proposed technique for CBIR.

The rest of this paper is organized as follows. Section 2 reviews related work, Section 3 gives problem setting, Section 4 presents the proposed framework and algorithm, Section 5 discusses experimental results, and section 6 concludes this work.

2. RELATED WORK

Our research work lies in the interplay between multimedia information retrieval and machine learning. We refer readers to some classical surveys of multimedia retrieval in [41, 28]. In the following, we focus on reviewing several categories of key related works.

2.1 Content-based Image Retrieval

CBIR has been extensively studied for several decades [28, 41], where conventional approaches usually choose rigid distance functions on some low-level features for similarity search, such as Euclidean distance or cosine similarity. The fixed rigid similarity or distance functions often fail to tackle the CBIR due to the complexity of visual image representation and the semantic gap challenge between the low-level visual features and high-level human perception. Recent years have witnessed a surge of active research efforts in designing various distance/similarity measures on some low-level features using machine learning techniques, among which some works focus on learning to hashing or compact codes [39, 34, 20, 7, 23], and some others can be categorized into distance metric learning (DML). Our work is also related to multimodal/multiview studies, which have been widely studied on image classification and object recognition [51, 1, 12]. However, it is usually hard to apply these techniques directly to CBIR because (i) image classes typically will not be given explicitly in CBIR tasks, (ii) even if classes can be given, the number can be very large, (iii) image datasets for CBIR tend to be much larger than those for classification tasks. We thus exclude the direct comparisons to such existing works.

2.2 Distance Metric Learning

Distance metric learning has been extensively studied in both machine learning and multimedia communities [50]. Existing DML studies can be grouped into different categories according to varied learning settings and methodologies. For example, in terms of training data formats, many DML studies in machine learning typically learn metrics directly from explicit class labels [47], while DML studies in multimedia mainly learn metrics from side information in the forms of either pairwise constraints [16, 15] or triplet constraints [8]. In terms of learning methodology, most existing DML studies generally follow batch machine learning methods, except that some recent DML studies begin to explore online learning techniques [19, 21]. All these studies generally address uni-modal DML, which differs from our multi-modal learning scheme. From another learning perspective, DML aims to learn an optimal linear projection that maps the input features into another feature space; by contrast, we aim to learn a nonlinear projection via deep neural networks. We also note that our work is different from some existing distance learning studies that learn nonlinear distance functions using kernel methods [16, 32], which are often poorly scalable and simply cannot scale up even for medium-scale applications. We thus cannot include the direct empirical comparisons to these existing works. Finally, we note that our work is very different from some existing multiview DML study [51] which is concerned with classification tasks by learning metrics on training data with explicit class labels, making it difficult to be directly compared with our method in experiments.

2.3 Multimodal Deep Learning

Our work falls into the category of deep learning (a.k.a. deep neural networks) methodology, which has been actively studied in machine learning recently. The goal of deep learning is to learn multiple levels of representations through a hierarchy of neural network architectures, where higher-level representation is expected to help define higher-level concepts. Many recent studies [14, 13] have found promising empirical results by applying deep learning to tackle a variety of tasks across different application domains, ranging from speech recognition [10], face recognition, to generic object recognition [27] and image classification [53, 26], etc. Some pioneering and representative studies of deep learning include Deep Belief Nets (DBN) [13], Auto Encoder (AE) [5], Stacked Denoising Autoencoder (SDA) [45], Deep Boltzmann Machine (DBM) [40] and Deep Energy Model (DEM) [33]. A more comprehensive introduction to deep learning can be found in [4] and references therein.

Recently, some studies [33, 43] have applied DBN or DBM to learn cross-modality/multimodal features, e.g., audio versus visual or textual versus visual. Our work differs considerably from these studies, at least in two aspects: (i) their approaches aim to learn a shared representation between modalities so as to infer some missing modality from others, e.g., to infer text from images; by contrast, our method aims to learn both the optimal nonlinear similarity function for each modality and their optimal combination; (ii) our problem setting is very different from the former studies [33, 43] which usually deal with classification tasks and fine-tune the deep neural networks using training data with explicit class labels; by contrast, we address retrieval tasks by fine-tuning the deep neural networks using triplet constraints. Due to the very different formulations, it is difficult and nontrivial to apply the existing techniques in our problem setting, and thus cannot compare with them directly in our empirical study. Finally, we note that our work is also different from some recent deep learning studies [34, 24] that apply deep learning to optimize hashing codes, making it difficult and unfair to be directly compared with our method.

2.4 Online Learning

In this paper, we explore online learning techniques to learn the multimodal similarity functions from the streams of triplet constraints. Online learning, a family of efficient and scalable machine learning algorithms, has been extensively studied for years. Unlike batch learning methods that usually suffer from expensive re-training cost whenever new training data arrive, online learning works in a sequential fashion by performing highly efficient (typically constant) updates for each new training data sequentially, making it highly scalable for large-scale applications. In literature, a variety of algorithm [6, 37, 9, 11, 52, 46] have been proposed for online learning. The most well-known algorithms is the Perceptron algorithm [37], which simply updates the weight vector of the learning model by adding the incoming instance with a constant weight whenever it is misclassified. In recent years, various algorithms [29, 9] have been proposed to improve the Perceptron,

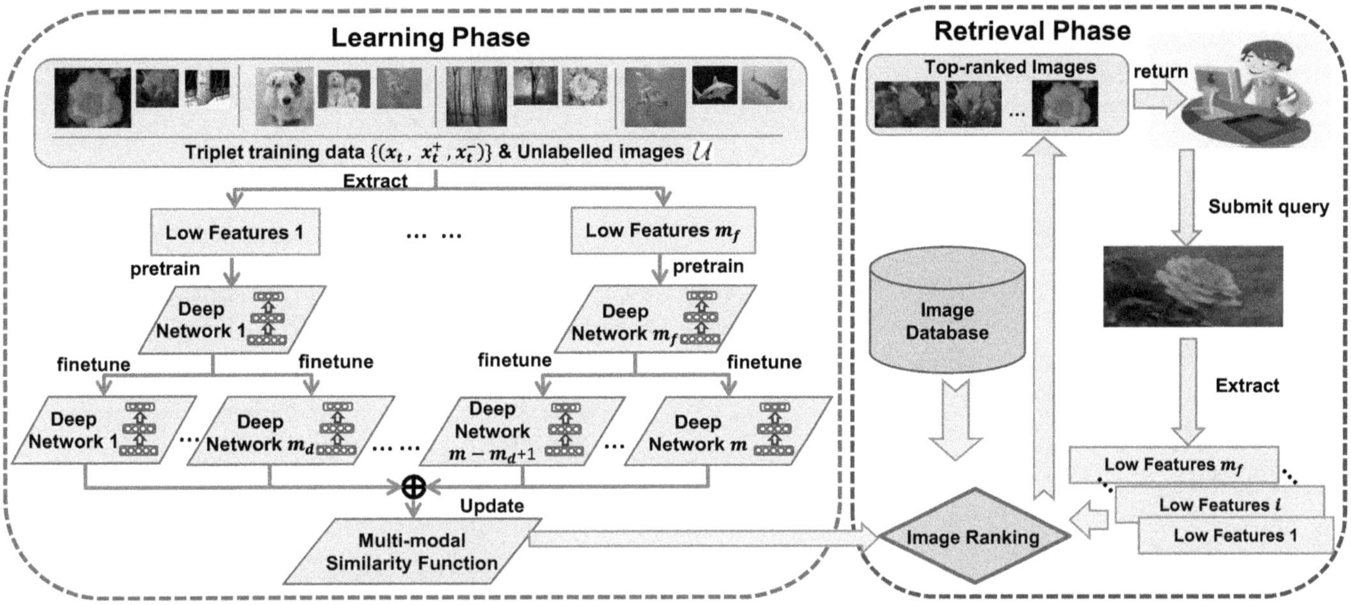

Figure 1: Overview of the proposed multimodal deep similarity learning scheme for image retrieval

many of them usually follow the principle of large margin learning. One notable approach is the Exponentiated Gradient online learning algorithm [6], which updates the classifier whenever it fails to produce a large margin on the received instance and meanwhile attempts to avoid too aggressive updates. In general, most existing online learning algorithms are designed for online classification tasks by learning models from a sequence of training data with class labels [18]. In this work, we apply the Exponentiated Gradient learning methodology to tackle the task of learning similarity functions from a sequence of triplet constraints.

3. PROBLEM SETTING

We address the fundamental problem of learning a pairwise similarity function for image retrieval from side information of pairwise/tripletwise image relationship. To formulate the learning task, we define the similarity function $S(\mathbf{x}_1, \mathbf{x}_2)$ for any two images $\mathbf{x}_1, \mathbf{x}_2 \in \mathbb{R}^n$, and assume a collection of training data instances is given (sequentially) in the forms of triplet, i.e.,

$$\{(\mathbf{x}_t, \mathbf{x}_t^+, \mathbf{x}_t^-), t = 1, \ldots, T\},$$

where each triplet indicates the tripletwise relationship of three images, i.e., image $\mathbf{x}_t$ is more similar to image $\mathbf{x}_t^+$ in contrast to image $\mathbf{x}_t^-$, and T is the total number of triplets. The goal is to learn a similarity function $S(\cdot, \cdot)$ that can always produce the similarity values satisfying the tripletwise constrain as follows:

$$S(\mathbf{x}_t, \mathbf{x}_t^+) > S(\mathbf{x}_t, \mathbf{x}_t^-), \quad (\mathbf{x}_t, \mathbf{x}_t^+, \mathbf{x}_t^-); \forall t; \tag{1}$$

The above discussion generally assumes similarity learning is performed on uni-modal data. We aim to generalize it for multi-modal data, where each image can be represented by different types of low-level feature descriptors (e.g., color, shape, or texture) and the similarity of any two images can be computed by defining multiple kinds of distance measures (e.g., cosine similarity, and Euclidean distance, etc.). In particular, we assume there are m_f types of feature descriptors and m_d kinds of measures, leading to a total of $m = m_f \times m_d$ modalities, each of which applies one kind of distance measure to compute the similarity of two images based on one type of feature descriptor.

The general idea of our multimodal similarity learning scheme is to learn optimal similarity functions $S_i(\cdot, \cdot)$ for each individual modality (with respect to one specific distance measure), and meanwhile identify an optimal combination of the m different modalities to obtain the final multimodal similarity function:

$$S(\mathbf{x}_1, \mathbf{x}_2) \equiv \sum_{i=1}^{m} \theta_i S_i(\mathbf{x}_1^{(i)}, \mathbf{x}_2^{(i)}), \tag{2}$$

where $\theta_i \in [0, 1]$ denotes the combination weight for the i-th modality and $\mathbf{x}_1^{(i)}$ denotes the feature space of the i-th modality. In the following, without loss of clarity, we will simplify notation $S_i(\mathbf{x}_1^{(i)}, \mathbf{x}_2^{(i)})$ as $S_i(\mathbf{x}_1, \mathbf{x}_2)$ by removing the superscript.

To simultaneously learn both the optimal combination weights $\theta = (\theta_1, \ldots, \theta_m)$ and the optimal individual similarity functions $\{S_i | i = 1 \ldots, m\}$, we cast the multimodal similarity learning problem into the following optimization task:

$$\min_{\theta \in \Delta} \min_{S_i} \frac{1}{2} \sum_{i=1}^{m} \|S_i\|^2 + C \sum_{t=1}^{T} \mathcal{L}_t((\mathbf{x}_t, \mathbf{x}_t^+, \mathbf{x}_t^-); S), \tag{3}$$

where $\Delta = \{\theta | \sum_{i=1}^{m} \theta_i = 1, \theta_i \in [0, 1], \forall i\}$, $\|S_i\|$ is a regularization term that limits the model complexity, $C > 0$ and

$$\mathcal{L}_t((\mathbf{x}_t, \mathbf{x}_t^+, \mathbf{x}_t^-); S) = \max(0, S(\mathbf{x}_t, \mathbf{x}_t^-) - S(\mathbf{x}_t, \mathbf{x}_t^+) + 1),$$

which implicitly impose the constraints in (1) by introducing a margin factor $+1$ to ensure a sufficiently large difference. The crux of the above multimodal similarity learning framework lies in how to effectively define or construct the set of individual similarity functions S_i and how to efficiently resolve the resulting and often challenging optimization task.

4. MULTIMODAL DEEP SIMILARITY LEARNING FRAMEWORK

4.1 Overview

Figure 1 illustrates the system flow of the proposed multimodal deep similarity learning scheme for image retrieval. The goal is to learn the similarity functions in the learning phase in order to facilitate the image ranking task in the retrieval phase. During the learning phase, we assume triplet training data instances arrive sequentially, which is natural for a real-world CBIR system where users' online relevance feedback are usually collected in a sequential manner [17].

Following the optimization framework in (3), one possible approach is to define S_i using traditional distance metric learning for optimizing the Mahalanobis distances:

$$S_i(\mathbf{x}_1, \mathbf{x}_2) = -(\mathbf{x}_1 - \mathbf{x}_2)^\top M^{(i)}(\mathbf{x}_1 - \mathbf{x}_2), \quad (4)$$

The optimization thus can be turned into the following:

$$\min_{\theta \in \Delta} \min_{M^{(i)} \succeq 0} \frac{1}{2} \sum_{i=1}^{m} \|M^{(i)}\|_F^2 + C \sum_{t=1}^{T} \mathcal{L}_t((\mathbf{x}_t, \mathbf{x}_t^+, \mathbf{x}_t^-); S), \quad (5)$$

where $\|\cdot\|_F^2$ denotes the Frobenius norm and $M^{(i)} \succeq 0$ enforce $M^{(i)}$ to be positive semi-definite (PSD) matrix.

By decomposing $M^{(i)} = A_i^\top A_i$, we reformulate Eqn.(4) as:

$$\begin{aligned} S_i(\mathbf{x}_1, \mathbf{x}_2) &= -(\mathbf{x}_1 - \mathbf{x}_2)^\top A_i^\top A_i(\mathbf{x}_1 - \mathbf{x}_2) \\ &= -(A_i\mathbf{x}_1 - A_i\mathbf{x}_2)^\top (A_i\mathbf{x}_1 - A_i\mathbf{x}_2) \\ &= -\text{Euclidean}(\phi_i(\mathbf{x}_1), \phi_i(\mathbf{x}_2))^2 \end{aligned}$$

where $\phi_i(\mathbf{x}) = A_i\mathbf{x}$. From this perspective, DML is equivalent to learning a *linear* projection A_i, which maps $\mathbf{x}$ into a new representation. Unlike the regular DML, in this paper, we aim to go beyond the linear projection by exploring deep neural networks to learn a non-linear projection. Figure 2 shows the proposed architecture of three-layer neural network, which works as follows: (i) we first adopt Stacked Denoising Autoencoder to pretrain neural networks for each feature space with unlabelled data for each modal, (ii) we then finetune these neural networks by investigating a novel unified twofold online learning scheme: (a) learning to optimize the parameters of neural networks on each individual modality; and (b) meanwhile learning to find the optimal combination of multiple diverse types of modality.

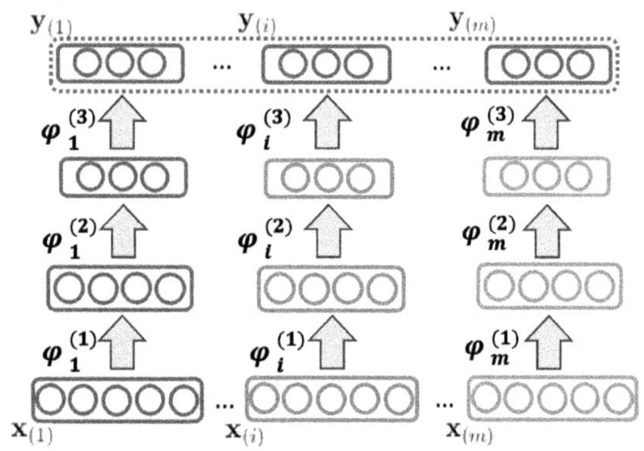

Figure 2: The proposed architecture of multimodal deep neural networks for learning multimodal similarity

4.2 Stacked Denoising Autoencoder

In this section, we briefly review Auto Encoder (AE) [5] and it extensions, including Denoising Autoencoder (DAE) [44] and Stacked Denoising Autoencoder (SDA) [45]. In our approach, we explore SDA to pretrain deep neural networks with unlabelled data.

Auto Encoder (AE), also called Auto Associator or Diabolo network, is trained to encode/map an input $\mathbf{x}$ to a hidden representation $\mathbf{y}$ such that $\mathbf{x}$ can be decoded/reconstructed from $\mathbf{y}$. Considering the hidden layer is encoded by a nonlinear one-layer neural network, we can set $\mathbf{y} = \varphi(\mathbf{x}) = s(W\mathbf{x} + b)$ and denote by $\mathbf{z} = \psi(\mathbf{y}) = s(W'\mathbf{y} + c)$ the reconstruction from $\mathbf{y}$, where $\mathbf{z}$ has the same shape as $\mathbf{x}$, and $s(\cdot)$ is a nonlinear function, e.g. the sigmoid. Depending on the distributional assumptions on the input given the code, we can apply diverse loss functions to measure the reconstruction error, e.g., if assuming the distribution of $p(\mathbf{x}|\mathbf{z})$ is Gaussian, we can adopt *squared error* as:

$$\mathcal{L}_{sq}(\mathbf{x}, \mathbf{z}) = \|\mathbf{x} - \mathbf{z}\|^2;$$

if we assume $\mathbf{x}$ is either binary or binomial probability, we can pose the loss function as the *cross-entropy* function:

$$\mathcal{L}_{ce}(\mathbf{x}, \mathbf{z}) = -\log P(\mathbf{x}|\mathbf{z}) = -\sum_i \mathbf{x}_i \log \mathbf{z}_i + (1 - \mathbf{x}_i)\log(1 - \mathbf{z}_i),$$

where $\mathbf{x}_i$ and $\mathbf{z}_i$ are the i-th entry of $\mathbf{x}$ and $\mathbf{z}$ individually. To minimize the above reconstruction error, AE seeks to learn the parameters W, W', b and c on the training dataset. In particular, the parameters are initialized randomly and then optimized by stochastic gradient descent. The part $(\mathbf{A})$ of Figure 3 illustrates the idea for auto encoder.

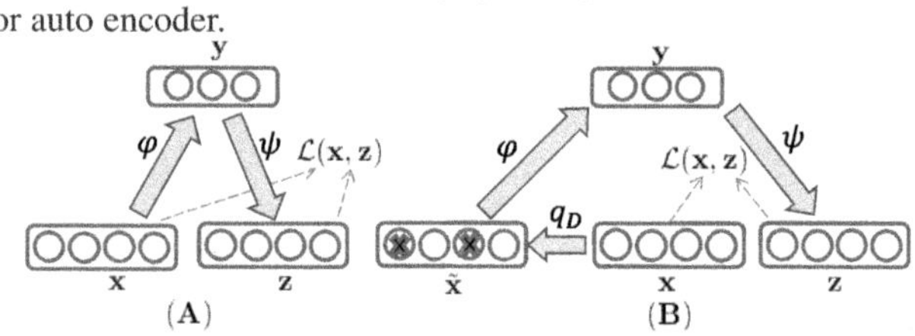

Figure 3: (A) Autoencoder; (B) Denoising Autoencoder

Denoising Autoencoder (DAE) is a simple variant of the basic autoencoder, which is trained to reconstruct a clean "repaired" input from its noisy version. Formally, we firstly construct $\mathbf{x}$'s noisy version $\tilde{\mathbf{x}}$ through a stochastic mapping $\tilde{\mathbf{x}} \sim q_D(\tilde{\mathbf{x}}|\mathbf{x})$, where q_D is a function to add noise into the original $\mathbf{x}$, which will be specified later. The noisy version $\tilde{\mathbf{x}}$ will be then mapped through AE to a hidden representation $\mathbf{y} = \varphi(\tilde{\mathbf{x}})$, where $\mathbf{y}$ is then used to reconstruct a clean version of $\tilde{\mathbf{x}}$ by $\mathbf{z} = \psi(\mathbf{y})$. Noted that the reconstruction error $\mathcal{L}(\mathbf{x}, \mathbf{z})$ but not $\mathcal{L}(\tilde{\mathbf{x}}, \mathbf{z})$ is minimized in DAE. The part $(\mathbf{B})$ of Figure 3 illustrates the idea for denoising autoencoder. To construct the map $\tilde{\mathbf{x}} \sim q_D(\tilde{\mathbf{x}}|\mathbf{x})$, Masking Noise strategy is exploited, where a fraction ν of the elements of $\mathbf{x}$ (chosen randomly for each example) is forced to 0.

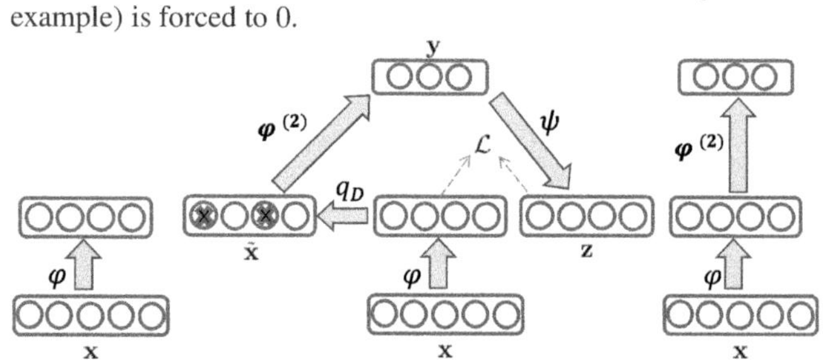

Figure 4: Stacking Denoising Autoencoder

Stacked Denoising Autoencoder (SDA) is utilized to initialize a deep network in the same way as stacking RBMs in deep belief networks. It is important to notice that input corruption is only used for the initial denoising-training of each individual layer, so that it may learn useful feature extractors. Once the mapping φ has thus been learnt, it will henceforth be used on uncorrupted inputs. In particular no corruption is applied to produce the representation that will serve as clean input for training the next layer. Figure 4 summarizes the complete procedure for learning and stacking serval layers of denoising autoencoders. Once a stack of encoders has thus been built, its highest level output representation can be used as input to a standalone supervised learning algorithm. The parameters of all layers can then be simultaneously fine-tuned using a gradient-based procedure such as stochastic gradient descent.

4.3 Online Learning Algorithms

After introducing Stacked Denoising Autoencoder, we now propose a novel method to tackle the optimization of the objective (3) with multiple deep models. Instead of directly solving the optimization task of Eqn. (3) in a batch learning fashion, in this section, we present an online learning algorithm to tackle the multi-modal similarity learning task. The key motivations are twofold: (i) solving Eqn.(3) directly can be computationally highly expensive for a large amount of training data; and (ii) more seriously, such a batch training process suffers from an extremely high re-training cost as whenever there is a new training data, the entire model has to be completely re-trained, making it non-scalable for a real-world CBIR application.

Specifically, the key challenge of our learning task is how to develop an efficient and scalable learning scheme that can optimize both the similarity functions on each individual modality and meanwhile optimize the combinational weights of different modalities. To this end, we propose to explore an online multi-modal similarity learning algorithm. In particular, after initializing a set of deep neural networks for m_f features by applying Denoising Autoencoder, we explore online learning techniques to update similarity function on each modality, i.e., once receiving a new arrived triplet, we finetune individual deep neural network based on the similarity functions, and then apply the Exponentiated Gradient online learning [6] to find the optimal combinational weights. We discuss each of the two learning tasks in detail below.

Let us denote $\mathbf{y} = \phi(\mathbf{x})$ the new representation of the image feature $\mathbf{x}$ in one single feature space, i.e., $\mathbf{y}$ is obtained by applying a nonlinear projection on $\mathbf{x}$ with an l-layer deep neural network, we can apply diverse approaches to define the similarity functions:

$$S_i(\mathbf{x}_1, \mathbf{x}_2) = \begin{cases} \frac{\mathbf{y}_1^T \mathbf{y}_2}{\|\mathbf{y}_1\| \|\mathbf{y}_2\|} & \text{(Cosine)} \\ -\|\mathbf{y}_1 - \mathbf{y}_2\|^2 & \text{(Euclidean)} \\ e^{\frac{-\|\mathbf{y}_1 - \mathbf{y}_2\|^2}{2\sigma}} & \text{(RBF Kernel)} \\ \mathbf{y}_1^T \mathbf{y}_2 & \text{(Linear Kernel)} \end{cases}$$

Then, we explore the hinge loss function as follows:

$$\mathcal{L}_t^{\gamma_s}((\mathbf{x}_t, \mathbf{x}_t^+, \mathbf{x}_t^-); S_i) = \max\{0, \gamma_s - S_i(\mathbf{x}_t, \mathbf{x}_t^+) + S_i(\mathbf{x}_t, \mathbf{x}_t^-)\}$$

where γ_s is the parameter of margin and $(\mathbf{x}_t, \mathbf{x}_t^+, \mathbf{x}_t^-)$ is the t-th training triplet received. By defining $(\mathbf{y}_t, \mathbf{y}_t^+, \mathbf{y}_t^-)$ as the new representation of $(\mathbf{x}_t, \mathbf{x}_t^+, \mathbf{x}_t^-)$ projected by deep neural networks, we can compute the derivation of $\mathcal{L}$ with respect to $\mathbf{y}_t, \mathbf{y}_t^+, \mathbf{y}_t^-$ individually as follows,

$$\frac{\partial \mathcal{L}}{\partial \mathbf{y}_t} = \begin{cases} -\frac{1}{\|\mathbf{y}_t^+\|\|\mathbf{y}_t\|}\mathbf{y}_t^+ + \frac{1}{\|\mathbf{y}_t^-\|\|\mathbf{y}_t\|}\mathbf{y}_t^- \\ \quad +(\frac{\mathbf{y}_t^T\mathbf{y}_t^+}{\|\mathbf{y}_t^+\|\|\mathbf{y}_t\|^3} - \frac{\mathbf{y}_t^T\mathbf{y}_t^-}{\|\mathbf{y}_t^-\|\|\mathbf{y}_t\|^3})\mathbf{y}_t & \text{(Cosine)} \\ -2\mathbf{y}_t^+ + 2\mathbf{y}_t^- & \text{(Euclidean)} \\ \frac{\mathbf{y}_t - \mathbf{y}_t^+}{\sigma} e^{\frac{-\|\mathbf{y}_t - \mathbf{y}_t^+\|^2}{2\sigma}} - \frac{\mathbf{y}_t - \mathbf{y}_t^-}{\sigma} e^{\frac{-\|\mathbf{y}_t - \mathbf{y}_t^-\|^2}{2\sigma}} & \text{(RBF Kernel)} \\ -\mathbf{y}_t^+ + \mathbf{y}_t^- & \text{(Linear Kernel)} \end{cases}$$

$$\frac{\partial \mathcal{L}}{\partial \mathbf{y}_t^+} = \begin{cases} -\frac{1}{\|\mathbf{y}_t\|\|\mathbf{y}_t^+\|}\mathbf{y}_t + \frac{\mathbf{y}_t^T\mathbf{y}_t^+}{\|\mathbf{y}_t\|\|\mathbf{y}_t^+\|^3}\mathbf{y}_t^+ & \text{(Cosine)} \\ -2\mathbf{y}_t + 2\mathbf{y}_t^+ & \text{(Euclidean)} \\ \frac{\mathbf{y}_t^+ - \mathbf{y}_t}{\sigma} e^{\frac{-\|\mathbf{y}_t - \mathbf{y}_t^+\|^2}{2\sigma}} & \text{(RBF Kernel)} \\ -\mathbf{y}_t & \text{(Linear Kernel)} \end{cases}$$

$$\frac{\partial \mathcal{L}}{\partial \mathbf{y}_t^-} = \begin{cases} \frac{1}{\|\mathbf{y}_t\|\|\mathbf{y}_t^-\|}\mathbf{y}_t - \frac{\mathbf{y}_t^T\mathbf{y}_t^-}{\|\mathbf{y}_t\|\|\mathbf{y}_t^-\|^3}\mathbf{y}_t^- & \text{(Cosine)} \\ 2\mathbf{y}_t - 2\mathbf{y}_t^- & \text{(Euclidean)} \\ \frac{\mathbf{y}_t - \mathbf{y}_t^-}{\sigma} e^{\frac{-\|\mathbf{y}_t - \mathbf{y}_t^-\|^2}{2\sigma}} & \text{(RBF Kernel)} \\ \mathbf{y}_t & \text{(Linear Kernel)} \end{cases}$$

We then follow the idea of Online Gradient Descent [54] to update the parameters $(\mathbf{W}^{(l)}, b^{(l)})$ of the last layer of l-layer neural network as follows:

$$\mathbf{W}_{t+1}^{(l)} \leftarrow \mathbf{W}_t^{(l)} - \eta \frac{\partial \mathcal{L}}{\partial \mathbf{W}^{(l)}} \tag{6}$$

$$b_{t+1}^{(l)} \leftarrow b_t^{(l)} - \eta \frac{\partial \mathcal{L}}{\partial b^{(l)}} \tag{7}$$

where $\frac{\partial \mathcal{L}}{\partial \mathbf{W}^{(l)}}$ and $\frac{\partial \mathcal{L}}{\partial b^{(l)}}$ are computed as follows, respectively:

$$\frac{\partial \mathcal{L}}{\partial \mathbf{W}^{(l)}} = \sum_{i=1}^{d} (\frac{\partial \mathcal{L}}{\partial \mathbf{y}_i}\frac{\partial \mathbf{y}_i}{\partial \mathbf{W}^{(l)}} + \frac{\partial \mathcal{L}}{\partial \mathbf{y}_i^+}\frac{\partial \mathbf{y}_i^+}{\partial \mathbf{W}^{(l)}} + \frac{\partial \mathcal{L}}{\partial \mathbf{y}_i^-}\frac{\partial \mathbf{y}_i^-}{\partial \mathbf{W}^{(l)}})|_{\mathbf{W}^{(l)}=\mathbf{W}_t^{(l)}}$$

$$\frac{\partial \mathcal{L}}{\partial b^{(l)}} = \sum_{i=1}^{d} (\frac{\partial \mathcal{L}}{\partial \mathbf{y}_i}\frac{\partial \mathbf{y}_i}{\partial b^{(l)}} + \frac{\partial \mathcal{L}}{\partial \mathbf{y}_i^+}\frac{\partial \mathbf{y}_i^+}{\partial b^{(l)}} + \frac{\partial \mathcal{L}}{\partial \mathbf{y}_i^-}\frac{\partial \mathbf{y}_i^-}{\partial b^{(l)}})|_{b^{(l)}=b_t^{(l)}}$$

where d is the dimension of the representation space, $(\mathbf{y}, \mathbf{y}^+, \mathbf{y}^-)$ is the t-th arrived triplet, and $\mathbf{y}_i$ is the i-th entry of $\mathbf{y}$. Finally, we can adopt backpropagation [38] to update the parameters of other layers of deep networks.

Another key task of multi-modal DML is to learn the optimal combinational weights $\theta = (\theta^{(1)}, \ldots, \theta^{(m)})$, where $\theta^{(i)}$ is set to $1/m$ at the beginning of the learning task. In our approach, we apply the Exponentiated Gradient online learning algorithm [6] to find the combinational weights sequentially. In particular, we define

$$\mathbf{s}_t = (S_1(\mathbf{x}_t, \mathbf{x}_t^+) - S_1(\mathbf{x}_t, \mathbf{x}_t^-), \ldots, S_m(\mathbf{x}_t, \mathbf{x}_t^+) - S_m(\mathbf{x}_t, \mathbf{x}_t^-))^T,$$

and formulate the optimization problem as follows:

$$\theta_{t+1} = \arg\min_{\theta} D_{KL}(\theta \| \theta_t) + \lambda \ell_t(\theta) \quad s.t. \ \theta \in \Delta \tag{8}$$

where $D_{KL}(\mathbf{u}\|\mathbf{v}) = \sum_i u_i \ln(\frac{u_i}{v_i})$ is the KL-divergence, and $\ell_t(\theta)$ is a hinge loss defined as:

$$\ell_t(\theta) = \max(0, \gamma - \theta^T \mathbf{s}_t).$$

The above optimization aims to trade off two major concerns: (i) the updated model should not be deviated too much from the previous model, which is measured by the KL-divergence between the two models; and (ii) the updated model suffers a small loss on the triplet training instance $(\mathbf{x}_t, \mathbf{x}_t^+, \mathbf{x}_t^-)$. The trade-off is essentially achieved by introducing the penalty cost parameter $C > 0$. In general, it is hard to derive a closed-form solution for the above optimization. To further simplify the optimization, we approximate the objective function by applying the first-order Taylor expansion of $\ell_t(\theta)$ at θ_t, and thus turn the optimization into the following:

$$\theta_{t+1} = \arg\min_{\theta \in \Delta} D_{KL}(\theta\|\theta_t) + \lambda[\ell_t(\theta_t) + \nabla\ell_t(\theta_t)(\theta - \theta_t)] \tag{9}$$

We can derive a closed-form solution in the following proposition.

PROPOSITION 1. *The closed-form solution to the optimization in (9) is:*

$$\theta_{t+1,i} = \frac{\theta_{t,i} e^{-\lambda \nabla \ell_t(\theta_t)_i}}{\sum_j \theta_{t,j} e^{-\lambda \nabla \ell_t(\theta_t)_j}}, i = 1, \ldots, m \tag{10}$$

where $\nabla\ell_t(\theta_t) = -s_t$ *if* $\ell_t(\theta_t) > 0$ *or* $\nabla\ell_t(\theta_t) = 0$ *if* $\ell_t(\theta_t) = 0$.

The above proposition can be obtained by following the idea of Exponentiated Gradient learning in [6]. We omit the detail proof because of the space limitation. From the results, we can see that θ remains unchanged if $\theta^T \mathbf{s}_t \geq \gamma$. That is, we will update the θ whenever the current θ fails to rank the order of $\mathbf{x}_t^+$ and $\mathbf{x}_t^-$ w.r.t. query $\mathbf{x}_t$ correctly at a sufficiently large margin.

Algorithm 1 OMDSL—Online Multimodal Deep Similarity Learning

INPUT:
- Unlabelled data: $\mathcal{U}$
- Training Triplets: $\{(\mathbf{x}_t, \mathbf{x}_t^+, \mathbf{x}_t^-)\}_{t=1,2,\dots}$

Initialize weights: $\theta_{1,i} = 1/m, \forall i = 1, \dots, m$
Pretrain m_f l-layer deep networks with unlabelled data for each feature space by adopting SDA (Fig. 4)
for $t = 1, 2, \dots$ **do**
  Receive: $(\mathbf{x}_t, \mathbf{x}_t^+, \mathbf{x}_t^-)$
  for $i = 1, 2, \dots, m$ **do**
    Update the parameters $(W_{(i)}^{(l)}, b_{(i)}^{(l)})$ of last layer of deep networks by Eqn 8.
    Adopt Backpropagation [38] to finetune other parameters $(W_{(i)}^{(1)}, W_{(i)}^{(l-1)}, b_{(i)}^{(1)}, \dots, b_{(i)}^{(l-1)})$
  end for
  Compute: $s_{t,i} = S_i(\mathbf{x}_t, \mathbf{x}_t^+) - S_i(\mathbf{x}_t, \mathbf{x}_t^-), i = 1, \dots, m$
  Compute: $\ell_t(\theta_t) = \max(0, \gamma - \theta_t^\top \mathbf{s}_t)$
  if $\ell_t(\theta_t) > 0$ **then**
    $\theta_{t+1,i} = \frac{\theta_{t,i} e^{-\lambda \nabla \ell_t(\theta_t)_i}}{\sum_{j=1}^m \theta_{t,j} e^{-\lambda \nabla \ell_t(\theta_t)_j}}, i = 1, \dots, m$
  end if
end for

Finally, Algorithm 1 summarizes the details of the proposed Online Multimodal Deep Similarity Learning (OMDSL) algorithm. The space complexity of the algorithm is $\mathcal{O}(\sum_{j=1}^m \sum_{i=1}^l d_{i-1}^{(j)} \times d_i^{(j)})$, where $d_0^{(j)} = D^{(j)}$ is the dimension of j-th feature space, and $d_i^{(j)} (i = 1, \dots, l)$ is the dimension of i-th hidden layer representation space of j-th deep networks. Because usually we choose $d_i^{(j)} \times d_{i-1}^{(j)} << D^{(j)} \times d_1^{(j)}; (i = 2, \dots, l)$, the first layer of deep network will dominate the space complexity. By denoting $D = \max(D^1, \dots, D^m)$ and $d = \max(d_1^{(1)}, \dots, d_1^{(m)})$, the worst-case space complexity is simply $\mathcal{O}(mDd)$, and the worst-case overall time complexity of the algorithm is $\mathcal{O}(TmDd)$, which is linear with respect to T — the total number of training triplets.

4.4 Theoretical Analysis

We now analyze the theoretical bounds of the proposed OMDSL algorithm. In particular, our goal is to bound the number of mistakes suffered by the proposed algorithm, denote by M, which measures the total number of cases where the model fails to predict the triplet constraints over the entire sequence, formally defined as:

$$M = \sum_{t=1}^T \mathbb{I}(S(x_t, x_t^+) < S(x_t, x_t^-)) \tag{11}$$

where $\mathbb{I}(\cdot)$ is an indicator function that output 1 when the statement holds and 0 otherwise. The following gives our theorem.

THEOREM 1. *Assume $\|\mathbf{s}_t\|_\infty \le C$ and the OMDSL algorithm runs with a learning rate of $\lambda = \sqrt{\frac{2 \ln m}{C^2 T}}$ over a sequence of triplets $(\mathbf{x}_1, \mathbf{x}_1^+, \mathbf{x}_1^-), \dots, (\mathbf{x}_T, \mathbf{x}_T^+, \mathbf{x}_T^-)$. Then, for any multimodal similarity function $S = \sum_{i=1}^m \theta_i S_i$ with $\forall \theta \in \Delta$, we have the following bound:*

$$M \le \frac{1}{\gamma} \sum_{t=1}^T \mathcal{L}_t^\gamma((\mathbf{x}_t, \mathbf{x}_t^+, \mathbf{x}_t^-); S) + \frac{C}{\gamma} \sqrt{\frac{T \ln m}{2}} \tag{12}$$

PROOF. The key idea of this proof follows the principle of similar proof in [6]. In particular, according to the definition of ℓ_t and its convexity property, we have

$$M = \sum_{t=1}^T \mathbb{I}(S(x_t, x_t^+) < S(x_t, x_t^-)) \le \frac{1}{\gamma} \sum_{t=1}^T \ell_t(\theta_t) \tag{13}$$

By applying the Taylor's theorem to ℓ_t, we can obtain

$$\ell_t(\theta_t) - \ell_t(\theta) \le -(\theta - \theta_t) \cdot \nabla \ell_t(\theta_t) \tag{14}$$

The next is to bound the right hand side of the above inequality. To facilitate the analysis, we denote $\mathbf{z} = \lambda \nabla \ell_t(\theta_t)$ and $\mathbf{v} = \theta_t \cdot \mathbf{z} - \mathbf{z}$. We then have the following:

$$\begin{aligned}
-(\theta - \theta_t) \cdot \mathbf{z} &= -\theta \cdot \mathbf{z} + \theta_t \cdot \mathbf{z} - \ln(\sum_{i=1}^m \theta_{t,i} e^{v_i}) + \ln(\sum_{i=1}^m \theta_{t,i} e^{v_i}) \\
&= -\theta \cdot \mathbf{z} - \ln(\sum_{i=1}^m \theta_{t,i} e^{-z_i}) + \ln(\sum_{i=1}^m \theta_{t,i} e^{v_i}) \\
&= \sum_{j=1}^m \theta_j \ln e^{-z_j} - \ln(\sum_{i=1}^m \theta_{t,i} e^{-z_i}) + \ln(\sum_{i=1}^m \theta_{t,i} e^{v_i}) \\
&= \sum_{j=1}^m \theta_j \ln(\frac{1}{\theta_{t,j}} \frac{\theta_{t,j} e^{-z_j}}{\sum_{i=1}^m \theta_{t,i} e^{-z_i}}) + \ln(\sum_{i=1}^m \theta_{t,i} e^{v_i}) \\
&= \sum_{j=1}^m \theta_j \ln \frac{\theta_{t+1,j}}{\theta_{t,j}} + \ln(\sum_{i=1}^m \theta_{t,i} e^{v_i}) \\
&= D_{KL}(\theta \| \theta_t) - D_{KL}(\theta \| \theta_{t+1}) + \ln(\sum_{i=1}^m \theta_{t,i} e^{v_i})
\end{aligned}$$

Plugging the above into (14) and summing over all t leads to:

$$\sum_{t=1}^T [\ell_t(\theta_t) - \ell_t(\theta)] \le \frac{1}{\lambda} [D_{KL}(\theta \| \theta_1) + \sum_{t=1}^T \ln(\sum_{i=1}^m \theta_{t,i} e^{v_i})] \tag{15}$$

where $-D_{KL}(\theta \| \theta_{T+1})$ is omitted. To bound the right hand side of the above inequality, we note that $D_{KL}(\theta \| \theta_1) \le \ln m$, since $\theta_1 = (1/m, \dots, 1/m)$. And we need bound the second term in the right hand side. Since $\|\mathbf{s}_t\|_\infty \le C$, then $|z_i| \le \lambda C$; by applying Hoeffding's inequality, we can get

$$\ln(\sum_{i=1}^m \theta_{t,i} e^{v_i}) \le \lambda^2 C^2 / 2 \tag{16}$$

As a result, we have the following

$$\sum_{t=1}^T [\ell_t(\theta_t) - \ell_t(\theta)] \le \frac{\ln m}{\lambda} + \frac{\lambda C^2 T}{2} = C \sqrt{\frac{T \ln m}{2}} \tag{17}$$

Re-arranging the above inequality concludes the theorem. □

The above theorem basically shows that the number of mistakes suffered by the proposed algorithm is bounded by the rate of $\mathcal{O}(\sqrt{T})$. Moreover, assume the best similarity function among all modalities is known in hindsight, e.g., assuming the i-th modality, we then have the following corollary.

THEOREM 2. *Assume $\|\mathbf{s}_t\|_\infty \le C$ and the OMDSL algorithm runs with a learning rate of $\lambda = \sqrt{\frac{2 \ln m}{C^2 T}}$ over a sequence of triplets $(\mathbf{x}_1, \mathbf{x}_1^+, \mathbf{x}_1^-), \dots, (\mathbf{x}_T, \mathbf{x}_T^+, \mathbf{x}_T^-)$, we then have*

$$M \le \frac{1}{\gamma} \sum_{t=1}^T \mathcal{L}_t^\gamma((\mathbf{x}_t, \mathbf{x}_t^+, \mathbf{x}_t^-); S_i) + \frac{C}{\gamma} \sqrt{\frac{T \ln m}{2}} \tag{18}$$

where S_i denotes the similarity function of the best modality.

The above follows immediately by setting $\theta_i = 1$ and $\theta_j = 0$ for $j \ne i$. This above result bounds the relationship between the total number of mistakes suffered by the proposed algorithm and the cumulative loss suffered by the best modality known in hindsight.

5. EXPERIMENTS

In this section, we conduct an extensive set of experiments to evaluate the efficacy of the proposed algorithm for similarity search on images with multimodal representations in CBIR.

5.1 Experimental Testbeds and Setup

We adopt four publicly available image data sets in our experiments, including COREL [16], Caltech101[1], Indoor [35][2], and ImageCLEF[3]. For each database, we randomly split it into three disjoint partitions: a test set of 500 images, a validation set of 500 images, and the rest images for training. Besides, to examine the scalability, we also include a large database "ImageCLEF+Flickr", which includes the ImageCLEF set as a ground-truth subset and additional 1-million Flickr images as background images.

To generate side information in the forms of triplet instances for learning the similarity functions, we sample the sequence of triplets from the images in the training set according to their ground truth class labels. Specifically, we generate a triplet instance by randomly sampling two images belonging to the same class and one image from another different class. In total, we generate 100K triplet instances for each standard dataset (except for the small-scale and large-scale experiments).

To fairly evaluate different algorithms, we choose their parameters using the same cross validation scheme. We adopt three-layer neural networks with $d_1 = 100$, $d_2 = 50$ and $d_3 = 50$ for all modalities on OMDSL, and set the maximum iteration to 500 for LMNN. To evaluate the retrieval performance, we adopt the standard mean Average Precision (mAP) and top-K retrieval accuracy.

5.2 Visual Features and Similarity Measures

We adopt both global and local feature descriptors for representing images. Before that, we have resized all the images to the scale of 500×500 pixels while keeping the aspect ratio unchanged. For global features, we extract five types of features to represent an image, including (1) color histogram and color moments (81 dimensions), (2) edge direction histogram (37 dimensions), (3) Gabor wavelets transformation (120 dimensions), (4) local binary pattern (59 dimensions), and (5) GIST features (512 dimensions). For local features, we extract the bag-of-visual-words representation [49] using two kinds of descriptors: (i) SIFT feature [30] and Hessian-Affine interest region detector with a threshold of 500; and (ii) SURF feature [3] and SURF detector with a threshold of 500. For the clustering step, we adopt a forest of 16 kd-trees and search 2048 neighbors to speed up the clustering task. By combining different descriptors (SIFT/SURF) and vocabulary sizes (200/1000), we extract four types of local features: SIFT200, SIFT1000, SURF200 and SURF1000. Finally, we adopt the TF-IDF weighing scheme to generate the final bag-of-visual-words. For all experiments, we normalize the feature vectors to the range of $[0, 1]$.

For each query-instance pair, we adopt four similarity functions to measure their similarity as described in Section 4.3, where we choose $\gamma_s = 0.25$ for Cosine similarity, $\gamma_s = 1$ for Euclidean, $\sigma = 2, \gamma_s = 0.25$ for RBF kernel, and $\gamma_s = 1$ for Linear kernel. Finally, we explore a total of 36 modalities to measure the overall image similarity for CBIR.

5.3 Comparison Algorithms

To extensively evaluate the efficacy of our algorithms, we compare the proposed OMDSL algorithm for image retrieval, against several representative distance metric learning algorithms, including RCA [2], LMNN [47], OASIS [8]. We also evaluate a heuristic baseline method with squared Euclidean distance, named as "EUCL-*". To adapt the existing DML methods for multimodal image retrieval, we have implemented several variants of each DML algorithm by exploring three fusion strategies [42, 25]: (i) "**B**est" — applying DML for each modality individually and then selecting the best modality, (ii) "**C**oncatenation" — an early fusion approach by concatenating features of all modalities before applying DML, and (iii) "**U**niform combination" — a late fusion approach by uniformly combining all modalities after metric learning.

5.4 Evaluation on Small-Scale Datasets

In this section, we build four small-scale data sets, named "Caltech101(S)", "Indoor(S)", "COREL(S)" and "ImageCLEF(S)", from the corresponding standard datasets by first choosing 10 object categories, and then randomly sampling 50 examples from each category. We adopt 5 global features described above as the multimodal inputs. To construct triplet constraints for online learning approaches, we generate all positive pairs (two images belong to the same class), and for each positive pair we randomly select an image from the other different classes to form a triplet. In total, about 10K triplets are generated for each dataset.

Table 1: Evaluation of the mAP performance.

Alg.	COREL(S)	Caltech101(S)	Indoor(S)	ImageCLEF(S)
Eucl-B	0.4431	0.4299	0.1726	0.4325
RCA-B	0.5097	0.4984	0.1915	0.4492
LMNN-B	0.4876	0.5462	0.1852	0.5231
OASIS-B	0.4445	0.5072	0.1884	0.4424
Eucl-C	0.5220	0.4306	0.1842	0.4431
RCA-C	0.6437	0.6156	0.2078	0.5927
LMNN-C	0.5816	0.5894	0.2027	0.5821
OASIS-C	0.5657	0.5441	0.2017	0.5618
Eucl-U	0.5220	0.4306	0.1842	0.4431
RCA-U	0.5625	0.4860	0.1894	0.4909
LMNN-U	0.6026	0.4282	0.2007	0.4647
OASIS-U	0.5679	0.5419	0.1989	0.5338
OMDSL	**0.7379**	**0.7136**	**0.2430**	**0.7552**

Table 1 summarizes the evaluation results on the small-scale data sets. The postfix "-B" indicates that we learn metrics on each modality (type of features) separately and then select the *best* single metric as the final similarity function via cross validation. The postfix "-C" indicates that we first *concatenate* all types of features together, and then learn the metric on the combined feature space, which is a kind of "early fusion" strategy. The postfix "-U" indicates we first learn an optimal metric for each modality, and then uniformly combine all distance functions for the final ranking, which is a kind of "late fusion" strategy. Table 2 shows the running time cost on the COREL(S) data set.

Table 2: Running time (in sec.) on COREL(S).

RCA-C	LMNN-C	OASIS-C	RCA-U
5.07	1442.66	404.35	2.91
LMNN-U	OASIS-U	OMDSL	—
858.94	376.77	300.27	—

We can draw several observations from the results in Table 1 and 2. First of all, the two kinds of fusion strategies, i.e., early fusion (with postfix"-C") and late fusion (with postfix"-U"), generally tend to outperform the best single metric approaches (with postfix"-B"). This is primarily because combining multiple types of features for retrieval could better explore the potential of all the features, which validates the importance of the proposed technique. Second, some of the uniformly combination algorithms (i.e., the

[1]http://www.vision.caltech.edu/Image_Datasets/Caltech101/

[2]http://web.mit.edu/torralba/www/indoor.html

[3]http://imageclef.org/

late fusion strategy) failed to outperform the best single metric approach in some cases, e.g., "RCA-U" (compared with "RCA-B") and "LMNN-U" (compared with "LMNN-B") on Caltech101(S). This implies that linear concatenation is not optimal to combine different kinds of features. Thus, it is critical to identify the effective features via machine learning and then assign them higher weights. Third, among all the compared algorithms, the proposed OMDSL significantly outperform the other algorithms, which validates that nonlinear learning with deep networks can learn more flexible similarity functions than traditional DML approaches. Finally, it is interesting to observe that OMDSL is even more efficient than most algorithms including OASIS, which is mainly because of the online learning strategy and the hidden layers of deep networks lying in intrinsic lower-dimensional space.

5.5 Evaluation on the Standard Datasets

We further evaluate the algorithms on standard-sized datasets. We exclude LMNN because of its extremely high computational cost. Following the standard setup with 5 global features and 4 local features, Table 3 summarizes the mAP results, and Figure 5 presents the top-K precisions on two randomly selected datasets.

Table 3: Evaluation of the mAP performance.

Alg.	COREL	Caltech101	Indoor	ImageCLEF
Eucl-B	0.1877	0.2187	0.0469	0.5523
RCA-B	0.2305	0.2837	0.0499	0.6010
OASIS-B	0.1958	0.3025	0.0522	0.6723
Eucl-C	0.2628	0.2259	0.0559	0.5752
RCA-C	0.2714	0.2473	0.0604	0.6272
OASIS-C	0.3202	0.3660	0.0726	0.7394
Eucl-U	0.2628	0.2259	0.0559	0.5752
RCA-U	0.2992	0.2413	0.0565	0.6161
OASIS-U	0.3594	0.3243	0.0705	0.6891
OMDSL	**0.4769**	**0.4476**	**0.0990**	**0.8387**

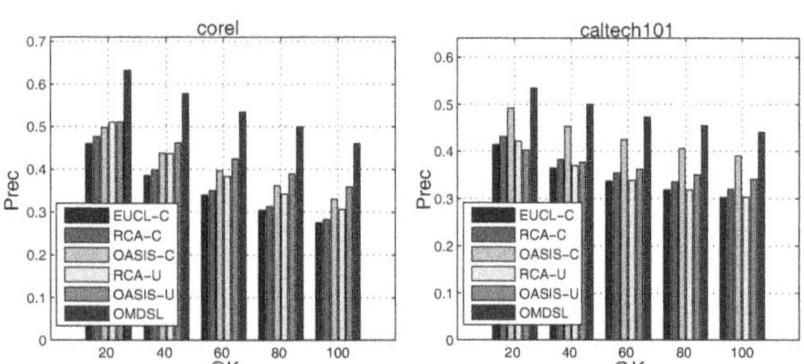

(a) *Corel* (b) *Caltech101*

Figure 5: Precision at Top-K results

From the results, we observed that the proposed OMDSL algorithm considerably surpasses all the other approaches for all cases, not only on mAP performance but also on top-K retrieval accuracy. This clearly validates the efficacy of the proposed algorithm for learning an effective similarity function on multi-modal data.

Table 4: Running time (in sec.) on "COREL".

RCA-C	OASIS-C	RCA-U	OASIS-U	OMDSL
468.19	65060.93	184.3	8781.54	3976.07

Finally, Table 4 summarizes the average running time cost on the COREL dataset with 100K triplet instances. The result shows that OMSDL is considerably more efficient and scalable than OASIS, making it practical for large-scale applications.

5.5.1 Deep Networks with Varied Numbers of Layers

To evaluate the impact of the number of layers in the deep networks for the proposed OMDSL algorithm, we construct five diverse deep networks with different numbers of layers, i.e., from 1-layer to 5-layer. Table 5 lists the dimensionality settings of the hidden layers configured for each of them individually.

Table 5: Dimensionality settings of the hidden layers.

1-layer	2-layer	3-layer	4-layer	5-layer
50	100, 50	100, 50, 50	100, 50, 50, 50	100, 50, 50, 50, 50

We evaluate mAP performance on four datasets in Table 6. It is interesting to observe that 3-layer and 4-layer deep networks tend to achieve the best, primarily because too high layer structure leads to overly flexible structure that might overfit the training data.

Table 6: Evaluation of the mAP of the proposed OMDSL with diverse deep networks using varied numbers of hidden layers.

Alg.	Caltech101	Indoor	ImageCLEF	COREL
1-layer	0.4374	0.0891	0.8155	0.4427
2-layer	0.4445	0.0982	0.8302	0.4698
3-layer	**0.4476**	0.0990	0.8387	0.4769
4-layer	0.4393	**0.0993**	**0.8395**	**0.4787**
5-layer	0.4390	0.0952	0.8381	0.4719

5.5.2 Evaluation of Pretraining

To examine the importance of pretraining, we conduct experiments by randomly initializing the parameters of deep networks with standard normal distribution, and then performing the same finetune stage to refine deep networks. Table 7 shows the results.

Table 7: mAP on OMDSL without pretraining stage.

Alg.	Caltech101	Indoor	ImageCLEF	COREL
2-layer w/o pre	0.3892	0.0786	0.7635	0.4123
3-layer w/o pre	0.3974	0.0774	0.7685	0.4203

Comparing Table 7 with Table 6, we observe that the performance drops significantly without pretraining, which proves stacked denoising autoencoder is helpful to initialize deep networks.

5.5.3 Analysis of Modality Weights

We now examine the combination weights of different modalities learned by the proposed algorithm. Figure 6 visualizes the results of weights θ for diverse modality learned on four different datasets. From the results, we observe that GIST and Surf1000 features are assigned much higher weights than the others on "Caltech101" and "ImageCLEF". This is primarily because "Caltech101" is an object dataset and "ImageCLEF" is a medical image dataset, which could be more sensitive to texture-related descriptors. By contrast, since "Indoor" and "Corel" contain many pictures about natural scenes and diverse categories, different modalities can make more or less contributions for different scenarios, further validating the importance of finding the optimal combination by our method.

5.6 Evaluation on the Large-scale Dataset

To test its scalability, we apply the proposed algorithm on a large-scale image retrieval application on "ImageCLEF+Flickr", which has over 1-million images and 300K triplet training data. Table 8 shows the mAP performance of the five algorithms. Clearly, our proposed algorithm OMDSL achieves the best mAP. Figure 7 presents the top-K precisions on ImageCLEF+Flickr. We can have the similar observation that our proposed methods significantly outperform the state of the art, in terms of precision. In short, the proposed algorithm significantly outperforms the state of the art, in terms of both mAP and retrieval accuracy performance measures.

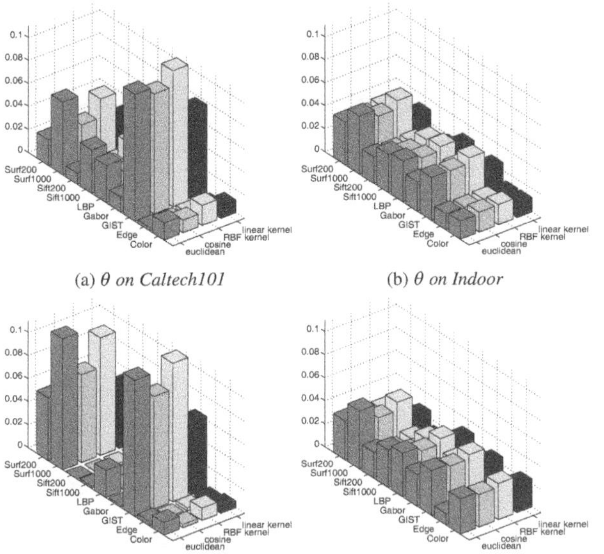

(a) θ on *Caltech101* (b) θ on *Indoor*

(a) θ on *ImageCLEF* (b) θ on *Corel*

Figure 6: The weights θ learned by OMDSL.

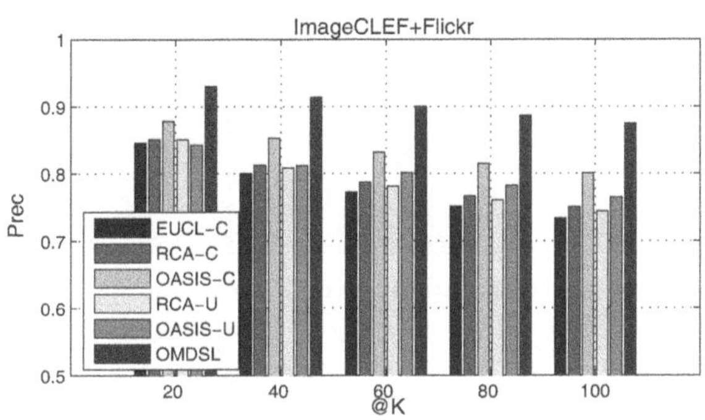

Figure 7: Precision at Top-K on "ImageCLEF+Flickr"

Table 8: mAP on "ImageCLEF+Flickr"

Eucl-C	RCA-C	OASIS-C	RCA-U	OASIS-U	OMDSL
0.5766	0.6163	0.7161	0.6219	0.7028	0.7592

5.7 Qualitative Comparison

Finally, to examine the qualitative retrieval performance, we randomly sample some query images from the query set, and compare the qualitative retrieval results. Figure 9 shows the qualitative results on "COREL" and "Caltech101" datasets. In each block, the first image is the query, and the results from the first to the fourth line represents "Eucl-C", "RCA-C", "OASIS-C", "RCA-U", "OASIS-U" and "OMDSL" respectively. The results show that OMDSL generally returns more relevant results than the others.

There are also some failure cases, as shown in Figure 8, where although all the returned images by "OMDSL" are facial images, only the second belongs to the query person, while Euclidean distance returns three correct images (1st, 2nd and 5th place of the top-5 list). We conjecture that the possible reasons include (i) the adopted features are generic but not face-specific features; (ii) the labeled data assume any two facial images belong to the same category, which cannot differentiate two different persons.

6. CONCLUSIONS

This paper investigated the fundamental problem of learning similarity functions for multimodal image retrieval. To address the limitations of regular DML approaches, we proposed a novel framework of Online Multimodal Deep Similarity Learning (OMDSL),

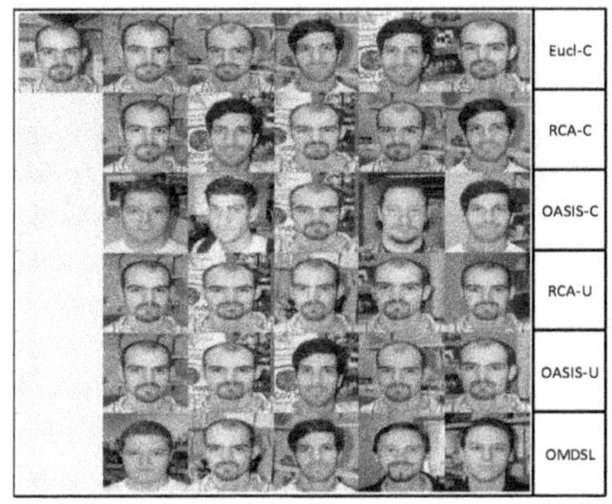

Figure 8: Example of a failure case from "Caltech101"

which integrates with multiple deep networks optimally through an efficient and scalable online learning scheme. In particular, OMDSL explores a unified two-stage online learning scheme by (i) learning a flexible nonlinear similarity function for each individual modality, and (ii) learning to find the optimal combination of multiple modalities simultaneously via a coherent online learning process. Extensive experiments were conducted on several public image datasets, in which the encouraging results showed that OMDSL is promising for multimodal similarity search. Although our current experiments were focused on image retrieval, this work is rather generic for any multimedia retrieval tasks. We plan to extend it to resolve other multimedia applications in the future.

Acknowledgments

This research was supported in part by MOE tier-1 project grant (RG33/11), and IDM/NRF Research Grant No.: MDA/IDM/2012/8/8-2 VOL 01.

7. REFERENCES

[1] S. Akaho. A kernel method for canonical correlation analysis. In *IMPS*. Springer-Verlag, 2001.

[2] A. Bar-Hillel, T. Hertz, N. Shental, and D. Weinshall. Learning distance functions using equivalence relations. In *ICML*, pages 11–18, 2003.

[3] H. Bay, T. Tuytelaars, and L. Van Gool. Surf: Speeded up robust features. In *ECCV*, pages 404–417. Springer, 2006.

[4] Y. Bengio. Learning deep architectures for AI. *FTML*, 2(1):1–127, 2009.

[5] Y. Bengio, P. Lamblin, D. Popovici, and H. Larochelle. Greedy layer-wise training of deep networks. In *NIPS*, pages 153–160. MIT Press, 2007.

[6] N. Cesa-Bianchi and G. Lugosi. *Prediction, Learning, and Games*. Cambridge University Press, New York, NY, USA, 2006.

[7] K. Chatfield, V. S. Lempitsky, A. Vedaldi, and A. Zisserman. The devil is in the details: an evaluation of recent feature encoding methods. In *BMVC*, pages 1–12, 2011.

[8] G. Chechik, V. Sharma, U. Shalit, and S. Bengio. Large scale online learning of image similarity through ranking. *JMLR*, 11:1109–1135, 2010.

[9] K. Crammer, O. Dekel, J. Keshet, S. Shalev-Shwartz, and Y. Singer. Online passive-aggressive algorithms. *JMLR*, 7:551–585, 2006.

[10] G. E. Dahl, D. Yu, L. Deng, and A. Acero. Context-dependent pre-trained deep neural networks for large-vocabulary speech recognition. *TASLP*, 20(1):30–42, 2012.

[11] M. Dredze, K. Crammer, and F. Pereira. Confidence-weighted linear classification. In *ICML*, pages 264–271, 2008.

[12] J. D. R. Farquhar, H. Meng, S. Szedmak, D. R. Hardoon, and J. Shawe-taylor. Two view learning: Svm-2k, theory and practice. In *NIPS*. MIT Press, 2006.

[13] G. Hinton and R. Salakhutdinov. Reducing the dimensionality of data with neural networks. *Science*, 313(5786):504 – 507, 2006.

[14] G. E. Hinton, S. Osindero, and Y.-W. Teh. A fast learning algorithm for deep belief nets. *NC*, 18(7):1527–1554, July 2006.

[15] S. C. Hoi, W. Liu, and S.-F. Chang. Semi-supervised distance metric learning for collaborative image retrieval. In *CVPR*, June 2008.

[16] S. C. Hoi, W. Liu, M. R. Lyu, and W.-Y. Ma. Learning distance metrics with contextual constraints for image retrieval. In *CVPR*, June 17–22 2006.

[17] S. C. Hoi, M. R. Lyu, and R. Jin. A unified log-based relevance feedback scheme for image retrieval. *TKDE*, 18(4):509–204, 2006.

[18] S. C. Hoi, J. Wang, and P. Zhao. *LIBOL: A Library for Online Learning Algorithms*. Nanyang Technological University, 2012.

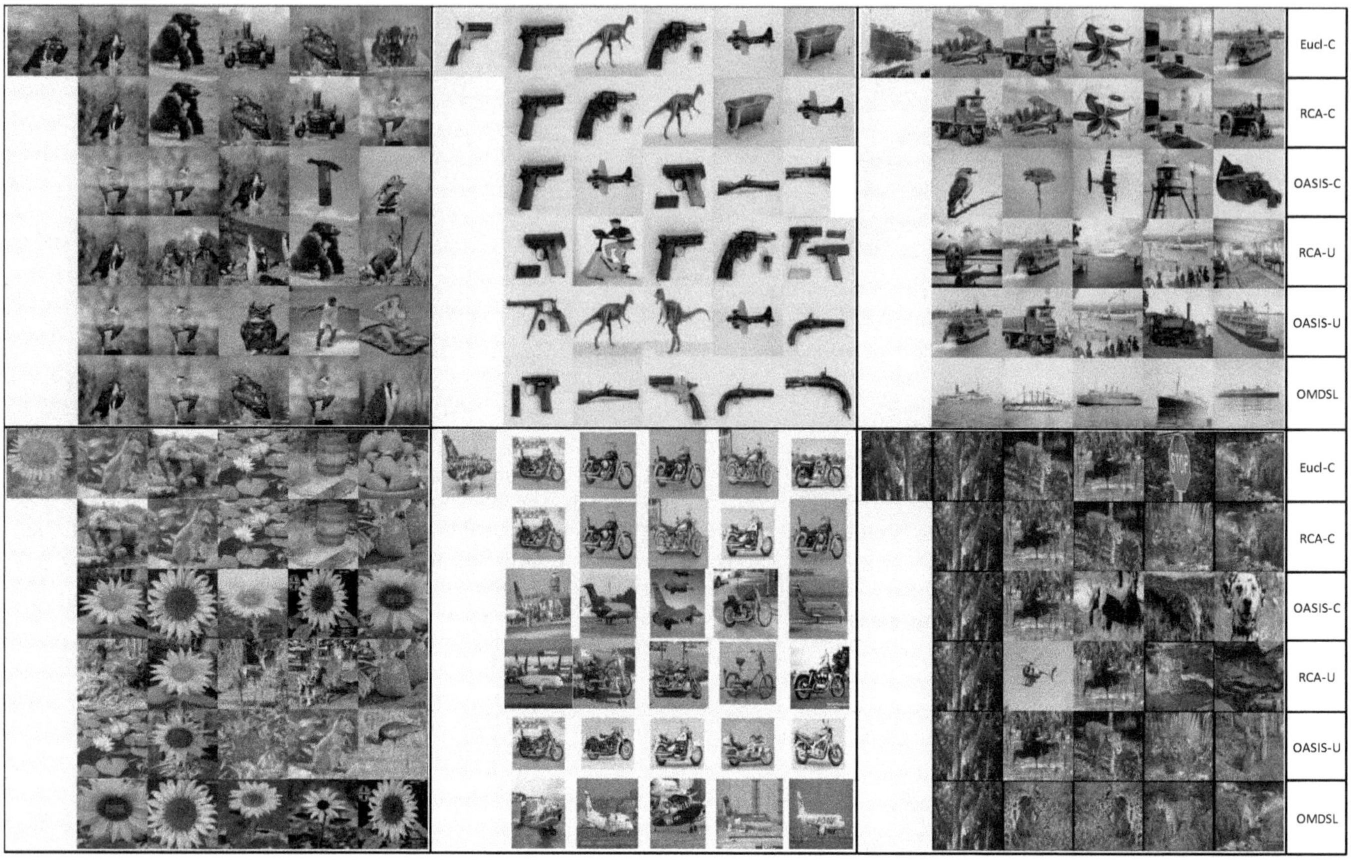

Figure 9: Qualitative evaluation of top-5 retrieved images. The first row is from "COREL" and the second is from "Caltech101".

[19] P. Jain, B. Kulis, I. S. Dhillon, and K. Grauman. Online metric learning and fast similarity search. In *NIPS*, pages 761–768, 2008.

[20] H. Jegou, F. Perronnin, M. Douze, J. Sanchez, P. Perez, and C. Schmid. Aggregating local image descriptors into compact codes. *TPAMI*, 34(9):1704–1716, Sept. 2012.

[21] R. Jin, S. Wang, and Y. Zhou. Regularized distance metric learning: Theory and algorithm. In *NIPS*, pages 862–870, 2009.

[22] Y. Jing and S. Baluja. Visualrank: Applying pagerank to large-scale image search. *TPAMI*, 30(11):1877–1890, 2008.

[23] A. Joly and O. Buisson. Random maximum margin hashing. In *CVPR*, pages 873–880, Washington, DC, USA, 2011.

[24] Y. Kang, S. Kim, and S. Choi. Deep learning to hash with multiple representations. In *ICDM*, pages 930–935, 2012.

[25] J. Kludas, E. Bruno, and S. Marchand-Maillet. Information fusion in multimedia information retrieval. *AMR*, pages 147–159, 2008.

[26] A. Krizhevsky, I. Sutskever, and G. Hinton. Imagenet classification with deep convolutional neural networks. In *NIPS*, pages 1106–1114. 2012.

[27] Q. V. Le, M. Ranzato, R. Monga, M. Devin, G. Corrado, K. Chen, J. Dean, and A. Y. Ng. Building high-level features using large scale unsupervised learning. In *ICML*, 2012.

[28] M. S. Lew, N. Sebe, C. Djeraba, and R. Jain. Content-based multimedia information retrieval: State of the art and challenges. *TOMCCAP*, 2(1):1–19, 2006.

[29] Y. Li and P. M. Long. The relaxed online maximum margin algorithm. In *NIPS*, pages 498–504, 1999.

[30] D. G. Lowe. Object recognition from local scale-invariant features. In *ICCV*, pages 1150–1157, 1999.

[31] B. S. Manjunath and W.-Y. Ma. Texture features for browsing and retrieval of image data. *TPAMI*, 18(8):837–842, 1996.

[32] B. McFee and G. Lanckriet. Learning multi-modal similarity. *JMLR*, 12:491–523, 2011.

[33] J. Ngiam, A. Khosla, M. Kim, J. Nam, H. Lee, and A. Y. Ng. Multimodal deep learning. In *ICML*, Bellevue, USA, June 2011.

[34] M. Norouzi, D. Fleet, and R. Salakhutdinov. Hamming distance metric learning. In *NIPS*. 2012.

[35] A. Quattoni and A. Torralba. Recognizing indoor scenes. In *CVPR*, 2009.

[36] R. Rahmani, S. A. Goldman, H. Zhang, S. R. Cholleti, and J. E. Fritts. Localized content-based image retrieval. *TPAMI*, 30(11):1902–1912, 2008.

[37] F. Rosenblatt. The perceptron: A probabilistic model for information storage and organization in the brain. *Psychological Review*, 65:386–407, 1958.

[38] D. E. Rumelhart, G. E. Hinton, and R. J. Williams. *Neurocomputing: foundations of research*. MIT Press, Cambridge, MA, USA, 1988.

[39] R. Salakhutdinov and G. Hinton. Semantic hashing. *IJAR*, 50(7), July 2009.

[40] R. Salakhutdinov and G. E. Hinton. Deep boltzmann machines. *AISTATS*, 5:448–455, 2009.

[41] A. W. M. Smeulders, M. Worring, S. Santini, A. Gupta, and R. Jain. Content-based image retrieval at the end of the early years. *TPAMI*, 22(12):1349–1380, 2000.

[42] C. G. Snoek, M. Worring, and A. W. Smeulders. Early versus late fusion in semantic video analysis. In *MM*, pages 399–402. ACM, 2005.

[43] N. Srivastava and R. Salakhutdinov. Multimodal learning with deep boltzmann machines. In *NIPS*. 2012.

[44] P. Vincent, H. Larochelle, Y. Bengio, and P.-A. Manzagol. Extracting and composing robust features with denoising autoencoders. In *ICML*, pages 1096–1103, 2008.

[45] P. Vincent, H. Larochelle, I. Lajoie, Y. Bengio, and P.-A. Manzagol. Stacked denoising autoencoders: Learning useful representations in a deep network with a local denoising criterion. *JMLR*, 11:3371–3408, Dec. 2010.

[46] J. Wang, P. Zhao, and S. C. H. Hoi. Exact soft confidence-weighted learning. In *ICML*, 2012.

[47] K. Weinberger, J. Blitzer, and L. Saul. Distance metric learning for large margin nearest neighbor classification. In *NIPS*, pages 1473–1480, 2006.

[48] L. Wu, S. C. Hoi, and N. Yu. Semantics-preserving bag-of-words models and applications. *TIP*, 19(7):1908–1920, 2010.

[49] J. Yang, Y.-G. Jiang, A. G. Hauptmann, and C.-W. Ngo. Evaluating bag-of-visual-words representations in scene classification. In *MIR*, pages 197–206, 2007.

[50] L. Yang and R. Jin. Distance metric learning: A comprehensive survey. *Michigan State Universiy*, pages 1–51, 2006.

[51] D. Zhai, H. Chang, S. Shan, X. Chen, and W. Gao. Multiview metric learning with global consistency and local smoothness. *TIST*, 3(3):53, 2012.

[52] P. Zhao, S. C. H. Hoi, and R. Jin. Double updating online learning. *JMLR*, 12:1587–1615, 2011.

[53] S.-h. Zhong, Y. Liu, and Y. Liu. Bilinear deep learning for image classification. In *MM*, pages 343–352, Scottsdale, Arizona, 2011.

[54] M. Zinkevich. Online convex programming and generalized infinitesimal gradientascent. In *ICML*, pages 928–936, 2003.

One-Man-Band: A Touch Screen Interface for Producing Live Multi-Camera Sports Broadcasts

Eric Foote
Disney Research
Pittsburgh, USA
efoote@nrec.ri.cmu.edu

Peter Carr
Disney Research
Pittsburgh, USA
carr@disneyresearch.com

Patrick Lucey
Disney Research
Pittsburgh, USA
pjlucey@disneyresearch.com

Yaser Sheikh
Carnegie Mellon University
Pittsburgh, USA
yaser@cs.cmu.edu

Iain Matthews
Disney Research
Pittsburgh, USA
iainm@disneyresearch.com

Generating live broadcasts of sporting events requires a coordinated crew of camera operators, directors, and technical personnel to control and switch between multiple cameras to tell the evolving story of a game. In this paper, we present an unimodal interface concept that allows one person to cover live sporting action by controlling multiple cameras and and determining which view to broadcast. The interface exploits the structure of sports broadcasts which typically switch between a zoomed out *game*-camera view (which records the strategic team-level play), and a zoomed in *iso*-camera view (which captures the animated adversarial relations between opposing players). The operator simultaneously controls multiple pan-tilt-zoom cameras by pointing at a location on the touch screen, and selects which camera to broadcast using one or two points of contact. The image from the selected camera is superimposed on top of a wide-angle view captured from a *context*-camera which provides the operator with periphery information (which is useful for ensuring good framing while controlling the camera). We show that by unifying directorial and camera operation functions, we can achieve comparable broadcast quality to a multi-person crew, while reducing cost, logistical, and communication complexities.

Keywords

Camera Control, Touch screen, Multiple Cameras

Categories and Subject Descriptors

H.5.2 [**Information Systems**]: Information Interfaces and Presentation—*User Interfaces*

General Terms

Human Factors

1. INTRODUCTION

ACM 978-1-4503-2404-5/13/10 ...$15.00.
http://dx.doi.org/10.1145/2502081.2502092.

Game-camera Iso-camera

Figure 1: (Top) To control the *game*-camera, the operator uses one finger to drag a box highlighting the portion of the court that the user wishes to frame, and two fingers to switch to the *iso*-camera. (Bottom) The output of our interface is a broadcast video produced by a single user (see accompanying video for full effect).

Creating production-quality broadcasts of live sporting events requires a coordinated crew of skilled individuals constantly aware of what is happening in the game and how the rest of the crew is cooperating to cover the action [11]. For popular team sports (e.g. professional football, basketball or hockey), a large broadcast crew is required to coordinate multiple cameras so that the broadcast can follow the fast-paced action on the field. There is also a much larger number of niche sporting events with a smaller, but devoted following, such as little-league, high school, and lower-divisional collegiate sports. Cost and logistical complexity preclude professional multi-camera setups, which is why these smaller events are typically webcast by a novice operator controlling a single camera. In this paper, we present a single operator interface that unifies the roles of director and camera operators, and allows a single user to create compelling broadcasts of live sporting events by simultaneously controlling and switching between multiple pan-tilt-zoom (PTZ) cameras.

The interface exploits the particular structure of focus and context between the different roles on a sports broadcast production crew. As live sport is fast moving and highly variable, there is a necessity for the interface to include both spatial and temporal contexts. In a typical setup, one camera operator controls the *game*-camera, which maintains a wide, zoomed-out shot to capture the team-level action. A second camera operator controls the *isolated*-camera (or iso-camera), which captures the emotion and drama of the play using a zoomed-in view for close-ups of players, coaches, or fans. Both camera operators focus on their viewfinder to ensure they have well composed shots. Simultaneously, their periphery vision gives them context of how the play is unfolding, which allows them to follow the action. The director relies on a bank of live monitors in a control room to select a series of camera angles to best focus on what is happening in the game. The director is in continual dialogue with the camera operators to get particular shots which will help place the action in context of the story the director is trying to tell. Thus, for a high-quality live broadcast to be obtained, the communication and understanding of instruction between the director and camera operators has to be very clear, which is hard to get achieve with an inexperienced team.

Our *One-Man-Band* (OMB) interface unifies the roles of director, game-camera operator, and iso-camera operator into an unimodal interface that allows one operator to produce a compelling broadcast of a sporting event. Our interface combines focus and context by superimposing video feeds from multiple robotic pan-tilt-zoom cameras onto video from a stationary fish-eye *context*-camera that captures the entire playing area (see Figure 1). The cameras are precisely calibrated and share a common vantage point. The overlay of the broadcast camera resembles a viewfinder, and the static context-camera mimics periphery vision. The user controls the game-camera by dragging the highlighted overlay to a new area of the touch screen using a single finger. To cut to the iso-camera, the user places a second finger on the screen. The view from the iso-camera is then displayed, and the iso-camera can be controlled in a similar fashion by dragging both fingers. To cut back to the game-camera, the user lifts one finger (so that only one finger is in contact with the touch screen) and the superimposed image returns to the game-camera. Thus, the interface focuses the user's attention on one of the camera roles at a time, while simultaneously providing live spatiotemporal context of the game, allowing the user to make timely cuts from one camera to the other, so that the evolving storyline of the game is captured in the broadcast[1].

We compare our touch interface concept against a traditional three-person crew, with two joystick operators for the game- and iso-cameras, and one director responsible for switching between views. To determine if there is any significant difference between the two approaches, we conducted two user studies and a perception study comparing the two methods. For the perception study, the users were asked to evaluate the two methods against three criteria: (1) action following: the quality of individual camera control, (2) appropriateness of cuts: the quality of cuts between cameras, and (3) overall quality: the quality of the final broadcast footage. In addition to the perception studies, we also carried out quantitative analyses which numerically shows how similar the approaches are in terms of the broadcast generated.

[1]In terms of a high-definition (HD) live broadcast, cropping the iso-camera view from the game-camera is not a reasonable option as the resolution will be substantially lower, and the iso-camera would be constrained to be taken from only within the confines of the game-camera view.

2. RELATED WORK

Interactive applications often require users to interact with more information than the screen can display. The *Focus + Context* interface scheme, introduced in the seminal work of Sarkar et al. [15] on fisheye lenses, enables users to interact with different level of details. More recently, Pietriga et al. [12] investigated a general framework for lenses that helped users in the navigation of large scenes, while Cockburn et al. [4] presented a general survey on Focus + Context techniques. We can apply a Focus + Context analogy to sport broadcasting with camera operators providing high resolution content through multiple view points. The director then requires an overview of all the video content in realtime and uses available visual information to decide the focus (i.e., select the appropriate camera viewpoint). Our system builds upon the Focus + Context interface scheme to provide both an overview of the area covered by the cameras and to enable the user to dynamically set the current area of interest.

Another approach is to use computer vision to automate the selection of current viewpoint. Some applications propose to remove the user from the decision process in the context of sport broadcasting [2, 13]. Compared to our system, which is generalizable to many sports, these approaches are often tailored specifically to a single sport. For example, Ariki et al. [2] proposed a system for producing a fully automated broadcast of a soccer game using computer vision and action recognition. Their application did not run in realtime, meaning the broadcast could only be generated as a post-processed recording rather than a live event.

Some methods have placed control of the broadcast in the hands of the viewer, instead of automating the broadcast. For example in [10], Matthews proposed a system allowing the viewer of a sporting event to select between multiple camera views, eliminating the need for a director, though still requiring the use of human operators to control each of the cameras. Free-Viewpoint Television [18] eliminated the need for camera operators with a system that uses an array of cameras to synthesize a view from any angle. Although this approach requires neither a director nor the use of any camera operators, the overhead involved in setting up the camera array is not suited for the low-budget scenario that we target with our system.

In the more general category of remote camera control, Liu et al. [9] proposed a system which, similar to the method proposed here, made use of a controllable pan-tilt-zoom camera plus a wider-angle view to provide the context. In this system, the views of both the context camera and the pan-tilt-zoom camera were displayed to the user on separate screens. The user would select a region to view by drawing a box on the context camera view, and the pan-tilt-zoom camera would position itself to view that region. Although our method makes similar use of a wider context camera for helping the user select a view, the "region-selecting" method in [9] requires the user to draw a new box each time they want to move the camera, and to continuously switch between the context and pan-tilt-zoom views. By contrast, our system displays both views on a single screen, and allows the user to drag the pan-tilt-zoom display region to respond more easily to a more fast-paced and dynamic scenario such as a sporting event. Our system also allows for the control of multiple cameras, while [9] uses only a single camera.

Other work on camera control has focused on the control of virtual cameras in a graphics or animation environment [3, 5, 16, 19, 20]. A common premise in each of these methods is that it is easier to control a camera by specifying the desired framing than it is to manipulate the degrees of freedom of the camera directly. For example, Singh et al. [16] presented a controller for manipulating a virtual camera by specifying the vanishing points and horizon line of the camera view. Manipulating the camera perspective would then affect the focal length, center of projection, or pose of the camera. Drucker and Zeltzer [5] proposed an interface for specifying constraints on the camera view, such as the size and/or position of one or more objects. Both [8] and [17] present a method for camera control by directly selecting an object for the camera to point at, and [17] also allowed users to control a virtual camera in a 3D graphics environment by specifying the framing of two points in the virtual world. In [6], Gleicher and Witkin proposed a virtual camera controller in which the user could "pin" one or more objects to sub-regions of the camera view, and using these constraints to solve for the time derivatives of the camera parameters.

A touch interface for controlling a remote camera was proposed by Kuzuoka et al. [8] as part of a system for remote collaboration. In this system, the camera view appeared on a touch screen display, and touching a displayed object would cause the camera to automatically center on that object. The interface also supported velocity control by holding a finger on the display. The velocity and direction of the resulting camera motion directly corresponded to the direction and distance from the touch position to the center of the display. However, the proposed controller did not allow for the use of multiple cameras, and did not provide a wider context view as our system does.

Other methods for making robotic camera control more intuitive have been proposed as well. Aiono et al. proposed a robotic camera that could be controlled by head movements, to be used by a doctor during surgical procedures [1]. Rui et al [14] proposed a system for remote viewing of meetings that used a 360 degree panorama view of the meeting room. Users would control a virtual pan/tilt camera that cropped the panorama to view only the portion that the user wanted to look at.

3. INTERFACE DESCRIPTION

Many elements for achieving simultaneous focus and context are common to both camera operation task (game- and iso-camera), so we describe these shared aspects first. A stationary *context*-camera with a fish-eye lens is used to display the entire area of play. The video from the active camera (either the game-camera or iso-camera) is superimposed on top of the context image in its correct location so that it appears as an inset on the context-camera view. To focus

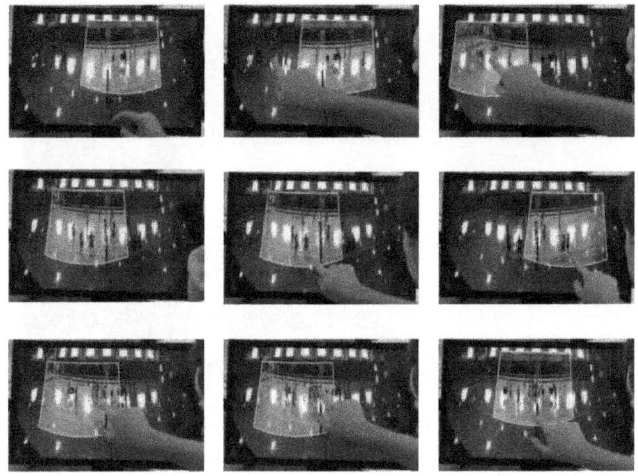

Figure 2: There are three ways to control the game camera from our interface. (Top Row) Touching a location at any point outside of the game-camera highlight box causes the camera to center on that location. (Middle Row) Touching and dragging any point inside of the game-camera box will move the camera relative to its current position. (Bottom Row) Touching the screen and then immediately releasing will also center the game camera on the point of contact, whether or not the user touched the screen inside the game-camera box.

the user's attention on the active camera, the image of the context camera is desaturated, and the superimposed image of the broadcast camera image is outlined with a solid color border (yellow for the game-camera and red for the iso-camera). All three cameras are calibrated and share the same vantage point. The views from all cameras are displayed and updated live.

Game-Camera Control.

The game-camera operator is responsible for covering the general action of the sporting match. For ball sports, this means that the ball should always be in shot as well as most of the players. If the game has a goal (or basket) then this should also be included, if possible. To accomplish these objectives, the game-camera operator maintains a wide-angle shot. As this view contains most of the information of interest, it will be used the majority of the time.

The three methods for controlling the game-camera are illustrated in Figure 2. In the first method (top row), the user touches a location on the screen outside the current view and the highlighted box containing the game-camera view will move to the center of that location. We call this the "tap-to-center" approach. The second method (middle row) or "click-and-drag" method is activated by touching the screen at any location inside the game-camera highlighted box and maintaining contact. With this form of control, the user drags his/her finger across the screen, and the game camera moves as needed to to maintain the same position relative to the user's finger. The third method of control (bottom row) is to touch and immediately release a location on the screen. The game-camera will center to that location,

Figure 3: **When the user switches to the iso-camera, the view is displayed in a highlighted red box and is also shown in the upper left corner of the interface to avoid occlusion from the user's hand.**

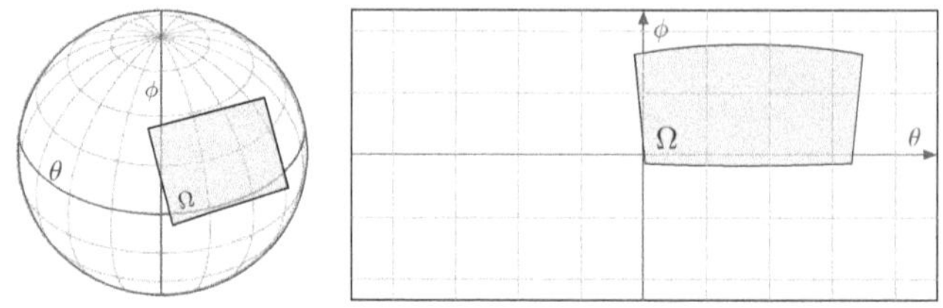

Figure 4: **The image plane of a PTZ camera can be considered as a tangent plane on a unit sphere, where the position of the tangent plane is determined by the pan and tilt angles of the camera, and the size is determined by the focal length (zoom) of the camera. In our interface, the surface area of the sphere is warped onto the flat plane of the display by sampling the spherical angles ϕ and θ uniformly (right). The viewable region in spherical coordinates remains mostly rectangular for small tilt angles and reasonably large focal lengths.**

regardless of whether it is currently in the highlighted box or not.

Iso-Camera Control.

The role of the iso-camera operator is to capture close-up shots when something interesting happens. This normally results in a zoomed-in shot of a player, coach or fan which illustrates the emotion and drama of the play that has just occurred. In the OMB interface, the user chooses and operates the iso-camera by placing a second finger on the screen. Like the game-camera view, the iso-camera view is displayed in a highlighted box on top of the context view, with its position corresponding directly to the position of the actual camera so that the views line up. The iso-camera controller also supports both the tap-to-center and click-and-drag control methods, using the midpoint of the user's fingers as reference.

The iso-camera is operated at a high zoom, since its purpose is to get close-up shots. As a result, when superimposed on the context image, the iso-camera image may appear quite small, making it difficult for the user to judge whether the shot is well composed. In addition, the user's hand may occlude the superimposed image. As a result, a virtual viewfinder image is superimposed in the top-left corner of the screen. Unlike the regular superimposed view, the virtual viewfinder image is not registered to the context view but simply inserted over top (See Figure 3).

Usage.

In a live sporting event, the user must constantly decide whether to broadcast the game-camera or the iso-camera. In this role, they are essentially the director, as they choose which view best conveys the story unfolding in the match. To make this easier, a series of simple rules can be applied. For instance, the main rule is to use the game-camera when the game is active, which occurs the majority of time. This view should include the ball and the majority of players in this view. When there is a break in play, it is then appropriate to cut to the iso-camera centered on a player/coach/fan who is reacting to recent events which have just transpired in the game. Examples of the system in use for basketball are given in the Experiments section.

4. SYSTEM DESCRIPTION

Our system uses a pair of Sony BRC-Z700 cameras for the game- and iso-cameras, and an Allied Vision GE 1910C for the context-camera with a fisheye lens. A 3M M2256PW touch screen monitor is connected to a Mac Pro, and a Gefen 4x1 video switcher toggles which broadcast signal is sent to the computer. Both Sony BRC-Z700 cameras and the Gefen video switcher are controlled by the Mac Pro via RS-232 serial links.

4.1 Graphical Display

The touch screen display always shows a composite of two live video feeds. The image of the currently broadcasting camera is aligned to and superimposed over the image of the context-camera by mapping both images onto the surface of a sphere. The necessary portion of the spherical surface is then displayed on the touch screen by plotting the composited image as a function of spherical angles (see Figure 4). This unwarping operation is computed by interpolating a spherical area of interest $\Omega = [\theta_{\min}, \theta_{\max}] \times [\phi_{\min}, \phi_{\max}]$ over the number of pixels in the display, and associating to every pixel location (u, v) a 3D point $\mathbf{M} = [M_x, M_y, M_z]$ on the surface of the unit sphere

$$M_x = \sin\theta\cos\phi \quad (1)$$

$$M_y = \sin\phi \quad (2)$$

$$M_z = \cos\theta\cos\phi. \quad (3)$$

The composited spherical image is computed by projecting each 3D point $\mathbf{M}$ into the context-, game- and iso-cameras to determine appropriate sampling locations $\mathbf{m}_c$, $\mathbf{m}_g$ and $\mathbf{m}_i$; in each camera for image interpolation (where the subscripts stand for **c**ontext, **g**ame and **i**so). Each camera has its own coordinate system, and the reference frame of the unit sphere is arbitrary. However, we assume the centers of projection (lenses) of all three cameras are located in approximately the same 3D position $\mathbf{C}$, and define this as the centre of the unit sphere. By convention, a camera coordinate system is defined such that the $\hat{\mathbf{z}}$ axis points in the direction the camera is looking, and the $\hat{\mathbf{x}}$ and $\hat{\mathbf{y}}$ directions correspond to the right and down directions on the image plane.

A camera's image plane is located one focal length f away from its center of projection $\mathbf{C}$ along its optical axis $\hat{\mathbf{z}}$. The principle point $\mathbf{p} = [p_u, p_v]$ corresponds to the intersection of the optical axis and the image plane, and is often assumed to coincide with the center of the image. The relationship between a 3D point $\mathbf{M}$ expressed in the camera coordinate system and its 2D projected location $\mathbf{m} = [m_u, m_v]$ on the image plane is governed through similar triangles (see Figure 5). Using homogeneous coordinates [7], the relationship is compactly expressed via matrix multiplication

$$\mathbf{m} = \mathtt{K}\mathbf{M}, \tag{4}$$

where

$$\mathtt{K} = \begin{bmatrix} f & 0 & p_u \\ 0 & f & p_v \\ 0 & 0 & 1 \end{bmatrix}. \tag{5}$$

The remainder of this discussion addresses how each 3D coordinate $\mathbf{M}$ is transformed from the coordinate system of the unit sphere to the coordinate system of each camera. Once $\mathbf{M}_c, \mathbf{M}_g$ and $\mathbf{M}_i$ are known, the projected image locations $\mathbf{m}_c, \mathbf{m}_g$ and $\mathbf{m}_i$ can be recovered from (4), where a particular $\mathtt{K}$ is used for each camera (since the cameras will have different focal lengths and principle points).

A PTZ camera has a camera coordinate system (as defined earlier) and a motor coordinate system. The camera coordinate system is determined by the camera's current pan and tilt angles, whereas the motor coordinate system remains fixed. For a given pair of pan/tilt angles, the mapping from motor to camera coordinate systems is governed by a 3D rotation

$$\mathtt{R}(\theta, \phi) = \begin{bmatrix} \cos\theta & 0 & -\sin\theta \\ \sin\theta\sin\phi & \cos\phi & \cos\theta\sin\phi \\ \sin\theta\cos\phi & -\sin\phi & \cos\theta\cos\phi \end{bmatrix}. \tag{6}$$

The orientations of the motor coordinate systems and focal lengths of the context-, game- and iso-cameras are determined from homographies [7] between the image planes and the world ground plane. Since each camera may not be in its home position ($\theta = 0, \phi = 0$) when the homography is estimated, the extracted orientation $\mathtt{S}$ describes the changeable camera coordinate system. As a result, the orientation $\mathtt{Q}$ of the camera's stationary motor coordinate system must take into account any non-zero pan θ_0 and tilt ϕ_0 angles at which the homography was estimated

$$\mathtt{Q} = \mathtt{R}^{-1}(\theta_0, \phi_0)\mathtt{S}. \tag{7}$$

Each 3D point $\mathbf{M}$ is transferred into the three camera coordinate systems by first rotating into each camera's motor coordinate system, and then rotating to the camera coordinate system for the camera's current pan/tilt angles

$$\mathbf{M}_c = \mathtt{Q}_c\mathbf{M} \tag{8}$$

$$\mathbf{M}_g = \mathtt{R}(\theta_g, \phi_g)\mathtt{Q}_g\mathbf{M} \tag{9}$$

$$\mathbf{M}_i = \mathtt{R}(\theta_i, \phi_i)\mathtt{Q}_i\mathbf{M}. \tag{10}$$

The context-camera is stationary, so it has no pan/tilt rotation matrix $\mathtt{R}$. As a result, the corresponding projected image locations are

$$\mathbf{m}_c = \mathtt{K}_c\mathtt{Q}_c\mathbf{M} \tag{11}$$

$$\mathbf{m}_g = \mathtt{K}_g\mathtt{R}(\theta_g, \phi_g)\mathtt{Q}_g\mathbf{M} \tag{12}$$

$$\mathbf{m}_i = \mathtt{K}_i\mathtt{R}(\theta_i, \phi_i)\mathtt{Q}_i\mathbf{M}. \tag{13}$$

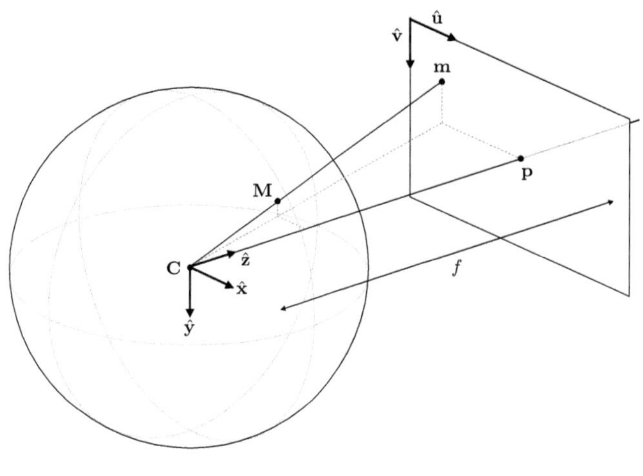

Figure 5: The composited spherical image is computed by transforming each pixel's corresponding 3D point M into the camera's coordinate system (shown here) and projecting onto the image plane. The resulting location m is determined by similar triangles and depends on the camera's focal length f and principal point p.

4.2 Interpreting Gestures

When the user touches the screen, we first determine the number of contact points. If there is only one point of contact, we display the view from the game-camera, and select this camera to control. If there are multiple points of contact, we display and control the iso-camera.

In the first case, we use the mapping described in Figure 5 to map the point of contact to a pan and tilt angle. As mentioned in the previous section, if the point of contact is outside of the camera view, or if the user lifts his/her finger within one second of making contact, then the game-camera will move to center on the point of contact. Otherwise, we measure the displacement from the initial point of contact as the user drags his/her finger across the screen. The necessary game-camera pan/tilt angles to maintain the relative displacement to the point of contact is determined by adding the relative displacement vector to the camera's position at initial contact.

In the second case involving multiple points of contact, we calculate the centroid of the contact points on the screen to determine target pan and tilt angles on the unit sphere. We then compute target pan/tilt angles in the iso-camera's motor coordinate system using $\mathtt{Q}_i$.

5. EXPERIMENT

We conducted two user studies and a perception study to determine whether a broadcast using the One-Man-Band (OMB) interface is comparable to a broadcast generated by a Three-Person-Crew (TPC). Our hypothesis was that: *"there is no significant difference in perceivable quality between broadcasts generated using the OMB interface and a conventional TPC."*

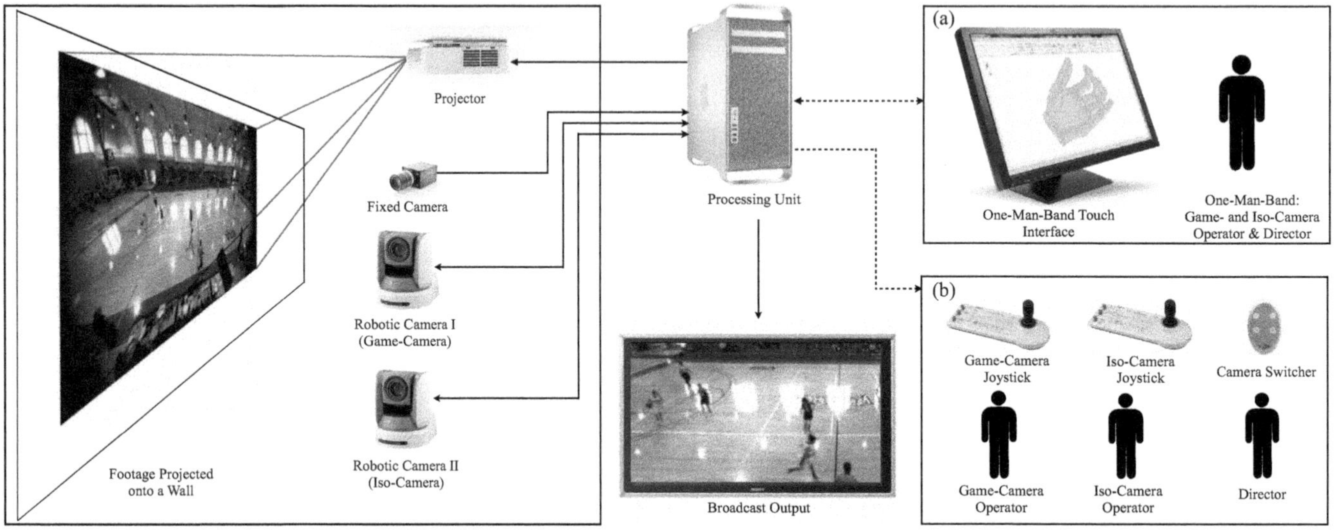

Figure 6: The setup used for both the OMB and the TPC experiments. A projector projects a full view of a basketball game onto a screen (left). Three cameras (two robotic and a fixed camera) are set up facing the wall with the following roles: i) one robotic camera captures the game view, ii) the other robotic camera captures the iso-view, and iii) the fixed camera records the whole field of view. Using this setup, we conducted two user studies: (a) For the OMB user study, all three cameras were connected to our touch screen interface. (b) For the TPC user study, each camera was connected to a joystick (i.e. game camera and iso camera) and the view was switched via a directors switching unit. Both studies yielded a broadcast video of the user studies which were stored, logged and analyzed to compare both setups.

5.1 User Study I: One-Man-Band

5.1.1 Participants and Apparatus

Thirty-three participants (15 females) aged 19-59 (mean 30.8) were recruited from a local university.

A schematic of the OMB system used in user study is shown in Figure 6(a). In order to create an experiment that was repeatable while being interesting for the participants, we first recorded a NCAA Division III college basketball game using a wide-angled camera. This view was wide enough to capture the entire court. Using a projector screen, we displayed the video from the camera in order to produce a repeatable live event. The two robotic pan-tilt-zoom cameras were pointed at the projector screen, with the field of view of the two broadcast cameras set such that they could only see a portion of the screen, which coincided with the zoom settings of the game- and iso-view camera. Using this setup, we allowed users to participate in a mock broadcast, using the cameras to capture the action on the screen just as they would with a live sporting event. By simulating the study in this way we could repeatedly generate identical conditions for the user studies.

5.1.2 Procedure

Participants were brought in individually and were tasked with simulating a broadcast using the OMB interface. To facilitate all studies, we edited out thirty-three (33) short clips from the wide angle video, ranging from 10 to 30 seconds long. Each clip contained a single "event" which would require the user to switch to the iso-view camera for a brief close-up. An "event" was defined as one of the following: (1) a player successfully scores a basket, (2) the ball goes out of bounds, or (3) a foul occurs.

Each participant first viewed the same short introductory video. This video explained: 1) the role of each person in a broadcast (i.e. director, game camera operator, iso-view camera operator), 2) how to use the interface, and 3) specific instructions for when to use the game camera and when to cut to the iso camera. Table 1 lists the specific instructions given to the users.

After receiving these instructions, each participant was shown a random assortment of twenty clips on the projector screen and used our OMB interface to record the action. The first ten clips were used as a practice run, so that the participants could get familiar to the interface. The second ten clips were recorded and used for analysis. Each study lasted approximately thirty minutes, and participants were compensated for their time.

5.2 User Study II: Three-Person-Crew Study

5.2.1 Participants

A different set of thirty-two participants (11 female) aged 20-55 (mean 24.9), were recruited to take part in the TPC study. We attempted to break these participants into groups of three, however due to four not showing up for the study, we ended up with eight groups of three (8×3) and four groups of two (4×2). To provide a fair comparison, we did not use the four groups of two. None participated in the One-Man-Band study.

5.2.2 Apparatus

The experiment used the same projector screen displaying a wide angle view of a basketball game, with cameras pointed at the screen. In this case, however, each of the robotic cameras was controlled by a separate joystick, and

1. The game-camera view (or wide-angled view) should capture a third of the court.
2. When the ball is moving from one side of the court to the other, frame the player with the ball on the last third of the frame (i.e., lead to where the play is going).
3. When the player with the ball arrives into the attacking third of the court, make sure that the hoop, backboard, and the player with the ball are all in view.
4. Cut to the iso-camera to get a close up of the player who either: (a) scored a basket, (b) touched the ball before it went out, (c) committed a foul or got fouled. If you are not sure who it was, give your best guess.

Table 1: The rules given to the participants for using the game-camera, iso-camera and when to cut between these two views.

the views from the two broadcast cameras were each displayed on their own monitor. A video switcher was used to change the view, which was used by the director. A diagram of the setup is given in Figure 6(b).

5.2.3 Procedure

Each group was shown the same introductory video as the previous study which explained the roles of production crew member (game-camera operator, iso-camera operator, and director), in addition to what each person should do when an "event" occurs. Using the setup depicted in Figure 6(b), one participant of the group was assigned to operate the game-camera, another to the iso-camera and the third to the role of the director. The director decided which view to broadcast and would give instructions to the other camera operators if desired.

For this study, a random assortment of forty clips were played on the projector screen for each group. As with the OMB study, the first ten were used as a practice run and data was not recorded. For the eight groups of three, during the practice run, the three participants rotated positions every three clips (leaving four clips for the last rotation), so that everyone was able to practice each role. Data was recorded for the last thirty (30) clips shown.

5.3 Perception Study: Method and Results

5.3.1 Participants

To gauge what naive observers thought of the resulting broadcasts that came from either the OMB and TPC user studies, thirty-one participants (12 females) aged 18-54 (mean 24.8) were recruited from a local university. None of these participants were used in either of the previous user studies.

5.3.2 Apparatus

Each participant viewed the broadcast videos from the OMB and TPC user studies. Two perception studies were conducted. The first used a computer program to display the videos and had three sliders underneath the viewing window which were used to indicate the viewer's ratings (i.e., 1-5 rating scale). The second study was to compare OMB and TPC videos generated for the same basketball clip, which were displayed side-by-side. A single slider underneath the videos was used to indicate preference, and a text box could be used to record comments.

5.3.3 Procedure

Each participant was shown an assortment of twenty recorded clips which were randomized each time. Ten were recorded by users in the OMB study, and ten from the TPC study. The clips were shown in random order, and participants rated each clip on a scale from 1 to 5 in three categories:

1. Overall quality,
2. Appropriateness of cuts, and
3. Game-camera smoothness.

Participants were shown examples of "good" and "bad" clips for each category before beginning the study. These examples were based on the opinion of an independent expert who did not know which interface was used.

For the second part of the study, participants viewed pairs of clips side by side. Both recordings were of the same game event, with one clip being taken from the OMB interface and the other from the TPC setup. Participants then selected which recording they thought was better at capturing the event.

5.3.4 Results

The results of the perception study are summarized in Table 2. These results were calculated from each participant's mean rating. T-tests were used to compare mean ratings for each group on the three questions.

	Overall Quality [1-5]	Cut Quality [1-5]	Game-Camera Smoothness [1-5]
OMB	2.87 (0.40)	2.70 (0.39)	3.28 (0.38)
TPC	3.08 (0.48)	2.65 (0.44)	3.52 (0.40)
p-value	0.061	0.599	0.016

Table 2: Mean (and stdev) and the p-value associated with the t-tests comparing the One-Man-Band to the three-person crew broadcast based on the perception ratings using a 5 point scale (1-5).

We see that for the categories of overall quality and cut appropriateness, the average ratings were not significantly different, and therefore the evidence indicates that a single user with our OMB interface can perform as well as a three-person crew with an existing interface. Only the category of game-camera smoothness showed a significant but slight preference for the three-person-crew results. For the side-by-side analysis, we compared the OMB to TPC clips and we found that participants selected the OMB produced clip 46% of the time, which is not significant ($p > 0.05$).

5.4 Quantitative Analysis: Results and Discussion

Prior to any user or perception studies, we first established "ground-truth" positions for each of the video clips.

The ground-truth positions were determined on a frame-by-frame basis for each clip using the rules given in Table 1. These rules define a "correct" way to film each clip [11]. The ground truth camera positions were generated according to these same rules; however, to eliminate the possibility of human error, we did not record the ground truth positions in realtime from a human camera operator. Instead, we stepped through each of the 33 sequences frame-by-frame, and determined the "text-book" camera position and selection for each frame. Although there is subjectivity in determining how "good" a broadcast is, we can use these results to get a relative indication on how close both interfaces are to a baseline broadcast.

After both user studies were conducted, we compared the position logs from both the OMB and TPC to our ground truth data. By comparing ground truth camera positions to those recorded by the user studies, we obtained some quantitative sense of how well users performed against an ideal broadcast.

	Correct Camera Selection [%]	Average Pan Error [°]	Average Tilt Error [°]
OMB	**79.01** (4.65)	5.17 (1.03)	**1.17** (0.24)
TPC	73.69 (10.87)	**4.51** (0.99)	1.48 (0.44)
p-value	0.015	0.011	<0.001

Table 3: Mean (and stdev) and the p-value associated with the t-tests comparing the OMB and the TPC to the ground-truth broadcast for: 1) the average number of frames the user selected the correct camera, 2) the average pan error per user, and 3) the average tilt error per user. Statistically significant results are highlighted in bold typeface.

The results of the quantitative analysis are summarized in Table 3 and visualized in Figure 7. Similar to the results reported in the perception studies, these results refer to the mean performance for each user. In the second column, the results describe the percentage of frames which coincided with the camera that was selected in the ground-truth data (i.e. the higher the percentage the better). From these results it can be seen that the OMB was better ($p < 0.05$) than the TPC for selecting the correct camera. This result suggests that the director in the TPC studies was not as good as the single operator using OMB; possibly due to a lack of engagement as the director was seldomly involved. In terms of average pan error, the TPC was better than the OMB ($p < 0.05$), which is understandable as there was a noticeable lag in the camera-control of the robotic cameras. However, in terms of tilt error, the OMB was better than the TPC ($p < 0.001$).

An example of the ground-truth broadcast, compared to the broadcasts generated via the OMB and TPC setups are given in Figure 8(a). In this example, key-frames showing the camera selection and position are shown in columns A through D. In Figure 8(b), the pan and tilt positions, as well as the camera selection are given as functions of time. Based on these measurements we were able to gain some quantitative result comparing the OMB to the TPC setup.

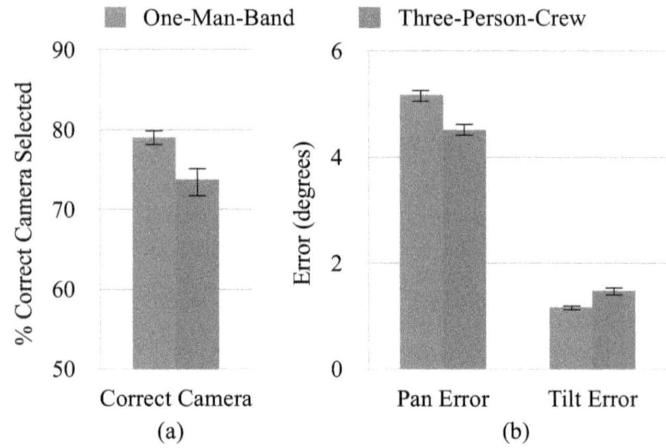

Figure 7: (a) The mean percentage of frames that users selected the correct camera. (b) The mean error in terms of pan and tilt across all the users for the OMB and TPC studies. The error bars on refer to the standard error.

6. SUMMARY AND FUTURE WORK

We present an interface which allows a single user to create a compelling broadcast of a sporting event by controlling multiple cameras simultaneously. Our experiments have shown that most novice users are able to learn the interface with very little practice, and can generate broadcasts that are approximately as good as those produced by a three-person-crew. Although the three-person-crew did slightly better in terms of camera smoothness, we showed that participants using our interface can do equally in terms of camera selection and pan-tilt positioning.

In the future, we plan to increase the number of cameras, as well as additional functionality such as replays and statistics. We will explore how these additional choices can be integrated into the touchscreen interface. For instance, while the user could still maintain direct control over the cameras (including when to switch between the game- and iso-views), the system could automatically suggest particulars cameras to cut to at opportune moments, or offer insightful statistical graphics during breaks in play.

7. REFERENCES

[1] S. Aiono, J. Gilbert, B. Soin, P. Finlay, and A. Gordon. Controlled Trial of the Introduction of a Robotic Camera Assistant for Laparoscopic Cholecystectomy. *Surgical Endoscopy*, 16(9):1267–1270, 2002.

[2] Y. Ariki, S. Kubota, and M. Kumano. Automatic production system of soccer sports video by digital camera work based on situation recognition. In *Multimedia, 2006. ISM'06. Eighth IEEE International Symposium on*, pages 851–860, 2006.

[3] M. Barange. Tabletop Interactive Camera Control. Master's thesis, INRIA, 2010.

[4] A. Cockburn, A. Karlson, and B. B. Bederson. A Review of Overview + Detail, Zooming, and Focus + Context Interfaces. *ACM Comput. Surv.*, 41:2:1–2:31, 2009.

[5] S. Drucker and D. Zeltzer. CamDroid: A System for Implementing Intelligent Camera Control. In

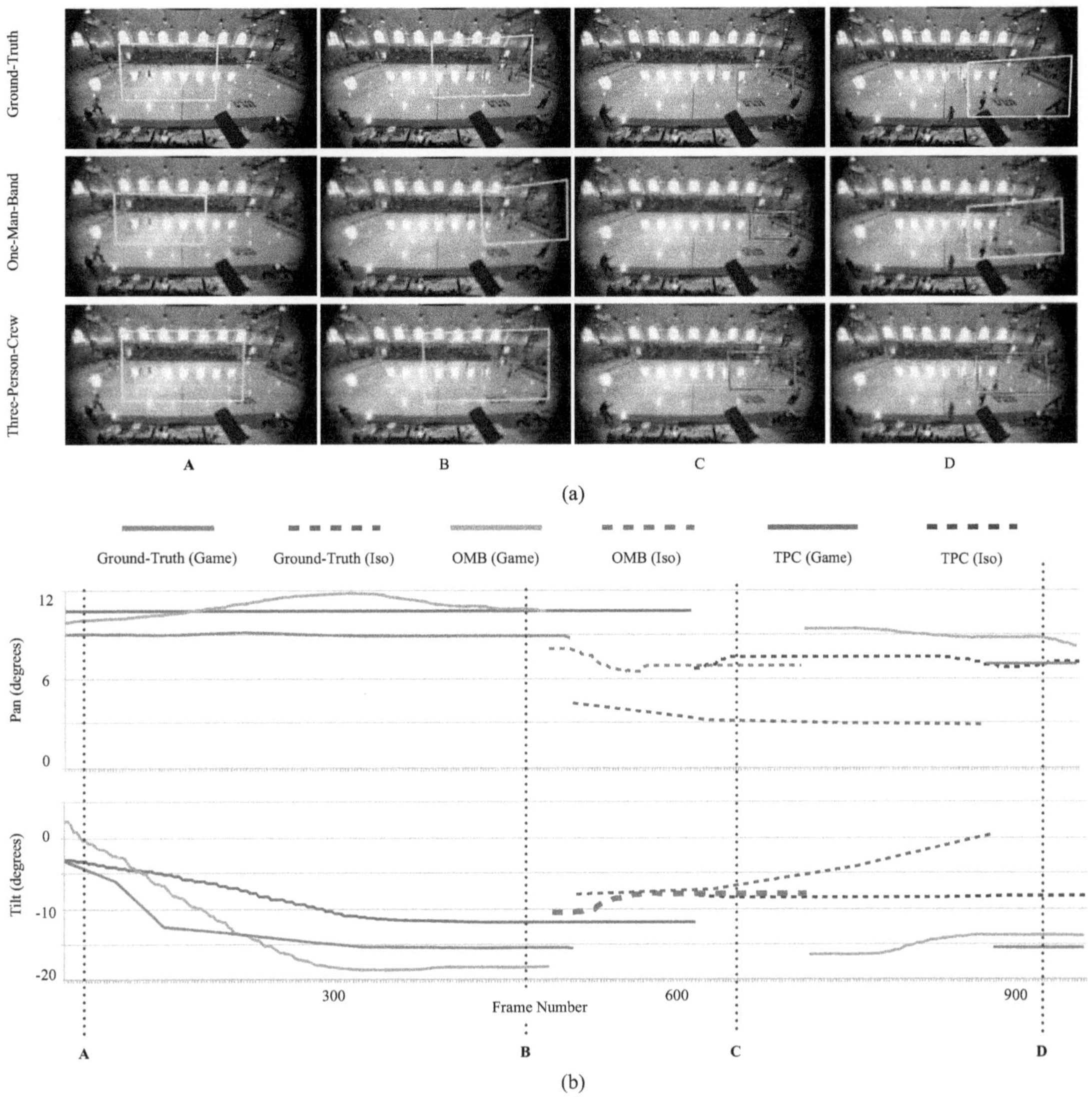

Figure 8: (a) Examples illustrating which camera and positions were selected for the various frames: (Top) ground-truth, (Middle) OMB, and (Bottom) TPC. (b) Curves comparing the camera pan (Top) and tilt (Bottom) angles for the ground-truth (blue), OMB (green), and TPC (red) results. The bold lines refer to the game-camera and the dotted refers to the iso-camera. The line going through the curves correspond to the example frames (A-D).

Symposium on Interactive 3D Graphics, pages 139–144. ACM, 1995.

[6] M. Gleicher and A. Witkin. Through-the-Lens Camera Control. In *SIGGRAPH*, volume 26, pages 331–340, 1992.

[7] R. Hartley and A. Zisserman. *Multiple View Geometry in Computer Vision*. Cambridge University Press, Cambridge, United Kingdom, 2002.

[8] H. Kuzuoka, T. Kosuge, and M. Tanaka. Gesturecam: A video communication system for sympathetic remote collaboration. In *Proceedings of the 1994 ACM Conference on Computer Supported Cooperative Work*, CSCW '94, pages 35–43. ACM, 1994.

[9] Q. Liu, D. Kimber, J. Foote, L. Wilcox, and J. Boreczky. Flyspec: a multi-user video camera system with hybrid human and automatic control. In *Proceedings of the tenth ACM international conference on Multimedia*, pages 484–492, 2002.

[10] J. H. Matthews. Interactive Television System and Method for Viewer Control of Multiple Camera Viewpoints in Broadcast Programming, 02 1997.

[11] J. Owens. *Television Sports Production*. Focal Press, 2007.

[12] E. Pietriga, O. Bau, and C. Appert. Representation-independent in-place magnification with sigma lenses. *IEEE Transactions on Visualization and Computer Graphics*, 16(03):455–467, 2009.

[13] G. Pingali, Y. Jean, and I. Carlbom. Real time tracking for enhanced tennis broadcasts. In *Computer Vision and Pattern Recognition, 1998. Proceedings. 1998 IEEE Computer Society Conference on*, pages 260–265, 1998.

[14] Y. Rui, A. Gupta, and J. J. Cadiz. Viewing Meetings Captured by an Omni-directional Camera. In *Proceedings of the SIGCHI Conference on Human Factors in Computing Systems*, pages 450–457, 2001.

[15] M. Sarkar and M. H. Brown. Graphical Fisheye Views. *Commun. ACM*, 37:73–83, 1994.

[16] K. Singh, C. Grimm, and N. Sudarsanam. The IBar: A Perspective Based Camera Widget. In *Proceedings of the 17th annual ACM symposium on User interface software and technology*, UIST '04, pages 95–98. ACM, 2004.

[17] P. S. Strauss, R. C. Zeleznik, and A. S. Forsberg. Two Pointer Input For 3D Interaction. In *Proceedings of the 1997 Symposium on Interactive 3D Graphics*, pages 115–120, 1997.

[18] M. Tanimoto. Free-viewpoint television. In *Image and Geometry Processing for 3-D Cinematography*, volume 5 of *Geometry and Computing*, pages 53–76. Springer Berlin Heidelberg, 2010.

[19] R. Turner, F. Balaguer, E. Gobbetti, and D. Thalmann. Physically-Based Interactive Camera Motion Control Using 3D Input Devices. In *Scientific Visualization of Physical Phenomena*, pages 135–145, 1991.

[20] R. C. Zeleznik and A. S. Forsberg. UniCam - 2D Gestural Camera Controls for 3D Environments, 1999.

Tele Echo Tube: Beyond Cultural and Imaginable Boundaries

Hiroki Kobayashi
Center for Spatial Information Science[1], The University of Tokyo
kobayashi@csis.u-tokyo.ac.jp

Michitaka Hirose
Cyber Interface Laboratory[2], The University of Tokyo
hirose@cyber.t.u-tokyo.ac.jp

Akio Fujiwara
Graduate School of Agricultural and Life Sciences[3],The University of Tokyo
akio@uf.a.u-tokyo.ac.jp

Kazuhiko Nakamura
Centre for Spatial Information Science[1], The University of Tokyo
k_nakamura@csis.u-tokyo.ac.jp

Kaoru Sezaki
Center for Spatial Information Science[1], The University of Tokyo
sezaki@csis.u-tokyo.ac.jp

Kaoru Saito
Graduate School of Frontier Sciences[4], The University of Tokyo
kaoru@nenv.k.u-tokyo.ac.jp

ABSTRACT
Currently, human-computer interaction (HCI) is primarily focused on human-centric interactions; however, people experience many nonhuman-centric interactions during the course of a day. Interactions with nature, such as experiencing the sounds of birds or trickling water, can imprint the beauty of nature in our memories. In this context, this paper presents an interface of such nonhuman interactions to observe people's reaction to the interactions through an imaginable interaction with a mythological creature. Tele Echo Tube (TET) is a speaking tube interface that acoustically interacts with a deep mountain echo through the slightly vibrating lampshade-like interface. TET allows users to interact with the mountain echo in real time through an augmented echo-sounding experience with the vibration over a satellite data network. This novel interactive system can create an imaginable presence of the mythological creature in the undeveloped natural locations beyond our cultural and imaginable boundaries. The results indicate that users take the reflection of the sound as a cue that triggers the nonlinguistic believability in the form of the mythological metaphor of the mountain echo. This echo-like experience of believable interaction in an augmented reality between a human and nature gave the users an imaginable presence of the mountain echo with a high degree of excitement. This paper describes the development and integration of nonhuman-centric design protocols, requirements, methods, and context evaluation.

Categories and Subject Descriptors
H.5.m. Information interfaces and presentation (e.g., HCI): Miscellaneous.

General Terms
Design, Human Factors.

MM'13, October 21–25, 2013, Barcelona, Spain.

http://dx.doi.org/10.1145/2502081.2502125

Keywords
HCBI (Human-Computer-Biosphere Interaction), Nature Interface, Sustainability, Sustainable Design.

1. INTRODUCTION
Human beings can imagine the mountain echo in a nature environment because our brain has the ability to record and store the creature as a cultural context of a textbook. Since each person's history and experience are different, the imagined presence of a mythological creature differs relative to the size, shape, and type of the cultures, as illustrated in Figure 1. A contemporary approach to observing the presence of "mountain Echo" is to sing out "YO-HOOOOO!" very lively on the mountain site. By listening to the reflection of the sound, we can observe and share the presence of the mythological creature in a cultural way. According to Greek mythology, Echo was the personification of echo.

This study has attempted to understand the processes of nonhuman-centric interaction between users and remote uninhabited environments through the use of information technologies and reveal new knowledge regarding such interactivity by examining the famous mythological phenomenon, "echo-sounding experience." In doing so, this study hopes to discover the cultural cognitive processes of our imagination mechanism. Such a discovery would help us design an interactive system that leverages the boundary of the real and virtual worlds by engaging a cultural cognition to perform a nonhuman-centric interaction with a culturally imaginable creature.

This paper will discuss the design, development, and evaluation of a system to tackle the previously mentioned mythological phenomenon in a contemporary real-world setting. First, on the basis of related studies, the author proposed a new concept for this study and will design a new experimental system based on related studies and methodologies. The method and requirements for developing the experiment system are also described. In addition, the imaginable process of the nonhuman-centric interactions of users is observed in the exhibition setting. Finally,

[1]5-1-5 Kashiwanoha, Kashiwa-Shi, Chiba, 277-8568, JAPAN; +81-4-7136-4291
[2]7-3-1 Hongo, Bunkyo-ku, Tokyo 113-8656, JAPAN; +81-3-5841-6369
[3]1-1-1 Yayoi, Bunkyo-ku, Tokyo 113-8657, JAPAN; +81-3-5841-5004
[4]5-1-5 Kashiwanoha, Kashiwa-Shi, Chiba, 277-8568, JAPAN; +81-4-7136-5874

on the basis of the observation results, the overall findings are discussed, including an explanation of the mythological phenomenon and possible applications of the system. This study is not intended to propose a solution to any one single technological or ecological problem; however, it proposes a new viewpoint of multidisciplinary HCI design and interfaces.

The structure of this paper is as follows. Section 2 details related studies and Section 3 describes the conceptual overview and the requirement of our proposed system. Section 4 describes the system requirement. Section 5 presents the results, and Section 6 discusses the discussion and application in detail. Section 7 summarizes the results, discusses future plans, and offers conclusions.

2. Related Studies

This study is based on the concept of human-computer-biosphere interaction (HCBI) [8], which is illustrated in Figure 2. HCBI is an extension of human-computer interaction (HCI) and human-computer-pet interaction (HCPI) [11]. Computer-supported cooperative work (CSCW) is based on computer-interaction paradigms to support specific activities. For example, we can exchange ideas, thoughts, theories, and messages by encoding them into transferable words, communicating them through computer systems, and then decoding them. However, in our daily lives, we implicitly exchange and share a great deal of additional nonverbal information to maintain our social relationships, such as messages acknowledging the presence and mood of others [6].

2.1 Human-Computer-Pet Interaction

The consideration of implicit (background) information opens up new possibilities for interaction through nonlinguistic, wearable computing devices, and nonverbal remote communication among different species. Wearable computing devices enable us to extend our spatial interactions and develop human-human communication beyond physical distance [16]. HCPI, illustrated in Figure 2, is a type of physical interaction paradigm that proposes the creation of a new form of media embodying symbiosis between humans and pets through Internet-connected computers [11]. "Botanicalls" was developed to provide a new way for plants and people to interact to develop better, longer-lasting relationships that go beyond physical and genetic distance [23]. Thus, computer systems became a medium through which a telepresence can be expressed among different species in the biosphere through nonlinguistic communication that is perceived and understood by individuals, thus violating the rules of linguistic science [20].

2.2 Cultural Interaction

However, no matter how advanced the technologies are, these remain human-centric interactions. We expect others to provide some perceivable feedback in response to our communication before we end an interaction. However, in our daily lives, there are many nonhuman-centric interactions, such as the sounds of singing birds, buzzing insects, swaying leaves, and trickling water in a beautiful forest. These implicitly imprints the beauty of nature in our minds. Recalling the beauty of nature can help us recover a sense of well-being when we are emotionally stressed. The crucial factor here is not the means of conveyance (words or language), but "something" hovering around, or an atmosphere that we cannot exactly identify. This type of interaction is consistent with the teachings of Zen Buddhism. Zen Buddhism originated in China in the 1st century A.D. after exposure to Indian Buddhism and is widely practiced in Japan [19].

Figure 1. "Yamabiko", ECHO in Japanese mythology. Left: "Yamabiko" in a collection of pictures "Hyakkai-Zukan" [18]. Right: The Illustrated Night Parade of A Hundred Demons [21].

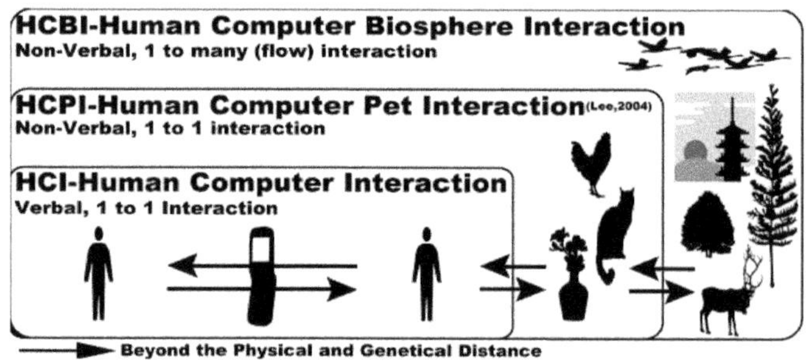

Figure 2. Human-computer-biosphere interaction (HCBI) concept, an extended concept from HCI (Human Computer Interaction) and HCPI (Human Computer Pet Interaction) [8].

2.3 Behavioral Science

The type of nonhuman-centric interaction described in the previous sections is reflected in the semiotic theories of Jakob von Uexküll [22]. Von Uexküll established the theory of Umwelt in Figure 3, from the German word meaning "environment" or "surrounding world." This theory suggests that all animals, from the simplest to the most complex, fit into their unique worlds with equal completeness. A simple world corresponds to a simple animal, and a well-articulated world corresponds to a complex one. Jakob von Uexküll stated that relations between subject and object are the "biological foundations that lie at the very epicenter of the study of both communication and signification in the human (and nonhuman) animal" [22].

2.4 Human-Computer-Biosphere Interaction

Kobayashi proposed that, much like elements of the concept of augmented reality, HCBI [8] can be extended to philosophical interactions from countable objects, such as pets and plants in space, to their "surrounding world," which is an uncountable, complex, nonlinguistic "something" that exists beyond our imagination. In the HCBI framework, the sounds of a forest or other natural environments are all information cues that help us to observe reality and build knowledge of reality. Thus, through HCBI, we can experience the marvel of all living beings and their relationships, including their interactions with elements of their reality. With HCBI, we can begin to interact with commonly inaccessible ecological systems.

2.5 Previous Studies

Development in three stages has been ongoing since year 1997. The first development stage was to build a networked Bio-acoustic Streaming and Recording System in the northern part of Iriomote Island (24°20'N, 123°55'E) in the southern Ryukyu Islands, Japan. The real-time streaming system has been upgraded several times over the years to improve long-term stability under unmanned operating conditions. This project received a Jury Recommended award at the Japan Media Arts Festival in 2002. Since 1997, real-time environmental sounds from Iriomote Island's subtropical forests have been monitored by networked microphones and transmitted via the website as "Live Sound from Iriomote Island" 24 hours a day, 365 days a year [8]. The technology behind this networked bio-acoustic streaming and recording system is also used for "AQUASCAPE: the stethoscope for the Earth's waters" through which Internet users are able to listen to sounds in real time, for example: the moving water of a pond in Tokyo, living creatures in a Japanese garden in Kyoto, and a street in Mumbai City, India [8].

The second development stage was in the first version of TET (island version) and was also installed in the northern part of Iriomote Island (24°20'N, 123°55'E) in the southern Ryukyu Islands, Japan. Based on the result of the first version the author developed a Wearable Forest system by which users are able to feel a sense of belonging to a subtropical forest on Iriomote Island, Japan from Los Angeles, USA, Vancouver, Canada and Mexico City[8], Mexico over 10,000 km distance away in real time.

The authors propose TET (mountain version), which extends the subject of interaction from countable objects, pets, and plants to their surrounding environment, which is an uncountable, complex, nonlinguistic, "something" surroundings, much like mythological elements in the Japanese case. This system, TET (mountain version), presents the possibility of more spatial interaction: remote interaction with a mountain echo located 1,200 m above sea level through a communication satellite at 36,000 km above sea level as a global-scale HCI with a cultural empasis.

2.6 Concept Overview

Tele Echo Tube (TET), shown in Figure 4, is a speaking tube that acoustically interacts with a deep mountain echo through the slightly vibrating lampshade-like interface. It is based on the previously mentioned HCBI concept [8], which is an extension of human-computer interaction (HCI) and human-computer-pet interaction (HCPI) [11]. TET allows users to interact with the mountain echo in real time through an augmented echo-sounding experience with the vibration over the satellite network, experiencing a distant mountain forest soundscape in immersive and ambient ways even in the midst of a modern city as shown in Figure 4.

2.7 Mountain Echo

Natural communities contain a spectrum of life forms that interact with each other. Many scientists agree with the judgment that the essence of ecology is the study of interactions among species in their native habitat [17]. In Japanese mythology, it was believed that there are many Yokai (literally demon, spirit, or monster. ECHO, mountain nymph in Greek mythology) living with other animals in the mountain forest environment. Japanese folklorists and historians mention Yokai as "supernatural or

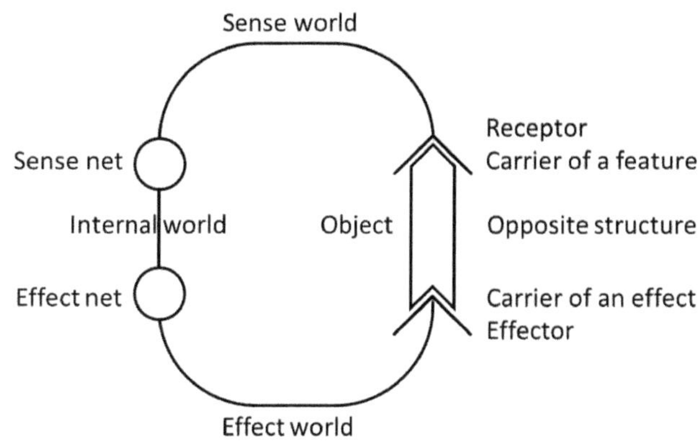

Figure 3. Functional cycle from von Uexküll's Umwelt theory [22].

Figure 4. TET (Island Version) remote system placed in an uninhabited subtropical forest on Iriomote Island, Japan (24°41'90.57"N,123°78'72.47"E)[7].
(note: the chair is not a part of this art work)

unaccountable phenomena to their informants" because Yokai generally have a sort of spiritual or supernatural power. In 1737, Sawaki Suushi, a Japanese artist in Edo Period Japanese, published a picture of a monster called "Yamabiko" in a collection of pictures, "Hyakkai-Zukan" [18], as shown in Figure 1. This is a well-known Yokai who creates a mountain echo. Based on this cultural and imaginable metaphor, TET creates cultural collaboration with "Yamabiko" and provides an echo-sounding experience for users in an imaginable way. TET aims to increase the mythological awareness in a traditional Japanese way through human-computer interaction .

2.8 System Requirement

The study was conducted in an uninhabited mountain forest at Chichibu University Forest, The University of Tokyo in Japan (35°56'17.28"N, 138°48'11.04"E, 150 km from Tokyo). Through ubiquitous technologies, it is generally considered that a typical environmental monitoring near urban areas can be performed effectively. However, in those remote areas, such as the home range of "Yamabiko," the availability of electric power and information infrastructures for monitoring wild animals is either limited or nonexistent. This is primarily because the profitability generated by infrastructure-based services is usually low in areas such as the sanctuary forest where the number of users is small in

Figure 5. Furthermore, in areas where no technological infrastructure is present, observation over a long duration (e.g., over several years) is difficult. Thus, it was necessary to develop methods that make TET happen while using the fewest possible resources. The following system specifications were defined for the development of a long-term observation tool.

1. The equipment must be able to operate in an extremely humid and hot subtropical forest environment.
2. The equipment must be highly stable to facilitate long-term unmanned operation.
3. The equipment must be remotely controllable to facilitate recovery from any unexpected system problems.
4. The equipment must facilitate the reduction of field observations and labor costs [15].

3. SYSTEM DESCRIPTION

TET (mountain version) consists of remote, communication, local, and interaction systems. The subsystem consists of the following four components, Remote System, Communication System Local System and Interaction System.

3.1 Remote System

The remote and local systems perform a remote interaction to create an echo-sounding experience with "Yamabiko" (ECHO, mountain nymph in Greek mythology) in Figure 1 through its live sound pipe through the satellite-networked Internet. The environmental sound and video in the mountain forest have been recorded and monitored by a landscape monitoring system since 1995. In addition, the real-time sound and video archives have been broadcast through an Internet website as "Cyber Forest Project," The University of Tokyo's Cyber Forest website [1], for every day since 2009. The real-time streaming system has been improved several times to achieve long-period stability under unmanned operating conditions. The remote system, shown on the left in Figure 4, is placed in an uninhabited mountain forest at the Cyber Forest Project site in Figures 5, 6, and 7. Networked microphones and speakers were placed to create the echo-sounding experience for 24 hours over 365 days. The weatherproof microphone consists of a nondirectional microphone wrapped in a sheet of thick waterproof sponge and a plastic hard mesh. The joint part of the microphone and an audio cable connecter are shielded by waterproof putty and tape to protect them from outside moisture. The microphone is tied onto a trunk of a tower in Figure 7. An A/D device converts the analog audio signal of the microphone (speaker) to a digital audio signal, and transfers the signal to an audio processing system with extremely low noises.

3.2 Communication System

The digital signal cable can be extended up to 10 kilometers without any digital distortion. Next, the digital audio signal is connected to the audio processing system. This audio signal is digitally processed to enhance its quality by remotely controlled real-time audio processing software. The processed audio signal is sent to the en-recording system, encoded into an MP3 live stream, and recorded as WAVE sound format files. The MP3 live stream is sent to a stream server at the Date Archive System directly through the Internet. The MP3 live stream is played on various MP3-based audio software at different locations all around the world simultaneously. The storage/analysis system stores WAVE

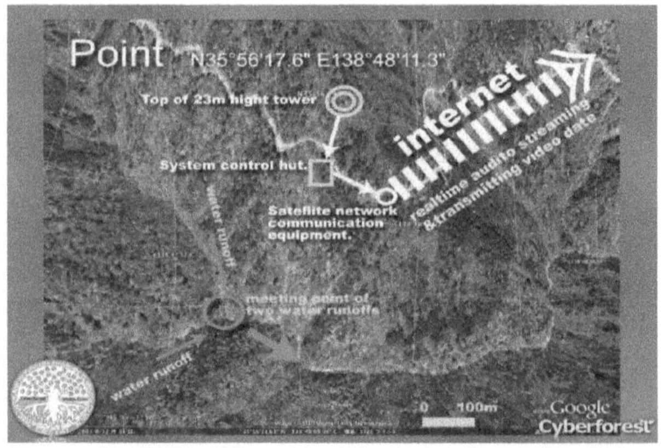

Figure 5. TET (Mountain Version) placed in Cyber Forest project site, located 1,200 m above sea level, The University of Tokyo Forests, Japan (35°56'17.28"N, 138°48'11.04"E).

Figure 6. The home range of "Yamabiko" in Cyber Forest project site.

Figure 7. Audio system, Weatherproof digital camera and solar panels placed in Cyber Forest project site.

Figure 8. Data Communication System: Satellite Internet dish, solar panels, and control house in Cyber Forest project site.

sound format files which are sent from an audio encoding/recording system into its storage system: it is capable of storing audio files which are recorded continuously for several decades. The Data Communication System provides a satellite-based internal computer network in the audio digitizing/streaming/recording system, and also provides Internet access to/from the system. Thus, all systems are remotely controllable through the Internet. Furthermore, a remotely placed monitoring system keeps track of all the system information through SysLog and SNMP software continuously. This management capability allows us to keep monitoring all the system information, from the input level on the microphone to the data traffic delay on the Internet connection over the satellite from the Data Communication System in Figure 8. The system continuously captures and transfers the live soundscape to a local system over the Internet within several seconds.

3.3 Local System

The local speaking tube system consists of networked microphones, speakers with a vibrator, and an echo canceller as described in Figures 9 and 10. An embedded CPU system receives the live soundscape data from the remote mountain via the satellite network, immediately performs echo cancelling on the sound signal, and sends it back to the remote site immediately in Figure 11. TET (mountain version) runs on a full-duplex audio pipe over the Internet and uses an echo-cancelling process for preventing the audio feedback in the loop.

3.4 Interaction System

The songs of small birds, the trickling of a stream, and the sounds of insects moving about in the mountain forest represent the arrival of spring in the mountain area in Figure 6. To interact with "Yamabiko," users can sing out "YO-HOOOOO!" in a very lively from the local speaking tube to the speakers on the mountain on the remote site, as described in Figure 12. The loopback call at the remote host occurs because the playback sound from the speaker is captured and transferred to the user by the remote host with a spontaneous network delay. When the users hear the loopback call, "their voices within the soundscape" from the mountain with the slight vibration from their hands through the interface in Figure 13, they recognize that the initial voices did actually travel through the mountain environment. This echo-sounding loop with the spontaneous network delay, which transfers live sounds bidirectionally from the remote and local sites, creates an echo-sounding effect, and in doing so, gives the user the opportunity to interact with the presence of "a fickle ECHO" on the deep mountain remotely. Those acoustic interactions indicate the nonlinguistic believability in a form of mythological metaphor of the mountain echo.

3.5 Interaction Measurement Design

First, we introduce some notations used in our interaction measurement. In the case of measuring "echo-sounding experience," performance conditions, or in this case, conditions related to transmission, network congestion, effect from temporary blackout and required buffer size in memory stack vary significantly. In situations where multiple units are deployed throughout the Internet from a remote to a local area operated for extended periods, system stability must be carefully controlled.

However, since the careful regulation of numerous units is unfeasible, developing a robust method with commercial products for a long time and continuous operation was considered essential. In this study, the system performance was addressed by measuring

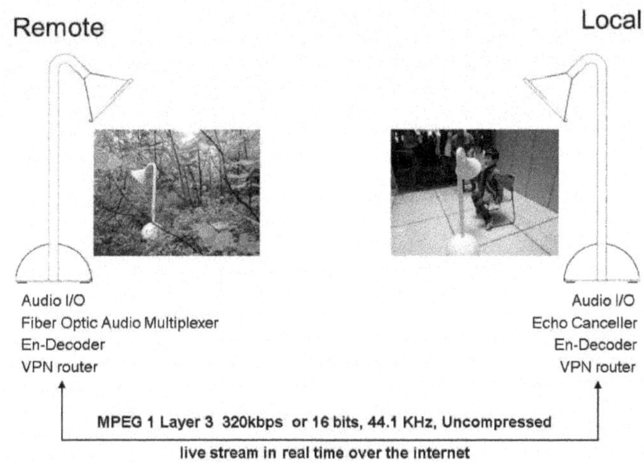

Figure 9. TET (island and mountain version). System diagram of remote and local installation.

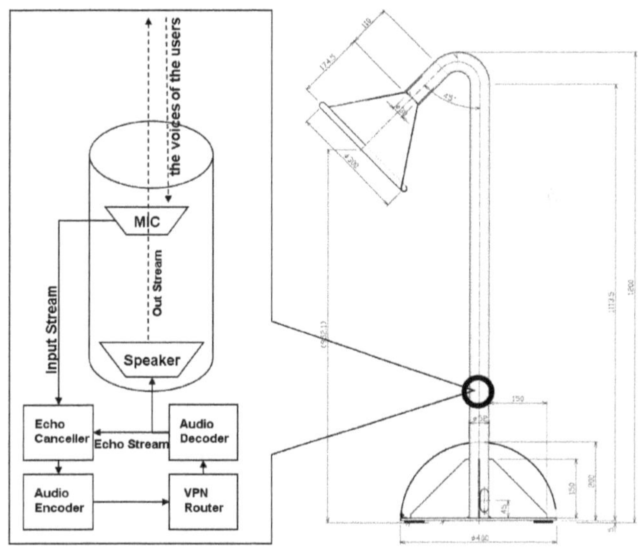

Figure 10. Tube diagram of TET (island and mountain version).

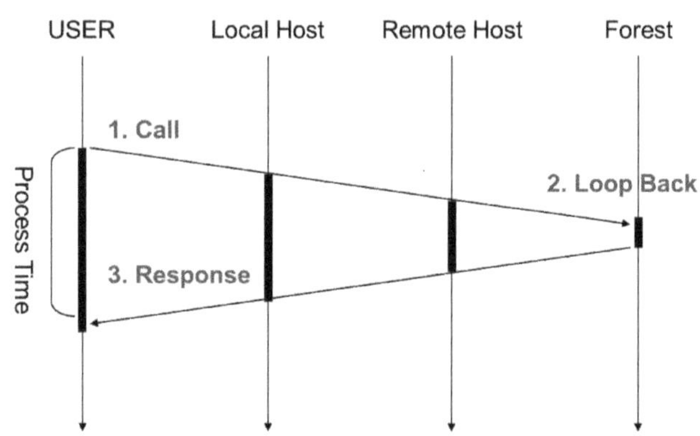

Figure 11. TET (island and mountain version). Diagram of nonverbal interaction between user and echo. This echo-sounding loop with the spontaneous network delay, which transfers live sounds bidirectionally from the remote and local sites, creates an echo-sounding effect.

the cumulative value of the network delay to create the presence of "a fickle ECHO" on the deep mountain remotely. In this study, the system performance was addressed by measuring the cumulative value of the network delay in a user's input using Equation *(1)* below:

$$T_p = T_c + T_l + T_r \qquad (1)$$

On the Tele Echo System, we have three stages, call, loopback, and response, as shown in Figure 11. T_p means the time of processing for a single echo-sounding experience. T_c means the time of calling process time while the user's calls travel from the local to the remote site. T_l means the time of calling process time while the user's call makes a loopback at the remote site in the forest. *True* means the time of responding from the remote to the local site. However, unlike the VoIP application, the MP3 live stream system is designed to transmit live stream data over a robust network with a large-size memory buffer. In addition, a special tuning on the TCP/IP stack to avoid network clipping is essential. Also, we used a commercial off-the-shelf product that can reduce operating cost to demonstrate the validity and usefulness of the time system.

3.6 System Configuration

System conditions fluctuate processing time T_p. Subjects were located in an isolated space. Stood or seated in front of the installation, they were faced by the installation in Figures 15 and 16. One speaker and microphone were placed inside the tube as in Figure 10, located 30 cm from the bottom. A single computer provided recording, communicating and processing with CUI-based operation. The setup comprised a Linux PC with 48 Kbps audio interface (EDIROL UA-25). Custom software was written in C++ using the Speex 1.3 set of open-source audio processing library which interfaced to our previously developed real-time sound streaming system from Iriomote island [8] and the Cyber Forest project site. The whole system was confirmed to operate for more than several years. Absolute 0 ms delay through the system was obtained via an analog bypass around the audio interface. Each trial with reaction from users was recorded as a movie. One of us (H.K.) listened to and watched all recorded digital files and calculated the processing time and observed the facial reactions of all users. To measure the interaction, we used a stopwatch to measure the amount of time elapsed from calling time to response time.

3.7 Trials

The Tele Echo Tube (island version) was selected to be included in the Artech Exhibition of International Conference on ASIAGRAPH 2008 at the National Museum of Emerging Science and Innovation, Tokyo, Japan. The Tele Echo Tube (mountain version) was selected to be included in the BASAL Exhibition, 2010, at the Museo Universitario de Arte Contemporáneo, Mexico. The processing time T_p. was varied over time and locations. Each subject performed each trial once only. Calling by singing out "YO-HOOOOO!" in each trial was randomly initiated by the subject. The subjects were ordered to wait for the reaction from the echo until the arrival of the response. Overall, one session took about one minute to complete. Subjected actions in the movie were analyzed visually and manually to measure

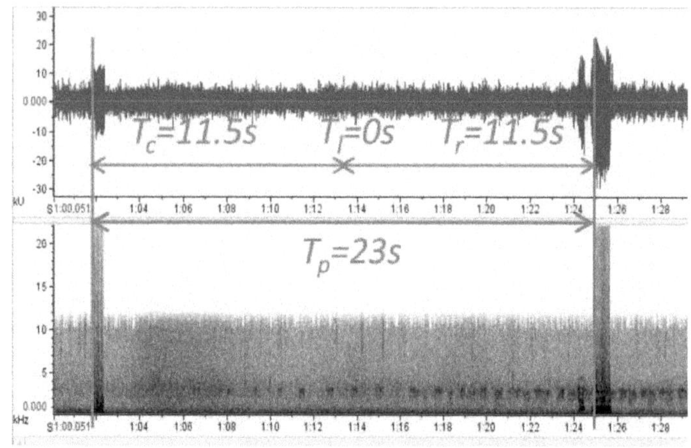

Figure 12. Visualization of echo-sounding interaction on ampitude vs time period (top) frequency vs time period (bottom).

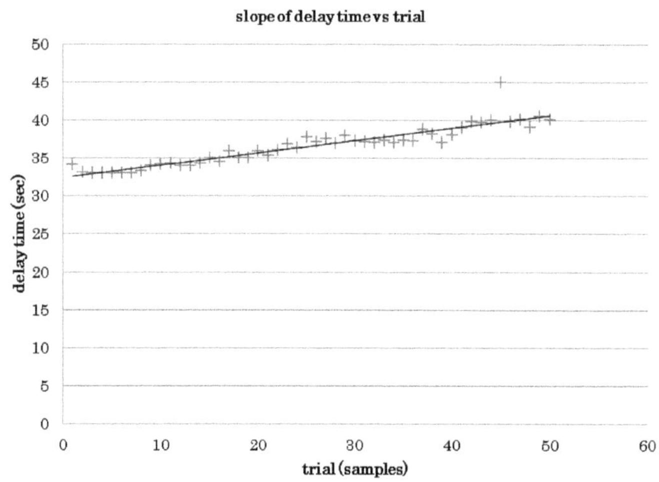

Figure 13. Change in time of echo-sounding interaction with a fickle ECHO over the robust network. Starting processing time T_p = 33 sec, ending processing time T_p = 40.1 sec.

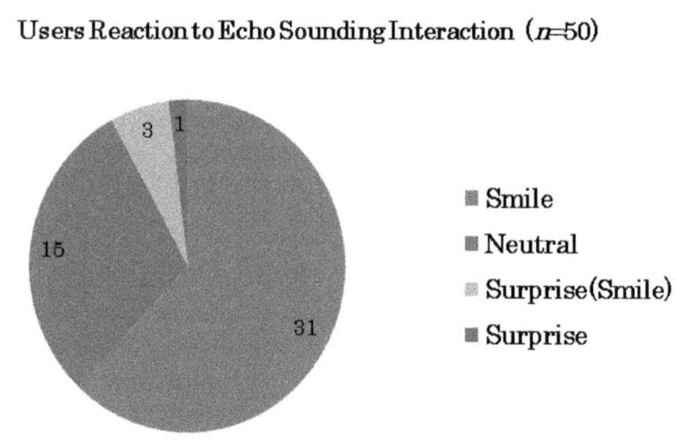

Figure 14. Users reaction to echo-sounding interaction in TET (island version) Artech Exhibition of International Conference on ASIAGRAPH 2008 at the National Museum of Emerging Science and Innovation, Tokyo, Japan.

performance time Tp as a summation of calling time T_c, loopback time T_l, *and* response time T_r per trial.

4. Analysis

The audience (n=50) was used as the subject of this experiment. The subject was placed and stood in front of the installation and change in the echo sounding was observed as a time in equation ***(1)***. Figure 13 shows that the estimated time of echo sounding was measured by the stopwatch when the subjects experienced and performed the integration. The figure result suggests that a change of time in echo sounding was detected in time and the cumulation of the changes caused by the network delay indicated the spontaneousness of the network delay. A comparison of the initial trial (T_p*=33sec*) and the last trial when the trial was ended (T_p*=40sec*) clearly reveals that the fickleness of the mountain echo had changed. Figure 14 shows a change in facial expression during the experiment. Thirty-one individuals out of 50 changed to a smile. One individual out of 50 returned a visible surprise on their face. Three individuals out of 50 returned visible surprise to smile on their faces. Fifteen individuals out of 50 returned a neutral expression on their faces.

5. Discussions

The results from this study can play an important role in the field of HCI by creating a new kind of interaction among humans, computers, and the biosphere beyond cultural and imaginable boundaries. There are a variety of applications that can be advanced through research by applying this information.

5.1 Technical Problems

Maintaining the system with high-quality streaming sound in operation for 24 hours over 365 days requires advanced computer engineering knowledge. The quality of the digital signal processed by the real-time audio processing software decreases as the recording systeuns for a longer period. In most of the cases, the processed signal contains many "clipping" sounds. The "clipping" sounds are caused by slowing down the computation power of a CPU (Central Processing Unit) which is located on the motherboard of the recording system.

Generally, the computational power being slowed down is caused by heat and memory leak. The heat is generated by the recording system itself as the recording system runs in an extremely high moisture and temperature environment in the subtropical forest. The memory leak, losing necessary memory blocks for a computational process, occurs on the recording system because the recording system runs for 24 hours over 365 days. Therefore, to solve the heat and memory leak problems, two identical recording systems are necessary which are placed to run separately for 12-hour shifts each. While the first system is in operation, the second system is not in operation. By following this time shift system, the CPU temperature of the two identical systems is decreased and the memory leak problem is solved.

However, this hardware switching mechanism is an extremely difficult function to run under unmanned conditions. To be exact, a detection of a system shutting-down process on one system followed by a system starting-up process on the other system every 12 hours is not easily detected under unmanned conditions. Because this system shutting-down process is not only caused by this 12-hour shift control software but could also be caused by a long-time power cut, software error could occur as well as other hardware problems. Therefore, to operate all the systems for a long period under unmanned conditions, an intelligent

Figure 15. TET (island version). The remote system is placed in an uninhabited subtropical forest on Iriomote Island, Japan (24°41'90.57"N,123°78'72.47"E) [7].
(note: the chair is not a part of this artwork).

Figure 16. TET (mountain version), selected work for the BASAL Exhibition, Museo Universitario de Arte Contemporáneo (MUAC), Mexico, (2010) [10].

autonomous control system is needed. All the systems were improved several times in the last nine years and finally the stability of the systems was gained. The latest software of all the systems has been operating under the unmanned conditions for the last two years, more than 17,520 hours without a single error.

5.2 Connection to the Concept of Umwelt

This echo-like experience of believable interaction in an augmented reality between a human and the mountain echo gave the users the imaginable presence of "Yamabiko" with a high degree of excitement in the country and overseas in Figure 13, in comparison to the previous work. The type of nonhuman-centric interaction described in this paper is reflected in the semiotic theories of Jakob von Uexküll [22]. Von Uexküll established the concept of Umwelt, from the German word meaning "environment" or "surrounding world," and suggested that all animals, from the simplest to the most complex, fit into their unique worlds with equal completeness. "Singing voice" corresponds to a single animal and a simple world; "A sign of presence" corresponds to a complex, well-articulated human world. Thus, a user's reaction to the sounds can be explained by the Umwelt theory. When users listen to live sounds from the invisible world through the Internet, they tend to pay attention to both a simple singing voice and the complex presence in Figure 17, even though no human exists in the forest.

5.3 Beyond Cultural and Imaginable Boundaries

A comparable type of complex presence existed in Japanese culture. For cultural and mythological reasons, in ancient times, interactions between nature and human societies were more balanced than the interactions that characterize modern society. Before human beings became capable of dramatically altering natural landscapes, humanity and nature were physically separated but spiritually and emotionally connected. Although Japanese farmers interacted with nature in their local environment, the mountainous wilderness areas of Japan were considered to be the domain of gods and mythological creatures. Japanese farmers prayed to the gods during seasonal festivals for favorable weather conditions to ensure successful crop production, and the general population was taught to respect the gods that resided in and protected the mountains. Consequently, wild animals and their habitats in the mountains were left undisturbed for the most part, and Japanese culture was characterized by respectful and benevolent interaction between nature and humanity.

5.4 Human-Computer-Biosphere Interaction

The Wearable Forest [9] in Figure 18, which is based on the HCBI hypothesis, uses the results of this study. The Wearable Forest is a garment that bioacoustically interacts with wildlife in a distant forest through a network of remote-controlled speakers and microphones. It is intended to emulate the unique bioacoustic beauty of nature by allowing users to experience a distant forest soundscape. This interaction between humans and nature can occur with minimal environmental impact. The Wearable Forest received first place in a juried selection process for the 12th IEEE International Symposium on Wearable Computers, 2008. To interact with wildlife, users can touch textile sensors that transfer the user-selected, prerecorded sounds of wildlife from the garment to the speakers in the forest. The bioacoustic loop, which transfers live sounds bidirectionally from the remote and local sites, gives the user the opportunity to interact with wildlife. For example, in a relatively quiet period after a brief rain shower in the subtropical

Figure 17. The nymph Echo in Greek mythology, (painting by Alexandre Cabanel, 1887 [5], A Collection of the Metropolitan Museum of Art, NY,USA.).

Figure 18. Wearable Forest clothing system : Beyond human-computer interaction [9].

forest, users in an urban location can play back the croaking of frogs through the remote speaker; in response, actual frogs might start croaking. If an appropriate sound is played back at an appropriate time, the actual wildlife might respond to the initial call. In this chorus-like experience, intraspecies communication in mixed reality between the user and the frogs could then possibly give the users a sense of belonging to nature in an experience similar to the peak experience in music therapy, which is triggered by choral singing [12].

The Wearable Forest system was exhibited and evaluated over five days during ACM SIGGRAPH 2008 in Los Angeles, USA, and over six days during ACM Multimedia 2008 in Science World British Colombia in Vancouver, Canada. During the first exhibition, the "out of synchronization" problem was confirmed [9]. The visitors were unable to identify a specific sound from other sounds on the audio live feed from the remote forest. This resulted in users' inability to recognize the potential auditory response from the wildlife, even if the response had occurred to the user in the distant forest. Therefore, even if no response is transferred from the wildlife after the loopback call of the initial call, other acoustical activities in the forest can be perceived as believable responses, such as the sounds of birdsong, buzzing insects, gently swaying leaves, and a tree falling. Those sounds indicate the nonlinguistic telepresence of entities in the forest. From a psychological aspect, participants who experienced the Wearable Forest in the ACM Multimedia 2008 art exhibition described "a sense of oneness" with the remote forest. They rated the episode on a number of scales indicating characteristics of transcendence [27], such as sense of union and timelessness. The result indicates that the Wearable Forest HCBI interface is able to create a sense of oneness between human beings and wildlife beyond physical and genetic distance. This type of nonhuman-centric interaction is consistent with the results reported in this paper.

5.5 Animal-Computer Interaction

The author and his associates initially introduced the concept of HCBI at HCI venues focused on environmental sustainability from 2009 [8] [7] [9] [10]. The theory, method, and evaluation of human and wildlife interaction were not discussed in detail because the research was not sufficiently well developed. However, the future direction of HCBI has been suggested by several researchers. In 2010, DiSalvo et al. [2] stated that HCBI points out the inherent contradiction in attempting to use technology to create more intimate connections with nature and Pereira et al. cited HCBI as an example of sustainable computing [14]. Giannachi [4] stated that HCBI clothing, for example the Wearable Forest system [9], facilitates the creation of a human-computer environment that enables new forms of communication. Mancini explored animal-computer interaction that aims to foster the relationship between humans and animals by enabling communication and promoting understanding between them and emphasized that the study of interactions between animals and computing technology has never entered the mainstream of computer science [13]. Mancini also organized the ACM CHI 2012 and hosted a Special Interest Group on Animal-Computing Interaction at CHI 2012 conference. The missing factors that would facilitate more robust studies of interactions between animals and computing technology are not knowledge or technologies. The missing factor is an interface that can facilitate human interaction with remote animals and the environment in a manner similar to the interactions with pets and their surrounding environment at home.

Figure 19. Scarecrows' gathering, near Lausanne, Switzerland (Rastplatz Bavois). This photo was taken by User:Gerbil from de.Wikipedia in July 2006 [3].

Before human beings became capable of levelling mountains with heavy construction vehicles, farmers prayed to gods in seasonal festivals with the tools in Figure 19 or the weather conditions needed to ensure successful crop production, and the general population was taught to respect the gods that resided in and protected the mountains in Figures 1 and 17. The sounds of singing birds, buzzing insects, swaying leaves, and trickling water in a mountain forest implicitly imprint the presence of nature in our cultural way. When we are away from the mountains, recalling the memory of a mountain takes us back to the same place. The crucial factor here is not the means of conveyance (words or language), but the "something" that hovers around; an atmosphere that we cannot identify exactly but that lasts beyond cultural and imaginable boundaries with information technology.

6. Conclusions

Recent technological and information advancements, including satellite imaging, have been unable to confirm the presence of mythological creatures in undeveloped natural locations, and very few humans now believe in the existence of the creatures that control the weather or other farming conditions. However, because we no longer embrace the presence of such cultural and imaginable metaphors in our daily lives, especially in city life, there has been little outcry at the severe materialism brought about by the globalization process. Tele Echo Tube (TET) aims to increase the mythological awareness in the midst of a modern city beyond our cultural and imaginable boundaries. It is a speaking tube installation that acoustically interacts with a deep mountain ECHO through a networked remote-controlled speaker and microphone. It allows users to interact with the ECHO in a sanctuary forest in real time through an augmented echo-sounding experience. In doing so, this novel interactive system can create an imaginable presence of the mythological creature in undeveloped natural locations.

7. ACKNOWLEDGMENTS

We would like to thank Mr. Nishimura, Mr. Kawasaki, Mrs. Nishimura, Mr. Murata, Mrs. Fujita, Mrs. Takaya, Dr. Kihara, Dr. Watanabe, Mr. Matsumoto, Mrs. Matsumoto, Dr. Izawa, Dr.

Nakanishi, Dr. Rokugawa, Dr. Matsushima, Dr. Kuramitsu, Mr. Yamane, Dr. Murayama, Dr. Takemura, Dr. Toyama, Dr. Tagawa, Dr. Abe and Dr. Hiyama for their support in preparing this research. I also appreciate the kindness of many friends who contributed to this research: Mr. Takagi, Mr. Suzuki, Mr. Kamiya, Mr. Hamatsu, and Mr. Arakawa in particular.

This research is supported by SoundExplorer participants, SoundBum participants, NTT-WEST Inc. Okinawa branch, IMS.JP Co. Ltd, the International Academic Research Grant Program of the University of Tokyo, and the Cyber Forest Project Research Group.

8. REFERENCES

[1] Akio, F. 2004. Concept Proposal and Evaluation of CyberForest: Multimedia Forestry Information System, The University of Tokyo., Tokyo, Japan.

[2] DiSalvo, C., Sengers, P., and Brynjarsdottir, H. 2010. Mapping the landscape of sustainable HCI. In *Proceedings of the SIGCHI Conference on Human Factors in Computing Systems* (Atlanta, Georgia, USA, 2010), ACM, 1753625, 1975-1984. DOI= http://dx.doi.org/10.1145/1753326.1753625.

[3] Gerbil 2006. Scarecrows' gathering, near Lausanne, Switzerland (Rastplatz Bavois). In *Category:Scarecrows* wikimedia.

[4] Giannachi, G., Kaye, N., and Shanks, M. 2012. *Archaeologies of Presence : Art, Performance and the Persistence of Being.* Routledge, London; New York.

[5] Hilaire, M., Cabanel, A., Amic, S., and Muse Fabre. 2010. *Alexandre Cabanel,1823-1889 : La Tradition du Beau.* Somogy Editions D'Art, Muse Fabre, Paris.

[6] Itoh, Y., Miyajima, A., and Watanabe, T. 2002. 'TSUNAGARI' communication: fostering a feeling of connection between family members. In *Proceedings of the CHI '02 Extended Abstracts on Human Factors in Computing Systems* (Minneapolis, Minnesota, USA, 2002), ACM, 506609, 810-811. DOI= http://dx.doi.org/10.1145/506443.506609.

[7] Kobayashi, H., Ito, R., and Hirose, M. 2010. Tele Echo Tube - augmented speaking tube for echo sounding experience in nature. In *9th International Conference on World Forum on Acoustic Ecology 2010*, Koli, Finland.

[8] Kobayashi, H., Ueoka, R., and Hirose, M. 2009. Human computer biosphere interaction: towards a sustainable society. In *Proceedings of the CHI '09 Extended Abstracts on Human Factors in Computing Systems* (Boston, MA, USA, 2009), ACM, New York, USA, 2509-2518. DOI= http://dx.doi.org/10.1145/1520340.1520355.

[9] Kobayashi H., Ueoka, R., and Hirose, M. 2009. Wearable forest clothing system: beyond human-computer interaction. In *Proceedings of the ACM SIGGRAPH 2009 Art Gallery* (New Orleans, Louisiana, 2009), ACM, New York, NY, 1-7. DOI= http://dx.doi.org/10.1145/1667265.1667267.

[10] Kobayashi, H.H. 2013. Tele Echo Tube. *Leonardo, 46,* 485-486. DOI= http://dx.doi.org/10.1162/LEON_a_00647.

[11] Lee, P., Cheok, D., James, S., Debra, L., Jie, W., Chuang, W., and Farbiz, F. 2006. A mobile pet wearable computer and mixed reality system for human poultry interaction through the Internet. *Pers Ubiquit Comput. 10*, 5, 301-317. DOI= http://dx.doi.org/10.1007/s00779-005-0051-6.

[12] Lowis, M.J. 2002. Music as a trigger for peak experiences among a college staff population. *Creativity Res J. 14*, 3-4, 351-359. DOI= http://dx.doi.org/Doi 10.1207/S15326934crj1434_6.

[13] Mancini, C. 2011. Animal-computer interaction: a manifesto. *Interactions, 18*, 4, 69-73. DOI= http://dx.doi.org/10.1145/1978822.1978836.

[14] Pereira, R., Lima, M., and Baranauska, M.C.C. 2010. Sustainability as a value in technology design. In *Proceedings of the First Interdisciplinary Workshop on Communication for Sustainable Communities* (São Carlos, São Paulo, Brazil2010), ACM, 1951495, 1-7. DOI= http://dx.doi.org/10.1145/1951493.1951495.

[15] Przeszlowska, A., Trlica, M.J., and Weltz, M.A. 2006. Near-ground remote sensing of green area index on the shortgrass prairie. *Rangeland Ecol Manag. 59*, 4 (Jul), 422-430

[16] Seymour, S. 2009. *Fashionable Technology : The Intersection of Design, Fashion, Science, and Technology*. Springer, Wien; New York.

[17] Smith, R.H. 1986. Ecology - individuals, populations and communities - Begon,M., Harper,J.L., Townsend., Eds. C.R. *Nature, 319*, 6056 (Feb 27), 809-809. DOI= http://dx.doi.org/Doi 10.1038/319809b0.

[18] Suushi, S. 1737. Hyakkai-Zukan: The illustrated volume of a hundred demons. paint on parchment scrolls, Fukuoka City Museum, Japan.

[19] Suzuki, D.T. 1959. *Zen and Japanese Culture*. Pantheon Books, New York.

[20] Thacker, E. 2001. The robot in the garden: Telerobotics and telepistemology in the age of the Internet. *Leonardo, 34*, 2, 162-163. DOI= http://dx.doi.org/DOI 10.1162/leon.2001.34.2.162.

[21] Toriyama, S. 2005. *The Illustrated Night Parade of a Hundred Demons*. Kadokawa Shoten Publishing Co., Ltd, Tokyo, Japan.

[22] Vonuexkull, J. 1992. A stroll through the worlds of animals and men - a picture book of invisible worlds. *Semiotica, 89*, 4, 319.

[23] Watanabe, S. and Kobayashi, H. 2007. Sound recording of vocal activity of animals inhabiting subtropical forest on Iriomote Island in the southern Ryukyus, Japan. *Advances in Bioacoustics II, 47*, 3.

eHeritage of Shadow Puppetry: Creation and Manipulation

Min Lin*[1], Zhenzhen Hu*[2], Si Liu[1], Meng Wang[2], Richang Hong[2], Shuicheng Yan[1]
[1]ECE Department, National University of Singapore
[2]School of Computer and Information, Hefei University of Technology
{mavenlin, huzhen.ice, eric.mengwang, hongrc.hfut}@gmail.com,
{dcslius, eleyans}@nus.edu.sg

ABSTRACT

To preserve the precious traditional heritage Chinese shadow puppetry, we propose the puppetry eHeritage, including a creator module and a manipulator module. The creator module accepts a frontal view face image and a profile face image of the user as input, and automatically generates the corresponding puppet, which looks like the original person and meanwhile has some typical characteristics of traditional Chinese shadow puppetry. In order to create the puppet, we first extract the central profile curve and warp the reference puppet eye and eyebrow to the shape of the frontal view eye and eyebrow. Then we transfer the puppet texture to the real face area. The manipulator module can accept the script provided by the user as input and automatically generate the motion sequences. Technically, we first learn atomic motions from a set of shadow puppetry videos. A scripting system converts the user's input to atomic motions, and finally synthesizes the animation based on the atomic motion instances. For better visual effects, we propose the sparsity optimization over simplexes formulation to automatically assemble weighted instances of different atomic actions into a smooth shadow puppetry animation sequence. We evaluate the performance of the creator module and the manipulator module sequentially. Extensive experimental results on the creation of puppetry characters and puppetry plays well demonstrate the effectiveness of the proposed system.

Categories and Subject Descriptors

J.5 [**Arts and Humanities**]: Arts, fine and performing

Keywords

Chinese shadow puppetry; face rendering; sparsity optimization over simplex; animation

1. INTRODUCTION

Shadow puppetry has a long history in China, Indonesia, India, Greece, etc. as a form of entertainment for both children and adults, and is also popular in many other countries around the world[1]. We focus on Chinese shadow puppetry in this work. Chinese shadow puppetry, as shown in Figure 1(a), is a traditional artistic form of theater performance with colorful silhouette figures. These figures are produced with puppets made of leather or paper. A traditional Chinese shadow puppet[2] is composed of a head part shown in Figure 1(b) and a body part shown in Figure 1(c). As an ancient form of storytelling, sticks and flat puppets are manipulated behind an illuminated background to create moving pictures [1]. By moving both the puppets and the light source, various effects can be achieved. But in the 21st century, shadow puppetry in China is on a steep and fast decline. Audiences and apprentices are evaporating at an alarming rate. To protect this ancient artistic heritage, China's State Council put Chinese shadow puppetry in the first list of National Intangible Cultural Heritage of China in 2006, and United Nations Educational, Scientific and Cultural Organization (UNESCO) listed the artistic form in Intangible Cultural Heritage in 2011[3].

Nowadays, the preservation of culture heritage attracts growing attentions of the world. Our artistic motivation is to develop a system by applying the latest multimedia technologies to aid preservation, interpretation, and dissemination of this ancient cultural heritage. To attract more people to be interested in shadow puppetry, we design two puppetry modules, including a **creator** module and a **manipulator** module that people all over the world can experience the fun of the puppet creating and performing by themselves.

The input of the creator module is two face images. One of the most important advantages of our creator module is *personalization*. The making process of a puppet includes seven steps which are all complex and ingenious [4]. Our creator module can *automatically* generate anyone's personalized puppet, and the process is almost *immediate*. We pay special attention to keeping the characteristics of the traditional puppet during the automatic creator process. For example, the puppet's face has long narrow eyes, a small mouth and a straight bridge of nose as shown in Figure 1(b). Technically, we extract the central profile curve from the profile face image and warp the reference puppet eye into

*indicates equal contribution

MM'13, October 21–25, 2013, Barcelona, Spain.
Copyright 2013 ACM 978-1-4503-2404-5/13/10 ...$15.00.
http://dx.doi.org/10.1145/2502081.2502104.

[1]http://en.wikipedia.org/wiki/Shadow_puppetry
[2]In this paper, we make puppet and puppetry interchangeable.
[3]http://www.unesco.org/culture/ich/index.php?lg=en&pg=00011&RL=00421
[4]http://www.travelchinaguide.com/intro/focus/shadow-puppetry.htm

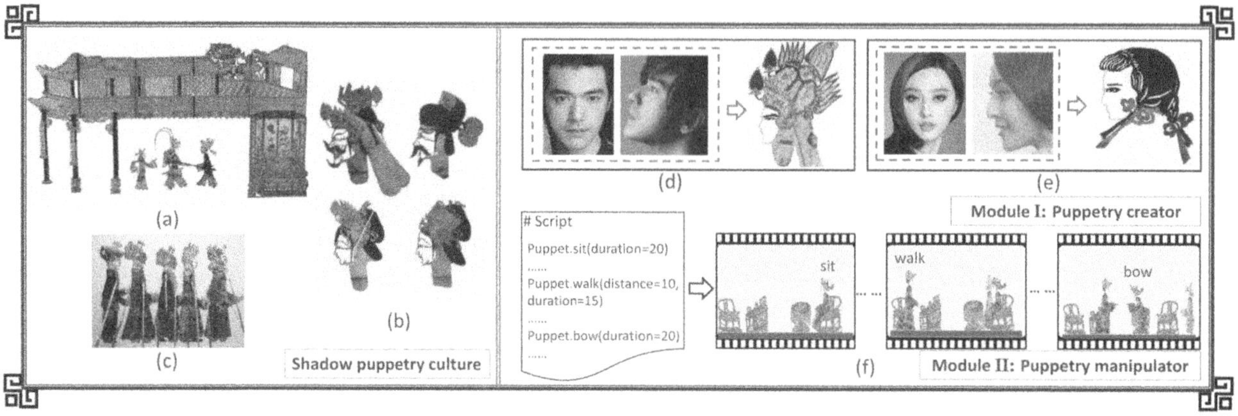

Figure 1: (a) A scene of traiditonal Chinese shadow puppetry. When light penetrates through a translucent sheet of cloth, the audience will see the "shadows", silhouettes in profile. (b) Faces of puppets are characterized by exquisite headdresses and representative facial features, such as thin eyebrows. (c) The puppets are manipulated with sticks through three keypoints, i.e., neck, left hand and right hand. (d) and (e) are two results of our puppetry creator module for male and female respectively. (f) is an exemplar sequence generated based on user-provided scripts by the puppetry manipulator module. All of the figures in this paper are best viewed in original PDF file.

the frontal view eye simultaneously. Then we transfer the puppet texture as the texture of the profile curve. One male and one female puppet generated by our creator module are shown in Figure 1(d) and Figure 1(e).

We also design a manipulator module. For this module, we aim to preserve the performance pattern of Chinese shadow puppetry during the shadow puppetry manipulation process. There are several basic puppet motion patterns (denoted as atomic actions afterwards), such as walk, dance, fight, nod, laugh, etc. Besides, as shown in Figure 1(c), the real puppet is controlled with three sticks which are fixed on the puppet's neck and two hands separately, and the motion pattern of other puppet parts is affected by gravity. Therefore, we need to simulate all the atomic actions in the puppet style. There are some existing research works on shadow puppets focusing on the user's body interaction with the virtual puppet, i.e., the puppet's motion imitates the user's motion [2],[3],[4]. But all of them cannot preserve the puppet's specific motion style. To the contrary, our module can convey this traditional artistic charm completely. Our manipulator module can directly accept text scripts as input and display the specified motions accordingly. The interface is shown in Figure 1(f). For manipulation, we identify atomic motions for the animation and collect instances from a set of shadow puppetry videos. A scripting system converts the user input into atomic motions, and finally synthesizes the animation using the collected instances.

The organization of the rest of this paper is as follows. In Section 2, we provide a review of related work. Section 3 makes an overview of our puppetry module: creator and manipulator. Next, in Section 4 and 5, more detailed step by step introduction of the modules is presented. The experimental results are shown later in Section 6. Finally, we conclude the paper in Section 7.

2. RELATED WORK

Our shadow puppetry system is built on several areas of related work.

2.1 eHeritage

Recently, for the propose of preserving cultural heritage through the application of advanced computing technologies, eHeritage becomes a hot research topic. The related literature is mainly divided into two categories: tangible cultural heritages and intangible cultural heritages. Tangible cultural heritages[5] include buildings and historic places, monuments, artifacts, etc. Anna Paviotti *et al.* [5] dealt with the problem of estimating the lighting field of the multispectral acquisition of frescoes by a variational method. Lior Wolf *et al.* [6] studied the task of finding the joins of the Cairo Genizah which is a precious collection of mainly Jewish texts. Tao Luo *et al.* [7] presented a multi-scale framework to generate 3D line drawing for archaeological illustration. Intangible culture heritage[6] includes traditional festivals, oral traditions, oral epics, customs, ways of life, traditional crafts, etc. Markus Seidl *et al.* [8] proposed a detection of gradual transitions in historic material. Anupama Mallik *et al.* [9] studied on the preservation of Indian classical dance. The shadow puppetry belongs to intangible cultural heritages.

2.2 Face Rendering

Digital image processing provides a solid foundation for building artistic rendering algorithms. All image-based artistic rendering approaches utilize image processing operations in some forms to extract information or synthesize results [10]. Non-photorealistic rendering focuses on enabling a wide variety of expressive styles of digital arts. Among these arts, cartoon and paper cutting are the most related to our work.

Cartoon: A cartoon is a form of two-dimensional illustrated visual art with a typically non-realistic or semi-realistic drawing or painting. CharToon system [11] provides special skeleton-driven components, an extensive set of building blocks to design faces and the support to reuse components and pieces of animations. Chen *et al.* [12] explored a Pictoon system that allows users to create a personalized cartoon and animation from an input face image based on sketch generation and cartoon stroke rendering.

Paper Cutting: Artistic paper cutting is also a traditional and popular Chinese decorative art which, usually

[5]http://www.unesco.org/new/en/cairo/culture/tangible-cultural-heritage/
[6]http://www.unesco.org/new/en/cairo/culture/intangible-cultural-heritage/

in a very concise two-tone form, has its unique beauty of expressive abstraction. Xu *et al.* [13] generated arrangements of shapes via a multilayer thresholding operation to compose digital paper cutting designs. M. Meng *et al.* [14] rendered paper cutting images from human portraits. They localized facial components and used pre-collected representative paper cutting templates. Then they obtained a synthesized paper cutting image by matching templates with the bottom-up proposals.

Our work differs from cartoon and paper cutting in that we only focus on the face rendering of shadow puppetry, which has its unique characteristics. Thus, very tailored image processing techniques are required.

2.3 Puppetry Animation

Developing an interactive and user-friendly interface for people of all skill levels, to create animation is a long-standing problem in computer graphics. Recently, a few works have been conducted on digital puppetry. As a visualization tool for traditional cinematic animation, digital puppetry transforms the movements of a performer to the actions of an animated character to provide live performance such as [15].

Shadow puppets are also used to produce animated films, but producing an animated film with shadow puppets, frame by frame, is laborious and time-consuming. The solution of animation performed by two-dimensional puppets appears only recently. Hsu *et al.* [16] introduced a motion planning technique which automatically generates the animation of 2D puppets. Barnes *et al.* [17] created a video-based animation interface. Users first create a cast of physical puppets and move these puppets to tell a story. They tracked the motions and rendered an animate video. Tan *et al.* [18] presented a method for interactive animation of 2D shadow play puppets by real-time visual simulating using texture mapping, blending techniques, and lighting and blurring effects. Kim *et al.* [19] controlled 3D avatars to create user-designed peculiar motions of avatars in real-time using general interfaces. ShadowStory [20] was a project created by Fei *et al.* for digital storytelling inspired by traditional Chinese shadow puppetry. The system allows children to design their own puppets and animate them with a tablet PC. Pan *et al.* [21] presented a 2D shape deformation of the triangulated cartoon which is driven by its skeleton and the animation can be obtained by retargeting the skeleton joints to the shape.

There are some websites where users can entertain with the puppetry, such as Puppet Parade[7], an interactive puppetry installation that animates puppets by tracking the arms of the puppeteers, or We Be Monsters[8], a collaborative puppet art installation that tracks multiple skeletons to animate a puppet. Although shadow puppetry is not a focus on these websites, the body motion is used to control the puppets. All these puppetry methods do not very accurately consider the unique motion style of shadow puppetry.

With the development and increasing popularity of Microsoft Kinect Camera, many researchers begin to explore how to achieve human-puppetry interaction via Kinect. Robert Held *et al.* [22] presented a 3D puppetry system that allows users to quickly create 3D animations by performing the motions with their own familiar, rigid toys, props, and puppets. During a performance, the puppeteer physically manipulates these puppets in front of a Kinect depth sensor. Leite *et al.* [23] presented an anim-actor technique. Anim-actor is a real-time interactive puppets control system using low-cost motion capture based on body movements of non-expert artists. Zhang *et al.* [4] proposed a general framework for controlling two shadow puppets, a human model and an animal model. Cooper S. Yoo *et al.* [24] created a tangible stage interface that can be used to control marionette without wires based on Kinect. Kinect camera can provide very accurate depth estimation which can greatly facilitate the animation process, but also limits the system.

[7]http://design-io.com/projects/PuppetParadeCinekid/

[8]http://wearemonsters.net/

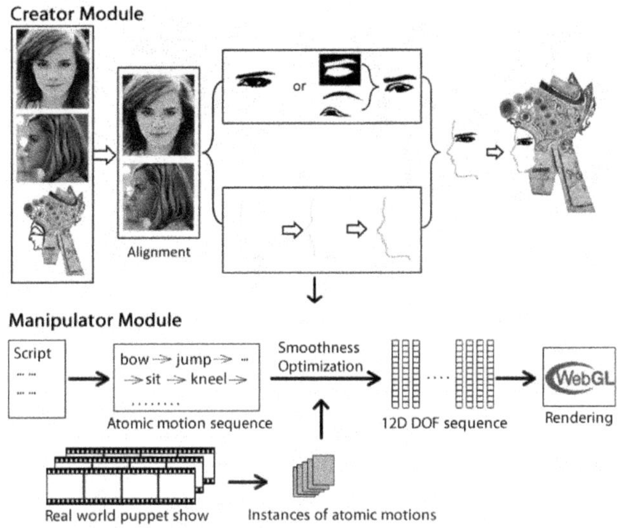

Figure 2: Illustration of the whole system framework. The upper panel is the creator module and the lower panel is the manipulator module.

3. OVERVIEW

In this section, we give an overview of the shadow puppetry system. As shown in Figure 2, the whole system contains two modules: creator module and manipulator module.

The first part is *creator* module. Since the real puppet face usually contains a profile (including forehead, nose, mouth, etc) and a frontal view eye, we require users to input one frontal view image and another profile view face image. First, we extract the eye and eyebrow from the frontal view image, and the puppet eye and eyebrow are deformed into the frontal view eye and eyebrow shape. Then the profile curve of the real profile face is extracted and deformed. Finally, the texture is transferred from a certain sample puppet to our generated puppet.

The second part is *manipulator* module. The objective of this part is to create a system that takes in a user script and outputs an animation sequence. To build this system, we collect puppetry show videos and manually define atomic motions as building blocks of the animation. Instances of the atomic motions are extracted from these videos. The script input by the user is first interpreted into an atomic motion sequence, which is then synthesized by weighted mean of the instances as later introduced.

4. MODULE I: PUPPETRY CREATOR

The design of Chinese shadow puppetry figures follows traditional aesthetics. There are mainly four kinds of puppetry faces: Sheng (male roles), Dan (female roles), Jing (roles with painted faces) and Chou (comic characters). These roles are mostly from classical plays and appearances are for-

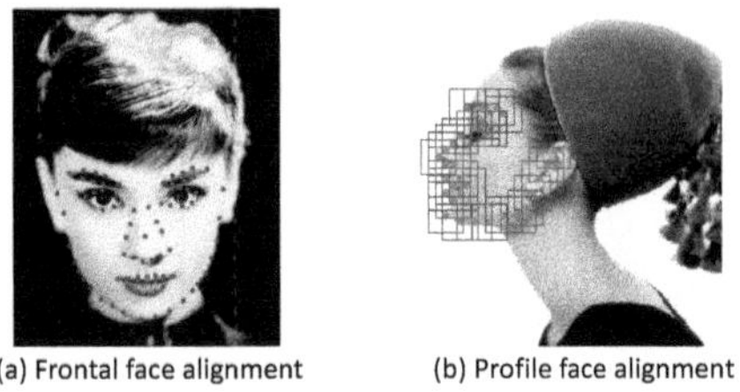

Figure 3: Aligned frontal and profile view faces.

malized. Since the procedures of puppetry making are very complicated and costly, it is hard for the user to create a specific puppetry figure. In this section, we will introduce the creator part of our system in details.

4.1 Face Alignment

Given a frontal view face image and a profile face image of the same person, we utilize the frontal view eye & eyebrow and the profile curve to create the head of a user-specific puppetry figure head.

Face Alignment: We process the face alignment of the frontal face and profile face separately. For a frontal view face, it is aligned by a commercial frontal face alignment algorithm [9]. The alignment of a profile face is performed based on the unified model proposed by Zhu *et al.* [25] for face detection, pose estimation, and landmark estimation in real-world, cluttered images. We show the aligned results of frontal and profile view respectively in Figure 3. After face alignment, we get the locations of a set of keypoints on face. Then based on these points, we extract the profile curve from the profile face and rotate the curve for direction adjustment. Similarly, eye and eyebrow areas are extracted from the frontal image.

4.2 Eye & Eyebrow Warping

In Chinese shadow puppetry, most of the figures' faces are in profile view. For describing features of characters, eyes and eyebrows are abstracted and exaggerated in an artistic way. For example, the eye of a puppet is stretched and the eyebrow is bent. The topology of the puppet eye is similar to the frontal view eye. To guarantee the similarity of the output figure face, given a target frontal view face image and a puppet face, we warp the puppet eye and eyebrow into the real eye and eyebrow shape.

Most state-of-the-art warping methods [26, 27] assume that the user provides explicit correspondences between the anchor points of the source and the target shape, and other points are mapped according to their relative positions with respect to the anchor points. Barycentric coordinates of triangles provide a convenient way to linearly interpolate the points within a triangle. Given a planar triangle $[v_1, v_2, v_3]$, any point v inside it has the unique Barycentric coordinates $[w_1, w_2, w_3]$ and:

$$\frac{w_1v_1 + w_2v_2 + w_3v_3}{w_1 + w_2 + w_3} = v. \quad (1)$$

The Barycentric coordinates are used as invariants to build the correspondences between two topologically equivalent polygons, characterized by the vertexes [27].

In our case, we first extract the contour points of puppet eye $C = \{c_1, \cdots, c_n\}$ by annotating landmarks and detect the contour points of real eye $P = \{p_1, \cdots, p_m\}$ automatically. In our setting, $n = m = 10$.

We consider puppet eye and real eye as two topologically equivalent polygons, characterized by C and P, and then build the correspondences based on Baryceentric coordinates between two eyes. The correspondences are used to warp reference puppet eye into the shape of real eye. Similarly, for eyebrow, we carry out the same process on puppet.

[9]http://www.omron.com/r_d/coretech/vision/okao.html

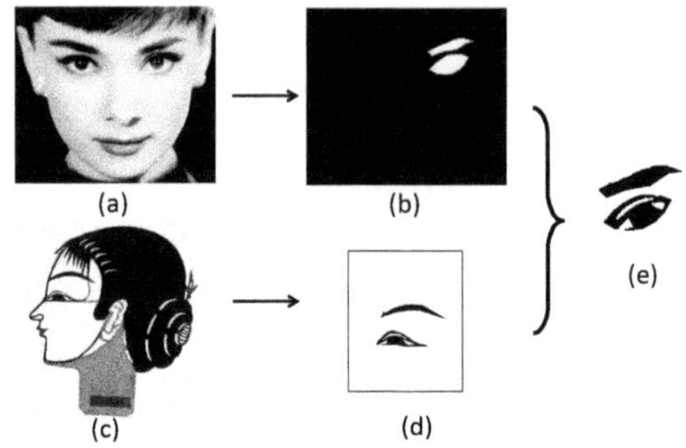

Figure 4: Eye & eyebrow warping. (a) Frontal face image, (b) extracted eye and eyebrow region after face alignment, (c) puppet face in our repository, (d) extracted eye and eyebrow of puppet, (e) eyes and eyebrows regions after warping puppet's eye and eyebrow to the real face shape.

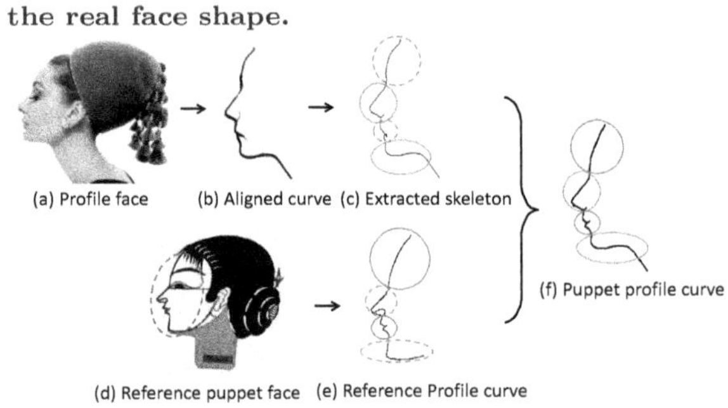

Figure 5: Profile curve generation. (a) The profile face provided by the users, (b) the extracted profile curve after rotated, (c) the skeleton of the profile curve, (d) the reference puppet face, (e) the reference profile curve skeleton and (f) the refined skeleton of profile curve after applying re-com.

One example of eye and eyebrow warping is shown in Figure 4. The original eye and eyebrow of the reference puppet in Figure 4(c) are warped to the shape of Audrey Hepburn's eye and eyebrow in Figure 4(b). The synthetic result is shown in Figure 4(e). The newly generated eye and eyebrow fuse the characteristics of Audrey Hepburn and the reference puppet: Audrey Hepburn's eyes are big and slightly turn upwards, and the reference puppet's eyes have obvious double eyelids.

4.3 Profile Curve Generation

Central profile curve is an important geometric feature. To generate an appropriate puppet profile, we will consider two aspects: 1) this profile should look like the input face and 2) this profile should have puppetry style. We keep the most unique parts of the profile curve and transform them into one with puppetry style.

4.3.1 Profile Abstraction

The central profile curve is highly discriminative. Some 3D facial research works use central profile curve as a significant feature for face maching [28] and face recognition [29]. To obtain a discriminative and puppet-like personalized puppet, we generate a profile curve which has the uniqueness of the input face and the characteristics of the reference puppet face. In order to estimate the uniqueness of

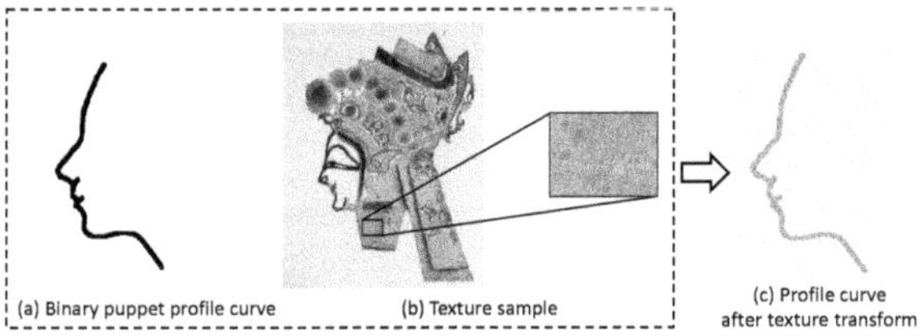

Figure 6: Texture Transfer

a real profile face, we collect a 90 degree profile face dataset including 500 images from the well-known MultiPIE benchmark [30].

Given a 90 degree profile face, we extract the edge of a profile face by using extended Difference of Gaussian (DOG) algorithm [31] and based on the face alignment result, we obtain the profile curve. A profile curve is separated into four parts: forehead, nose, mouth and jaw. We aim to preserve unique parts and replace others with the corresponding parts of the reference puppet, which are manually annotated offline.

First, we process this curve area by binary morphology tools and extract the binary skeleton line with only one pixel width [32] and then for each part, we extract histogram of oriented gradients (HOG) [33] feature as a vector. For each part, based on the MultiPIE dataset, we calculate the average distance $\overline{d}$, and the importance of the part from the input face is measured by the ratio of d, which is the mean of its distances to the K-Nearest-neighbors ($k = 3$ in our implement), over $\overline{d}$. The two most unique parts are kept and the other two parts are replaced by the corresponding parts of shadow puppetry profile.

From the profile image as shown in Figure 5(a), we get the direction adjusted profile curve in Figure 5(b). The parts in green circles are the two most unique parts and retained as shown in Figure 5(c). The parts in gray circles are replaced with the parts in red circles in Figure 5(e) extracted from Figure 5(d). Finally, we recombine these selected parts and generate a puppet profile curve in skeleton form.

4.3.2 *Profile Texture Transfer*

After previous steps, we obtain a profile skeleton which is like both the real face and the puppet face. Then we dilate this line till the same profile width of the reference puppet as shown in Figure 6(a). To be more like a puppet, we transfer the leather texture to the profile area. Efros *et al.* [34] presented a simple image quilting algorithm of generating novel visual appearance in which a new image is synthesized by stitching together small patches of existing images. Given a piece of leather sample in Figure 6(b), the texture for the profile curve can be synthesized by the image quilting method [34]. In Figure 6(c), we show an example of texture transfer result.

4.4 Post Processing

In shadow puppetry play, there are a lot of vivid props, including architecture, furniture, plants and animals, designed with distinct dynastic features. Some representative examples are shown in Figure 7(a). To make the roles more artistically charming, puppets are decorated with exquisite headdresses, which are classified into male style and female style. We can match the generated puppet with the proper headdresses, and some results are shown in Figure 7(b).

5. MODULE II: PUPPETRY MANIPULATOR

Traditional Chinese shadow puppet is created by hinging together nine parts: head, upper body, left & right arm, left & right hand, lower body, front & rear foot. Although there are variants replacing lower body with two upper legs, the nine-part design dominates. In a real puppet show, each puppet is controlled with three stick manipulators. The major manipulator is attached to the neck, clipping together the head and the upper body. Each of the other two manipulators is hinged to one hand. Based on this control model, shadow puppets have their own distinguished pattern of motion. In this section, we describe a system that is able to animate shadow puppets in their own styles learned from real world puppet shows.

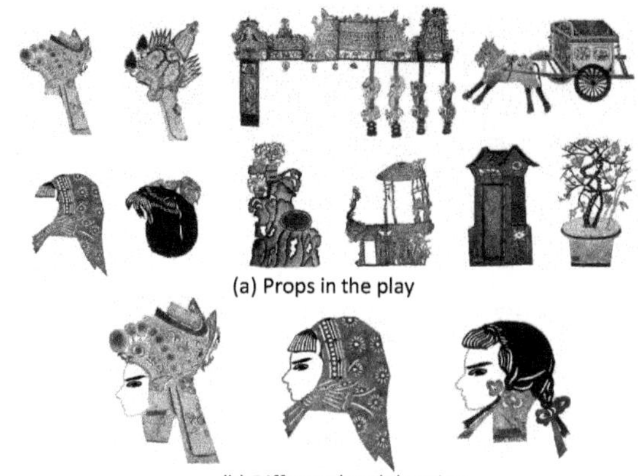

(a) Props in the play

(b) Different head dressing

Figure 7: Props in the puppetry and different head dressing.

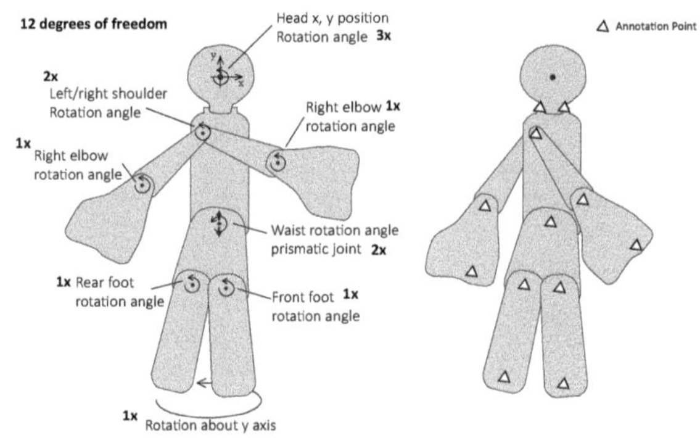

(a) Degrees of freedom (b) Annotation point for DOF infering

Figure 8: Degrees of freedom and annotation points.

5.1 Control Model

In our system we adopt the nine-part puppet design, i.e. the digital puppet consists of nine parts linked by 7 joints and in total has 12 degrees of freedom (DOF), as depicted in Figure 8(a). The 7 joints are named according to their positions: left & right shoulder, left & right elbow, waist and front & rear knee. All the 7 joints are revolute joints, except waist, which has an additional prismatic joint along vertical axis of the upper body. Therefore, among the 12 DOFs, seven describe the rotation angles at each of the joints; three of them describe the x and y coordinates and the rotation angle of the head center (we choose head center as descriptor of puppet position because the major manipulator is located near the head); the rest two DOFs are the rotation angle about y axis in the 3D scene which is used to flip the puppet, and the displacement of prismatic joint on the waist which is for undulation of upper body.

The conformation of the puppet is controlled by assigning values to the 12 DOFs. Animation can thus be synthesized by feeding a sequence of DOFs. The method to generate DOF sequence is described in the next sections.

5.2 Motion System

5.2.1 Identification of Atomic Motions

Based on five videos of popular real world puppet show, i.e. "Tale of the White Snake Madam", "Emperor Xuanzong of Tang", "Yanfei Wonder Woman", "Yang Saga", "Green Dragon Sword", it can be observed that the animation of puppets can be decomposed into smaller building blocks, which we call atomic motions. Eight atomic motions identified from the videos are listed in Table 1.

5.2.2 Data Preparation and Processing

After the atomic motions are identified, we manually extract video chunks that contain atomic motions from the puppet shows. For each of the atomic motions, we extract 50 video chunks which we call instances of that atomic motion. Each frame in the video chunks are labeled with 12 key points that describe the conformation of the puppet as shown in Figure 8(b). From the key points, we can easily calculate the DOFs information for each frame. Thus each instance of the atomic motion is finally converted to an instance matrix, with each column being the DOFs of the corresponding frame.

However, shaking defect is observed when the DOFs are applied directly to our digital puppets, because the available videos are generally of low quality and the point labeled by hand will introduce a high frequency shaking defect, which compromises the annotation accuracy. To overcome this defect, we apply locally weighted scatterplot smoothing to the rows of the DOF matrix. Later experiments show that the smoothing improves the visual experience significantly.

After smoothing, the instances of the same atomic motion are then temporally realigned by linear interpolation. For example, the atomic motion **A** has n instances, each converted to a matrix A_i. The A_is are linearly interpolated to have the same column number as the matrix with the most columns, denoted by A_i's. We consider the weighted mean of the aligned instances as eligible variants of that atomic motion:

$$A_{new} = A_1'w_1 + A_2'w_2 + \cdots + A_n'w_n \tag{2}$$

$$\sum_{i=1}^{n} w_i = 1, \quad w_i > 0.$$

Unlimited variants of the atomic motion can be generated which form a rich set of ingredients for building complex animations.

5.2.3 Recombination of Atomic Motions

Atomic motions captured from the videos have limited types. One way to increase their number is through recombination. Each atomic motion can be decomposed into independent parts. For example, the upper body motion is independent of the lower body motion. We can thus combine upper body motion of "bow" with lower body motion of "kneel" to form a new atomic motion "kowtow".

5.2.4 Composite Motions

While atomic motion provides high flexibility for animation synthesis, composite motion offers convenience. Composite motion consists of sequential atomic motions. It is defined for easier usage of the scripting interface. For instance, composite motion "talk for 10 minutes" means "breathe" continuously and "point" sometimes for 10 minutes. In this case, it will take much more efforts if we input atomic motions one by one. The scripting system will handle the conversion of composite motions to atomic motions. Composite motion is an addition to atomic motion which gives users higher level control of the puppet.

Table 1: Atomic motions

Atomic Motion	Meaning
jump	the whole body move forward for some distance, which represents walking in shadow puppet show
bow	To lower the head or upper body as a social gesture
sit	Sitting on the chairs in the scene
kneel	Kneel down on the ground
point	A hand gesture frequently appearing during speech, indicates the puppet is talking.
swing	The forward and backward motion of hands
breathe	Undulation of upper body, in puppet show, this motion indicates the puppet is talking
turn	Flipping the puppet about the y axis of the scene, changing its facing direction

5.3 Animation Generation

The animation of puppets can be decomposed to smallest building blocks called atomic motions. Based on atomic motions, composite motions are synthesized as larger building blocks. In this work we render the animation using browser based webgl for ease of sharing with others, each puppet has a corresponding javascript object. Through the scripting interface, manipulators of the digital puppet invokes different functions on the object. For each atomic or composite motion, we define a corresponding function. The manipulator can easily control the puppet by invoking the function with parameters like time duration and spatial distance. For example, puppet.walk(10,15) tells puppet to walk 10 units in the defined 2D world in 15 frames' time. Through script, the manipulator can also place props like chair to specific locations, the locations of the props can then be used in the script. The manipulator can either do scripting on-line by inputing one motion after the other or off-line by writing done all the scripts and feed to the puppet. The on-line system is mainly for the user to experience the individual motions. For an entire animation sequence generation, off-line is preferred because it offers better control of timing. In the rest part of this section, we will present the method for off-line animation generation.

The off-line animation generation system takes in a sequence of atomic & composite motions as input from a scripting interface. A preprocessing step on the input motion sequence decomposes the composite motions into atomic motions, which makes the motion sequence monotonously atomic. The DOF sequence is finally created by converting each atomic motion into DOFs. As mentioned in Section 5.2.2, atomic motions are generated by weighted means of their instances. Reusing a limited number of the instances makes the animation monotonous; by taking different weight vector, infinite variants of one atomic motion can be generated from its limited instances. The aesthetic of the animation is greatly influenced by the smoothness of the animation. The visual experience is discounted if two adjacent frames differ a lot. Thus, minimizing the position gap between atomic motions is the criterion in selecting the weight vectors.

5.3.1 Weights Selection

The smoothness of the animation sequence can be measured by the position gap between consecutive atomic motions, namely the distance from the last frame of one atomic motion to the first frame of the next. Smoothing the whole motion sequence can be achieved by optimizing the following problem:

$$\min_{\{w_i\}} s(\{w_i\}) = \sum_{i=1}^{N-1} \|F_{i+1}w_{i+1} - L_i w_i\|_2^2 \tag{3}$$

$$s.t. \quad \sum_j w_{ij} = 1, \quad w_{ij} \geq 0, \quad i \in \{1, 2, \cdots, N\}.$$

For better explanation, we introduce the instance matrix M_j^k, which means the jth instance of the atomic motion k. k is in the set of atomic motions listed in Table 1. $k(i)$ denotes the atomic motion type of the ith atomic motion in the motion sequence. F_i is formed by taking the first columns of $M_j^{k(i)}$ for each j. L_i is formed by taking the last columns. w_i is the weight vector for the ith atomic motion. For an given atomic motion, the weights are constrained to be non-negative, and sum to one.

Due to the imperfectness of instances realignment, weighted recombination of the instances has shaking defect if too many instances are combined together. To reduce shaking defects, we impose a sparsity constraint on the weight vectors, so that a minimum number of instances are selected. The following optimization problem is formed:

$$\min_{\{w_i\}} s(\{w_i\}) + \lambda \sum_{i=1}^{N} \|w_i\|_0 \tag{4}$$

$$s.t. \quad \sum_j w_{ij} = 1, \quad w_{ij} \geq 0, \quad i \in \{1, 2, \cdots, N\}.$$

Generally, the l_0-norm is relaxed into l_1-norm to solve for computational efficiency. However, the l_1-norm heuristic does not work here because the constraint makes l_1-norm of the weight vector equal to 1, namely constant.

We utilize another relaxation method to handle this sparsity on probability simplex problem proposed in [35]. The l_0-norm can be lower bounded by reciprocal of infinity norm when the corresponding l_1-norm is a constant. For any x constraint to probability simplex:

$$\|x\|_1 = \sum_{i=1}^{n} |x_i| \leq \|x\|_0 \max_i |x_i| \leq \|x\|_0 \|x\|_\infty \tag{5}$$

Because $\|x\|_1 = 1$,

$$\frac{1}{\|x\|_\infty} \leq \|x\|_0. \tag{6}$$

Then we resort to solve the following problem:

$$\min_{\{w_i\}} s(\{w_i\}) + \lambda \sum_{i=1}^{N} \frac{1}{\|w_i\|_\infty} \tag{7}$$

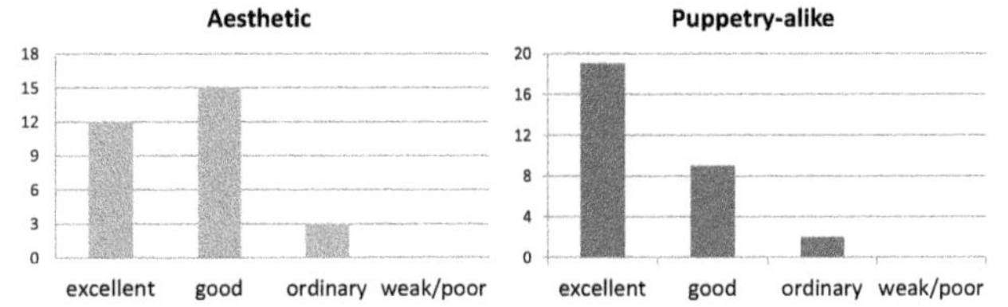

Figure 9: Evaluation of our creator results from the 30 subjects. Results of aesthetic and puppetry-alike level of assessment are shown sequentially. The horizontal axis corresponds to the different evaluation levels, the vertical axis is the number of persons.

We show here a single variable version of this problem:

$$\begin{aligned} &\min_x s(x) + \lambda \frac{1}{\|x\|_\infty} \\ &= \min_x s(x) + \min_i \frac{\lambda}{x_i} \\ &= \min_i \min_x s(x) + \frac{\lambda}{x_i}. \end{aligned} \tag{8}$$

$\min_x s(x) + \frac{\lambda}{x_i}$ is convex optimization if $s(x)$ is convex, since $\frac{\lambda}{x_i}$ is a convex function when $x_i > 0$. The convex optimization is done for each $i \in \{1, 2, \cdots, N\}$ using exponentiated gradient descent [36]. By solving the n convex problems (n is the length of vector x), the single variable version of this problem can be globally optimized.

Equivalently, (4) is converted to:

$$\min_{k_1} \cdots \min_{k_N} \min_{w_i, i \in \{1,2,\cdots,N\}} s\{w_i\} + \frac{\lambda}{w_{1k_1}} + \cdots + \frac{\lambda}{w_{Nk_N}} \tag{9}$$

Each of the convex problem can be solved by alternatively applying exponentiated gradient to each of the variables.

However, the number of convex problems grows exponentially as the variable number increases. In our case, the variable number is N, which is the number of atomic motions in the motion sequence. Thus it is not practical to solve the weights for the whole motion sequence in one shot. Therefore, we employ a scanning window method: each time we only optimize a segment of the motion sequence. In this way the complexity is linear to the sequence length.

After the weights are obtained by optimization described above, we calculate the whole DOF sequence by using Equation 2 for each atomic motion.

6. EXPERIMENTS

In this section, we first evaluate the performance of the creator module and manipulator module sequentially. Then we comprehensively show the results of the our system in a so-called "love story with puppetry" scenario to show the combination effectiveness of creator results and manipulator results.

For the user studies in this section, 30 subjects (7 females and 23 males) ranged from 22 to 40 years old (μ=27.3, σ=3.9) are invited to participate in our experiments.

6.1 Results on Creator Module

6.1.1 Quantitative Results: User Study

Here we discuss the properties of the creator puppet in the following three aspects: aesthetic, puppetry-alike and discrimination.

Aesthetic: Whether the result looks elegant?

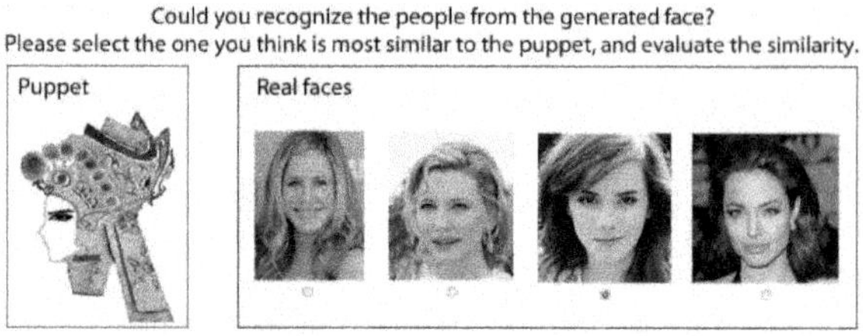

Figure 10: The exemplar user interface of our discriminative evaluate tool.

Table 2: ANOVA analysis of comparing smoothed and original atomic motions

F-statistics	p-value
1025.49	5.02281e-121

Puppetry-alike: Does the generated face keep the characteristics of puppet?

In these two questions, we set five values for subjects to choose: excellent, good, ordinary, weak and poor. We present 10 creator puppet images to subjects and the results are shown in Figure 9. We can see that our puppet module has achieved very high score in both evaluation metrics.

Discrimination: Could you recognize the people from the generated face? We evaluate this index by several single-choice questions. For example, we show a puppetry of Emma Watson to the subjects, in the same time, we show four face images: one is Emma Waston and the other three are random choices. An example of user study interface is shown in Figure 10. The subjects choose which face image among the four candidates most looks like the puppet. We test 10 creator results and summarize the subjects' feedback. The average precision is 71.1%. The precision is not quite high because the generated puppet images are all in profile view, but the candidates are in frontal view. However, the precision of 71.1% is much higher than random guess (25%).

6.1.2 *Qualitative Results*

Here we show some result examples of the creator module. As shown in Figure 11, the first column are input frontal view face images, the second column are input profile face images of the same person. The creator results are shown in the third column and results decorated with headdress are shown in the forth column.

6.2 Results on Manipulator Module

6.2.1 *Atomic Motion*

Here we evaluate the result of applying locally weighted scatterplot smoothing to the instance matrices of atomic motions. For each type of atomic motion, one instance is randomly selected and smoothed. The subjects are presented both the original and smoothed version of the atomic motion instances. For each original and smoothed pair of the instances, the subjects are required to evaluate their smoothness on the 5-point Likert scale without prior knowledge which one is smoothed. One randomly selected instance for all eight types of atomic motions are evaluated. We show the notched box plot of the result in Figure 12(a). One way ANOVA analysis is also performed on the data shown in Table 2. The results show that locally weighted scatterplot can significantly improve the smoothness of the atomic motions.

6.2.2 *Animation Smoothness Evaluation*

The smoothness of generated animation is not only dependent on the smoothness of atomic motion itself, but also on the transition of adjacent atomic motions. To evaluate the weight selection method, we generated five animation sequences each about 30s in length consisting of random atomic motions. Two versions of the animations are generated, one with weights selected using our method described in Section 5.3.1 and the other with randomly selected weights. Subjects are given the same options as in the evaluation of atomic motion smoothness. Figure 13(a) and Figure 13(b) compare the transitions selected from the animation sequences generated with smoothness optimized weights and random weights. It can be observed the position gap between consecutive atomic motions is smaller when smoothness optimized weight is used.

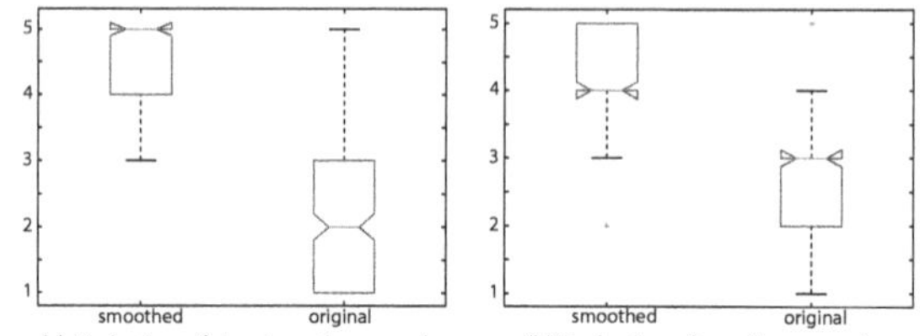

(a) Evaluation of atomic motion smoothness (b) Evaluation of transition smoothness

Figure 12: Notched box plot of smoothness evaluation.

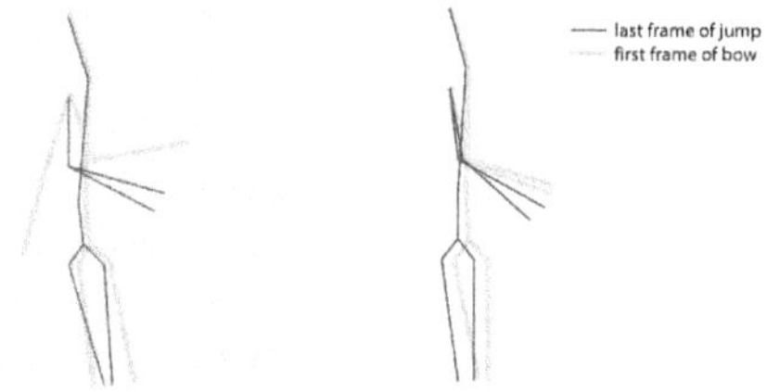

(a) random (b) smooth

Figure 13: Smoothing result

The notched box plot of the result is shown in Figure 12(b), and the one way ANOVA analysis is shown in Table 3. The results show that optimized weights using our method is significantly better in transition smoothness than randomly selected weights.

6.2.3 *Short Video Evaluation*

Two video chunks about one minute in length is selected from the puppetries "Tale of the White Snake Madam" and "Green Dragon Sword". Using the scripting interface, we reproduced those two videos. The subjects in this study are required to watch the original and reproduced videos, then answer questions regarding three aspects of the synthesized videos. The questions are answered on a 5-point Likert scale from "very bad" (1) to "very good" (5). The mean and standard deviation of the scores are calculated and displayed in Table 4. From the results, conclusion can be made that the puppetries generated from our system preserve the motion pattern of real puppetry, and successfully convey the information to the subjects. The subjects are satisfied with the resolution of the generated puppetry, which is expected because videos captured from real puppetries are limited in the capturing condition and are usually low in quality.

6.3 Love Story with Puppetry

To demonstrate the usage of both the creator and manipulator module, we make a short video that tell a love story

Table 3: ANOVA analysis of comparing animation sequence generated using weights from smoothness optimization and randomly selection

F-statistics	p-value
327.53	6.60827e-50

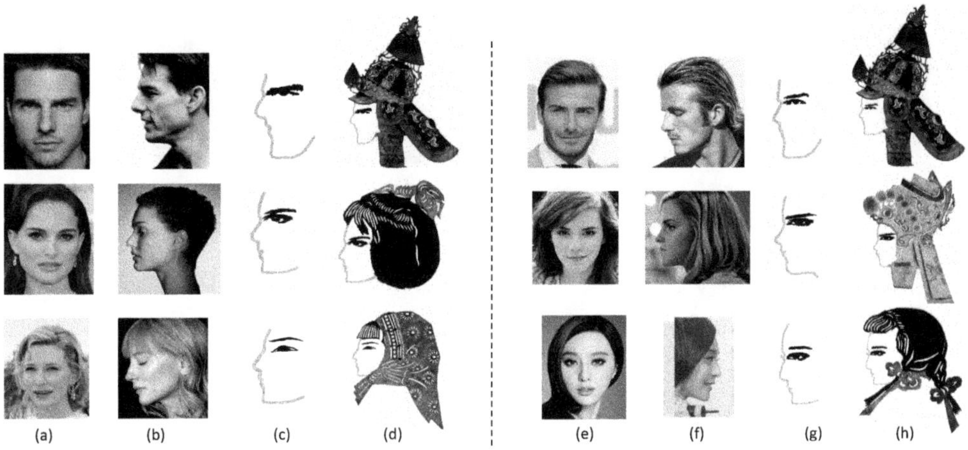

Figure 11: Examples of creators module. The first two columns correspond to the frontal and profile images provided by users. The third column is the generated puppet, and the last column is the puppet after adding head dress.

Table 4: Evaluation of short video as compared to the original video

Question	Mean	Stdev
Q1. Does the generated video preserve the motion pattern of real puppet?	4.3333	0.6609
Q2. How is the information conveyed?	4.2333	0.6789
Q3. How is the resolution?	4.6667	0.6065

Table 5: The evaluate of the "love story with puppetry"

Question	Mean	Stdev
Q1: Does the video convey information? Could you understand the whole story by watching the video?	4.14	0.9438
Q2: Do you like the style of interaction between physical space and virtual space?	4.00	0.8459
Q3: Can you recognize the person generated by our puppet creator module?	4.01	1.0184
Q4: Does the generated puppet preserve the traditional puppet style?	4.37	0.6897
Q5: Does the generated action pattern preserve the traditional puppet style?	4.31	0.6311
Q6: Through the practical operation with the manipulator module, do you think it is convenient to use it?	4.27	0.9131
Q7: Do you think our work can help preserve the traditional Chinese shadow puppet culture?	4.35	0.9632
Q8: Do you want to see similar product in the puppet museum?	4.60	0.6547

between a man and a female puppet. The animations of the puppets in this video are generated using our manipulator module. The man in this story finally becomes a puppet, which is generated by our creator module.

Story Synopsis: A boy named Ryan was a PhD student. He was sad because he was still single. One day, a miracle happened, a very beautiful puppet girl appeared and said to him: "Would you come to my world?" So he was changed into a puppet and entered the girl's world. They got married and lived happily ever since. Some example frames are displayed in Figure 14. The full video can be watched online [10] and also included in the supplementary materials.

[10]http://www.youtube.com/watch?v=lxJUw3mKF18yA

We designed 8 questions and asked all the subjects to watch and evaluate the video on a 5-point Likert scale: very good, good, normal, bad and very bad from score 5 to score 1. Besides watching the video, the subjects also tried the manipulator module by typing the script themselves and experiencing the play creation. Then we count the average score of each question, and the results are shown in Table 5. Q1 and Q2 are related to the user friendliness of our system. Q3 and Q4 are related to the performance of the creator module while Q5 and Q6 are related to the performance of the manipulator module. Q7 and Q8 are related to our initial motivation.

From the results we can conclude that most subjects agree that both the generated puppet (mean score 4.37) and its action pattern (mean score 4.31) can well preserve the traditional puppet style. And most subjects think our work can help preserve the traditional Chinese shadow puppet culture (mean score 4.27), and want to see similar product in the puppet museum (quite high score 4.60). Due to the limitation of the profile face, people cannot always recognize the puppet generated by our creator module (score 4.01). We leave refining this part as our future work. The subjects also provided some suggestions. One subject commented, "The idea is quite good, and I look forward to more wonderful puppetry videos". Some of the subjects thought that more atomic actions should be added. One subject thought we should enhance the soundtracks of the puppet.

7. CONCLUSIONS AND FUTURE WORK

In this paper, we proposed the eHeritage of shadow puppetry, including a creator module and a manipulator module. The creator module can generate a puppet for one person based on his/her frontal view face image and profile face image. The manipulator module can automatically generate the motion sequences based on the script provided by the user. We conduct extensive experiments on puppetry creator and manipulator module, and the results show the effectiveness of the proposed system. Currently our system mainly focuses on the visual effect of the puppetry. In future, we would like to take more consideration to the audio parts, such as automatic vocal style transfer from human singing to puppetry style singing.

8. ACKNOWLEDGMENT

This research is partially supported by the Singapore National Research Foundation under its International Research

Figure 14: Some representative frames of the "love story with puppetry".

Centre @Singapore Funding Initiative and administered by the IDM Programme Office; and also partially supported by State Key Development Program of Basic Research of China 2013CB336500, in part by the Natural Science Foundation of China (NSFC) under grant 61172164.

9. REFERENCES

[1] F. Chen, "Visions for the masses: Chinese shadow plays from shaanxi and shanxi," *Pacific Science*, 2012.

[2] L. Leite and V. Orvalho, "Shape your body: control a virtual silhouette using body motion," in *Proc. ACM Annual Conference Extended Abstracts on Human Factors in Computing Systems Extended Abstracts*, 2012.

[3] S. Y. Lin, C. K. Shie, S. C. Chen, and Y. P. Hung, "Action recognition for human-marionette interaction," in *Proc. ACM International Conference on Multimedia*, 2012.

[4] H. Zhang, Y. Song, Z. Chen, J. Cai, and K. Lu, "Chinese shadow puppetry with an interactive interface using the kinect sensor," in *Proc. the 12th European Conference on Computer Vision Workshop*, 2012.

[5] A. Paviotti and D. A. Forsyth, "A lightness recovery algorithm for the multispectral acquisition of frescoed environments," in *IEEE 12th International Conference on Computer Vision Workshops*, 2009.

[6] L. Wolf, R. Littman, N. Mayer, N. Dershowitz, R. Shweka, and Y. Choueka, "Automatically identifying join candidates in the cairo genizah," in *IEEE 12th International Conference on Computer Vision Workshops*, 2009.

[7] T. Luo, R. Li, and H. Zha, "3d line drawing for archaeological illustration," *International Journal of Computer Vision*, 2011.

[8] M. Seidl, M. Zeppelzauer, and C. Breiteneder, "A study of gradual transition detection in historic film material," in *Proc. the second workshop on eHeritage and digital art preservation*, 2010.

[9] A. Mallik, S. Chaudhury, and H. Ghosh, "Preservation of intangible heritage: a case-study of indian classical dance," in *Proc. the second workshop on eHeritage and digital art preservation*, 2010.

[10] B. Gooch and A. Gooch, *Non-photorealistic rendering*, 2001.

[11] Z. Ruttkay and H. Noot, "Animated chartoon faces," in *Proc. the 1st International Symposium on Non-photorealistic animation and rendering*, 2000.

[12] H. Chen, N. N. Zheng, L. Liang, Y. Li, Y. Q. Xu, and H. Y. Shum, "Pictoon: a personalized image-based cartoon system," in *Proc. the 10th ACM International Conference on Multimedia*, 2002.

[13] J. Xu, C. S. Kaplan, and X. Mi, "Computer-generated papercutting," in *15th Pacific Conference on Computer Graphics and Applications*, 2007.

[14] M. Meng, M. Zhao, and S. C. Zhu, "Artistic paper-cut of human portraits," in *Proc. the International Conference on Multimedia*, 2010.

[15] A. Mazalek, M. Nitsche, C. Rébola, A. Wu, P. Clifton, F. Peer, and M. Drake, "Pictures at an exhibition: a physical/digital puppetry performance piece," in *Proceedings of the 8th ACM conference on Creativity and cognition*, 2011.

[16] S. W. Hsu and T. Y. Li, "Planning character motions for shadow play animations," *Proc. the International Conference on Computer Animation and Social Agents*, 2005.

[17] C. Barnes, D. E. Jacobs, J. Sanders, D. B. Goldman, S. Rusinkiewicz, A. Finkelstein, and M. Agrawala, "Video puppetry: a performative interface for cutout animation," in *ACM Transactions on Graphics*, 2008.

[18] K. Tan, A. Talib, and M. Osman, "Real-time simulation and interactive animation of shadow play puppets using opengl," *International Journal of Computer and Information Engineering*, 2010.

[19] D. H. Kim, M. Y. Sung, J.-S. Park, K. Jun, and S.-R. Lee, "Realtime control for motion creation of 3d avatars," in *Advances in Multimedia Information Processing-PCM 2005*, 2005.

[20] F. Lu, F. Tian, Y. Jiang, X. Cao, W. Luo, G. Li, X. Zhang, G. Dai, and H. Wang, "Shadowstory: creative and collaborative digital storytelling inspired by cultural heritage," in *Proc. the 2011 Annual Conference on Human Factors in Computing Systems*, 2011.

[21] J. Pan and J. Zhang, "Sketch-based skeleton-driven 2d animation and motion capture," *Transactions on edutainment VI*, 2011.

[22] R. Held, A. Gupta, B. Curless, and M. Agrawala, "3d puppetry: a kinect-based interface for 3d animation," in *Proc. the 25th Annual ACM Symposium on User Interface Software and Technology*, 2012.

[23] L. Leite and V. Orvalho, "Anim-actor: understanding inter with digital puppetry using low-cost motion capture," in *Proc. the 8th International Conference on Advances in Computer Entertainment Technology*, 2011.

[24] M. D. G. Cooper Sanghyun Yoo, "Digital puppet: a tangible, interactive stage interface," in *Proceedings of the SIGCHI Conference on Human Factors in Computing Systems*, 2011.

[25] X. Zhu and D. Ramanan, "Face detection, pose estimation, and landmark localization in the wild," in *IEEE Conf. Computer Vision and Pattern Recognition*, 2012.

[26] J. Gomes, *Warping and morphing of graphical objects*. Morgan Kaufmann, 1999.

[27] K. Hormann and M. S. Floater, "Mean value coordinates for arbitrary planar polygons," *ACM Transactions on Graphics*, 2006.

[28] G. Pan, Y. Wu, Z. Wu, and W. Liu, "3d face recognition by profile and surface matching," in *Proc. the International Joint Conference on Neural Networks*, 2003.

[29] T. Nagamine, T. Uemura, and I. Masuda, "3d facial image analysis for human identification," in *Proc. 11th IAPR International Conference on Pattern Recognition, Conference A: Computer Vision and Applications*, 1992.

[30] R. Gross, I. Matthews, J. Cohn, T. Kanade, and S. Baker, "Multi-pie," *Image and Vision Computing*, 2010.

[31] H. Winnemöller, "Xdog: advanced image stylization with extended difference-of-gaussians," in *Proc.the ACM SIGGRAPH/Eurographics Symposium on Non-Photorealistic Animation and Rendering*, 2011.

[32] J. Serra, *Image analysis and mathematical morphology*, 1982.

[33] N. Dalal and B. Triggs, "Histograms of oriented gradients for human detection," in *IEEE Conf. Computer Vision and Pattern Recognition*, 2005.

[34] A. A. Efros and W. T. Freeman, "Image quilting for texture synthesis and transfer," in *Proc. the 28th Annual Conference on Computer Graphics and Interactive Techniques*, 2001.

[35] M. Pilanci, L. E. Ghaoui, and V. Chandrasekaran, "Recovery of sparse probability measures via convex programming," in *Advances in Neural Information Processing Systems 25*, 2012.

[36] J. Kivinen and M. K. Warmuth, "Exponentiated gradient versus gradient descent for linear predictors," *Information and Computation*, 1997.

Hybrid Robotic/Virtual Pan-Tilt-Zoom Cameras for Autonomous Event Recording

Peter Carr
Disney Research
Pittsburgh, USA
carr@disneyresearch.com

Michael Mistry
University of Birmingham
Birmingham, UK
m.n.mistry@bham.ac.uk

Iain Matthews
Disney Research
Pittsburgh, USA
iainm@disneyresearch.com

ABSTRACT

We present a method to generate aesthetic video from a robotic camera by incorporating a virtual camera operating on a delay, and a hybrid controller which uses feedback from both the robotic and virtual cameras. Our strategy employs a robotic camera to follow a coarse region-of-interest identified by a realtime computer vision system, and then resamples the captured images to synthesize the video that would have been recorded along a smooth, aesthetic camera trajectory. The smooth motion trajectory is obtained by operating the virtual camera on a short delay so that perfect knowledge of immediate future events is known.

Previous autonomous camera installations have employed either robotic cameras or stationary wide-angle cameras with subregion cropping. Robotic cameras track the subject using realtime sensor data, and regulate a smoothness-latency trade-off through control gains. Fixed cameras post-process the data and suffer significant reductions in image resolution when the subject moves freely over a large area.

Our approach provides a solution for broadcasting events from locations where camera operators cannot easily access. We can also offer broadcasters additional actuated camera angles without the overhead of additional human operators. Experiments on our prototype system for college basketball illustrate how our approach better mimics human operators compared to traditional robotic control approaches, while avoiding the loss in resolution that occurs from fixed camera system.

Categories and Subject Descriptors

I.2.9 [**Artificial Intelligence**]: Robotics; I.4.8 [**Image Processing and Computer Vision**]: Scene Analysis

General Terms

Experimentation, Theory

Keywords

Camera, control, tracking, planning

MM'13, October 21–25, 2013, Barcelona, Spain.

ACM 978-1-4503-2404-5/13/10 ...$15.00.
http://dx.doi.org/10.1145/2502081.2502086.

Figure 1: Hybrid Camera. We first use a robotic pan-tilt-zoom camera to follow the centroid of player positions estimated by a realtime person detector. After a short delay, we then resample the image to generate the video frame of a virtual camera (highlighted) which has a smooth camera motion trajectory because the path planning algorithm can take into account how the players will move in the immediate future (see accompanying video for full effect).

1. INTRODUCTION

Robotic cameras which can record live events autonomously have the potential to streamline and improve current broadcast production models. For example, the optimal shooting location may be impractical for a human operator (which arises often in sports) or the cost of hiring a professional camera operator may not justify the benefit of an additional perspective. In these instances, methods to improve or automate the control of robotic cameras would be extremely useful. Automatically planning where the camera should look is a key challenge [14], especially when the source information is noisy sensor data. Fundamentally, the camera must be controlled to ensure it tracks the intended target. Although path planning and camera control are separate tasks, the two are highly coupled: there is no point planning a motion path which the camera is physically unable to follow.

The camera should also move smoothly and purposefully to avoid disorienting the viewer. Although smooth motion can be achieved through low control gains (which limit changes in acceleration), the resulting system will be unable to follow dynamic object trajectories. Instead, the autonomous camera should mimic human behavior and plan a trajectory which balances smooth motion against tracking error. As a result, planning requires anticipating object motion, or as Owens writes: "understanding the intricacies of the event ... gives camera operators the ability to predict how they should be moving their cameras" [20].

An online, realtime system is preferable because the event can then be broadcast live. Furthermore, if the sensor data can be processed in realtime, a robotic pan-tilt-zoom (PTZ) camera can follow the subject of interest and capture high-resolution images using all pixels from its image sensor. However, to output aesthetic video, the system must also be able to anticipate future object locations so that a smooth trajectory can be planned. Previous online autonomous robotic camera systems have only been employed in environments with limited dynamic motion such as lecture halls and video conference facilities. We handle

Team sports, on the other hand, have highly dynamic object motions. As a result, all implementations to date have employed non-realtime offline resampling approaches. In the resampling framework, one or more high-definition stationary cameras capture live action, and video from a virtual camera is synthesized after the fact by resampling the pixels from the fixed cameras (often by simply cropping a rectangular subregion). As Gleicher and Masanz [11] point out, the offline approach is attractive because complex non-realtime algorithms can be used to plan the camera trajectory, and more importantly, there is no need to accurately anticipate future object motions because the true future motion information is readily available. Similarly, there are no control issues because the virtual camera can move anywhere immediately. The downside of resampling is that only a fraction of the system's resolution is used in the output. For instance, in a sport like basketball, all players typically occupy only half the court at any given time. Therefore, with a set of fixed cameras covering the entire court, at least half the recorded pixels would never be used in the output video. In addition, it is impossible to gain high-resolution close-up images.

In this work, we propose a hybrid robotic/virtual camera which balances the strengths and weakness of both online and offline approaches: a robotic PTZ camera is equipped with a wide angle lens and tracks sports players in realtime, and a second virtual camera resamples the original source video in realtime, but on a short temporal delay (see Fig. 1). Our proposed solution has several interesting properties:

- The hybrid camera remains an online, realtime system with small latency, but gains the offline benefit of perfect knowledge about future events (up to the duration of the induced temporal delay).
- The synthesized video of the virtual camera exhibits minimal loss in image resolution (unlike offline resampling systems) because the robotic camera follows the action.
- The hybrid camera is a redundantly actuated system, which presents certain control issues.

The amount of delay is a critical design factor which regulates the hybrid nature of the system: zero delay produces a completely online system, and infinite delay produces a completely offline system. A longer delay improves the virtual camera's ability to plan a good trajectory because it has knowledge about events further into the future. However, the robotic camera must be controlled in realtime to ensure the virtual camera remains within the frame boundary so that the resampling process has sufficient information to synthesize the image that would have been captured had the robotic camera looked where the virtual camera is now looking. Longer delays make the controlling feedback loop more unstable. As a result, our hybrid camera has a suitable delay which balances the benefits of improved planning against the drawbacks of more difficult control.

We demonstrate the effectiveness of our proposed hybrid robotic/virtual camera through a prototype system deployed for broadcasting college basketball games. Our experiments demonstrate how the introduction of a small delay improves the system's ability to plan a smooth and purposeful path for the virtual camera using a hysteresis filter which appears to anticipate state changes because of knowledge about the immediate future. The robotic camera is controlled to follow a live prediction of where the virtual camera is expected to look, as well as monitoring where the virtual camera is actually looking. As expected, we show how the control stability of the robotic camera decreases as delay increases. Our supplementary video shows how a hybrid camera is able to produce live footage which more closely resembles the work of a human operator.

2. RELATED WORK

Autonomous Cameras

Previous work in autonomous camera systems for sports production [1,3,4,7] has employed a common framework: one or more high-resolution fixed cameras capture the game, and features such as player and ball locations are extracted offline. The output broadcast is then generated as a post process by determining the optimal subregion of the appropriate fixed camera at each time instant. There has been significant variety in how the optimal subregion is determined at each time instant. Daigo and Ozawa [7] augment player features with audience gaze angles. Images of the three fixed cameras are stitched together using cylindrical projection and a rotational offset based on player and audience gaze features. Ariki *et al.* [1] considered three different shot sizes depending on the estimated game situations. A smooth path was achieved using a Schmitt trigger which only put the camera in motion when the ball neared the edge of the frame. Chen and De Vleeschouwer [3] generated a virtual camera trajectory for basketball using an MRF chain to balance smoothness against deviating from the optimal virtual camera state at each time instant.

In addition to sports, autonomous camera systems have been deployed in lecture halls, video conferences, and television production stages. In these situations, the motion of subjects is significantly less dynamic than team sports, and a range of camera solutions has been employed. Pinhanez and Bobick [21] demonstrated how a user-supervised autonomous camera system could automatically frame shots for a cooking show. Various vision algorithms were deployed depending on the type of shot as requested by the human director. Yokoi and Fujiyoshi [24] used a fixed 1080i camera to record a lecturer. A cropping window was computed from frame differencing, and the authors investigated both bilateral filtering and human specified control points for a learned acceleration model to smooth the noisy input signal. Sun *et al.* [23] controlled a virtual camera to record a lecturer. The motion of the virtual camera was regulated using a Kalman filter augmented with a three state rule-based post filtering technique to prefer a stationary cameras unless the lecturer was moving significantly. Zhang *et al.* [25] use a fixed camera to estimate a saliency map of the video conference room and computed an optimal cropping window which balanced a loss of information from aperture and resolution effects. Instead of cropping from the wide-angle camera, the desired subregion is used to control a robotic PTZ camera.

Our work is most similar to Zhang *et al.* [26] who also used a hybrid robotic/virtual camera. The robotic camera tracked a lecturer and moved as necessary to keep the subject in the center of the image. A subregion of the image was then cropped to compensate for motor control errors. There was no delay between the virtual and robotic cameras. In effect, the virtual camera was to used to achieve ideal perfect control by compensating for any discrepancy between the plan for where the physical camera was supposed to look, and where the physical camera was actually looking. In a more complex environment, such as basketball, accurate prediction of object motion is necessary for generating aesthetic video. Instead, we operate a virtual camera on a delay to avoid the need to anticipate player movements.

Path Planning and Control

Determining where the cameras should look is a key component of any autonomous system. Additionally, the planned trajectory must be smooth, which means the process to decide where the camera should look at any given time instant must take into account where the camera should be looking during a temporal window which spans both before and after the current time instant.

Camera planning continues to be a popular topic in computer graphics (see the recent survey by Christie *et al.* [5]). However, computer graphics algorithms rarely consider incomplete and noisy data generated from computer vision and other sensing modalities.

The tasks of moving a physical camera to keep an object of interest within the field of view is referred to as *visual servoing* in the robotics literature. Stanciu and Oh [22] employed a proportion-only feedback control algorithm to adjust the pan-tilt angle of a camera mounted on the end of a human operated boom to keep a target object in the center of the camera image. When multiple targets are tracked, control algorithms often monitor features derived from the point set, such as mean and standard deviation. Farag and Abdel-Hakim [9] use proportion-only control to position the centroid of detected image features near the centers of the images of a stereo camera pair. Gans *et al.* [10] use task-priority kinematic control to keep a set of interest points within the camera field of view. They showed how the mean and variance are independent objectives: pan-tilt values are modified to keep the mean near the center of the image, and zoom is regulated to keep the standard deviation within the image boundary.

Two recent works in machine learning and computer vision have examined the problem of determining where cameras should look based on player motions. Dearden *et al.* [8] used a K nearest neighbor classifier to learn the relationship between features (such as player position) and the PTZ state of cameras operated by professionals. Kim *et al.* [17] track individual players using a particle filter and extrapolate a global motion vector field on the ground plane using Gaussian process regression. The authors show how convergence regions in the vector field correlate with actual broadcast camera movements.

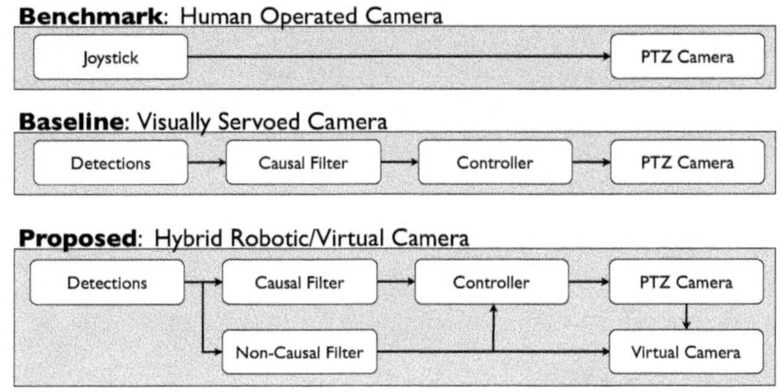

Figure 2: Camera Operation Techniques. We compare our proposed hybrid robotic/virtual camera operation technique to an autonomous camera operated using visual servoing. Our objective is to mimic human operation, so we express the performance of both the baseline and proposed autonomous systems relative to the benchmark of a human operated camera.

Finally, both robotics and computer vision have examined the problem of planning smooth trajectories for cameras. Nieuwenhuisen and Overmans [19] use a probabilistic roadmap to generate an initial estimate of linear segments which link the current camera state to the desired future camera state. The path is refined by fitting circular arcs between segments and computing a smooth velocity plan which depends on path curvature. Gleicher and Liu [12] developed a video stabilization technique by estimating the trajectory of a hand held camera using inter-frame homographies, and identifying segments of constant velocity linked together with ease in/out curves. Grundmann *et al.* [13] refine a noisy trajectory using a linear program which generates a trajectory preferring constant postion or constant velocity segments.

3. EXPERIMENTAL DESIGN

In this work, we investigate two critical aspects of robotic camera operation: path planning and motor control. A planning algorithm generates a saliency signal $\mathbf{s}(t) = [\hat{\phi}, \hat{\theta}, \hat{\dot{\phi}}, \hat{\dot{\theta}}]^\mathsf{T}$ specifying a desired instantaneous pan-tilt position $(\hat{\phi}, \hat{\theta})$ and velocity $(\hat{\dot{\phi}}, \hat{\dot{\theta}})$ for the camera at every time instant. The control algorithm regulates the speed of the pan-tilt motors so that the camera follows the planned state space trajectory $\mathbf{s}(t)$ as best as possible.

To gauge the success of our proposed hybrid robotic/virtual camera solution, our experimental set-up consist of three different camera operation techniques (see Fig. 2):

Benchmark Our objective is to mimic a human operator. Therefore, we measure the performance of a human operator using a joystick with direct control over the pan-tilt motor speeds.

Baseline We use a standard visual servoing implementation as our baseline: a realtime, zero-latency moving average causal filter generates a saliency signal from noisy player detections. An instantaneous position error proportion-only controller is used to regulate the pan-tilt motor speeds.

Figure 3: Experimental Setup. Two Allied Vision GX 1920C machine vision cameras mounted near the ceiling of the gym are used to detect and track the basketball players (see Fig. 4). Three Sony EX3 cameras situated behind the spectator seating at center court capture the broadcast video. Each camera is mounted on a FLIR D48-E robotic pan-tilt head. The motion of each camera is determined from either a human operated joystick, or an autonomically generated plan based on the realtime analysis of the player positions (see Fig. 5).

Proposed Our proposed solution employs a zero-latency causal filter for the robotic camera, and an M second delay inducing non-causal filter for the virtual camera. The position errors of both the robotic and virtual cameras are used to regulate the speeds of the pan-tilt motors or the robotic camera.

Because each technique regulates the pan-tilt motor speeds in a different way, our experimental setup (see Fig. 3) includes three Sony EX3 cameras mounted on FLIR D48-E robotic pan-tilt units. As a result, we are able to compare the three operation techniques on the same live data. The benchmark camera requires a human operator, whereas the baseline and proposed autonomous techniques both rely on a realtime computer vision system to detect the (x, y) locations of basketball players. Therefore, our setup includes two Allied Vision GX 1920C machine vision cameras mounted near the ceiling. We use the method of Carr *et al.* [2] to detect players at 25fps with one frame latency (see Fig. 4).

Changes in tilt are highly unaesthetic, so we employ a constant tilt angle for all three Sony EX3 broadcast cameras. For simplicity, the remainder of the paper only refers to the planning and control aspects of each camera's instantaneous pan position and velocity, but the theory and techniques which will be discussed shortly apply equally well to tilt. Similarly, we only consider the X coordinate of locations on the basketball court (corresponding to the lengthwise axis).

We first describe how a path is planned in each of the three scenarios, and examine how planning improves with increased delay. We then discuss the details of the resampling algorithm used to synthesize the images of the virtual camera. Finally, we detail how the robotic pan-tilt motors are controlled for each operation technique, and demonstrate how increased delay reduces the controllability of the hybrid camera.

Figure 4: Player Detections. Example frames from the machine vision cameras and corresponding detections.

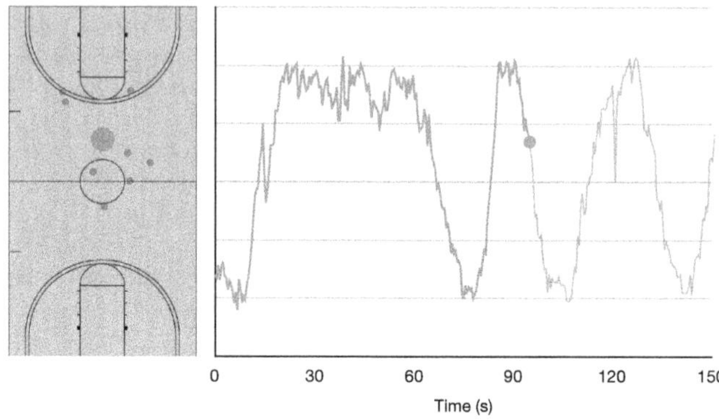

Figure 5: Centroid of Players. The vision system outputs a set of player locations (blue circles) for a given time instant. The centroid (green circle) approximates the appropriate fixation point. The trace of the centroid $\mathbf{r}(t)$ over time is shown on the right, where the current time is ~ 90 seconds.

4. PATH PLANNING

In this work, planning refers to the problem of generating the saliency signal $\mathbf{s}(t)$ from the detected player positions output by the vision system. It is equivalent to framing a shot in cinematography. The first task is to identify the subject(s) of interest, which in basketball corresponds to the players, ball and nets. Afterwards, the rules of shot composition [14, 16, 20] then dictate how the camera should be operated such that objects of interest appear in salient regions of the image (see Fig. 6). It is important to compose the shot such that the viewer can draw the correct interpretation. In basketball, the shot should be framed based on the current and anticipated player positions.

Perfect tracking of the players and ball is not yet possible in either online or offline approaches. Therefore, the autonomous understanding of the scene in realtime includes missed players and false detections. As a result, we employ assumptions common in visual servoing [9, 10] and approximate the camera fixation point as the centroid $\mathbf{r}(t) = [X, \dot{X}]$ of detected player positions.

PTZ Projection

The vision system outputs a fixation point $\mathbf{r}(t)$ in the world coordinate system, but the path planning algorithm must generate a trajectory $\mathbf{s}(t) = [\hat{\phi}, \hat{\dot{\phi}}]^\mathsf{T}$ in each camera's pan-tilt coordinate system. Before describing how an suitable camera path can be extracted from $\mathbf{r}(t)$, we briefly describe how a target location in the world coordinate system is converted into the pan-tilt coordinate system of a PTZ camera.

Figure 6: Rule of Thirds. Camera operators frame shots such that important objects fall on imaginary lines which divide the image into thirds. Objects in motion should have 'lead room' to illustrate where the object is going.

The PTZ cameras are calibrated using point correspondences between the ground plane and image plane (and assuming square pixels) [15]. The 3×4 projection matrix $\mathtt{P}$ maps a homogeneous 3D world point $\mathbf{X} = [X, Y, Z, 1]^\mathsf{T}$ to a homogeneous 2D image point $\mathbf{x} = [u, v, w]^\mathsf{T}$ via

$$\mathbf{x} = \mathtt{P}\mathbf{X}. \tag{1}$$

The projection matrix factors into matrices representing projective $\mathtt{K}$ (3×3), rotation $\mathtt{R}$ (3×3) and position parameters $\mathbf{C}$ (3×1)

$$\mathtt{P} = \mathtt{KR}[\mathtt{I} | -\mathbf{C}]. \tag{2}$$

The intrinsic matrix $\mathtt{K}$ contains the focal length f and principal point (u_0, v_0)

$$\mathtt{K} = \begin{bmatrix} f & 0 & u_0 \\ 0 & f & v_0 \\ 0 & 0 & 1 \end{bmatrix}. \tag{3}$$

The rotation matrix of each Sony EX3 camera changes as its corresponding robotic head moves. As a result, we factor $\mathtt{R}$ into two rotation matrices $\mathtt{Q}$ and $\mathtt{S}$ such that

$$\mathtt{R} \stackrel{\text{def}}{=} \mathtt{QS}. \tag{4}$$

The rotation matrix $\mathtt{S}$ represents the rotational aspects of the transformation from the world coordinate system to the home (0,0) pan-tilt position and remains fixed. The matrix $\mathtt{Q}$ is the 3D rotation for the current pan-tilt position (ϕ, θ) relative to the coordinate system of the pan-tilt motor axes and must be recomputed whenever the robotic head moves

$$\mathtt{Q}(\phi, \theta) = \begin{bmatrix} \cos(\phi) & 0 & -\sin(\phi) \\ -\sin(\phi)\sin(\theta) & \cos(\theta) & -\cos(\phi)\sin(\theta) \\ \sin(\phi)\cos(\theta) & \sin(\theta) & \cos(\phi)\cos(\theta) \end{bmatrix}. \tag{5}$$

Oracle

The purpose of the path planning algorithm is to generate a saliency signal $\mathbf{s}(t)$ defined in each camera's pan-tilt coordinate system based on the centroid $\mathbf{r}(t)$ of player locations as observed by the vision system. We begin by evaluating the assumption that the centroid of player positions is a reasonable approximation for the true fixation point.

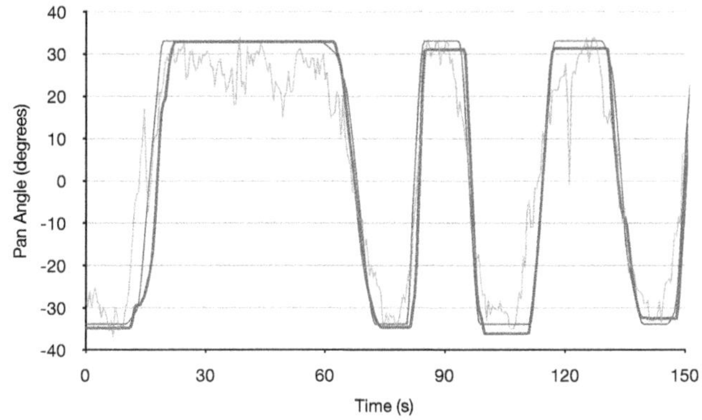

Figure 7: Human and Oracle Signals. The human operated joystick (red) reasonably tracks the oracle signal (blue), although it lags on occasion and misses the optimal pan angle at each end of the court. The raw player detections centroid (green) also follows the oracle signal, but with substantially more noise, and tends to lead and lag the oracle signal more than the human controlled camera.

We generate a ground truth *oracle* saliency signal $\mathbf{s}^\star(t)$ for the first half of a basketball game by manually identifying key pan positions every second which generate well composed shots. For example, the player with the ball is placed on the appropriate third so that the majority of the image shows where the ball may go next, while at the same time, the amount of visible court area is maximized.

Over the same period of the game, the human operated camera reasonably traces the oracle signal (see Fig. 7). In addition, the centroid of player positions also tracks the oracle signal reasonably well, although it does lag or lead significantly at times. The centroid is not a good approximation in certain basketball situations such as fast breaks, or slow approaches by the point guard (when the defending team falls back to half court defense). However, it is a reasonably good fixation point the majority of the time.

Error Measure

Good camera operation should follow the target of interest with smooth, purposeful motion. Therefore, when comparing a saliency signal $\mathbf{s}(t)$ to the oracle $\mathbf{s}^\star(t)$ signal we evaluate discrepancies between position (for accurate tracking), velocity (for smooth motion) and changes in direction (for purposeful motion). We arbitrarily assign equal importance to these three factors, although one could tailor the weighting for a specific preference. Additionally, we normalize the measured discrepancy with respect to the oracle based on the performance of the human operated camera.

Causal Filtering

Online systems require causal filters which only depend on current and previous values. Our benchmark implementation of visual servoing uses a moving average filter to smooth out the noise in the pan angles from the noisy centroid of player positions. The filter buffers the pan angles previously computed over the last N seconds and outputs the average of the buffered values (see Fig. 8). As N increases, the filtered signal $\mathbf{s}_N(t)$ becomes more smooth, and changes in direction are reduced. However, the filter performance saturates for large N because any gain in smooth and purposeful motion is offset by tracking errors arising from significant filter lag.

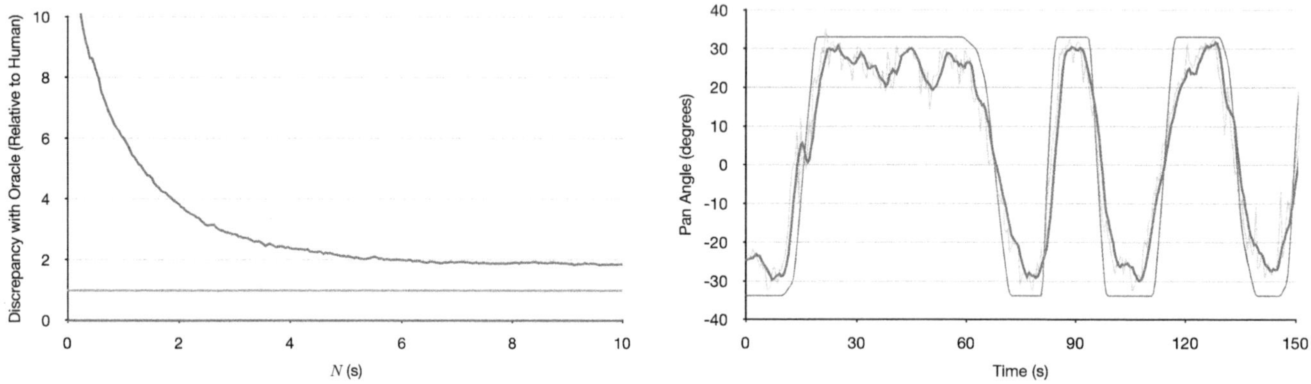

Figure 8: Causal Filter. Left: The performance of moving average causal filter (red) as a function of buffer size is plotted relative to the human operated camera (green) and oracle (blue). A larger buffer size produces smoother and more purposeful camera motion, but struggles to track a rapidly moving target, which is why performance saturates at roughly 2×. **Right:** The filter for $N = 2.0$s produces a slightly smother output than the noisy input signal (green) without introducing significant lag with respect to the oracle (blue).

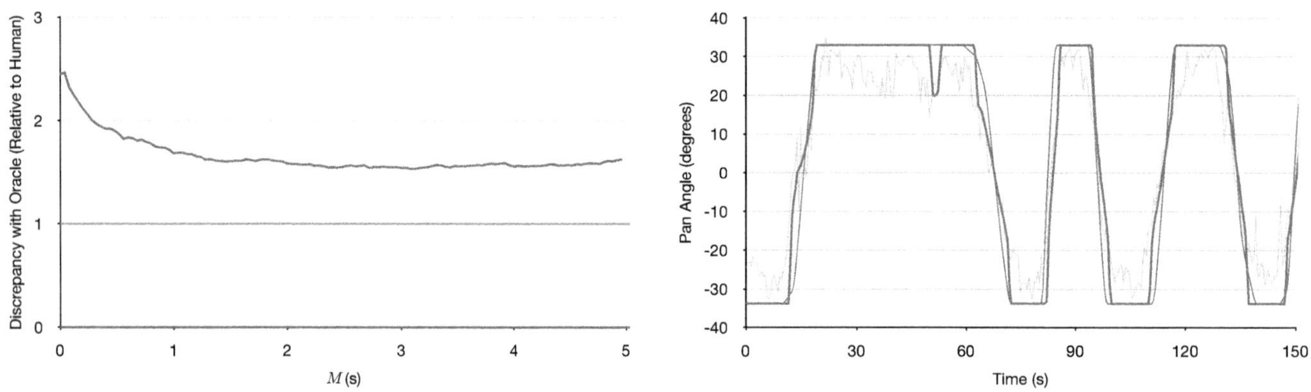

Figure 9: Non-Causal Filter. Left: The performance of the L1 trend non-causal filter (red) increases with a larger induced delay M. In effect, the filter is able to look further into the future before determining whether the camera should maintain its current trajectory or transition to a different trajectory. **Right:** The filter for $M = 2.0$s generates a reasonable approximation of the oracle signal (blue). For clarity, the filter output has been shifted M seconds into the future in order to align temporally with the raw input (green) and oracle signals.

Non-Causal Filtering

Offline and delayed online systems can use non-causal filters which consider previous, current and future values to output a filtered response at the current time. We buffer $N = 10.0$s into the past and M seconds into the future. We begin by approximating the buffered signal as a series of constant velocity segments using L1 trend filtering [18]. The filtered pan positions at the current time and up to four seconds into the future are examined by a Schmitt trigger to produce a hysteresis effect (moving the camera when tracking error is large, and stopping the camera when tracking error is small). If the Schmitt trigger anticipates a change in state, the filter applies a fourth-order polynomial to ease-in/out from the current position/velocity to the anticipated position/velocity [6].

We evaluate the non-causal filter's performance for different values of M (see Fig. 9). The hysteresis aspect of the filter produces a dramatic improvement in purposeful camera movement. As expected, the filter exhibits diminishing returns for larger and larger values of M because distant future events should not significantly impact the decision of how the camera should be moved at the current time instant. Unlike the causal filter, the non-causal filter does not introduce any lag dependent on N because the L1 trend filter fits constant velocity segments to the raw signal (and knowledge about future events prevents the constant velocity model from overshooting).

Although the non-causal filter produces a trajectory that is similar to the oracle, the filtering process is unable to remove the systematic errors associated with the assumption that the centroid of player positions is an adequate proxy for the correct camera fixation point. Quite often the centroid leads the oracle signal when easing out of a stationary state (since the defending team often falls back to half court defense). To overcome these systematic measurement errors, more complex feature extraction and planning algorithms would be needed.

5. SPHERICAL RESAMPLING

The non-causal filter generates a trajectory $\mathbf{s}_{N,M}(t)$ for the virtual camera operating on a delay of M seconds. The video of the virtual camera must be synthesized from the video of the robotic camera. The virtual camera is operating on a delay of M seconds, and we denote its current time t. To generate the current virtual image, we must resample the image $\mathbf{I}(t - M)$ captured by the robotic camera M

Figure 10: Spherical Resampling. The image captured by the robotic camera (left) at pan $\phi_{\text{robotic}}(t-M)$ is resampled to synthesize the image of the virtual camera (right) oriented at $\hat{\phi}_{\text{virtual}}(t)$. Here, the virtual camera is looking further to the right than where the robotic camera had looked, which is why only pixels from the right side of the image are used for resampling.

seconds ago. At that time, the robotic camera was at pan position $\phi_{\text{robotic}}(t-M)$. The non-causal filter will generate a target pan angle $\hat{\phi}_{\text{virtual}}(t)$ for the virtual camera, which should be similar to both the planned $\hat{\phi}_{\text{robotic}}(t-M)$ and actual $\phi_{\text{robotic}}(t-M)$ robotic camera positions.

Similar to [7, 11, 12], we synthesize the video of virtual PTZ camera via a projective warping (see Fig. 10). In this situation, the mapping from virtual image plane to the robotic image plane is governed by a purely rotational homography [15]

$$\mathtt{H}_{\text{real}\rightarrow\text{virt}} = \mathtt{K}_{\text{virtual}}\mathtt{R}_{\text{virtual}}\mathtt{R}_{\text{robotic}}^{-1}\mathtt{K}_{\text{robotic}}^{-1} \quad (6)$$

which can be obtained by substituting $\hat{\phi}_{\text{virtual}}(t)$ and $\phi_{\text{robotic}}(t-M)$ into (5). If the video of the virtual PTZ is synthesized by cropping a rectangular subregion from a stationary camera, the resulting video no longer has its optical axis near the center of the image which makes the camera appear as though it is translating left/right on a track or up/down on pedestal.

It is important to note that the size of the image generated by (6) remains constant regardless of any change in focal length between the robotic and virtual cameras. However, as the focal length of the virtual camera increases, the number of pixels sampled from the robotic camera decreases; lowering the effective resolution of the virtual camera. Additionally, we currently assume there is no significant motion blur in the images captured by the robotic camera, and do not render blur effects into the synthesized images of the virtual camera based on its virtual motion.

If there is a large discrepancy between the virtual camera's planned position $\hat{\phi}_{\text{virtual}}(t)$ and the actual state $\phi_{\text{robotic}}(t-M)$ of the robotic camera, it is entirely possible that (6) will map all or part of the virtual camera's image beyond the boundary of the robotic camera's image. In this situation, the system can clamp the planned state of the virtual camera to ensure it remains within the field of view of the robotic camera, or render empty/black regions in the virtual camera image. Neither solution is ideal. Clamping the virtual camera motion will induce jitter into the smooth trajectory, and black regions rendered in the images of the virtual camera are unaesthetic. In the next section, we mitigate these non-ideal boundary effects by controlling the pan-tilt motors to balance the deviation of the virtual camera from the center of the robotic camera's image against the deviation of the robotic camera from its planned state space trajectory $\mathbf{s}_N(t)$.

6. CAMERA CONTROL

With plans for the robotic and virtual cameras established, the final task is to operate the robotic camera such that the virtual camera is able to follow its planned trajectory as much as possible (since the broadcast video originates from the virtual camera, not the robotic camera). We first discuss the control aspects of each camera individually, and then address the issues of controlling both cameras in a holistic fashion.

Robotic Control

Each FLIR pan-tilt unit is operated with a 30Hz control loop that gets the current pan-tilt positions $(\phi_{\text{robotic}}, \theta_{\text{robotic}})$ and sets the pan-tilt velocities $(\dot{\phi}_{\text{robotic}}, \dot{\theta}_{\text{robotic}})$. In traditional visual servoing, the task of getting the robotic camera to follow the trajectory $\mathbf{s}_{\text{robotic}}(t)$ generated by the causal filter is regulated based on the residual $e_{\text{robotic}}(t)$ between the actual pan position and the desired position

$$e_{\text{robotic}}(t) = \hat{\phi}_{\text{robotic}}(t) - \phi_{\text{robotic}}(t). \quad (7)$$

We employ proportion-only feedback

$$\dot{\phi}_{\text{robotic}}(t) = \dot{\hat{\phi}}_{\text{robotic}}(t) + \kappa\, e_{\text{robotic}}(t). \quad (8)$$

Virtual Camera

The virtual camera represents an infinitely fast, massless system which compensates for the deviation between the current planned position generated by the non-causal filter, and where the robotic camera was looking M seconds ago

$$e_{\text{virtual}}(t) \stackrel{\text{def}}{=} \hat{\phi}_{\text{virtual}}(t) - \phi_{\text{robotic}}(t-M). \quad (9)$$

If the deviation is large, it is entirely possible the virtual camera will move beyond the boundary of the image captured by the robotic camera M seconds ago. One possibility is to restrict $|e_{\text{virtual}}(t)| \leq \Delta\phi$ by modifying $\hat{\phi}_{\text{virtual}}(t)$. Another possibility is to increase the zoom of the virtual camera. In our experiments, we define the focal length of the virtual camera to be equal to that of a Sony EX3 camera equipped with a standard lens (so that we can make side-by-side comparisons between the video synthesized by the virtual camera and that captured by a visual servoed camera).

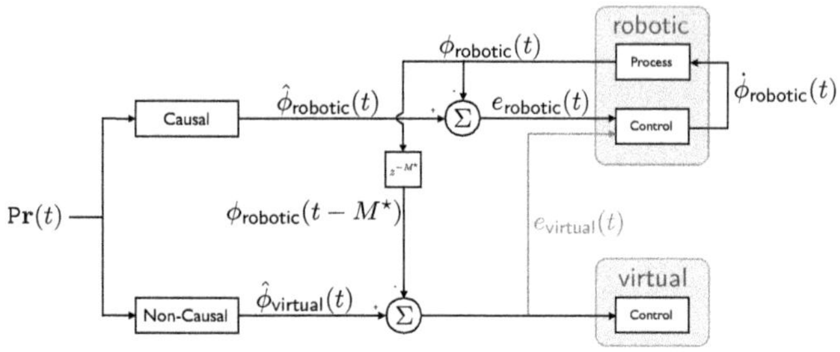

Figure 11: We control the hybrid camera by modifying the control of the robotic camera to consider not only the discrepancy $e_{\text{robotic}}(t)$ of where the robotic camera should look (determined by the output of the causal filter) but also the discrepancy $e_{\text{virtual}}(t)$ (highlighted in red) of where the virtual camera should look (determined by the non-causal filter). The robotic camera's feedback control loop contains delayed values which decreases the stability of the system as the delay grows in magnitude.

The change in focal length between the virtual and robotic cameras is equivalent to a 1.5× zoom factor applied to the wide angle lens of the robotic camera. The robotic camera has a horizontal field of view of $\sim 80°$, and the virtual camera $\sim 60°$. As a result, the virtual camera can deviate $\pm\Delta\phi = 10°$ before hitting the frame boundary. If the focal length of the virtual camera is increased, the deviation $\Delta\phi$ would increase as well, with exact values determined by (6).

Arbitrarily restricting the virtual camera to remain within the image captured by the robotic camera may create an erratic motion path. Ideally, the non-causal filter should take deviation limits into account when planning the trajectory. However, even if a maximum deviation $\Delta\phi$ were enforced in the non-causal filter, the system would not be correcting the error in the robotic camera, and the virtual camera may drift further from the planned trajectory. In this work, we investigate an alternative solution: as the virtual camera deviates from the center of the captured image, we incorporate an addition term into the robotic camera's velocity controller (8) to induce motion which pushes the virtual camera back to the center of the image (or equivalently pulls the robotic camera to follow the plan of the virtual camera).

Hybrid Camera

We control the robotic and virtual cameras in a holistic fashion by defining the deviation of the hybrid camera as a linear combination of the robotic and virtual camera deviations

$$e_{\text{hybrid}}(t) = e_{\text{robotic}}(t) + \gamma\, e_{\text{virtual}}(t) \tag{10}$$

The robotic deviation indicates how the robotic camera should move to follow $\hat{\phi}_{\text{robotic}}(t)$. The virtual deviation indicates how the robotic camera should move to return the virtual camera to the center of the image.

$$= \hat{\phi}_{\text{robotic}}(t) - \phi_{\text{robotic}}(t) + \gamma\hat{\phi}_{\text{virtual}}(t) - \gamma\phi_{\text{robotic}}(t - M) \tag{11}$$

Substituting $e_{\text{hybrid}}(t)$ for $e_{\text{robotic}}(t)$ in (8) results in a proportional feedback control

$$\dot{\phi}_{\text{robotic}}(t) = \dot{\hat{\phi}}_{\text{robotic}}(t) + \kappa\, e_{\text{hybrid}}(t) \tag{12}$$

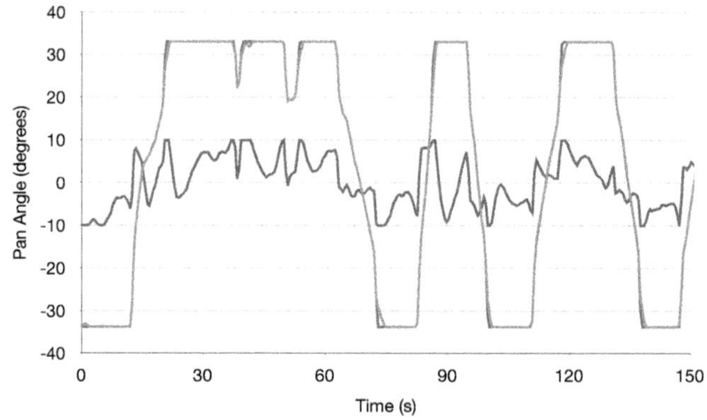

Figure 12: Independent Control. In the above scenario, the virtual camera operates on a 1.0 second delay and is restricted to remain within the image plane of the robotic camera. There is no feedback between the virtual camera and the robotic camera (i.e. the signal $e_{\text{virtual}}(t)$ in Fig. 11 is not sent to the robotic controller). As a result, the relative position (blue) of the virtual camera with respect to robotic camera fluctuates between $\pm 10°$. When the virtual camera hits either of its pan limits, there is a deviation between where the virtual camera is looking (green) and where the non-causal filter had planned for it to look (red).

which balances how well the robotic and virtual cameras follow their plans while encouraging the robotic camera to deviate from its plan to ensure the virtual camera does not go outside the image boundary. The challenge with the proposed formulation is that the hybrid feedback includes a delayed term $\gamma\phi_{\text{robotic}}(t - M)$ which decreases the stability of the system (see Fig. 11).

Stability Analysis

We evaluate the hybrid camera's ability to follow the plan generated by the non-causal filter for a variety of values of γ and M (the two parameters introduced into our proposed control loop). We limit the virtual camera's movement to remain within the field of view of the robotic camera — i.e. ϕ_{virtual} must be within $\pm 10°$ of ϕ_{robotic}.

We consider the case of $\gamma = 0$ as our baseline because there is no delayed feedback from the virtual camera in this situation. Effectively, the robotic and virtual cameras are controlled independently. The performance of this configuration for $M = 1.0$s is shown in Figure 12. The relative pan angle (blue) of the virtual camera with respect to the robotic camera illustrates the situations when the virtual camera reaches the frame boundary of the robotic camera (for example, saturating at $+10°$ at roughly 20 seconds). When this occurs, the tracking performance deteriorates and the virtual camera (green) is no longer able to follow the desired non-causal plan (red). Over this 150s sequence, the virtual camera was at the frame boundary 10.5% of the time, which resulted in an average per-frame control error (the deviation from the non-causal filter output) of 0.21° per frame. On average, the virtual camera was looking 5.9° from where the robotic camera had looked M seconds ago.

Next, we examine the situation when delayed feedback from the virtual camera is incorporated into the control loop. The hybrid camera's performance when $\gamma = 0.5$ and $M = 1.0$s is shown in Figure 13. In this configuration, the

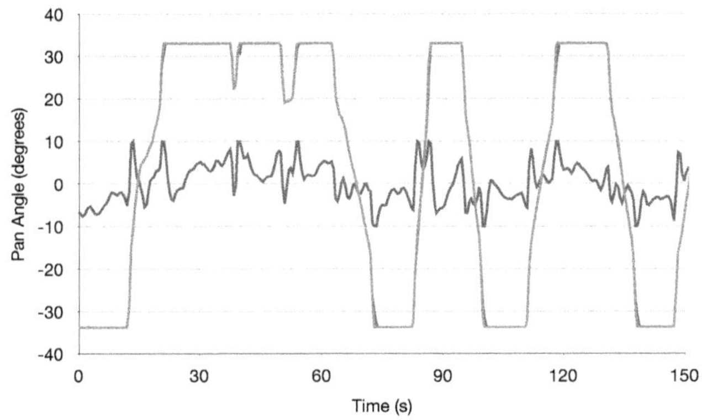

Figure 13: Stable Hybrid Control. The simulation now incorporates a delay $M = 1.0$s, and the relative position of the virtual camera $e_{\text{virtual}}(t)$ is incorporated into the robotic camera's control algorithm. As the virtual camera moves away from the center of the robotic camera's image, the robotic controller will adjust the robotic camera's speed to drive the virtual camera back to the image center. Similarly, the resulting path of the hybrid camera (green) more closely follows its plan (red).

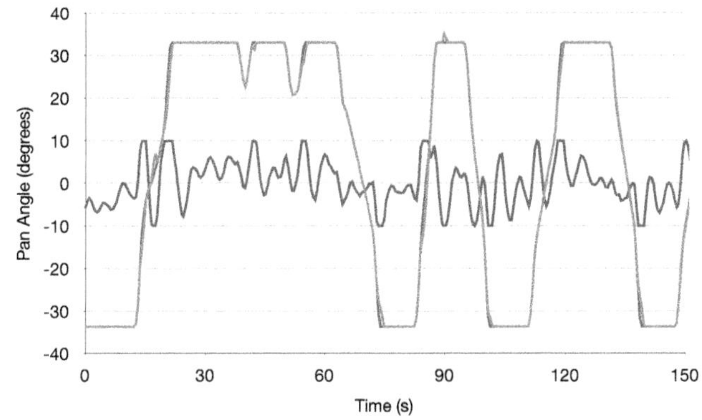

Figure 14: Unstable Hybrid Control. When $\kappa = 0.75$ and $M = 2.0$s, we see the adverse effects of incorporating too much gain and delay in the feedback signal. The robotic camera oscillates around its target trajectory, and the virtual camera oscillates from one frame boundary to the other. As a result, the virtual camera exceeds the 33° pan limit at $\sim$ 90s.

virtual camera is able to track the plan generated by the non-causal filter quite well. Over the same 150s sequence, the virtual camera was only at the frame boundary 5.1% of the time (roughly a 2× improvement over independent control). Similarly, the average per-frame deviation was reduced to 0.11°. Furthermore, the hybrid controller was able to balance the errors of both cameras so that the virtual camera remained closer to the center of the robotic camera's image at all times: the average discrepancy in pan angles was reduced to 4.6°. Qualitatively, hybrid control has increased the frequency of the virtual camera's relative pan angle (blue), but has reduced its overall energy.

However, if the feedback gain γ is too high, or the delay M becomes too large, the resulting control loop may be unstable. Figure 14 shows how a hybrid controller configured with $\gamma = 0.75$ and $M = 2.0$s begins to exhibit signs of an unstable system: the virtual camera begins to oscillate rapidly from one side of the robotic camera's frame to the other. Similarly, the robotic camera also oscillates because the controller is attempting to regulate the robotic camera's pan angle to keep the virtual camera in the center of the frame. For the same 150s sequence (although the non-causal plan is slightly different since the value of M has changed), the virtual camera now spends 12.6% of its time at the frame boundary, which results in an average per-frame tracking error of 0.30°. Furthermore, at 90s, the impact of unstable control becomes evident: the magnitude of the robotic camera's oscillation about a constant pan angle is so large, the virtual camera is unable to fully compensate, and the virtual camera exceeds the soft 33° pan limit.

7. SUMMARY

Autonomous camera systems have traditionally been implemented with either robotic cameras or virtual cameras resampled from fixed cameras. The offline resampling process can generate smooth aesthetic trajectories because the algorithm has full information about all future events. However, because the physical cameras do not move, the resolution of the system is limited. In addition, it is impossible to broadcast a live event. Robotic cameras, on the other hand, generate plans in realtime with no information about future events. Aesthetics aspects are often neglected because it is extremely difficult to track and accurately anticipate object motions in realtime and zero latency. In this work, we propose a hybrid system which operates a virtual camera on a delay (so that it can plan smooth purposeful motion based on perfect knowledge about immediate future events) and controls a robotic camera to follow the live action (which maximizes the resolution of the synthesized broadcast video). As we have shown, the amount of delay is a crucial design parameter. Longer delay improves the path planning process, but makes stable robotic control more difficult.

We employ hysteresis to generate purposeful camera motion; it is better to maintain the camera's current trajectory than to deviate slightly to make a small improvement in shot composition. Incorporating hysteresis into a zero latency system is difficult because switching from one state to another may generate a discontinuous plan or introduce temporary latency while the system transitions between states. However, by operating a virtual camera operating on a delay, our non-causal hysteresis filter is able to anticipate state changes based on actual future information.

If the operating delay is sufficiently short, controlling the robotic camera to keep the virtual camera within its field of view is advantageous. However, if the delay becomes too large, the system may become unstable. In this situation, the robotic camera should be controlled in a traditional visual servoing manner with no delayed feedback; the video can still be resampled with an independently controlled virtual camera operating on a delay. Although our example prototype system is geared towards autonomous cameras, the idea of a hybrid robotic/virtual camera can apply to robotic cameras with remote human operators.

8. REFERENCES

[1] Y. Ariki, S. Kubota, and M. Kumano. Automatic production system of soccer sports video by digital

camera work based on situation recognition. In *International Symposium on Multimedia*, 2006.

[2] P. Carr, Y. Sheikh, and I. Matthews. Monocular object detection using 3D geometric primitives. In *ECCV*, 2012.

[3] F. Chen and C. D. Vleeschouwer. Personalized production of basketball videos from multi-sensored data under limited display resolution. *CVIU*, 114(6), 2010.

[4] K. Choi, S. W. Lee, and Y. Seo. Automatic broadcast video generation for ball sports from multiple views. In *International Workshop on Advanced Image Technology*, 2009.

[5] M. Christie, P. Olivier, and J.-M. Normand. Camera control in computer graphics. *Computer Graphics Forum*, 27(8):2197–2218, 2008.

[6] J. Craig. *Introduction to Robotics: Mechanics and Control.* Prentice Hall, third edition, 2004.

[7] S. Daigo and S. Ozawa. Automatic pan control system for broadcasting ball games based on audience's face direction. In *ACM Multimedia*, 2004.

[8] A. Dearden, T. Demiris, and O. Grau. Learning models of camera control for imitation in football matches. In *International Symposium on Imitation in Animals and Artifacts*, 2007.

[9] A. Farag and A. Abdel-Hakim. Virtual forces for camera planning in smart video systems. In *WACV*, 2005.

[10] N. R. Gans, G. Hu, and W. E. Dixon. Keeping multiple objects in the field of view of a single ptz camera. In *American Control Conference*, 2009.

[11] M. Gleicher and J. Masanz. Towards virtual videography. In *ACM Multimedia*, 2000.

[12] M. L. Gleicher and F. Liu. Re-cinematography: improving the camera dynamics of casual video. In *ACM Multimedia*, 2007.

[13] M. Grundmann, V. Kwatra, and I. Essa. Auto-directed video stabilization with robust l1 optimal camera paths. In *CVPR*, 2012.

[14] M. Haigh-Hutchinson. *Real-Time Cameras.* Morgan Kaufmann, 2009.

[15] R. Hartley and A. Zisserman. *Multiple View Geometry in Computer Vision.* Cambridge University Press, second edition, 2004.

[16] S. Katz. *Film Directing Shot by Shot.* Michael Wiese Productions, 1991.

[17] K. Kim, D. Lee, and I. Essa. Detecting regions of interest in dynamic scenes with camera motions. In *CVPR*, 2012.

[18] S.-J. Kim, K. Koh, S. Boyd, and D. Gorinevsky. L1 trend filtering. *SIAM Review*, 51(2), 2009.

[19] D. Nieuwenhuisen and M. Overmars. Motion planning for camera movements. In *ICRA*, 2004.

[20] J. Owens. *Television Sports Production.* Focal Press, 2007.

[21] C. Pinhanez and A. Bobick. Intelligent studios: Using computer vision to control TV cameras. In *IJCAI Workshop on Entertainment and AI*, 1995.

[22] R. Stanciu and P. Oh. Designing visually servoed tracking to augment camera teleoperators. In *IROS*, 2002.

[23] X. Sun, J. Foote, D. Kimber, and B. S. Manjunath. Region of interest extraction and virtual camera control based on panoramic video capturing. *IEEE Transactions on Multimedia*, 7(5), 2005.

[24] T. Yokoi and H. Fujiyoshi. Virtual camerawork for generating lecture video from high resolution images. In *ICME*, 2010.

[25] C. Zhang, Z. Liu, Z. Zhang, and Q. Zhao. Semantic saliency driven camera control for personal remote collaboration. In *International Workshop on Multimedia Signal Processing*, 2008.

[26] C. Zhang, Y. Rui, J. Crawford, and L.-W. He. An automated end-to-end lecture capture and broadcasting system. *ACM Transactions on Multimedia Computing, Communications and Applications*, 4(1), 2008.

Social Life Networks: A Multimedia Problem?

Amarnath Gupta
San Diego Supercomputer Center
Univ. of California San Diego
La Jolla, USA
a1gupta@ucsd.edu

Ramesh Jain
Computer Science
Univ. of California Irvine
Irvine, CA 92617
jain@ics.uci.edu

ABSTRACT

Connecting people to the resources they need is a fundamental task for any society. We present the idea of a technology that can be used by the middle tier of a society so that it uses people's mobile devices and social networks to connect the needy with providers. We conceive of a world observatory called the Social Life Network (SLN) that connects together people and things and monitors for people's needs as their life situations evolve. To enable such a system we need SLN to register and recognize situations by combining people's activities and data streaming from personal devices and environment sensors, and based on the situations make the connections when possible. But is this a multimedia problem? We show that many pattern recognition, machine learning, sensor fusion and information retrieval techniques used in multimedia-related research are deeply connected to the SLN problem. We sketch the functional architecture of such a system and show the place for these techniques.

Categories and Subject Descriptors

H.4 [**Information Systems Applications**]: Miscellaneous; D.2.8 [**Software Engineering**]: Metrics—*complexity measures, performance measures*

General Terms

Multimedia, Situation model, Social Networks

Keywords

Situation Recognition, Event Monitoring

1. INTRODUCTION

Connecting people to the resources they need is a fundamental task for any society. Connecting patients to the appropriate health care facility, farmers to the right people in the right agricultural advice centers, disaster victims to the best shelters, are actions that every society and its societal agents (Government, Military, non-profit organizations) carry out on a regular basis. In developing countries, the needs for security, food, water, health care, education, and basic transportation are still unsolved. [9] argued that one can think of the world population as a pyramid. the large middle section of the pyramid can, with sufficient technology support, be assisted to find the connections they need to improve their lives. Their lack of current, factual information creates many problems, including ineffective resource distribution, wasted aid, and poor living quality. With the right technology infrastructure, the MOP segment of the human society can be connected to the resources they need.

We imagine a new world where all people are connected in a giant social network, where every node is a real-life entity (people, organizations, facilities, equipment, ...) and every edge is a local connection between a node pairs that are spatially, emotionally, or logically close to them. This would include their neighbors, doctors, their local grocery stores and police stations, their homes and workplaces as well as things in their homes and workplaces, their local transportation and places in their villages and cities. This social network, accessible from their simple and smart phones and computers, is always keeping up to date information about the physical entities they represent. The whole network acts as a "world observatory", and yet provides only information to people related to their "circles". We call such a world-status-bearing network a *Social Life Network* (SLN). Although such an idealized, abstract network does not exist today, we postulate that if we unite all social networks and interconnected mobile devices capturing every moment of our lives, web sites tracking our browsing behavior, electronic commerce transactions we make every day, and bring them under a single network, it is not too far-fetched to see that we are already very close to having an SLN.

The SLN is, by definition, a dynamic entity. It is designed to be always current and constitutes a model of the evolving world; it captures events and situations in the life of each person or thing and collective events and situations that affect any segment of the human society represented in the SLN. Therefore, an SLN has a fundamental difference compared to standard social networks. In an SLN, properties (and hence nodes and edges) of the graph are always evolving; therefore paths between two nodes might emerge or disappear as the model evolves. This gives rise to a generic problem that we refer to as the *SLN Problem*: "Can we connect a person node in an SLN to a resource node as the person's situation evolves and needs to be connected to the resource node?" In other words, can we connect a person to a matching resource as and when the person's situation

MM'13, October 21–25, 2013, Barcelona, Spain.
Copyright 2013 ACM 978-1-4503-2404-5/13/10 ...$15.00.
http://dx.doi.org/10.1145/2502081.2502279.

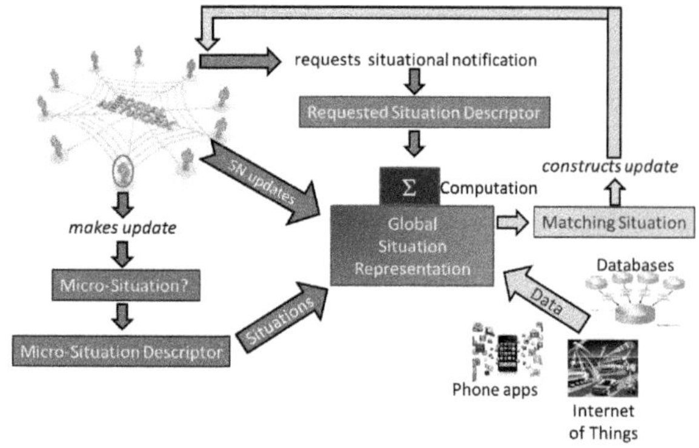

Figure 1: A schematic sketch of a Social Life Network

evolves? To our knowledge, this is a new unsolved problem for the next generation of social networks.

At this point, it would seem that this next-generation social networks problem is completely unrelated to multimedia systems. We however argue that multimedia systems should not be narrowly defined as a discipline that operates on sensory signals like audio, images and video to extract semantics. Rather, it should be viewed as a wealth of representational and computational techniques that model the real world in terms of multidimensional signals and applies some specific classes of operations on them – if any engineering problem can make effective use of these techniques, it falls within the purview of multimedia systems. In the case of the SLN problem we posit that today's social network solutions do not adequately capture the spatiotemporal dependencies of real world situations in a way that multimedia representations can and therefore, we should be able to use multimedia techniques for this problem. Based on this postulation, we intuitively hypothesize that *one can automatically derive a media-representation of the evolving properties of the SLN model, and utilize it for situation detection that enables a solution for the SLN problem by using computing techniques from multimedia systems.*

The Intuition. A Social Life Network can be pictorially represented as shown in Figure 1. It builds on a social network, defined in a broader sense, where not only people, but other objects like mobile applications, databases, and the Internet of Things (e.g., household appliances and cars) also provide information. All of these information sources send their "signals" to a separate Situation Management Module. This module monitors the updates made by the members of the social network as well as other information from the networked world, and determines if any of the updates may qualify as a potential micro-situation, based on some criteria set by the administrators of the system; if an update passes the qualification test, it gathers contextual information about the update and constructs a micro-situation object, which it sends to a global Situation Processor. On the other hand, another member posts a request for situations it would like to be notified on. This request is also converted into a desired Situation Description, and sent to the same processor. The processor matches the situation request with the already-ingested situation updates, and upon finding a successful match, constructs a suitable update message, and dispatches it to the appropriate requesters.

As we have seen in Situation Recognition Systems [25, 26], the computation preformed inside the processor can make use of spatial, temporal and semantic representations used by multimedia techniques. The primary intuition behind a multimedia representation is simple. *If real-world events can be captured using a suitable combination of human and electronic sensors, then interesting situations can be recognized as the occurrence of spatiotemporal patterns in the combined sensor-space. These pattern computations can be performed by first computing application dependent features from these combined sensors, and then applying appropriate matching techniques on these feature sets.* In the next section, we elaborate on this intuitive principle.

2. SITUATION DETECTION: MULTIMEDIA *VIS À VIS* SLN

Currently, most multimedia situation detection systems (including our own [25, 26]) go through the following generic workflow:

(a) Acquire signals from a few "media" sources like videos, image collections.

(b) Acquire signals from auxiliary sources (e.g., a GPS).

(c) Represent the signals in some novel, interesting way.

(d) Extract novel features that are geared toward object recognition, concept recognition, or action recognition.

(e) Use a classifier to group and categorize the features into some known situation categories.

Since it attempts to solve a larger problem, the SLN setting goes far beyond solving situation recognition problems in several important ways.

(i) We can conceptualize the input to SLN as *messages* – in a sense they form the "raw signals" from which the situations have to be assessed and acted upon. These messages can come from people who actively post them. However, they could also come from sensors (GPS location) that "post" on a user's behalf, from global information sources (rainfall from a weather station, regional drought statistics from a Government agency) or from software applications that transmit highly focused complex data (e.g., prescription refills from a doctor's office; heart rate, activity level from a mobile application).

(ii) The messages would often be partly structured text and semi-structured data from sensors and applications respectively, but they will also contain labeled images, videos and voice information related to messages.

(iii) The situation understanding process must extract, integrate and correlate the relevant information produced by the multiplicity of diverse and complex messages, which will come in asynchronously, following different formats and protocols. This correlation must be computed both at the level of single person's messages (micro-situations as shown in Fig. 1) and at the global situation processor that assimilates micro-situations as well as global situations to determine actions.

(iv) The SLN has to be able to handle multiple representations and sometimes joint representations that facilitates feature extraction and situation recognition. A well-studied analogy is the widespread use of both

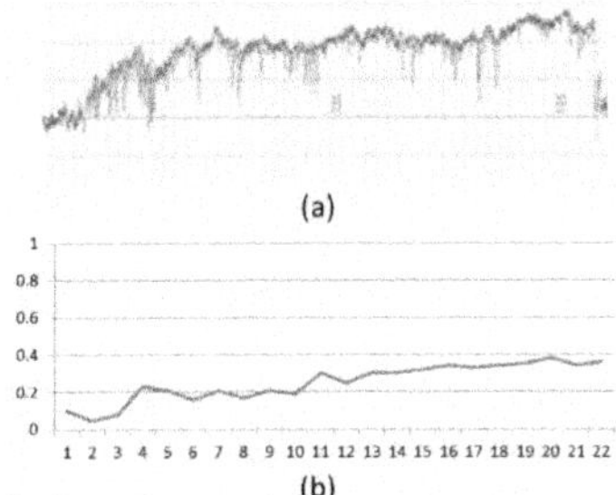

Figure 2: (a) The heart rate of a person as she types a message, (b) the emotionality measurement of the same person

time and frequency domain representations for signal processing and interpretation. These representations are useful for different problems, and hence are equally valuable. An interesting example of joint representation is a spectrograph which is a time-plot of short-term Fourier coefficients computed over small intervals.

(v) Unlike a multimedia information retrieval system, there need not be any explicit query in SLN. The evolving situation of the SLN member *is* a continuous query posed to the rest of the system. However, the processor needs to produce an action only when the combination of the member's micro-situation and the global state of the world "match" in some well-defined way.

(vi) Tasks like "matching" situations and classifying situation-related features will possibly be a combination of automated and human-powered (e.g., through crowdsourcing) because the time-to-response may sometimes be critical for actions like rescuing a flood victim.

Despite these distinctive characteristics of SLN situation processing compared to standard multimedia situation detection, they are deeply connected.

2.1 Signal Formation in SLN

In standard multimedia problems, the signals are a given – one starts with signals from the media source(s), and possibly supplements it with additional data sources. In SLN however, *signals need to be constructed* from asynchronous, multivariate, mixed-modality information coming from possibly uncoordinated source. Often the construction itself is a computational process, and depends on the application in which the situation recognition occurs. In this sense, we blur the distinction between what is called a feature in traditional multimedia system and what we are calling situation-depicting signals in our current setting. As a simple, somewhat unrealistic example, consider the time-series (a) and (b) in Figure 2. The first time-series is measured from the online activity in a network, and depicts the burstiness of activity measured an SLN member on a specific site. The second time-series is measured by a wearable device from the same member, and represents the member's heart rate. As shown in the figure, the member's site activity is frequent, and the heart rate has a moderate elevation. These two indicators, taken individually, say nothing about the member's state or situation. Taken together, they might signify a level of increasing stress in the member as she interacts at the web site, and hence may be considered as the components that can construct a "virtual", semantic *signal* by combining these two measurable signals. The difficult part is making the decision that these signals jointly constitute an event-level signal. Once the decision is made, the problem transfers to the realm of existing or emerging multimedia techniques (e.g., sensor fusion) for the actual construction process. In [21] the authors perform cooperative localization, i.e., accurately detect the actual positions of vehicles based upon the vehicular velocity and yaw-rate reported at 50 Hz, combined with GPS coming through a Global Navigation Satellite System (GNSS) reported at 4Hz. The latter signal however is prone to ambiguity because it gets impacted by the buildings around the vehicle. The technique in [21] uses a Bayes filtering technique to handle the GNSS ambiguity, and then uses raytracing from building models to eliminate undesirable GNSS signals. Coupled with the vehicle motion signals, they construct the "virtual" (fused in their terminology) positional signal. Mapping to our example, combining the message and time-series signals can be achieved if it can be shown that they are generated by the same time-dependent point process (or processes that last for a duration [10]), i.e., the probability of their co-occurrence can be predicted by a single generative model. The details of such combination modeling is beyond the scope of this "ideas" paper.

2.2 An Analysis of SLN Signals

It is evident from the prior discussion that a primary design problem for situation processing in SLN is to identify and characterize the classes of virtual signals that need to be constructed. Here, we define a starting analysis of such signals that we have identified from the current multimedia-related literature.

An SLN signal is by definition a temporal entity that depicts the existence of a complex state, entering into and exiting a state, a state transition with transition parameters (like delays), or a declaratively definable pattern over the states and transitions. The states, transitions, and patterns can be thought of in terms of the following axes.

There is a wide diversity among the observed situation-depicting variables that define SLN signals. Roughly, we can think of them as measurements, derived measurements, references, reference-based measurements, aggregates, relationships and propagations. A measurement is a direct observation (e.g., GPS coordinates) that is used to compute states (of entities, or phenomena or locations), and is often subject to stability and accuracy issues. To construct a situation signal from a measurement one often goes through a discretization or robust estimation process before it is actually used. In [17], McGovern *et al* use a SAX-based [24] discretization technique for detecting situations in two different scenarios. In the first an individual's state of motion (going up the stairs vs. down the stairs) is computed from discretized measurements of joint trajectories; in the second, the states of supercell thunderstorms are recognized using wind speed, barometric pressure and so forth. A derived measurement is computed from one or more measurements. Frequency of a single signal, the joint probability of a multivalued signal are classical derived measurements used for situation detection. A reference is the mention of one entity (or event) in another entity. Attaching a picture to a message, citing an event in a tweet are examples of references. The entity (or event) in question can either be the concept of the entity (or event), or a concrete instance thereof. For example, a bag of words based feature description associated with a concept name is a reference to a concept; on the other hand, referring to a specific labeled event (e.g., a much discussed violent crime) is an example of the latter. From a multimedia viewpoint, this mention and its temporal behavior can be viewed as a situation-depicting signal. As a simple example, just counting the number of occurrences of "Boston Marathon" (an instance of a `marathon race` concept) in messages and pictures over time starting April 2013 will determine that an evolving situation has occurred about this event. In a more complex case, [23] have developed a traffic situation detection method, where a vehicle specifies its own state (e.g., stopped at an intersection) by referencing the other entities and events in its vicinity (e.g., entity:car-in-front c, event:c "suddenly-stopped"). Reference-based measurements are variables derived from references. Continuing the traffic metaphor, a time-plot of the number of cars in a highway segment (a contextual locational variable) that entered a `stopped` state because the `car-in-front` had a `suddenly-stopped` event designates the onset of a traffic jam, and perhaps an accident situation. The last two examples also show the use of aggregates in the construction of a situation-depicting signal. But we would like to specially mention aggregates because they are always parameterized over a collection mechanism. In the Eventshop system [25, 26] the aggregate structure comes in the form of a spatial grid that stores the aggregate of messages based on a theme at every time-point. The situation detection occurs by specifying a tree of algebraic operations that compute patterns on the spatial grid. A relationship conforms to the notion of a "relational feature" in multimedia systems; with this category of "signals", a situation emerges because of the interaction between multiple-parties, where a party can be any combination of entities, locations and events. The traffic situation example above can be viewed as a rudimentary relationship. A more suitable case has been developed in [2] where multi-party situations are analyzed by classifying the state of each person with an SVM, computing the motion of a person through sensors, and the distances between people as a proxy for interaction (they do not consider non-physical interaction like conversation or electronic communication). These virtual signals are fused to detect situations like "introduction" or "game playing". Finally, propagation refers to signals that arise due a *flow* over a structure. Two well-researched examples are optical flow [19], and network flow that are widely used in literature as models of an evolving situation. As a concrete example, a road segment network is a network that is laid over a spatial grid, and traffic flow, measured from vehicle location and velocity as well as from inductive loops can be measured over segments of the network. The situation-depicting flow signal is computed using an origin-destination flow model in this case by combining road-segment data (i.e. data from the edges of the network) with spatiotemporally acquired data through Emage operations [25]. The propagation is then measured by observing the variation of the flow over the structure of the network, i.e., as a time series at every node of the road network.

In the beginning of this section, we noted the importance of combining multiple "raw signals" to create situation-depicting signals. Most of the efforts described in the foregoing paragraphs and systems like them make use of one or more combination technique. We describe some of them.

The EventShop system [5] achieves this integration in two stages. In the first stage a *stel*, i.e., a spatiotemporal element that aggregates the count of some physical variable (collected from one or more data sources) is created on a single semantic theme at a single time point. More generally, however, it can use any other aggregation function that constructs the stel-value. A spatial grid (an array) of stels constructs what is called an *Emage*. A sequence of spatial grids (i.e., a time-series of arrays with application-defined spatial and temporal resolutions) constitute an Emage-sequence for a single variable. In stage 2, when multiple variables need to be combined, the system lets the user define a tree of algebraic operations that create a new Emage sequence from existing Emage sequences. Emutem, a healthcare application described in [18] aims to combine signals from microphones, physiological parameter sensors (e.g., pulse rate) and infrared occupation sensors to detect situations like fall and heart attack. Since all signals are continuous, they use a Gaussian mixture model to specify each type of signal and then use a fuzzy information combination model with Gaussian membership functions. At a more symbolic level, [19] creates an activity recognition system for healthcare – it uses an SVM to classify the individual activity signals and then apply a rule-based information combination method on the results of classification. In a smart home application, [3] uses an ontology-driven rule engine to real-time, continuous recognition of household activities like making coffee and watching TV. Finally, [8] constructs "logical sensors" by combining the outputs of hardware sensors using subjective logic, which is a modification of the well-known Dempster-Shafer model for belief propagation.

We note that the foregoing discussion is not about how the SLN should operate, but to establish the intuition that many of the current representation and analysis machinery used by the multimedia, pattern recognition and pervasive computing communities can be viewed through the glasses of situation processing. Next, we turn our attention to the actual information processing in an SLN as we see it.

3. SITUATION PROCESSING IN ACTION

3.1 Three Use Cases

We present three uses cases with distinct foci to develop the mechanics of situation processing within the SLN system. In the first two cases, assume that the SLN works atop a social network S which has individual, group and system type members. For every member, the SLN provides a special "friend" called the *Situation Box*, which can be treated just as another member of the network – when desired, the user will post messages to the Situation Box, tag it in pictures, other entities and events, send voice messages to it, and respond to any information that is posted by the Situation Box. The Situation Box, which is run by the SLN, can also provide messages to the human member. If the member so desires, she can direct her mobile device applications to post information to this situation box on her behalf. An application like Moves (`http://www.moves-app.com/`) could, for instance, auto-post the location and activity on behalf of the member if desired. Whenever the Situation Box receives any user input, it is registered by the SLN as a user event. For non-human members, however, every posting made is considered to be a contributing event. For the third case, assume that the SLN works on the Internet of Things and vehicular ad-hoc networks (VANET).

Elderly Person in a Disaster. Sue, an elderly member of the SLN, lives by herself and has difficulty walking, a complaint she has often made to the Situation Box. Sue has environmental allergies from multiple allergens including dust and mold, and often suffers from allergy-induced asthma. Whenever she suffers an allergy attack, usually after cleaning her house, she complains to the Situation Box, but usually feels better in a day or two. At the time of our interest, Sue is aware of an impending hurricane predicted to sweep over her town. In her repeated and increasingly anxious complaints to the Situation Box, she says she is concerned about her house flooding. She also expresses deep concern that she will have severe mold allergy, like she had five years ago, if her house gets flooded. The SLN should assess her situation and connect her with family, or an evacuation team or emergency medication services to help her.

Insect Infestation in India. Dr. Thomas Reinhardt, an agricultural entomologist in Berlin studies south Asian insects, especially insects that infest agricultural plants. His maintains two circles on this SLN, personal and professional. The professional circle consists of his colleagues, and a special entity called "Problems", where he expects to gather interesting real-world problems related to his area of interest. He links his "Problems" node to the Situation Box, which gathers situations as requested by people who post "Desired Situations" on the board, with the expectation that the SLN will find *matching situations* and respond to the posts. Far away, in a few states of Northwest India, farmers are experiencing an unexplained problem with the crop they are growing – the leaves are discoloring and the plants are dying. They have started using their phones to send updates to their Situation boxes. These updates include pictures and steps they have already taken. The SLN is expected to have Dr. Reinhardt be interested in the case, and perhaps contact the Government to offer his expertise.

Situation-aware Vehicular Network. An non-human SLN is built on top of a VANET, where the members are cars, traffic sensors on freeways, including inductive loops, periodic reports from emergency roadside services, and mobile traffic applications like Waze (`www.waze.com`). For this SLN, information updaters are smart cars whose positions on a road segment, velocities, accelerations are known at every k seconds, and dynamic relationships are formed between a car and other cars within a d distance. Let us assume every car wants a notification if it is heading toward an impending traffic jam or accident situation (i.e., this "query" is made by every car) based on status updates by its neighbors and then wants to connect to a car at the nearest exit to enquire about the local traffic situation. The SLN also has access to traffic volume and speed estimates, historical average and peak traffic for any time of the day, and weather reports. The expectation from the SLN is that it will update potentially affected cars within a reasonable time so that they can advise the drivers of a different route.

3.2 Overall Functionality of the SLN

Let us recapitulate the primary situation processing tasks in a social life network through our use cases.

(a) For every registered member of the SLN, it must *record and monitor the events generated by the member* based on (i) information offered by the member and (ii) the output on any devices and applications that monitor the member's state. These user events must be transformed to situation-depicting signals and must be interpreted in context to derive what we call a *micro-situation* in Figure 1. In the elderly person's case, the SLN must derive a progressive sequence of micro-situations. In the case of the Indian farmers, the micro-situations sent by every farmer can be gathered into a *macro-situation*, a data structure to hold an aggregate view of the total crisis. As we will see, the techniques of situation-depicting signal generation in Sec. 2.2 will be used here.

(b) The SLN also records, maintains and monitors the *interest and capability* declared by any member that can play the role of a resource provider. The SLN converts this declaration to a **match target**, which is notionally like a continuous query plan in a data stream management system, but with an important distinction. Provider capabilities and interests are not static, define-once structures. They evolve over time, sometimes based on dynamically changing situations, and sometimes just with time. For the elderly lady, the nearest rescue center may have to change its plans as it gets filled up as more people seek shelter; but the shelter five miles away has just expanded its capacity.

(c) It assimilates, computes and monitors the *state of the world* (i.e., the world within the SLN's purview), by collecting contextual information sent by physical, social, Internet etc. from a large body of external information resources (e.g., weather, news, police advisories). However, the information from these resources can show wide variability in their timeliness, frequency of update, accuracy, coverage and granularity. If the Vehicular Network gets the information that the police has just closed an exit 2 miles down the freeway, it must adjust its computation of traffic jam likelihood. Most of the information combination techniques from Section 2.2 apply here.

(d) It must *match the micro and macro situations to the declared interests and capabilities* of the resource providers. Since both these factors evolve with time, the matching process must be time aware. Techniques for situation matching will use algorithms from database, information retrieval and multimedia communities. Further, since the quality of match strongly depends on the contextual data like location of the situation, conditions under which the situations occur and any other correlated data will play a significant role in the matching process.

(e) Finally, once the match has occurred, *the result of the match must be delivered back* to the members whose situations can be addressed – it is desirable that this delivery of result is always accompanied by a concrete action. In the case on Indian Farmers, the SLN will have to construct semi-structured multimedia summary packet of the evolving state of the ailing crops (and their environment) that is comprehensive enough for Dr. Reinhardt.

These five components form the basic building blocks of the SLN architecture. The next section discusses the operations of these components in more detail.

4. FUNCTIONAL ARCHITECTURE OF SITUATION PROCESSING IN SLN

The members in an SLN can have three roles – they can be

solution seekers (SS), solution providers (SP) or information providers (IP). A single member can serve in any of the three roles, but may have only one role at a time. Any transaction with the SLN (e.g., through the Situation Box) must be identified as one of these roles. In the following we refer to member actions with respect to their roles.

4.1 Formation of Micro and Macro-Situations

To create a micro-situation from an SS member's member events, the SLN uses a basic situation constructor and a number of specialized situation constructor modules that work cooperatively. These constructors operate on the messages and related information, and creates/updates one or more *situation description structures* (SDS), data structures that are shared by all situation handling modules.

The Analyzer. The activity analyzer takes as input a member activity and analyzes it for augmentation. The most common activity is sending messages. A text message `M` has an optional `[object, [tag]]` portion that depicts a list of objects (e.g., pictures) that can be posted and the list of tags that can be associated with each object. The tag may be assigned by the user or maybe assigned by an automatic or human algorithm. In the Indian farmers case, people can attach the tag "severe discoloration" to the picture of the wheat plan leaves. `M` is always analyzed for content and references. Every content analysis function assigns one or more *scores* to the message, which are then attached to the message. For example, entity and emotion detection algorithms can be applied to `M`, producing a referred entity list, and a list of {`emotion, strength`} pairs. The entity (e.g., "flood water") will be recognized using a relevant ontology and the emotions (e.g., `[(fear, 0.6), (sadness, 0.2)]`) will be recognized using techniques described in [14, 1]. Specifically, techniques like [14] relates the emotional (e.g., fear) to the causing entity (e.g., mold-allergy). An activity like adding a description to a picture is treated like a new message with the picture as the reference. An entity (e.g., a voice recording) with no textual tag will only be algorithmically analyzed.

SDS Objects. For every member the SLN Analyzer creates an *ECPS(event context parameter space)* instance, a multidimensional structure that is updated for every member activity. Based upon prior research that analyzes temporal statements about states and events [11] we can view the event e (e.g., posting a high-fear message, attaching pictures of one's body with the label "rash") in terms of the ECPS:

- $TIM(e)$, the mean time-of-occurrence of e
- $LOC(e)$, the location of e, if available
- $DUR(e)$, the duration of e
- $CAT(e)$, the category(-ies) of e based on some ontology
- $ENT(e)$, the set of entities related to e
- $EVT(e)$, events occurring within $\pm\Delta T$ of e
- $AFR(e)$, the average frequency if e occurs repeatedly
- $AGE(e)$, the length of time since the first event like e

The parameter $CAT(e)$ is assigned by a classification algorithm (e.g., [13, 29, 15, 16]) that analyzes `M` and labels it with a known term from an ontology. The labeling is crucial because depending on the event category, it can be sent to a special handler that performs deeper situational analysis of the event. For example, medical-events (e.g., allergy and asthma in our example) are dispatched to a medical micro-situation generator (discussed next). In general $CAT(e)$ is multi-valued because more than one category can be assigned to e. The emotional classification of messages, for instance, can be a second category associated with e. Parameters $TIM(e), LOC(e), DUR(e), AGE(e)$ should be viewed at multiple levels of granularity. The frequency of occurrence should be represented by the minute, hour, day, the time of the day (e.g., evening), and so forth because the event pattern for constructing the reference model can be found at any level of granularity. Parameters $ENT(e)$ and $EVT(e)$ are computed only from the content of the augmented message `M` and its history for the current member, and not on any global situations.

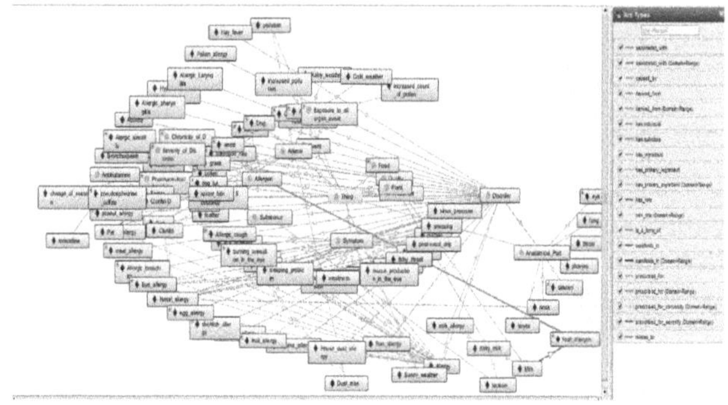

Figure 3: A portion of the Allergy Asthma Ontology

When the categories are more specific, the micro-situation detector can produce a much richer situation description using the relevant ontologies. Figure 3 shows a portion of the allergy-asthma ontology. This ontology contains the knowledge diseases and their classifications, symptoms, drugs for different forms of allergies, allergens that are responsible for different symptoms and so forth. When Sue's messages are passed to this disease aware situation handler, it now navigate the ontology to elicit additional information by posting messages back to Sue's Situation Box – it can ask whether Sue has the requisite medication to last long enough, extract the response and place it in the micro-situation it constructs for Sue.

A secondary SDS object used by the SLN is an *evolving subspace cluster tracker (ESCT)*. Based on the *ECPS*, we compute subspace clusters (assuming a finite set of event and entity categories) over the above parameters for a finite duration of time, followed by a cluster transition tracking technique. Subspace clustering techniques have been heavily used in signal processing [28], multimedia research [4, 22]. Cluster transition analysis has been used in multimedia applications ([7] for audio signal segmentation), and data mining [27, 12], where cluster transitions are categorized into external transitions (new cluster, cluster survival, cluster split, cluster absorption, cluster death) and internal transitions (no change, size change, compactness change, location change). If Sue posts a high-strung emotional message most Thursday mornings complaining about an allergy attack with a general reference to the housecleaning event, and reports a relief message by Friday afternoons, we will soon see a steady cluster in the (allergy-ThursdayMorning-housecleaning) subspace, and another steady cluster (relief-FridayPostMorning-AllergyMedication) subspace. The steady occurrence of these two time-delayed clusters will form a *ref-*

erence pattern for some of Sue's posting behavior. However, during the flood situation we will witness high-strung fearful postings that are more random in time, but more clustered in entities **flood, water, mold** – this shift in the clustering structure will be reflected through a set of *interestingness metrics* that compare clusters. Cluster survival is measured by testing if the two cluster means in the same region but at two different time points differ by less than half standard deviation. To detect compactness transitions, we use the difference of the standard deviations of the clusters X, Y. Cluster absorption is measured by absorption ratio, the portion of clusters of time t_i absorbed by clusters of time t_{i+1}. Cluster location shift is measured by a *skewness* metric [20]:

$$\gamma(X) = \frac{\frac{1}{|X|} \cdot \Sigma_{x \in X}(x - \mu(X))^3}{\frac{1}{|X|} \cdot (\Sigma_{x \in X}(x - \mu(X))^2)^{3/2}}$$

Micro-situation constructor. The concrete construction process of a micro-situation is performed as follows. For every SDS touched by a user activity (more generally, a set of user activities), there is a scoring mechanism that evaluates the *importance score* of the current activity. Different SDS objects and activity type combinations compute the score in different ways. For the cluster tracker SDS, the importance score can be computed by creating a union of conjunctive rules over the different measures of interestingness described above. Thus one can state that the importance score grows linearly if either the external or the internal transition score exceeds the threshold of 0.5, and is the higher of the two scores beyond 0.5. When the importance score is beyond a second threshold, the SDS objects are passed on to the Situation Matching module.

Macro-situation constructor. A macro-situation is processed the same way as a micro-situation except that in this case the system tracks SDS objects like ECPS and ECST for multiple members instead of individual members. But macro-situations often have a spatial variability that is captured by location-aware SDS object. We use Emage, the grid-like structure used in Eventshop [5, 25] as explained in Section 2.2 as a spatial SDS object. Each Emage is associated with the collection of messages from which it was derived, and is therefore connected to other SDS objects that are related to the same set of member-events.

4.2 Construction of a Match Target

Let us now look at Situation Processing from the SP-members' standpoint. In the simplest case, an SP-member uses a simple user interface to specify the nature of service or interest she can provide. Depending on the specified service, the SLN uses an ontology to acquire more information about the service. If a disaster shelter provides an accommodation service to 50 people, the SLN will simply ask for the location of the shelter, and create a variable to count the remaining capacity of the shelter at any point in time. The location information will be used to match potential victims using a distance measure between a victim and the shelter.

In a more complex case, the SLN offers a formal notification language to specify more complex conditions the situations of interest must satisfy. The full language is out of the scope of this paper, but as a simple SLN specification, Dr. Reinhardt's interest on recent south Asian insects infesting agricultural plants can be declared formally as follows.

```
WITH myInterest m                                  (1)
WHERE m.topic IN (instance*(O,insect-category-
1))                                                (2)
NOTIFY                                             (3)
WHEN                                               (4)
OCCURS SITUATION s AND                             (5)
s.ISABOUT m AND                                    (6)
S.occursDuring([Now-6,*],month) AND                (7)
S.severity > 0.6                                   (8)
```

Lines 1-2 specify a variable `m` of built-in type `myInterest` whose `topic` attribute can be any transitively derived instance of a specific insect category in an ontology `O`. The `NOTIFY` clause states that the provider should receive the notification. The notification condition uses the built-in expression `OCCURS SITUATION` and assigns the situation a variable `s`. The rest of the declaration specifies properties of the desired situation. Line 6 uses the special property `ISABOUT` to depict the approximate theme of the situation. The difference between `topic` and theme is that the former is a narrow subject associated with an SLN node, while the latter is associated with the aggregated topics of a collection of nodes, and hence has a broader scope. Line 7 uses the system-defined property `occursDuring` to specify the timespan of situation `s` and states that it should be at most 6 months old. Finally, line 8 uses a property `severity` between 0 and 1 and is set to be at least 0.6 in this declaration. The `severity` condition, as we will see, will get converted to the importance score discussed in Section 4.1. The declaration does not use any spatial condition about the situation because it can come from any place.

To convert this declaration into a representation that the situation processor may handle, it needs to be transformed into an automata structure that sits on top of SDS objects and monitors their changing states. We sketch the basic rationale of transformation process without giving the complete algorithm. 1) The ontological condition in the `WITH` clause gets unfolded, and the possible values of `m.topic` gets enumerated; in other words, `m.topic` is replaced by a list of k insects. 2) Since "topic" is known to be an entity reference, and entities are handled by the ESCT objects, the SLN creates a cluster tracking object for each insect so that it can track how cluster properties change with time. Further, it notes that the severity (in fact, an importance score) threshold should be OR-ed over the k clusters, i.e., the condition is satisfied if *any* of the k cluster severity values exceeds 0.6. Since this condition is only on a single entity, it should only use the intrinsic cluster transitions. Specifically, a set of rules will be used to identify that cluster size transition is the only interestingness metric that can be used here. Thus the conditions `s.ISABOUT m` and `s.severity > 0.6` transforms into `importanceScore(insect1.cluster.sizeTransition(deltaT)) > 0.6 OR ... (k times)`, where the `deltaT` parameter specifies the time period over which the size transition is observed, and can be nominally calculated as a fraction of the total period of observation (6 months in our case). Thus, if the fraction is 10%, the transition should be observed over some 18 days. A simple implementation of the `importanceScore` function can be to interpret it as % growth, thus a 60% growth over 18 days will satisfy the condition. 3) All user activities contributing to the qualify cluster elements are chosen (i.e., it gets the activity IDs of every user activity that satisfied condition in the previous step). 4) For these activities, get all other SDS objects (e.g., the Emage) (recall that a situation is physically represented as several different SDS objects). 5) Determine which of these SDS objects have a high importanceScore. 6) Create a SituationObject with information collected from the previous step.

The steps above represent a recipe for detecting the *candidate situation(s)* that Dr. Reinhardt maybe interested in. They still need to be evaluated and scored for their recency and overall severity as described in Section 4.4.

The above discussion should not give the impression that setting up the match target is not dependent on the global situation processor. Many times the interest specification of a provider would be dependent an evolving situation that is unrelated to member activities. If the disaster shelter loses power or accessibility, the interest specification might become useless. This information cannot be determined if only user activities are explored. In general, the match target should also inspect the *state of the world.*

4.3 Assimilation of World-State

The "world" in SLN refers to the physical reality represented through a collection of potentially real-time information sources that relevant for an application domain. These sources act as IP-members or are created virtually, by aggregating information from SS-members. Different weather stations can be IP-members that stream a vector of data every minute. On the other hand, for the Vehicular Network, one can construct an "average traffic speed" source that is computed from all cars for each road segment. Since they are not individual specific, they are modeled along the fundamental axes of any situation, namely time, location, thematic metadata, and optionally, any intrinsic observation structure over which the application domain can be interpreted. In many applications, the intrinsic observation structure may be space itself as in the case of [25]. But in our Vehicular Network use case, the road network is a more logical choice to interpret some of the situation dynamics. To allow for this, the SLN framework must admit multiple representations to serve different purposes within the same application, so long as they are in synchrony with one another. The framework also allows multi-resolution information in space and time so that different IP-members can provide information at different resolutions. It is the SLN system's task to keep them aligned with each other, and provide roll-up aggregation, and interpolation operations on the data so that any downstream operator (like convolution) can view all data at the same resolution.

Since there is large variety of information in an SLN network, it must allow multiple models of information assimilation depending on the data. In the case of the Vehicular Network, the likelihood of congestion will depend on external factors like the weather, and it makes sense to develop an estimate of the weather impact $w(r)$ on an arbitrary road segment r. If the weather information is provided by multiple weather stations, then $w(r)$ can be computed as an estimation problem using techniques like Kalman filtering combined with a spatial process like inverse distance weighting or Thessian polygon averaging. On the other hand, if each car also had an environment sensor and could measure rainfall, then $w(r)$ could be computed by a simpler aggregation model. Now consider police reports as an world event source that provides events like accidents, road blocks, police giving a ticket on the roadside and so on. To estimate its impact factor $p(r)$ on road segment r, we have to model it using a network propagation model that will predict (perhaps using machine learning) the spread of congestion probabilities for each event type and then aggregate all such probabilities using a suitable fusion mechanism like a Bayesian network. The takeaway point is that the assimilation model in SLN will never have a single solution, but must be crafted for each application using the same library of techniques predominantly used by the multimedia community. In our own research, we have designed Eventshop [5], where we have adopted a "design studio" approach to developing world assimilation models. Here, the designer will chooses representation models from a model library, data manipulation operators from an operator library, spatial and temporal process models from a process library and so forth, and compose them into an assimilation model to test it on sample data we collect.

Once the appropriate assimilation models are constructed, the SLN needs to combine it with both the micro (and macro) situations, as well as the interest and capability models that demonstrate situation dependency. For the Elderly Person use case, this means that the model of hurricane's effect, including estimates for accessibility, water damage, likelihood of mold damage, and so forth must be computed for Sue's house. If other specific parameters are needed for these computations, they must be obtained, often by direct communication with Sue through her Situation Box. For the shelter provider in the same hurricane situation, the situation model will be used to compute a number of *viability measures* for the provider's offer. If a long power outage occurs, the viability measure can use prior data from the current and similar providers to determine how long they have been operational without power, and then predict a time-based estimate of how long the shelter would be operational. In general, a vector of such situation-influence measures will be added to the interest profile of the predictor, and will be exercised upon a situation match.

4.4 Situation Matching

The fundamental task in Situation Matching is some combination of the following: deciding which providers' offerings and interests is of maximal use to a specific member (Elderly Person case), deciding which member-presented situations should be packaged for a provider to give him maximal situation information (Indian Farmer case) deciding what situational summary is most useful to a specific member (Vehicular Network case). All these tasks need some form of matching, which is a central capability of many different kinds of systems. In classical information retrieval (including multimedia), matching corresponds to a similarity computation between a query object and a feature object based on multiple criteria, and then a rank computation that aggregates the similarity scores into a total score. In many recommendation systems a match corresponds to a combination of two rank computations – content-based ranking based on item similarity, and collaborative filtering that ranks items used by users with similar profiles. Some modern search engines treat matching as a multi-stage decision process instead of a straightforward similarity based ranking computation. Situation matching in an SLN is an open problem where lessons can be learnt from several research communities. In this paper, we offer some general principles for the problem.

Severity Criteria. Contrary to retrieval and recommendation systems, a unique characteristic of the situation matching is that the member situations that need to find match targets may come with one or more severity criteria that imposes an urgency (i.e., a priority or a time-bound) condition on the match finding process. The severity measures need to be computed based on component-level measures. In Section 4.2, the provider's query uses the `importanceScore` function to compute one measure of severity based on the rate of growing references to the insects affecting the crop. In general, the estimated level of distress expressed in the micro-situations, the spatial extent of the macro-situations, the prior statistics of comparable infestations from the world-state assimilation models, will each compute a severity score. If the situation matching process is implemented as a decision process, it may compute the composite severity score by an evidence accumulation model.

Multi-Match. It is important to recognize that a single situation may satisfy multiple providers. Sometimes these providers will be in competition (i.e., only one shelter is needed for member), and sometimes they can be independently satisfied. For the Indian Farmers, a bank can provide a low-interest loan to the infestation victims independently of Dr. Reinhardt's possible suggestion of the correct plant and soil treatment. This introduces the issue of multi-query optimization because both "queries" can share several situation processing steps to gain overall efficiency. For example, both the bank and the entomologist will utilize the severity metric of estimated distress level and the spatial coverage estimate of the infestation problem. Therefore all computations leading up to these two estimates can be reused. Such reuse is vital to maintain the performance of SLN if it must be applied on an Internet scale. Although the general multi-query optimization is a known NP-complete problem, the SLN system is likely to provide enough contextual constraints on the problem to make it more tractable.

Hybrid Matching. It is now established that for many hard and time-critical information management tasks, completely automated solutions are less practical and less optimal than mixed mode operations that involve more user interaction and crowdsourcing to people. We expect that many situation matching problems need to balance automated matching with human-in-the-loop methods. The interesting questions are when the SLN should decide to consult a human, whom should it consult, and how it would use human-provided input to complete the matching task. In the Indian Farmer case, there is an image interpretation step that determines that discolored and disfigured portions of the leaf images need tagging (to identify potential insect names). So, it is reasonable to have automated techniques to classify images that need to be human tagged, and crowdsource the images or highlighted image regions for actual tagging. Since there might be uncertainty in the user responses, this crowdsourcing task would need to send the correct number of sample images to the correct number of people and aggregate results using mixture of experts model.

4.5 Result Formation and Delivery

Let us revisit the expected result when member situations and providers' offers and interests match in our use cases. For the Elderly Person, the provider(s) must get a member status report and the member needs to get a confirmation that the provider will contact her. For the Indian Farmers, the providers get a comprehensive summary of the situation without necessarily getting the details of any member's status. For the Vehicular Network case, every car gets a "personalized" report that contains a summary of the nearby congestion situation sorted by the its current distance from the congestion point. The common task here is to construct a *situation summary.* As in any summarization task, the objective is to preserve the overall thread of events, and provide more detail on only the salient fragments of the situations ordered in time. Further, whenever an important subevent of the situation occurs, it must be instantiate with sample "cases" which is a composition of "raw" content like messages, images, and voice recordings, but also their situational interpretations defined in terms of the important changes observed in the SDS objects. In the Indian Farmers case, the sudden jump in the photograph submission along with the most dominant increase in the spatial expansion of the infestation situation will be considered a salient situational feature – thus, plots of cluster sizes and before/after snapshots of spatial coverage at these salient time intervals should be part of the summary. Recently [30] have developed an integer programming based approach for video summarization that might be generalized for situation summarization. Comparable approaches have been used for other summarization tasks for news, scholastic text, and other forms of multimedia. We believe this is a particularly suitable subproblem to benefit from multimedia techniques.

5. CONCLUSION

The primary goal of this "ideas paper" is to present a complex, socially relevant problem to the multimedia community rather than offer a definite solution. We show different aspects of the problem and establish that it requires an amalgamation of techniques rather than a fixed approach; further, we identify and address several 'multimedia' related problems required to build emerging systems like the SLN. We have tried to highlight that the information representation methods, feature extraction and comparison algorithms, object and event recognition techniques, learning principles, retrieval strategies, semantic approaches and so forth that are currently developed by the community, can be effectively used for many parts of this problem. However, they must be extended and re-evaluated to meet the timeliness and appropriateness criteria for specific SLN applications.

Testing the idea. We have started creating an experimental testbed for the situation specification and matching problem. In this testbed, microsituations are generated using mobile apps, and world situations are monitored using Eventshop. However, the system is not yet connected to a messaging platform such as the SMSim [6]. This, alongwith scalability testing, is part of our future work.

The Morality Question. An obvious concern with the proposed system is its "big brother" flavor. There are legitimate security and privacy concerns in sending members' personal situations to a central matching machinery, and the potential threat that same situation matching machinery can be used for illegal profiling and immoral exploitation. We recognize the importance this issue and the need to engage in discussions on it, but consciously leave the topic outside the scope of this introductory paper. However, this should not limit other more restricted applications of the same idea. In a personal finance application, tracking the current and expected spending pattern of a family (playing the role of a society) the system may be able to connect a family member to a more reasonable store for buying a certain product. Here, while the state of the world (store prices) is assimilated and used, the information remains "local" to the family. Similarly, in an academic application, a new researcher (defined through a research and interest profile) can be helped by connecting her with the right professionals when attending a conference.

Finally, we thank the reviewers for their insightful comments, which have improved the paper significantly.

6. REFERENCES

[1] A. Balahur, J. M. Hermida, and A. Montoyo. Building and exploiting emotinet, a knowledge base for emotion detection based on the appraisal theory model. *IEEE Trans. on Affective Computing*, 3(1):88–101, 2012.

[2] O. Brdiczka, J. L. Crowley, and P. Reignier. Learning situation models in a smart home. *IEEE Trans. Sys. Man Cyber. Part B*, 39(1):56–63, Feb. 2009.

[3] L. Chen, C. D. Nugent, and H. Wang. A knowledge-driven approach to activity recognition in smart homes. *IEEE Trans. Knowl. Data Eng.*, 24(6):961–974, 2012.

[4] E. Elhamifar and R. Vidal. Sparse subspace clustering. In *Proc. of the IEEE Conf. on Comp. Vision and Pat. Recog.(CVPR) 2009.*, pages 2790–2797, 2009.

[5] M. Gao, V. K. Singh, and R. Jain. Eventshop: from heterogeneous web streams to personalized situation detection and control. In *Proc. of the 3rd Ann. ACM Web Science Conf.*, pages 105–108, 2012.

[6] M. Gatti, A. P. Appel, C. Pinhanez, C. dos Santos, D. Gribel, P. Cavalin, and S. B. Neto. Large-scale multi-agent-based modeling and simulation of microblogging-based online social network. In *Proc. of Int. Work. on Multi-Agent-based Simul.*, May 2013.

[7] M. M. Goodwin and J. Laroche. Audio segmentation by feature-space clustering using linear discriminant analysis and dynamic programming. In *IEEE Workshop on Applications of Signal Processing to Audio and Acoustics*, pages 131–134, 2003.

[8] G. Groh, C. Fuchs, and A. Lehmann. Combining evidence for social situation detection. In *Proc. of 3rd IEEE Conf. on Social Comput.*, pages 742–747, 2011.

[9] R. Jain and D. Sonnen. Social life networks. *IT Professional*, 13(5):8–11, 2011.

[10] M. Karsai, K. Kaski, A.-L. Barabási, and J. Kertész. Universal features of correlated bursty behaviour. *Scientific reports*, 2, 2012.

[11] Z. Kozareva and E. H. Hovy. Learning temporal information for states and events. In *Proc. of the 5th IEEE Int. Conf. on Semantic Computing (ICSC)*, pages 424–429, 2011.

[12] C. Lauschke and E. Ntoutsi. Monitoring user evolution in twitter. In *IEEE/ACM Int. Conf. on Advances in Social Networks Analysis and Mining*, pages 972–977, 2012.

[13] K. Lee, D. Palsetia, R. Narayanan, M. M. A. Patwary, A. Agrawal, and A. N. Choudhary. Twitter trending topic classification. In *IEEE Data Mining Workshops at ICDM*, pages 251–258, 2011.

[14] S. Y. M. Lee, Y. Chen, and C.-R. Huang. A text-driven rule-based system for emotion cause detection. In *Proc. of the NAACL HLT Workshop on Comput. Approaches to Analysis and Generation of Emotion in Text*, pages 45–53, 2010.

[15] C. Li, A. Sun, and A. Datta. Twevent: segment-based event detection from tweets. In *Proc. of the 21st ACM Int. Conf. on Information and Knowledge Management, CIKM*, pages 155–164, 2012.

[16] H. Liu, B. Luo, and D. Lee. Location type classification using tweet content. In *11th Int. Conf. on Machine Learning and Applications (ICMLA)*, pages 232–237, 2012.

[17] A. Mcgovern, D. H. Rosendahl, R. A. Brown, and K. K. Droegemeier. Identifying predictive multi-dimensional time series motifs: an application to severe weather prediction. *Data Min. Knowl. Discov.*, 22(1-2):232–258, Jan. 2011.

[18] H. Medjahed. *Distress Situation Identification by Multimodal Data Fusion for Home Healthcare Telemonitoring.* PhD thesis, Institute National des Telecommunications, Jan 2010.

[19] Y. Nam, S. Rho, and C. Lee. Physical activity recognition using multiple sensors embedded in a wearable device. *ACM Trans. Embed. Comput. Syst.*, 12(2):26:1–26:14, Feb. 2013.

[20] I. Ntoutsi, M. Spiliopoulou, and Y. Theodoridis. Tracing cluster transitions for different cluster types. *Control and Cybernetics*, 38(1):239–259, 2009.

[21] M. Obst, S. Bauer, P. Reisdorf, and G. Wanielik. Multipath detection with 3d digital maps for robust multi-constellation gnss/ins vehicle localization in urban areas. In *IEEE Intelligent Vehicles Symposium (IV)*, pages 184–190, 2012.

[22] G. Petkos, S. Papadopoulos, and Y. Kompatsiaris. Social event detection using multimodal clustering and integrating supervisory signals. In *Proc. of 2nd ACM Int. Conf. on Multimed. Retriev.*, page 23, 2012.

[23] M. Platho, H.-M. Groß, and J. Eggert. Traffic situation assessment by recognizing interrelated road users. In *Proc. of the 15th Int. IEEE Conf. on Intell. Transp. Systems*, pages 1339–1344, 2012.

[24] J. Shieh and E. Keogh. iSAX: indexing and mining terabyte sized time series. In *Proc. of the 14th ACM SIGKDD Int. Conf. on Knowl. Discovery and Data Mining*, pages 623–631, 2008.

[25] V. K. Singh, M. Gao, and R. Jain. Social pixels: genesis and evaluation. In *Proc. of the ACM Int. Conf. on Multimedia*, pages 481–490, 2010.

[26] V. K. Singh, M. Gao, and R. Jain. Situation recognition: an evolving problem for heterogeneous dynamic big multimedia data. In *Proc. of the 20th ACM Multimedia Conf.*, pages 1209–1218, Nov. 2012.

[27] M. Spiliopoulou, I. Ntoutsi, Y. Theodoridis, and R. Schult. Monic: modeling and monitoring cluster transitions. In *Proc. of the 12th ACM Int. Conf. on Knowledge discovery and data mining (SIGKDDD)*, pages 706–711, 2006.

[28] R. Vidal. Subspace clustering. *IEEE Signal Processing Magazine*, 28(2):52–68, 2011.

[29] S. R. Yerva, Z. Miklós, and K. Aberer. Entity-based classification of twitter messages. *IJCSA*, 9(1):88–115, 2012.

[30] Z. Yuan, T. Lu, D. Wu, Y. Huang, and H. Yu. Video summarization with semantic concept preservation. In *Proc. of the 10th Int. Conf. on Mobile and Ubiquitous Multimedia*, pages 109–112, 2011.

Unveiling the Multimedia Unconscious: Implicit Cognitive Processes and Multimedia Content Analysis

Marco Cristani[1]
Alessandro Vinciarelli[2,3]
[1]University of Verona (Italy)
[2]University of Glasgow (UK)
marco.cristani@univr.it
vincia@dcs.gla.ac.uk

Cristina Segalin[1]
Alessandro Perina[4]
[3]Idiap Research Institute (Switzerland)
[4]Microsoft Research (USA)
cristina.segalin@univr.it
alperina@microsoft.com

ABSTRACT

One of the main findings of cognitive sciences is that automatic processes of which we are unaware shape, to a significant extent, our perception of the environment. The phenomenon applies not only to the real world, but also to multimedia data we consume every day. Whenever we look at pictures, watch a video or listen to audio recordings, our conscious attention efforts focus on the observable content, but our cognition spontaneously perceives intentions, beliefs, values, attitudes and other constructs that, while being outside of our conscious awareness, still shape our reactions and behavior. So far, multimedia technologies have neglected such a phenomenon to a large extent. This paper argues that taking into account cognitive effects is possible and it can also improve multimedia approaches. As a supporting proof-of-concept, the paper shows not only that there are visual patterns correlated with the personality traits of 300 Flickr users to a statistically significant extent, but also that the personality traits (both self-assessed and attributed by others) of those users can be inferred from the images these latter post as "favourite".

Categories and Subject Descriptors

H.3.1 [**Information Storage and Retrieval**]: Content Analysis and Indexing—*Indexing methods*; I.4.10 [**Image Processing and Computer Vision**]: Image Representation—*Statistical*; J.4 [**Social and Behavioral Sciences**]: *Psychology*

Keywords

cognitive processing; feature extraction; flickr; image representation; personality traits

1. INTRODUCTION

Until a few years ago, production and diffusion of multimedia data required skills and infrastructure that were the privilege of a few individuals and organizations (archives, digital libraries, online repositories, etc.) [39]. Nowadays, technologies as ubiquitous and user-friendly as smartphones and tablets allow one to easily create multimedia material (pictures, videos, soundbites, text and their combinations) and share it with others - typically through social media or other online technologies - by simply pushing a button. In such a technological landscape, multimedia data is not just a way to transmit knowledge and information - as it used to be traditionally for any type of data [6, 42] - but one of the channels through which we interact with others.

The core idea of this article is that, in such an unprecedented scenario, *the exchange of multimedia data has become a form of human-human communication and, therefore, it should involve the cognitive phenomena typically observed in human-human interactions.* This applies in particular to implicit cognitive processes that take place outside our conscious awareness, but still shape to a large extent our perception of the world and our behavior [24], namely the tendency to express and attribute to others goals, values, intentions, traits, beliefs and any other type of socially relevant characteristics [50].

To have a measure of how much multimedia data have become a means of communication between people, it is sufficient to consider a few statistics available on Youtube at the moment this article is being written[1]: while uploading every day 12 years of video material, Youtube users access the popular on-line platform one trillion times per year, an average of 140 visits per person on Earth (the figure refers to 2011). In other words, there seems to be no multimedia sample produced by one person that is not consumed by someone else. Unlike a mere few years ago, creation, diffusion and sharing of multimedia data is no longer the exclusive prerogative of skilled professionals, but the everyday practice of the lay person. Multimedia data are no longer, or no longer exclusively, the carefully crafted product of creativity and communication skills, but the spontaneous expression of common individuals involved in everyday social interactions.

The problem is that our cognitive processes are the result of a long evolutionary history and cannot change at the pace of technology. Therefore, our cognition keeps following patterns that were shaped during times when technology was far from existing [33]. In particular, a large body of evidence shows that our cognition constantly works to make sense of the world around us and that this happens, to a large extent, "*effortlessly, and even unintentionally*" [49]. This means that the information we gather and process through

[1]`http://www.youtube.com/yt/press/statistics.html`

MM'13, October 21–25, 2013, Barcelona, Spain.

ACM 978-1-4503-2404-5/13/10 ...$15.00.
http://dx.doi.org/10.1145/2502081.2502280.

our conscious attention - the typical realm of current multimedia technologies - is only one of the factors that drive our reactions towards the environment, the others being "*implicit, even automatic processes: implicit attitudes, inferences, goals and theories, and the affect and behaviors they produce*" [50], where the word "*implicit*" means outside our conscious awareness.

To the best of our knowledge, multimedia approaches neglected so far to a large, if not full, extent the phenomena above. Most of the current technologies take into account only information that can be automatically detected in the data (*e.g.*, objects in pictures) or inferred from it (*e.g.*, genre from music). The few attempts to take into account implicit cognitive processes focused on observable effects, including emotional, behavioral and physiological reactions, used, *e.g.*, for retrieval [1] and tagging purposes [37]. However, such reactions might be difficult to detect, especially in settings where social norms impose behavioral limitations (*e.g.*, public spaces). Furthermore, observable reactions are nothing else than effects that follow the actual changes in the user, namely those that concern "*implicit attitudes, inferences, goals and theories*" (see above).

The possible solution to such a state of affairs is that cognitive changes behind observable reactions are not random, but tend to follow, according to the *Brunswik Lens* [5], stable and predictable patterns. The Brunswik Lens, one of the most effective models developed in cognitive psychology, provides a framework suitable for investigating how multimedia data can be adopted as an observable evidence of "attitudes, inferences, goals and theories" (see above) of data producers. Symmetrically, the model helps to explain how data consumers attribute "attitudes, inferences, goals and theories" to data producers.

This paper shows that cognitive effects are detectable at least in the case of the interplay between Flickr pictures and personality traits of Flickr users.

The results, obtained over PsychoFlickr (a novel image dataset of 60,000 images posted by 300 individuals), show not only that there is a statistically significant correlation between personality traits of the users and features extracted from the images they post, but also that the same features are correlated with the traits that picture observers assign to the users, even if observers and users have never been in contact. Furthermore, both associations are sufficiently stable to be learned by supervised statistical classifiers. This opens up to a set of applications like, *e.g.*, automatic attribute prediction: given a pool of images, the goal is to infer personal characteristics of its owner. This goal is performed here by projecting images on low-dimensional manifolds and exploiting sparse regression.

The rest of this paper is organized as follows: Section2 surveys research trends relevant to this work, Section 3 describes the Brunswik Lens model, Section 4 presents the dataset used for the experiments, Section 5 reports on experimental evidence supporting the core-idea of this paper, Section 6 presents application domains that can benefit from this work and the final Section 7 draws some conclusions.

2. NEIGHBORING AREAS

The key-idea of this article is that the exchange of multimedia data has become a form of human-human communication and, therefore, it should give rise to the same cognitive phenomena (*e.g.*, see [49, 50]) typically observed in any human-human interaction. To the best of our knowledge, this article is the first attempt to adopt such a perspective in multimedia technologies. However, several domains consider neighboring issues that, while being different from the ones proposed in this article, still include aspects relevant to this work.

The application of the *sociotechnical* perspective in studying the use of digital libraries - until a few years ago the most common infrastructure for the exchange of multimedia data - is one of the earliest attempts to take into account social issues in technological applications: "*To understand, use, plan for and evaluate digital libraries, we need to attend to social practice, which we define as people's routine activities that are learned, shaped, and performed individually and together*" [39]. The main difference between the sociotechnical perspective and the research direction proposed in this work is that the former focuses on use and usability issues (especially in professional and institutional settings) while the latter targets the communication between individuals, a step made possible only by recent technologies (social media, mobile devices, etc.).

In parallel, several efforts were done to improve multimedia technologies by automatically detecting and understanding emotional, behavioral and physiological reactions of data consumers (*e.g.*, if a person watching a video laughs, then the video can be tagged as "*funny*") [1, 26, 37]. The core-idea of these trends is that the content of the data produces observable changes in data consumers, then the observation of these latter provides information about the data. The main difference with respect to this article is that the accent is on the data content, like in most of the multimedia technologies, and not on the communication process underlying the data exchange between individuals.

More recently, some works investigated the interplay between observable characteristics of multimedia data and cognition [27, 55]. The first work [27] considers images tagged as "*favourite*" by a certain person as an expression of her aesthetic preferences and shows that, given a certain amount of pictures tagged as "*favourite*" by a certain individual, it is possible to predict whether the same will happen for another picture or set of pictures. The second work [55] investigates the characteristics of abstract paintings that stimulate certain emotional reactions rather than others. Both works shift the attention from the bare content of images to their potential role in a communication process, namely a person expressing aesthetic preferences in [27] and a painter eliciting emotions in [55]. However, unlike the perspective advocated in this article, both works take into account only one of the parties involved in the communication process.

To the best of our knowledge, the only two works that seem to consider multimedia data as a form of communication are in [12, 15]. The work in [15] studies the perception of profile pictures on social media and, in particular, the agreement between the actual personality traits of profile holders and traits attributed by others based on the profile picture. The work in [12], does a similar analysis, but it considers all elements that can appear in a profile. Not surprisingly, these works focus on social media, an interaction-oriented technology that allow users to use multimedia material to communicate with others. However early, the approaches in [12, 15] seem to confirm the action of implicit cognitive processes when using multimedia data in a communication scenario, the key-idea advocated in this article. Still, both

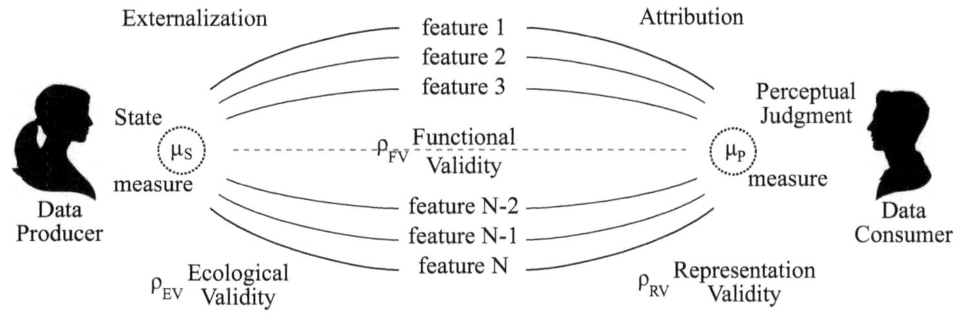

Figure 1: The picture shows a simplified version of the Brunswik Lens Model adapted to the exchange of multimedia data between a Data Producer and a Data Consumer.

works focus on a specific case and do not try to identify the underlying perspective that can be applied to many different cases.

3. THE MULTIMEDIA LENS MODEL

This section provides a conceptual framework that illustrates the perspective proposed in this article, namely a simplified version of the *Brunswik's Lens* (see Figure 1), the model originally proposed in [5] and successively modified to investigate, among other interaction phenomena, the influence of nonverbal behavior in face-to-face interactions [44] or the judgment of rapport [3].

In the model of Figure 1, the multimedia data is considered a form of communication between "*Data Producers*" (DP) and "*Data Consumers*" (DC). The key-idea of this article is that the process includes not only the exchange of content, a problem that the multimedia indexing and retrieval community has extensively investigated for at least two decades, but also implicit cognitive processes typical of any human-human interaction like, *e.g.*, the spontaneous attribution of socially relevant characteristics (attractiveness, trustworthiness, etc.) or the development of impressions.

The DP is always assumed to be in a certain *state* that can be either *transient* (*e.g.*, emotions, attitudes, goals, physiological conditions etc.) or *stable* (*e.g.*, personality traits, values, social status, etc.). In operational terms, the states are defined as quantitative measures (identified as μ_S in Figure 1) to be obtained via objective processes depending on the particular case under observation. For example, in the case of the social status, the measure can be the yearly income of the DP, while for the physiological condition it can be the heart rate or the galvanic skin conductance. In many cases, the states correspond to psychological constructs (*e.g.*, personality traits or interpersonal attractiveness) and the measures are the outcome of psychometric questionnaires. These latter are typically administered to the DPs and include questions associated to *Likert* scales (see Section 5 for an example).

According to the model, the multimedia data are an *externalization* of the DP state, i.e. an observable effect of it. Furthermore, the data is all the DCs know about a DP. From an operational point of view, the data correspond not only to the actual multimedia material (*e.g.*, pictures, video, soundbites, etc.), but also to any *feature* that can be extracted, manually or automatically, from the material itself. The empirical covariation of state measures and features quantifies the *ecological validity* of these latter, i.e. their effectiveness in accounting for the DP state. In Figure 1, the ecological validity is indicated with ρ_{EV} and, typically, it corresponds to the correlation or the Spearman coefficient between features and μ_S.

When the DCs consume the data, they attribute the DP a state of measure μ_P. The process is called *attribution* and μ_P is referred to as *perceptual judgment*. For example, the DCs can attribute a certain yearly income to the DP based on the pictures and videos this latter shows. In the case of the psychological constructs (see Section 5), the attribution process is typically unconscious and it takes place spontaneously, whether the DC needs it (wants it) or not [49, 50]. In principle, μ_S and μ_P should have the same value (or at least similar values), but communication processes are always noisy, especially when the communication takes place through ambiguous channels like multimedia data are. The empirical covariation between features and perceptual judgments accounts for the *representation validity* of the features (identified as ρ_{RV}), i.e. for the influence these latter have on the attribution process. Like in the case of ρ_{EV}, the most common measurements of ρ_{RV} are correlation and Spearman coefficient.

The cognitive processes this paper focuses on are active in particular at the perceptual judgment stage, when DCs unconsciously develop an impression about the DP even if all they know about this latter is the multimedia data they are consuming. However, the processes are important for the DP as well because, in a communication scenario, there is no data production without an attempt to convey an impression, i.e. to ensure that μ_S and μ_P are close to each other. The empirical covariation of μ_S and μ_P (identified as ρ_{FV} in Figure 1) accounts for the latter aspect and it is called *functional validity*. Furthermore, the full version of the Brunswik Lens [5] allows one to include contextual information. This makes it possible the integration of the technologies proposed in this article into context aware approaches [2].

4. THE PSYCHOFLICKR DATASET

We experimented the core-idea of this paper on Flickr[2], one of the most popular online photo-sharing platforms. To this purpose we collected a corpus, dubbed *PsychoFlickr*, that reflects the Lens Model and includes both pictures and personality assessments. The corpus is publicly available at [*the dataset will be made available in case of acceptance*] and was collected as follows: we contacted 300 random "*pro*" users, i.e. individuals that pay a yearly fee in order to access privileged Flickr functionalities. These users are expected to be, on average, more adept than others to photography

[2] `www.flickr.com`.

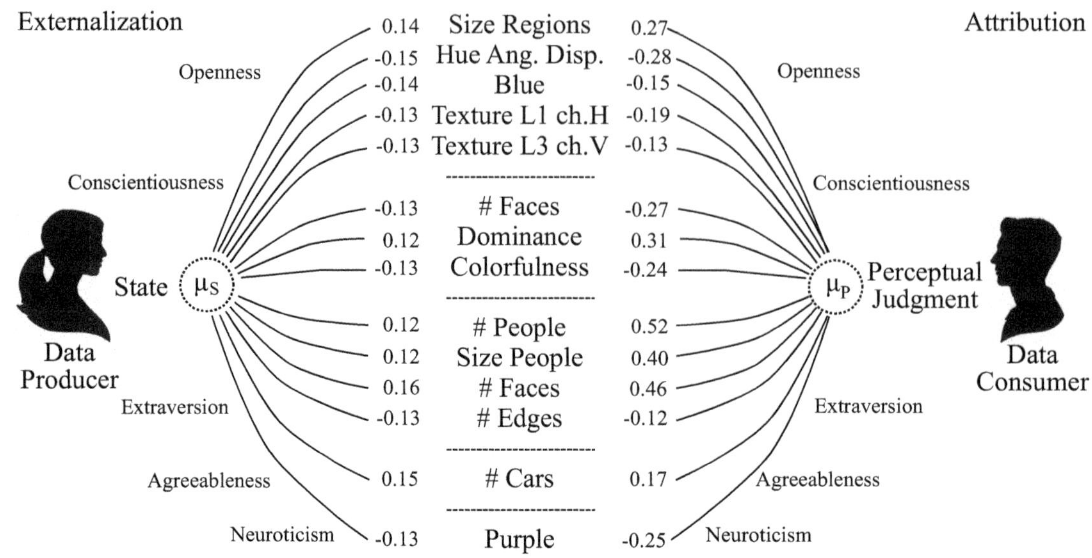

Figure 2: The picture shows the Brunswik Lens model for the PsychoFlickr dataset, where the state corresponds to the Big Five traits (as per assessed with the BFI-10). Ecological and Representation validities are measured with the Spearman Coefficient and the picture shows (for each trait) features for which both values are statistically significant ($p < 5\%$).

language and techniques. For each of these 300 users, we collected the 200 latest pictures made by others they labeled as *"favourite"*, for a total of 60,000 images. Furthermore, each user filled the BFI-10 (Big Five Inventory 10) [40], a personality questionnaire aimed at measuring the personality of an individual in terms of the *Big Five*, five broad dimensions shown to capture most of the individual differences [43]. The outcome of the BFI-10 is a five dimensional vector where each component measures how high an individual is with respect to each of the Big Five traits, namely *Openness* (tendency to be intellectually open, curious and have wide interests), *Conscientiousness* (tendency to be responsible, reliable and trustworthy), *Extraversion* (tendency to interact and spend time with others), *Agreeableness* (tendency to be kind, generous, etc.) and *Neuroticism* (tendency to experience the negative aspects of life, to be anxious, sensitive, etc.). In particular, for each trait, we have an integer which goes from -4 (low tendency) to 4 (high tendency).

Finally, we hired eight *assessors* that looked at the set of 200 favorite images provided by each of the users and, for each of them, filled the BFI-10 questionnaire. However, while the Flickr users adopted the self-assessment version of the BFI-10, the assessors used the other-assessment version. In other words, the users rated statements like *"I am a reserved person"*, while the assessors rated statements like *"This person is reserved"*, where by "person" is meant the user that has labeled the images under examination as *"favourite"*. Each of the 8 assessors filled the personality questionnaires for each of the 300 users. The users and the assessors were never in contact and, furthermore, the images were the only information the assessors had at disposition about the users under exam. The 8 personality ratings produced by the different assessors about the same user were averaged to obtain the *perceptual judgment* (according to experimental psychology practices [40]).

The agreement among the assessors was measured with the Krippendorff's α [23], a reliability coefficient suitable for a wide variety of assessments (binary, nominal, ordinal,

	O	C	E	A	N
α	0.07	0.16	0.23	0.19	0.20

Table 1: Krippendorff's α for the Big Five traits.

interval etc.), and robust to small sample sizes. Table 1 reports the α values for the different traits. The values are statistically significant and comparable to those observed in the literature for zero acquaintance scenarios [4], i.e. situations where assessors and subjects being rated do not have any personal contact (like it in the *PsychoFlickr* corpus).

In terms of the Lens Model, the *"pro"* users are the Data Producers, the assessors are the Data Consumers, the personality is the state and the outcome of the BFI questionnaire is the state measure (see Section 3 for more details).

5. MULTIMEDIA LENS AND FLICKR

This section measures, in quantitative terms, whether implicit cognitive processes are actually at work in the scenario underlying the PsychoFlickr corpus or not. In particular, the section addresses the following questions:

- Is there a consistent relation between features extracted from sets of "favourite" images and personality traits of Flickr users (both self-assessed and attributed)?
- If yes, is the relation sufficiently stable to automatically predict the personality traits of Flickr users (both self-assessed and attributed) based on sets of "favourite" images?

If the key-idea of this work holds, and implicit cognitive processes influence the exchange of multimedia data (according to the Lens Model), then the answer should be positive in both cases.

5.1 Features and Personality

We adopted a wide, though not exhaustive, spectrum of features, here grouped into two families (see Table 2). On one side, we have the cues that focus on aesthetic aspects [10,

Category	Name	L	Short Description
Aesthetics	Use of light	1	Average pixel intensity of V channel [10]
	HSV statistics	4	Mean of S channel and standard deviation of S, V channels [28]; *Hue angular dispersion* in IHLS color space [31]
	Emotion-based	3	Amount of *Pleasure, Arousal, Dominance* [28, 51]
	Colorfulness	1	Colorfulness measure based on Earth Mover's Distance (EMD) [10, 28]
	Color Name	11	Amount of *Black, Blue, Brown, Green, Gray, Orange, Pink, Purple, Red, White, Yellow* [28]
	Entropy	1	Image entropy [27]
	Wavelet textures	12	Level of spatial graininess measured with a three-level (L1,L2,L3) Daubechies wavelet transform on the HSV channels [10]
	Tamura	3	Amount of *Coarseness, Contrast, Directionality* [47]
	GLCM-features	12	Amount of *Contrast, Correlation, Energy, Homogeneity* for each HSV channel [28]
	Edges	1	Total number (#) of edge points, extracted with Canny [27]
	Level of detail	1	Number of regions (after mean shift segmentation) [7, 17]
	Regions	1	Average *size* of the regions (after mean shift segmentation) [7, 17]
	Low depth of field (DOF)	3	Amount of focus sharpness in the inner part of the image w.r.t. the overall focus [10, 28]
	Rule of thirds	2	Mean of S,V channels in the inner rectangle of the image [10, 28]
	Image parameters	2	Size of the image [10, 27]
Content	Objects	28	Objects detectors [13]: we kept the number of instances (#) and their average bounding box *size*
	Faces	2	Number (#) and *size* of faces after Viola-Jones face detection algorithm [52]
	GIST descriptors	24	Level of openness, ruggedness, roughness and expansion for scene recognition [36].

Table 2: Summary of all features. The column 'L' indicates the feature vector length for each type of feature.

28]: the reason is that the PsychoFlickr corpus includes pictures posted as "*favourite*", i.e. likely to represent the aesthetic preferences of the users under examination. On the other side, we focused on the content of the images; to this end, we employed robust probabilistic object detectors [13] (for a complete list of all detectable objects see [13]); we also retained the average area (the algorithm gives also the bounding box of the detected objects). In addition, we focused on the faces, adopting the standard Viola-Jones face detection algorithm [52] implemented in the OpenCV libraries. Finally, we adopted the GIST scene descriptors, which amounts to apply a set of oriented band-pass filters.

Figure 2 shows the features with higher ecological (covariation of self-assessment and features) and representation (covariation of features and perceptual judgment) validity with respect to the Big Five traits. The covariations, measured with the Spearman Coefficient, are statistically significant ($p < 5\%$). Therefore, *implicit cognitive processes seem to be actually at work when Flickr users share their set of favourite images.* The answer to the first question at the beginning of this section is positive. Further confirmation comes from Figure 3, showing a random selection of images labeled as "favourite" by extravert (collage "a") and introvert (collage "b") subjects. The former appear to picture people way more frequently than introvert ones (80% and 17% of the images in the collage, respectively).

5.2 Personality Prediction

Ecological and representation validity values of Figure 2 seem to suggest that predicting personality traits (both self-assessed and attributed) using "favourite" images is possible. The problem was cast as a regression instance on the traits of the users, considering users as the sets of their preferred images (see appendix A for a description of the regression approach). The performance was measured with the Spearman correlation coefficient between actual and predicted personality traits, the higher the coefficient, the closer the prediction to the true value. The results are reported in Table 3 where the first column shows the trait, the second explains whether the predicted trait is self-assessed or attributed by the assessors, "Max ρ" is the maximum correlation found across the tests (i.e. the various configurations of the regression approach), "Mean (Std)" are mean value and standard deviation computed on correlations with p-values $< 5\%$, and "% s.s" is the percentage of different configurations of the regression approach that resulted in a statistically significant result.

In line with the literature on personality computing [29], the performances achieved over self-assessed traits are lower than those obtained over attributed ones. The reason is that the former depend on an individual assessment and tend to be more noisy while the latter, resulting from the consensus among different assessors, tend to correlate better with measurable characteristics of the data. In particular, for the attributed traits, all configurations of the regression approach tested in the experiments led to statistically significant results, while for the self-assessed traits this happens only for Openness. The best performance is achieved, for the attributed assessments, for Extraversion and Conscientiousness. The same applies to most of the works on personality computing presented in the literature and the reason is that Extraversion and Conscientiousness are the two traits people perceive more quickly and effectively [20]. In the case of this work, the performance is satisfactory for Neuroticism and Agreeableness as well. The trait for which the performance is lower is Openness. The probable explanation is that the distribution of the users along such trait is peaked around high values (Openness is the trait of creativity and "pro" Flickr users are, not surprisingly, higher than the average along the trait).

The results presented in Table 3 are statistically significant ($p < 5\%$) and, therefore, the answer to the second question of the beginning of this section is positive. In other words, implicit cognitive processes seem to influence the attribution of personality traits in Data Consumers watching "favourite" pictures on Flickr.

6. POTENTIAL APPLICATIONS

Section 2 surveys areas that share some aspects with the perspective proposed in this article while still showing substantial differences. This section focuses on application domains that involve the exchange of multimedia data and, therefore, might benefit from taking into account the cogni-

(a) (b)

Figure 3: Collage (a) and (b) are a random selection of "favourite" pictures of subjects high and low in Extraversion (as per attributed by the assessors), respectively. The most important difference is that extrovert individuals show a preference for pictures portraying people (80% of the samples in the collage) while introvert show the opposite preference (17% of the pictures in the collage).

Trait	Label	Max ρ	Mean (Std) ρ	% s.s.
O	Self	0.25	0.17 (0.04)	100%
	Attributed	0.35	0.32 (0.04)	100%
C	Self	0.24	0.22 (0.03)	44%
	Attributed	0.57	0.49 (0.05)	100%
E	Self	0.28	0.19 (0.05)	88%
	Attributed	0.62	0.55 (0.03)	100%
A	Self	0.20	0.17 (0.03)	55%
	Attributed	0.52	0.45 (0.05)	100%
N	Self	0.14	0.12 (0.07)	7%
	Attributed	0.60	0.54 (0.04)	100%

Table 3: Prediction Results. ρ is the Spearman Correlation Coefficient

tive processes that, according to the results presented above, seem to influence such type of process.

Understanding and modeling of cognitive processes involved in multimedia data consumption are likely to be beneficial for Human Information Interaction (HII), the domain studying the "*relationship between people and information*" [14]. HII researchers are particularly interested in modelling people *proflections*, i.e. individual's conscious and unconscious projections on information objects (*e.g.*, pictures) and the reflections that other people and machines create to those projections (*e.g.*, links and annotations) [30]. This applies in particular to multimedia retrieval technologies that might be enhanced by taking into account not only the data content (like most of current technologies do [26]), but also the interplay between content and perceptual judgments (personality, values, goals, intentions, etc.).

The role of cognitive biases can be of interest for Digital Humanities as well, especially for what concerns the effort towards "*new modes of knowledge formation enabled by networked, digital environments*" and the focus on "*distinctive modes of producing knowledge and distinctive models of knowledge itself*" [6]. In particular, Digital Humanities investigate the impact of media authoring technologies on the transmission of knowledge and information, a phenomenon likely to involve implicit cognitive processes like those described in this work. In a similar vein, the perspective adopted in this article can be useful in Big Data Analytics - the domain aimed at making sense of large amounts of unstructured data [32] - one of the most important challenges technology faces today. In particular, there is consensus among Big Data experts that no useful information can be extracted from large databases without associating automatic mining approaches and human interpretation [35]. This latter is likely to be influenced by cognitive processes similar to those illustrated in the experiments of this work.

Viral marketing, the "*diffusion of information about the product and its adoption over the network*" [25], is an advertisement technique aimed at spreading information as widely as possible through (mostly online) *word of mouth* mechanisms. The previous part of this paper has shown that the exchange of multimedia data, being a form of human-human communication, can be thought of as a form of word of mouth. Therefore, implicit cognitive processes might contribute to explain and enhance virality. In the same vein, communication strategies based on social media can benefit from the prediction of perceptual judgments likely to be attributed to a given multimedia message diffused through online social platforms [21].

According to the European Consumer Commissioneer, "*Personal data is the new oil of the internet and the new currency of the digital world*" [16]. The "states" of data producers (see Section 3) often correspond to personal characteristics of potential interest for different bodies (*e.g.*, companies trying to model their customers or governments interested in gathering information about the population). Approaches like those presented in this work can help to obtain such information by analyzing publicly available data that people usually post on personal home pages, Youtube, Facebook, etc. [22]. In parallel, the development of technologies capable of going beyond the mere content and infer personal characteristics of data producers require a redefinition of the concept of privacy and a careful analysis of ethical issues [9].

A peculiar form of communication through multimedia material is the participation in online games where several participants interact via avatars or animated characters. The choice of a particular character or particular gaming strategies and options is likely to convey information about the player "states" (see, *e.g.*, the approaches in [18, 54, 56] for the case of personality). In a similar way, computer mediated communication can be influenced by implicit cognitive processes via interface characteristics like the profile picture of Skype users.

Creating and viewing photographs as a process of self-insight and personal change is the main principle of *phototherapy* and *therapeutic photography* [53, 46], two recent psychology perspectives; for the therapists, "*Images provide an undercurrent of emotion and ideas that enrich interpersonal dynamics, often on a level that is not fully conscious or capable of being verbalized*". Of particular interest for these fields is how the language of composition and visual design intersects with the language of unconscious primary cognitive processes, including emotional/ideational association. Our study suggests that answers to these questions may be found with the help of computers.

Last, but not least, it is apparent the crucial role that image processing and machine learning would have; at the same time, our study delineates new challenges for these areas; for example, discovering visual patterns that correlate with personal traits in a stronger way than ordinary features or fit better cognition processes could be a research mission for the field of deep learning and feature learning [45]. Generative modeling can also be involved, looking for new models that mimic the way diverse visual features should be combined together to communicate a certain personal trait. An immediate example applies to the Counting Grid used in Section A.1: in this paper, we employed CG as a mere dimensionality reduction strategy, without accounting the traits label. Including this information may lead to a low-dimensional embedding where nearby images exhibit similar features *and* personal traits.

The list presented in this section is far from being exhaustive, but it is representative of the scenarios where the investigations proposed in this article can be relevant, namely those where individuals produce, exchange and consume (possibily multimedia) data.

7. CONCLUSIONS

This article advocates the idea that the exchange of multimedia data has become a human-human communication scenario and, therefore, it involves the same cognitive phenomena of any other form of interaction between people, especially when it comes to expression and mutual attribution of socially relevant characteristics (attractiveness, social status, personality, goals, values, intentions, etc.). As a supporting evidence, the paper proposes experiments on the interplay between personality traits and Flickr pictures. The results show that the personality of an individual can be predicted, to a statistically significant extent, through the pictures she labels as "*favourite*". Furthermore, the experiments show that the images can be used to predict the traits that others attribute to such an individual. Therefore, at least for what concerns personality, the exchange of images via Flickr seems to work according to the *Brunswik Lens* (see Section 3), the cognitive model underlying social interactions. In other words, the key-idea proposed in this work appears to hold.

To the best of our knowledge, such a perspective has never been adopted in a multimedia technology context before. The probable reason is that multimedia data became an interaction channel only recently, when the diffusion of appropriate technologies for data production (cameras, smartphones, tablets, etc.) and consumption (social media, digital libraries, etc.) made it possible to exchange multimedia data as easily as we previously exchanged written material (letters, messages, etc.) [6].

This new scenario opens several research questions (the list is not exhaustive):

- Is it possible to improve multimedia technologies by taking into account implicit cognitive processes?
- Do implicit cognitive processes influence our behavior as multimedia technology users?
- Does multimedia technology need to change to accomodate implicit cognitive processes? If yes, how?
- Can traditional multimedia technologies contribute to understand the influence of cognitive processes in data production and consumption? If yes, how?
- What do we reveal about ourselves when we share multimedia data?
- What is the effect of the multimedia data we share on the impression others develop about us?

It can be expected that the perceptual judgments we make about those who produce the data we consume end up influencing our perception of the data. For example, we might tend to like more or to find more relevant data produced by people we perceive as more similar to us. If actually observed, such an effect (known in psychology as "*similarity-attraction*" [8]), might not only improve retrieval technologies, but also contribute to explain our behavior as users and, in ultimate analysis, lead to higher technology usability and effectiveness. Similar considerations apply to any technology that involves the consumption of data.

Symmetrically, the increasing amount of multimedia information we produce and share (Instagram pictures, Tweets including pointers to video and audio data, etc.) is probably contributing to a larger and larger extent to our "*appearance*", one of the characteristics that influence most the impression others develop about us (an effect known as the "*halo-effect*" psychology [34]). However, while we know how to manage our appearance in face-to-face interactions, in most cases we are still not aware of the way others see us through the lens of the multimedia data we produce.

The two examples above show how cognitive and technological issues are tightly intertwined in everyday scenarios involving production and consumption of multimedia data. The two cases focus on specific aspects, but the perspective proposed in this work might show that the full range of phenomena taking place in face-to-face interactions (see [11] for a monograph) take place through multimedia data as well. If true, the door would be open towards new multimedia applications as well as novel findings in cognitive sciences.

APPENDIX

A. THE REGRESSION APPROACH

To apply a standard regression approach is problematic because there are multiple images associated to the same target. Straightforward algorithms like, *e.g.*, summing all the image descriptors of each user, and then perform regression, does not work because such process adds noise to a weak signal. Multiple instance regression [41] is also unadvisable because of its high computational complexity, especially when the number of images for each user is large.

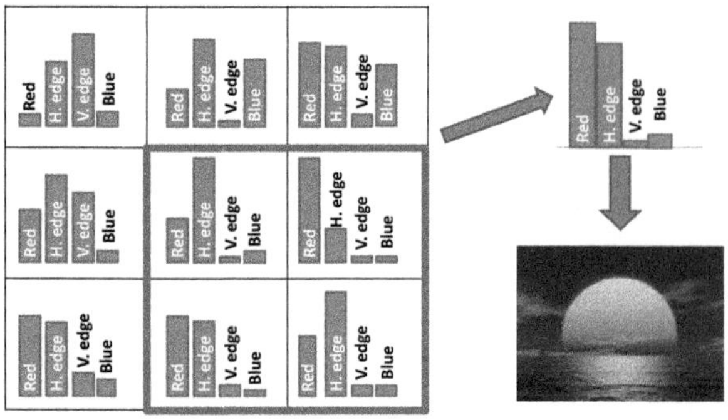

Figure 4: Generating an image from a simple 3×3 counting grid: given a 2×2 window on the grid, we average the feature counts, obtaining a bag of features which corresponds to the final image. V. edge and H. edge are toy features meaning vertical and horizontal edges, respectively.

Therefore, we propose an alternative approach composed by the following three steps:

1. **Feature Extraction and Normalization**. We first extract from all the images the set of features listed in Section 5.1; since each z-th cue expresses the level of presence of a given quantity, i.e. a count c_z, we can think each image as an histogram of counts $\{c_z\}$, or bag-of-features (BoF). After that, we normalize each c_z to ensure that each feature takes values in the same range. This avoids some features (*e.g.*, number of edges) to overcome others (*e.g.*, GIST, amount of coarseness)
2. **Clustering**. After dividing the users in training and testing users, we consider all the images of the training users. By means of a clustering algorithm, we learn a low-dimensional representation that maps each t-th image (i.e. its BoF) in a 2-dimensional location ℓ^t, lying on a smooth manifold. As clustering method we employed the *Counting Grid* [38], a recent generative model which embeds BoF representations in N-dimensional manifolds[3]. This way, each user u becomes a set of locations $L^u = \{\ell^t\}$ on the manifold.
3. **Regression and Trait Prediction**. Considering the training users, we train a regressor to the personality traits. In specific, for each user u we have a five-dimensional target that characterizes the Big Five personality traits $p \in \{O, C, E, A, N\}$, where each trait is described by a value $y_p^u \in [-4, 4]$. As regression method, we used Lasso [48]. Trait prediction amounts to test the regressor on the test users.

In the following, we will detail the latter two steps of the process.

A.1 Clustering: the Counting Grid Model

The counting grid (CG) is a generative model recently introduced in [38] for analyzing images collections. It assumes that images are represented as histograms $\{c_z\}$ or bags of features, where c_z counts the occurrences of feature z.

[3]Here we decide $N = 2$ for the sake of clarity; other dimensions can be explored. In addition, we tried different dimensionality reduction approaches (Mixtures of Dirichlet distributions), leading to inferior performances.

Considering its two-dimensional version, a CG is a 2D finite discrete grid where each location $\mathbf{i} = (x, y)$ contains a normalized count of features $\pi_{\mathbf{i},z}$. Under this model, an image (i.e. its BoF $\{c_z\}$) could be thought as produced by the following generative process: a small window is located in the grid, averaging the feature counts within it to obtain a local probability mass function over the features, and then generating from it an appropriate number of features in the bag (see Fig. 4). In other words, unlike a straightforward embedding (e.g. PCA) that links an image with a point location, the counting grid forces the image to link with a small window of locations. Given that the size $E_1 \times E_2$ of a counting grid is usually small compared to the number of images, this also forces windows linked to different images to overlap, and to co-exist by finding a shared compromise in the feature counts located in their intersection. The overall effect of these constraints is to produce locally smooth transitions between strongly different feature counts by gradually phasing features in/out in the intermediate locations.

In practice, local neighborhoods in the grid represent similar concepts and images mapped in close locations are somehow similar.

Formally, the counting grid $\pi_{\mathbf{i},z}$ is a 2D finite discrete grid, spatially indexed by $\mathbf{i} = (x, y) \in [1 \dots E_1] \times [1 \dots E_2]$, and containing normalized counts of features indexed by z. Thus, we have $\sum_z \pi_{\mathbf{i},z} = 1$ everywhere on the grid. A given BoF $\{c_z\}$ is generated by selecting a certain location $\mathbf{k}$, calculating the distribution $h_{\mathbf{k},z} = \frac{1}{W_n} \sum_{\mathbf{i} \in W_{\mathbf{k}}} \pi_{\mathbf{i},z}$ by averaging all the words counts within the window $W_{\mathbf{k}}$ (with area W_n) that starts at $\mathbf{k}$, and then drawing features counts from this distribution.

In other words, the position of the window $\mathbf{k}$ in the grid is a latent variable; given $\mathbf{k}$, the likelihood of $\{c_z\}$ is

$$p(\{c_z\}|\mathbf{k}) = \prod_z (h_{\mathbf{k},z})^{c_z} = \alpha \prod_z \Big(\sum_{\mathbf{i} \in W_{\mathbf{k}}} \pi_{\mathbf{i},z} \Big)^{c_z}, \qquad (1)$$

where α is a fixed normalization factor.

To learn a counting grid, we need to maximize the likelihood over all training images T, that can be written as

$$p(\{\{c_z^t\}, \mathbf{k}^t\}_{t=1}^T) \propto \prod_t \prod_z \Big(\sum_{\mathbf{i} \in W_{\mathbf{k}^t}} \pi_{\mathbf{i},z} \Big)^{c_z^t}, \qquad (2)$$

which is intractable, much like in mixtures; therefore, it is necessary to employ an iterative EM algorithm. Starting from a random initialization of the counting grid π, the E-step aligns all bags of features to grid windows, to match the bags' histograms, inferring where each bag maps on the grid, i.e.

$$q^t(\mathbf{i}) \propto \exp \sum_z c_z^t \cdot \log h_{\mathbf{i},z} \qquad (3)$$

In the M-step the model parameter, i.e. the counting grid π, is re-estimated. For details on the learning algorithm and on its efficiency, the reader can refer to the original papers [38, 19]. For our purposes, the most interesting outputs are the posterior probabilities q^t's, the position in the grid of each image. Summing over the entire grid the contributes $q^t(\mathbf{i})$, which are due to the images of a user, provides a signature L^u. Essentially, it is a 2D matrix, of the same dimension of the grid, where some locations $\{\mathbf{i}\}$ are weighted by the q^t's, indicating that in such locations there are some images of the user u.

A.2 Regression and Trait Prediction

To assess the validity of our prediction method, we used the Leave-One-User-Out paradigm. We considered CGs of various complexities with size $E = [20 \times 20, 25 \times 25, \ldots 65 \times 65]$ and window $W = [5 \times 5]$ and we learnt a model with all the images belonging to the training users. Then, we computed L^u for each user, and used this representation to regress on the profile y_p^u. We learned the regression weight vector $\mathbf{w}$ by minimizing the error function

$$E(\mathbf{w}) = \sum_{\mathbf{i}=1}^{L} \left(\mathbf{y_p} - \mathbf{w}^T \cdot L^u(\mathbf{i})\right)^2 \tag{4}$$

where L indicates the number positions in the grid. We solved the problem using Lasso [48], a shrinkage and selection method for linear regression which enforces the sparsity on coefficients $\mathbf{w}$ by bounding the sum of the absolute values of the coefficients. The bound is a constraint that has to be taken into account when minimizing the error function. At this point the training phase is completed and to predict the personality train of the held out (test) user, we 1) infer the mappings of its images on the counting grid (Eq.3), 2) compute is latent description $L^{test}(\mathbf{i})$ and 3) by calculating

$$\hat{y}_p^{test} = \mathbf{w}^T \cdot L^{test}, \tag{5}$$

we predict the trait.

B. REFERENCES

[1] I. Arapakis, J.M. Jose, and P.D. Gray. Affective feedback: an investigation into the role of emotions in the information seeking process. In *Proceedings of the ACM SIGIR Conference on Research and Development in Information Retrieval*, pages 395–402. ACM, 2008.

[2] M. Baldauf, S. Dustdar, and F. Rosenberg. A survey on context-aware systems. *International Journal of Ad Hoc and Ubiquitous Computing*, 2(4):263–277, 2007.

[3] F.J. Bernieri and J.S. Gillis. Judging rapport: Employing brunswik's lens model to study interpersonal sensitivity. In J.A. Hall and F.J. Bernieri, editors, *Interpersonal Sensitivity. Theory and Measurement.* Lawrence Erlbaum, 2001.

[4] J.C. Biesanz and S.G. West. Personality coherence: Moderating self-other profile agreement and profile consensus. *Journal of Personality and Social Psychology*, 79(3):425–437, 2000.

[5] E. Brunswik. *Perception and the representative design of psychological experiments.* University of California Press, 1956.

[6] A. Burdick, J. Drucker, P. Lunenfelds, T. Presner, and J. Schnapp. *Digitial Humanities.* MIT Press, 2012.

[7] D. Comaniciu and P. Meer. Mean shift: a robust approach toward feature space analysis. *IEEE Transactions on Pattern Analysis and Machine Intelligence*, 24(5):603 – 619, 2002.

[8] J.W. Condon and W.D. Crano. Inferred evaluation and the relation between attitude similarity and interpersonal attraction. *Journal of Personality and Social Psychology*, 54(5):789, 1988.

[9] R. Cowie. The good our field can hope to do, the harm it should avoid. *IEEE Transactions on Affective Computing (to appear)*, 2013.

[10] R. Datta, D. Joshi, J. Li, and J. Wang. Studying aesthetics in photographic images using a computational approach. In *Proceedings of the European Conference on Computer Vision*, volume 3953 of *Lecture Notes in Computer Science*, pages 288–301. Springer Verlag, 2006.

[11] J. Elster. *Explaining Social Behavior.* Cambridge University Press, 1997.

[12] D.C. Evans, S. D. Gosling, and A. Carroll. What elements of an online social networking profile predict target-rater agreement in personality impressions. In *Proceedings of the International Conference on Weblogs and Social Media*, pages 45–50, 2008.

[13] P. F. Felzenszwalb, R. B. Girshick, and D. McAllester. Discriminatively trained deformable part models, release 4. http://www.cs.brown.edu/~pff/latent-release4/, 2010.

[14] R. Fidel. *Human Information Interaction.* MIT Press, 2012.

[15] S. Fitzgerald, D.C. Evans, and R.K. Green. Is your profile picture worth 1000 words? Photo characteristics associated with personality impression agreement. In *Proceedings of AAAI International Conference on Weblogs and Social Media*, 2009.

[16] World Economic Forum. Personal data: the emergence of a new asset class. Technical report, World Economic Forum, 2011.

[17] C.M. Georgescu. Synergism in low level vision. In *Proceedings of the International Conference on Pattern Recognition*, pages 150–155, 2002.

[18] D. Johnson and J. Gardner. Personality, motivation and video games. In *Proceedings of the Conference of the Computer-Human Interaction Special Interest Group of Australia on Computer-Human Interaction*, pages 276–279, 2010.

[19] N. Jojic and A. Perina. Multidimensional counting grids: Inferring word order from disordered bags of words. In *Proceedings of Uncertainty in Artificial Intelligence*, pages 547–556, 2011.

[20] C.M. Judd, L. James-Hawkins, V. Yzerbyt, and Y. Kashima. Fundamental dimensions of social judgment: Unrdestanding the relations bteween judgments of competence and warmth. *Journal of Personality and Social Psychology*, 89(6):899–913, 2005.

[21] A.M. Kaplan and M. Haenlein. Users of the world, unite! The challenges and opportunities of social media. *Business Horizons*, 53(1):59–68, 2010.

[22] M. Kosinski, D. Stillwell, and T. Graepel. Private traits and attributes are predictable from digital records of human behavior. *Proceeedings of the National Academy of Sciences*, 110(15):5802–5805, 2013.

[23] K. Krippendorff. Reliability in content analysis. *Human Communication Research*, 30(3):411–433, 2004.

[24] Z. Kunda. *Social cognition: Making sense of people.* The MIT Press, 1999.

[25] J. Leskovec, L. Adamic, and B. Huberman. The dynamics of viral marketing. *ACM Transactions on the Web*, 1(1):5, 2007.

[26] M.S. Lew, N. Sebe, D. Chabane, and R. Jain. Content-based multimedia information retrieval: State of the art and challenges. *ACM Transactions on Multimedia Computing, Communications, and Applications*, 2(1):1–19, 2006.

[27] P. Lovato, A. Perina, N. Sebe, O. Zandoná, A. Montagnini, M. Bicego, and M. Cristani. Tell me what you like and I'll tell you what you are: discriminating visual preferences on Flickr data. In K.M. Lee, Y. Matsushita, J.M. Rehg, and Z. Hu, editors, *Proceedings of the Asian Conference on Computer Vision*, volume Lecture Notes in Computer Science 7724. Springer Verlag, 2012.

[28] J. Machajdik and A. Hanbury. Affective image classification using features inspired by psychology and art theory. In *Proceedings of the ACM International Conference on Multimedia*, pages 83–92, 2010.

[29] F. Mairesse, M. A. Walker, M. R. Mehl, and R. K. Moore. Using linguistic cues for the automatic recognition of personality in conversation and text. *Journal of Artificial Intelligence Research*, 30:457–500, 2007.

[30] G. Marchionini. Human–information interaction research and development. *Library & Information Science Research*, 30(3):165–174, 2008.

[31] K.V. Mardia and P.E. Jupp. *Directional Statistics*. Wiley Series in Probability and Statistics. Wiley, 2009.

[32] M. Minelli, M. Chambers, and A. Dhiraj. *Big Data, Big Analytics*. Wiley, 2013.

[33] C. Nass and S. Brave. *Wired for speech: How voice activates and advances the Human-Computer relationship*. The MIT Press, 2005.

[34] R.E. Nisbett and T.D. Wilson. The halo effect: Evidence for unconscious alteration of judgments. *Journal of Personality and Social Psychology*, 35(4):250–256, 1977.

[35] F.J. Olhorst. *Big Data Analytics*. Wiley, 2013.

[36] A. Oliva and A. Torralba. Modeling the shape of the scene: A holistic representation of the spatial envelope. *International Journal of Computer Vision*, 42(3):145–175, 2001.

[37] M. Pantic and A. Vinciarelli. Implicit Human-Centered Tagging. *IEEE Signal Processing Magazine*, 26(6):173–180, 2009.

[38] A. Perina and N. Jojic. Image analysis by counting on a grid. In *Proceedings of the International Conference on Computer Vision and Pattern Recognition*, pages 1985–1992, 2011.

[39] A. Peterson Bishop, N.A. van House, and B.P. Buttenfields, editors. *Digital Library Use*. MIT Press, 2003.

[40] B. Rammstedt and O. P. John. Measuring personality in one minute or less: A 10-item short version of the Big Five Inventory in English and German. *in Journal of Research in Personality*, 41:203–212, 2007.

[41] S. Ray. Multiple instance regression. In *Proceedings of the International Conference on Machine Learning*, pages 425–432, 2001.

[42] D. Rosenberg. Data before the Fact. In L. Gitelman, editor, *Raw data is an oxymoron*, pages 15–40. MIT Press, 2013.

[43] G. Saucier and L.R. Goldberg. The language of personality: Lexical perspectives on the five-factor model. In J.S. Wiggins, editor, *The Five-Factor Model of Personality*. 1996.

[44] K.R. Scherer. Personality markers in speech. In *Social markers in speech*, pages 147–209. Cambridge University Press, Cambridge, 1979.

[45] K. Sohn, D.Y. Jung, H. Lee, and A.O. Hero. Efficient learning of sparse, distributed, convolutional feature representations for object recognition. In *IEEE International Conference on Computer Vision*, pages 2643–2650, 2011.

[46] J. Suler. The psychotherapeutics of online photosharing. *International Journal of Applied Psychoanalytic Studies*, 6(4):339–344, 2009.

[47] H. Tamura, S. Mori, and T. Yamawaki. Texture features corresponding to visual perception. *IEEE Transactions on Systems, Man and Cybernetics*, 8(6), 1978.

[48] R. Tibshirani. Regression shrinkage and selection via the lasso. *Journal of the Royal Statistical Society, Series B*, 58:267–288, 1994.

[49] J.S. Uleman, L.S. Newman, and G.B. Moskowitz. People as flexible interpreters: Evidence and issues from spontaneous trait inference. In M.P. Zanna, editor, *Advances in Experimental Social Psychology*, volume 28, pages 211–279. Elsevier, 1996.

[50] J.S. Uleman, S.A. Saribay, and C.M. Gonzalez. Spontaneous inferences, implicit impressions, and implicit theories. *Annual Reviews of Psychology*, 59:329–360, 2008.

[51] P. Valdez and A. Mehrabian. Effects of color on emotions. *Journal of Experimental Psychology General*, 123(4):394–409, 1994.

[52] P.A. Viola and M.J. Jones. Robust real-time face detection. *International Journal of Computer Vision*, 57(2):137–154, 2004.

[53] J. Weiser. *Phototherapy techniques: Exploring the secrets of personal snapshots and family albums*. Jossey-Bass San Francisco, 1993.

[54] C.Y. Yaakub, N. Sulaiman, and C.W. Kim. A study on personality identification using game based theory. In *Proceedings of the International Conference on Computer Technology and Development*, pages 732–734, 2010.

[55] V. Yanulevskaya, J. Uijlings, E. Bruni, A. Sartori, E. Zamboni, F. Bacci, D. Melcher, and N. Sebe. In the eye of the beholder: employing statistical analysis and eye tracking for analyzing abstract paintings. In *Proceedings of the ACM international conference on Multimedia*, pages 349–358, 2012.

[56] N. Yee, N. Ducheneaut, L. Nelson, and P. Likarish. Introverted elves & conscientious gnomes: The expression of personality in World of Warcraft. In *Proceedings of the Annual Conference on Human Factors in Computing Systems*, pages 753–762, 2011.

Large-scale Visual Sentiment Ontology and Detectors Using Adjective Noun Pairs

Damian Borth [1] Rongrong Ji [2] Tao Chen [2] Thomas Breuel [1] Shih-Fu Chang [2]

[1]University of Kaiserslautern, Germany [2]Columbia University, USA
{d_borth, tmb}@cs.uni-kl.de {rrji, taochen, sfchang}@ee.columbia.edu

ABSTRACT

We address the challenge of sentiment analysis from visual content. In contrast to existing methods which infer sentiment or emotion directly from visual low-level features, we propose a novel approach based on understanding of the visual concepts that are strongly related to sentiments. Our key contribution is two-fold: first, we present a method built upon psychological theories and web mining to automatically construct a large-scale Visual Sentiment Ontology (VSO) consisting of more than 3,000 Adjective Noun Pairs (ANP). Second, we propose SentiBank, a novel visual concept detector library that can be used to detect the presence of 1,200 ANPs in an image. The VSO and SentiBank are distinct from existing work and will open a gate towards various applications enabled by automatic sentiment analysis. Experiments on detecting sentiment of image tweets demonstrate significant improvement in detection accuracy when comparing the proposed SentiBank based predictors with the text-based approaches. The effort also leads to a large publicly available resource consisting of a visual sentiment ontology, a large detector library, and the training/testing benchmark for visual sentiment analysis.

Categories and Subject Descriptors

H.3.3 [**Information Storage and Retrieval**]: Information Retrieval and Indexing

Keywords

Sentiment Prediction, Concept Detection, Ontology, Social Multimedia

1. INTRODUCTION

Nowadays the Internet, as a major platform for communication and information exchange, provides a rich repository of people's opinion and sentiment about a vast spectrum of topics. Such knowledge is embedded in multiple facets, such as comments, tags, browsing actions, as well as shared media objects. The analysis of such information either in the area of opinion mining, affective computing or sentiment analysis plays an important role in behavior sciences, which aims to understand and predict human decision making [26] and enables applications such as brand monitoring, stock market prediction, or political voting forecasts.

So far, the computational analysis of sentiment mostly concentrates on the textual content [26]. Limited efforts have been conducted to analyze sentiments from visual content such as images and videos, which is becoming a pervasive media type on the web. For example, two of the most popular tweets in 2012 (see Fig. 1) conveying valuable sentiment information primarily visually[1]. Thus, an open issue in sentiment analysis research is the need of visual content analysis.

This problem poses a set of unique challenges as it addresses abstract human concepts in the sense of emotion and affect. Typically, semantic concept detection in images is concerned with the physical presence of objects or scenes like "car" or "building". On the other hand sentiment could differ among persons as the stimuli evoked human responses are naturally subjective. In some sense, this is analogous to the differentiation between content-based image retrieval (CBIR) and emotional semantic image retrieval (ESIR) [33]. There exists an *affective gap* in ESIR [21] between low-level features and the emotional content of an image reflecting a particular sentiment, similar to the well-known *semantic gap* in CBIR between low-level features and image semantics. To fill the semantic gap, mid-level representations based on visual concepts have been proposed. In this paper, we propose to discover and detect a set of visual concepts that can be used to fill the affective gap and automatically infer the sentiments reflected in an image. Note, that our mid-

Figure 1: Tweets from the "2012 Year on Twitter" collection: Barack Obamas reelection tweet (left) and a tweet capturing the destruction caused by Hurricane Sandy (right). Both tweets are characterized by a short text ("four more years" and "rollercoaster at sea" respectively) and conveying the sentiment visually.

[1]Please note that, throughout the paper we will define sentiment similarly to [26], as the polarity of an opinion item which either can be *positive, neutral or negative*

MM'13, October 21–25, 2013, Barcelona, Spain.

http://dx.doi.org/10.1145/2502081.2502282.

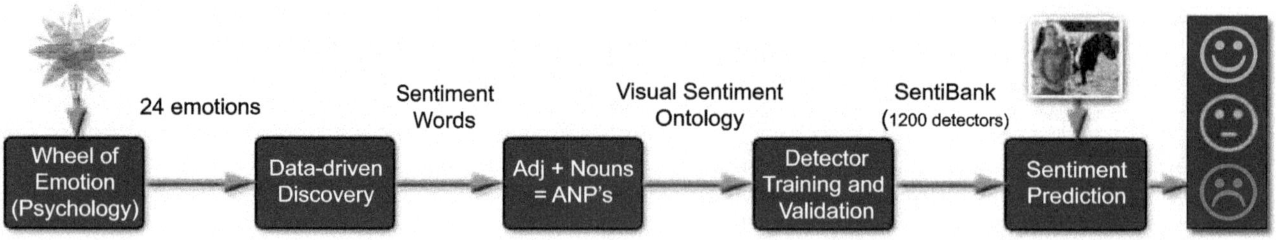

Figure 2: Overview of the proposed framework for constructing the visual sentiment ontology and SentiBank. Applications in multimodal sentiment prediction is also shown.

level representation is much expressive than the ones (e.g., color schemes or geometric shapes) described in [33] and has a better capability for explaining sentiment prediction results.

We apply the psychological theory, Plutchik's Wheel of Emotions [27], as the guiding principle to construct a large-scale **visual sentiment ontology** (VSO) that consists of more than 3,000 semantic concepts. Our construction criteria ensure that each selected concept **(1)** reflects a strong sentiment, **(2)** has a link to emotions, **(3)**is frequently used in practice, and **(4)** has a reasonable detection accuracy. To satisfy these conditions, we introduce **Adjective Noun Pairs (ANP)** such as "beautiful flower" or "disgusting food". The advantage of using ANPs, compared to nouns or adjectives only, is its capability to turn a neutral noun like "dog" into an ANP with strong sentiment like "cute dog" by adding an adjective with a strong sentiment. Such combined phrases also make the concepts more detectable than adjectives (like "beautiful"), which are typically abstract and difficult to detect. Building upon the VSO we introduce **SentiBank**, a library of trained concept detectors providing a mid-level visual representation. We show - through extensive experiments - that useful detector performance can be achieved for 1,200 ANP concepts, which form the released detector library SentiBank. Further, we demonstrate the usefulness of the proposed approach towards sentiment prediction on image tweets as it outperforms text-based prediction approaches by a very large margin. In summary, our contributions are - **first**, a systematic, data-driven methodology for the construction of a visual sentiment ontology from user-generated content and folksonomies on the web; **second**, the large-scale Visual Sentiment Ontology founded by a well-known psychological model; **third**, a mid-level representation built on automatic detectors of the discovered concepts in order to bridge the *affective gap* mentioned earlier; and, **forth**, the public release of the VSO including its large-scale dataset, the SentiBank detector library, and the benchmark for visual sentiment analysis.

In the rest of the paper, we first discuss related work (Sec.2) and show an overview of the proposed framework (Sec. 3). Then, the design and construction methodology of the VSO (Sec.4) and SentiBank, the proposed mid-level visual concept representation (Sec.5) are discussed. Finally, application in image tweet sentiment prediction is presented (Sec.6).

2. RELATED WORK

The challenge of automatically detecting semantic concepts such as objects, locations, and activities in visual data, referred to as video annotation [1], concept detection [28], semantic indexing [25] or multimedia event detection [20], has been studied extensively over the last decade. In benchmarks like TRECVID [25] or the PASCAL visual object challenge [10], the research community has investigated a variety of features and statistical models. In addition, there also has been much work in creating large ontologies and datasets [7, 14, 29]. Typically, such vocabularies are defined according to utility for retrieval, coverage, diversity, availability of training material, and its detectability by automatic detection systems [23, 25]. Recent approaches have also turned towards web portals like Flickr and YouTube as information sources for visual learning, employing user-generated tags as an alternative to manual labels [16, 31]. Aligned with the aforementioned trend, our approach also exploits large-scale image tags available on the web. Our focus, however, is less on concept detection itself but rather on the construction of an ontology of visually detectable ANPs serving as mid-level representation of sentiment attributes of visual content. In contrast, the prior works focus on physical concepts corresponding to objects, scenes, location but not concepts that characterize sentiment visually.

With respect to sentiment analysis, much progress has been achieved in text analysis [9, 30] and textual dictionary creation [9, 35]. However, efforts for visual analysis fall far behind. The closest that comes to sentiment analysis for visual content is the analysis of aesthetics [6, 15, 22], interestingness [12], and affect or emotions [13, 21, 37, 36]. To this end, either low-level features are directly taken to predict emotion [18, 13], or indirectly by facial expressions detection [32] or user intent [11]. Similarly [34], which introduced a high-level representation of emotions, is limited to low-level features such as color based schemes. Please refer to [15, 33] for a comprehensive study of aesthetics and emotions in images. Compared to the above works, our proposed approach is novel and ambitious in two ways. First, we build a large-scale ontology of semantic concepts correlated with strong sentiments like "beautiful landscape" or "dark clouds" as a complement to a textual sentiment dictionary [9, 35]. Such an ontology is the first of its kind and would open new research opportunities for the multimedia community and beyond. Second, from such an ontology and a publicly shared detector library a mid-level visual representation can be learned for the purpose of robust sentiment prediction.

Only a few small datasets exist today for affect / emotion analysis on visual content. A prominent one is the *International Affective Picture System* (IAPS) [17] providing normative ratings of emotion (pleasure, arousal, dominance) for a set of color photographs. The dataset consists of 369 photos covering various scenes showing insects, puppies, children, poverty, diseases and portraits, which are rated by 60 participants using affective words. Similarly, the *Geneva Affective Picture Database* (GAPED) [4] provides

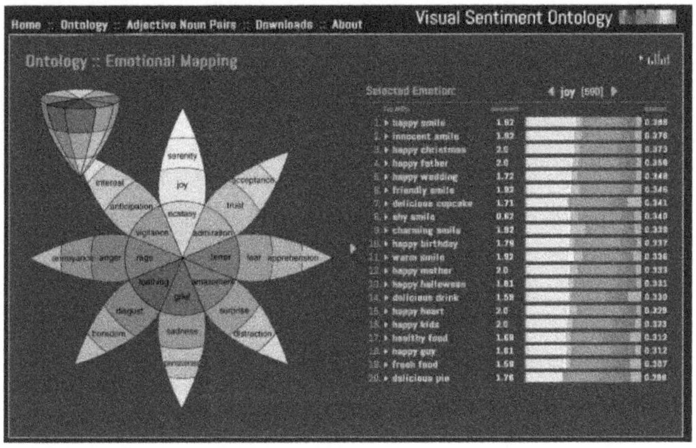

Figure 3: Plutchik's Wheel of Emotions and the visualization interface of the ontology based on the wheel.

730 pictures including negative (e.g., spiders, snakes, scenes containing human rights violation), positive (e.g., human and animal babies, nature sceneries) and neutral pictures. All pictures were rated according to valence, arousal, and the consistency of the represented scenes. In [21], the *Affective Image Classification Dataset* includes two separate datasets of abstract painting (228 paintings) and artistic photos (807 photos), which are labeled with 8 basic emotions through a crowd-sourcing procedure. In contrast to the above mentioned datasets our work provides a significantly larger dataset (about 0.5 million) of images crawled from social media and labeled with thousands of ANP concepts. In addition, we created a separate image dataset from Twitter for a sentiment prediction benchmark.

3. FRAMEWORK OVERVIEW

An overview of the proposed framework is shown in Fig. 2. The construction process is founded on psychological principles such as *Plutchik's Wheel of Emotions* [27]. During the first step, we use each of the 24 emotions defined in Plutchik's theory to derive search keywords and retrieve images and videos from Flickr and YouTube. Tags associated with the retrieved images and videos are extracted - for example "joy" leads to "happy", "beautiful", and "flower". These tags are then analyzed to assign sentiment values and to identify adjectives, verbs, and nouns. The set of all adjectives with strong sentiment values and all nouns is then used to form adjective noun combinations or **Adjective Noun Pairs (ANP)** such as "beautiful flowers" or "sad eyes". Those ANPs are then ranked by their frequency on Flickr and sampled to form a diverse and comprehensive ontology containing more than 3,000 ANP concepts. We then train individual detectors using Flickr images that are tagged with an ANP and keep only detectors with reasonable performance to form **SentiBank**. This detector library consists of 1,200 ANP concept detectors providing a 1,200 dimension ANP detector response for a given image. As a sample application, we apply SentiBank and train classifiers to predict sentiment values of image tweets and demonstrate a superior performance over conventional sentiment prediction using text only.

4. VISUAL SENTIMENT ONTOLOGY

In this section we outline the design and systematic construction of the proposed Visual Sentiment Ontology (VSO). Here we focus on sentiment or emotion expressed by the content owner shared on social media such as Twitter. We assume the sentiments of the receivers (i.e., viewers of the visual content), though not directly addressed in this paper, are strongly related to those of the content owners. Our goal is to construct a large-scale ontology of semantic concepts, which **(1)** reflect a strong sentiment, **(2)** have a link to an emotion, **(3)** are frequently used and **(4)** have reasonable detection accuracy. Additionally, the VSO is intended to be comprehensive and diverse enough to cover a broad range of different concept classes such as *people, animals, objects, natural or man-made places*, and so on.

joy	terror	amazement	disgust
joy	terror	amazing	disgusting
happy	horror	beautiful	gross
love	zombie	nature	food
smile	fear	wonder	nasty
beautiful	dark	light	sick
flowers	street	love	dirty
light	halloween	sky	dead
nature	war	eyes	face
kids	undead	clouds	blood
christmas	bomb	landscape	insect

Figure 4: Example top tags for different emotions. Colors of the boxes (green, grey, red) indicate different sentiments (positive, neutral, negative).

4.1 Psychological Foundation

To establish a solid foundation for the construction of the VSO we utilize a well-known emotion model derived from psychological studies. There are several well-known early works such as Darwin's evolutionary motivation of emotions [5], Ekman's facial expression system [8] and Osgood's appraisal and valence model [24]. Here, focus on *Plutchnik's Wheel of Emotions* [27] as seen in Fig. 3 is organized into 8 basic emotions, each with 3 valences. Beginning from the top we have:

1. ecstasy → joy → serenity
2. admiration → trust → acceptance
3. terror → fear → apprehension
4. amazement → surprise → distraction
5. grief → sadness → pensiveness
6. loathing → disgust → boredom
7. rage → anger → annoyance
8. vigilance → anticipation → interest

Why Plutchnik's Emotion Model? The model is inspired by chromatics in which emotions elements are arranged along a wheel and bi-polar emotions are opposite to each other - a useful property for the construction of a sentiment ontology. Further, it maps well to psychological theories such as Ekman, where 5 basic emotions are the same (anger, disgust, fear, sadness, surprise) while Ekman's "happiness" maps well to Plutchnik's "joy". Compared to the emotional model utilized in [21], Plutchnik basic emotions correspond to all 4 negative emotions but have slightly different positive emotions. In contrast, Plutchnik introduced two additional basic emotions (interest, trust) and organizes each of them into 3 intensities providing a richer set of different emotional valences. Statistics of our crawled

Table 1: Statistics of the Visual Sentiment Ontology construction process

(a)	Flickr	YouTube
# of emotions	24	24
images or videos	150,034	166,342
tags	3,138,795	3,079,526
distinct top 100 tags	**1,146**	**1,047**
(b)	**Sentiment Words**	
distinct top 100 tags	**1,771**	
pos+neg adjectives	268	
neutral adjectives	0	
total adjectives	**268**	
pos+neg nouns	576	
neutral nouns	611	
total nouns	**1,187**	
(c)	**VSO Statistics**	
ANP concept candidates	320k	
ANPs (with non-empty images)	47k	
ANPs included in VSO	**3k**	
top pos. adjectives	beautiful, amazing, cute	
top neg. adjectives	sad, angry, dark	
top nouns	face, eyes, sky	

dataset confirm useful contribution of each emotion group in Plutchik to the final VSO.

4.2 Sentiment Word Discovery

Initial Image & Video Retrieval: For each of the 24 emotions we retrieve images and videos from Flickr and YouTube respectively and then extract their distinct associated tags by the Lookapp tool [2]. In total we retrieve about 310k images and videos and about 6M tags, which are made of a set of 55k distinct tags. An overview of this step can be seen in Tab. 1 (a).

Tags Analysis: For tag analysis we first remove stopwords and perform stemming. For each emotion, we perform tag frequency analysis to obtain the top 100 tags. Examples of such top tags can be seen in Fig. 4. Finally, the sentiment value of each tag is computed using two popular linguistics based sentiment models, SentiWordNet [9] and SentiStrength [30]. In this work, each word is assigned a sentiment value ranging from -1 (negative) to +1 (positive). Overall, as shown Tab. 1 (b), we are able to retrieve 1146 distinct tags from Flickr and 1,047 distinct tags from YouTube forming the final set of 1,771 distinct tags with 1,187 nouns (576 positive and negative ones and 611 neutral ones) and 268 positive or negative adjectives. Note that we ignore verbs in this work because of the current focus on still images.

4.3 Adjective Noun Pair (ANP) Construction

Looking closer at the results of the previous step we can see that the 576 discovered nouns with positive or negative sentiment would satisfy the first concept selection condition mentioned above for ontology construction (reflecting strong sentiment), but in this case we would not be able to include the 611 neutral nouns. As for the adjectives, all 268 have either a positive or negative sentiment value (satisfying condition **(1)**) but probably we would not be able to satisfy condition **(4)**: reasonable detection accuracy. Visual learning

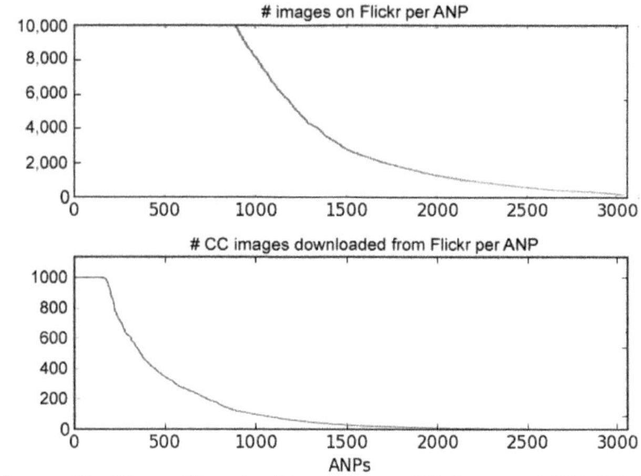

Figure 6: Top: Count of images on Flickr per ANP. **Bottom:** count of CC images downloaded per ANP (limited to max of 1000 images per ANP).

of adjectives is understandably difficult due to its abstract nature and high variability. Therefore, we propose adjective nouns combinations or **Adjective Noun Pairs (ANP)** to be the main semantic concept elements of the VSO. The advantage of using ANPs, as compared to nouns or adjectives only, is the feasibility of turning a neutral noun into a strong sentiment ANP. Such combined concepts also make the concepts more detectable, compared to adjectives only. The above described ANP structure shares certain similarity to the recent trend in computer vision and multimedia concept detection, i.e. *bi-concepts* [19] or TRECVID's *concept pairs* [25].

Candidate Selection: The set of all strong sentiment value adjectives and the set of all nouns are now used to form ANPs such as "beautiful flower" or "disgusting food". After ANP concepts are formed, an extra text analysis step is employed to avoid ANPs that correspond to named entities with meaning changed (e.g., "hot" + "dog" leads to a named entity instead of a generic concept). Obviously, during the construction of ANPs we also have to fuse the sentiment value of the adjective and the noun. This is done by applying a simple model to sum up the corresponding sentiment values $s(ANP) = s(adj) + s(noun)$ where the sentiment value $s(ANP)$ is between -2 and +2. Obviously, with this model we have to be careful with cases like "abused" being negative and "child" being positive forming the ANP "abused child", which reflects definitely a strong negative sentiment. We address this issue, by identifying ANPs that include an adjective and a noun with opposite sentiment values. We observed that in such cases the adjective usually has a stronger impact on the overall ANP sentiment than the noun and thus let the ANP inherits the sentiment value of the adjective.

Candidate Ranking: Those ANPs candidates (about 320k) are then ranked by their frequency on Flickr to remove meaningless or extremely rare constructions like e.g. "frightened hat" or "happy happiness". Having this ranked list of ANP frequencies (characterized by a long tail as seen in Fig. 6 (top)), we dismiss all ANPs with no images found on Flickr. This leads to a remaining set 47k ANP candidates. In this step we also eliminate cases where both, the singular and plural forms of an ANPs exists in the VSO. In such a case we take the more frequent one.

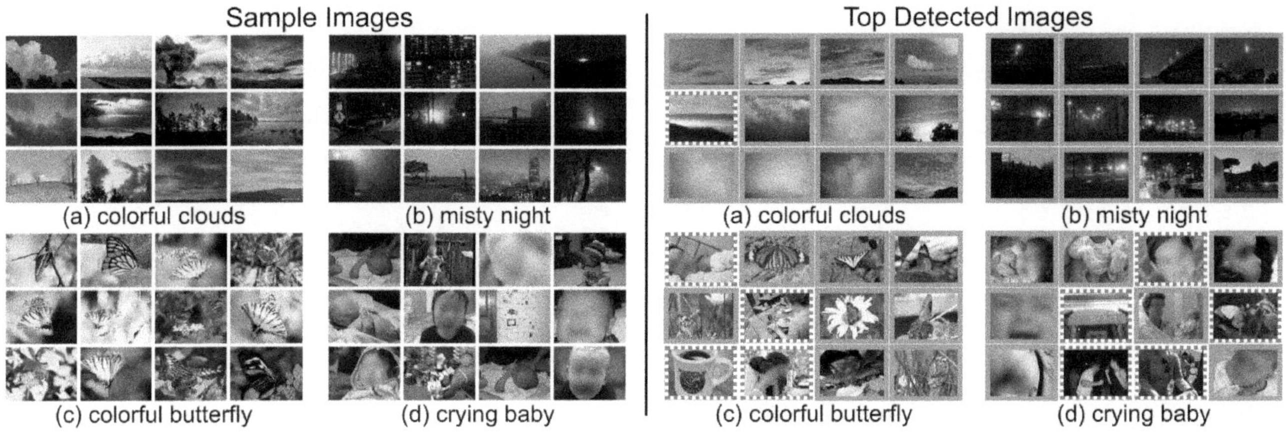

Figure 5: Left: Selected images for four sample ANPs, **(a)**,**(c)** reflecting a positive sentiment and **(b)**, **(d)**, a negative one. **Right:** top detected images by SentiBank ANPs with high detection accuracy (top) and low accuracy (bottom). Correct detections are surrounded by green and thick frames and incorrect ones by red and dashed frames. Faces in the images are blurred.

Table 2: Top 3 ANPs for basic emotions.

Emotion	Top ANPs
joy	happy smile, innocent smile, happy christmas
trust	christian faith, rich history, nutritious food
fear	dangerous road, scary spider, scary ghost
surprise	pleasant surprise, nice surprise, precious gift
sadness	sad goodbye, sad scene, sad eyes
disgust	nasty bugs, dirty feet, ugly bug
anger	angry bull, angry chicken, angry eyes
anticipation	magical garden, tame bird, curious bird

Ontology Sampling: The final step is to subsample the concepts in a diverse and balanced way and include those with a high frequency only. To avoid dominance by just a few popular adjectives, we partition candidate concepts into individual adjective sets and sample from each adjective a subset of ANPs. Further we only take ANPs if they have sufficient (currently > 125) images found on Flickr.

Link back to Emotions: We are interested in how the discovered ANPs are related to the basic emotions used in the very first retrieval step. Here, we measure the counts of images that have both the emotion term and the ANP string in their meta-data and normalize the resulting 24 dimension histogram to unit sum. This way a two-directional connection between an emotion and an ANP can be established. For example, the most dominant emotion for "happy smile" ANP is "joy" and for the emotion "disgust" the popular ANP is "nasty bugs". More examples can be seen in Table 2.

The final VSO contains more than 3,000 ANP concepts with 268 adjectives and their corresponding ANPs. Some of top ranked APNs are: "happy birthday", "beautiful flower", and "little girl" being positive and "dark night", "heavy rain", and "broken window" being the negative counterpart.

4.4 Flickr CC Dataset & Visualization Tool

An essential part of the VSO is its image dataset representing each ANP. The images are used for SentiBank detector training (Sec. 5). We used the Flickr API to retrieve and download Creative Common (CC) images for each ANP (limited to 1000 images by the API service) and include only images that contain the ANP string either in the title, tag or description of the image. With this we were able to download a sufficient amount of CC images for 1,553 of the 3,000 ANPs (in total about 500k images). The distribution of image count per ANP can be seen in Fig. 6 (bottom). Selected images of four example ANPs are show in Fig. 5 (left).

To help visualize the VSO and the associated dataset, we have developed two novel visualization techniques, one based on Wheel of Emotion (shown in Fig. 3) and the other the well-known TreeMap hierarchical visualization method (Fig. 8). The Emotion Wheel interface allows users to view and interact with the Plutchik 24 emotions directly and then zoom in to explore specific ANP concepts and associated images. The TreeMap interface offers a complementary way of navigating through different levels of VSO - emotion, adjective, noun, and ANPs. At each level, the map shows statistics and summaries of information from the level below. Interactive demos of these tools are available online[2].

5. SENTIBANK

Given the Visual Sentiment Ontology constructed above, we propose *SentiBank*, a novel visual sentiment analysis framework using the output of ANP detectors as a mid-level concept representation for each image. Its objective is to detect ANP concept presence and to characterize the sentiment reflected in visual content. To this end, we address several key issues, namely ANP label reliability, design of individual ANP detectors, detector performance, and coverage.

5.1 Reliability of ANP labels

It is known that web labels may not be reliable [7, 31]. Using Flickr tags directly as pseudo labels of ANPs might incur either *false positive*, i.e. an image is labeled by an ANP but actually does not show the ANP, or *false negative*, i.e. if an image is not labeled with an ANP it does not imply the ANP is not present in the image.

Dealing with Pseudo Labels: Considering the potential of *false positive*, we further evaluate the ANP labels by an Amazon Mechanical Turk (AMT) experiment. We ran-

[2]`http://visual-sentiment-ontology.appspot.com/`

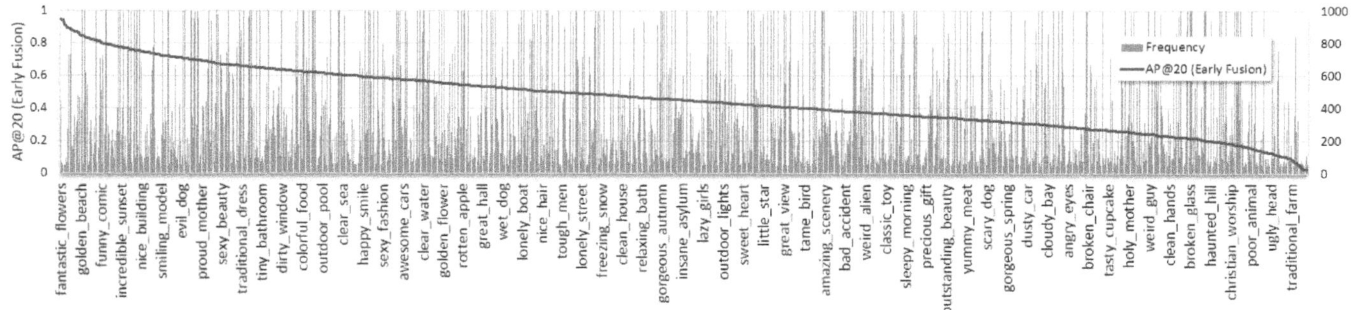

Figure 7: AP@20 (avg. over 5 runs of the reduced testsets) vs. frequency of 1,553 ANP detectors ranked by detector performance. Note only a subset of ANP names are shown due to space limit.

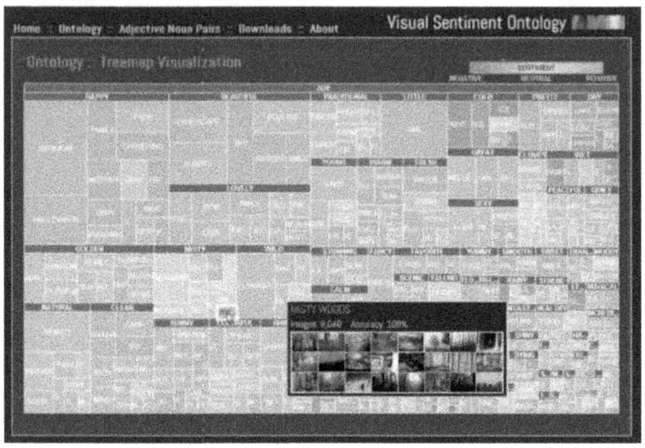

Figure 8: VSO visualization interface using Treemap.

domly sample images of 200 ANP concepts to manually validate their actual presence, namely using AMT crowdsource to check whether an image indeed contains the corresponding ANP. Each image label is validated by 3 Turkers and is treated as "correct" only if at least 2 Turkers agree that an image contains the given ANP label. Results of this experiment show that 97% of AMP image labels are actually "correct", which indicates that false positive is not a major issue.

Unfortunately, for the *false negative* issue, such a label validation procedure is prohibitive since it would require to fully label all images for all ANPs. This is also an open issue for existing crowdsourced visual recognition benchmarks such as ImageNet LISVRC2010-2012 and ObjectBank. In this work, we resolve this by randomly sampling positives of other ANPs (except those containing the same adjective or noun) when forming the negative set for each ANP class. This way we can minimize the probability of false negative, while avoiding the prohibitive task of labeling the entire dataset over every ANP concept.

Training and Testing Partitions: For training we sample 80% of pseudo positive images of each ANP and twice as many negative images using the subsampling scheme described above. For testing, we prepare two different testsets, denoted as the *full* and *reduced* testsets. Both use the remaining 20% of pseudo positive samples of a given ANP as positive test samples. But the negative samples are different - the full testset includes 20% pseudo positive samples from each of the other ANPs (except those with the same adjective or noun). This leads to a balanced training set and a large and diverse testset for individual detector performance evaluation. However, the prior of the positive in each testset is very low, only about 1/1,553. The reduced testset, intended for fast implementations and balanced test sample distributions, includes much less negative samples - the number of negative test samples for each ANP is just twice as many the positive samples. To avoid testset bias, we also generate 5 runs of the reduced testset, each of which includes different negative samples while keeping the positive samples fixed. We will use performance average over these 5 runs in later experiments (Fig. 7, 9, 10) in the paper and leave the performance details over the full testset in supplementary materials.

5.2 Training ANP Detectors

With the partition of training and test data for each ANP, detectors for individual ANPs can be readily trained.

Visual Feature Design: Following the feature design for state-of-the-art visual classification systems such as ObjectBank [38], we first include generic visual features: a 3×256 dimension Color Histogram extracted from the RGB color channels, a 512 dimension GIST descriptor [40] that has been shown to be useful for detecting scenes like "beautiful landscape", a 53 dimension Local Binary Pattern (LBP) descriptor suitable for detecting textures and faces, a Bag-of-Words quantized descriptor using a $1,000$ word dictionary with a 2-layer spatial pyramid and max pooling, and finally a $2,000$ dimensional attribute [39] useful for characterizing abstract ANPs. Additional features specialized for detecting objects, faces, or aesthetics will be presented later in Sec. 5.5.

ANP Detector Training: Due to the large amount of ANPs in the ontology, we employ Linear SVMs to train ANP detectors in order to ensure high efficiency. Parameter tuning of SVM was performed by cross-validation optimizing Average Precision at rank 20 (AP@20), a performance measure focusing on the accuracy of the top ranked samples. Detector performance was also measured by the Area Under Curve (AUC), estimating the probability of ranking a random positive sample higher than a random negative one. Finally, our third measure is F-Score, describing the harmonic mean between precision and recall. All three measures are standard metrics for detector evaluation.

Detector performance using various features can be seen in Fig. 9. Here we can observe a clear dominance by the attribute features followed by Bag-of-Words (BOW). Considering feature fusion, both early and late fusions are evaluated. The former refers to merging and normalizing different feature vectors into a single vector. The latter refers to the fusion of detector scores after classification. We have evaluated different fusion methods including *Early*

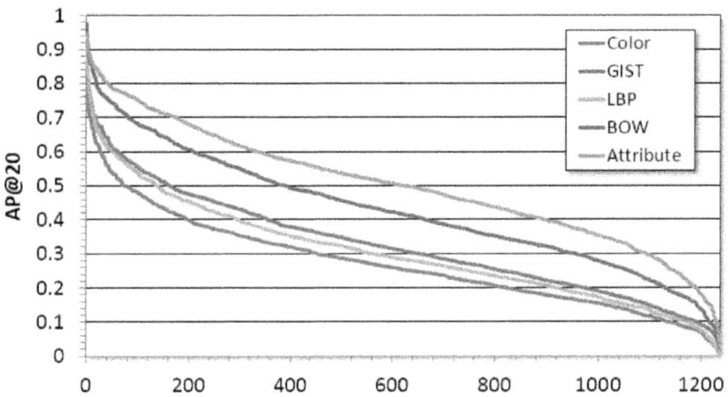

Figure 9: Comparison of ANP detectors using different features. Performance computed by avg. over 5 runs of the reduced testsets.

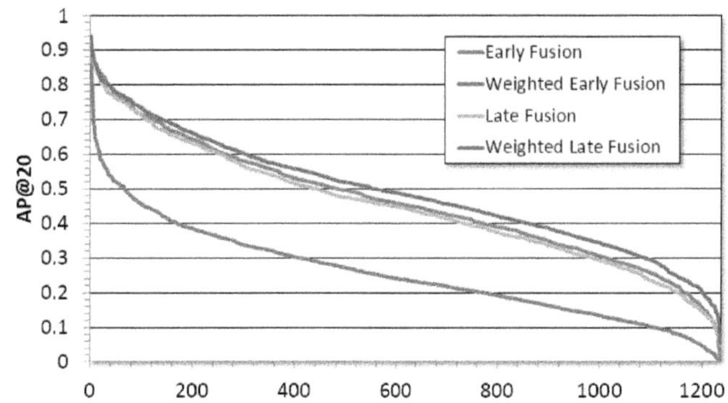

Figure 10: AP@20 of ANP detectors using different fusion approaches. Performance computed by avg. over 5 runs of the reduced testsets.

Fusion, Weighted Early Fusion, Late Fusion, and Weighted Late Fusion[3]. As shown in Fig. 10, Weighted Late Fusion out-performs other fusion schemes by a small margin, while the performance of early and late fusion is quite close. For implementation simplicity, we use the early fusion approach in the released SentiBank detectors.

5.3 Ontology Structure

An ontology consists of not only concepts but also relations that can be used for browsing and reasoning about concepts within a domain. To construct such ontological structures, we have conducted an interactive process in which multiple subjects were asked to combine the 1,200 ANP concepts in SentiBank into distinct groups, so that each group shares coherent semantics among group members. Consensus among subjects was reached through result comparison and discussion. We perform grouping processes for adjectives and nouns in the VSO separately. Such separate processes allow exploitation of relations unique for adjectives or nouns. For example, a hierarchical structure for nouns (a total of about 520) was found to include six levels and 15 nodes at the top level, such as person, place, object, food, and abstract concept. The adjectives (a total of about 260) were grouped to two levels with 6 nodes at the top level. The standard hyponym-hypernym ("is-a") relations were found in the noun hierarchy, while special relations like exclusive ("sad" vs. "happy") and strength order ("nice" vs. "great" vs. "awesome") were found among adjectives. We also found special conditions for combining adjectives and nouns into ANPs. For example, some adjectives are only applicable to certain noun groups, such as people, place, food, and objects. In other words, adjective groups can be considered as facets of specific types of nouns - a practice often used in ontology construction.

Comparison of the constructed noun taxonomy and the well-known ImageNet shows 59% of the VSO nouns being mapped to ImageNet synsets. This leads to 41% of VSO nouns not covered by ImageNet, although they can still be found in WordNet. These concepts unique to VSO are mainly related to abstract concepts such as "violence" or "religion", which reflect strong emotions or sentiments. This confirm the unique focus on emotions and sentiments in the concept discovery process of VSO, as described earlier in this section. Due to the space limit, we refer for more details to the technical report [3]

[3]weights are also tuned by cross-validation

5.4 ANP Detectability and Coverage

ANP Detectability Overview: An important step in building SentiBank is to select only ANPs with reasonable detection accuracy. To this end, we rank the ANP detectors based on the previously described performance measures such as F-Score, AUC, or AP@20. It is worth noting that using different performance metrics only slightly affect the relative orders of the ANP detectors. At the end, we choose 1,200 ANP detectors, all of which have non-zero AP@20 and most have F-score greater than 0.6, when evaluated over the reduced testset. It's interesting to see (as shown in Fig. 7) that there is no correlation between the detectability of an ANP and its occurrence frequency. Instead, the difficulty in detecting an ANP depends on the content diversity and the abstract level of concept. We show some examples of the best and worst ANPs based on AP@20 in Figure 5.

Generalizability and Coverage: Are the selected SentiBank ANP detectors generalizable to different data domains? It would be useful to check the performance degradation if we apply SentiBank detectors to new data domains, such as TRECVID or PASCAL VOC. In the next section, we answer this question indirectly by predicting the sentiment of image tweets which have different characteristics than the Flickr images. In addition, as discussed in Sec. 5.3, the scope of the constructed VSO is broad, covering many categories in other well-known visual ontologies, such as LSCOM [23] and ImageNet [7]. This will help to address a common out-of-vocabulary problem when applying small-sized detectors to general domains.

5.5 Special Visual Features

Other than the generic features, we also test several special features for training the SentiBank detectors. First, since many of the ANP concepts are associated with objects, we utilize object detection techniques to localize the concept within an image. We choose 210 ANPs that are associated with detectable objects such as people, dog, or cars. We apply the object detection tools from [38] and combine multi-scale detection results to form a spatial map for constraining the image region from which the visual features described in Sec. 5.2 are extracted. Another option is to take the object detection response scores directly as features. Secondly, we evaluate facial features on 99 ANPs with nouns like face, smile, tears, etc. These include the detected face count, relative face size, relative facial marker position

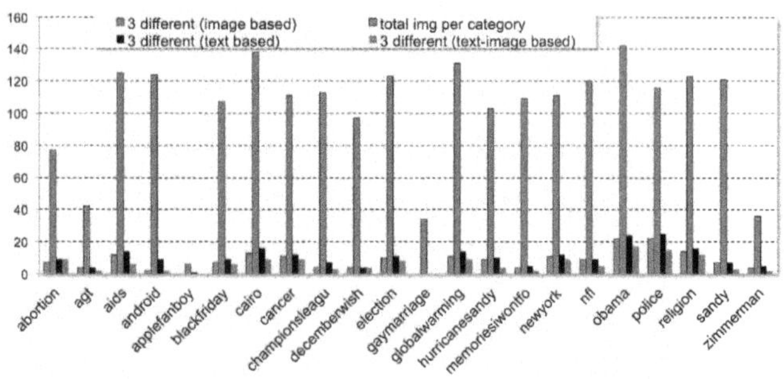

Figure 11: The volumes and label disagreements for different hashtags. For each hashtag, the total number of images is shown, in addition to the number of images receiving complete disagreement among Turkers (i.e., 3 different sentiment labels: positive, negative and neural), while labeling is done using text only, image only, and joint image-text combined.

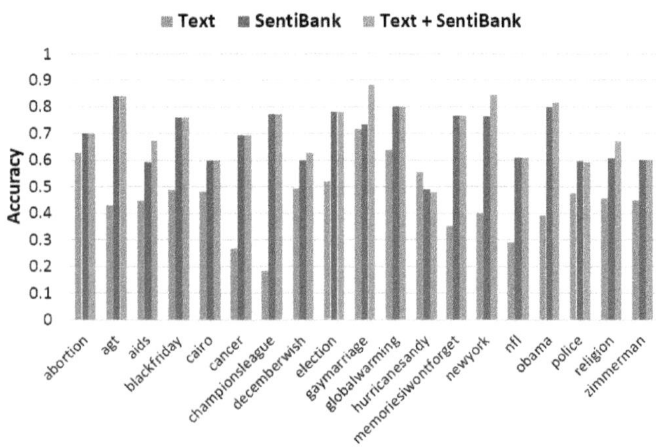

Figure 12: Phototweet sentiment prediction accuracy over different hashtags by using text only (SentiStrength), visual only (SentiBank), and combination. Accuracy averaged over 5 runs.

and Haar features at the markers. Thirdly, we test aesthetics related features on all of the ANPs. These features from [41] include dark channel and luminosity feature, sharpness, symmetry, low depth of field, white balance, etc. The above three groups of features increase the mean AP@20 score of selected ANP sets by 10.5%, 13.5% and 9.0% (relative gains) respectively on the reduced testset and the mean AP@100 by 39.1%, 15.8% and 30.7% on the full testset. Based on the above comparisons, we conjecture that the generic features offer a competitive solution for detecting ANP visual sentiment concepts, while special features offer great potential for further improvements.

6. SENTIBANK APPLICATIONS

In this section we demonstrate potential applications of SentiBank. Since our initial motivation to construct the VSO and create SentiBank is to capture the sentiment reflected in visual content, our first application focuses on sentiment prediction in image tweets[4]. Additionally, we evaluate SentiBank against a well-known emotion dataset of art photos [21].

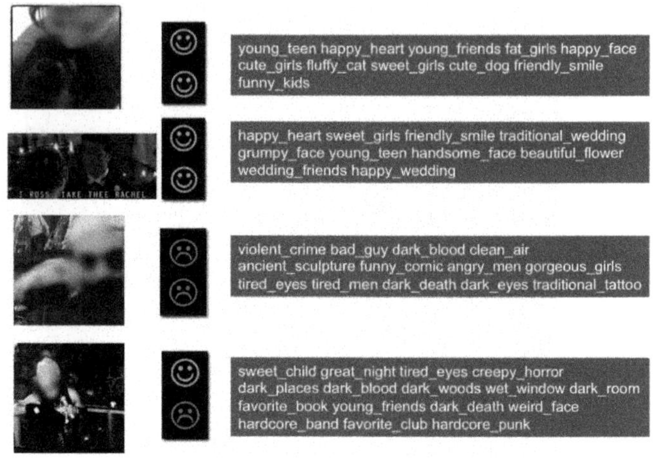

Figure 13: Sentiment prediction results using SentiBank as features (top icon in each box in the middle: ground truth sentiment, bottom icon: predicted sentiment). On the right the top responding ANPs found in the prediction.

6.1 Sentiment Prediction

For sentiment prediction, state-of-the-art approaches typically rely on text-based tools such as SentiWordNet [9] or SentiStrength [30]. However, due to the length restriction of 140 characters in tweets, such approach is limited and often unable to correctly discern the sentiment of the text content. To overcome this issue, we use the proposed visual sentiment analysis tool, SentiBank, to complement and augment the text features in sentiment prediction.

Hashtag Selection: We collect tweets containing images from the PeopleBrowsr API using the following popular hashtags: *Human:* #abortion, #religion, #cancer, #aids, #memoriesiwontforget, *Social:* #gaymarriage, #police, #nuclearpower, #globalwarming, *Event:* #election, #hurricanesandy, #occupywallstreet, #agt (america got talent), #nfl, #blackfriday, #championsleague, #decemberwish, *People:* #obama, #zimmerman, *Location:* #cairo, #newyork, *Technology:* #android, #iphonefan, #kodak, #androidgame, #applefan. The resulting dataset consists of 20 to 150 images per hashtag, crawled during November 2012.

Ground Truth Labeling: To obtain sentiment ground truth for the collected image tweets, we conduct three labeling runs using AMT, namely *image-based*, *text-based*, and joint *text-image based*. They correspond to image only inspection, text only inspection, and full inspection using both image and text contained in the tweet. Each run is assigned to 3 randomly assigned Turkers, but no Turkers are asked to annotate the same tweet under different modality settings. Fig. 11 shows the labeling statistics, where we define an image as "agreed", if more than 2 Turkers assign the same label (either positive, negative or neutral). From the results, we clearly see that, joint *text-image based* labels are the most consistent ones, following by *image-based* labels and then the *text-based* labels. This indicates the limitation of text-based sentiment analysis for Twitter and highlights the potential for a holistic sentiment analysis using both the image and text analysis. At the end, we include only the image tweets that receive unanimously agreed labels among three Turkers from the image-text annotation as the final benchmark set.

[4] Sentiment is often measured in a particular domain such as movies, food, or politics. For this study we adopt a generic definition across different tweet topics without topic-specific differentiation

Table 3: Tweet Sentiment Prediction Accuracy (Visual Based Methods)

	Linear SVM	**Logistic Regr.**
Low-level Features	0.55	0.57
SentiBank	0.67	**0.70**

It includes 470 positive tweets and 133 negative tweets over 21 hashtags, among which 19 hashtags each with more than 10 samples are shown in Fig. 12.

Visual-based Classifier: As mentioned before, SentiBank serves as an expressive mid-level representation of visual concept. For each image, SentiBank provides a 1,200 dimension ANP response, which is used as an input feature for the sentiment classification. Here, we employ linear classifiers such as Linear SVM and Logistic Regression. To this end, we are not only aiming to predict the sentiment being reflected in images but also to provide an explanation of the prediction result. This is achieved by providing a list of top responding ANP detectors in addition to the sentiment prediction label.

We first compare the proposed SentiBank mid-level representation with low-level features, using two different classification models, LinearSVM and Logistic Regression. For low-level features, we use the same set as those described in Sec. 5.2 (color histogram, GIST, LBP, BoW, and attributes). Prediction accuracy is shown in Table 3 - confirming the significant performance improvement (more than 20% relatively) achieved by the SentiBank features. The logistic regression model is also found to be better than Linear SVM.

In a separate experiment, we have also confirmed the superiority of SentiBank using Adjective-Noun Pairs over the concepts of nouns only, adjectives only, or their union. This again verifies the advantage of using ANP concepts to build out SentiBank representations.

Text Based Classification: We adopt two text-based sentiment predictors:

`(1) Naive Bayesian text-based Sentiment Classifier:`

$$Score = \frac{1}{M}\sum_{m=1}^{M} Frequency_m \times Score_m \qquad (1)$$

in which *Score* is the sentiment prediction score normalized to [-1,1], M the number of unique words after stemming and stop words removal, $Frequency_m$ the frequency of word m, and $Score_m$ is the individual sentiment score of word m obtained from SentiStrength.

`(2) SentiStrengh API:` We directly use the sentiment prediction by the publicly available SentiStrength API[5] to compute the sentiment score for the entire tweet text. Our experiment has shown that SentiStrenght API prediction accuracy based on the entire tweet text is higher than the one combining scores of individual words using the Naive Bayesian method.

Joint text-image Classification Performance: Finally, we compare the accuracy using text only (SentiStrength), visual only (SentiBank), and their combination. From Tables 3 and 4, we find visual based methods using SentiBank concepts are significantly better than the text only (70% vs. 43%). By further analyzing the results, we find most of the

[5]http://sentistrength.wlv.ac.uk/

Table 4: Comparison of Tweet Sentiment Prediction Accuracy

text only (SentiStrength)	**text + visual (SentiBank LinearSVM)**	**text + visual (SentiBank Logistic Regr.)**
0.43	0.68	**0.72**

text contents in the tweets are short and neutral, explaining the low accuracy of text-based methods in predicting the sentiment. In such cases, the sentiment values of the visual content predicted by the SentiBank-based classifiers play a much more important role in predicting the overall sentiment of the tweet.

Fig. 12 shows comparison of sentiment prediction accuracy for each individual hashtag. Here, we find the visual-based approach using SentiBank concepts consistently outperforms the text-based method using SentiStrength API, except only one hashtag ("hurricanesandy"). It's also very encouraging to see combining text and SentiBank features further improves accuracy for several hashtags, despite the low accuracy of the text-based method.

Results of a few sample images can be seen in Fig. 13. Here, SentiBank's capability in explaining predictions is illustrated by showing a list of top ANPs detected in each test image.

6.2 Emotion Classification

Although our initial motivation was to predict sentiment reflected in images, an evaluation of the proposed method in emotion classification (similar to the task in [21]) might be of interest. Especially since our VSO construction process starts with web search using emotions as search terms. The dataset is based on ArtPhotos retrieved from DeviantArt.com and contains 807 images from 8 emotion categories. Such evaluation poses a set of challenges such as domain change. SentiBank is trained on a different set of images than the testset. Further, our emotion categories are slightly different, not mentioning our focus is on a framework with generic visual features rather than the specialized affective features used in [21]. We follow a similar process to select SentiBank ANPs as features for each emotion category, combined with the Naive Bayesian classifier. Results are reported in Fig. 14. Even in such a challenging setting, SentiBank compares well to [21] when using the same classification model (Naive Bayesian) and even slightly outperforms the best results in [21] when using the Logistic Regression model. This demonstrates the potential of SentiBank for applications in different domains.

7. DISCUSSION

In this paper we have presented an approach towards the prediction of sentiment reflected in visual content. To reach this goal we propose a systematic, data-driven methodology to construct a large-scale sentiment ontology built upon psychology and web crawled folksonomies. Further, we present SentiBank, a concept detector library based on the constructed ontology to establish a novel mid-level representation for bridging the *affective gap*. Finally, we release the concept ontology, dataset, the detector library, and the benchmark for tweet sentiment analysis to stimulate research in this direction.

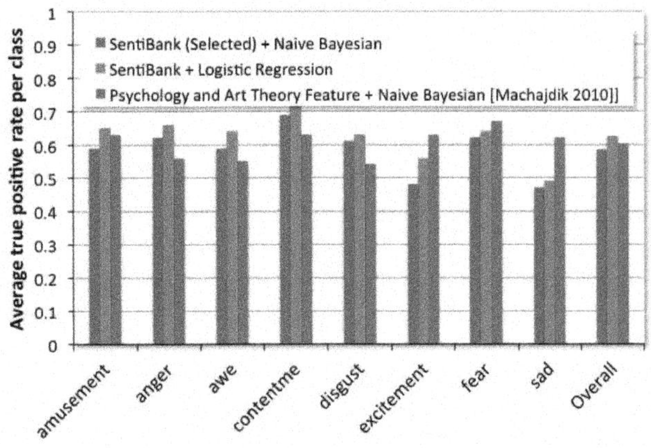

Figure 14: Emotion classification performance.

Several exciting directions are open for investigation. First, the cultural influence on expressing sentiment and emotion is of interest. Further, as shown earlier the application of special features such as aesthetic features used in [21] and face expression features offers interesting potential for further improvement. Additionally, other applications such as advertising, games, virtual reality are promising when the cross-domain performance of the detectors is studied in more depth. Another important task is the extension of VSO and SentiBank to video applications.

8. ACKNOWLEDGEMENT

Research was sponsored in part by the U.S. Defense Advanced Research Projects Agency (DARPA) under the Social Media in Strategic Communication (SMISC) program, Agreement Number W911NF-12-C-0028. The views and conclusions contained in this document are those of the author(s) and should not be interpreted as representing the official policies, either expressed or implied, of the U.S. Defense Advanced Research Projects Agency or the U.S. Government. The U.S. Government is authorized to reproduce and distribute reprints for Government purposes notwithstanding any copyright notation hereon.

9. REFERENCES

[1] H. Aradhye, G. Toderici, and J. Yagnik. Video2Text: Learning to Annotate Video Content. *Internet Multimedia Mining*, 2009.

[2] D. Borth, A. Ulges, and T.M. Breuel. Lookapp - Interactive Construction of web-based Concept Detectors. *ICMR*, 2011.

[3] D. Borth and S-F. Chang. Constructing Structures and Relations in SentiBank Visual Sentiment Ontology. *Technical Report #CUCS-020-13, Columbia University, Computer Science Dep.*, 2013.

[4] E. Dan-Glauser et al. The Geneva Affective Picture Database (GAPED): a new 730-picture database focusing on valence and normative significance. *Behavior Research Methods*, 2011.

[5] Charles Darwin. *The Expression of the Emotions in Man and Animals.* Oxford University Press, USA, 1872 / 1998.

[6] R. Datta, D. Joshi, J. Li, and J. Wang. Studying Aesthetics in Photographic Images using a Computational Approach. *ECCV*, 2006.

[7] J. Deng et al. ImageNet: A Large-Scale Hierarchical Image Database. *CVPR*, 2009.

[8] P. Ekman et al. Facial Expression and Emotion. *American Psychologist*, 48:384-384, 1993.

[9] A. Esuli and F. Sebastiani. SentiWordnet: A publicly available Lexical Resource for Opinion Mining. *LREC*, 2006.

[10] M. Everingham, et al. The Pascal Visual Object Classes (VOC) Challenge. *Int. J. of Computer Vision*, 88(2):303-338, 2010.

[11] A. Hanjalic, C. Kofler, and M. Larson. Intent and its Discontents: the User at the Wheel of the Online Video Search Engine. *ACM MM*, 2012.

[12] P. Isola, J. Xiao, A. Torralba, and A. Oliva. What makes an Image Memorable? *CVPR*, 2011.

[13] J. Jia, S. Wu, X. Wang, P. Hu, L. Cai, and J. Tang. Can we understand van Gogh's Mood?: Learning to infer Affects from Images in Social Networks. *ACM MM*, 2012.

[14] Y.-G. Jiang, G. Ye, S.-F. Chang, D. Ellis, and A. Loui. Consumer Video Understand.: Benchmark Database and an Eval. of Human and Machine Performance. *ICMR*, 2011.

[15] D. Joshi, R. Datta, E. Fedorovskaya, Q. Luong, J. Wang, J. Li, and J. Luo. Aesthetics and Emotions in Images. *Signal Processing Magazine*, 28(5):94-115, 2011.

[16] L. Kennedy, S.-F. Chang, and I. Kozintsev. To Search or to Label?: Predicting the Performance of Search-based Automatic Image Classifiers. *MIR Workshop*, 2006.

[17] P. Lang, M. Bradley, and B. Cuthbert. International Affective Picture System (IAPS): Technical Manual and Affective Ratings, 1999.

[18] B. Li, et al. Scaring or Pleasing: Exploit Emotional Impact of an Image. *ACM MM*, 2012.

[19] X. Li, C. Snoek, M. Worring, and A. Smeulders. Harvesting Social Images for Bi-Concept Search. *IEEE Transactions on Multimedia*, 14(4):1091-1104, 2012.

[20] N. Codella et al. IBM Research and Columbia University TRECVID-2011 Multimedia Event Detection (med) System. *NIST TRECVID Workshop*, 2011.

[21] J. Machajdik and A. Hanbury. Affective Image Classification using Features inspired by Psychology and Art Theory. *ACM MM*, 2010.

[22] L. Marchesotti, F. Perronnin, D. Larlus, and G. Csurka. Assessing the Aesthetic Quality of Photographs using Generic Image Descriptors. *ICCV*, 2011.

[23] M. Naphade, J. Smith, J. Tesic, S. Chang, W. Hsu, L. Kennedy, A. Hauptmann, and J. Curtis. Large-Scale Concept Ontology for Multimedia. *IEEE MultiMedia*, 13(3):86-91, 2006.

[24] C. Osgood, G. Suci, and P. Tannenbaum. *The Measurement of Meaning*, volume 47. University of Illinois Press, 1957.

[25] P. Over et al. Trecvid 2012 – An Overview of the Goals, Tasks, Data, Evaluation Mechanisms and Metrics. *TRECVID Workshop*, 2012.

[26] B. Pang and L. Lee. Opinion Mining and Sentiment Analysis. *Information Retrieval*, 2(1-2):1-135, 2008.

[27] Robert Plutchik. *Emotion: A Psychoevolutionary Synthesis.* Harper & Row, Publishers, 1980.

[28] C. Snoek and M. Worring. Concept-based Video Retrieval. *Foundations and Trends in Inf. Retrieval*, 4(2), 2009.

[29] S. Strassel et al. Creating HAVIC: Heterogeneous Audio Visual Internet Collection. *LREC*, 2012.

[30] M. Thelwall et al. Sentiment Strength Detection in Short Informal Text. *J. of the American Soc. for Information Science and Tech.*, 61(12):2544-2558, 2010.

[31] A. Ulges, C. Schulze, M. Koch, and T. Breuel. Learning Automatic Concept Detectors from Online Video. *Journal on Comp. Vis. Img. Underst.*, 114(4):429-438, 2010.

[32] V. Vonikakis and S. Winkler. Emotion-based Sequence of Family Photos. *ACM MM*, 2012.

[33] W. Wang and Q. He. A Survey on Emotional Semantic Image Retrieval. *IEEE ICIP*, 2008.

[34] X. Wang, J. Jia, P. Hu, S. Wu, J. Tang, and L. Cai. Understanding the Emotional Impact of Images. *ACM MM*, 2012.

[35] T. Wilson et al. Recognizing Contextual Polarity in phrase-level Sentiment Analysis. *HLT/EMNLP*, 2005.

[36] V. Yanulevskaya et al. In the Eye of the Beholder: Employing Statistical Analysis and Eye Tracking for Analyzing Abstract Paintings. *ACM MM*, 2012.

[37] V. Yanulevskaya et al. Emotional Valence Categorization using Holistic Image Features. *IEEE ICIP*, 2008.

[38] Li et al. ObjectBank: A high-level Image Rep. for Scene Classification and Semantic Feature Sparsification. *NIPS*, 2010.

[39] F. Yu, et al Designing Category-level Attributes for Discriminative Visual Recognition. *CVPR*, 2013.

[40] A. Olivai and A. Torralba. Modeling the Shape of the Scene: a Holistic Representation of the Spatial Envelope. *Int. J. of Computer Vision*, 42(3):145-175, 2001.

[41] S. Bhattacharya and B. Nojavanasghari and T. Chen and D. Liu and S.-F. Chang and M. Shah. Towards a Comprehensive Computational Model for Aesthetic Assessment of Videos. *ACM MM*, Grand Challenge, 2013.

Indexing Billions of Images for Sketch-based Retrieval

Xinghai Sun[†]*, Changhu Wang[‡], Chao Xu[†], Lei Zhang[‡]
[†]Key Laboratory of Machine Perception (Ministry of Education), Peking Univ., Beijing, P. R. China
[‡]Microsoft Research Asia, Beijing, P. R. China
{sunxh, xuchao}@cis.pku.edu.cn, {chw, leizhang}@microsoft.com

ABSTRACT

Because of the popularity of touch-screen devices, it has become a highly desirable feature to retrieve images from a huge repository by matching with a hand-drawn sketch. Although searching images via keywords or an example image has been successfully launched in some commercial search engines of billions of images, it is still very challenging for both academia and industry to develop a sketch-based image retrieval system on a billion-level database. In this work, we systematically study this problem and try to build a system to support query-by-sketch for two billion images. The raw edge pixel and Chamfer matching are selected as the basic representation and matching in this system, owning to the superior performance compared with other methods in extensive experiments. To get a more compact feature and a faster matching, a vector-like Chamfer feature pair is introduced, based on which the complex matching is reformulated as the crossover dot-product of feature pairs. Based on this new formulation, a compact shape code is developed to represent each image/sketch by projecting the Chamfer features to a linear subspace followed by a non-linear source coding. Finally, the multi-probe Kmedoids-LSH is leveraged to index database images, and the compact shape codes are further used for fast reranking. Extensive experiments show the effectiveness of the proposed features and algorithms in building such a sketch-based image search system.

Categories and Subject Descriptors

H.3.1 [**Information Storage and Retrieval**]: Content Analysis and Indexing

General Terms

Algorithm, Design, Experimentation

*This work was performed at Microsoft Research Asia.

MM'13, October 21–25, 2013, Barcelona, Spain.

http://dx.doi.org/10.1145/2502081.2502281.

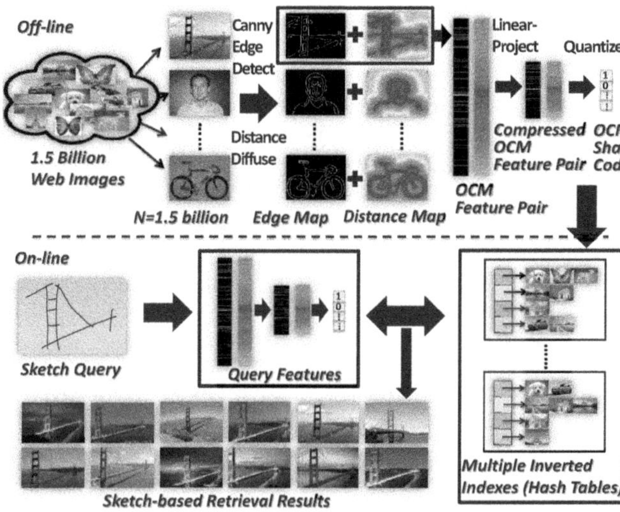

Figure 1: The outline of the sketch-based image retrieval system. Upper part: off-line engine building procedure, including image preprocessing, feature pair extraction, dimension reduction, shape codes generation and index construction. Lower part: the online retrieval.

Keywords

Sketch-based Image Retrieval, Billion Scale, Chamfer Matching, Product Quantization, Indexing

1. INTRODUCTION

Image content analysis has long been a fundamental research problem in the computer vision and multimedia communities. Although much progress has been made in analyzing texture-rich natural images, the understanding of textureless *shape*, which plays an essential role in human vision, is still a challenging problem. Most previous efforts in shape analysis were constrained within small databases, which seriously limit potential discoveries and practical applications. Stepping into the era of big data, the explosive growth of web images motivates us to restudy this problem in a very large scale. We believe a web-scale image data set can provide a great potential to solving many traditionally unsolvable problems. To efficiently utilize billions of images, the first step is to efficiently access the data set. Therefore, in this work, we target at the retrieval problem: to retrieve images similar to a hand-drawn sketch (in terms of shape) from 1.5 billion images in real time. Based on the success of this capability, other shape/sketch understanding problems, e.g. sketch recognition, shape modeling, shape detection, sketch suggestion, will become possible.

- The Bless of Big Data

We are embracing the era of big data. The exploding amount of web data have revolutionized our daily lives and reshaped the scientific research, including image retrieval and understanding in both academia and industry. Before 2000, most research in multimedia was conducted in thousand-level databases, in which diverse features and sophisticated models were explored. It then moved to its million-era owning to the growth of web images and the development of content-based image retrieval (CBIR). Some challenging problems such as image annotation were studied in a data-driven way[17], and superior performance shows the power of big data. Torralba et al [15] collected 80 million tiny images and showed the great value of data-driven methods in several computer vision tasks. Since 2008, CBIR has moved into a billion-era, and come into commercial use, e.g. query by image examples in TinEye and Google.

- Large-scale Sketch-based Image Retrieval

Finding images by drawing a sketch is a highly desired feature, especially with the popularity of touch-screen devices. Different from keyword-based and example-based methods, sketch-based image retrieval (SBIR) targets at finding images similar to a user's drawing in terms of major shapes. This new retrieval scheme provides a flexible and natural way for users to express their search intentions, which can be combined with other schemes in a complementary way. However, search by sketch is a very challenging task, since the flexibility of the drawing makes the query space very huge. In a small database, it is almost impossible to find an acceptable image if we do not constrain a user's drawing.

As a crucial part of SBIR, shape matching was intensively studied in 1990s in small databases of hundreds to thousands of images, and used in small-scale vertical applications, such as hand-gesture recognition, mould, clip-art and other simple pattern retrieval. To enable an arbitrary drawing as a query, in 2010, we proposed an *edgel-index* structure, based on which a real-time sketch-based search engine *MindFinder*[4, 3] was built on two million natural images. The result was promising, since the system can find similar images for a large portion of simple hand-drawn sketches. However, we also observed that two million images are still far from sufficient to cover the query space. Thus, encouraged by the use of query-by-example technology in commercial search engines such as Google and TinEye, in this work we attempt to advance the state-of-the-art sketch-based image search to the scale of billion-level.

- Algorithm Design

There are two major challenges to build a sketch-based image search engine on a billion-level database: 1) robust shape matching between a hand-drawn sketch and a real image; and 2) efficient index structure and compact representation to support such a large-scale matching. Moreover, these two aspects are intimately coupled with each other, making the problem even more challenging.

To bridge the representation gap, most methods first extract representative contours from real images; some statistical features, e.g. gradient/edge histogram[6], shape context[1], GF-HoG[8], sketch-HoG[7], are further used along with global or bag-of-local-feature representation. Some work designed complex topology models which are however difficult to scale up. Chamfer Matching[2] is another effective way to deal with such a global matching. It measures the similarity of two edge maps by minimizing geometric distance of two edge point sets. To evaluate their effectiveness, we conducted experiments on sketch classification and sketch-based image retrieval to test these representation and matching methods. The experiments showed that Oriented Chamfer Matching[13] (OCM) achieves very competitive performance. Thus, we base our further design on OCM.

Besides shape matching, scalability remains the major issue in a practical system. Most existing sketch-based work can hardly scale up to billion-level databases. The brute-force linear-scan used in small databases is impossible to support such a large-scale task. The edgel-index structure in MindFinder system would require 5TB memory space and cost several minutes for a single query if indexing 1.5 billion images. Other inverted index structure for bag-of-feature (e.g. SHoG) representation also requires more than 3TB memory cost using the recommended number of local features. All of these methods are impractical and unacceptable with only a few common servers. Moreover, Oriented Chamfer Matching is much more time-consuming than L-2 global feature matching, due to the minimization process[1], which makes the problem more challenging.

To make OCM more efficient, we proposed a compact feature representation, whose on-line matching is tens of thousands of times faster than OCM (with on-line DT). The OCM distance is first transformed into the dot-product of two high-dimensional vectors (edge-map vector and distance transform (DT) vector), which is a novel way to look at OCM, as shown in Fig.1. Since DT vector is intrinsically low-dimensional, we linearly project the two vectors onto this low-dimensional subspace without much information loss in dot-product calculation. Product quantization[9] are further utilized to reduce the representation. Finally, each image is represented by 288 bytes, possible to be stored in memory and used for fast near-accurate OCM computation.

Based on this representation, an efficient index structure is built. We turn to hashing techniques in large-scale approximate nearest neighbor search. Since the unstructured k-means hash[11] outperforms many structured hash methods, we utilize k-medoids hashing for fast but only coarse indexing (Fig.1). By leveraging this hashing structure, a relatively small portion of OCM distances need to be computed for reranking. The reranking stage is very efficient, since based on the compact representation, we only need to calculate the dot-product between two short vectors. It could support 2×10^6 OCM computations within a second in one common server. Based on this design, a system was built using 10 common servers, each of which indexes $100 \sim 200$ million images with approximately 60GB memory cost, supporting real-time response. The outline of this system is shown in Fig.1. Intensive experiments have shown the effectiveness of the proposed features and methods in building a billion-scale sketch-based retrieval system.

The rest of the paper is organized as follows: Section 2 introduces the compact feature representation and matching approach. The index structure is presented in Section 3. Po-

[1] A distance-transform(DT) map could be constructed, which actually uses memory storage to reduce time cost, but is still impractical for billions of images.

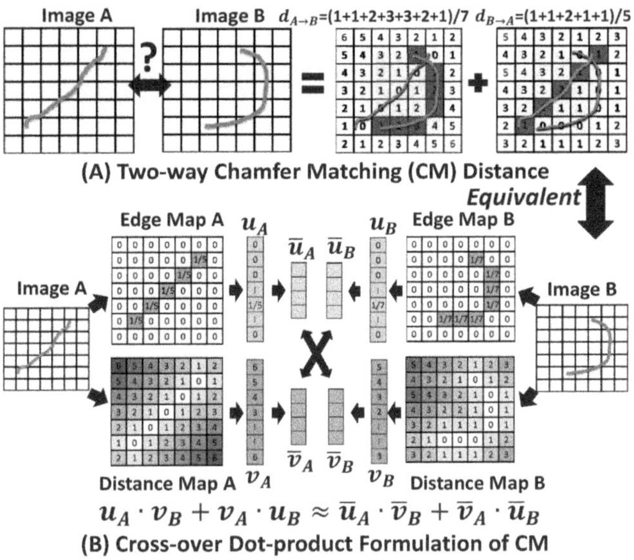

Figure 2: The crossover dot-product reformulation for Chamfer matching. (a) Two-way Chamfer matching (CM). (b) Crossover dot-product reformulation of CM. Each image is represented by a Chamfer feature pair: edge-map vector u and distance-map vector v. The classic two-way Chamfer matching distance is equivalent to the crossover dot-product of the feature pairs, facilitating further dimension compression (ū and v̄) and compact shape codes generation.

tential applications and extensive experiments are provided in Section 4 and 5, followed by the conclusion in Section 6.

2. COMPACT SHAPE CODING AND MATCHING

In this section, we first introduce the basic feature representation and matching approach adopted in this work, i.e. Oriented Chamfer Matching (OCM)[13] for edge maps. Then, a new reformulation for OCM is proposed, based on which a compact representation and matching is introduced. Finally, we present the multi-layer source coding for OCM to further compress the representation.

2.1 Feature Representation and Matching

Developing an effective shape feature and its corresponding matching method is a fundamental and preliminary problem to any shape-related tasks. Intensive research efforts have been spent on this problem, including local and global features based on gradient/edge histogram[6], shape context[1], sketch-HoG[7], and corresponding *bag-of-visual-word* representations to organize local features. Different features will correspond to different matching methods, such as histogram intersection for bag-of-visual-words, and Chamfer Matching[2, 3] for raw edge matching.

In this work, to choose an appropriate feature and matching method as a basic representation, we conducted experiments on sketch classification and sketch-based image retrieval to evaluate these representation and matching methods. Experiment results (in Sec.5.1) show that OCM achieves very competitive performance in these two sketch-related tasks. Thus we build our retrieval algorithm and system on OCM, which will be briefly introduced below.

Oriented Chamfer Matching

Chamfer matching[2] is a basic shape matching method proposed in the early 1990s. Different from the statistical information in histogram-like features, Chamfer matching bases its matching process on pixel-level: it measures the geometric distances of two edge-pixel sets from two images. Let $\mathcal{I}_{\mathcal{A}} = \{\mathbf{x}_a\}$ and $\mathcal{I}_{\mathcal{B}} = \{\mathbf{x}_b\}$ denote the edge pixel sets of images A and B, where $\mathbf{x}_a = (x_a, y_a)$ is the geometric coordinates of edge pixels. The one-way Chamfer distance from $\mathcal{I}_{\mathcal{A}}$ to $\mathcal{I}_{\mathcal{B}}$ is defined as:

$$D^{CM}_{A\to B} = \frac{1}{|\mathcal{I}_{\mathcal{A}}|} \sum_{\mathbf{x}_a \in \mathcal{I}_{\mathcal{A}}} \min_{\mathbf{x}_b \in \mathcal{I}_{\mathcal{B}}} \parallel \mathbf{x}_a - \mathbf{x}_b \parallel_2, \quad (1)$$

and the final two-way Chamfer Distance is given by:

$$D^{CM}_{A,B} = \frac{1}{2}(D^{CM}_{A\to B} + D^{CM}_{B\to A}). \quad (2)$$

To encode the orientation information of curves at edge pixels, Oriented Chamfer Matching (OCM)[13] was proposed to quantize the orientation of edge pixels into different channels and perform the basic Chamfer matching on each channel. Assume each edge set is represented by $|\mathcal{I}_{\mathcal{A}}{}^{\theta}|$ sub-sets with different orientations: $\mathcal{I}_{\mathcal{A}} = \{\mathcal{I}_{\mathcal{A}}{}^{\theta} \mid \theta \in \Theta\} = \{\{\mathbf{x}^{\theta}_a\} \mid \theta \in \Theta\}$, where Θ is a quantized orientation set, $\mathcal{I}_{\mathcal{A}}{}^{\theta}$ is a subset with edge pixels $\mathbf{x}^{\theta}_a$ of quantized orientation $\theta \in \Theta$. Oriented Chamfer Matching is defined by:

$$D^{OCM}_{A\to B} = \frac{1}{|\mathcal{I}_{\mathcal{A}}|} \sum_{\theta\in\Theta} \sum_{\mathbf{x}^{\theta}_a \in \mathcal{I}_{\mathcal{A}}{}^{\theta}} \min_{\mathbf{x}^{\theta}_b \in \mathcal{I}_{\mathcal{B}}} \parallel \mathbf{x}^{\theta}_a - \mathbf{x}^{\theta}_b \parallel_2, \quad (3)$$

with its two-way form similar to Eqn.2. In this work, the edge pixel's orientation is quantized into 6 bins, i.e. $-15^\circ \sim 15^\circ, 15^\circ \sim 45^\circ, \ldots, 135^\circ \sim 165^\circ$.

2.2 Compact Representation for OCM

In spite of good matching performance, OCM's matching function requires intensive computation and large memory cost. By leveraging an edge-pixel-based inverted index structure (Edgel Index) to speed up searching, we have built a real-time sketch-based image search engine[4, 3] based on Chamfer matching on a two-million image database. However, to save the memory cost, in [3] the two-way OCM was simplified to a one-way OCM search followed by a two-way OCM reranking for the top 5000 resulting images. However, when the database is enlarged by 750 times to 1.5 billion, this reranking scheme will not work since the recall will be quite low using one-way OCM search. On the other hand, even the one-way OCM search cannot work here since the whole index will cost 5TB memory, which is unaffordable for common servers. It should be noted that it is also impractical to only store the coordinates of edge pixels of each image, since on the one hand, it will also take 3TB memory space (assuming 1000 edge pixels per image), and more importantly, it is intractably inefficient to generate the distance-maps on-line for all the database images. Thus, a more compact representation for raw edges and their efficient OCM are highly desired.

Crossover Dot-Product Reformulation for OCM

Distance transformation (DT) is often used to speed up the on-line Chamfer distance computation. Assuming to

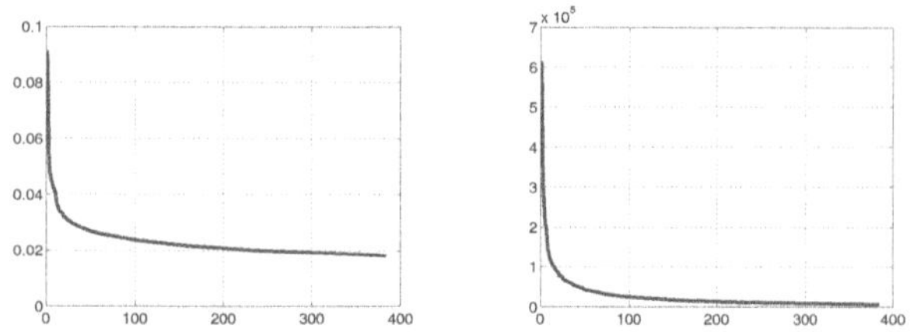

(a) Edge-map Vector $\mathbf{u}$ (b) Distance-map Vector $\mathbf{v}$

Figure 3: Spectrums of a) edge-map vector u: intrinsically high-dimensional, and b) distance-map vector v: intrinsically low-dimensional.

calculate $D^{OCM}_{A \to B}$, we first compute a distance-map $DT^{\theta}_{\mathcal{I}_B}$ for each channel of $\mathcal{I}_B = \{\mathcal{I}_B{}^1, \mathcal{I}_B{}^2, \dots, \mathcal{I}_B{}^\theta\}$. The distance-map value for each geometric location $\mathbf{x}$ measures the minimal distance from this location to an edge in $\mathcal{I}_B{}^\theta$:

$$DT^{\theta}_{\mathcal{I}_B}(\mathbf{x}) = \min_{\mathbf{x}^{\theta}_b \in \mathcal{I}_B{}^{\theta}} \| \mathbf{x} - \mathbf{x}^{\theta}_b \|_2, \tag{4}$$

Then Eqn. 3 is equal to:

$$D^{OCM}_{A \to B} = \frac{1}{|\mathcal{I}_A|} \sum_{\theta \in \Theta} \sum_{\mathbf{x}^{\theta}_a \in \mathcal{I}_A{}^{\theta}} DT^{\theta}_{\mathcal{I}_B}(\mathbf{x}^{\theta}_a). \tag{5}$$

When $DT(\cdot)$ is computed off-line, the complexity of online matching could be reduced from $\mathcal{O}(|\mathcal{Q}| \times |\mathcal{D}|)$ to $\mathcal{O}(|\mathcal{Q}|)$, with the cost of increased storage of distance-maps. Assuming the size of an image is 160×160 and the orientation is quantized into 6 bins, the distance maps for each image have to be stored with 0.6 MB ($160 \times 160 \times 6 \times 4$ bytes) and for 1.5 billion images it will cost 900 TB, which is difficult to be stored on disks of common servers, let alone to load them in memory for fast access.

To develop a more compact representation and speed up the matching, we first convert a sketch/image to a vector representation, based on which the OCM can be conducted by the dot-product of vectors.

Therefore, two vectors are defined: 1) **edge-map vector** (denoted as $\mathbf{u}$), by concatenating edge-map matrixes ED^{θ} of all the orientation channels, and 2) **distance-map vector** (denoted as $\mathbf{v}$), by concatenating distance-map matrixes DT^{θ} of all the $|\Theta|$ orientation channels:

$$ED^{\theta} = [e_{ij}],\ e_{ij} = \begin{cases} 1/|\mathcal{I}|, & \text{if } \mathbf{x}^{\theta}_{ij} \in \mathcal{I}^{\theta}; \\ 0, & \text{otherwise.} \end{cases} \tag{6}$$

$$\mathbf{u}^{\theta} = \text{vec}(ED^{\theta}), \quad \mathbf{u} = [\mathbf{u}^1, \mathbf{u}^2, \dots, \mathbf{u}^{\theta}]^{\mathrm{T}}, \tag{7}$$

$$\mathbf{v}^{\theta} = \text{vec}(DT^{\theta}), \quad \mathbf{v} = [\mathbf{v}^1, \mathbf{v}^2, \dots, \mathbf{v}^{\theta}]^{\mathrm{T}}, \tag{8}$$

where $\text{vec}(\cdot)$ denotes the vectorization operation on matrix. Both $\mathbf{u}$ and $\mathbf{v}$ are of 153,600 ($160 \times 160 \times 6$) dimensions, with $\mathbf{u}$ being sparse and $\mathbf{v}$ being dense.

Then, the one-way OCM can be simply written as the dot-product of these two vectors:

$$D^{OCM}_{A \to B} = \mathbf{u}^{\mathrm{T}}_B \mathbf{v}_A. \tag{9}$$

The two-way (symmetric) OCM is given by:

$$D^{OCM}_{A,B} = \frac{1}{2}(\mathbf{u}^{\mathrm{T}}_B \mathbf{v}_A + \mathbf{v}^{\mathrm{T}}_B \mathbf{u}_A), \tag{10}$$

where $(\mathbf{u}_A, \mathbf{v}_A)$ and $(\mathbf{u}_B, \mathbf{v}_B)$ are Chamfer feature pairs of $\mathcal{I}_A$ and $\mathcal{I}_B$. The two-way OCM is taken as the crossover dot-product form of the Chamfer feature pairs, as illustrated in Fig.2.

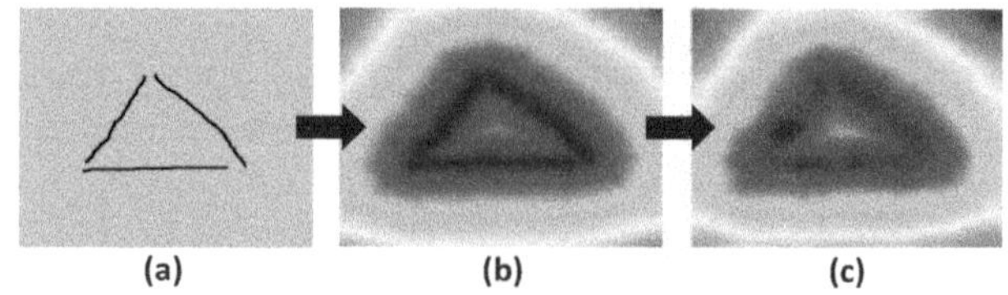

(a) Distance-map Reconstruction

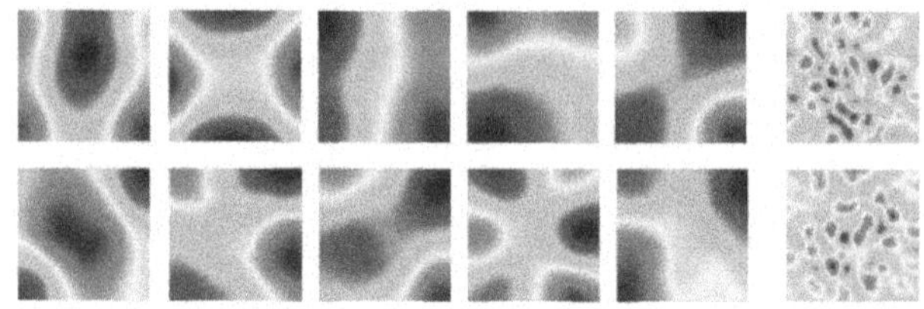

(b) Bases for Reconstruction

Figure 4: Illustration for distance-map reconstruction with principle component bases. (a) From left to right, edge map of an example sketch, original distance-map, reconstructed distance map with 256 principle components. (b) Eigen-maps of distance transform maps. The left five columns show the top ten principle components of the distance-transform map, serving as some of the reconstruction bases for compressing the distance-transform map. The last column shows the 300th and 301st components of the distance-transform map, containing high-frequency information.

The crossover dot-product formulation of Oriented Chamfer distance is a new way to look at the classic OCM, making it easier for further compression and analysis.

Linear Subspace Projection

It is impractical to directly store and compute $\mathbf{u}$ and $\mathbf{v}$ in large-scale tasks, since both vectors are high-dimensional. We perform PCA analysis on these two vectors, and found that $\mathbf{v}$ is intrinsically low-dimensional while $\mathbf{u}$ is not. The sorted eigenvalues of the covariance matrix of sampled $\mathbf{u}$ and $\mathbf{v}$ vectors are shown in Fig.3(a) and Fig.3(b). It can be seen that the distance-map vector $\mathbf{v}$ are intrinsically distributed in a linear subspace of much lower dimension: only about two hundred principal axes can cover most variations in the original feature space. Notice that the Chamfer matching distance is already represented as crossover dot-product of $\mathbf{u}$ and $\mathbf{v}$ (in Eqn.9). Although $\mathbf{u}$ is not intrinsically low-dimensional, we can preserve the dot-product between $\mathbf{u}$ and $\mathbf{v}$, by projecting them onto $\mathbf{v}$'s subspace.

Let us denote $U_{D \times d}$ as the orthogonal projection matrix learned by PCA analysis for sampled vectors $\mathbf{v}$ (D is the original dimension number and d is the reduced dimension number, $d \ll D$). We project both $\mathbf{u}$ and $\mathbf{v}$ to the subspace using $U_{D \times d}$ to generate a compact representation $\bar{\mathbf{u}}$ and $\bar{\mathbf{v}}$:

$$\bar{\mathbf{u}}_{d \times 1} = U^T_{D \times d} \mathbf{u}_{D \times 1}, \tag{11}$$

$$\bar{\mathbf{v}}_{d \times 1} = U^T_{D \times d} \mathbf{v}_{D \times 1}. \tag{12}$$

We now show that the dot-product between $\mathbf{v}$ and $\mathbf{u}$ is preserved under the new representation. $\mathbf{v}$ and $\mathbf{u}$ can be

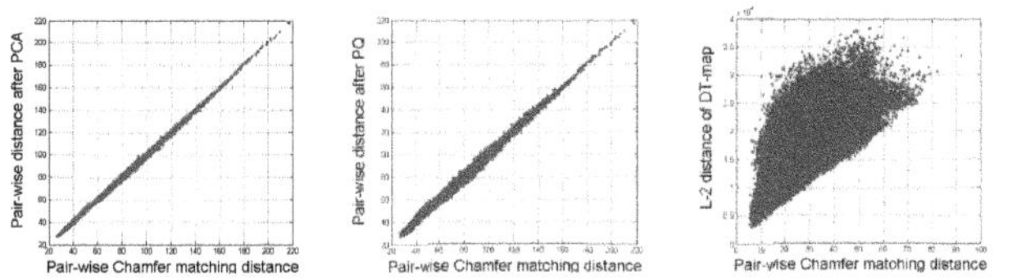

(a) PCA-reduced (b) PQ-Coding (c) L2 of DT-map

Figure 5: Pair-wise distances comparison. We sampled one million pairs of images and compared different distances against the groundtruth OCM distances. The X-axis represents the OCM distances, while the Y-axis represents: a) OCM after the PCA dimension reduction, b) OCM after product quantization coding (in Sec.2.3), and c) the L-2 distances of distance-transform (DT) map[16]. Figure (a) and (b) show good linear correlations with very minor distance distortion; Figure (c) have very big distance distortions, showing that the L-2 distances of DT-map is inconsistent with Chamfer matching.

written as below:

$$\mathbf{u} = U\bar{\mathbf{u}} + \mathbf{e}_u, \quad (13)$$
$$\mathbf{v} = U\bar{\mathbf{v}} + \mathbf{e}_v, \quad (14)$$

where $\mathbf{e}_v$ is a residual vector, which is very small. Although $\mathbf{e}_u$ is not small, it is orthogonal to the projected subspace. Thus we have,

$$\begin{aligned} \mathbf{u}^T\mathbf{v} &= (\bar{\mathbf{u}}^T U^T + \mathbf{e}_u^T)(U\bar{\mathbf{v}} + \mathbf{e}_v) & (15) \\ &= \bar{\mathbf{u}}^T U^T U \bar{\mathbf{v}} + (\mathbf{e}_u^T U)\bar{\mathbf{v}} + \bar{\mathbf{u}}^T(U^T\mathbf{e}_v) + \mathbf{e}_u^T\mathbf{e}_v & (16) \\ &= \bar{\mathbf{u}}^T\bar{\mathbf{v}} + \mathbf{e}_u^T\mathbf{e}_v & (17) \end{aligned}$$

Since $|\mathbf{e}_u^T\mathbf{e}_v| \leq |\mathbf{e}_u||\mathbf{e}_v| \leq |\mathbf{u}||\mathbf{e}_v| \leq |\mathbf{e}_v|$ and $|\mathbf{e}_v|$ is negligible, the dot-product of two high-dimensional features $\mathbf{u}$ and $\mathbf{v}$ are well preserved under the dot-product of new low-dimensional features $\bar{\mathbf{u}}$ and $\bar{\mathbf{v}}$.

Now we have a more compact representation for the Chamfer distance between a sketch and an image using their vector-based representation:

$$D_{A,B}^{OCM} = \frac{1}{2}(\bar{\mathbf{u}}_B^{\mathrm{T}}\bar{\mathbf{v}}_A + \bar{\mathbf{v}}_B^{\mathrm{T}}\bar{\mathbf{u}}_A), \quad (18)$$

with $\bar{\mathbf{u}}$ and $\bar{\mathbf{v}}$ are only d-dimensional ($d \ll D$). d is typically set to be 256. The distance distortion of the compression is illustrated in Fig.5, from which we can see that the sampled pair-wise distances are mostly preserved when the vector dimensions are reduced from 153,600 to 256, amounting to only 0.17%. Quantitative analysis is provided in Sec.5.2.

Such a compression is actually like a low-pass filter. The top 10 linear principle components of the distance-map are illustrated in the left part of Fig.4(b), while the 300th and 301st principle components are in the right part. It can be seen that top principle components usually capture the informative low-frequency information of the distance map, while the remaining components contain more noisy high-frequency part. After truncating the high-frequency component tails, these principle ***eigen-maps*** are adequate to build a group of bases to reconstruct original distance maps, as shown in Fig.4(a).

This dot-product reformulation and the compression technique greatly simplify the classic Chamfer matching in both computation and memory cost. It essentially converts the intensive on-line computation (e.g. seeking the closest edge point) to off-line (e.g. generating distance-transform map and projecting) while cutting down the feature dimension. Currently, each Chamfer matching only requires several hundred on-line multiplication, much faster than the original $\mathcal{O}(|\mathcal{Q}| \times |\mathcal{D}|)$ geometric distance calculation.

2.3 Non-linear Multi-layer Source Coding

For each image, the low dimensional features $\{\bar{\mathbf{u}}, \bar{\mathbf{v}}\}$ (e.g. 256 dimensional) still require a huge memory cost for a large database. For example, for 1.5 billion images, it will cost 3T-B memory space with "float" type, which cannot be stored in memory and have to be read from disk on-the-fly. However, the relatively low speed of random disk accessing severely limits the number of images that could be online ranked (or re-ranked), and in that case an accurate indexing structure is needed to avoid large number of reranking.

Some recent approximate nearest-neighbor (ANN) search techniques inspired by source coding goes another way, such as product quantization[9], which is proved to achieve state-of-the-art ANN performance and outperforms LSH in terms of the trade-off between memory usage and accuracy[9]. Product quantization focuses on explicitly approximating vectors using short codes, so that a large number of compressed codes can be loaded into memory to support a very large portion of reranking after only a coarse indexing. We utilize this technique to further quantize both $\bar{\mathbf{u}}$ and $\bar{\mathbf{v}}$ vectors of database images, and encode them to a more compact code, which can be stored in memory for fast reranking for a large number of images obtained by a coarse index (Sec.3).

In this section, we will first introduce product quantization for OCM, followed by the multi-stage residue coding.

Product Quantization

Product quantization[9] decomposes the vector space into a Cartesian product of low-dimensional subspace, and quantizes each subspace separately, which achieves a good balance between compression rate and learning difficulty.

We briefly introduce the product quantization[9] below. Denote $x \in \mathcal{R}^d$ as the vector to be quantized. x is first split into m subvectors[2] $x^1, \ldots, x^m \in \mathcal{R}^{d/m}$. For each subvector x^i, a sub-quantizer $q^i(\cdot)$ is learned by k-means, mapping the real-value subvector x^i to one of the k_s quantization centroids $c_i = q^i(x^i)$. Then the global product quantizer is:

$$q(x) = (q^1(x^1), q^2(x^2), \ldots, q^m(x^m)). \quad (19)$$

We utilize product quantization to generate compact codes for Chamfer features. In the off-line stage, each image is encoded by a vector of sub-quantizer's IDs:

$$s(x) = (s^1(q^1), s^2(q^2), \ldots, s^m(q^m)), \quad (20)$$

in which $s^i(q^i) \in [0, k_s - 1]$, is the ID of the quantization centroid $q^i(x^i)$.

Although k_s is typically set to a small value (e.g. 256 or 4096) for fast learning and quantization, the number of possible values of $q(x)$ is large, i.e. $(k_s)^m$, since the centroid codebook of the whole vector is the Cartesian product of the centroids of the m sub-quantizers. Such a large number of quantization centroids provide explicit approximation of the original vectors. The centroid index value for each vector

[2]In practice, vectors are multiplied by a random orthogonal matrix prior to quantization to balance the energy of each subvector. Query vectors are also multiplied by the matrix.

could be encoded with $\lceil m \log_2(k_s) \rceil$ bits. Thus, memory space is saved a lot.

Here **Asymmetric Distance Computation** (ADC)[9] is adopted: the database image feature x is encoded to be $s(x)$, but the query feature y is not encoded. Then, the distance $d^{cm}(x, y)$ is approximated by $d^{cm}(q(x), y)$. Thus, there is no approximation error in the query side.

In the on-line retrieval, $d^{cm}(q(x), y)$ could be computed using the decomposition:

$$d^{cm}(q(x), y) = q(x)^T y = \sum_{j=1,\ldots,m} q^j(x^j)^T y^j, \quad (21)$$

where y^j is the jth subvector of the query y. For each j, we calculate the dot-product between y^j to k_s quantization centroids of $q^j(\cdot)$ to construct a look-up table $t(1), ..., t(k_s)$. Then, for each database image, we check its shape code $s(x)$, and sum up all the corresponding values in the look-up table as the final distance to the query y:

$$d^{cm}(q(x), y) = \sum_{j=1,\ldots,m} t(s^i). \quad (22)$$

Multi-stage Residue Coding

Inspired by the work of [9, 10], we refine the first-stage quantization by re-coding their residues. Since the residues often contain lower energy/information than raw vectors, encoding the residue is easier than encoding the original data vector. The residue vector after the quantization is:

$$r(x) = x - q(x), \quad (23)$$

which is further quantized by another quantizer q_r learned on a sampled set of residue vectors. Thus, an improved estimation $\hat{x}$ of x is the sum of approximated vector and the encoded residue vector:

$$\hat{x} = q(x) + q_r(r(x)). \quad (24)$$

Notice that increasing the centroid number k_s of each sub-quantizer can also improve the quantization accuracy. However, a larger k_s will severely increase the computation burden in both learning and quantization processes. With residue encoding, the quantization error is greatly reduced while the computation cost is only linearly increased.

In this work, we perform two-stage residue encoding. At each stage, we set k_s to 4096, and jointly quantize every eight dimensions, which achieves a good balance among compression rate, accuracy and computation cost. Detailed experiments are shown in Sec.5.2.

Finally, the Chamfer features $\bar{\mathbf{u}}$ and $\bar{\mathbf{v}}$ are encoded with $3 \times \log_2(4096) \times 256/8$ bits, and thus each image costs 288 bytes. This feature will be used in the fast reranking stage.

3. MULTI-PROBE KLSH FOR CHAMFER INDEXING

Although the proposed compact shape codes can be stored in memory and support 2×10^6 shape matchings per second on a common server, for a real-time search task of 1.5 billion images, an effective indexing structure is still necessary to prune the obviously unrelated images.

In this work, we build Kmeans-LSH (KLSH)[11] index[3] for images with the dissimilarity defined as the Chamfer distance in Eqn.18. Although Chamfer distance is actually not a metric (does not satisfy the triangle inequality), the experiments showed the effectiveness of KLSH in our system. Details are provided in Sec.5.3. Below we will briefly introduce KLSH, followed by implementation details.

Multi-Probe KLSH

KLSH utilizes unstructured k-means quantizers as hash functions:

$$h_i(x) = \arg\min_{j=1,\ldots,k} d(x, c_j^i), \quad i = 1, \ldots, l. \quad (25)$$

where k is the cluster number of the k-means quantizer and also the number of hash buckets; $d(\cdot, \cdot)$ is the dissimilarity metric; c_j is the cluster centroids. Each hash value $h_i(\cdot)$ represents a hash bucket and all database objects are put into one of the buckets according to their hash values. Thus, each h_i function forms a hash table, and the objects falling in the same bucket will have a larger likelihood of being nearest neighbors than those disseminated in different buckets. Then, multiple (l) hash tables/functions (with different k-means initiates) are constructed to reduce the probability that a vector is missed, as in the LSH framework. When a user draws a query sketch and triggers the search, the hash value of query object y is obtained by $h_i(y)$, and the objects in the bucket of the value $h_i(y)$ in each hash table are returned as the resulting short-list for further reranking.

Since the memory cost increases with the number of hash tables[4] l, to reduces memory usage, multi-probe KLSH[11] is used here to retrieve several (m_p) buckets per hash table, instead of only one. Then for each query, the total number of buckets retrieved becomes $l \times m_p$. Therefore, for a fixed number of buckets, the number of hash tables is reduced by a factor of m_p, so is the memory cost.

Implementation Details

We built the sketch-based image retrieval system with 10 common servers to support a realtime search on 1.5 billion images. Each server indexes $100 \sim 200$ million images with about 60GB memory cost. The memory cost includes two parts: KLSH index and the shape codes. For the hash index, we constructed $l = 5$ hash tables each of which consists of $k = 8192$ hash buckets and the total index will cost 4GB. For the shape codes part, we truncated both u and v to be of 256 dimensions, and every eight dimensions were jointly quantized and encoded with $4.5 (= 3 \times 1.5)$ bytes. The total memory cost for 200 million images is 54GB. Given a query, the hash index in each server returns a list of 2×10^6 images, which are further reranked with Chamfer shape codes. The response time for each query is $0.5 \sim 1.5$ seconds.

4. POTENTIAL APPLICATIONS

Based on this billion-scale sketch-based image retrieval system, many applications which were thought very challenging or even impossible might become easier and feasible.

1. Sketch Recognition (Fig.6(a)) In the era of touch screens, automatically recognizing a hand-drawn sketch has become an important research problem, and will benefit many touch-related applications. Most existing methods mainly focus on recognizing simple shapes in specific domains, or classifying sketches to a limited number of cate-

[3]The k-medoids clustering was used instead of k-means clustering, since we have to deal with a space only defined by dissimilarity.

[4]l hash tables will cost $n \times l \times 4$ bytes, where n is the number of indexed objects. When $n = 1.5 \times 10^9$, each single hash table will cost 6GB memory.

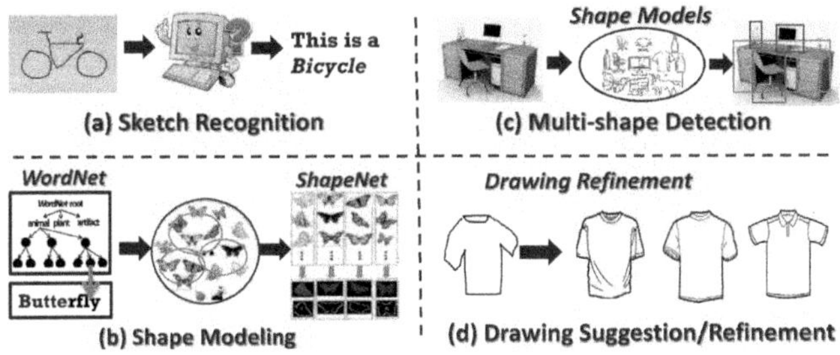

Figure 6: Four potential applications that could be advanced by the retrieval system.

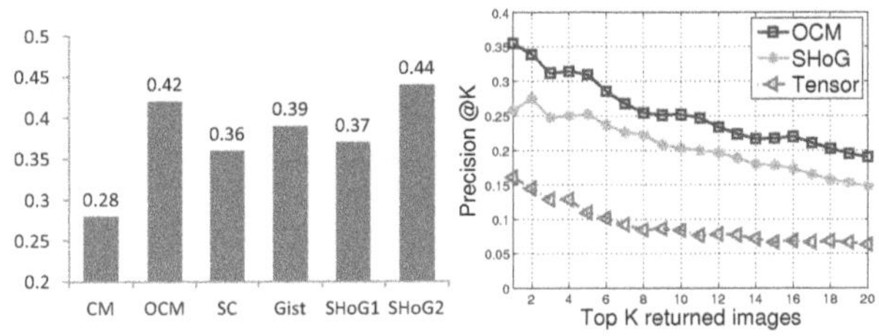

(a) Sketch Classification (b) Image Retrieval

Figure 7: Results of different shape features on sketch classification and sketch-based image retrieval tasks. (a) Sketch classification accuracy of CM[2], OCM[13], SHoG[5], Shape Context (SC)[1], and Gist[12]. (b) Sketch-based image retrieval performance (Precision@K) of OCM[13], SHoG[7] and Tensor[6].

gories. To recognize an arbitrary drawing, we have developed a data-driven method[14] based on one million clipart images. However, million-scale images are still far from sufficient to cover the query space. We believe that with the help of 1.5 billion images and the sketch retrieval techniques, sketch recognition will become more practical.

2. Shape Modeling (Fig.6(b)) Automatically mining and modeling shapes for an arbitrary concept is a fundamental problem in visual concept modeling in computer vision. Most existing work only focuses on modeling a very limited number of objects. Based on this system and its backend index structure, it becomes possible to model any concept with meaningful shapes, which will be useful to many computer vision problems.

3. Multi-Shape Detection (Fig.6(c)) Object detection is another important problem in computer vision. Most existing work focuses on detecting a single object, such as face, human body, and car. Once we collect a large number of shape models, it might be possible to conduct multi-shape or multi-object detection. For example, if we have typical shape models for vehicles, persons, houses, trees, etc., it will be helpful for detecting related objects in a natural image by combining with other features.

4. Drawing Suggestion & Refinement (Fig.6(d)) Drawings from non-experts are usually unartistic, and sometimes even ugly. By recognizing a user's partial sketch and mining possible shape intentions, the system can suggest better drawings to help the user quickly get an elegant drawing, which is useful for kids education and quick interaction.

5. EXPERIMENTS

Extensive experiments were conducted to evaluate the entire system as well as different components including feature selection, dimension reduction, product quantization, and indexing structure. We explore the impact of data scale in sketch-based retrieval, showing the promising advantages coming along with the increasing growth of data scale.

5.1 Feature Comparison

Several representative shape features were evaluated on two different sketch-related tasks, i.e. sketch classification and sketch-based image retrieval.

Sketch classification was conducted on the 20K hand-drawn sketch data set[5] (20K sketches in 250 categories), and five representative features for shape matching were compared, i.e. CM[2], OCM[13], Shape Context[1], Gist[12] and SHoG[5] [5] (SHoG1 learns the codebook only on the training set, while SHoG2 learns it on the whole data set as in [5]). We used 3-fold cross-test: the data set was randomly partitioned into three parts, in which one was used as testing set and the remaining two as training set. The accuracies averaged over all three folds are reported in Fig.7(a).

Sketch-based image retrieval was conducted on the 102K image dataset with 31 hand-drawn sketches[7], on which SHoG was proved outperforming other local features in [7]. We compared OCM[13], SHoG[7], and Tensor[6], all of which were successfully leveraged in sketch-based image retrieval systems. The Precision@K curves are shown in Fig.7(b).

The experimental results showed the competitiveness of OCM compared with other features in these two tasks, and thus we base this system on OCM.

5.2 Compression Loss Analysis

In this section, we evaluate the loss of both compression components of PCA dimension reduction and product quantization under different parameter configurations.

Metric for Compression Loss

We use the following metrics to evaluate the compression loss:

1) **Root Mean Square Error (RMSE)**: is defined as $\sqrt{\sum_i (d_i - \hat{d}_i)^2}$, where d_i is the OCM distance and $\hat{d}_i$ is the approximated distance after compression. 10^7 pairs of images were randomly sampled for this test.

2) **Precision-Recall (PR) & MAP for NN-search**: based on nearest-neighbor search, we consider images within an OCM proximity (k-NN, e.g. k=100) of each query as "positive" while the rest "negative". By recalling images based on the approximated distances, the precision-recall curves (PR) and mean average precision (MAP) for the approximated distance can be plotted.

3) **Precision @K for SBIR**: Retrieval Precision @K directly evaluates how the compression procedure impacts the final retrieval performance. We perform this experiment in the same 102K dataset with 31 queries as aforementioned in Sec.5.1. The top 20 results were labeled as "related" or "unrelated" to the query sketch in terms of shape, based on which Precision@K is evaluated for retrieval performance.

PCA Dimension Reduction

As explained in Sec.2.2, the dimension of Chamfer features is reduced by projecting **u** and **v** onto a subspace of

[5]The local feature in [5] is named as SHoG here, which is a little different from that in [7].

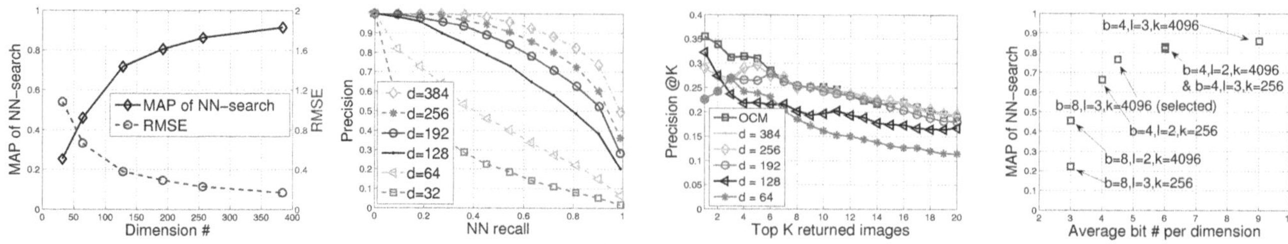

(a) RMSE & MAP of PCA (b) PR-Curves of PCA (c) Prec@K of PCA (d) MAP of PQ

Figure 8: Compression loss analysis. (a-c) The compression loss for PCA dimension reduction ($d = 32, 64, 128, 256, 384$ for $\bar{\mathbf{u}}$ and $\bar{\mathbf{v}}$), evaluated by RMSE, MAP, precision-recall curves of nearest-neighbor search, Precision@K curves of real retrieval performance; (d) The loss in product-quantization coding, evaluated by MAP of NN-search, under different parameter configurations about joint quantization dimension number b_s, encoding layers n_l and number of quantization centroids k_s.

$\mathbf{v}$ to preserve their dot-product value $\mathbf{u}^T\mathbf{v}$. Small distance distortion might occur during the reduction. With the aforementioned metrics, we evaluated how the Chamfer distance distorts when vectors are reduced to different dimensions. Fig.8(a-c) show the results under the metric of RMSE, PR curves, and Precision@K with different vector dimensions. Note that vectors of more than 256 dimensions no longer lead to significant accuracy improvements. Thus, the dimension of $\bar{\mathbf{u}}$ and $\bar{\mathbf{v}}$ is set to 256 to achieve a reasonable balance between memory cost and approximation accuracy.

Product Quantization Coding

$\bar{\mathbf{u}}$ and $\bar{\mathbf{v}}$ are further encoded into short bits by product quantization as introduced in Sec.2.3. Factors that impact the quantization performance include the dimension number for joint quantization b_s, the quantization centroid number k_s, and the encoding layer number n_l. Large k_s and n_l with small b_s will increase the actual allocated bit number per dimension, and thus reduce the quantization error at the cost of more total bits; a large k_s helps improve the quantization performance at the cost of increasing computation cost during quantizer learning and coding process. We evaluated several parameter configurations, as shown in Fig.8(d). To balance the memory cost, accuracy, and computation cost, we choose $b_s = 8$, $n_l = 3$, and $k_s = 4096$.

5.3 Impact of KLSH

In this section, we measure the quality of the k-medoids hashing structure in terms of *selectivity-recall curve*[11]. *Selectivity* represents the ratio of the total selected images (for further reranking) among the indexed corpus. The *recall* measures the ratio of recalled k-NN images among k. Here k is set to 200. The experiment was performed on the introduced hash structure which indexes 200 million images[6].

The index quality is mainly related to two factors: the number of hash buckets k and the number of hash tables l. The selectivity-recall curves with $l = 5$ and different k are shown in Fig.9(a), while curves with $k = 8192$ and different l in Fig.9(b). It is observed that a larger k or l will improve the index quality. However, a larger k increases the off-line computation cost for constructing the index, and a large l increases the index's memory cost by a factor of l. It should be noted that, as aforementioned, since the reranking process are significantly accelerated by the proposed shape codes, a large portion of images (e.g. 2×10^6 images per second per server) are possible to be reranked. Therefore, we only need a coarse index. We choose $k = 8192$ and $l = 5$ in our system, with which 10^{-2} selectivity can obtain 68% recall of the 200-NN images, at a relatively small cost for off-line index building.

[6]This is because in our system each server indexes less than 200 million images, as introduced in Sec.3

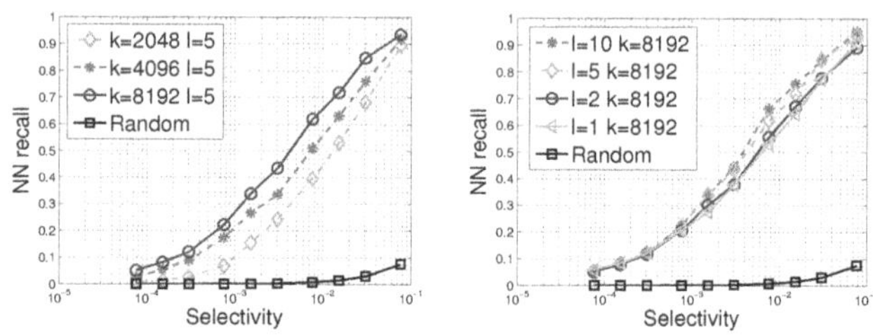

(a) Different k (b) Different l

Figure 9: Evaluations of the effectiveness of Kmeans-LSH in Chamfer matching distance space with sensitivity-recall curves at different k and l.

5.4 Evaluations for the Whole System

To evaluate the sketch-based retrieval system, we conducted a series of experiments on a large image corpus consisting of 1.5 billion images. We show how the system performance varies with increasing image set size, showing the necessity of studying billion-scale SBIR. We show that the traditional keyword-based image search results could be significantly enhanced when cooperating with sketch-based search. Besides, we also analyze how the quality of user-drawn sketch queries impacts the system performance.

Sketch-500 Query Set & 1.5-Billion Image Set

The *Sketch500* data set [14] were used as the query set. It consists of 500 hand-drawn sketches (see Fig.10(a)) built based on a list of 1000 commonly-used non-abstract nouns collected for elementary education[7]. These sketches were drawn by a graduate student based on top results returned from a commercial keyword-based image search engine. By removing some non-entity words that are difficult to depict, such as "earthquake", "storm", and "dust", 500 sketches were finally collected together with their keyword texts.

1.5 billion thumbnails randomly sampled from Bing were utilized to build the search system. Some text information

[7]http://www.free-teacher-worksheets.com/support-files/list-of-nouns.eps

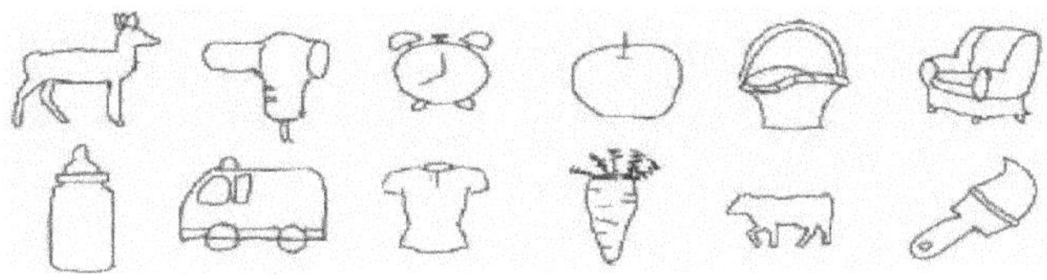

(a) Examples in Sketch500 dataset

(b) Illustrations for the strict labeling rule

Figure 10: (a) Examples of hand-drawn sketches in Sketch500 query set. (b) Examples of labeling rule — both shape and concept consistency. the 1st column shows example queries; the 2nd and 3rd columns are images labeled with "correct" since their shapes and concepts are consistent with the queries'; column 4∼7 are "incorrect" due to their incorrect concepts or dissimilar shapes.

such as image titles and surrounding texts together with *tfidf* ranking were leveraged for keyword-based search.

Evaluation Measurement and Labeling Methodology
Since it is impossible to manually label all the 1.5 billion images, we adopted a strategy commonly used in [3, 6]: only label the top 20 returned search results for each query and measure the retrieval performance with Precision@K (the ratio of the "correct" images in top K returned images). This is consistent with the observed fact that users usually care about the top results returned by a search engine. For labeling principles, we set a strict rule: only images that meet the following two requirements were labeled as "correct": 1) of similar shape to the query sketch and 2) of consistent concept with the query. As illustrated in Fig.10(b), images with either obvious shape dissimilarity or concept inconsistency were labeled as "incorrect". Note that, if the requirement of concept consistence is relaxed, the retrieval performance will be much higher than what appears in our experiments.

Performance on Different Image Set Scale
A series of experiments were conducted on 5 different scales of random image subsets: 0.2 million, 2 million, 20 million, 200 million and 1.5 billion. The Precision@K curves were averaged over all 500 queries, which is shown in Fig.11(a). Fig.11(b) illustrates how *Precision@10* value changes with the growth of image sets — when the image data set grows up, the sketch-based retrieval performance improves significantly. This is reasonable, since more images provide a wider coverage of our visual world and can respond better to users' uncontrollable drawings.

Enhancement on Keyword-based Image Retrieval
Since each query in *Sketch500* is associated with a keyword, which can be taken as a keyword query in a keyword-based search, we compared the retrieval performances on the 1.5 billion image data set under three schemes: **Text**, **Sketch** and **Sketch+Text**. As shown in Fig.12(a), **Sketch+ Text** significantly outperformed both **Text** and **Sketch**. For pure keyword-based search, since no shape information is considered, users are hard to find desired images with a particular shape. For pure sketch-based search, the "polysemy" of shapes will bring much noisy images with similar shapes but inconsistent concepts. E.g., the shape of a standing dog is very close to that of a standing horse (see Fig.12(b)). By combining both the shape and text, the search engine might satisfy those users who have more specific search intentions. The top results for some query sketches under these three schemes are compared in Fig.14.

Influence of Hand-drawn Sketch Quality
Since there might be large intra-class variations in human drawings, we'd like to see how the sketch quality impacts the system performance. We distorted the sketch queries by randomly and independently offsetting all strokes of a sketch to different directions. The moving distance is a parameter multiplied by the longer side of the sketch, and this parameter is called "variance" in this work. 100 sketches were randomly sampled from *Sketch500* in this experiment. Fig.13(b) shows the retrieval performances with distorted sketches under different distortion variances. We can see that, the retrieval performance consistently dropped as the increase of variance, which is not a surprise since sometimes even human vision are not easy to tell the distorted sketches very well, as shown in Fig.13(a).

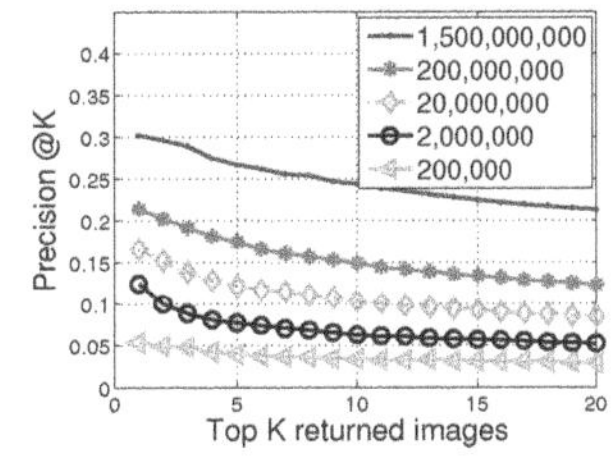

(a) Precision@K

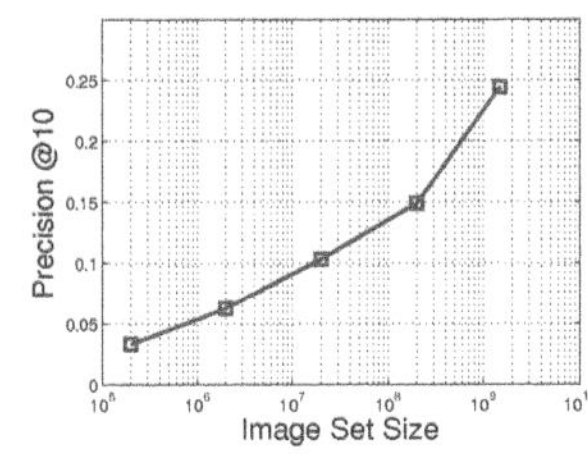

(b) P@10 vs. Image Number

Figure 11: Retrieval performance vs. image set size. (a) Precision@K was evaluated for five randomly sampled data sets of 0.2M, 2M, 20M, 200M, and 1.5B images. (b) The plot shows how Precision@10 (in (a)) increases as the data set grows up.

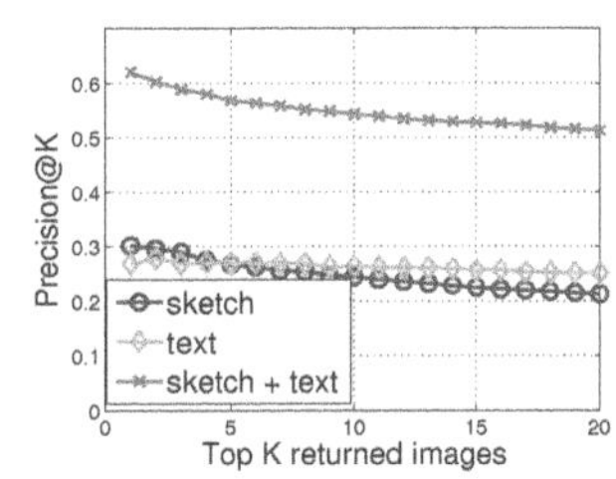

(a) Precision@K

(b) Shape Polysemy

Figure 12: Enhancement on keyword-based image search. (a) Retrieval performance under Text, Sketch, Sketch+Text schemes. (b) Illustrative examples for "shape polysemy": since many objects might share similar shapes, image search purely based on the sketch often leads to ambiguous results. This can explain why combining both shape and keyword could significantly enhance retrieval accuracy.

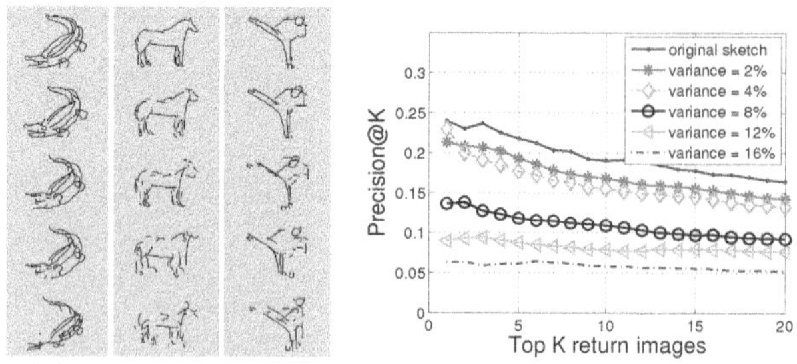

(a) Sketch Qualities (b) Precision@K

Figure 13: Retrieval performance under different sketch qualities. (a) Three example columns indicating 5 different sketch quality levels with distorted variations ±2%, ±4%, ±8%, ±12%, ±16%. (b) Precision@K curves under different variations.

6. CONCLUSIONS

In this paper, we have presented our study on how to build a practical system to support sketch-based image search on a billion-level database, which might be the first attempt in both academia and industry. To achieve this goal, we systematically studied related problems such as feature selection, compact feature representation, fast matching and indexing, with particular considerations to some practical issues such as computation cost, memory cost, and retrieval speed. Currently this system is sensitive to affine translation. We will continue improving this system, based on which we hope other shape/sketch related applications which were thought very challenging might become feasible.

7. ACKNOWLEDGEMENTS

The work of Xinghai Sun and Chao Xu was partially supported by NBRPC 2011CB302400, NSFC 60975014, 61121002 and NSFB 4102024.

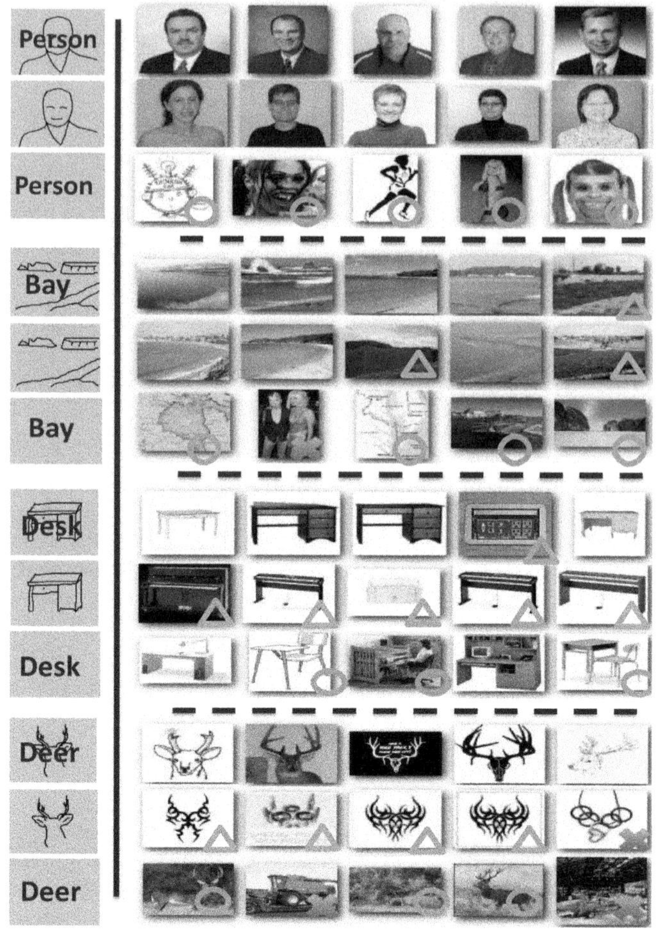

Figure 14: Example queries and corresponding top results (from 1.5 billion images) for Tag+Sketch, Sketch, Tag. The green circle and blue triangle indicate the images that are not consistent with the query in terms of shape and concept respectively. The red cross indicate neither of them are consistent. It is clear that the results are greatly enhanced when combing the two search modalities.

8. REFERENCES

[1] S. Belongie, J. Malik, and J. Puzicha. Shape context: A new descriptor for shape matching and object recognition. *NIPS*, 2001.

[2] G. Borgefors. Hierarchical chamfer matching: A parametric edge matching algorithm. *PAMI*, 1988.

[3] Y. Cao, C. Wang, L. Zhang, and L. Zhang. Edgel index for large-scale sketch-based image search. In *CVPR*, 2011.

[4] Y. Cao, H. Wang, C. Wang, Z. Li, L. Zhang, and L. Zhang. Mindfinder: Interactive sketch-based image search on millions of images. In *ACM MM*, 2010.

[5] M. Eitz, J. Hays, and M. Alexa. How do humans sketch objects? *SIGGRAPH*, 2012.

[6] M. Eitz, K. Hildebrand, T. Boubekeur, and M. Alexa. An evaluation of descriptors for large-scale image retrieval from sketched feature lines. *Computers & Graphics*, 2010.

[7] M. Eitz, K. Hildebrand, T. Boubekeur, and M. Alexa. Sketch-based image retrieval: Benchmark and bag-of-features descriptors. *TVCG*, 2011.

[8] R. Hu, M. Barnard, and J. Collomosse. Gradient field descriptor for sketch based retrieval and localization. In *ICIP*, 2010.

[9] H. Jégou, M. Douze, and C. Schmid. Product quantization for nearest neighbor search. *PAMI*, 2011.

[10] H. Jégou, R. Tavenard, M. Douze, and L. Amsaleg. Searching in one billion vectors: re-rank with source coding. In *ICASSP*, 2011.

[11] L. Paulevé, H. Jégou, and L. Amsaleg. Locality sensitive hashing: A comparison of hash function types and querying mechanisms. *Pattern Recognition Letters*, 2010.

[12] C. Siagian and L. Itti. Rapid biologically-inspired scene classification using features shared with visual attention. *PAMI*, 2007.

[13] B. Stenger, A. Thayananthan, P. Torr, and R. Cipolla. Model-based hand tracking using a hierarchical bayesian filter. *PAMI*, 2006.

[14] Z. Sun, C. Wang, L. Zhang, and L. Zhang. Query-adaptive shape topic mining for hand-drawn sketch recognition. In *ACM MM*, 2012.

[15] A. Torralba, R. Fergus, and W. T. Freeman. 80 million tiny images: A large data set for nonparametric object and scene recognition. *PAMI*, 2008.

[16] K.-Y. Tseng, Y.-L. Lin, C.-Y. Hsiu, and W. H. Hsu. Sketch-based image retrieval on mobile devices using compact hash bits. In *ACM MM*, 2012.

[17] C. Wang, F. Jing, L. Zhang, and H.-J. Zhang. Scalable search-based image annotation of personal images. In *ACM MIR*, 2006.

Clickage: Towards Bridging Semantic and Intent Gaps via Mining Click Logs of Search Engines

Xian-Sheng Hua, Linjun Yang, Jingdong Wang, Jing Wang
Ming Ye, Kuansan Wang, Yong Rui, Jin Li
Microsoft Corporation, One Microsoft Way, Redmond WA 98052, USA
{xshua; linjuny; jingdw; v-wangji; mingye; kuansanw; yongrui; jinl}@microsoft.com

ABSTRACT

The semantic gap between low-level visual features and high-level semantics has been investigated for decades but still remains a big challenge in multimedia. When "search" became one of the most frequently used applications, "intent gap", the gap between query expressions and users' search intents, emerged. Researchers have been focusing on three approaches to bridge the semantic and intent gaps: 1) developing more representative features, 2) exploiting better learning approaches or statistical models to represent the semantics, and 3) collecting more training data with better quality. However, it remains a challenge to close the gaps.

In this paper, we argue that the massive amount of click data from commercial search engines provides a data set that is unique in the bridging of the semantic and intent gap. Search engines generate millions of click data (a.k.a. image-query pairs), which provide almost "unlimited" yet strong connections between semantics and images, as well as connections between users' intents and queries. To study the intrinsic properties of click data and to investigate how to effectively leverage this huge amount of data to bridge semantic and intent gap is a promising direction to advance multimedia research. In the past, the primary obstacle is that there is no such dataset available to the public research community. This changes as Microsoft has released a new large-scale real-world image click data to public. This paper presents preliminary studies on the power of large-scale click data with a variety of experiments, such as building large-scale concept detectors, tag processing, search, definitive tag detection, intent analysis, etc., with the goal to inspire deeper researches based on this dataset.

Categories and Subject Descriptors

H.3.1 [**Information Storage and Retrieval**]: Content Analysis and Indexing - *abstracting methods, dictionaries, indexing methods.* Information Search and Retrieval - *retrieval model, search process, relevance feedback.*

MM'13, October 21–25, 2013, Barcelona, Spain.

ACM 978-1-4503-2404-5/13/10 ...$15.00.
http://dx.doi.org/10.1145/2502081.2502283.

Keywords

Image search, image understanding, dataset

1. INTRODUCTION

It was estimated that there were more than 6 billion photos on Flickr, at least 690 million videos on YouTube and 220 billion or more photos on Facebook. Content-aware multimedia managing, understanding, searching and consuming is a key technology to deal with the explosion of images and videos available on the Internet, desktops and mobile devices.

However, visual content analytical technologies have not been extensively exploited in real-world applications such as tagging, searching, advertising and recommendation. The primary barrier is that current media content understanding technologies are still not mature enough to bridge the "semantic gap" (the gap between the low-level features and high-level semantics) and the "intent gap" (the gap between the representation of users' query/demand and the real intent of the users), in terms of accuracy, scalability and coverage. The technologies are still not there to effectively power real-world applications, especially when the data volume is large and data complexity is high [7, 12].

There are three possible directions to bridge these gaps: 1) to develop more representative visual features from the pixels in images or video frames, 2) to invent better learning approaches and/or statistical models to model and learn the semantics, and 3) to collecting more training data with better quality. Considerable efforts on the first two approaches have been made in the past decades (though the "gaps" remain). For the third, the key barrier is the availability of high quality and large scale dataset.

Though there are already quite a few labeled image datasets available to model and learn semantics for visual content, such as ImageNet [5], the coverage (in terms of both labels and images) of those datasets are far from being able to infer semantics for real-world applications. A good dataset for this purpose should not only contain large-scale data, but also reveals the challenges in solving real-world problems, enables creative researches to solve the challenges, and verifies the right solutions that are able to power real-world applications. We argue that the click data from commercial search engines meets these requirements.

Click data has been studied for some time in Web search area. But to the best of our knowledge, only a few limited research that is using large-scale click image data to bridge semantic and intent gap can be found in literature [10]. In this paper, we will discuss why and how large-scale click data

Table 1: Comparison of different image datasets.

	# of images***	# of labels	Construction	Coverage	Ext.**	Acc.**	Avail.**	Seg.**
MSRC	Small: 591	23	Manual	Low: 23 object categories	Low	High	Yes	Yes
Caltech101	Small: 9K	101	Search + Manual	Low: 101 object categories	Low	High	Yes	No
PASCAL 2012	Small: 27K	20	Search + Manual	Low: 20 categories	Low	High	Yes	No
Caltech256	Small: 30k	256	Search + Manual	Low: 256 object categories	Low	High	Yes	No
Corel	Small: 30K	98	Manual	Low: 98 categories	Low	High	Yes	No
LabelMe	Small: 30K	183	Crowdsourcing	Low: 183 categories	Medium	High	Yes	Yes
ImageCLEF	Middle: 250K	-*	Search Engine	Medium: English Dictionary	High	Low	Yes	No
NUS-Wide	Middle: 270K	5,018	Social Media	Medium: 5K generic tags	High	Medium	Yes	No
ESP	Large: 10+M	-*	Crowdsourcing (ESP)	Medium: generic manual tags	Medium	High	No	No
TinyImage	Large: 80M	75K	Search Engine	Medium: 75K from WordNet	High	Low	Yes	No
ImageNet	Large: 14M	22K	Search + Crowdsourcing	Medium: 22K synset (WordNet)	Medium	High	Yes	No
Clickture	Large: 40M	73.6M	Search Log	High: Queries of Users	High	High	Yes	No

* Not available in public literature.

** Ext. = Extensibility; Acc. = Label Accuracy; Avail. = Public Availability; Seg. = Segmented。

*** Using the largest number that we can find in literature.

can be used to bridge semantic gap and intent gap in a variety of image applications. We call this direction "Clickage", which means the use of large-scale click data to build the linkage among visual content, semantics and search intents. In [9], a large-scale click based image dataset, Clickture, is introduced. All the data used in this paper can be accessed at a central website (http://www.clickture.info). Table 1 shows a summary of commonly used image datasets and Clickture. More details of the unique features, construction processes, and properties of Clickture can be found in [9]. This paper will focus on experiments on Clickture to explore what this large-scale click-based dataset can provide and to show that the idea of "Clickage" is a promising direction to advance content-aware multimedia research.

The main purpose of this paper is not to present the "best" solutions to the research problems discussed below, but to introduce baselines for a variety of existing and new research topics by using the Clickture dataset, as well as to inspire deeper and more sophisticated studies based on this new real-world image dataset.

We will briefly review the properties of the Clickture dataset in Section 2. For the next three sections (3 to 5), we present three sets of exemplary research problems on the dataset, including query modeling, graph-based image analysis, and query intent analysis. Extensive experimental results will be reported and a dedicated "discussion" sub-section is included in each section. We conclude the paper in Section 6 with a highlight on a few additional research directions using the Clickture dataset.

2. THE NEW DATASET: WHAT AND WHY

To make the paper self-contained, in this section, we briefly review what are included in the Clickture dataset and then summarize the unique properties of this dataset. As aforementioned, more details can be found in [9].

2.1 The Datasets

The dataset, named Clickture, was sampled from one-year click log of a commercial image search engine. It consists of a big table with 212.3 million triads:

$$Clickture = \{\langle K, Q, C\rangle\}. \quad (1)$$

A triad $\{\langle K, Q, C\rangle\}$ means that the image "K" was clicked "C" times in the search results of query "Q" in one year (maybe by different users at different times). Image K is represented by a unique "key" which is hash code generated from the image URL, together with the original URL. Query "Q" is a textual word or phrase, and click count C is an integer which is no less than one. One image may correspond with to one or more entries in the table. One query may also appear in multiple entries triads that are associated with different images. There are 40 million unique (in terms of URLs) image keys, that is, images in the dataset, and 73.6 million unique queries (based on textual string comparison in lower case) in the Clickture.

Table 2: Basic numbers of Clickture-Full and Clickture-Lite.

	Full	Lite
# of images	40M	1M
# of image/query pairs	212.3M	23.1M
# of unique queries	73.6M	11.7M
# of unique terms	4.0M	915K
# of clicks	405M	82.3M
# of queries per image (average)	5.3	23.1
# of images per query (average)	2.9	2.0
# of clicks per image	10.1	82.3

Through users' click action during When doing image search, a user often clicks one or more images that are relevant to the query, thus mostly the query Q in the triad is relevant linked to the image K. In general, the bigger the click count C is, the higher probability that the corresponding query is relevant to the image. For convenience, we call Q a "clicked query" of Image K, and K a "clicked image" of query Q, and call $\langle K, Q\rangle$ a "clicked image-query pair", and the triad $\langle K, Q, C\rangle$ as "click data". We also call "clicked queries" of an image as "labels" of the image.

To enable the use of Clickture by a wide range of research organizations and individuals with different computing, networking, storage and programing capacities, a subset of Clickture images (1 million images and 11.7 million queries), is provided. We call this set Clickture-Lite and the full $40M$ dataset Clickture-Full (or in brief Clickture). The $1M$ images in Clickture-Lite are randomly sampled from the $40M$ image dataset (based on click frequency). Table 2 shows the basic numbers of Clickture-Full/-Lite, in which "terms" means individual words in a query. For example, query *white dog* contains two terms: *white* and *dog*.

Figure 1 shows the distributions of query lengths (i.e., number of words in a query) of Clickture (for clarity of the figure, only the percentage numbers for the Full set are shown). It is observed that most queries have 3 or 4 words (around 53% for both sets) and more than 83% queries have 2 to 5 words. Less than 2% of the queries only have one word. Around 15% queries have six of more words, which maps to $1.7M$ and $11.3M$ queries in Clickture Lie and Full sets, respectively. These queries give us sufficient data to study the challenge of both long and short queries in image search.

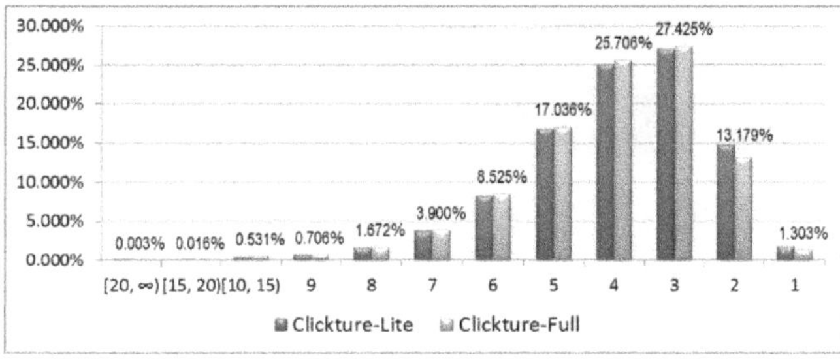

Figure 1: Query length distribution.

Table 3: Top 5 domains.

	Full	Lite
1	blogspot.com	blogspot.com
2	wordpress.com	wordpress.com
3	photobucket.com	photobucket.com
4	staticflickr.com	staticflickr.com
5	deviantart.net	fanpop.com

Table 3 shows the top 5 domains where the image URLs come from. We can see that top domains are all from social media websites (including blog websites and photo sharing websites), which is accordant to the fact that social media now is receiving increasing attention from Internet users. At the same time, it also shows that Clickture provides sufficient data to facilitate researches on social media data.

2.2 The Advantages of Click Data

Most existing image datasets consist of limited number of images, which in general have relatively high accuracy but lower coverage in terms of both images and labels. Usually it only contains hundreds of object categories and is far from revealing the real-word complexities and meeting the needs of real-word applications, which needs to deal with millions of objects. Datasets based on social media sharing websites (for example, NUS-Wide [3], in which the user-input tags on Flickr were regarded as the labels of the images) typically contain big noises as well as the problem that the labels are often too generic because users generally tend not to spend too much time on labeling [5]. TinyImage [18] and ImageCLEF (the part for scalable image annotation) use the results returned by search engines directly [1], which are very noisy. ImageNet improved the label quality by using crowdsourcing labeling, which reaches 99.7% precision in average. ESP dataset [21] and LabelMe [19] are also constructed through crowdsourcing, one through ESP image labeling game and the other through volunteered online labeling. LabelMe only has 183 categories because manually labeling regions is still tedious even by leveraging online volunteers. Labels generated through ESP game are mostly "basic level" semantics as humans tend to label easily accessible semantics, although they are accurate. The labels in ImageNet are based on WordNet hierarchy, which have better coverage than ESP data. However, its overlap with the queries that people are using in daily search is very low. For example, it only covers 0.01% of the distinct queries in Clickture [9].

Figure 2: Random examples in click data

The primary shortcoming of existing image datasets is the low coverage of real-world semantic to reveal and verify the real-world challenges and complexities, thus the researches based on those datasets still have a large gap from being capable of powering real-world applications. On the contrary, Clickture was constructed by a totally different approach: using search engine click logs. As a byproduct of commercial image search engines, and with the increase of the image indexed as well as the number users that are using image search, Clickture can potentially grow both in amount of data collected and its coverage, and be extended unlimitedly. It also reflects common users' searching and consuming interests and covers the semantics (textual queries) that people desire to search in daily life. Labels in Clickture are more accurate than datasets that are using search results from search engines or user-input tags in Flickr, though less accurate than manual labeling. Figure 2 shows a few random exemplary images with top three clicked queries. We observe that the quality of the label is generally high, though noises can also be observed. Figure 3 shows the top 100 clicked images of query *chair*, which contains a variety of chairs with diverse appearances.

Figure 3: Top 100 clicked images of query "chair".

3. EXAMPLARY RESEARCH (I): QUERY MODELING

In this section, we will use Clickture as "labeled" data for semantic "concept" (a.k.a., "queries" in this paper) modeling and classification and then use the classification results to improve the ranking of image search. Throughout the section, for each image in the dataset, we use a 1000-dimensional feature vector, which includes color histogram, color wavelet, gradient histogram, face, etc.

3.1 Top Query Modeling

In this experiments, we evaluate statistical models learned from Clickture for queries with relatively larger number of clicked images. For Clickture-Lite, we filter out queries with less than 100 clicked images and form a "top query list", which contains 6891 queries. We also use this list for the Clickture-Full. Table 4 shows the distribution of the number of clicked images of these queries in the Full and Lite datasets. A few examples can be found in Figure 4 and 6.

Table 4: Number of clicked images for top queries.

# of images	# of queries (Lite)	# of queries (Full)
[100, 200)	4955	115
[200, 300)	1081	558
[300, 500)	596	1748
[500, 1000)	216	2695
[1000, infinity)	43	1775
Total	6891	6891

Table 5: Top query modeling performance on Clickture-Lite.

Model	Acc.	P. Prec.	P. Recall	N. Prec.	N. Recall	T. Train	T. Test
SVM (n=1)	0.7710	0.7690	0.7822	0.7818	0.7598	14.61	4.33
SVM (n=2)	0.7665	0.7633	0.7842	0.7823	0.7488	12.74	3.78
FRC (n=1)	**0.7846**	**0.7816**	**0.7931**	**0.7923**	**0.7760**	10.22	3.43
FRC (n=2)	0.7646	0.7610	0.7788	0.7729	0.7503	6.41	2.15
PM (n=1)	0.7670	0.7604	0.7833	0.7798	0.7507	2.21	0.74
PM (n=2)	0.7537	0.7480	0.7732	0.7707	0.7342	1.94	0.65
AP (n=1)	0.7367	0.7346	0.7539	0.7564	0.7195	1.13	0.61
AP (n=2)	0.7190	0.7184	0.7453	0.7482	0.6926	1.12	0.60
LR (n=1)	0.7734	0.7678	0.7869	0.7837	0.7598	3.27	0.24
LR (n=2)	0.7627	0.7572	0.7793	0.7764	0.7461	2.63	0.19

Acc.: Accuracy; P.: Positive; Prec.: Precision; T.: Time Cost (in machine-hour); FRC: Fast Rank Classification; PM: Parameter Mixer; AP: Averaged Perception; LR: Logistic Regression.

Table 6: Top query modeling performance on Clickture-Full.

Model	Acc.	P. Prec.	P. Recall	N. Prec.	N. Recall	T. Train	T. Test
SVM (n=1)	0.7811	0.7861	0.7897	0.7953	0.7722	22.72	6.73
SVM (n=2)	0.7875	0.7870	0.7993	0.7999	0.7752	17.83	5.28
FRC (n=1)	**0.8246**	**0.8215**	**0.8317**	**0.8299**	**0.8172**	21.14	7.10
FRC (n=2)	0.8124	0.8093	0.8216	0.8181	0.8028	15.15	5.09
PM (n=1)	0.8030	0.7966	0.8156	0.8115	0.7901	5.09	1.71
PM (n=2)	0.7920	0.7849	0.8080	0.8038	0.7757	3.35	1.13
AP (n=1)	0.7745	0.7700	0.7868	0.7859	0.7618	1.37	0.74
AP (n=2)	0.7632	0.7586	0.7825	0.7815	0.7434	1.26	0.68
LR (n=1)	0.8057	0.7997	0.8173	0.8134	0.7939	7.42	0.55
LR (n=2)	0.8094	0.8008	0.8259	0.8216	0.7925	5.25	0.41

Abbreviations are the same as Table 5.

In the first set of experiments, we regard clicked images with click count equal to or greater than n as "real" positive samples for the corresponding query in the top query list. The larger the n is, the more accurate the training data is. The tradeoff is that there are fewer training samples satisfying the accuracy criteria. We selected negative samples by randomly sampling from the rest of the dataset, with the images that do not contain the target query in the clicked query list.

(a) "backsplash designs"

(b) "bunk beds"

(c) "lifted trucks"

Figure 4: Top query modeling examples (upper row: training data; lower row: top predicted positive).

Five learning algorithms are applied on the top query dataset in Table 4, with 6891 top queries with their clicked images: Linear SVM [16], Fast Rank Classification (Boosting Decision Trees) [6], Parameter Mixer [15], Averaged Perception [4] and Logistic Regression [2]. Two-fold cross validation is used to evaluate the performance of the algorithms. Parameters of those algorithms are fine-tuned on a randomly sampled query set with 50 queries. All the learning and prediction are carried out on a low-end cluster with 12 machines (Quad-Core 2.1 GHz CPU, 8G RAM, Windows Server 2008).

Table 5 and 6 shows the performance numbers (accuracy, positive precision/recall, and negative precision/recall) of those five algorithms on Clickture-Lite and -Full respectively, including training and test time costs of each experiment.

From the two tables, we can see Fast Rank Classification perform the best in all metrics. Moreover, when is set to 1, the results are almost always better than those when $n = 2$, which shows that more data generates better results though at the same time more noises are brought in.

Figure 4 shows the randomly selected three queries with accuracies larger than 0.95, on the Clickture-Full dataset when $n = 1$, using the best learning algorithm in Table 6 (i.e., Fast Rank). The top ten positive training samples (according to click counts) are shown in the first row and the top ten images from the test part which have the highest prediction confidence (though may not be correct) are shown in the second row.

3.2 Image Annotation by Query Modeling

In the above experiment, we used clicked images as both training data and ground-truth for evaluation. In this section, we apply the models learned in Section 3.1 to annotate a different set of images.

From the top 6891 queries, we randomly select 100 queries with accuracy higher than 0.90, and then for each query model, top 50 search results of the corresponding query from a search engine are used for evaluation. The 100 best classifiers (from the aforementioned five algorithms, retrained using all the click data) are applied on 5K images. The accuracy, positive precision/recall, and negative precision/recall are 0.8412, 0.8292, 0.8590, 0.8541 and 0.8233, respectively. Figure 5 shows a few prediction results.

Figure 5: Examples of image annotation by top query modeling. The query is "cars". Images with blue, green and orange borders mean: true positive, true negative and false negative, respectively. No false positive is found in this example query.

3.3 Rank Learning

We investigate how Clickture can be used to improve image search ranking. The development set in the MSR-Bing Image Retrieval Challenge 2013 [9] is used for testing, which contains around $80K$ image-query pairs. The task is to estimate the relevance of the image and the query for each query-image pair, and then for each query, we order the images based on the prediction scores returned by the trained classifiers.

As in [9], Discounted Cumulated Gain (DCG) [11] is applied to measure ranking results against the manually labeled ground-truth,

$$DCG_p = \alpha_p \sum_{k=0}^{p} \frac{2^{rel_k} - 1}{\log_2(k+1)} \quad (2)$$

where $p = 25$, $\alpha_p = 0.01757$, rel_k is graded relevance score of the result in position k in the labeled dataset, and $rel_k = \{Excellent = 3; Good = 2; Bad = 0\}$. And last, the average of the DCGs on all the queries is the final evaluation result.

In this experiment, we discard queries in the development set that do not intersect in the Clickture. In total 352 and 546 queries intersect with Clickture-Lite and -Full, respectively. We randomly select 100 shared queries from these two intersections for evaluation. Fast Rank Regression [6] is used to learn a ranking function, and all the clicked images of the selected queries are used as training data. Two settings were tried: Setting 1: regarding the ranking label of all clicked images as "relevant" and randomly selected negative samples as "irrelevant"; Setting 2: regarding images with click count greater, equal, less than m as "Excellent", "Good", and "Average", respectively and negative samples as irrelevant (m is set to 3 in this experiment).

For Setting 1, DCG numbers on the Full and Lite sets are 0.474 and 0.482, respectively. The DCGs increased to 0.483 and 0.493 for Setting 2, which shows more training data generates better results, and grading click counts also further improve the DCG numbers. In Section 5, we will see that query intent estimation from click data will improve these results.

3.4 Discussion

3.4.1 *Applications of Query Modeling*

Experiments in this section showed promising results on annotating images with queries. When the number of queries (labels) is small, the annotations cannot improve the search quality in any significant way due to only a small portion of the images in the index will be impacted by those classifiers, as well as that sufficient number of Web images in general already have textual meta-data that are relevant to those categories. However, those small number of classifiers may significantly assist personal photo search because personal photos in general are lack of text descriptions. In Section 5, we will show that small-scale classification helps general web image search when the categories are sufficiently broad and when they are combined with query intent estimation.

3.4.2 *Large-Scale Query Modeling*

In 3.3, we only evaluated queries that can be found in the training datasets, and only trained classifiers for those top queries. In real search systems, this will not improve the search quality too much as it cannot cover queries that are not in the top query list. Two possible approaches can be applied: query modeling and n-gram modeling. The most difficult aspect here is handling the scalability issue, that is, training large-number of classifiers efficiently and predicting labels over large-number of labels in real-time [9, 8].

3.4.3 *Completeness of Clicked Queries*

The primary purpose of "query modeling" is to use click data to connect image content with semantics. The advantage of using click data is that it conveys a very wide range of "semantics" through a variety of "queries". Though those "queries" are not a "complete" list of textual descriptions of the image content, we believe it covers most "semantics" that average users care in their daily search. At the same time, the study of the completeness of the clicked query list of an image is a separate research topic which is very interesting and challenging.

3.4.4 *Modelability of Queries*

We first tried to model "query" with large number of clicked images and also discussed possible approaches to model every queries and n-grams with clicks. However, not every query can be modeled through the low-level features that we extracted and the statistical models that we choose. For example, the 10 queries with the worst accuracy (less than 0.61) under the best experimental setting in Table 6 are: *images quotes, crazy, s* (letter "s"), *image, cool stuff, pictures of stuff, image of art, funny animated pictures, fun,* and *Chinese.*

Figure 6 shows a few exemplar clicked images for some of these queries. We can hardly find any "patterns" to model. It is also difficult to design specific features to model them. We plan to investigate on identification of those tough to model queries, and investigate their feature discovery and selection in a future work.

A large number of queries in Clickture only have very limited number of images, which are very difficult to be well modeled. We plan to investigate the modelling of such query by leveraging other semantically-similar queries and returned images in our future work as well.

3.4.5 *Handling Noises*

Though clicked queries are in general relevant to the corresponding image, noises exist in Clickture. Some images may be clicked by mistake as they attracted users' attention for whatever reason (for example, very unique or strange images, even though they are not relevant to the current query). Clicked labels may also contain typos. As search engines typically are tolerant to "typos", they show indexed im-

Figure 6: Queries that are difficult to model (top: "crazy"; middle: "fun"; bottom: "cool stuff").

ages of the (automatically) corrected query to users. Therefore, some clicked images may be associated with queries with typos. The query count is a good indicator for the confidence or relevance of the label to the image. By grouping multiple visually duplicate and/or similar images into a cluster, it is possible to reduce the noises in the clicked queries. Reduction of noise will be discussed more in Section 4.

3.4.6 Leveraging Correlations among Queries

Quite a few similar clicked queries will appear for "popular" images (images with a large number of clicked queries). For example, "cat", "cats", "cat picture", "image of cats", "image of cat", "cats images", "kitten", "image of kitten", etc., may be clicked queries of the same image. A preprocessing step of removing non-essential phrases, such as "picture", "image", "image of", and "picture of" from the query labels, will combine clicked images of semantically-equal queries into one single set.

In addition, if the "correlations" of queries can be discovered, for example, if we know "labradoodle dog" is a kind of "dog", and "dog" is a kind of animal, the clicked images of those queries can be leveraged upon each other to enhance query modeling. WordNet provides such an ontology. The shortcoming is that it only covers a limited number of queries. Researchers have also found ways to automatically create term ontologies, such as Needle Seek [27], which can be applied here.

4. EXAMPLARY RESEARCH (II): GRAPH-BASED IMAGE UNDERSTANDING

In this section, we will build a similarity graph on the 40 million Clickture-Full dataset and then use it to do "tag processing", image search and image annotation. Experimental results and discussion remarks will be presented at the end of this section.

4.1 Building Image Graph and Image Index

We represent each image with a 768-dimensional float vector. Mixture of Gaussian models are used to generate 12 representative colors in the color space [22], and for each RGB color, we compute a probability histogram indicating its similarity to the 12 colors. For each image, we divide it into a 9×9 grid. A color histogram is generated for each 2×2 cells. As a result, we get 64 histograms, from which a 768-dimensional feature vector is produced by concatenation.

As in [23], a hierarchical partition tree partitions the whole data set into one million clusters, and then a similarity graph is built for the one million cluster centers. Each cluster center is assigned with a unique ID and then regarded as a "visual word" to describe the image. We build up an inverted index structure that maps each cluster ID (a.k.a. visual word) to its member images in Clickture-Full.

For each image in Clickture-Full, we then search over the inverted index to obtain the nearest 100 images to the query image as the initial similar images. Finally, we re-rank those images using the Euclidean distance between the original features of the images and the query image [23]. By this way, we have generated a 100-NN graph on the $40M$ Clickture-Full dataset.

4.2 Tag Processing

Here "tag" means a clicked query of an image in Clickture-Full dataset. As aforementioned, noises exist in the dataset and the clicked queries are not complete, tag processing will reduce the noises as well as adding more tags to the images.

4.2.1 Tag Ranking

Tag ranking is to rank the tags of an image according to their relevance or importance to the image [14, 13]. Different from the work in [14, 13], tag ranking here not only ranks existing tags of the image, but also enriches tags from its neighbors, and this can be done in a unified way, as below.

Suppose the nearest neighbor list of query image x_0 is $\{\langle x_i, d_i\rangle, 0 \le i \le m\}$, among which x_i is an image, d_i is the distance of x_i to the query image, with $d_0 = 0$. Then a tag t's weight to x_0 is

$$w_t = \sum_{i=0}^{m} ClickCount(x_i, t) \cdot e^{-\alpha d_i} \quad (3)$$

where $ClickCount(x_i, t)$ is the click number of image x_i under query t, and α is a parameter to adjust the importance of image distance.

In equation (3), click count is used to indicate the confidence of a tag. To avoid to be dominated by images with very high click counts, we clip click counts to T ($T = 25$ in this paper). At the same time, to suppress the possible noises in neighbors, when computing the weight of each tag, we only use the nearest M candidates that have that tag. For each image, besides re-weighting the existing tags of the target image, we enrich at most 5 tags from its neighbors (M is set to 20 here).

4.2.2 Definitive Tag Generation

In many scenarios, it is beneficial to generate one most representative tag for the image. We call this tag the *definitive* tag of the image. For example, in "search by image" scenario, a "best guess" of the user uploaded image is to show the definitive tag. Moreover, "search by image" can then search over the image database using both the definitive tag and the query image's visual features, which will lead to improved quality of the search results comparing with searching by only visual features.

Based on "tag ranking" in 4.2.1, the top one tag of the image can be regarded as "definitive tag". A more sophisticated approach can take into account the balance of "generality" and "specificity" of tags to find a more representative tag. For example, "dog" is a correct tag for an image of a labradoodle dog, but "labradoodle dog" is more specific thus a more informative tag than the generic tag "dog".

4.3 Annotation by Nearest Neighbor Search

After tag processing over the graph, the tag quality of the images in Clickture is greatly improved. Then, can we use this "graph" to annotate images that are not in Clickture? In Section 3, we have shown that this can be done by building statistical models for queries and then applying the learned models on the image to get annotations. However, when we have built a large image graph with quality tags, a different approach can be employed.

Actually, this can be done easily by using the same approach of tag processing, where the difference is that the query image does not have any initial tag. First, we extract visual words using the approach mentioned in Section 4.1 from the "out-of-database" image, then get a list of nearest neighbors from the inverted index. And last, use equation (3) to get the tags for the target image.

4.4 Similar Image Search

To search for similar image of a given image, we first find its nearest neighbors based on only image features (that is, visual words matching through the inverted index and then re-ranking based on the original image features). This is the baseline results of similar image search.

4.4.1 Re-Ranking by Tag Filtering

When the query image is in the database and it has some tags, we can improve the similar image search result simply by applying a tag filter. After the baseline image list is obtained, we check each of the image on whether it shares a common tag with the query image. We move all images that do not share a common tag with the query to the end of the image list.

4.4.2 Re-Ranking by Tag Ranking

Using the equation of tag ranking, we can re-rank the baseline "similar image list" by

$$Sim(x_i) = e^{-\alpha d_i} \sum_{j=1}^{k} w_{t_j} \cdot ClickCount(x_i, t_j) \tag{4}$$

where $w_(t_j)$ is the weight of tag t_j to image x_i, $1 \leq j \leq K$. In (4), both click counts and tag ranks/weights are applied to re-rank the baseline similar image list.

4.5 Definitive Image Generation

For a given "tag" or query, what are its most representative images? After tag ranking, the tag weight measures the relevance of a tag/query to an image. For all images that contains a certain tag, we can sort the image by the tag weight to rank images and identify the most representative images.

More sophisticated approaches can take the balance of diversity, visual quality, representativeness, freshness and completeness into account in ranking the images and generating representative images.

4.6 Experimental Results

We randomly sampled 1000 images from Clickture-Full dataset to evaluate the approaches presented in this section. In case the query image should not be included in Clickture (a.k.a. "out-of-database" images) in an experiment (for example, annotation by NN search, definitive tag for images that are not in Clickture, etc.), to save labeling cost, we use the same 1000 images but remove their tags and at the same time remove them from Clickture.

Table 7 lists the average numbers of tags or accuracy of image search with the following definitions:

- *Number of Original Tags*: number of tags with the query image
- *Number of Original Useful Tags*: number of tags that are strongly connected to the query, labeled manually
- *Number of Enriched Tags*: number of tags got from the candidate neighbors. Always 5 in this experiments
- *Number of Enriched Useful Tags*: number of tags got from the candidate neighbors that are strongly connected to the query
- *Number of Good Definitive Tag*: for each image, we regarded the tag with the largest weight as the definitive tag, and count how much percentage of the primary tag can well represent the sematic content of the image
- *Rate of Baseline Relevant Images*: number of the image with same sematic content in the first 20 images after ranking by only image features
- *Rate of Relevant Image After Tag Filtering*: number of the image with same sematic content in the first 20 images after tag filtering
- *Rate of Relevant Image After Tag Ranking*: number of the image with same sematic content in the first 20 images after refinement

From the table, on average, tag ranking adds 1.18 strong relevant tags for in-database images. The number increased to 2.04 for out-of-database images. The reason is that the in-database images already contain 1.89 strongly relevant tags (on average) so there is less room to add more high-quality tags.

Table 7: Tag precessing evaluation.

#/Rates	In Database	Out of Database
Number of Original Tags	4.8	n/a
Number of Original Useful Tags	1.89	n/a
Number of Enriched Tags	5	5
Number of Enriched Useful Tags	1.18	2.04
Number of Good Definitive Tag	0.91	0.89
Rate of Baseline Relevant Images	0.3945	0.3945
Rate of Relevant Image After Tag Filtering	0.5145	n/a
Rate of Relevant Image After Tag Ranking	0.6110	0.5905

It is also observed that, for in-database images, tag filtering improves the relevance 12 points compared with the baseline (in terms of percentage of relevant images in top 20 returned results), and tag ranking improves more than 21 points. For out-of-database image, tag ranking improves 19.6 points (tag filtering will not work in this case). Figure 7 and 8 shows a few exemplar results of in-database and out-of-database image queries, respectively. The third result in Figure 7 is an example with worse result after tag ranking. The reason is that a few images about music notes have a

(a) Ranked High Confidence Tags: *Cocker, Spaniel, Puppies*

(b) Ranked High Confidence Tags: *Jeep, Jeeps, Orange*

(c) 'Ranked High Confidence Tags: *Shoes, Music, Notes*

Figure 7: Three In-Database Example. Each example has three sets of results shown and (top-left image is the query image): top row: baseline search results; middle row: re-ranking by tag filtering; bottom row: re-ranking by tag ranking. The ranked high confidence tags are shown under each result set and the first one is the detected "definitive tag".

very similar shape with a shoe, thus the tags of music notes are wrongly propagated to the shoe image. Figure 9 shows more results of definitive tag detection.

To evaluate definitive image detection, we randomly sampled 1000 queries and compare the top one definitive images for the following two settings: (1) based on original click counts only; (2) based on ranks after tag ranking. Table 8 shows the evaluation results and Figure 10 shows a few examples.

4.7 Discussion

It is possible to use different features and distance metrics to build graphs. Different tags (clicked queries) may be more effectively and precisely propagated on different features and/or distance metrics.

After tag filtering and refinement over graphs, the noise in the clicked log reduces. We may be able to build better statistical models upon them.

Building sub-graphs on certain domains is another idea to more effectively using the correlations among images. Images within a specific domain, for example, people, landmarks, animals, etc., generally have denser and more trustable connections.

Going one step further, connecting image graph with web page graph (which is constructed through in-links and out-links on the web pages), and query/label ontologies is another promising direction to infer more accurate semantics.

(a) Definitive Tag is "House Family".

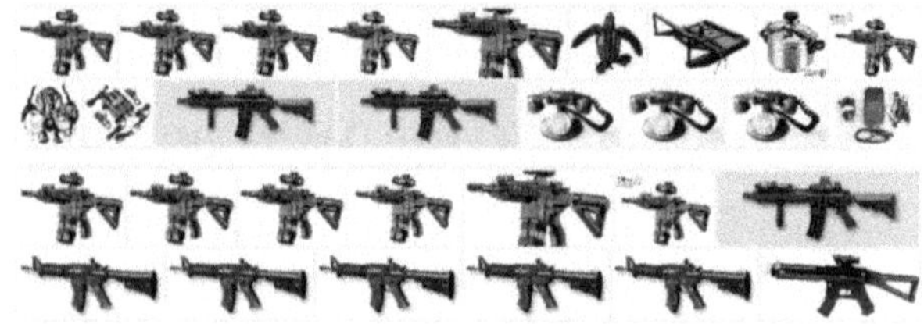

(b) Definitive Tag: "AR Rifles Gun"

(c) Definitive Tag: "Watch Spiral Rolex"

Figure 8: Three out-of-database examples. For each example, first row: baseline results; second row: re-ranking by tag ranking. The first image of each result is the query image.

Table 8: Definivtive image evaluation.

	Average Precision
Using Click Counts	0.8020
Using Ranks after Tag Ranking	0.9300

This may blur the boundary between image semantic understanding and image search, as they are leveraging each other to achieve better understanding/search performance.

5. EXAMPLARY RESEARCH (III): QUERY INTENT ANALYSIS

Preliminary intent analysis has been reported in [26]. Besides revealing the connections between image content and semantics, click data also reflect users' query intents. Through image categorization and click data analysis, we may be able to discover users' search intent of a query.

Search intent of a query (or "query intent" in brief) can be described by categories in different levels. For example, in a relatively higher level, we may say the search intent of

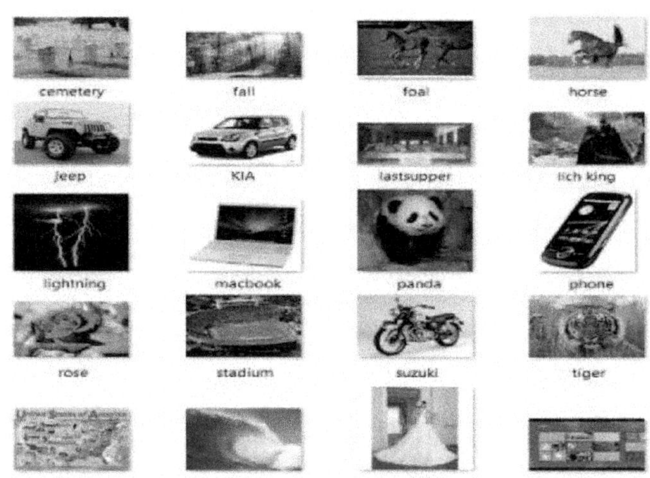

Figure 9: Example of definitive tag detection.

Figure 10: Examples of definitive images (top five in order). From top to bottom: forest, jeep, lighting, shoes, and stadium.

"Canon 60D" is "searching images of a product", while in a relatively lower level, the intent can be described as "searching images of a camera", or "searching images captured by cameras of a certain model". If the intent of a query is known, the search results can be ranked better accordingly.

Query intents can also be "implicit", which we can also call it query "types". For example, for an image query of "World War II", most people would like to see real World War II pictures, instead of pictures in a movie about World War II. As all real World War II pictures are mostly in black and white, then "black and white" can be an implicit or hidden "query intent". This kind of "type/intent" categorization can also help ranking. For example, we will not rank color images high for query "World War II" when we know the query intent of this query is "black and white".

One thing we should point out is that "query intents" are not necessarily exclusive to each other. For example, query "World War II Criminals" can be classified as "black and white" and at the same time "people".

After define a set of "query intent" categories, search intent of a query can be learned from labeled data. Alternatively, if we can classify the images into corresponding image categories, users' search intent can be mined from click data. For example, if we can detect whether an image contains people's face, we can classify whether a query's intent is looking for people or not.

5.1 Query Intent Estimation

In this experiment, we estimate a set of implicit or explicit query intents that the corresponding image type classification approaches are relatively mature, which include 11 non-exclusive categories: *black & white, portrait photo, clipart, high visual quality, line drawing, indoor, outdoor, cityscape, landscape, human full body,* and *head & shoulder.* Exemplary approaches to extracting those features can be found in [17, 24, 20, 25]. These classifiers were built on separate annotated datasets. The output of each classifier is either 1 (positive) or -1 (negative), or 0 if cannot be categorized into either of them.

To estimate query intent, we first apply image classifiers on all the images in the Clickture datasets to get images types. For a certain query q, suppose its clicked images are $\{\langle x_i, C_i, f_i\rangle, 1 \leq i \leq n\}$, where x_i is the image, C_i is the corresponding click count under this query, and f_i is the output of an image classifier of type t. Then the correspondence between query q and image type t can be estimated as

$$R(q,t) = \sum_{i=1}^{n} \frac{g(C_i) f_i}{g(C_i)} \tag{5}$$

where $g(C_i)$ is a weighting function to adjust the importance of click counts. In our experiments, we empirically set $g(C_i)$ to $\sqrt{C_i}$. Then the correspondence between q and t is formulated by

$$R(q,t) \begin{cases} \geq \delta & Positve \\ \in (-\delta, \delta) & Nocorrespondence \\ \leq -\delta & Negative \end{cases} \tag{6}$$

Figure 11 shows a few examples of clicked images for a few exemplar queries, together with the estimated query types.

(a) Query: "Nicole Kidman". Positive Intent/Image Type: Portrait, High Visual Quality, Human Full Body, Head and Shoulder. Negative Intent/Image Type: Clipart, Line Drawing.

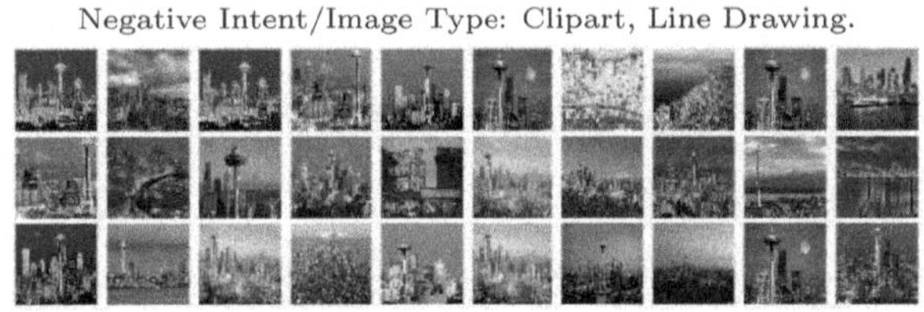

(b) Query: "Seattle". Positive Intent/Image Type: Outdoor, Cityscape, High Visual Quality. Negative Intent/Image Type: Clipart, Line Drawing, Human Full Body, Black & White.

(c) Query: "Word War II". Positive Intent/Image Type: Outdoor, Back '& White. Negative Intent/Image Type: High Visual Quality, Clipart, Human Full Body.

Figure 11: Examples of detected query intent types.

5.2 Search Re-Ranking by Query Intent

To verify whether query intent categorization help relevance ranking, we apply a re-ranking step on the results obtained in Section 3.3. Suppose the relevance prediction of image I and query q is r, the image type vector is $\{t_i\}$ and the query type vector is $\{q_i\}$. Then the updated relevance prediction of I and q is

$$r' = ReRank(r, \sum t_i q_i) \tag{7}$$

where $ReRank(\cdot)$ is a re-ranking function combining the original relevance prediction with the correspondence between image types and query types. Different re-ranking functions can be designed. In our experiment, we set the re-ranking function as

$$ReRank(r, s) = r + \frac{\alpha s}{\|\{t_i\}\|} \tag{8}$$

where α is a balancing weight. After applying query intent based re-ranking, the DCG on the 100 selected queries used in Section 3.3 is increased to 0.494 on Clickture-Lite and 0.505 on Clickture-Full (under Setting 2), where we can see obvious improvements (1.1 and 1.2 points, respectively) compared with the original DCG results.

5.3 Discussion

This section demonstrates only a preliminary query intent analysis and its application on search re-ranking. There is still rooms to exploit along this direction.

Similar to generating ontologies from clicked queries that we discussed in Section 3, ontologies for query intent is also important for query understanding. In the above exemplary study, we generate a few query intents/types manually. To support large-scale query intent analysis, automatic approach is desired. In addition, building connections between query ontologies and intent ontologies is another topic to be explored.

The query intents of a specific query can be complex. Different people may have different intents when a query is issued. Even the same person may have different intents at different time with the same query. For example, "Oscar" could be a person's name, or the academy awards, or a film, etc. When a person queries this word during the Oscars ceremony time in 2013, then the intent mostly could be the pictures of the ceremony and pictures of awarded actors and actresses in Oscar 2013. Studying and modeling the shifting and revolution of query intents through click data analysis can be another interesting research topic.

6. CONCLUSIONS AND FUTURE WORK

In this paper, we show how Clickage can advance multimedia research by doing extensive experiments on a number of existing and new research problems based on a click-based dataset. We argue that the growth of click data has the potentials of bridging semantic and intent gap in search and search related applications, and makes it highly valuable to advance the state-of-the-art of multimedia research.

Besides the ideas we presented in the "discussion" part of Section 3, 4 and 5, a variety of other research topics can be carried out based on the Clickage idea, for example,

Distance Metric Learning: Clicked queries provide large-scale additional and powerful hints to build a better distance metric between images.

Image Clustering: Clicked queries can be used as features to facilitate image clustering. The distance metric learned through clicked data can also be applied to aid image clustering.

Visualization and Browsing: Through semantic learned from Clickture, we may be able to build better methods to visualize and/or browse of search results and/or the entire image corpus.

Other Image Related Applications: Such as image advertising, image recommendation, image completion, super-resolution, compression, etc.

In addition, researchers may also use click data to study whether a query, label or tag is learnable, or how difficult to learn a specific label or a specific type of labels. New image visual features may also be invented to model different types of labels. Label relationship or ontology (for example, label graph or label hierarchy) may also be built based on the click data.

7. REFERENCES

[1] Image retrieval in clef, http://imageclef.org/2012/photo-web.

[2] G. Andrew and J. Gao. Scalable training of l1-regularized log-linear models. In *ICML*, 2007.

[3] T.-S. Chua, J. Tang, R. Hong, H. Li, Z. Luo, and Y. Zheng. Nus-wide: a real-world web image database from national university of singapore. In *CIVR*, 2009.

[4] M. Collins. Discriminative training methods for hidden markov models: Theory and experiments with perceptron algorithms. pages 1–8, 2002.

[5] J. Deng, W. Dong, R. Socher, L.-J. Li, K. Li, and F.-F. Li. Imagenet: A large-scale hierarchical image database. In *CVPR*, pages 248–255, 2009.

[6] J. H. Friedman. Greedy function approximation: A gradient boosting machine. *Annals of Statistics*, 29:1189–1232, 2000.

[7] A. Hanjalic, R. Lienhart, W. Y. Ma, and J. R. Smith. The Holy Grail of Multimedia Information Retrieval: So Close or Yet So Far Away? *Proceedings of the IEEE*, 96(4):541–547, Apr. 2008.

[8] X.-S. Hua. Looking into "msr-bing image retrieval challenge". In *Microsoft Research Technical Report MSR-TR-2013-76*, April 2013.

[9] X.-S. Hua and et al. Clickture: A large-scale real-world image dataset. In *Microsoft Research Technical Report MSR-TR-2013-75*, August 2013.

[10] V. Jain and M. Varma. Learning to re-rank: Query-dependent image re-ranking using click data. In *Proceedings of the International World Wide Web Conference*, March 2011.

[11] K. Järvelin and J. Kekäläinen. Cumulated gain-based evaluation of ir techniques. *ACM Trans. Inf. Syst.*, 20(4):422–446, 2002.

[12] M. S. Lew, N. Sebe, C. Djeraba, and R. Jain. Content-based multimedia information retrieval: State of the art and challenges. *TOMCCAP*, 2(1):1–19, 2006.

[13] X. Li, C. G. M. Snoek, and M. Worring. Learning social tag relevance by neighbor voting. *IEEE Transactions on Multimedia*, 11(7):1310–1322, 2009.

[14] D. Liu, X.-S. Hua, L. Yang, M. Wang, and H.-J. Zhang. Tag ranking. In *WWW*, pages 351–360, 2009.

[15] G. Mann, R. T. McDonald, M. Mohri, N. Silberman, and D. Walker. Efficient large-scale distributed training of conditional maximum entropy models. In *NIPS*, pages 1231–1239, 2009.

[16] S. Shalev-Shwartz, Y. Singer, N. Srebro, and A. Cotter. Pegasos: primal estimated sub-gradient solver for svm. *Math. Program.*, 127(1):3–30, 2011.

[17] M. Szummer and R. W. Picard. Indoor-outdoor image classification. In *CAIVD*, pages 42–51, 1998.

[18] A. Torralba, R. Fergus, and W. T. Freeman. 80 million tiny images: A large data set for nonparametric object and scene recognition. *IEEE Trans. Pattern Anal. Mach. Intell.*, 30(11):1958–1970, 2008.

[19] A. Torralba, B. C. Russell, and J. Yuen. Labelme: Online image annotation and applications. *Proceedings of the IEEE*, 98(8):1467–1484, 2010.

[20] P. A. Viola and M. J. Jones. Rapid object detection using a boosted cascade of simple features. In *CVPR (1)*, pages 511–518, 2001.

[21] L. von Ahn and L. Dabbish. Esp: Labeling images with a computer game. In *AAAI Spring Symposium: Knowledge Collection from Volunteer Contributors*, pages 91–98, 2005.

[22] J. Wang, J. Wang, X.-S. Hua, and S. Li. Scalable similar image search by joint indices. In *ACM Multimedia*, pages 1325–1326, 2012.

[23] J. Wang, J. Wang, G. Zeng, Z. Tu, R. Gan, and S. Li. Scalable k-nn graph construction for visual descriptors. In *CVPR*, pages 1106–1113, 2012.

[24] R. Yan, Y. Liu, R. Jin, and A. Hauptmann. On predicting rare classes with svm ensembles in scene classification. In *ICASSP*, pages 21–24, 2003.

[25] Z. Yang, M. Li, and H. Ai. An experimental study on automatic face gender classification. In *ICPR (3)*, pages 1099–1102, 2006.

[26] Z.-J. Zha, L. Yang, T. Mei, M. Wang, Z. Wang, T.-S. Chua, and X.-S. Hua. Visual query suggestion: Towards capturing user intent in internet image search. *TOMCCAP*, 6(3), 2010.

[27] F. Zhang, S. Shi, J. Liu, S. Sun, and C.-Y. Lin. Nonlinear evidence fusion and propagation for hyponymy relation mining. In *ACL*, pages 1159–1168, 2011.

Latent Feature Learning in Social Media Network

Zhaoquan Yuan[1], Jitao Sang[1], Yan Liu[2], Changsheng Xu[1]
[1]National Lab of Pattern Recognition, Institute of Automation, CAS, Beijing 100190, China
[2]Department of Computing, The Hong Kong Polytechnic University, Hong Kong, P.R. China
[1]{zqyuan, jtsang, csxu}@nlpr.ia.ac.cn, [2]csyliu@comp.polyu.edu.hk

ABSTRACT

The current trend in social media analysis and application is to use the pre-defined features and devoted to the later model development modules to meet the end tasks. In this work, we claim that representation is critical to the end tasks and contributes much to the model development module. We provide evidence that specially learned feature well addresses the diverse, heterogeneous and collective characteristics of social media data. Therefore, we propose to transfer the focus from the model development to latent feature learning, and present a general feature learning framework based on the popular deep architecture. In particular, following the proposed framework, we design a novel relational generative deep learning model to test the idea on link analysis tasks in the social media networks. We show that the derived latent features well embed both the media content and their observed links, leading to improvement in social media tasks of user recommendation and social image annotation.

Categories and Subject Descriptors

H.3.m [**Information Storage and Retrieval**]: Miscellaneous

General Terms

Algorithms, Experimentation, Performance

Keywords

Feature learning, Deep learning, Social media, Link analysis

1. INTRODUCTION

1.1 Challenges in Social Media Network

Recently, with the explosive growth of user generated data on the web, social media has become one of the most popular web applications, and play an important role in related multimedia applications, including image and video annotation [1], multimedia retrieval [2, 3], user recommendations [4], target advertisement [5], etc. Social media is defined as the means of interactions among people in which they create, share, and exchange information and ideas in virtual communities and networks [6]. It is an umbrella term to describe various social interactions, among which social media network, e.g., Flickr, Youtube, Twitter, is the main focus in the multimedia community.

MM'13, October 21–25, 2013, Barcelona, Spain.

http://dx.doi.org/10.1145/2502081.2502284.

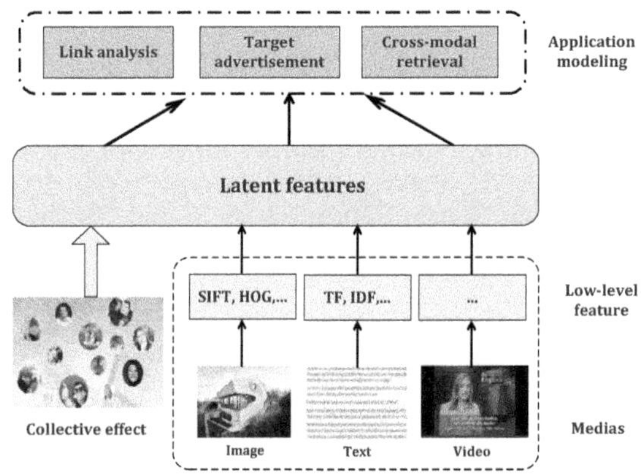

Figure 1: Framework of latent feature learning-based social media analysis.

Social media network exhibits unique characteristics when compared with traditional media forms, which poses practical challenges to social media analysis and applications. 1) From the perspective of generation, social media data are noisy and diverse. The user-generated mechanism gives rise to their low quality and large quantity. Users with various background use social media to record their daily life, resulting in subjective social media data and featuring a wide array of attributes like resources, appearance and degree of diffusion. The diversity characteristic makes the basic social media analysis tasks, such as social image classification difficult. Images describing the same concept may show much different appearances, leading to notorious intra-variance problem to traditional classification algorithms. 2) From the perspective of distribution, social media data are heterogeneous. It is very common that multiple forms of data, e.g., text, image and video, exist simultaneously on the same social media platforms. Data with different structures and distributions prevent from integrated social media understanding. Take user modeling as example, to understand user preferences from his/her online activities, viable solutions need to model heterogeneous user data, e.g., registration profile, browsing history, shared images and videos, added comments and annotations, in a principled way. 3) From the perspective of interaction, social media data are interconnected. We refer to it as the "collective" effect that social media data do not exist independently but interact with each other. The collective effect is either explicit or implicit, e.g., the interaction of observed user-user relation to their online behaviors is explicit, while the interaction of collaborative annotation to derive the final tag metadata is implicit. The collective effect among social media data violates the independently and identically distributed assumption in most statistical machine learning algorithms. Both content and collective information need to be considered for solutions.

1.2 Current Research Efforts

To address the above challenges, many research efforts have been conducted, which can be generally categorized into three lines. 1) Social media data preprocessing. The basic idea of this kind of approach is to address the first challenge, by removing noise from user-generated content to obtain clean and refined data, before application-specific algorithms are designed for solutions [7]. Typical research topics include video duplicate detection [8], image tag refinement [9] and social media organization [10]. 2) Social media semantic understanding. The basic idea is to address the second challenge, by extracting semantics for each type of data via multimedia content analysis, and gaining overall understanding of heterogeneous data in the derived semantic space. Typical research topics include cross-modal retrieval [11], topic and event identification [12], and social media knowledge mining [13]. 3) Social media network analysis. The basic idea is to address the third challenge, by embedding the interconnected social media data into tensors [14] or social graphs [5], where social network analysis methodology and metric is exploited for solution. Typical research topics include community detection [15], contextual social media analysis [16], etc.

Most of the current research efforts are devoted to the high-level model development, while representation learning, one of the fundamental problems in machine learning, is largely ignored. Much recent work in machine learning has focused on learning good feature representations which are targeted for end tasks [17]. Feature learning has been shown effective especially in dealing with high-dimensional data for complicated tasks [18]. It is demonstrated that the performance of machine learning algorithms heavily depends on the choice of data representation on which they are applied [19]. The importance of feature learning is far from being emphasized in current social media community, and we believe that it is a promising research line to take advantage of feature learning to address the challenges from unique characteristics in social media networks.

1.3 Brave New Idea

In this paper, we present a brave new idea on the latent feature learning to solve the higher-level tasks in social media networks. The basic premise is that, if we can consider the collective effect and learn a unified feature representation for various social media data, later tasks of social media analysis or application could be solved with off-the-shelf machine learning algorithms, and the performances are expected to be improved. The idea is illustrated in Fig. 1. The latent features which is kind of latent representation for medias in social media network are learned by 1) composing and decomposing structure-specified low-level features; and 2) integrating the collective effect from interconnected social media data. Higher-level social media tasks, e.g., link analysis, cross-media retrieval, are performed based on the derived latent feature space. Positioned in the middle-level, the latent feature representation involves with feature fusion from low-level features and captures the dependency between interconnected data. Moreover, since the latent feature is data-driven and learned automatically rather than pre-defined, the robustness is guaranteed.

Recall the challenges in social media networks, feature learning for social media data is quite different from that for traditional data, and it is not a trivial task. Deep learning framework, which models the learning task using deep architectures composed of multi-layer nonlinear modules, rises up to the challenges and provides a proper tool for automatic feature learning. The ability of deep learning in high-level abstraction and distributed representation has been validated in many classical machine learning problems, such as computer vision [20], natural language processing [21], information retrieval [22]. Recently, its advantage has also received attentions in social media related problems, like multi-modal fusion [23], multi-view learning [24], tag-aware image classification [25], etc. The reason that we utilize the deep learning framework for feature learning solutions is two-fold: 1) The mechanism of bottom-up greedy unsupervised pre-training and find-tuning well fits to the social media data characteristics of diverse and heterogeneous. The final feature representation is learned via a feature hierarchy, where higher-level features are formed by composition and decomposition of the lower-level features. Follow this layer-wise learning structure, the derived features are expected to capture the dependency and interaction in the raw features and explain more abstract and robust semantics. 2) Deep learning could be explained from multiple related machine learning perspectives, such as neural network, probabilistic graphical model, etc. This theoretical flexibility makes it possible to solve the feature learning of social media data and final social media applications under a unified framework. We emphasize that, to address the collective effect we summarized in the challenges, it may be necessary to combine deep learning models with the conventional machine learning models like matrix factorization and non-parametric Bayesian statistics.

To verify the idea, we design a Relational Generative Deep Belief Nets(RGDBN) model to solve the link analysis problem for social media network analysis. In the RGDBN model, we assume that the observed links between data are generated from the interactions of latent features. By integrating a flexible non-parametric Bayesian model named Indian buffet process into the modified Deep Belief Nets [26], we learn the optimal latent features that best embed both the media content and their explicit collective effects. The model is capable of analyzing the links between heterogeneous as well as homogeneous data, with effectiveness validated from social media applications in social image annotation and user recommendation.

The rest of the paper is organized as follows. In Section 2, more theoretical and experimental proofs will be provided to elaborate the advantages of latent feature learning in

(a) Example images with tag "flower"

(b) Example images with tag "running"

Figure 2: Example images from Flickr to demonstrate the diversity characteristic of social media data.

addressing the social media challenges. In Section 3, we describe our proposed RGDBN model to test the idea of latent feature learning in solving social media link analysis problems. Related work in link analysis and feature learning is discussed in Section 4. We conclude the paper with an outlook on future work and challenges to be tackled in Section 5.

2. IDEA JUSTIFICATION

To further justify the idea of latent feature learning for social media network analysis and application, and motivate the possible solutions, in this section, in correspondence to the summarized challenges, we present three standpoints to elaborate the advantages of deep learning-based latent feature learning.

Standpoint 1: Learned latent feature is discriminative to represent homogeneous social media data.
As discussed in the introduction, user-generated social media data are noisy and diverse. The homogeneous data expressing the same concept may vary much from each other, making discriminative representation very challenging. Fig. 2 shows some example images from Flickr by issuing the keywords "flower" and "running", respectively. With the images in Fig. 2(a) expressing the same concept, their appearances are very different, and for Fig. 2(b) is the same. Representations based on the pre-defined low-level features, e.g., Scale-invariant Feature Transform (SIFT), color moment, Local Binary Pattern (LBP), are likely to fail in discriminating such images. In this case, a common solution is to directly map the low-level features onto an invariant space to find more discriminative representations. Linear Discriminant Analysis (LDA) and Principal Component Analysis(PCA) are such the widely used dimension reduction methods. LDA explicitly attempts to model the difference between the classes of data, and PCA is capable of identifying the directions with the greatest variances, along which the low-level raw data points are projected to obtain the new representation.

However, as reported in [27], the representation derived from linear PCA achieves much worse discriminative ability than that from a deep learning-based model in representing images of the same concept. Likewise, [28] indicates that deep learning methods significantly outperforms LDA on discriminative tasks. These evidences well demonstrate the advantage of deep learning-based latent feature learning in discriminating homogeneous social media data.

Figure 3: A visual image of flower associated with several related textual tags. The joint representation for multi-modal visual and textual data could be learned by Deep Restricted Boltzmann Machine(DRBM).

Standpoint 2: Deep learning is capable of learning joint representation for heterogeneous social media data.
We have discussed in the second challenge that, social media data are very heterogeneous. Social media data expressing the same concept are not only diverse in homogeneous form, but in heterogeneous forms. For example, user-generated content usually involves with data from different modalities. Fig. 3 shows a visual image of flower associated with several related textual tags. Since social media data of different modalities carry much different statistical distributions, the latent feature structure is quite complicated. This makes it very challenging for the traditional methods to obtain a joint representation, especially for the unlabeled data. Fortunately, a recent deep learning model called Deep Restricted Boltzmann Machine(DRBM [23]) succeeds in learning the joint representation of heterogeneous social media data. It first uses separate modality-friendly latent models to learn low-level representations for each modality, and then fuse into joint representation along the deep architecture in the higher-level. The DRBM model has reported state-of-the-art performance in image classification tasks by obtaining 12% improvement compared with traditional shallow methods. Recently, it is also successfully applied to social media applications of cross-media retrieval, even when some data modalities are absent [25]. From this discussion, we have investigated and proved the ability of deep learning in obtaining joint representations for the heterogeneous social media data.

Standpoint 3: It is reasonable and feasible to integrate the collective effect into the learned latent feature.
Recall that social media data are interconnected, where the collective effect captures the dependency among the medias and plays an important role in data generation and relationship understanding. This presents the rationality of integrating the collective effect into the latent feature. In order to model the collective effect in the deep learning framework, a feasible solution is to combine with the Bayesian methods. With the collective effect modeled as prior for the latent feature, the observed data can be viewed as generated from the latent feature through a deep architecture as shown in Fig. 4. The collective effect defines the prior distribution $P(\mathbf{z})$ of latent feature $\mathbf{z}$, and the deep gener-

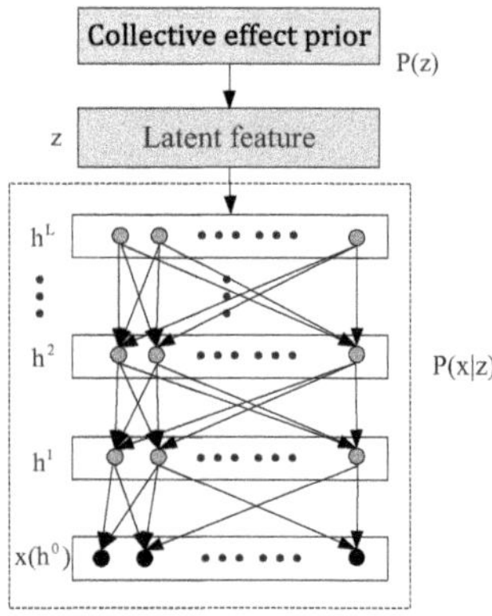

Figure 4: Integrating the collective effect prior into unified latent feature.

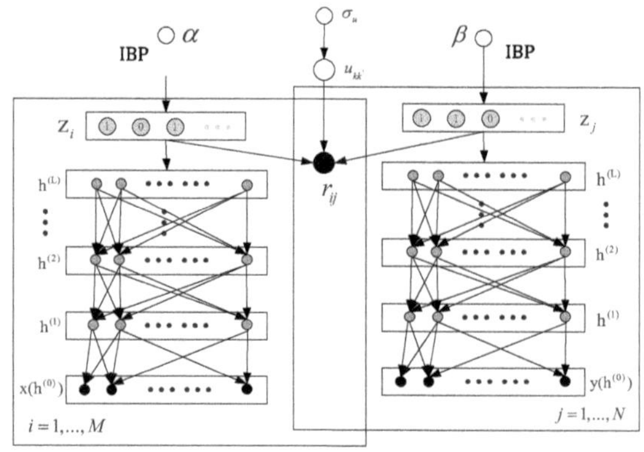

Figure 5: The Framework of Relational Generative Deep Belief Nets.

ative process determines the condition distribution $P(\mathbf{x}|\mathbf{z})$. In this way, we are able to combine the collective effect and media content in a unified framework. Actually, the strategy to define the collective effect prior is task-specific. For example, for the tasks of topic detection or community discovery with dynamic media content of changing scale, it is better to combine with the non-parametric Bayesian methods, e.g., using Dirichlet Process [29] as the collective effect prior.

In order to verify the advantage of integrating collective effect prior into latent feature learning within the proposed latent feature learning framework, we design a relational generative deep learning model to test the advantage of feature learning in solving social media link analysis problems which aim to predict potential links between items based on existing relationship and media information in social media network. Details will be discussed in section 3.

3. LATENT FEATURE LEARNING FOR LINK ANALYSIS

In this section, we address the important link analysis problems in social media network so as to illustrate the latent feature learning methods for social media analysis. Due to the heterogeneity characteristic and collective effect discussed in the introduction section, link analysis is a challenging problem. Within the latent feature learning framework, we propose a novel Relational Generative Deep Belief Nets(RGDBN) model to handle this problem. In the RGDBN model, the link between items is generated from the interactions of their latent features. By integrating the Indian buffet process into the modified Deep Belief Nets, we learn the latent feature that best embeds both the media content and observed media relationships. The model is able to analyze the links between heterogeneous as well as homogeneous data.

3.1 Relational Generative Deep Belief Nets

Assume we observe the two kinds of set of items "$\mathcal{A}$" and "$\mathcal{B}$" with the raw feature matrices $\mathbf{X}$, $\mathbf{Y}$, where each row $\{\mathbf{x}_i\}_{i=1}^M$ and $\{\mathbf{y}_j\}_{j=1}^N$ denote the raw feature vector of the ith and jth item respectively, and their link relationship matrix between them $\mathbf{R} \in \mathbb{R}^{M\times N}$, where, $r_{ij} = 1$ if we observe a link between the item i and j, and $r_{ij} = 0$ if we observe that there is no link. Unobserved links are unfilled, where M and N denote the number of items in category "$\mathcal{A}$" and "$\mathcal{B}$" respectively. Our goal is to learn a model to predict unfilled values based on the raw features of items and their observed links. Note that "$\mathcal{A}$" and "$\mathcal{B}$" may be heterogeneous or homogeneous in our model.

In our RGDBN model which is shown in Fig. 5, we assume that each of the two kinds of items is represented by a set of latent features. Let $\mathbf{Z}^{\mathcal{A}}$ and $\mathbf{Z}^{\mathcal{B}}$ be the binary matrices to represent the latent features of the two kinds of items, where each row correspondents to an item and each column correspondents to a feature such that $z_{ik} = 1$ if the ith item has the feature k and $z_{ik} = 0$ otherwise. Let $\mathbf{z}_i^{\mathcal{A}}$ and $\mathbf{z}_j^{\mathcal{B}}$ denote the feature vectors corresponding to the ith item in "$\mathcal{A}$" item and jth item in the "$\mathcal{B}$" item. For simplicity, we use $\mathbf{z}_i$ and $\mathbf{z}_j$ to represent them.

In the proposed generative model, The prior distribution over the latent features $P(\mathbf{Z}^{\mathcal{A}})$ and $P(\mathbf{Z}^{\mathcal{B}})$ specify the number of features and their probabilistic distributions, while the distributions over observed low-level features conditioned on those latent features $P(\mathbf{X}|\mathbf{Z}^{\mathcal{A}})$, $P(\mathbf{Y}|\mathbf{Z}^{\mathcal{B}})$ and relationships $P(\mathbf{R}|\mathbf{Z}^{\mathcal{A}}, \mathbf{Z}^{\mathcal{B}})$ determine how these latent features generate the observed raw features and their relationships.

On one hand, the latent features will generate the relation links in the proposed generative model, and the probability of having a link from item i to j is entirely determined by the combined effect of all pairwise latent feature interactions. Let $\mathbf{U}$ be a real-valued weight matrix where $u_{kk'}$ is the weight that affects the probability of there being a link from item i to item j if item i has feature k and item j has feature k'. We assume that links are independent conditioned on $P(\mathbf{Z}^{\mathcal{A}})$, $P(\mathbf{Z}^{\mathcal{B}})$ and $\mathbf{U}$, and only the features of item i and j influence the probability of a link between those items. This defines the likelihood:

$$P\left(\mathbf{R}|\mathbf{Z}^{\mathcal{A}}, \mathbf{Z}^{\mathcal{B}}, \mathbf{U}\right) = \prod_{i,j} P\left(r_{ij}|\mathbf{Z}^{\mathcal{A}}, \mathbf{Z}^{\mathcal{B}}, \mathbf{U}\right) \quad (1)$$

where the product ranges over all pairs of items. Given the feature matrix $\mathbf{Z}^{\mathcal{A}}$, $\mathbf{Z}^{\mathcal{B}}$ and weight matrix $\mathbf{U}$, the probability that there is a link from item i to item j is:

$$\Pr\left(r_{ij} = 1|\mathbf{Z}^{\mathcal{A}}, \mathbf{Z}^{\mathcal{B}}, \mathbf{U}\right) = \sigma\left(\mathbf{z}_i \mathbf{U} \mathbf{z}_j^T\right) \quad (2)$$

where $\sigma(.)$ denotes the logistic function, and we give a prior on $\mathbf{U}$ with $\mathcal{N}(0,\sigma_u^2)$ for each u_{ij} independently.

On the other hand, motivated by that there should be strong relationship for items with similar content features and the content information plays an important role in link analysis between items, the latent features also generate the observed raw low-level content features $\mathbf{x}_i$ and $\mathbf{y}_j$. We use a modified Deep Belief Nets [26] to model a deep generative process with multiple non-linear transactions to learn the high-level representation. Different from the DBN where the top two layers constitute a Restricted Boltzmann Machine(RBM) [30], our deep generative multi-layer networks composed of multiple layers $\{\mathbf{h}^{(0)},\mathbf{h}^{(1)},...,\mathbf{h}^{(L)}\}$ as illustrated in Fig. 5 where the data are generated in a top-down way directly. This generative process for $\mathbf{x}_i$ is represented as follows (the generative process for $\mathbf{y}_j$ is in a similar way):

$$P\left(\mathbf{x}_i|\mathbf{h}^{(1)},\ldots,\mathbf{h}^{(L)},\mathbf{z}_i\right) = P(\mathbf{z}_i)\left(\prod_{1=1}^{L-1} P\left(\mathbf{h}^{(l)}|\mathbf{h}^{(l+1)}\right)\right) P(\mathbf{x}_i|\mathbf{h}^{(1)})P(\mathbf{h}^{(L)}|\mathbf{z}_i) \quad (3)$$

The units in each layer are independent given the values of the units in the layer above and the parametrization of these conditional distributions is:

$$\Pr\left(h_s^{(l)}=1|\mathbf{h}^{(l+1)}\right)=\sigma\left(b_s^{(l)}+\sum_t W_{s,t}^{(l+1)}h_t^{(l+1)}\right) \quad (4)$$

where $h_s^{(l)}$ is the binary activation of hidden unit s in layer l, $\mathbf{h}^{(l)}$ is the vector $\left(h_1^{(l)},h_2^{(l)},\ldots\right)$, and $b_s^{(l)}$ and $W_{s,t}^{(l+1)}$ denote the bias and weight between unit s in layer l and unit t in layer $l+1$ respectively. The transaction way from $\mathbf{z}_i$ to $\mathbf{h}_i^{(L)}$ is the same as equation 4.

In our cases, as the input feature $\mathbf{x}_i$ (also for $\mathbf{y}_j$) is real-value rather than binary, the Gaussian RBM [31] is used to model the generative process in the lowest layer :

$$P\left(x_s|\mathbf{h}^{(1)}\right)=\mathcal{N}\left(b_s+\sigma_s\sum_t W_{s,t}^{(1)}h_t^{(1)},\sigma_s^2\right) \quad (5)$$

where σ_s^2 denotes the variance of the unit s. We would like the model to give high probability to generate the training data.

As the deep architecture re-uses and extracts the features in a layer-wise way in the learning process, after the learning process is completed, the "invariant" and "abstract" representation of features in lower layers is learned and lies in the top layer of architecture which preserves the latent feature representation for the media contents.

In our model, the latent features are the key factor that determine the link relationship. However, on one hand, the existence of collective effect leads to that the social media data do not exist independently but influence with each other, which means that what latent features an item has are not only influenced by the content of the item itself, but also the features the other items possess. For example, an item should possess some "popular" features that most of items have with high probabilities though these features are not reflected from its content information. Therefore, the collective effect should be considered into the latent features for each item. On the other hand, from the model expressivity angle, if the number of the latent features is fixed in advance, the model is less flexible. Based on the above ideas, we want to seek a prior for the latent feature to allow us to simultaneously infer the number of features at the same time we learn which items have each feature. The Indian buffet process (IBP) is such a prior, and it offers hopes to integrate the collective effect into the unified latent features for our model.

IBP [32] is a stochastic process defining a probability distribution on binary matrices with a finite number of rows and an unbounded number of columns. A feature matrix drawn from it for a finite number of items will only have a finite number of non-zero features. The generative process to sample matrices from the IBP can be described through a culinary metaphor. Each row of $\mathbf{Z}$ corresponds to a diner at an Indian buffet and each column corresponds to a dish at the infinitely long buffet. If a customer takes a particular dish, then the entry that corresponds to the customer's row and the dish's column is 1 and the entry is 0 otherwise. The culinary metaphor describes how people choose the dishes. In the IBP, the first customer chooses a Poisson(α) number of dishes to sample, where α is a parameter of the IBP. The ith customer tries each previously sampled dish with probability proportional to the number of people that have already tried the dish and then samples a Poisson(α/i) number of new dishes.

We use the IBP prior on $\mathbf{Z}^{\mathcal{A}}$ and $\mathbf{Z}^{\mathcal{B}}$ respectively by regarding the items corresponding to the customers, and latent features corresponding to the dishes. If some features are possessed by a number of items, then the current item also has the features with probability proportional to the number of items. We describe this prior as:

$$\mathbf{Z}^{\mathcal{A}} \sim \text{IBP}(\alpha) \quad (6)$$

$$\mathbf{Z}^{\mathcal{B}} \sim \text{IBP}(\beta) \quad (7)$$

where α and β control the growth rate of the new features.

Combining the IBP prior and deep generative learning process under the Bayesian framework, the collective effect and media content information are integrated into the unified latent features $\mathbf{Z}^{\mathcal{A}}$ and $\mathbf{Z}^{\mathcal{B}}$ which are just what we emphasize in this paper for social media network analysis.

3.1.1 *Inference and Learning*

Exact inference for our model is intractable. For simplicity's sake, we firstly learn the high-level representation(in layer $\mathbf{h}^{(L)}$) from the content feature for each item, and then do the posterior inference on $\mathbf{Z}^{\mathcal{A}}$, $\mathbf{Z}^{\mathcal{B}}$ and $\mathbf{U}$ using the approximate Markov Chain Monte Carlo [33] algorithm.

The learning of the high-level representation from content feature is mainly to learn the parameters(including weights between adjacent layers and biases). Similar to the DBN, the whole unsupervised learning processes include layer-wise pre-training and a following fine-tuning stage.

The greedy layer-wise pre-training is the phase of constructing the deep architecture based on Restricted Boltzmann Machine, which is an undirected graphical model with a hidden layer $\mathbf{h}\in\{0,1\}^F$ and another visible layer $\mathbf{v}\in\{0,1\}^D$, where D and F are the number of units in the visible layer and hidden layer respectively. The conditional distribution of hidden unit t with value 1 given the states of visible units is:

$$Q(h_t = 1|\mathbf{v}) = \sigma\left(b_t + \sum_s v_s W_{s,t}\right) \quad (8)$$

where $\sigma(x)$ denotes the logistic function. v_s and h_t are the binary states of the visible unit s and the hidden unit t, and a_s and b_t are their biases. W_{st} denotes the symmetric weight.

Similarly, the probability on visible units given the hidden units:

$$P(v_s = 1|\mathbf{h}) = \sigma\left(a_s + \sum_t h_t W_{s,t}\right) \quad (9)$$

There is no closed solution for the parameters of RBM, but they can be obtained by alternating Gibbs sampling. For simplicity, a contrastive divergence [26] is carried out, which is an approximate version of Gibbs sampling:

$$\triangle W_{s,t} = \epsilon(< v_s h_t >_{data} - < v_s h_t >_{recon}) \quad (10)$$

where ϵ is the learning rate. $< . >_{data}$ and $< . >_{recon}$ are the expectation with respect to the data distribution and the expectation with respect to the reconstruction distribution after running k steps of Gibbs sampling. The biases parameters could be updated in a similar way.

For the Gaussian RBM in the lowest layer, the probability on visible units given the hidden units is given by equation 5, and the corresponding conditional distribution on hidden layer given the visible layer is:

$$Q\left(h_t^{(1)} = 1|\mathbf{x}\right) = \sigma(\mu_t + \sum_s W_{s,t}^{(1)} \frac{x_s}{\sigma_s}) \quad (11)$$

where μ_t denotes the mean of unit t, and the update of the parameters is as follows:

$$\triangle W_{s,t}^{(1)} = \epsilon(\frac{1}{\sigma_s} < v_s h_t >_{data} - \frac{1}{\sigma_s} < v_s h_t >_{recon}) \quad (12)$$

Multiple layers deep network is built in a bottom-up fashion. Each pair of two adjacent layers can be regarded as a RBM by taking the lower layer as visible layer $\mathbf{v}$ and the upper layer as hidden layer $\mathbf{h}$.

After having greedily pre-trained the deep multiple layers, we use the wake-sleep algorithm to adjust the parameters of all the layers globally in the fine-tuning stage. In this training process, the "recognition" weights that are used for inference are untied from the "generative" weights that define the model. In the "wake" phase, units are driven by bottom-up recognition connections, and top-down generative connections are adapted to increase the probability that they would reconstruct the correct activity vector in the layer below. In the "sleep" phase, units are driven by generative connections and recognition connections are adapted to increase the probability that they would produce the correct activity vector in the layer above.

For the posterior inference on $\mathbf{Z}^{\mathcal{A}}$, $\mathbf{Z}^{\mathcal{B}}$ and $\mathbf{U}$, we illustrate the process by taking the $\mathbf{Z}^{\mathcal{A}}$ for example, and the process for $\mathbf{Z}^{\mathcal{B}}$ is also in a similar way. Given $\mathbf{U}$, and the parameters Θ (weights and biases) between layer $\mathbf{Z}^{\mathcal{A}}$ and $\mathbf{h}^{(L)}$, we sample the $\mathbf{Z}^{\mathcal{A}}$ by starting with an arbitrary binary matrix, and then iterate through the rows of the matrix. For non-zero columns k and row i,

$$\begin{aligned}
&\Pr\left(z_{ik} = 1|\mathbf{Z}_{-ik}, \mathbf{z}_j, \mathbf{h}_i^{(L)}, \mathbf{h}_j^{(L)}, R\right) \\
&\propto \Pr(z_{ik} = 1|\mathbf{Z}_{-ik},) P\left(r_{ij}, \mathbf{h}_i^{(L)}|z_{ik} = 1, \mathbf{Z}_{-ik}, \mathbf{z}_j, \mathbf{U}, \Theta\right) \\
&\propto \Pr(z_{ik} = 1|\mathbf{Z}_{-ik},) P(r_{ij}|z_{ik} = 1, \mathbf{Z}_{-ik}, \mathbf{z}_j, \mathbf{U}) P\left(\mathbf{h}_i^{(L)}|\mathbf{z}_i, \Theta\right) \\
&\propto m_k \cdot P(r_{ij}|z_{ik} = 1, \mathbf{Z}_{-ik}, \mathbf{z}_j, \mathbf{U}) P\left(\mathbf{h}_i^{(L)}|\mathbf{z}_i, \Theta\right)
\end{aligned} \quad (13)$$

where m_k denotes the number of non-zero columns entries in column k excluding row i, and $\mathbf{Z}_{-ik}$ is the set of assignments of other items, not including i, for feature k. Note that equation 13 indicates the three parts we try to model: $\Pr(z_{ik} = 1|\mathbf{Z}_{-ik},)$ captures the collective effect, while the term $P(r_{ij}|z_{ik} = 1, \mathbf{Z}_{-ik}, \mathbf{z}_j, \mathbf{U})$ makes the latent more likely to generate the relationship, and the part $P\left(\mathbf{h}_i^{(L)}|\mathbf{z}_i\right)$ to generate the raw content feature along the deep architecture. Similarly the number of new features associated with item i should be drawn from a Poisson(α/M) distribution. Given the $\mathbf{Z}^{\mathcal{A}}$ and $\mathbf{Z}^{\mathcal{B}}$ to sample $\mathbf{U}$, we simply use the method in [34] to use a Metropolis-Hastings step for each weight in which we propose a new weight from a normal distribution centered around the older one.Given $\mathbf{Z}$, we update values of Θ in the same way as in contrastive divergence algorithm.

3.1.2 Prediction

Based on the results of posterior inference, it is easy to predict the missing data values given the observed link. we collect T samples $\{\mathbf{Z}^{\mathcal{A},(t)}, \mathbf{Z}^{\mathcal{B},(t)}, \mathbf{U}^{(t)}\}_{t=1}^{T}$, and estimate the predictive distribution of a unfilled link values as the average of the predictive distributions for each of the collected samples. Assuming that we want to predict the missing link r_{ij} between items i and j, the approximate predictive distribution will be as follows:

$$\begin{aligned}
&\Pr(r_{ij} = 1|\mathbf{R}_{train}, \mathbf{x}_i, \mathbf{y}_j) \\
&\approx \frac{1}{T} \sum_t \Pr\left(r_{ij} = 1|\mathbf{z}_i^{(t)}, \mathbf{z}_j^{(t)}, \mathbf{U}^{(t)}\right)
\end{aligned} \quad (14)$$

In conclusion, the proposed Relational Generative Deep Belief Nets model is summarized in Algorithm 1.

3.2 Experiments

In order to evaluate the effectiveness of the novel RGDBN model, we conduct a series of experiments on both self-developed dataset from Flickr for homogeneous user-user relationship and public MIRFlickr-25000 dataset [35] for heterogeneous image-tag relationship.

For both experiments of link prediction, we trade it positive sample if we observe $r_{ij} = 1$ in the dataset, and negative sample if $r_{ij} = 0$. The prediction results are ranked in increasing sequences according to the prediction probabilities. AUC, the area under the ROC (Receiver Operating Characteristic) curve, serves as the performance metric, which is calculated by the following equation:

$$\text{AUC} = \frac{S_0 - n_0(n_0 + 1)/2}{n_0 n_1}$$

where n_0 and n_1 are the number of positive and negative samples respectively, and $S_0 = \sum Pos(q)$, where $Pos(q)$ is the rank position of qth positive example in the ranked list.

Algorithm 1: RELATIONAL GENERATIVE DEEP BELIEF NETS

Input: Initial relation matrix $\mathbf{R}$; low level features matrix of "$\mathcal{A}$" items $\mathbf{X}$; low level features matrix of "$\mathcal{B}$" items $\mathbf{Y}$; Number of deep network layers L; Random initial bias parameters for units in layer $\mathbf{h}^{(0)}, \mathbf{h}^{(1)}, \ldots, \mathbf{h}^{(L)}$; Random initial weight parameters $W^{(0)}, W^{(1)}, W^{(2)}, \ldots, W^{(L-1)}$; Random initial latent feature matrix $\mathbf{Z}^{\mathcal{A}}$; Random initial latent feature matrix $\mathbf{Z}^{\mathcal{B}}$.

Output: Unfilled link values r_{ij} of $\mathbf{R}$

for *each layer from* $\mathbf{h}^{(1)}$ *to* $\mathbf{h}^{(L)}$ **do**
- Greedy layer-wise pre-training by learning a RBM at a time;

wake-sleep algorithm for fine-tuning the parameters of deep nets;

for *a number of iterations* **do**
- **for** *each row* i *in* $\mathbf{Z}^{\mathcal{A}}$ **do**
  - sample z_{ik};
- **for** *each row* j *in* $\mathbf{Z}^{\mathcal{B}}$ **do**
  - sample z_{jk};
- sample $\mathbf{U}$;
- sample $\mathbf{\Theta}$;

for *each test entriy* r_{ij} **do**
- **for** *collection number* T **do**
  - collect $\mathbf{z}_i^{(t)}$ *and* $\mathbf{z}_j^{(t)}$;
  - collect $\mathbf{U}^{(t)}$;

Return test unfilled link values $r_{ij} = \frac{1}{T}\sum_t \Pr\left(r_{ij} = 1|\mathbf{z}_i^{(t)}, \mathbf{z}_j^{(t)}, \mathbf{U}^{(t)}\right)$;

It means that AUC is a way to measure the quality of ranking, as the more positive examples are ranked higher (with higher probability of being a positive example), the higher the term S_0, which is a better measure than accuracy.

3.2.1 link analysis between homogeneous items

We first conduct the experiment about link prediction applied in user recommendation between the homogeneous items. In our experiment, we crawl 3,500 users' data from Flickr, and the data information include user's name, contact list, tag list in his profile, uploaded and "like" photos and related tags for each photo. In our experiment, we use the tags in user's profile and that associated his/her uploaded and "like" photos as raw representation to describe the user and only the 1,000 most frequent tags are considered. The TF-IDF is as the low level feature for each user. In the contact list of user i, if user j is in it, we set $r_{ij} = 1$, if there is user j in it and also there are not common tag for them, we set $r_{ij} = 0$. The remaining entries of matrix $\mathbf{R}$ are left as unfilled. The contact number distribution for users is shown in Fig. 6, from which we can see most of the users have contact number less than 100. Note that, the matrix $\mathbf{R}$ is not symmetrical, and it indicates that user i is in the contact list of user j, which does not means that user j is in the contact list of user i. We hold out 20% of the data during training and report the AUC results for the hold-out data.

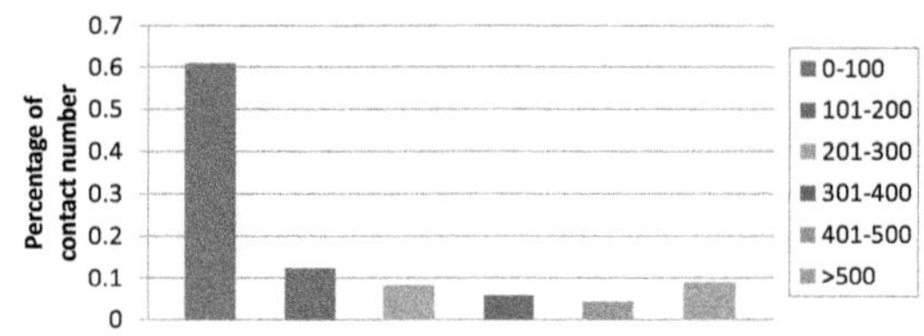

Figure 6: Histogram of contact number for users.

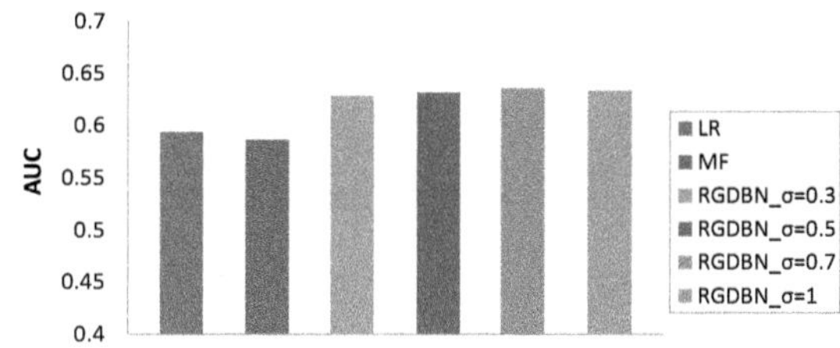

Figure 7: AUC results for link prediction between user-user relationship.

In the proposed RGDBN model, we set the hyper-parameter both α and β as 1. There are 4 layers in the deep architecture, and the number of units for layer $\mathbf{h}^{(0)}$, $\mathbf{h}^{(1)}$, $\mathbf{h}^{(2)}$, $\mathbf{h}^{(3)}$ is 1000, 800, 500, 300 respectively.

We then compare our model against Logistic regression which regards the link problem as supervised binary classification problem and classic collaborative method matrix factorization(MF). In Logistic regression(LR), each data point corresponding to a pair of users. Similar with the related work [36], the features include the number of common tags, sum of tags, Jaccard's cofficient, shortest distance, and Katz, etc. For RGDBN, we conduct the experiments with different σ_u values 0.3, 0.5, 0.7, 1 for the prior on $\mathbf{U}$, and the AUC results are illustrated in Fig. 7.

We observe that the proposed RGDBN model outperforms the matrix factorization and classification-based method using the topographical features and proximity features. From the view of features used in these models, we think that the features in classification-based method are raw features extracted from the graph topology and attribute, and those in matrix factorization could be considered as a shallow learned feature based on the low-rank approximation, while the latent features learned in RGDBN model are deep learned and more representative.

3.2.2 link analysis between heterogeneous items

We also conduct the experiment for link analysis applied in social image annotation between heterogeneous items for image-tag relationship on public collection dataset [35]. The data set consist of 25,000 annotated images which are collected from Flickr along with their tags. The average number of tags per image is 8.94. It includes 24 labeled categories and each image may belong to multiple categories. Fig. 8 shows some sample images from the dataset.

In our experiment, we consider analyzing the image-tag relationship. For image i, if it is associated with groundtruth label or tag j, we set $r_{ij} = 1$, otherwise $r_{ij} = 0$. Only the 800 most frequent tags are considered. For the hold-out data, we select 20% of training data associated with the labels.

In the our proposed RGDBN model, we set the hyper-parameter $\alpha = 1$ and $\beta = 0.5$ respectively. There are 4

Figure 8: Sample images from MIRFLICKR-25000 dataset.

layers for the image deep architecture, and the number of of units is 1024, 500, 200, 50 respectively, while for the tag deep architecture, we only use 3 layers with the number of of units 800, 200, 50 respectively. The reasons are two-fold. First, we think that the tag and the low-level visual feature are not in the same semantic level. Tag is closer to the learned latent feature level with respect to visual feature. Second, in the experimental dataset, the number of tag training samples is less than that of images. Reducing the number of layers leads to less number of parameters to train. We use HOG as raw feature for images, while for the tags, we consider the co-occurrence patterns among the tags and take the normalized co-occurrence counts of tags as features.

For comparison experiments, other than classic matrix factorization(MF) method, we regard the image-tag link prediction as an image classification problem where we take each image as a data point. If image i is classified into tag j, we regard there is a link between image i and tag j. The Logistic regression(LR) model is used. We also conduct the experiments with different σ_u values 0.3, 0.5, 0.7, 1 for the prior on $\mathbf{U}$, and the AUC results are shown in Fig. 9.

We see that though our RGDBN outperforms the matrix factorization and image classification based method, the whole performance is worse than that in the experiment with homogeneous items. In our opinions, other than the reason of heterogeneity, the link sparsity is also an important factor. The fact that the average number of tags per image is less than 10 indicates that most of the entries in $\mathbf{R}$ is zero. Since we expect the model to produce high probability in generating the observed relationship, the derived low probability in equation 2 results in a small number of latent features to be learned in the posterior sample process. Under such circumstance, the advantage of the latent feature is limited.

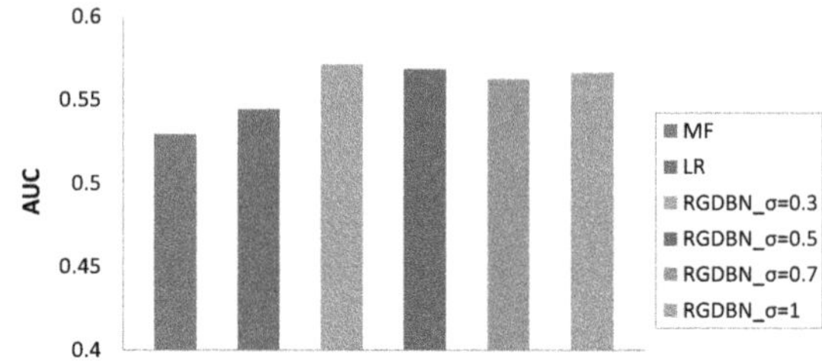

Figure 9: AUC results for link prediction between image-tag relationship.

4. RELATED WORK

In this section, we give a brief review of the related work about link analysis in social media network and latent feature learning methods.

4.1 Link analysis in social media network

The existing link analysis techniques in social media network can be roughly divided into graphical topology-based, low-rank approximation-based, and Bayesian relational methods.

In the graphical topology-based methods, the proximity features including common keywords [36] and topological features [37, 38, 4]. such as shortest distance, common neighbors, Katz are usually extracted to represent linked pairwise items. Then these features could be used in conventional models. For example, [36] utilizes these feature for supervised pairwise classification.

Low-rank approximation-based methods represent the observed links into graph adjacency matrices, and utilize matrix factorization techniques to reconstruct the original matrices by low-rank approximation [39]. This kinds of methods can be regarded as the special case of latent feature learning , i.e., with only one layer..

Bayesian relational models assume that there are some latent factors to generate the observed links. The basic idea is to set prior on these factors, with typical works of include Infinite Relational Model [40], Mixed Membership Stochastic Blockmodel [41], Nonparametric Latent Feature Model [34], etc. These models are of some flexibility for modeling the observed links. However, in these models, the latent factors are not in the unified semantic level, which can not handle the complex links in social media network, especially for the heterogeneous ones.

4.2 Latent feature learning

Feature learning is a classical problem in machine learning, with extensive efforts devoted to it. Besides the deep learning research line, we review several other feature learning algorithms.

One kind of latent feature learning methods aim to find a low-rank approximation for raw features, including sparse coding [42], PCA [43], ICA [44], etc. They map the raw data to a lower-dimensional representation based on the assumption that the data lies (approximately) in a underlying low-dimensional linear subspace.

Another kind of feature learning methods is based on the the single-layer network , e.g., RBM, auto-encoder, and K-means clustering. [45] shows that large numbers of hidden nodes and dense feature extraction are critical to achieving high performance for these methods.

In addition, topic models [46], can also be regarded as a solution of latent feature learning. They aim to discover the abstract "topics" that occur in a collection of raw data and take the "topics" distributions as the semantic representation of the raw data.

From the perspective of depth of the model architecture, all the above methods are shallow models. Shallow models are recognized as encountering the curse of dimensionality, and having limited capability in learning the distributed representation in complex situations [47].

5. CONCLUSION

The novel idea of this work is to tackle the analysis and applications in social media network with latent features automatically learned from a specially designed deep architecture. This goes against the current trend which advocates the use of pre-defined features and focuses on higher-level model development. Based on the discussions on the characteristics in social media data and challenges in social media analysis, we justify why it is necessary to bring attention to this new research line and what benefits of this new research line may bring to the social media community and the broader social media applications.

We introduced a fully generative framework to integrate deep learning with non-parametric Bayesian, where the defined "collective" effect is modeled as the priors for latent feature generation. To test the idea and the proposed framework, we design a novel RGDBN model and apply it in the link analysis tasks. Our analysis confirmed that the feature learning process preserves sufficient information to capture the interactions between heterogeneous as well as homogeneous data. We showed that the learned latent feature is more representative to embed the linked media content, and more effective to generate the observed links, which outperforms non-feature learning methods in user recommendation and image annotation tasks.

For the future work, firstly, we will focus on refining the idea and improving the framework by presenting a general scheme to integrate the collective effect priors into the deep architecture, and more reasonable and complex forms of latent features will be considered. Scondly, since the reasoning and inference are critical to a practical probabilistic graphical model, we are working towards developing more efficient posterior inference techniques for model learning. Thirdly, the idea and framework should be evaluated in more social media tasks and applications, investigating in particular whether the derived latent feature is helpful to represent the complexly interconnected social media data. Aslo, more comparisons will be made with state-of-the-art existing approaches and other feature learning algorithms.

6. ACKNOWLEDGEMENTS

This work is supported in part by National Basic Research Program of China (No. 2012CB316304), National Natural Science Foundation of China (No. 61225009), and Beijing Natural Science Foundation (No. 4131004). This work is also supported by the Singapore National Research Foundation under its International Research Centre @ Singapore Funding Initiative and administered by the IDM Programme Office.

7. REFERENCES

[1] Liangliang Cao, Jie Yu, Jiebo Luo, and Thomas S Huang. Enhancing semantic and geographic annotation of web images via logistic canonical correlation regression. In *Proceedings of the 17th ACM international conference on Multimedia*, pages 125–134. ACM, 2009.

[2] Jitao Sang and Changsheng Xu. Right buddy makes the difference: An early exploration of social relation analysis in multimedia applications. In *Proceedings of the 20th ACM international conference on Multimedia*, pages 19–28. ACM, 2012.

[3] Zheng-Jun Zha, Meng Wang, Yan-Tao Zheng, Yi Yang, Richang Hong, and Tat-Seng Chua. Interactive video indexing with statistical active learning. *Multimedia, IEEE Transactions on*, 14(1):17–27, 2012.

[4] Yuxiao Dong, Jie Tang, Sen Wu, Jilei Tian, Nitesh V Chawla, Jinghai Rao, and Huanhuan Cao. Link prediction and recommendation across heterogeneous social networks. In *Data Mining (ICDM), 2012 IEEE 12th International Conference on*, pages 181–190, 2012.

[5] Dong Liu, Guangnan Ye, Ching-Ting Chen, Shuicheng Yan, and Shih-Fu Chang. Hybrid social media network. In *Proceedings of the 20th ACM international conference on Multimedia*, pages 659–668. ACM, 2012.

[6] Toni Ahlqvist. *Social media roadmaps: exploring the futures triggered by social media*. VTT, 2008.

[7] Huiji Gao, Xufei Wang, Jiliang Tang, and Huan Liu. Network denoising in social media. In *ASONAM2013*, 2013.

[8] Xiao Wu, Alexander G Hauptmann, and Chong-Wah Ngo. Practical elimination of near-duplicates from web video search. In *Proceedings of the 15th international conference on Multimedia*, pages 218–227. ACM, 2007.

[9] Guangyu Zhu, Shuicheng Yan, and Yi Ma. Image tag refinement towards low-rank, content-tag prior and error sparsity. In *Proceedings of the international conference on Multimedia*, pages 461–470. ACM, 2010.

[10] Gerald Friedland, Oriol Vinyals, and Trevor Darrell. Multimodal location estimation. In *Proceedings of the international conference on Multimedia*, pages 1245–1252. ACM, 2010.

[11] Yue Gao, Meng Wang, Zheng-Jun Zha, Jialie Shen, Xuelong Li, and Xindong Wu. Visual-textual joint relevance learning for tag-based social image search. *Image Processing, IEEE Transactions on*, 22(1):363–376, 2013.

[12] Lu Liu, Lifeng Sun, Yong Rui, Yao Shi, and Shiqiang Yang. Web video topic discovery and tracking via bipartite graph reinforcement model. In *Proceedings of the 17th international conference on World Wide Web*, pages 1009–1018. ACM, 2008.

[13] Hari Sundaram, Lexing Xie, Munmun De Choudhury, Y-R Lin, and Apostol Natsev. Multimedia semantics: Interactions between content and community. *Proceedings of the IEEE*, 100(9):2737–2758, 2012.

[14] Jitao Sang, Changsheng Xu, and Jing Liu. User-aware image tag refinement via ternary semantic analysis. *Multimedia, IEEE Transactions on*, 14(3):883–895, 2012.

[15] Yu-Ru Lin, Jimeng Sun, Hari Sundaram, Aisling Kelliher, Paul Castro, and Ravi Konuru. Community discovery via metagraph factorization. *ACM Transactions on Knowledge Discovery from Data (TKDD)*, 5(3):17, 2011.

[16] Guo-Jun Qi, Charu Aggarwal, Qi Tian, Heng Ji, and Thomas S Huang. Exploring context and content links in social media: A latent space method. *Pattern*

Analysis and Machine Intelligence, IEEE Transactions on, 34(5):850–862, 2012.

[17] Honglak Lee. *Unsupervised Feature Learning Via Sparse Hierarchical Representations*. Stanford University, 2010.

[18] Huan Liu and Lei Yu. Toward integrating feature selection algorithms for classification and clustering. *Knowledge and Data Engineering, IEEE Transactions on*, 17(4):491–502, 2005.

[19] Yoshua Bengio, Aaron C Courville, and Pascal Vincent. Unsupervised feature learning and deep learning: A review and new perspectives. *CoRR abs/1206.5538*, 2012.

[20] Quoc V Le, Marc'Aurelio Ranzato, Rajat Monga, Matthieu Devin, Kai Chen, Greg S Corrado, Jeff Dean, and Andrew Y Ng. Building high-level features using large scale unsupervised learning. *arXiv preprint arXiv:1112.6209*, 2011.

[21] Ronan Collobert and Jason Weston. A unified architecture for natural language processing: deep neural networks with multitask learning. In *Proceedings of the 25th international conference on Machine learning*, pages 160–167. ACM, 2008.

[22] Ruslan Salakhutdinov and Geoffrey Hinton. Semantic hashing. *International Journal of Approximate Reasoning*, 50(7):969–978, 2009.

[23] Nitish Srivastava and Ruslan Salakhutdinov. Multimodal learning with deep boltzmann machines. In *Advances in Neural Information Processing Systems 25*, pages 2231–2239, 2012.

[24] Yoonseop Kang and Seungjin Choi. Restricted deep belief networks for multi-view learning. In *Machine Learning and Knowledge Discovery in Databases*, pages 130–145. Springer, 2011.

[25] Nitish Srivastava and Ruslan Salakhutdinov. Learning Representation for Multimodal Data with Deep Belief Nets. In *International Conference on Machine Learning Workshop*, 2012.

[26] Geoffrey E Hinton, Simon Osindero, and Yee-Whye Teh. A fast learning algorithm for deep belief nets. *Neural computation*, 18(7):1527–1554, 2006.

[27] G. E. Hinton and R. R. Salakhutdinov. Reducing the dimensionality of data with neural networks. *Science*, 313:504–507, 2006.

[28] Grégoire Mesnil, Yann Dauphin, Xavier Glorot, Salah Rifai, Yoshua Bengio, Ian Goodfellow, Erick Lavoie, Xavier Muller, Guillaume Desjardins, David Warde-Farley, et al. Unsupervised and transfer learning challenge: a deep learning approach. In *Unsupervised and Transfer Learning Workshop, in conjunction with ICML*, 2011.

[29] Yee Whye Teh. Dirichlet process. *Encyclopedia of machine learning*, pages 280–287, 2010.

[30] P Smolensky. *Information processing in dynamical systems: Foundations of harmony theory*, volume 1, pages 194–281. MIT Press, 1986.

[31] Yoshua Bengio, Pascal Lamblin, Dan Popovici, and Hugo Larochelle. Greedy layer-wise training of deep networks. *Advances in neural information processing systems*, 19:153, 2007.

[32] Thomas Griffiths and Zoubin Ghahramani. Infinite latent feature models and the indian buffet process. *SciencesNew York*, 18(GCNU TR 2005-001):475, 2005.

[33] Christian P Robert and George Casella. *Monte Carlo statistical methods*, volume 319. Citeseer, 2004.

[34] Kurt Miller, Michael I Jordan, and Thomas L Griffiths. Nonparametric latent feature models for link prediction. In *Advances in neural information processing systems*, pages 1276–1284, 2009.

[35] Mark J Huiskes and Michael S Lew. The mir flickr retrieval evaluation. In *Proceedings of the 1st ACM international conference on Multimedia information retrieval*, pages 39–43. ACM, 2008.

[36] Mohammad Al Hasan, Vineet Chaoji, Saeed Salem, and Mohammed Zaki. Link prediction using supervised learning. In *SDM' 06: Workshop on Link Analysis, Counter-terrorism and Security*, 2006.

[37] Hisashi Kashima and Naoki Abe. A parameterized probabilistic model of network evolution for supervised link prediction. In *Data Mining, 2006. ICDM'06. Sixth International Conference on*, pages 340–349. IEEE, 2006.

[38] David Liben-Nowell and Jon Kleinberg. The link-prediction problem for social networks. *Journal of the American society for information science and technology*, 58(7):1019–1031, 2007.

[39] Aditya Krishna Menon and Charles Elkan. Link prediction via matrix factorization. In *Machine Learning and Knowledge Discovery in Databases*, pages 437–452. Springer, 2011.

[40] Charles Kemp, Joshua B Tenenbaum, Thomas L Griffiths, Takeshi Yamada, and Naonori Ueda. Learning systems of concepts with an infinite relational model. In *AAAI*, volume 3, page 5, 2006.

[41] Edoardo M Airoldi, David M Blei, Stephen E Fienberg, and Eric P Xing. Mixed membership stochastic blockmodels. *The Journal of Machine Learning Research*, 9:1981–2014, 2008.

[42] Honglak Lee, Alexis Battle, Rajat Raina, and Andrew Y Ng. Efficient sparse coding algorithms. *Advances in neural information processing systems*, 19:801, 2007.

[43] Harold Hotelling. Analysis of a complex of statistical variables into principal components. *The Journal of educational psychology*, pages 498–520, 1933.

[44] Pierre Comon. Independent component analysis, a new concept? *Signal processing*, 36(3):287–314, 1994.

[45] Adam Coates, Honglak Lee, and Andrew Y Ng. An analysis of single-layer networks in unsupervised feature learning. *Ann Arbor*, 1001:48109, 2010.

[46] David M Blei, Andrew Y Ng, and Michael I Jordan. Latent dirichlet allocation. *the Journal of machine Learning research*, 3:993–1022, 2003.

[47] Yoshua Bengio. Learning deep architectures for ai. *Foundations and trends® in Machine Learning*, 2(1):1–127, 2009.

Learning Latent Spatio-Temporal Compositional Model for Human Action Recognition

Xiaodan Liang
Sun Yat-Sen University, China
xdliang328@gmail.com

Liang Lin*
Sun Yat-Sen University, China
linliang@ieee.org

Liangliang Cao
IBM Research, U.S.
liangliang.cao@us.ibm.com

ABSTRACT

Action recognition is an important problem in multimedia understanding. This paper addresses this problem by building an expressive compositional action model. We model one action instance in the video with an ensemble of spatio-temporal compositions: a number of discrete temporal anchor frames, each of which is further decomposed to a layout of deformable parts. In this way, our model can identify a Spatio-Temporal And-Or Graph (STAOG) to represent the latent structure of actions *e.g.* triple jumping, swinging and high jumping. The STAOG model comprises four layers: (i) a batch of leaf-nodes in bottom for detecting various action parts within video patches; (ii) the or-nodes over bottom, *i.e.* switch variables to activate their children leaf-nodes for structural variability; (iii) the and-nodes within an anchor frame for verifying spatial composition; and (iv) the root-node at top for aggregating scores over temporal anchor frames. Moreover, the contextual interactions are defined between leaf-nodes in both spatial and temporal domains. For model training, we develop a novel weakly supervised learning algorithm which iteratively determines the structural configuration (*e.g.* the production of leaf-nodes associated with the or-nodes) along with the optimization of multi-layer parameters. By fully exploiting spatio-temporal compositions and interactions, our approach handles well large intra-class action variance (*e.g.* different views, individual appearances, spatio-temporal structures). The experimental results on the challenging databases demonstrate superior performance of our approach over other methods.

Categories and Subject Descriptors

I.5 [**Computing Methodologies**]: Pattern Recognition; I.4 [**Computing Methodologies**]: Image Processing and Computer Vision

General Terms

Algorithms, Experimentation, Performance

*Corresponding author is Liang Lin. This work was supported by the 863 Program of China (no.2012AA011504), the National Natural Science Foundation of China (no. 61173082), and the Special Project on the Integration of Industry, Education and Research of Guangdong Province (no. 2012B091100148), and the Guangdong Science and Technology Program (no. 2012B031500006).

Keywords

Video Understanding, Action Recognition, Structural Learning, And-Or Graph

1. INTRODUCTION

With the popularity of personal video cameras and multi-view video capturing devices, we are entering an era with rich amount of multimedia documents surrounding us. To interact with these videos, there have been increasing demands of understanding human activities in these videos. Although many research studies [45, 41, 19, 46, 23, 5, 30, 37, 32, 8] have been carried out to understand and retrieve large scale video contents, these works focus on high level semantics instead of describing human activities. There still exists a need to recognize fine-grained information for human activities, *e.g.* body poses and temporal motions.

This paper targets on the challenge of understanding spatial and temporal variances of video phenomenons. More specifically, we are considering the following difficulties:

- A human body is composed of multiple parts, and different parts are associated with different motions.
- Both the short term and long term motions may be fused by different background movement or camera motion, which brings the difficulties of accurately modeling the temporal characteristics for actions.
- In real world videos, human actions often happen with uncertainties: some happen along with occlusions, some are caused by view/pose variance, or due to diverse actor appearances and motions.

Due to these difficulties, it is crucial to reduce the spatio-temporal ambiguity when modeling the human actions. Most of the previous studies were built on simplified action models while overlooking the detailed spatio-temporal structure information. Of these works, a large amount of studies were based on spatio-temporal interest points [16, 42, 33]. Some researchers proposed to enrich the action model with the appearance information or context information [40, 34]. Some other researchers learned temporal structures for action recognition [29, 35]. However, none of these works provides an effective model which can unify spatial and temporal information to infer the structure of human motion.

We aims to develop an effective configurable model, namely the Spatio-Temporal And-Or Graph (STAOG) for action recognition, which addresses the problems mentioned above. Our idea is partially motivated by the image grammar model [47], which hierarchically decomposes an image pattern with mixed and-nodes and or-nodes, as well as modeling rich structural variations of parts.

The challenges of generalizing And-Or graphs for action recognition are two-folds. First, the traditional And-Or graphs are lim-

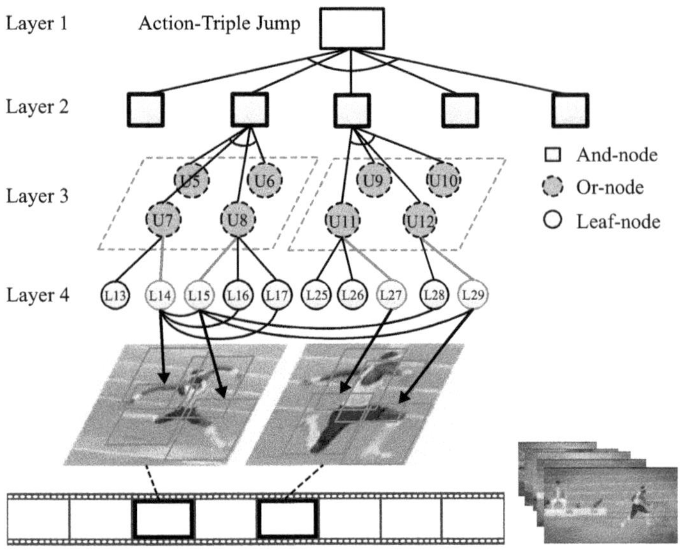

Figure 1: An example of the Spatio-Temporal And-Or Graph model, where the and-nodes represent compositions in either time or space, the or-nodes indicate structural alternatives, and the leaf-nodes (at the bottom) correspond to local part detectors. The links between leaf-nodes represent spatio-temporal contextual interactions.

ited in modeling the hierarchical configuration of spatio-temporal information. Because actions in videos are often more complicated than images, we need more powerful models for video problems. Second, videos require more efficient models that can be effectively learned from large amount of video information without elaborate supervision and initialization.

To handle the first challenge, our STAOG model extends the traditional deformable graphical models by introducing switch variables in hierarchy, *i.e.* or-nodes that explicitly specify structural reconfiguration. Both spatial and temporal interactions between action parts can be simultaneously learned. One action in the video can be treated as an ensemble of spatio-temporal compositions: a number of discrete temporal anchor frames, each of which is further decomposed into a layout of deformable parts. An example of the proposed STAOG model is illustrated in Fig. 1. There are four layers in our model from bottom to top:

(1) The *leaf-nodes* in the bottom layer represent a batch of local classifiers for detecting various action parts in every anchor frame, which are denoted by the solid circles in Fig. 1. During detection, location displacement is allowed for each leaf-node to tackle the part deformation.

(2) The *or-nodes* over the bottom are "switch" variables specifying the activation of their children leaf-nodes, denoted by the dashed circles. Each or-node is used to specify an appropriate selection from candidate action parts detected by the associating children leaf-nodes. In this way, by explicitly switching selections over leaf-nodes, the or-nodes make our model reconfigurable during the inference, which is the key to handle large action variabilities.

(3) The *and-nodes* verify the holistic appearance of action within the anchor frame, (the rectangles in layer 2), and we thus consider it as the spatial and-node. It includes two aspects: (i) a global classifier with bag-of-features, and (ii) aggregated scores from its children or-nodes.

(4) The *root-node* in the top can be viewed as an and-node in time, (the rectangle in top). Its definition is similar to the spatial and-node: (i) a classifier with global features in observed frames, (ii) aggregated scores over candidate temporal anchor frames, plus penalty for anchor frame displacements.

(5) The *spatio-temporal contextual interactions*, *e.g.* the curves (graph edges) among leaf-nodes in Fig. 1, are defined based on informative contextual pairwise relations in either spatial or temporal domain. Note that the collaborative edges are imposed between leaf-nodes that are associated with different action parts. Their effectiveness will be particularly demonstrated in the experiments.

To overcome the second challenge, we present a novel weakly supervised learning algorithm for model training, inspired by the non-convex optimization techniques [43, 38]. This algorithm trains the model in a dynamic manner: the model structure (*e.g.* the configuration of leaf-nodes and or-nodes) is iteratively generated and reconfigured on the training data, with optimizing the multi-layer parameters. The other structure attributes (*e.g.* the activation of leaf-nodes, and temporal deformation of anchor frames) are modeled with the latent variables and optimized simultaneously.

In the testing stage, we present an algorithm of cascaded search and verification for recognizing actions with the trained STAOG model. We first generate a set of hypotheses in both spatial and temporal compositions. (i) Spatial testing via the and-nodes. Within the input frame, all candidate action parts are found by leaf-nodes and several possible configurations (*i.e.* spatial compositions of action parts) are produced with different specifications via the or-nodes. These configurations are also weighted via the and-node. (ii) Temporal testing via the root-node. The scores proposed by the and-nodes are aggregated via the root-node for a possible temporal composition. Several possible configurations are then produced as hypotheses represented by different latent variables. Finally, each hypothesis is globally verified with the spatial and temporal edges in the model.

This paper is organized as follows. Section 2 gives a brief review of related work. Then we present our STAOG model in Section 3, followed by a description of the inference procedure in Section 4. Section 5 presents a description for structural learning of our model. The experimental results and comparisons are exhibited in Section 6. Section 7 concludes this paper.

2. RELATED WORK

Traditional works for action recognition focused on developing informative features, such as spatio-temporal descriptors [16, 7, 46],3D Gradient [15], 3D SIFT descriptors [30] and motion features [14, 18], and the action classifier can be trained with labeled data. Most of these methods, however, are limited to periodic actions with clean background, such as running and jogging.

To address complex actions with cluttered background, several compositional or expressive models were proposed and achieve very impressive results [24, 5, 28, 39, 13, 6]. For example, Wang et al. [39] modeled the human action by a flexible constellation of parts conditioned on image observations and learned the parameters of an HCRF model in a max-margin framework, motivated by the recent progresses in object recognition and detection, *e.g.* the deformable part model by Felzenszwalb et al. [10]. Yao et al. [40] proposed to generate spatio-template action templates with the information projection method. Sadanand et al [28] adopted high-level representations with a bank of individual action detectors. However, actions in video often involve much more information in both spatial and temporal domain, compared with image-based object recognition, and most of these studies do not explicitly localize parts of actions (actors) due to the computational burden. Moreover, structural configurations of these models are usually fixed, including a fixed number of part detectors as well as the predefined composition.

One unique characteristic of human action recognition problem lies in the temporal structure. A lot of works were proposed to build temporal structure models [9, 25, 35, 4] based on discriminative and interesting motion segments of the video. Raptis et al. [26] extracted clusters of trajectories and proposed a graphical model to incorporate constraints for individual and group events. Albanese et al. [1] represented temporal relations of activities using the probabilistic Petri Nets and integrated high-level reasoning approaches. Different from these approaches, we do not treat the whole temporal frames as units.Instead, we model temporal structure based on action parts with explicit relations and presents a solution to find both spatial and temporal configurations for dynamic activities.

Recently, the And-Or graph models [47] have been discussed for several vision tasks such as object recognition [21] and shape modeling [20]. These works mainly focused on images instead of videos and do not take the temporal dynamic structure into account. The very recent work by Amer et al. [3] proposed to recognize activities with the spatio-temporal And-Or graph model, but they over-simplified the model training by manually fixing the model structure (*i.e.* the layout of graph nodes).

It is worth mentioning that this paper learn the spatio-temporal graph without using any extra annotations or scripts. Research works which utilize rich annotation for event parsing and interpretation are beyond the scope of this work. In contrast, Marszalek et al. [24] explored the action contexts of natural dynamic scenes with movie scripts. Gupta et al. [11] proposed to learn a visually grounded storyline model from annotated videos, and Pei et al. [31] studied the event grammar model for daily activities based on a predefined set of unary and binary relations. Extra annotations are required for these studies.

3. SPATIO-TEMPORAL AND-OR GRAPH

The STAOG model is defined as $\mathcal{G} = (\mathcal{V}, \mathcal{E})$, where $\mathcal{V}$ represents the four types of nodes and $\mathcal{E}$ the graph edges as Fig. 1. The root node in top verifies the temporal composition, which aggregates scores over anchor frames. Each and-node represents a temporal anchor frame for verifying spatial composition. The or-nodes are derived from each and-node, which are "switch" variables for specifying the activation of their children leaf-nodes. The number of leaf-nodes for each or-node is dynamically learned with an upper limit number m. For simplicity, we use $t = 1, \ldots, T$ to index all and-nodes in the whole STAOG model, $i = 1, \ldots, Z$ for or-nodes and $j = 1, \ldots, n$ for leaf-nodes. We also index the child or-node of and-node A_t as $i \in ch(t)$, and index the child leaf-node of or-node U_i as $j \in ch(i)$. The spatio-temporal graph edges(*i.e.* interactions) are defined between the leaf-nodes associated with different or-nodes. In this section, we describe two factors in detail: the spatio-temporal compositions, and the contextual interactions in both spatial and temporal domains.

3.1 Spatio-Temporal Compositions

We employ Laptev's 3-D corner detector [16] to detect interest points in video sequences, and each interest point is described by HoG (histogram of gradient) and HoF (histogram of optical flow) [17]. Furthermore, we generate a dictionary of spatio-temporal interest points' descriptors, clustered by the k-means method in training stage. Given a video sequence X, we first equally divide it into T temporal segments. The center frame in each video segment is chosen as an initial anchor frame. Each anchor frame is further decomposed into a number of action parts. In our method, we define the action parts based on the video patch representation,

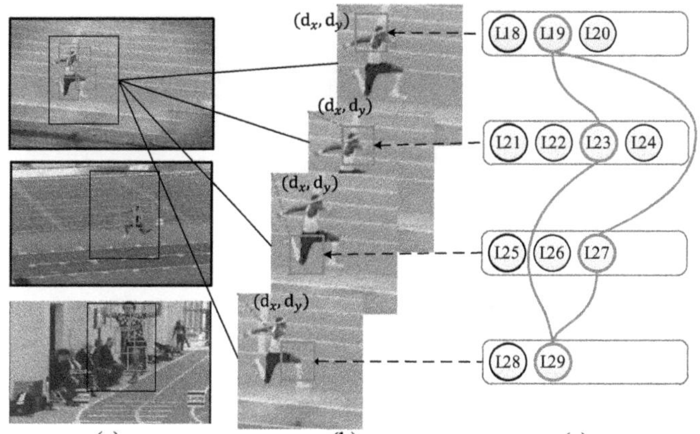

(a) (b) (c)

Figure 2: Illustration of spatial compositions. (a) The black boxes denote the initial positions of action parts. (b) The parts are exhibited which are associated with a set of leaf-nodes. Each (d_x, d_y) indicates the location displacement determined by the model. (c) The activated leaf-nodes are highlighted by red and spatial contextual interactions are defined between the pairwise spatial adjacent leaf nodes.

i.e. 3-D volumes spanning ρ consecutive frames. Thus, for each anchor frame I_t, we observe a sequence of frames centered at I_t, and the sequence denoted as Λ_t is treated as the input for anchor frame processing.

Leaf-node: Each leaf-node L_j represents a local classifier for detecting action parts within video patches and includes two terms: an appearance feature ϕ^l and the spatial displacement feature ϕ^s. Within an anchor frame I_t, the features of action parts are described by the BoW histogram based on the generated dictionary. Assume the action part detected by L_j is localized at position $p_j = (p_j^x, p_j^y)$, then $\phi^l(\Lambda_t, p_j)$ is denoted as the appearance feature. During detection, the locations of action parts are allowed to be perturbed to tackle the spatial deformation. We incorporate the spatial displacement $\phi^s(q_j, p_j) = (d_x, d_y)$ for each action part, which can be computed by maximizing the response of L_j during inference; q_j, representing the initialized position of L_j, is set according to the center-point of the frame. Thus the spatial displacement is defined as $\phi^s(q_j, p_j) = (d_x, d_y)$, where (d_x, d_y) is the displacement.The response of L_j is defined as,

$$R_j^l(\Lambda_t, p_j) = \omega_j^l \cdot \phi^l(\Lambda_t, p_j) - \omega_j^s \cdot \phi^s(q_j, p_j), \qquad (1)$$

where ω_j^l is the parameter for the appearance feature and ω_j^s corresponds to the spatial deformation parameter.

Or-node: Each or-node U_i is proposed to specify an appropriate candidate from its children leaf-nodes. For each leaf-node L_j of U_i's children, the indicator variable $v_j \in \{0, 1\}$ represents whether it is activated or not and each or-node only selects one leaf-node. Briefly, we utilize the indicator vector $\mathbf{v}_i$ for the or-node U_i and each element of $\mathbf{v}_i$ is an indicator variable v_j of the leaf-node L_j. Intuitively, the significant intra-class variance caused by views, background clutters or actors can be captured by different spatial configurations that are determined with the or-nodes. The response of the or-node U_i is defined as,

$$R_i^u(\Lambda_t, \mathbf{v}_i) = \sum_{j \in ch(i)} R_j^l(\Lambda_t, p_j) \cdot v_j, \qquad (2)$$

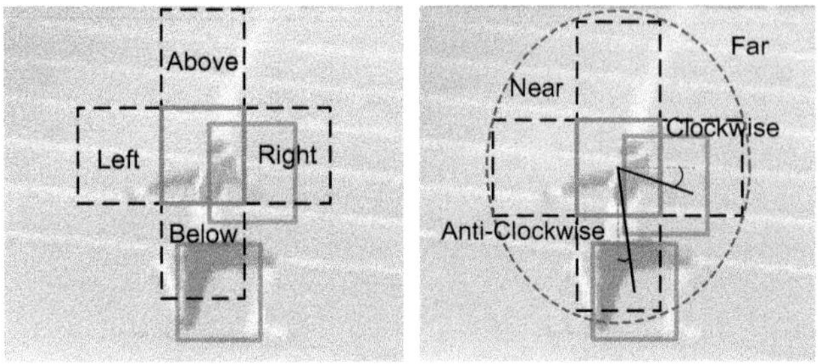

Figure 3: Illustration of the contextual relations for defining spatial edges in the STAOG model. We define the edges between spatial adjacent leaf-nodes with 8 relations according to their spatial layout: above, below, left, right, near, far, clockwise and anti-clockwise.

And-node: Each and-node A_t verifies the holistic appearance of action for the anchor frame I_t, and spatial composition of the or-nodes in its children. We define the configuration vector V_t for all leaf-nodes within the anchor frame, which includes all indicator vectors $\mathbf{v}_i$ corresponding to its children or-nodes U_i. The response of the and-node A_t is defined as,

$$R_t^a(\Lambda_t, V_t) = \omega^a \cdot \phi^a(\Lambda_t) + \sum_{i \in ch(t)} R_i^u(\Lambda_t, \mathbf{v}_i), \tag{3}$$

where $\phi^a(\Lambda_t)$ is the BOW histogram globally extracted from the 3-D volume Λ_t centered at I_t. The second term aggregates the response scores from all or-nodes of A_t's children.

Root-node: The root-node is a global potential function that verifies the temporal compatibility of model, including three terms: the global BoW histogram of the video clip, aggregated scores of its children and-nodes, and temporal displacements of anchor frames. Fig. 4 illustrates the temporal composition by the root-node. We employ the root-node for searching for the best localizations of T anchor frames. We introduce the latent variable Δ_t to indicate the temporal displacement of each anchor frame I_t, calculated during the inference. This implicitly carries the temporal ordering constraints, which are crucial for discriminating human activities.

In particular, the temporal displacement penalty ξ_t punishes the position of the and-node A_t (*i.e.* one anchor frame) shifting far away from the initial anchor point τ_t in time. Once Δ_t is optimized, the position of each anchor frame can be determined by $\tau_t + \Delta_t$ accordingly. We define ξ_t by,

$$\xi_t = -\omega_t^\tau \cdot \Delta_t, \tag{4}$$

where ω_t^τ is the corresponding parameter. The response of the root-node can be then defined as,

$$R^r(X, \mathbf{V}, \boldsymbol{\Delta}) = \omega^r \cdot \phi^r(X) + \sum_{t=1}^{T} R_t^a(\Lambda_t, V_t) + \xi_t, \tag{5}$$

where $\phi^r(X)$ is the BoW histogram feature extracted from the whole video sequence X. $\mathbf{V} = (V_1, \cdots, V_T)$ and $\boldsymbol{\Delta} = (\Delta_1, \cdots, \Delta_T)$ are latent variables in the model for specifying the spatial and temporal configurations.

3.2 Contextual Interactions

Spatial interactions. We impose spatial contextual interactions, *i.e.* spatial edges, between pairwise spatially adjacent leaf-nodes in each anchor frame, as Fig. 2(c) illustrates. Note that we only link the edges between a pair of leaf-nodes that are respectively associated with two different or-nodes.

For one edge connecting two leaf-nodes $(L_j, L_{j'})$, we define it with a set of informative relations, *i.e.* a 8-bin binary feature $\varphi^s(L_j, L_{j'})$: *above, below, left, right, near, far, clockwise* and *anti-clockwise* between two adjacent leaf-nodes. The relations are visualized in Fig. 3. Suppose one edge connects two leaf-nodes $(L_j, L_{j'})$ which detect action parts at positions p_j and $p_{j'}$ respectively. The centered red rectangle represents the location p_j, and the other red rectangles represent the adjacent parts. In the right chart of Fig. 3, the dashed line represents the initial layout of the two leaf-nodes, and the black solid line the adjusted actual layout during inference. Then we define the relations as,

- *near* or *far*: If $p_{j'}$ is fallen into the outer dashed ellipse, it is near to p_j, *i.e.* the bin of near is activated (*i.e.* set as 1); otherwise it is far to p_j.
- *above, below, left* or *right*: The corresponding bin is set as 1 only if the center of $p_{j'}$ is inside the corresponding dashed rectangles.
- *clockwise* or *anti-clockwise*: one of the two relations is activated (*i.e.* set as 1) according to the angle between the dashed line and the black solid line.

The relations intuitively encode the spatial contexts of two action parts detected via the two leaf-nodes with respect to two different or-nodes. The response of the pairwise potentials can be parameterized as,

$$\Gamma_{jj'}^s = \beta_{jj'}^s \cdot \varphi^s(L_j, L_{j'}), \tag{6}$$

where $\beta_{jj'}^s$ is the corresponding 8-bin parameter vector.

Temporal interactions. We also impose the edges in temporal domain in our model to represent the temporal interactions of action parts. The edges connect temporally adjacent leaf-nodes, illustrated in Fig. 4. The edges are connected between any pair of leaf-nodes $(L_j, L_{j'})$ that belong to the same part within the two adjacent anchor frames respectively. A set of temporal relations are collected to concatenate a 4-bin binary feature vector $\varphi^\tau(L_j, L_{j'})$.

Specifically, we adopt four predicates: *intersect, after, meets, interrupt*, inspired by Allen's temporal predicates [2] [27]. These predicates describe relations between two time intervals. The action part detected by one leaf-node L_j for a specific anchor frame is described by the feature ϕ^l extracted from a 3-D volume with time span ρ. Note that we ignore some predicates of ordering such as *before* and *equals*, as the order of temporally adjacent anchor frames is supposed to be fixed. Assume that leaf-node L_j is associated with the anchor frame localized at $\tau_t + \Delta_t$, (initial position plus displacement). The starting and ending time $(f_{L_j}^{start}, f_{L_j}^{end})$ of L_j can be calculated as,

$$\begin{aligned} f_{L_j}^{start} &= \tau_t + \Delta_t - \frac{\rho}{2}, \\ f_{L_j}^{end} &= \tau_t + \Delta_t + \frac{\rho}{2}. \end{aligned} \tag{7}$$

Then we can define the four temporal predicates for the two temporal adjacent leaf-nodes $(L_j, L_{j'})$ as,

$$\begin{aligned} \textit{intersect}(L_j, L_{j'}) &\Longleftrightarrow f_{L_{j'}}^{start} < f_{L_j}^{end}, \\ \textit{after}(L_j, L_{j'}) &\Longleftrightarrow f_{L_j}^{end} < f_{L_{j'}}^{start} < f_{L_j}^{end} + \rho, \\ \textit{meets}(L_j, L_{j'}) &\Longleftrightarrow f_{L_{j'}}^{start} = f_{L_j}^{end}, \\ \textit{interrupt}(L_j, L_{j'}) &\Longleftrightarrow f_{L_j}^{end} + \rho < f_{L_{j'}}^{start}. \end{aligned} \tag{8}$$

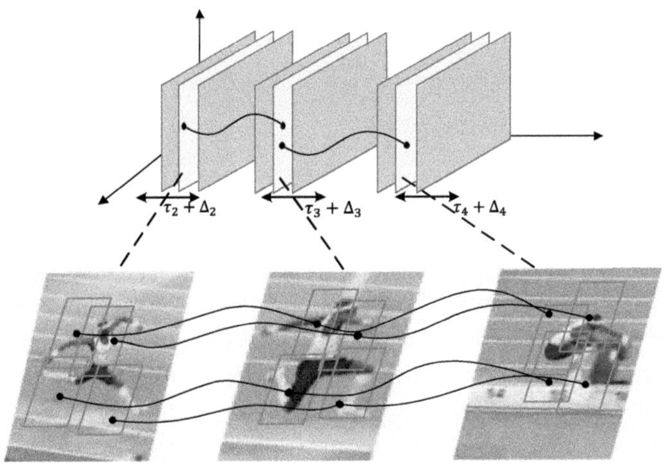

Figure 4: Illustration of temporal compositions. The input video is decomposed into a number of discrete temporal anchor frames. The optimal position of each anchor frame is localized in $\Delta_t + \tau_t$, *i.e.* the temporal displacement Δ_t plus the initial anchor point τ_t. The temporal contextual interactions are defined in temporally adjacent action parts.

Thus, we define the response of one temporal edge linking two leaf-nodes accordingly,

$$\Gamma^{\tau}_{jj'} = \beta^{\tau}_{jj'} \cdot \varphi^{\tau}(L_j, L_{j'}), \tag{9}$$

where $\beta^{\tau}_{jj'}$ is the corresponding 4-bin parameter. If the pairwise leaf-nodes $(L_j, L_{j'})$ satisfies the specific predicate, the corresponding bin is set to 1, otherwise 0.

Therefore, the overall response of the STAOG model is:

$$R^g(X, \mathbf{V}, \mathbf{\Delta}) = R^r(X, \mathbf{V}, \mathbf{\Delta}) + \sum_{j}^{n}\Big(\sum_{j' \in \gamma^s(j)} \Gamma^{s}_{jj'} \cdot v_j \cdot v_{j'} + \sum_{j' \in \gamma^{\tau}(j)} \Gamma^{\tau}_{jj'} \cdot v_j \cdot v_{j'}\Big), \tag{10}$$

where $(\mathbf{V}, \mathbf{\Delta})$ are the hidden variables in the STAOG model. The second term defines the spatio-temporal contextual interactions between the leaf-nodes. $\gamma^s(j)$ is denoted as the set of leaf-node L_j's neighbors which are spatially adjacent to the leaf-node L_j, and $\gamma^{\tau}(j)$ is introduced for the leaf-nodes which are temporally adjacent to the leaf-node L_j. Intuitively, spatial interactions between action parts guarantee the spatial coherence, as well as temporal interactions embedding the temporal contextual relations. Briefly, we refer $\mathcal{L} = (\mathbf{V}, \mathbf{\Delta})$ as the latent variables in the following. The Eq.10 can be briefly written as:

$$R^g(X, \mathcal{L}) = \psi \cdot \Phi(X, \mathcal{L}), \tag{11}$$

where ψ includes the complete parameters of the STAOG model, and $\Phi(X, \mathcal{L})$ denotes the overall feature vector.

4. INFERENCE

The inference task is to detect T optimal temporal anchor frames for one video instance as well as the spatial composition of action parts within each anchor frame. In our approach, we perform a cascaded search that integrates three steps: spatial testing, temporal testing and global verification to maximize the global potential $R^g(X, \mathcal{L})$ defined in Eq.10.

Step 1. Spatial Testing via the and-nodes.

The subgraph of the STAOG model, rooted at one and-node, can be viewed as the spatial composition classifier for localizing action parts in one frame. We first use all existing leaf-nodes to search for candidate actions parts. Assume the leaf-node L_j associated with the frame I_t detects the action part at the position p_j^* by maximizing the response in Eq.1. Each or-node is allowed to activate only one leaf-node, then a possible configuration consisting of action parts is decided by the indicator variables of the or-node, (*i.e.* $\mathbf{v}_i$ for or-node U_i, indicating which leaf-node is activated). In this way, a set of possible configuration hypotheses $\{V_t\}$ are generated for further testing, which ensemble the hypotheses proposed by the or-nodes for the frame I_t. In practice, we limit the maximum number of hypotheses by setting a threshold on $R^a_t(\Lambda_t, V_t)$ in Eq.3.

Algorithm 1 Inference Algorithm

Input:
A learned STAOG model G, the action parts detected by all leaf-nodes by maximizing the response in Eq.1.
Initialization:
The set of possible hypotheses $l_t = \{\}$ for all $t \in 1, \ldots T$ anchor frames.
Iteration:
for all $t = 1 \cdots T$ **do**
  For each and-node A_t, a set of temporal displacement steps Σ is predefined for sliding the possible anchor frames.
  for all $\Delta_t \in \Sigma$ **do**
  (a) initialize the set of pair terms $Q = \{Q_1, \ldots, Q_K\}$ for all or-nodes of A_t's children.
  (b) generate a set of pair terms Q_i for each or-node U_i.
  • **for all** $U_i, i \in ch(t)$ **do**
    for all $L_j, j \in ch(i)$ **do**
      $Q_i = Q_i \cup (i, j)$.
    end for
  • **end for**
  (c) obtain possible hypotheses $V_t = (\mathbf{v}_1, \ldots, \mathbf{v}_K)$ by assembling the indicator variables of K or-nodes according to the set Q.
  (d) The set of possible hypotheses for each specific displacement Δ_t is constructed as $l_t = l_t \cup (\{V_t\}, \Delta_t)$.
  end for
end for
Assemble these hypothesis $\{l_t\}$ for all T anchor frames orderly to generate the set of hypotheses sequence l. Each possible configuration $(\mathbf{V}, \mathbf{\Delta})$ belongs to the set l. The global response of STAOG model can be calculated by Eq.12.
Output:
The latent variables $\mathbf{V}, \mathbf{\Delta}$ and the final score $S_{\psi}(X)$.

Step 2. Temporal Testing via the root-node.

We apply the spatial testing with the and-nodes to localize a number of candidate anchor frames over several frames. The s-cores over candidate anchor frames (proposed by the and-nodes) are aggregated via the root-node for a possible temporal composition. For efficiency, we utilize a fixed number of discrete steps Σ for searching each anchor frame. Several possible hypotheses are then produced with different anchor frame determinations by sliding the discrete steps Σ. In addition, we re-weight the hypotheses at the root-node in Eq.5 by considering the temporal displacements of anchor frames as well as the the global features over the video clip. Intuitively, the hypotheses are represented by the specified latent variables $(\mathbf{V}, \mathbf{\Delta})$.

Step 3. Global Verification.

Given all the hypotheses from the root-node, we apply the global potential function defined in Eq.10 to validate the optimal detection. The objective of the global verification is to cope with the noisy local detections on leaf-nodes. It combines the score of the root-node with the responses of spatial and temporal contextual interactions (edges).

The optimal response $S_\psi(X)$ of the model as well as the latent variables $(\mathbf{V}, \mathbf{\Delta})$ can be calculated as,

$$S_\psi(X) = \max_{\mathbf{V},\mathbf{\Delta}}(\psi \cdot \Phi(X, \mathbf{V}, \mathbf{\Delta})). \quad (12)$$

Algorithm 1 summarizes the overall algorithm of the inference.

5. STRUCTURAL LEARNING

We formulate the structural learning of STAOG model as a joint optimization task for model structure and parameters. We solve this model by a novel latent learning method extended from the CCCP framework [43]. This algorithm iterates to train the model in a dynamic manner: the leaf-nodes can be automatically created or removed to reconfigure the model structure. The model structure is determined by latent variables $\mathcal{L} = (\mathbf{V}, \mathbf{\Delta})$ that are inferred in each step.

Let $D = ((X_1, y_1), (X_2, y_2), \ldots, (X_N, y_N))$ be a set of labeled training samples, with $y_k \in \{1, -1\}$. The feature vector for each sample (X, y) is defined as,

$$\Phi(X, y, \mathcal{L}) = \begin{cases} \Phi(X, \mathcal{L}) & \text{if } y = +1, \\ 0 & \text{if } y = -1. \end{cases} \quad (13)$$

The temporal anchor frames and spatial configurations for each frame can be optimized by maximizing $R^g(X, \mathcal{L})$ in the inference procedure. We refer to $\mathcal{L} = (\mathbf{V}, \mathbf{\Delta})$ as the latent variables, then we redefine Eq.12 as,

$$S_\psi(X) = \max_{y,\mathcal{L}}(\psi \cdot \Phi(X, y, \mathcal{L})), \quad (14)$$

The optimization of this function can be solved by the latent structural SVM framework,

$$\begin{aligned} \min_\psi \frac{1}{2}\|\psi\|^2 + C\sum_{k=1}^{N}[&\max_{y,\mathcal{L}}(\psi \cdot \Phi(X_k, y, \mathcal{L}) + h(y_k, y)) \\ &- \max_{\mathcal{L}}(\psi \cdot \Phi(X_k, y_k, \mathcal{L}))], \end{aligned} \quad (15)$$

where C is a penalty parameter set as 0.003 empirically and $h(y_k, y)$ is the cost function, where $h(y_k, y) = 0$ if $y_k = y$, otherwise 1. The optimization problem described above is not convex in general. Following the CCCP framework, we convert the function in Eq.15 into a convex and concave form as,

$$\begin{aligned} &\min_\psi[\frac{1}{2}\|\psi\|^2 + C\sum_{k=1}^{N}\max_{y,\mathcal{L}}(\psi \cdot \Phi(X_k, y, \mathcal{L}) + h(y_k, y))] \\ &- [C\sum_{k=1}^{N}\max_{\mathcal{L}}(\psi \cdot \Phi(X_k, y_k, \mathcal{L}))] \\ &= \min_\psi[f(\psi) - g(\psi)], \end{aligned} \quad (16)$$

where $f(\psi)$ represents the first two terms, and $g(\psi)$ the last term. This leads to an iterative learning algorithm that alternates estimating model parameters and the hidden variables $\mathcal{L}$. However, we still need to dynamically determine the graph configuration, *i.e.* the production of leaf-nodes associated with or-nodes. An additional step for dynamically reconfiguring structure is added between the two original steps. The procedure is presented as follows.

(I) The model parameter ψ_t obtained in the previous iteration is fixed. We find a hyperplane q_t to upper bound the concave part $g(\psi)$ in Eq. 16. Specifically, q_t is the derivative of $g(\psi)$. Thus, we have $-g(\psi) \leq -g(\psi_t) + (\psi - \psi_t) \cdot q_t, \forall\psi$. The optimal latent

Algorithm 2 Learning algorithm for STAOG model

Input:
Training samples,$D = ((X_1, y_1), (X_2, y_2), \ldots, (X_N, y_N))$.
Output:
The trained STAOG model .
Initialization:
1. Initialize the positions of action parts and anchor frames for all samples.
2. Initialize the latent variables $\mathcal{L}$ and parameters ψ.

repeat
1. Estimate the latent variable $\mathcal{L}_k^* = (\mathbf{V}_k^*, \mathbf{\Delta}_k^*)$ for each positive sample (X_k, y_k) during inference.
2. (a) Localize the anchor frames and action parts using the current latent variables $(\mathbf{V}^*, \mathbf{\Delta}^*)$.
   (b) For each or-node U_i, we obtain a set of feature vectors of its children leaf-nodes for positive samples, and regroup the feature vectors by Spectral clustering.
   (c) Reconfigure leaf-nodes according to clustering results to generate a new structure. Calculate the energy Eq. 17 as $E(\psi_t^d)$.
3. **– if** $E(\psi_t^d) < E(\psi_t)$ **then**
   Accept the new model structure and estimate the parameters $\psi_{t+1} = argmin_\psi(f(\psi + \psi \cdot q_t^d))$.
   – else
   keep the previous model structure. Estimate the parameters $\psi_{t+1} = argmin_\psi(f(\psi + \psi \cdot q_t))$.
   – end if

until The optimization function defined in Eq. 15 converges.

variable $\mathcal{L}_k^*$ is calculated by $\mathcal{L}_k^* = argmax_{\mathcal{L}}(\psi_t \cdot \Phi(X_k, y_k, \mathcal{L}))$ for each positive example. Then the hyperplane is constructed as $q_t = -C\sum_{k=1}^{N}\Phi(X_k, y_k, \mathcal{L}_k^*)$.

(II) In the second step, the STAOG model is adjusted by structural reconfiguration with applying the current model on training examples. The reconfiguration is performed for each part, *i.e.* or-node, independently, with the fixed latent variable $\mathcal{L}_k^* = (V_k^*, \Delta_k^*)$. Note that each action part detected by one leaf-node is mapped to several feature bins at specific positions in the vector $\Phi(X_k, y_k, \mathcal{L}_k^*)$.

For each or-node U_i, we apply its children leaf-nodes for detecting parts in all positive samples. Assume that leaf-node L_j detects an action part on the k-th sample using the feature vector π_j^k, which is a sub-vector of the complete feature vector of k-th sample, $\Phi(X_k, y_k, \mathcal{L}_k^*)$. And we obtain a set of feature vector $\{\pi_j^k\}$ for all samples. The vectors detected by the same leaf-node are first grouped into one cluster, *i.e.* one cluster for one leaf-node. We denote the cluster for the j-th leaf-node as Ω_j. Then we perform the spectral clustering algorithm with the Euclidean distance on vectors of all leaf-nodes of or-node U_i's children for all positive samples, and the similar vectors are grouped together. We re-arrange the feature vectors for all samples based on the newly generated partition. For example, if the feature vector π_j^k is grouped from Ω_j into another cluster Ω_j', we adjust the position of π_j^k in $\Phi(X_k, y_k, \mathcal{L}_k^*)$, *i.e.* by moving the feature bins into the position representing j'-th leaf-node. If Ω_j' is a newly generated cluster, we thus create a new leaf-node accordingly. By analogy, we remove one leaf-node if few samples are grouped into the corresponding cluster. In this way, the structure of U_i is reconfigured with the feature vector rearrangement. In practice, we constrain the extent of structural reconfiguration, *i.e.* only few leaf-nodes can be created or removed in one iteration. We present a toy example in Fig.5 for illustration. In Fig.5(a), a leaf-node associated with the or-node U_7 is created to better handle the intra-class variance; A leaf-node is removed if there is another similar one, (*e.g.* the leaf-node associated with the

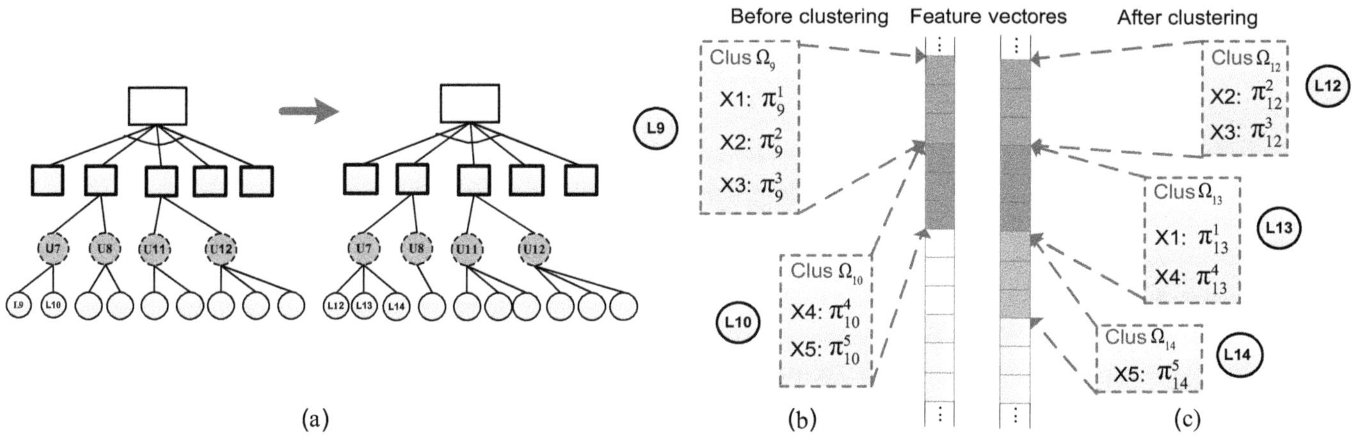

Figure 5: Illustration of discriminative structural learning. We reconfigure the model structure by re-arranging the feature vector, as the example illustrated. Parts of the STAOG model reconfigured in two iterations are shown in (a), where the left one represents the original model and the other one the new model. During this step, the new leaf-node associated with U_7 and U_{11} are created and a leaf-node associated with U_8 is removed. Assume that we use 5 samples, $X_1, \ldots, X_5$, for the structure learning. (b) shows the feature vectors detected by the same leaf-node are first grouped into one cluster, *i.e.* one cluster for one leaf-node. (c) illustrates the feature rearrangement after clustering. For example, the feature vector of sample X_1 is grouped from cluster Ω_9 into cluster Ω_{13}, we move the feature bins π_9^1 into the bins corresponding to the leaf-node L_9. Cluster Ω_{14} is a newly generated cluster, we thus create a new leaf-node accordingly.

or-node U_8). The sub-vector of π_9^1 of sample X_1 is grouped from cluster Ω_9 to cluster Ω_{13}, then the feature bins are moved from π_9^1 to π_{13}^1 as Fig.5(b) shows.

After this structure reconfiguration, we obtain the new feature vector for each sample, $\Phi^d(X_k, y_k, \mathcal{L}_k^*)$, and the hyperplane is re-calculated as $q_t^d = -C\sum_{k=1}^N \Phi^d(X_k, y_k, \mathcal{L}_k^*)$, accordingly.

(III) The newly generated model structure can be represented by the feature vector $\Phi^d(X_k, y_k, \mathcal{L}_k^*)$. The model parameters can be learned by solving $\psi_t^d = argmin_\psi(f(\psi + \psi \cdot q_t^d))$. The optimization task in Eq.15 becomes,

$$\min_{\psi} \frac{1}{2}\|\psi\|^2 + C\sum_{k=1}^{N}[\max_{y,\mathcal{L}}(\psi \cdot \Phi(X_k, y, \mathcal{L}) + h(y_k, y)) - \psi \cdot \Phi^d(X_k, y_k, \mathcal{L}_k^*))]. \quad (17)$$

This is a standard structural SVM problem, which can be solved in the cutting plane method and Sequential Minimal Optimization. The energy Eq.17 can be calculated by $E(\psi_t^d) = f(\psi_t^d) - g(\psi_t^d)$. We accept the new model structure until $E(\psi_t^d) < E(\psi_t)$ and $\psi_{t+1} = \psi_t^d$. Otherwise, we keep the model structure as in the previous iteration and the parameter vector is calculated by $\psi_{t+1} = argmin_\psi(f(\psi + \psi \cdot q_t))$. Thus, we ensure that the optimization function will decrease in each iteration. We repeat the 3-step iteration until convergence. Algorithm 2 summarizes the overall algorithm of learning a STAOG model. In the case of multi-class classification, we use a one-against-rest approach and select the class with the highest score.

6. EXPERIMENTS

We test our STAOG model on two different action recognition databases: UCF YouTube [22] and Olympics Sports [25]. The video resolution is normalized to 320×240. The YouTube dataset contains 11 action categories, which is challenging due to large variation in camera motion, object appearance, pose/view and large intra-class variability. We follow the standard setup using leave-one-out cross validation for a pre-defined set of 25 folds.Average accuracy over all classes is reported as performance measure. The Olympic Sports dataset consists of 16 different sports classes that contain complex motions going beyond simple punctual or repetitive actions. The challenges of Olympic sports arise from background clutters, viewpoints and complex sequence of primitive actions. Each action is performed only by a single actor and represents a temporal sequence of primitive actions (*e.g.* triple-jumping, pole-vault and diving). We use the same train-test split setup and the average precision (AP) for each of the action classes as in [35].

6.1 Implementation

We fix the number of and-nodes (anchor frames) in the STAOG model as $T = 3$ for UCF YouTube dataset, and $T = 5$ for Olympic Sports dataset empirically. We need more anchor frames for Olympic dataset because the actions are more complex and last over more frames. The parameter T can be roughly estimated by the action temporal complexity in general. The number of spatial layout for each anchor frame is fixed as 2×2, and thus $K = 4$ or-nodes for each anchor frame. There are at most $m = 4$ leaf-nodes associated to each or-node. We extract the interest points described by the HOG and HOF features by utilizing the code published in [17] beforehand. The size of one action part (within a 3-D volume) is empirically set to 60×60 pixels spanning $\rho = 15$ frames. The dimension of the generated dictionary is set as 300 for describing action parts in each anchor frame and the global features of the anchor frames. We set the discrete temporal steps searching for anchor frames: $\Sigma = [\pm 2, \pm 4, \pm 6, \pm 8, \pm 10]$. The convergence of our learning algorithm usually takes $9 \sim 10$ iterations.

The experiments are carried out on a PC with Core I5 3.0GHZ CPU and 4GB memory. The average CPU-time used to process a video from Olympic Sports dataset is 200 seconds and 150 for a video in the UCF YouTube dataset. In particular, it takes 7 seconds for processing one frame in Olympic Sports dataset, and 4 seconds for each frame in the UCF YouTube dataset on average. The efficiency of our method is slightly diverse with the densities of the feature points in the video sequence.

	Liu et al [22].	Zhang et al [44].	Ikizler-Cinbis et al [12].	Dense trajectories [36].	Ours-1	Ours-2	Ours(full)
b_shoot	53.0%	**98.0%**	48.5%	43.0%	58.4%	62.0%	77.9%
bike	73.0%	74.0%	75.2%	**91.7%**	82.1%	87.3%	88.6%
dive	81.0%	80.0%	95.0%	**99.0%**	98.4%	98.6%	98.8%
golf	86.0%	68.0%	95.0%	97.0%	95.7%	95.3%	**97.4%**
h_ride	72.0%	65.0%	73.0%	85.0%	81.3%	86.0%	**88.0%**
s_juggle	54.0%	67.0%	53.0%	76.0%	66.0%	81.6%	**82.2%**
swing	57.0%	71.0%	66.0%	**88.0%**	85.2%	84.1%	85.4%
t_swing	80.0%	68.0%	77.0%	71.0%	69.6%	80.0%	**80.7%**
t_jump	79.0%	80.0%	93.0%	94.0%	90.2%	94.7%	**95.8%**
v_spike	73.3%	77.0%	85.0%	95.0%	89.7%	90.6%	**96.4%**
walk	75.0%	54.0%	66.7%	87.0%	85.2%	86.2%	**87.4%**
Accuracy	71.2%	72.9%	75.2 %	84.2%	82.0%	**86.0%**	**88.9%**

Table 1: Accuracy per action class and average accuracy for all classes on the YouTube dataset [22].

Figure 6: Example inference results on three different action models *e.g.* basketball-layup (a), clean-and-jerk (b) and triple-jump(c) learned on the Olympic Sports dataset and each of action category includes two instances. The red boxes in each frame represent the discovered discriminative action parts. Our model successfully localizes the accurate anchor frames across the instances in the long action videos. In addition, it is noticed that the large intra-class variabilities can be captured by our model.

	Nicbles et al [25].	Tang et al [35].	Ours(full)
h-jump	27.0%	18.4%	**35.6%**
l-jump	71.7%	81.8%	**86.4%**
t-jump	10.1%	16.1%	**36.2%**
p-vault	**90.8%**	84.9%	84.3%
g-vault	**86.1%**	85.7%	83.1%
s-put	37.3%	43.3%	**56.8%**
snatch	54.2%	88.6%	**89.0%**
c-jerk	70.6%	78.2%	**83.3%**
j-throw	**85.0%**	79.5%	78.1%
h-throw	71.2%	70.5%	**75.4%**
d-throw	47.3%	48.9%	**53.3%**
d-platform	**95.4%**	93.7%	92.8%
d-board	**84.3%**	79.3%	76.5%
basketball	82.1%	85.5%	**86.7%**
bowling	53.0%	**64.3%**	62.0%
t-serve	33.4%	49.6%	**62.3%**
mAP	62.5%	66.8%	**71.4%**

Table 2: Average Precision(AP) values on the Olympic Sports dataset [25].

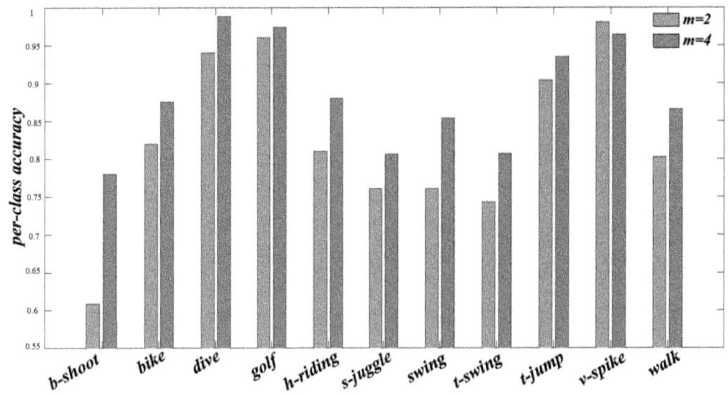

Figure 7: Empirical analysis for different settings of spatial compositions, where we set different maximum numbers m of leaf-nodes under the or-nodes. Each pillar represents the accuracy for one action category. The color indicates the results with different settings, $m = 2$ or $m = 4$.

6.2 Results and Comparisons

Compared with the recently proposed methods on the YouTube dataset, our model outperforms the state-of-the-art: we achieve the accuracy of 88.9% in YouTube dataset, the reported results of the competing algorithms are: 71.2% in [22], 72.9% in [44],75.2% in [12] and 84.2% in [36]. The accuracy scores for all categories are reported in Table 1. Our method outperforms on 7 out of the 11 categories which have relatively large intra-class variance or background disturbance. In the Olympic Sports dataset, we obtain better AP scores for 10 out of the 16 categories, and overall AP score 71.4%, better than the previous methods [35, 25]. The competing method proposed by Tang et al. [35] utilizes the variable-duration HMM for learning the temporal structure. Our results show that our compositional model with the explicit spatial and temporal relations can achieve better performance. The detailed results are reported in Table 2.

Figure. 6 illustrates the inference results on three action categories from the Olympic Sports dataset, each of which includes two instances. Our model also localizes the action parts in the anchor frames, as they are discriminative in appearance and motion. These results demonstrate well the capability of our model, since the scenarios of actions contain the very realistic challenges in video action recognition. The spatial compositions defined over the and-nodes enable us to handle pose/view variations and background disturbances. The temporal compositions are effective to localize anchor frames in videos against various motion frequency, temporal locations and video length.

For further evaluation, we conduct three empirical analysis in different model settings as follows.

(I) We simplify the temporal compositions by discarding the displacement Δ_t for each anchor frame, *i.e.* fixing the temporal structure. We report AP scores of this model setting in the fourth column of Table 1, named as "Ours-1". The average accuracy is 82%,6.9% less than our complete model.

(II) We also evaluate the benefit of spatio-temporal contextual interactions. Our model can be simplified into a tree structure by removing the interactions. The accuracies are shown in the sixth column of Table 1, named as "Ours-2". We can observe that the contextual interactions make the accuracies increase 2.9% on average. The increased performance also speaks in favour for our model, as it shows that through better associations between the anchor frames and action parts, it is possible to achieve better accuracies.

(III) One may be interested in how the performances are improved by introducing the or-nodes in spatial compositions, which is one of the key components in the STAOG model. In this experiment, we set different maximum numbers m of leaf-nodes under the or-nodes, *i.e.* how many leaf-nodes at most can be created for the model. We compare the results on the YouTube dataset in Fig. 7, and observe that $m = 4$ achieves the better results in general than $m = 2$, 82.4%. In practice, the number m is not sensitive, as the exact number of leaf-nodes is decided by the clustering on data during the structural learning.

7. CONCLUSION

This paper studies a novel hierarchical model for human action recognition, in the form of a configurable Spatio-Temporal And-Or Graph. This model is shown to handle well realistic challenges in action recognition. Moreover, we consider two aspects to improve our method. First, the model can be integrated with high level semantic information to represent multi-agent complex events. Second, we plan to speed up the algorithm for large-scale processing.

8. REFERENCES

[1] M. Albanese, R. Chellappa, N. P. Cuntoor, V. Moscato, A. Picariello, V. S. Subrahmanian, and O. Udrea. A constrained probabilistic petri net framework for human activity detection in video. *IEEE Transactions on Multimedia*, 10(6):982–996, 2008.

[2] J. F. Allen and G. Ferguson. Actions and events in interval temporal logic. *J. Log. Comput.*, 4(5):531–579, 1994.

[3] M. R. Amer, D. Xie, M. Zhao, S. Todorovic, and S. C. Zhu. Cost-sensitive top-down/bottom-up inference for multiscale activity recognition. In *ECCV (4)*, pages 187–200, 2012.

[4] W. Brendel and S. Todorovic. Learning spatiotemporal graphs of human activities. In *ICCV*, pages 778–785, 2011.

[5] L. Cao, Z. Liu, and T. S. Huang. Cross-dataset action detection. In *CVPR*, pages 1998–2005, 2010.

[6] W. Choi, K. Shahid, and S. Savarese. Learning context for collective activity recognition. In *CVPR*, 2011.

[7] P. Dollár, V. Rabaud, G. Cottrell, and S. Belongie. Behavior recognition via sparse spatio-temporal features. In *VS-PETS*, October 2005.

[8] X. Duan, L. Lin, and H. Chao. Discovering video shot categories by unsupervised stochastic graph partition. *IEEE Transactions on Multimedia*, 15(1):167–180, 2013.

[9] T. V. Duong, H. H. Bui, D. Q. Phung, and S. Venkatesh. Activity recognition and abnormality detection with the switching hidden semi-markov model. In *CVPR (1)*, pages 838–845, 2005.

[10] P. F. Felzenszwalb, R. B. Girshick, D. A. McAllester, and D. Ramanan. Object detection with discriminatively trained part-based models. *IEEE Trans. Pattern Anal. Mach. Intell.*, 32(9):1627–1645, 2010.

[11] A. Gupta, P. Srinivasan, J. Shi, and L. S. Davis. Understanding videos, constructing plots learning a visually grounded storyline model from annotated videos. In *CVPR*, pages 2012–2019, 2009.

[12] N. Ikizler-Cinbis and S. Sclaroff. Object, scene and actions: Combining multiple features for human action recognition. In *ECCV (1)*, pages 494–507, 2010.

[13] L. Jiang, A. G. Hauptmann, and G. Xiang. Leveraging high-level and low-level features for multimedia event detection. In *ACM Multimedia*, pages 449–458, 2012.

[14] Y.-G. Jiang, Q. Dai, X. Xue, W. Liu, and C.-W. Ngo. Trajectory-based modeling of human actions with motion reference points. In *ECCV (5)*, 2012.

[15] A. Kläser, M. Marszalek, and C. Schmid. A spatio-temporal descriptor based on 3d-gradients. In *BMVC*, 2008.

[16] I. Laptev. On space-time interest points. *International Journal of Computer Vision*, 64(2-3):107–123, 2005.

[17] I. Laptev, M. Marszalek, C. Schmid, and B. Rozenfeld. Learning realistic human actions from movies. In *CVPR*, 2008.

[18] Z. Li, Y. Fu, T. S. Huang, and S. Yan. Real-time human action recognition by luminance field trajectory analysis. In *ACM Multimedia*, pages 671–676, 2008.

[19] L. Lin, H. Gong, L. Li, and L. Wang. Semantic event representation and recognition using syntactic attribute graph grammar. *Pattern Recognition Letters*, 30(2):180–186, 2009.

[20] L. Lin, X. Wang, W. Yang, and J. Lai. Learning contour-fragment-based shape model with and-or tree representation. In *CVPR*, pages 135–142, 2012.

[21] L. Lin, T. Wu, J. Porway, and Z. Xu. A stochastic graph grammar for compositional object representation and recognition. *Pattern Recognition*, 42(7):1297–1307, 2009.

[22] J. Liu, J. Luo, and M. Shah. Recognizing realistic actions from videos. In *CVPR*, pages 1996–2003, 2009.

[23] Z. Ma, Y. Yang, Y. Cai, N. Sebe, and A. G. Hauptmann. Knowledge adaptation for ad hoc multimedia event detection with few exemplars. In *ACM Multimedia*, pages 469–478, 2012.

[24] M. Marszalek, I. Laptev, and C. Schmid. Actions in context. In *CVPR*, 2009.

[25] J. C. Niebles, C.-W. Chen, and F.-F. Li. Modeling temporal structure of decomposable motion segments for activity classification. In *ECCV (2)*, pages 392–405, 2010.

[26] M. Raptis, I. Kokkinos, and S. Soatto. Discovering discriminative action parts from mid-level video representations. In *CVPR*, pages 1242–1249, 2012.

[27] M. S. Ryoo and J. K. Aggarwal. Spatio-temporal relationship match: Video structure comparison for recognition of complex human activities. In *ICCV*, pages 1593–1600, 2009.

[28] S. Sadanand and J. J. Corso. Action bank: A high-level representation of activity in video. In *CVPR*, pages 1234–1241, 2012.

[29] S. Satkin and M. Hebert. Modeling the temporal extent of actions. In *ECCV (1)*, pages 536–548, 2010.

[30] P. Scovanner, S. Ali, and M. Shah. A 3-dimensional sift descriptor and its application to action recognition. In *ACM Multimedia*, pages 357–360, 2007.

[31] Z. Si, M. Pei, B. Yao, and S.-C. Zhu. Unsupervised learning of event and-or grammar and semantics from video. In *ICCV*, pages 41–48, 2011.

[32] Y. Song, L.-P. Morency, and R. Davis. Multi-view latent variable discriminative models for action recognition. In *CVPR*, pages 2120–2127, 2012.

[33] Y. Song, S. Tang, Y.-T. Zheng, T.-S. Chua, Y. Zhang, and S. Lin. Exploring probabilistic localized video representation for human action recognition. *Multimedia Tools Appl.*, 58(3):663–685, 2012.

[34] J. Sun, X. Wu, S. Yan, L. F. Cheong, T.-S. Chua, and J. Li. Hierarchical spatio-temporal context modeling for action recognition. In *CVPR*, pages 2004–2011, 2009.

[35] K. Tang, F.-F. Li, and D. Koller. Learning latent temporal structure for complex event detection. In *CVPR*, pages 1250–1257, 2012.

[36] H. Wang, A. Kläser, C. Schmid, and C.-L. Liu. Action recognition by dense trajectories. In *CVPR*, pages 3169–3176, 2011.

[37] S. Wang, Y. Yang, Z. Ma, X. Li, C. Pang, and A. G. Hauptmann. Action recognition by exploring data distribution and feature correlation. In *CVPR*, pages 1370–1377, 2012.

[38] X. Wang and L. Lin. Dynamical and-or graph learning for object shape modeling and detection. In *NIPS*, pages 242–250, 2012.

[39] Y. Wang and G. Mori. Hidden part models for human action recognition: Probabilistic versus max margin. *IEEE Trans. Pattern Anal. Mach. Intell.*, 33(7):1310–1323, 2011.

[40] B. Yao and S. C. Zhu. Learning deformable action templates from cluttered videos. In *ICCV*, pages 1507–1514, 2009.

[41] G. Yu, J. Yuan, and Z. Liu. Real-time human action search using random forest based hough voting. In *ACM Multimedia*, pages 1149–1152, 2011.

[42] J. Yuan, Z. Liu, and Y. Wu. Discriminative video pattern search for efficient action detection. *IEEE Trans. Pattern Anal. Mach. Intell.*, 33(9):1728–1743, 2011.

[43] A. L. Yuille and A. Rangarajan. The concave-convex procedure. *Neural Computation*, 15(4):915–936, 2003.

[44] Y. Zhang, X. Liu, M.-C. Chang, W. Ge, and T. Chen. Spatio-temporal phrases for activity recognition. In *ECCV (3)*, pages 707–721, 2012.

[45] X. Zhou, X. Zhuang, S. Yan, S.-F. Chang, M. Hasegawa-Johnson, and T. S. Huang. Sift-bag kernel for video event analysis. In *ACM Multimedia*, pages 229–238, 2008.

[46] G. Zhu, M. Yang, K. Yu, W. Xu, and Y. Gong. Detecting video events based on action recognition in complex scenes using spatio-temporal descriptor. In *ACM Multimedia*, pages 165–174, 2009.

[47] S. C. Zhu and D. Mumford. A stochastic grammar of images. *Foundations and Trends in Computer Graphics and Vision*, 2(4):259–362, 2006.

Exploring Discriminative Pose Sub-Patterns for Effective Action Classification*

Xu Zhao*† zhaoxu@sjtu.edu.cn
Yuncai Liu* whomliu@sjtu.edu.cn
Yun Fu† yunfu@ece.neu.edu

*Department of Automation
Shanghai Jiao Tong University, Shanghai, 200240

†Department of ECE
Northeastern University, Boston, MA 02115

ABSTRACT

Articulated configuration of human body parts is an essential representation of human motion, therefore is well suited for classifying human actions. In this work, we propose a novel approach to exploring the discriminative pose sub-patterns for effective action classification. These pose sub-patterns are extracted from a predefined set of 3D poses represented by hierarchical motion angles. The basic idea is motivated by the two observations: (1) There exist representative sub-patterns in each action class, from which the action class can be easily differentiated. (2) These sub-patterns frequently appear in the action class. By constructing a connection between frequent sub-patterns and the discriminative measure, we develop the SSPI, namely, the Support Sub-Pattern Induced learning algorithm for simultaneous feature selection and feature learning. Based on the algorithm, discriminative pose sub-patterns can be identified and used as a series of "magnetic centers" on the surface of normalized super-sphere for feature transform. The "attractive forces" from the sub-patterns determine the direction and step-length of the transform. This transformation makes a feature more discriminative while maintaining dimensionality invariance. Comprehensive experimental studies conducted on a large scale motion capture dataset demonstrate the effectiveness of the proposed approach for action classification and the superior performance over the state-of-the-art techniques.

Categories and Subject Descriptors

I.5.4 [**Pattern Recognition**]: Applications; H.2.8 [**Database Applications**]: Data Mining

Keywords

Action classification; sub-pattern mining; feature transform

*This work is supported in part by the NSF CNS award 1135660 and 1314484, Office of Naval Research award N00014-12-1-0125 and N00014-12-1-1028, Air Force Office of Scientific Research award FA9550-12-1-0201, U.S. Army Research Office grant W911NF-13-1-0160, National Basic Research Program (973) under No. 2011CB302206 and NSFC grant under No. 61273285.

MM'13, October 21–25, 2013, Barcelona, Spain.

http://dx.doi.org/10.1145/2502081.2502094.

1. INTRODUCTION

Human Motion Analysis (HMA) has been an interdisciplinary research topic for decades and is attracting continuing interests from multimedia, computer vision, computer graphics and medical research communities, due to the potential applications in human-computer interaction, clinical studies, content-based video indexing, intelligent surveillance, assisted living and so on [15, 24]. Action classification is an important research thread of HMA and constructs the basis for many of the above mentioned applications.

Most of the action classification works focus on recognizing actions using visual appearance features extracted from videos [14, 27, 23] or still images [32, 22, 34]. Only a small number of early works [31, 16] and recent works [22, 12, 32] introduce pose as a cue, not straightforwardly, for action classification. Although extracting low level appearance features is much easier than obtaining high-level pose parameters, we argue that human body pose, the articulated configuration of human body parts, is essential to explain the inherent nature of human motion, and therefore contains more discriminative information for action classification.

The critical role of pose information for action recognition had been validated by the Johansson experiment [20], which shows that using 10-12 bright spots, describing the motions of the main joints of a living body, can evoke a compelling impression of human walking, running, dancing, etc. In comparison, appearance features are noisy and not robust to the change in external imaging condition. Most importantly, appearance is not an essential description of human motion. Furthermore, recent advances in human pose estimation [29, 11, 33, 5, 4] facilitate the use of pose as input for action recognition in a practical vision system. Motivated by the above facts, in this work, we focus on using human pose as a feature and exploring its potential effectiveness for the action classification task.

Different from visual features of which each component carries few explicit semantical meaning about human motion, pose feature has several noticeable properties: (1) *Physicality*. Each component of the pose feature has corresponding physical significance. In this work, hierarchical motion angles are introduced to represent body pose (see Section 5.1). (2) *Clarity*. Pose feature is concise and noise free; therefore it is well suited for revealing the implicit relationship between pose components and action classes. (3) *Visibility*. The intermediate and final results can be visualized to show the correlation between pose patterns and action classes through qualitative analysis. Such properties enlighten us about the different ways that pose features can be utilized. The idea is inspired by how human beings perceive actions.

As the common human experience, action class information can be easily captured from partial observations, for example, with some parts of the body occluded. If a whole body pose is viewed as

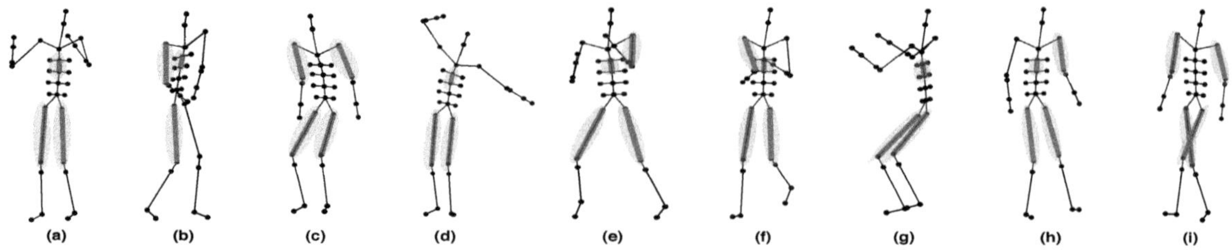

Figure 1: Body pose randomly selected from 9 action classes: chicken dance, golf swing, jump, cartwheel, boxing, run, motorcycle, pick up and walk respectively from (a) to (i). The ellipse occluded red parts are the representative pose sub-patterns. We aim at exploring the discriminative power of the sub-patterns and employing them for efficient action classification.

a full pattern, the partial observation corresponds to a sub-pattern, which is a physical configuration of some local body parts. Then, there exist representative sub-patterns in each action class, which can be used to differentiate it from other classes. As can be seen from Figure 1, one can recognize the actions very likely by just seeing the ellipse occluded body parts. To effectively utilize pose sub-pattern for action classification, however the following critical questions need to be further addressed.

- How to find the representative pose sub-patterns for a specific action class?
- How the pose sub-patterns can help improve the classification performance?
- How to evaluate the discriminative power of pose sub-patterns within the context of action classification?

In this paper, we answer the above questions systematically and provide solutions using a novel feature transform framework.

Extracting sub-patterns from full poses is an exponential complexity problem. Fortunately, benefiting from the physicality property of pose features, existing frequent pattern mining algorithm can be used to generate Support Sub-Patterns (SSP). This is motivated by the fact that the representative sub-patterns of a particular action class appear more frequently than other sub-patterns in that action class. For example, for action "Boxing", the typical sub-pattern "arms held up to defend" appears most frequently therefore it is recognized as SSP. Seeing just this sub-pattern can provide lots of valuable information about the entire action "Boxing" (see Figure 9). Thus, by mining frequent patterns, the scalability issue for classification in large pose databases could be solved.

Employing the obtained sub-patterns to make classification is the heart of this work. We propose a Support Sub-Pattern Induced (SSPI) feature transform framework. As a completely new approach, SSPI differs from two typical feature transform frameworks, namely, feature combination and feature reduction. These frameworks map the features to a higher and lower dimensional space respectively to increase the discriminative power of the transformed features. In contrast, SSPI does not change the feature dimensionality and the transform occurs in the bits correlated with the corresponding SSP. Namely, if a full pose pattern contains a SSP, this SSP will dominate a change to the original full pattern. In other words, SSPs perform like a series of fixed "magnetic centers" on the surface of a normalized feature super-sphere. Each center leads to a moving of the full pattern along the surface and the resultant force from all the SSPs forms the final transformed feature. As far as we know, this is the first work conducting feature transform in this way.

During the feature transformation, there are two critical issues. (1) What's the criterion for evaluating such a transform? (2) How much "force" from the SSPs should be acted on the full pattern? Because our final aim is to improve the accuracy of action classification, Fisher score is chosen as the criterion to construct the objective function. And, each SSP is coupled with a weight, which is used to calculate the strength of the attraction. The weights are the parameters of the Fisher score function and can be learned from pose data by maximizing the objective function. Once the weights are determined, the feature will be transformed using the Fisher score optimum. One can also evaluate the discriminative power of a SSP according to its impact on the objective function.

To summarize, the main contributions of this work are as the follows:

First, utilizing the "physicality", "clearness" and "visibility" properties of pose data , we introduce frequent pattern mining to explore Support Sub-Patterns. The SSPs are representative sub-patterns of the action classes and can be applied to action classification, even action search, pose estimation and human detection.

Secondly, we propose a SSP induced feature transform approach, through which the feature keeps the original dimensionality but is converted into a more discriminative formation for classification via SSP induced feature learning. This framework could be applied to more general feature transform applications.

Thirdly, for the SSPI framework, we construct the objective function using the Fisher score optimum. An efficient two-phases optimal algorithm for searching the optimal weights of the SSPs is developed. Experiments on large scale pose databases demonstrate the superior performance of the proposed algorithm on the action classification task.

2. RELATED WORK

Action Classification. A large number of methods have been proposed for recognizing human actions. Here we focus on methods most related to our proposed work. Readers interested in more details can refer to some recent reviews [1, 24] on this topic.

Methods that use pose as a feature for action classification usually exploit the space-time trajectories to interpret human activities. Campbell et al. [6] recognized human actions by representing them as curves in low-dimensional phase spaces. Template matching is used to find action labels. Similar methodologies can be found in [26, 35, 28, 3], where either trajectories formed by joints [28, 35, 3] or curvature patterns of trajectories formed from body parts [26] are treated as features. Slightly different from the explicit trajectory based methods, in [31], motion of body parts is treated as a set of signals to describe sequential changes of feature values. In a much earlier work [30], Siskind animated a line-drawing of a person as pose input and classified actions such as dropping, throwing, picking up, and putting down by analyzing the event logic.

In sum, a common practice of these types of work is to mainly consider the temporal behaviors of body pose but not the relationship between the spatial configuration of poses and action classes.

In this work, the proposed idea of SSPs is used for mining the internal correlation between spatial sub-patterns and action labels.

Another recent research trend to employ pose as a cue in action recognition is closely related to the concept of "poselets" [22, 12, 32]. The basic idea is that semantically similar actions or poses should belong to clusters defined by the same poselets, no matter what the appearance looks like. In doing so, pose becomes an efficient and complementary cue of appearance features for action recognition. These kind of methods are advantageous in that they combine more sources of information. However, the noisy nature of image data and the required manual annotation make it difficult to explore the relationship between pose patterns and action class labels in a meaningful way.

Pattern Based Classifcation. Pattern based classification is a focused research topic in data mining field, where the discriminative frequent patterns usually are taken as features to build high quality classifiers [21, 8, 9, 13]. Frequent sub-patterns reveal the associations between data attributes, therefore carrying rich semantic information about the data. The importance of frequent pattern in classification tasks has been thoroughly investigated in [8].

The construction of a feature representation using frequent patterns is the core of pattern based classification. Cheng et al. [8, 9] achieved this by feature combination, namely, mapping the original features into a higher dimensional space by combing the frequent patterns with the original single features. The critical part of this procedure is feature selection, by which the most discriminative frequent patterns are selected to construct the final feature representation. In [8], feature selection is separately conducted from the generation of frequent patterns. To speed up the algorithm and mine highly discriminative patterns, direct discriminative pattern mining approaches are proposed in [9, 13, 21].

Besides aforementioned methods, associative classification is another class of frequent pattern based classification approaches. It is rule based and the association between frequent patterns and class label is used for classification [19]. It's also worth mentioning that Yuan et al. [36] found the visual patterns with semantic correlations by mining frequent patterns from image databases.

Our work is different from above approaches in the following aspects: (1) Feature transform is not a simple feature combination. Changes occurr only in the bits correlated with the corresponding frequent patterns and the feature is length invariant. (2) Feature selection is implicitly integrated into the feature transform procedure by learning the transform weights of the frequent patterns. (3) The discriminative power of the frequent patterns can be explicitly evaluated according to the learned transform model.

3. PROBLEM FORMULATION

In the context of action classification, assume a pose dataset has k categorical attributes, each of which is a motion angle and has a set of values. These pose data points fall into m action classes $\mathcal{C} = \{c_1, \cdots, c_m\}$. Thus, each $(angle, value)$ pair can be mapped to a distinct item in $\mathcal{P} = \{o_1, \cdots, o_d\}$. Since pose angles are represented by continuous numerical attributes, the values should first be discretized. Here we adopt binary coding. Suppose a pair $(ang, val) \mapsto o_i$, where ang is a joint angle and val is a value. Let $\mathbf{x}$ be the pose vector of a data point s. Then $x_i = 1$ if $ang(s) = val$; $x_i = 0$ if $ang(s) \neq val$. In this way, the dataset is represented in $\mathbf{B}^d$ as $D = \{\mathbf{x}_i, y_i\}_{i=1}^n$, where $\mathbf{x}_i \in \mathbf{B}^d$, $y_i \in \mathcal{C}$ and $x_{ij} \in \mathbf{B} = \{0, 1\}$, $\forall i \in [1, n], j \in [1, d]$. Therefore, after discretization and binary mapping, a pose data point is mapped to a binary pattern, which is a convenient form to use for sub-pattern exploration. For the ease of analysis, in the following we define some related concepts built on the basis of pose patterns [8].

Definition 1. (Sub-Pattern) A sub-pattern $\alpha = \{o_{s_1}, \cdots, o_{s_k}\}$ is a subset of $\mathcal{P}$, where $s_i \in \{1, \cdots, d\}$, $\forall i \in [1, k]$. A single pattern $o_i \in \mathcal{P}$ is the special case of sub-pattern. Therefore, given a dataset $D = \{\mathbf{x}_i\}$, the set of data points that contains sub-pattern α is denoted as $D_\alpha = \{\mathbf{x}_i | x_{is_j} = 1, \forall o_{s_j} \in \alpha\}$. An equal-length binary expression of a sub-pattern α is noted as $\mathbf{x}_\alpha \in \mathbf{B}^d$ with $x_\alpha = 1$ for $\forall o \in \alpha$ and $x_\alpha = 0$ for $\forall o \notin \alpha$.

In this work, we aim to explore the discriminative pose sub-patterns for action classes. The support sub-patterns related to the action class c are defined as:

Definition 2. (Support Sub-Pattern (SSP)) For a dataset D_c with class label c, a sub-pattern α is supportive for this class if $\theta = \frac{|D_{\alpha,c}|}{|D_c|} \geq \theta_0$, where θ_0 is the minimum support threshold with $0 \leq \theta_0 \leq 1$, hence θ is the relative support of α. The set of support sub-patterns of class c is denoted as $\mathcal{SP}_c$.

SSP actually defines the sub-patterns that most frequently appear in each action class as the supportive patterns for classification. This is consistent with our daily observation that there exist some typical poses in each action class, which can describe the action very well. Additionally, these poses often occur with high frequency while any subject performs the action. Therefore these poses, or more precisely, the pose sub-patterns, are discriminative and representative of the action class. Very often one can recognize an action class by just observing a local pose, for example, a pose of a leg or an arm when other parts of the human body are occluded. The observed sub-parts that can help people recognize actions correspond to the SSP. We will make further explorations of SSPs in the following section.

4. FEATURE TRANSFORM

In this section, we focus on the feature transform for effective classification based on SSPs. Here, feature transform is an operation performed on the original pose data points. For a data point $\mathbf{x}$, a feature transform could be any function $\{f : \mathbf{x} \mapsto \mathbf{x}', f \in \mathbb{F}\}$ from functional space $\mathbb{F}$. After the transformation, one can expect much better classification performance in the transformed feature space than the original one. We examine two kinds of feature transform methods in the following sections.

4.1 Conventional SSP Based Feature Combination

As introduced in [8], the conventional frequent patterns based feature transform is a form of non-linear feature combination over the set of single features. Under this transform, given a dataset $D = \{\mathbf{x}_i, y_i\}_{i=1}^n$ and a set of frequent sub-patterns $\mathcal{SP}$ collected from all the classes, D is mapped to a higher dimensional feature space, by integrating the SSP and the original items. Hence the feature space $\mathbf{B}^d$ ($d = |\mathcal{P}|$) is enlarged to $\mathbf{B}^{d'}$ with features taken in $\mathcal{P} \cup (\cup_{i=c_1}^{c_m} \mathcal{SP}_i)$. After the transform, the data is denoted as $D' = \{\mathbf{x}_i', y_i\}_{i=1}^n$, where $\mathbf{x}_i' \in \mathbf{B}^{d'}$ and

$$d' = |\mathcal{P} \cup (\cup_{i=c_1}^{c_m} \mathcal{SP}_i)|. \quad (1)$$

Then, what is the philosophy behind the conventional frequent pattern based classification? To make the picture more clear, we summarize the motivations as follows according to [8].

- The discriminative power of a SSP is much higher than the original single features because they capture more underlying semantics of the data. It's true for human action classification, as explained in Section 3.

- The dimensionality of feature space is increased to d' from d (see Eq. (1)). This will also likely increase the chance of including discriminative features.
- The discriminative power of low frequency sub-patterns is confined by a small value because of their limited coverage in the dataset. Symmetrically, it's true for the very high frequency sub-patterns due to their commonness in the data.

The implementation of the conventional SSP based feature combination is straightforward. The detailed description is given in Algorithm 1. One can refer to [8] for the proof of the above statements and the procedures for feature selection mentioned in the Algorithm 1.

Algorithm 1 Conventional SSP Based Feature Combination

```
Input: Original dataset D = {x_i, y_i}_{i=1}^n, min_sup : θ_0
Output: Transformed dataset D' = {x'_i, y_i}_{i=1}^n
for c_i = c_1 to c_m do
    SP_{c_i} = Apriori(D_{c_i}, θ_0)
    ▷ Apriori represents the algorithm of frequent pattern mining
end for
SP_s = FeatureSel(∪_{i=c_1}^{c_m} SP_i, param)
    ▷ FeatureSel functionalized as the procedure for feature selection, param is the related parameters.
for all x_i ∈ D do
    x'_i = CheckSPP(x_i, SP_s), |x'_i| = |x_i| + |SP_s|
    ▷ CheckSPP checks whether the SPPs appear in x_i or not. If appear, the corresponding additional indicator bit is set as 1; if not, set it as 0.
end for
return D' = {x'_i, y_i}_{i=1}^n
```

4.2 SSP Induced Feature Transform

SSP based feature combination improves the classification performance by explicitly adding additional bits. It extends the features to a much higher space meanwhile loads more computational burden onto classifier. To avoid explicit feature combination and feature selection, we propose a novel SSP Induced (SSPI) feature transform algorithm, by which the feature length is kept invariant and the feature selection is implicitly incorporated into the learning process for feature transform.

4.2.1 *Fisher Score Oriented Feature Learning*

Fisher score is a general measure for feature selection [17]. However, in our algorithm, it is used as an orientation for learning based feature transform. Given the original pose data set $D = \{\mathbf{x}_i, y_i\}_{i=1}^n, \mathbf{x}_i \in \mathbf{B}^d$. The Fisher score is defined as

$$F(\mathbf{X}) = \mathrm{tr}\{(\tilde{\mathbf{S}}_b)(\tilde{\mathbf{S}}_t + \gamma\mathbf{I})^{-1}\}, \tag{2}$$

where $\mathbf{X} \in \mathbf{B}^{d \times n}$ and γ is a positive regularization parameter. $\tilde{\mathbf{S}}_b$ is called between-class scatter matrix and $\tilde{\mathbf{S}}_t$ is called total scatter matrix, which are respectively defined as follows

$$\begin{aligned} \tilde{\mathbf{S}}_b &= \sum_{k=1}^{m} n_{c_k}(\tilde{\boldsymbol{\mu}}_{c_k} - \tilde{\boldsymbol{\mu}})(\tilde{\boldsymbol{\mu}}_{c_k} - \tilde{\boldsymbol{\mu}})^T \\ \tilde{\mathbf{S}}_t &= \sum_{i=1}^{n}(\mathbf{x}_i - \tilde{\boldsymbol{\mu}})(\mathbf{x}_i - \tilde{\boldsymbol{\mu}})^T, \end{aligned} \tag{3}$$

where $\tilde{\boldsymbol{\mu}}_{c_k}$ and n_{c_k} are the mean vector and the size of the k-th class respectively. $\tilde{\boldsymbol{\mu}} = \sum_{k=1}^{m} n_{c_k}\tilde{\boldsymbol{\mu}}_{c_k}$ is the overall mean vector. To statistically improve the classification performance, we can maximize the distance between data points in different classes, while minimizing the distance between data points in the same class. This can be achieved by maximizing the Fisher score in Eq. (2). To this end, we need to find a feature transform $f(\cdot)$ for all data points such that $f : \{\mathbf{x}_i\}_{i=1}^n \mapsto \{\mathbf{x}'_i\}_{i=1}^n$ and satisfy

$$\max_{f(\cdot)} F(\mathbf{X}') = \mathrm{tr}\{(\tilde{\mathbf{S}}_b)(\tilde{\mathbf{S}}_t + \gamma\mathbf{I})^{-1}\}, \tag{4}$$

where $\mathbf{x}_i, \mathbf{x}'_i$ are with the same dimensionality d in our work and $\tilde{\mathbf{S}}_b, \tilde{\mathbf{S}}_t$ are constructed using the transformed data $\{\mathbf{x}'_i\}_{i=1}^n$. Assume we collect k SSPs: $\{\mathcal{SP}_j\}_{j=1}^k$ from all the classes by frequent pattern mining using the same parameter min_sup. Since the SSPs contain discriminative class information, the feature transform of any data point $\mathbf{x} \in \mathbf{B}^d$ will be SSP induced and can be formulated as follows

$$\mathbf{x}'_j = \begin{cases} (\mathbf{x}_{\mathcal{SP}_j} \oplus \mathbf{x}) \cdot \phi_j, x'_{js_i} = 1, \forall o_{s_i} \in \mathcal{SP}_j & \text{if } \mathbf{x} \in D_{\mathcal{SP}_j} \\ \mathbf{x} & \text{otherwise} \end{cases} \tag{5}$$

$$\mathbf{x}' = \frac{1}{k}\sum_j \mathbf{x}'_j \tag{6}$$

where $\mathbf{x}_{\mathcal{SP}_j}$ is the equal-length binary expression of sub-pattern $\mathcal{SP}_j$ and $D_{\mathcal{SP}_j}$ is the dataset containing $\mathcal{SP}_j$, as defined in Definition 1. $\mathbf{x}'_j$ is the transformed feature under the function of $\mathcal{SP}_j$. $\mathbf{x} \in D_{\mathcal{SP}_j}$ ensures that feature transform is performed only when $\mathbf{x}$ contains the SSP. "$\oplus$" is the exclusive OR operation on two binary strings for checking the bit difference between $\mathbf{x}$ and $\mathbf{x}_{\mathcal{SP}_j}$. $o_{s_i} \in \mathcal{P}$ is an item of $\mathbf{x}$. After the "$\oplus$" operation, the bits of $\mathbf{x}$ with value "1" corresponding to the items of $\mathcal{SP}_j$ are unexpectedly changed to "0". We need to set them back to original "1". By doing this, change will only take place in the bits where $\mathbf{x}$ is "1" whereas $\mathbf{x}_{\mathcal{SP}_j}$ is "0". ϕ_j is the weight parameter coming up with $\mathcal{SP}_i$, which indicates the "force" of $\mathcal{SP}_i$ on the data points containing it or $\mathcal{SP}_i$'s impact on the Fisher score. The final transformed feature $\mathbf{x}'$ is the resultant of the individual "forces" from all the SSPs.

Then, after Eq. (5) and (6) are plugged into Eq. (4), the Fisher score becomes a function with respect to $\Phi = [\phi_1, \phi_2, \cdots, \phi_k]$. We are going to find the optimum Φ^* to maximize the Fisher score $F(\Phi)$

$$\Phi^* = \underset{\Phi=[\phi_1,\phi_2,\cdots,\phi_k]}{\mathrm{argmax}} F(\Phi). \tag{7}$$

Due to the complex non-linear transform operation, it's difficult to derive the derivation $\frac{\partial F}{\partial \phi}$ analytically. However, the property of the objective function is well defined and the optimum searching can be efficiently performed using non-gradient based optimization algorithms. Our optimization scheme and the implementation of feature transform procedure are introduced in the next section.

4.2.2 *Algorithm Implementation*

Implementation of Feature Transform. The implementation of the proposed feature transform algorithm is summarized in Algorithm 2. It's worth pointing out that after feature transform, the data points are not with binary format anymore, because the bit value has been mapped to real domain. The efficiency of the algorithm is sufficient to be utilized on large scale datasets because the computational complexity of the SSPI feature transform procedure is linear with regards to the size of dataset.

Optimization. In Algorithm 2, after going through feature transform, the new dataset $\hat{D}'$ turns into the function of parameters

Algorithm 2 SSP Induced Feature Transform

```
Input: Training dataset $D = \{\mathbf{x}_i, y_i\}_{i=1}^{n}, \{\mathcal{SP}_j\}_{j=1}^{k}$
Output: Transformed dataset $D' = \{\mathbf{x}'_i, y_i\}_{i=1}^{n}, \Phi^*$
for $i = 1$ to $n$ do
    for $j = 1$ to $k$ do
        if $\mathbf{x}_i \in D_{\mathcal{SP}_j}$ then
            $\hat{\mathbf{x}}'_{ij} = (\mathbf{x}_{\mathcal{SP}_j} \oplus \mathbf{x}_i) \cdot \phi_j$
            $\hat{x}'_{is.} = 1, \forall o_{s.} \in \mathcal{SP}_j$
            ▷ reset the bits of $\hat{\mathbf{x}}'_{ij}$ corresponding to items of $\mathcal{SP}_j$ as "1".
        else
            $\hat{\mathbf{x}}'_{ij} = \mathbf{x}_i$
        end if
    end for
    $\hat{\mathbf{x}}'_i = \text{mean}(\hat{\mathbf{x}}'_{ij})$
                                        ▷ mean takes the average over all $j$
end for
$F = F(\hat{D}')$
                                        ▷ plug $\hat{D}' = \{\hat{\mathbf{x}}'_i\}_{i=1}^{n}$ into Eq. (4)
$[\Phi^*, D'] = \text{optimize}(F)$
                                        ▷ maximize Fisher score function w.r.t $\Phi$
```

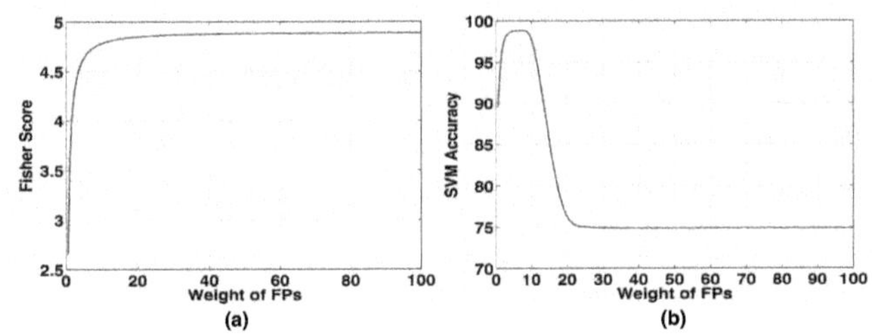

Figure 2: (a) Relationship between common SSI weight and the Fisher score. (b) Relationship between common SSI weight and the final classification accuracy.

$\Phi = [\phi_1, \phi_2, \cdots, \phi_k]$. As the weights of the SSPs, the parameters $[\phi_1, \phi_2, \cdots, \phi_k]$ determine how and what extent of the "forces" from SSPs will act on the input data points. Under the meaning of Fisher score maximization, the optimal Φ^* will lead to the best classification performance. To search the Φ^*, it's intractable to use gradient based optimal algorithm because the highly non-linear feature transform operation makes it hard to get the analytical formation of the objective function with regards to Φ. However, the interesting property of the objective function allows us to find an efficient two-phases optimal algorithm for this problem.

To check the property of the objective function which is closely related to the action classification problem, we conduct the analysis on the human pose data. We first set the weights of all the SSPs as identical[1]. By doing this, the multiple dimensional optimization turns into one-dimensional optimization, which makes it much easier to check the property of the objective function. The relationship between the common weight ϕ and Fisher score can be found in Figure 2(a). As can be seen, the functional relationship is unimodal and the objective function is convex. So conventional one dimensional optimization algorithm is sufficient to find the optimum. In this work, we use golden section search [25].

From Figure 2(b), however, it can be seen that after reaching at the top point of the objective function, in the flat domain, an abrupt decrease in classification accuracy will happen if the value of the common weight keeps increasing. Due to the monotonous increasing of the common weight, the feature vector is changed continuously; therefore it has difficulty converging to the best classification accuracy. For this reason we switch to the second phase, where the multiple constraints on the different weights can form a well-shaped convex objective function.

[1] The weights are initialized randomly within the interval [1, 10] in our problem.

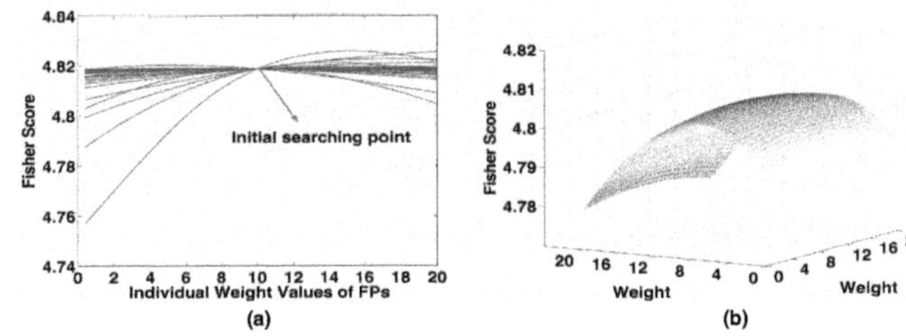

Figure 3: (a) F-W curves formed by fixing the weights of other SSPs at the common optimal weight and changing the weight of one SSP. (b) 3D visualization of the objective function.

The aim of the second phase optimization is to find the optimal individual weights for each SSP, starting from the initial searching point obtained in the first phase optimization. To this end, we analyze the property of the objective function with respect to the individual weights. In Figure 3(a), we plot the curves of Fisher score about the individual SSP weights. We call the curves as F-W curve, which is formed by fixing the weights of other SSPs at the common optimal value and changing the weight of a SSP. It's obvious that the curves are parabola-like and convex. Furthermore, for a more clear and intuitive visualization, we plot the 3D shape of the objective function in Figure 3(b). As we can see, the function is also very smooth. In view of the convexity property of the objective function, we employ the downhill simplex method [25] as the searching strategy. Benefitting from the convexity of the objective function and the given starting guess obtained from the first phase, the optimal searching converges quickly.

The two-phase optimization process is described in Algorithm 3.

Algorithm 3 Two-Phase SSP Weights Optimization Algorithm

```
Input: Training dataset $D = \{\mathbf{x}_i, y_i\}_{i=1}^{n}, SSP = \{\mathcal{SP}_i\}_{i=1}^{k}$
Output: Optimized weights $\Phi^* = [\phi_1^*, \phi_2^*, \cdots, \phi_k^*]$
$\Phi = [1, 1, \cdots, 1] \cdot \phi$
                              ▷ set the weights of SSPs as common weight
$\hat{D}'$ = FeatureTrans($D$, $SSP$, $\Phi$)
      ▷ transformed dataset parameterized by $\phi$ by Algorithm 2
$F = F(\hat{D}')$
$\phi^* = \text{SectionSearch}(F)$
      ▷ Phase 1: golden section search for one dimensional optimization
$SimplexPoint = \text{GenerateSimplex}(\phi^*, para)$
      ▷ generate the initial guess for simplex search, $para$ is the related parameters
repeat
    $\hat{D}'$ = FeatureTrans($D$, $SSP$, $SimplexPoint$)
    $F = F(\hat{D}')$
    $SimplexPoint = \text{SimplexSearch}(F)$
      ▷ Phase 2: simplex search for multiple dimensional optimization
until <converge> return $\Phi^* = SimplexPoint$
```

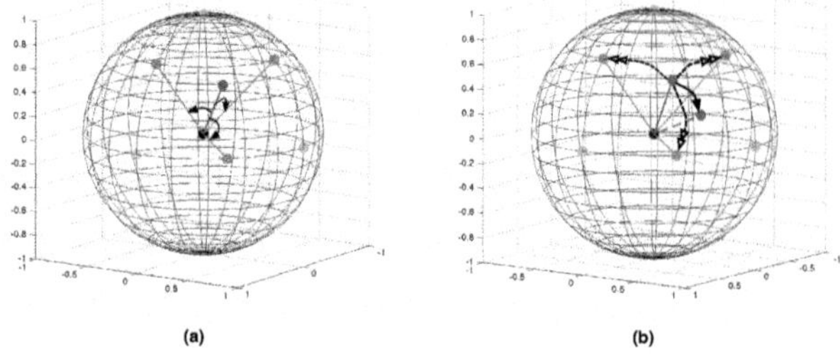

Figure 4: (a) Full pattern "111" (blue) and several sub-patterns before feature transform. (b) "111" pattern transformed (dashed blue pattern) to another place under the forces from the sub-patterns.

4.2.3 Geometric Interpretation

The proposed feature transform approach can be intuitively explained from the geometric viewpoint, as can be seen in Figure 4. For visualization, we take three-dimensional data as example.

Suppose we have a binary pattern "111" (the blue point in Figure 4(a)) and several sub-patterns "110", "101", "011" (red points) and "001", "010", "100" (green points). For simplicity, we just consider the impacts of the sub-patterns denoted by the red color. All the patterns can be easily normalized to reside on the surface of a unit 3D sphere. Then, the feature transform is actually a redistribution of the data points along the surface of the 3D sphere. One can imagine the sub-patterns as fixed magnetic centers scattered on the surface of the sphere and the data points can move freely along the surface. Since the pattern "111" contains all the sub-patterns, all the sub-patterns will have "magnetic attractive force" on it. If the force of a sub-pattern is powerful enough for pattern "111", the angle between them will be reduced and the "111" pattern will be attracted to approaching the sub-pattern. In Fig. 4, we can see that finally the pattern "111" is transformed to another point under the composition of forces from all the three sub-patterns.

For a practical problem, such as pose based action classification, the sub-patterns actually contain rich information about action classes because they frequently appear in the specific action classes. So when a sub-pattern appears in a data point, it gives partial evidence that this point contains part of the "gene" for that action class. It makes sense that we move a step further to decrease the distance between the pattern and the sub-pattern by a feature transform. Statistically speaking, this kind of "approaching" will result in the improvement of that feature's discriminative power. The geometric viewpoint is helpful to deepen the understanding of the SSPI approach theoretically and to construct a more general feature learning model. This is a direction of our future work.

5. EXPERIMENTS

In this section, we report our empirical study of the proposed approach for action classification and sub-pattern analysis of pose data. By conducting the experimental evaluation, we hope to get the answers to two main concerns: (1) Starting from the SSP of pose data, what is the performance of the proposed feature transform framework for action classification? (2) In the process of feature transform, what kind of sub-patterns are extracted and how about their discriminative power to action classification? By conducting experimental evaluations on a large scale human pose dataset, for the first concern, we examine the effectiveness of the SSPI feature transform approach and make comparison with the state-of-the-art approaches. For the second concern, we visually check the SSPs for all the action classes and evaluate their discriminative power quantitatively under the feature transform framework.

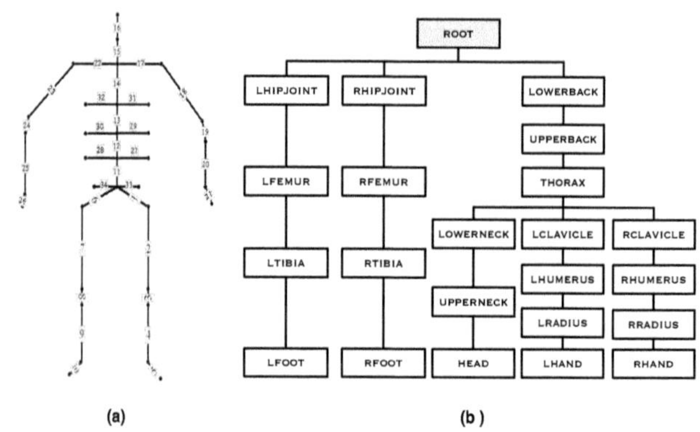

Figure 5: (a) Human body model with 34 bones. (b) Defined hierarchical structure of human body.

5.1 Experimental Setup: Data and Dataset

Human Pose Data. In this work, we work on human pose data. The human body pose is represented in the Acclaim format (ASF, AMC). With this format, human body is defined by a full body model which is consisted of 34 bones with hierarchical structures. The pose is specified by the motion angles of body bones, which describe the dynamic relationships between parent and children bones, as well as the global motion of the full body. See Figure 5 for the visualized body model and the definition of hierarchical structure. The original full body Degree of Freedoms (DOFs) are 62. However, to reduce the computational burden, we discard some unimportant joint angles, such as fingers, thumb, toes and so forth in the experiments. Finally, we select 19 body angles which cover the DoFs of humerus (left and right), radius (left and right), femur (left and right), tibia (left and right) and the upper back.

In this work, our approach is built on the basis of sub-pattern analysis, therefore the continuous pose data first needs to be quantized. To this end, we constrain the value of the motion angles into the interval $[-180°, 180°]$ and then perform 10 levels quantization to each angle within their respective ranges. By doing this, each pose data point is turned into a 190-bit binary pattern, which is used as the basic pose feature in the following experiments.

Experimental Setup of The Dataset. To conduct comprehensive evaluations, we perform experiments on the motion capture dataset collected at CMU [10], which is very large and includes dozens of actions performed by over one hundred subjects. From the whole database, we choose the MoCa data of 9 action classes performed by diverse number of subjects respectively. The 9 action classes include walk, run, jump, pick-up, sitting on a motorcycle, cartwheel, boxing, chicken dance and golf swing. Because the total frame number of the different action classes are different in the original dataset, different percentages are adopted when taking the data frames from the action classes. In doing so, each class will roughly have the same number of data frames. This avoids the class imbalance problem. In our experimental setup, there are in total of 169975 frames for the 9 classes, from which we randomly select 52482 frames for each experiment. Some portion of the 52482 data frames are used for training and the remainder for testing. In most of our experiments we divided this set in half.

Table 1: **Accuracy (%) of action classification on different pose features. See texts for the abbreviations.**

Action	**Pose Features**							
	RQ	BQ4	BQ10	PCA(BQ10)	LDA(BQ10)	BQFP[8, 9]	BQFP-S[8]	**SSPI**
Walk	84.00	92.03	89.27	84.09	82.92	91.02	91.14	**97.39**
Run	77.66	88.92	89.43	70.32	79.10	88.68	93.96	**99.00**
Jump	87.05	95.02	92.93	84.53	85.30	93.36	96.03	**99.02**
Pick-up	73.47	87.80	87.89	82.19	76.15	87.64	93.08	**98.12**
Motorcycle	99.40	99.45	99.32	99.75	98.42	99.70	99.45	**100.0**
Cartwheel	77.54	93.08	92.72	74.66	79.93	92.76	94.24	**99.30**
Boxing	86.08	95.13	94.73	98.18	90.62	96.16	95.96	**99.37**
Chicken-dance	91.21	95.64	96.47	84.51	90.00	96.09	96.58	**99.69**
Golf-swing	99.92	**100.0**	99.92	90.19	99.35	99.92	**100.0**	**100.0**
Average	86.26	94.12	93.63	85.38	86.87	93.92	95.60	**99.10**

5.2 Classification Performance

In this part, working on the MoCa data, we evaluate the effectiveness of the proposed feature transform algorithm for action classification. By comparing with several different methods, the performance of our approach is checked from different perspectives, which are important to have a comprehensive understanding to the SSPI feature transform framework.

Experimental Setup of the Classifier. In this work, SVM is used as the classifier. The LIBSVM [7] is chosen as the software implementation of SVM and we use RBF as the kernel of SVM. For each prediction model, before model training, a grid search is conducted to find the optimum of the parameters C, γ of RBF using 5-folds cross-validation. The model is trained also using a 5-folds cross-validation on the training dataset using the optimal C, γ. In all the classification experiments, the final accuracy is reported by averaging on 10 executions of the SVM prediction procedure, using training and test subsets randomly taken from the full dataset. One advantage of doing this is to avoid over-fitting.

Selected Approaches for Comparison. To evaluate the performance of our approach, we compare with seven methods. Among them, three coding strategies, namely, real number coding, 4-bit coding and 10-bit coding are evaluated. To work on pattern based classification, quantization of the original continuous data is required. Real-number Quantization (RQ) maps each feature dimensionality to a discrete real value which is obtained by 10-level quantization of the original single features. Using binary coding scheme, 4 bits (BQ4) and 10 bits (BQ10) coding map each feature dimensionality to a 4-bit and 10-bit binary code respectively, so the original feature vector is turned into either a 76-bit or 190-bit binary string.

We use the methods proposed in [8], which we call BQFP and BQFP-S, as the key comparison for validating our proposed SSPI feature transform algorithm. There are three reasons for selecting these algorithms: (1) Both SSPI and BQFPs work on Frequent Pattern (FP) based classification. The BQFP and its upgraded version, BDFP-S, which adds an additional step for feature selection, are the state-or-the-art techniques. (2) BQFPs use non-liner feature combination scheme, which maps the feature to a higher dimensional space. In doing so, the performance gets improved but computational burden for classifier is increased. However, the SSPI does not change the dimensionality of the features. (3) BQFP-S explicitly chooses its features, while SSPI does so implicitly using SSP weight learning. We therefore want to compare the differences mentioned in (2) and (3) quantitatively by experimental evaluations.

Furthermore, because SSPI keeps feature's dimensionality invariant whereas BQFPs increase it, it will be interesting to see if reducing the dimensionality results in better performance. So, the conventional PCA and LDA are used for this purpose. We select LDA because it is similar to SSPI, in that it also uses Fisher score as the internal criteria for dimensionality reduction. Notice that both PCA and LDA work on BQ10 coding scheme.

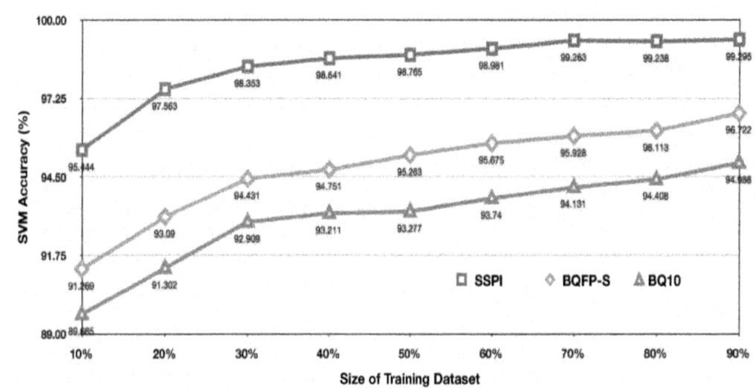

Figure 6: Classification accuracy as a function of the size of training dataset. The SSPI, BQFP-S and BQ10 are compared.

Results and Analysis. In Table 1, we report the classification accuracy of the pose features generated by different methods. For the three coding strategies, it can be seen that the performance of RQ is significantly worse than BQ4 and BQ10. This is due to its simple quantization scheme performed in real domain. BQ4 and BQ10 have close performance because they use similar binary coding scheme. However, in our problem, we prefer to use BQ10 as the basic quantization method, because each bit in BQ10 has a very clear physical meaning and the obtained SSPs are specified by the local human poses and can be easily visualized. It satisfies our requirements of "physicality" and "visibility" to pose data.

Notice that the performances of BQFP and BQ10 are very similar for all the action classes. This result is consistent with [8]. It confirms the hypothesis that for frequent pattern based classification, without feature selection, the performance of feature combination schemes can be very poor. As can be seen, after adding feature selection module to the BQFP algorithm, BQFP-S achieves much better performance. It's worth pointing out that for the pose data,

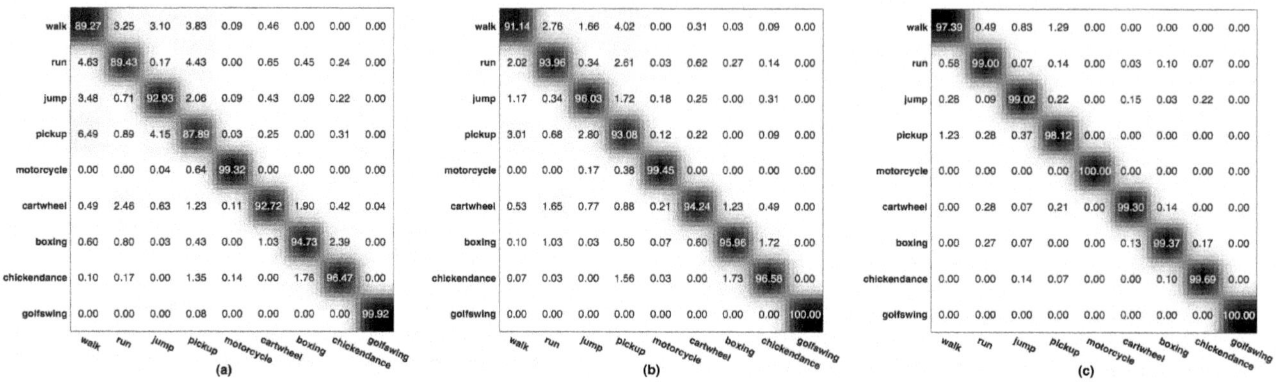

Figure 7: Confusion matrices of (a) BQ10, (b) BQFP-S and (c) SSPI for action classification, with mean classification accuracy of 93.63%, 95.6% and 99.10% respectively. Notice that many confusions are removed or relieved in the SSPI feature transform framework, especially for the action class "walk", "run", "pick-up" and "cartwheel".

even a small increase in classification accuracy is important and not easy to achieve. So the superior performance of BQFP-S over BQFP is significant. Compared with BQFPs and BQ10, the performance of PCA and LDA is discouraged. It may be caused by the information loss combined with the dimensionality reduction.

It's encouraging that SSPI significantly outperforms all the other methods in classification accuracy, for almost all the action classes except the identical 100% performance with BQ4 and BQFP-S for the action class"golf-swing". Overall, SSPI outperforms the state-of-the-art technique, BQFP-S, by 4% in classification accuracy, which is quite remarkable for pose pattern based classification. It's also worth noting that for the most confused action classes "walk", "run", "pick-up" and "cartwheel", SSPI achieves significant performance improvements on SVM accuracy compared to all the other methods (5-7% and 8-11% improvement compared to BQFP-S and BQ10 respectively), as indicated in Table 1. The four actions are prone to confuse because many "walk-like" frames are contained in these actions. From Figure 7, it can be seen that many confusions are removed or relieved in the SSPI feature transform framework, especially for the four confusing actions. The potential cause for resulting in such kind of improvement of SSPI is that under the "force" of SSPs, the bits corresponding to the "walk-like" attribute are changed so that the confusion can be mitigated accordingly.

For a more comprehensive evaluation to SSPI, we also investigate the robustness of SSPI algorithm to the sizes of training and test datasets. The results are shown in Figure 6. For clearness, we just select the BQFP-S and BQ10 for comparisons[2]. It can be seen that with the increase of training dataset size (indicated by the ratio of training data), the performance of all the three methods is improved. It also can be observed that SSPI obviously outperforms the other two methods during the change of data size.

From the experimental results, we can draw several observations. First of all, the proposed SSPI feature transform framework achieves remarkable overall better performance than the state-of-the-art techniques. Its effectiveness is demonstrated. Second, the SSPI feature transform mechanism is beneficial to remove the confusion appeared between the classes with overlapped attributes. Finally, the performance of SSPI is robust and can be applied to the datasets with different scales.

In terms of the computational expense, the mining process is quite efficient and it takes less than half a second for mining 300 SSPs from nearly $30,000$ training samples. The most time consuming part is on the weights optimization. It takes 10 minutes or so to complete the optimum searching on the training data, using a 3.1G core i5 machine with 4G memory.

[2]There is a slight difference between the numbers in Table 1 and Fig. 6 (50% case), as we select data randomly for each execution.

5.3 Evaluation On Support Sub-Patterns

SSPI feature transform is demonstrated quite effective to action classification. The functionality of the SSP, however, is not just constrained to classification. Thanks to the good properties of human pose data, we can visualize the SSPs and intuitively build the correspondence between the SSP represented local pose and its discriminative power, which can be computed explicitly within the framework of feature transform. By doing this, the utilization of SSP can be extended to much wider scenarios, such as action search, pose estimation, event understanding and so forth. Therefore, in this part, we conduct comprehensive evaluation to the SSP.

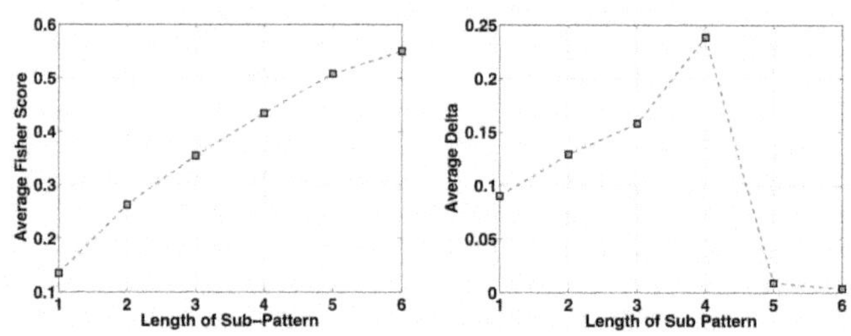

Figure 8: (a) Fisher score as a function of the pattern length. The Fisher score is averaged over all the SSPs with the same length. (b) Average discriminative power of the SSPs is compared, with regards to the pattern length.

SSP Mining. To generate SSPs, frequent pattern mining algorithm is an effective solution. In this work, we use Apriori algorithm [2, 18] to mine the frequent items from quantized human pose data, namely, the BQ10 binary string introduced in Section 5.2. There is only one parameter which needs to be specified in the Apriori algorithm, say, the minimum support threshold (min_sup) defined in Definition 1. We apply the same min_sup to all the action classes and empirically set it as 0.55 in this work.

In our experiments, for each action class, about dozens of the SSPs are generated and the length of the SSP ranges from 1 to 6. After merging the same SSP from different classes, near 300 SSPs are employed for feature transform. The same number also comes

Table 2: Top six SSPs ranked by their discriminative power and listed in descending order from left to right.

SSP_i	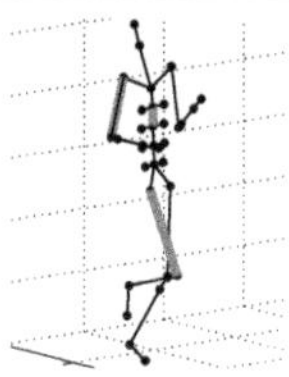	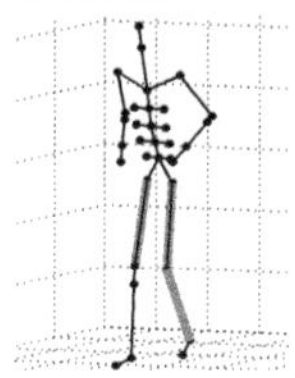	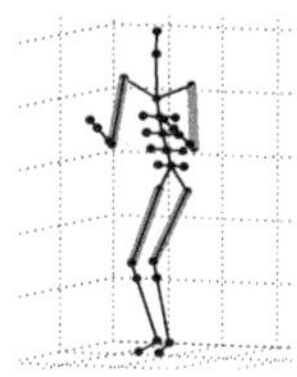	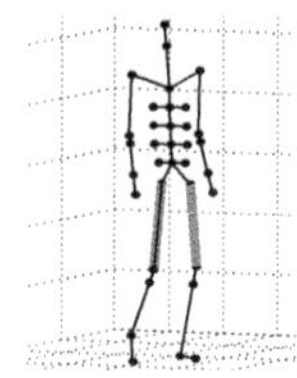	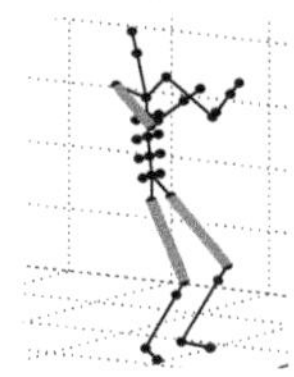	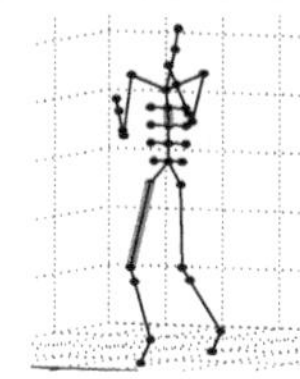
$\frac{\partial F}{\partial \phi_i}$	1.7185	0.8406	0.5798	0.4758	0.3918	0.2809

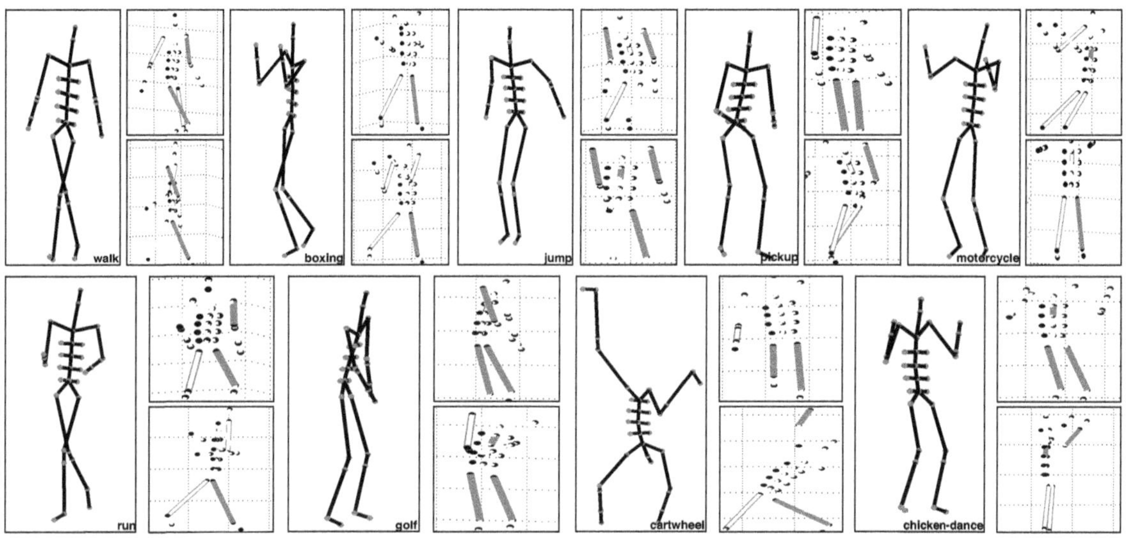

Figure 9: Sample poses and their corresponding two SSPs. Both pose and SSP are randomly selected from the 9 action classes. The SSPs are generated for each action class respectively. The actions are walk, boxing, jump, pick-up, motorcycle pose, run, golf-swing, cartwheel and chicken dance from left to right and top to bottom.

up with the dimensionality of the weight vector Φ. In Figure 9, we show the pose samples randomly selected from the 9 action classes and two corresponding SSPs in their right sides. As can be seen, the visualization of the SSP presents us an intuitive observation that the SSP is the representative local pose and can be viewed as the "signature" of the corresponding action class.

Analysis on SSP's Discriminative Power. SSP plays important role in feature transform. However, in this process, the importance of different SSPs is unequal. One critical advantage of the SSPI feature transform framework is that the "importance", namely the discriminative power of the SSPs can be quantitatively evaluated. To this end, we define the Discriminative Power (DP) of the SSP as: $\frac{\partial F}{\partial \phi_i}$, where F is the Fisher score function and ϕ_i is the weight parameter associated with the i-th SSP.

We can see that the DP actually measures the sensitivity of the Fisher score function to the change of ϕ corresponding to the SSP. In our implementation, we compute the $\frac{\partial F}{\partial \phi_i}$ in this way: when calculating the DP of the i-th SSP, we first fix the weights of other SSPs at their optimal values and then change the values of ϕ_i within a scope, which is taken as $[0, 20]$ in our experiments, to measure the change of Fisher score function ΔF. Because the objective function is convex according to the analysis in Section 4.2.2, ΔF is taken as the difference between peak value and valley value of the objective function within the scope.

As a SSP actually corresponds to a feature subset, it can be evaluated with Fisher score based feature selection method [17]. To evaluate the DP of the SSP, we first check the Fisher score of the SSP by taking the SSP as the selected feature subset. The average Fisher score with regards to different pattern length is compared in Figure 8(a). As can be seen, with the increase of pattern length, the Fisher score is monotonously increasing. It's reasonable because long patterns contain more information than the shorter ones when they are used as feature subset. However, when SSP is adapted into the SSPI feature transform framework, it is no longer treated as feature subset and it plays more like a "force" to induce the change of feature. Therefore the pattern length is not the dominant factor to determine SSP's DP. In Figure 8(b), the DP of SSPs with different pattern lengths are compared. The DP is computed by averaging on all the SSPs with the same pattern length. It can be found that the SSP with length 4 become the most discriminative sub-patterns and the length 5, 6 degrade to the worst comparing with Figure 8(a).

We also rank the SSPs according to their DPs. The result is shown in Table 2, where the figures of the top 6 SSPs and their corresponding DPs are presented. Although the SSP is plotted just on the pose of one class, actually they may appear in multiple action classes. Statistically speaking, the higher the rank of a SSP, the greater the contribution it makes for action classification. Therefore, essentially under the framework of SSPI, the SSPs are selected by an implicit way according to their DPs, which is different from the explicit manner for feature selection presented in [8].

Potentially, the results of quantitative evaluation on SSP can be used for action search, action retrieval and pose estimation. For example, the DP of a SSP can be viewed as a confidence of classifying a pose to a specific action class represented by the SSPs.

6. CONCLUSION

In this paper, we propose a new feature transform framework for pose based action classification. Utilizing the properties of pose data, we introduce frequent pattern mining to explore the Support Sub-Patterns (SSP), which are representative sub-patterns of the action class and can be applied for effective action classification. Based on the sub-patterns, the original pose feature can be converted into a more discriminative formation for classification, by SSP induced feature learning. In this framework, we construct the objective function under the meaning of Fisher score optimum. A two-phases efficient optimal algorithm for searching the optimal weights of SSPs is developed. By applying the learned optimal weights on feature transform, the discriminative feature for classification is obtained. Experimental studies demonstrate the superior performance of the proposed approach over the state-of-the-art techniques on the task of action classification. Furthermore, the discriminative power of the SSP can be explicitly evaluated within the feature transform framework. It could derive many interesting applications within the field of human motion analysis.

7. REFERENCES

[1] J. K. Aggarwal and M. S. Ryoo. Human activity analysis: A review. *ACM Computing Surveys*, 2011.

[2] R. Agrawal, R. Srikant, et al. Fast algorithms for mining association rules. In *VLDB*, 1994.

[3] S. Ali, A. Basharat, and M. Shah. Chaotic invariants for human action recognition. In *ICCV*, 2007.

[4] M. Andriluka, S. Roth, and B. Schiele. Pictorial structures revisited: People detection and articulated pose estimation. In *CVPR*, 2009.

[5] A. Bissacco, M. Yang, and S. Soatto. Fast human pose estimation using appearance and motion via multi-dimensional boosting regression. In *CVPR*, 2007.

[6] L. W. Campbell and A. F. Bobick. Recognition of human body motion using phase space constraints. In *ICCV*, 1995.

[7] C.-C. Chang and C.-J. Lin. LIBSVM: A library for support vector machines. *ACM Transactions on Intelligent Systems and Technology*, 2:27:1–27:27, 2011. Software available at http://www.csie.ntu.edu.tw/ cjlin/libsvm.

[8] H. Cheng, X. Yan, J. Han, and C. Hsu. Discriminative frequent pattern analysis for effective classification. In *ICDE*, 2007.

[9] H. Cheng, X. Yan, J. Han, and P. Yu. Direct discriminative pattern mining for effective classification. In *ICDE*, 2008.

[10] CMU. http://mocap.cs.cmu.edu.

[11] S. Corazza, L. Mündermann, E. Gambaretto, G. Ferrigno, and T. Andriacchi. Markerless motion capture through visual hull, articulated icp and subject specific model generation. *International Journal of Computer Vision*, 87(1):156–169, 2010.

[12] C. Desai and D. Ramanan. Detecting actions, poses, and objects with relational phraselets. In *ECCV*, 2012.

[13] W. Fan, K. Zhang, H. Cheng, J. Gao, X. Yan, J. Han, P. Yu, and O. Verscheure. Direct mining of discriminative and essential frequent patterns via model-based search tree. In *KDD*, 2008.

[14] J. Gall, A. Yao, N. Razavi, L. Van Gool, and V. Lempitsky. Hough forests for object detection, tracking, and action recognition. *Pattern Analysis and Machine Intelligence, IEEE Transactions on*, 33(11):2188–2202, 2011.

[15] D. Gavrila. The visual analysis of human movement: A survey. *Computer Vision and Image Understanding*, 73(1):82–98, 1999.

[16] D. Gavrila, L. Davis, et al. Towards 3-d model-based tracking and recognition of human movement: a multi-view approach. In *International workshop on automatic face and gesture recognition*, 1995.

[17] Q. Gu, Z. Li, and J. Han. Generalized fisher score for feature selection. In *UAI*, 2011.

[18] J. Han, H. Cheng, D. Xin, and X. Yan. Frequent pattern mining: current status and future directions. *Data Mining and Knowledge Discovery*, 15(1):55–86, 2007.

[19] J. Han and M. Kamber. *Data mining: concepts and techniques*. Morgan Kaufmann, 2006.

[20] G. Johansson. Visual perception of biological motion and a model for its analysis. *Attention, Perception, & Psychophysics*, 14(2):201–211, 1973.

[21] H. Kim, S. Kim, T. Weninger, J. Han, and T. Abdelzaher. Ndpmine: efficiently mining discriminative numerical features for pattern-based classification. *Machine Learning and Knowledge Discovery in Databases*, pages 35–50, 2010.

[22] S. Maji, L. Bourdev, and J. Malik. Action recognition from a distributed representation of pose and appearance. In *CVPR*, 2011.

[23] H. Ning, T. Han, D. Walther, M. Liu, and T. Huang. Hierarchical space-time model enabling efficient search for human actions. *Circuits and Systems for Video Technology, IEEE Transactions on*, 19(6):808–820, 2009.

[24] R. Poppe. A survey on vision-based human action recognition. *Image and Vision Computing*, 28(6):976 – 990, 2010.

[25] W. H. Press, S. A. Teukolsky, W. T. Vetterling, and B. P. Flannery. *Numerical recipes 3rd edition: The art of scientific computing*. Cambridge University Press, 2007.

[26] C. Rao, A. Yilmaz, and M. Shah. View-invariant representation and recognition of actions. *International Journal of Computer Vision*, 50(2):203–226, 2002.

[27] S. Sadanand and J. Corso. Action bank: A high-level representation of activity in video. In *CVPR*, 2012.

[28] Y. Sheikh, M. Sheikh, and M. Shah. Exploring the space of a human action. In *ICCV*, 2005.

[29] J. Shotton, A. Fitzgibbon, M. Cook, T. Sharp, M. Finocchio, R. Moore, A. Kipman, and A. Blake. Real-time human pose recognition in parts from single depth images. In *CVPR*, 2011.

[30] J. M. Siskind. Grounding language in perception. *Artificial Intelligence Review*, 8(5):371–391, 1994.

[31] Y. Yacoob and M. J. Black. Parameterized modeling and recognition of activities. In *ICCV*, 1998.

[32] W. Yang, Y. Wang, and G. Mori. Recognizing human actions from still images with latent poses. In *CVPR*, 2010.

[33] Y. Yang and D. Ramanan. Articulated pose estimation with flexible mixtures-of-parts. In *CVPR*, 2011.

[34] B. Yao and L. Fei-Fei. Action recognition with exemplar based 2.5d graph matching. In *ECCV*, 2012.

[35] A. Yilma and M. Shah. Recognizing human actions in videos acquired by uncalibrated moving cameras. In *ICCV*, 2005.

[36] J. Yuan, Y. Wu, and M. Yang. From frequent itemsets to semantically meaningful visual patterns. In *SIGKDD*, 2007.

Human Activities Recognition using Depth Images

Raj Gupta[1] Alex Yong-Sang Chia[2*] Deepu Rajan[1]

[1]School of Computer Engineering, Nanyang Technological University - Singapore
[2]Rakuten Inc. - Japan
{rajk0005, asdrajan}@ntu.edu.sg, alex.chia@mail.rakuten.com

ABSTRACT

We present a new method to classify human activities by leveraging on the cues available from depth images alone. Towards this end, we propose a descriptor which couples depth and spatial information of the segmented body to describe a human pose. Unique poses (i.e. codewords) are then identified by a spatial-based clustering step. Given a video sequence of depth images, we segment humans from the depth images and represent these segmented bodies as a sequence of codewords. We exploit unique poses of an activity and the temporal ordering of these poses to learn subsequences of codewords which are strongly discriminative for the activity. Each discriminative subsequence acts as a classifier and we learn a boosted ensemble of discriminative subsequences to assign a confidence score for the activity label of the test sequence. Unlike existing methods which demand accurate tracking of 3D joint locations or couple depth with color image information as recognition cues, our method requires only the segmentation masks from depth images to recognize an activity. Experimental results on the publicly available Human Activity Dataset (which comprises 12 challenging activities) demonstrate the validity of our method, where we attain a precision/recall of 78.1%/75.4% when the person was not seen before in the training set, and 94.6%/93.1% when the person was seen before.

Categories and Subject Descriptors

I.4.8 [**Image Processing and Computer Vision**]: Scene Analysis

Keywords

Human activity detection; depth image segmentation

*Part of this work was done while Alex Yong-Sang Chia was with Institute for Infocomm Research - Singapore.

Figure 1: Silhouettes ambiguities in poses. Pose differences (due to different hand positions) cannot be seen from silhouettes in (a), but are readily visible from three-dimensional shape information in (b).

1. INTRODUCTION

Human activities recognition is useful in many applications like surveillance, action/event centric video retrieval and patient monitoring systems. A large majority of activity recognition works focuses on gray or RGB video sequences, and exploits spatio-temporal interest points or silhouettes as recognition cues. Here, a significant challenge is to sieve out image/video features that are representative of the activity in which background clutter, illumination changes and camera motion could easily corrupt these features. Also, given that these features incorporate only spatial x-y and temporal information, they often fail to fully resolve the silhouette ambiguity in poses under self occlusion [27].

There is an emerging consensus that depth information is a more reliable recognition cue for classifying human activities. It is color/texture/intensity invariant and hence is robust towards appearance variations of the humans performing the action. More importantly, recent depth cameras (e.g. Kinect) offer substantial depth resolutions of a few centimeters and thus provide very good estimation of the three-dimensional geometry of the scene. Unlike gray/color images acquired with traditional 2D cameras which provides spatial x-y image information, depth images afford another important spatial dimension (z-component) which can be exploited to help resolve silhouettes ambiguities in poses. For example, consider Fig. 1(a) which shows silhouettes of a person lying on the ground and moving his arms. Due to self-occlusion, the difference in poses is not evident. However, in Fig. 1(b), which shows the corresponding depth images, the outline of the hands is visible facilitating pose description.

In this paper, we present a method which harnesses *only* depth images to recognize very complex human activities such as brushing teeth, cooking - chopping and cooking - stirring. Our method does not demand knowledge of body joints locations, but only requires segmentation mask of the human silhouette to be available. We propose an algorithm

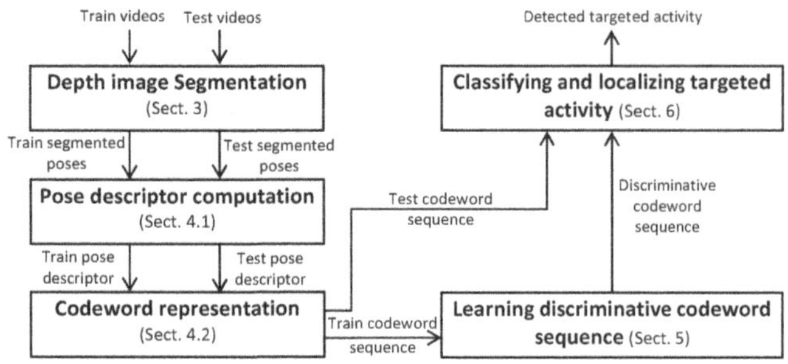

Figure 2: Block diagram of the proposed algorithm.

to extract the human silhouette from depth images. A scale and depth invariant descriptor is developed to represent the 3D pose of a segmented silhouette. We extract the descriptors from training images depicting a wide array of poses, and cluster these descriptors to find a set of compact clusters. Here, we propose a spatial based clustering step to ensure cluster members are well represented by its medoids, and consider each medoid as a codeword. Collectively, these codewords represent the range of unique body poses that are exhibited by the humans in the training images.

Fig. 2 shows the block diagram of the proposed algorithm. For a given training depth video sequence (and its activity label), we segment the human from the video sequence, and represent the sequence of segmented bodies as a sequence of codewords. Discriminative subsequence of codewords that model unique poses and the distinguishing temporal ordering of these poses are then learned with a boosting framework. Each discriminative subsequence has a variable number of codewords, and is termed in this paper as *x-subsequence-codewords* or *xSC*. Both the *xSC*, its window size and weight are learned automatically, and represent the most discriminative subsequences for the activity class. At test time, we adopt a sliding window approach to align each *xSC* to overlapping windows of the test sequence. Each *xSC* acts as a classifier and we learn a boosted ensemble of *xSC* to give a confidence score for the activity label of the test sequence. We evaluated our method on the Human Activity Detection database [30] which comprises 12 challenging activities, and obtain state-of-the-art recognition results. Additionally, we also applied our method on the task of activity detection where we localize all instances of a targeted activity from a test video sequence. Accurate localizations of targeted activities are demonstrated.

2. RELATED WORK

Majority of human activity recognition works [2] exploit gray/color cues, with the use of depth cues attracting interest only in recent years. Here, we first discuss the more representative recognition works which exploit gray/color videos, before discussing those that exploit depth images.

Human activity recognition works mainly employ either a holistic representation or a part-based representation. In holistic representation methods, Bobick *et al.* [6] developed the motion energy and motion history images to encode short spans of motions efficiently. Hu moments [12] extracted from these images are then exploited as activity descriptors. Efros *et al.* [9] exploited optical flow measurements to compute spatio-temporal descriptors, and demonstrated the power of these descriptors in recognizing activities seen in low resolution videos. Yilmaz *et al.* [32] tracked moving 2D contours to generate a 3D spatio-temporal volume, and extracted differential geometry features from the surfaces of the volumes to recognize various activities. Although their method achieved very good activity recognition accuracy, it demands robust tracking of the contours and fails when contours cannot be tracked (e.g. under self-occlusion). Parameswaran *et al.* [23] used 3D joint locations to model the geometry of an action, and represented an activity in terms of its static canonical poses and dynamic trajectories in 2D invariance space. A limitation of this work is the need for accurate 3D joint locations.

Motivated by the success in the object classification domain, part based representations for activity recognition have gained strong traction in the research community. The majority of these methods employ sparse interest point descriptors such as [15, 8, 20] to recognize human actions. For example, Schuldt *et al.* [26] represented each video sequence by a bag-of-word representation, in which they employed STIP features [15] as the underlying features. A support vector machine is then learned for classifying test video sequences. Very good results have been demonstrated on videos depicting simple actions like running and walking. Dollar *et al.* [8] applied separate linear filters in the spatial and temporal dimensions to detect interest points that have local maxima value in both dimensions. A classifier is then learned in a similar way as [26] to recognize a test activity. The above methods use a histogram representation of features and ignore the temporal ordering between features. To preserve the temporal ordering, Nowozin *et al.* [20] improved on the histogram representation and proposed a sequential representation to preserve the temporal ordering between words. The PrefixSpan subsequence mining algorithm is exploited to find discriminative representation of an activity. Their method does not model the global geometry of human body joints when performing an activity, and instead considers them as a simple bag of features.

The above methods exploit appearance (color/texture) information as the key recognition cues and are often easily corrupted by variations in illumination and appearance of the human body. More importantly, such features encode the spatial (x-y) information, and cannot fully resolve silhouette ambiguity seen in self-occlusion [27]. To overcome these problems, recent works use depth cues to recognize human activities. Ni *et al.* [19] and Zhao *et al.* [34] used multi-modality sensor combination (e.g. color and depth) to compute Depth-Layered Multi-Channel STIPs and three dimensional motion history images for human activity recognition. Hao and Parker [33] extended Dollar's method [8] using depth images and constructed a 4D hyper cuboid for feature extraction. While these methods demonstrated improved performance gained by these depth extended feature representations, the use of color images affect the performance of these algorithms due to the reasons discussed earlier. Li *et al.* [17] proposed the first work that uses only depth information to recognize human activities. Here, they sampled a bag of 3D points from depth images, and project these points into a 2D space. An action graph is constructed from the training points to encode the actions to be recognized. Although their method achieves good recognition accuracy, the use of 2D projections of key poses can lead to sub-optimal feature representations. To describe the pose of

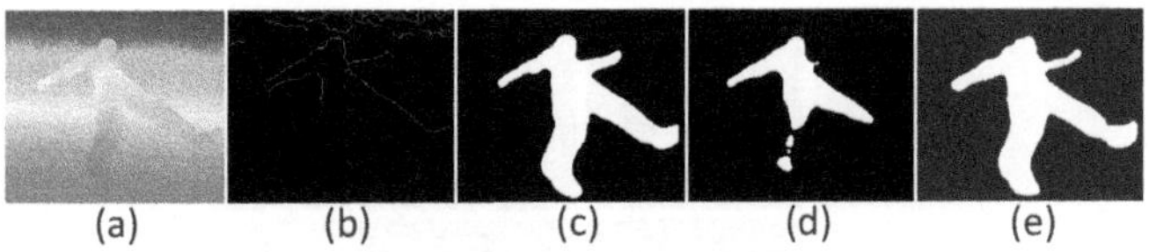

Figure 3: Depth image segmentation. (a) Depth image where an object is very near to the background. (b) Edge map extracted from (a). (c)-(d) Segmentation masks obtained by applying background subtraction [35] on color image and depth image respectively. (e) Mask obtained with our method which is able to extract the object completely (similar to (c)) with depth image alone.

human, Shotton *et al.* [27] exploited decision trees and artificially rendered humans to estimate 3D joint locations from a single depth image. This method was further extended by Holzer *et al.* [11] in which regression trees were used to learn interest points from depth images. Excellent joins/interest point detection were shown in [27, 11], though application of detected joints/points to human activity recognition tasks were not demonstrated. Sung *et al.* [29, 30] directly used the orientations and 3D joint locations to learn a model based on maximum-entropy Markov model. To deal with inaccurate joint locations, Wang *et al.* [31] used *local occupancy pattern* around each joint location detected by the tracker. While [29, 30, 31] yield very good classification of complex activities, it require the detection of body joint locations. This limits their applicability.

3. DEPTH IMAGE SEGMENTATION

The segmentation of moving objects from a depth image is an important problem. While standard segmentation approaches [18, 35, 28] that are developed for RGB images can also be used for depth images, these approaches often fail to extract objects that are very close to the background (e.g. person lying on the ground/bed, objects very near to wall) and require additional information like color for proper segmentation. Fig. 3 shows such an example where the person is lying on the ground. Since the object is very near to the background, the object boundaries become ambiguous in the depth map. This is illustrated in Fig. 3(b), which shows the edge map of Fig. 3(a) obtained by the Canny edge detector. Fig. 3(c) and 3(d) show the segmentation results obtained after applying a popular background subtraction method [35] on color and depth images, respectively, where segmentation masks obtained from depth image is noticeably weaker. To address this issue, we propose a method that computes the spatiograms [5] of the depth image along with the projections of its surface normals in xy, yz and zx planes for both images (background image and object+background image) and then compares these spatiograms to compute the similarity scores [21]. These similarity scores are used to segment the foreground object as shown in Fig. 3(e).

3.1 Extraction of surface normals

We briefly review the method to extract surface normals as described in [25]. Let the position vectors of points in an image be given as a function of $(s,\ t)$ coordinates of the parametric space (image coordinates). We define $\vec{X}_s$ and $\vec{X}_t$

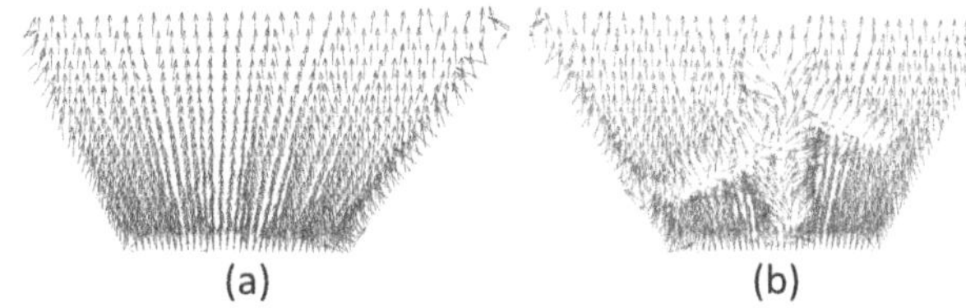

Figure 4: Visualization of surface normals computed on (a) background depth image and (b) the object+background depth image (shown in Fig. 3(a)).

as the partial derivatives of $\vec{X}$ with respect to s and t,

$$\vec{X} = \begin{pmatrix} x(s,\ t) \\ y(s,\ t) \\ z(s,\ t) \end{pmatrix};\ \vec{X}_s = \begin{pmatrix} x_s(s,\ t) \\ y_s(s,\ t) \\ z_s(s,\ t) \end{pmatrix};\ \vec{X}_t = \begin{pmatrix} x_t(s,\ t) \\ y_t(s,\ t) \\ z_t(s,\ t) \end{pmatrix}. \quad (1)$$

For each of the functions $x(s,\ t)$, $y(s,\ t)$, and $z(s,\ t)$ a local least squares polynomial function fit is evaluated. This polynomial function is then differentiated to compute the derivatives $\vec{X}_s$ and $\vec{X}_t$. Given a function $f(s,\ t)$, the derivatives are evaluated as [4]: $f_s = D_s * S * f$ and $f_t = D_t * S * f$ where $*$ denotes convolution and S is a smoothening operator. D_s and D_t are given respectively as $\vec{C_0}\ \vec{C_1}^T$ and $\vec{C_1}\ \vec{C_0}^T$, where $\vec{C_0} = \frac{1}{7}\ [1\ 1\ 1\ 1\ 1\ 1\ 1]^T$ and $\vec{C_1} = \frac{1}{28}\ [-3\ -2\ -1\ 0\ 1\ 2\ 3]^T$. The surface normal is then computed as the cross product of the partial derivatives $\vec{X}_s$ and $\vec{X}_t$,

$$\hat{n} = \frac{\vec{X}_s \times \vec{X}_t}{\parallel \vec{X}_s \times \vec{X}_t \parallel}. \quad (2)$$

Fig. 4(a) shows the surface normals computed for a background image, while Fig. 4(b) shows the surface normals computed on Fig. 3(a), which contains both the foreground object and the background. For each of these surface normals, the projections onto the xy-plane, the yz-plane, and the zx-plane are used to compute the spatiograms [5].

3.2 Spatiogram computation and matching

A spatiogram [5] is a generalization of histogram in which feature distribution information of a histogram is combined with spatial layout information (mean and covariance of the spatial position of all pixels that fall into each bin). This allows spatiograms to capture higher-order spatial moments of each attribute bin. To compute the histogram for an image of N pixels, the histogram bin count n_b of bin b can be written as:

$$n_b = C \sum_{i=1}^{N} \delta_{ib}, \quad (3)$$

where C is a normalizing constant and

$$\delta_{ib} = \begin{cases} 1 & \text{if } i^{th} \text{ pixel falls in } b^{th} \text{ bin} \\ 0 & \text{otherwise.} \end{cases} \quad (4)$$

Let $X_i = [x_i, y_i]^T$ be the spatial position of pixel i, in which the spatial co-ordinates in the image are normalized to $[-1, +1]$. For each bin, we compute the spatial mean (μ_b) and covariance (Σ_b) as:

$$\mu_b = \frac{1}{\sum_{j=1}^{N} \delta_{jb}} \sum_{i=1}^{N} X_i \delta_{ib}, \quad (5)$$

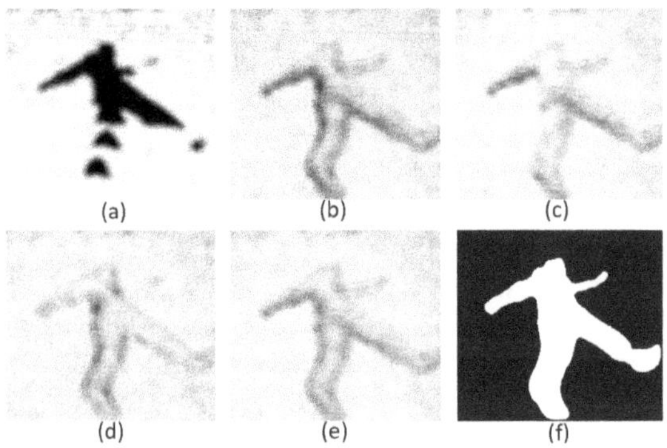

Figure 5: Illustration of similarity between spatiograms obtained for background only image and object+background image. The spatiograms are computed for (a) depth image, and projections of surface normals onto (b) xy, (c) yz and (d) zx planes. (e) Average similarity score of surface normal projections. (f) Segmentation mask obtained using similarity maps (a) and (e).

$$\Sigma_b = \frac{1}{\sum_{j=1}^{N} \delta_{jb}} \sum_{i=1}^{N} (X_i - \mu_b)(X_i - \mu_b)^T \delta_{ib}, \quad (6)$$

Given a background image and an object+background image, we compute spatiogram $S = \{n, \mu, \Sigma\}$ for their depth images and for the projections of their surface normals in xy, yz and zx planes. Let $S = \{n, \mu, \Sigma\}$ and $S' = \{n', \mu', \Sigma'\}$ denote respectively the spatiograms for the background image and object+background image respectively. The similarity (ρ) between the two spatiograms is then computed as [21]

$$\rho = \sum_{b=1}^{B} \sqrt{n_b n'_b} \left[8\pi |\Sigma_b \Sigma'_b|^{1/4} N(\mu_b; \mu'_b, 2(\Sigma_b + \Sigma'_b)) \right], \quad (7)$$

where $N(X; \mu, \Sigma)$ represents a normalized Gaussian evaluated at X. The similarity is computed at every pixel between spatiograms obtained for background depth image and object+background depth image. Similarities are also computed for the spatiograms obtained from the projections of the surface normals onto the three planes with the similarity computed, as before, between background only and object+background cases. The similarity maps ρ_d, ρ_{xy}, ρ_{yz} and ρ_{zx} for the depth image and all three projections of its surface normals in xy, yz and zx planes are shown in Fig. 5(a)-(d) respectively. Darker pixel represents higher dissimilarity between a background only image and an object+background image. These similarity maps are then combined together to detect the object position as follows:

$$mask = \begin{cases} 1 & \min(\rho_d,\ \rho_{xyz}) \leq T \\ 0 & \text{otherwise.} \end{cases} \quad (8)$$

where T is a threshold and the value of ρ_{xyz} is

$$\rho_{xyz} = (\rho_{xy} + \rho_{yz} + \rho_{zx}) \;/\; 3, \quad (9)$$

and is illustrated in Fig. 5(e). The final segmentation mask, shown in Fig. 5(f), is obtained after morphological operations to fill holes and to smoothen object boundaries.

3.3 Segmentation results

In this section, we compare the performance of the proposed algorithm with a popular background subtraction method [35]. To compute the similarity score at pixel p, we compute the spatiograms over a neighborhood of p for background and object+background images and then find the similarity between these two spatiograms using Eq. (7). In our experiments, we fix the neighborhood size and number of bins to 15×15 and 24, respectively. The threshold value T (in Eq. 8) has been chosen empirically and was fixed to 0.86 in all our experiments.

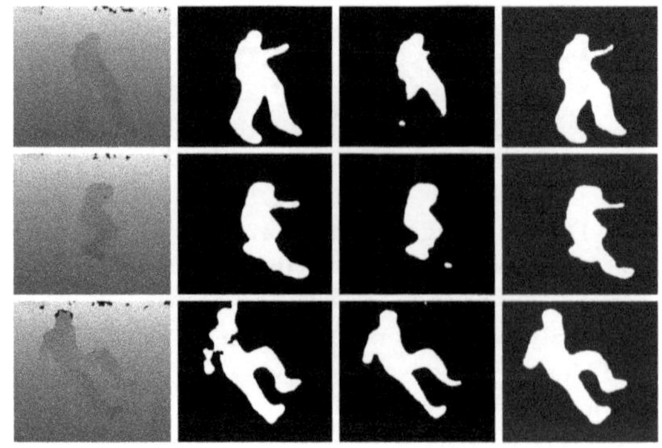

Figure 6: Results of depth image segmentation. First column: Input depth image. Second and third columns: Segmentation mask obtained after applying standard background subtraction method [35] on color and depth images respectively. Fourth column: Segmentation mask obtained by our algorithm.

Fig. 6 shows segmentation results obtained by our method and by [35]. Here, we use depth images as input for the proposed method while we apply [35] on both color and depth images to demonstrate the effectiveness of the proposed algorithm. Input depth images are shown in the first column of Fig. 6. We show segmentation masks obtained by applying [35] on color and depth images in the second and third columns of Fig. 6 respectively. The segmentation masks obtained by our method are shown in the fourth column of Fig. 6. It can be seen that the proposed method is able to extract the complete objects from the depth images that are very close to the background.

4. CODEBOOK OF HUMAN POSES

We build a codebook of body poses from training images, and represent a human pose shown in a video frame by its most similar codeword. Here, explicit effort is made to learn codewords which not only have coherent appearances with a large number of poses (i.e. can represent most poses well), but also have substantial different appearances from other codewords (i.e. effectively covers the range of poses seen in the training set). To learn this codebook, we segment the human body from training depth images, and represent each segmented silhouette by a scale, depth and translation invariant descriptor. We apply a spatial-based clustering method to these descriptors, and consider the medoid of each resulting clusters as a codeword.

4.1 Computing pose descriptors

We require a framework to compare poses. A naive method is to consider a segmented depth image to be a 3D point cloud and compare two poses by the alignment of their 3D point clouds [24]. The alignment of 3D point clouds is a registration problem, which has high computational demands.

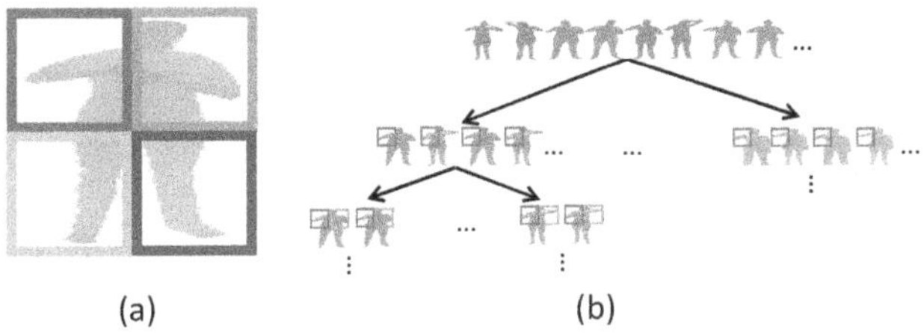

Figure 7: **Spatial-based clustering. (a) Division of bounding box of a segmented body into 4 quadrants. (b) Clustering proceeds in the form of a hierarchical tree, in which we apply clustering on descriptor values of cells belonging to a quadrant at each tree level. Note that members in each sub-cluster have similar sub-poses within the processed quadrants (shown color coded in (b)).**

For better efficiency, we extract descriptors from training images depicting a wide array of body poses, and exploit these descriptors to compare between poses. To ensure a descriptor is translation and scale invariant, we first segment the human from the background using the method presented in Sect. 3, and resize the segmented body to a canonical size prior to computing the descriptor. To describe the segmented body, a straightforward option would be a histogram of normalized depth values computed over the body, which is a simple bag of features representation. However, we can empower the descriptor with greater discriminative potential by encoding the spatial layout of the normalized depth values. Here, we define a dense grid over the bounding box of the segmented body, and compute the average normalized depth value for each cell in the grid. Additionally, we also compute the fraction of the body that is within each cell in the grid. The former incorporates depth information into the descriptor, while the latter encodes the spatial layout of the pose. The concatenation of these two values across all cells yields the pose descriptor.

4.2 Spatial-based clustering to learn codewords

We cluster the set of descriptors that are extracted from the training set, and compute the medoid of each cluster as a codeword. Here, we seek codewords which are sufficiently flexible such that each codeword can well represent poses that have similar appearances, but yet are substantially distinct from each other to ensure they cover the possible variations of poses. One approach to clustering is to consider each descriptor in its entirety during the the clustering step. However, such an approach considers every dimension in the descriptor *simultaneously*. Consequently, sharp differences between two descriptors in a few dimensions may be mitigated by small differences in other dimensions, so that dissimilar poses are grouped together into the same cluster.

To improve the quality of the clustering, we propose a spatial-based clustering step which explicitly incorporates pose information during clustering. We divide the bounding box of the segmented body into four quadrants (see Fig. 7), and cluster the descriptors based on their values within each quadrant separately. Here, we first apply clustering on the descriptor values of cells in the first quadrant to find sub-clusters whose members have similar poses within the first quadrant of the segmented body. The clustering step continues in the form of a hierarchical tree, in which each subsequent node of the tree corresponds to a sub-cluster formed from the previous clustering step, and we cluster on descriptor values from cells of quadrant i at level i of the tree. Consequently, each leaf node of the tree includes descriptors which have similar values in every quadrant, and hence are more likely to have similar poses. In our work, we apply the robust mean-shift clustering to the set of descriptors. Given that we apply mean-shift clustering on separate dimensions of the descriptors (as opposed to the entire dimensions collectively), and each application of mean-shift at a node of the tree is evaluated on sub-clusters with fewer members than its parent node, clusters can thus be efficiently found.

We apply the above method on the Human Action dataset [29, 30], and plot a histogram of the Euclidean distances between the cluster medoids (i.e. codewords) and its members (intra-cluster distances) in Fig. 8(a). For comparison, we show the histogram obtained by direct application of mean-shift clustering on the descriptor values in Fig. 8(b). Note that while both possess the same number of clusters, the proposed method finds much more compact clusters as shown by the smaller mean value (a t-test shows that this smaller mean value to be significant, $p < 10^{-15}$). Fig. 8(c) shows the histogram of the Euclidean distances between the cluster medoids found by the spatial-clustering method (inter-cluster distances), and Fig. 8(d) shows those obtained with direct application of mean-shift clustering. The proposed method finds codewords that are substantially distinct from each other, as shown by the higher mean Euclidean distance between codewords ($p < 10^{-12}$). We show codewords selected by our method in Fig. 9. As observed, salient and unique poses exhibited by the human, e.g. sitting, standing and drinking water are well represented.

5. DISCRIMINATIVE SUBSEQUENCES OF CODEWORDS

In this section, we describe our method to learn discriminative subsequences of video codewords (termed xSC in this paper) that are unique to a targeted activity. Inference at test time for the targeted activity is achieved by aligning these xSC to the test video codeword sequence with a sliding window approach, and computing the weighted sum of the confidence score at each window. Here, we first detail the learning of these activity-specific subsequence of codewords before discussing how they are exploited at test time.

We seek a discriminative xSC which models the distinguishing poses of a human when performing an activity, and the distinctive temporal ordering of these poses to reliably recognize an activity. The former incorporates pose/appearance features as recognition cues, while the latter encodes important temporal information that are unique to the activity. The alignment of these discriminative xSC to a window of a test sequence can thus be exploited to localize the activity within the test sequence with a sliding window approach. A key challenge here is on the *alignment* of a xSC to the test window. Specifically, a person may exhibit poses at test time that are slightly different from those seen during training, even when performing the same activity. Hence, the test video will be represented by a codeword sequence that is different from the xSC learned during training. More importantly, a person may perform a same activity with different speeds during training and testing. Such temporal variations are typically inconsistent across the activity (e.g. faster actions in initial phase of the activity, and slower

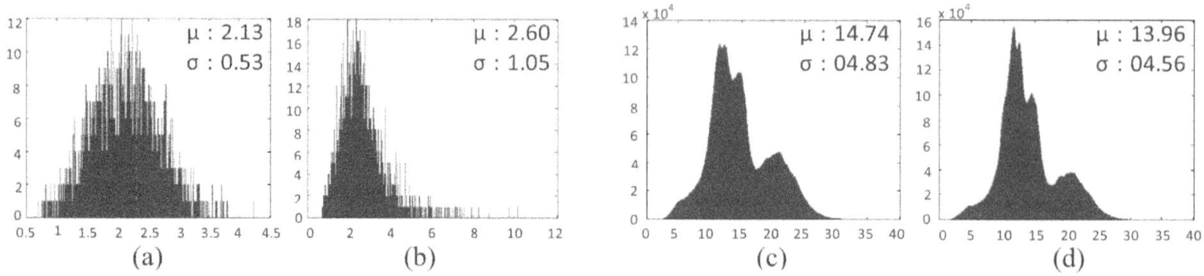

Figure 8: Comparison of clustering quality. Histogram of the Euclidean distances between codewords and its members obtained by our method and by direct application of mean-shift are shown in (a) and (b) respectively. Histograms of the Euclidean distances between codewords obtained by our method and by mean-shift are shown in (c) and (d) respectively. Notice that the proposed method finds more compact clusters, while learning codewords which have more diverse appearances. T-tests show the improvements to be statistically significant, ($p = 10^{-15}$ for comparison between (a) and (b), and $p = 10^{-12}$ for comparison between (c) and (d)).

Figure 9: Codeword exemplars obtained for Human Activities dataset [29].

actions thereafter). This makes temporal ordering of the codewords in a xSC a potentially less reliable recognition cue. Here, we first describe our alignment method which addresses these two issues in a unified framework, before discussing how an ensemble of boosted xSC are learned.

5.1 Aligning xSC to a test window codewords

Motivated by recent successes of DNA sequences alignment in the bioinformatics field [14], we formulate the problem of video codewords alignment as a DNA sequence alignment problem where we consider a codeword of a video sequence to be analogous to a codon in a DNA sequence. Correspondingly, given a discriminative xSC and a test window of codewords, we compute the optimum alignment between the two sequences by the semi-global sequence alignment method [3]. Unlike the global alignment method, the semi-global alignment method ignores leading and trailing gaps in the sequence alignment process and is well suited for our problem in which a xSC may be longer than the test window codewords. Additionally, unlike local sequence alignment which finds *subsequences* of xSC within the test window, semi-global alignment searches for the presence of the *entire* xSC within the test window and hence fully exploits the discriminative potential of the xSC. In the following, we first describe the semi-global sequence alignment method, before addressing how this method gives robust alignment under pose and temporal variations in the video sequence.

Let P denotes a window of codewords, $P = \{p_1, \ldots, p_m\}$, where p_i is the ith codeword in the sequence, and let $Q = \{q_1, q_2, \ldots, q_n\}$ denote a discriminative xSC. The optimum semi-global alignment between P and Q can be obtained by first computing a $(m+1) \times (n+1)$ score matrix M, where

$$M(i+1, j+1) = \min \begin{cases} M(i,j) + d(p_i, q_j) \\ M(i, j+1) + g \\ M(i+1, j) + g \end{cases} . \qquad (10)$$

Here, $d(p_i, q_j)$ denotes the Euclidean distance between the pose descriptors of codewords p_i and q_j, and g is a gap penalty which represents the cost of inserting a gap in the alignment. In all experiments, we set g to be equal to the standard deviation of the distances computed between every codeword. Given matrix M, we identify the entry $M(x, y)$ in the last row/column which has the minimum value as ϕ. It denotes the misalignment score between the two sequences. The optimum alignment is then found by keeping track of the elements that contribute the minimum distance at each step i.e. backward transversal of a path from $M(x, y)$ to $M(1, 1)$. As illustration, Fig. 10(a) shows an example xSC that is learned for the open-bottle activity, and its alignment to a positive window, where the xSC and window codewords corresponds to different persons. Misalignment score ϕ obtained is given in the same figure. We show the alignment of the same xSC to a random negative window (drinking-water activity) in Fig. 10(b). As observed, a higher misalignment score is obtained when xSC is paired to a negative window.

The formulation of the sequence alignment in the above share similarities to the classical time warping, but has an important difference in that time warping considers the distances of vector pairs taken from a common k-dimensional feature space, whereas sequence alignment considers the distances of codewords taken one each from each sequence [1]. Here, insertion and deletion of gaps in the alignment is similar to lengthening (slowing-down) and shortening (speeding-up) of the activity in the video sequence, and empowers the alignment procedure to be robust to temporal variations of an activity. Additionally, we compute the optimum alignment based on the pose differences between the codewords (rather than demanding the exact matching of codewords). This affords us much flexibility when aligning sequences with slight pose variations. In this aspect, we attempt to strike a winning tradeoff: exploit the appearance and temporal orderings of the codewords encoded in a xSC to empower it with strong discriminative potential to recognize an activity, and leveraging on an alignment framework which affords an xSC with sufficient flexibility to align to test sequences with slight pose and temporal variations.

5.2 Learning discriminative xSC

We learn a boosted ensemble of xSC from positive and negative training sequences for each target activity. These xSC are aligned to test video codeword sequence with a slid-

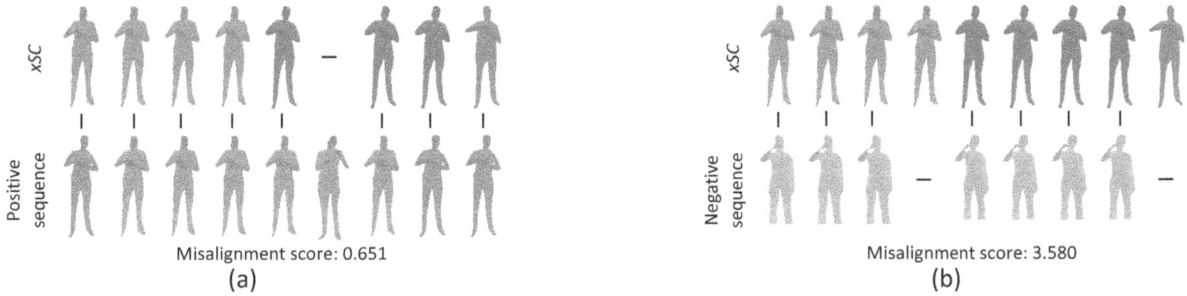

Figure 10: Alignment of example positive and negative window codewords on the same xSC that is learned for the open-container activity. Vertical and horizontal lines between codewords denote the alignment of the codewords and the gaps inserted to obtain the optimum alignment, respectively. Misalignment scores (ϕ) are show for each alignment.

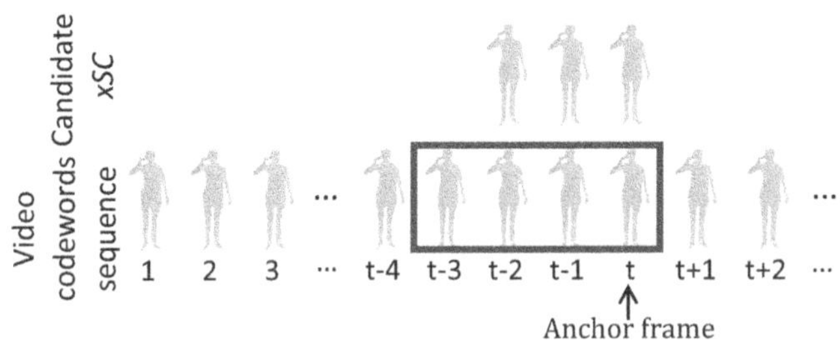

Figure 11: Aligning a candidate xSC to a video codeword sequence. We show the window by the blue rectangle, and also depict the anchoring frame for the window. Candidate xSC assigns a misalignment score to each image frame of the video codeword sequence at the anchoring frame of the window.

ing window approach at inference, where weighted sum of the confidence score at each window is used as the overall confidence measure for the targeted activity at the window. We first present our method to learn a single discriminative xSC, before discussing how a boosted ensemble of discriminative xSC is learned.

We require a discriminative xSC to align well to positive window codewords but not to the negative. In this work, we exploit validation video sequences for discriminative learning of xSC. Specifically, we select a random subsequence of codewords from a positive training codeword sequence as a candidate xSC, and align it to positive and negative validation codeword sequences with a sliding window approach. Rather than assigning a fixed size window for every candidate xSC, we pair each candidate xSC with a window of random size, and anchor each window to a video frame in the validation sequence (see Fig. 11). The anchoring frame provides the reference for the current window. The use of sliding windows enables our method to not only recognize human activities (i.e. classification task), but more importantly empower it with an ability to find a targeted activity within a video sequence (i.e. localization task). We consider the misalignment score (defined as ϕ above) for each window as a feature value of the window, where the class label for the window is $+1$ if its corresponding anchoring image frame is from a positive validation sequence, and -1 otherwise. The set of feature values and class labels, together with the weights of the windows (initialized according to the number of positive and negative validation video frames) are then used to learn a weak decision stump[13] which maximizes the weighted accuracy on the set of validation windows. The prediction of the decision stump classifier based on the learned xSC at a window w is,

$$xSC\left[w\right] = \begin{cases} +1 & \text{if } \phi < \tau \\ -1 & \text{otherwise} \end{cases}, \tag{11}$$

where τ is a learned parameter. We learn an ensemble of discriminative xSC by AdaBoost [10], where each boosting round outputs an xSC, its weight, window size, and a corresponding decision stump. All xSC learned by AdaBoost are then combined to form a boosted ensemble, where the overall confidence measure of an activity in a window w is

$$H\left[w\right] = \sum_{j=1} \alpha_j \times xSC_j\left[w\right], \tag{12}$$

with α_j as the weight of xSC_j and is learned during boosting. In this paper, we pick candidate xSC by selecting random subsequences from positive training data, and assign its window size a random value between 75% to 125% its length. We sample windows of the validation sequences (both positive and negative) at every frame, and apply 300 boosting rounds to learn the boosted ensemble.

6. HUMAN ACTIVITIES CLASSIFICATION AND LOCALIZATION

In this section, we describe how the learned boosted ensembles are used to recognize human activities (i.e. classification task), and how they are exploited to find human activities within a test video (i.e. localization task). The only image information used by the ensemble is the depth image information, obtained with the Kinect sensor.

To classify the activity depicted in a test video, we learn a boosted ensemble for each activity, and capitalize on these ensembles to recognize the activity-label of the test video. Specifically, we apply the boosted ensemble $H_i\left[\cdot\right]$ which was learned for the ith activity to the test video in a sliding window approach. The sliding step is the same as that used for training. Each window in the test video is assigned a score based on Eq. (12), and we consider the median score of all windows within the test video for the classification confidence of the video as activity i. To localize the ith activity, we apply the boosted ensemble $H_i\left[\cdot\right]$ on all windows of the test video, and employ the powerful mean shift mode estimation technique [7] on the confidence measure of each window, similar to [16]. Mean shift models the non-parametric distribution with the kernel density estimator,

$$P(\mathrm{w}) \propto \sum_{w_j \in W} H_i[w_j] G\Big(\frac{\mathrm{w} - w_i}{b_w}\Big) \tag{13}$$

where the Gaussian kernel G uses bandwidth b_w. Mean shift efficiently finds modes within the sequence which are then used as the final set of detections. Here, we used the density estimated at each mode as the confidence value of the detection.

7. EXPERIMENTAL RESULTS

7.1 Classification results

We evaluate our technique on the challenging Human Activity dataset [29] and compare against the best (to our knowledge) classification results obtained so far on this dataset. We used only depth information in our method and adhere to the same evaluation protocols as those used by other methods. This dataset comprises 12 challenging activities (see Table 1) performed by 4 persons. We note that humans in the dataset are located away from the background. Moreover, since the background images are also not available with the dataset, we can not use our proposed method for segmentation. Hence, we apply a simple depth threshold value to segment the human from the background. In our work, we use the Otsu's method [22] to learn an optimum depth threshold value to extract the foreground human. Following [29], we separate the 12 activities into five different environments of office, kitchen, bedroom, bathroom, and living room, and evaluate under two settings: 'new-person' and 'person-seen-before'.

In the 'new-person' setting, we evaluate the boosted ensemble learned for each activity on video sequences in which the ensemble has not previously seen the person carrying out the activity. We used leave-one-out cross validation to test each person data whereby the ensemble was trained on the data of three persons and tested on the fourth person. To learn an ensemble for an activity-class, we pick the positive sequence of one person (randomly chosen) as the training sequence, and use the sequences (both positive and negative) of the other two persons for validation. To evaluate the ensemble, we apply it on data of the person not used for training/validation, in which all activities of the person are used for testing. In this aspect, each activity is searched for in video sequences of *every* activity class. In the 'person-seen-before' setting, we evaluate the boosted ensemble on video sequences for which the ensemble has previously seen the person carrying out the activity. Here, we report two-fold cross validation classification accuracy, in which we split the video sequence of each person into two equal halves, used one half for training/validation, and the other for testing.

We first discuss classification results for the 'new-person' setting. Fig. 12(a) reports the confusion matrix of the activities irrespective to different environments. Turning to incorrect classifications, it can be seen that activities brushing-teeth and talking-phone are often misclassified. This is due to the similar body poses for both activities which is further complicated by little hand motions in both activities. Consequently, our method which exploit the appearance and temporal cues fail to achieve accurate classification on these activities. On the other hand, our method attain high accuracies for activities which have unique poses (e.g. working-on-computer) and unique temporal pose ordering (e.g. rinsing-mouth). We compare results obtained by our method with *Naive Classifier (multi-class support vector machine)*, *One-level MEMM*, *two-level MEMM*[29] in Table 2. Our method is able to detect and classify the activities performed in different environments with an overall average precision/recall measure of 78.1%/75.4% which is better than 67.9%/55.5% obtained by Sung *et al.* [30] under this setting (bottom row of Table 2). It has to be mentioned that [30] exploits the pose information obtained with robust tracking of body joints locations, while our method uses silhouettes that are (crudely) segmented from depth images. This demonstrates the power of our learned ensemble to recognize complex activities.

Fig. 12(b) reports the confusion matrix for the 'person-seen-before' setting. It can be seen that the boosted ensemble has sharp improvement in performance. This is not surprising, since this experiment setting allows the boosted ensemble to directly exploit the unique characteristic of the person performing the activity to learn the *xSC*, but does highlight the capability of our method to hone in on these characteristics. Here, our algorithm is able to detect and classify the activities performed in different environments with an overall average precision/recall measure of 94.6%/ 93.1% which is better than 84.7%/83.2% obtained by Sung *et al.* [30] for the same setting (bottom row of Table 2). To our knowledge, this is the best result published so far for this dataset.

Table 1: Activities in Human Activity dataset [29].

ID	Activity	ID	Activity
1.	Brushing teeth	7.	Talking on phone
2.	Rinsing mouth	8.	Drinking water
3.	Wearing contact lenses	9.	Opening container
4.	Working on computer	10.	Talking on couch
5.	Cooking - Chopping	11.	Relaxing on couch
6.	Cooking - Stirring	12.	Writing on whiteboard

(a) Detected (columns) / Ground truth (rows)

	1	2	3	4	5	6	7	8	9	10	11	12
1	.25						.75	.25				
2		1										
3			1									
4				1								
5					.75	.50						
6					.25	.50						
7	.50						.25	.25		.25		
8	.25							.50	.25			
9									.75			
10										.50		
11										.25	1	
12												1

(b) Detected (columns) / Ground truth (rows)

	1	2	3	4	5	6	7	8	9	10	11	12
1	1						.25	.13				
2		1										
3			1						.13			
4				1								
5					1							
6						1						
7							.38					
8							.25	.88				
9							.13		.88			
10										.75		
11										.25	1	
12												1

Figure 12: Confusion Matrices for each activity are shown in (a) and (b) respectively. Results for "new-person" setting are shown in (a), and "person-seen-before" setting in (b) irrespective to different activity environments. Indices in first row and column of each table corresponds to those in Table 1.

Figure 13: Example sequence of training images used to localize the *left-leg-kicking* activity from a test sequence.

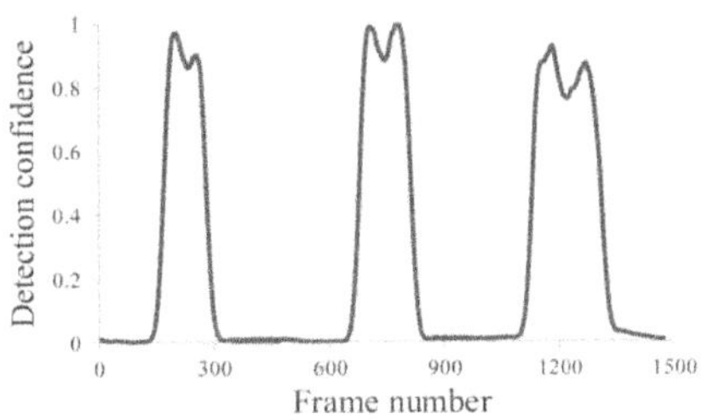

(a)

(b)

Figure 14: Activity localization. (a) Plot of detection confidence against frame number, obtained by applying the boosted ensemble of the test video using the sliding window approach. (b) Detections obtained by our method, where each row correspond to a detection and number indicate frame index. Red bounding boxes within segmented body correspond to detected modes.

7.2 Localization results

In this section, we demonstrate our method to localize a targeted activity from a test sequence. Here, a human is very near to the background (lying on the ground) and hence we use the proposed method to extract the foreground. We define the targeted activity as the kicking motion of the left leg, and show an example training sequence of the activity in Fig. 13. We test our method on a test sequence which shows a person performing the targeted activity at three separate times within the sequence. Specifically, this activity were performed at frames f_{175} to f_{280}, f_{676} to f_{847} and f_{1120} to f_{1325}. Frames f_1 to f_{174}, f_{281} to f_{675}, f_{848} to f_{1119} and f_{1326} to f_{1478} comprise random activities perform by the person. We show example frames from each interval in Fig. 15. We learn a boosted ensemble of xSC for the target activity, and plot the detection confidence for each sliding window in Fig. 14(a). Detections obtained by mean shift mode estimation corresponds to the three peaks in the graph. We show these detections in Fig. 14(b), where the fourth frame in each detection corresponds to the detected modes. These detections accurately localize the left-leg-kicking activity, and demonstrate the activity localization capability of our method.

8. CONCLUSION

We presented a method which uses only depth images for activity classification and localization. Towards this end, we proposed a descriptor to represent a human pose, and exploited a spatial-based clustering method to find unique human poses (i.e. codewords). Given a training video, we represent the video as a sequence of codewords and learn subsequences of codewords (termed xSC) that model both the discriminative poses of a human when performing an activity, as well as the distinctive temporal ordering of these poses. We identify such a discriminative xSC as one which aligns well only in positive test videos. Here, we formulate the problem of alignment of xSC with a test window codewords as the DNA alignment problem, and exploit the semi-global alignment method to find the optimum alignment. The insertion/deletion of gaps in the alignment represents the slowing-down/speeding-up of the targeted activity in the videos, and affords the alignment to be robust towards temporal variations in the activity. At the same time, robustness to pose variations is achieved since the optimum alignment is computed from the pose differences of the codewords (rather than demanding the exact matching of codewords). Activity classification and localization results on test videos demonstrate the effectiveness of our approach, in which for the Human Activity dataset, we achieved improvement over the best results published so far for the dataset.

Acknowledgements: We thank the anonymous reviewers for their valuable input. This work is supported by Institute for Infocomm Research and by Microsoft Research Asia.

9. REFERENCES

[1] J. Aach and G. M. Church. Aligning gene expression time series with time warping algorithms. *Bioinformatics*, 17(6):495–508, 2001.

[2] J. Aggarwal and M. Ryoo. Human activity analysis: A review. *ACM Computing Surveys*, 43, 2011.

[3] T. Attwood and D. Parry-Smith. Introduction to bioinformatics, 1999. Addison Wesley Longman.

[4] P. J. Besl. *Surface in Range Image Understanding*. Springer-Verlag New York, Inc. New York, 1989.

[5] S. T. Birchfield and S. Rangarajan. Spatiograms versus histograms for region-based tracking. *CVPR*, 2005.

[6] A. F. Bobick and J. W. Davis. The recognition of human movement using temporal templates. *Trans. on Pattern Analysis and Machine Intel.*, 23:257–267, 2001.

[7] D. Comaniciu and P. Meer. Mean shift: A robust approach toward feature space analysis. *Trans. on Pattern Analysis and Machine Intel.*, 24(5), 2002.

[8] P. Dollar, V. Rabaud, G. Cottrell, and S. Belongie. Behavior recognition via sparse spatio-temporal features. *In: ICCCN, IEEE*, pages 65–72, 2005.

[9] A. A. Efros, A. C. Berg, E. C. Berg, G. Mori, and J. Malik. Recognizing action at a distance. *ICCV*, 2003.

[10] Y. Freund and R. E. Schapire. A decision-theoretic generalization of on-line learning and an application to boosting. *J. of Comp. and System Sc.*, 55:119–139, 1997.

[11] S. Holzer, J. Shotton, and P. Kohli. Learning to efficiently detect repeatable interest points in depth data. *Eurpoean Conf. on Comp. Vision*, 2012.

[12] M.-K. Hu. Visual pattern recognition by moment invariants. *IRE Trans. on Info. Theory*, 8, 1962.

[13] W. Iba and P. Langley. Induction of one-level decision trees. *Int. Workshop on Machine Learning*, 1992.

[14] S. Kumar and A. Filipski. Multiple sequence alignment: In pursuit of homologous dna positions. *Genome Research*, pages 127–135, 2007.

[15] I. Laptev. On space-time interest points. *Int. Journal on Computer Vision*, 64:107–123, 2005.

[16] B. Leibe, A. Leonardis, and B. Schiele. Combined object categorization and segmentation with an implicit shape model. *Eurpoean Conf. on Comp. Vision Workshop*, pages 17–32, 2004.

[17] W. Li, Z. Zhang, and Z. Liu. Action recognition based on a bag of 3d points. *Comp. Vision and Pattern Recognition workshops*, 2010.

[18] A. Monnet, A. Mittal, N. Paragios, and V. Ramesh. Background modeling and subtraction of dynamic scenes. *ICCV*, 2003.

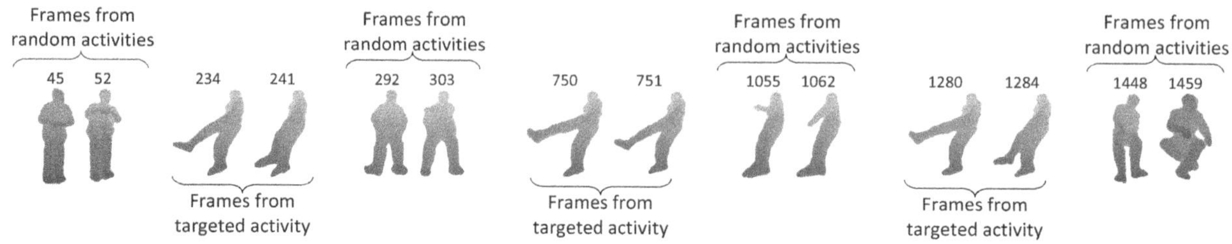

Figure 15: Example frames from different intervals of the test video sequence. Intervals shown belong to both targeted and random activities.

Table 2: ***Precision*** **and** ***Recall*** **scores of** ***Naive Classifier (multi-class support vector machine)***, ***One-layer MEMM*** **model,** ***Two-layer MEMM*** **model, and** ***Our method*** **in each environment.**

Location	Activity	new-person								person-seen-before							
		Naive Classifier		One-layer MEMM		Two-layer MEMM		Our Method		Naive Classifier		One-layer MEMM		Two-layer MEMM		Our Method	
		Prec	*Rec*	*Prec*	*Rec*	*Prec*	*Rec*	*Prec*	*Rec*	*Prec*	*Rec*	*Prec*	*Rec*	*Prec*	*Rec*	*Prec*	*Rec*
bathroom	rinsing mouth	77.7	49.3	71.8	63.2	51.1	51.4	**100**	**100**	73.3	49.7	70.7	53.1	61.4	70.9	**100**	**100**
	brushing teeth	64.5	20.5	83.3	57.7	88.5	55.3	**100**	**75.0**	81.5	65.1	81.5	75.6	96.7	77.1	**100**	**100**
	wearing contact lens	82.0	89.7	81.5	89.7	78.6	88.3	**80.0**	**100**	87.8	71.9	87.8	71.9	79.2	94.7	**100**	**100**
	Average	**74.7**	**53.1**	**78.9**	**70.2**	**72.7**	**65.0**	**93.3**	**91.6**	**80.9**	**62.2**	**80.0**	**66.9**	**79.1**	**90.9**	**100**	**100**
bedroom	talking on phone	82.2	32.6	82.0	32.6	63.2	48.3	**60.0**	**75.0**	70.2	67.2	70.2	69.0	88.7	90.8	**100**	**62.5**
	drinking water	19.2	12.1	19.1	12.1	70.0	71.7	**50.0**	**50.0**	64.1	31.6	64.1	39.6	83.3	81.7	**80.0**	**100**
	opening container	95.6	65.9	95.6	65.9	95.0	57.4	**100**	**75.0**	48.7	52.3	48.7	54.8	93.3	77.4	**88.8**	**100**
	Average	**65.6**	**36.9**	**65.6**	**36.9**	**76.1**	**59.2**	**70.0**	**66.7**	**61.0**	**50.4**	**61.0**	**54.5**	**88.4**	**83.3**	**89.6**	**87.5**
Kitchen	cooking (chopping)	33.3	56.9	33.2	57.4	45.6	43.3	**60.0**	**75.0**	78.9	28.9	78.9	29.0	70.3	85.7	**100**	**100**
	cooking (stirring)	44.2	29.3	45.6	31.4	24.8	17.7	**50.0**	**50.0**	44.6	45.8	44.6	45.8	74.3	47.3	**100**	**100**
	drinking water	72.5	21.3	71.6	23.9	95.4	75.3	**75.0**	**75.0**	52.2	51.5	52.2	52.4	88.8	86.8	**100**	**100**
	opening container	76.9	6.20	75.8	6.20	91.9	55.2	**100**	**75.0**	17.9	62.4	17.9	62.4	91.0	77.4	**100**	**100**
	Average	**56.8**	**28.4**	**56.6**	**29.7**	**64.4**	**47.9**	**71.2**	**68.7**	**48.4**	**47.2**	**48.4**	**47.4**	**81.1**	**74.3**	**100**	**100**
living room	talking on phone	69.7	0.90	83.3	25.0	51.5	48.5	**50.0**	**75.0**	34.1	67.7	34.1	67.7	88.8	90.6	**100**	**75.0**
	drinking water	57.1	53.1	52.8	55.8	54.3	69.3	**66.7**	**50.0**	80.2	48.7	71.0	53.8	80.2	82.6	**80.0**	**100**
	talking on couch	71.5	35.4	57.4	91.3	73.2	43.7	**100**	**50.0**	91.4	50.7	91.4	50.7	98.8	94.7	**100**	**62.5**
	relaxing on couch	97.2	76.4	95.8	78.6	31.3	21.1	**80.0**	**100**	95.7	96.5	95.7	96.5	86.8	82.7	**72.7**	**100**
	Average	**73.9**	**41.5**	**72.3**	**62.7**	**52.6**	**45.7**	**74.2**	**68.7**	**75.4**	**65.9**	**73.1**	**67.2**	**88.7**	**87.7**	**88.2**	**84.4**
office	talking on phone	60.5	31.0	60.6	31.5	69.4	48.2	**60.0**	**75.0**	80.4	52.2	80.4	52.2	87.6	92.0	**100**	**75.0**
	writing on whiteboard	47.1	73.3	45.2	74.1	75.5	81.3	**100**	**100**	42.5	59.3	42.5	59.3	85.5	91.9	**100**	**100**
	drinking water	41.1	12.4	51.2	23.2	67.1	68.8	**66.7**	**50.0**	53.4	36.7	53.4	36.7	82.3	81.5	**80.0**	**100**
	working on computer	93.5	76.8	93.5	76.8	83.4	40.7	**100**	**100**	89.2	69.3	89.2	69.3	89.5	93.8	**100**	**100**
	Average	60.5	48.4	62.6	51.4	73.8	59.8	**81.7**	**81.2**	66.4	54.4	66.4	54.4	86.2	89.8	**95.0**	**93.7**
Overall Average		**66.3**	**41.7**	**67.2**	**50.2**	**67.9**	**55.5**	**78.1**	**75.4**	**66.4**	**56.0**	**65.8**	**58.1**	**84.7**	**83.2**	**94.6**	**93.1**

[19] B. Ni, G. Wang, and P. Moulin. Rgbd-hudaact: A color-depth video database for human daily activity recognition. *Int. Conf. on Comp. Vision Workshops*, 2011.

[20] S. Nowozin, G. Bakir, and K. Tsuda. Discriminative subsequence mining for action classification. *ICCV*, pages 1–8, 2007.

[21] C. O'Conaire, N. E. O'Connor, and A. F. Smeaton. An improved spatiogram similarity measure for robust object localisation. *ICASSP*, pages 15–20, 2007.

[22] N. Otsu. A threshold selection method from gray-level histograms. *Trans. on Sys., Man and Cyber.*, 9(1), 1975.

[23] V. Parameswaran and R. Chellappa. View invariance for human action recognition. *Int. J. on Comp. Vision*, 66:83–101, 2006.

[24] R. B. Rusu, N. Blodow, Z. C. Marton, and M. Beetz. Aligning point cloud views using persistent feature histograms. *Intelligent Robots and Systems*, 2008.

[25] B. Sabata, F. Arman, and J. K. Aggarwal. Segmentation of 3d range images using pyramidal data structures. *Int. Conf. on Computer Vision*, 1990.

[26] C. Schuldt, I. Laptev, and B. Caputo. Recognizing human actions: A local svm approach. *ICPR*, pages 32–36, 2004.

[27] J. Shotton, A. FItzgibbon, M. Cook, T. Sharp, M. Finocchio, R. Moore, A. Kipman, and A. Blake. Real-time human pose recognition in parts from single depth images. *CVPR*, 2011.

[28] P. Spagnolo, T. Orazio, M. Leo, and A. Distante. Moving object segmentation by background subtraction and temporal analysis. *Image and Vision Computing*, 24(5):411–423, 2006.

[29] J. Sung, C. Ponce, B. Selman, and A. Saxena. Human activity detection from rgbd images. *AAAI workshop on Pattern, Activity and Intent Recognition*, 2011.

[30] J. Sung, C. Ponce, B. Selman, and A. Saxena. Unstructured human activity detection from rgbd images. *Int. Conf. on Robotics and Automation*, 2012.

[31] J. Wang, Z. Liu, Y. Wu, and J. Yuan. Mining actionlet ensemble for action recognition with depth cameras. *CVPR*, 2012.

[32] A. Yilmaz and M. Shah. Actions sketch: A novel action representation. *CVPR*, 1:984–989, 2005.

[33] H. Zhang and L. E. Parker. 4-dimensional local spatio-temporal features for human activity recognition. *Int. Conf. on Intelligent Robots and Systems*, 2011.

[34] Y. Zhao, Z. Liu, L. Yang, and H. Cheng. Combining rgb and depth map features for human activity recognition. *APSIPA ASC*, 2012.

[35] Z. Zivkovic. Improved adaptive gaussian mixture model for background subtraction. *ICPR*, pages 28–31, 2004.

We Are Not Equally Negative: Fine-grained Labeling for Multimedia Event Detection

Zhigang Ma
DISI, University of Trento
Trento, Italy
ma@disi.unitn.it

Yi Yang
SCS, Carnegie Mellon
University, Pittsburgh, USA
yiyang@cs.cmu.edu

Zhongwen Xu
CCST, Zhejiang University
Hangzhou, China
zhongwen@zju.edu.cn

Nicu Sebe
DISI, University of Trento
Trento, Italy
sebe@disi.unitn.it

Alexander G. Hauptmann
SCS, Carnegie Mellon
University, Pittsburgh, USA
alex@cs.cmu.edu

ABSTRACT

Multimedia event detection (MED) is an effective technique for video indexing and retrieval. Current classifier training for MED treats the negative videos equally. However, many negative videos may resemble the positive videos in different degrees. Intuitively, we may capture more informative cues from the negative videos if we assign them fine-grained labels, thus benefiting the classifier learning. Aiming for this, we use a statistical method on both the positive and negative examples to get the decisive attributes of a specific event. Based on these decisive attributes, we assign the fine-grained labels to negative examples to treat them differently for more effective exploitation. The resulting fine-grained labels may be not accurate enough to characterize the negative videos. Hence, we propose to jointly optimize the fine-grained labels with the knowledge from the visual features and the attributes representations, which brings mutual reciprocality. Our model obtains two kinds of classifiers, one from the attributes and one from the features, which incorporate the informative cues from the fine-grained labels. The outputs of both classifiers on the testing videos are fused for detection. Extensive experiments on the challenging TRECVID MED 2012 development set have validated the efficacy of our proposed approach.

Categories and Subject Descriptors

H.3.1 [**Information Search and Retrieval**]: Content Analysis and Indexing; I.2.10 [**Vision and Scene Understanding**]: Video analysis

Keywords

Multimedia Event Detection (MED); Fine-grained Labeling; Multi-source Attributes; Attribute Representation; Attribute Selection

MM'13, October 21–25, 2013, Barcelona, Spain.
Copyright 2013 ACM 978-1-4503-2404-5/13/10 ...$15.00.
http://dx.doi.org/10.1145/2502081.2502119.

1. INTRODUCTION

Multimedia collections have been proliferating, which requires effective multimedia content analysis for indexing, retrieval and management. The analysis is essentially a task of abstracting the semantics of multimedia data, for which we need to bridge the semantic gap between the low-level features and the high-level descriptions [11][14].

Recently, the focus on multimedia analysis has been gradually shifting from image analysis towards video analysis due to the rich semantic information in videos [31][20][19][18]. Existing works on video analysis cover several topics among which detection is an emerging one. Detection identifies the occurrence of a class of interest from a set of infinite classes. As it is impossible to know all the infinite classes during the training process, building up a discriminative classifying hyperplane is difficult, which in turn makes detection a challenging task. Detection is closely related to many real-world applications. For example, when a user submits an enquiry of *parkour* to Youtube, the media portal actually detects this from its tremendous video archives and provides the user with the results.

A plethora of works are about detecting simple objects (*e.g. car*), scenes (*e.g. indoor* and *outdoor*) or human actions (*e.g. running*) in videos. However, users are usually more interested in more meaningful multimedia events such as *parkour*. Multimedia events are higher level descriptions of multimedia data which build upon necessary objects, scenes and human actions. For example, the event *parkour* includes several attributes such as *people*, *outdoor*, *building*, and *running*, *jumping*, *etc.* These attributes are the semantic concepts of objects, scenes and human actions. Detection of these multimedia events is formidably difficult as they contain many objects, various actions, multiple scenes and have significant intra-class variations. Additionally, they usually take place in much longer video clips where many frames can be uninformative so it is unlikely to infer an event with a single image or a few video frames. The research on detecting this kind of events remains in its infancy, though we have seen some pioneering works recently [20][19][18] promoted by the TRECVID MED task. The definition of MED task from National Institute of Standards and Technology (NIST) is: "detect the occurrence of an event within a video clip based on an Event Kit, which contains some text description about the concept and some example videos." Existing works on MED treat negative examples equally. However, given closer investigation, we would find out that negative videos actually have different degrees of "negativeness." To better illustrate our argument, we give an ex-

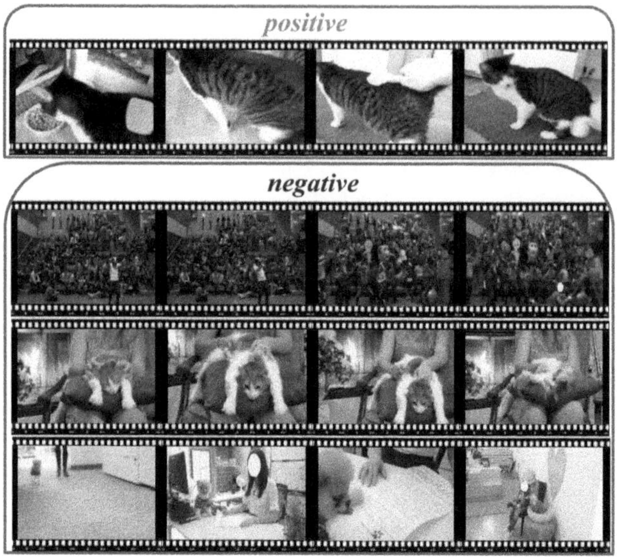

Figure 1: An example showing that negative videos for an event are not equally negative.

ample using the event *Grooming an animal* in Figure 1. We can see that the first negative video, which is *Harlem Shake*, is quite clear to be negative. In contrast, it is very difficult to differentiate the second negative video representing *Massaging an animal* from the positive one. We find many common attributes between this video and the positive video such as *animal* and *hand* (object), *touching* (action). The last negative video is also ambiguous as it has *animal* and *hand* but does not look exactly like *Grooming an animal*. In fact, it is about *A day in the life of a cute dog*. As suggested by the example in Figure 1, negative videos for an event are not equally negative. Some are definitely negative so using 0 as their labels during the classifier learning is precise. Some have positive attributes so assigning them labels with different values between 1 and 0, *a.k.a.* fine-grained labels in this paper, may better characterize them. But manually assigning the fine-grained labels is laborious, subjective and possibly not accurate enough. Hence, in this paper, we focus on how to adaptively assign fine-grained labels to negative videos, based on which we obtain extra information cues for classification. It is worth pointing out that the research on MED includes several directions such as discriminative feature design, speeding up feature extraction, parallel and so on. Nonetheless, we particularly focus on fine-grained labeling in the classifier learning. To the best of our knowledge, we are the first to tackle this issue for multimedia event detection.

As mentioned before, the fine-grained labels of negative examples depend on the amount of positive attributes they have. Hence, our approach first represents MED videos with a variety of attributes. Then we learn a decisive attribute set to evaluate the "negativeness" of the negative videos and initialize the fine-grained labels accordingly. The fine-grained labels are exploited in our framework which jointly optimizes the knowledge from the visual features (*e.g.*, STIP) of MED videos, the attributes based representations and the fine-grained labels. We consequently obtain two kinds of classifiers, one based on visual features and one based on attribute representations, which both benefit from the extra information cues uncovered from the fine-grained labels. The two kinds of classifiers are combined for multimedia event detection.

The main contributions of our work are as follows:

- We propose to leverage attributes to evaluate the "negativeness" of the negative examples.
- We conduct the first MED exploration of adaptively assigning fine-grained labels to negative examples.
- We design a framework that jointly optimizes the knowledge from the visual features, the attributes based representation, and the fine-grained labels, through which two kinds of classifiers are obtained for multimedia event detection.

2. RELATED WORK

In this section, we briefly review the related works on multimedia event detection and visual attributes.

2.1 Multimedia Event Detection

Most existing works have focused on detecting simple events which can be characterized by a single shot or a few frames. Adam *et al.* have proposed an algorithm using multiple local monitors for detecting unusual events in surveillance videos [3]. Wang *et al.* have designed a new motion feature based on motion relativity and visual relatedness for detecting simple events such as *dancing* [24]. Xu *et al.* have studied detecting sport events like *goal* by using web-casting text and broadcast video [28]. A multi-resolution, multi-source and multi-modal bootstrapping framework has been proposed for detecting news events like *riot* in [25]. The focused events in above works are simple, last for short time and have small intra-class variations. In contrast, we focus on the multimedia events which are complicated, occur in much longer videos and have huge intra-class variations.

Recently, how to detect more complicated multimedia events has attracted more research interest [5][6][20][19][21][29][22][18]. In [5][6], SVM is used for detection and shows good performance. In [19], a classifier-specific intermediate representation learned by leveraging external video resources is developed for MED. In [20], Ma *et al.* have proposed to use video attributes to boost MED performance. Some other works have focused on novel video representations for boosted event detection performance. For example, a multi-channel shape-flow kernel descriptors is proposed for event detection in [21]; Yang *et al.* design an approach that discovers date-driven concepts from multi-modality signals, based on which a sparse video representation is learned for event detection [29]; Natarajan *et al.* propose to combine multiple features from different modalities to improve multimedia event detection [22]. Transfer learning has been exploited by Ma *et al.* for multimedia event detection when there are only few positive examples [18].

These aforementioned works have contributed to multimedia event detection in different ways. However, no study has been conducted on how to more effectively utilize negative examples for boosted performance. In this paper, we dwell in the usage of negative examples. Multimedia events usually happen in long video clips. The negative examples may resemble the positive examples in many frames, which justifies fine-grained labels that reflect the different degrees of "negativeness" of negative examples. We therefore propose to uncover extra informative cues from the fine-grained labels to boost the MED performance.

2.2 Visual Attributes

Using visual attributes to represent multimedia data has been popular recently. Farhadi *et al.* have introduced them as the describable properties of objects [9]. For instance, a *tennis ball* has attributes like *round* and *green*. Usually, attributes reflect the parts, shape or texture of objects at a local level and are both machine-detectable and human-understandable. Wang *et al.* have proposed a discriminative model leveraging attributes for object recognition [27]. A method to learn visual attributes and object classes together has

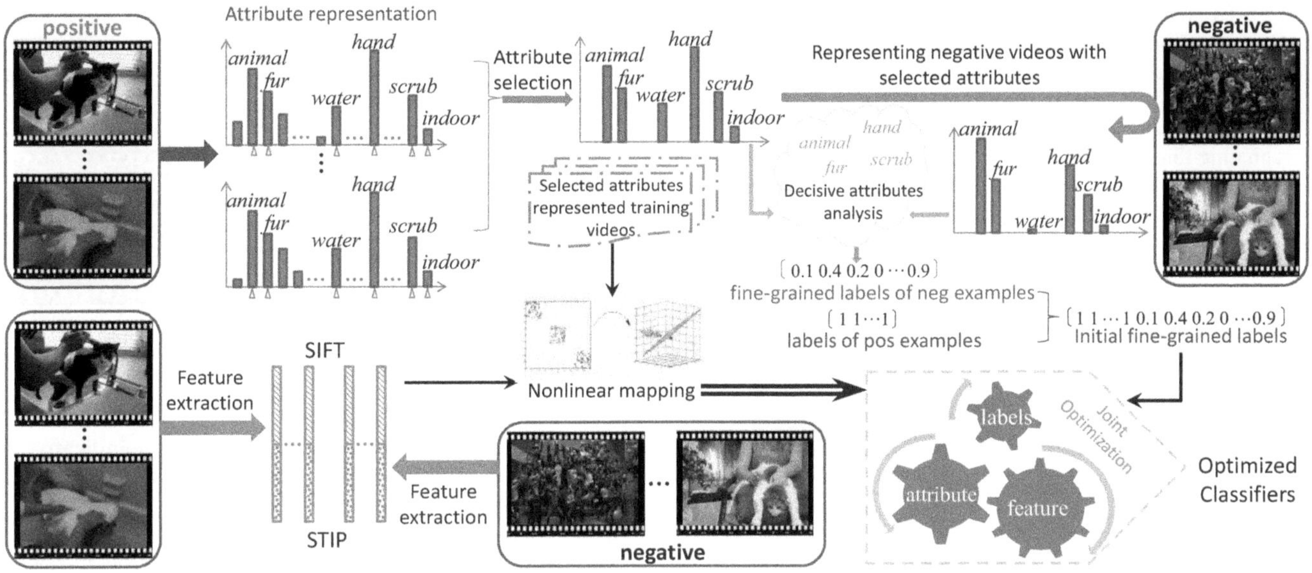

Figure 2: Our framework for multimedia event detection (MED). We first use other video sources to train the attribute representations for the MED videos. The attribute representations of positive examples are exploited to select the particularly indicative attributes. Based on the indicative attributes, we evaluate the "negativeness" of the negative examples and initialize the fine-grained labels accordingly. Meanwhile, we perform a nonlinear mapping for the visual features and the indicative attributes representations of training videos. The nonlinear representations and the initialized fine-grained labels are incorporated into our learning model. The model jointly optimizes the knowledge from the visual features, the attributes representations and the fine-grained labels. Two kinds of optimized classifiers, one from attributes and the other from features, are then obtained for MED.

been presented in [26]. Hwang *et al.* have proposed to explore the shared features between objects and their attributes for animal and scene classification [12]. Dhar *et al.* have leveraged high level describable attributes for selecting high aesthetic quality images and interesting ones from large image collections [7]. Ma *et al.* have presented the idea of video attributes and used them to get extra informative cues which are then incorporated into the event detector for improved accuracy [20].

As Hauptmann has suggested [10], proper usage of semantic concepts is likely to boost the performance of video analysis. Further, recent works on multimedia event recounting show that considering elementary concepts of multimedia videos as the evidences is helpful for explaining why a particular event prediction has been made [8]. The semantic concepts usually cover objects, scenes and human actions which are the elements of meaningful events. It is also convenient because we have many labeled object, scene and action datasets publicly available, *e.g.*, HMDB [15]. Hence, we propose to treating the semantic concepts of these data as attributes and learn the attribute representations of multimedia events. The attribute representations can be exploited to evaluate the "negativeness" of negative examples, resulting in the fine-grained labels.

3. FRAMEWORK OVERVIEW

Figure 2 demonstrates our framework for MED using *Grooming an animal* as an example. We briefly introduce each step of our approach as follows and leave the details in the next section.

Step 1: We leverage other video sources related to objects, scenes (*e.g.*, some concepts defined in TRECVID Semantic Indexing Task) and actions to train the attribute representations of the MED videos. We propose to use multi-source multi-feature attributes, in other words, multiple video sets represented by different features as our attribute sources.

Step 2: For a specific event, some attributes are particularly indicative while others may be not. Therefore, we select and leverage these indicative attributes to evaluate the "negativeness" of negative examples.

Step 3: We represent both the positive and negative videos with the indicative attributes. Among these indicative attributes, we learn a decisive attribute set which is decisive enough to evaluate the "negativeness" of negative examples. Specifically, we calculate the distances of the negative examples to the positive ones based on the decisive attribute set. The initial fined-grained labels are then allocated from 0 to 1 *w.r.t.* the distances.

Step 4: Multiple visual features are combined to represent each MED video. As nonlinear mapping is an effective way for video analysis [32], we perform full rank principal component analysis [23] for the feature representations to achieve nonlinear mapping similarly to [18]. In *Step 2* we obtain the indicative attributes based representation of the training videos. We also apply full rank principal component analysis on this representation.

Step 5: The nonlinear representations and the initial fine-grained labels (including the labels of positive examples) are incorporated into our learning model. In our model, the knowledge from the visual features, the attributes based representations and the fine-grained labels are jointly optimized. The optimized fine-grained labels help us discover extra useful information for classifier learning. Our model results in two types of classifiers based on the features and attributes respectively. Then we combine them for prediction.

4. PROBLEM FORMULATION

In this section, we detail how to initialize fine-grained labels, how to adaptively optimize them, and how to obtain the two kinds of classifiers.

The first step is to evaluate the "negativeness" of the negative examples. We realize it by utilizing visual attributes, *i.e.*, representing event videos by visual attributes that are semantic concepts of objects, scenes and human actions. A specific event is usually characterized by several indicative attributes which are capable of differentiating this event from others. Hence, if a negative example has low "negativeness," the negative example should also have many of these indicative attributes. Inspired by this, we seek to discover the indicative attributes of an event followed by assessing the "negativeness" of the negative examples.

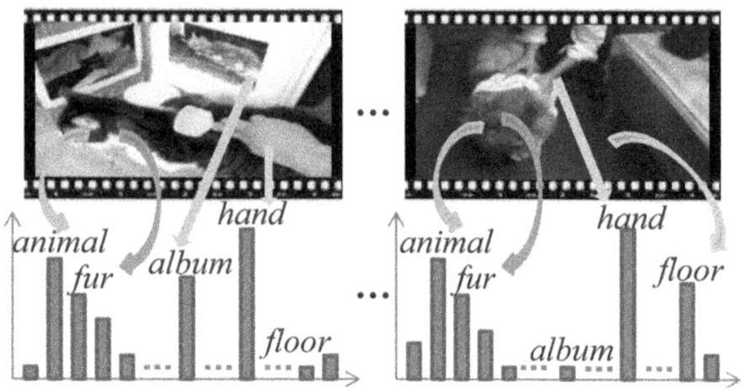

Figure 3: An example showing that the indicative attributes for an event should have consistently higher values. Attributes with small differences, *e.g.*, *fur* are indicative while those with big differences, *e.g.*, *album* are not.

What attributes are indicative for a specific event? Suppose we have n_p positive examples $A_p = [a_p^1, a_p^2, ..., a_p^{n_p}] \in \mathbb{R}^{d_{attr} \times n_p}$ represented by attributes. The indicative attributes should be those who have consistently higher values over all the positive examples. Let us see an exemplar event *Grooming an animal* in Figure 3. The indicative attributes for this event could be *animal*, *fur*, *hand*, *etc.* which are very informative. Consequently, all the positive examples would have consistently higher values on these attributes. There are also some attributes that are not relevant to the event, *e.g.*, *photo* and *floor* in the example and they would show large variance among positive examples. The observation from Figure 3 indicates that if we calculate $\sum_{(a_p^i, a_p^j) \in A_p} (a_p^i - \frac{1}{n_p}\sum_{i=1}^{n_p} a_p^i)^T (a_p^j - \frac{1}{n_p}\sum_{j=1}^{n_p} a_p^j)$, the dimensions corresponding to the indicative attributes should have lower values (ideally close to zero). Meanwhile, we define an attribute selection matrix S that is supposed to be sparse for selecting the indicative attributes. Thus, we propose the following objective function for attribute selection:

$$\begin{aligned} &\min_S Tr\left[S^T \left(\sum_{(a_p^i, a_p^j) \in A_p} (a_p^i - \frac{1}{n_p}\sum_{i=1}^{n_p} a_p^i)^T (a_p^j - \frac{1}{n_p}\sum_{j=1}^{n_p} a_p^j) \right) S\right] \\ &+\lambda \|S\|_{2,1} \qquad (1) \\ &\Rightarrow \min_S Tr(S^T A_p H A_p^T S) + \lambda \|S\|_{2,1} \\ &\qquad s.t. \quad S^T S = I \end{aligned}$$

where $\|\cdot\|_{2,1}$ is the $\ell_{2,1}$-norm, H is a centering matrix and λ is a parameter. The solution of the above function is similar to the optimization approach proposed in [30].

After the attributes are selected, we use them to represent the videos. Then we evaluate the "negativeness" of the negative examples. We again take the event *Grooming an animal* as an example to demonstrate our idea. In Figure 4, the indicative attributes for *Grooming an animal* are *animal*, *fur*, *water*, *hand*, *scrub*, *indoor* and *etc.* The negative video *Massaging a horse* as shown on the right is similar to the positive video. Only a few attributes such as *animal*, *fur*, *hand* and *scrub* existing in the negative video make it look like *Grooming an animal* whereas other attributes, *e.g.*, *water* and *indoor* are not important.

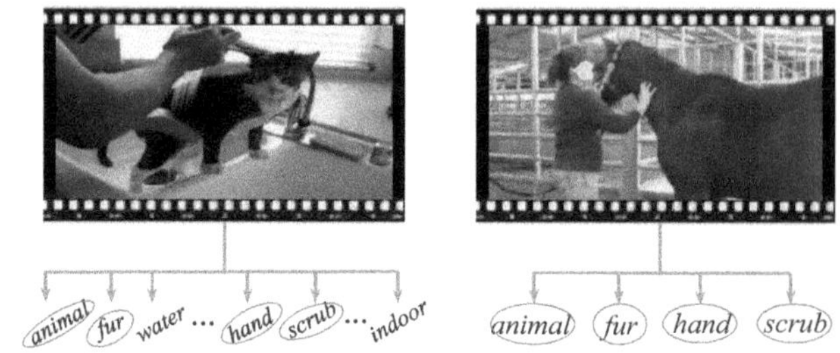

Figure 4: An example showing that a few of the indicative attributes would be decisive enough for evaluating the "negativeness" of negative videos.

In light of this, we learn a decisive attribute set from the indicative attributes. The decisive attribute set is used for evaluating the "negativeness" of the negative examples. Suppose k attributes are considered to be decisive. We sort the indicative attributes of the negative videos and select the top k attributes. Next we need to initialize the fine-grained labels for the negative examples. We formulate our strategy based on the fact that negative examples are not equally negative. For instance, suppose *animal* and *hand* are the decisive attributes for *Grooming an animal.* The two negative examples in Figure 5 both have these two attributes. However, the first video looks very much like *Grooming an animal* but we can judge more easily that the second one is not *Grooming an animal.* Hence, to reflect such differences, we calculate the distances between negative examples and positive examples based on the k-decisive attribute representations. After that, we assign fine-grained labels, *e.g.*, 0, 0.1,...,0.9 to negative examples according to their distances to the positive examples. Higher value indicates that they have lower "negativeness," in other words, they resemble positive examples. Remind that we use attributes from multiple datasets to represent the event videos. Hence, multiple groups of fine-grained labels of negative videos are obtained. Combining these labels and the labels of positive examples (all ones), we get the initial fine-grained labels and denote them as $g_i|_{i=1}^m$.

Figure 5: An example showing that the negative examples have different "negativeness" even if they have the same decisive attributes.

However, the initial fine-grained labels may be not accurate enough to reflect the "negativeness" of negative examples. As a robust classifier depends on the label information, we consider adaptively optimizing the fine-grained labels together with the classifier learning. Consequently, they are mutually beneficial for achieving a better classifier as well as more accurate fine-grained labels.

We denote the adaptively assigned fine-grained labels as $f_i|_{i=1}^m$ and propose to jointly optimize $f_i|_{i=1}^m$ and the classifiers based on attributes representations. The idea is summarized by the following function:

$$\min_{w_i,p_i,f_i} \sum_{i=1}^m \|(\tilde{X}_i^T w_i - p_i) \odot f_i\|_2^2 + \gamma \sum_{i=1}^m \|f_i - g_i\|_2^2 \tag{2}$$

where $\tilde{X}_i|_{i=1}^m$ denotes the multi-source attributes based nonlinear representations of the training data, $w_i|_{i=1}^m$ and $p_i|_{i=1}^m$ denote the corresponding classifiers and predicted labels respectively. $\odot$ is the Hadamard operator. For two matrices U and V with the same dimensions, the Hadamard product of them is give by $(U \odot V)_{i,j} = (U)_{i,j}(V)_{i,j}$. In the above function, the first term makes the optimization of $w_i|_{i=1}^m$, $p_i|_{i=1}^m$ and $f_i|_{i=1}^m$ mutually influential and the second term guarantees that $f_i|_{i=1}^m$ does not deviate drastically from $g_i|_{i=1}^m$ initialized by our labeling strategy.

The fine-grained labels bring extra perks for MED. Essentially, the low-level visual features like STIP should be exploited as the primary information cues. Hence, we propose to capture the knowledge from the visual features by minimizing $\|\tilde{X}^T w - p\|_2^2$ where $\tilde{X}^T$ is the nonlinear representations of the visual features, w and p are the corresponding classifier and predicted labels respectively. The predicted labels p_i and p should be consistent with each other as well as the ground truth, which can be realized by minimizing $\sum_{i=1}^m \|p_i - p\|_2^2$. Now we incorporate the knowledge from visual features, attributes based representations and fine-grained labels into a joint model through the following objective function:

$$\begin{aligned}\min_{w_i,w,p_i,p,f_i} & \sum_{i=1}^m \|(\tilde{X}_i^T w_i - p_i) \odot f_i\|_2^2 + \|\tilde{X}^T w - p\|_2^2 \\ & + \alpha(\sum_{i=1}^m \|p_i - p\|_2^2 + \|p - y\|_2^2) + \beta(\sum_{i=1}^m \|w_i\|_2^2 + \|w\|_2^2) + \gamma \sum_{i=1}^m \|f_i - g_i\|_2^2\end{aligned} \tag{3}$$

In Eq. (3), α, β and γ are regularization parameters and $\beta(\sum_{i=1}^m \|w_i\|_2^2 + \|w\|_2^2)$ is added to avoid over-fitting. The joint optimization enables us to add extra useful information from fine-grained labels to the two types of classifiers, *i.e.*, $w_i|_{i=1}^m$ and w.

Once w_i and w are obtained, we apply them to the testing videos and fuse the prediction scores as the final decision values. Our method is able to incorporate extra informative cues from fine-grained labels to the learning process of two types of classifiers based on different modalities. We therefore name it Graining for Multi-Modal Classifiers (GMMC).

5. OPTIMIZATION

We propose an alternating approach to solve Eq. (3).

(1) Fixing f_i to optimize w, p, w_i and p_i:

By defining a diagonal matrix D_i whose diagonal elements $D_i^{jj} = f_i^j$, the problem in Eq. (3) converts to:

$$\begin{aligned}\min_{w_i,p_i} & \sum_{i=1}^m \|D_i(\tilde{X}_i^T w_i - p_i)\|_2^2 + \|\tilde{X}^T w - p\|_2^2 \\ & + \alpha(\sum_{i=1}^m \|p_i - p\|_2^2 + \|p - y\|_2^2) + \beta(\sum_{i=1}^m \|w_i\|_2^2 + \|w\|_2^2) + \gamma \sum_{i=1}^m \|f_i - g_i\|_2^2\end{aligned} \tag{4}$$

By setting the derivative of Eq. (4) *w.r.t.* w_i to 0, we have:

$$w_i = (\tilde{X}_i D_i^2 X_i^T + \beta I_i)^{-1} \tilde{X}_i D_i^2 p_i = K_i \tilde{X}_i D_i^2 p_i \tag{5}$$

where $I_i \in \mathbb{R}^{d_i \times d_i}$ is an identity matrix and $K_i = (\tilde{X}_i D_i^2 \tilde{X}_i^T + \beta I_i)^{-1}$. Substituting Eq. (5) into Eq. (4) and setting its derivative *w.r.t.* p_i to 0, we have:

$$p_i = \alpha J_i p \tag{6}$$

$$\tag{7}$$

where $J_i = \left((D_i^2 \tilde{X}_i^T K_i \tilde{X}_i - I) D_i^2 (\tilde{X}_i^T K_i \tilde{X}_i D_i^2 - I) + \alpha I + \beta I\right)^{-1}$ and $I \in \mathbb{R}^{n \times n}$ is an identity matrix. By setting the derivative of Eq. (4) *w.r.t.* w to 0, we have:

$$w = (\tilde{X}\tilde{X}^T + \beta I_d)^{-1} \tilde{X} p = M \tilde{X} p \tag{8}$$

where $I_d \in \mathbb{R}^{d \times d}$ is an identity matrix and $M = (\tilde{X}\tilde{X}^T + \beta I_d)^{-1}$. Substituting w_i, p_i and w into Eq. (4) and setting its derivative *w.r.t.* p to 0, we obtain:

$$\begin{aligned}p = \alpha[& \sum_{i=1}^m \alpha^2 J_i (D_i^2 - D_i^2 \tilde{X}_i^T K_i \tilde{X}_i D_i^2) J_i + (\tilde{X}^T M \tilde{X} - I)^2 + \alpha \sum_{i=1}^m (\alpha J_i - I)^2 \\ & + \alpha I + \beta \tilde{X}^T M^2 \tilde{X}]^{-1} y\end{aligned} \tag{9}$$

(2) Fixing w, p, w_i and p_i to optimize f_i:

The problem equals to:

$$\min_{f_i} \sum_{i=1}^m \left\|(\tilde{X}_i^T w_i - p_i) \odot f_i\right\|_2^2 + \gamma \sum_{i=1}^m \|f_i - g_i\|_2^2 \tag{10}$$

Denoting $X_i^T w_i - p_i = [z_i^1, \ldots, z_i^n]^T$, we define a diagonal matrix Q_i with its diagonal elements $Q_i^{jj} = z_i^j$. In this way, we can rewrite Eq. (10) as:

$$\min_{f_i} \sum_{i=1}^m \|Q_i f_i\|_2^2 + \gamma \sum_{i=1}^m \|f_i - g_i\|_2^2 \tag{11}$$

By setting the derivative of Eq. (11) *w.r.t.* f_i to 0, we obtain:

$$f_i = \gamma (Q_i^2 + \gamma I)^{-1} g_i \tag{12}$$

Next, we propose Algorithm 1 to solve the objective function in Eq. (3). It can be proved that the objective function value monotonically decreases in each iteration until convergence using Algorithm 1. Due to the space limit, we omit the proof. The computational complexity is discussed as follows. For training, the most complex part of Algorithm 1 is calculating the inverse of a few matrices: $O(d_i^3)$ for updating w_i; $O(n^3)$ for updating p_i; $O(d^3)$ for updating w; $O(n^3)$ for updating p and $O(n^3)$ for updating f_i. Thus, the complexity is $O(max(d_i, d, n)^3)$. During testing, computing kernels between the testing data and the training data is the most expensive process. Suppose there are n_{te} testing videos, we need to compute nn_{te} kernels. Each datum is d_i or d dimensional so the complexity is $O(max(d_i nn_{te}, dnn_{te}))$.

6. EXPERIMENTS

In this section, we present the experiments on multimedia event detection. The comparison to several algorithms is performed to show the efficacy of GMMC.

6.1 Datasets

The TRECVID MED 2012 development set (MED12) is used in our experiments. MED12 consists of 50328 video clips which are related to 20 events. The 20 events and their examples are displayed in Figure 6. We extract two features, *i.e.*, SIFT [17] and STIP [16] for MED videos as showcase. Then we use 1x1, 2x2 and 3x1 spatial grids to generate the spatial BoW representation. For each grid, we use standard BoW representation with 4,096 dimensions, thus resulting in 32,768 dimension spatial BoW feature for SIFT/STIP to represent each video.

Algorithm 1: Optimization procedure for GMMC

Input:

$\tilde{X}_i \in \mathbb{R}^{d_i \times n}|_{i=1}^{m}$, $\tilde{X} \in \mathbb{R}^{d \times n}$ and $y \in \mathbb{R}^{n \times 1}$;

$g_i \in \mathbb{R}^{n \times 1}|_{i=1}^{m}$;

Parameters α, β and γ.

Output:

Optimized $w_i \in \mathbb{R}^{d_i \times 1}|_{i=1}^{m}$ and $w \in \mathbb{R}^{d \times 1}$;

1: Set $t = 0$, initialize $f_i \in \mathbb{R}^{n \times 1}|_{i=1}^{m}$ randomly;

2: **repeat**

Compute the diagonal matrix D_i^t according to $D_i^{jj} = f_i^j$;
Update w_i^{t+1} according to Eq. (5);
Update p_i^{t+1} according to Eq. (6);
Update w^{t+1} according to $w = (\tilde{X}\tilde{X}^T + \beta I_d)^{-1}\tilde{X}p$;
Update p^{t+1} according to Eq. (9);
Compute $\tilde{X}_i^T w_i - p_i = [z_i^1, ..., z_i^n]^T$;
Compute the diagonal matrix Q_i^t according to $Q_i^{jj} = z_i^j$;
Update f_i^{t+1} according to $f_i = \gamma(Q_i^2 + \gamma I)^{-1} g_i$;
$t = t + 1$.

until *Convergence*;

3: Return w_i and w.

Figure 6: Sample frames of the 20 events in TRECVID MED 2012: (from left to right, column wise) *Birthday party*, *Changing a vehicle tire*, *Flash mob gathering*, *Getting a vehicle unstuck*, *Grooming an animal*, *Making a sandwich*, *Parade*, *Parkour*, *Repairing an appliance*, *Working on a sewing project*, *Attempting a bike trick*, *Cleaning an appliance*, *Dog show*, *Giving directions to a location*, *Marriage proposal*, *Renovating a home*, *Rock climbing*, *Town hall meeting*, *Winning a race without a vehicle* and *Working on a metal crafts project*.

The development set from TRECVID 2012 semantic indexing task (SIN12) [1] and the HMDB dataset [15] are used for training the attribute representations of MED videos. SIN12 contains 346 concepts of objects, scenes and actions whereas HMDB is a dataset with 51 action categories. We use the concept labels of SIN12 and HMDB as the attributes and train classifiers for them. Then we map MED data to the attribute space to get the attribute-based representation. We extract SIFT features for SIN12 and STIP features for HMDB considering that SIN12 generally contains static concepts while HMDB is an action dataset.

6.2 Comparison Algorithms

SVM has been widely used by several research groups for TRECVID MED and has shown its robustness [5][6], so we use it as one of the comparison algorithms. In TREVID MED 2012 competition, the champion team combined attribute and feature representations to train the SVM model [32]. Hence, we use SVM on both the visual features and the selected attributes representations to train the models. The predicted scores of the testing videos from different models are fused to generate the final decision values. This is consistent with the prediction way of GMMC.

We have knowledge from multiple sources, *i.e.*, two attribute representations and one visual feature representation of the MED videos. Multi-task learning is an effective way to leverage multiple sources. Hence, we additionally compare GMMC to the followig multi-task learning algorithms: Dirty Model (DM) [13], Clustered Multi-task Learning (CMTL) [33] and Joint Feature Learning (JFL) [4]. Similarly, the predicted scores based on different sources are fused to have the final decision values.

For GMMC and the comparison algorithms, we uniformly use the χ^2 kernel.

6.3 Setup

For each event, we randomly choose 100 positive examples and 1000 negative examples from MED12 to form the training set. The remaining data are used as the testing set. We do not use the official training and testing sets in TRECVID MED 2012 competition as the labels of the testing set are not provided so we cannot evaluate the performance.

There are three types of parameters. The first one is the size of the decisive attribute set, *i.e.*, k. We observe that the performance is usually good when it is 8 to 15, though there is variation, so we empirically set it as 10 in the experiment. The second type is the parameter for kernel calculation. It is fixed to the mean of the pairwise distances among the training samples, which is widely done in the literature. The third type includes the regularization parameters. We tune them from $\{0.001, 0.1, 10, 1000\}$ for all the algorithms and report the best result for each algorithm.

Two evaluation metrics are used. The first one is Minimum NDC (MinNDC) which is the official metric defined by NIST [2]. Note that lower MinNDC indicates better performance. The second one is Average Precision (AP). Higher AP indicates better performance.

6.4 MED Results

Figure 7 and Figure 8 show the MED results of different algorithms. It can be seen that our proposed method GMMC is the most robust algorithm. SVM is generally the second competitive classifier, which is in accordance with the existing works on TRECVID MED. Other algorithms have varying degree of success on different events.

Specifically, GMMC gets the best detection performance for 15 events with both evaluation metrics. Zooming into details, we find that SVM only has huge advantage over GMMC for *Rock climbing* whereas it is slightly better for other 4 events. For *Rock climbing*, GMMC performs rather poor probably due to the following reason: when a video has the attributes like *rock* and *climbing*, it is quite likely to be a positive video. To illustrate this analysis more clearly, we give a detailed example. We have searched videos in Youtube using two attributes *climbing* and *rock* (note that we typed in "climbing", "rock" to avoid the retrieval using exactly the event description *Rock climbing*) and display the top 10 retrieved videos in Figure 9. It can be seen that all the retrieved videos are actually positive examples, indicating that it is rare for a negative video to feature different "negativeness" by having positive attributes such as *climbing* and *rock*. Hence, our adaptive labeling strategy may be

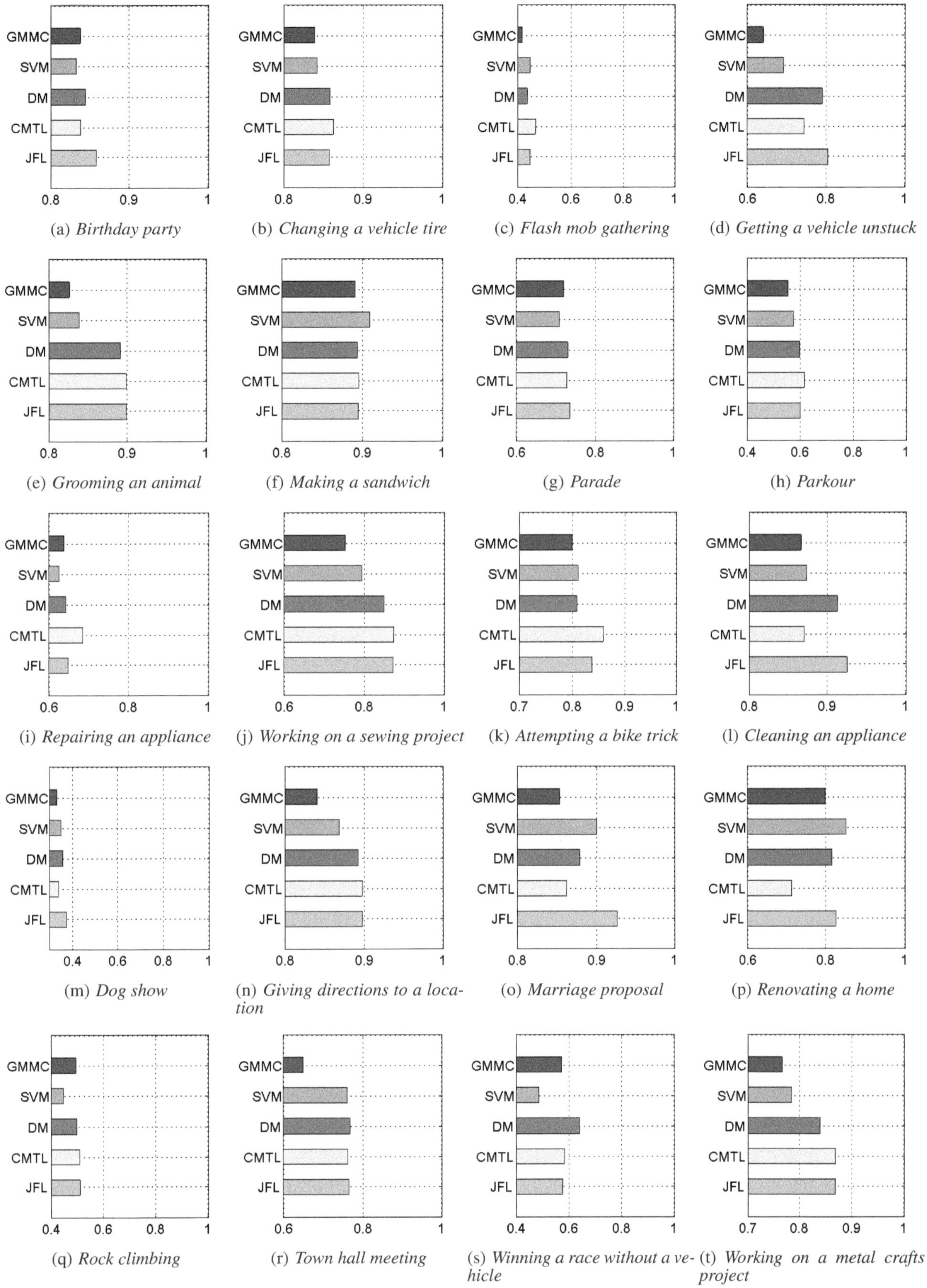

(a) *Birthday party* (b) *Changing a vehicle tire* (c) *Flash mob gathering* (d) *Getting a vehicle unstuck*

(e) *Grooming an animal* (f) *Making a sandwich* (g) *Parade* (h) *Parkour*

(i) *Repairing an appliance* (j) *Working on a sewing project* (k) *Attempting a bike trick* (l) *Cleaning an appliance*

(m) *Dog show* (n) *Giving directions to a location* (o) *Marriage proposal* (p) *Renovating a home*

(q) *Rock climbing* (r) *Town hall meeting* (s) *Winning a race without a vehicle* (t) *Working on a metal crafts project*

Figure 7: Performance comparison between different algorithms in terms of MinNDC. Note that LOWER MinNDC indicates BETTER performance.

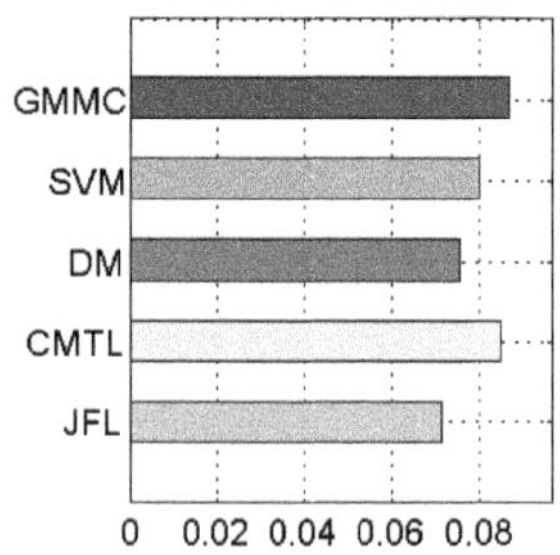

(a) *Birthday party*

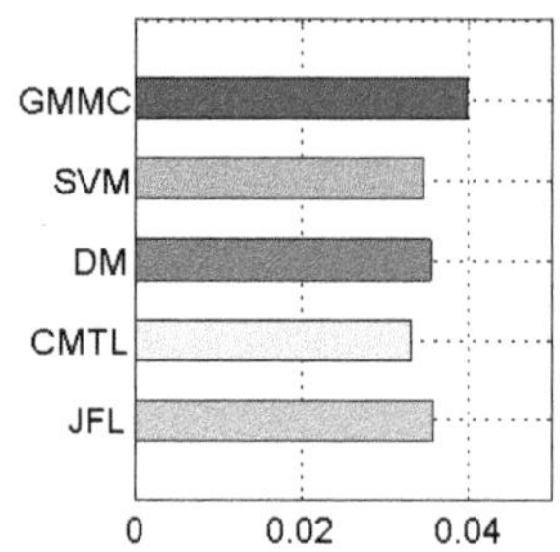

(b) *Changing a vehicle tire*

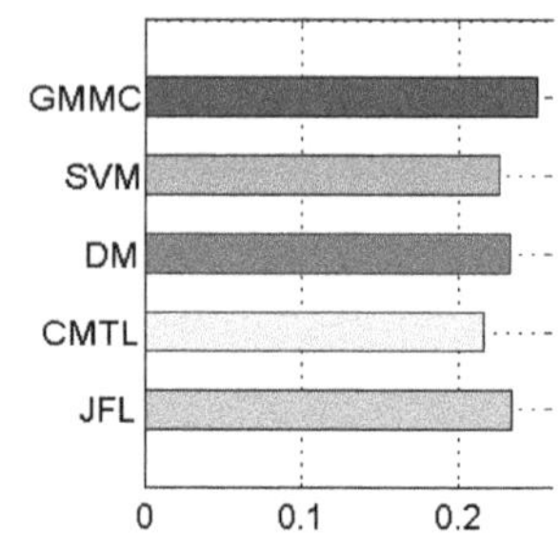

(c) *Flash mob gathering*

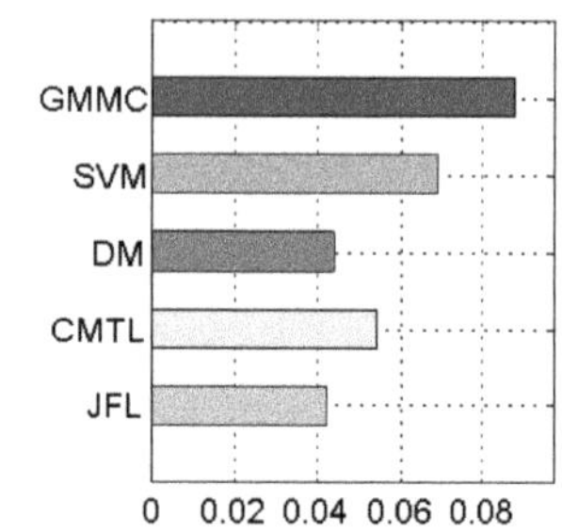

(d) *Getting a vehicle unstuck*

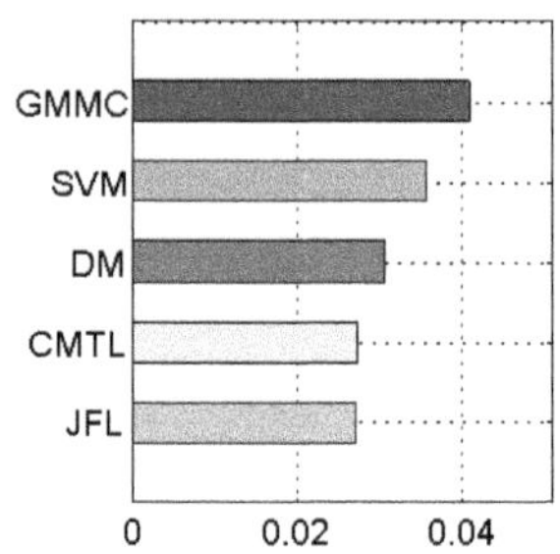

(e) *Grooming an animal*

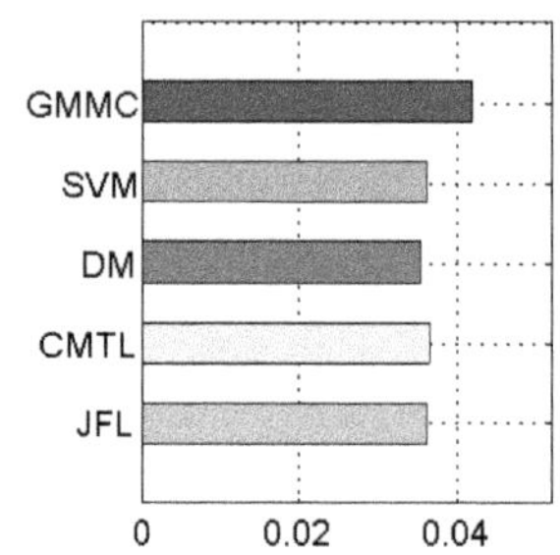

(f) *Making a sandwich*

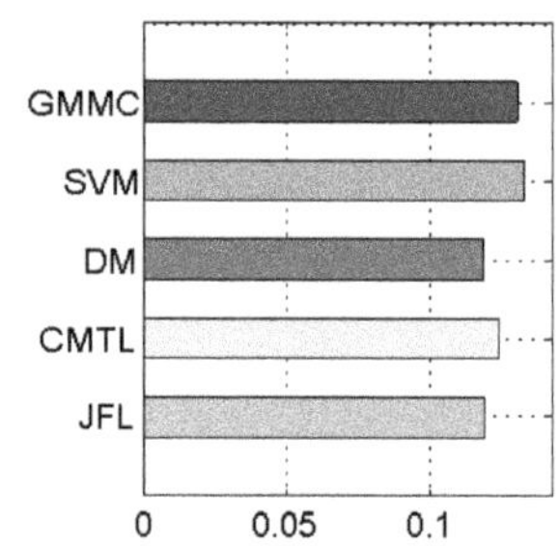

(g) *Parade*

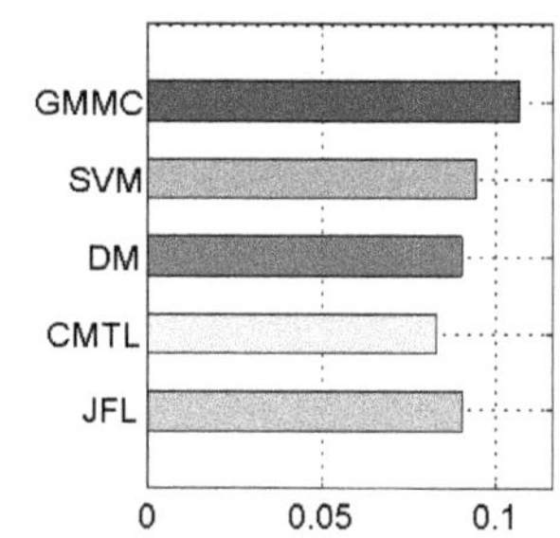

(h) *Parkour*

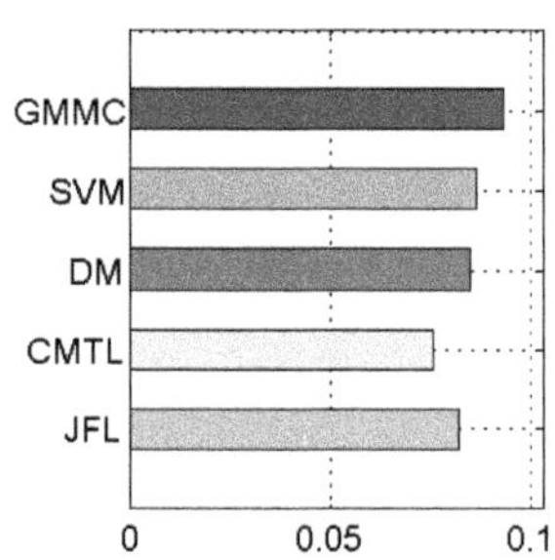

(i) *Repairing an appliance*

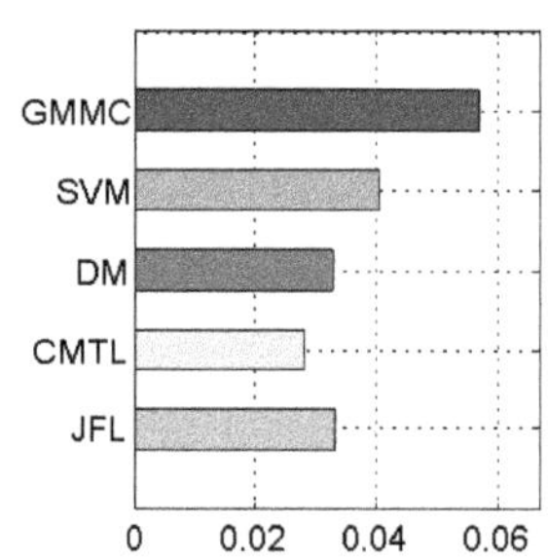

(j) *Working on a sewing project*

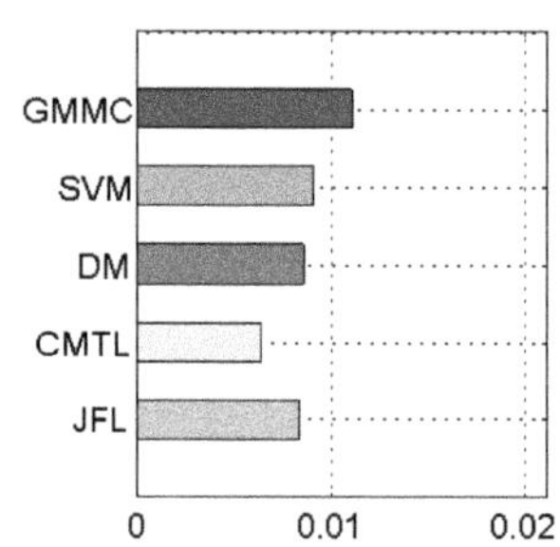

(k) *Attempting a bike trick*

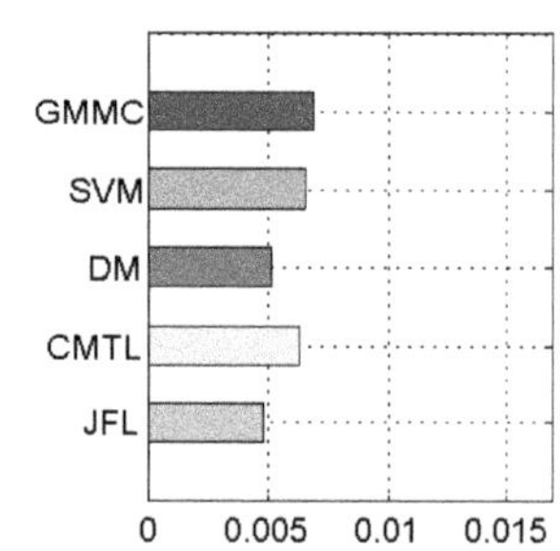

(l) *Cleaning an appliance*

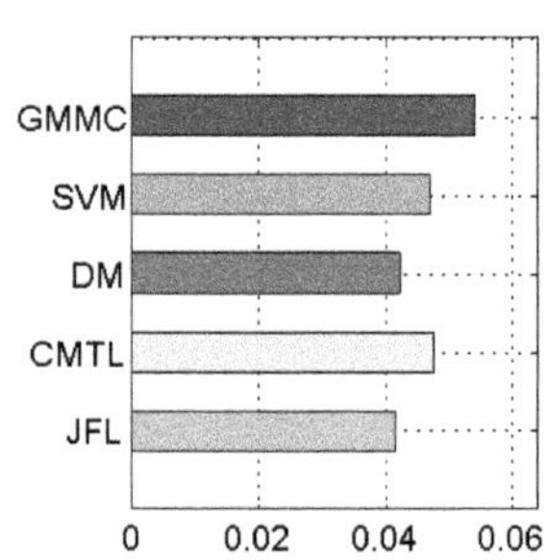

(m) *Dog show*

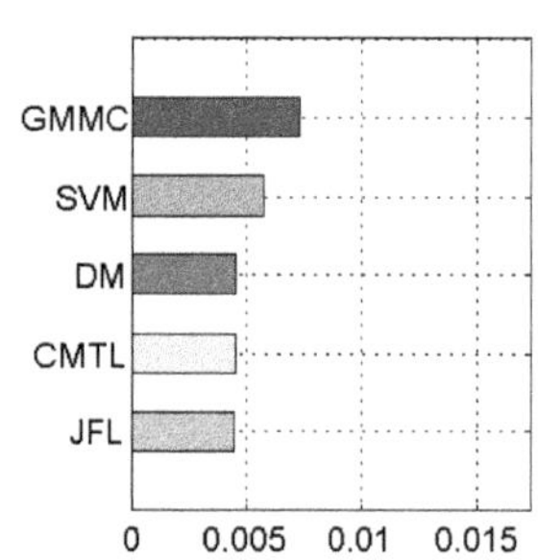

(n) *Giving directions to a location*

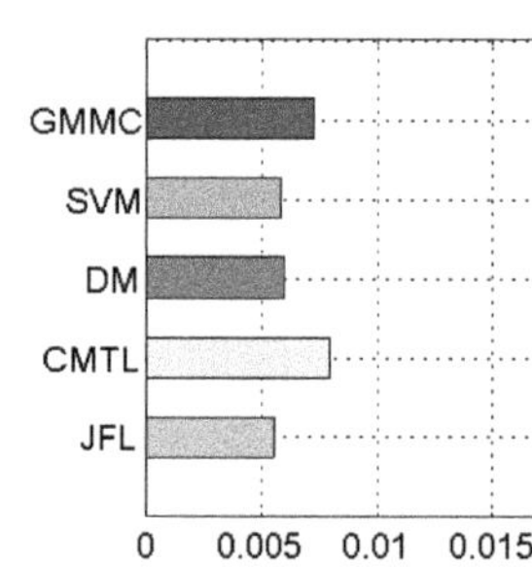

(o) *Marriage proposal*

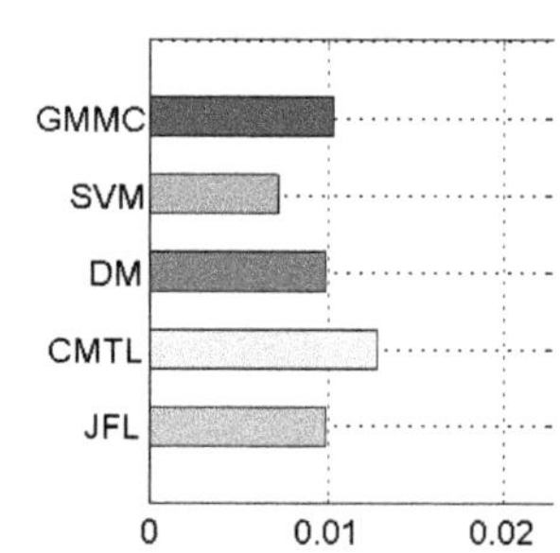

(p) *Renovating a home*

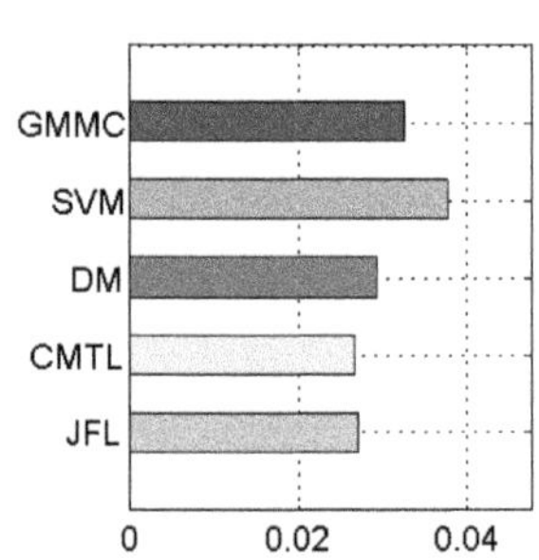

(q) *Rock climbing*

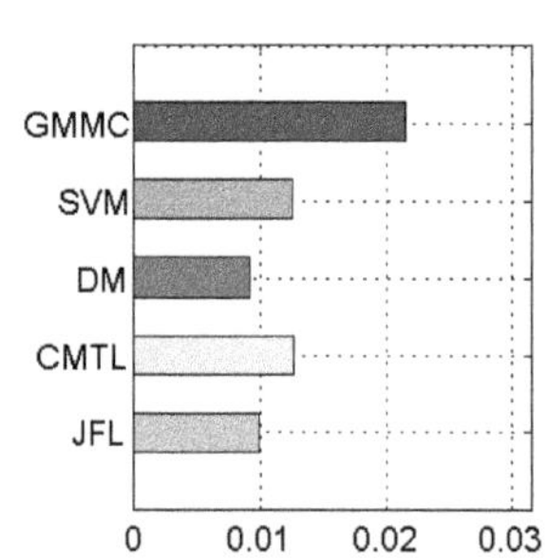

(r) *Town hall meeting*

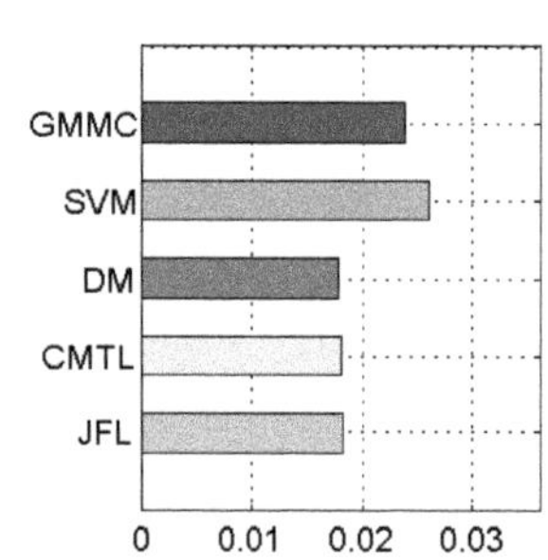

(s) *Winning a race without a vehicle*

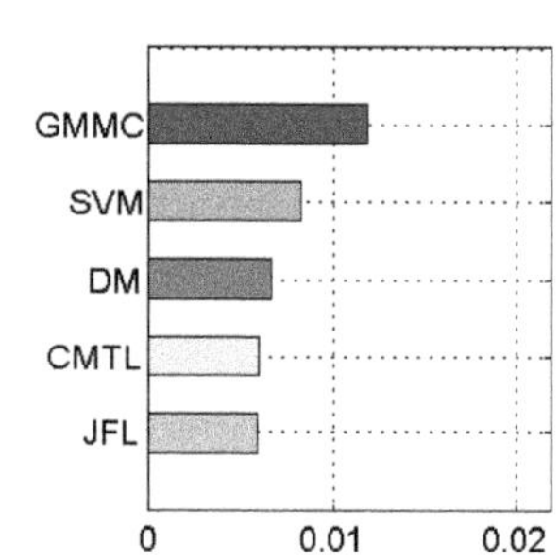

(t) *Working on a metal crafts project*

Figure 8: Performance comparison between different algorithms in terms of AP. Note that HIGHER AP indicates BETTER performance.

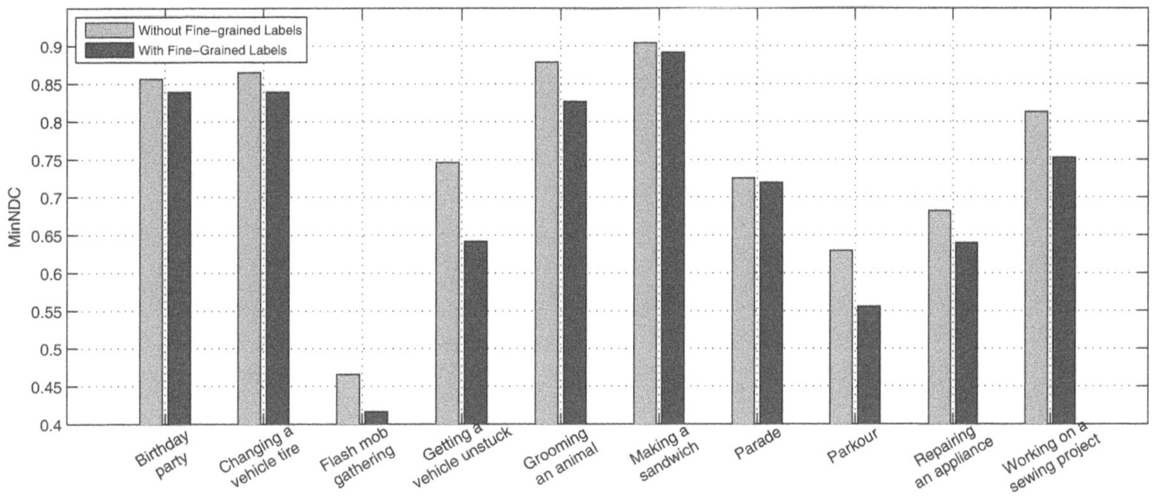

Figure 10: Performance comparison between leveraging fine-grained labels and not leveraging them in terms of MinNDC. The LOWER, the BETTER. Judged by the t-test, using fine-grained labels is significantly better than not using them over the 10 events.

not justified for this event, *i.e.*, using 0 to indicate all negative examples is more precise. In contrast, for the events on which GMMC outperforms SVM, the advantage is generally remarkable. With AP as metric, GMMC outperforms SVM by about 8% to 68%. For instance, GMMC is 40.1%, 68% and 43.9% better than SVM for *Working on a sewing project*, *Town hall meeting* and *Working on a metal crafts project*, respectively. The MED results have validated the effectiveness of our approach.

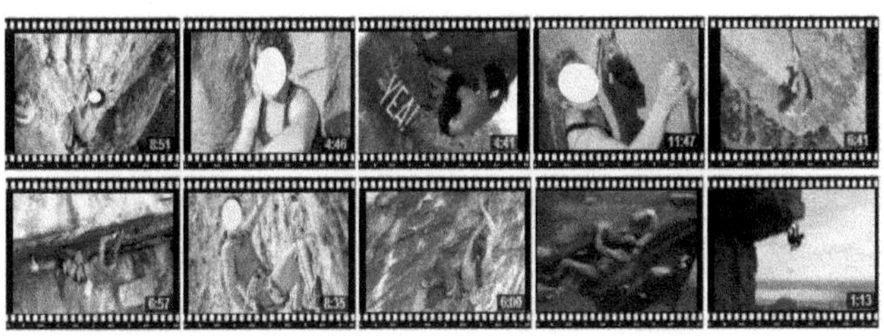

Figure 9: An example showing that for the event *Rocking climbing*, it is rare for a negative video to have the positive attributes.

6.5 Without Fine-Grained Labels?

We have leveraged the fine-grained labels to help the classifier learning. How would the performance vary if our formulation does not leverage fine-grained labels, *i.e.*, all the negative examples are treated equally with label 0? We re-implemented our algorithm in this scenario and display the experimental results in Figure 10 in comparison with the results obtained by exploiting fine-grained labels. Due to the space limit, we only show the comparison on the first 10 events in terms of MinNDC. It can be seen that using fine-grained labels clearly contributes to the performance gain. This experiment validates that the proposed fine-grained labeling is helpful for MED.

6.6 Influence of Attribute Selection

In our framework, the first step is to select the indicative attributes for an event. We have used a sparse model as illustrated by Eq. (1). The parameter λ is supposed to affect the selected attributes, thus also affecting the consequent steps. Hence, we show the MED performance variation *w.r.t.* λ in Figure 11. The first three

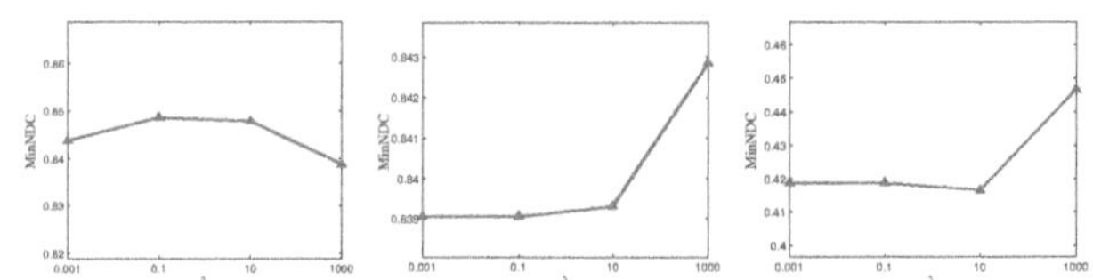

(a) *Birthday party* (b) *Changing a vehicle tire* (c) *Flash mob gathering*

Figure 11: Performance variation *w.r.t* to λ.

events are taken as showcases and MinNDC is used. We can see that different λ does result in different detection accuracy, meaning that the attribute selection in our framework is important.

7. CONCLUSION

In this paper, we have introduced the first exploration on adaptively assigning fine-grained labels to negative videos to better characterize their properties. As a result, more useful informative cues can be obtained, which are incorporated into the classifier learning for MED. Our approach is summarized by the following steps: attribute representation using multiple video sources; indicative attributes selection; evaluation of "negativeness," and joint optimization of fine-grained labels, attribute representation based classifiers and visual features based classifier. The two kinds of classifiers are applied to the testing videos and their output are fused to get the decision values. In this way, we have added useful knowledge from the fine-grained labels to the classification. We have conducted experiments on the challenging TRECVID MED 2012 development set. The comparison with several approaches has shown the effectiveness of our method. We should point out that our method depends on attribute representation but current attribute detectors are not yet reliable, which could restrain the performance of our method. Should we develop more accurate attribute detectors in the future, better MED performance can be expected.

8. ACKNOWLEDGMENTS

This paper was partially supported by the xLIME FP7 project, the S-PATTERNS FIRB project and the Intelligence Advanced Research Projects Activity (IARPA) via Department of Interior National Business Center contract number D11PC20068. The U.S. Government is authorized to reproduce and distribute reprints for Governmental purposes notwithstanding any copyright annotation thereon. Disclaimer: The views and conclusions contained herein are those of the authors and should not be interpreted as necessarily representing the official policies or endorsements, either expressed or implied, of IARPA, DoI/NBC, or the U.S. Government.

9. REFERENCES

[1] http://www-nlpir.nist.gov/projects/tv2012/tv2012.html#sin.

[2] http://www.nist.gov/itl/iad/mig/upload/med11-evalplan-v03-20110801a.pdf.

[3] A. Adam, E. Rivlin, I. Shimshoni, and D. Reinitz. Robust real-time unusual event detection using multiple fixed-location monitors. *IEEE Trans. Pattern Anal. Mach. Intell.*, 30(3):555–560, 2008.

[4] A. Argyriou, T. Evgeniou, and M. Pontil. Multi-task feature learning. In *NIPS*, pages 41–48, 2006.

[5] L. Bao, L. Zhang, S.-I. Yu, Z. zhong Lan, L. Jiang, A. Overwijk, Q. Jin, S. Takahashi, B. Langner, Y. Li, M. Garbus, S. Burger, F. Metze, and A. Hauptmann. Informedia @ TRECVID2011. In *NIST TRECVID Workshop*, 2011.

[6] L. Cao, S.-F. Chang, N. Codella, C. Cotton, D. Ellis, L. Gong, M. Hill, G. Hua, J. Kender, M. Merler, Y. Mu, A. Natsev, and J. R. Smith. IBM Research and Columbia University TRECVID-2011 Multimedia Event Detection (MED) System. In *NIST TRECVID Workshop*, 2011.

[7] S. Dhar, V. Ordonez, and T. L. Berg. High level describable attributes for predicting aesthetics and interestingness. In *CVPR*, pages 1657–1664, 2011.

[8] D. Ding, F. Metze, S. Rawat, P. F. Schulam, S. Burger, E. Younessian, L. Bao, M. G. Christel, and A. G. Hauptmann. Beyond audio and video retrieval: towards multimedia summarization. In *ICMR*, 2012.

[9] A. Farhadi, I. Endres, D. Hoiem, and D. A. Forsyth. Describing objects by their attributes. In *CVPR*, pages 1778–1785, 2009.

[10] A. G. Hauptmann. Lessons for the future from a decade of informedia video analysis research. In *CIVR*, pages 1–10, 2005.

[11] A. G. Hauptmann, R. Yan, W.-H. Lin, M. G. Christel, and H. D. Wactlar. Can high-level concepts fill the semantic gap in video retrieval? a case study with broadcast news. *IEEE Transactions on Multimedia*, 9(5):958–966, 2007.

[12] S. J. Hwang, F. Sha, and K. Grauman. Sharing features between objects and their attributes. In *CVPR*, pages 1761–1768, 2011.

[13] A. Jalali, P. D. Ravikumar, S. Sanghavi, and C. Ruan. A dirty model for multi-task learning. In *NIPS*, pages 964–972, 2010.

[14] Y.-G. Jiang, J. Yang, C.-W. Ngo, and A. G. Hauptmann. Representations of keypoint-based semantic concept detection: A comprehensive study. *IEEE Transactions on Multimedia*, 12(1):42–53, 2010.

[15] H. Kuehne, H. Jhuang, E. Garrote, T. Poggio, and T. Serre. Hmdb: A large video database for human motion recognition. In *ICCV*, pages 2556–2563, 2011.

[16] I. Laptev and T. Lindeberg. Space-time interest points. In *ICCV*, 2003.

[17] D. G. Lowe. Distinctive image features from scale-invariant keypoints. *International Journal of Computer Vision*, 60(2):91–110, 2004.

[18] Z. Ma, Y. Yang, Y. Cai, N. Sebe, and A. G. Hauptmann. Knowledge adaptation for ad hoc multimedia event detection with few exemplars. In *ACM Multimedia*, pages 469–478, 2012.

[19] Z. Ma, Y. Yang, N. Sebe, K. Zheng, and A. G. Hauptmann. Multimedia event detection using a classifier-specific intermediate representation. *IEEE Transactions on Multimedia*, 2013.

[20] Z. Ma, Y. Yang, Z. Xu, S. Yan, N. Sebe, and A. G. Hauptmann. Complex event detection via multi-source video attributes. In *CVPR*, 2013.

[21] P. Natarajan, S. Wu, S. N. P. Vitaladevuni, X. Zhuang, U. Park, R. Prasad, and P. Natarajan. Multi-channel shape-flow kernel descriptors for robust video event detection and retrieval. In *ECCV (2)*, pages 301–314, 2012.

[22] P. Natarajan, S. Wu, S. N. P. Vitaladevuni, X. Zhuang, S. Tsakalidis, U. Park, R. Prasad, and P. Natarajan. Multimodal feature fusion for robust event detection in web videos. In *CVPR*, pages 1298–1305, 2012.

[23] B. Schölkopf, A. J. Smola, and K.-R. Müller. Nonlinear component analysis as a kernel eigenvalue problem. *Neural Computation*, 10(5):1299–1319, 1998.

[24] F. Wang, Y.-G. Jiang, and C.-W. Ngo. Video event detection using motion relativity and visual relatedness. In *ACM Multimedia*, pages 239–248, 2008.

[25] G. Wang, T.-S. Chua, and M. Zhao. Exploring knowledge of sub-domain in a multi-resolution bootstrapping framework for concept detection in news video. In *ACM Multimedia*, pages 249–258, 2008.

[26] G. Wang and D. A. Forsyth. Joint learning of visual attributes, object classes and visual saliency. In *ICCV*, pages 537–544, 2009.

[27] Y. Wang and G. Mori. A discriminative latent model of object classes and attributes. In *ECCV (5)*, pages 155–168, 2010.

[28] C. Xu, J. Wang, K. Wan, Y. Li, and L. Duan. Live sports event detection based on broadcast video and web-casting text. In *ACM Multimedia*, pages 221–230, 2006.

[29] Y. Yang and M. Shah. Complex events detection using data-driven concepts. In *ECCV (3)*, pages 722–735, 2012.

[30] Y. Yang, H. T. Shen, Z. Ma, Z. Huang, and X. Zhou. $l_{2,1}$-norm regularized discriminative feature selection for unsupervised learning. In *IJCAI*, pages 1589–1594, 2011.

[31] Y. Yang, J. Song, Z. Huang, Z. Ma, N. Sebe, and A. G. Hauptmann. Multi-feature fusion via hierarchical regression for multimedia analysis. *IEEE Transactions on Multimedia*, 15(3):572–581, 2013.

[32] S.-I. Yu, Z. Xu, D. Ding, W. Sze, F. Vicente, Z. Lan, Y. Cai, S. Rawat, P. Schulam, N. Markandaiah, S. Bahmani, A. Juarez, W. Tong, Y. Yang, S. Burger, F. Metze, R. Singh, B. Raj, R. Stern, T. Mitamura, E. Nyberg, and A. Hauptmann. Informedia e-lamp @ TRECVID2012: Multimedia event detection and recounting med and mer. In *NIST TRECVID Workshop*, 2012.

[33] J. Zhou, J. Chen, and J. Ye. Clustered multi-task learning via alternating structure optimization. In *NIPS*, pages 702–710, 2011.

Joserlin: Joint Request and Service Scheduling for Peer-to-Peer Non-linear Media Access

Zhen Wei Zhao
NUS Graduate School for Integrative Sciences and Engineering
National University of Singapore, Singapore
zhaozhenwei@nus.edu.sg

Wei Tsang Ooi
School of Computing
National University of Singapore, Singapore
ooiwt@comp.nus.edu.sg

ABSTRACT

A peer-to-peer non-linear media streaming system needs to schedule both on-demand and prefetch requests carefully so as to reduce the server load and ensure good user experience. In this work, we propose, Joserlin, a joint request and service scheduling solution that not only alleviates request contentions (requests compete for limited service capacity), but also schedules the prefetch requests by considering their contributions to potential reduction of server load. In particular, we propose a novel request binning algorithm to prevent self-contention among on-demand requests issued from the same peer. A service and rejection policy is devised to resolve contention among on-demand requests issued from different neighbors. More importantly, Joserlin employs a gain function to prioritize prefetch requests at both requesters and responders, and a prefetch request issuing algorithm to fully utilize available upload bandwidth. Evaluation with traces collected from a popular networked virtual environment shows that Joserlin leads to 20%~60% reduction in server load.

Categories and Subject Descriptors: C.4 [**Performance of Systems**]: Design studies; C.2.4 [**Computer-Communication Networks**]: Distributed Systems - Distributed applications
General Terms: Algorithms, Design, Performance
Keywords: Non-linear access pattern, peer-to-peer, scheduling, service scheduling, on-demand request, prefetch request

1. INTRODUCTION

Peer-to-peer (P2P) techniques have been widely adopted for media streaming. The application of these techniques, however, mainly focuses on linear media, such as video, where user interactions are limited. As new classes of interactive media applications emerge, researchers have started to investigate the use of P2P techniques on streaming these interactive media content, including networked virtual environment (NVE) [9, 18] and zoomable video [21].

User interaction leads to non-linear user access pattern. We say that an access pattern is non-linear if different users may access different sequences of media objects. For instance, in zoomable video, users may choose to zoom into different regions; in an NVE, users may choose to navigate the rooms in a different order. Non-linear access pattern creates *uncertainty* in user accesses: given the current set of media objects accessed, more than one possible set of objects can be accessed next. Such non-linear access pattern poses many new challenges on P2P streaming systems [35], one of which is the request and service scheduling, the focus of this paper.

In a typical P2P media streaming system, peers navigate in the media resource space, consisting of all accessible media objects. Objects not in a peer's cache when they are needed will be requested from neighbors. We call such requests *on-demand requests*. Each on-demand request is associated with a deadline. If the requested object has not been retrieved from a neighbor by the deadline, the request is sent to the server as a last resort. To reduce object retrieval time, prefetching is commonly used. Prefetching predicts objects needed in the future and issue *prefetch requests* to neighbors to retrieve them. Prefetch requests are not sent to the server to reduce the server load.

Our goal in this paper is to schedule on-demand and prefetch requests to reduce the amount of content requested from the server. This goal is equivalent to reducing the number of requests sent to the server, assuming same-size media objects.

We call scheduling activities at the requester side (the peer that sends the request) *request scheduling* and call those at the responder side (the peer that receives the request) *service scheduling*. Request scheduling decides: **(i)** which neighbor a request should be sent to, **(ii)** the requesting order of prefetch requests, and **(iii)** when and at what rate prefetch requests should be sent out. Service scheduling decides: **(i)** which request to serve and which request to reject (referred to as *rejection policy*) and **(ii)** the serving order of requests (referred to as *service policy*).

Request and service scheduling has been studied extensively in the context of P2P VoD streaming systems. In VoD, however, video chunks are accessed mostly sequentially. Seeks are rare (average of 1.6−3.4 seeks for movies [14] and 9.3 for sports videos [7]), and thus the access pattern is mostly linear. Existing solutions would not work well for non-linear access patterns, due to the following characteristics of interactive media streaming systems:

(i) Data availability changes quickly. Even if a peer A currently holds a media object needed by peer B, the next object needed by B may not be available at A. Existing scheduling solutions that fail to factor in this cannot work well with non-linear access scenarios. For instance, bandwidth reservation-based service scheduling solutions [30, 13, 26] are inefficient, as the reserved bandwidth at a peer A may not be used to serve another peer B if peer A does possess the objects requested by peer B later.

(ii) Prefetch misses frequently. Non-linear access pattern leads to a clear difference between on-demand and prefetch requests – on-demand requests are caused by prefetch misses and have much

MM'13, October 21–25, 2013, Barcelona, Spain.
Copyright 2013 ACM 978-1-4503-2404-5/13/10 ...$15.00.
http://dx.doi.org/10.1145/2502081.2502090.

tighter deadlines. Many existing works do not distinguish the two [26, 29, 18, 28], and thus on-demand requests' deadlines are often missed due to unnecessary contentions with prefetch requests. Solutions that consider the two separately [2] do not study the interplay between the two systematically, particularly how scheduling of prefetch requests can benefit on-demand requests. Existing prefetch request scheduling solutions have been largely heuristic or best-effort, leading to limited benefits to on-demand requests.

To address the aforementioned challenges, we propose Joserlin, a joint request and service scheduling scheme designed for peer-to-peer non-linear media access systems. Joserlin performs request-level scheduling, which is more flexible than the bandwidth reservation-based approaches. Moreover, Joserlin assigns priorities to both on-demand requests (based on urgency) and prefetch requests (based on a derived gain function) to avoid contentions. The derived prefetch gain function factors in prefetch requests' contribution to potential on-demand requests from neighbors that request for the prefetched object, in terms of reducing their probability to be sent to the server. As a result, Joserlin co-schedules on-demand and prefetch requests to reduce the server load due to on-demand requests.

Joserlin encompasses four major contributions: **(i)** We propose a novel request binning algorithm that helps avoid self-contention among on-demand requests from the same peer; **(ii)** We conduct an analytical study on the on-demand request rejection policy; **(iii)** We systematically study the interplay between on-demand and prefetch requests, based on which a gain function is derived to prioritize prefetch requests at both requesters and responders; **(iv)** We propose a prefetch request issuing algorithm that fully utilizes peers' upload bandwidth and respect prefetch requests' relative priority.

The rest of this paper is organized as follows: Sec. 2 discusses related works. Some preliminary preparations are presented in Sec. 3. Sec. 4 investigates on-demand requests. Sec. 5 studies prefetch requests and their interplay with on-demand requests. Evaluation is carried out in Sec. 6 by comparison with existing solutions. Finally, Sec. 7 concludes and presents our future work.

2. RELATED WORK

We now present existing work on request and service scheduling in P2P media streaming, focusing on video and NVE systems.

In P2P live video streaming, *chunk scheduling* (also called *piece selection*) strategies, such as rarest-first [34], random [22], and the hybrid approach [32], are well studied and understood. Guo et al. [11] proposed an optimal scheduling strategy exploiting forward queues. Liang et al. showed that P2P live streaming performance is insensitive to scheduling only when the streaming rate is low or the playback delay is long [17]. Bonald et al. analytically studied the trade-off by a few peer and chunk selection polices in push-based epidemic live streaming systems [6]. They pointed out that the combination of random peer and latest useful chunk selection policy can achieve the optimal dissemination rate within an optimal delay bound. PRIME requests packets from parent peers either randomly or proportionally with respect to their upload bandwidth [20].

For service scheduling, Bertinat et al. [5] proposed a network-flow based service scheduling scheme. Chen et al. [8] proposed a scheduling policy based on Interest-Offer-Accept/Decline. With this approach, responders have to reserve their bandwidth and wait until requesters send back an Accept/Decline message, resulting in long content retrieval latency and a waste of upload bandwidth. These scheduling schemes, however, do not apply to non-linear media access, where different peers access different objects in an asynchronous manner. Furthermore, prefetching, an important consideration in Joserlin, does not exist in live streaming.

In P2P VoD, chunk scheduling strategies such as rarest-first [25, 3] and hybrid approaches [15, 14, 27] are widely adopted by literatures. Apart from that, some works proposed the partition-based method, in which peers' downloading window is partitioned into urgent, normal, and prefetch sections [24]. Peers request data in each section with different probabilities. Kiraly et al. [16] proposed a deadline-based scheduling scheme to prioritize streams of different importances in push-based overlays. Ying et al. [29] assigned requests proportionally to each neighbor's historical throughput.

As for service scheduling in VoD, Zhou et al. [36] investigated strategies such as fair sharing and fixed bandwidth allocation. Yu et al. [30], Huang et al. [13], and Wang et al. [26] proposed their respective service scheduling schemes based on network-flow reservation, which, however, does not fit well with non-linear access scenarios as discussed in Sec. 1. Abbasi et al. [2] used two separate queues: an on-demand queue with earliest deadline first (EDF) service policy and a prefetch queue with FIFO service policy. Their work, however, only provides best-effort scheduling of prefetch requests. Zhang et al. [31] used super nodes to allocate bandwidth, resulting in priority inversion during online scheduling. Zhang et al. [33] proposed a first-aid service scheduling scheme, which allows high priority requests to preempt low priority ones. The work does not deal with prefetch requests and the preempted on-demand requests. Yang et al. [28] suggested sending requests to the least loaded neighbor and using EDF to serve incoming requests. Requests that cannot be served by their deadlines are dropped early. They, however, do not distinguish between on-demand and prefetch requests, leading to contention of the two at the responder side. Furthermore, their do not study the rate at which prefetch requests are issued. These solutions for VoD are not adequate to address the new challenges posed by non-linear accesses, as discussed in Section 1.

Apart from P2P video streaming, several researchers also studied request and service scheduling in P2P NVE streaming. For instance, Chien et al. [9] proposed a reservation-based service scheduling scheme, which is not suitable for non-linear access scenarios (Sec. 1). Moreover, this work does not distinguish on-demand and prefetch requests. Liang et al. [18] used FIFO queue as a service policy. A request that cannot be served before its deadline is rejected and resubmitted to another neighbor until its deadline is reached. The FIFO queue, however, does not factor in the timeliness requirement of requests. Each time a request is resubmitted, it joins the end of the queue, making it even unlikely to be served on time. Another drawback is that the work does not distinguish prefetch requests from on-demand requests. Sung et al. [23] proposed that a peer should send requests to neighbors that are close to its current position with higher probability, and far neighbors with lower probability to alleviate request congestions. By doing this, the method cannot exploit far neighbors that are under-loaded.

Our work differs from existing ones by clearly distinguishing on-demand and prefetch requests, prioritizing them to avoid unnecessary contentions at both requesters and responders, and co-scheduling them to gain from the interplay between the two classes of requests. Moreover, majority of existing solutions treat request and service scheduling as separate, leading to scheduling efficiency loss [28]. We unify the request and service scheduling through a global prioritization policy.

3. PRELIMINARIES

In this section, we characterize a peer's mobility, explain its responsibility as both a requester and responder, and outline assump-

p	a peer
u	the upload bandwidth of a peer
s	the object size, a constant.
q, r	a request (r denotes on-demand request and q denotes prefetch request).
t_r	remaining time until a request r's deadline
C_r	the candidate set of on-demand request r
M_r	the set of neighbors, of the peer that issues request r, possessing the object requested by r, but has not received r. $\|M_r\|$ is the size.
w_r	the number of remaining retries for request r
ρ	the probability that each serving slot is *unavailable*.
H	random variable for upload bandwidth of a neighboring peer
κ_r	the log-likelihood that request r cannot join any other queue in M_r without rejecting another request.
τ	the prefetch interval size, a constant.
δ_q	the estimated access probability of the object requested by q at the peer that issues q, during the current prefetch interval
ϕ	the access probability threshold to distinguish prefetching gain due to contributions **C1** and **C2**.
B_r	total upload bandwidth of peers in M_r.
g_q	the gain function of a prefetch request q
χ	number of prefetch requests to send to a neighbor at one time, to replenish the queue at that neighbor.

Table 1: Symbol table.

tions made. Table 1 summarizes major symbols used in this paper, and others will be introduced when encountered.

All accessible media objects constitute an n-dimensional media resource space, where peers navigate following their respective paths. We characterize peers' navigation path with (i) its virtual position and (ii) its interest window, centered at the virtual position.

We consider mesh-based P2P protocol, where each peer maintains a list of neighbors. A peer moves around in the resource space to access media objects. A media object that falls within its interest window but is not present in the cache is fetched with an on-demand request, sent to one of its neighbors. Each on-demand request has a timeout value, which is generally short to ensure good user experience. For instance, Claypool et al. [10] reported that the acceptable latency in online interactive games varies from $0.3s$ to $1s$. We model the timeout value as a function of the distance between the requested object and the peer's current virtual position. An on-demand request that cannot be served by the neighbors within its deadline is sent to the server. Furthermore, a peer also prefetches objects from its neighbors.

To serve other peers, each peer maintains a priority queue, where incoming requests are inserted according to a service policy. The peer ensures that all requests in this queue meet their deadlines. Otherwise, one or more requests are rejected from the queue according to a rejection policy. On-demand and prefetch requests may have different service and rejection policies, which will be studied respectively in Sec. 4 and 5. Since on-demand requests have much tighter deadlines, they enjoy higher priority.

Next, we outline assumptions made to simplify the analysis in the remaining of this paper. We assume that media objects are of the same size, denoted by s. Typically, large media objects are often quantized into smaller chunks, each of which can be treated as an independent requestable object. Thus, the same-size object assumption is reasonable. We further assume that each request retrieves one object. In practice, multiple objects can be requested by a single request message.

Joserlin is independent of the access probability prediction algorithm, and we assume that such an algorithm already exists. Moreover, we do not consider incentive mechanism and assume that peers are cooperative. Guo et al. [12] pointed out that some incentive mechanisms such as tit-for-tat is not suitable for streaming systems where peers access media content asynchronously.

4. ON-DEMAND REQUESTS

For on-demand requests, which object to request and when to request are determined by user interactions, rather than by the scheduling scheme. Hence, the on-demand request scheduling scheme only needs to decide: **(Q1)** which neighbor an on-demand request should be sent to? The service scheduling scheme at the responder side needs to decide: **(Q2)** what is the appropriate service and rejection policy?

Since requesters independently issue on-demand requests without consensus among each other, some responders may get overloaded, and others are underloaded. We adopt the reject-and-retry technique used by Liang et al. [18] and Yang et al. [28] to balance the load across neighbors: when an on-demand request is rejected, the requester can quickly retry it to other neighbors until either the request is served or its deadline is reached, by when the request is sent to the server as a last resort. The reject-and-retry technique can effectively balance the load at neighbors, but it does not perform scheduling. Specifically, it does not answer **(Q1)** and **(Q2)**.

Furthermore, on-demand requests often contend for the limited service capacity at responders. Such request contention problem is not addressed by the reject-and-retry technique. For instance, when the system is under heavy load, a portion of the requests have to resort to the server due to capacity deficit at neighbors. With the reject-and-retry technique, however, these requests will be retried multiple times until either timeout or there are no more neighbors to retry, leading to excessive message overhead. Generally speaking, contending requests from the same requester can be avoided at the requester side. Contending requests from different requesters are hard to avoid at responders without introducing significant communication overhead. Therefore, we rely on the request rejection process at the responder side to resolve contention. Joserlin chooses which request to reject carefully, considering both data availability and deadlines of requests.

In the rest of this section, we answer the aforementioned two questions for on-demand requests. More specifically, we propose a request binning algorithm in Sec. 4.1 that decides which neighbor an on-demand request should try, by avoiding self-contention among requests issued from the same requester. Sec. 4.2 studies the service and rejection policy to resolve contentions among requests at the responder side.

4.1 Request Binning Algorithm

Given a set of on-demand requests, the request binning algorithm decides where each request should be sent to. It is designed to alleviate request contention at the requester side, preventing requests issued by the same peer from stepping on each other, i.e., causing a request from itself to be rejected.

We say a set of requests is *contention-free* with respect to a peer p, if all their deadlines can be satisfied by p when there is no other requests at p. The binning algorithm assigns each request in a given set R to either a neighbor or the server. All requests assigned to a neighbor form a *bin* such that requests in the same bin are contention-free with respect to that neighbor. Consider a set of requests. If adding a request r to this set does not cause the deadline of any request (including r) in the set to be violated (with respect to the service policy), we say that this addition is *safe*. We only add a request to a bin if it is safe. Furthermore, for each request $r \in R$, the algorithm produces a candidate set C_r. If r is rejected, the requester only retries it to peers in C_r, even if other peers outside C_r may possess the requested object. A neighbor is in C_r if (i) it possesses the object that r is requesting and (ii) adding r to the bin of this neighbor is safe. Alg. 1 sketches the binning algorithm at a generic requester.

The candidate sets allow requests to stop retrying earlier, especially when the system load is heavy. Heavy system load increases the number of requests in each bin, and reduces the size of the candidate sets accordingly. Since we only send rejected requests to neighbors in their respective candidate sets, the number of retries would be small. Our evaluation in Sec. 6 shows that the binning algorithm reduces the retrying message overhead significantly.

Algorithm 1: On-demand Request Binning Algorithm

Let N be the set of the requester's neighbors;
Let R be the set of on-demand requests need to be issued;
Let λ_p be the total time used by requests at a neighbor p;
Let u_p be the upload bandwidth of a neighbor p;
Let Γ_p be the set of requests (the bin) assigned to a neighbor p;
foreach $p \in N$ **do** $\lambda_p \leftarrow 0$;
while *R is not empty* **do**
  Remove request r with smallest timeout from R;
  Let N_r be a subset of neighbors in N that possess the object o requested by r;
  Let t_r be the remaining time until r's deadline;
  while *N_r is not empty* **do**
    Remove a peer p from N_r;
    Let $|o|$ denotes the size of the requested object o;
    if $\lambda_p + |o|/u_p \leq t_r$ **then**
      Add r to Γ_p;
      $\lambda_p \leftarrow \lambda_p + |o|/u_p$;
      break;
  if *r has not been assigned to any peer* **then**
    Assign r to the server;
Let C_r be the candidate set of a request r;
foreach *request r that is not assigned to the server* **do**
  foreach $p \in N_r$ **do**
    if *$r \notin \Gamma_p$ and the insertion of r into Γ_p is safe* **then**
      Add p into C_r;

4.2 Service Policy and Rejection Policy

The service queue of a peer can be modeled as a non-preemptive priority queue, where requests in service cannot be preempted. Since object size is usually small due to chunking of large objects, the non-preemptive priority queue converges to a preemptive priority queue, where the EDF service policy is optimal [19]. We therefore adopt EDF as our service policy for on-demand requests. Note that EDF is also adopted by Yang et al. [28] and Abbasi et al. [2].

We now analyze the rejection policy. Any on-demand request that arrives at peer p and can be safely inserted into the service queue of p (with respect to EDF) will be accepted for service by p. Otherwise, some request r' misses its deadline after the insertion of the newly arrived request as shown in Fig. 1. Let V be the set of requests in the service queue of p that have a earlier or equal deadline than r'. To restore the service queue to a state where each request's deadline is satisfiable, we have to reject one request from V (only one is needed since we assume same-size objects).

We have two naive choices: (i) Reject the newly arrived request, resulting in a drop-tail policy. The drawback of this policy is that, if the newly arrived request's deadline is almost up, it would have insufficient time to be retried at other neighbors and has to be sent to the server. (ii) Reject the request r' whose deadline is violated. Note that r' has the largest remaining time to deadline in V, thus can be retried more times. This choice, however, may cause r' to resort to the server prematurely, if the data availability within its requester's neighborhood is poor (e.g, not many neighbors possess the requested object).

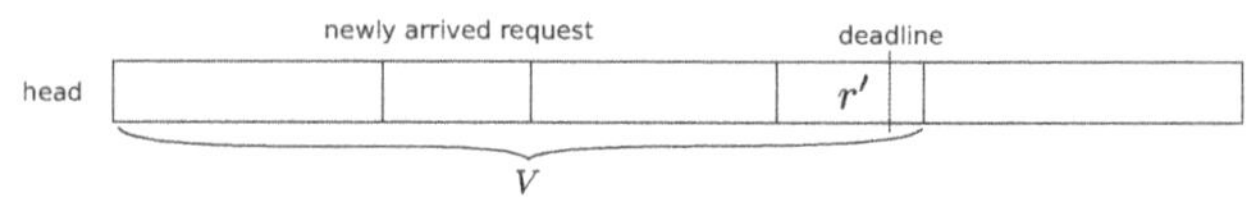

Figure 1: The illustration of V.

Deciding which request to reject needs to factor in both the deadline and the data availability. In general, the rejection policy should reject the request that is most likely to be served from other peers before its deadline. Next, we analyze how these different factors affect the rejection policy.

Consider an on-demand request r that is rejected and needs to be re-sent to another peer. We calculate the log-likelihood that r *cannot* join any other peer's service queue without rejecting a request from them. Let M_r be the neighbors of the requester of r that possess the object requested by r, but has not been tried. Due to the binning algorithm in Sec. 4.1, M_r is a subset of r's candidate set. For tractability purpose, we assume the round-trip time between r's requester and its neighbors is the same, denoted by RTT.

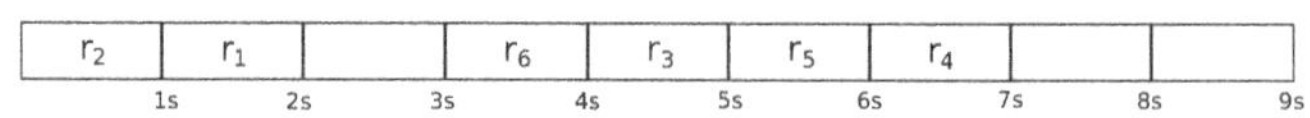

Figure 2: Service queue re-arrangement for on-demand requests. Suppose the original service queue has on-demand requests $\{r_1, r_2, r_3, r_4, r_5, r_6\}$ with remaining time to deadline $\{2s, 2s, 5s, 7s, 7s, 7s\}$ respectively. Rearrangement starts with r_1 being inserted into an available slot that is closest but before its deadline (the second slot in this case). Then r_2 is inserted using the same rule (into the first slot). The rest of requests are inserted in similar fashion.

We denote $x(u, t)$ as the probability that an on-demand request *cannot* join a service queue whose upload bandwidth is u without rejecting a request from that queue, when the request's remaining time to deadline is t. To derive the equation for $x(u, t)$, we divide the time into equal-sized slots. Each slot is the time taken to serve one request. For expository convenience, we re-arrange the service queue in the following manner: iterate through all on-demand requests from the head of the queue, and insert each request into an available slot that is closest to, but before its deadline. We assume that deadlines are always aligned at slot boundaries. A queue re-arrangement example is shown in Fig. 2. After the re-arrangement, we can see that $x(u, t)$ is equal to the probability of not finding an available slot before the request's deadline. Let the probability that each slot is *unavailable* be ρ, then

$$x(u, t) = \rho^{\frac{tu}{s}} \qquad (1)$$

Note that ρ depends on the current system load (the number of on-demand requests). The current system load, however, is hard to characterize as each request has their respective deadlines. Moreover, ρ also depends on the upload capacity, data availability, and peers' access pattern. Modeling ρ is going to be complex, and thus we treat ρ as a constant in this paper.

If the on-demand request r is rejected, the requester randomly selects another neighbor from M_r to retry until r either gets accepted or timeouts. Randomization is necessary to avoid the synchronization effect. The upload bandwidth of the neighbor that r is re-sent to, is therefore a random variable, denoted by H. The number of retries w_r is constrained by $|M_r|$ and the remaining time to deadline t_r:

$$w_r = min\left\{|M_r|, \left\lfloor\frac{t_r}{RTT}\right\rfloor\right\} \quad (2)$$

To calculate the probability that r cannot join any queues in M_r without rejecting another request, consider what needs to happen: r needs to be re-sent to neighbors in M_r, one after another, until r's deadline is up or M_r is exhausted. Every time r is re-sent and rejected, the remaining time t_r reduces by RTT. We can therefore derive the log-likelihood that r cannot join any other queue without rejecting a request as:

$$\kappa_r = E\left[log\left(\prod_{i=1}^{w_r} x(H, t_r - i \times RTT)\right)\right]$$

$$= E\left[log\left(\rho^{\frac{H}{s}\sum_{i=1}^{w_r}(t_r - i \times RTT)}\right)\right] \quad (3)$$

$$= \frac{log(\rho)}{s} \times \varphi_r \quad (4)$$

where $E[\cdot]$ denotes the expectation and

$$\varphi_r = E[H] w_r \left(t_r - \frac{(w_r+1)RTT}{2}\right) \quad (5)$$

With this analysis, we can now describe the rejection policy. The serving peer should pick the request r with the smallest κ_r to reject. Since $log(\rho) < 0$, this selection is equivalent to choosing the request r with the largest φ_r.

$|M_r|$ and $E[H]$ correspond to availability of the object requested by r and t_r corresponds to the remaining time to r's deadline. In general, we should reject requests that have both good data availability and large remaining time. The remaining time, however, is usually the bottleneck if the data availability condition is good. For instance, when $|M_r| \geq \lfloor\frac{t_r}{RTT}\rfloor$, $w_r = \lfloor\frac{t_r}{RTT}\rfloor$ and t_r becomes the dominant factor with a degree of two. Only under poor data availability, factoring in $|M_r|$ and $E[H]$ would help. As the data availability bottleneck is going to be alleviated with prefetch requests in Sec. 5, we find that t_r is usually the bottleneck in the sense that the request r with the largest φ_r is most likely to be the one with the largest remaining time. This observation suggests that the naive rejection policy, which rejects the request whose deadline is violated, would suffice. Therefore, Joserlin uses this as the rejection policy.

5. PREFETCH REQUESTS

Any residual upload bandwidth remaining after serving on-demand requests should be fully utilized to prefetch objects outside the current interest window. On-demand request scheduling only needs to decide which neighbor (or server) an on-demand request should be sent to, as which object to request and when to request are determined by user interactions. Unlike on-demand request scheduling, prefetch request scheduling also needs to decide which object to prefetch and when to prefetch, leading to two additional scheduling dimensions.

As stated in Sec. 3, we assume that there exists a prediction algorithm that assigns each object a probability that the object will be accessed by the peer within a given period of time. Due to user interactions, such prediction algorithms are usually more accurate when this time period is short. Therefore, Joserlin slots time into small prefetch intervals of length τ (typically in the order of seconds) and each peer recomputes objects' access probability at the beginning of each prefetch interval. Each prefetch request therefore has a timeout value of τ. Unlike on-demand request, the deadline for a prefetch request exists to ensure that: (i) the prefetch request is not obsolete due to recomputation of access probability after every prefetch interval, and (ii) the requester gets a chance to re-send the request to another neighbor if the current neighbor is overloaded. Note that, for a prefetch request, it is rejected if the serving peer cannot *start* serving it by the deadline, while for an on-demand request, it is rejected if the serving peer cannot *finish* serving it by the deadline. This minor modification is to prevent scenarios where the remaining time to the next prefetch interval cannot fit in a prefetch request, leading to wasted bandwidth.

With the preceding prefetching framework, there are still two questions unanswered: **(Q3)** How to decide the requesting and serving order of prefetch requests? **(Q4)** When and at what rate should prefetch requests be issued so as to fully utilize the available upload bandwidth? To answer **(Q3)**, Sec. 5.1 derives a gain function, which is used to prioritize prefetch requests at both requesters and responders. In Sec. 5.2, a prefetch request issuing algorithm is devised to answer **(Q4)**.

5.1 Prefetch Gain Function

We associate each prefetch request q with a gain function g_q to prioritize them for both issuing and serving order. This gain function reflects the contributions of q to server load reduction. Higher gain leads to higher priority.

In general, a prefetched object contributes to reducing the server load in three ways: **(C1):** it eliminates on-demand requests for the same object (if the prefetch is a hit) at the prefetching peer. **(C2):** it increases data availability and, therefore, increases the chances that a neighbor of the prefetching peer can successfully fetch the object via on-demand requests. **(C3):** it increases data availability and, therefore, increases the chances that a neighbor of the prefetching peer can prefetch the object via prefetch requests. **C3** can be extended to multiple hops.

Both **C2** and **C3** help to reduce the number of on-demand requests sent by neighbors to the server: **C2** allows a neighbor's on-demand requests to be met, and **C3** suppresses an on-demand request in case the prefetch request for the same object hits. However, we do not consider **C3** in our gain function, since it is hard to tell if a missing object will be requested on-demand or prefetched by a neighbor. But, in the worst case, if prefetch requests fail to retrieve the object and the object is needed, an on-demand request will be issued by the neighbor anyway. It is therefore more important to consider **C2**. Henceforth, we will only consider **C1** and **C2** when designing the gain function.

Among **C1** and **C2**, we give priority to **C1** over **C2**, since if we can eliminate on-demand requests in the first place, there is no need for the second type of contribution. Furthermore, prefetch hit leads to better user experience compared to on-demand requests.

Consider a prefetch request q. Let δ_q be the access probability of the object requested by q at the peer that issues q within the current prefetch interval, as estimated by the prediction algorithm. If δ_q is larger than a threshold ϕ, we treat the corresponding prefetch request q as having significant gain due to **C1**. Otherwise, its gain due to **C1** is negligible, and we should consider its contribution

C2. If $\delta_q > \phi$, the contribution of q can be modeled using the access probability δ_q:

$$g_1(q) = \delta_q \tag{6}$$

If $\delta_q \leq \phi$, the gain due to **C2** is not obvious, and its derivation requires a comprehensive analysis of the effect that this prefetch request may potentially have on a neighbor's on-demand request. In Eqn. 4, we have derived the log-likelihood that an on-demand request r cannot be served by any neighbor without rejecting an existing on-demand request in their service queues. We can regard κ_r as a function of $|M_r|$ and $B_r = E[H]|M_r|$, where B_r is the total upload bandwidth of peers in M_r.

$$\kappa_r(|M_r|, B_r) = \frac{log(\rho) B_r}{s|M_r|} w_r \left(t_r - \frac{(w_r+1)RTT}{2} \right)$$

Note that when r have not been sent to any peer, the remaining time to deadline t_r is equal to its timeout value.

Now consider what would happen when one neighbor of the prefetching peer sends an on-demand request r for the prefetched object: M_r is going to expand with the prefetching peer by 1, and B_r is going to increase by u, which is the upload bandwidth of the prefetching peer. As a result, r will have a higher chance of being served. We can quantify this increment with the decrease in log-likelihood

$$\kappa_r(|M_r|, B_r) - \kappa_r(|M_r|+1, B_r+u) = -\frac{log(\rho)}{s} \times \theta_r^u \tag{7}$$

where

$$\theta_r^u = \begin{cases} t_r u - \frac{RTT}{2}(B_r + |M_r|u + u) & \text{if } |M_r| < \lfloor \frac{t_r}{RTT} \rfloor \\ \frac{t_r^2}{2RTT} \times \frac{|M_r|u - B_r}{|M_r|(|M_r|+1)} & \text{otherwise} \end{cases} \tag{8}$$

Note that we ignore some boundary conditions for the sake of simplicity in Eqn. 8. As the term $-log(\rho)/s$ is positive and is a constant, we factor it out and use θ_r^u as the gain function for prefetching the object that would be needed by a neighbor's on-demand request r.

Note that θ_r^u could be negative – i.e., prefetching the object actually "hurts" the neighbors' on-demand requests. This scenario can occur, for instance, when the prefetching peer's upload bandwidth u is very small. A peer with small upload bandwidth may not help much in serving on-demand requests, but may cause a peer to waste one RTT, increasing the chance of timeout. We, however, want to bound the gain to non-negative values only. This is reasonable, since after a peer prefetches an object, it can opt not to announce itself as the content provider for that object (e.g., if its upload bandwidth is too small).

We can now derive the gain of a prefetch request q due to **C2**. Let u be the upload bandwidth of the prefetching peer that issues q, and let N_q be neighbors of the prefetching peer that do *not* possess the object requested by q. If a neighbor already possesses an object, it would not issue any on-demand request for it. Consider each peer $p \in N_q$ and their corresponding on-demand request r_p for the same object requested by q. The gain function can be written as:

$$g_2(q) = \sum_{p \in N_q} max(0, \theta_{r_p}^u). \tag{9}$$

To compute g_2, the prefetching peer reports its upload bandwidth to each of its neighbors p. For each object that is missing from p's cache, p collects the number of content providers for the object in its neighborhood, the total upload bandwidth of the content providers, and the average RTT between itself and these content providers. The timeout value of an on-demand request is only known when it is issued. The average timeout value of historical on-demand requests, however, can be used as approximation. With these information, p computes the gain of the prefetch request q to the on-demand request that is issued from itself and requests for the same object using Eqn. 8, and then sends it back to the prefetching peer. The prefetching peer aggregates potential gains from all of its neighbors and computes g_2 using Eqn. 9.

Finally, we combine the two contributions and yield the prefetch gain function for a prefetch request q as

$$g_q = \begin{cases} g_1(q) & \text{if } \delta_q > \phi \\ \frac{g_2(q)}{G_{max}} \times \phi & \text{otherwise} \end{cases} \tag{10}$$

G_{max} is a constant, denoting the maximum possible value of g_2. The purpose of introducing this constant is to normalize g_2 to the range of [0, 1].

After receiving a prefetch request, the serving peer inserts it into the same service queue as on-demand requests. On-demand requests have higher priority over prefetch requests in the service queue. Within on-demand requests, priority is given to the one with earlier deadline, and within prefetch requests, priority is given to the one with larger gain value. Ties are broken based on the objects' distance to the prefetching peers' current virtual positions.

5.2 Prefetch Request Issuing Algorithm

We now discuss Joserlin's prefetch request issuing algorithm that decides when and where a prefetch request should be sent to. The algorithm aims to: (i) fully utilize peers' upload bandwidth, (ii) respect the relative priority of prefetch requests issued from different peers, and (iii) incur small overhead.

Fully utilizing peers' upload bandwidth is not difficult if peers issue prefetch requests quickly. This behavior, however, would create serious problem if prefetch requests are not prioritized properly at the responder side. For instance, if prefetch requests are served using the FIFO policy [2], aggressively issuing prefetch requests would starve other peers. In contrast, if prefetch requests are issued conservatively, peers' upload bandwidth may be under utilized. In Joserlin, since peers serve prefetch requests in decreasing order of priority (based on the gain function in Sec. 5.1), how fast a neighbor's prefetch requests get served depends on how much gain they bring to the system compared to prefetch requests from other neighbors, not how fast they arrive. Thus, there is no point in issuing prefetch requests aggressively. A peer in Joserlin therefore should issue prefetch requests at a rate that matches the serving rate at each of its neighbors.

Noticing that peers' upload bandwidth gets fully utilized as long as their service queues are not empty, our idea is that each peer should ensure that it has at least one prefetch request awaiting in each of its neighbors' service queue *at any point of time* (except special cases, such as when the peer has no prefetch requests to issue). Ensuring this property also allows the serving peer to respect the "global" priority, i.e., serve prefetch requests in decreasing order of priority *as computed across multiple prefetching peers*.

Note that a peer with upload bandwidth of u can serve up to $\varpi = \lceil \frac{u \times RTT}{s} \rceil$ number of prefetch requests from a neighbor within an RTT. To retain the system at a valid state, a neighbor should issue new prefetch requests to the service queue, whenever it realizes the number of its pending prefetch requests at the service queue drops below ϖ.

Based on the aforementioned observations, we design Joserlin's prefetch request issuing algorithm as follows: at the beginning of each prefetch interval, a prefetching peer builds a priority queue of all prefetch requests it will send, using the gain function as the priority. Then, for each of the peer's neighbors (in random order), the peer picks up to $\varpi+\chi$ ($\chi\geq 1$) highest priority prefetch requests for objects available at that neighbor, and send these requests to it. For every χ prefetched objects received from a neighbor, the prefetching peer issues another χ prefetch requests to this neighbor. χ is the replenishing unit. Rejected prefetch requests are re-inserted into the priority queue. The prefetching peer stops sending prefetch requests to a neighbor that rejects a prefetch request until the next prefetch interval. In practice, χ prefetch requests can be bundled into a single message. Small χ causes more request message overhead. Large χ, however, causes more rejection message overhead. Joserlin uses $\chi=\varpi$ to adapt to RTT and upload bandwidth of the neighbors.

6. EVALUATION

In this section, we evaluate Joserlin with traces collected from a well-known NVE called Second Life and a simulator implemented on top of Oversim [4]. We choose NVE as the application to base our evaluation on because (i) it is a typical non-linear access scenario; (ii) there are many existing work on peer-to-peer NVE, allowing us to compare our methods; and (iii) user traces are available and not difficult to collect.

6.1 Trace Collection and Parameter Settings

The traces include both avatar mobility traces(we do not distinguish avatar and peer in the rest of this paper) and texture traces collected from the Second Life region Freebies and Sunland. The size of both regions is $256m\times 256m$. The mobility traces sample avatar's position every $10s$, and we interpolate the positions in between to obtain traces that sample every $1s$. The Freebies trace is 2.5 hours long and the Sunland trace is 2.2 hours long. The media objects that avatars need to retrieve while moving around are textures. There are 1782 textures in the Freebies region and 2197 in the Sunland region. Each texture has a position and size value. Large textures are quantized into units of 64KB. After quantization, the number of texture objects becomes 3422 and 5747, respectively.

We use the same bandwidth trace as the one used by Liang et al. [18], which is collected from dslreports.com [1]. The startup latency is set to 5s. Each peer maintains between 10 and 15 neighbors. If the number of neighbors drops below 10, the peer should request new neighbors from a tracker. Both bitmap exchange and gain update intervals are set to 10s.

The interest window in our model corresponds to the Area-of-Interest in NVE, which we set to a circle with a radius of 20m (the interest window size, ψ). The deadline to retrieve a texture is set to be a linear function of d, the distance between the texture and the peer's current position:

$$f(d)=t_{min}+\frac{d}{\psi}(t_{max}-t_{min}) \tag{11}$$

where t_{min} and t_{max} are the minimum and maximum timeout value for on-demand requests. By default, we set t_{min} to 0.3s and t_{max} to 1s.

The prefetch interval size τ is set to 5s. To predict which media object is needed (for prefetching), we assume that a peer continues to move in the same direction and with the same speed for the next τ seconds. The predicted distance moved is thus τ times the current moving speed. A cap of 30m is put on the predicted distance moved to prevent exceedingly large instantaneous moving speed, caused by user interactions such as teleportation. Based on the predicted movement, a predicted interest region can be computed. Textures that fall within the predicted region are considered to have predicted access probabilities larger than the threshold ϕ. All other textures have access probabilities less than ϕ.

Within the predicted region, textures that are further away from the peer's current position have smaller access probabilities. To model this, we set a texture's access probabilities to $\frac{d}{D_{max}}(\phi-1)+1$, where d denotes the texture's distance from the peer's current position, and D_{max} is the maximum possible value of d (used to normalize d to the range of [0, 1]). This function restricts the access probability of any texture within the predicted region to be in the range of [ϕ, 1]. Note that the value for ϕ does not matter for our evaluation, as it is not necessary to know the exact predicted access probability. Knowing the relative access probability is sufficient to break ties among different prefetch requests. Furthermore, note that we need not model the access probability for textures outside of the predicted region (Eqn. 10).

In our simulations, serving peers serve one request at a time. Although in practice, peers may serve several requests concurrently. Furthermore, network layer details such as congestion and packet loss are not captured in the simulations.

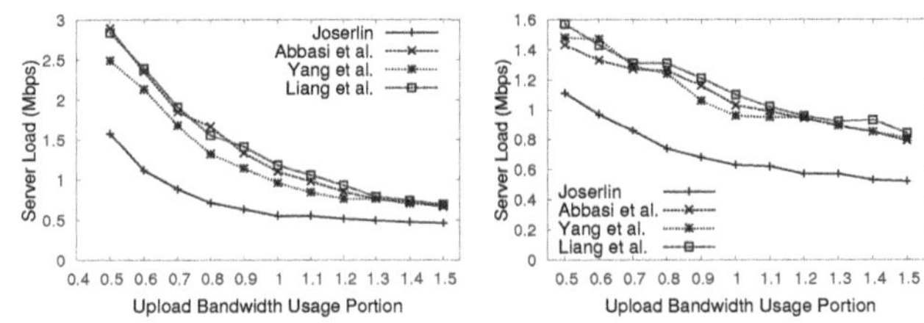

(a) Freebies (b) Sunland

Figure 3: Vary the upload bandwidth.

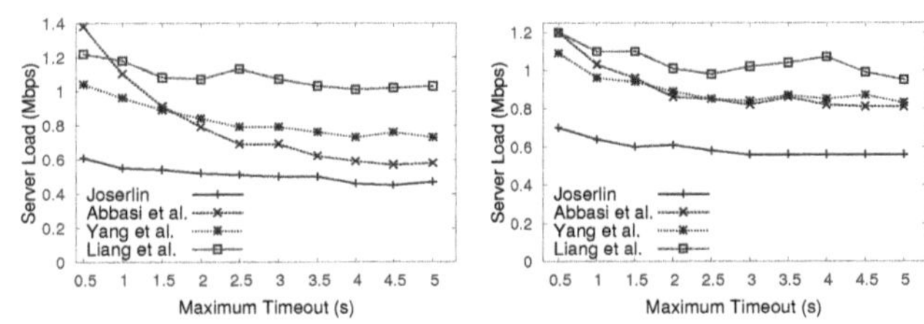

(a) Freebies (b) Sunland

Figure 4: Vary the timeout value.

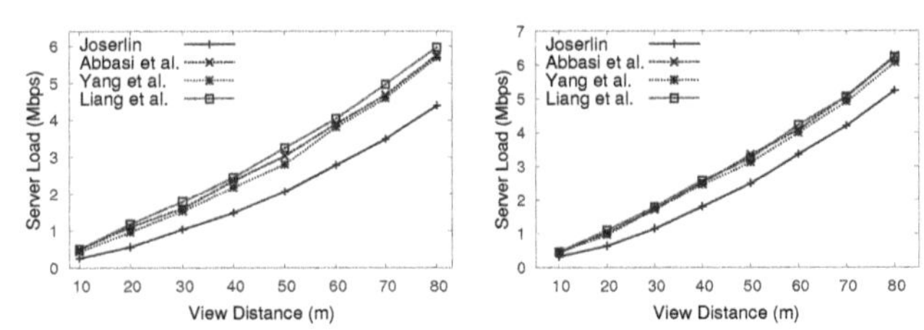

(a) Freebies (b) Sunland

Figure 5: Vary the interest window size.

6.2 Performance Comparison

We compare our request and service scheduling scheme with solutions proposed by Liang et al. [18], Yang et al. [28], and Abbasi et al. [2]. We use the same parameter settings for all four schemes, including the prefetch prediction algorithm.

Abbasi et al. [2] use cooperative prefetching, with which textures inside the predicted region are prioritized over those outside. Ties among objects that fall into the predicted region are broken based on their distance to peers' current positions. The rarest-first policy is used for objects outside the region. Liang et al. [18]'s and Yang

		default settings		50% of upload band.		timeout range [0.3, 2]		40m view distance		30s inter-arrival time	
		timeout	data avail.	timeout	data avail.	timeout	data avail.	timeout	data avail.	timeout	data avail.
Freebies	Yang et al.	614	20,023	936	52,474	174	17,411	825	44,922	444	26,270
	Liang et al.	1,026	25,479	1,676	61,277	547	23,426	1,857	52,947	1,239	34,961
	Abbasi et al.	318	22,511	691	57,829	44	16,540	891	47,557	345	27,781
	Joserlin	203	12,242	1,106	31,587	95	11,760	379	31,768	496	14,292
Sunland	Yang et al.	744	18,178	1,265	28,289	403	17,008	1,580	45,694	229	25,209
	Liang et al.	1,189	21,190	753	31,450	912	19,640	2,399	49,873	279	28,047
	Abbasi et al.	920	19,031	296	27,696	348	16,412	1,454	46,926	641	25,622
	Joserlin	362	12,123	751	20,866	115	11,946	396	34,818	207	18,728

Table 2: Number of requests sent to the server and their respective reasons.

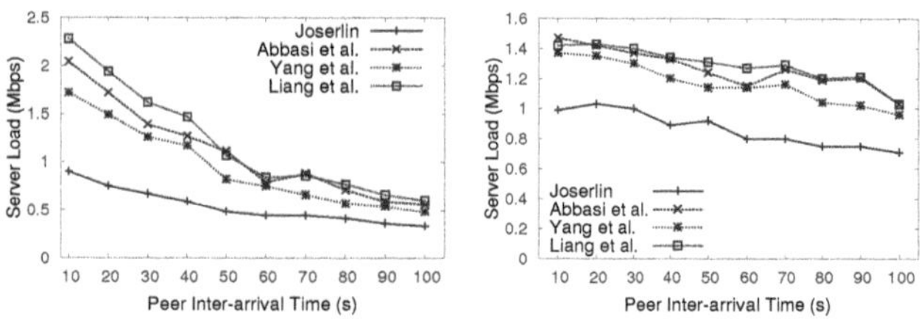

(a) Freebies (b) Sunland

Figure 6: Vary the peer arrival rate.

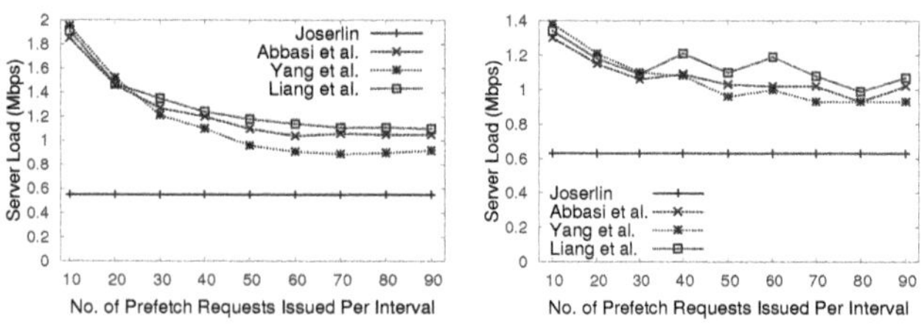

(a) Freebies (b) Sunland

Figure 7: Vary the number of prefetched objects per prefetch interval.

et al. [28]'s solutions do not prioritize prefetch requests, so we augment them with one: Textures in the predicted region are given higher priority. Within each category (textures within or outside the predicted region), closer textures get higher priority.

The three schemes that we are comparing against do not have a complete prefetch request issuing algorithm. Yang et al. [28] proposed that each peer can send n requests to each of its neighbors periodically, but did not hint on how large n should be. To ensure a fair comparison, for these three schemes, each peer sends 50 prefetch requests to its neighbors at the beginning of each prefetch interval. Ignoring the data availability bottleneck, 50 prefetch requests is enough to fully utilize the available upload bandwidth. We vary this number as well in our performance comparison to study its effect on these schemes. Note that the three schemes have their respective service policy for prefetch requests: Liang et al. [18] and Abbasi et al. [2] use FIFO policy; Yang et al. [28] use EDF policy. Moreover, we augment Abbasi et al.'s scheme with reject-and-retry, even though this technique is not in their proposed solution.

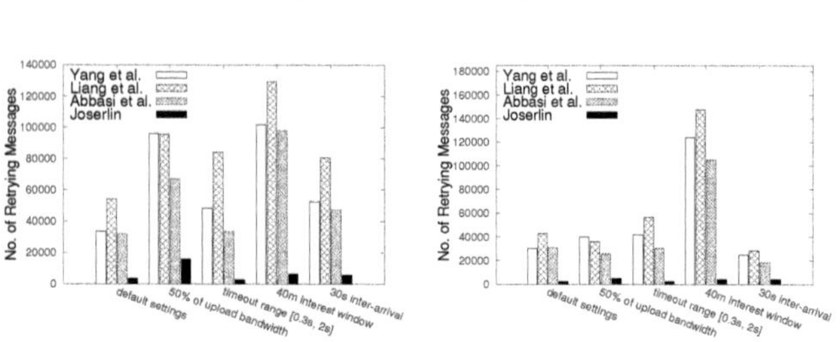

(a) Freebies (b) Sunland

Figure 8: Number of retrying messages.

Upload Bandwidth. In Fig. 3, we vary peers' upload bandwidth from 50% to 150% of their default values and plot the average server load with respect to the upload bandwidth. As expected, the server load decreases as the upload bandwidth increases. Joserlin achieves a performance gain of 30%∼50% for the Freebies trace and 25%∼40% for the Sunland trace, in comparison to the other three schemes. In Fig. 3(a), as the upload bandwidth decreases, the server load of the other three schemes increases much faster than Joserlin's. This observation suggests that Joserlin is particularly good at handling relatively heavy system load (with respect to the available upload bandwidth). As the upload bandwidth increases, the four schemes converge in Fig. 3(a). This is because the system performance will be insensitive to scheduling when there is excessive upload bandwidth available. In Fig. 3(b), such trend is less obvious, as the user access pattern in the Sunland trace is bursty, leading to higher instantaneous system load.

Timeout. Fig. 4 keeps the t_{min} value unchanged and varies the maximum timeout value t_{max}. Joserlin achieves a performance gain of 35%∼40% over Yang et al.'s scheme, 50%∼55% over Liang et al.'s scheme, 55% over Abbasi et al.'s scheme when timeout is small and 20% when timeout is large for the Freebies trace. As for the Sunland trace, the performance gain is 30%∼35% over Yang et al.'s scheme, 40%∼47% over Liang et al.'s scheme, 40% over Abbasi et al.'s scheme when timeout is small and 30% when timeout is large.

It is worth noticing that Joserlin's server load only increases slightly as t_{max} decreases. The server load for each of the other three schemes, however, either remains high or increases quickly when t_{max} decreases. In general, the significance of prefetch requests to on-demand requests is much larger when the timeout value is small. With our carefully designed prefetch gain function and issuing algorithm, Joserlin successfully exploits the interplay between prefetch and on-demand requests, thus incurs much less server load when the timeout value is small.

In Fig. 4(a), the performance of Yang et al.'s and Liang et al.'s schemes does not change much with respect to the timeout value, since they do not differentiate on-demand and prefetch requests, causing contentions between the two. Abbasi et al.'s scheme incurs a large server load when the timeout value is small due to their simple prefetch scheduling policy. As the timeout value increases, Abbasi et al.'s scheme, which differentiates on-demand and prefetch requests, beats the other two and converges to Joserlin's performance. Most media streaming systems, however, demand short timeout value to ensure good user experience.

Interest Window Size. The interest window size is varied in Fig. 5. As the interest windows size increases, instantaneous system load increases as the more objects need to be fetched on-demand when prefetch misses occur. The performance gain of Joserlin over the other three schemes decreases from 40% to 20% for the Freebies trace, and decreases from 35% to 15% for the Sunland trace, as the interest window size increases. When the instantaneous system load is high, scheduling becomes insignificant, as there is insufficient upload capacity to serve the requests anyway. Note that there is no contradiction with the observation in Fig. 3(a), where Joserlin can handle relatively heavy system load better than other schemes. When the system load is light, we do not need sophisticated scheduling, and when the system load is too heavy, scheduling becomes insignificant. The scheduling scheme makes a difference only when the system load is somewhere in between.

Peer Arrival Rate. We separate the two traces into one mobility sequence per peer, and each sequence is fed into the simulator following a Poisson peer arrival rate with different average inter-arrival time, until they are drained. In Fig. 6(a), Joserlin achieves a performance gain of $50\%\sim60\%$ compared to the other schemes when the peer arrival rate is large. When peer arrival rate is small, the performance gain decreases to $30\%\sim45\%$. This observation suggests that Joserlin is good at dealing with large peer populations. In Fig. 6(b), the performance gain is $20\%\sim30\%$.

Number of Prefetch Requests. In Fig. 7, we vary the number of prefetch requests issued by Yang et al's, Liang et al.'s and Abbasi et al.'s scheme per prefetch interval. Note that this parameter is not used in Joserlin's prefetch request issuing algorithm. Instead, Joserlin automatically adopts its prefetch request issuing rate to the serving rate. Joserlin, whose results are shown as a horizontal lines in the figure, beats the other three schemes when we vary the aggressiveness of prefetching. We can see that the server load suffers when fewer prefetch requests are issued per interval, due to under utilization of peers' upload bandwidth. As more prefetch requests are issued, the server load, however, stabilizes. These two figures indicate that simply sending more prefetch requests to saturate peers' upload bandwidth is not enough. Sophisticated scheduling for prefetch requests is needed.

Causes of Server Load. Next, we select five representative scenarios to investigate the causes of server load and the retrying message overhead. These five representative scenarios are the default setting, 50% of upload bandwidth, timeout range of $[0.3, 2]$, $40m$ viewing distance, and $30s$ peer inter-arrival time.

In Table 2, we inspect the causes of server load by investigating why each request is sent to the server in the five representative scenarios. The reason is either "timeout", if the request's deadline is reached, or "data availability", if the neighbors either do not possess the requested object or have insufficient upload capacity to serve the request. Joserlin significantly reduces the number of on-demand requests sent to the server due to "data availability", which is the sole major cause of the server load. The prefetch gain function in Sec. 5.1 and prefetch request issuing algorithm in Sec. 5.2 contribute to this reduction.

Number of Retries. We compare the number of retries in Fig. 8. Our scheme incurs significantly fewer retrying messages under all scenarios. In particular, comparing the scenario with timeout range of [0.3s, 2s] to the default setting, the retrying message overhead for both Yang et al.'s and Liang et al.'s schemes increases due to request contentions. The larger timeout value causes requests to retry more times before timeout. When larger interest window size is used, all other three schemes incur excessive retrying message overhead due to the heavier system load. The reject-and-retry mechanism retries many requests repeatedly until timeout, as there is insufficient service capacity. Joserlin avoids this problem with the on-demand request binning algorithm sketched in Alg. 1, thus incurs much less overhead. For instance, in the Freebies trace with timeout range of $[0.3s, 2s]$ scenario, Joserlin's retrying message overhead is approximately 7.5%, 5.3%, and 3% of that incurred by Abbasi et al.'s, Yang et al.'s, and Liang et al.'s respectively.

Neighborhood Sizes. We further use the Freebies trace with $30s$ inter-arrival time scenario to inspect the effect of neighborhood

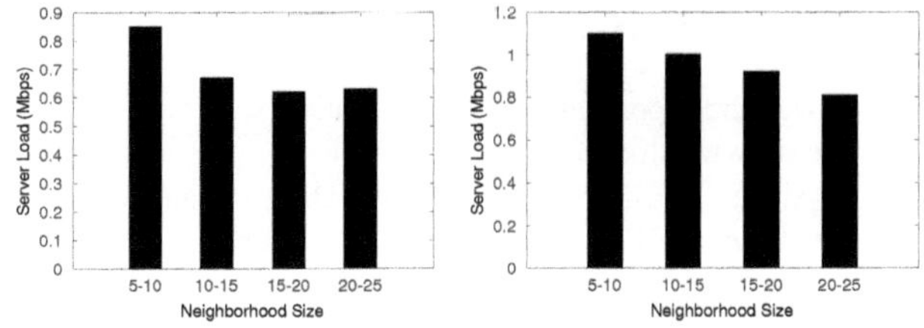

(a) Freebies (b) Sunland

Figure 9: Effect of different neighborhood sizes.

size. The server load is compared between neighborhood sizes distributed between $5-10$, $10-15$, $15-20$, and $20-25$. In Fig. 9(a), the server load incurred by neighborhood size of $10-15$, $15-20$, and $20-25$ are very similar. In Fig. 9(b), however, the server load decreases as the neighborhood size increases. We believes that this phenomenon is due to the higher instantaneous system load in the Sunland trace, and thus more neighbors are needed to absorb the burst of on-demand requests. A general guideline for the neighborhood size would be to use large neighborhood size if the instantaneous system load is higher. Otherwise, small neighborhood size would suffice, helping reduce the message overhead for neighborhood maintenance and bitmap exchange.

Protocol Overhead. The protocol overhead is mainly caused by the underlying distributed computation of gain, which requires exchanges of θ. The interval for recomputation of the gain function is set to $10s$. Thus, if the neighborhood size is between $10-15$, each peer needs to send $1-1.5$ update messages per second. By our measurement, the average value is 1.23/s. Each update message should include the computed θ value (Eqn. 8) for missing objects. Note, however, that a peer does not need to report the θ value to its neighbor under the following circumstances: (i) the object is present in its cache or has been requested, (ii) the θ value does not change since last report, and (iii) its neighbor already has the object in its cache. This observation allows us to significantly prune the number of gain values reported in each update message. Further, each gain value can be encoded with $2-4$ bytes depending on the quantization and accuracy. In our simulations, we measured 26.18 values per message on average for the Freebies trace and 22.61 for the Sunland trace, using default settings.

7. CONCLUSION AND FUTURE WORK

To conclude, Joserlin is a joint request and service scheduling scheme for P2P non-linear media streaming systems that avoids request contention through request binning and exploits the interplay between on-demand and prefetch requests to prioritize prefetch requests at both requesters and responders. Joserlin issues prefetch requests to fully utilize peers' upload bandwidth, without violating requests' relative priorities. Our evaluation compares Joserlin with three existing solutions using traces collected from Second Life and finds that Joserlin outperforms these solutions in all scenarios.

For future work, we would like to investigate how to maintain neighborhood in the P2P overlay to further improve streaming efficiency and reduce the server load. If neighbors of a powerful peer have prefetched enough content, we should restructure the overlay so that this peer can become a neighbor of other more needy peers. Such restructuring adds a new optimization dimension to our joint request and service scheduling.

Acknowledgments: This research is supported by the Singapore National Research Foundation under its International Research Centre @ Singapore Funding Initiative and administered by the IDM Programme Office.

8. REFERENCES

[1] Broadband reports and speed test statistics. http://www.dslreports.com/archive.

[2] U. Abbasi, G. Simo, and T. Ahmed. Differentiated chunk scheduling for P2P video-on-demand system. In *CCNC'11*, pages 622–626, Las Vegas, NV, January 2011.

[3] S. Annapureddy, S. Guha, C. Gkantsidis, D. Gunawardena, and P. R. Rodriguez. Is high-quality VoD feasible using P2P swarming? In *WWW'07*, pages 903–912, Banff, Canada, May 2007.

[4] I. Baumgart, B. Heep, and S. Krause. OverSim: A flexible overlay network simulation framework. In *IEEE Global Internet Symposium, 2007*, pages 79–84. IEEE, 2007.

[5] M. E. Bertinat, D. Padula, F. R. Amoza, P. Rodríguez-Bocca, and P. Romero. Optimal bandwidth allocation in mesh-based peer-to-peer streaming networks. In *INOC'11*, pages 529–534, Hamburg, Germany, June 2011.

[6] T. Bonald, L. Massoulié, F. Mathieu, D. Perino, and A. Twigg. Epidemic live streaming: optimal performance trade-offs. *SIGMETRICS Perform. Eval. Rev.*, 36(1):325–336, June 2008.

[7] A. Brampton, A. MacQuire, I. A. Rai, N. J. P. Race, L. Mathy, and M. Fry. Characterising user interactivity for sports video-on-demand. In *NOSSDAV'07*, pages 99–104, Urbana-Champaign, IL, June 2007.

[8] Z. Chen, K. Xue, and P. Hong. A study on reducing chunk scheduling delay for mesh-based P2P live streaming. In *Grid and Cooperative Computing (GCC'08)*, pages 356–361, Shenzhen, China, October 2008.

[9] C.-H. Chien, S.-Y. Hu, J.-R. Jiang, and C.-W. Cheng. Bandwidth-aware peer-to-peer 3D streaming. *Int. J. Adv. Media Commun.*, 4(4):324–342, Nov. 2010.

[10] M. Claypool and K. Claypool. Latency and player actions in online games. *Commun. ACM*, 49:40–45, November 2006.

[11] Y. Guo, C. Liang, and Y. Liu. AQCS: adaptive queue-based chunk scheduling for P2P live streaming. In *IFIP-TC6 Networking Conference (NETWORKING'08)*, pages 433–444, Singapore, May 2008.

[12] Y. Guo, S. Mathur, K. Ramaswamy, S. Yu, and B. Patel. Ponder: Performance aware P2P video-on-demand service. In *GLOBECOM'07*, pages 225–230, Washington, DC, Nov. 2007.

[13] C. Huang, J. Li, and K. W. Ross. Peer-assisted VoD: Making Internet video distribution cheap. In *IPTPS'07*, Bellevue, WA, Feb. 2007.

[14] Y. Huang, T. Z. J. Fu, D. M. Chiu, J. C. S. Lui, and C. Huang. Challenges, design and analysis of a large-scale P2P VoD system. In *SIGCOMM'08*, pages 375–388, Seattle, WA, Aug. 2008.

[15] K.-W. Hwang, V. Misra, and D. S. Rubenstein. Stored media streaming in BitTorrent-like P2P networks. Technical Report CUCS-024-08, Columbia University, New York, April 2008.

[16] C. Király, R. L. Cigno, and L. Abeni. Deadline-based differentiation in P2P streaming. In *GLOBECOM'10*, pages 1–6, Miami, FL, Dec. 2010.

[17] C. Liang, Y. Guo, and Y. Liu. Is random scheduling sufficient in P2P video streaming? In *ICDCS'08*, pages 53–60, Beijing, China, June 2008.

[18] K. Liang, R. Zimmermann, and W. T. Ooi. Peer-assisted texture streaming in metaverses. In *MM'11*, pages 203–212, Scottsdale, AZ, Nov. 2011.

[19] C. L. Liu and J. W. Layland. Scheduling algorithms for multiprogramming in a hard-real-time environment. *J. ACM*, 20(1):46–61, Jan. 1973.

[20] N. Magharei and R. Rejaie. PRIME: peer-to-peer receiver-driven mesh-based streaming. *IEEE/ACM Trans. Netw.*, 17(4):1052–1065, Aug. 2009.

[21] A. Mavlankar, J. Noh, P. Baccichet, and B. Girod. Peer-to-peer multicast live video streaming with interactive virtual pan/tilt/zoom functionality. In *ICIP'08*, pages 2296–2299. IEEE, 2008.

[22] V. Pai, K. Kumar, K. Tamilmani, V. Sambamurthy, and A. E. Mohr. Chainsaw: Eliminating Trees from Overlay Multicast. In *IPTPS'05*, pages 127–140, Ithaca, NY, Feb. 2005.

[23] W.-L. Sung, S.-Y. Hu, and J.-R. Jiang. Selection strategies for peer-to-peer 3D streaming. In *NOSSDAV'08*, pages 15–20, Braunschweig, Germany, May 2008.

[24] A. Vlavianos, M. Iliofotou, and M. Faloutsos. BiToS: Enhancing BitTorrent for supporting streaming applications. In *INFOCOM'06*, pages 1–6, Barcelona, Spain, Apr. 2006.

[25] N. Vratonjić, P. Gupta, N. Knežević, D. Kostić, and A. Rowstron. Enabling DVD-like features in P2P video-on-demand systems. In *P2P-TV'07*, pages 329–334, Kyoto, Japan, Aug. 2007.

[26] J. Wang, C. Huang, and J. Li. On ISP-friendly rate allocation for peer-assisted VoD. In *MM'08*, pages 279–288, Seattle, WA, Aug. 2008.

[27] X. Yang, M. Gjoka, P. Chhabra, A. Markopoulou, and P. Rodriguez. Kangaroo: Video seeking in P2P systems. In *IPTPS'09*, Boston, MA, Apr. 2009.

[28] Y. Yang, A. L. H.Chow, L. Golubchik, and D. Bragg. Improving QoS in BitTorrent-like VoD systems. In *INFOCOM'10*, pages 2061–2069, San Diego, CA, Mar. 2010.

[29] L. Ying and A. Basu. pcVOD: Internet peer-to-peer video-on-demand with storage caching on peers. In *International Conference on Distributed Multimedia Systems (DMS'07)*, pages 218–223, San Francisco, CA, Sept. 2007.

[30] Q. Yu and D. Chen. Optimal data scheduling for P2P VoD streaming systems. In *ICPADS'10*, pages 817–822, Shanghai, China, Dec. 2010.

[31] M. Zhang and B. Feng. A P2P VoD system using dynamic priority. In *Malaysia International Conference on Communication*, pages 518 – 523, Kuala Lumpur, Malaysia, Dec. 2009.

[32] M. Zhang, Y. Xiong, Q. Zhang, and S. Yang. On the optimal scheduling for media streaming in data-driven overlay networks. In *GLOBECOM'06*, San Francisco, CA, Nov. 2006.

[33] T. Zhang, F. Ren, and X. Cheng. First-aid mechanism for peer-to-peer streaming. In *ICNP'08*, Orlando, FL, Oct. 2008.

[34] X. Zhang, J. Liu, B. Li, and T.-S. P. Yum. CoolStreaming/DONet: A data-driven overlay network for peer-to-peer live media streaming. In *INFOCOM'05*, pages 2102–2111, Miami, FL, Mar. 2005.

[35] Z. W. Zhao. Challenges in supporting non-linear and non-continuous media access in P2P systems. In *MM'12*, pages 1397–1400, Nara, Japan, Nov. 2012.

[36] Y. Zhou, T. Z. J. Fu, and D. M. Chiu. A unifying model and analysis of P2P VoD replication and scheduling. In *INFOCOM'12*, pages 1530–1538, Orlando, FL, Mar. 2012.

FlashStream: A Multi-tiered Storage Architecture for Adaptive HTTP Streaming

Moonkyung Ryu
College of Computing
Georgia Institute of Technology
Atlanta, GA, USA
mkryu@gatech.edu

Umakishore Ramachandran
College of Computing
Georgia Institute of Technology
Atlanta, GA, USA
rama@cc.gatech.edu

ABSTRACT

Video streaming on the Internet is popular and the need to store and stream video content using CDNs is continually on the rise thanks to services such as Hulu and Netflix. Adaptive HTTP streaming using the deployed CDN infrastructure has become the de facto standard for meeting the increasing demand for video streaming on the Internet. The storage architecture that is used for storing and streaming the video content is the focus of this study. Hard-disk as the storage medium has been the norm for enterprise-class storage servers for the longest time. More recently, multi-tiered storage servers (incorporating SSDs) such as Sun's ZFS and Facebook's flashcache offer an alternative to disk-based storage servers for enterprise applications. Both these systems use the SSD as a cache between the DRAM and the hard disk. The thesis of our work is that the current-state-of-the art in multi-tiered storage systems, architected for general-purpose enterprise workloads, do not cater to the unique needs of adaptive HTTP streaming. We present *FlashStream*, a multi-tiered storage architecture that addresses the unique needs of adaptive HTTP streaming. Like ZFS and flashcache, it also incorporates SSDs as a cache between the DRAM and the hard disk. The key architectural elements of FlashStream include optimal write granularity to overcome the write amplification effect of flash memory SSDs and a QoS-sensitive caching strategy that monitors the activity of the flash memory SSDs to ensure that video streaming performance is not hampered by the caching activity. We have implemented FlashStream and experimentally compared it with ZFS and flashcache for adaptive HTTP streaming workloads. We show that FlashStream outperforms both these systems for the same hardware configuration. Specifically, it is better by a factor of two compared to its nearest competitor, namely ZFS. In addition, we have compared FlashStream with a traditional two-level storage architecture (DRAM + HDDs), and have shown that, for the same investment cost, FlashStream provides 33% better performance and 94% better energy efficiency.

MM'13, October 21–25, 2013, Barcelona, Spain.

http://dx.doi.org/10.1145/2502081.2502122

Categories and Subject Descriptors

D.4.2 [**Operating Systems**]: Storage Management—*Storage hierarchies*; H.5.1 [**Information Interfaces And Presentation**]: Multimedia Information Systems—*Video*

General Terms

Design, Performance, Measurement

Keywords

Video-on-Demand, Storage, Flash Memory, Solid-State Drive, Adaptive HTTP streaming

1. INTRODUCTION

Hulu [3] a web service that streams premium contents such as news, TV series, and shows, and Netflix [6] the largest subscription service for DVD rental and streaming video over the web are huge successes. In November 2011, Hulu had more than 30 million unique viewers in the U.S. [4]. Netflix currently has 20 million subscribers in the U.S., and they consume 30% of North American Internet traffic during the peak time [7].

Adaptive HTTP streaming (AHS) is a new paradigm of video streaming over the web currently being used by major content distributors, including Netflix. AHS does not depend on specialized video servers. Instead, AHS exploits off-the-shelf web servers. The advantage of this paradigm is that it can easily exploit the widely deployed content distribution network (CDN) infrastructure for the scalable video streaming service, and the firewall and NAT traversal problems can be greatly simplified. On the other hand, its weakness is that there is no QoS mechanism on the server side to guarantee video delivery. It relies on the large resource provisioning (i.e., CPU, RAM, storage capacity, storage and network bandwidth, etc.) that is customary with CDNs. This approach achieves simple system design, scalability, and jitter-free video streaming at the cost of large resource over-provisioning.

In the 90's and early 2000's, Internet-based video streaming for high-bitrate video was challenging due to technological limitations. In that era, every component of the video server needed to be carefully optimized to meet the volume of clients, the data rate of video, and the real-time guarantees for jitter-free video delivery. For example, real-time scheduling was needed to allocate precious CPU, disk, and network resources for the simultaneous video streams; efficient memory caching was needed to ensure that the disks are not overloaded; data placement strategy over multiple disks was needed to evenly distribute the disk load; and an admission control mechanism was needed to ensure that quality of service guarantees can be met without overloading the various system components. However, most of these software solutions have become less important with the remarkable hardware improvements over the past two decades. There is 100× speedup in CPU speeds; RAM capacity has increased by 1,000×; hard disk drive (HDD) capacity has grown by 10,000×; and network bandwidth has improved 10,000×. The only thing that has been stagnant is the access latency of the HDD. The access latency has *only* improved four times over the last two decades! [2]

The video streaming system requires a number of HDDs both for capacity (to store the video library) and for bandwidth (to serve the video library). While the cost per gigabyte of HDDs has decreased significantly, the cost per bits-per-second of HDDs has not. Moreover, an array of HDDs consumes a lot of power (approx. 5-15 watts per drive) and generates a large amount of heat; therefore, more power is required for cooling a data center hosting a large array of disks. The amount of user generated content (UGC) and the corresponding number of viewers are increasing explosively on the web. In addition, the AHS approach requires storage bandwidth over-provisioning for reliable video streaming service; therefore, the cost of storage for a large scale service is significant. For these reasons, the storage component of the video streaming system needs researchers' attention again for more throughput, lower power consumption, and lower cooling costs.

Solid-State Drive (SSD) is a new storage technology that is comprised of semiconductor memory chips (e.g., DRAM, Flash Memory, Phase Change Memory) to store and retrieve data rather than using the traditional spinning platters, a motor, and moving heads found in conventional magnetic disks. Among various types of SSDs, flash-based SSDs currently have the maximum penetration into modern computer systems. The advantages of flash-based SSDs are fast random read, low power consumption (approx. 0.1-1.3 watts per drive), and low heat dissipation due to the absence of the mechanical components. On the other hand, its high cost per gigabyte compared to magnetic disks, poor small random write performance, and limited lifetime are major concerns compared to the disks.

Though flash-based SSDs are attractive as an alternative to HDDs for video storage for all the above reasons, the cost per gigabyte for SSD is still significantly higher than HDDs. Moreover, despite the increasing affordability of SSDs, the ratio of capacity costs of SSD to HDD is expected to remain fairly constant in the future since the bit density of HDDs is also continuously improving. Therefore, a viable architecture is to use the flash-based SSDs as an intermediate level between RAM and HDDs for caching hot contents. One interesting characteristic of video service is that only a small number of videos relative to the entire collection is accessed frequently. Therefore, we can serve frequently accessed hot contents using flash-based SSDs, serve cold contents by slow HDDs, and store the entire video library in HDDs. In this way, we can build a high-performance Video-on-Demand (VoD) system cost-effectively.

Recently, Facebook introduced flashcache, and Sun Solaris introduced ZFS, both of which are multi-tiered storage systems using SSDs as an intermediate cache between the DRAM and the hard disk. Our prior study [27] analyzing these two systems for use as a storage server for adaptive HTTP streaming showed that both systems do not perform well and presented design guidelines for building a high-performance multi-tiered video storage system using flash memory SSDs. The design guidelines can be summarized as follows. First, while low-end flash memory SSDs are well-suited to serve the caching needs of videos in an HTTP streaming server, it is of paramount importance to avoid small random writes to the flash memory SSDs due to the unique performance characteristic of flash memory. Second, SSD write operations should not be in the critical path of serving missed video segments (brought from the hard disk) to the clients. Third, SSD read operations should have higher priority than SSD write operations because the former needs to be served before their deadline to the clients, while the latter is not time critical.

In this paper, we propose *FlashStream*, a multi-tiered storage architecture incorporating flash memory SSDs that caters to the needs of adaptive HTTP streaming. The unique contributions of our work are the following:

1. To minimize write amplification, writes to SSDs are always requested at the granularity of an optimal block size and aligned on the optimal block size. In addition, we present a novel reverse-engineering technique to find out the optimal block size for any flash-based SSDs. This accomplishes the first design guideline.
2. Utilization-aware SSD admission and ring buffer mechanisms control the write request rate to SSDs and give higher priority to read requests. We adopt ZFS's evict-ahead policy to avoid SSD write operations from the critical path of serving missed data. This fulfills the second and third design guidelines.
3. Metadata for video segments are embedded in the SSD blocks to quickly restore data in SSD upon power failure.

We have built FlashStream as a web server based on pion-net [9] open source network library. We have experimentally evaluated the performance of FlashStream and compared it to both ZFS and flashcache. We show that FlashStream outperforms both these systems for the same hardware configuration.

The rest of the paper is organized as follows. Section 2 explains the background about flash memory SSDs. We describe the FlashStream architecture for adaptive HTTP streaming using flash memory SSDs in Section 3, and discuss our implementation in Section 4. Section 5 presents extensive experimental results comparing FlashStream with other systems. Related work is presented in Section 6 and the final section presents our concluding remarks.

2. BACKGROUND

In this section, we briefly review a technology central to the problem being addressed in this paper: a Flash Memory SSD.

2.1 Flash Memory SSD

Flash memories, including NAND and NOR types, have a common physical restriction, namely, they must be erased before being written [11]. Flash memory can be written or read a single page at a time, but it has to be erased in an *erase block* unit. An erase block consists of a certain number of pages. In NAND flash memory, a page is similar to a HDD sector, and its size is usually 2 to 4 KBytes, while an erase block is typically 128 pages or more.

Flash memory also suffers from a limitation on the number of erase operations possible for each erase block. In SLC NAND flash memory, the expected number of erasures per

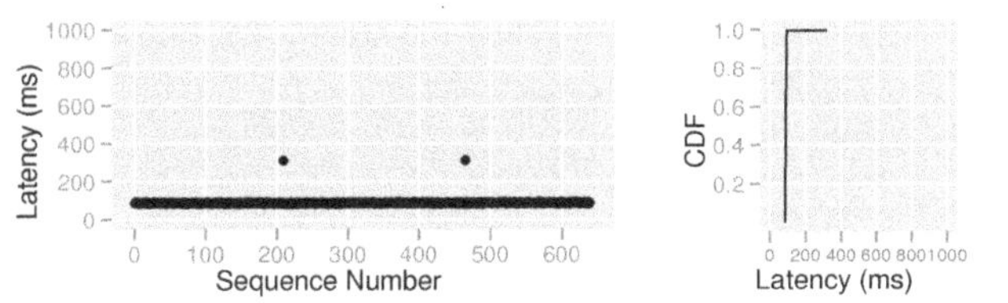

(a) Latency sequence for sequential writes (b) Latency CDF for sequential writes

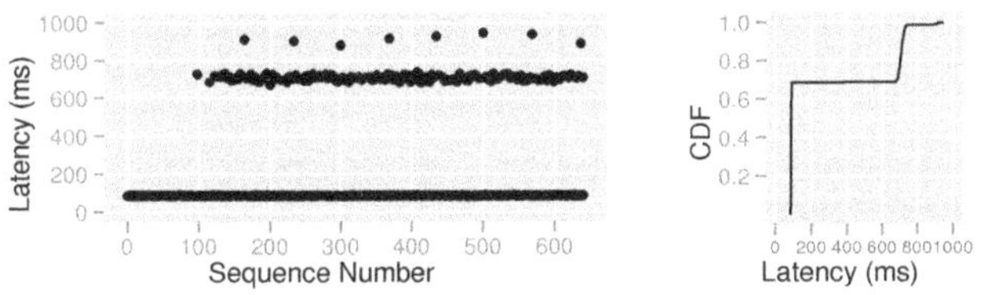

(c) Latency sequence for random writes (d) Latency CDF for random writes

Figure 1: Latency distribution for sequential/random writes with 8 MB request size. OCZ Core V2 is used for the measurement.

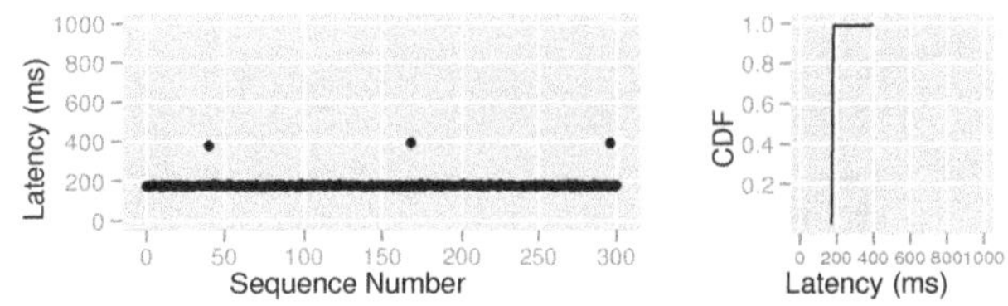

(a) Latency sequence for sequential writes (b) Latency CDF for sequential writes

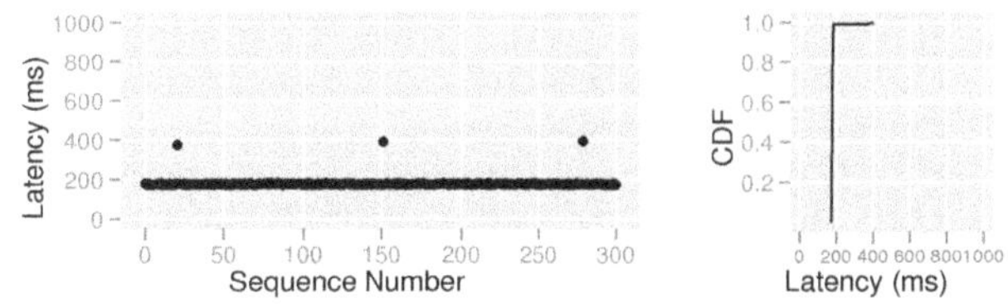

(c) Latency sequence for random writes (d) Latency CDF for random writes

Figure 2: Latency distribution for sequential/random writes with 16 MB request size. OCZ Core V2 is used for the measurement.

block is 100,000 but is only 10,000 in two-bit MLC NAND flash memory.

An SSD is simply a set of flash memory chips packaged together with additional circuitry and a special piece of software called the Flash Translation Layer (FTL) [16, 17, 24]. The additional circuitry may include a RAM buffer for storing meta-data associated with the internal organization of the SSD and a write buffer for optimizing the write performance of the SSD.

To avoid erasing and re-writing an entire block for every page modification, an FTL writes data out-of-place, remapping the logical page to a new physical location and marking the old page invalid. This requires maintaining some amount of free blocks into which new pages can be written. These free blocks are maintained by erasing previously written blocks to allow space occupied by invalid pages to be made available for new writes. This process is called *garbage collection.* FTL tries to run this process in the background as much as possible while the foreground I/O requests are idle, but it is not guaranteed, especially when a new clean block is needed instantly to write a new page. Due to random writes emanating from the upper layers of the operating system, a block may have valid pages and invalid pages. Therefore, when the garbage collector reclaims a block, the valid pages of the block need to be copied to another block. Thus, an external write may generate some additional unrelated writes internal to the device, a phenomenon referred to as *write amplification.*

3. FLASHSTREAM ARCHITECTURE

We build on our prior work reported in [27] wherein we presented design guidelines for building a high-performance multi-tiered video storage system using flash memory SSDs. Keeping the guidelines in mind, we describe the architecture of *FlashStream* in the following subsections. We use MLC SSDs instead of SLC because the SSDs are used as cache in FlashStream, not for permanent storage. Therefore, we do not need the better reliability of SLC. Moreover, MLC is significantly cheaper than SLC.

3.1 Optimal Block Size

As we discussed in Section 2.1, the reasons for the poor performance of flash memory for small random writes are two fold: (a) a block has to be erased before a page within it can be written, and (b) an erase block consists of several pages, valid pages in the block being erased must be copied to other clean pages before erasing the block (*write amplification*), and page write and block erasure are inherently slow operations. Due to the write amplification effect, small random writes not only degrade the SSD performance but also reduces the flash memory lifetime.

One way to completely eliminate both "write amplification" and poor performance due to random page writes is to ensure that write requests to the SSD are always in multiples of the block size of the flash memory that is used in the SSD, and that the writes are aligned on block boundaries. This strategy will also have the additional benefit of fast garbage collection (due to the elimination of write amplification) and longer flash memory lifetime. However, there is a catch.

SSD manufacturers put great efforts to fully exploit all available hardware resources and features to improve performance, and they use different designs [11]. In addition, the internal organization of an SSD and their techniques are proprietary and not readily available. How do we choose the right write granularity in the software architecture of the storage system when we do not know the internal architecture of the SSD? To this end, we define the *optimal block size* for write requests to the SSD as the minimum write size that makes the random write performance similar to the sequential write performance.

To determine the optimal block size, we do a reverse-engineering experiment on any given flash-based SSD. The idea is to perform random writes with different request sizes until the performance matches that with a sequential workload. To illustrate the technique, we use an OCZ Core V2 flash-based SSD. Figure 1 shows the latency of 640 write operations for sequential and random workloads when the request size is 8 MB on this SSD. For the random writes (see Figure 1(c)), we notice frequent high latencies (i.e., 800-1000 ms) due to the write amplification effect. On the other hand, when the request size is 16 MB (see Figure 2), the latency distributions

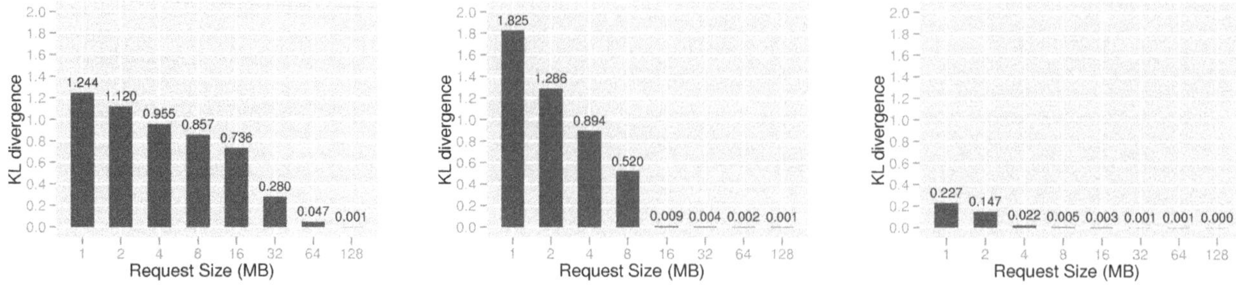

(a) INTEL X25-M G1 (b) OCZ Core V2 (c) SAMSUNG SLC MCCOE64G5MPP

Figure 3: KL divergence values for different request sizes and SSDs. The optimal block size for INTEL SSD is 64 MB, that for OCZ SSD is 16 MB, and that for SAMSUNG SSD is 4 MB.

for the sequential write and the random write workloads are very similar. Figures 1(b) and 1(d) show the CDF graphs for the 8 MB request size; Figures 2(b) and 2(d) show the CDF graphs for the 16 MB request size. While the CDF graphs are useful to visually see the similarity of two distributions, we need a quantitative measure to determine the similarity. Kullback-Leibler (KL) divergence [19] is a fundamental equation from information theory that quantifies the proximity of two probability distributions: the smaller the KL value the more similar the two distributions. In flash memory SSDs, write operation latency is a random variable and hard to estimate because it is affected by various factors such as mapping status, garbage collection, and wear-leveling. We use the KL divergence value as the metric for comparing the similarity of the latency distributions obtained with the sequential and random write workloads.

Figure 3 shows how the KL divergence value changes with different request sizes for three different SSDs. For all the SSDs, the KL divergence value converges to zero as the request size increases. We let the optimal block size be the request size where the KL divergence value becomes lower than a threshold that is close to zero. The threshold is a configuration parameter. A lower threshold can give a block size that shows more similar latency between sequential writes and random writes. We choose 0.1 for the threshold because Figure 3 shows the KL divergence value quickly converges to zero once it becomes lower than 0.1. Therefore, 64 MB is the optimal block size for INTEL X25-M G1, 16 MB for OCZ Core V2, and 4 MB for SAMSUNG SLC MCCOE64G5MPP. The optimal block size is a function of the internal architecture of the SSD (page size, block size, available internal parallelism for access to the flash memory chips, etc.). However, this experimental methodology allows us to reverse-engineer and pick a write size that is most appropriate for a given SSD. Once the optimal block size has been determined, FlashStream divides the logical address space of flash memory into identical allocation blocks that are of the same size as the optimal block size determined with the experimental methodology.

3.2 System Design

In adaptive HTTP streaming systems, a segment is a basic unit for accessing videos. Accordingly, FlashStream organizes its storage structure at segment granularity. Figure 4 depicts the FlashStream architecture. The first cache layer is a RAM cache. The RAM buffer pool is an array of memory blocks, and each block stores data for a video segment file. Because segments have different sizes, the size of each block in the RAM buffer pool is different. The second cache layer is an SSD cache. The SSD's address space is divided into equal-sized blocks (same as the optimal block size). All write operations to the SSD are requested with the optimal block size aligned on the block boundary. All segment requests that miss the two caches are served by disks. The segments read from the disks are pushed into the RAM buffer pool, and then they are returned to the CPU. On the other hand, the segments read from the SSD are not inserted into the first-level cache (RAM buffer pool) but they are directly returned to the CPU (i.e., DMA'ed into its memory). In this way, we can maximally utilize the capacity of the first-level RAM cache and the second-level SSD cache because we avoid the same segment from being stored in both levels. One of our design goals is to minimize the I/O requests sent to the disks since the hard disk is the slowest element in the three-level hierarchy of FlashStream, and thus could hurt real-time streaming performance. By storing data either in the DRAM or the SSDs (but not both), FlashStream maximizes the cumulative cache hit ratio in the first two levels and minimizes the read requests sent to the disks.

3.2.1 RAM Buffer Pool

The RAM buffer pool is the first-level in the three level hierarchy of FlashStream. Segments cached in the buffer are ordered according to the replacement policy used. For example, when a least recently used (LRU) replacement policy is employed, the most recently used segment will be at the head of the buffer pool and the least recently used segment will be at the tail. LRU is the default replacement policy for the RAM buffer pool because it is simple and works well in most cases. However, it should be noted that other replacement policies (such as LRU-Min and GDS [26]) can be easily used for the RAM buffer pool without affecting the design decisions in the other components of FlashStream. Whenever a new segment is inserted into the pool and the pool has insufficient space, then segments at the end of the pool are evicted until the pool has space to host the new segment. A RAM monitor thread periodically monitors the tail part of the RAM buffer pool (Figure 4). This tail portion of the pool is called the *monitor room*. The size of the monitor room is a system configuration parameter, and we use 10% of the total number of segments in the RAM buffer pool for the monitor room size by default. When the thread finds segments in the monitor room that are not in the SSD cache, then those segments are copied to a ring

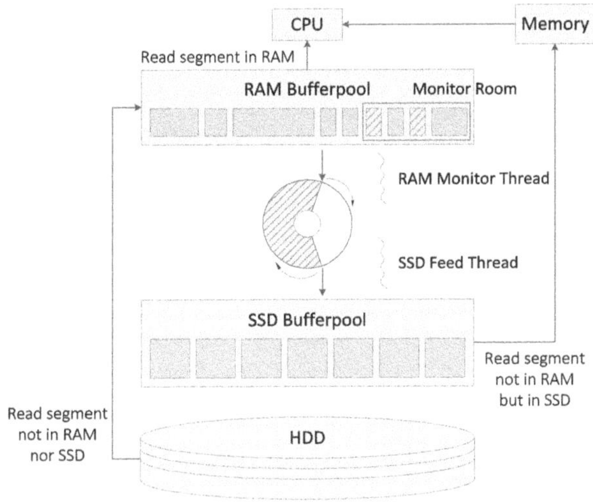

Figure 4: FlashStream Architecture. A finite-sized RAM buffer serves as the first-level cache of the server. SSD is the second-level cache. Upon a miss in the first-level cache, the data is served from the SSD (i.e., it is not copied into the first-level cache). A miss in both the caches results in reading the missing segment from the hard disk and into the first-level RAM buffer cache.

buffer. In Figure 4, such segments are shown as shaded squares in the monitor room. Segments that are in the ring buffer are candidates for being written into the second level cache. The monitor thread simply throws away the segments in the monitor room to make room for new segments coming from the disk even if they have not been copied into the ring buffer by the monitor thread. This is similar to the *evict-ahead policy* used in the ZFS file system. We assume that the video data is immutable and thus read-only (e.g., DB of movies stored at Netflix). When a video object is updated (e.g., new version of a movie is distributed to the CDN servers by the content provider), the cached copies of the segments pertaining to the old version of the video object will simply be removed from the memory hierarchy of FlashStream. This is an out-of-band administrative decision outside the normal operation of FlashStream and does not interfere with the evict-ahead policy for managing the buffer pool. The advantage of the evict-ahead policy is that it can avoid flash write operations from the critical path for handling cache miss [27]. On the other hand, the drawback of the evict-ahead policy is that there is no guarantee that the evicted segments will be written to the second level cache (i.e., SSD). When a segment misses both the RAM and SSD caches, it is read from the disks and placed in the RAM buffer pool. A thread that is inserting a segment into the RAM buffer pool does not have to wait for a victim segment (in the monitor room) to be copied into the ring buffer (for writing eventually to the SSD). The hope is that the victim would have already been copied into the ring buffer by the monitor thread *ahead of time*.

3.2.2 SSD Buffer Pool

Segments that are to be written to the SSD are buffered in the ring buffer between the RAM buffer pool and the SSD buffer pool. While the RAM monitor thread fills up the ring buffer, an SSD feed thread consumes the ring buffer and writes data to the SSD in units of the optimal block size (Section 3.1). In addition, the SSD feed thread employs a simple admission mechanism. For a video streaming system, read operations have higher priority than write operations. Therefore, when the SSD is busy for serving read requests, the SSD feed thread should not make write requests to the SSD. Details of the admission mechanism are presented in Section 4.4. If the second-level cache (SSD) is full, the victim block chosen for eviction from the SSD is simply thrown away since the block is already present in the disk, and we are always dealing with read-only data in the storage server.

3.2.3 SSD Block Replacement Policies

A *Least Recently Used (LRU)* replacement policy and a *Least Frequently Used (LFU)* replacement policy are appropriate for evicting blocks from the SSD cache. However, there is an interesting design dilemma. Recall that our unit of management of the second-level SSD cache is the optimal block size of the SSD. Since segments can be of variable sizes, a single block in the SSD cache (of optimal block size) may hold multiple segment sizes. How do we update the LRU list of blocks when a segment that is a small part of a block is accessed? How do we maintain the LFU book-keeping for multiple segments that may be in the same SSD block? We suggest three different replacement policies:

1. Least Recently Used Block (LRU): In this policy, a segment access is considered the same as an access to the containing SSD block. Therefore, when any segment in a block is accessed, the block is moved to the front of an LRU list. When a block needs to be evicted, the last block in the list is chosen as a victim.
2. Least Frequently Used Block on Average (LFU-Mean): This scheme keeps track of the access count for each segment. When a block needs to be evicted, the average access count of the segments in a block is calculated, and the block with the least average count is chosen as a victim.
3. Least Frequently Used Block based on Median (LFU-Median): Similar to the LFU-Mean policy, this scheme keeps track of the access count for each segment as well. Because the mean is not robust to outliers, this policy uses median of the access counts of the segments in a block.

The performance of these SSD block replacement policies are evaluated in Section 5.

3.2.4 Difference from ZFS

FlashStream employs an evict-ahead policy similar to the ZFS file system, however, there are fundamental differences between the two.

1. ZFS uses FIFO replacement policy for the SSD. The motivation is same as FlashStream; FIFO replacement policy generates sequential writes to the SSD and avoids small random writes to the SSD. However, the FIFO replacement policy of ZFS shows a low hit ratio. On the other hand, FlashStream employs different kinds of block replacement policies, and it shows a lot higher hit ratio than ZFS. The results are presented in Section 5.2.
2. ZFS does not differentiate the priority of writes and reads to/from the SSD because it is not designed for a video streaming system. Therefore, reads which would be hits in the SSD cache get queued up behind ongoing writes, and miss the deadline that reads need to be serviced. On the other hand, FlashStream uses an

Segment Id		
Video Id	Segment Number	Bitrate

Table 1: Each video segment is uniquely identified by a tuple: {Video Id, Segment Number, Bitrate}.

admission policy for writes to the SSD to give a higher priority for read requests.

3. FlashStream decouples monitoring the RAM buffer and writing evicted segments in the ring buffer to the SSD. These two functions are inter-twined in ZFS, and it could lead to lost opportunity. Recall that the evict-ahead policy used in ZFS will simply throw away pages from the RAM buffer even if they have not been written to the SSD. Thus, if the RAM insertion rate from the disk is faster than the rate at which evicted pages can be written to the SSD, then a larger population of evicted pages will be thrown away. On the other hand, in FlashStream, the monitor thread and the SSD feed thread cooperate through the ring buffer and thus there is an opportunity for more evicted segments to be cached in the SSD (despite the evict-ahead policy) even during periods when the RAM insertion rate is higher than the SSD write throughput. The amount of time taken to fill the SSD cache for both systems is presented in Section 5.2.

4. IMPLEMENTATION

In this section, we describe the details of FlashStream implementation. We have built our FlashStream web server based on *pion-net* [9] open source network library. FlashStream directly manipulates a flash memory SSD as a raw device. In addition, FlashStream bypasses the operating system's page cache and manages the RAM for caching segment files on its own. Each video segment is uniquely identified by a tuple: {video id, segment number, bitrate} (see Table 1). The tuple represents the id of a segment. Buffer Manager and SSD Manager are the two most import components, and their details are explained in the following subsections.

4.1 RAM Buffer Manager

A buffer manager manipulates the available RAM buffer for caching segments. Figure 5(a) shows data structures used by the buffer manager. It keeps a pool of cached segments in RAM. For fast lookup, a hash table (key, value store) is maintained in RAM. The key is a segment id, and the value is a tuple: {memory address of the block in RAM, size of the block}. The segment list maintains a list of segment ids for victim selection. The buffer manager uses an LRU replacement policy. A hit in the RAM results in the segment being moved to the head of the segment list. The last element of the segment list is a victim. When a new segment read from the disk is inserted to the RAM buffer pool, a new entry is inserted into the hash table, and the id of the new segment is inserted at the head of the segment list. If needed, a victim is evicted from the buffer pool and the entry for the victim in the hash table is removed.

4.2 SSD Manager

An SSD manager manipulates the available SSD blocks for caching segments. Figure 5(b) shows the data structures used by the SSD manager. SSD's address space is divided into equal-size blocks, and the block is same as the optimal block size (see Section 3.1). A block hash table (another key, value store) is maintained to lookup the segments that

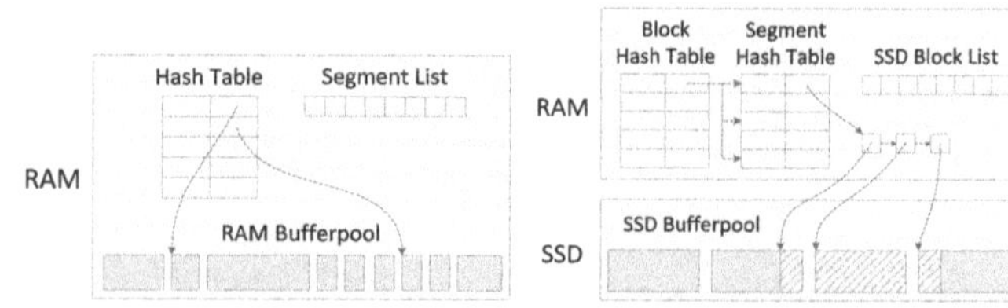

(a) RAM Buffer Manager (b) SSD Manager

Figure 5: Data structures used by the RAM Buffer Manager and the SSD Manager. Replacement from the RAM buffer is in units of variable-sized video segments.

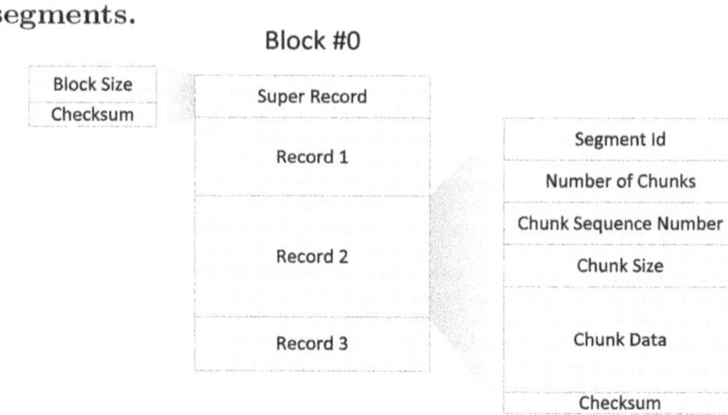

Figure 6: Data structure of an SSD block: An SSD block is composed of records, with each record containing the metadata as well as the data pertaining to the segment id. Block #0 (the first block) of the SSD is special in that it contains a super record in addition to the data records.

are stored in a block. The key is an SSD block number, and the value is a list of segment ids that are stored in the same block. A segment hash table is used to lookup the logical block address of the SSD for a segment. When the segment size is larger than the size of an SSD block, then the segment is stored using multiple blocks. In addition, a part of a segment can be written at the end of a block and the rest can be written in the front of another block. We call such partial data of a segment a *chunk* of the segment. Therefore, the value field in the segment hash table is a list of tuples; each tuple contains {SSD block number, offset into the block, size of a segment chunk}. In Figure 5(b), the shaded blocks in the SSD buffer pool represents a single segment stored in multiple SSD blocks. An SSD block list maintains a list of block numbers for victim selection. The block hash table, the segment hash table, and the SSD block list data structures are stored in physical memory (i.e., RAM) for fast access.

4.3 SSD Block Data Layout

Flash memory SSDs provide capacity from hundreds of gigabytes to a few terabytes in a single drive these days. After a system crash or administrative downtime, warming up such a large capacity SSD takes a long time. Since flash memory is non-volatile, a warmed up SSD can still serve as a second-level cache despite power failures as long as we have metadata for the segments stored in the SSD as well. To recover the stored data, FlashStream embeds metadata in the SSD blocks. Figure 6 shows the data layout in the SSD blocks. The first SSD block (block number 0) has a special record, namely, *super record*. The super record includes information about the block size and its checksum. Only the first

	SSD A	SSD B
Model	INTEL X25-M G1	OCZ Core V2
Capacity	80 GB	120 GB
4KB Random Read Throughput	15.5 MB/s	14.8 MB/s
4KB Random Write Throughput	3.25 MB/s	0.02 MB/s

Table 2: MLC Flash Memory SSDs that are used for our experiments. SSD A shows significantly better random write performance than SSD B. We intentionally use a very low-end SSD (SSD B) to show how well FlashStream works with low-end SSDs.

SSD block has the super record, and the other SSD blocks do not. Following the super record, a series of records are stored. Each record represents a chunk of a segment. The record consists of *segment id*, *number of chunks*, *chunk sequence number*, *chunk size*, *chunk data*, and *checksum*. From the segment id, the system can figure out the segment that the chunk belongs to. The number of chunks tells how many chunks the segment is divided into, and the chunk sequence number tells the order of the chunk in its segment. Checksum is used to verify the integrity of each record. After system crash, by scanning sequentially all SSD blocks, FlashStream can reconstruct the in-memory data structures of the SSD manager (i.e., block hash table and segment hash table).

4.4 Utilization-Aware SSD Admission

The SSD feed thread employs an admission mechanism to avoid writes to the SSD when the SSD is busy for serving reads. To measure how busy the SSD device is, we use */proc/diskstats* wherein the Linux kernel reports information for each of the storage devices. */proc/diskstats* provides the amount of time (in milliseconds) spent doing I/O for each storage device. We read the number at the beginning of a certain epoch and again at the end of the epoch. Because this is an accumulated number, the difference between the two readings gives the time spent in I/O for that device for the current epoch. The ratio of the time spent in I/O to the periodicity of the epoch serves as a measure of the storage device utilization for that epoch. The SSD feed thread stops writing data to the SSD when the SSD utilization exceeds a threshold λ, and the default value for the threshold is 60%.

5. EVALUATION

In this section, we evaluate the performance of the FlashStream system. We would like to mimic the request pattern that is fielded and serviced by an HTTP server (i.e., a CDN server) that is serving video segments to distributed clients under the adaptive HTTP streaming mechanism. To this end, the workload offered to the FlashStream server is a large number of independent requests from clients. To measure the storage subsystem performance exactly and to avoid network subsystem effects, the workload generator program and the FlashStream server run on the same machine communicating via a loop-back interface. The machine has Xeon 2.26 GHz Quad core processor with 8 GB DRAM, and Linux kernel 2.6.32 is installed on it. We use a 7200 RPM HDD, and the capacity of the HDD is 550 GB. We have evaluated five system configurations. In addition to our FlashStream system with three SSD cache replacement policies, we have measured the performance of two state-of-the-art multi-tiered storage systems (that use flash memory caching), namely, ZFS [10] and flashcache [1]. Table 3 shows the web server and the file system that are used for each system configuration. The version of Apache web server is 2.2.14, and the version of ZFS is zfs-fuse 0.6.0-1. The flash memory SSDs we used for our experiments are listed in Table 2. Note that we intentionally use a very low-end SSD (SSD B) to show how well FlashStream works with low-end SSDs. In our evaluation, FlashStream and ZFS have worked slightly better with SSD B while Flashcache has worked better with SSD A. Therefore, we present only results of FlashStream and ZFS used with SSD B and results of flashcache used with SSD A. We use only 75 GB out of the total capacity for both SSDs for fair comparison.

Configuration	Web Server	File System
FlashStream(LRU)	FlashStream	EXT4
FlashStream(LFU-Mean)	FlashStream	EXT4
FlashStream(LFU-Median)	FlashStream	EXT4
ZFS	Apache	ZFS
Flashcache	Apache	EXT4

Table 3: Five system configurations used for our evaluation.

5.1 Workload

Zipf distribution is generally used in modeling the video access pattern of a video-on-demand (VoD) system, and typically a parameter value between 0.2 and 0.4 is chosen for the distribution [23]. We use 0.2 for the parameter in our study. Dynamic Adaptive Streaming over HTTP (DASH) [5] is an ISO/IEC MPEG standard of the adaptive HTTP streaming paradigm. We use a DASH dataset [20] for our test which is available in the public domain. As shown in Table 4, the dataset comprises six distinct video objects with five different bitrates for each video. However, for our experimentation we needed to create a larger dataset comprising of 2000 distinct videos. We have generated the 2000 videos by uniformly using the six videos and five bitrates. The total size of our dataset is 545 GB. Since we use five different bitrates and videos are encoded with variable bitrate (VBR), the segments of our generated dataset have very different sizes.

In every t seconds (which is the inverse of the request rate), the workload generator selects a video object according to the zipf distribution. Next, it chooses a segment of the video object according to a uniform distribution; each segment of the video object has the same probability. The reason behind the uniform distribution is as follows. A large scale adaptive HTTP video streaming service like Netflix relies on the CDN infrastructure that widely deploys web cache servers near the edge networks. For an effective load balancing, a video segment (or object) is replicated to a number of web cache servers, and a client's request for the segment is directed to a web server holding the segment via a request routing technique. There are many different request routing techniques such as DNS routing, HTML rewriting [12], and anycasting [25]. For this reason, there is no guarantee that a client who downloaded a segment i of a video will download the next segment $i+1$ from the same server. The next segment request may be directed to a different web server that holds a replica. Therefore, it is reasonable to assume that the probability that a web server gets a request for a segment of a video object is totally random.

The workload generator sends an HTTP request for the chosen segment to the web server. When the segment request is

Name	Bitrates	Segment Length	Source Quality	Length	Genre
Big Buck Bunny	200/400/700/1500/2000 Kbps	10 sec	1080p YUV	09:46	Animation
Elephants Dream	200/400/700/1500/2000 Kbps	10 sec	1080p YUV	10:54	Animation
Red Bull Playstreets	200/400/700/1500/2000 Kbps	10 sec	1080p 6Mbit AVC	01:37:28	Sport
The Swiss Account	200/400/700/1500/2000 Kbps	10 sec	1080p 6Mbit AVC	57:34	Sport
Valkaama	200/400/700/1400/2000 Kbps	10 sec	1080p 6Mbit AVC	01:33:05	Movie
Of Forest and Men	200/400/700/1400/2000 Kbps	10 sec	SD	10:53	Movie

Table 4: Source DASH dataset that is used to generate our 2000 videos.

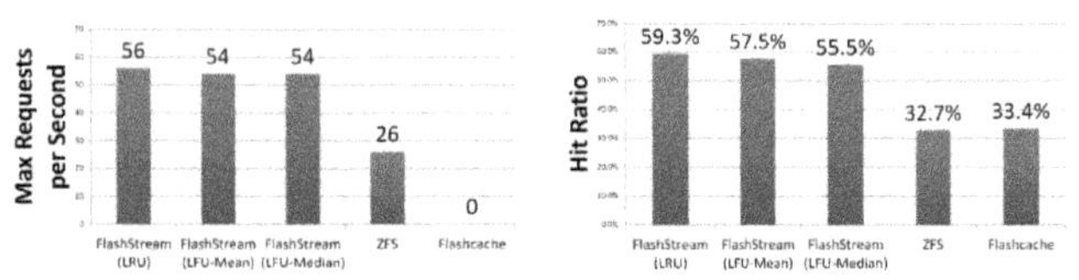

(a) Maximum Request Rate (b) Cache Hit Ratio

Figure 7: Maximum request rate and SSD cache hit ratio of the 5 different system configurations with a warmed up cache for 0% segment miss ratio. FlashStream performs 2 times better than ZFS.

not satisfied (i.e., it is not downloaded to the client) within the segment's play-out time (10 seconds for our test video), the client counts it as a segment deadline miss. We choose the 10 second segment size because it is the default size used by Apple HTTP Live Streaming [13]. We measure the segment miss ratio against different request rates. *Segment miss ratio* is defined as the ratio of the number of segment deadline misses to the total number of segment requests for a given request rate. Therefore, the *requests per second* is a control parameter, and the segment miss ratio is the measured figure of merit of the storage subsystem.

5.2 Performance Comparison

In this section, we measure the maximum request rate that the five systems can support when the cache is warmed up. This is the best performance each of the systems can provide. We have fully filled up the SSD cache by running the workload generator for a sufficient amount of time before each measurement. FlashStream (regardless of replacement policy) takes 94 minutes to fully fill up the 75 GB SSD cache while ZFS takes 1200 minutes (20 hours) and flashcache takes 1320 minutes (22 hours) for the same amount of SSD cache. We assume the QoS requirement for video streaming is 0% segment miss ratio. By increasing the request rate gradually, we measure the segment miss ratio for each request rate until the segment miss ratio gets higher than 0%. In this way, we can get the maximum request rate for 0% segment miss ratio. We run each measurement with a different request rate for an hour.

Figure 7(a) shows that FlashStream performs two times better than ZFS. Different SSD cache replacement policies of FlashStream perform similarly while LRU is slightly better than the other two. ZFS is able to support a maximum of 26 requests per second, and flashcache cannot support even 1 request per second.

Next, we measure the SSD cache hit ratio of the five systems with a warmed up cache when the request rate is the maximum request rate that the systems can support. Each measurement is run for an hour. Figure 7(b) shows that FlashStream with LRU SSD cache replacement policy has the best hit ratio. The other two policies (i.e., LFU-Mean and LFU-Median) show slightly lower hit ratio than LRU. ZFS's lower maximum request rate compared to FlashStream correlates directly with ZFS's lower SSD cache hit ratio. Page reads that miss the SSD cache of ZFS go to disks, makes the disks overloaded, and the reads from the disks miss their deadline. This result tells us, for the SSD cache, block-level replacement policies (that FlashStream uses) are able to achieve a higher hit ratio than FIFO replacement policy (that ZFS uses), and results in a higher maximum request rate. The reason for the poor performance of flashcache is due to the fact that SSD write operations are in the critical path of serving read operations that miss the SSD cache. Thus though the observed hit ratio for flashcache is 33.4%, it does not translate to performance (as measured by the maximum request rate) due to the fact that SSD cache reads could be backed up behind long latency SSD cache write operations. FlashStream and ZFS systems address this problem by the evict-ahead mechanism (see Section 3.2.1). For a more detailed analysis of the poor performance of ZFS and flashcache, please refer to our prior study [27].

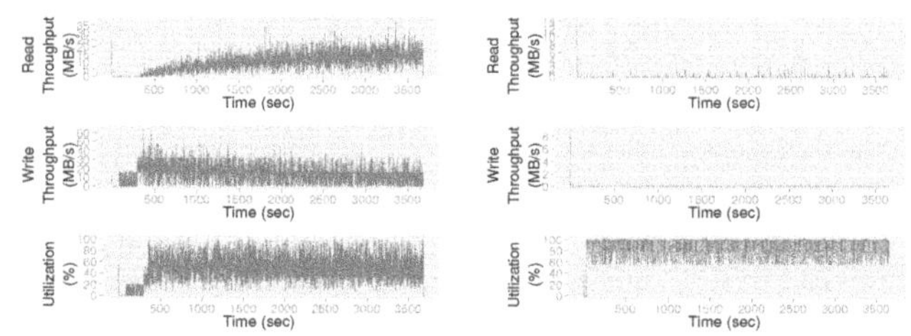

(a) 16MB Block Size (b) 4KB Block Size

Figure 8: Effect of different block sizes on Read throughput, Write throughput, and Utilization of the SSD (second-level cache of FlashStream). When the block size matches the optimal block size (Figure 8(a)), the SSD is not overloaded (i.e., there is no write amplification), and the system fills segments gradually, and serves the segments that hit the SSD. When the block size is 4KB (Figure 8(b)), the SSD is overloaded (due to write amplification), and shows very low read and write throughput.

5.3 Effect of Block Size

In this section, we measure how the choice of the SSD block size affects the FlashStream performance. We run FlashStream with a cold cache for an hour using SSD B. Even though the SSD cache is empty, for this experiment, we intentionally make FlashStream return random free blocks (not in a sequential order) when the SSD feed thread needs to write a block of data to the SSD. It is because we want to see quickly the effect of the SSD writes with random offsets without fully filling up the SSD cache. This is for a quick

Configuration	DRAM	SSD	HDD	RPS	$\frac{\text{Requests}}{\text{Joule}}$
FlashStream	2GB	100GB	1	64	2.91
Traditional A	12GB	-	1	34	0.57
Traditional B	2GB	-	2	48	1.50

Table 5: Three system configurations for energy efficiency comparison. SSD is a low-end SSD and HDD is 7200 RPM. RPS represents the maximum request rate.

measurement and it does not harm the correctness of the results. As we have shown in Figure 3, the optimal block size of SSD B is 16MB. Figure 8(a) shows read throughput, write throughput, and utilization (top to bottom) of the SSD for an hour. From the write throughput graph (middle), we notice that the system gradually fills segments into the SSD cache. The read throughput graph (top) shows that the read throughput increases as segment requests hit the SSD cache. The utilization graph (bottom) tells us that the SSD device is not overloaded during this period.

On the other hand, Figure 8(b) presents the same SSD's read throughput, write throughput, and utilization when the block size is 4KB. SSD B is a low-end SSD that shows very low performance with small random writes (see Table 2). Due to the write amplification triggered by the small block writes with random offsets, the SSD is overloaded during the whole period (100% utilization), and hence provides very low read and write throughput.

When the block size is 16MB, during the one hour period, 70.4% of the total capacity of the SSD is filled, and the SSD hit ratio is 34.4%. On the contrary, when the block size is 4KB, only 0.08% of the total SSD capacity is written and the SSD hit ratio is 0.65%. To make matters worse, 3% of the read requests that hit the SSD miss their deadline due to the poor read throughput. This experiment underscores the importance of using the optimal block size for the SSD to achieve good performance.

5.4 Energy Efficiency

In this section, we compare the energy efficiency for three different systems: FlashStream and two "traditional" systems (one for more DRAM and another for more disks). Table 5 shows the hardware configuration of the three systems. FlashStream has 2 GB DRAM, 100 GB SSD, and a single 7200 RPM 1 TB HDD. Traditional A has 12 GB DRAM and a single 7200 RPM 1 TB HDD. Traditional B has 2 GB DRAM and two 7200 RPM 1 TB HDDs striped per Linux's software RAID-0 configuration. Compared to FlashStream, Traditional A uses more DRAM for caching instead of SSDs, while Traditional B uses more HDDs for more disk throughput via parallel access. All three systems have the similar total capital cost according to the capital cost of devices in Table 6 (Traditional B is $10 more expensive than the other two). Apache web server is used for traditional systems. Table 6 shows the energy cost of each device in the active state. Each DRAM module in our test machine has 2 GB; 12 GB DRAM corresponds to 6 DIMMs. For FlashStream, we measure the maximum request rate after the SSD is filled up. For traditional systems, we warm up for an hour that is sufficiently long to fill up the given DRAM. We use the same workload as in Section 5.1.

Table 5 shows that FlashStream achieves the best energy efficiency. FlashStream serves 64 requests per second with 0% segment miss ratio and its energy efficiency is 2.91 requests per joule. For Traditional configurations, using additional HDD (i.e., Traditional B) is better than using more

	Capital Cost	Energy Cost
DRAM	$8/GB	8W/DIMM
Low-end SSD	$0.8/GB	2W/drive
7200RPM 1TB HDD	$90/drive	12W/drive

Table 6: Capital cost and energy cost of devices. Data comes from the specification of commodity DRAM, SSDs, and HDDs that are commercially available [8].

DRAM (i.e., Traditional A). FlashStream is 94% more energy efficient than Traditional B. Moreover, Traditional B wastes disk capacity because it uses more HDDs only for more throughput; the dataset size is 545 GB while Traditional B has 2 TB HDDs in total. In addition, we ignore the cooling cost and the cost associated with rack space in a datacenter. FlashStream that uses less DRAM and HDDs but more flash-based SSDs would generate less heat and occupy less volume in a rack. We do not consider these benefits in this analysis.

6. RELATED WORK

FlashStore [14] is a high throughput key-value storage that uses flash memory as a cache between the RAM and the hard disk. Kgil, et al. [18] have studied energy efficient web server using flash memory as an extended system memory. Their work is based on simulations with text and image workloads. Lee, et al. [22, 21] have researched the application of flash memory SSD as a database server. The authors claim that a single enterprise class SSD can be on par with or far better than a dozen hard drives with respect to transaction throughput, cost effectiveness, and energy consumption. Do, et al. [15] have proposed three different design alternatives that use an SSD to improve the performance of a database server's buffer manager. They empirically have shown that they could speedup 3-9 times than the default HDD configuration depending on system parameters. Singleton et al. [28] have shown how much power can be saved when flash memory is used as a write buffer along with hard disks for mobile multimedia systems.

Different from the all previous works, FlashStream shows how to construct a high-performance and energy efficient multi-tiered storage system for adaptive HTTP streaming through the judicious use of flash memory SSDs as an intermediate level in the storage hierarchy.

7. CONCLUSIONS

In this paper, we have proposed a set of guidelines for effectively incorporating flash memory SSDs for building a high throughput and power efficient multi-tiered storage system for adaptive HTTP streaming. We have implemented FlashStream based on these guidelines and have evaluated its performance using realistic workloads. We have compared the performance of FlashStream to two other system configurations: Sun's ZFS, and Facebook's flashcache. Similar to FlashStream, the two configurations also incorporate flash memory SSDs in their respective storage hierarchy. FlashStream performs twice as well as its closest competitor, namely, the ZFS configuration, using segment miss ratio as the figure of merit for comparison. In addition, we have compared FlashStream with a traditional two-level storage architecture (DRAM + HDDs), and have shown that, for the same investment cost, FlashStream provides 33% better performance and 94% better energy efficiency.

There are several avenues for future research building on our novel multi-tiered storage system with flash memory SSDs for adaptive HTTP streaming. Discrepancy of the caching granularity (i.e., optimal block size) and the access granularity (i.e., segment size) of the SSD cache opens up new research opportunities for effective cache replacement algorithms. We proposed three initial algorithms for the purpose, but more studies are warranted. We used storage device's utilization as an indicator for finding opportune moments to schedule caching related I/O requests to the SSD. We would like to explore other dynamic indicators as this technique requires the threshold value for device utilization to be chosen statically by a system administrator, which could lead to the under-utilization or overloading of the SSDs if the threshold is not chosen properly. Lastly, given the promise shown by FlashStream, we would like to develop a distributed video server using the multi-tiered storage approach. Such a server will open up a host of new research issues including initial placement of video objects, migration policies for load balancing, etc.

8. ACKNOWLEDGMENTS

We thank our shepherd Prof. Cheng-Hsin Hsu and the anonymous reviewers for their valuable and constructive comments to improve the quality of this paper.

9. REFERENCES

[1] Flashcache. `http://www.facebook.com/note.php?note_id=388112370932`.

[2] Hdd technology trends. `http://www.storagenewsletter.com/news/disk/hdd-technology-trends-ibm`.

[3] Hulu. `http://www.hulu.com`.

[4] Hulu viewers. `http://www.comscore.com/Press_Events/Press_Releases/2011/12/comScore_Releases_November_2011_U.S._Online_Video_Rankings`.

[5] ISO/IEC DIS 23009-1.2. Information technology - Dynamic adaptive streaming over HTTP (DASH) - Part 1: Media presentation description and segment formats.

[6] Netflix. `http://www.netflix.com`.

[7] Netflix traffic. `http://www.techspot.com/news/46048-netflix-represents-327-of-north-americas-peak-web-traffic.html`.

[8] Newegg. http://www.newegg.com.

[9] pion-net. `http://www.pion.org/projects/pion-network-library`.

[10] Zettabyte file system. `http://solaris-training.com/classp/200_HTML/docs/zfs_wp.pdf`.

[11] N. Agrawal, V. Prabhakaran, T. Wobber, J. D. Davis, M. Manasse, and R. Panigrahy. Design tradeoffs for ssd performance. In *ATC'08: USENIX 2008 Annual Technical Conference on Annual Technical Conference*, pages 57–70, Berkeley, CA, USA, 2008. USENIX Association.

[12] A. Barbir, B. Cain, R. Nair, and O. Spatscheck. Known content network (cn) request-routing mechanisms. RFC 3568, `http://tools.ietf.org/html/rfc3568`.

[13] A. C. Begen, T. Akgul, and M. Baugher. Watching video over the web: Part1: Streaming protocols. *IEEE Internet Computing*, 15(2):54–63, 2011.

[14] B. Debnath, S. Sengupta, and J. Li. Flashstore: High throughput persistent key-value store. In *Proceedings of the 36th International Conference on Very Large Data Bases*, Singapore, September 2010.

[15] J. Do, D. Zhang, J. M. Patel, D. J. DeWitt, J. F. Naughton, and A. Halverson. Turbocharging dbms buffer pool using ssds. In *Proceedings of the 2011 ACM SIGMOD International Conference on Management of data*, SIGMOD '11, pages 1113–1124, 2011.

[16] Intel Corporation. Understanding the Flash Translation Layer (FTL) Specification. White Paper, `http://www.embeddedfreebsd.org/Documents/Intel-FTL.pdf`, 1998.

[17] A. Kawaguchi, S. Nishioka, and H. Motoda. A flash-memory based file system. In *USENIX Winter*, pages 155–164, 1995.

[18] T. Kgil and T. Mudge. Flashcache: a nand flash memory file cache for low power web servers. In *Proceedings of the 2006 international conference on Compilers, architecture and synthesis for embedded systems*, CASES '06, pages 103–112, 2006.

[19] S. Kullback and R. A. Leibler. On information and sufficiency. *The Annals of Mathematical Statistics*, 22(1):79–86, March 1951.

[20] S. Lederer, C. Müller, and C. Timmerer. Dynamic adaptive streaming over http dataset. In *Proceedings of the third annual ACM conference on Multimedia Systems*, MMSys '12, pages 89–94, Chapel Hill, North Carolina, USA, February 2012.

[21] S.-W. Lee, B. Moon, and C. Park. Advances in flash memory ssd technology for enterprise database applications. In *Proceedings of the ACM SIGMOD*, pages 863–870, June 2009.

[22] S.-W. Lee, B. Moon, C. Park, J.-M. Kim, and S.-W. Kim. A case for flash memory ssd in enterprise database applications. In *Proceedings of the ACM SIGMOD*, pages 1075–1086, June 2008.

[23] T. R. G. Nair and P. Jayarekha. A rank based replacement policy for multimedia server cache using zipf-like law. *Journal of Computing*, 2(3):14–22, 2010.

[24] C. Park, W. Cheon, J. Kang, K. Roh, W. Cho, and J.-S. Kim. A reconfigurable ftl (flash translation layer) architecture for nand flash-based applications. *Trans. on Embedded Computing Sys.*, 7(4):1–23, 2008.

[25] C. Partridge, T. Mendez, and W. Milliken. Host anycasting services. RFC 1546, `http://tools.ietf.org/html/rfc1546`.

[26] S. Podlipnig and L. Böszörmenyi. A survey of web cache replacement strategies. *ACM Comput. Surv.*, 35(4):374–398, December 2003.

[27] M. Ryu, H. Kim, and U. Ramachandran. Why are state-of-the-art flash-based multi-tiered storage systems performing poorly for http video streaming? In *Proceedings of the 22nd SIGMM Workshop on Network and Operating Systems Support for Digital Audio and Video*, Toronto, Ontario, Canada, June 2012.

[28] L. Singleton, R. Nathuji, and K. Schwan. Flash on disk for low-power multimedia computing. In *Proceedings of the ACM Multimedia Computing and Networking Conference*, January 2007.

Early Event-Driven (EED) RTCP Feedback for Rapid IDMS

Mario Montagud, Fernando Boronat
Universitat Politècnica de València (UPV)
Calle Paranimf, 1, 46730
Grao de Gandia (Valencia), SPAIN
+34 962849341
{mamontor@posgrado, fboronat@dcom}.upv.es

Hans Stokking
TNO
Netherlands Organisation for Applied Scientific Research
Brassersplein 2, Delft (the Netherlands)
+31 88 86 67278
hans.stokking@tno.nl

ABSTRACT
Inter-Destination Media Synchronization (IDMS) is essential in the emerging media consumption paradigm, which is radically evolving from passive and isolated services towards dynamic and interactive group shared experiences. This paper concentrates on improving a standardized RTP/RTCP-based solution for IDMS. In particular, novel Early Event-Driven (EED) RTCP feedback reporting mechanisms are designed to overcome latency issues and to enable higher flexibility, dynamism and accuracy when using RTP/RTCP for IDMS. The faster reaction on dynamic situations (e.g., detection of asynchrony or channel change delays) and a finer granularity for synchronizing media-related events, while preserving the RTCP bandwidth bounds, are validated through simulation tests.

Categories and Subject Descriptors
C.2.4 [**Computer-Communication Networks**]: Distributed Systems; H.5.1 [**Information Interfaces and Presentation**]: Multimedia Information Systems.

General Terms
Performance, Design, Experimentation.

Keywords
Event-Driven, IDMS, RTP/RTCP, Simulation, Synchronization.

1. INTRODUCTION
Nowadays, we are witnessing a real transition from physical togetherness towards networked togetherness around media content. Traditionally, users have gathered at a single location for consuming media (e.g., for watching TV content). The typical scenario is a group of friends watching a live football match at a friend's home. But recent advances on media streaming and on social networking, in conjunction with the proliferation of connected devices, lead to a new media consumption landscape. Novel forms of shared media experiences are gaining momentum [1], allowing geographically distributed users to socially interact (e.g., using text, audio or video chat, or combinations thereof) within the context of simultaneous content consumption. The co-located friends in the above example can now watch the football match from their own home, while being able to converse, discuss about its evolution, and cheer together when goals are scored.

MM'13, October 21–25, 2013, Barcelona, Spain.

http://dx.doi.org/10.1145/2502081.2502114

However, realizing those shared interactive services faces a lot of challenges [2]. In particular, this paper focuses on the provisioning of synchronized playout in all the involved consumer devices. This process is commonly referred to as Inter-Destination Media Synchronization (IDMS), and its relevancy is increasing in a large number of use cases, such as networked multi-player games, synchronous e-learning, or Social TV [1]. For instance, in the above *"watching apart together"* scenario, being aware of a goal through the cheering of a friend via the chat channel, before the goal sequence is displayed on the local screen, can be very frustrating and would spoil the shared experience [3].

The main technological barrier for IDMS is the end to end (e2e) delay variability when delivering media to distributed clients. Different sources of delay in the distribution chain can contribute to that variability, which can range from few milliseconds up to several seconds, depending on the technology in use [1, 3-5]. For instance, the measurements in [5] showed that the e2e delays for the shortest and longest paths of an IPTV scenario can differ up to 6 s. Without intervention, such different delays lead to differences in playout timings, thus preventing seamless and coherent interactions in these networked environments.

The need for IDMS for supporting interactive shared TV experiences has been reported in previous works [3, 6, 7]. For instance, controlled experimental setups have analyzed the effect of de-synchronization on the Quality of Experience (QoE) in Social TV scenarios [7, 3]. In [7], distributed users watched a quiz show, while interacting via voice and text chat. It was concluded that delay differences up to 1 s might not be noticeable by users, but differences over 2 s really become annoying for most of them (i.e., both text and voice chatters). Similar results were obtained in [3] by recreating the football watching experience. These user perception tests provide initial empirical evidence that actual delay differences lead to a severe QoE degradation. Moreover, Social TV is not, by far, the most restrictive IDMS use case, and other scenarios require stringent synchronization (sync, hereafter) levels [1]. Consequently, this motivates the development of adaptive and accurate IDMS solutions to compensate such e2e delay variability.

Due to the increased relevancy of IDMS, several works have addressed this topic up to now. Some illustrative papers discuss a number of use cases [1], report on working prototype implementations (e.g., [2, 8-11]), and provide a taxonomy of existing IDMS solutions [12]. Among them, a noteworthy approach consists of extending the RTCP capabilities [13] to provide useful feedback information for IDMS (e.g., [10, 11]). Using RTP/RTCP [13] for IDMS is advantageous due to several reasons. First, the use of RTCP as a feedback channel allows for continuous monitoring and control processes of the overall IDMS timings. This differs from other basic solutions that uniquely rely on synchronizing specific control events. Accordingly, these solutions provide a coarse sync process, with lower accuracy, because of the continuous and unpredictable e2e delay variability during a media session's lifetime. Second, the IDMS problem can be tackled above the transport layer, based on the current presentation times of each client. This way, the e2e delay variability can be compensated for. This allows the achievement of more accurate sync levels than the ones in specific solutions based only on compensating the network delay variability, because the media content is also significantly delayed in different manners at the client side [1, 3-5]. Third, the current standardization efforts within the ETSI [14] and IETF [15] to provide RTP/RTCP-based technology for IDMS will help to ensure interoperability and to promote deployment in real environments (e.g., in IPTV). In contrast, most of the existing solutions (surveyed in [12]) define proprietary protocols that may increase the network load and make compatibility between third-party implementations more difficult. Further benefits of using RTP/RTCP for IDMS include: i) the widespread use and support of those protocols; ii) the inclusion of timestamps in the media delivery units (i.e., RTP packets); iii) the support for intra- and inter-stream sync; iv) the adaptability and scalability of RTCP (see next Section); v) the ability of negotiating the use of common wall-clock sources [16]; vi) the inherent rate adaptive mechanisms; etc.

Acknowledging the suitability of and last advancements on RTP/RTCP-based technology for IDMS, we still foresee a key limitation: the proposed RTCP messages for IDMS [15] are exchanged in a pre-scheduled manner, uniquely based on preserving the allowed traffic bounds specified in [13]. This cannot provide efficient IDMS control, because there is no provisioning for timely feedback that would allow to repair or to manage dynamic events of interest close to their occurrence.

The goal of this paper is to overcome those issues, by making the use of the RTCP channel for IDMS more efficient. Novel standard compliant RTCP reporting rules and messages, which in conjunction we call Early Event-Driven (EED) RTCP Feedback, are presented for achieving a more rapid, flexible, dynamic and accurate IDMS control, while being backward compatible with standardized RTP/RTCP solutions [13-18], and still adhering to the RTCP traffic bounds specified in [13]. In particular, the EED RTCP Feedback for IDMS provides the three following advantages. First, asynchrony situations can be repaired earlier than using the Regular RTCP reporting rules [13] adopted up to now. Second, the use of EED RTCP Feedback enables the concurrent presentation of dynamic media-related events in a fine-grained synchronized way with the piece of content they refer to. Third, the latency from the instant at which receivers join RTP (multicast) sessions until they achieve IDMS (referred to as IDMS latency) can be significantly reduced. The proposed RTCP extensions for IDMS are applicable to and can have a potentially high impact on a wide spectrum of scenarios with demanding IDMS characteristics [1], such as IPTV, networked multi-player games, synchronous e-learning, etc.

Through simulation tests we aim to provide evidence of the ability of the proposed EED RTCP Feedback to achieve faster reaction and more accurate responsiveness to dynamic situations in IDMS-enabled sessions, thus overcoming important limitations of existing RTP/RTCP-based IDMS solutions [10, 11, 15].

The remainder of the paper is structured as follows. The next section presents an overview of the standardized RTCP timing rules. Section 3 discusses related work. Then, the novel aspects of the EED RTCP Feedback for enhancing the IDMS performance are presented in Section 4. Section 5 gives performance results, and, finally, in Section 6 we draw some conclusions, summarize our contributions and discuss future work.

2. STANDARD RTCP REPORTING RULES

In this section, an overview of the RTCP reporting rules specified in different IETF standards is provided. This is important to help understanding (the benefits of) the EED RTCP Feedback for IDMS proposed in this paper.

2.1 Regular RTCP Feedback (RFC 3550)

The participants of an RTP Session regularly exchange RTCP reports to inform mainly about Quality of Service (QoS) statistics [13]. On the one hand, a low frequency of feedback reporting can lead to faulty behavior owing to outdated statistics. On the other hand, excessive reports can be redundant and cause unnecessary control traffic. Also, if the RTCP reports were exchanged at a constant rate, the control traffic would grow linearly with the number of participants. Therefore, a trade-off between up-to-date information and the amount of control traffic must be met. To do so, the RTCP feedback rate must be dynamically adjusted according to the estimated population of the session.

The total amount of control traffic added by RTCP should be limited to a small (so that the primary function of media data transport is not impaired) and known (so that each participant can independently calculate its share) fraction of the allocated RTP session bandwidth ($BW_{session}$). A fraction of 5 % is recommended in [13]. If the proportion of senders constitute less than one quarter of the membership (i.e., $n_{senders} \leq \frac{1}{4} \cdot n_{participants}$, where $n_{participants} = n_{senders} + n_{receivers}$), this percentage is further divided into two parts, where 25 % must be dedicated to active senders and the remaining can be consumed by receivers. Otherwise, the RTCP bandwidth is equally shared between senders and receivers. Accordingly, the RTCP report interval is deterministically computed, $T^{3550}_{RTCP\_d}$, based on the allocated $BW_{session}$, the average size of all received and sent RTCP packets ($RTCP_{size}$), the number of participants in the session and their role (senders or receivers). These formulas are in Eqs. (a) of Fig. 1[1].

However, $T^{3550}_{RTCP\_d}$ should have a lower bound to avoid having bursts of RTCP packets. The recommended value in [13] for the minimum interval, $T^{3550}_{RTCP\_d\_min}$, is 5 s (see Eq. (b1) of Fig. 1). In some cases (e.g., if the data rate is high and the application demands more frequent RTCP reports), an implementation may scale $T^{3550}_{RTCP\_d\_min}$ to a smaller value given by 360 divided by $BW_{session}$ (in kbps), as shown in Eq. (b2) of Fig. 1. This yields an interval smaller than 5 s when $BW_{session}$ becomes greater than 72 *kbps*. Accordingly, the minimum value between $T^{3550}_{RTCP\_d}$ and the selected option for $T^{3550}_{RTCP\_d\_min}$, will be used for the RTCP report interval, as shown in Eq. (c) of Fig. 1. After that, the interval between RTCP packets is varied randomly over the range [0.5, 1.5] times that minimum RTCP report interval, as shown in Eq. (d) of Fig. 1, to prevent floods of RTCP reports.

[1] We have placed all the Eqs. in Fig.1 to provide a schematic view of the stepwise calculation process for the RTCP report interval.

$$n_{participants} = n_{senders} + n_{receivers}$$

$$\text{(a)} \begin{cases} \text{if } (n_{senders} \leq \frac{1}{4} n_{participants}) \begin{cases} \text{senders: } T^{3550}_{RTCP\_d} = \dfrac{n_{senders} \cdot avg(RTCP_{size})}{0.25 \cdot 0.05 \cdot BW_{session}} \\ \text{receivers: } T^{3550}_{RTCP\_d} = \dfrac{n_{receiverss} \cdot avg(RTCP_{size})}{0.75 \cdot 0.05 \cdot BW_{session}} \end{cases} \\ \text{else, } \quad T^{3550}_{RTCP\_d} = \dfrac{n_{participants} \cdot avg(RTCP_{size})}{\underbrace{0.05 \cdot BW_{session}}_{BW_{RTCP}}} \end{cases}$$

Regular RTCP Feedback (RFC 3550)

$$\text{(b)} \begin{cases} \text{(b1)} \quad T^{3550}_{RTCP\_d\_\min} = 5 \ s \\ \text{(b2)} \quad T^{3550}_{RTCP\_d\_\min} = \dfrac{360}{BW_{session}(kbps)} \end{cases}$$

$$\text{(c)} \quad T^{3550}_{RTCP\_d\_\min} = \min(T^{3550}_{RTCP\_d\_\min}, T^{3550}_{RTCP\_d})$$

$$\text{(d)} \quad T^{3550}_{RTCP\_random} = (0.5 + rand()) \cdot T^{3550}_{RTCP\_d\_\min} \in [0.5, 1.5] \cdot T^{3550}_{RTCP\_d\_\min}$$

$$\text{(e)} \quad T^{3550}_{RTCP\_recons} = T^{3550}_{RTCP\_random} / (e - 3/2)$$

Early RTCP Feedback (RFC 4585)

$$\text{(f)} \quad T^{4585}_{RTCP} = (0.5 + rand()) \cdot (\text{"} trr - \text{int"} + T^{3550}_{RTCP\_d} / (e - 3/2))$$

Figure 1. Calculation Steps of the RTCP Report Interval.

Additionally, *"timer reconsideration"* algorithms are introduced in [13] to allow for a more rapid adaptation of the RTCP report interval in large-scale sessions, where the membership can largely vary. To compensate for the fact that the *"timer reconsideration"* algorithms converge to a lower value than the intended average RTCP bandwidth, the computed report interval is finally divided by e-3/2=1.21828, as shown in Eq. (e) of Fig. 1.

2.2 Early RTCP Feedback (RFC 4585)

In [17], further RTCP reporting mechanisms are specified to enable receivers to provide, statistically, more immediate RTCP feedback to the senders. This Early RTCP Feedback profile, which is known as RTP Audio-Visual Profile with Feedback (RTP/AVPF), allows for short-term adaptation and efficient feedback-based repairing mechanisms to be implemented, while maintaining the RTCP bandwidth constraints and preserving scalability to large groups. The RTCP report interval specified in [13] is denoted as Regular RTCP interval in [17]. In addition, it is specified in [17] that RTCP reports can be reported earlier than the next scheduled Regular RTCP transmission time if a receiver detects the need to inform about events of interest about the media stream (e.g., picture or slice loss) close to their occurrence[2].

The reporting rules for Regular RTCP packets in [17] are similar than the ones in [13]. However, $T^{3550}_{RTCP\_d\_min}$ is dropped in [17]. Instead, an optional attribute, called *trr-int*, is specified as an offset parameter (in ms) to $T^{3550}_{RTCP\_d}$, as shown in Eq. (f) of Fig.1. Note that providing *trr-int* as an independent variable is meant to minimize the frequency of Regular RTCP packets (i.e., saving RTCP bandwidth), while allowing more flexibility to transmit Early RTCP packets (i.e., using the saved RTCP bandwidth) in response to dynamic events. This could not be achieved by reducing the overall RTCP bandwidth, because the Early RTCP packets would be affected as well. Values between 4 and 5 s for *trr-int* are recommended in [17] to assure interworking with RTP entities only using Regular RTCP Feedback [13]. However, as *trr-int* is an optional attribute, it may be set to zero (default value) if a specific application would benefit from a higher frequency of Regular RTCP packets. In such a case, the only difference between Regular [13] and Early RTCP Feedback [17] for transmitting Regular RTCP packets resides in the minimum value for the report interval, which is dropped in [17].

2.3 Rapid Inter-Stream Sync (RFC 6051)

In multimedia streaming services, the inter-stream sync delay refers to the time difference between the instant at which a user joins a multicast session, probably involving different media (e.g., audio and video, or when using layered and/or multi-description codecs) carried in separate streams, and the instant at which these correlated streams can be synchronously presented to that user [18]. The aim in RFC 6051 [18] is to minimize the inter-stream sync delay when using RTP/RTCP for media delivery. The motivation is that a receiver cannot synchronize playout until a compound RTCP packet, including a Source Description or SDES packet (source identification) and a Sender Report or SR (timing correlation parameters) [13], is received for all the involved RTP sessions. If there is no packet loss, this gives an expected delay equal to the average time for receiving the first RTCP packet from the RTP Session with the longest RTCP report interval[3].

RFC 6051 [18] introduces three backward compatible extensions to RTP/RTCP [13] to reduce the inter-stream sync delay. First, the RTCP timing rules are updated to allow Single Source Multicast (SSM) senders [19] the immediate transmission of an initial RTCP packet upon joining each RTP session in a multimedia session. The rationale for not allowing the transmission of immediate RTCP packets to SSM receivers is to avoid feedback implosion if lots of receivers join the session almost simultaneously. Second, a new RTP/AVPF transport layer feedback message [17] is defined to allow receivers to request the generation of an Early RTCP SR from the media sender. This enables rapid (re-)sync in case that an RTCP SR has not been received for a long period (e.g., packet loss), or to allow latecomers to achieve inter-stream sync as soon as possible. Finally, new RTP header extensions are defined to enable the inclusion of in-band sync metadata with RTP data packets.

3. RELATED WORK

In this section, some implementations making use of the above-described standardized RTP/RTCP reporting rules to increase the video quality (Section 3.1) and to reduce the inter-stream sync delay (Section 3.2) are presented. As these proofs of concept provided better QoE in streaming services, this motivates the design and development of novel EED reporting mechanisms (Section 4) to enhance the responsiveness of existing RTP/RTCP-

---

[2] A suppression mechanism is adopted, in which receivers wait for a random dithering interval to avoid RTCP feedback implosion (i.e., lots of receivers reporting on the same event) [17].

[3] Note that the inter-stream sync delay depends on the specific instant at which a user joins the multimedia session or each RTP session (e.g., the user may first receive the RTCP packets from the RTP session with the longest RTCP interval), as well as on the impact of the randomization processes in all the involved RTP sessions.

based solutions for IDMS using a centralized approach (Section 3.3). To conclude this section, previous works on event-based IDMS are briefly described in Section 3.4.

3.1 Use of Early RTCP Feedback

The work in [20] showed that the proposed RTCP extensions in [17], in conjunction with temporal video adaptation mechanisms, resulted in a significant video quality gain under lossy conditions. Also, the use of RTP/AVPF [17] allowed a better performance of a proposed error-resilient video coding technique in [21].

3.2 Reduction of Zapping and Sync Delay

Reducing channel-change (i.e., zapping) delays is a major concern for IPTV services. This involves optimizing several components of IPTV systems [22], such as media (trans-)coding, multicast (join/leave) procedures, predictive tuning methods, acquisition of the necessary reference information from the stream to start its consumption, buffering techniques, etc. Up to now, several solutions have been devised to overcome the zapping latency by using RTP/RTCP mechanisms (e.g., [22-24]). However, in conjunction with the above techniques, the RTCP timing rules from [18] should be provided to enable rapid (inter-stream) sync. This is because media will not be played out until the associated sync info is available, and the sync process should not contribute to further increase the channel-change delay. As an example, the works in [23, 24] made use of a rapid acquisition technique (by employing an auxiliary retransmission server), combined with enhanced RTCP reporting mechanisms, to decrease zapping (and sync) delays when joining on-going RTP multicast sessions.

3.3 RTP/RTCP for IDMS

Previous studies have shown the feasibility of RTP/RTCP for IDMS, in both real [10] and simulated environments [11]. Based on the initial idea in [10], standardization processes have been undertaken to provide RTP/RTCP-based technology for IDMS [14, 15]. Two additional RTCP messages for IDMS have been specified in [15]. First, an RTCP XR (Extended Report) block for IDMS, called IDMS report, enables clients in the IDMS session (i.e., Sync Clients) to provide feedback about reception and/or presentation times for specific RTP packets. Second, a new RTCP IDMS packet type, called IDMS Settings packet, is used to provide guidance on when to play out the media.

The above RTP/RTCP-based IDMS solutions adopted a centralized Sync Maestro Scheme (SMS) as the communication process between the involved sync entities [1]. The operation of SMS is sketched in Fig. 2. First, each Sync Client sends (unicast) IDMS reports to a single Sync Manager. Based on the collected IDMS reports, the Sync Manager computes the delay differences among the Sync Clients and, if the detected asynchrony exceeds a specific threshold, it will send (multicast) an IDMS Settings packet to notify the Sync Clients of the required adjustments to achieve IDMS.

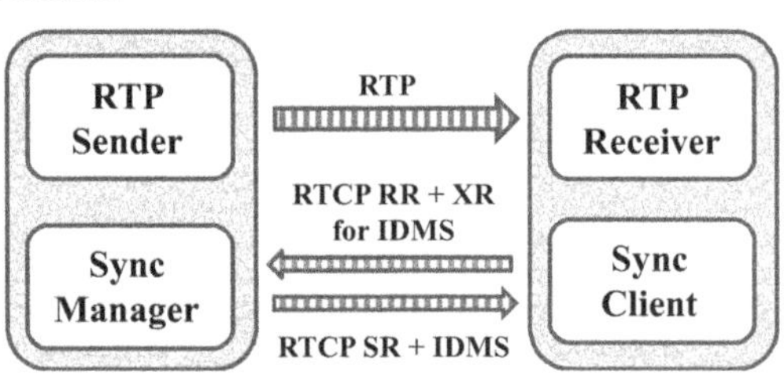

Figure 2. RTP/RTCP-based IDMS Solution Using SMS.

An exhaustive qualitative comparison between the existing control schemes for IDMS is provided in [1]. This study pointed out that SMS is, in general, best suited for IDMS. Concretely, SMS is preferable in such use cases in which consistency, coherence and security aspects must be ensured. Likewise, SMS can provide a satisfactory responsiveness in terms of flexibility, traffic overhead, causality and fairness. However, two main downsides of using SMS for IDMS were identified: scalability and interactivity. On the one hand, scalability-wise there are no significant differences between a centralized and a distributed architecture with respect to the IDMS control. This is due to the fact that in both approaches all the IDMS reports converge either to the Sync Manager (in SMS) or to each one of the involved Sync Clients (in a distributed architecture). Moreover, two mechanisms help to partially mitigate scalability issues of SMS when using RTP/RTCP for IDMS. First, the RTCP report interval is dynamically adjusted according to the number of active Sync Clients and the available bandwidth in the session (see Section 2.1) [13]. Second, the Sync Clients can be divided into logical groups, which facilitates the IDMS management to the Sync Manager [11, 15]. On the other hand, interactivity is an especially relevant limitation of SMS when using an RTP/RTCP-based IDMS solution. This is because of the required bidirectional communication process to exchange the IDMS information (see Fig. 2): first, the Sync Manager must collect the IDMS reports from all the Sync Clients; second, the Sync Manager must adhere to bounded timing rules [13] to be able to send a new RTCP IDMS Settings packet; and third, this packet has to be received by all the Sync Clients. The interactivity constraints could limit the implementation of an SMS-based IDMS solution in those use cases in which very high sync granularity and timely responsiveness to dynamic events (e.g., avoidance of asynchrony situations, rapid channel change delays, etc.) are required [1].

3.4 Event-Based Sync

Two different approaches for media sync can be distinguished: axis-based and event-based [12]. On the one hand, axis-based solutions aim to continuously align the presentation of media streams along either a virtual or a wall-clock timeline axis. On the other hand, event-based solutions handle the sync of media streams over a discrete set of reference points or events. These events can be either specific occurrences in time within the media stream or state modifications (e.g., user generated actions), either sporadic or periodic, and either inserted into the media stream or sent in parallel using another communication channel.

Event-based sync solutions have been traditionally used in networked games [12] and in Collaborative Virtual Environments [25] to keep a consistent shared session. In [2], a popular event-based sync algorithm for networked games [8] was adapted to be used for shared video watching. The goal was to achieve a concurrent sync of specific user actions at all the clients. The algorithm consists of two parts: i) *local lag* to compensate for short term inconsistencies; and ii) *time warp* to undo inconsistencies that may still occur due to extreme delay variability.

Mostly, event-based sync solutions have adopted a distributed receiver-based approach [1, 12, 25]. This requires the availability of a multicast channel among all involved users to be able to exchange events, which is not feasible when using specific streaming technologies, such as Source Specific Multicast (SSM) with unicast feedback [19], because only the Distribution Source can transmit data in a multicast way. This is not an issue when using SMS, because the feedback reports for IDMS are sent by the Sync Clients in a unicast way to the Sync Manager.

Moreover, in this work we are not dealing with updates of the media stream content, state or position by the Sync Clients, but with dynamic events in the session (e.g., detected or triggered by the Sync Manager) that need to be handled in a timely fashion. The intention is to take advantage of the flexibility, dynamism and interactivity features provided by event-based (distributed) approaches, while still adhering to the benefits of using an axis-based (centralized) solution for IDMS [1, 12].

4. EED RTCP FEEDBACK FOR IDMS

To date, the existing RTP/RTCP-based IDMS solutions using SMS (e.g., [10, 11]) have used Regular RTCP Feedback [13]. Consequently, there may be a variable time lag (according to Eqs. in Fig. 1) between detecting an event and being able to send an appropriate RTCP packet to handle it. Furthermore, the RTCP reports may even not be received at the target side, since RTCP is sent over UDP and thus it is not a reliable control channel. This section describes the novel EED RTCP reporting mechanisms we propose to overcome these issues, thus enabling higher flexibility, dynamism, interactivity and accuracy when using SMS for IDMS.

4.1 Immediate Initial RTCP IDMS Settings

The same rationale for reducing the inter-stream sync delay in [18] (Section 2.3) can be used for IDMS purposes. When using SMS in an RTP/RTCP-based solution, it would also be desirable to transmit a nearly-immediate[4] RTCP IDMS Settings packet by the Sync Manager upon establishing a multimedia session. This would ensure a reduction of the IDMS latency experienced by the Sync Clients in a shared session.

If the Sync Manager is integrated within the Media Server (Fig. 2), it must send the IDMS Settings packet in parallel with the initial RTP data packets. If the Sync Manager is co-located within a Sync Client or a third party entity, it must send the IDMS Settings packet as soon as it receives the initial RTP data packets from the Media Server. In either case, as the Sync Manager is a single centralized RTP entity, it must also be allowed to transmit Early RTCP packets [18]. This way, the Sync Clients can start synchronously consuming the media earlier.

4.2 Dynamic EED RTCP IDMS Settings

During the media session's lifetime, if Regular RTCP Feedback is used, the Sync Manager may have to wait a nearly-complete RTCP reporting interval to be able to send a new compound RTCP packet (including an IDMS Settings packet) after detecting an out-of-sync situation, which might potentially take several seconds (up to 5 s or even more) [13]. This is illustrated in Fig. 3. In such a case, if an out-of-sync situation is detected just after the transmission of an RTCP packet (at instant $t_{r(1)}$), the next RTCP packet cannot be sent until the next randomized RTCP transmission time (at instant $t_{r(2)}$). The figure shows the worst case, in which the randomized RTCP report interval is near the upper limit, i.e.:

$$t_{r(2)} - t_{r(1)} \approx 1.5 \cdot [t_{d(2)} - t_{r(1)}] \quad (1)$$

Where:

- $t_{d(n)}$: *n-th* Scheduled (Deterministic) RTCP Transmission Time.
- $t_{r(n)}$: *n-th* Real (Randomized) RTCP Transmission Time.

Therefore, the contribution of the Sync Manager delay (i.e., the time interval since an event is detected and an IDMS Settings packet is sent) to the total IDMS latency in case of an out-of-sync situation (see Fig. 3) becomes a serious barrier for those use cases requiring stringent sync levels (e.g., networked video walls, networked loudspeakers, or networked games) [1].

To overcome this issue, the Sync Manager is allowed to send Early RTCP packets as a response to dynamic events. Figure 4 illustrates this process, in which an IDMS Settings packet is sent just after the detection of an event, despite that this moment is earlier than the next scheduled Regular RTCP transmission time (faster/immediate reaction of the Sync Manager). Consequently, the IDMS latency is significantly reduced, mainly due to the fact that the Sync Manager delay has been minimized.

Note that if *trr-int* is set to zero, only one Early RTCP packet can be transmitted between two consecutive Regular RTCP packets in order to preserve the RTCP traffic bounds [17]. It means that an Early RTCP packet can only be sent if the previous transmitted RTCP packet was a Regular RTCP packet. Hence, after sending an Early RTCP packet, the RTCP reporting engine must schedule the sending time for the next RTCP packet by delaying (i.e., skipping) one more Regular RTCP report interval (see dotted arrows in Fig. 4).

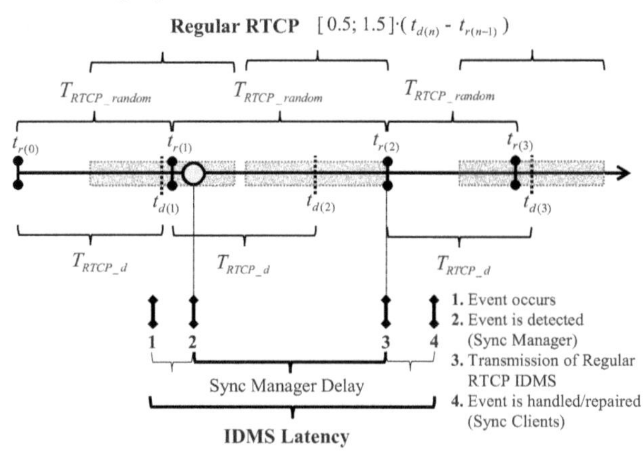

Figure 3. Regular RTCP Feedback.

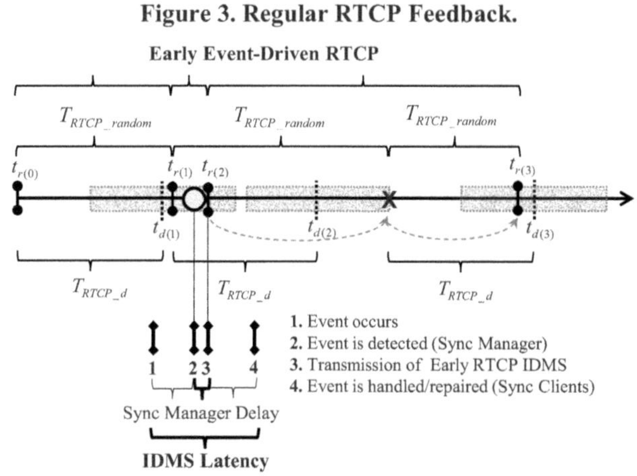

Figure 4. Early Event-Driven (EED) RTCP Feedback.

[4] Note that in this work, the terms (nearly-)immediate, close-to-instant and Early are used as synonymous. This is because the Sync Manager is a single centralized entity in the media session, and the Early RTCP packets can be sent immediately by this entity without requiring a contention algorithm, as required for receivers in [17].

This can also be very useful to provide playout hints for specific events that must be presented to all the involved users in a fine-grained synchronized way with the piece of content they refer to. Those events can be media-related events whose timing can be known in advance (e.g., commercials, start of the match in a sports event, etc.); but if the RTP/RTCP implementation somehow has direct access to the application layer, the events' timing can be even unknown (e.g., a goal in a football match, etc.) or dynamically triggered by users (e.g., shared service control, interactive instant messaging, a TV quiz show, in-game actions, etc.). In this case, the use of EED RTCP Feedback for IDMS implies the triggering of content- or action-based adjustments. Accordingly, a synchronous link between the application layer (i.e., operator generated events) and the transport/control layer (i.e., RTP/RTCP) is needed to align them in terms of timestamps. This is not a severe issue, since the Sync Manager will be co-located with the Media Server most of the times.

In case of a high frequency of events, setting an offset value for the RTCP report interval, by means of using the *trr-int* attribute, can help to save RTCP bandwidth (by restraining the transmission of too frequent Regular RTCP packets) while being able to use the (saved) bandwidth when events occur. This situation, however, is not considered in this paper (left for future study).

A similar mechanism exists in HBBTV[5]. It consists of inserting *"do it now"* events as elementary streams into the MPEG-TS to allow sync of dynamic events from extra applications (e.g., a question in an interactive quiz TV show, time-sensitive subtitles, etc.) with the live DVB content. However, the proposed EED RTCP Feedback is not only valid to dynamically trigger local inter-stream sync (even though this is not tested in this work), but also to enforce global IDMS adjustments in all the participants.

4.3 Rapid (Re-)Sync Request

If the initial compound RTCP packet (including SR, SDES and IDMS Settings) is lost, a Sync Client will not be able to synchronize the media playout until the next RTCP packet can be sent. This is undesirable. RFC 6051 [18] defines a new RTP/AVPF transport layer feedback message [17] to request the generation of an Early RTCP SR, allowing rapid inter-stream (re-)sync. A similar mechanism is proposed in this paper to be applied for IDMS purposes. A new RTP/AVPF transport layer feedback message [17], called RTCP-IDMS-REQ, is introduced to request the rapid generation (and transmission) of an RTCP IDMS Settings packet from the Sync Manager (see Fig. 5). The Payload Type (PT) of this RTCP message should be 205 [17], the Frame Message Type should be assigned by IANA (*Internet Assigned Numbers Authority*), and its length must be equal to 3. The *SSRC of the packet sender* field must indicate the Sync Client that is unable to synchronize, while the *SSRC of the media source* field must indicate the source of the media stream that the Sync Client is unable to synchronize. In contrast to the RTCP-SR-REQ [18], in which the *Feedback Control Information* (FCI) part is kept empty, in the RTCP-IDMS-REQ it must carry the Sync Group Identifier to which the sender of this message belongs [15].

Once a new RTCP-IDMS-REQ is received by the Sync Manager, it must generate an Early RTCP IDMS Settings packet. This mechanism can also be employed if a Sync Client has not received IDMS Settings in a (configurable) long time interval. Even though this mechanism is similar to the one in [18] to request rapid SRs, it is especially necessary since, in most implementations (e.g., [10, 11]), the IDMS Setting packets are only sent when the detected asynchrony exceeds an allowed threshold, and not regularly in each RTCP report interval as SRs.

4.4 Reduction of Channel Change Delays

The support for and rapid accommodation of latecomers are key issues to enable dynamic IDMS sessions. This is another useful applicability of the proposed RTCP-IDMS-REQ message. Once a latecomer joins an IDMS-enabled session, it must send an RTCP-IDMS-REQ message to the Sync Manager, which must send an Early RTCP IDMS Settings packet to rapidly bring the latecomer up-to-date. Upon receiving the IDMS Settings packet, the latecomer has the necessary sync info to start playing out the media stream in a time synchronized way with the other Sync Clients (thus preventing from either long annoying startup delays or initial playout inconsistencies). The timing diagram for the RTCP exchange processes in this SMS-based IDMS solution is illustrated in Fig. 6. It can be seen that, using EED RTCP Feedback, the IDMS latency for latecomers (i.e., the time interval between joining and acquiring IDMS) can be significantly reduced mainly due to the fact that the Sync Manager delay (Δt_2 in Fig. 6) is minimized. Two additional mechanisms could contribute to further reduce the latency for receiving the IDMS info (see Fig. 6). The first one consists of employing priority mechanisms for the transport of RTCP messages, e.g., by adopting a Differentiated Services (DiffServ) policy, as in [24]. This would help to decrease the Round Trip Time (RTT) delays and the loss probability for RTCP packets (out of the scope of this paper).

0–1	2	3–7	8–15	16–31
V=2	P	FMT=TBD	PT = RTPFB	length
SSRC of packet sender				
SSRC of media source				
Media Stream Correlation Identifier (SyncGroupID)				

(TBD: To Be Determined)

Figure 5. RTCP IDMS-REQ Feedback Message.

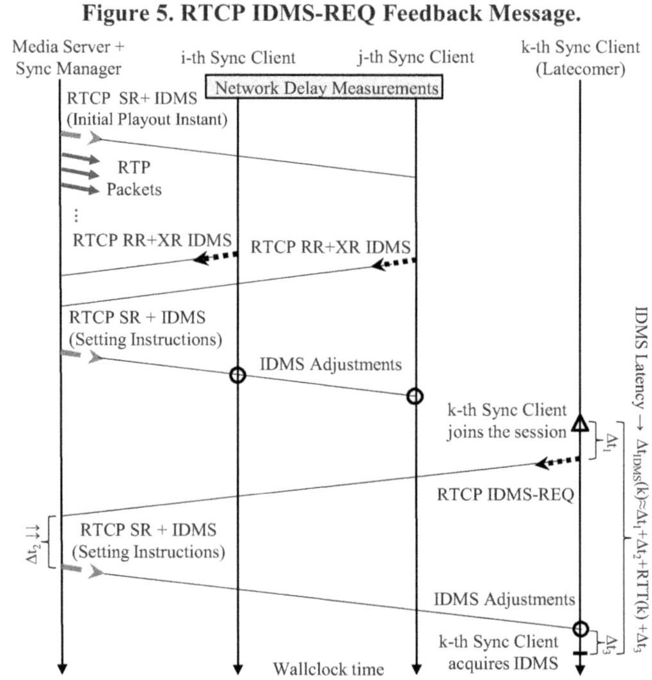

Figure 6. RTCP Message Exchanges for IDMS using SMS.

[5] Hybrid Broadcast Broadband (HBB) TV, http://www.hbbtv.org/.

The second one is based on the transmission of Early RTCP-IDMS-REQ messages by latecomers upon joining the session. According to [18], the delay since joining and sending an RTCP-IDMS-REQ message (Δt_1 in Fig. 6) should not be reduced to avoid flooding of requests at specific time instants (e.g., at the time a broadcasted sport event begins). While in this paper we adhere to this standard compliant rule, we will analyze in future research if this flash crowd effect is a real limiting issue in different large-scale SSM scenarios (e.g., networked quiz shows, gaming, IPTV, etc.). Our initial assumption is that the upstream bandwidth availability by the Sync Clients (which is not used for other purposes) and the aggregation and re-distribution mechanisms by Feedback Targets [19] do not entail a real constraint for allowing the transmission of Early RTCP-IDMS-REQ by Sync Clients. Moreover, it is assumed in [18] that all Sync Clients switch channels simultaneously, but even though using automated procedures (e.g., through notifications via the Electronic Program Guides in IPTV), this would not be a matter of a few seconds, but of minutes.

5. EVALUATION

Modeling and simulations were conducted using NS-2. The EED RTCP Feedback for IDMS was tested in a multicast scenario (Fig. 7) with four distributed Sync Clients belonging to the same logical group (Group 1 or G1) [11, 15], and with variable delays, and therefore Round Trip Times (RTTs), to the Media Server (see Table 1). All the links were bidirectional, their propagation delays were set to 10 ms, and their capacity was configured as shown in the figure. The Sync Manager was co-located with the Media Server which transmitted with a specific rate of θ=25 Media Units (i.e., video frames) per second (MU/s). Apart from the RTP/RTCP traffic, heavy and fluctuating background traffic (different cross-traffic flows following FTP/TCP, Pareto/UDP, CBR/UDP patterns) was configured over the network topology in order to cause significant different network jitter for each Sync Client, by forcing full usage of the links' capacities at some instants during the simulations. The scheduler clock of the simulator was used as a reference wall-clock in all the involved sync entities, thus ensuring the availability of a common clock source in all of them (as achieved by using a clock sync mechanism [16], such as NTP, in real setups). Additionally, significant playout rate deviations (skews and drifts) [11] were set (see Table 1) in order to force higher asynchronies between the Sync Clients, and to test if they could be successfully handled by our IDMS solutions[6].

In all the simulation tests, smooth playout adjustments were employed to acquire IDMS since, as it was shown in [11], this reactive technique outperforms the aggressive playout adjustments (*skips & pauses*) policy, because of the ability of achieving a more fine-grained sync, while minimizing the occurrence of long-term (annoying) playout disruptions.

5.1 Interactivity Comparison between Regular and EED RTCP Feedback

Figure 8 illustrates the playout (e2e) delay evolution for 3 Sync Clients to acquire IDMS when using EED RTCP Feedback, by employing the "sync to the mean playout point" policy [11]. First, it can be observed that all the Sync Clients were perfectly synchronized at the initial playout instant, despite of jitter and the e2e delay variability between them, because of the reception of an Immediate Initial IDMS Settings packet (Section 4.1). After that, it can be seen that the asynchrony between them progressively increased, mainly due to the configured deviations in their playout processes (Table 1). Every time an asynchrony exceeding τ_{max} (configured to 80 ms) was detected by the Sync Manager, it sent (multicast) an Early RTCP IDMS Settings packet to make the Sync Clients to get in sync with the selected IDMS reference (mean playout point among them [11]).

The same situation when using Regular RTCP Feedback was also simulated. The graphs for both cases were very similar. To clarify the differences among them, zoom views of the playout adjustment processes in each case are presented in Fig. 9. It can be observed that the asynchrony situation was corrected later when using Regular RTCP (left graph) than when using EED RTCP (right graph). This way, this figure shows that the IDMS latency was reduced when using EED RTCP Feedback, because of the minimization of the Sync Manager delay. As can be observed in both graphs, the playout adjustments did not start simultaneously in all the Sync Clients (due to the variable network delays to the Media Server, as shown in Table 1), but all of them finished their adjustments almost simultaneously at the target playout point included in the IDMS Setting packet (high performance in terms of coherence of SMS [1]).

In our simulated scenario, the Sync Manager was implemented within the single Media Server resources (i.e., $n_{senders}=1$) and the bandwidth for the RTP Session was configured to $BW_{session}=200$ *kbps*. Assuming an approximate value of $avg(RTCP_{size})\approx 1000$ bits (including the IDMS messages, plus transport and network layer headers, e.g. UDP and IP), and according to formulas in Fig. 1, a delay of up to 0.6 seconds could be accumulated between the instant at which an asynchrony situation is detected by the Sync Manager and the instant at which it can transmit an IDMS Settings packet. This gives the maximum Sync Manager delay because of the bounded RTCP reporting rules. Even though the maximum playout asynchrony may slightly increase during this additional Sync Manager delay, the issue here is that, when using Regular RTCP Feedback, the out of sync situation will not be corrected during this time interval.

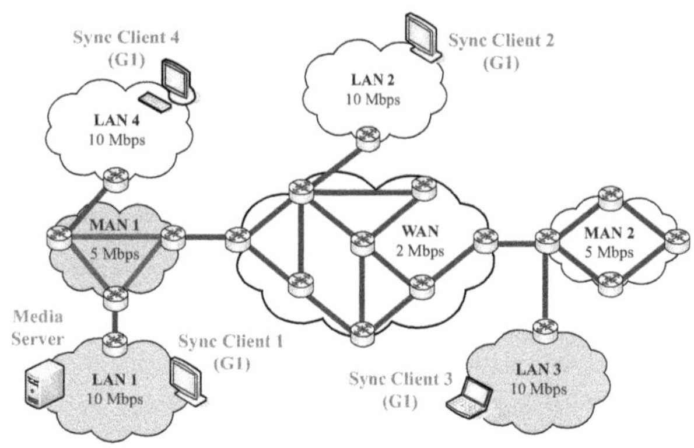

Figure 7. Simulated Scenario.

Table 1. Sync Clients' Parameters

Sync Client	Mean RTT	Rate Skew	Rate Drift
SC1 (LAN1)	~10 ms	$\gamma_1 = 0.05$ %	$\varepsilon_1 = 0.02$ %
SC2 (LAN2)	~125 ms	$\gamma_2 = -0.02$ %	$\varepsilon_1 = 0.02$ %
SC3 (LAN3)	~288 ms	$\gamma_3 = -0.05$ %	$\varepsilon_3 = 0.02$ %
SC4 (LAN4)	~125 ms	$\gamma_4 = 0.015$ %	$\varepsilon_4 = 0.02$ %

[6] The effect of the playout rate imperfections over the local and global media sync (especially IDMS) can be found in [11].

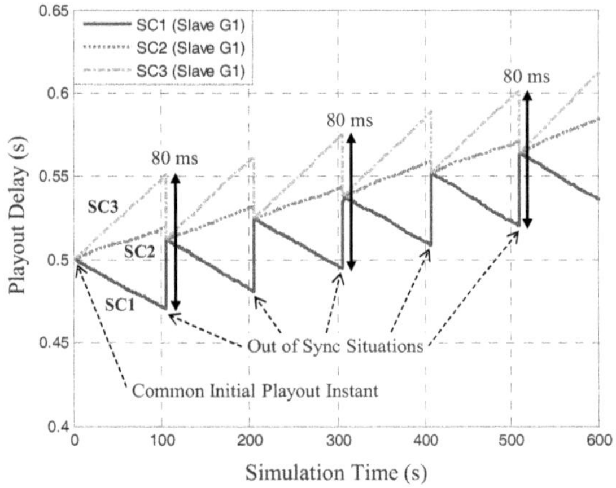

Figure 8. Playout (e2e) Delay Evolution when using EED RTCP Feedback for IDMS.

Note that, even without considering either the $T^{3550}_{RTCP\_d\_min}$ or the *trr-int* attribute, the differences between Regular and EED RTCP Feedback in terms of interactivity are significant, especially for those IDMS use cases with stringent sync requirements [1]. These differences would have been significantly larger (up to 5 s or even more, according to the Eqs. in Fig. 1 [13]) if any of the above mechanisms ($T^{3550}_{RTCP\_d\_min}$ or *trr-int*) were adopted due to the following two reasons. The first one is because of the larger Sync Manager delays. The second one is because of the larger delays needed to gather the IDMS reports from all Sync Clients, since their RTCP report interval would be lower in such a case. Therefore, asynchrony situations would be detected later.

Also, it is important to emphasize that these delay differences occur when using any of the policies for choosing a master IDMS reference presented in [11], although only the evaluation of one of them (sync to the mean playout point) is included in this paper due to space limitations.

Moreover, according to the Eqs. in Fig. 1, such delay differences would be much larger if the Sync Manager functionality would have been implemented as a part of an RTP receiver in a large-scale session (i.e., involving lots of Sync Clients), as can be inferred from the value of the RTCP report interval in Fig. 10, or if there were multiple senders in the session. Therefore, the proposed EED RTCP Feedback for IDMS would be even more beneficial if the Sync Manager were implemented as a part of a Sync Client (left for further study), provided that multicast feedback capabilities were available to that Sync Client.

To corroborate the benefits of using EED RTCP Feedback for IDMS, the fraction of MUs that were played out in all Sync Clients with an asynchrony larger than the allowed threshold was assessed, for different threshold values, when using both Regular and EED RTCP Feedback. Figure 11 shows the average results of 10 simulation runs (with different seeds for the random variables in each iteration). The following asynchrony threshold values were employed: sub-frame accuracy ($1/(2\cdot\theta)$=20 ms), frame accuracy ($1/\theta$=40 ms), 2 frames accuracy ($2/\theta$=80 ms) and 4 frames accuracy ($4/\theta$=160 ms).

It can be appreciated that the fraction of out of sync MUs when using EED RTCP Feedback is not as dependent on the allowed threshold as when Regular RTCP Feedback is used, since a less steep slope can be observed in the graph. Indeed, we can see that despite the fact that the differences are not very high for the upper threshold (160 ms), they become relevant when the threshold is reduced. For example, the fraction of out of sync MUs is almost double for a frame accurate threshold (40 ms), whilst it is more than double for the lowest threshold, comparing Regular to EED RTCP Feedback. This corroborates the better performance in terms of interactivity, because of the earlier correction of out of sync situations when using EED RTCP Feedback for IDMS. This is especially relevant for the IDMS use cases with stringent sync requirements [1]. Also, it is important to mention that although the percentages of out of sync MUs seem quite high, this fact does not mean that those asynchrony situations are annoying to human perception, because it is sufficient with setting an allowed threshold slightly lower than the normally noticeable asynchrony limits. For example, the maximum asynchrony value when using Regular RTCP Feedback for τ_{max}=80 ms in all simulations was 82.3 ms (higher than when using the EED RTCP), which confirms this assumption.

5.2 Fine-Sync for Media-Related Events

Figure 12 illustrates the same situation as in Fig. 8 when media-related events were triggered by the Media Server (through the Sync Manager) with a frequency of one event per 150 s (although they could be triggered dynamically or sporadically). In such a case, the Sync Manager sent IDMS Settings packets both as a response to the detection of out of sync situations (occurring in a non-deterministic way) and to the occurrence of media-related events (e.g., from application-dependent actions, such as post-advertisements, start of a football match, a penalty shot, etc.), despite that the asynchrony at that moment was lower than the allowed threshold. Table 2 shows the sync granularity with which those events were presented in the involved Sync Clients when using both Regular and EED RTCP Feedback (mean value and standard deviation of 10 simulation runs). It can be seen that the asynchrony for media-related events can range from a perfect sync (i.e., no delay differences) to the allowed threshold (or a slightly superior value) when using Regular RTCP, because there is no provisioning for syncing dynamic events. The asynchrony values from Table 2 for Regular RTCP can be checked through the graphical representation of the playout delays in Fig. 8. In contrast, it can be seen that those media-related events were presented with highly accurate sync levels when using EED RTCP Feedback. The obtained sync granularity is not perfect (i.e., asynchrony equal to zero), as expected, due to the configured playout rate deviations (Table 1).

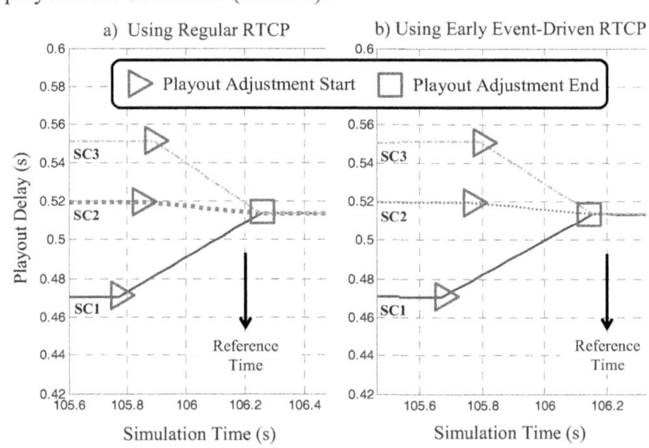

Figure 9. Zoom View of the Playout Adjustments to Achieve IDMS: Regular vs EED RTCP Feedback.

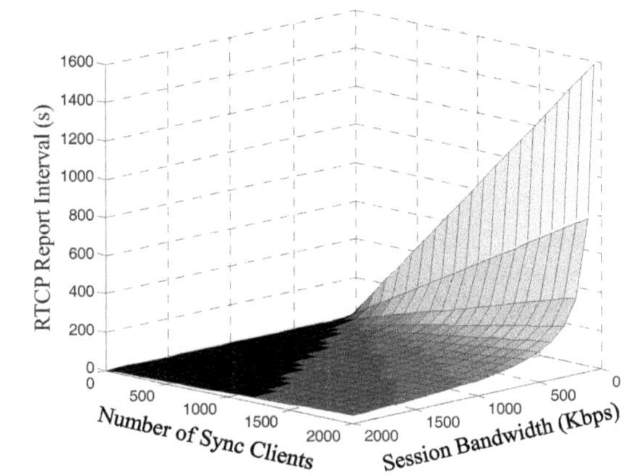

Figure 10. RTCP Report Interval for Sync Clients.

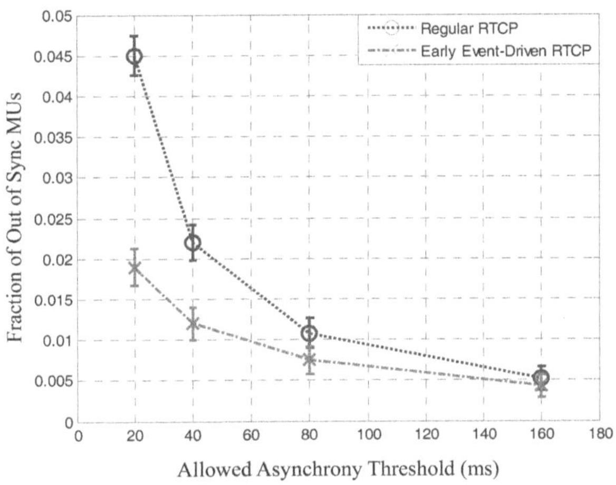

Figure 11. Interactivity Comparison between Regular and EED RTCP Feedback for IDMS.

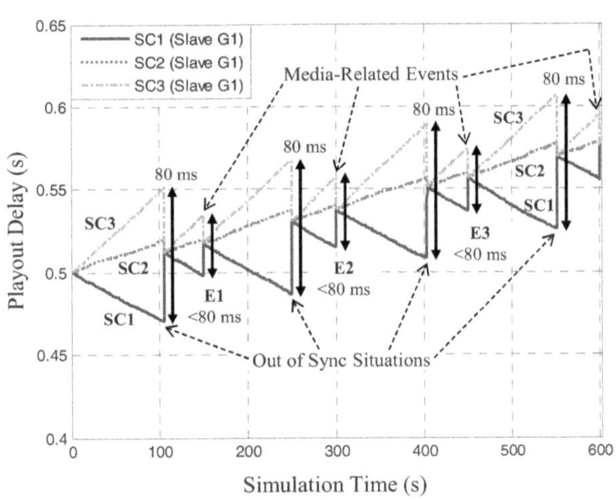

Figure 12. Playout (e2e) Delay Evolution when using EED RTCP for IDMS (with Media-Related Events).

Table 2. Sync Accuracy for Media-Related Events

Event (s)	ASYNCHRONY (ms)	
	Regular RTCP	EED RTCP
E1 (150)	38.5 ± 0.627	0.080 ± 0.022
E2 (300)	77.0 ± 0.804	0.073 ± 0.017
E3 (450)	29.5 ± 0.832	0.066 ± 0.019
E4 (600)	70.7 ± 0.799	0.071 ± 0.018

5.3 Rapid Accommodation of Latecomers

Figure 13 illustrates the same situation as in Fig. 8 when a latecomer (SC4) joined the session in progress at second 60. At that moment, SC4 sent an RTCP-IDMS-REQ message, and started buffering the incoming RTP packets. Once the Sync Manager received the RTCP-IDMS-REQ message, it sent an Early IDMS Settings packet to allow SC4 to become synchronized as soon as possible. Once SC4 received the IDMS Settings packet, it scheduled its playout controller to be able to synchronize (assuming SC4 is already able to start consuming the media stream because of the adoption of some of the techniques in [22-24]). Depending on the target playout point included in the IDMS Settings packet, it could be possible that some buffered media data need to be discarded by the latecomer when starting its playout process. In the simulated cases, SC4 experienced a maximum IDMS latency of 2.1 s (Δt_1 = 0.8 s, RTT = 0.125 s, Δt_2 = 0.6 s, Δt_3 = 0.575 s, see Fig. 6) when using Regular RTCP Feedback, whilst the one when using EED RTCP Feedback was decreased to 1.5 s (i.e., 2.1 – 0.6), mainly due to the fact that the Sync Manager delay (Δt_2 in Fig. 6) was minimized. Therefore, as discussed earlier, the use of EED RTCP Feedback can also significantly contribute to decrease the zapping delays in those media sessions requiring IDMS. Further research will be addressed to analyze the feasibility of reducing the other sources of delay (i.e., RTT, Δt_1 and Δt_3) when zapping in IDMS-enabled sessions. The first two (RTT and Δt_1) have been discussed in Section 4.3, whilst the third one (Δt_3) implies optimizing both the operation of the Sync Manager (IDMS target playout point calculation) and of the latecomer (buffering techniques and/or retrospective interpretation of the IDMS Setting packets).

5.4 Traffic Overhead

The same amount of RTCP packets were sent by the Sync Manager (co-located with the Media Server) during the 10-minutes session (around 1300-1320 packets, depending on the initial seed in each simulation) when using both Regular and EED RTCP Feedback, always adhering to the allowed RTCP traffic bounds [13]. Note that any differences were only originated at the initial playout instant and after detecting an event (e.g., an out-of-sync situation or a latecomer joins). In these cases, an Early IDMS Settings packet was sent using EED RTCP Feedback, but the next Regular RTCP transmission time was skipped (see Fig. 4). Therefore, the total number of sent RTCP packets did not differ.

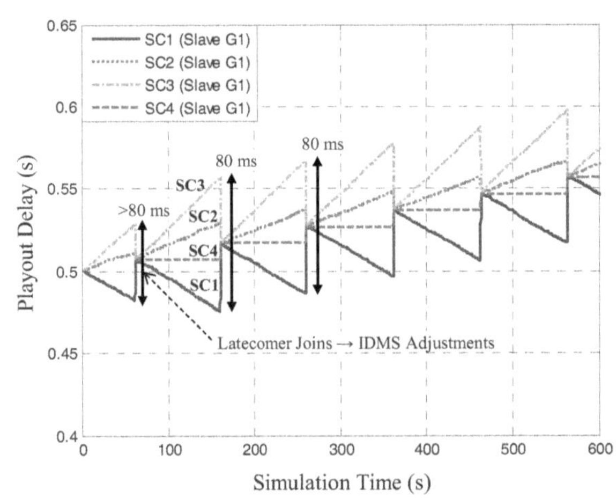

Figure 13. Rapid Accommodation of Latecomer (SC4).

6. CONCLUSIONS

In this paper, we have presented novel EED RTCP reporting mechanisms that enable higher interactivity (i.e., lower IDMS latency), flexibility, dynamism and accuracy when using a standardized RTP/RTCP-based solution for IDMS [15]. The simulation results provide evidence of the ability of the designed EED RTCP Feedback to achieve faster reaction to specific situations (e.g., an out of sync, or channel change delays) in IDMS-enabled sessions, as well as a finer granularity for syncing dynamic application-to-media events in all Sync Clients, compared to using Regular RTCP Feedback, while still adhering to the RTCP traffic bounds [13].

As future work, we plan to evaluate the benefits of the EED RTCP Feedback for IDMS by implementing a prototype in a real media framework (GStreamer). This will enable us to perform real-world assessments in present-day network environments, analyzing the effects on the user experience (QoE) of different levels of out of sync situations and how they are avoided by using our IDMS solution. Additional research will be focused on analyzing and optimizing the different sources of delay to further decrease the IDMS latency when zapping (see Fig.6). Moreover, as can be inferred from Fig. 10, future research will also be needed to enable a really scalable IDMS solution involving lots of Sync Clients, such as Internet Radio or IPTV distribution channels. Otherwise, the RTCP report interval for the Sync Clients will increase up to the point that their IDMS reports will be sent with a very low frequency, thus probably providing outdated and unusable IDMS statistics.

7. ACKNOWLEDGMENTS

This work has been financed, partially, by Universitat Politècnica de València (UPV) under its R&D Support Program in PAID-01-10 & PAID-00-12 Projects, and by FP7/2007-2013 under grant agreement no. ICT-2011-7-287848 (HBB-NEXT project). We also want to thank Pablo Cesar and the paper's shepherd, Hermann Hellwagner, for their helpful comments.

8. REFERENCES

[1] Montagud, M., Boronat, F., Stokking, H., van Brandenburg, R., Inter-destination multimedia synchronization: schemes, use cases and standardization, *Multimedia Systems*, 18(6), 459-482, November 2012.

[2] Vaishnavi, I., et al., From IPTV to synchronous shared experiences challenges in design: Distributed media synchronization, *Signal Processing: Image Communication*, 26(7), 370-377, August 2011.

[3] Mekuria, R., Cesar, P., Bulterman, D., Digital TV: the effect of delay when watching football, *EuroiTV '12*. Berlin (Germany), July 2012.

[4] ITU-T G.1050. Network model for evaluating multimedia transmission performance over Internet Protocol, 2007.

[5] van Deventer, O., et al., Advanced Interactive Television Service Require Synchronization, *IWSSIP'08*, Bratislava, June 2008

[6] Shamma, D.A., Bastea-Forte, M., Joubert, N., Liu, Y.: Enhancing online personal connections through synchronized sharing of online video, ACM CHI'08 Extended Abstracts, Florence (2008).

[7] Geerts, D., et al., Are we in sync? Synchronization requirements for watching online video together, *CHI 2011*, New York (USA), May 2011.

[8] Mauve, M., et al., Local-Lag and Timewarp: Providing Consistency for Replicated Continuous Applications, *IEEE Transactions on Multimedia*, 6(1), February 2004.

[9] Hashimoto, T., Ishibashi, Y., Group Synchronization Control over Haptic Media in a Networked Real-Time Game with Collaborative Work, *Netgames'06*, Singapore, October 2006.

[10] Boronat, F., Guerri, J.C., Lloret., J., An RTP/RTCP based approach for multimedia group and inter-stream synchronization, *MTA Journal*, 40(2), 285–319, 2008

[11] Montagud, M., Boronat, F., Enhanced adaptive RTCP-based Inter-Destination Multimedia Synchronization approach for distributed applications, *Computer Networks Journal*, 56(12), 2912-2933, August 2012.

[12] Boronat, F., Lloret, J., García, M., Multimedia group and inter-stream synchronization techniques: A comparative study, *Inf. Syst*, 34(1), 108-131, March 2009.

[13] Schulzrinne, H., et al., RTP: A Transport Protocol for Real-Time Applications, *RFC 3550*, July 2003.

[14] ETSI TS 183 063 V3.5.2, Telecommunications and Internet converged Services and Protocols for Advanced Networking (TISPAN); IMS-based IPTV stage 3 specification, 2011.

[15] van Brandenburg, R., et al., "RTCP for inter-destination media synchronization", draft-ietf-avtcore-idms-08, IETF Internet Draft, January 2013.

[16] Williams, A., et al., RTP Clock Source Signalling, draft-williams-avtcore-clksrc-02, IETF Internet Draft, Feb. 2013.

[17] Ott, J., et al., Extended RTP Profile for Real-time Transport Control Protocol (RTCP)-Based Feedback (RTP/AVPF), RFC 4585, July 2006.

[18] Perkins, C., Schierl, T., Rapid Synchronization of RTP Flows, RFC 6051, November 2010.

[19] Ott, J., Chesterfield, J., Schooler, E., RTP Control Protocol (RTCP) Extensions for Single-Source Multicast Sessions with Unicast Feedback, RFC 5760, February 2010.

[20] Kropfberger, M., Hellwagner, H., Evaluation of RTP immediate feedback and retransmission extensions, *ICME 2004*, 1751-1754, Taipei (Taiwan), June 2004.

[21] Liu, C., et al., RTP/AVPF compliant feedback for error resilient video coding in conversational applications, *ISCIT 2009*, 218-223, Incheon (Korea), September 2009.

[22] Ramos, F., et al., Reducing channel change delay in IPTV by predictive pre-joining of TV channels, *Signal Processing: Image Communication, 26(7)*, 400-412, August 2011.

[23] Begen A. C., Glazebrook N., Ver Steeg W., Reducing Channel-Change Times with the Real-Time Transport Protocol, *IEEE Int. Computing*, 13(3), 40-47, June 2009.

[24] Begic Z., Kos, M., Rapid synchronization of RTP multicast sessions, *International Journal of Computer Science and Network Security*, 10(9), pp. 42-47, September 2010.

[25] Fleury, C., Duval, T., Gouranton, V., Arnaldi, B., Architectures and Mechanisms to Efficiently Maintain Consistency in Collaborative Virtual Environments, *SEARIS 2010*, Massachussets (USA), March 2010.

Orchestration: TV-Like Mixing Grammars applied to Video-Communication for Social Groups

Marian F Ursu[1], Martin Groen[1], Manolis Falelakis[1], Michael Frantzis[1], Vilmos Zsombori[1], Rene Kaiser[2]

[1]Narrative Interactive Media Group
Department of Computing
Goldsmiths, University of London, UK

[2]Joanneum Research
Institute for Information and Communication Technologies, Graz, Austria

m.ursu@gold.ac.uk

ABSTRACT

This paper reports research into video-mediated synchronous communication within social groups. The ultimate aim of the research is to create a more natural medium for interaction, aware of the context in which it operates, able to continuously adapt itself to the communication needs and optimise the way in which it captures and transmits aspects of the communication. This, is hypothesised, can be achieved by equipping each of the various locations involved in the communication with multiple controllable video cameras and microphones, and mixing the resulting content through techniques similar to those used in television—a process referred to as "orchestration". Through orchestration, each location should be able to receive the appropriate perspectives and levels of detail, thus generating experiences in which the spatial separation between participants is minimised. The paper defines the concept of orchestration and presents two major evaluation experiments that provide supporting evidence for the main assumption and motivate further research, in richer interaction contexts, into this concept.

Categories and Subject Descriptors

H.4.3. [**Information Systems Applications**] Communications Applications – *computer conferencing, teleconferencing and videoconferencing.*

Author Keywords

Video, Mediated, Communication, Conferencing, Interaction, Telepresence, Social, Group, Orchestration

1. INTRODUCTION

Video has already entered the informal space of synchronous social communication and its popularity is rapidly increasing [1], [2]. However, the current video communication systems available for social interaction are still quite primitive and display significant limitations related to the set-ups in which they can be used and the communication topologies they can support. In particular, they are poor at supporting *distributed group* conversation, *movement* in the physical space (by forcing people to fit in the frames of the static cameras) [12], and at conveying messages through subtle and nuanced *body language*, *facial expressions* and *voice intonations* [3]. All these are aspects that seem to inherently require *dynamically-adaptable* communication systems.

Recent commercial products start to provide basic solutions that implement dynamic reconfiguration, by attempting to focus on the important or relevant parts of group communication. For example, in point-to-point group communication, Polycom Eagle Eye Director[1] and Xbox Video Kinect employ close-ups by using a secondary moving camera or cropping from a wide shot, respectively. In multipoint group communication, Skype and Google+ Hangouts signal, at all the other locations, the location with the dominant audio level, by using a visual cue or by displaying it in a larger window, respectively. Such approaches, though useful, are mere acknowledgements that group social communication requires novel solutions.

The overarching question that drives the research reported here is: can video conferencing systems be developed for *groups* of people, connecting two or possibly more physical locations, where immersion, presence, social presence, naturalness [14] and other such factors are optimized, and where, ultimately, the medium becomes transparent and the spatial separation unnoticeable? The scope of the enquiry is restricted to informal contexts of social interaction between friends and family but extensions to other communication contexts are easy to foresee.

The main hypothesis corresponding to the research question is that such group communication experiences could be achieved by capturing the necessary perspectives and levels of detail of the overall interaction through automatically controllable multiple cameras and microphones installed in each location, and by automatically mixing the available content, for each location, through techniques akin to those used in television. The control and mixing processes are referred here as *communication orchestration* or simply *orchestration.* Orchestration is similar to compiling a live TV transmission, but it has to address communication rather than narrative needs and is required concurrently for each of the locations participating in the

MM '13, October 21 - 25 2013, Barcelona, Spain
Copyright 2013 ACM 978-1-4503-2404-5/13/10…$15.00.
http://dx.doi.org/10.1145/2502081.2502118.

[1] The description of the products listed in this paragraph can easily be found through search engines on the Web so explicit references will not be provided.

communication. Orchestration is a reasoning, a decision making process. It relies on the capabilities for audio and video processing of the communication infrastructure, such as camera control and audio-visual composition, but it does not include them.

A more focused hypothesis can now be formulated, namely that orchestration can improve the quality of social group video-mediated communication (when members of the group are dispersed in different physical locations). We first approached this hypothesis by delegating the orchestration decision making to human operators, thereby exploring the concept. A positive result would establish a benchmark and would further motivate the research into the concept's implementation, i.e. addressing the question of whether automatic processes could resemble sufficiently closely manual orchestration. This paper reports on the conceptual investigation: it provides evidence, gathered from two major end-user experiments, that orchestration *can* improve the quality of video-mediated communication between groups. At the same time it highlights the need for further research into this complex concept.

Orchestration is applicable to multi-camera multi-microphone communication between many locations, but the experiments reported here have been carried out between two locations only. Orchestration is a reasoning process that controls the mixing and composition of both video and audio, but in this paper its scope was restricted to video mixing only. The communication platform used in experimentation employed beyond state of the art low-delay high-definition audio and video and also provided real-time video-mixing capabilities for each location through dedicated tools.

2. ORCHESTRATION: WORKED EXAMPLE

Let us first introduce the *concept* of orchestration. To reiterate, why would a physical space (room) require a multi-camera set up at all? There can be simple pragmatic reasons, such as not being able to fit the whole room in the widest shot of one single camera or needing to provide better levels of visual detail than the ones realized through a static wide. A more adventurous but credible assumption is that the level of engagement and immersion could increase as a result of mixing sources that provide different perspectives and levels of detail (compare the quality of experience between a well-produced television programme or film and a typical Skype video chat).

Assume that two groups of three friends, each group located in a different room, are to meet over a multi-camera video-communication link, intending to enjoy each other's company and relax by playing a game of Pictionary and having an idle chat. The two rooms are typical living rooms. Each is equipped with a large HD TV screen—functioning as the visual communication window to the other room—and with 4 controllable cameras (PTZ) able to provide for 6 predefined shots (see Figure 1), which are available for mixing on the screen in the other room. These predefined shots are mixed in response to particular events or sequences of events in the interaction between the two groups (e.g. a dialogue between two people or someone drawing on the Pictionary board). For simplicity, it can be assumed that there are no split screens—i.e. each individual shot is shown in full screen—and there are no transitions between shots—i.e. only cuts are used. The remainder of this section describes the purpose of the different shots and how they might be employed, assuming some dynamic reframing for all the cameras, following a sequence of play.

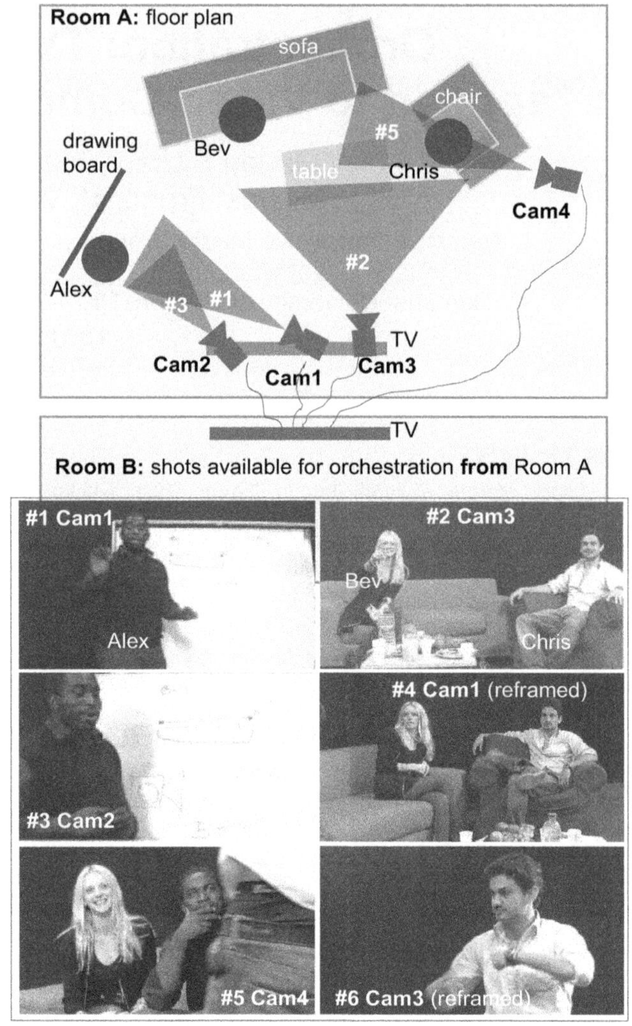

Figure 1. Shots used in orchestrated communication.

Shot #1 Alex is at the drawing board for his turn at Pictionary, interacting mainly with the group in the other room, where the ones actively involved in guessing are. This shot represents a point of view (POV) for the opposite room: it shows Alex and the board, but it also allows Alex to directly address his friends in the other room.

Shot #2 This wide shot is used while Bev and Chris are passive, as a short cutaway, to re-enforce their presence to the other room, but also when they have short interventions for the other room, that is for across-screen communication.

Shot #3 Alex is still at the drawing board, but most of the conversation is now happening between him and Bev and Chris. The POV shot used previously (#1) is no longer the best one to show Alex, as he is now looking at his friends in the same room and not the screen. This shot is now used to convey his side of the conversation (mixed with Shot #4)

Shot #4 The group in the remote location is currently not actively involved in the conversation, so they can be viewed as "spectators". The conversation between Alex, Bev and Chris is covered in a manner similar to representing a discussion on TV by employing reverse angles, i.e. by mixing this shot with Shot #3. This shot is obtained by reframing Camera 1.

Shot #5 Moving ahead in time, the friends decide to switch Pictionary with Charades: Chris is now miming. Alex and Bev in the same room are one guessing team and the group in the other room the other guessing team. Alex and Bev are very animated. Here, again, the reverse angle idea is employed using this shot and Shot #6.

Shot #6 This shot is generated by reframing Camera 3, previously used for Shot #2 (by zooming on Chris). It represents the other half of the reverse angle set up in Shot #5. This shot can also serve a similar remote-room POV purpose as Shot #1, but for Chris, as he can address the other room directly through this shot.

3. ORCHESTRATION: GENERALITIES

Inherently, a multi-camera video communication system must be aware of the context in which it operates—context including the people and their interaction, the configuration of the physical space, the peripheral devices and network capabilities. It has to be able to take decisions in order to best mediate the communication as it progresses: i.e. at each point in the conversation it has to decide what each participant is going to see and hear, from the multitude of available sources, in order to create, for each, a meaningful, rewarding and natural communication experience. The control is exerted on input devices (mobile cameras and microphones) as well as on output devices (screen composition and spatial sound). This decision making process is defined as *orchestration*.

Orchestration must observe two general and interrelated principles:

- A more *pragmatic* principle, related to *conversation management*, that dictates how messages should *correctly* and *effectively* be conveyed from originators to receivers, in order to ensure, for example, dialogue continuity, transmission of social cues and visibility of conversation markers.
- A more *aesthetic* principle, related to the creation of *engaging and immersive experiences*, which dictates how messages should be framed in *suitable narrative structures*, similar to cinematic or TV grammars.

The orchestration decisions respond with particular configurations of the communication medium to aspects of the communication semantics, such as communication topology, conversation rhythm, and social interaction cues. Communication semantics does not refer to understanding *what* is being discussed, but rather to the extraction of meaningful information *about* the conversation and *the way it is conducted*.

The general functional architecture of a video-mediated communication system that supports orchestration is depicted in Figure 2. The a/v input and output devices (cameras, speakers, TVs and mics) from each room connect to each other via a *configurable communication infrastructure*. This includes components for capture and encoding, network transmission and processing, and composition and rendering, which can be controlled by the orchestrator. Such a communication infrastructure has been implemented to support this research. This has been a significant challenge on its own, as it aimed to provide low-delay high-definition audio and video [9], but at the same time to ensure continuity of video mixing. The link between the *orchestrator* and the communication infrastructure is made through two components: *feature extractor* and *command dispatcher*. The former is able to extract meaningful information from the a/v streams and possibly sensors, such as position of people in the physical space, face position and orientation, and direction of audio activity. A sample of such features is described in [13]. These constitute the primitive information cues used by the orchestrator to refine aspects of the communication semantics. For example, from audio activity associated with the people involved in the conversation, the orchestrator can infer conversation turn taking [18]. The decisions of the orchestrator regarding the (re)configuration of the communication infrastructure are translated into actual commands to the physical components by a command dispatcher. The orchestrator's ability to reason about the communication context is obviously restricted by what primitive information is available through the system's *perception tools*—the feature extractors. At the other end, its decisions are constrained by the (dynamic) capabilities of the communication infrastructure—upload and download capacities for each location, network transmission delays, capabilities for encoding, decoding and composition, and also by their capabilities for reconfiguration.

The orchestrator's *intelligence* or *knowledge* can be represented as a set of interlinked rules that associate particular *communication contexts* with particular *configurations* of the communication infrastructure. The definitions of "context" and "configuration" are purposely left vague for now. For example, there may be rules which associate singular communication events with instant configuration decision, such as, with reference to the above example, "If person at the drawing board is gesticulating then use Shot #1". There may be rules which associate communication topologies with camera setups, such as "If the person at the drawing board is talking to the people in the same room, with the ones in the other room silent, then use Cam3 and Cam2 framed as Shots #3 and #4 (reversed angles) in conveying their discussion to the other room"; more particular rules which decide the mixing method will then operate within the scope of this one. And so on.

The orchestration rules have different levels of generality with regards to the settings in which they are applicable. For example, a formal debate is different from a casual social conversation. In the former, the participants should be allowed sufficient time to convey an argument whilst at the same time ensuring that all those who want to express an idea can do so, whereas the latter may be less pragmatically constrained and may have more aesthetic requirements. Social game-play can lead to different requirements

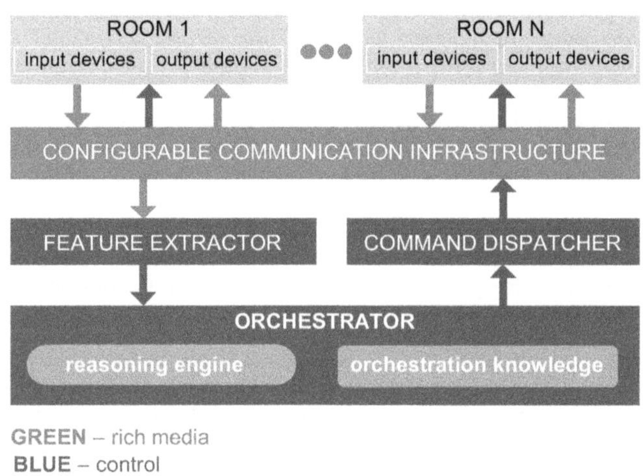

Figure 2. Architecture of an orchestrated video communication system.

compared to a therapy group. The former can require seeing each player in close-up, whereas the latter may require close-ups to be avoided. However, rules related to conversation turns may be applicable across many settings.

Orchestration knowledge does not yet exist, neither in written nor in tacit form, as there are no platforms capable of orchestrated communication. TV and film techniques provide inspiration, but they are not readily transferable to direct communication. They are motivated by storytelling, by relating events to an audience that has no means to intervene in the narration. In video communication, each party is actively involved in the process. Research into conversation analysis provides insights with regards to, say, conversation conventions and social cues that ought to be observed, but they do not recommend the video manipulation techniques required for such messages to be correctly conveyed across multi-camera video links.

4. RELATED WORK

In an early survey [21], users of video conferencing were asked for the reasons why they used it. 89% of the 76 respondents indicated that they liked having regular visual contact with remote collaborators. A more recent study [20] reported that people preferred video-conferencing systems because it enabled them to check on emotions and facial expressions of their dialogue partners and it enabled them to communicate the tone of voice by, for example, smiling when a message was conveyed. Aligned with this, the study in [17] investigated the effects on empathy of showing only the head, in video-mediated communication, as opposed to showing the whole upper body. The results indicated that empathy was lower for participants that met in the head-only framing condition as compared to the upper-body framing condition. We can infer from these results that there is scope for improvement in terms of the versatility of the video-mediated communication systems, particularly with regards to their ability to transmit more sophisticated social messages (e.g. facial expressions, gestures, body language). Orchestrated video communication has this space as one of its main targets.

Users also have the ability to adapt their normal face-to-face behavior to accommodate the limitations of video-mediated communication systems [12]. This could be interpreted as suggesting that less is fine. However, the impact of such "adapted" behavior over longer interaction periods has not been assessed, and, even so, a common sense question still remains: why adapt to a lesser medium when the medium could be improved? The study of home users regarding their uses of and attitudes towards video-mediated communication systems reported in [11] is aligned with this direction of enquiry. The study highlights the artful ways in which users appropriate such systems to reconcile a desire for closeness with those with whom they communicate. The study concludes with a discussion on how next generation video communication systems might be designed to account for the understanding of human values in communicative practice. Orchestration is a concept aligned with this line of thinking.

The study reported in [5] aimed for a richer understanding of human-to-human communication in the presence of shared visual content. It presents a computational model that integrates visual and linguistic cues to enable reference in a shared visual space, during tightly-coupled task-orientated interactions. The integrated model, which focuses on resolving pronouns (e.g. "this"), outperformed the language- and visual-only models. Although the shared visual content consisted of computer generated, thus referable, graphical objects, therefore significantly easier to manage than shared video streams, the study is still very relevant to video communication systems, which should be able to correctly adapt, through orchestration, to the utterance of such pronouns accompanied by gestures, such as pointing by hand or by gaze, the later accompanied by a head gesture (nodding).

Studies have also been carried out with regards to the physical characteristics of video-conferencing systems. For example, a study reported in [24] found that participants assessed video-conferencing capabilities much higher when they were presented via television sets than via PC/webcam combinations. Another study [11] conducted a series of interviews and observations and reported recommendations that would improve the user experience with video-conferencing systems. Among others, users indicated that they would want the system to be mobile, to allow them to walk around the house and to focus on specific objects. Users also indicated that they would like video-conferencing systems to support multiparty use. These requirements are well accounted for by our proposition. With regards to mobility, however, we propose a different solution: a static but multi-camera system, which should allow people to move freely in the space and should also have the ability to focus on objects of interest.

Single camera video-conferencing systems introduce spatial distortion effects when they are used by groups of people. Irrespective of the angle from which the remote participants view the display, they will all experience a shared but incorrect perspective. That is, they will all have the impression that the person on the other side of the video link is looking at them. This phenomenon is known as 'perceptual invariance' [22]. A related phenomenon is the 'Mona Lisa Effect', referring to the eerie effect of Mona Lisa's eyes following you as you walk around. The study reported in [16] investigated the effect of multiple cameras placed in a configuration aimed to counteract perceptual invariance. The result was that the multiple-camera configuration generated higher levels of trust, whereas the single camera configuration affected trust negatively: a clear case for multi-camera communication.

As a related issue, certain information vanishes due to the spatial distortion of communicating via video-conferencing technology. One attempt to reduce such information loss is to provide augmented reality technology on top of video-conferencing technology. A study reported in [23] investigated the effects of augmenting the imagery provided on a remote location with additional visual information that could be manipulated with a Nintendo Wiimote game controller. This technology could thus be used to mimic the effect of pointing, as in a face-to-face communication setting. Results showed that the augmented reality 'pointing' had an effect that could be considered as similar to pointing in face-to-face settings. Spatial distortion occurs also with regards to head and body sizes, when people observe each other via classical video-conferencing systems. People further away from the camera appear to be smaller. In a study reported in [15] a technique was developed to adjust head-size to take the spatial distortion effects into account. Users indicated a preference for the adjusted head size option as compared to non-adjusted one. Both of these studies present clear requirements for Orchestration.

A study reported in [7] investigated the effect of spatial audio and spatial video on user assessments of conversation quality, engagement in the conversation, and the ability to keep track of the conversation. Spatial audio refers to the manipulation of sound to create the illusion of different origins in the 3D space. Spatial video refers to the placement of different video streams in a simulated 3D space of the screen. The study was carried out with a dedicated camera, microphone and display for each remote participant. The results showed that participants assessed the spatial video as having a significantly larger added value than spatial audio. Engagement in the conversation was significantly better and it was significantly easier to identify who was talking in the spatial video condition. This could suggest that Orchestration can do so much more at this end. But at the same time, there is a warning: incorrect mixing could harm the experience.

Closely related to our work is the meeting capture system reported in [19] whose aim was to apply TV production principles to capture and present videos of small group meetings. It uses a motion capture system and headbands with markers to locate people in the meeting space. Based on the cues extracted automatically, such as 'speaker change', 'posture change' and 'head orientation', a set of editing rules was developed and tested. E.g. whenever there was a speaker change detected, the system showed a close-up shot of the new speaker. When multiple speakers started to speak at the same time or took turns quickly, the system cut to an overview or wide shot that showed all three participants. Whenever a participant's posture changed from sitting to standing or walking, the system showed the overview shot to convey the posture change. The initial results were monotonous and highly predictable, but they became better as the behavior was fine-tuned and the camera placement was improved. For evaluation the authors compared automatic versus professional decisions. This work is different from our research as 'meeting capture' implies a narration from the meeting room to passive viewers, whereas we concentrate on inter-communication, in which all the participants are actively involved.

Well aligned with our work is the research that attempted to employ TV-like methods to improve video-conferencing between groups in a work setting, described in [8]. TV debate programs were studied with a view to refining shot categories according to the roles of the *actors* (speaker, listener, 3rd party) and the number of people involved in the debate (8 shots being refined) and transition and duration probability matrices for the inferred shots. A number of rules for videoconferencing were refined using the same concepts and they were applied in a setup consisting of 2 rooms, 4 people per room and 1 camera per room. We are conducting similar research, but in more complex physical and interaction spaces, with more complex communication equipment (e.g. multiple cameras), and with a stronger focus on the less structured social communication.

To summarise, although the literature appears to strongly motivate it, the area of *context-aware* video communication that we label *orchestrated communication*, has barely been touched. The effects of different types of shots upon communication have been investigated, but in *static* setups—i.e. they were not changed (through mixing or editing) during the communication session. Editing techniques have been proposed, but for *off-line recounting* rather than synchronous interaction. *Real-time mixing* techniques have been proposed, but in very restricted setups and with no rigorous evaluation of the communication experiences. We are reporting here a rigorous evaluation of social-group orchestrated communication experiences through a context-aware multi-camera system able to adapt in real-time (through manual intervention) to the communication needs. According to our knowledge, this is the first study of this kind.

5. DECISIONS REGARDING EXPERIMENTS DESIGN

Recall the hypothesis behind this research, namely that orchestration can improve the quality of multi-camera video-mediated communication between groups in informal social setups. This is a far too encompassing statement to be investigated as a whole—there are far too many variables such as the number of locations linked by the communication system, their physical layout, the equipment set up in each location, the size and distribution of the social groups, the social activities undertaken and, not least, the orchestration intelligence employed. The scope of the enquiry reported here was restricted to two living rooms and four friends, two in each room, playing the game of Pictionary and having a relaxed time. This setting was investigated through two major experiments.

The type, number and placement of the cameras varied between experiments, but the cameras were static, i.e. not dynamically reframed. Each room used one HD 50 inch TV screen and stereo sound was also a constant across experiments. The communication infrastructure was a prototype low-delay high-definition video-conferencing system, but the transmission was over the intranet. Only video was dynamically mixed. Orchestration was performed by two film professionals, collocated in a separate control room. Each had a video connection to one of the rooms, heard the audio from both rooms, and mixed the available shots from the room they were observing onto the other room's screen, which they could also see. This control setup for manual orchestration was built on top of the system's communication infrastructure.

Three experimental conditions of equal length were used in all the sessions of both experiments: *orchestrated*, *static* and *randomly mixed*. Their order was counterbalanced. In the *orchestrated* condition the human operators mixed a number of predefined shots in response to social interaction states and events, on the basis of a well-described set of rules—i.e. the orchestration knowledge. All the rules of the set were formulated such that a way to implementation for automatic reasoning could reasonably be foreseen. This meant that the social interaction states and events employed in the rules' conditions were feasibly regarded as inferable from primitive information provided by state of the art feature extractors or by expected extensions thereof. Also, the rule set was optimized to be sufficiently simple to allow the human operators to assimilate and apply the respective knowledge accordingly and consistently, but also sufficiently rich to be expected to determine rewarding communication experiences. There were no perceivable delays from the moment of issuing a mixing decision to its actual realization on the screen, as all the necessary shots were rendered in parallel. The *static* condition consisted of showing on each screen a static wide shot of the other room. To avoid an otherwise potential advantage through design of the orchestrated condition, the physical room layout was set up such that the wide shot covered all the relevant events and activities in the room. In the *randomly mixed* condition, the predefined shots used in the orchestrated condition were automatically randomly mixed, but with the rhythm of mixing set to mimic that of the human editors' in the *orchestrated* condition: cuts were done at random times ranging from the quickest to the slowest cut as performed by human editors.

In order to provide for a setting in which social interaction could take place, the participants were selected such that the members of each Pictionary team were either friends or good acquaintances. In order to stimulate communication across screen, each of the team members was placed on the opposite side of the video connection. The rules of the game had also been slightly amended. After the normal period allowed to the active team to guess (1 min) and in case of no correct guess, another period of 1 minute was allowed in which the other team could also guess and so "steal" the game turn. This stimulated both local and across-screen interaction. The participants were briefed that it was their choice of how they combined game-play with idle chats. Refreshments were also provided. To ensure sufficient time for social interaction, but at the same time to avoid making the overall experience tedious, the length of interaction in each condition was 20 minutes.

The quality of communication was assessed via two measures: an objective one, based on *social task efficiency*, and a subjective one, using a validated questionnaire based on the "sense of presence inventory" [14], that allowed the assessment of four qualitative factors: immersiveness, naturalness, presence and social presence. The notion of "task efficiency" might seem somewhat out of place in the context of idle chat and play of social games. However, the number of correct guesses across screen, and the number of games completed with no win, considered in the context of the overall number of games played, is a good indication of how successful the medium is in conveying meaningful information. Task efficiency was defined accordingly.

To ensure maximum objectivity of their assessment, the participants were briefed neither of the capabilities of the communication medium nor of the experimental conditions.

6. FIRST ORCHESTRATION EXPERIMENT

In the first experiment [6] (March-April 2011), Pictionary was played on drawing pads. The experimental setup is illustrated in Figure 3. Each room had 1 main HD camera (Sony EVI-HD1), providing one wide shot and 2 mid-shots through virtual cropping, and 2 auxiliary HD web cameras (Logitech), providing 2 reverse angle mid-shots (Figure 4). As they were not dynamically reframed, they were framed wider in order to allow some movement of the participants. The main principles considered in orchestration were to alternate between the wide and the mid-shots provided from the main camera for across-screen

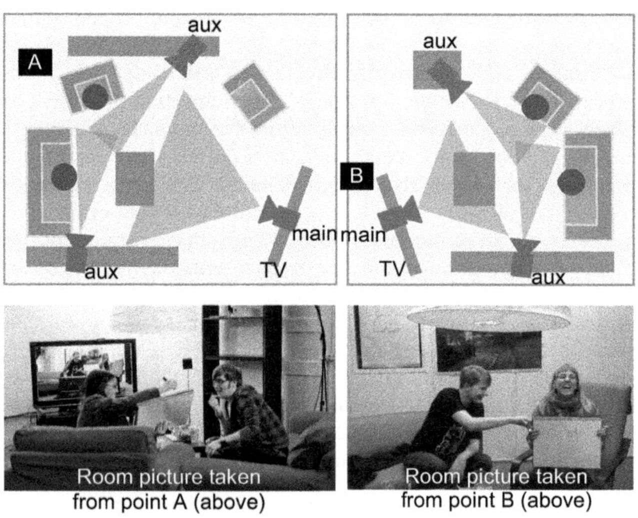

Figure 3. Setup of first orchestration experiment.

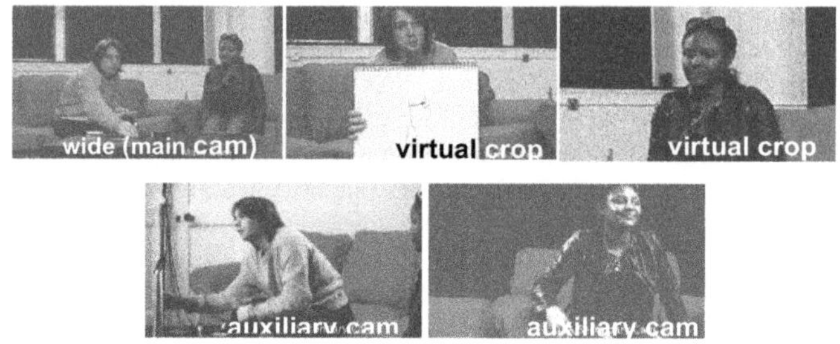

Figure 4. Predefined shots in first orchestration experiment.

communication, and to use the other two shots (reverse angles) for conveying in-room interaction. The more detailed orchestration rules are sketched in Table 1. The *static* condition used the same wide as the *orchestrated* condition.

Table 1. Orchestration rules in first experiment

prioritize communication over narrative requirements
use the corresponding virtual crop when a person has a more sustained communication across screen or when s/he shows the drawing board
when both people in a room communicate at the same time or through quick turns with the other room, use the wide
if the above condition is too long, use the virtual crop on the person drawing (not applicable in the room where there is no drawing)
use the auxiliary cameras to render scenes in which there is manly local interaction, similar to TV mixing of dialogues
the wide can also be used for the same function (above)
use the auxiliary (side) cameras when the drawing board pad is in view
use virtual crops to animate the wide after longer periods of use
use the wide whenever in doubt, as a fallback

8 interaction sessions were carried out with a total of 32 participants—a session being defined by a group (4 people) undertaking all three conditions, in approximately 2 hours of overall experimentation (including briefing and filling-in questionnaires in between conditions), of which 60 minutes (3x20) was time of effective conversation and interaction.

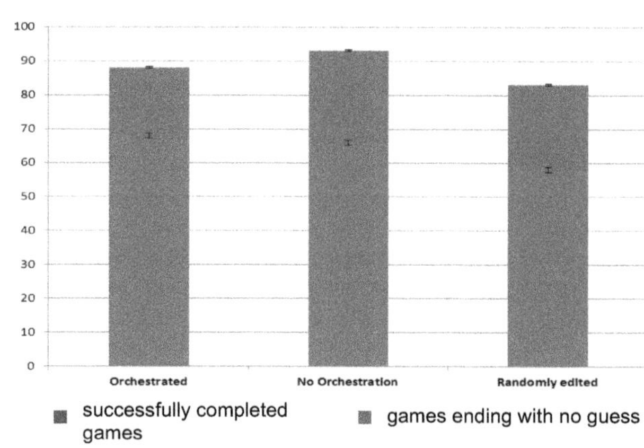

Figure 5. Task efficiency results.

The objective evaluation results are illustrated in Figure 5. There were more games played in the *static* condition (93) than in the *orchestrated* (88) and *random* (83). However, there were overall more successfully completed games in the *orchestrated* condition (68) than in *static* (66) and *random* (58). The game success rate in the *orchestrated* condition (.77) was significantly higher than in the other two conditions (.70), with p=.007. This is clear evidence that, in this instance, participants were more effective when their communication was orchestrated and, therefore, that orchestration *can* lead to more effective communication experiences. The result is even more significant, as the communication setting did not necessarily require orchestration: the wide HD shot shown on the large TV screen (*static* condition) showed everything from the other room, therefore being able to be regarded as a transparent wall to the other room and so possibly more appropriate and "natural" than mixing different angles of the room. Yet, the experiment led to a different conclusion, favoring orchestration. It appears sensible to assume that more complex communication settings (e.g. three or more rooms, with wide shot not being able to capture everything) would benefit even more from orchestration, but such hypotheses have yet to be rigorously tested.

Regarding the subjective evaluation, the results were inconclusive when comparing the *orchestrated* condition with the *static*—there were no statistically significant differences in the experience of the four assessed factors, although the average assessment was higher in all for the *static* condition. Certain aspects of the experimental setup might have had an impact. For example, there were significant variations in picture quality between the wide shot, the shots of the auxiliary cameras and the virtual crops. They were clearly noticeable and affected visual continuity. There were also problems regarding framing. The reverse angle shots and the virtual crops could not be framed as tightly as required by their assigned communication and narrative functions, as the auxiliary cameras had no lens control and the virtual crops degraded quickly with the cropping size.

Orchestration used five *static* shots (i.e. not reframed during interaction). Almost all of the interaction sessions were quite animated, with the participants moving comfortably in the room. Thus, some of the static shots lost their function, as there was no possibility of dynamic reframing.

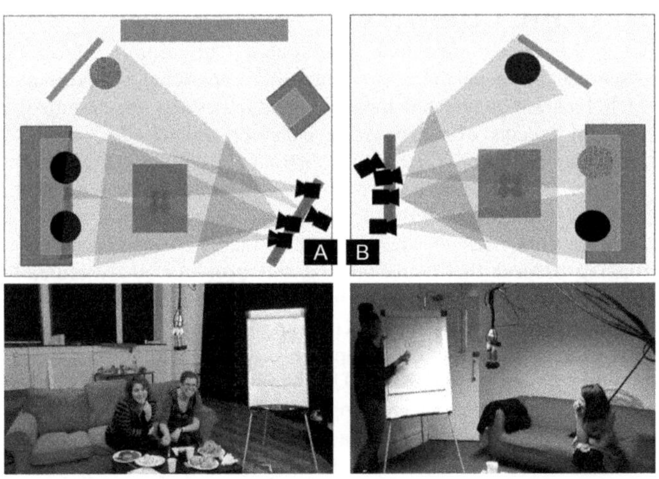

Room picture taken from point A (above)

Room picture taken from point B (above)

Figure 6. Setup of second orchestration experiment.

Figure 7. Predefined shots in the *orchestrated* condition.

A second experiment, addressing these issues, was setup to reassess the subjective evaluation. The orchestration rules were also revised.

7. SECOND ORCHESTRATION EXPERIMENT

In the second experiment (January 2012), Pictionary was played on drawing boards (one available in each room). The experimental setup is illustrated in Figure 6. There were two *sitting positions* on the sofa and one *standing position* at the drawing board. Each room was equipped with 4 HD cameras (Sony EVI-HD1), providing the following 4 predefined shots: wide, one mid-shot showing the person drawing and the drawing board, and one tight mid-shot on each sitting position (see Figure 7). As they were not dynamically reframed, they were framed wider in order to allow some movement of the participants. The wide used in the non-orchestrated condition was wider than the orchestrated wide – the latter included the drawing board in the frame, the former did not. The orchestration rules employed the definitions presented in **Table 2**. The rules for orchestration for the "guessing room" are presented in Table 3. The rules for orchestration for the "drawing room" are presented in Table 4.

Table 2. Definitions used in orchestration rules

conversation turn ≡ starts with a person starting voice activity and ends when the person stops the continuous speech activity
game turn ≡ starts with person drawing and ends when the game sessions ended
communicative turn ≡ a conversational or a game turn
cross talk ≡ a communicative turn has not ended and another one (in the same room) started

Table 3. "Guessing room" orchestration rules

For the first half of the game, prioritize the "guesser" in cross talk situations.
For the second half of the game, if applicable, treat both persons equally, in terms of the logic, in cross talk situations.
For the first half of the game, prioritise the "guesser" even when the other person in the room holds the conversational turn, to ensure a meaningful conversation between the two people actively involved in guessing
When a conversational turn shift first appears, give it priority.

Show the mid-shot corresponding to the person who has the conversational turn.
If no person has an active communicative turn then show wide or alternate between the mid-shots.

Table 4. "Drawing room" orchestration rules

Overall, prioritize the game turn over the conversational turn.
"Drawing person" arriving at the board has full priority.
Prioritize a conversational turn when it first happens over a game turn.
Do not consider a conversational turn over a game turn more than three times.
When a communicative turn is identified, show the corresponding mid-shot.
When there is no communicative turn, but "drawing person" is still at the board, alternate between the corresponding mid-shots. If "drawing person" is seated, show the wide.
Before the "drawing person" reaches the board (preparatory stage), show the wide.
If a conversation starts in the "preparatory stage", show mid-shots according to the conversational turns.

9 interaction sessions were carried out with a total of 36 participants – the definition of a session being the same as in the previous experiment.

The questionnaire used in the participants' assessment of the 4 factors—naturalness, immersiveness, presence and social presence—of the communication and interaction experiences used a Likert scale ranging from 1 (strongly disagree) to 5 (strongly agree). Orchestration affected the assessment of only two of the four conditions (Pillai's Trace = .22, $F(8, 206) = 3.28$, $p = .002$, $\eta p2 = .11$). "Immersiveness" received an average assessment score of 4.10 (SD = .62) in the *orchestrated* condition, 3.88 (SD = .73) in the *static* condition and 3.46 (SD = .93) in the *randomly mixed* condition. Only the difference between the *orchestrated* and the *randomly mixed* condition was significant, $p = .002$ (Bonferroni corrected)—i.e. no significant difference between *static* and *randomly mixed.* The assessments of "social presence" were significantly higher in both the *orchestrated* condition (M = 3.67, SD = .60) and in the *static* condition (M = 3.62, SD = .70) in comparison with the *randomly mixed* condition, $p < .001$ (Bonferroni corrected), but not between them. The corresponding graphs are depicted in Figure 8. These results provide evidence, but less compelling, for orchestration being able to improve the perception of video-mediated communication experiences.

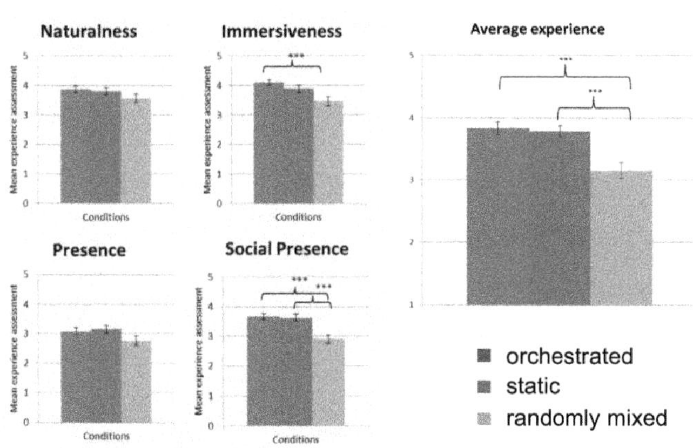

Figure 8. Results of subjective evaluation

Interestingly, for "immersiveness", the *static* condition was not evaluated as significantly different, statistically, from the *randomly mixed* condition. This renders the behavior of the system in the latter condition as meaningful and satisfying. This is not surprising, as all the shots used in this condition were the same as the ones used in the orchestrated condition, and so, each carried meaningful information. Furthermore, as the set of available shots was not large and the mixing rhythm mimicked that of the human operators, the probability that the randomly mixed stream was "meaningful" was high—in other words, orchestrating by randomly mixing (sic!) appears somewhat sufficient in this setting. Therefore, having "informed orchestration" assessed as significantly better than "random mix" sheds a positive light upon orchestration as such.

As already mentioned, the *static shot* in the chosen experimental setting (only 2 rooms, the wide capturing everything relevant, HD video, large TV screen) may be regarded as providing a transparent wall between the rooms—quite close to the collocated experience. Having orchestration on a par with it with regards to "social presence" (both outperforming the *randomly mixed* condition) can also be interpreted as a positive result, particularly noting that in this setting orchestration is not *necessarily required.*

Finally, the assumptions made when framing (recall that the cameras were not dynamically reframed) with regards to the position of the participants and the drawing board have not been complied with entirely. There have been a few situations when the drawing board was moved closer to the screen in the *static* condition or when some of the available cameras were covered (playfully) in the *orchestrated* and *randomly mixed* conditions to prevent the other room from guessing, or simply when people moved out of the frame of the tighter shots. This could have been enforced through briefing, but the preference was not to do so and leave it as an inherent part of the experiment setup (see *decisions regarding the experiment design* section).

8. CONCLUSIONS

In *group* video-mediated interaction, subgroups might be dispersed in more than two physically separated locations and each location may need many a/v input devices to capture the relevant aspects of the people's behavior and to allow them to move naturally in the space, unconstrained by the communication medium. This generates the problem of dealing, in each location, with the multiple audio and video sources originating from the other locations. *Orchestration* was defined here as the decision making process that could address this problem by dynamically adapting the communication infrastructure to the continuously changing interaction context. The hypothesis behind this research was that orchestration can improve the quality of group video-communication experiences. The hypothesis was tested in two major experiments, by carrying out orchestration manually, by human operators. They acted according to a clear set of rules—orchestration knowledge—which could reasonably be expected to be implemented in automatic processes. Partial implementations of such knowledge have been reported in [13], [10], [4].

The experiments provided evidence for a positive answer. With reference to *task efficiency* (experiment 1), and *social presence* and *immersiveness* (experiment 2), orchestration outperformed the other two conditions (with statistical significance). There are no cases in which any of the other two conditions outperformed orchestration. Therefore, in this particular basic setup, orchestration has improved the quality of group communication. But, more importantly, we interpret this result as persuasive motivation to continue this line of work: orchestration has the potential to improve group communication experiences, in more complex settings. On one hand, it outperformed, in some aspects, static communication (via a wide), which, in the basic experimental setting employed here—2 locations, 2 people per location, small number of shots, fixed framing— would appear to be more than sufficient. On the other hand, it outperformed random mixed communication, which, in the way employed here—same shots, all meaningful at all times, and similar mixing rhythm as in orchestrated communication—would appear to be a meaningful form of orchestration. More complex settings, thus, could be expected to benefit more from orchestration.

9. ACKNOWLEDGEMENTS

This work was supported in part by funding from the European Community's Seventh Framework Programme grant agreements ICT-2007-214793 and ICT-2011-287760.

10. REFERENCES

[1] Ames, M. G., Go, J., Kaye, J. J., & Spasojevic, M. (2010). Making love in the network closet: the benefits and work of family videochat *Proc ACM CSCW*, 145-154.

[2] Ballagas, R., Kaye, J. J., Ames, M., Go, J., & Raffle, H. (2009). Family communication: phone conversations with children *Proc ACM IDC,* 321-324.

[3] Doherty-Sneddon, G., Anderson, A., Omalley, C., Langton, S., Garrod, S., & Bruce, V. (1997). Face-to-face and video-mediated communication: A comparison of dialogue structure and task performance. *Journal of Experimental Psychology-Applied, 3*(2), 105-125

[4] Falelakis, M., Groen, M., Kaiser, R., and Ursu M.F. (2012). Automatic orchestration of video streams to enhance group communication. In Proceedings of the *International Workshop on Socially Aware Multimedia, associated* with *ACM MM 2012*, Nara, Japan.

[5] Gergle, D., Rose, C.P., Kraut, R.E (2007). Modeling the impact of shared visual information on collaborative reference. In *Proc ACM CHI*, 1543-1552.

[6] Groen, M., Ursu, M.F., Michalakopoulos, S., Falelakis, M., and Gasparis, E. (2012). Improving video-mediated communication with Orchestration. *Computers in Human Behaviour (28)*, 1575-1579.

[7] Inkpen, K., Hegde, R., Czerwinski, M., & Zhang, Z. (2010). Exploring spatialized audio and video for distributed conversations. *Proc ACM CSCW*, 95-98.

[8] Inoue, T., Okada, K. and Matsushita, Y. (1995). Learning from TV programs: Application of TV presentation to a videoconferencing system. *Proc. ACM UIST*, 147-154.

[9] Jansen, J., Cesar, P., Bulterman, D., Stevens, T., Kegel, I., & Issing, J. (2011). Enabling composition-based video-conferencing for the home. *IEEE Transactions on Multimedia* 13(5), 869-881.

[10] Kaiser, R., Weiss, W., Falelakis, M., Michalakopoulos, S., and Ursu, M.F. (2012). A rule-Based Virtual Director Enhancing Group Communication. In *2012 IEEE Conference on Multimedia and Expo Workshops (ICMEW)*, Melbourne, Australia, 187-192.

[11] Kirk, D. S., Sellen, A., & Cao, X. (2010). Home video communication: mediating 'closeness'. *Proc ACM CSCW,* 135-144.

[12] Kleij, van der, R., Schraagen, J.M., Werkhoven, P., & De Dreu, C.K.W. (2009). How Conversations Change Over Time in Face-to-Face and Video-Mediated Communication. *Small Group Research 40(4)*, 355-381.

[13] Korchagin, D., Duffner, S., Motlicek, P., and Scheffler, C. (2012). Multimodal Cue Detection Engine for Orchestrated Entertainment. In *Proceedings of the International Conference on Multi-Media Modeling (MMM) 2012*, Klagenfurt, Austria, 662-670.

[14] Lessiter, J., Freeman, J., Keogh, E., & Davidoff, J. (2001). A cross-media presence questionnaire: The ITC-Sense of Presence Inventory. *Presence: Teleoperators and Virtual Environments, 10*(3), 282-297.

[15] Liu, Z. C., Cohen, M., Bhatnagar, D., Cutler, R., & Zhang, Z. Y. (2007). Head-size equalization for improved visual perception in video conferencing. [Article]. *IEEE Trans. on Multimedia, 9*(7), 1520-1527.

[16] Nguyen, D. T., & Canny, J. (2007). Multiview: improving trust in group video conferencing through spatial faithfulness *Proc ACM CHI*, 1465-1474.

[17] Nguyen, D. T., & Canny, J. (2009). More than face-to-face: empathy effects of video framing *Proc ACM CHI* 423-432.

[18] Psathas, G. (1995). Conversation Analysis, The Study of Talk-in-Interaction (Qualitative Research Methods), Sage.

[19] Ranjan, A., Birnholtz, J. and Balakrishnan, R. (2008). Improving Meeting Capture by Applying Television Production Principles with Audio and Motion Detection. *Proc. ACM CHI*, 227-236.

[20] Scholl, J., Parnes, P., McCarthy, J. D., & Sasse, A. (2005). Designing a large-scale video chat application *Proc ACM MM,* 71-80.

[21] Tang, J. C., & Isaacs, E. (1992). Why Do Users Like Video?: Studies of Multimedia-supported Collaboration: Sun Microsystems Laboratories.

[22] Vishwanath, D., Girshick, A. R., & Banks, M. S. (2005). Why pictures look right when viewed from the wrong place. *Nature Neuroscience,* 8(10), 1401-1410.

[23] Walkowski, S., Dörner, R., Lievonen, M., & Rosenberg, D. (2011). Using a game controller for relaying deictic gestures in computer-mediated communication. *International Journal of Human-Computer Studies, 69*(6), 362-374.

[24] Wheatley, D. J., & Basapur, S. (2009). A comparative evaluation of TV video telephony with webcam and face to face communication. *Proc EuroITV 2009*, 1-8.

The Space Between the Images

Leonidas J. Guibas
Stanford University
Computer Science Department
Stanford, CA 94305 USA
guibas@cs.stanford.edu

ABSTRACT

Multimedia content has become a ubiquitous presence on all our computing devices, spanning the gamut from live content captured by device sensors such as smartphone cameras to immense databases of images, audio and video stored in the cloud. As we try to maximize the utility and value of all these petabytes of content, we often do so by analyzing each piece of data individually and foregoing a deeper analysis of the relationships between the media. Yet with more and more data, there will be more and more connections and correlations, because the data captured comes from the same or similar objects, or because of particular repetitions, symmetries or other relations and self-relations that the data sources satisfy. This is particularly true for media of a geometric character, such as GPS traces, images, videos, 3D scans, 3D models, etc.

In this talk we focus on the "space between the images", that is on expressing the relationships between different mutlimedia data items. We aim to make such relationships explicit, tangible, first-class objects that themselves can be analyzed, stored, and queried -- irrespective of the media they originate from. We discuss mathematical and algorithmic issues on how to represent and compute relationships or mappings between media data sets at multiple levels of detail. We also show how to analyze and leverage networks of maps and relationships, small and large, between inter-related data. The network can act as a regularizer, allowing us to to benefit from the "wisdom of the collection" in performing operations on individual data sets or in map inference between them.

We will illustrate these ideas using examples from the realm of 2D images and 3D scans/shapes -- but these notions are more generally applicable to the analysis of videos, graphs, acoustic data, biological data such as microarrays, homeworks in MOOCs, etc. This is an overview of joint work with multiple collaborators, as will be discussed in the talk..

Categories and Subject Descriptors

J.0. [**Computer Applications**]: General

General Terms

Algorithms, Theory

Keywords

Geometric data analysis, shape analysis, image co-segmentation

MM'13, October 21–25, 2013, Barcelona, Spain.
ACM 978-1-4503-2404-5/13/10.
http://dx.doi.org/10.1145/2502081.2509857

Lecture Video Segmentation by Automatically Analyzing the Synchronized Slides

Xiaoyin Che
Hasso Plattner Institute
Prof.-Dr.-Helmert-Str. 2-3,
14482 Potsdam, Germany
xiaoyin.che@hpi.uni-potsdam.de

Haojin Yang
Hasso Plattner Institute
Prof.-Dr.-Helmert-Str. 2-3,
14482 Potsdam, Germany
haojin.yang@hpi.uni-potsdam.de

Christoph Meinel
Hasso Plattner Institute
Prof.-Dr.-Helmert-Str. 2-3,
14482 Potsdam, Germany
christoph.meinel@hpi.uni-potsdam.de

ABSTRACT

In this paper we propose a solution which segments lecture video by analyzing its supplementary synchronized slides. The slides content derives automatically from OCR (*Optical Character Recognition*) with an approximate accuracy of 90%. Then we partition the slides into different subtopics by examining their logical relevance. Since the slides are synchronized with the video stream, the subtopics of the slides indicate exactly the segments of the video. Our evaluation reveals that the average length of segments for each lecture is ranged from 5 to 15 minutes, and 45% segments achieved from test datasets are logically reasonable.

Categories and Subject Descriptors

H.3.1 [**Information Storage and Retrieval**]: Content Analysis and Indexing—*Abstracting methods, Indexing methods*; K.3.1 [**Computers and Education**]: Computer Uses in Education—*Distance learning*

Keywords

Video Segmentation, Slides Content Analysis, OCR

1. INTRODUCTION

With the prosperity of online video lecture, the knowledge can break through the wall of campus and benefit the people around the world. However, it is not comfortable for people to stare at a computer screen for a long lecture, especially when they just have interest in some parts of the lecture rather than the whole. As a result, to segment the lecture video becomes nessecary.

Manual segmentation has no doubt the best result, but it is also a huge consumption for the time or/and money. And due to the specialty of lecture videos (*commonly no scene change*), the segmentation methods for natural videos[1, 4] are no longer proper. Instead, many research for lecture video segmentation base on blackboard writing[2, 6], speech recognition[5, 7] or additional lecture transcript[3]. But unfortunately, people use blackboard less recently while speech, regardless of the accuracy problem, is always too flexible to be concluded as certain topics. And additional transcript exists only in some special cases. All those facts drive us to look for some new ideas of segmenting lecture videos.

In recent years, many lecturers use slides when giving lectures, instead of blackboard. Meanwhile many E-Learning systems also include the slides as well as the lecture videos. Slides are generally the outline of the lecture or presentation. By analyzing slides content properly, the whole lecture or presentation can be logically divided into several subtopics, in other words, segments. If the slides are synchronized with the relevant lecture video, no matter recorded in a second video stream(*tele-TASK*[1] *e.g.*) or just stored as a sequence of time-related pictures (*VideoLectures.NET*[2] *e.g.*), the slides segments can be perfectly treated as the video segments.

Based on this idea, we propose a new segmentation method for lecture videos by analyzing the synchronized slides content from OCR results. OCR technology enables us to extract textual data from pictures or videos, and for the slides of lecture video, the accuracy is fairly high that over 92% characters and 85% words can be extracted correctly and saved in text-lines, which contain both text data and location info[8]. Then we can reconstruct the content structure of each slide. After that we will first figure out whether there are special slides can be recognized as subtopics border, which is the foundation of global segmentation. Furthermore, we also search for index-pages or generate virtual index-pages by exploring the shared words between titles of continuous slides, which enables partial segementation. Finally a default time segmentation process is included.

The rest of this paper will be organized as follow: Section 2 illustrates our detailed solution while Section 3 and Section 4 show the evaluation results and conclusion respectively.

2. DETAILED SOLUTION

2.1 Solution Framework

Figure 1 illustrates the framework of proposed solution. With OCR results as input, the whole procedure is fundamentally divided into two parts: Intra-Slide Reconstruc-

[1]http://www.tele-task.de/
[2]http://videolectures.net/

MM'13, October 21–25, 2013, Barcelona, Spain.
Copyright 2013 ACM 978-1-4503-2404-5/13/10 ...$15.00.
http://dx.doi.org/10.1145/2502081.2508115.

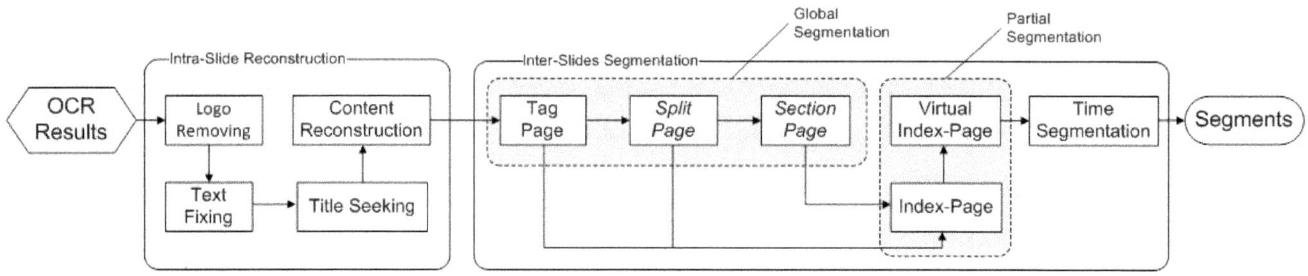

Figure 1: Diagram of proposed solution framework

tion and Inter-Slides Segmentation, which will be further explained in Chapter 2.2 and Chapter 2.3.

2.2 Intra-Slide Reconstruction

2.2.1 *Preparation*

Firstly, we will try to remove the logo. When existing, the logo appears in the same position of almost every slide, commonly in a corner. But it is totally meaningless or even harmful for our solution.

Next, we will try to fix the error occurred in OCR results. Text-lines will be checked by splitting into words. If the average word length is shorter than 2 characters, this text-line will be deleted entirely. Otherwise, a text-line can also be shortened by eliminating ill-recognized words with an abnormally long length or containing too much symbols.

All further steps will build on the remaining texts, along with their location info.

2.2.2 *Title Seeking*

Title is the most important content for a slide. Generally, the title has 3 features: bold, locating in the upper part of the slide and being separated with other texts. Sometimes, the title can be so long that have to occupy multiple physical rows. And because of the OCR accuracy problem, text in one physical row may probably be recognized as several text-lines when the gap between two words is large. In addition, potential subtitle will be included as a part of the title in our approach. So we will search for at most 3 text-lines as candidates. Finally they will be sorted by the location logic and combined together as the title.

When seeking a title candidate, a lot of factors have to be considered. But if a text-line can match all the requirements below, it seems very likely to be selected as a title candidate (*with slide resolution 1024× 768*):

1. *Higher than the average or 30 pixels.*
2. *Vertically locates in the top 1/3 of the slide.*
3. *Horizontally locates in the left 2/3 of the slide.*
4. *Not closer than 10 pixels to any border.*
5. *If it is not the only text-line matching requirements above, not far from the previous one, neither vertically nor horizontally.*

2.2.3 *Content Reconstruction*

To organize a group of text-lines in order is a big challenge, especially when the slide contains pictures, charts or tables. But first of all, we will connect those long descriptions occupying multiple physical rows, just like what we do when seeking title. Then we will go through all the text-lines to explore potential hierarchy among them, based on their locations and sizes. As a result, up to 3 levels will be found, according to the custom that most presenters write their slides content from the left horizontally and from the top vertically.

2.3 Inter-Slides Segmentation

2.3.1 *Global Segmentation*

The aim of global segmentation is to segment the lecture or presentation by its main structure. Most presentations are indeed consisted by several subtopics, but unfortunately only some of them have apparent signs which can be considered as subtopic borders. In this step we attempt to figure out all possible such 'border' and generate segments based on them. We name this kind of segment as GLS (*Globally Logical Segment*).

In our research, 3 kind of slide can be identified as GLS basis: tag-page, split-page and section-page. This order also affects the priority when more than 1 kind of GLS basis exists. And at least two slides of same kind should be found before they get utilized as GLS basis. Figure 2 shows examples of these 3 kind of special slides.

Tag-Page:

A tag-page in fact is an outline of the whole slides, with a special title such as 'Agenda', 'Topics' or 'Outline', and its content containing most or all the subtopics. For each time, one certain text-line is highlighted to indicate that this subtopic will be discussed in the following slides until the next appearance of the tag-page. The OCR process cannot recognize the feature of 'highlighted topic' and a tag-page may contain more text-lines than the real number of subtopics (*sub-subtopic e.g.*), but the correct subtopic must be found as the annotation to this GLS. As a result, to get a correct mapping relation between the multi-slides sections and their corresponding subtopics in the tag-page becomes vitally important.

In our research, we try to match the subtopics in the tag-page to the titles in following common slides. However, we have to be very tolerant about the matching requirements, approximately 50%, because in content the subtopics are much more general than the following titles. Even so, not all sections can be matched to a subtopic, so we have to use the already matched ones as reference and assign those 'free' sections around them. Finally several GLSs will be achieved, noticed that the last slide with special title such as 'Thanks' will be separated from the last GLS.

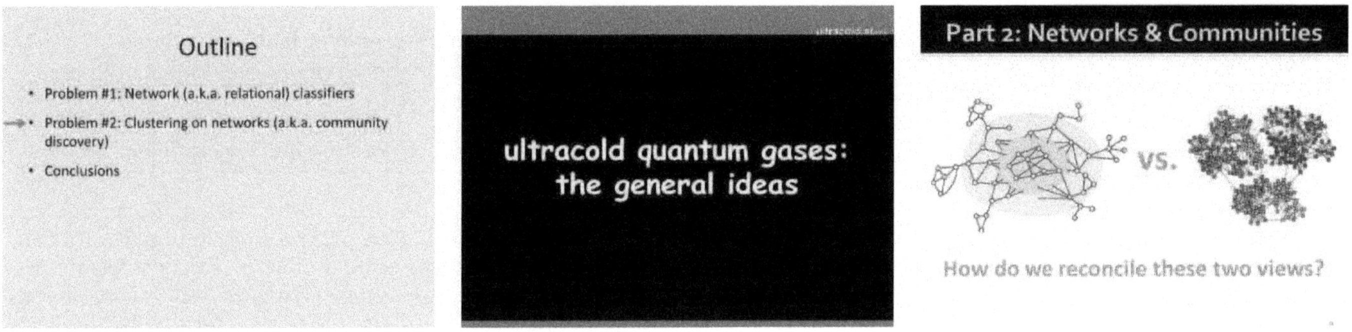

Figure 2: Examples of tag-page, split-page and section-page

Split-Page:

Split-page is another kind of widely used 'border' by the lecturer or presenter. Generally the only content in a split-page is a prompt of the following slides, and for most cases, locates in the center of the slide rather than the title position. In other words, a split-page doesn't have a title after our intra-slide reconstruction process, which is a main prerequisite when we search for it.

The text we get from the split-page, obviously, is the best annotation text for this GLS. So there is no such 'matching' procedure required like what we do when dealing with tag-page.

Section-Page:

Not like tag-page or split-page above, section-page is more than a border. A section-page has all the features a common slide may have, expressing definitions, explaining algorithms or showing pictures. The only difference is in the title, which contains some special border words such as 'Part 1:', 'Theme two' or 'Topic III' e.g. Only if when we find at least two slides with special title words in same format, then they can be acknowledged as section-pages.

The section-page title, after removing the special border words, will be applied in annotation.

2.3.2 *Partial Segmentation*

For those presentations without recognizable subtopic border, or the slides locating before the first GLS, we propose a partial segmentation process to explore the logical correlation among several neighboring slides. Under partial segmentation, PLS (Partially Logical Segment) will be found out, by which some slides with continuous or relevant content can be gathered together. Compared to GLS, PLS is less convincing, but still reasonable. In our research, partial segmentation process affects in 2 steps: index-page and virtual index-page.

Index-Page:

Index-page looks like partial tag-page. The content of an index-page is a preview of a sequence of following common slides, so it is natural to combine all these slides together as a PLS. The method of index-page searching is also similar to the tag-page, by exploring the similarity of text-lines in the potential index-page and titles from following slides. But the threshold of 'matching' here is higher, at least 75%, because this kind of partial correlation is always direct.

Due to the independency of index-page, every slide in a non-GLS presentation, or before the first GLS, has a chance to be an index-page. We have to go over all of them with a floating search window. If over half text-lines in the current can match some following titles, this slide will be marked as index-page and its text-lines will connect those corresponding slides. And similar to tag-page, those unmatched slides will be assigned to the text-lines by position. After that, the search window will jump to the end of the newly generated PLS. If the current slide is not an index-page, the search window will just move to the next.

Finally, one text-line in the index-page may connect to a single following slide or a sequence. And the title of the index-page will be directly adopted as the annotation text of the PLS.

Virtual Index-Page:

Virtual index-page derives from a series of continuous slides sharing some words in their titles. In this case, those slides are very likely describing similar topics, and can be packaged as a whole. In our approach, we only consider nouns longer than 3 characters as candidates, and the noun must appears in half slides inside the counting interval, and at least 3 times, to be finally adopted.

This process is also running inside a floating window, just like the one searching real index-page. And to improve the accuracy, both the plural and the punctuation problem get well solved. At the end, the annotation text of the PLS generated from the virtual index-page will consist of all the possible shared words.

2.3.3 *Default Time Segmentation*

A time segmentation procedure is reserved to apply for the rest of the presentation except the GLSs and PLSs, by which all segments will not be too long. The length of TS (*Time Segment*) depends on the average length of logical segments in the same presentation, or else, if there is neither GLS nor PLS found, a time segment should not longer than 1/4 of the whole presentation. The annotation text of a TS adopts the title of the slide in this segment with longest duration.

3. EVALUATION

To evaluate the result of our approach, the diversity of test videos is very important. So we collect 10 extra lecture or presentation videos as an additional dataset, along with 10 videos from public dataset (*Videos with slides only*). All videos have different lecturers and both their contents and styles are totally independent with each other.

In our experiments, we just focus on our own method rather than do comparison between methods, according to 2

Table 1: Segments Overview of Public Dataset

Video	Borders	Segs	GLS	PLS	TS	AveLength
d-g-u	Yes	4	3	0	1	13:29
k-e-d	No	7	0	1	6	05:53
k-k-s	No	6	0	1	5	08:41
k-r-n	Yes	5	3	0	2	12:27
k-s-n	Yes	3	2	0	1	15:02
s-d-s	No	4	0	2	2	11:45
s-e-r-c	Yes	4	2	0	2	14:12
s-k-s	No	5	0	0	5	09:26
s-l-n	Yes	5	2	1	2	09:44
s-w-i	Yes	7	2	2	3	05:06

Table 2: Segments Overview of Additional Dataset

Video	Borders	Segs	GLS	PLS	TS	AveLength
5626	No	5	0	1	4	08:05
6011	No	4	0	0	4	07:11
6031	No	5	0	2	3	06:06
6098	Yes	6	4	0	2	07:58
6102	Yes	6	3	1	2	03:19
6104	No	5	0	1	4	07:12
6106	Yes	5	4	0	1	06:22
6196	No	8	0	4	4	07:20
6201	No	3	0	2	1	16:26
6212	Yes	6	2	1	3	10:21

reasons. Firstly, we have to manually achieve ground truth data before comparing, but this may be too subjective to convince people. Secondly, it is not fair to compare results if they derive from completely different resources, especially when the accuracy of OCR is much better than ASR (*Automatic Speech Recognition*), which is well acknowledged.

The overview segmentation result of the public and additional dataset are depicted in Table 1 and Table 2 respectively. For public dataset, we use the initials of the folder as the video name in 'Video' column, while a series number for the video from additional dataset. 'Border' means whether the synchronized slides of this video contain obvious subtopic border, which is obtained manually. Next we present the numbers of total segments, GLS, PLS and TS generated by our solution. And finally an average length of the segments in each lecture video is calculated.

From the segments overview we can easily find out that a presentation gets commonly split into 3∼8 segments, with the average length controlled inside 5∼15 minutes. It means that a presentation will never be cut too fragmentary, for which each segment will keep plenty of information as complete knowledge points, and the duration of a segment is comfortable for the learners behind the screen, neither too long to feel tired, nor too short to be confused.

Based on the test datasets, the proposed segmentation method is well capable in exploring the subtopics border when they exist (*10 in 10*). According to the further analysis showed in Table 3, over 50% segments we got from this kind of videos is GLS, in addition with almost 10% PLS, makes the segmentation result highly logical. For other videos, there are also over 1/4 segments achieved as PLS, from in fact comparatively lineal organized or discrete consisted presentations. In general, nearly half segments derived from our 20-videos dataset are logical.

Table 3: Segments Ratio Analysis

Video Type	GLS	PLS	All LS	TS
with Border	52.9%	9.8%	62.7%	37.3%
no Border	-	26.9%	26.9%	73.1%
All	26.2%	18.4%	44.6%	55.4%

And to be noticed, each presentation automatically contains one TS because the first slide is always a front cover and never a part of any logical structure. And many presentations will have one more TS at the end due to the large probability that the presenter will use the final slide to express the gratitude. Regarding these two facts, the actual ratio of logical segments should be even higher.

4. CONCLUSION

The proposed solution for lecture video segmentation has been proven effective by the evaluation results. Mainly by comparing text, we have successfully explored lots of logical correlation between slides and apply them into segmentation process. To go further in the future, the method of analyzing must involve more artificial intelligence factor, which is what we will attempt next.

5. REFERENCES

[1] V. Badrinarayanan, I. Budvytis, and R. Cipolla. Semi-supervised video segmentation using tree structured graphical models. *IEEE Transactions on Pattern Analysis and Machine Intelligence*, page 1, 2013.

[2] G. Friedland and R. Rojas. Anthropocentric video segmentation for lecture webcasts. *Journal on Image and Video Processing*, 2008:9, 2008.

[3] A. S. Imran, L. Rahadianti, F. A. Cheikh, and S. Y. Yayilgan. Semantic tags for lecture videos. In *Semantic Computing (ICSC), 2012 IEEE Sixth International Conference on*, pages 117–120. IEEE, 2012.

[4] I. Koprinska and S. Carrato. Temporal video segmentation: A survey. *Signal processing: Image communication*, 16(5):477–500, 2001.

[5] M. Lin, J. F. Nunamaker Jr, M. Chau, and H. Chen. Segmentation of lecture videos based on text: a method combining multiple linguistic features. In *System Sciences, 2004. Proceedings of the 37th Annual Hawaii International Conference on*, pages 9–pp. IEEE, 2004.

[6] M. Onishi, M. Izumi, and K. Fukunaga. Blackboard segmentation using video image of lecture and its applications. In *Pattern Recognition, 2000. Proceedings. 15th International Conference on*, volume 4, pages 615–618. IEEE, 2000.

[7] N. Yamamoto, J. Ogata, and Y. Ariki. Topic segmentation and retrieval system for lecture videos based on spontaneous speech recognition. In *European Conference on Speech Communication and Technology*, pages 961–964, 2003.

[8] H. Yang, M. Siebert, P. Luhne, H. Sack, and C. Meinel. Lecture video indexing and analysis using video ocr technology. In *Signal-Image Technology and Internet-Based Systems (SITIS), 2011 Seventh International Conference on*, pages 54–61. IEEE, 2011.

Activity-Aware Adaptive Compression

A Morphing-Based Frame Synthesis Application in 3DTI

Shannon Chen, Pengye Xia, and Klara Nahrstedt
Department of Computer Science, University of Illinois at Urbana-Champaign
{cchen116, pxia3, klara}@illinois.edu

ABSTRACT

In view of the different demands on quality of service of different user activities in the 3D Tele-immersive (3DTI) environment, we combine activity recognition and real-time morphing-based compression and present the Activity-Aware Adaptive Compression. We implement this scheme on our 3DTI platform: the TEEVE Endpoint, which is a runtime engine to handle the creation, transmission and rendering of 3DTI data. User study as well as objective evaluation of the scheme show that it can achieve 25% more bandwidth saving compared to conventional 3D data compression as *zlib* without perceptible degradation in the user experience.

Categories and Subject Descriptors

H.1.2 [**Information Systems**]: Models and Principles – *human factors;* H.4.3 [**Information Systems Applications**]: Communications Applications – *Computer conferencing, teleconferencing, and videoconferencing;* I.4.2 [**Image Processing and Computer Vision**]: Compression (Coding) – *Approximate methods*

Keywords

3D Tele-Immersion; Compression; Morphing; Frame Rate; Adaptation

1. INTRODUCTION

During the past decade, the potential of 3D Tele-immersive (3DTI) services has gained its attention from both academia and industry. While most commercial 3D systems are specialized for sole purpose, the trend of development of 3DTI platforms is towards multi-purpose, multi-sites, and multi-modal platforms [1-2] to enable a variety of user activities including e-learning, collaborative art performance, and exergaming [4].

Inevitably, with its great potential, the resource demand of 3DTI rises due to its interactive characteristic, complexity of 3D rendering, and delivery of media-rich content [2]. From previous observations [5], we see that 3DTI users can have very different tolerance to quality degradation when participating in different types of user activities. Thus, we present the Activity-Aware Adaptive Compression (A3C), which is a real-time compression scheme that combines activity recognition and morphing-based compression on the 3DTI content.

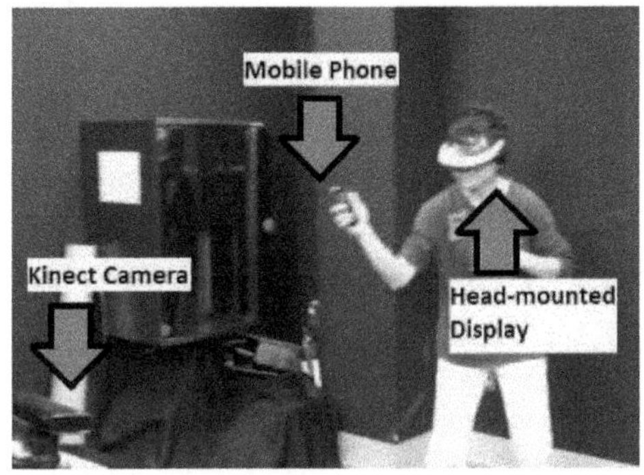

Figure 1. User interface of TEEVE Endpoint.

A3C adopts the Morphing-based Frame Synthesis (MBFS) as its compression scheme. Taking advantage of the unique properties of 3DTI scenes, the MBFS technique allows the content receiver to boost up the video frame rate by injecting synthesized frames into the received content. Thus, the transmission frame rate of the content producer can be reduced to save substantial amount of bandwidth for content delivery. With MBFS, the deducted frames will be synthesized and restored at the receiver side, hence the perceived quality can be preserved.

To maximize the effectiveness of MBFS compression, we apply activity recognition to identify the motion characteristics of current user activity and to assign suitable compression parameters (e.g., the Synthesized Frames per Second, which will be introduced later in Section 3.2.) The visual quality of synthesized frames depends heavily on the motion level of the content. For high motion content, the graphical difference between captured frames is large and the sharpness degrades due to motion blur. These effects increase the artifacts introduced by feature-based morphing, making the synthesis unnatural and more detectable to viewers. Therefore, we combine the compression scheme with user activity recognition to dynamically fine-tune the compression scheme and achieve high visual quality and optimum resource saving.

We implement the A3C scheme on our 3DTI platform: the TEEVE Endpoint, which is a runtime engine to handle the creation, transmission and rendering of 3DTI data. The user interface of the TEEVE Endpoint includes Kinect camera, head-mounted display, and the user's mobile phone (Figure 1.) The Kinect camera and the accelerometers embedded in the display capture the head position and the view direction of user. To provide a vivid immersive experience, the information is used in the construction of the 3DTI scene to synchronize the view point and view direction of user in the virtual space with those in the physical user space. The user's mobile phone serves both purposes of a control console and an auxiliary on-body motion sensor for activity recognition. With a downloadable app, the accelerometer in the phone would be connected to the endpoint and provide sensing data to aid the immersive experience.

MM'13, October 21–25, 2013, Barcelona, Spain.

ACM 978-1-4503-2404-5/13/10…$15.00.
http://dx.doi.org/10.1145/2502081.2508116

We evaluate our total solution via objective compression ratio as well as subjective user study. Using four common user activities with distinctive motion characteristics, the former shows a bandwidth saving up to 25% more than conventional compression scheme adopted by existed 3DTI platforms. The user study, on the other hand, is conducted via interviewing the players of a 3DTI virtual fencing game built upon the TEEVE Endpoint. Results show that A3C does not introduce perceptible degradation to the gameplay experience with its substantial resource saving.

The remainder of this paper is organized as follows. In the next section, an overview of the TEEVE Endpoint is provided as a background for the introduction of A3C in Section 3. Section 4 covers the evaluation of A3C, which includes both objective and subjective aspects. Finally, in Section 5 we conclude.

2. SYSTEM COMPONENTS

2.1 TEEVE Endpoint

The TEEVE Endpoint is our runtime engine to handle the 3DTI data and it provides application programming interfaces (APIs) to developers to easily create 3DTI applications. As shown in Figure 2, the architecture of the runtime engine contains several modules. The *capturing module* takes the raw data from 3D camera and generates 3DTI data in real-time. The *resource management module* takes the 3DTI data to compose 3DTI frames which are disseminated over the network to the remote sites through the *transmission module*. The 3DTI data is passed to the *rendering module* for displaying the visual feedback. The *3DTI game engine* sits on top of the rendering module to control the rendering behavior in response to the events detected within the system. These events include system state changes, collision detection, and user-interaction input. The 3DTI game engine further provides API to the developers to register callback functions for those events to define the rendering behavior.

2.2 Tele-immersive User Interface

The user interface of our solution includes Kinect camera, mobile phone and head-mounted display. The three devices collaborate with each other as part of the UI module to provide 3D visual data input, user perspective input, user control input and user activity input, which are coordinated by the game engine. The *3D visual data input* is captured by the Kinect camera. Each 3DTI site is equipped with one Kinect camera. With the depth information, the scene is captured and represented as a point cloud. The *User perspective input* represents the view point and view direction of the user. The position and rotation of the head are tracked by the Kinect and the motion sensor embedded in the head-mounted display, respectively. The *User control input* is retrieved from the translational movement and rotational movement of the user's hand. The former is tracked by the Kinect camera while the latter is tracked by user's mobile phone when being held as a console. The *User activity input* is continuously fetched by the mobile phone when it is not being used as a console. The triaxial accelerometer embedded in the phone provides motion data to the endpoint for activity recognition.

3. ACTIVITY-AWARE ADAPTIVE COMPRESSION

Our total solution of A3C can be broken down into three major components: activity recognition, frame deduction, and frame amendment (Figure 3.) The first two components reside in the resource management module at the producer endpoint, while the last component resides in the rendering module at the receiver endpoint. In the following sections, we introduce the design of these components.

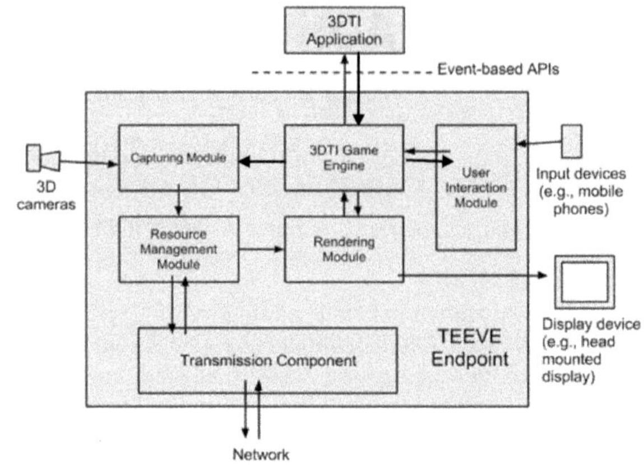

Figure 2. TEEVE Endpoint Architecture.

3.1 Activity Recognition

As the first component of our system, we build a SVM-based [6] mapping from motion data acquired from user's mobile phone to user activities. Each common user activity in 3DTI environment has its motional and postural uniqueness. Thus, by monitoring the motion data from the on-body mobile phone, the activities can be classified in real-time with a machine leaning approach. The activities we are targeting and their motional/postural characteristics are listed as follows.

- Storytelling: User is *sitting* in the center of the 3DTI environment with most of her action concentrate on facial area. Occasional gesture is expected.
- Speech: User is *standing* in the center of the 3DTI environment. Facial movement is expected along with occasional gestural and body movement.
- Exercise learning: Slow and gross-motor movements of all body parts are expected from the user.
- Gaming: Both posture and position of user change rapidly. Fast and gross-motor movements are expected.

To build up a mapping from sensor data to user activity for real-time classification, we apply the Support Vector Machine [6]. The features (e.g., positions, speed, changing frequency,) fed into the machine, are deducted from the variation of acceleration in the time domain and the power spectrum in the frequency domain. The former is acquired by sliding window analysis on the data compiled while the latter is acquired by Fast Fourier Transform.

We recruited 10 participants to perform all four activities in the 3DTI environment. Due to the size of regular smart phones, all participants naturally place the phone in their pants pocket when asked to carry it on-body. 200-minute record containing all four activities in equal lengths was compiled. With this training data, the SVM is able to generate a user activity classifier for our system which takes current motion data as input, and output the type of user activity in real-time. The accuracy of the trained machine is 91.5% (10-fold cross-validation,) which provides a solid foundation to the consecutive procedures of A3C.

3.2 Frame Deduction and Amendment

The design of the morphing-based compression mechanism is to deduct a certain amount of frames at the resource management module of the producer site before they are sent to the transmission module. The deduction will then be amended at the

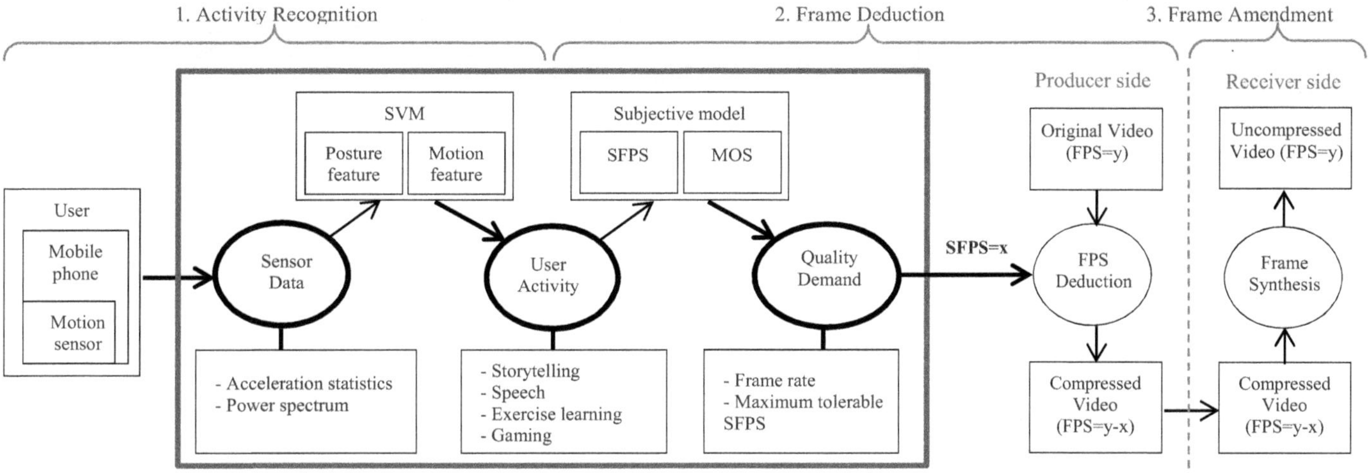

Figure 3. Overview of user activity-based resource adaptation for 3DTI videos.

receiver site in its rendering module. Synthesized frames will be created based on the received content and injected into the video. These synthesized frames replace the deducted one and restore the frame rate. Figure 3 shows an example where x frames are deducted/amended in the compression/decompression of a video which originally contains y frames per second.

The amount of frames deducted is described by a compression parameter: the Synthesized Frames per Second (SFPS), which also stands for the number of synthesized frames injected in the final uncompressed result. In the following, we first introduce the technique of frame amendment: the Morphing-Based Frame Synthesis (MBFS) before we detail the decision of SFPS adjustment based on user perception and activity characteristics.

3.2.1 Morphing-Based Frame Synthesis

With the frame synthesis technique, 3DTI visual content has more flexibility on frame rate adaptation compared to conventional 2D videos. 3DTI bears some properties that make MBFS possible:

- With the depth information, only the subjects are captured to be put into the virtual space. The background is discarded.
- Common subjects in 3DTI are human bodies, which have fair sizes that take major portion of the scene.
- Number of subjects is limited by the interactive characteristic and the size of the display. This lowers the graphical complexity of each scene.

Combining these properties, we propose to create synthesized frames by graphic morphing [7], which is a special effect in motion pictures that transit one image to another based on predefined feature pairs. Figure 4 shows an example of applying morphing technique for frame synthesis. The first and the last frames in the figure are the only real frames captured by a camera, while the ten frames in-between are synthesized.

We use graphical feature matching [10-11] and skeleton detection to mark the feature pairs in two captured frames. Due to the limited number of subjects and their fair sizes, the graphical feature matching can provide a meaningful number of matching pairs. In addition, human bodies are the most common subjects in the scene. Thus, we also include the joints detected by skeleton detection of Kinect as matching feature pairs. For image processing after the feature pairs are acquired, the paper of Beier and Neely [7] provides extensive details. As a result, with the morphing technique we can insert extra synthesized frames to boost up the original frame rate.

3.2.2 Activity-Aware Frame Deduction

Due to different motion characteristics, for different user activities, the optimum adjustment of SFPS is very different. The prominence of synthesized frames depends heavily on the motion of the visual content. For relatively static activities, the difference between frames is small, which makes the morphing result very similar to the deducted frame. On the other hand, for activities that contain intense body movements, the high motion introduces motion blur to the captured frames, which raises the bar of graphical feature matching and skeleton detection. These disadvantages increase the possibility of feature mismatch, which renders the synthesis unnatural and more detectable by the viewer.

To explore this complication, we conduct user tests and ask 15 participants to rate sequences of pre-recorded 3DTI visual content of the four types of 3DTI user activities (Section 3.1.) Each sequence contains video clips of the same activity compressed with different SPFS settings. The participants are requested to view these clips and give a Mean Opinion Score (MOS) to represent the Quality of Experience (QoE.) From the feedback of the participants, we are able to pinpoint the Just Noticeable Difference (JND) perceptual thresholds [8] of SFPS for all activities. The thresholds represent the SPFS that separate noticeable degradation from unnoticeable ones for each activity. These thresholds are built into the frame deduction component of A3C so that the system can adaptively compress the visual content without affecting its perceptual quality.

4. EVALUATION

4.1 Objective Metric: Compression Ratio

The purpose of adaptive compression is to find the lowest compression ratio for the 3DTI activity without comparable degradation of the QoE. Thus, we setup two resource saving modes with different levels of QoE degradations: imperceptible mode (targeting 90% of QoE of the original reference clip) and acceptable mode (targeting 80% QoE.) Table 1 shows the adjustment of SPFS in both modes and the resulting compression ratio (CR) of each scenario (due to space limit, detailed analysis of these results can be found in [1]). We also include the compression ratio of *zlib* [9], which is a popular compression scheme adopted by previous 3DTI systems. The result shows that the proposed A3C scheme can achieve up to 25% more bandwidth saving comparing to *zlib*.

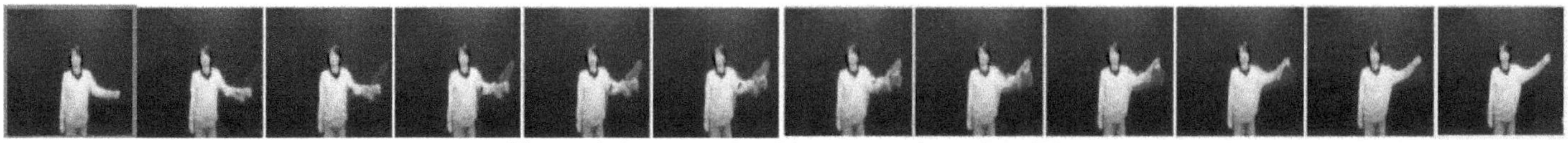

Figure 4. An example of frame rate boosting. [1]

Note that Table 1 only shows the results of each activity separately. To achieve adaptive compression, A3C utilizes the activity recognition component (Section 3.1) to classify current movement and reconfigure the SFPS according to Table 1. For example, when user leaves her chair and starts to exercise, A3C automatically tunes the SFPS from 2.5 to 1.0 (assuming acceptable mode.) In practice, A3C reduces the 4.1 Mbps bandwidth consumption of 3DTI visual stream by 2.0~2.5 Mbps.

Table 1. Activity-based resource adaptation

User Activity			Story	Speech	Exercise	Game
A3C	Imper. mode	SFPS	1.4	0.0	0.0	2.5
		CR	2.1:1	1.8:1	1.9:1	2.4:1
	Accept. mode	SFPS	2.5	2.5	1.0	2.5
		CR	2.4:1	2.4:1	2.2:1	2.4:1
zlib		CR	1.8:1	1.8:1	1.9:1	1.9:1

4.2 Subjective Metric: Gameplay Experience

In order to evaluate the perceptual effect introduced by A3C, we choose the activity with the highest motion level: exergaming, as a medium of the subjective test. As we mentioned previously, high motion content is more likely to introduce artifacts under morphing-based compression. Thus, the quality of exergaming is the most vulnerable one to compression among other activities.

We implement a virtual fencing game on the TEEVE Endpoint as an experiment testbed. The game includes two sites connected within the campus network. Each site contains one Kinect camera to capture the 3D scene. The 3D data of each player is transmitted to the other site and rendered in the virtual world. Player in each site wears a head-mounted display embedded with accelerometers and sees from her first person's perspective in the virtual world. The players hold their mobile phone as game consoles. When the phone is used as a game console, the activity recognition of A3C component classifies current activity as "gaming." The SFPS is adaptively tuned to the value stated in Table 1. A sword is rendered in the virtual world at the hand of the player with the sword direction synchronized with the rotational movement of the phone. The objective of the game is to hit the remote player (the opponent) with your weapon. Player's score decreases as hit by one another. A player wins when her opponent's score decreases to zero. Figure 5 shows a sample game screen.

Table 2. Interview Questions and Average Scores

	A3C Enabled	A3C Disabled
Q1: Are you satisfied with the graphical resolution of the game?	3.3	3.3
Q2: How is the responsiveness of the game control?	4.4	4.1
Q3: Do you consider the game realistic?	3.4	3.7
Q4: Do you enjoy the immersive experience?	4.6	4.6

(Score: 5 being the most and 1 being the least)

Among the two 3DTI sites, only one of them has the A3C scheme enabled. We recruit seven real players to participate in the game in pairs. After a five-minute gameplay, we interview each player about their gameplay experience. After that, the players are asked to switch sites, play the game for another five minutes, and being interviewed again. The interview questions are listed in Table 2,

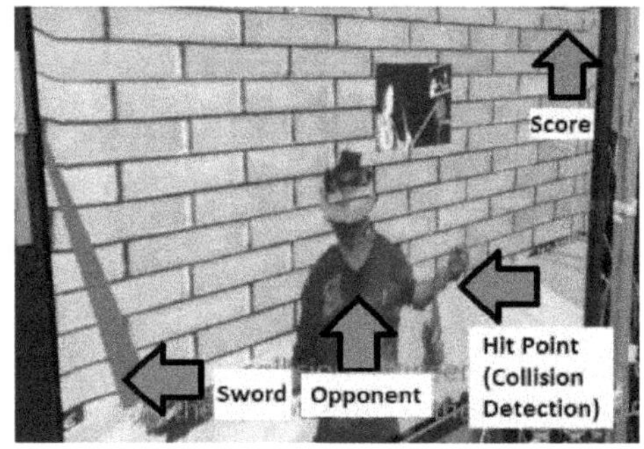

Figure 5. Game screen of the virtual fencing.

which focus on the sensory immersion of gameplay experience [3]. The players are asked to answer the questions on a 5-point Likert scale. The result suggests that the experience within both sites do not have significant difference. The similarity of the two sites is supported by two-way ANOVA test ($F<0.01$, $p=1$).

5. CONCLUSION

In this work, we propose a solution for 3DTI applications to reduce its bandwidth consumption without degrading the user experience. We present the Activity-Aware Adaptive Compression (A3C) scheme, which combines activity recognition and morphing-based compression. The scheme is implemented on the TEEVE Endpoint and evaluated via both objective and subjective metrics. Result shows that A3C brings 25% more bandwidth saving comparing to existed compression scheme of 3DTI without compromising the user experience.

6. ACKNOWLEDGMENTS

This material is based upon work supported by NSF Grant CNS 10-12194, CNS09-64081KN.

7. REFERENCES

[1] S. Chen et al. Activity-based synthesized frame generation in 3DTI Video. ICME, 2013.

[2] Z. Yang et al. Enabling multi-party 3D tele-immersive environments with ViewCast. TOMCCAP, 2009.

[3] L. Ermi et al. Fundamental components of the gameplay experience: analyzing immersion. DIGRA, 2005.

[4] M. Renata et al. Advancing interactive collaborative mediums through tele-immersive dance (TED): a symbiotic creativity and design environment for art and computer science. MM, 2008.

[5] Z. Huang et al. Towards the understanding of human perceptual quality in tele-immersive shared activity. MMSys, 2012.

[6] C.-C. Chang et al. LIBSVM: a library for support vector machines. TIST, 2011.

[7] T. Beier et al. Feature-based image metamorphosis. SIGGRAPH, 1992.

[8] G. Gescheider. Psychophysics: the fundamentals. Psychology Press, 3/e, 1997.

[9] zlib. http://www.zlib.net/

[10] M. Muja et al., Fast approximate nearest neighbors with automatic algorithm configuration, VISAPP , 2009.

[11] H. Bay et al., SURF: speeded up robust features, CVIU, 2008.

Flickr-tag Prediction using Multi-modal Fusion and Meta Information

Yu-Chuan Su, Tzu-Hsuan Chiu, Guan-Long Wu
Chun-Yen Yeh, Felix Wu, Winston H. Hsu
National Taiwan University, Taipei, Taiwan

ABSTRACT

We present our evaluation and analysis on Yahoo! Large-scale Flickr-tag Image Classification dataset. Our evaluations show that combining multi-features and different classification models, the MAP of tag prediction can be significantly improve over ordinary linear classification. Further analysis shows that some tags are given not because of the visual content but the meta information of images. Our experiments show that we can make more accurate prediction on certain tags using meta information without any training process, compared with visual content based classifiers. Combine the meta information, multi-features and multi-models fusion, we achieve significantly better performance than simple linear classification. We also evaluate the performance of various mid-level feature, and the results suggest that "Concept Bank" feature may be a promising direction for the task.

Categories and Subject Descriptors

I.4.8 [**Image Processing and Computer Vision**]: Scene Analysis

Keywords

Multi-features Fusion; Meta data; Concept Bank

1. INTRODUCTION

Targeting on ACM Multimedia 2013 Yahoo! Large-scale Flickr-tag Image Classification Grand Challenge, we evaluate various classification models and features, both low-level and mid-level ones, on the dataset. The main challenge of the task is the intra-class visual diversity. Unlike existing image classification datasets which contain many classes with small number of visually consistent images, the proposed dataset consists of only 10 classes with 150k images for each class, and the visual content of the 150k images are so diverse that some of them might not share any visual similarity. Therefore, traditional image classification approach may not apply well on the dataset.

MM'13, October 21–25, 2013, Barcelona, Spain.
Copyright 2013 ACM 978-1-4503-2404-5/13/10 ...$15.00.
http://dx.doi.org/10.1145/2502081.2508117.

To overcome the difficulty, we propose to adopt high dimensional image feature along with multi-features and models fusion. By combining multiple features and models, we are able to capture more diverse visual content. In particular, we believe fusing with classification models that are resistant to intra-class diversity, such as nearest neighbor (NN) classifier, can significantly improve the performance. Beside features and models fusion, we also propose to adopt meta information for tag-prediction. Our observations indicate that some tags are given mainly based on the meta information rather than the visual content. Without meta information, some tags are doomed to be ill predicted by visual content.

We also evaluate the performance of various mid-level features. With the higher level semantic embedded in mid-level features, they should be more robust to visual content diversity. In particular, we examined human face feature and "Concept Bank" feature on the dataset. Our results suggest that "Concept Bank" feature is a promising direction for the task, but a larger concept space is necessary for competitive performance, where the 136 dimensional concept space in our experiment is not big enough.

The outline of our evaluation on the dataset is as follows. First, we perform linear classification and multi-features fusion (section 3) following state-of-the-art image classification systems [1]. Second, we examine the performance of k-nearest neighbor (kNN) model (section 4). The results motivated the use of meta information for tag prediction, as presented in section 5. Finally, we evaluate the efficacy of mid-level features (section 6).

2. RELATED WORK

Linear support vector machine (SVM) is the most common classifier in large scale image classification. Among all variants of linear SVM solver, LIBLINEAR [4] is the most popular one; the solver, however, does not handle large data that does not fit into memory well. A common approach to overcome the problem is to use stochastic gradient descend (SGD) for optimization; alternatively, Yu et. al. proposed a block optimization approach that solve the SVM problem in batch manner [9]. The approach shows better performance on several datasets, and the training time is comparable with SGD solver.

The most popular dataset for large scale visual recognition is ImageNet [2]. Unlike the Yahoo! Grand Challenge dataset, ImageNet is a dataset with large number of concepts, where each concept contains relatively small number of images with higher visual consistency. Based on the

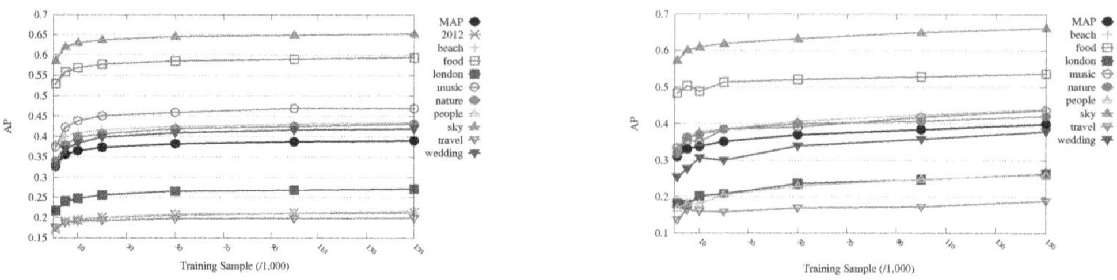

(a) Linear SVM

(b) k-Nearest Neighbor (kNN)

Figure 1: The AP of each tag with different classification models using Dense SIFT. Tags that are ill predicted by linear SVM also have poor AP using kNN classifier (k=10), which indicates that visual content is not discriminative for those tags.

dataset, the ImageNet Large Scale Visual Recognition Challenge (ILSVRC) [1] is a contest that requires the recognition of 1,000 image categories with a total of 1.2 million training images.

In state-of-the-art large scale image classification systems, high dimensional descriptors based on local features such as Vector of Locally Aggregated Descriptors (VLAD) [5] and Locality onstraint Linear Coding (LLC) [8] have become the standard features. Following [7, 8, 5], we adopt the following four features in our experiments:

- Hessian Affine SIFT + VLAD (HA) [5]
- Grid Color Moment + VLAD (CM) [7, 5]
- Dense SIFT + LLC (Dense) [8]
- LBP + LLC (LBP) [8]

For color moment, we extract the 96 dimensional grid color moment (4×4 grid, 1st and 2nd moment in HSV color space) from dense sampled image patches and use it as local feature to aggregate VLAD feature. For LBP, the 59 dimensional LBP is extracted from 32×32 dense sampled patch as local feature.

3. LINEAR SVM CLASSIFIER

Following state-of-the-art large scale image classification systems [1], we perform 10-classes linear classification and use the normalized decision value to rank the test images. 1-against-all strategy is used for the multi-class classification, and the decision value is first scaled by logistic function and then L1-normalized over the 10-classes. When the training image number from each tag is less than 10k, we use the primal space solver in LIBLINEAR; however, when the training image number is more than 10k, the entire training set is too large to fit into memory, so we use an alternative solver from LIBLINEAR that handles training data by batch [9]. The

Table 1: MAP with bagging algorithm. The training sets are randomly sampled without replacement to ensure the total number of training samples. Using the same number of training samples, the performance of bagging classifier is inferior to single classifier trained with all samples.

1k samples Single Classifier	1k samples 100 Classifiers	100k samples Single Classifier
0.304	0.319	0.364
5k samples Single Classifier	5k samples 30 Classifiers	150k samples Single Classifier
0.330	0.345	0.366

AP of each tag and overall MAP using Dense SIFT are in fig. 1a, which shows that increasing training data improves the performance.

Following the observation, we examine that given a fixed number of training data, can bagging strategies achieve similar or even better performance than using all training data to train one single classifier. If bagging classifier performs well, the scalability of the training process would become free from the hardware constraints of single machine and more training samples can be used. To answer the question, we perform bagging with 1,000 and 5,000 randomly sampled training image for each base classifier; the output of bagging classifier is the average of 100 and 30 classifiers respectively. To control the exact number of training samples, the random sample is done without replacement The results are shown in table 1, where the significant performance gap between single classifier and bagging classifier with the same number of training samples indicates that we should train the base classifier with as many training sample as possible.

To further improve the performance, we perform multi-features fusion. We use late fusion strategy by simply add the decision score of different classifiers, and the resultant performances are in fig. 2. The performances are significantly improved by multi-features fusion, although ill predicted tags such as "travel" still has AP lower than 0.3. In fact, the relative performance of tags are the same over all features and fusion results, which means that "hard tags" are general for all features. Therefore, we turn the focus to exploiting the power of classification model next.

4. K-NEAREST NEIGHBOR CLASSIFIER

The main difficulty of the dataset is claimed to be the intra-class diversity, where single classifier might not be able to capture the visual appearance of all the sub-classes under the same tag. Theoretically, NN based classifiers can overcome the problem by nature, because the algorithm requires

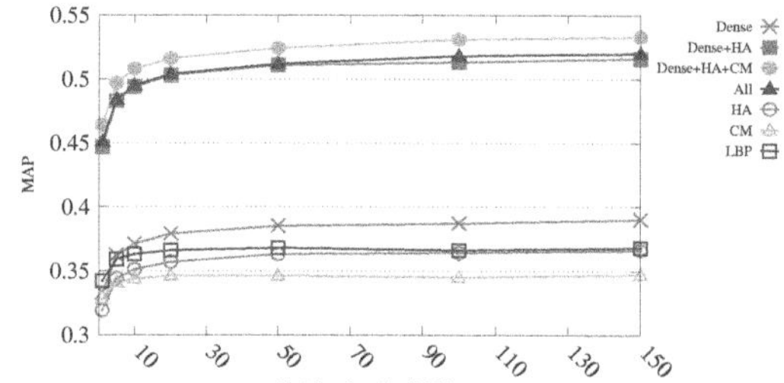

Figure 2: Multi-features fusion. Performance is significantly improved with late fusion which simply average the prediction score of different classifiers.

Table 2: MAP of late fusion on both features and models. By fusing different models, the overall MAP shows significant improvement over single model and feature. Note the MAP is computed without tag "2012."

	Dense	Dense+HA	Dense+HA+CM
SVM	0.409	0.543	0.553
kNN	0.406	0.517	0.568
Both	0.413	0.541	0.582

only the existence of similar samples with correct tag instead of the intra-class similarity. It is also shown that kNN classifier performs well when the dataset is large enough [3]. Therefore, we focus on classification by retrieval in this section.

When we apply kNN classifier directly on the dataset, we found that the retrieval results are dominant by tag "2012." Combined with the poor AP of tag "2012" with linear classification, we believe the visual content of "2012" is so diverse that it is actually a superset of other tags. To overcome the problem, we removed images with tag "2012" from the training set in the following experiments (test set is left unchanged).

The experiment settings are as followed. For the kNN classifier, L2 distance is used for retrieval, and the retrieval depth k is set to 10. The raw decision score of test image i on tag t is defined as

$$\tilde{i}_t = \sum_{k=1}^{10} \frac{\delta^t_{t_k}}{d^2_{ik}}, \tag{1}$$

where t_k is the tag of the kth nearest image and d_{ik} is the distance between the two images. $\tilde{i}$ is then L1-normalized, where the normalized decision score is used to rank test images, following the procedure in linear classification. The results are shown in fig. 3.

We can see from the results that kNN generally performs worse than linear SVM, especially when the number of training samples is small. However, when the training set grows larger, the performance difference becomes smaller; for color moment and LBP, kNN even outperforms linear SVM when the training set is large enough. More importantly, while the performance of linear SVM shows only minor improvement with more than 20k training samples per class, the performance of kNN doesn't seem to saturate even with 150k training images per class. Therefore, we believe that kNN has the potential to outperform linear SVM using all features with more training samples per class.

We also show the AP of each tag in fig. 1b. We can see that the relative performance of each tag is similar to that of linear SVM, which indicates that tags such as "London," "people" and "travel" are indeed less discriminative using visual content regardless of the model.

Finally, we perform late fusion on linear SVM and kNN. Because kNN performs well only with large training set, we only show the result using the entire training set in table 2. By combining both model and three features, the MAP can reach nearly 0.6.

5. PREDICTION WITH META DATA

In previous section, we ignore tag "2012" because of its intra-class visual diversity and visual content overlap with other tags. Combined with the tag name, we postulate that the tag was given based on the context instead of the content of images. More specifically, we argue that the tag "2012" was given because of the taken time of the photo. To justify the argument, we perform experiments as follow.

Table 3: The result of prediction tag "2012" with upload year. Because the prediction does not require any training, the experiment is perform on both training and test set. The AP of purely using upload year predictor is better than the optimal AP using visual content.

	Precision	Recall	AP
Training	0.530	0.966	0.470
Testing	0.529	0.966	0.470

First, we predict tag "2012" using only the upload time. More precisely, we predict positive for tag "2012" if the image is uploaded in 2012 and negative otherwise. The results are shown in table 3. We can see the results on training set and test set are almost the same, and the precision is 5 times higher than random guess; more importantly, the recall is close to 1.0. To further compare the AP, we randomly permute the image order of positive and negative images respectively and take the 10 times average. The AP is higher than the optimal result we can achieve using visual content.

Next, we examine whether visual content can further improve the result. Because the recall of upload year prediction is close to 1.0, we focus only on positive images. For the training set, we only retain images uploaded in 2012, and we keep the ratio of positive and negative to 1:1; for testing, we randomly permute the negative images and use the classifier to rank the positive images. HA feature is used for the experiments. The MAP with different numbers of training images are in fig. 4. By combining meta information and visual content, the originally ill predicted tag "2012" can achieve AP higher than the overall MAP.

The above results indicate that some tags are given mainly due to the context, rather than the visual content of the image. We believe the same argument apply to other tags such as "London" that are not well predicted by pure visual content. Therefore, the meta information of an image is crucial for tag prediction.

6. MID-LEVEL FEATURES

In this section, we present our experiments on two mid-level features. By casting images into a high level semantic space, we believe mid-level features are more resistant to intra-class visual diversity, compared with ordinary low level visual features. In practice, we examined human face feature and "Concept Bank" feature in our experiments.

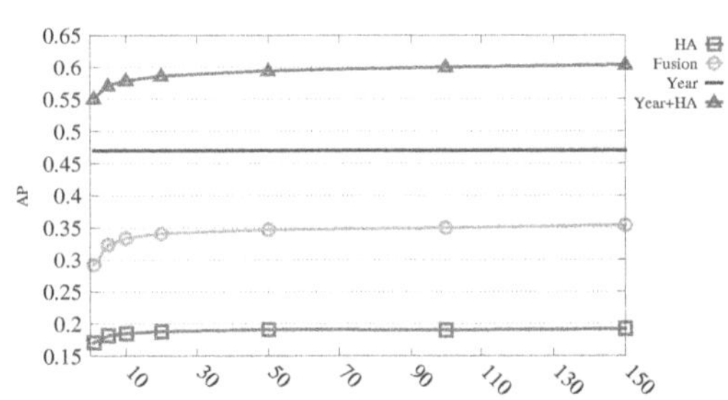

Figure 4: AP for tag "2012". We can see the meta information significantly outperform visual content, while combining both shows further improvement.

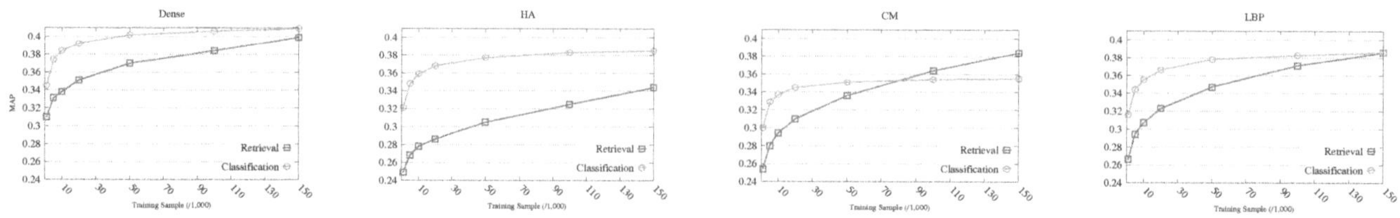

Figure 3: Result of kNN classifier. Although the perform is worse than that of linear SVM under small training set, the performances are comparable when all training data are used. More importantly, kNN classifier shows higher potential of improvement with more training samples, which suggests it would eventually outperform linear SVM.

6.1 Human Face Feature

Motivated by the success of upload year predictor for tag "2012," we try to improve the prediction of tag "people" with face detector. In practice, we use the Omron face detector for face detection. Unlike upload year, however, the existence of human face is not a good indicator for tag "people." In fact, more than half of the training images contain human face except tag "beach" and "sky," and human face are actually more common in tag "music" and "wedding" than in tag "people." Therefore, the existence of human face is not helpful for the prediction of tag "people."

6.2 Concept Bank Feature

Inspired by "Object Bank" [6], we cast each image onto a set of "concepts" and use the response of the concepts as feature for tag prediction. In practice, we randomly select 136 concepts from ILSVRC2012 for the concept space; for each concept, we use all the training data (about 1,000 images) in ILSVRC2012 as positive samples and randomly select the same number of images from the training set of Yahoo! dataset as negative samples, using Hessian affine feature. A logistic regression predictor is trained for each concept, and the normalized response on the predictors is used as the new concept bank feature.

Using the new concept bank feature, we perform logistic regression with the same setups as previous linear SVM classification. For comparison, we perform the same experiment on 136 dimension signatures generated by random projection. The results are shown in fig. 5. The performance of concept bank is significantly better than random projection even if the concepts are selected randomly, which justify the efficacy of concept bank feature. Although concept bank feature does not perform as good as original feature, the training time and feature size is significantly reduced because the feature dimension is reduced from 8,192 to 136. It is worth noting that the performance saturates around 5k of training samples per tag, which is much faster than the original feature. We believe extending the concept space can further improve the performance and is a promising direction for the task.

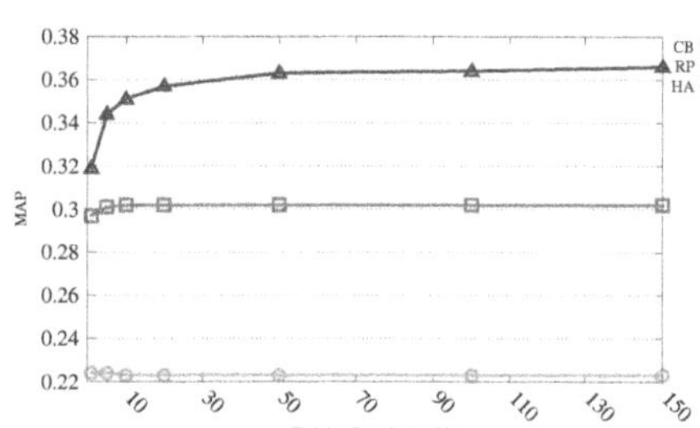

Figure 5: MAP of concept bank (CB) feature. We train 136 concepts randomly selected from ILSVRC2012 and represent each image using the response on the concepts. Hessian affine (HA) feature is used for concept detection. CB significantly outperforms random projection (RP) under same dimension (136). Although the original HA still performs the best, CB significantly reduce feature dimension (8192→136), which in turn reduce data size and training time.

7. CONCLUSIONS

In this paper, we present our evaluation and analysis on the Flickr-tag Image Classification dataset. Our results show that combining multi-features and models can significantly improve the tag prediction performance. However, our analysis also shows that some tags are given due to the meta information of the image instead of its visual content. The most obvious example is the tag "2012," which is better predicted by the upload year than the visual content. For such tags, visual content along can not yield satisfactory performance and meta information is essential for prediction. In fact, we believe the main difficulty of the dataset comes from these visually indiscriminable tags rather than the diverse visual content.

We also examined the "Concept Bank" feature, which cast each image into a concept space representation for classification. Although the new feature does not perform as well as the original feature in our experiments, it significantly reduced the feature dimension and training time while the performance is nearly 50% better than random projection. By increasing the concept space and possibly with selection, the "concept bank" feature has great potential on the task.

8. REFERENCES

[1] A. Berg et al. Large scale visual recognition challenge 2010, 2010.

[2] J. Deng et al. Imagenet: A large-scale hierarchical image database. In *CVPR*, 2009.

[3] J. Deng et al. What does classifying more than 10,000 image categories tell us? In *ECCV*, 2010.

[4] R.-E. Fan et al. LIBLINEAR: A library for large linear classification. *JMLR*, 9, 2008.

[5] H. Jégou et al. Aggregating local descriptors into a compact image representation. In *CVPR*, 2010.

[6] L.-J. Li et al. Object bank: A high-level image representation for scene classification and semantic feature sparsification. In *NIPS*, 2010.

[7] F. Perronnin et al. Improving the fisher kernel for large-scale image classification. In *ECCV*, 2010.

[8] J. Wang et al. Locality-constrained linear coding for image classification. In *CVPR*, 2010.

[9] H.-F. Yu et al. Large linear classification when data cannot fit in memory. In *KDD*, 2012.

Structured Exploration of Who, What, When, and Where in Heterogeneous Multimedia News Sources

Brendan Jou*, Hongzhi Li*, Joseph G. Ellis*,
Daniel Morozoff-Abegauz and Shih-Fu Chang

Digital Video & Multimedia Lab, Columbia University

ABSTRACT

We present a fully automatic system from raw data gathering to navigation over heterogeneous news sources, including over 18k hours of broadcast video news, 3.58M online articles, and 430M public Twitter messages. Our system addresses the challenge of extracting "who," "what," "when," and "where" from a truly multimodal perspective, leveraging audiovisual information in broadcast news and those embedded in articles, as well as textual cues in both closed captions and raw document content in articles and social media. Performed over time, we are able to extract and study the trend of topics in the news and detect interesting peaks in news coverage over the life of the topic. We visualize these peaks in trending news topics using automatically extracted keywords and iconic images, and introduce a novel multimodal algorithm for naming speakers in the news. We also present several intuitive navigation interfaces for interacting with these complex topic structures over different news sources.

Categories and Subject Descriptors

H.5.1 [**Information Interfaces and Presentation**]: Multimedia Information Systems; H.5.4 [**Information Interfaces and Presentation**]: Hypertext/Hypermedia

Keywords

Multimedia Analysis; Topic Linking; Speaker Diarization

1. INTRODUCTION

News today is arguably foundationally driven by just four of the five "W's" – *Who*, *What*, *When*, and *Where*. What happened? When did it happen? Where did it happen? Who was involved? Who said what? This natural progression of questions is a classic example of what one might ask about an event. Without any one of these questions, the story would fall flat and quickly become less captivating. For example, what is a story about a bombing without a mention of location and time? Each of the four W's are necessary to tell a full story.

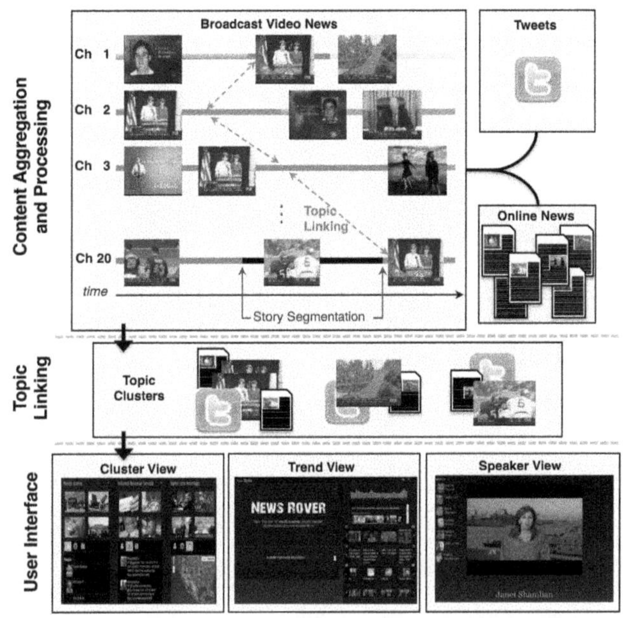

Figure 1: System Overview.

What about "Why" though – the fifth W? The goal of most news agencies and journalists is to bring as many facts as possible surrounding an event to the surface. As a result, *the why* tends to be relegated to opinion commentaries and post-event interview coverage. Further, the question of who, what, when and where an event happened precedes the question of why it happened. And so, our key motivating question was whether we could capture this principle quartet of W's, using each as a pillar toward a foundational platform to study and explore news in all its multimodal mediums.

Several works in academia and industry have been proposed to address similar challenges. Perhaps one of the most notable is the NIST TRECVID challenges, where from 2003 to 2006 there was a large focus on analyzing news productions and from 2007 to 2009 on more unconstrained news rushes. The goal in all these was to extract "name of the person/place/thing/event in the image/video" [12], that is, the four W's. However, the be-all-end-all in these experiments was exclusively video, and the breadth of topics is limited to those that get chosen for video broadcast. Instead, we expand the heterogeneity of our news sources in our system. Similarly, in the information extraction (IE)

*Denotes equal contribution.

MM'13, October 21–25, 2013, Barcelona, Spain.
Copyright 2013 ACM 978-1-4503-2404-5/13/10 ...$15.00.
http://dx.doi.org/10.1145/2502081.2508118.

community, a significant effort has been focused on detecting events and topics in newswire documents [11] and social media [2]. Another recent challenge called REPERE [10] is also focused on answering the questions, "Who is speaking? Who is present in the video? What names are cited? What names are displayed?" for European broadcast news. Our focus here will be not only on the persons or names, but also on the larger scope of the events and topics themselves, utilizing the full set of information in U.S. broadcast news which naturally differs programmatically from European news. We propose a unified framework where *both* news articles and social media posts, namely from Twitter, *and* broadcast video intersect, where events and entities are indexed regardless of media type by extracted topic structures. An overview of our system can be seen in Fig. 1

Our key contributions include (1) a recording architecture that archives and processes over 700 hours of video and 72k online articles per week, (2) a hierachically organized topic structure indexing who, what, when, and where, (3) a topic trend summarization method, (4) a novel approach to named multimodal speaker diarization and transcription, and (5) several novel user interfaces to navigate heterogeneous multimodal news.

2. SYSTEM ARCHITECTURE

2.1 Data Collection

Recording and Crawling. A major component of our system is recording and processing a variety of news content available through broadcast and cable news outlets. We use 12 cable tuners with on-chip encoding to simultaneously record. We currently have the capability to record news from about 100 U.S. English-speaking channels. To maximize our news recording coverage, we developed an automatic scheduling program that finds news programs using an online electronic program guide, and automatically queues them for recording by available tuners.

Along with our broadcast video recording capabilities, we also developed crawlers for Google News and Twitter feeds. Our Google News crawler searches every five minutes for new articles and indexes each document by the topic ontology defined by Google News. By retaining the topics from Google News and not just the articles, we are able to incorporate current trending topics as well as define a separate set of long-term topics we wish to track. In particular, there are 2,000 popular long-term news topics, such as the "Syrian Revolution" and "North Korea," that we always search for regardless of if they make the front page of Google News. Our Twitter crawler takes a similar approach, finding and retaining Twitter trends and popular hashtags. We index these Twitter trends and their associated "tweets", while also maintaining a list of 2,000 long-term popular topics on Twitter. Weekly recording statistics are in Table 1.

Table 1: Average Estimates of Data Per Week.

Programs recorded	700	Online articles	72,000
Hours of video	700	Google topics	4,000
Stories segmented	7,000	Twitter trends	3,500

Story Segmentation. The news programs we record are often 30 minutes to one-hour long and contain news commentary or reporting on a variety of different stories as well as commercials. Our news recording and processing system automatically finds the boundaries between these story segments and cuts up the original program into individual story segments that can be linked to topics and more easily consumed by an end user.

Closed captions (CC) are required by law to be made available for all U.S. news programs and many CC transcripts include special markers that denote the end of a story segment, >>>, and speaker changes, >>. Closed captions often lag the actual audiovisual content of the program by 10-15 seconds. And so, to acquire an accurate boundary detection for story segments we perform Automatic Speech Recognition (ASR) on the entire news program and then temporally align the CC transcript with the output of ASR using dynamic time warping. We further refine the boundary precision by aligning the story marker to the closest detected shot boundary. In cases where special markers do not exist in CC, we will apply our previous work using multimodal segmentation [7] that proved a F1 score performance of 0.76.

2.2 Topic Structures

News media is hierarchical in nature and generally characterized by a group of documents, often from different sources and media types, surrounding a single event. A news topic can be these single, one-off events, but can also be a concept or a collection of events. For example, one might imagine the 2012 Olympics as a topic of news-worthy discussion, but the Olympics itself, as a collection of events and concept, could be a topic as well. Topics form the "what" of news.

To discover and mine topics in the news, many previous works have employed Latent Dirichlet Allocation (LDA) and its variants. However, today, there are also a number of commercial platforms that apply proprietary topic discovery algorithms using implicit, but strong signals like user traffic. Google News extracts trending topics from the online articles largely using search logs and click-through traffic [4]. Twitter mines hot trends from tweets by potentially leveraging content sharing (i.e. re-tweets) and publish-throughput via hashtags. Our system collects trending topics from these sources, including Google News, Google Search Statistics and Twitter, and combines them into a generic pool. We keep an active list of these trending topics, continuously assigning incoming tweets, articles, and video to topics.

Given our gathered topics and their associated articles and tweets, we then need to link in the video news stories. We use a multi-modal topic linking method to assign each video news story to a topic. As shown in Fig. 2, we extract keyframes from each video and perform near-duplicate image matching to topic-organized images crawled from the online news articles and tweets. We also use the CC transcript from the story segments for text matching using a term-frequency inverse-document-frequency (TF-IDF) model.

Entity Extraction. From each story segment's CC transcript we perform named entity extraction [6], including persons, locations, and organizations. This naturally gives us the "who" and "where" that are associated with stories and topics. As our CC transcript is time-aligned with ASR, accurate time stamps are known for each word, and therefore we know when each entity is mentioned in each story segment. Since CC names are not always accurate, and often times people are referred to by only their first name, we use community-edited databases like DBpedia and Wikipedia to perform name co-referencing over all news stories and topics.

Topic Trend Visualization & Representation. Hav-

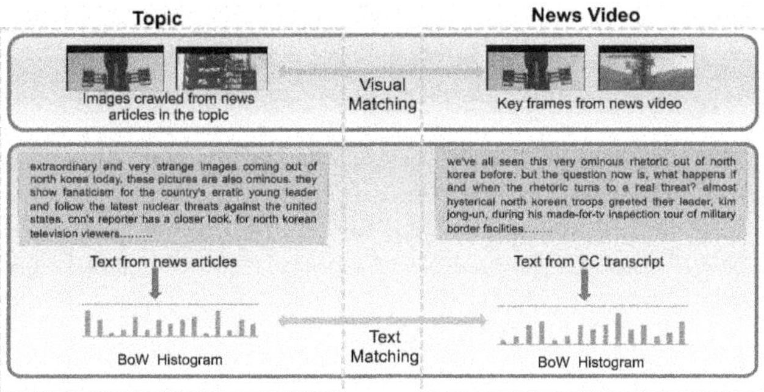

Figure 2: Topic Matching Process.

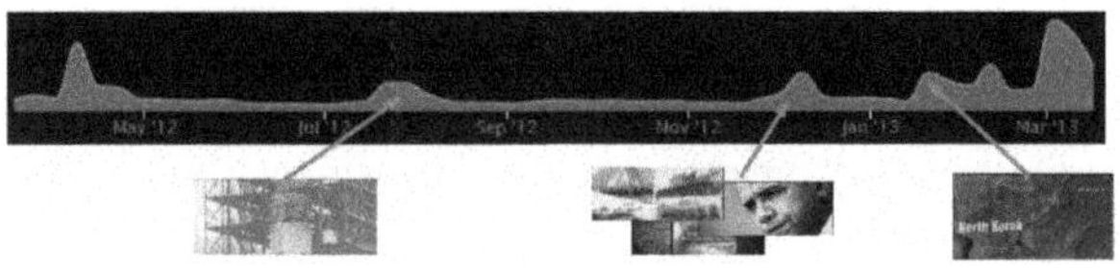

Figure 3: Example Trend for "North Korea" Topic.

ing collected data for the "long-term" topics over the past three months, we are able to track the news coverage a single topic receives over time. A "traffic" curve for a topic is visualized as in Fig. 3, where the y-axis represents the volume of news content we have linked to this topic versus publish time. In the trend, we observe visible peaks for times when there is heightened news coverage on this topic.

The question then is how we can quickly understand what happened "when," for each of these peaks or (sub-)events. We approach this summarization problem in two ways. In one approach, we extracted keywords and phrases from articles appearing often within each peak [3] and simply used the most commonly occurring words or phrases. However, we noted that certain pictures or scenes in the news are often repeated by multiple news programs during important events. These iconic images are highly descriptive, conveying information in a succinct and complete way that text cannot. To quickly detect these reoccurring images we have implemented a near-duplicate detection algorithm to find these reoccurring scenes or images. Example results of extracted representative images are shown in Fig. 3.

3. WHO SAID WHAT

"Talking heads" are a critical facet of news reporting. As we have addressed the challenge of extracting the four W's, deeper and interesting structures can be explored in the relationship between two or more of these W's. We begin to study these relationships by tackling the combination of *who* and *what* in broadcast news. In particular, we seek to address the question of "who said what," that is, naming speaking persons and determining their respective quotes.

The problem of speaker diarization is the closest to our setting. Speaker diarization seeks to answer the question of "who spoke when," often by clustering detected speech and mapping clusters to names [1]. Recently, [13] explored multimodal speaker diarization using a Dynamic Bayesian Network in both the business meeting and broadcast news videos. Several works extending from [5], have tried to tackle a similar problem using multimodal information for television shows but rely on the a priori presence of fully annotated transcripts that have names mapped to spoken text.

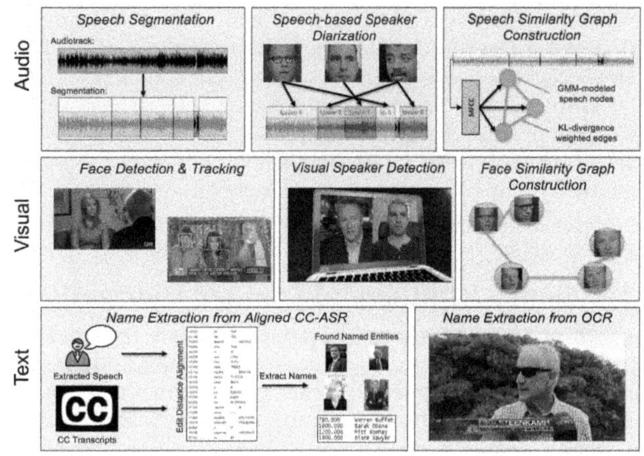

Figure 4: "Who Said What" Features.

Such transcripts are not available in broadcast news and make it far more challenging without this supervision.

Our approach differs from these previous approaches in one fundamental way: we have a more stringent definition of "who." For a useful system, we require that "who" does not simply mean a class or cluster number but rather an actual name, and to do so without manual intervention. We also exploit the multimodal aspect of the "who said what" problem by using audio, visual, and textual cues.

3.1 Speaker Representation

Visual/Facial. We perform face detection on the news stories using OpenCV's Haar-like cascade and then extract SIFT features from detected landmark points within each detected face [15]. We generate face tracks by exploiting temporal and spatial continuity within the detected faces. Finally, we compute the similarity between face tracks using a Gaussian Kernel distance between every pair of faces in the tracks, and then average the distance in the top face pairs.

We also perform text detection on sampled frames from the stories to extract on-screen person names. These names from optical character recognition (OCR), along with those from CC, are combined and normalized to form the set of candidate name labels during the prediction stage.

Audio/Speech. As our basic visual unit is the *face track*, our basic audio unit is a *speech segment*. Speech segments denote contiguous speech by one or more persons without extended silence. We extract segments by applying the segmentation tool in [8]. On average, detected speech segments are 2.3 seconds long. To measure the similarity between segments, we extract MFCCs from each audio segment and model each as a multivariate Gaussian. The distance between speech segments is measured by the symmetric Kullback-Leibler (KL) divergence over the multivariate Gaussian distributions [14], and then a Gaussian kernel over the KL-distances normalized by the standard deviation of all the distances in a story segment.

Multimodal. In order to link the audio and visual features, we use a variant of the visual speaker detection in [5]. This knowledge of who is visually speaking allows us to disambiguate from whom speech is coming from when there is more than one person on-screen. Instead of a pure visual speaker detection, we take a hybrid multimodal approach to detecting visual speakers. Using the facial landmarks, we affine-align the face, determine the mouth region and perform template matching to detect whether the face is speaking. Repeating this over the entire face track, we get a series of best template matches which correspond to the smallest sum of square differences for "inter-frames" or frame pairs. Following [5], two thresholds are used to predict if the "inter-frame" is non-speaking, reject and speaking. We use majority voting within face tracks that overlap speech segments to predict if the face is visually speaking.

3.2 Named Multimodal Speaker Diarization

Given our multimodal speaker identity cues, we position our problem in a transductive learning setting and use label inference over a heterogeneous graph with weak labels, which correspond to the names automatically extracted from the news video. We create a visual subgraph consisting of face tracks and an audio subgraph consisting of speech segments, both constructed using b-matching [9]. Cross-modal edges are formed between vertices of the two subgraphs if a face track temporally overlaps a speech segment and is detected as speaking via our multimodal speaker detection algorithm.

We apply the extracted names from CC and OCR as weak labels on our constructed graph. Two approaches to weak label assignment have proven effective in our experiments. First, if a face track temporally overlaps with an occurrence of an OCR name on-screen we assign the name to that face node. Second, if a new face track appears on screen up to 10 seconds after a CC name appears in the transcript, we assign the CC name to this face node.

These weak labels are then propagated on the graph using local and global consistency [9], enforcing smoothness using the normalized Laplacian and softly constraining the solution to the labels since they are weak. We set the highest scoring label and its corresponding name as the prediction for each node in the graph. Given the predicted names for speakers, getting the "what," or quote, related to them is now trivial because we have their associated speech segments and simply extract the portion of closed captions that is time-locked with the speech.

To evaluate our performance, we collected annotations using Amazon's Mechanical Turk over 225 detected face tracks from NBC Nightly News and News 4 New York over an average of 5 to 7 unique names per story. We limited our face tracks to a subset of mostly frontal tracks by performing a second pass of face detection using a higher threshold. When considering all identities, including those who never spoke, we correctly labeled 105 face tracks for a total accuracy of 0.475, using the extracted CC and OCR names as weak labels. This represents a significant improvement over simply using CC or OCR names as weak labels alone, which give accuracies of 0.284 and 0.40, respectively. Additionally, as our goal is to name speakers, if we limit to speaking non-anchors appearing on-screen, we achieve an accuracy of 0.619.

4. NAVIGATION INTERFACE

We have developed three novel interfaces that showcase the hierarchy of our extracted topics from the story linking capability to individual topics, and who-said-what speaker identification. First, our "topic cluster" interface shows a user the major news topics or stories of the day as well as a quick summary of each topic via "who," "what," and "where." Second, our "topic exploration" interface allows exploration of news videos, articles, tweets, and people involved in a particular topic. The content shuffles and rearranges dynamically based on user clicks over the trend indicating the "when" of a topic, and we present our visual summarization of the topic as well. Last, our "who said what" interface showcases a video and dynamically changing name display, including biographical information like a Wikipedia page and image. Screenshots of these interfaces are in Fig 1.

5. CONCLUSION

We have presented a unique and novel system integrating heterogeneous multimodal news sources including broadcast news, online articles, and Twitter tweets. Extracting topics over time we are able to generate trends, observe peaks in each topic, and summarize each (sub-)event per trend by keywords and iconic images. In addition, we presented a novel multimodal speaker diarization framework using label propagation that is able to directly infer names in broadcast video automatically without manual intervention for class-name assignment. We also showed several intuitive interfaces that streamline the navigation of these modalities and gives a fresh look at news past and present. In the future, we plan to pursue a user study to evaluate the utility of our system for understanding and structuring the news.

6. REFERENCES

[1] X. Anguera Miro, S. Bozonnet, N. Evans, C. Fredouille, G. Friedland, and O. Vinyals. Speaker diarization: A review of recent research. *ASLP*, 2012.

[2] H. Becker, M. Naaman, and L. Gravano. Beyond trending topics: Real-world event identification on Twitter. In *ICWSM*, 2011.

[3] E. L. Bird, Steven and E. Klein. *Natural Language Processing with Python*. O'Reilly Media Inc., 2009.

[4] A. S. Das, M. Datar, A. Garg, and S. Rajaram. Google News personalization: Scalable online collaborative filtering. In *WWW*, 2007.

[5] M. Everingham, J. Sivic, and A. Zisserman. Taking the bite out of automated naming of characters in TV video. *Image Vision Computing*, 2009.

[6] J. R. Finkel, T. Grenager, and C. Manning. Incorporating non-local information into information extraction systems by gibbs sampling. In *ACL*, 2005.

[7] W. Hsu, L. Kennedy, C.-W. Huang, S.-F. Chang, C.-Y. Lin, and G. Iyengar. News video story segmentation using fusion of multi-level multi-modal features in TRECVID 2003. In *ICASSP*, 2004.

[8] M. Huijbregts. *Segmentation, Diarization, and Speech Transcription: Suprise Data Unraveled*. PhD thesis, University of Twente, 2008.

[9] T. Jebara, J. Wang, and S.-F. Chang. Graph construction and b-matching for semi-supervised learning. In *ICML*, 2009.

[10] J. Kahn, O. Galibert, L. Quintard, M. Carre, A. Giraudel, and P. Joly. A presentation of the REPERE challenge. In *CBMI*, 2012.

[11] Q. Li, S. Anzaroot, W.-P. Lin, X. Li, and H. Ji. Joint inference for cross-document information extraction. In *CIKM*, 2011.

[12] National Institute of Standards and Technology. Text REtrieval Conference (TREC): VIDeo track (TRECVID).

[13] A. Noulas, G. Englebienne, and B. J. A. Kröse. Multimodal speaker diarization. *PAMI*, 2012.

[14] M. A. Siegler, U. Jain, B. Raj, and R. M. Stern. Automatic segmentation, classification and clustering of broadcast news audio. In *DARPA Speech Recogn. Workshop*, 1997.

[15] M. Uřičář, V. Franc, and V. Hlaváč. Detector of facial landmarks learned by the structured output SVM. In *VISAPP*. SciTePress, 2012.

Towards a Comprehensive Computational Model for Aesthetic Assessment of Videos

Subhabrata Bhattacharya
subh@cs.ucf.edu

Behnaz Nojavanasghari
behnaz@eecs.ucf.edu

Tao Chen
taochen@ee.columbia.edu

Dong Liu
dongliu@ee.columbia.edu

Shih-Fu Chang
sfchang@ee.columbia.edu

Mubarak Shah
shah@cs.ucf.edu

ABSTRACT

In this paper we propose a novel aesthetic model emphasizing psycho-visual statistics extracted from multiple levels in contrast to earlier approaches that rely only on descriptors suited for image recognition or based on photographic principles. At the lowest level, we determine dark-channel, sharpness and eye-sensitivity statistics over rectangular cells within a frame. At the next level, we extract Sentibank features (1,200 pre-trained visual classifiers) on a given frame, that invoke specific sentiments such as "colorful clouds", "smiling face" etc. and collect the classifier responses as frame-level statistics. At the topmost level, we extract trajectories from video shots. Using viewer's fixation priors, the trajectories are labeled as foreground, and background/camera on which statistics are computed. Additionally, spatio-temporal local binary patterns are computed that capture texture variations in a given shot. Classifiers are trained on individual feature representations independently. On thorough evaluation of 9 different types of features, we select the best features from each level – dark channel, affect and camera motion statistics. Next, corresponding classifier scores are integrated in a sophisticated low-rank fusion framework to improve the final prediction scores. Our approach demonstrates strong correlation with human prediction on 1,000 broadcast quality videos released by NHK as an aesthetic evaluation dataset.

Category and Subject Descriptors: H.4 [Information Systems Applications] : Miscellaneous

Keywords: Video Aesthetics, Affect features, Camera motion features, Cinematography, Low Rank late fusion

1. INTRODUCTION

Automatic aesthetic ranking of images or videos is an extremely challenging problem as it is very difficult to quantify beauty. That said, computational video aesthetics [4, 7–11, 13, 14] has received significant attention in recent years. With the deluge of multimedia sharing websites, research in this direction is expected to gain more impetus in future, apart from the obvious intellectual challenge in scientific formulation of a concept as abstract as *beauty*.

MM'13, October 21–25, 2013, Barcelona, Spain.
Copyright 2013 ACM 978-1-4503-2404-5/13/10 ...$15.00.
http://dx.doi.org/10.1145/2502081.2508119.

Figure 1: **Video aesthetic assessment: Top row shows frames from videos ranked from** $1-5$ **and bottom row shows the bottom** 5 **ranked videos in the NHK video aesthetic dataset, using the proposed approach. Numbers in parentheses indicate deviation from ground truth rankings. Our approach correctly predicts video** 0431 **(bottom right) to be the lowest ranked.**

Since there is no well-defined set of rules following which any image or video can be deemed as beautiful, the problem can be posed appropriately in machine learning paradigm. In this vein, the authors of [4, 7] propose the use of low-level statistical features e.g., hue count, blur, saturation to predict aesthetic appeal. [9] insinuated using these properties for foreground regions, which intuitively is a more reasonable approach. However it involves segmentation. Later these are circumvented using visual saliency maps [22] or dedicated content based classifiers [8].

In contrast to these customized statistics that are believed to capture some aspects of aesthetics, the authors of [10] propose the use of image descriptors popular in object recognition literature to assess beauty of photographs. Except for a few earlier efforts [9, 11, 13], most research efforts are concentrated on modeling aesthetic in still images. While features proposed in [4, 7, 8, 10, 14] demonstrate some success for images, we argue that these do not necessarily apply to videos. For example, rule of thirds – a composition guideline used to assess photography, requires foreground to be aligned to 4 specific locations in an image frame [8, 9]. Videos captured with such constraints, tend to have non-moving foreground and lead to viewer dissatisfaction [13]. Also, cinematographic techniques – camera motion, lighting changes etc. are often introduced in produced videos to increase their aesthetic appeal, which cannot be captured using aesthetics based on single images.

Motivated by the above, we propose a hierarchical framework encapsulating aesthetics at multiple levels which can be used independently or jointly to model beauty in videos. Our contributions are: (1) We extract motion statistics that latently encode cinematographic principles, specific to foreground and background or camera, superior to approaches proposed in [9, 11, 13], (2) We introduce application of human sentiment classifiers on image frames that capture vital affective cues which are directly correlated with visual aesthetics and are semantically more interpretable than [8], (3) We employ a relatively small set of low-level psychovisual [15, 18] features as opposed to [4, 7, 9, 10, 14] and encode them efficiently into descriptors that capture spatial variations within video frames, and finally, (4) We exploit a more sophisticated fusion scheme [21] that show consistent improvement in overall ranking when compared to methods used in [10, 11, 13]. Section 2 discusses computation of these features in detail.

2. VIDEO AESTHETICS

We analyze a video at multiple granularities employing three strategies, each catering to specific aspects of aesthetics. Each video is divided into shots and for each shot, keyframes are selected uniformly. Following this, features are selected at three levels – cell, frame and shot.

2.1 Cell-level

At this level, each keyframe in a shot is divided into $m \times m$ grids of rectangular cells. Each cell ($\{A_j\}_{j=1}^{m\times m}$) is further described using the following statistics, thus providing a mean to analyze low-level aesthetics in different spatial regions: (a) The **Dark-channel** statistics, proposed in [5] and used in [8], is essentially a minimum filter on RGB channels which reflects local clarity, saturation, and hue composition in a given image (I) subjected to a neighborhood, $\Omega(i)$ around i-th pixel. For j-th, cell the dark channel feature is computed in Eqn. (1) as:

$$F_{dc}(j) = \sum_{(i)\in A_j} \frac{\min\limits_{c\in R,G,B}\big(\min\limits_{i'\in\Omega(i)} I_c(i')\big)}{\sum\limits_{c\in R,G,B} I_c(i)}, \tag{1}$$

with each real valued numbers normalized by the cell area. (b) **Sharpness** statistics are derived from squared root of the product of spectral map (α_{x_j}) and sharpness map computed over 8-pixel row (x_j^r) and column neighborhoods (x_j^c) of the gray-scale equivalent (x_j) of a cell from a color frame (A_j). The simplified formulation from [19] as given in Eqn. (2)

$$F_{sp}(j) = \left[\left(1 - \frac{1}{1+e^{-3(\alpha_{x_j}-2)}}\right)\left(\frac{1}{4}\max_{r,c}\frac{\sum\limits_{r,c}|x_j^r - x_j^c|}{255}\right)\right]^{\frac{1}{2}}, \tag{2}$$

captures the perceived sharpness of j-th cell, indicating the amount of detail in each cell. (c) **Eye-sensitivity** is one of the oldest known aesthetic attribute known to humans, which is associated with the visual cortex's sensitivity to colors of certain wavelength in the visible spectrum. We obtain this by building a weighted color histogram for a given cell using the corresponding color sensitivity scores predefined in [18]. The peak of the histogram represents the sensitivity score with respect to the human eye, for a given cell and is used as our final cell level statistics ($\mathbf{F_{es}}$).

2.2 Frame-level

Global frame-level descriptors as used in [10] are more suited in for recognition of scenes or objects, primarily due to their invariance towards pose, viewpoints, illuminance condition under which images are captured etc. We hypothesize that such properties are not desired in the current problem context and resort to detection of a more abstract concept – *human affect* present in a given video frame. We apply a large set of affect based classifiers from a recent work by Borth and colleagues [2], hereafter being referred to as SentiBank Detectors. These detectors are founded on a psychological research known as Plutchik's Wheel of Emotions [15].

To train this detector library, a Visual Sentiment Ontology is firstly built by data-driven discovery from Internet: adjective and noun tags are extracted from Flickr and Youtube based on their co-occurrence with each of the 24 emotions defined in Plutchik's theory. These tags are then assigned with sentiment values and used to form Adjective Noun Pairs (ANP) such as "cold winter" or "happy baby". More than $3,000$ ANPs are then selected to form the ontology based on their frequency ranking on Flickr and semantic coverage. For each ANP of the ontology a detector is trained from Flickr images that are tagged with this ANP and only $1,200$ ANP concept detectors are selected according to the detector performance to form the SentiBank detectors library, which we apply on video frames to generate a $1,200$ dimensional ANP detector response, hereafter referred to as $\mathbf{F_{af}}$. Fig. 2 demonstrates the results of applying a small subset of these detectors on 4 different keyframes from $1,000$ videos in the NHK video aesthetics dataset. In each case, we observe direct correlation between the sentiment invoked in a viewer with the individual detector's confidence, which argues in favor of their applicability in this context.

Figure 2: Results of applying sentiment classifiers on 4 different keyframes from the NHK dataset. A subset of 10 unique classifiers listed on the right of the figure, are applied on the keyframes shown above. Detection confidence for each of these classifiers for all 4 images are shown as a barchart.

2.3 Shot-level

This is the final level of our feature hierarchy where we compute three different statistics from a video shot based on (a) **Foreground** and (b) **Background motion** and (c) **Texture dynamics**. To accomplish the former two tasks, we track distinctive points [16] from a sequence of frames in a shot, to get meaningful trajectories. Since trajectories can either belong to moving foreground objects and either non-moving background or moving camera, we further apply a Bayesian spatio-temporal saliency detection algorithm [22] based on natural image statistics, employing priors from viewer's eye fixation. This generates a coarse map for every frame with regions corresponding to foreground with high saliency and those to background with low saliency. Using this coarse map, trajectories are labeled whether they are emanated from either foreground or background.

For both types of trajectories, we independently perform a low-rank matrix decomposition using [3] to find dominant trajectories belonging to both motion classes. The low-rank assumption is based on the observation that: all trajectories belonging to either foreground or background, when stacked together, form a matrix which can be factorized into a low-rank component and a noise component. This step ensures further refining of trajectories obtained initially. First k-components of the low-rank matrix identify the dominant trajectories. Finally each dominant trajectory is described using statistically invariant features listed as: mean, standard deviation, range, minimum, maximum, l_1 and l_2 norm. Thus, in this case, a 2 dimensional x, y trajectory of arbitrary length, is reduced to a 2×7 dimensional vector, denoted as $\mathbf{F_{fg}}$ or $\mathbf{F_{bg}}$ depending on its source (foreground or background/camera).

In addition, we also represent a shot based on its texture dynamics. For this purpose, we employ a spatio-temporal local-binary pattern algorithm [23], for describing volumetric texture variations in videos. The spatio-temporal LBP descriptor is computed by binning LBP codes along a small spatio-temporal neighborhood in three orthogonal planes: $x-y$, $x-t$ and $y-t$. Hence the final descriptor for a shot is given by a histogram ($\mathbf{F_{tx}}$) of 3×2^n, n indicating the spatial-pixel neighborhood in x, y plane.

All descriptors are further clustered independently using a fast k-means clustering algorithm [12] to create vocabularies of different sizes. Thereafter, each video is described using separate bag-of-X representations obtained by standard vector quantization. Here X denotes a particular feature type from our pool of features: $\mathbf{F_{dc}}$ (dark channel), $\mathbf{F_{sp}}$ (sharpness), $\mathbf{F_{es}}$ (eye-sensitivity), $\mathbf{F_{af}}$ (affect), $\mathbf{F_{fg}}$ (foreground motion), $\mathbf{F_{bg}}$ (background motion), and $\mathbf{F_{tx}}$ (texture dynamics). Finally, bag-of-X representations for a particular feature type, are used in a ranking SVM framework [6] to learn an aesthetic model for the given feature type. In the next section, we discuss how individual models generated from complementary features, can be efficiently fused to produce a final aesthetic model.

2.4 Rank Fusion

We employ the Low-Rank Late Fusion (LRLF) scheme [21] to fuse the ranking scores from m ranking SVM models, each of which is trained with one specific aesthetic feature. The advantage of this fusion scheme is that it is not only isotonic to the numeric scales of scores from different models but also removes the prediction errors from each model. Given a ranking score vector $\mathbf{s}^i = \{s_1^i, \ldots, s_n^i\}$ from the i-th model, where n is the number of videos and each s_j^i denotes the ranking score of the j-th video predicted by the i-th model. We convert it into an comparative relationship matrix T^i such that $T_{jk}^i = 1$ if $s_j^i > s_k^i$, $T_{jk}^i = -1$ if $s_j^i < s_k^i$ and $T_{jk}^i = 1$ if $s_j^i = s_k^i$. In this way, the real-valued score vector is encoded as an integer matrix, which gets rid of the numeric scale variances among scores from different models. Taking the comparative relationship matrices $\{T^i, i = 1, \ldots, m\}$ as input, LRLF scheme seeks a shared rank-2 matrix through which each T^i can be decomposed into a common rank-2 matrix and a sparse error matrix. Our hypothesis behind the rank-2 matrix is that if ideal score vector $\mathbf{s}^*$ exists, the real-valued comparative relation matrix T^* is a rank-2 matrix formed by $T^* = \mathbf{s}^*\mathbf{e}^\top - \mathbf{e}\mathbf{s}^{*\top}$, where $\mathbf{e}$ is a all-one vector. LRLF considers the reverse problem: Based on the inferred rank-2 matrix $\hat{T}$, it performs rank-2 factorization of $\hat{T}$ such that $\hat{T} = \hat{\mathbf{s}}\mathbf{e}^\top - \mathbf{e}\hat{\mathbf{s}}^\top$. Finally, the recovered $\mathbf{s}^\top$ can be used as final fused score for video aesthetic ranking.

3. EXPERIMENTS

We evaluate our algorithm on the recently released "NHK - Where is beauty?" dataset, consisting of $1,000$ broadcast quality videos, aesthetically ranked from best (1) to worst ($1,000$) by humans. In our setup, each keyframe from a video is divided into 3×3 grids containing a total number of 9 cells. Empirically, $m = 3$ implicitly mandates one of the composition rules proposed in [1, 4, 9] – the rule of thirds, hence a natural choice. Sharpness for a cell, described using minimum, maximum, mean and standard deviation of the S_3 map discussed in Eqn. (2) leads to a 9×4 dimensional vector i.e, $\mathbf{F_{sp}} \in \mathbb{R}^{36}$. Dark channel and eye-sensitivity are measured described using the mean and maximum values for a given cell, respectively, implying $\mathbf{F_{dc}} \in \mathbb{R}^9$ and $\mathbf{F_{es}} \in \mathbb{R}^9$. For frame level features, we replicate the experimental setup in [2]. For shot-level features, k is empirically set to 5 to select top 5 dominant trajectories from each of the two motion classes. Finally, while computing the texture dynamics descriptor based on [23], we consider a $5 \times 5 \times 5$ neighborhood yielding $\mathbf{F_{tx}} \in \mathbb{R}^{96}$ ($3 \times 2^5 = 96$).

In addition, we implemented two independent baselines inspired from [10] whose performance are recorded in top two rows in Tab. 1. The two baselines are generated on generic image [17] (BL-I) and video [20] (BL-V) descriptors, widely used in recognition tasks. All descriptors are randomly sampled from 200 videos to construct vocabularies with different sizes $(128, 256, 512, 1024)$ and subsequently for every vocabulary-feature combination, bag-of-X representations are generated for all videos. We use SVM rank [6] on linear kernels using the 1-slack (dual) with constraint cache optimization algorithm, to train separate models for each setting. We employ a 5-fold cross validation scheme to select the cost parameter for each SVM. Once parameters are selected, we use the regular query setting with $80\% - 20\%$ (training - testing) split, ensuring testing samples do not appear during the training phase for a particular split. Thus with 5 splits, we can generate the ranks for all videos in the dataset. Finally, evaluation is performed using the Kendall (τ) and Spearman's (ρ) rank correlation coefficients:

$$\tau = \frac{N_c - N_d}{\frac{1}{2}N(N-1)}, \text{and} \quad \rho = 1 - \frac{6\sum d_i^2}{N(N^2-1)}, \qquad (3)$$

where N_c and N_d denote the number of concordant and discordant pairs respectively, N being total number of samples $= 1000$, and d_i being the difference of between the ground truth and predicted ranks. Both τ and ρ can take values between $[-1, 1]$, where -1, 1 indicating ground truth rank and predicted ranks are completely reverse, and same, respectively, while 0 signifies no-correlation between the two rank sets.

Feature	Kendall's coefficient (τ) 128	256	512	$1,024$	Spearman's coefficient (ρ) 128	256	512	$1,024$
BL-I	-0.011	0.001	0.006	-0.002	-0.041	0.014	-0.013	0.012
BL-V	0.001	-0.021	0.012	0.001	0.001	0.001	-0.002	-0.049
$\mathbf{F_{dc}}$	0.014	**0.017**	0.016	0.013	0.039	**0.025**	0.045	0.044
$\mathbf{F_{sp}}$	-0.018	0.017	0.014	0.023	-0.027	-0.003	0.026	0.031
$\mathbf{F_{es}}$	0.003	0.004	0.006	0.001	-0.004	-0.004	0.004	-0.002
$\mathbf{F_{af}}$	0.028	0.021	0.034	**0.030**	0.035	0.041	0.045	**0.046**
$\mathbf{F_{fg}}$	0.009	**0.005**	0.011	0.013	0.015	**0.008**	0.013	0.021
$\mathbf{F_{bg}}$	**0.027**	0.041	0.039	-0.016	**0.039**	0.044	0.047	-0.018
$\mathbf{F_{tx}}$	-0.001	-0.001	-0.002	**-0.000**	0.001	-0.004	-0.003	**-0.003**
FUSED	0.0861				0.1266			

Table 1: Summary of experiments using classifiers trained on different Bag-of-X representations of baseline features from [17] (BL-I) and [20] (BL-V), followed by our proposed features (labeled as $\mathbf{F_{xx}}$). The row labeled FUSED shows the best fusion results obtained after combining 5 different feature combinations (indicated in bold) using [21].

Tab. 1 summarizes all our experiments. For every feature - vocabulary combination, both Kendall(τ) and Spearman (ρ) are reported. Our proposed psychovisual features perform significantly better than the baselines reported as BL-I and BL-V in top two rows. Thus, classifiers trained on generic image level descriptors such as colorSIFT [17] and video level descriptors such as MBH [20] are not suited for quantifying video aesthetics. Intuitively, this can be explained from the following observations: (a) colorSIFT descriptors on high-quality images capture more detail (Flickr images as shown in [10]) as compared to low-resolution 640×360 video frames from the NHK dataset, and (b) MBH [20] descriptors are unable to differentiate between motion originating from background or foreground, which is necessary for describing motion based aesthetics, resulting into generation of suboptimal aesthetic models.

The last row in Tab. 1 (FUSED), shows fusion [21] results obtained from a two-step process: first we use cross validation to select top 5 features (which may use different vocabulary sizes) based on high ρ and τ values. Next we use various late fusion methods (score averaging, normalized rank, and low-rank fusion [21]) to fuse these independent 5 scoring models. Thus selecting an optimal algorithm for fusing knowledge from individual models, boosts overall performance. More detailed analysis of fusion is provided in Fig. 4. It is evident that models built on shot-level features: camera/background motion perform well with smaller vocabulary sizes, in comparison to the ones that are trained using texture descriptors and sentibank features - which perform better with larger vocabularies.

We also observe that, shot level features : camera/background and foreground motion statistics outperform all other features in most cases. It is also interesting to note that frame-level sentibank features also perform equally well. Among cell-level features, dark channel based statistics demonstrate best performance. This is further supported by the scatter plot in Fig. 3(a). Ideally, the dots in the figures are expected to be along the line that connects $(1, 1)$ to $(1000, 1000)$, indicating no discordance between ground truth rank and predicted rank. We notice that magenta dots, corresponding to dark channel features are more aligned to the line, than those belonging to sharpness or eye-sensitivity.

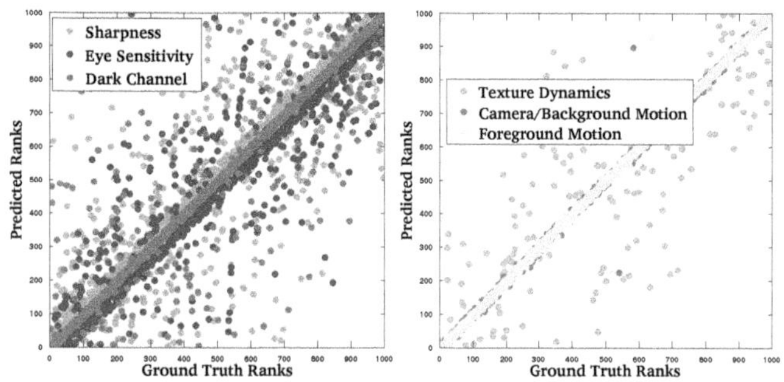

(a) (b)

Figure 3: Scatter plot showing label disagreement between (a) Cell-level (Dark channel – Magenta , Sharpness – Green, Eye-sensitivity – Blue), and, (b) Shot-level (Foreground motion – Yellow, Camera/Background motion – Cyan, Texture dynamics – Red) feature based classifiers (Best viewed when zoomed). Each dot is plotted according to Cartesian pairs (Ground Truth Rank, Predicted Rank).

However, in case of shot level features, we observe a larger degree of agreement between the ground truth and the prediction, in comparison to the cell-level features. This is reflected in Fig. 3(b). Finally, in Fig. 4, we provide some results using classifiers trained on frame-level affect based features (Orange). Except for a few ($< 5\%$), we see strong label agreement between ground truth and prediction - similar to the shot-level features. This encourages us to fuse the individual classifier outcomes in 3 different settings. These results are also shown in Fig. 4. Fusion of classifiers trained on affect and dark channel based features are indicated in Turquoise. These results are further improved after adding classifiers trained on camera/background motion (Lime green). Ultimately fusion results from classifiers trained on top 5 features is shown in Pink. We notice strong level of concordance in this setting.

4. CONCLUSION

We proposed a novel model for assessing beauty of broadcast quality videos, emphasizing on statistics from multiple granularities i.e. cells within keyframes, entire frame and shots. Specifically, we introduced three novel features – affect statistics at frame level, and motion statistics of foreground and background at shot level. Through extensive experiments, we demonstrated that using only a handful of carefully selected features, and efficiently fusing models learned on top them, can greatly increase the performance of aesthetic evaluation over previously published approaches. Although

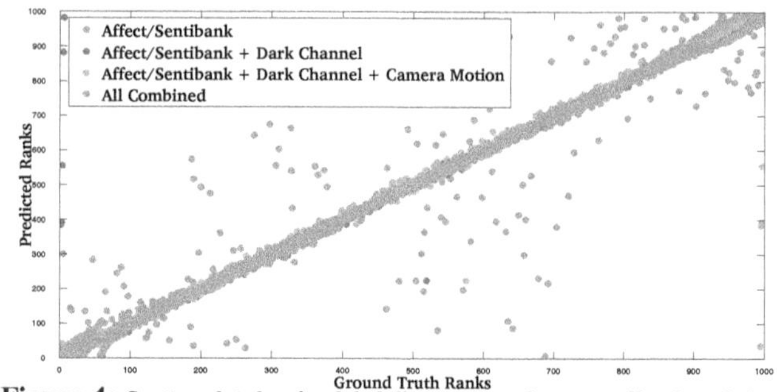

Figure 4: Scatter plot showing label disagreement between affect based classifier results (Orange) versus ground truth. Fusion results are also shown : affect + dark channel (Turquoise), affect + dark channel + camera/background motion (Lime green), and top 5 features combined (Pink). Refer to Fig. 3 for details on interpretation.

our results indicate significant performance gain over prior work, we conjecture that there is still plenty of scopes for further improvement. Since research in aesthetic quality assessment of videos is currently at an inchoate stage, we intend to explore how knowledge from different domains images, audio, text etc. can be exploited in this direction, as part of our future work.

5. REFERENCES

[1] S. Bhattacharya, R. Sukthankar, and M. Shah. A holistic approach to aesthetic enhancement of photographs. *TOMCCAP*, 7(Supplement):21, 2011.

[2] D. Borth, R. Ji, T. Chen, T. Breuel, and S.-F. Chang. Large-scale visual sentiment ontology and detectors using adjective noun pairs. In *ACM MM*, 2013.

[3] E. J. Candès, X. Li, Y. Ma, and J. Wright. Robust principal component analysis? *J. ACM*, 58(3):11:1–11:37, June 2011.

[4] R. Datta, D. Joshi, J. Li, and J. Z. Wang. Studying aesthetics in photographic images using a computational approach. In *ECCV*, pages 288–301, 2006.

[5] K. He, J. Sun, and X. Tang. Single image haze removal using dark channel prior. *TPAMI*, 33(12):2341–2353, 2011.

[6] T. Joachims. Optimizing search engines using clickthrough data. In *ACM KDD*, pages 133–142, 2002.

[7] Y. Ke, X. Tang, and F. Jing. The design of high-level features for photo quality assessment. In *CVPR*, pages 419–426, 2006.

[8] W. Luo, X. Wang, and X. Tang. Content-based photo quality assessment. In *ICCV*, pages 2206–2213, 2011.

[9] Y. Luo and X. Tang. Photo and video quality evaluation: Focusing on the subject. In *ECCV*, pages 386–399, 2008.

[10] L. Marchesotti, F. Perronnin, D. Larlus, and G. Csurka. Assessing the aesthetic quality of photographs using generic image descriptors. In *ICCV*, pages 1784–1791, 2011.

[11] A. K. Moorthy, P. Obrador, and N. Oliver. Towards computational models of the visual aesthetic appeal of consumer videos. In *ECCV*, pages 1–14, 2010.

[12] M. Muja and D. G. Lowe. Fast approximate nearest neighbors with automatic algorithm configuration. In *VISAPP*, pages 331–340. INSTICC Press, 2009.

[13] N. Murray, L. Marchesotti, and F. Perronnin. Ava: A large-scale database for aesthetic visual analysis. In *CVPR*, pages 2408–2415, 2012.

[14] M. Nishiyama, T. Okabe, I. Sato, and Y. Sato. Aesthetic quality classification of photographs based on color harmony. In *CVPR*, pages 33–40, 2011.

[15] R. Plutchik. Harper & Row Publishers, 1980.

[16] J. Shi and C. Tomasi. Good features to track. In *CVPR*, pages 593–600, 1994.

[17] K. van de Sande, T. Gevers, and C. Snoek. Evaluating color descriptors for object and scene recognition. *TPAMI*, 32(9):1582–1596, 2010.

[18] J. J. Vos. Colorimetric and photometric properties of a 2-deg fundamental observer. *Color Research and Application*, 1978.

[19] C. Vu, T. Phan, and D. Chandler. S3: A spectral and spatial measure of local perceived sharpness in natural images. *TIP*, 21(3):934–945, 2012.

[20] H. Wang, A. Klaser, C. Schmid, and C.-L. Liu. Action recognition by dense trajectories. In *CVPR*, pages 3169–3176, 2011.

[21] G. Ye, D. Liu, I.-H. Jhuo, and S.-F. Chang. Robust late fusion with rank minimization. In *CVPR*, pages 3021–3028, 2012.

[22] L. Zhang, M. H. Tong, T. K. Marks, H. Shan, and G. W. Cottrell. SUN: A bayesian framework for saliency using natural statistics. *J Vis*, 8(7):32.1–20, 2008.

[23] G. Zhao and M. Pietikainen. Dynamic texture recognition using local binary patterns with an application to facial expressions. *TPAMI*, 29(6):915–928, June 2007.

Multi-factor Segmentation for Topic Visualization and Recommendation: the MUST-VIS System

Chidansh Bhatt
Idiap Research Institute
Martigny, Switzerland
cbhatt@idiap.ch

Andrei Popescu-Belis
Idiap Research Institute
Martigny, Switzerland
apbelis@idiap.ch

Maryam Habibi
Idiap and EPFL
Martigny, Switzerland
mhabibi@idiap.ch

Sandy Ingram
Klewel SA
Martigny, Switzerland
sandy.ingram@klewel.com

Stefano Masneri
Heinrich Hertz Institute
Berlin, Germany
stefano.masneri@hhi.fraunhofer.de

Fergus McInnes
University of Edinburgh, UK
fergus.mcinnes@ed.ac.uk

Nikolaos Pappas
Idiap and EPFL
Martigny, Switzerland
npappas@idiap.ch

Oliver Schreer
Heinrich Hertz Institute
Berlin, Germany
oliver.schreer@hhi.fraunhofer.de

ABSTRACT

This paper presents the MUST-VIS system for the MediaMixer/VideoLectures.NET Temporal Segmentation and Annotation Grand Challenge. The system allows users to visualize a lecture as a series of segments represented by keyword clouds, with relations to other similar lectures and segments. Segmentation is performed using a multi-factor algorithm which takes advantage of the audio (through automatic speech recognition and word-based segmentation) and video (through the detection of actions such as writing on the blackboard). The similarity across segments and lectures is computed using a content-based recommendation algorithm. Overall, the graph-based representation of segment similarity appears to be a promising and cost-effective approach to navigating lecture databases.

Categories and Subject Descriptors

H.3.1 [**Information Storage and Retrieval**]: Content Analysis and Retrieval; H.5.1 [**Information Interfaces and Presentation**]: Multimedia Information Systems

Keywords

lecture segmentation, lecture recommendation

1. INTRODUCTION

The MUST-VIS system presented in this paper is our solution to the ACM Multimedia 2013 Grand Challenge on Temporal Segmentation and Annotation proposed by MediaMixer and VideoLectures.NET. MUST-VIS stands for multi-factor segmentation for topic visualization and recommendation, because the system first performs lecture segmentation using audio, text and visual information, and then uses techniques inspired from recommender systems to connect segments. The goal is to improve access to repositories of audio-visual recordings of lectures, through segmentation and recommendation of segments, unlike many existing methods that are limited to entire lectures only.

MUST-VIS introduces a multi-modal algorithm for lecture segmentation based on video and audio/text, and annotates segments using keyword clouds, which offer direct access to the information content, while taking into account the major speaker actions. While these annotations make segments searchable by users, an efficient way to access lecture content is via recommendations of segments and lectures. This technique is demonstrated in MUST-VIS with a prototype interface, as visualization is essential for exploring large amounts of data at various levels of granularity. The MUST-VIS processing algorithms are time-efficient and scale well to large repositories. Moreover, segments and recommendations can all be computed offline rather than at search time. We also sketch evaluation methods for the system.

The paper is organized as follows. In Section 2, we describe how users interact with the MUST-VIS system. In Section 3, we present the system components, and in Section 4 we present some evaluation results.

MM'13, October 21–25, 2013, Barcelona, Spain.
Copyright 2013 ACM 978-1-4503-2404-5/13/10 ...$15.00.
http://dx.doi.org/10.1145/2502081.2508120.

2. MUST-VIS: THE USERS' VIEW

The users of lecture databases such as VideoLectures.NET, YouTube.com/edu or KhanAcademy.org are faced with the challenge of efficient search and browsing, especially when searching for specific pieces of information, such as a fact, a proof or argument, or a reference. In addition, obtaining the gist of a lecture without entirely watching it is another challenge. We assume here that the priority of end-users is to explore the most semantically-relevant information contained within audio-visual lecture recordings.

The MUST-VIS system presents to its users a graphical user interface (GUI) shown in Fig. 1. The goal is to provide an insight into the content of each of the topical segments of lectures, using keyword clouds, which are magnified when hovering over them with the mouse. The segments of a lec-

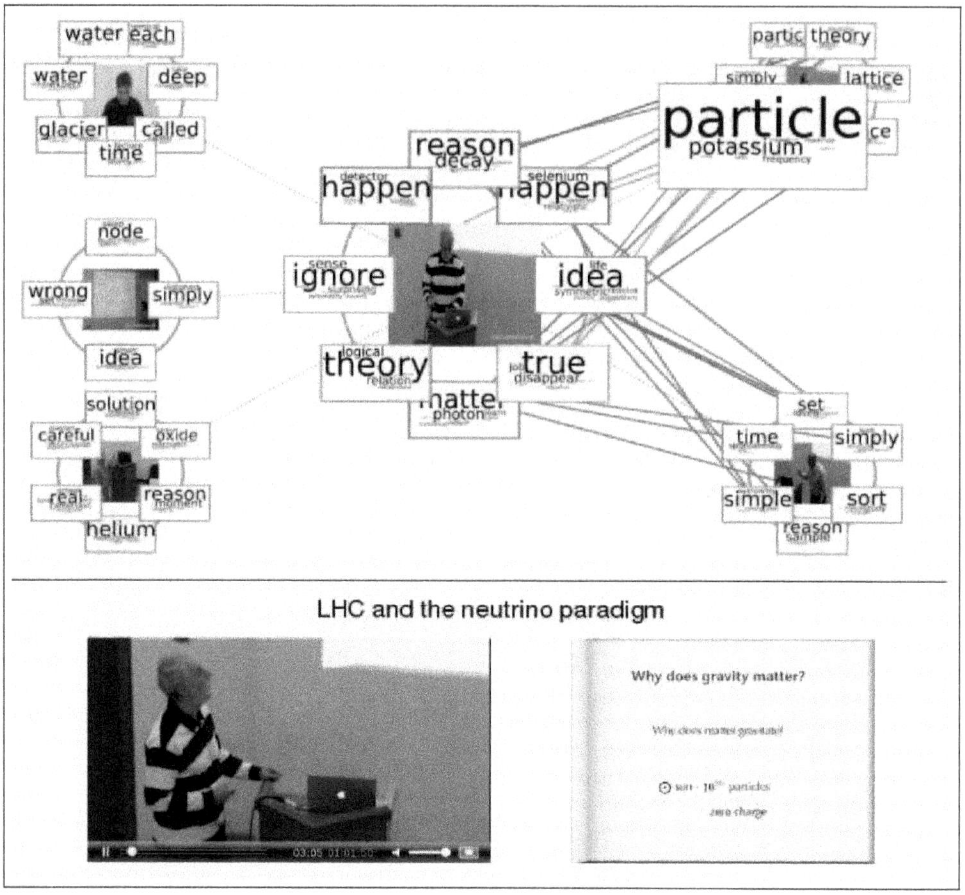

Figure 1: The MUST-VIS navigation graph (top) and video/slide player (bottom). Each lecture is represented with a keyframe and keyword clouds for each segment around it. The lecture in focus (center: LHC and the Neutrino Paradigm) is surrounded by lectures with related segments (e.g., on the right, Ultracold Atoms, and Bioinspired Nanostructured Materials).

ture are ordered by starting time in a clockwise circular manner around the keyframe provided in the lecture repository. The lecture featured at the center of the screen is considered to be in focus and can be played (audio/video plus slides) by clicking on its center or on a segment.

Using content-based recommendation techniques, each segment and each lecture are related to the most similar ones, forming a *navigation graph*, which for simplicity is limited to the five most related lectures. We assume for now that the lecture from which navigation starts is found either directly (by URL) or through keyword-based search. Depending on user preferences, the GUI displays either segment-to-segment similarity links, or lecture-to-lecture ones, or it can zoom from one type to the other. In Fig. 1, the two most similar lectures to the one in focus are shown with segment-to-segment links, while three additional lectures are shown only with lecture-to-lecture links. Each of the segments of the lecture in focus and its links have a unique color code, to facilitate tracing segment-to-segment links. A mouse click on one of the recommended lectures or segments brings it in focus (allowing the user to play it) and redraws the graph to show its own set of recommendations.

3. COMPONENTS OF THE SYSTEM

To compute the navigation graph, MUST-VIS makes use of state-of-the-art multimodal processing of audio, video and text. The fully-automatic components, shown in Fig. 2, are run offline for temporal segmentation and keyword extraction from lectures. Similarity across lectures and segments is then computed using a state-of-the-art content-based recommendation algorithm.

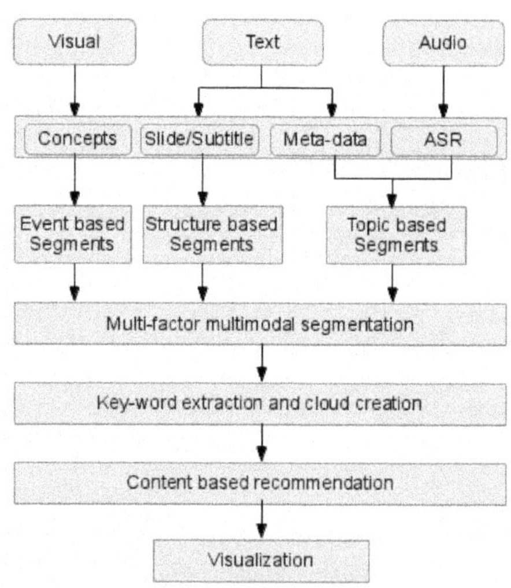

Figure 2: Lecture processing in MUST-VIS.

3.1 Video Processing for Segmentation

We implemented a classical frame-based temporal segmentation algorithm [9] with four possible classes: 'talk' (video representing the speaker), 'slide presentation' (only the slide show is visible in the video), 'mixed' (both speaker and screen are visible, including when the camera is moving from one to the other), and 'blackboard' (speaker writing on the blackboard). In MUST-VIS, we use the segmentation based on temporal boundaries derived from these four semantic-level action detection in the video, rather than traditional shot boundary detection. This is because shot boundary does not provide the same semantic information as the four classes above, and is not applicable to lectures that are recorded with a single shot.

An SVM classifier was trained using 51 features: the number of detected faces, the width of the largest face, its horizontal position, and the 48 values of 16-bin histograms on the three color channels. A training dataset was created manually by labeling one frame every second in the first ten minutes of each video. Classification is performed for each frame, but to avoid over-segmentation, we merge every 50 frames and choose the majority class. Two lectures from the 20 provided by the Grand Challenge organizers were annotated as test data ('geanakoplos_ lec18' and 'ekaykin_drilling'). The classification accuracy of our method was 79% for the first one and 87% for the second one, over respectively 432K and 323K frames. Two sources of error have been identified: the first and most important is the classification of 'talk' frames as 'mixed', which may happen if the detected face is small. The second one is due to small shifts in starting times, appearing when merging frames; being lower than 0.5 s, this does not impact MUST-VIS.

3.2 Audio Processing and Speech Recognition

Speech/non-speech segmentation and speaker diarization were performed using components from the AMIDA system [7], incorporating the programs 'shout_segment' and 'shout_ cluster' from the SHoUT toolkit [8]. Speech recognition was performed using a system [1] trained primarily over TED talks as used for the IWSLT 2012 ASR evaluation. The system has two passes of decoding, both using hybrid models in which HMM observation probabilities are computed using a deep neural network. The second pass incorporates speaker adaptation through a CMLLR transform. Both passes used a trigram language model (LM), and the final transcriptions were obtained by word lattice re-scoring with a 4-gram LM. The LMs were derived by interpolating in-domain models trained on TED talk transcripts with multiple out-of-domain models trained on Europarl, News Crawl and News Commentary data and the LM from the AMIDA system [7]. The performance of the system, as shown in [1] (Table 4, fifth line of results), is around 18% word error rate.

3.3 Text-Based Segmentation and Keywords

The automatic transcripts or the subtitles of each lecture of the dataset are topically segmented using the TextTiling algorithm implemented in the NLTK toolkit [2]. Then the words in the each topic segment are ranked using a recent diverse keyword extraction technique [6], which selects keywords so that they cover the maximum number of topics mentioned in each segment. Finally, word cloud representations are generated using WordCram (`www.wordcram.org`) for each segment and also for entire lectures. Words ranked higher become graphically emphasized in the word cloud.

3.4 Multimodal Segmentation

State-of-the-art video segment detection methods use multiple modalities only infrequently [4]. When cross-modal alignment is performed, it is generally at a lower-level of granularity than needed here. In MUST-VIS, the three available types of segmentation information (from words, video and slides) are combined using a novel segmentation method that is inspired from multimodal alignment. Let $\mathcal{V}$ be the set of 20 lectures provided for the Grand Challenge. One subset, noted $V_{slide} = \{V_1, \ldots, V_{10}\}$, is accompanied by slides, while the other, $V_{subtitles} = \{V_{11}, \ldots, V_{20}\}$, is accompanied by subtitles.

For a given video $V \in \mathcal{V}$, ASR-based segments are noted $S_{ASR} = \{SA_1, \ldots, SA_I\}$ where I depends on V. For a given video $V \in V_{slide}$, segments with text from each slide are noted $S_{slide} = \{SS_1, \ldots, SS_J\}$, where J depends on V. And, for a given video $V \in V_{subtitles}$, the text from the subtitles is mapped onto the temporal boundaries computed by video segmentation and noted $S_{subtitle+visual} = \{SV_1, \ldots, SV_K\}$ (K depends on V). In practice, $I < J$ and $I < K$. For each segment S, S^{start} is its start time, S^{end} its ending time, and S^{text} is the text contained within it.

The multimodal segmentation algorithm has parameters σ, ρ and Δt. Here, σ (initialized to 1) represents the starting index and similarly ρ (initialized to 1) represents the ending index of the segment in S_{slide} that matches the segment in S_{ASR}. The number of segments considered for computing the cosine similarity around the segment index $\tau \in S_{slide}$ is Δt. In practice, $\Delta t = 3$ for V_{slides} and $\Delta t = 5$ for $V_{subtitle+visual}$. The segments of S_{ASR} are considered as principal, due to size and availability.

<u>Input</u>: $S_{ASR}, S_{slide}, \Delta t$ <u>Output</u>: SAS
$\sigma, \rho \leftarrow 1$
for each segment SA_i in S_{ASR} **do**
  $\tau \leftarrow \arg\min_{j \in [\rho, J]} dist(SA_i^{end}, SS_j^{end})$
  $\rho \leftarrow \arg\max_{x \in [\tau - \Delta t, \tau + \Delta t]} sim(SA_i^{text}, SS_{[\sigma:x]}^{text})$
  $SAS_i^{text} \leftarrow SA_i^{text} \bigcup SS_{[\sigma:\rho]}^{text}$
  $SAS_i^{start} \leftarrow SS_\sigma^{start}, SAS_i^{end} \leftarrow SS_\rho^{end}$
  $\sigma \leftarrow \rho + 1$
end for

For each SA_i^{end}, the algorithm first identifies the segment index τ of the nearest segment SS_j^{end}. As the individual SA_i is usually larger, it aligns with multiple SS_j. The segment alignment boundary is selected after identifying the index ρ of the segment in SS_j which has the maximum cosine similarity between the combined text content of all the segments from $SS_{[\sigma:\rho]}$ and the text content of SA_i^{text}. The value of ρ is constrained to be within $[\tau - \Delta t, \tau + \Delta t]$ to avoid the situation where a smaller number of segments from S_{slide} is aligned to S_{ASR}, leaving behind many unallocated segments from S_{slide}. All the segments SA_i are thus aligned by order of start time to ordered groups of segments from SS_j.

Between 4 and 10 segments are found for each of the lectures in the dataset, a value that was aimed for so that segments are easily grasped through the GUI (with equal sizes for now). Depending on user requirements, finer-grained segments can be easily obtained.

3.5 Recommending Lectures and Segments

While keyword-based search in annotated lectures and segments is now well-understood, we propose here to recommend to viewers new segments and lectures, as an alternative to search which improves the accessibility of a lecture database. We use techniques from content-based recommender systems, and compute similarity between items based on their content descriptors, through standard vector space models based on TF-IDF weighting, which have been shown to perform well for multimedia recommendation [10]. In addition to the words from the above-mentioned features, we used all available meta-data such as titles, speaker names, descriptions, subtitles, and slide titles with start time. We thus generated for each segment a ranked list of the most similar other segments.

An additional goal is to generate segment-to-segment recommendations which, when integrated over all segments of a lecture, are coherent with the lecture-level recommendations obtained directly. To achieve this, we generated from the segment-to-segment similarity matrix a summation matrix considering all possible pairings of segments from two talks, which was normalized. Based on these scores, we generate the top recommendations for each lecture, then select only the best segment-to-segment links from them. In Section 4, we show experiments with various selection cut-offs to increase the coherence between the two levels of recommendations.

3.6 Visualization: GUI

The GUI presented in Section 2 was implemented using the D3 JavaScript library for manipulating documents [3], allowing interactive visualization and exploration using force-directed graphs. This allowed us to position the nodes of the graph in a two-dimensional space so that all the edges are of equal length and there are as few crossing edges as possible, by assigning forces among the set of edges and the set of nodes, and minimizing the potential energy.

4. RESULTS AND DISCUSSION

As no ground-truth annotations are available for the Grand Challenge dataset, and evaluation in use is a costly alternative, we provide the following quality indicators for the MUST-VIS system. The use of all multimodal features for recommendation, in addition to standard metadata, increases the vocabulary by about 35% and the average similarity scores for segments by about 0.1. This is unlike recent observations that multimodal features decreased performance on a hyperlinking task [5]. In our case, the average increase in similarity scores for segments with slides is higher than for those with subtitles, indicating that slides are (predictably) a more useful complement to ASR than subtitles.

In a pilot experiment, two of the authors have assigned ground-truth recommendations to each of the 20 lectures in the dataset. Table 1 compares the ground-truth rankings versus automated methods in several configurations, using Mean Reciprocal Rank (MRR) and Mean Average Precision (MAP). The highest agreement is between the two annotators, followed very closely by the agreement between lecture-to-lecture (LL) and averaged segment-to-segment similarities (SS). Therefore, the possibility of "smooth zooming" between LL and SS recommendations is validated. The lecture-level recommendation is slightly closer to the ground-truth than the averaged segment-level one, though both are at some distance with respect to inter-coder agreement. Such distance can be reduced with the help of hybrid recommendation systems, using collaborative filtering based on user-log information, when available, along with the proposed content-based method. The random recommendation performs poorly compared to other methods.

Table 1: Comparison of ground-truth recommendations (A1, A2) with automated ones: lecture-to-lecture (LL), segment-to-segment (SS) and random (R, as baseline, 500 draws), using MAP (a) and MRR (b) over 1–5 top recommendations.

	A1		A2		LL		SS		R	
	(a)	(b)	(a)	(b)	(a)	(b)	(a)	(b)	(a)	(b)
A1	1.0	1.0	.91	.54	.33	.14	.28	.10	.13	.03
A2	-	-	1.0	1.0	.31	.15	.22	.10	.10	.02
LL	-	-	-	-	1.0	1.0	.91	.52	.29	.11
SS	-	-	-	-	-	-	1.0	1.0	.30	.11
R	-	-	-	-	-	-	-	-	1.0	1.0

5. CONCLUSION

The MUST-VIS system performs segmentation and annotation of lectures based on features from several modalities, and displays the results in a novel GUI, which enables navigation based on recommended lectures and segments. With respect to current recommender systems, MUST-VIS offers clearer justifications of its recommendations, through the number of links and the keyword clouds, and facilitates access to relevant parts within lectures. Both features should thus help answering the Grand Challenge on Temporal Segmentation and Annotation of Lectures.

6. ACKNOWLEDGMENTS

This work was supported by the Swiss National Science Foundation through the AROLES project n. 51NF40-144627 and by the European Union through the inEvent project FP7-ICT n. 287872 (`www.inevent-project.eu`).

7. REFERENCES

[1] P. Bell, P. Swietojanski, and S. Renals. Multi-level adaptive networks in tandem and hybrid ASR systems. In *Proc. ICASSP*, 2013.

[2] S. Bird. NLTK: the natural language toolkit. In *Proc. COLING-ACL*, pages 69–72, 2006.

[3] M. Bostock and al. D3 data-driven documents. *IEEE Tran. Vis. Comput. Gr.*, 17(12):2301–2309, 2011.

[4] M. Del Fabro and L. Boszormenyi. State-of-the-art and future challenges in video scene detection: a survey. *Multimedia Systems*, pages 1–28, 2013.

[5] M. Eskevich and al. Multimedia information seeking through search and hyperlinking. In *Proc. ICMR*, pages 287–294, 2013.

[6] M. Habibi and A. Popescu-Belis. Diverse keyword extraction from conversations. In *Proc. ACL*, 2013.

[7] T. Hain and al. Transcribing meetings with the AMIDA systems. *IEEE Tran. ASL*, 20(2), 2012.

[8] M. Huijbregts. *Segmentation, Diarization and Speech Transcription: Surprise Data Unraveled.* PhD thesis, Centre for Telematics and Information Technology, University of Twente, Enschede, Nov. 2008.

[9] I. Koprinska and al. Temporal video segmentation: A survey. *Sig. Proc.: Image Comm.*, 16(5), 2001.

[10] N. Pappas and A. Popescu-Belis. Combining content with user preferences for TED lecture recommendation. In *Proc. CBMI*, 2013.

Beauty is Here: Evaluating Aesthetics in Videos Using Multimodal Features and Free Training Data

Yanran Wang, Qi Dai, Rui Feng, Yu-Gang Jiang
School of Computer Science, Fudan University, Shanghai, China
{11210240061, daiqi, fengrui, ygj}@fudan.edu.cn

ABSTRACT

The aesthetics of videos can be used as a useful clue to improve user satisfaction in many applications such as search and recommendation. In this paper, we demonstrate a computational approach to automatically evaluate the aesthetics of videos, with particular emphasis on identifying beautiful scenes. Using a standard classification pipeline, we analyze the effectiveness of a comprehensive set of features, ranging from low-level visual features, mid-level semantic attributes, to style descriptors. In addition, since there is limited public training data with manual labels of video aesthetics, we explore freely available resources with a simple assumption that people tend to share more aesthetically appealing works than unappealing ones. Specifically, we use images from DPChallenge and videos from Flickr as positive training data and the Dutch documentary videos as negative data, where the latter contain mostly old materials of low visual quality. Our extensive evaluations show that combining multiple features is helpful, and very promising results can be obtained using the noisy but annotation-free training data. On the NHK Multimedia Challenge dataset, we attain a Spearman's rank correlation coefficient of 0.41.

Categories and Subject Descriptors

I.2.10 [**Artificial Intelligence**]: Vision and Scene Understanding—*Video analysis*

Keywords

Video aesthetics, beautiful scenes, free training data, multimodal features, attributes.

1. INTRODUCTION

Estimating the aesthetic quality of videos has many practical applications. In video search or recommendation, among videos with similar relevance scores, people would prefer to view aesthetically more appealing ones. It also can help broadcasting organizations to quickly select better materials out of normally very huge databases (see example clips in Figure 1).

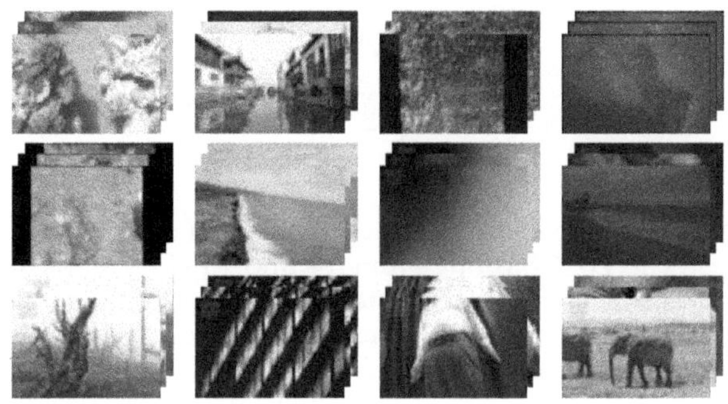

Figure 1: Example clips of the NHK broadcast video footage. This paper presents an approach to automatically identify aesthetically more appealing clips.

There have been several studies focusing on the estimation of image aesthetics [3, 5, 8, 4]. Various features and classifiers have been evaluated in this context, with a general conclusion that using multiple features is helpful. A few researchers have also exploited video aesthetics [7, 9, 1, 11]. In [7], Moorthy et al. evaluated several low-level features on a small dataset of 160 consumer videos, and observed promising results by combining seven features. Niu and Liu [9] designed a few features to distinguish professionally edited videos from amateur raw videos, assuming that professional videos have better visual quality. In [1], Chan et al. adopted cinemagraphs to determine beautiful scenes using basically motion information. Redi and Merialdo [11] assumed that beauty is highly related to interestingness. They trained models using images on Flickr, which provides a ranking criterion called interestingness.

In this paper, we present a computational approach to evaluate video aesthetics, which is different from the above works in two aspects. First, we consider a large variety of features including not only low-level features that have been widely used, but also mid-level semantic attributes and style descriptors. Second, as there is very limited training data publicly available, we propose to directly make use of resources from several domains without doing any manual annotation. This is based on our observations that images and videos on a few media-sharing websites such as DPChallenge and Flickr are mostly aesthetically appealing, while some old materials like documentary videos are much less

MM'13, October 21–25, 2013, Barcelona, Spain.
ACM 978-1-4503-2404-5/13/10 ...$15.00.
http://dx.doi.org/10.1145/2502081.2508121.

Figure 2: *Free* training data from different sources, where the DPChallenge images and Flickr videos are used as positive samples (aesthetically more appealing) and the Dutch documentary videos are used as negative samples.

pleasing. Different from [11] where Flickr images with low interestingness scores were used as negative training samples, we observe that even some of those images are beautiful and therefore do not use any Flickr images as negative data. Note that this is critical as the selection of training data affects the final results significantly. Through extensive experiments using the *free* training data, we also provide valuable insights on the selection of useful features for evaluating video aesthetics.

In the following we first introduce our training data, and then describe the evaluated features and discuss results.

2. FREE TRAINING DATA

One of the reasons that video aesthetics has not been extensively studied is that very few training samples with manual labels are publicly available. We therefore propose to construct two annotation-free training datasets by assuming that images/videos on certain websites are mostly beautiful, particularly those highly rated ones.

The first training set uses images from DPChallenge.com as positive samples. From the AVA dataset released in [8], we select 60,000 images with high ratings as indicated by DPChallenge. 50,000 frames from 1,400 Dutch documentary videos are uniformly extracted as negative examples. These videos were obtained from the past U.S. NIST TRECVID evaluations[1].

The second training set uses Flickr videos as positive samples and the 1,400 Dutch documentary videos as negative data. The Flickr videos are collected using 10 interestingness-enabled searches (keywords: animal, beach, flower, food, mountain, nature, night, ocean, street, and sunset), and the top 200 videos are downloaded from each search, leading to a set of 2,000 pseudo-positive samples.

[1]http://trecvid.nist.gov/

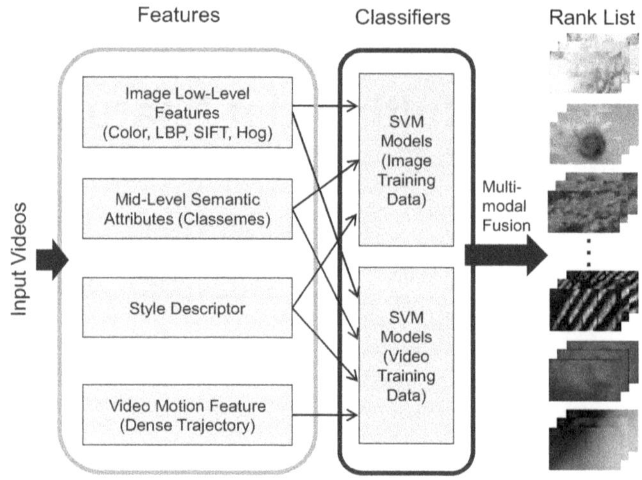

Figure 3: Overview of our system framework for evaluating the aesthetic quality of videos.

Figure 2 gives a few examples of our training data. As can be seen, the DPChallenge and Flickr data are mostly beautiful, while the documentary videos are much less appealing aesthetically.

3. THE COMPUTATIONAL APPROACH

Figure 3 shows our framework, where we adopt SVM classifiers to predict aesthetic quality due to their overwhelming performances in many applications. A large number of features are evaluated. We briefly describe each of them below.

Color Histogram in HSV space is the first feature to be tested. We compute a histogram on each sampled frame (from every 2 second window) and use the averaged histogram to represent a video.

LBP (Local Binary Pattern [10]) is a popular texture feature that describes the local pattern of one pixel to its neighboring pixels. A standard setting of 8 neighbors are used, leading to a representation of 256 dimensions.

SIFT (Scale Invariant Feature Transform [6]) is a very popular local descriptor. We follow the traditional process described in [6], where salient local patches are detected by DoG (Differences of Gaussian). We adopt the bag-of-words representation using a spatial pyramid with a codebook of 500 words.

HOG (Histogram of Oriented Gradients [2]) feature has been popular in several applications such as human detection. We compute HOG descriptors over densely sampled patches, and convert the descriptors to a bag-of-words representation with a codebook of 4,000 words.

Dense Trajectory feature [13]) is a state-of-art motion-based representation. Densely sampled local patches are tracked over time and several descriptors are used to describe the local volume around each trajectory. These descriptors are converted into bag-of-words representations. We use the source codes provided by the authors of [13].

Classemes [12] is a mid-level attribute feature, where each dimension is the prediction score of a semantic class. 2,659 semantic concept classifiers are used, leading to a representation of 2,659 dimensions. The classifiers were trained using external data on the Web [12]. Classemes is one of the most popular attribute features, and it is interesting to study whether such mid-level representations are useful for estimating aesthetics.

Style Descriptor [8] is formed by concatenating 14 photographic style predicting scores, including complementary colors, image grain, motion blur, and vanishing point, etc. These have been proved effective for evaluating the aesthetics of images. We use SIFT, LBP and Color Histogram as features to train 14 models, using the training data provided by [8].

Among the above features, the first five are low-level visual features. The Classemes is a mid-level semantic representation as mentioned earlier, and the Style Descriptor was specially designed for predicting visual aesthetics. Note that audio features are not considered here since the targeted NHK test videos focus more on visual scenes and most of them do not have audio soundtracks. However, in a more general setup of evaluating video aesthetics we conjecture that audio features are also useful.

We use χ^2 kernel for all the features except that Classemes uses RBF kernel since it has negative feature values. For the combination (fusion) of multiple features, we adopt kernel-level fusion with equal fusion weights, where kernels computed from each of the features are averaged to form a fused kernel. Note that using adaptive fusion weights may lead to (normally marginally) better performance.

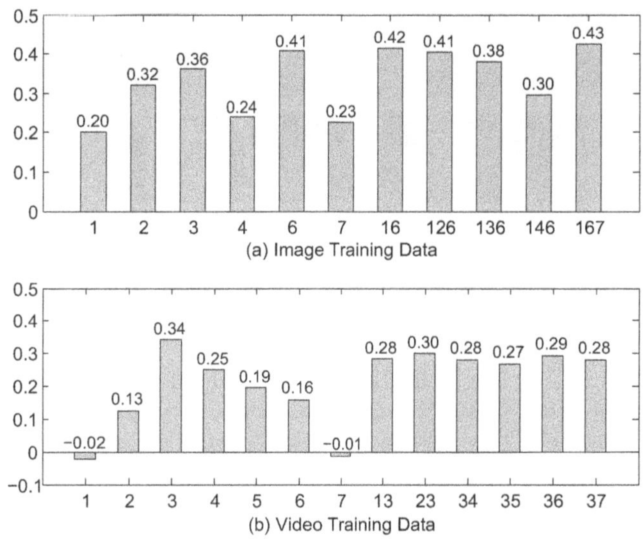

Figure 4: Evaluation results on 500 NHK clips using our annotations, measured by Spearman's rank correlation coefficients. We report results of both individual features and their fusion (1. Color Histogram; 2. LBP; 3. SIFT; 4. HOG; 5. Dense Trajectory; 6. Classemes; 7. Style). See texts for more explanations on the feature fusion setups.

4. EXPERIMENTS

4.1 Test Data and Evaluation Measure

The test dataset consists of 1,000 clips of broadcast video footage provided by NHK, with an average duration of around 1 minute. These clips cover a wide range of contents such as landscapes and creatures. With models trained by both our image- and video-based training sets, rank lists of the test clips can be generated according to aesthetic quality. Spearman's rank correlation coefficient is used as the evaluation measure, which is a value between -1 and 1, indicating the degree of correlation between the ground-truth ranking and the predicted ranking.

Since the official ground-truth ranking of the NHK test dataset is not publicly available for self evaluation[2], we manually annotated half of the test clips to assign an integer score between 0 and 10 to each clip. This allows us to perform more evaluations, so that it is possible to provide more detailed result analysis and insights in this paper. As will be discussed later, we find that the expected best result submitted to NHK is not from the actual optimal feature choices.

4.2 Results and Analysis

Let us now evaluate the results of all the features and their fusion. Results on the 500 NHK clips evaluated based on our annotations are summarized in Figure 4. Since there can be many feature combinations, we adopt a simple strategy to reduce the number of evaluated results: Starting from the best individual feature, we incrementally add in other features and a feature is dropped immediately if it does not help in a fusion experiment.

We first discuss results using the image-based training data. As shown in Figure 4(a), among all the low-level visual features, SIFT is the best performer, achieving a Spearman's coefficient of 0.36. Color has the worst performance, indicating that color information is less useful in predicting visual aesthetics. Overall, features focusing more on texture structures like the SIFT and LBP tend to be more effective. The mid-level semantic attribute feature Classemes offers the best single-feature result (0.41). This indicates that the semantic contents of images play an important role in aesthetic quality evaluation, which is an interesting observation. The style descriptor, which was observed to be very useful for evaluating image aesthetics, is not as good as expected. However, it may be used in combination with other features for improved performance, as discussed in the following feature fusion experiments.

The fusion of multiple features can further improve results in the image-based training experiment. As shown on the right side of Figure 4(a), the best result is attained by fusing Color Histogram, the Classemes, and the Style Descriptor (Spearman's coefficient 0.43). Adding Color over Classemes (the bar marked by "16" in the figure) also improves results marginally. Although LBP, HOG and SIFT perform well individually, they are not complementary when combined with Color or Classemes.

Next we discuss results obtained by the video-based training data. As shown in Figure 4(b), overall the results are much worse than that from the image-based training. This is not surprising as the NHK video clips focus more on scenes, for which it is intuitively sufficient to purely use images for model training. We believe that video based training is necessary and effective if the targeted application domain is broader. Among the individual features, SIFT is the best, with a Spearman's coefficient of 0.34. The Dense Trajectory motion feature, which is very powerful in human action recognition, performs poorly on this task. This is due to the

[2]Only a maximum of five result runs can be submitted to NHK for evaluation.

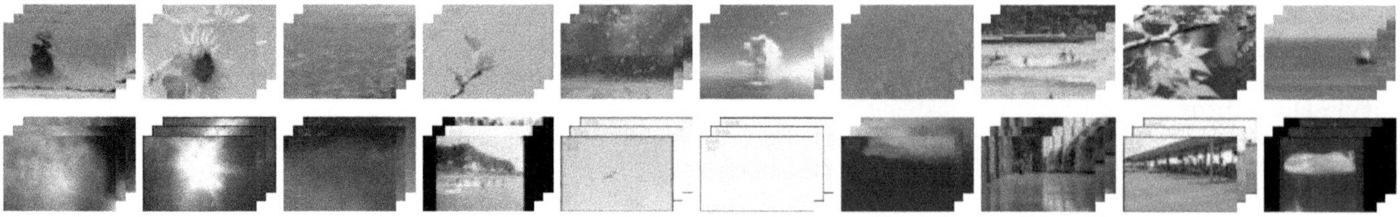

Figure 5: The top and bottom rows show the most and the least beautiful 10 videos respectively, identified by our best submitted run (image-based training data with Color Histogram and Classemes features).

Table 1: Evaluation results of our five submitted runs using the NHK ground-truth. "Image+Video" means the late fusion (average prediction scores) of the two runs using the image- and video-based training data respectively.

Training Data	Image	Video	Image+Video
Color+Classemes	**0.41**	0.03	0.39
Color+Classemes+SIFT	0.37	0.19	—

fact that very few foreground object motions exist in the NHK footage, and the aesthetically quality of scenes is intuitively not highly related to motion. In the feature fusion experiments using the video-based training data, we do not observe any performance gain, probably because the results of the other features are much worse than that of the SIFT.

Finally, we report the performances of our five submitted result runs, which were measured over the entire test set using NHK's official ground-truth labels. As shown in Table 1, the best result is also from the image-based training data, using Color Histogram and Classemes. This is similar to that reported in Figure 4(a) using half of the test data and our own labels. According to our analysis earlier, we expect that slightly better performance may be obtained on this entire test set if the Style Descriptor is further added. Figure 5 shows the top and bottom 10 clips identified by our best submitted run.

5. CONCLUSIONS

We have presented an approach for evaluating aesthetics in videos. Since there is limited labeled training data available, we constructed two annotation-free training datasets by making use of image and video data from various sources (e.g., Flickr and DPChallenge). Our results suggest that the image-based training is more suitable for the scenario of the NHK Challenge, where the focus is mainly on identifying beautiful scenes. However, for a more broader task of evaluating video aesthetics, this conclusion may not hold.

We also evaluated several off-the-shelf features, including not only low-level visual features, but also mid-level semantic attribute features and a photographic style descriptor. Results show that all these three types of features are useful, and among them the semantic attribute feature gives superior performance.

6. ACKNOWLEDGEMENT

This work was supported in part by two grants from the National Natural Science Foundation of China (#61201387 and #61228205), two grants from the Science and Technology Commission of Shanghai Municipality (#13PJ1400400 and #12511501602), a National 863 Program (#2011AA010604), and a New Teachers' Fund for Doctoral Stations, Ministry of Education (#20120071120026), China.

7. REFERENCES

[1] Y.-T. Chan, H.-C. Hsu, P.-Y. Li, and M.-C. Yeh. Automatic cinemagraphs for ranking beautiful scenes. In *Proceedings of ACM International Conference on Multimedia*, 2012.

[2] N. Dalal and B. Triggs. Histograms of oriented gradients for human detection. In *Proceedings of IEEE Conference on Computer Vision and Pattern Recognition*, 2005.

[3] R. Datta, D. Joshi, J. Li, and J. Z. Wang. Studying aesthetics in photographic images using a computational approach. In *Proceedings of European Conference on Computer Vision*, 2006.

[4] S. Dhar, V. Ordonez, and T. L. Berg. High level describable attributes for predicting aesthetics and interestingness. In *Proceedings of IEEE Conference on Computer Vision and Pattern Recognition*, 2011.

[5] Y. Ke, X. Tang, and F. Jing. The design of high-level features for photo quality assessment. In *Proceedings of IEEE Conference on Computer Vision and Pattern Recognition*, 2006.

[6] D. G. Lowe. Distinctive image features from scale-invariant keypoints. *International Journal of Computer Vision*, 60(2):91–110, 2004.

[7] A. K. Moorthy, P. Obrador, and N. Oliver. Towards computational models of visual aesthetic appeal of consumer videos. In *Proceedings of European Conference on Computer Vision*, 2010.

[8] N. Murray, L. Marchesotti, and F. Perronnin. AVA: A large-scale database for aesthetic visual analysis. In *Proceedings of IEEE Conference on Computer Vision and Pattern Recognition*, 2012.

[9] Y. Niu and F. Liu. What makes a professional video? a computational aesthetics approach. *IEEE Transactions on Circuits and Systems for Video Technology*, 22(7):1037–1049, 2012.

[10] T. Ojala, M. Pietikäinen, and D. Harwood. A comparative study of texture measures with classification based on featured distributions. *Pattern Recognition*, 29(1):51–59, 1996.

[11] M. Redi and B. Merialdo. Where is the interestingness? retrieving appealing video scenes by learning flickr-based graded judgments. In *Proceedings of ACM International Conference on Multimedia*, 2012.

[12] L. Torresani, M. Szummer, and A. Fitzgibbon. Efficient object category recognition using classemes. In *Proceedings of European Conference on Computer Vision*. 2010.

[13] H. Wang, A. Klaser, C. Schmid, and C.-L. Liu. Action recognition by dense trajectories. In *Proceedings of IEEE Conference on Computer Vision and Pattern Recognition*, 2011.

Metadata Enrichment For News Video Retrieval – A Graph-based Propagation Approach

Kong-Wah WAN, Wei-Yun YAU, and Sujoy ROY
Institute for Infocomm Research
1 Fusionopolis Way, Singapore 138632
kongwah@i2r.a-star.edu.sg, wyyau@i2r.a-star.edu.sg, sujoy@i2r.a-star.edu.sg

ABSTRACT

This paper summarizes our contribution to the Technicolor Rich Multimedia Retrieval from Input Videos Grand Challenge. We hold the view that semantic analysis of a given news video is best performed in the text domain. Starting with a noisy text obtained from applying Automatic Speech Recognition (ASR), a graph-based approach is then used to enrich the text by propagating labels from visually similar videos culled from parallel (YouTube) News sources. From the enriched text, we next extract salient keywords to form a query to a news video search engine, retrieving a larger corpus of related news video. Compared to a baseline method that only uses the ASR text, significant improvement in precision has been obtained, indicating that retrieval has benefited from the ingestion of the external labels. Capitalizing on the enriched metadata, we find that videos are more amenable to the Wikipedia-based Explicit Semantic Analysis (ESA), resulting in better support for subtopic news video retrieval. We apply our methods to an in-house live news search portal, and report on several best practices.

Categories and Subject Descriptors

H.3.3 [**Information Search and Retrieval**]: Retrieval models

Keywords

Multimedia Search

1. INTRODUCTION

Motivated by recent advances in visual analytics, the Technicolor Challenge aims to forward the search paradigm to the retrieval of unstructured multimedia based on video queries. The challenge scenario is as follows: given a short news video, output and analyse a corpus of relevant documents such as other videos or text articles on the same or related story, summarizing and elucidating their semantic links and relationships. In this paper, we propose a metadata enrichment method to address parts of this scenario.

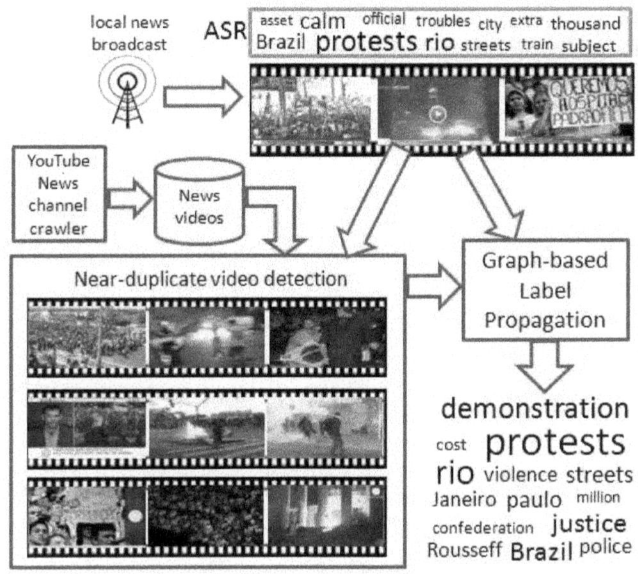

Figure 1: A short news video is used to retrieve similar videos from parallel YouTube sources, the labels of which are fed into a label propagation algorithm for textual enrichment.

The fundamental thrust in our work is that semantic analysis of content is best done in the textual domain, and that meaningful retrieval of multimedia content can only come about from the improvement in the quality of its textual description. Towards this goal, we adopt a graph-based propagation approach to enrich the textual content of a news video. Figure 1 shows the schematics of the computation in an in-house news retrieval system we have implemented. Short news video stories are first segmented from a live news broadcast. A rudimentary text representation can then be obtained by Automatic Speech Recognition (ASR). Concurrently, visually similar YouTube news videos are matched using a near-duplicate detection engine. The YouTube videos are crawled from a predefined list of official News channels, where many have proper labels, tags and short synopsis. These external labels are input to a label propagation algorithm to enrich the ASR text. The intent for this enrichment step is two-fold: missing words are recovered and important words have their prominence increased.

MM'13, October 21–25, 2013, Barcelona, Spain.

http://dx.doi.org/10.1145/2502081.2508122 .

The enrichment procedure is our differentiation from many existing news indexing systems [6], which base their retrieval engine solely on the ASR text. While keywords are mostly picked up by ASR, personal names and important related words are often missed, and finer-grained analysis such as subtopic retrieval [9], is severely limited by the inherent noise in these ASR text. In contrast, using our enrichment process, we show how the resulting text can facilitate such semantic retrieval. In what follows, we describe details of the enrichment step in Section 2 and how it facilitates subtopic retrieval in Section 3, before concluding in Section 4.

2. METADATA ENRICHMENT

Our metadata enrichment follows the general framework of image label refinement [4], which has received considerable attention in the computer vision community. However, there have been few attempts, if any, to address video label refinement. The two main challenges are: (a) video has a temporal dimension, and labels cannot be directly associated to any segment in the video; (b) deriving a good measure of video content similarity. We circumvent the former by a bag-of-labels approach, and adopt a near-duplicate video detection approach to resolve video content similarity. We describe these in the next two sub-sections.

2.1 Graph-based Label Propagation

The basic idea in label propagation is that videos that are similar in content are more likely to also be similar in semantic meaning. A direct application of this is to first compute the pairwise similarity between videos and then to approximate the labels of an input video by its nearest neighbours. In this work, we adopt the graph-based label propagation algorithm in [11]. This is a semi-supervised learning process wherein adjacent nodes (videos) exchange an amount of information (labels) proportional to the weight (similarity) of the edges. A cost function is optimized to ensure that at the convergent state, labels are smooth amongst nearby nodes and do not deviate too much from their initial assignment.

Treat the ASR words in the ith video V_i as its labels. Let the initial label assignment of n videos $\{V_i\}_{i=1}^{n}$ and m labels from a vocabulary $\{w_j\}_{j=1}^{m}$, be represented by the label matrix $Y \in \{0,1\}^{n \times m}$, such that $Y_{ij} = 1$ if the ASR word w_j is found in V_i. The goal is to produce an enriched label matrix $A \in \mathbb{R}^{n \times m}$ such that A_{ij} denotes the confidence score of the label w_j being assigned to V_i:

$$A = (1 - \alpha)(\mathbb{I} - \alpha S)^{-1} Y, \qquad (1)$$

where $S = D^{-1/2} W D^{-1/2}$ is the Laplacian matrix; W is the affinity matrix (see Section 2.2) where W_{ij} is a similarity score between V_i and V_j, $W_{ii} = 0$ to prevent self-reinforcement; D is the diagonal matrix $D_{ii} = \sum_{j \neq i} W_{ij}$; $\alpha \in [0, 1]$ is a parameter controling the rate of propagation.

2.2 Video Similarity

Despite the abundance of literature on the subject, searching for visually similar videos remains a very challenging problem. Recent works can be broadly categorized into the use of global versus local features. In the former, global features derived mainly from color, texture, etc, are suitable for identifying near-identical videos, while local features comprising of scale-invariant keypoints are found to be more robust and effective for detecting near-duplicate videos. In this work, we adopt the local features based approach for near-duplicate video detection [10].

As the number of keypoints detected in an image can be very large, we first cluster them into a visual dictionary of size C. Each keypoint in an image is then mapped to the nearest *visual word*. We form a histogram of these words as the final bag-of-visual-words (bovw) representation of the video. The similarity between two images I_i and I_j is given by the cosine similarity of their histograms $h(.)$:

$$sim_{image}(I_i, I_j) = \frac{\sum_{k=1}^{C} h_k(I_i) h_k(I_j)}{\sqrt{\sum_{k=1}^{C} h_k(I_i)^2} \sqrt{\sum_{k=1}^{C} h_k(I_j)^2}} \qquad (2)$$

We use an inverted file index to speed up the matching of the sparse histograms. Each entry in the index is a visual word and stores the links to the images containing the word. Hence, each cosine similarity is evaluated only for a small subset of the images and for the non-zero entries in the bovw.

Given two videos V_i and V_j and their keyframes, a simple way to compute the video similarity between V_i and V_j is to first exhaustively perform the image similarity scoring between all keyframe pairs, and then aggregating them. However, this does not take into account of the fact that the matching keyframe pairs must also be aligned temporally. We address this problem by a 2-D Hough Transform-like voting histogram. For each candidate video V_k matching to a query video V_q, we use k as an index along the first dimension of the 2-D histogram H_{2d}, and perform image level similarity $Sim_{image}(I_k, I_q)$ (equation 2) to retrieve all matching keyframe pairs. For each keyframe pair I_k and I_q, with corresponding timestamp t_k and t_q, we first quantize their time lag $lag = t_k - t_q$, and using it as an index along the second dimension in H_{2d}, write $Sim_{image}(I_k, I_q)$ into the bin $H_{2d}[k, lag]$. As a result, a peak $H_{2d}[k, lag]$ in the 2-D histogram indicates that keyframe segments in V_k around the timestamp lag have high matching scores in terms of local features and temporal alignment. The video similarity score is given by:

$$sim_{video}(V_k, V_q) = \max_{lag}(H_{2d}[k, lag]) \qquad (3)$$

2.3 Evaluation

We perform two experiments on a dataset provided by [7]. It comprises of 127K news video + ASR-text, and 16 topical queries [1] with manually labeled ground truth. A total of 54K YouTube videos were crawled from 8 channels over the two years spanning these queries. To expedite near-duplicate detection, only the YouTube videos within a neighboring time window of each ASR video are considered for similarity matching.

2.3.1 Advantage of Label Propagation

The first experiment assesses the impact of label propagation on retrieval precision. Given an input news video, we can perform salient keyword extraction separately on the ASR text and the enriched text, to respectively generate two new text queries, denoted as Q_{ASR} and Q_{ENR}. Then, each

[1] The queries are: 1. Air France AF447, 2. Caspian Air Crash, 3. Environment Issues, 4. Italy Earthquake, 5. Pakistan Taliban, 6. US Airways Hudson River, 7. Yemenia Air Crash, 8. beijing olympics, 9. H1N1 flu, 10. mas selamat, 11. mumbai attack, 12. myanmar protest, 13. cyclone nargis, 14. obama presidential election, 15. sichuan earthquake, 16. tamil tigers.

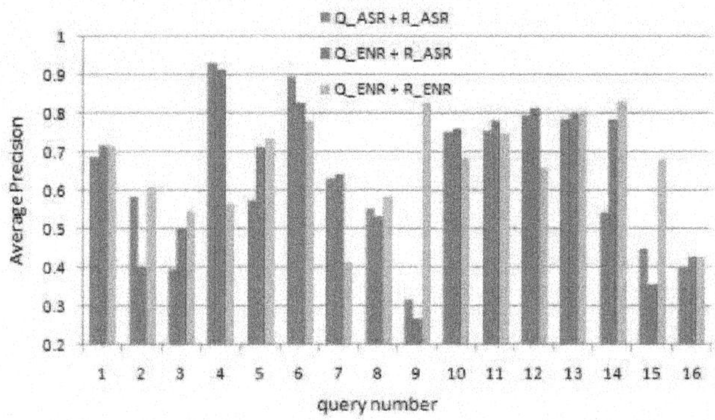

Figure 2: Comparative Average Precision results. Best viewed in color.

of these queries can in turn be issued to a text-based news retrieval engine, where we use the returned videos to calculate retrieval precision. The idea is that the higher the quality of a text, one would expect the better the extracted keywords and resultant query, ultimately leading to retrieved results that are more relevant. For this experiment, keywords are extracted based on a standard $tf.idf$ algorithm. Each word is weighted by $tf \times idf$, where tf is the frequency of the word in the video corpus, and idf is the inverse of the number of documents in which the word appears. The two words with the largest weight are returned as the query.

Two more additional combinations are factored in the comparison: the text-based news retrieval engine may be indexed using the original ASR text (denoted by R_{ASR}), or indexed using the enriched text (denoted by R_{ENR}). Empirically, the parameter α has little effect on the label propagation, and so is set to 0.5 for all experiments. Figure 2 shows the comparative Average Precision (AP) results. The overall Mean AP for $Q_{ASR} + R_{ASR}$, $Q_{ENR} + R_{ASR}$ and $Q_{ENR} + R_{ENR}$ are respectively 0.48, 0.61 and 0.66. As expected, the retrieval results using the ASR text issuing to an indexing system based also on ASR text performs the worst. With just label propagation, results are significantly improved, with further improvement coming from re-indexing all videos with the enriched text.

2.3.2 Noise Resilience

The second experiment assesses the impact of noise to retrieval performance. For each word in the video text, with a probability rate r, it is randomly deleted or a random word (chosen uniformly from the vocabulary) inserted. In Figure 3, we plot the Mean Average Precision (MAP) against noise. Even though our noise model is clearly simplistic and does not capture the underlying language model, the results are instructive. The propagation framework is resilient to small levels of noise. Beyond the noise rate of 0.25, the MAP deteriorates and the method performs worse than the ASR-based baseline. This indicates that the label propagation algorithm is very dependent on the initial label assignment. The direct implication of this result is that we should do a targeted search for videos with higher quality text that facilitate label propagation. For example, we can manually identify a few official YouTube News channels with good quality labels and synopsis from which videos are crawled.

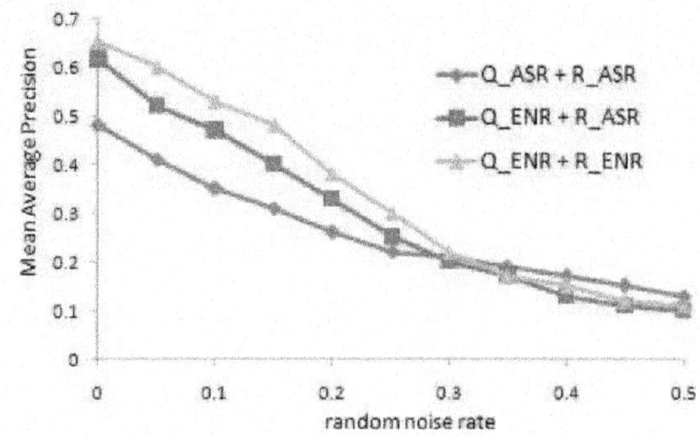

Figure 3: Comparative Average Precision results under different noise rates. Best viewed in color.

3. SUBTOPIC RETRIEVAL

. In this section, we describe another application that has been made more amenable by the enrichment of news video text – subtopic retrieval. The problem of subtopic retrieval was introduced in [9] to study how a retrieval system can best support a user gather information about the different *aspects* or *subtopics* of a topic. It is akin to search result clustering and the removal of near-duplicates, with the goal of presenting a diversified list of results catering to the varying information needs of the users.

To elucidate subtopics in documents, many topic modeling based methods have been proposed [1]. However, a critical issue with the resulting topics is the lack of human interpretability [3]. In this work, we follow the approaches of [7] and develop an algorithm to model a news story as a distribution over Wikipedia pages. For example, a news story on "The re-capture of Mas Salemat" will be modeled by a weighted distribution over related articles like "Mas Salemat", "JI", "Internal Security Act", etc.

The motivation of our approach is three-fold. First, by interpreting each news story in terms of its affinity with a collection of Wikipedia concepts, the resulting topic model is grounded in human cognition and "explicit semantics" [5], as opposed to "latent topics" derived by Bayesian methods such as the Latent Dirichlet Allocation (LDA) [1]. Second, Wkipedia as the space of reference articles gives us the added advantage of tapping into a resource that is almost complete and up-to-date. Third, the editorial content of each Wikipedia page is organized into a taxonomic Table-of-Content (TOC) structure which not only readily elucidates the needed perspectives or aspects of the topic, but also allows a non-linear search and facilitates exploratory learning.

All that remains is to map a given video text to the related Wikipedia TOC content. To do this efficiently, each Wikipedia page is first XML-parsed to extract the TOC entries. Short TOC entries (<30 unique non-stop words) are merged with an adjacent TOC entry. An inverted index is then built that maps each word to a list of TOCs in which it appears. Given a story text, we iterate over each word, retrieves the corresponding TOCs from the inverted index, and count-aggregate them into a weighted vector of concepts, such that each feature in the vector encodes the relevance of the corresponding Wikipedia concept. To compare between two vectors, we compute the Cosine similarity $Cosine_{wiki}$. Clearly, the better the quality of the input video text, the more accurate is the mapping to the concepts.

Table 1: **Comparative S-recall results (using MMR).**

	$S\text{-}rec@20$
ASR baseline ($Q_{ASR} + R_{ASR}$)	0.277
Enrichment-1 ($Q_{ENR} + R_{ASR}$)	0.318
Enrichment-2 ($Q_{ENR} + R_{ENR}$)	0.327

3.1 Evaluation

The goal of subtopic retrieval is to include in the early ranks, documents that cover as many different subtopics as attested in the corpus. More formally, given the set of known subtopics f_i underlying the videos related to a query video V_q, and a set of videos $\{V_1, V_2, \ldots, V_k\}$ retrieved up to rank k, subtopic retrieval is evaluated by *S-recall* [9]:

$$S\text{-}rec@k = \frac{1}{n_q} \sum_{i=1}^{n_q} I(f_i \in \{V_1, V_2, \ldots, V_k\}) \quad (4)$$

where n_q is the number of subtopics of q, and $I(\cdot)$=1 if f_i appears in any of the videos ranked 1 to k, and 0 otherwise. At any k, $S\text{-}rec@k$ rewards returning a list of k videos that contain as many of the n_q subtopics as possible.

We implement a diversity retrieval model called Maximal Marginal Relevance (MMR) [2]. This is a greedy method that selects the ith video V_i according to a combination of its similarity to the video query V_q and its similarity to all higher-ranked videos at position 1 to k-1:

$$\begin{aligned} \mathbf{MMR}(V_i, V_q) &= \beta Cosine_{wiki}(V_i, V_q) - \\ &\quad (1-\beta) \max_{1 \le j < i} Cosine_{wiki}(V_i, V_j) \quad (5) \end{aligned}$$

where $\beta \in [0, 1]$ is a trade-off parameter. We set $\beta = 0.5$.

At the time of this writing, we used as queries a small collection of 33 topic ground truths [2] provided by [8], which are based on the TRECVID-2005 dataset. For subtopic retrieval evaluation, three human assessors further annotated subtopics on these video topics [3]. As per the evaluation methodology in Section 2.3.1, we apply keyword extraction to the original ASR text and enriched text to generate two new queries Q_{ASR} and Q_{ENR}. These are issued to the two video indices R_{ASR} (based on ASR text) and R_{ENR} (based on enriched text). Table 1 shows the S-recall measures on the respective returned videos. It is clear that the text enrichment process has improved subtopic retrieval.

Figure 4 shows a snapshot of our system UI. Given a user query, returned news videos are organized according to the Wikipedia TOC (right panel). The videos in each TOC group are playback in reverse chronological order. Users can click on any TOC group for non-linear browsing.

4. CONCLUSIONS

There is a general anticipation that recent advances in visual search can bring much progress to the domain of multimedia search. However, it is our view that the semantic gap issue remains unsolved, and that text processing still holds the best prospects for progress in semantic analysis of content. In this paper, we describe a label propagation method that enriches the textual content of videos. We show that with proper targeting of external video resources with good quality labels, raw videos become more amenable to search, and finer-grained semantic analysis such as subtopic retrieval can be facilitated. Specific future works include investigating the use of bigrams in the label propagation.

[2]Sample topics: "Bush visits Canada", "Arafat-health", etc.

[3]We are in the process of creating a larger corpus of 400 topic queries, fully annotated with subtopics, and available upon request. We will also report subtopic retrieval lresults on this corpus in a later publication.

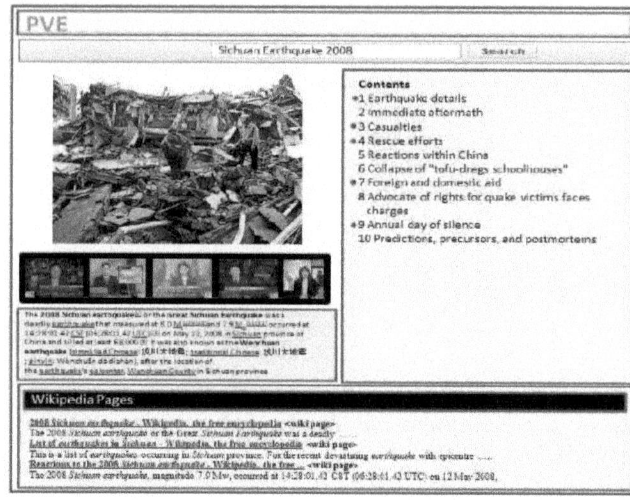

Figure 4: UI of News subtopics browser. See text.

5. REFERENCES

[1] D. Blei, A. Ng, and M. Jordan. Latent dirichlet allocation. *Journal of Machine Learning Research*, 3:993–1022, 2003.

[2] J. Carbonell and J. Goldstein. The use of MMR, diversity-based reranking for reordering documents and producing summaries. *Proc SIGIR conf on Research and development in informaion retrieval*, pages 335–336, 1998.

[3] J. Chang, J. Boyd-Graber, C. Wang, S. Gerrish, and D. Blei. Reading tea leaves: How humans interpret topic models. In *Advances in Neural Information Processing Systems*, 2009.

[4] L. Dong, X. Hua, M. Wang, and H. Zhang. Image retagging. In *Proc ACM Multimedia*, pages 491–500, 2010.

[5] E. Gabrilovich and S. Markovitch. Computing semantic relatedness using wikipedia-based explicit semantic analysis. In *Proc Int'l Joint Conf on Artifical Intelligence*, pages 1606–1611, 2007.

[6] J. Law-To, G. Grefenstette, and J. Gauvain. Voxaleadnews: robust automatic segmentation of video into browsable content. In *Proc ACM Multimedia*, pages 1119–1120, 2009.

[7] S. Roy, M. Mak, and K. Wan. Wikipedia based news video topic modeling for information extraction. In *Proc Multimedia Modeling*, pages 411–420, 2011.

[8] X. Wu, A. Hauptmann, and C. Ngo. Novelty detection for cross-lingual news stories with visual duplicates and speech transcripts. In *Proc Multimedia*, pages 168–177, 2007.

[9] C. Zhai, W. Cohen, and J. Lafferty. Beyond independent relevance: methods and evaluation metrics for subtopic retrieval. In *Proc SIGIR conf on Research and development in informaion retrieval*, pages 10–17, 2003.

[10] W. Zhao, X. Wu, and C. Ngo. On the Annotation of Web Videos by Efficient Near-Duplicate Search. *IEEE Transactions on Multimedia*, 12:448–461, 2010.

[11] D. Zhou, O. Bousquet, T. N. Lal, J. Weston, and B. Schlkopf. Learning with local and global consistency. In *Advances in Neural Information Processing Systems 16*, pages 321–328, 2004.

Human Action Recognition by Fast Dense Trajectories

Zongbo Hao
University of Electronic Science and Technology of China
No.4 Section2, North Jianshe Road, 610054, Chengdu, Sichuan, China
Tel: +86 28 6183 0580
zbhao@uestc.edu.cn

Qianni Zhang
Queen Mary, University of London
Mile End Road
London E1 4NS, U.K.
Tel: +44 20 7882 7138
qianni.zhang@eecs.qmul.ac.uk

Ebroul Ezquierdo
Queen Mary, University of London
Mile End Road
London E1 4NS, U.K.
Tel: +44 20 7882 5354
ebroul.ezquierdo@eecs.-qmul.ac.uk

Nan Sang
University of Electronic Science and Technology of China
No.4 Section2, North Jianshe Road, 610054, Chengdu, Sichuan, China
Tel: +86 28 6183 0581
sn@uestc.edu.cn

ABSTRACT
In this paper, we propose the fast dense trajectories algorithm for human action recognition. Dense trajectories are robust to fast irregular motions and outperform other state-of-the-art descriptors such as KLT tracker or SIFT descriptors. However, the use of dense trajectories is time consuming. To improve the efficiency, we extract feature trajectories in the ROI rather than in the whole frames, and we use the temporal pyramids to achieve adaptable mechanism for different action speed. We evaluate the method on the dataset of Huawei/3DLife – 3D human reconstruction and action recognition Grand Challenge in ACM Multimedia 2013. Experimental results show a significant improvement over the dense trajectories descriptor in real-time, and adaptable to different speed.

Categories and Subject Descriptors
I.2.10 [**Vision and Scene Understanding**]: Video analysis; I.4.8 [**Scene Analysis**]: motion

Keywords
Fast dense trajectories; human action recognition; adaptable to different speed; real-time

1. INTRODUCTION
The recognition of human action and motion using computer vision has recently gained more and more interest in recent years [14][10][7]. The key point is detecting, tracking, recognizing humans from the video by the computer vision, and then understanding and characterizing their actions [16]. Action recognition has broad application prospect and potential economic value in the field such as intelligent surveillance, smart appliances, human machine interface, and content-based image retrieval. Because of individual differences, the diversity and complexity of actions, and complex backgrounds, action recognition is a challenging problem. We know the challenges in action recognition mainly are: (1) person localization in cluttered or dynamic environment; (2) lighting condition; (3) observed from different viewpoint or with the dynamic background or with the moving camera. At the same time, a robust human action recognition algorithm should be invariant to different rates of execution [14].

From the viewpoint of application, action recognition can be divided into three types: (1) intelligent surveillance; (2) human machine interface and (3) automatic video annotation. There are two stages in human action recognition by computer vision: Action representation and classification of these representations. Action representations encode the human actions in the first stage, and have great affect on the second stage. An ideal representation should not only take into account the influence of the size of human body, the complex background, different viewpoint and the speed of the action, but also comprise sufficient information for the classifier to differentiate the actions. An effective classifier is expected to be able to distinguish existing and new action types.

Action recognition can be categorized in three general approaches: the approaches based on local features, based on global features and the systematic approach. The local feature based approach represents actions using the local spatial-temporal information [13][9][6]. For instance, [4]used an unsupervised learning method similar to bag-of-words approach to learn the probability distribution of the spatial-temporal interested points. The methods proposed in [12] obtained the activities model using the data captured from the joint movement to recognize the actions. These two methods failed to combine the local features as a whole in recognition. The global methods use global features, for example the optical flow, to represent motion. In [2], Histogram of Optical Flow (HOF) was used to recognize the movement of the athletes. In [11][3], 3D spatial-temporal models were used to represent human actions. Yet these methods did not build a model for the dynamic time features. In the systematic approach, a dynamic system is built to recognize human actions according to the feature changes of the human movement. So the dynamic features are taken into account. In [1] the trajectories of the joint

MM'13, October 21–25, 2013, Barcelona, Spain.

movement and the counters of the shape were used to represent the features. In [15] a nonlinear model was built according to the trajectories. However these systems suffer from the shortcoming of inadequate local representations.

In this paper, we propose a fast dense trajectories algorithm to recognize human actions. The algorithm of dense trajectories performs well in human action recognition, yet it makes heavy calculation load and not suitable for real-time systems. We extract foreground first and track the feature points in the foreground area to reduce the calculation significantly. Another contribution of this paper is using the temporal pyramid when tracking the trajectory, which makes our approach adaptable to the action speed.

This paper is organized as follows. In section 2, we describe the fast dense trajectories and the use of spatial-temporal points to distinguish recursive actions. In section 3, we employ the temporal pyramid to make the algorithm adaptable to action speed. In section 4 we test our approach on the dataset of ACM Multimedia 2013, and compared it with the dense trajectories algorithm. At last in section 5 is the conclusion of the research.

2. FAST DENSE TRAJECTORIES

Dense trajectories contain rich information of movement [8], but the dense optical flow introduces heavy calculation load, and is not suitable for the real-time application. In this paper, we employ a fast method for dense trajectories which can significantly reduce the calculation, and thus makes dense trajectories applicable in real-time.

2.1 Fast Dense Trajectories

Dense trajectories are the sequences of the dense feature points in the video. Let the optical flow for the Image I_t be $\omega_t = (u_t, v_t)$, feature point in I_t be $p_t = (x_t, y_t)$,then

$$A = \sum \omega(x - x_t, y - y_t) \begin{pmatrix} I_x^2 & I_x I_y \\ I_y I_x & I_y^2 \end{pmatrix} \quad (1)$$

where I_x, I_y is the gradient on the x and y directions respectively. The Eigen value for matrix A is λ_1, λ_2, then the qualified feature point p_t should satisfy

$$\max(\lambda_1, \lambda_2) > T_{eig} \quad (2)$$

T_{eig} is the threshold. Its speed should satisfy

$$\|\omega_t(x_t, y_t)\|_2 > T_v \quad (3)$$

T_v is the threshold for the moving speed. If the feature point p_t satisfies conditions in (2) and (3), it will be selected as the seed and be tracked by optical flow, which means the small movements, which are usually caused by noise, will be abandoned. We track the seeds using the method as proposed in [8] on median filtering.

$$P_{t+1} = (x_{t+1}, y_{t+1}) = (x_t, y_t) + (M * \omega)|_{(\bar{x}_t, \bar{y}_t)} \quad (4)$$

where M is the median filtering kernel, and $(\bar{x}_t, \bar{y}_t)$ is the rounded position of (x_t, y_t). Because of the calculation errors, long term tracking will fail and drift away the real trajectories. Thus, we limit the trajectory length to L frames as [8]. That is, when the length of the trajectory exceeds L frames, we stop tracking that trajectory, in order to avoid tracking with the accumulated error.

Figure.1 illustrates the dense trajectories of the action knocking. The circles indicate the current positions of the feature points, and the connecting lines are the trajectories. We can see that the trajectories are continuous, by which we can calculate the gradient and predict the next position so as to reduce the calculation and improve the property of real-time.

Figure 1 Illustration of the dense trajectories

We notice that in the dataset provided by the Huawei/3DLife – 3D human reconstruction and action recognition Grand Challenge, only the corresponding limbs that perform the actions make movement while other parts of the body keep still. Based on this observation, in the first step, we extract the foreground in the video sequences. Then the trajectories are tracked only in the foreground. This approach allows reducing the calculation load significantly, and moreover, it helps improving the recognition performance by removing the noise in the videos. Here foreground extraction is achieved using a threshold-difference background subtraction method.

2.2 SPATIAL-TEMPORAL POINTS

In the video series used in our experiments, we observe that the same action is often repeated for several times, but with different speed. As we can see in the knocking video, the knocking action is performed first slowly and the speed of action increases. As a result, the same action has different trajectories length. It is necessary to distinguish real action from a mixture of several recursive trajectories as one action. So we employ the spatial-temporal points to ensure each repeating action is clearly separated from others.

Spatial-temporal interest points are the points with the local space-time features that correspond to interesting events in video data whose neighborhood are with high spatial-temporal variation or the "space-time corners". Usually we can find spatial-temporal points at the end of an action sequence. For example, when the football player heading the ball, the ball's trajectory will change, we can get the spatial-temporal point, as show in figure 2 [9].

Similarly, we can get spatial-temporal points at the connection spot between two recursive actions in the sequences. Here we use the approach proposed in [13]. First the frames are filtered by the Gaussian filter in spatial, and then by the 1D Gabor filter in temporal. The intensity value of each point can be calculated as:

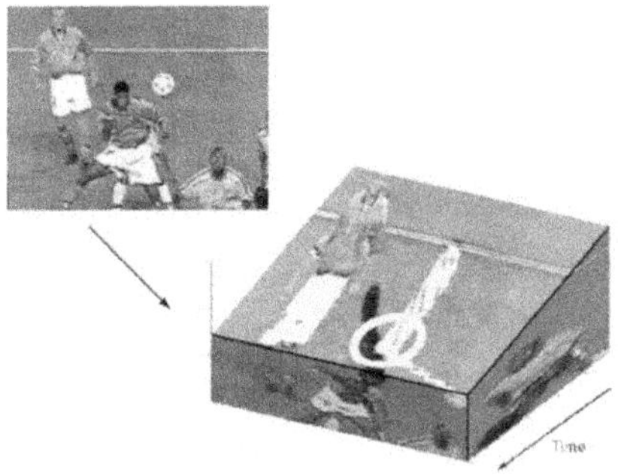

Figure 2 Spatial-temporal points

$$R = (I * g * h_{ev})^2 + (I * g * h_{od})^2 \tag{5}$$

where $g(x, y; \sigma)$ is two-dimensional spatial Gaussian smoothing kernel, h_{ev} and h_{od} are two orthogonal one-dimensional Gabor filters. Here $g(x, y; \sigma^2) = \frac{1}{2\pi\sigma^2} e^{-(x^2+y^2)/2\sigma^2}$, $h_{ev}(t; \tau, \omega) = -\cos(2\pi t\omega) e^{-t^2/\tau^2}$, $h_{od}(t; \tau, \omega) = -\sin(2\pi t\omega) e^{-t^2/\tau^2}$.

2.3 DISTINGUISH BETEEN SIMILAR ACTIONS

Some actions are similar, for example, head scratching, eye rubbing and touching one's face. They all have the action putting the hands on the head, which makes the trajectories look alike. The biggest difference is what the hands touch with on the spatial-temporal points. So we recognize the hand and its connecting body parts using the haar cascade classifier. To some extend it helps improve the recognition accuracy.

3. TEMPORAL PYRAMID

The same action performed by different executors may take unequal time. For example, the kicking action requires the person first lift one of his leg, and then stretches it out, at last back it and stand straight. Such a series of actions may take different time. In order to ensure the proposed method is adaptable to the action speed, temporal pyramid is employed. In the pyramid, the top level $j = 0$ is a histogram over the full temporal extent of trajectories of the actions acquired as explained in section 2 and 3. The next level is the concatenation of two histograms obtained by temporally segmenting the action clip into two halves, and so on. We can get a coarse-to-fine representation by concatenating all such histograms together

$$x^j = \frac{2^{j-1}}{|T|} \sum_{t \in T^j} f^t \tag{6}$$

where T^j is the temporal extent on the j'th of the pyramid and x^j is the feature on that segment. The scale factors define an implicit correspondence based on the finest temporal resolution at which a model feature matches a video feature. This allows us to extract the trajectories in an adaptable manner. The same action with different speed can be correctly recognized.

We train a classifier with the public SVM implementation of [5]

$$x = \min([x^0 \dots x^j \dots x^L]^T, 0.02) \tag{7}$$

Several histogram kernels have been considered in our experiments, but we found a simple linear kernel defined on an L1-normalized feature works well.

4. EXPERIMENTS

We tested our approach on the dataset of Huawei/3DLife – 3D human reconstruction and action recognition Grand Challenge in ACM Multimedia 2013. There are 26 kinds of gestures/movements in the dataset, among which 5 are static gestures, and the others are more dynamic. Each gesture/movement is performed by 7 individuals being recorded from six different viewpoints. We tested our algorithm on the 21 dynamic action types, and compared with the dense trajectories, as shown in Table1. Table 1shows that the clapping, pushing and walking actions have the highest recognition accuracy, because the trajectories are easy to distinguish from others. While eye movement and facial expression has the worst score, for they are somewhat static because only the eyeballs and the muscles on the face are moving, which are hard to track. And the two approaches perform basically equal for these actions. Our approach outperforms dense trajectories significantly for actions of the head scratching, eye rubbing and touching one's face.

In both our approach and the dense trajectories, the neighborhood size of the feature point has great influence on the recognition efficiency. In figure 3 the top row is the dense trajectories with different neighborhood size, and the bottom row is for our approach. The number indicates the size. We can see that when the size is small (D5 compared with F5), there are many useless feature points for fast dense trajectories. And when the size gets bigger, the feature points become less (D20 and F20). The calculation time gets smaller, as shown in figure 4. For fast dense trajectories, the size s=10 is the optimal option, and s=17 is the best for dense trajectories.

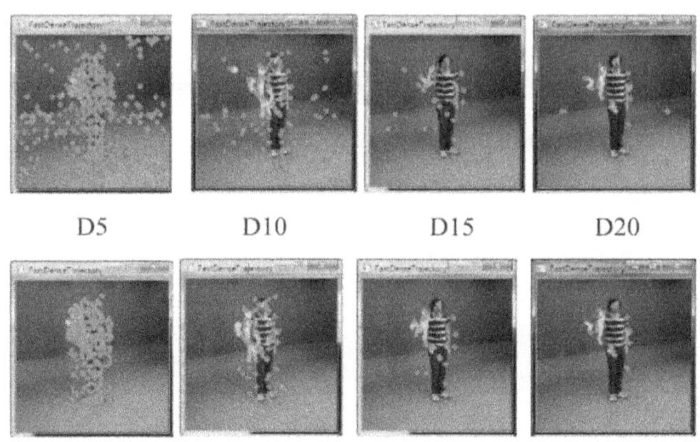

D5 D10 D15 D20

F5 F10 F15 F20

Figure 3 Influence of the neighborhood size of feature points

5. CONCLUSION

This paper has presented a fast dense trajectories algorithm for human action recognition. Dense trajectories perform well in action recognition. However it is time consuming. We extract the foreground first, and then track the feature points in the ROI instead of in the entire frame, which can improve the recognition efficiency greatly. Then we employ the temporal pyramid to make the algorithm adaptable to different action speed. For the similar actions, we use the interacting objects to distinguish. Our approach outperforms the dense trajectories in the efficiency, and more robust to different action speed.

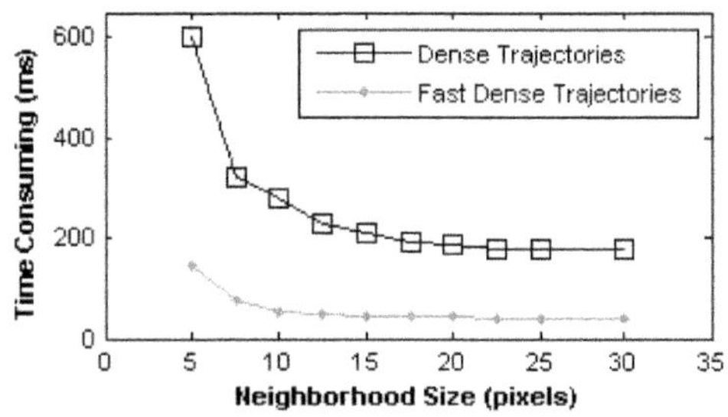

Figure 4 the neighborhood size feature

Table 1 Recognition performance

	Recognition accuracy (%)			**Recognition accuracy (%)**	
actions	Our approach	Dense trajectory	actions	Our approach	Dense trajectory
clapping	92.3	94.1	knocking the door	82.8	83.3
crossing the arms	87.7	88	lifting an object	88.6	88.8
crossing the legs	90.6	91.3	nodding	86.7	90.1
eye rubbing	88.4	83.7	punching/boxing	86.3	88.2
eye movement and facial expression	73.1	70.3	pushing away with both hands	91.3	93.6
fingers motion	83.5	83.2	bending the knees and standing up	89	91.1
fist clenched	77	81.1	throwing	87.6	89.3
head scratching	87.1	82.5	Touching one's face	91.1	87.9
head shaking	89.1	91.2	Walking on a treadmill	90.2	93.4
head tilting	88.7	89.1	waving one hand	84.2	84.5
kicking and punching	87.2	90.1			

6. REFERENCES

[1] Bissacco, A., Chiuso, A., and Soatto, S., 2007. Classification and recognition of dynamical models: The role of phase, independent components, kernels and optimal transport. *Pattern Analysis and Machine Intelligence, IEEE Transactions on 29*, 11, 1958-1972.

[2] Efros, A.A., Berg, A.C., Mori, G., and Malik, J., 2003. Recognizing action at a distance. In *Computer Vision, 2003. Proceedings. Ninth IEEE International Conference on* IEEE, 726-733.

[3] Yilmaz, A. and Shah, M., 2005. Actions sketch: A novel action representation. In *Computer Vision and Pattern Recognition, 2005. CVPR 2005. IEEE Computer Society Conference on* IEEE, 984-989.

[4] Niebles, J.C., Wang, H., and Fei-Fei, L., 2008. Unsupervised learning of human action categories using spatial-temporal words. *International Journal of Computer Vision 79*, 3, 299-318.

[5] Fan, R.-E., Chang, K.-W., Hsieh, C.-J., Wang, X.-R., and Lin, C.-J., 2008. LIBLINEAR: A library for large linear classification. *The Journal of Machine Learning Research 9*, 1871-1874.

[6] Willems, G., Tuytelaars, T., and Van Gool, L., 2008. An efficient dense and scale-invariant spatio-temporal interest point detector. In *Computer Vision–ECCV 2008* Springer, 650-663.

[7] Pirsiavash, H. and Ramanan, D., 2012. Detecting activities of daily living in first-person camera views. In *Computer Vision and Pattern Recognition (CVPR), 2012 IEEE Conference on* IEEE, 2847-2854.

[8] Wang, H., Klaser, A., Schmid, C., and Liu, C.-L., 2011. Action recognition by dense trajectories. In *Computer Vision and Pattern Recognition (CVPR), 2011 IEEE Conference on* IEEE, 3169-3176.

[9] Laptev, I., 2005. On space-time interest points. *International Journal of Computer Vision 64*, 2-3, 107-123.

[10] Liu, J., Kuipers, B., and Savarese, S., 2011. Recognizing human actions by attributes. In *Computer Vision and Pattern Recognition (CVPR), 2011 IEEE Conference on* IEEE, 3337-3344.

[11] Blank, M., Gorelick, L., Shechtman, E., Irani, M., and Basri, R., 2005. Actions as space-time shapes. In *Computer Vision, 2005. ICCV 2005. Tenth IEEE International Conference on* IEEE, 1395-1402.

[12] İkizler, N. and Forsyth, D.A., 2008. Searching for complex human activities with no visual examples. *International Journal of Computer Vision 80*, 3, 337-357.

[13] Dollár, P., Rabaud, V., Cottrell, G., and Belongie, S., 2005. Behavior recognition via sparse spatio-temporal features. In *Visual Surveillance and Performance Evaluation of Tracking and Surveillance, 2005. 2nd Joint IEEE International Workshop on* IEEE, 65-72.

[14] Poppe, R., 2010. A survey on vision-based human action recognition. *Image and vision computing 28*, 6, 976-990.

[15] Ali, S., Basharat, A., and Shah, M., 2007. Chaotic invariants for human action recognition. In *Computer Vision, 2007. ICCV 2007. IEEE 11th International Conference on* IEEE, 1-8.

[16] Hu, W., Tan, T., Wang, L., and Maybank, S., 2004. A survey on visual surveillance of object motion and behaviors. *Systems, Man, and Cybernetics, Part C: Applications and Reviews, IEEE Transactions on 34*, 3, 334-352

Scalable Training with Approximate Incremental Laplacian Eigenmaps and PCA

Eleni Mantziou
CERTH-ITI
Thessaloniki, Greece
lmantziou@iti.gr

Symeon Papadopoulos
CERTH-ITI
Thessaloniki, Greece
papadop@iti.gr

Yiannis Kompatsiaris
CERTH-ITI
Thessaloniki, Greece
ikom@iti.gr

ABSTRACT

The paper describes the approach, the experimental settings, and the results obtained by the proposed methodology at the ACM Yahoo! Multimedia Grand Challenge. Its main contribution is the use of fast and efficient features with a highly scalable semi-supervised learning approach, the Approximate Laplacian Eigenmaps (ALEs), and its extension, by computing the test set incrementally for learning concepts in time linear to the number of images (both labelled and unlabelled). A combination of two local visual features combined with the VLAD feature aggregation method and PCA is used to improve the efficiency and time complexity. Our methodology achieves somewhat better accuracy compared to the baseline (linear SVM) in small training sets, but improves the performance as the training data increase. Performing ALE fusion on a training set of 50K/concept resulted in a MiAP score of 0.4223, which was among the highest scores of the proposed approach.

Categories and Subject Descriptors

I.5 [**Pattern Recognition**]: Design Methodology

General Terms

Experimentation, Measurement, Performance, Algorithms

Keywords

Concept Detection, Laplacian Eigenmaps, Large-scale Annotation, Machine Learning

1. INTRODUCTION

This document describes our participation in the ACM Yahoo! Multimedia Grand Challenge 2013. The competition introduces a new challenging dataset that features 10 noisy concepts with $150K$ images per concept.

In recent years, the available online content constantly increases. In this context, semi-supervised learning is a promising approach for concept detection since it can benefit from the inclusion of unlabelled images in the training process. More specifically, *manifold learning* approaches rely on the assumption that there is an underlying image manifold, wherein semantically similar images are placed close to each other and semantically dissimilar images are positioned far from each other. Typically, *manifold learning* is implemented by means of constructing a similarity graph between labelled and unlabelled images and leveraging the graph to estimate the labels of the unlabelled images by considering the labels of neighbouring labelled images. Considering the beneficial results of using a manifold learning method in a concept detection problem, we choose to employ an approximate semi-supervised method for this challenge. However the manipulation of such large graphs is computationally costly, which is impractical for large datasets. Also, once new images are observed the graph must be updated.

Our approach, described in Section 2, tackles the scaling problem by constructing approximate eigenvectors based on the density structure of the data and by updating the eigenvectors of the test set incrementally. This is implemented with the use of the marginal distribution by building a density histogram to compute the eigenfunctions considering the limit as the number of points go to infinity. After computing the eigenfunctions, we interpolate them at each of the data points to extract the first k-approximate eigenvectors with the smallest eigenvalues. We will refer to this approach as Approximate Laplacian Eigenmaps (ALE) [1]. Extending the ALE, we devise an incremental method, in which once a new image is inserted, we interpolate its feature vector based on the eigenfunctions and eigenvalues of the training images. In this paper, we construct features that are easy to manipulate especially in large scale problems, by combining SIFT and RGB-SIFT with the VLAD feature aggregation.

2. OVERVIEW OF METHOD

Our approach is based on Semi-Supervised Learning (SSL) by constructing Laplacian Eigenmaps (LEs) approximately and incrementally. We use the LEs as new features to train concept classifiers. SMaL is a **S**calable **Ma**nifold **L**earning framework [3] on top of ALE, which is linear to the number of images, making possible to use the graph Laplacian in large-scale problems. SMaL makes use of the Vectors of Locally Aggregated Descriptors (VLAD), and reduces their dimensionality by PCA.

VLAD [2] is a simplified non-probabilistic version of the Fisher Vector for feature aggregation, which uses a codebook of size μ_K computed using k-means. By applying nearest

MM'13, October 21–25, 2013, Barcelona, Spain.

http://dx.doi.org/10.1145/2502081.2508124 .

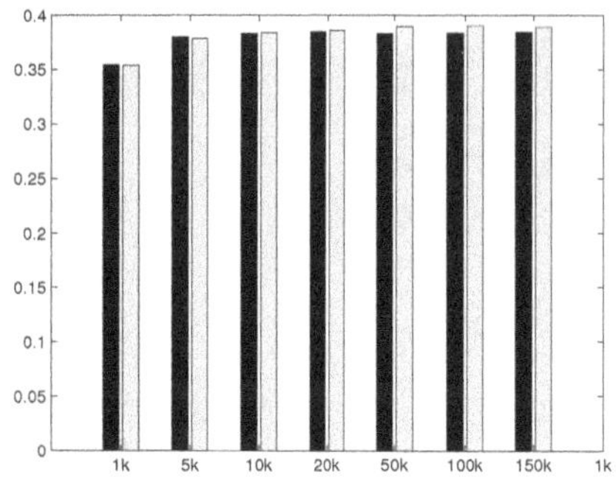

(a) SIFT

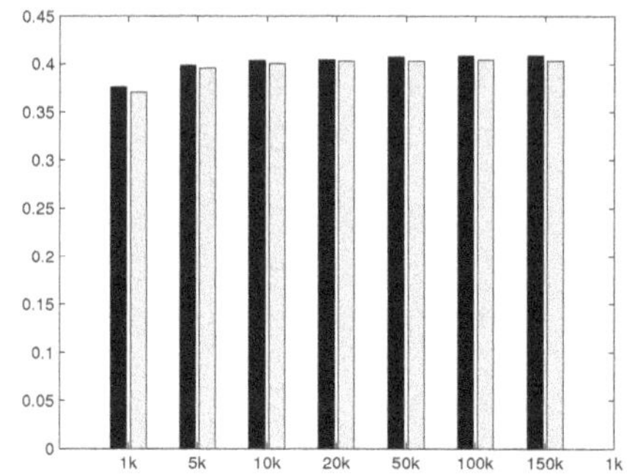

(b) RGB-SIFT

Figure 1: Comparison of MiAP between SVM (**black**) and SMaL (**light gray**).

neighbour (NN) search, each local descriptor x_t is associated with its nearest centroid. Then, the differences between the descriptors x_t and the centroid μ_i are accumulated to u_i. The d-dimensional vector of each feature is concatenated with u_i constructing the Kd dimensional final VLAD vector.

As mentioned above, in order to construct the LEs, we need to build a $n \times n$ similarity matrix between labelled and unlabelled images (n is the number of labelled and unlabelled images together). A matrix like this is very costly to compute in large collections. In SMaL, we tackle this problem based on the approximate computation of LEs by estimating a smaller covariance matrix, as suggested in [1], where it is hypothesized that the data $x_i \in \Re^d$ are samples from a distribution $p(x)$. Rotating the data to be as independent as possible, $s = Rx$, can result in a $B \times B$ histogram of bins, using only marginal distributions that approximate the density $p(s)$ of the rotated data.

Then, instead of computing the eigenvectors of the similarity matrix between the original data ($n \times n$), one can define eigenfunctions g corresponding to the eigenvalues of the rotated data s ($B \times B$), which can be seen as approximations of the LEs of the original data when $n \rightarrow \infty$. This is considerably faster, since typically $B \ll n$. These are recovered by solving the following equation:

$$\left(\tilde{D} - P\tilde{W}P\right) g = \sigma P\hat{D}g \quad (1)$$

where $\tilde{W}$ is the affinity between the B discrete points, P is a diagonal matrix whose diagonal elements give the density at the discrete points, $\tilde{D}$ is a diagonal matrix whose diagonal elements are the sum of the columns of $P\tilde{W}P$, and $\hat{D}$ is a diagonal matrix whose diagonal elements are the sum of the columns of $P\tilde{W}$. An interpolation step follows to the target dimension C_D (described in [1]) and in the end, the $n \times C_D$ approximate LE vectors are derived.

To tackle the Yahoo! challenge which does not allow the use of test data during training, we devised an online implementation by computing the eigenvectors of unlabelled data incrementally. We build the $B \times B$ matrix based on the histogram bins of labelled data. From this matrix the eigenfunctions and the eigenvalues of the eigenfunctions are derived. We use these values to interpolate both the labelled and unlabelled data separately.

In the final step, the LEs are used to define a smoothness operator that takes into account the unlabelled data. The key idea is to find functions f, which agree with the labelled

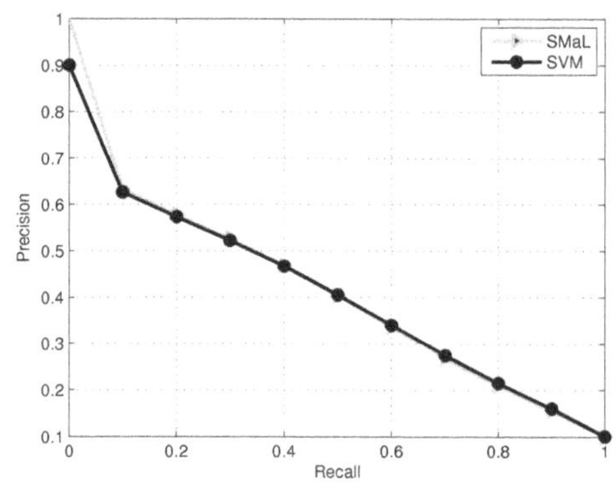

Figure 2: Precision-Recall curve at 50K/Concept between SMaL and Linear SVM, when SIFT & RGB-SIFT are fused.

data and are also smooth with respect to the graph. To avoid the trivial solution $f = 1$, a combination of smoothness vector and the training error loss is minimized [1]. The smoothness of an eigenvector ϕ has the form

$$f = \Sigma_i \alpha \phi_i \quad (2)$$

Thus, smooth vectors are linear combinations of the eigenvectors with small eigenvalues. In our implementation, we define f as $f = U\alpha$. Thus, the minimization problem reduces to the minimization of α, defined as

$$(\Sigma + U^T \Lambda U)a = U^T \Lambda y \quad (3)$$

where Σ are the smallest eigenvalues, U is the $n \times C_D$ approximate LE vectors, Λ is a diagonal matrix, whose diagonal elements are $\Lambda_{ii} = \lambda$ if i is labelled, otherwise $\lambda = 0$, and y are the labels.

3. EXPERIMENTAL SETUP

Training Set Creation: As suggested by the organizers, we evaluate our results on 1K, 5K, 10K, 20K, 50K, 100K and 150K training images per concept. For better consistency of the results, we take random sets and use 10 repetitions at each split (except 150K/concept since it uses all the training data and cannot be split).

Feature Extraction: We have used the SIFT ($d = 128$) and RGB-SIFT ($d = 384$) local descriptors [6] as features.

	SMaL			SVM	
	Train	*Test*		*Train*	*test*
	$B \times B$, g, U	f		*Model*	*Prediction*
1K	5.3 sec	10 mins	1K	23 sec	2.5 sec
50K	59 sec	10 mins	50K	19 mins	2.5 sec
150K	3 mins	10 mins	150K	71 mins	2.5 sec

Table 1: Time Trade-Off between SMaL and linear SVM in three different splits. Times refer to one repetition

We use a dense regular grid with a spacing of 6 pixels and perform K-means clustering with a vocabulary size of $K = 64$ centroids for better performance as proposed in [2]. The clustering was performed on an independent set of 10,000 images, randomly sampled from the MIRFLICKR-1M dataset [4]. The final VLAD vectors are power-and L2-normalized and then reduced from $D = Kd$ to $D' = 512$ and L2-normalized again [7]. The choice of D only marginally affects accuracy as observed experimentally. We tested the BoW features, provided by the organizers, with our implementation, but with inferior results. Probably, BoW would also need to be reduced by PCA to perform well with SMaL due to the hypothesis that the data must be as separate as possible [1]. However, we could not apply PCA on BoW, since we would need to extract BoW features for an independent set of images (we did not have access to the BoW extraction software).

SMaL Optimization: In ALE, no variable needs optimization, since it was observed that different values of B and C_D did not affect accuracy. Thus, we choose to set $B = 50$ for computational efficiency reasons. For the number of eigenvectors and the Smooth Functions the best results were obtained with $C_D = 500$ and $\Lambda = 100$ respectively. All values were experimentally defined using the ImageCLEF 2012 dataset [5].

Incremental Learning: Our approach performs incremental learning in batches. We assume that the unlabelled data come in batches (e.g. 1000 images). We chose to include 1000 images in a batch (instead of one) for time efficiency reasons, making sure that the accuracy was unaffected. At first, the algorithm builds the histogram of the selected training set. From this histogram, we derive the $B \times B$ matrix, the eigenfunctions (g) and the eigenvalues of the eigenfunctions (σ). After computing the g and σ, we interpolate g at each of the training data to extract U_{train} and Σ. The $B \times B$ and g, are then used to compute the eigenvectors of the unlabelled data (U_{test_i}) for each batch, by interpolating g of the training set to the batch data. U_{train} and U_{test} are then concatenated to produce U.

To measure accuracy, we use the Mean interpolated Average Precision (MiAP) measure as proposed by the organizers. The MiAP scores reported in Section 4 are the average scores from 10 repetitions at each split. Finally, as baseline a linear SVM was trained using the same local descriptors as input. A linear SVM was chosen as a smore competitive method than a kNN algorithm, since it typically achieves better results in concept detection problems. Also, we could not use a non-linear SVM (i.e. RBF) due to the excessive computational cost.

All experiments were coded in Matlab and executed on an 8-core (Intel Quad Core i7-950 @3.07Ghz, 12G RAM) and a 24-core (an Intel Xeon Q6600 @2.0Ghz, 128G RAM) machine. The reported execution times (Table 1) were obtained from measurements on the 24-core machine.

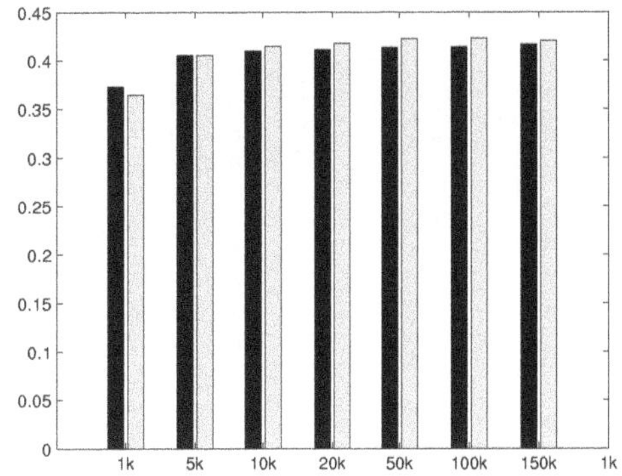

Figure 3: Comparison of MiAP between SVM (**black**) and SMaL (**light gray**) in case of fusion.

4. DESCRIPTION OF RESULTS

In this section, we provide the experimental results of our submission. As mentioned above, our method is benchmarked against a linear SVM classifier. Figure 1 presents the MiAP of these two methods, as measured using the SIFT and RGB-SIFT respectively. When using SIFT, it is observed that as the training set increases, SMaL performs better than the linear SVM. For instance, if 1K/concept are used, SMaL yields a MiAP score of 0.3537, while the linear SVM yields a score of 0.3543, but if 10K/concept are used, MiAP in SMaL is 0.3842, instead of linear SVM which is 0.3831.

The main observation is that the execution time of SMaL remains almost unaffected as the training set increases as illustrated in Table 1. For example, if a 50K/concept training set is used, SMaL needs 59 secs for training and 10 mins to predict the 500K test set in batches, while linear SVM needs 19 mins for training and 2.5 secs for prediction. Moreover, if 150K/concept is used SMaL needs 3 mins to compute the training variables ($B \times B$, g and U) and 10 mins for prediction, while linear SVM needs about 71 mins to learn the model and 2.5 secs for prediction. This capability of SMaL, gives us the advantage of using as many training images as possible, since the computation of eigenvectors is linear to the number of images and the computation of each batch is consistent in each split. On the other hand, we report that SMaL does not perform as well when the RGB-SIFT descriptor is used.

Table 2 depicts the Mean interpolated Precision (MiP) for each concept in the smallest (1K) and the biggest split (150K). Generally, we hypothesize that some concepts like *Sky* are more visually coherent, while some others, like *Nature* or *2012*, are more noisy. According to this hypothesis, we observe that SMaL can predict better than linear SVM the more noisy concepts. More specifically, in the $1K$ set in the *Nature* concept SMaL performs 0.3535, while SVM 0.3387. Another example is the concept *2012*, where the MiP of SMaL is 0.1967 and of the linear SVM is 0.1849. These differences increase as we use more training examples. In $150K$, in the concept *Nature* SMaL performs 0.3987, while the linear SVM yields a MiP of 0.3674. For the concept *2012* the MiP in SMaL is 0.2572 and in linear SVM it is 0.2246. The best performance for both methods is attained for the concept *Sky*, which is much more coherent than the other

SIFT				
Concept	#	$1K$	$150K$	**Diff**
Nature	SMaL	0.3535	0.3987	0.0452
	SVM	0.3387	0.3674	0.0287
Food	SMaL	0.5122	0.5460	0.0338
	SVM	0.5146	0.5499	0.0352
People	SMaL	0.2146	0.2623	0.0477
	SVM	0.2189	0.2605	0.0416
Wedding	SMaL	0.3925	0.4319	0.0394
	SVM	0.3993	0.4436	0.0442
Music	SMaL	0.4064	0.4406	0.0342
	SVM	0.4078	0.4342	0.0264
Sky	SMaL	0.5856	0.6101	0.0245
	SVM	0.5943	0.6235	0.0292
London	SMaL	0.2686	0.2961	0.0275
	SVM	0.2710	0.2903	0.0193
Beach	SMaL	0.4118	0.4392	0.0274
	SVM	0.4154	0.4430	0.0276
2012	SMaL	0.1967	0.2572	0.0605
	SVM	0.1849	0.2246	0.0397
Travel	SMaL	0.1947	0.2104	0.0157
	SVM	0.1981	0.2070	0.0090

RGB-SIFT				
Concept	#	$1K$	$150K$	**Diff**
Nature	SMaL	0.3897	0.4234	0.0337
	SVM	0.3812	0.4313	0.0501
Food	SMaL	0.5492	0.5786	0.0293
	SVM	0.5527	0.5785	0.0258
People	SMaL	0.2034	0.2301	0.0268
	SVM	0.2123	0.2644	0.0520
Wedding	SMaL	0.4115	0.4507	0.0392
	SVM	0.4181	0.4563	0.0383
Music	SMaL	0.4239	0.4557	0.0319
	SVM	0.4271	0.4617	0.0346
Sky	SMaL	0.6143	0.6376	0.0232
	SVM	0.6236	0.6501	0.0266
London	SMaL	0.2665	0.3071	0.0406
	SVM	0.2775	0.3059	0.0284
Beach	SMaL	0.4404	0.4656	0.0252
	SVM	0.4436	0.4735	0.0300
2012	SMaL	0.2073	0.2616	0.0543
	SVM	0.2136	0.2564	0.0428
Travel	SMaL	0.2001	0.2299	0.0298
	SVM	0.2094	0.2121	0.0027

Table 2: Comparison of MiP scores between $1K$ and $150K$.

concepts. On the other hand, one of the most difficult concepts proves to be the *Travel* concept, which in most cases has a MiP under 0.20. However, RGB-SIFT seems to yield good performance in this concept at 150K, as depicted in Table 2.

Fusion: Within SMaL, fusion takes place at the level of the Laplacian Eigenmap vectors. As a result, we obtained improved efficiency and better results than SVM. As illustrated in Figure 3, SVM performs better than SMaL in 1K, but as the training set increases, SMaL improves its accuracy. In 50K, MiAP in SMaL is 0.4223, while in SVM it is 0.4133. Figure 2 illustrates the performance comparison between SMaL and SVM in terms of Precision-Recall curve. Figure 4 illustrates the top 18 results of the test set (ranked by prediction score) for four concepts of the GC dataset.

5. CONCLUSIONS

In this paper, we proposed an approximate incremental semi-supervised learning approach, leveraging VLAD vectors, with the goal of learning very general concepts with high noise. Our framework significantly decreases the computational requirements of training in view of large amounts of training data, while improving the performance. Our experiments demonstrate that the proposed framework gives slightly better results compared to the baseline method, while achieving large computational gains. In the future, we plan to further investigate the behaviour of our method to better manage the noisy labels.

Figure 4: Top 18 images for the concepts: Nature, Food, Beach and Travel (top-to-bottom) on a 150K training set: SVM (left), SMaL (right).

6. ACKNOWLEDGMENTS

This work was supported by the SocialSensor project, partially funded by the European Commission, under the contract number FP7-287975.

7. REFERENCES

[1] R. Fergus, Y. Weiss, and A. Torralba. Semi-supervised learning in gigantic image collections. In *NIPS*, pages 522–530. 2009.

[2] H. Jégou, M. Douze, C. Schmid, and P. Pérez. Aggregating local descriptors into a compact image representation. In *IEEE Conf. on, CVPR*, pages 3304–3311, 2010.

[3] E. Mantziou, S. Papadopoulos, and I. Kompatsiaris. Large-scale semi-supervised learning by approximate laplacian eigenmaps, VLAD and pyramids. In *WIAMIS*, 2013.

[4] B. T. Mark J. Huiskes and M. S. Lew. New trends and ideas in visual concept detection: The MIR FLICKR retrieval evaluation initiative. In *MIR '10*, pages 527–536, New York, NY, USA, 2010. ACM.

[5] B. Thomee and A. Popescu. Overview of the clef 2012 flickr photo annotation and retrieval task. in the working notes for the CLEF 2012 labs/workshop. Rome, Italy, 2012.

[6] K. E. A. van de Sande, T. Gevers, and C. G. M. Snoek. Empowering visual categorization with the GPU. *IEEE Transactions on Multimedia*, 13(1):60–70, 2011.

[7] E. S. Xioufis, S. Papadopoulos, I. Kompatsiaris, G. Tsoumakas, and I. P. Vlahavas. An empirical study on the combination of SURF features with vlad vectors for image search. In *WIAMIS*, 2012.

Estimating Beauty Ratings of Videos using Supervoxels

Gökhan Yildirim
School of Computer and Communication Sciences
EPFL, Switzerland
gokhan.yildirim@epfl.ch

Appu Shaji
School of Computer and Communication Sciences
EPFL, Switzerland
appu.shaji@epfl.ch

Sabine Süsstrunk
School of Computer and Communication Sciences
EPFL, Switzerland
sabine.susstrunk@epfl.ch

ABSTRACT

The major low-level perceptual components that influence the beauty ratings of video are color, contrast, and motion. To estimate the beauty ratings of the NHK dataset, we propose to extract these features based on *supervoxels*, which are a group of pixels that share similar color and spatial information through the temporal domain. Recent beauty methods use frame-level processing for visual features and disregard the spatio-temporal aspect of beauty. In this paper, we explicitly model this property by introducing supervoxel-based visual and motion features.

In order to create a beauty estimator, we first identify 60 videos (either beautiful or not beautiful) in the NHK dataset. We then train a neural network regressor using the supervoxel-based features and binary beauty ratings. We rate the 1000 videos in the NHK dataset and rank them according to their ratings. When comparing our rankings with the actual rankings of the NHK dataset, we obtain a Spearman correlation coefficient of 0.42.

Categories and Subject Descriptors

I.2.10 [**Artificial Intelligence**]: Vision and Scene Understanding—*Video analysis*; I.4.6 [**Image Processing and Computer Vision**]: Segmentation—*Region growing, partitioning*

Keywords

Video beauty; supervoxel; video ranking

1. INTRODUCTION

Rating any visual stimulus as "beautiful" is highly subjective and very personal. What some person might find beautiful another might be indifferent to or even find ugly. Yet, there are many images and videos that most of us find beautiful, which follow some perceptual arrangement that is pleasing to the majority of us. Thus, estimating beauty ratings does not always require high-level perceptual cues, such as objects, people, and action recognition, but can often be modeled by low-level features, such as color, contrast, and motion.

In this paper, we attempt to estimate the beauty ratings of the videos in the Japan Broadcasting Corporation (NHK) dataset[1]. In the dataset, there are 1000 videos with an average duration of one minute and a resolution of 640×360 pixels. Most of them are very simple videos, are composed of only a few shots and contain little action. A video *shot* is a stack of frames where the video recording is not interrupted. As each shot can have its own content, the less shots there are, the simpler it is to understand a video. The videos in the NHK dataset have three shots on average, are short and thus much simpler compared to a regular movie or even a YouTube video. We thus believe that a low-level approach will be sufficient to achieve a good rating estimation.

We select our features based on recent research in image and video beauty, which has shown that low-level visual features, such as composition, colorfulness, lightness, and contrast [3, 8, 9, 10], are successful in estimating image aesthetics. Video beauty is also related to camera motion stability [8, 9, 10]. While the low-level features are calculated for each video frame, motion stability is measured by matching image patches or keypoint descriptors from one frame to the next, which might fail on uniform areas.

The main drawback of the above methods are that they calculate the low-level visual features and the motion features with frame-level processing. We claim that there is a combined, spatio-temporal dimension to beauty. Thus, in our method, we jointly extract low-level visual and motion features from **supervoxels**. A supervoxel, which is a 3D extension of a superpixel, is a group of pixels sharing similar color and spatial information along the temporal axis. Supervoxels allow us to summarize and simplify the content of a video through its color/texture and motion components. They have been used in biological applications, such as motion estimation on microscopy data [2] and mitochondria segmentation [7], as well as in video retrieval [6]. We use Achanta et al.'s method [1] to compute the supervoxels of every video shot. In comparison to the state-of-the-art methods, our visual features are able to represent the video on a shot level. In addition, our motion features are based on the velocity of the supervoxels throughout a video shot and the initial and final positions of the supervoxels. They successfully measure the motion profile and the spatial composition of both uniform and textured image regions.

MM'13, October 21–25, 2013, Barcelona, Spain.
Copyright 2013 ACM 978-1-4503-2404-5/13/10 ...$15.00.
http://dx.doi.org/10.1145/2502081.2508125.

[1]http://acmmm13.org/submissions/call-for-multimedia-grand-challenge-solutions/task-where-is-beauty/

In our rating algorithm, supervoxel features are used to train a neural network-based regressor, which estimates the "beauty" of a given video. In order to establish a ground truth, we select 60 videos from the NHK dataset, which are either beautiful or not in a collective sense. Our neural network is regressed over these binary ratings so that it can learn the distinctive properties of video beauty. We test our algorithm on 1000 videos in the NHK dataset and obtain a Spearman correlation coefficient of 0.42 with respect to the actual NHK challenge ground truth.

2. SUPERVOXELS AND TRAJECTORIES

We summarize the visual and motion features of a video with supervoxels. As different parts of a video can have different contents or viewpoints, we need to detect the individual shots that are visually consistent for proper supervoxel extraction.

2.1 Shot Detection

A video, $\mathbf{V}$, contains several shots. We can extract individual shots by detecting the discontinuities in optical flow in a video. In our paper, we use Horn-Shunck's optical flow method [5]. For shot detection, we only need to identify the sudden changes in the magnitude of the optical flow.

$$\begin{aligned} \mathbf{d}(t) &= \frac{1}{Z}\sum_{x}\sum_{y}\sqrt{\mathbf{O_u}(t)^2+\mathbf{O_v}(t)^2} \\ \mu &= \alpha \times \text{median}(\mathbf{d}) \end{aligned} \quad (1)$$

Here, $\mathbf{O_u}(t)$ and $\mathbf{O_v}(t)$ are the optical flow vector components in the horizontal and the vertical directions at frame t, respectively. $\mathbf{d}(t)$ is the average optical flow for frame t, Z is the total number of pixels in one video frame, x and y are the spatial coordinates, μ is the threshold for shot detection, and α is a constant to modify the threshold. A shot is detected if the optical flow is greater than this threshold. The median provides an average motion value that is resistant to extreme values. We found α equal to 10 provides the best shot detection for the NHK dataset.

An example of shot detection on a bowling video (0113.mp4 in the NHK dataset) is given in Figure 1. As we can see from Figure 1(a) and 1(b), the video includes two shots illustrated with a sharp optical flow jump at frame #242.

After shot detection, we have visually consistent stacks of video frames, such as Figure 1(c) and 1(d), that have the visual consistency we require to extract supervoxels and their properties.

2.2 Supervoxel Extraction

Oversegmenting a single object into multiple supervoxels is acceptable, provided that the segment size is large enough to benefit from pixel grouping, i.e. the resultant supervoxels have similar visual and motion features. However, undersegmentation might cause mixtures between irrelevant objects, which is not desirable. Thus, we select a spatial size for supervoxels by assuming that the minimum size for an object of interest is equal to 20 pixels (recall from Section 1 that videos have a size of 640×360 pixels). We choose the longest possible temporal size to capture the motion of an object throughout the video shot.

We can see an example of supervoxel extraction in Figure 2. We represent each supervoxel with their average color (averaged in L*a*b* space) in Figure 2(b).

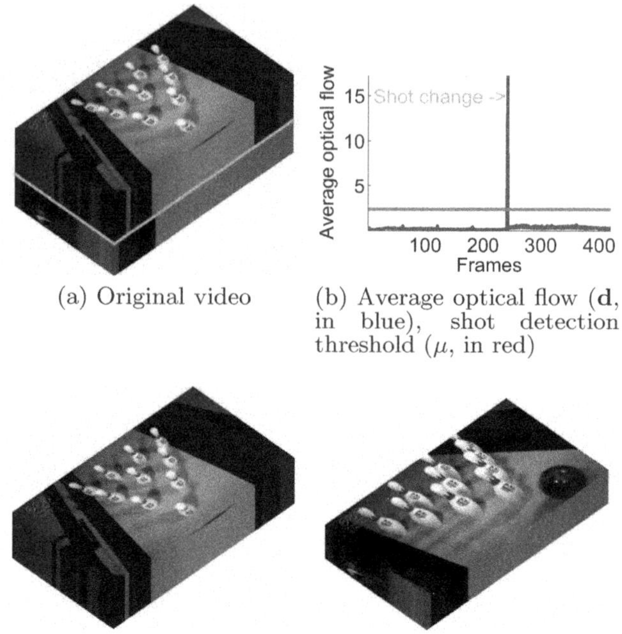

(a) Original video

(b) Average optical flow ($\mathbf{d}$, in blue), shot detection threshold (μ, in red)

(c) First shot

(d) Second shot

Figure 1: Shot detection on a video with two shots. Shot change is depicted with a green line in (a)

(a) Second shot

(b) Supervoxels of second shot

Figure 2: Supervoxel extraction.

2.3 Feature Extraction

In order to *learn* the relationship between video features and beauty, we use the visual and motion features of the supervoxels and their trajectories.

2.3.1 Visual Features

We employ visual features similar to the ones in the state-of-the-art methods that judge video beauty [3, 8, 9, 10], with one important difference: we compute them from the supervoxels. The explanation of the ten visual features ($f_1 - f_{10}$) we use are given in Table 1.

2.3.2 Motion Features

In order to express the motion inside a supervoxel, we calculate the supervoxel trajectories through a video shot by computing the center of mass of a supervoxel on each frame. Supervoxel $\mathbf{X}_{jk}$ represents the kth supervoxel of jth shot.

$$\begin{aligned} \mathbf{r}^x_{jk}(t) &= \frac{1}{|x \in \mathbf{X}_{jk}(t)|}\sum_{x\in\mathbf{X}_{jk}(t)} x \\ \mathbf{r}^y_{jk}(t) &= \frac{1}{|y \in \mathbf{X}_{jk}(t)|}\sum_{y\in\mathbf{X}_{jk}(t)} y \end{aligned} \quad (2)$$

Table 1: **Visual features computed over supervoxels.**

Feature	Comment
Brightness	Average value of the Y channel of the YCbCr color space
Contrast	Average brightness difference between a supervoxel and the rest of the supervoxels
Saturation	Average value of the S channel of the HSV color space
Saturation Contrast	Average saturation difference between a supervoxel and the rest of the supervoxels
Colorfulness	Colorfulness measure in [4] between a supervoxel and the rest of the supervoxels
Average Color	Average value of L*, a* and b* channels of the CIELab color space (3 features)
Saliency	Average color difference between a supervoxel and the rest of the supervoxels (over L*a*b*)
Normalized Voxel Size	The number of pixels in a supervoxel normalized by the size of the shot cube

Here, $\mathbf{r}^x_{jk}(t)$ and $\mathbf{r}^y_{jk}(t)$ are the (x, y) coordinates of the center of mass of the supervoxel $\mathbf{X}_{jk}$ at frame t. The computed coordinates form the trajectories. The trajectories of the supervoxels in Figure 2(b) are illustrated in Figure 3(a) and 3(b). For didactic purposes, we illustrate stationary and moving trajectories separately.

We can observe from Figure 3(a), for this video, the supervoxels that are close to the frame border have negligible motion. The progression of the bowling pins and the bowling ball are illustrated in Figure 3(b).

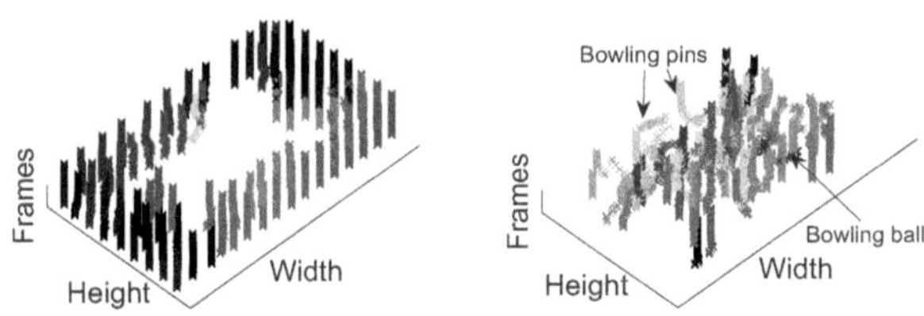

(a) Stationary trajectories (b) Moving trajectories

Figure 3: Supervoxel trajectories.

To compute our motion features, we calculate the velocity of the supervoxel trajectories at each frame as follows:

$$\begin{aligned} \mathbf{l}^x_{jk}(t) &= \mathbf{r}^x_{jk}(t+1) - \mathbf{r}^x_{jk}(t) \\ \mathbf{l}^y_{jk}(t) &= \mathbf{r}^y_{jk}(t+1) - \mathbf{r}^y_{jk}(t) \\ \mathbf{l}_{jk}(t) &= \sqrt{\left[\mathbf{l}^x_{jk}(t)\right]^2 + \left[\mathbf{l}^y_{jk}(t)\right]^2} \end{aligned} \quad (3)$$

Here, $\mathbf{l}^x_{jk}(t)$ and $\mathbf{l}^y_{jk}(t)$ are horizontal and vertical velocity components of the trajectory at frame t, respectively, $\mathbf{l}_{jk}(t)$ is the magnitude of the trajectory velocity for supervoxel $\mathbf{X}_{jk}$ at frame t. In order to profile the motion of a supervoxel, we create a 20-bin histogram using $\mathbf{l}_{jk}$. The maximum velocity is equal to 19 pixels per frame, because the expected spatial size for supervoxels is 20 pixels (see Section 2.2). After normalizing with $||\mathbf{l}_{jk}||_1$, a trajectory gives us 20 features in total ($f_{11} - f_{30}$).

The distribution represents how smooth a supervoxel is advancing inside a shot. For example, a concentrated histogram as illustrated in Figure 4(a) corresponds to a stationary supervoxel. Conversely, a distributed histogram as shown in Figure 4(b) corresponds to a moving supervoxel, in this case a bowling pin (see Figure 3(b)).

In addition to a velocity histogram, we also use the normalized initial and final spatial trajectory positions (4 features in total, $f_{31} - f_{34}$) of the supervoxels as motion-based features. The normalization is performed using the dimensions of the video frame, so that the feature values vary in

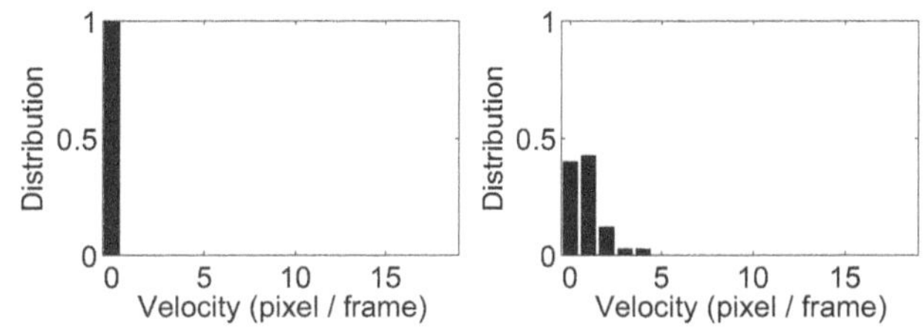

(a) Velocity histogram of a stationary supervoxel (b) Velocity histogram of a bowling pin

Figure 4: Velocity histograms of two supervoxel trajectories in the bowling video.

the interval $[-0.5, 0.5]$. These positions are related to the composition of supervoxels in the shot.

3. VIDEO RANKING RESULTS

It is possible to define heuristic rules to estimate the beauty of a video. For example, people might consider colorful videos with high contrast and smooth movements as beautiful. However, we choose to discover those rules, if they exist, by regressing our features over video ratings.

We select 60 videos from the NHK dataset, half of which can be considered as collectively "beautiful" (with rating = 1) and the rest as "not beautiful" (with rating = 0). Instead of having a continuous rating, we create a binary ground truth to properly learn the separation between good and bad videos. We then train a neural network-based regressor (with one hidden layer of 10 neurons) for rating estimation. As video beauty is a subjective concept, parametrizing the joint distribution of the input features and the beauty is prone to errors. Thus, we choose a discriminative regression model instead of a generative model. The input of the network is the supervoxel feature vector ($f_1 - f_{34}$) of all supervoxels in all of the training videos and the ground truth is the binary beauty ratings.

In order to estimate the rating of a video, we extract its supervoxel features and pass them through the neural network. The rating of a video is calculated by averaging the ratings of its supervoxels as shown in (4).

$$R_{\mathbf{V}} = \frac{1}{N} \sum_{\forall \mathbf{F_{kj}} \in \mathbf{V}} \psi(\mathbf{F_{kj}}) \quad (4)$$

Here, $R_{\mathbf{V}}$ is the final rating of the video $\mathbf{V}$, N is the number of supervoxels in $\mathbf{V}$, $\psi(.)$ is the neural network function, and $\mathbf{F}_{jk}$ is the feature vector of supervoxel $\mathbf{X}_{jk}$.

We rank the videos in the NHK dataset with respect to their estimated final ratings. The correlation coefficients of our ranking and the user study-based ranking obtained by the NHK challenge is given in Table 2.

Table 2: Correlation between estimated and ground truth rankings.

Feature Type	Correlation Type	Value
Motion only	Spearman	0.052
Visual only	Spearman	0.387
Both	Spearman	**0.424**
Motion only	Kendall	0.036
Visual only	Kendall	0.264
Both	Kendall	**0.290**

As we can see from Table 2, the main contribution is provided by visual features. Another observation is that the sum of the individual performances of visual and motion features is very similar to their combined performances. This shows that our supervoxel-based features are successful to decouple the visual and motion properties of a video.

In Figure 5, we show example frames from the top- and bottom-ranked videos in the NHK dataset. These ranking results are obtained using both visual and motion-based supervoxel features. We can observe that the top-ranked videos are more colorful than the bottom-ranked ones. We refer the reader to the NHK video website for judging motion related performance.

4. CONCLUSION

We show that low-level supervoxel-based features are successful in estimating the beauty rating of short and simple videos in the NHK dataset. The supervoxels accurately represent and separate the coupling between the visual and motion aspects in a video. Because, different than the state-of-the-art techniques, our method regards the spatio-temporal aspect of the beauty by involving shot-level processing.

We build a neural network regressor to learn the relationship between the perceptual components of a video and its beauty. We then use this regressor to automatically rate and rank the videos in the NHK dataset and obtain a moderate amount of correlation.

We collect binary ground truth ratings for only 60 videos of the NHK dataset. A larger training set will significantly enhance the ranking performance. Moreover, the potential of additional supervoxel-based features can be investigated not only in the context of video beauty but also, in general, video processing. For practical purposes, we might need a scalable learning method, such as a stochastic neural network, in order to perform online learning. In addition, new features can be enabled or disabled by activating or deactivating corresponding neurons.

5. ACKNOWLEDGEMENTS

This work was supported by the Swiss National Science Foundation under grant number 200021_143406 / 1.

6. REFERENCES

[1] R. Achanta, A. Shaji, K. Smith, A. Lucchi, P. Fua, and S. Süsstrunk. SLIC superpixels compared to state-of-the-art superpixel methods. *IEEE Transactions on PAMI*, 34(11):2274–2282, 2012.

[2] F. Amat, E. W. Myers, and P. J. Keller. Fast and robust optical flow for time-lapse microscopy using super-voxels. *Bioinformatics*, 29(3):373–380, 2013.

[3] S. Bhattacharya, R. Sukthankar, and M. Shah. A framework for photo-quality assessment and enhancement based on visual aesthetics. In *Proc. of the International Conference on Multimedia*, pages 271–280, 2010.

[4] D. Hasler and S. Süsstrunk. Measuring colorfulness in natural images. In *Proc. SPIE Human Vision and Electronic Imaging*, volume 5007, pages 87–95, 2003.

[5] B. K. P. Horn and B. G. Schunck. Determining optical flow. *Artificial Intelligence*, 17:185–203, 1981.

[6] R. Hu, S. James, T. Wang, and J. Collomosse. Markov random fields for sketch based video retrieval. In *Proc. of ACM Multimedia Retrieval*, pages 279–286, 2013.

[7] A. Lucchi, K. Smith, R. Achanta, G. Knott, and P. Fua. Supervoxel-based segmentation of mitochondria in em image stacks with learned shape features. *IEEE Transactions on Medical Imaging*, 31(2):474–486, 2012.

[8] Y. Luo and X. Tang. Photo and video quality evaluation: Focusing on the subject. In *Proc. of ECCV*, volume 3, pages 386–399, 2008.

[9] A. Moorthy, P. Obrador, and N. Oliver. Towards computational models of the visual aesthetic appeal of consumer videos. In *Proc. of ECCV*, volume 6315, pages 1–14, 2010.

[10] Y. Niu and F. Liu. What makes a professional video? a computational aesthetics approach. *IEEE Transactions on Circuits and Systems for Video Technology*, 22(7):1037–1049, 2012.

Figure 5: Frames from the videos in the NHK dataset that are top-ranked (16 images above) and bottom-ranked (16 images below) by our algorithm.

Action Recognition using Invariant Features under Unexampled Viewing Conditions

Litian Sun Kiyoharu Aizawa
Department of Information and Communication Engineering
The University of Tokyo, Japan
{sun1101,aizawa}@hal.t.u-tokyo.ac.jp

ABSTRACT

A great challenge in real-world applications of action recognition is the lack of sufficient label information because of variance in the recording viewpoint and differences between individuals. A system that can adapt itself according to these variances is required for practical use. We present a generic method for extracting view-invariant features from skeleton joints. These view-invariant features are further refined using a stacked, compact autoencoder. To model the challenge of real-world applications, two unexampled test settings (NewView and NewPerson) are used to evaluate the proposed method. Experimental results with these test settings demonstrate the effectiveness of our method.

Categories and Subject Descriptors

I.2.10 [**Artificial intelligence**]: Vision and scene understanding—*Motion*; I.5.4 [**Pattern recognition**]: Applications—*Computer vision*

General Terms

Algorithms; Experimentation

Keywords

Grand Challenge; 3DLife; Action recognition; Unexampled test setting; View-invariant feature; Autoencoder

1. INTRODUCTION

Recognition of human actions has attracted much attention because of its wide applications, including surveillance and monitoring systems, video indexing and retrieval, and human–computer interaction. Video sequences obtained by traditional color cameras are sensitive to illumination changes, clothing variations, and background clutter. Emerging low-cost depth sensors could effectively reduce the influence of such variances by providing the 3D structure of the scene. Tasks such as background subtraction, segmentation, and tracking are thus significantly simplified. However, it remains challenging to recognize actions recorded from different viewpoints and performed by different people.

Most previous work has used spatiotemporal patterns of appearance or motion in human actions for recognition tasks. Some studies extracted features from the appearance of the human body, such as 3D points sampled from contour projections in [3], and 4D surface-normal vectors in [6]. Other studies have considered skeleton joint information to be more compact and useful in representing human actions [8, 9].

Although most of these methods are quite powerful in recognizing actions from similar viewpoints, their performance in real-world applications may fall off dramatically, because the user's actions are often not recorded from the expected viewpoint, and similar actions may look very different when observed from different angles, even when these angles deviate only slightly from the original viewpoint. Transfer learning methods [1, 4] learn the relationship between different viewpoints from training data, and apply the learned relationship to recognize the testing actions. For this approach, collecting labeled data from all the target viewpoints is required, which makes it impractical for real-world applications.

Session 2 of the first dataset provided by the Huawei/3DLife Grand Challenge contains RGB-depth videos captured by two Microsoft Kinect sensors from front and side views, including 17 classes of actions performed by 14 subjects. We address this challenge in two unexampled test settings: NewView and NewPerson. For the NewView test setting, we use videos captured from either the front or side for training and predict the action classes for videos from the other view. For the NewPerson test setting, we use videos captured from 13 subjects for training and perform the tests on the remaining subject.

A view-invariant feature extraction framework was developed to transform the original skeleton information expressed in the camera's coordinate system to a user-defined coordinate system. Orientation information is as view-dependent as position, because it is expressed as a quaternion, which is a linear combination of bases in the camera's coordinate system. Directional velocity and angular velocity are calculated and expressed in the same coordinate system. These view-invariant features were further refined using a stacked, compact autoencoder (SCAE). We adopt the neural network method, because its nonlinear operations and architecture with hidden layers allow it to find patterns in data. Consequently, the refined features are quantized and summarized

MM'13, October 21–25, 2013, Barcelona, Spain.

http://dx.doi.org/10.1145/2502081.2508126.

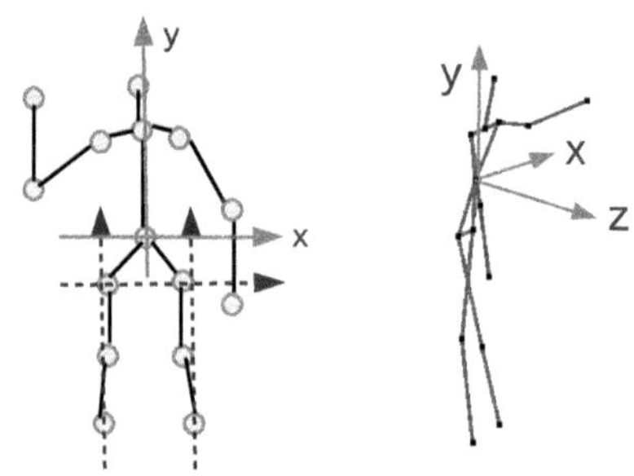

Figure 1: User-defined coordinate system. The left part shows how the axes are determined (reference lines are shown as dotted blue lines, and the x- and y-coordinates are shown as solid pink lines); the right part shows the action "throwing" and the corresponding user-defined coordinate system (rotated for better visualization).

into histograms of visual word frequencies, and a linear support vector machine (SVM) is employed for training.

Our contribution is threefold. 1) We propose a generic coordinate transformation framework to extract view-invariant features from skeleton information. 2) Experimental results reveal that, using our method, features extracted from the orientation and angular velocity of skeleton joints could be almost as discriminative as position and velocity; this has been neglected in previous work [8, 11]. 3) We showed that the SCAE can be efficiently applied to dense features such as positions and orientations for further refinement. In contrast to the sparseness constraints in sparse autoencoders [5, 10], which expect the ratio of activated units in the hidden layer to be less than 0.1 and even close to 0, the reasonable range of our compact constraint ρ is between 0.4 and 0.7. This is because the input data in our case contain dense information, rather than the sparse information conveyed by image or video patches [2]. For these reasons, we called the autoencoder that we trained the SCAE.

The remainder of this paper is organized as follows. The proposed algorithm is described in detail in Section 2, and experimental results are presented and discussed in Section 3. Finally, conclusions are given in Section 4.

2. PROPOSED METHOD

An action can be described as the continuous evolution of a rigid skeleton. The human body tracking system NITE [7] provided by PrimeSense can extract the position and orientation information of 15 skeleton joints frame by frame in real time. We first set up a user-defined coordinate system from the skeleton joints, and transform the positions and orientations into that coordinate system. Velocity and angular velocity are calculated from the converted positions and orientations. These four features constitute the view-invariant descriptor for the skeleton joints. An SCAE is employed to optimize the features further. Finally, a Bag-of-Words (BoW) scheme is adopted, and an SVM is used as the classifier.

2.1 View-invariant feature extraction

To analyze the motion of the human body, we set up a user-defined coordinate system from the skeleton in the starting frame of the action. We take the torso joint as the origin. The x-axis is defined as the line from left hip to right hip, and the y-axis is defined as the average of the left and right leg lines. Figure 1 shows these reference lines as dotted blue lines. The z-axis is perpendicular to the plane determined by the x- and y-axes. In some situations in which the hip line may not be perpendicular to the leg line, we make the x-axis perpendicular to the plane determined by the y- and z-axes. The transformation matrix M is used to transform from XYZ (camera's coordinate system) to UVW (user-defined coordinate system) coordinates.

$$M = \begin{bmatrix} U_x & U_y & U_z \\ V_x & V_y & V_z \\ W_x & W_y & W_z \end{bmatrix} \tag{1}$$

2.1.1 Coordinate transformation

We define $P_{id}(t) = (p_{id,x}(t), p_{id,y}(t), p_{id,z}(t))$ as the joint position at time t ($t \in [t_s, t_e]$). id refers to a specific skeleton joint, such as the head, neck, torso, and left and right shoulder, elbow, hand, hip, knee, and foot. We set the origin as the torso joint in the starting frame. The positions of the other joints relative to the new origin are calculated by $P'_{id} = P_{id} - P_{torso}(t_s)$. To process the data of different human body sizes, we normalize the joints' positions to the average distance between the torso joint and the feet joints in the starting frame. The position in the new coordinate system $P' = (p_u, p_v, p_w)$ is calculated by $(P'')^T = M(t_s) * (P')^T$. Here we omit the joint id and time t subscript indexes for simplicity.

Similarly, we define $Q = (q_w, q_x, q_y, q_z)$ as the joint orientation, which is expressed as a quaternion. We calculate the relative orientation of each joint by abstracting the torso orientation in the starting frame using $Q'_{id} = Q_{id} * Q^*{}_{torso}(t_s)$, in which Q^* is the conjugate of Q. Notice that the quaternion is expressed in the XYZ coordinate system, which is not view invariant. We adjust the quaternion expression as follows.

$$\begin{aligned} Q' &= (q'_w, q'_x, q'_y, q'_z) = (cos(\theta'/2), \vec{q}'_{xyz} sin(\theta'/2)) \\ Q'' &= (cos(\theta'/2), \vec{q}''_{uvw} sin(\theta'/2)) \\ (\vec{q}''_{uvw})^T &= M(t_s) * (\vec{q}'_{xyz})^T \end{aligned} \tag{2}$$

The θ' information is contained in the last three elements of the final quaternion, so we represent the orientations of the joints by those last three elements.

2.1.2 Velocity calculation

Velocity is calculated from the joint positions in the user-defined coordinate system. We use two sets of velocity calculations with different temporal intervals. As well as the scalar velocities in UVW coordinates, the magnitude of the velocity also matters. Thus, a four-dimensional vector is used to represent one velocity feature.

$$\begin{aligned} \vec{v_1}(t) &= (P''(t+1) - P''(t-1))/(T_{t+1} - T_{t-1}) \\ \vec{v_2}(t) &= (P''(t+2) - P''(t-2))/(T_{t+2} - T_{t-2}) \end{aligned} \tag{3}$$

The angular velocities of the joints can be calculated similarly using the two settings, although the detailed calculations concerning the quaternion are different, as follows.

$$\begin{aligned} Q''_{diff} &= Q''(t+\delta) * (Q''(t-\delta))^* \\ &= (cos(\beta/2), \vec{q}''_{uvw} sin(\beta/2)) \\ \beta &= cos^{-1}(2 \times Q''_{diff}) \end{aligned} \tag{4}$$

$$\alpha = \frac{Q''_{diff}}{2\delta} = \frac{\beta}{2\delta} \frac{\vec{q}''_{uvw}}{\sqrt{q_u''^2 + q_v''^2 + q_w''^2}} \quad (5)$$

2.2 Feature refinement

For each frame, NITE provides position information for all 15 joints, while orientation information is detected for only 11 joints (the exceptions being the left and right hand and foot). Thus, a $15 \times (3+4\times 2) + 11 \times (3+3\times 2) = 264$-dimensional feature is used to represent one frame. Four consecutive frames are treated as a temporal volume with a sampling interval of two frames; thus, each volume has a $264 \times 4 = 1056$-dimensional vector as descriptor. In this section, we show how these vectors are refined using the SCAE.

An autoencoder is a two-layer neural network that learns nonlinear codes to represent the input data. Specifically, we want to learn the weight and bias parameters from the input data $\{x^{(i)}\}_{i=1}^{m}$ to build a network, so that the encoded hidden-layer representation $h = \sigma(Wx + b_h)$ is decoded (or reconstructed) to $y = \sigma(W^T h + b_y)$, which approximates the input. We define the cost function using an L_2 norm as, as follows.

$$E(W,b) = \frac{1}{2}\sum_{i=1}^{m} \|y^{(i)} - x^{(i)}\|_2^2 \quad (6)$$

To learn the substantial information held by the feature vector, we impose a compact constraint on the hidden units. Thus, the proportion of activated units in the hidden layer is trained to approximate the compactness parameter ρ using KL divergence. A weight-decay part is added to the cost function for better generalization. A back-propagation technique is employed for training using the minibatch stochastic gradient descent (SGD) algorithm.

$$\begin{aligned} E(W,b) =& \frac{1}{2}\sum_{i=1}^{m} \|y^{(i)} - x^{(i)}\|_2^2 + \frac{\lambda}{2}\|W\|^2 \\ &+ \sum_{j=1}^{n} D_{KL}(\rho \| \frac{1}{m}\sum_{i=1}^{m} h_j(x^{(i)}, W, b)) \end{aligned} \quad (7)$$

Compact autoencoders can be stacked to form a multilayer system in which each layer takes the hidden units of the preceding layer as input. The efficient way to train a multilayer autoencoder system is to perform greedy layer-wise training first and then optimize all the layers during fine-tuning. In our case, as there are no labeled data at this stage, we unfold the multilayer autoencoder and train the network to minimize the error between the reconstructed result and the input using back propagation.

We developed a two-layer compact autoencoder, with a structure of $1056- > 1200- > 600$, which means that the input feature vectors have 1056 elements, the first layer has 1200 hidden units, and the second layer has 600 hidden units. The compactness parameter is set as 0.6 for both layers. We have designed architectures of different sizes with different compactness parameters, and this architecture gave the best performance.

3. EXPERIMENTS

We evaluated the proposed view-invariant descriptor on Session 2 of Dataset 1 provided by the Huawei/3DLife Grand Challenge. There are 17 action classes: A_{01} *Hand waving;* A_{02} *Knocking on a door;* A_{03} *Clapping;* A_{04} *Throwing;* A_{05} *Punching;* A_{06} *Pushing away;* A_{07} *Jumping jacks;* A_{08} *Lunges;* A_{09} *Squats;* A_{10} *Punching and kicking;* A_{11} *Weight lifting;* A_{12} *Golf drive;* A_{13} *Golf chip;* A_{14} *Golf putt;* A_{15} *Tennis forehand;* A_{16} *Tennis backhand; and* A_{17} *Walking on a treadmill.* Each action was performed by 14 subjects, and repeated at least five times by each subject. We conducted experiments with two test settings: NewView and NewPerson.

Table 1: Performance comparison of action recognition in the NewView test setting, with and without coordinate transformation, and with different combinations of features.

	Side view test			**Front view test**		
No CT	VelM	AVelM	Both	VelM	AVelM	Both
	53.2	27.5	44.2	62.8	25.2	48.4
CT	Pos +Vel	Ori+ AVel	All	Pos +Vel	Ori+ AVel	All
A_{01}	74.4	93.8	83.3	86.1	87.3	91.1
A_{02}	90.1	59.2	83.1	53.5	81.7	93.0
A_{03}	98.8	78.3	97.1	98.8	79.7	95.7
A_{04}	74.3	72.9	70.0	80.0	68.8	91.4
A_{05}	80	64.3	75.7	78.8	82.9	85.7
A_{06}	85.7	65.7	84.3	88.8	52.9	78.8
A_{07}	100	89.9	100	100	100	100
A_{08}	90.0	80.0	90.0	91.4	71.4	81.4
A_{09}	92.0	66.7	80.0	96.0	98.7	98.7
A_{10}	89.9	75.4	89.9	100	56.5	100
A_{11}	94.3	78.8	94.3	87.1	92.0	94.3
A_{12}	54.3	44.3	52.9	65.7	48.8	65.7
A_{13}	55.4	47.3	52.7	60.8	37.5	52.7
A_{14}	69.3	68.0	68.0	68.0	73.3	86.7
A_{15}	87.1	74.3	85.7	92.0	72.9	82.9
A_{16}	81.2	85.5	87.0	79.7	59.4	78.3
A_{17}	85.7	71.4	92.9	92.0	100	100
Average	**82.1**	**71.5**	**80.1**	**82.9**	**73.2**	**86.1**

Table 1 shows the performance comparison of action recognition with the NewView test setting with and without coordinate transformations. Experimental results for different combinations of view-invariant features are also included. We first performed the action recognition without coordinate transformation ("No CT"), using the magnitudes of the velocity (VelM) and angular velocity (AVelM), which are considered to be view invariant and are widely used. For the results with "CT", we transformed the skeleton joint information to the user-defined coordinate system. Position and velocity (Pos+Vel), orientation and angular velocity (Ori+AVel), and all four features (All) were used as descriptors for action recognition.

We first evaluated the coordinate transformation without the autoencoder. The descriptors were quantized into visual words. The size of the codebook was set to guarantee that clusters had 60 members on average. In the NewView test setting, the dictionary size turned out to be about 350. The skeleton joint information of an action was represented by a BoW. A temporal pyramid-matching scheme was adopted here. Besides the BoW representation for the whole skeleton sequence, we also divided the action into three temporal subsequences and calculated their BoW representations. Finally, a linear SVM was used for classification.

In general, the performance in the front view test was better than that in the side view test. This is natural, be-

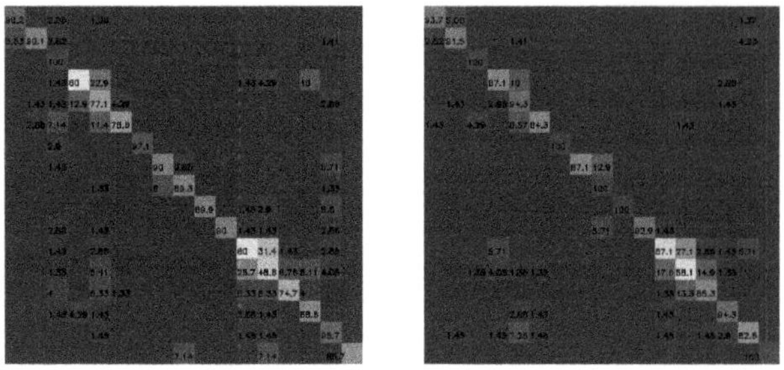

(a) Side view test (b) Front view test

Figure 2: Confusion matrices of NewView tests (All+SCAE). The average accuracy rates are 82.8% (a) and 88.1% (b).

cause the skeleton joints' information in the side view is not as accurate as that detected in the front view. Some joints are occluded from detection, and some are wrongly identified. Comparing the average accuracy rates of the experiments with and without coordinate transformations, the proposed coordinate transformation and view-invariant feature extraction method achieved at least 20% improvement. It is interesting that with the coordinate transformation method, the average accuracy rate achieved using orientation together with the angular velocity (Ori+AVel) is only about 10% lower than that achieved using position and velocity (Pos+Vel). Considering that the orientation information for four nodes (left and right hands and feet) is not detected by NITE, while position information is detected, this performance indicates that orientation information could be almost as discriminative as position information. Furthermore, the results with "CT" reveal that orientation and position information have some complementary properties, and combining them leads to better performance. This is shown in, for instance, A_{01} Hand waving, A_{02} Knocking on a door,A_{16} Tennis backhand, and A_{17} Walking on a treadmill in the side view test, and A_{02} Knocking on the door and A_{14} Golf putt in the front view test.

Figure 2 shows the confusion matrices of the NewView test using all four features and further refined by the SCAE (All+SCAE). The average accuracy rates for the side view and front view tests are 82.8% and 88.1%, respectively. Compared with the results shown in Table 1, actions are predicted better, except A_{12} Golf drive and A_{13} Golf chip. This is because those two actions are both poorly represented by the skeleton joints because of the considerable overlapping of body parts. We compare the proposed SCAE with principle component analysis (PCA) in the feature refinement stage. The PCA is set to reduce the feature dimension from 1056 to 600, the same as in SCAE. The average accuracy rates (All+PCA) for the side and front view tests are 81.5% and 86.4%, respectively. The proposed SCAE thus performed better than PCA.

In the NewPerson test, skeleton data from 13 subjects were used for training, and the test was conducted on the remaining subject. We obtained average accuracy rates of 77.5% (All), 77.9% (All+PCA), and 79.78% (All+SCAE). This improvement comes mainly from the high variance duration of the autoencoder network. Our experiments showed that setting the compactness parameter to 0.1 (as in the sparse autoencoder) lowered the performance.

4. CONCLUSIONS

We have addressed the Huawei/3DLife Grand Challenge component of action recognition under unexampled viewing conditions. We proposed a generic framework to extract view-invariant features from the position and orientation information of skeleton joints. We developed a stacked, compact autoencoder network for feature refinement. The original positions and orientations of skeleton joints are transformed to a user-defined coordinate system, and velocity and angular velocity are then calculated in the new coordinate system.

The proposed method was evaluated under two unexampled test settings: NewView and NewPerson. We showed that the view-invariant property of the features extracted by our method was efficient in the NewView test. In addition, the experimental results show that the view-invariant orientation and angular velocity features play an important role in action recognition. The experimental results also show that the SCAE could refine dense features and improve the classification performance.

5. REFERENCES

[1] C.-H. Huang, Y.-R. Yeh, and Y.-C. F. Wang. Recognizing actions across cameras by exploring the correlated subspace. In *Computer Vision–ECCV 2012. Workshops and Demonstrations*, pages 342–351. Springer, 2012.

[2] Q. V. Le, W. Y. Zou, S. Y. Yeung, and A. Y. Ng. Learning hierarchical invariant spatio-temporal features for action recognition with independent subspace analysis. In *CVPR2011*, pages 3361–3368. IEEE.

[3] W. Li, Z. Zhang, and Z. Liu. Action recognition based on a bag of 3d points. In *CVPRW2010*, pages 9–14. IEEE.

[4] J. Liu, M. Shah, B. Kuipers, and S. Savarese. Cross-view action recognition via view knowledge transfer. In *CVPR2011*, pages 3209–3216. IEEE.

[5] J. Ngiam, A. Coates, A. Lahiri, B. Prochnow, A. Ng, and Q. V. Le. On optimization methods for deep learning. In *Proceedings of the 28th International Conference on Machine Learning (ICML-11)*, pages 265–272, 2011.

[6] O. Oreifej and Z. Liu. Hon4d: Histogram of oriented 4d normals for activity recognition from depth sequences. *CVPR2013*.

[7] PrimeSense. http://www.openni.org/files/nite/.

[8] J. Sung, C. Ponce, B. Selman, and A. Saxena. Unstructured human activity detection from rgbd images. In *Robotics and Automation (ICRA), 2012 IEEE International Conference on*, pages 842–849. IEEE, 2012.

[9] C. Wang, Y. Wang, and A. L. Yuille. An approach to pose-based action recognition. *CVPR2013*.

[10] Y. Wong, M. T. Harandi, C. Sanderson, and B. C. Lovell. On robust biometric identity verification via sparse encoding of faces: holistic vs local approaches. In *Neural Networks (IJCNN), The 2012 International Joint Conference on*, pages 1–8. IEEE, 2012.

[11] L. Xia, C.-C. Chen, and J. Aggarwal. View invariant human action recognition using histograms of 3d joints. In *CVPRW2012*, pages 20–27. IEEE.

Search-Based Relevance Association with Auxiliary Contextual Cues

Chun-Che Wu, Kuan-Yu Chu, Yin-Hsi Kuo, Yan-Ying Chen, Wen-Yu Lee, Winston H. Hsu
National Taiwan University, Taipei, Taiwan

ABSTRACT

In this work, we target at solving the Bing challenge provided by Microsoft. The task is to design an effective and efficient measurement of query terms in describing the images (image-query pairs) crawled from the web. We observe that the provided image-query pairs (e.g., text-based image retrieval results) are usually related to their surrounding text; however, the relationship between image content seems to be ignored. Hence, we attempt to integrate the visual information for better ranking results. In addition, we found that plenty of query terms are related to people (e.g., celebrity) and user might have similar queries (click logs) in the search engine. Therefore, in this work, we propose a relevance association by investigating the effectiveness of different auxiliary contextual cues (i.e., face, click logs, visual similarity). Experimental results show that the proposed method can have 16% relative improvement compared to the original ranking results. Especially, for people-related queries, we can further have 45.7% relative improvement.

Categories and Subject Descriptors

H.3.3 [**Information Storage and Retrieval**]: Information Search and Retrieval—*Retrieval models*

Keywords

Image retrieval; Name detection; Identity bank

1. INTRODUCTION

Aiming at the Bing Grand Challenge, in this work, we are dealing with the relevance of each image-query pair. That is, given a tag and a list of images (cf. Figure 2), we need to measure the relevance of the images according to the tag. And the database contains 23 millions of tag-image pairs with their corresponding click number log. Both the queries and database are real data from Microsoft. This challenge might be related to visual re-ranking [2][4][7] or image search result refinement [5]; hence, it is essential to bridge the semantic gap between visual and textual information [6]. In addition, the response time (latency) of the proposed method should be take into account for online image-query relevance measurement. Hence, in this work, we investigate the effectiveness of different auxiliary contextual cues which seldom be considered in the prior work.

To deal with the large scale real data, we adopt three major strategies. First, the search-based system consists of

MM'13, October 21–25, 2013, Barcelona, Spain.

http://dx.doi.org/10.1145/2502081.2508127.

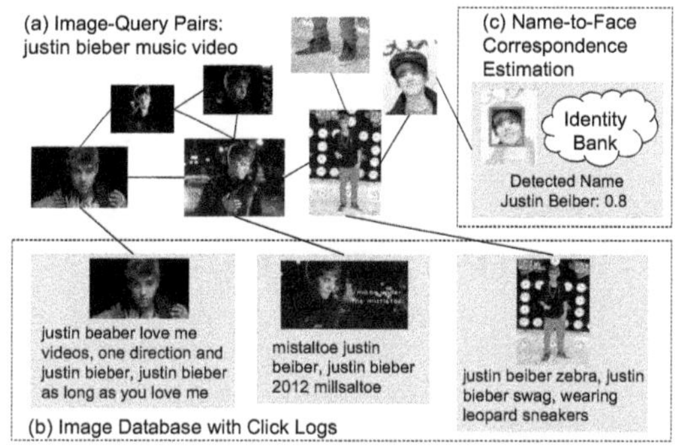

Figure 1: The proposed search-based relevance association with auxiliary contextual cues. We observe that the provided image-query pairs are usually related to the query tag; however, the relationship between image content seems to be ignored. Therefore, to tackle this challenge, we propose to measure the relevance via auxiliary contextual cues (i.e., face, click logs, visual similarity).

two parts, images search and tag similarity association. For each image-query pair, similar images are retrieved based on visual content (tag). Then the relevance is measured by the tag (visual) similarities (cf. Figure 1(b)). Further, we observe that a significant portion of the image-query pairs in Bing dataset comprise faces in images and names in their tags (as an example image-query pair in Figure 3). If we only look at the 1,000 unique tags in development set, around 318 (31.8%) unique tags consist of at least one name (either given name or family name).[1] Thus, we believe the correspondence between face in image and name in the tag will benefit measuring image-query relevance. Therefore, as Figure 1(c) shows, once an image-query pair contains at least a face and a name, the relevance of this query will be measured by the proposed name-to-face correspondence estimation.

Third, as Figure 2 shows, another observation is that the provided image-query pairs might be the text-based search results. That is, relevant (users' desired) images might be the majority in the list corresponding to the tag. Further, the desired images usually have similar visual content in the image-query pairs (cf. Figure 4). As a result, we find the classical PageRank algorithm [10] can solve the problem. As Figure 1(a) shows, the graph is constructed for each query. And each image in the list is a node and the weights of the edges are set by the visual similarities. Finally, we integrate the results from each model and provide extensive experiments to support our methods and arguments. In conclusion, we propose three models to measure the relevance of image-query pairs. Our methods demonstrate their effectiveness, and achieve 16% and 45.7% relative improvement in all queries and people-related queries, respectively.

[1]For celebrity, there exists 8.98% image-query pairs, and 86.20% of them contain at least one face in image content.

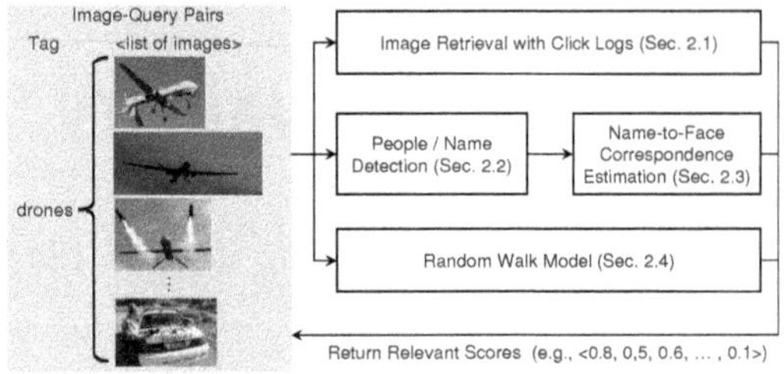

Figure 2: A system diagram of the proposed method. iven a list of image-query pairs, we integrate three different approaches to measure the relevant scores for each image-query pair.

2. RELEVANCE ASSOCIATION WITH AUXILIARY CONTEXTUAL CUES

Initially, this challenge aims to predict scores for each image-query pair individually. However, we observe that the image-query pairs should be related to each other. Thus, we slightly modified the problem as follows. Given a tag and a list of images related to that tag, a list of (re-ranked) relevance scores should be returned. Our system flow is shown in Figure 2. Image-query pairs are first fed into three different scoring methods, which are content-based method (Sec. 2.1), human-based method (Sec. 2.2 and 2.3) and query-association method (Sec. 2.4). The output scores are fused together as the final relevant scores.

2.1 Image Retrieval with Click Logs (IRCL)

The most intuitive way to measure the relevance score of an image-query pair is to retrieve visually and textually similar images from database (cf. Figure 1(b)). To efficiently retrieve similar images, we can first retrieve visually similar images (IRCLV) and calculate tag similarity from the top-ranked images. Similarly, we can retrieve textually similar images (IRCLT) and then calculate visual similarity from the top-ranked images. Therefore, the most critical steps is to effectively retrieve similar images by applying content- or text-based image retrieval.

1) Content-based image retrieval (IRCLV). To efficiently retrieve similar images from large-scale database, we apply the state-of-the-art bag-of-words (BoW) model with 1M vocabulary [11]. We first extract the visual features for the query image, and retrieve similar database images under the inverted indexing structure. Based on the top-ranked visually similar images, we can calculate the tag similarity between the query tag and click logs. To avoid misspelling (e.g., "fridsy") and synonym issues, we apply the standard pre-precessing before calculating the similarity.

2) Query tag expansion from hash tags in Twitter (IRCLT). For text-based image retrieval, we further apply tag expansion for query and tag clustering for database to ensure the quality of the top-ranked images. For tags in database images, we apply affinity propagation [1] for better representation. For each query tag, we first retrieve similar tweets from Twitter and then extract top frequently appeared hash tags as the query expansion results. We found that the hash tags are succinct with less noise than other methods such as snippet from search engine, and created by the users so its more close the what users really expect. Based on the expansion results, we can efficiently retrieve textually similar images. Eventually, we combine the textual and visual similarity as the final relevant scores.

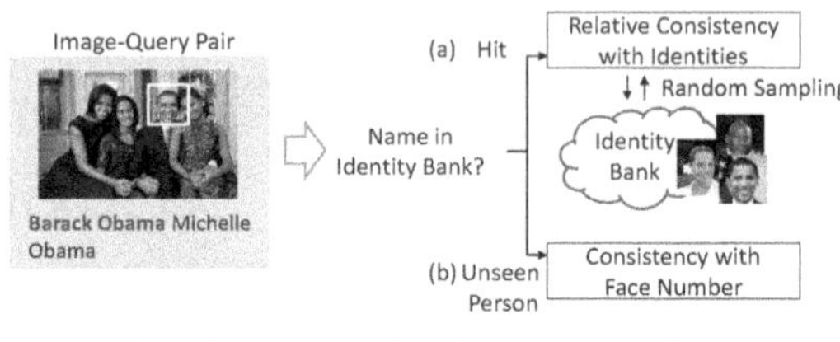

Figure 3: The framework of name-to-face correspondence estimation. iven an image-query pair, if the name in the tag is included in Identity Bank, the relevance will be measured by its corresponding identity model and its ranking in the results of randomly sampled models (as (a)). We also measure the consistency between the number of faces in image content and the number of names in its tag, which can deal with persons without training data (as (b)).

2.2 People/Name Detection

As mentioned in Sec. 1, a significant portion of image-query pairs comprise names; hence, it is essential to detect whether the image-query pair contains a name. We propose two name detection methods as follows:

1) Name list method (NLM). We first collect a list of celebrity names from http://www.posh24.com/celebrities/, which is denoted as $\mathbb{L}$ later. For each multiple-word celebrity name in $\mathbb{L}$, the first and the last words of the name are added into the $FirstNameSet$ and $LastNameSet$ respectively. After constructing these information, for each new coming tag, if it contains a name in the name list $\mathbb{L}$, we said a name is detected. However, unseen names cannot be handled by using this method only. For that reason, an additional method is applied to enhance the recall. That is, a detection is also claimed if we can find two consecutive words, in which the first and the second words are in the $FirstNameSet$ and $LastNameSet$ respectively.

2) Social media method. After using tag snippets returned by the search engine as query expansion, an interesting observation has been found. If a query tag contains names, it has higher probability that social media website can be found in the title of top-10 related website, such as Linkedin, Twitter and Facebook.

2.3 Name-to-Face Correspondence Estimation

There arises two challenges in finding name-to-face correspondence in large-scale wild photos on the internet: first, how to efficiently train and test identity models for as many persons as possible; second, how to deal with unseen persons - the identities never appeared in training images. In the following paragraphs, we first explain how we train the visual-based face identity models - *Identity Bank* - to discover name-to-face correspondences. Based on Identity Bank, we can further improve correspondence measurement by comparing with the other identity models through efficient random-sampling strategy as shown in Figure 3(a). Then, we measure the consistency between the number of faces in image content and the number of names in query tag, which delivers informative cues for finding unseen person's name-to-face correspondence (Figure 3(b)).

1) Relative Consistency with Identity Bank (IB). Firstly, we address how Identity Bank is constructed and used for name-to-face correspondence measurement. Given a set of image-query pairs, we leverage face detection [9] and name detection (cf. Sec. 2.2) to collect training face images and their name annotations. Only the image-query

Figure 4: Images expected by the users usually have similar visual content but are not directly the same as the semantic of the tag. "Waldo Alabama" is often not referred to the town but the covered bridge famous in the town.

pairs with exact one face and name are included for the purpose of reducing ambiguity in multiple name-to-face correspondences and ensuring correct name annotations. Each face identity model is trained by SVMs with 295-dimensional Pyramid Local Binary Patterns extracted from training faces. Totally, Identity Bank consists of 6,762 identity models trained by 35,092 face images from Bing training dataset. Two factors may decline correspondence measurement by Identity Bank, 1) noisy labels - the training data are crawled from web rather than manually annotated; 2) insufficient training data - only 9.14% identities have at least 10 training images. To reduce uncertainties, we randomly sample more models from Identity Bank for testing and use the multiple test results to confirm the confidence of correspondence measurement. As an image-query pair example in Figure 3, we will choose the model of "Barack Obama" for measuring the name-to-face correspondence probability. Meanwhile, we randomly select another two models, e.g., "Angelina Jolie" and "Michael Jordan" and obtain their test results as background model. The correspondence probability of "Barack Obama" will be further adjusted by its rank among the three test results. Higher confidence scores will be derived if the target name is more salient than the background ones.

2) Consistency with Face Number (FN). Further, it is critical to deal with unseen persons for an online system because it should adapt to incrementally updated data. From our statistics in Bing development set, around 29.96% image-query pairs are with names (persons) never shown in any training image and thus without corresponding models in Identity Bank. To tackle the problem, we propose to measure the consistency by matching the number of faces in image content and the number of names in its tag. In this scenario, no training images are required so it is applicable to the unseen persons. Their names can be detected via the Name List and Social Media as mentioned in Sec. 2.2. Two criteria for consistency measurement are addressed. Firstly, if a name is detected in a tag, the associated image should comprise at least one face. Secondly, we consider the word "and" after a name, for example, Justin Bieber and his mother. In this case, the number of faces should greater than one though only one name is detected. The image-query pairs following the two rules will be given higher relevance; otherwise, the relevance will be decreased.

2.4 Random Walk Model

We observe the given image-query pairs might come from text-based image retrieval results (may also on user's click through). Thus, we assume that the majority of retrieved images are relevant to the query. Furthermore, relevance depends on what users really want, which usually focuses on a few famous features directly/indirectly regarding to the tag.

Table 1: The performance of content-based method (IRCL) and name-to-face correspondence measurement. The proposed method (IB+FN) can reach 45.71% relative improvement for the name of queries appeared in Identity Bank (I), The results confirm the benefits from the proposed name-to-face correspondence estimation for relevance measurement.

Full queries	Initial	IRCLV (+FN)		IRCLT	Ideal
DCG@25 (A)	0.469	0.484 (0.489)		0.495	0.684
Name queries	Initial	IB	FN	IB+FN	Ideal
DCG@25 (N)	0.481	0.496	0.508	0.516	0.702
DCG@25 (I)	0.350	0.496	0.500	0.510	0.672

Table 2: The performance of name detection with auxiliary social media keywords in the snippets from the search engine.

	NLM	Facebook	Linkedin	Twitter
Precision	0.967	0.73	0.959	0.795
Recall	0.279	0.585	0.438	0.509

Hence, the image-query pairs often contain similar visual content, frequently grouping into some clusters as shown in Figure 4. Although "Waldo Alabama" is a town in the U.S., what most users really like to see from tag is the famous covered bridge in Alabama. Thus, the relevant images often contain certain the famous covered bridge in Alabama and form some clusters. As a result, if an image in the list is relevant to the tag, there should be some other images with strong visual similarities. In short, those having strong visual connections with others deserve more relevance scores.

As a result, it is reasonable to assign the relevance score to an image based on its connections (similarities) with others. The stronger the connections are, the higher the score should be. The concept is highly related to the website ranking based on the connection of hyperlinks. Thus, inspired by the PageRank, the relevance scores ($\mathbf{s}$) are formulated as $\mathbf{s} = (\alpha\mathbf{P} + (1-\alpha)\mathbf{v}\mathbb{1}^{\mathbf{T}})\mathbf{s}$, where $\mathbb{1}$ is a vector of one, and $\mathbf{v}$ is encoded with initial normalized prior ($\mathbb{1}$) or prior knowledge from previous sections. Corresponding to our observation, the transition probability ($\mathbf{P}$) is equivalent to the normalized similarity between image-query pairs (i.e., $P(i,j) = sim(i,j)/\sum_i sim(i,j)$). Obviously, the solution is the eigenvector corresponding to the largest eigenvalue.

3. EXPERIMENTAL SETUP AND RESULTS

1) ataset and valuation. We use the entire dataset provided by Bing challenge, which contains 1M images with 23M click logs. In addition, they also provide a development set that contains 1,000 query terms with around 80K images. To tackle this challenge, we extract different kinds of visual features—bag-of-words (BoW) [12], the vector of locally aggregated descriptors (VLAD) [3], grid color moment (GCM), and local binary pattern (LBP) [8] for facial images. We evaluate the relevant scores of the same query terms by Discounted Cumulated Gain at 25 (DCG@25) as defined by the challenge. The averaged DCG@25 of the original ranking (Initial) and the ideal ranking is 0.469 and 0.684, respectively. Because some queries are less than 25 excellent images, the averaged DCG@25 will not be 1.

2) Performance of IRCL. We first evaluate the performance of the entire queries (A) by content-based method that considers both visual and tag similarities. As the first row of Table 1 shows, the proposed IRCLV (0.484) is better than the initial ranking (0.469). This is because users might have similar types of queries (e.g., poster, logo) in the

Table 3: **The performance of query-association method on three different features. Our method has 16% relative improvement compared to the original ranking (0.469), and demonstrate our arguments in Sec. 2.4.**

Method	Average Similarity			Random Walk (RW)			RW with Prior	RW with Late Fusion
Feature	GCM	VLAD	BoW	GCM	VLAD	BoW	BoW	BoW
DCG@25 (A)	0.492	0.538	0.541	0.490	0.527	0.543	0.543	0.544

search engine. Therefore, by considering both visual and tag similarities, we can obtain partial knowledge from the provided database. In addition, as mentioned in Sec. 2.3, the query might contain the name so we should also consider the number of faces in images. Hence, we can further improve the accuracy to 0.489 (IRCLV+FN). Then we expand query tags by Twitter. Each query tag is viewed as a hash tag of Twitter. We use the hash tag of Twitter to find related tags to the corresponding query tag. In our experiments, this approach (IRCLT) can improve the accuracy to 0.495. Nevertheless, the accuracy is still far from the ideal case (0.684) because most of queries are quite different from the database. Thus, the relationship between the query images will be considered in the later paragraph.

3) People Name etection Results. Table 2 shows the performance of name detection results. With the auxiliary social media keywords, the recall of detection will increase obviously. As the recalls improve, more queries can perform the human-based model for further relevance association. Although "Facebook" provides the largest improvement in recall, which shows its popularity among the world, it hurts the precision most. According to our observation, the reason is that "Facebook" is not only for people. Clubs, companies, even pets will have their own "Facebook" account. Therefore, there are many false positives. On the other hand, The accounts of "Linkedin" almost owned by real people, so the precision barely drops. In short, the auxiliary social media keywords will boost the recall of name detection under tolerant sacrifice of precision, and then further improve the relevance association results.

4) Name-to-Face Correspondence stimation. To evaluate the effect from name-to-face correspondence estimation, we conduct the experiments on the test queries with at least one name detected (dataset (N)), totally 7,180 image-query pairs, which corresponds to around 9% of the whole test queries in Bing dataset. The baseline for comparison is assigning each query with the same relevance. As shown in Table 1 (N), relevance measurement by Identity Bank (IB) and by Face Number (FN) report 1.5% improvement and 2.7% improvement compared with the baseline (0.481), respectively. In addition, their late fusion (0.516) surpasses the baseline with 3.5% improvement. We also conduct the experiments on the test queries with names included in Identity Bank (I), that is, the identities with training data. As shown in Table 1 (I), these test queries are more challenging because the DCG@25 in Ideal case (0.672) is lower than that for dataset (N) (0.702) and the result of baseline decreases to 0.350. In these challenging queries, the result of proposed method (IB+FN), 0.510, substantially outperforms the result of baseline with 16% improvement, that is, 45.71% relative improvement. In summary, the proposed name-to-face correspondence measurement can deal with celebrities (with training images) as well as unseen persons (without training images) and obviously improves image-tag relevance measurement in the queries with names.

5) Random Walk Model. Table 3 shows the experiments on query-association method (Sec. 2.4). First, we measure the relevance directly based on the average similarity of each query image (i.e., $s = \sum_j sim(i,j)$). The experiment manifests our observations in Sec. 2.4. That is, more similar images the one has, higher relevance score the one deserves. We can further improve the accuracy to 0.543 by random walk model; however, the prior from other models (RW with Prior) does not help. The reason might be that, in some cases, it needs lots of iterations to converge to the stationary points. The weight of the image network will decrease exponentially, so if the convergence costs many iterations, the results will bias to the results of prior models which is worse than the results of original random walk model. On the other hand, if we apply the late fusion, which will ensure the weight of the other models is relatively small, the performance will have slightly improvement. Therefore, we can have 16% (from 0.469 to 0.544) relative improvement in entire queries (A).

4. CONCLUSIONS AND FUTURE WORK

We propose a search-based relevance association framework to measure the relevance of image-query pairs. By utilizing different auxiliary contextual cues, we propose three methods - content-based, human-based, and query-association - to conquer the challenge. The preliminary experiments manifest the effectiveness of our proposed methods, which successfully uplift the image-query relevance measurement in Bing challenge. In the future, we will investigate how to integrate different methods and further leverage semantic knowledge for image matching.

5. REFERENCES

[1] B. J. Frey and D. Dueck. Clustering by passing messages between data points. *Science*, 2007.

[2] W. H. Hsu et al. Video search reranking via information bottleneck principle. ACM MM, 2006.

[3] H. Jégou et al. Aggregating local image descriptors into compact codes. *IEEE TPAMI*, Sept. 2012.

[4] W. Liu et al. Noise resistant graph ranking for improved web image search. In *CVPR*, 2011.

[5] J. Lu et al. Image search results refinement via outlier detection using deep contexts. In *CVPR*, 2012.

[6] H. Ma et al. Bridging the semantic gap between image contents and tags. *IEEE TMM*, 12(5):462–473, 2010.

[7] N. Morioka and J. Wang. Robust visual reranking via sparsity and ranking constraints. In *ACM MM*, 2011.

[8] T. Ojala et al. Multiresolution gray-scale and rotation invariant texture classification with local binary patterns. *IEEE TPAMI*, 24(7):971–987, 2002.

[9] Omron. Okao vision. 2008. `http://www.omron.com/r_d/vision/01.html`.

[10] L. Page et al. The pagerank citation ranking: Bringing order to the web. Technical report, 1999.

[11] J. Philbin et al. Object retrieval with large vocabularies and fast spatial matching. In *CVPR07*.

[12] J. Sivic et al. Video Google: A text retrieval approach to object matching in videos. In *ICCV*, 2003.

Image Search by Graph-based Label Propagation with Image Representation from DNN

Yingwei Pan [§], Ting Yao [†], Kuiyuan Yang [‡], Houqiang Li [§],
Chong-Wah Ngo [†], Jingdong Wang [‡], Tao Mei [‡]
[§] University of Science and Technology of China, Hefei, P. R. China
[†] City University of Hong Kong, Kowloon, Hong Kong
[‡] Microsoft Research Asia, Beijing, P. R. China
{panyw, tingyao}.ustc@gmail.com; lihq@ustc.edu.cn;
cscwngo@cityu.edu.hk; {kuyang, jingdw, tmei}@microsoft.com

ABSTRACT

Our objective is to estimate the relevance of an image to a query for image search purposes. We address two limitations of the existing image search engines in this paper. First, there is no straightforward way of bridging the gap between semantic textual queries as well as users' search intents and image visual content. Image search engines therefore primarily rely on static and textual features. Visual features are mainly used to identify potentially useful recurrent patterns or relevant training examples for complementing search by image reranking. Second, image rankers are trained on query-image pairs labeled by human experts, making the annotation intellectually expensive and time-consuming. Furthermore, the labels may be subjective when the queries are ambiguous, resulting in difficulty in predicting the search intention. We demonstrate that the aforementioned two problems can be mitigated by exploring the use of click-through data, which can be viewed as the footprints of user searching behavior, as an effective means of understanding query.

The correspondences between an image and a query are determined by whether the image was searched and clicked by users under the query in a commercial image search engine. We therefore hypothesize that the image click counts in response to a query are as their relevance indications. For each new image, our proposed graph-based label propagation algorithm employs neighborhood graph search to find the nearest neighbors on an image similarity graph built up with visual representations from deep neural networks and further aggregates their clicked queries/click counts to get the labels of the new image. We conduct experiments on MSR-Bing Grand Challenge and the results show consistent performance gain over various baselines. In addition, the proposed approach is very efficient, completing annotation of each query-image pair within just 15 milliseconds on a regular PC.

MM'13, October 21–25, 2013, Barcelona, Spain.
Copyright 2013 ACM 978-1-4503-2404-5/13/10 ...$15.00.
http://dx.doi.org/10.1145/2502081.2508128.

Categories and Subject Descriptors

H.3.3 [**Information Storage and Retrieval**]: Information Search and Retrieval—*Search process*

Keywords

Image search, deep neural networks, neighborhood graph search, click-through data.

1. INTRODUCTION

The rapid development of Web 2.0 technologies has led to the surge of research activities in image search. Since the query is provided as text rather than image, it is difficult to directly bring image visual features into play and build on advances in computer vision research. As a result, while visual documents are rich in image visual content and user-supplied texts, commercial image search engines to date mostly perform retrieval by employing static and textual features extracted from the image's parent web page and surrounding text, respectively. This kind of visual search approach may not always achieve satisfying results as textual information is sometimes noisy and even unavailable. Moreover, image rankers trained on query-image pairs labeled by human experts may lead to poor generalization performance due to the label noise problem and difficulty associated with understanding the user's intent [9].

To address the above issues, we explore user searching behavior through click-through data, which is largely available and freely accessible by search engines, for connecting image visual content with semantic textual queries as well as user's search intent. Accordingly, a novel graph-based label propagation approach is proposed. For a given query-image pair, we firstly identify approximate nearest neighbors (ANNs) of the given image from the set of previously clicked images by using neighborhood graph search. Specifically, an image neighborhood graph is constructed using image representations generated by deep neural networks, which have been proven effective in speech recognition and image classification recently. An iterated neighborhood graph search is efficiently performed to find the nearest neighbor images with the mechanism of avoiding unnecessary neighborhood expansions and local optimum. Next, the clicked queries to these ANNs are aggregated and propagated to predict the relevance score for the given query-image pair.

Our proposed method tackles the two issues highlighted above as follows. First, the image graph is built on only visual features extracted directly from the previously clicked images. As a result, images that are visually similar to the new image in terms of measured color, texture, and edge properties are located as ANN candidates. It is worth noting that our approach does not require any textual information and any priori knowledge about the user intent.

Second, we consider exploring user click-through data to shed some light on bridging semantic gap and user intention gap for image search. In general, image rankers obtain training data by manually labelling the relevance of query-image pairs. However, it is difficult to fathom the user's intent based on the query keywords alone especially for those ambiguous queries. For example, given the query "guitar factory," experts tend to label images of guitar manufacturing base as being highly relevant. However, empirical evidence suggests that most users wish to retrieve images of a guitar with brand "guitar factory." Expert labels might therefore be erroneous. Such factors bias the training set and the ranker is learnt to be sub-optimal. Our click-based method provides a useful alternative aimed at tackling this problem directly. As in image search, users browse image thumbnails before selecting the images to click. The decision to click is likely dependent on the relevancy of an image. Therefore, click data can serve as a reliable feedback potentially useful for image search. We hypothesize that, most of the clicked images are relevant to the given query judged by the real users.

In summary, this paper makes the following contributions:

- We study the problem of image search by leveraging user click-through data.
- We propose a graph-based label propagation approach to predict query-image relevance score and the algorithm is demonstrated on a real-world user click data collected from Bing image search engine.

The remaining sections are organized as follows. Section 2 describes the related work on use of click data. Section 3 presents the graph-based label propagation method for image search, while Section 4 provides empirical evaluations, followed by the conclusions in Section 5.

2. RELATED WORK

Click-through data has been studied and analyzed widely with different Web mining techniques for improving search engines' efficacy and usability in recent years. In [1], the authors introduced another vectorial representation for the queries without considering the content information. Queries were represented as points in a high dimensional space, where each dimension corresponds to a unique URL. The weight assigned to each dimension was equal to the click frequency. Poblete *et al.* [10] proposed the query-set document model by mining frequent query patterns to represent documents rather than the content information of the documents. Li *et al.* [8] presented the use of click graphs in improving query intent classifiers. There are also several approaches that have tried to model the representation of queries or documents on the click-through bipartite. In addition, click-through data has also been used to learn the rank function. Joachims *et al.* [6] did an eye tracking experiment to observe the relationship between clicked links and the relevance of the target pages. For image search, click-through data has been found to be very reliable [3][5]. In [3], the method built a query-image click graph and performed backward random walks to determine a probability distribution over images conditioned on the given query which can be used for ranking. Jain *et al.* [5] reranked the image search results so as to promote images that are likely to be clicked to the top of the ranked list. Later in [11], an in-depth analysis of several ranking algorithms was performed on Flickr user log data to investigate the importance of many factors, including the internal and external image popularity, the overall attentions, diversity, semantic categories and visual appearance. In another work by Yao *et al.* [13], by combining click-through and video document features for deriving a latent space, the dot product of the mappings in the latent space is taken as the similarity between videos and the similarity is further applied for video tagging tasks.

3. GRAPH-BASED LABEL PROPAGATION

In this section, we first describe the image representation used in this paper, followed by the neighborhood graph search for finding ANNs on the image neighborhood graph. Then, a label propagation algorithm is proposed to further aggregate and propagate ANNs' queries/click counts to predict new query-image relevance score.

3.1 Image Representation

Recently, deep neural networks (DNN) has demonstrated its effectiveness to learn image representation and classifier simultaneously with a large number of training data. The learned image representation from DNN is close to semantics, and ever exceeds current estimate of Inferior Temporal (IT) representation performance in macaque's visual cortex [2]. Inspired by the success of DNN, we use it to generate image representation in this paper, which is a 1024-dimensional feature vector. Similar to [7], the used DNN architecture is denoted as $Image - C64 - P - N - C128 - P - N - C192 - C192 - C128 - P - F4096 - F1024 - F1000$, which contains five convolutional layers (denoted by C following the number of filters) while the last three are fully-connected layers (denoted by F following the number of neurons); the max-pooling layers (denoted by P) follow the first, second and fifth convolutional layers; local contrast normalization layers (denoted by N) follow the first and second max-pooling layers. The weights of DNN are learned on ILSVRC-2010, which is a subset of ImageNet dataset with 1.26 million training images from 1,000 categories. For an image, its representation is the neuronal responses of the layer $F1024$ by input the image into the learned DNN.

3.2 Neighborhood Graph Search

After building the image neighborhood graph on image representations, an iterated neighborhood graph search approach is exploited to locate the ANNs. We apply a recent query-driven iterated neighborhood graph search algorithm [12], to conduct the search process. The basic procedure is outlined in Algorithm 1.

GenerateInitialSolution(q, T) searches over trees T, which are constructed to index the reference images. The initial solution contains a small amount of initial NN candidates that have high probabilities to be near true NNs. Following the implementation in [12], we use kd-trees in our experiments. LocalNGSearch(P_0, G) starts from a set of seeds P_0 and searches over G by conducting neighborhood expansions in a best-first manner. Perturbation(R^*, q, T,

Algorithm 1 Query-driven iterated neighborhood graph search

$P_0 \leftarrow$ GenerateInitialSolution(q, T)
$R^* \leftarrow$ LocalNGSearch(P_0, G)
repeat
  $P' \leftarrow$ Perturbation(R^*, q, T, *history*)
  $R^{*'} \leftarrow$ LocalNGSearch(P', G, *history*)
  $R^* \leftarrow$ AcceptanceCriterion(R^*, $R^{*'}$)
until termination condition met

history) generates new seeds from trees T according to the search history and previously selected NNs (R^*), to avoid unnecessary neighborhood expansions. LocalNGSearch(P', G, *history*) is slightly different from LocalNGSearch(P_0, G) as the search history, i.e., the NNs discovered up to the current iteration are considered in neighborhood expansion. Readers can refer to [12] for technical details.

3.3 Label Propagation

For a new query-image pair (q, I), we conduct the neighborhood graph search to get new image's Top K nearest visually similar images and aggregate their clicked queries/click counts to predict the relevance score of the new query-image. Specifically, for the new image I, let the Top K nearest neighbor in the image neighborhood graph be $I_i, 1 \leq i \leq K$. For each neighbor image I_i, let $q_i^j, 1 \leq j \leq M_i$ be the previously clicked query set to image I_i and f_i^j be the click counts of image I_i in response to query q_i^j. Then, the relevance $r(q, I)$ of query q to image I becomes

$$r(q,I) = \sum\nolimits_{i=1}^{K} simi(I,I_i) \sum\nolimits_{j=1}^{M_i} \frac{|q_i^j \cap q|}{|q_i^j \cup q|} \log f_i^j, \quad (1)$$

where $simi(I, I_i)$ stands for the visual similarity between image I and its neighbor I_i which is calculated on the visual feature representation. $|q_i^j \cap q|$ and $|q_i^j \cup q|$ indicate the number of common terms between q_i^j and q, and the total unique term number of the two queries, respectively. We use the logarithm of click counts in this paper, which is verified to be effective.

The spirit of label propagation is to give a higher relevance score for query-image pair (q, I) if the visually similar neighbor images are highly clicked by queries in close semantic proximity with query q.

4. EXPERIMENT

We conduct experiments on the MSR-Bing Image Retrieval Challenge [4], which contains a training dataset and a dev dataset. Both of them are sampled from Bing user click log. In total, there are 11,701,890 distinct queries and 1,000,000 different images in training dataset, while the dev dataset consists 1,000 queries and 79,665 images.

In our experiments, we adopt the whole training dataset as our training data and the evaluations are conducted on all 1,000 queries in dev dataset.

4.1 Experimental Settings

Compared Approaches: We compare the following approaches for performance evaluation:

- N-Gram SVM Modeling (N-Gram SVM). We use all the clicked images of a given query as positive samples and randomly select negative samples from the rest of the training dataset to build a SVM model for each query, and then use this model to predict the relevance of the query to a new image. In addition, in order to extend the capability of the training data to model queries that are not covered in the dataset, n-gram modeling, which attempts to model each n-gram as a "query", is used. In other words, if a query is not in the training set, but its n-grams appear in some queries of the training set, we can generate the model by linearly fusing the SVM models of these queries. In our experiments, we use bigram and unigram. The five runs using different visual features, including color moments (CM), wavelet texture (WT), edge histogram (EDH), bag of visual words (BoW), and DNN feature, are finally reported.
- Graph-based label propagation (GLP). We design five runs for our proposed graph-based approach, each based on one of the aforementioned five visual features.

Table 1: The NDCG@25 of different approaches with different individual visual features.

Method	WT	EDH	CM	BoW	DNN
N-Gram SVM	0.4878	0.4829	0.4873	0.4845	0.4899
GLP	0.4931	0.4866	0.4896	0.4848	0.5050

Evaluation Metrics: Following the measurements in the challenge's industrial track, for each query, we use Discounted Cumulated Gain (DCG) to evaluate the performance of top 25 images. Given an image ranked list based on the score, the DCG for each query is calculated as

$$DCG@25 = 0.01757 \sum_{i=1}^{25} \frac{2^{rel_i} - 1}{\log_2^{i+1}}, \quad (2)$$

where $rel_i = \{Excellent = 3, Good = 2, Bad = 0\}$ is the manually judged relevance for each image with respect to the query, and 0.01757 is a normalizer factor to make the score for 25 Excellent results 1. The final metric is the average of $DCG@25$ for all queries in the test set. Note that for the queries with less than 25 images in the dev dataset, we simply grade relevance score of all the supplemental positions as *Bad*. Moreover, the run time of our graph-based method is also compared and discussed.

4.2 Performance Comparison

Table 1 shows the NDCG performance of ten runs averaged over 1,000 test queries. Overall, the results across different visual features consistently indicate that GLP leads to a performance boost against N-Gram SVM modeling. Particularly, the DCG@25 performance of GLP on DNN feature can achieve 0.5050, which improves the N-Gram SVM model by 3.1%. In addition, when only evaluating the performance on the queries with more than 25 images in the dev dataset, GLP model on DNN feature (DCG@25 = 0.6339) can lead to better performance gain than N-Gram SVM model by 4.6%. This somewhat reveals the weak use of click data in training SVM model, where all the clicked images are used as positive training samples no matter how many times they have been clicked. As such, some non-relevant distracting images, which might have received only a single, or very few, clicks will also be considered as positive, thereby bringing some

Table 2: **Run time (ms) of N-Gram SVM and GLP on five different visual features. The experiments are conducted on a regular PC (Intel dual-core 3.33GHz CPU and 8 GB RAM).**

Method	WT	EDH	CM	BoW	DNN
N-Gram SVM	900	890	860	6800	7500
GLP	9.9	9.8	11	15.8	14.8

label noise. GLP, in contrast, is benefited from the way of taking into account the absolute click counts for relevance prediction, which should be more accurate.

Compared to global and local visual features, DNN feature achieves both the best performance by using N-Gram SVM modeling and GLP, which verifies the effectiveness of DNN feature in semantic-level similarity measurement.

Figure 1 shows the top ten images for query "portable cd player insigna" by using GLP method based on five individual features, respectively. We can easily see the results with DNN features get all excellent images, followed by WT for nine excellent images, EDH and BoW for eight excellent images, and CM for seven excellent images.

4.3 Run Time

The complexity of our method is $O(P\log^2 n + (1-P)\log^3 n)$, where n denotes the number of search seeds and P represents the probability of starting from an ideal seed. Table 2 listed the detailed run time on each feature for the two compared methods. Our approach is extremely efficient, completing relevance prediction of each image-query pair within 15 milliseconds on average. This is much faster than N-Gram SVM modeling which needs beyond 800 milliseconds.

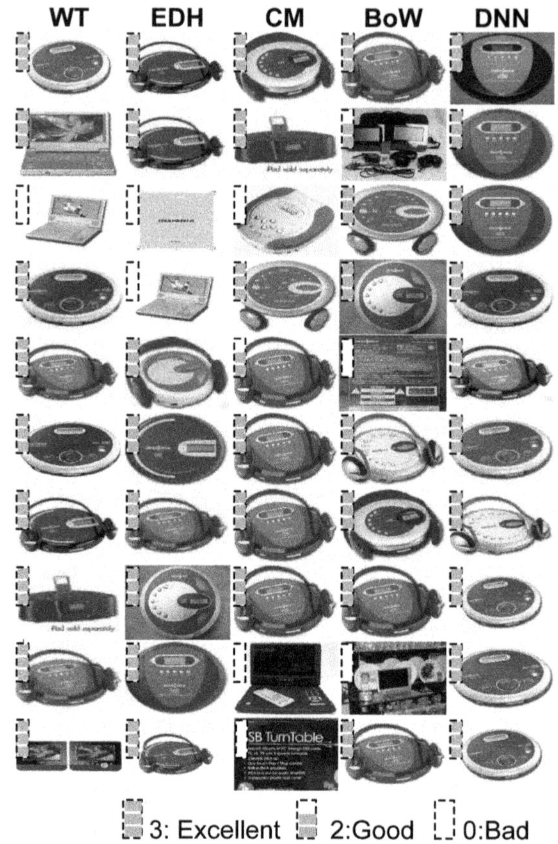

Figure 1: The exemplary list of top ten images for query "portable cd player insigna" ranked by GLP method based on five different visual features.

5. CONCLUSION

In this paper, we tackled two major limitations of existing image search rankers - not incorporating visual features and learning from training data with label noise. By using user click data as a "bridge" to connect image visual content with textual queries as well as user intents, we propose a graph-based label propagation approach to tackle the two issues. The extensive experiments evaluated on 564 test queries show that our proposed GLP algorithm gave consistently better results than SVM-based method on different visual features. Moreover, an important property of GLP method is its speed, which is very efficient and can provide instant response. This aspect makes it a good candidate for online image search applications.

6. ACKNOWLEDGMENTS

This work was supported in part by a grant from the Research Grants Council of the Hong Kong SAR (CityU 119610) and Microsoft Research Asia Windows Phone Academic Program FY12-RES-OPP-107.

7. REFERENCES

[1] R. A. Baeza-Yates and A. Tiberi. Extracting semantic relations from query logs. In *KDD*, 2007.

[2] C. F. Cadieu, H. Hong, D. Yamins, N. Pinto, N. J. Majaj, and J. J. DiCarlo. The neural representation benchmark and its evaluation on brain and machine. In *ICLR*, 2013.

[3] N. Craswell and M. Szummer. Random walks on the click graph. In *SIGIR*, 2007.

[4] X.-S. Hua, L. Yang, J. Wang, J. Wang, M. Ye, K. Wang, Y. Rui, and J. Li. Clickage: Towards bridging semantic and intent gaps via mining click logs of search engines. In *ACM MM*, 2013.

[5] V. Jain and M. Varma. Learning to re-rank: Query-dependent image re-ranking using click data. In *WWW*, 2011.

[6] T. Joachims, L. Granka, B. Pan, H. Hembrooke, F. Radlinski, and G. Gay. Evaluating the accuracy of implicit feedback from clicks and query reformulations in web search. *ACM Trans. on Information Systems*, 25(2), 2007.

[7] A. Krizhevsky, I. Sutskever, and G. E. Hinton. Imagenet classification with deep convolutional neural networks. In *NIPS*, 2012.

[8] X. Li, Y.-Y. Wang, and A. Acero. Learning query intent from regularized click graphs. In *SIGIR*, 2008.

[9] T. Mei, Y. Rui, S. Li, and Q. Tian. Multimedia search reranking: A literature survey. *ACM Computing Surveys*, to appear.

[10] B. Poblete and R. A. Baeza-Yates. Query-sets: using implicit feedback and query patterns to organize web documents. In *WWW*, 2008.

[11] M. Trevisiol, L. Chiarandini, L. M. Aiello, and A. Jaimes. Image ranking based on user browsing behavior. In *SIGIR*, 2012.

[12] J. Wang and S. Li. Query-driven iterated neighborhood graph search for large scale indexing. In *ACM MM*, 2012.

[13] T. Yao, T. Mei, C.-W. Ngo, and S. Li. Annotation for free: Video tagging by mining user search behavior. In *ACM MM*, 2013.

Real-time Salient Object Detection

Chia-Ju Lu Chih-Fan Hsu Mei-Chen Yeh

Dept. of Computer Science and Information Engineering
National Taiwan Normal University, Taipei, Taiwan
{lcjptg, hsuchihfan}@gmail.com, myeh@csie.ntnu.edu.tw

ABSTRACT

Salient object detection techniques have a variety of multimedia applications of broad interest. However, the detection must be fast to truly aid in these processes. There exist many robust algorithms tackling the salient object detection problem but most of them are computationally demanding. In this demonstration we show a fast salient object detection system implemented in a conventional PC environment. We examine the challenges faced in the design and development of a practical system that can achieve accurate detection in real-time.

Categories and Subject Descriptors

I.5.4 [**Pattern Recognition**]: Applications – *Computer Vision.*

Keywords

Object detection, Saliency.

1. INTRODUCTION

The objective of salient object detection is selecting image regions, usually specified using a rectangle, that best catch human perceptual attention. This technique can be used for a wide range of multimedia systems and applications. For example, it can benefit content-aware image retargeting which aims to resize an image while preserving important regions [4]; the technique can also be utilized for creating a beautiful picture collage from a group of photos [5]. However, the detection must be fast to truly aid in these tasks. Real-time salient object detection is practical but difficult because salient objects in images can have a wide variability in appearance, and we usually do not know the location, the shape, and the size they may have.

Most salient object detection approaches tackle the problem by two steps: saliency map extraction and salient object localization. To achieve a good detection performance, the saliency map is usually derived by combining multiple features. Then, a dense-sampling approach that examines a large number of regions is applied to localize the salient region. Both steps are computational expensive, and, thus, hinder the usage of this technique for real-time applications. Such robust approaches consider high accuracy more importantly than execution efficiency. For example, it takes on average seconds to minutes to process a 400×300 image reported in [2].

In this demonstration we show a real-time salient object detection system. Designing algorithms that can achieve both effectiveness and efficiency is the main concern in creating our system. In particular, we explore the use of the efficient subwindow search (ESS) approach [1], which is primarily designed for generic object detection, to significantly speed up the detection process. To reach

MM'13, October 21–25, 2013, Barcelona, Spain.
ACM 978-1-4503-2404-5/13/10.

Figure 1. Example outcomes of our system. Salient objects in the images are localized in real-time.

great detection accuracy, we apply the novel features proposed in [2] for describing a salient object. Therefore, the salient object detection is viewed as an optimization problem that seeks a best image region based on the measurement in [2], and the problem is then efficiently solved by ESS. To summarize, we modify and integrate the state-of-the-art approach [2] into the ESS framework. The fast algorithm returns accurate detection results — some examples are shown in Fig. 1.

In the following we describe in detail our system design, including the system framework and the algorithms, and the demonstration setup.

2. SYSTEM OVERVIEW

Figure 2 illustrates our system framework. Given an input image, we first construct an integral image of the color spatial distribution map and an integral histogram from the image [3]. Both reduce the time complexity of feature extraction from an image region to $O(1)$. However, the evaluation of all possible sub-regions is still computational expensive. Therefore, the localization is performed using ESS, which applies a branch-and-bound scheme. We design the quality function that considers several novel salient features in [2] (Section 2.1), and the search is efficiently conducted using ESS (Section 2.2). Finally, we obtain one (or more) rectangles that contain salient objects.

2.1 Salient Features

We did a survey on saliency representation and modified the approach in [2] for developing our system. Liu *et al.* proposed three types of novel features—namely, center-surround histogram, color spatial distribution, and multi-scale contrast. In particular, we used the former two features as the localization step would search regions with multiple scales. The center-surround histogram computes the dissimilarity of a rectangle and its surrounding frame. A larger dissimilarity value implies a bounding box is distinct from its surrounding area and is likely to be a salient object. The χ^2 distance between histograms of RGB color is used as the dissimilarity value. However, this regional

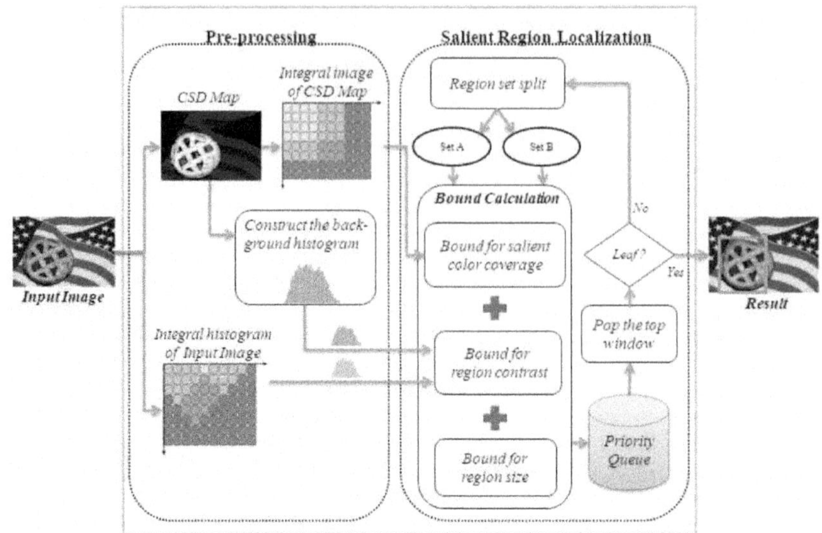

Figure 2. System framework.

feature is not readily integrated in a branch-and-bound scheme as it is not trivial how to derive a good bound in a rectangle set if we do not use an exhaustive search approach. Therefore, we compute the dissimilarity of a region and the background (i.e. a static feature vector for a region set) instead.

The background is estimated by computing the color histogram of the whole image. Next, each bin values are adjusted based on the color spatial distribution—if a color is widely distributed in the image, it is less likely contained in a salient object. Therefore, the background histogram somewhat disables those bins which have a dense pixel set. Similar to Liu's implementation, the spatial distribution of a color is computed as the sum of the variances of x- and y- coordinates of pixels being the color. This feature is further normalized and weighted considering the distance to the image center. Finally, we impose restrictions on the size of salient objects by assuming that the region should not be either too large or too small.

To summarize, our system is designed considering three factors. It searches for a best region that is dissimilar to background, contains salient colors as many as possible, and has a reasonable size. We used equal weights to combine these features.

2.2 Salient Region Localization

We use the ESS approach [1] to efficiently find a region that has the exact maximum of our objective function. The approach hierarchically splits the search space into disjoint subsets and examines the one that looks most promising. This is achieved by computing a bound given a region set. The bound of a region set is used to organize the candidate sets in a priority queue in a best-first manner. We always examine the region set that looks most promising in terms of its bound, and decide if a region set should be discarded if its value is not better than the best solution seen so far. Interesting readers may refer to [1] for more details.

2.3 Runtime and Detection Results

We have evaluated our system using the MSRA salient object database [2]. In particular, the image set B that contains 5000 images was used. Without any parameter tunings, we obtained a satisfactory detection result with precision 0.65 and recall 0.77, which are slightly worse than the results reported in [2]. By learning the weights for combing the features, it seems reasonable to expect this approach would yield even better results. The detection is fast—70% of the images in the database take less than 0.5 seconds to process, and over 90% can be done within 1 second, while the approach in [2] takes seconds to even minutes to process one image, running non-optimized C++ codes on a machine with a 1.8 GHz CPU and 4GB of RAM. Comparing with the state-of-the-art approaches [2], our system has a comparable detection result with considerably lower computational complexity.

3. DEMONSTRATION SETUP

In this paper, we present a fast and accurate salient object detection system. The speed improvement is achieved by integrating state-of-the-art approaches into the ESS framework. The demonstration has the form of stand-alone software. The system reads images in a specified folder system and sequentially displays the image as well as the detection result on screen when activated. We will also provide a simple interface for receiving input images from conference attendants for a live demonstration of our system. We will demonstrate the system's ability to execute real-time and accurate detection of salient objects in images.

4. ACKNOWLEDGMENT

This work was supported in part by the National Science Council, Taiwan, under Grants NSC 101-2221-E-003-023.

5. REFERENCES

[1] C. H. Lampert, M. B. Blaschko, and T. Hofmann, "Efficient Subwindow Search: A Branch and Bound Framework for Object Localization," *IEEE TPAMI*, 31(12), pp. 2129-2142, December, 2009.

[2] T. Liu, J. Sun, N. N. Zheng, X. Tang and H. Y. Shum, "Learning to Detect A Salient Object," *IEEE TPAMI*, 33(2), pp. 353-367, February, 2011.

[3] F. Porkili, "Integral Histogram: A Fast Way to Extract Histograms in Cartesian Spaces," *Proc. IEEE CVPR*, 2005.

[4] F. Stentiford, "Attention Based Auto Image Cropping," *Proc. IEEE ICCV*, 2007.

[5] J. Wang, L. Quan, J. Sun, X. Tang, and H.-Y. Shum, "Picture Collage," *Proc. IEEE CVPR*, 2006.

Kanji Snap – an OCR-based Smartphone Application for Learning Japanese Kanji Characters

Korpi Kiia [1]
Dept. of Information and Communication Eng.
University of Tokyo
7-3-1 Hongo, Bunkyo-ku,
Tokyo 113-8656, Japan
(+81) 80-4406-6063
kiia@hal.t.u-tokyo.ac.jp

Aizawa Kiyoharu
Dept. of Information and Communication Eng.
University of Tokyo
7-3-1 Hongo, Bunkyo-ku,
Tokyo 113-8656, Japan
(+81)-3-5841-6651
aizawa@hal.t.u-tokyo.ac.jp

ABSTRACT

As optical character recognition techniques improve, new opportunities to improve existing systems open up. There are for example OCR reading aids for the visually impaired and applications for translating foreign text by capturing photos with smartphones. But one field that hasn't made use of the advancing technology is the learning environment. This demo concentrates on incorporating optical character recognition into a smartphone application for learning Japanese kanji characters. With the application users can take photos of kanji in their everyday environment and look up detailed information and translations easily. Users can practice those kanji with vocabulary lists and quizzes and track their study progress.

Categories and Subject Descriptors

I.7.5 [**Document and Text Processing**]: Document Capture – *Optical character recognition (OCR).*

Keywords

Mobile multimedia, OCR, Japanese, kanji, learning

1. INTRODUCTION

Japanese kanji characters are adopted from the Chinese logographic writing system and approximately 2000 to 3000 characters are in common use in Japan. Foreigners trying to master the language see a high amount of kanji characters passively every day, but they tend to ignore most of them and concentrate on learning from textbooks and flashcards instead. Learning could be sped up significantly if the students made use of the kanji that they see over and over again, like street signs, restaurant menus or household items. The main reason why students do not do this, is that looking up characters that you cannot read by searching for individual radicals that make up the character or through handwriting recognition is slow and cumbersome. Sometimes handwriting recognition will fail, if the stroke order is unknown to the student.

MM '13, Oct 21-25 2013, Barcelona, Spain
ACM 978-1-4503-2404-5/13/10.
http://dx.doi.org/10.1145/2502081.2502241

Figure 1. Highlighting of an OCR result(a), which can be saved for later revision (b)

2. PROPOSED SYSTEM

Kanji Snap aims to change the users everyday environment into a learning environment by providing a way to translate and display detailed information about kanji that the user can take photos of. The user will also be prompted to create their own vocabulary lists from the kanji they see regularly and also add photos of the occurrences to each vocabulary list entry. Adding contextual information like this will help in memorizing and recalling the characters. The kanji can be revised through the saved images in the application either by using them as flashcards or by answering small quizzes that ask for readings or meanings of the kanji. The application also features challenges that will engage the user to scan their environment. The proposed system has the following functions:

- optical character recognition of photos taken by user, where kanji characters will be highlighted in the image
- displaying of detailed information of recognized kanji, e.g. different readings, meanings, words containing the kanji and example sentences
- saving of kanji and photos with recognition results into vocabulary lists created by the user
- revision of vocabulary lists, quizzes and small challenges requiring the user to take photos
- game-like statistics that keep track of the users study progress and award points for completing quizzes and challenges

[1] Department of Media Technology, Aalto University

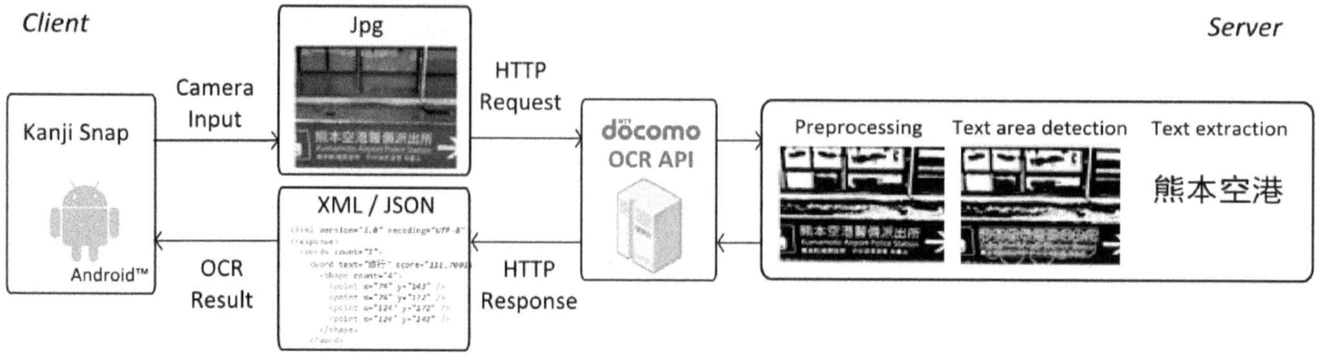

Figure 2. The framework of the OCR based learning application

3. PROTOTYPE

3.1 Web-based OCR service

Kanji Snap is based on a optical character recognition API for Japanese characters provided by the company NTT DOCOMO[2]. The service is specialized in extracting text from landscape images and in addition to this also provides a mode for recognition from one line of text for increased accuracy and speed. Through the API images can be sent as HTTP requests to the web server for recognition. The server will preprocess the image, identify the text regions and finally extract the words. To improve accuracy the results will be compared against a dictionary database with more than one million entries. The recognition result is sent back as HTTP response, including a scored list of extracted words and the location of the each word on the image.

3.2 Dictionaries

To give the user access to useful information on the recognized text, two dictionaries provided by Jim Breen are used[1]. The first is a kanji dictionary file, converted to a SQLite database, containing detailed information about single kanji characters. The second dictionary is a Japanese-English online dictionary with different features, e.g. single word look-ups, text glossing and example sentences. The online dictionary can be accessed through a API which enables simple searches to be initiated via URL query strings.

3.3 Android application

The mobile-based client is developed as Android application. The application is divided into three main parts: the main screen, image capture and vocabulary list views. The main screen displays user statistics like points and progress in addition to changing challenges that require the user to take photos of kanji, e.g. "find the following kanji character and take a photo of it" or "take photos of three different kanji with the reading 'shi'".

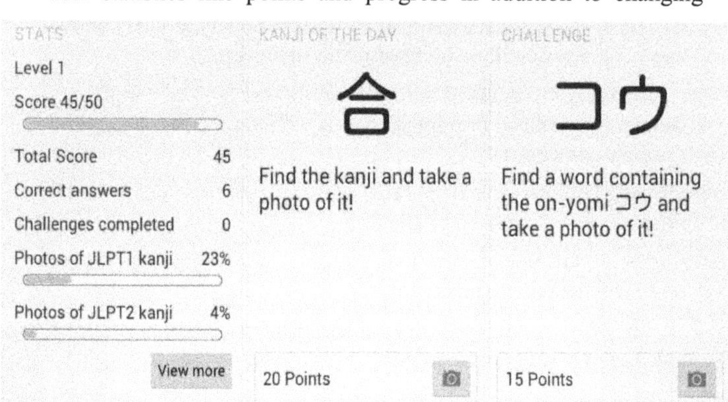

Figure 3. Home screen with statistics and challenges

Through the image capture interface the user can either just scan, translate and study kanji or save both the kanji and images including recognition results to their vocabulary lists. After taking a picture, the user can choose between two OCR modes, recognition from the whole image or cropping one line of text from the image. Recognized kanji will be marked in the image and made clickable for displaying more information. There is also an option to highlight kanji by the Japanese-Language Proficiency Test levels, so the user can easily see what kanji correspond to their current learning level.

The vocabulary list view lets the user add and modify lists and view a single list's contents. New kanji can be added to lists through images, text input or language test level vocabulary lists. Through the kanji detail views images can be added and the same functionality as in the image capture interface is provided. Lists can be reviewed by browsing through flashcard like details of kanji in the list. An option to quiz a list is also available, where users will be asked Japanese readings and English meanings of the kanji. To add a game-like element to the application, correct answers will be awarded points.

4. CONCLUSION

This demo presents a new learning technique for the study of Japanese kanji characters utilizing optical character recognition. Rather than learning from text books, the user can learn the most frequently seen kanji from their real context. In the future this application could be expanded to incorporate exiting flash card sets and their spaced repetition algorithms for timed revision.

5. ACKNOWLEDGMENTS

Our thanks go to NTT DOCOMO for providing their OCR API free of charge and Jim Breen for providing both original dictionary files and backdoor access to his online dictionary service.

6. REFERENCES

[1] Breen, J. Jim Breen's Japanese Page, 2013. Retrieved April 12, 2013, from Japanese Studies Centre, Monash University: http://www.csse.monash.edu.au/~jwb/japanese.html.

[2] Mojininshiki API, 2012. Retrieved April 12, 2013, from NTT DOCOMO Inc., http://recognize.jp/.

Mobile Video Browsing with the ThumbBrowser

Marco A. Hudelist
Institute of Information Technology
Alpen-Adria-University Klagenfurt
9020 Klagenfurt, Austria
marco@itec.aau.at

Klaus Schoeffmann
Institute of Information Technology
Alpen-Adria-University Klagenfurt
9020 Klagenfurt, Austria
ks@itec.aau.at

Laszlo Boeszoermenyi
Institute of Information Technology
Alpen-Adria-University Klagenfurt
9020 Klagenfurt, Austria
laszlo@itec.aau.at

ABSTRACT
In this work we propose an early prototype of a video browser for mobile devices with touchscreens. We concentrate on utilizing the thumbs because of the natural posture used with the devices when watching videos in landscape mode. The controls are only displayed when the user touches the screen and automatically rearrange themselves depending on the position of the thumbs. A combination of a radial menu and an extended seeker control with hierarchical browsing and bookmarking features enables the user to navigate quickly through videos.

Categories and Subject Descriptors
H.3.3 [**Information Storage and Retrieval**]: Information Search and Retrieval

Keywords
Video Browsing, Mobile devices, Touchscreens, Natural User Interfaces

1. INTRODUCTION
Mobile devices like Tablet PCs and smartphones are easy to use, increasingly capable and always available. Therefore, more and more people use them to watch and record video at home and on the go, in private but also in professional use cases. It is also very easy to show videos to friends and colleagues. But the longer the video files the more difficult it is to navigate and filter out interesting scenes. This is especially true on mobile devices with touchscreens where the provided controls are still reminiscent of the early VCR-days.

In this work we propose an early prototype for improved video browsing on tablet PCs focusing on thumb-friendly [10] controls. The usual way of watching videos on tablets is holding them in landscape orientation to maximize screen space usage. In this configuration the thumbs become especially important as they can be used to interact with the device without leaving the comfortable holding position. We therefore propose a combination of a radial menu [3] and an extended seeker bar control that can be used from the sides of the device. They only appear when the user touches the screen and automatically reorient themselves based on the position of the thumb(s).

MM '13, Oct 21-25 2013, Barcelona, Spain
ACM 978-1-4503-2404-5/13/10.
http://dx.doi.org/10.1145/2502081.2502242

2. RELATED WORK
For a general overview of proposals of new video browsing interfaces see [11]. Examples for video browsing tailored for mobile devices are given in [8], concentrating on skimming through a video at different speeds, and [7] where users are able to browse videos hierarchical by using a storyboard-like arrangement. To realize a fine control of seeking speeds, swipe and dragging gestures on the sides are utilized in [4]. Further, using swipe gestures in [5], videos can be navigated between key frames (horizontal swipes) and between interrelated videos (vertical swipes). A way to navigate through videos on a smartphone with just one thumb is shown in [9]. Further examples for touch and gesture based video navigation can be found in [2] where the user is able to switch between channels and navigate inside a video. In our own related work we also proposed improved image and video browsing interfaces utilizing gestures in in [6] and [1].

3. INTERFACE
In the default view of our interface all available screen space is utilized for displaying the video. All controls are hidden from the user. To make the controls visible the user has to place one or both of her thumbs on the sides of the touchscreen (see Figure 1).

Figure 1: The two main controls of the ThumbBrowser.

If the user places the right thumb on the screen an extended vertical seeker control appears. This control consists of a vertical timeline and a magnifying glass with additional information areas. The top of the timeline is mapped to the beginning of the video, the bottom to the end of the video. The magnifying glass follows the position of the thumb as the user drags it up or down the timeline. It shows the user the corresponding frame that resides at the location on the timeline (see Figure 2b). In the top information area the time code of the currently selected frame by the magnifying glass is shown. If users decide to jump to the selected position in the video they just have to lift their right thumb. This triggers the video jump and the control is faded out. In the case that users don't want to jump they

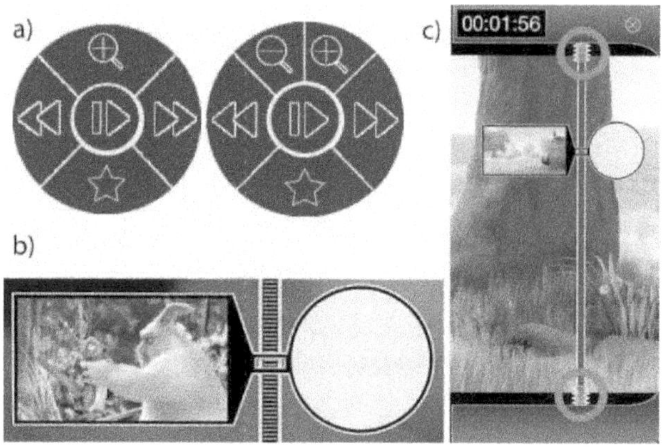

Figure 2: Controls of the ThumbBrowser: a) Radial menus (default and zoomed-in); b) Magnifying glass; c) Squeezed timeline after zoom op.

have to drag the magnifying glass to the right and lift their thumb. This cancels the jump and hides the control.

When the user places the left thumb on the screen a radial menu appears (see Figure 2a). It offers options to fast forward, fast revert, make a timeline zoom (plus sign) and to create a bookmark (star sign). For fast forwarding and fast reverting it is enough to drag the thumb over the respective option. The magnifying glass on the timeline, now showing the current position in the video, adjusts its position accordingly as the video is fast forwarded/reverted in the background. Playback continues at normal speed as soon as the thumb is lifted. The options of timeline zoom and creating a bookmark can be selected by dragging the thumb over the option and lifting it. After the thumb is lifted the control is faded out. A single tap with the left thumb without selecting any option on the menu switches between pausing the video and normal playback.

The timeline zoom option enables hierarchical browsing. For this, the user has to position the magnifying glass at the appropriate position on the timeline and then activate the option on the left radial menu. The timeline is then "expanded" around the selected position, which is indicated by a squeezing animation at the top and the bottom of it (see Figure 2c). A new time window is created around the current position of the magnifying glass (+/- 20 seconds in the first zoom operation). Users can now scan through this section of the video in finer detail as all of the timeline now corresponds to a much smaller time range. As the video continues to play this window is adjusted accordingly so that the current position is always located in the center of the timeline. The user can repeat the process to further zoom-in or choose to zoom-out and return to the original timeline-mapping.

To undo any unwanted jump a stack-like jump history is used. Users can undo every jump one by one by swiping from the left side into the screen. Additionally, users can also add custom bookmarks by using the appropriate option on the radial menu, which adds the current position to the jump history.

4. FUTURE WORK

In future work we will evaluate our interface in a user study to contrast its performance with the default video search tools of current tablet PCs (e.g., video players) in Known-Item-Search (KIS) scenarios. Further, we plan to extend the ThumbBrowser to incorporate results of content analysis (e.g., face recognition, color distribution, etc.) to speed up search for specific search scenarios.

ACKNOWLEDGMENTS

This work was funded by the Federal Ministry for Transport, Innovation and Technology (bmvit) and the Austrian Science Fund (FWF): TRP 273-N15 and the European Regional Development Fund and the Carinthian Economic Promotion Fund (KWF), supported by Lakeside Labs GmbH, Klagenfurt, Austria.

5. REFERENCES

[1] Ahlström, D., Hudelist, M. A., Schoeffmann, K. and Schaefer, G. 2012. A user study on image browsing on touchscreens. In *Proc. of the 20th ACM international conference on Multimedia (MM '12)*. ACM, New York, NY, USA, 925-928.

[2] Buchinger, S., Hotop, E., Hlavacs, H., De Simone, F. and Ebrahimi, T. 2010. Gesture and touch controlled video player interface for mobile devices. In *Proc. of the international conference on Multimedia (MM '10)*. ACM, New York, NY, USA, 699-702.

[3] Callahan, J., Hopkins, D., Weiser, M. and Shneiderman, B. 1988. An empirical comparison of pie vs. linear menus. In *Proc. of the SIGCHI Conference on Human Factors in Computing Systems (CHI '88)*, J. J. O'Hare (Ed.). ACM, New York, NY, USA, 95-100.

[4] Ganhör, R. 2012. ProPane: fast and precise video browsing on mobile phones. In *Proc. of the 11th International Conference on Mobile and Ubiquitous Multimedia (MUM '12)*. ACM, New York, NY, USA, Article 20, 8 pages.

[5] Huber, J., Steimle, J., Lissermann, R., Olberding, S. and Mühlhäuser, M. 2010. Wipe'n'Watch: spatial interaction techniques for interrelated video collections on mobile devices. In *Proc. of the 24th BCS Interaction Specialist Group Conference (BCS '10)*. British Computer Society, Swinton, UK, UK, 423-427.

[6] Hudelist, M.A., Schoeffmann, K., Boeszoermenyi, L. Mobile Video Browsing with a 3D Filmstrip. In *Proc. of the International Conference on Multimedia Retrieval*, ACM, New York, NY, USA, 2013. Currently under review.

[7] Hürst, W. and Darzentas, D. 2012. HiStory: a hierarchical storyboard interface design for video browsing on mobile devices. In *Proc. of the 11th International Conference on Mobile and Ubiquitous Multimedia (MUM '12)*. ACM, New York, NY, USA, Article 17, 4 pages.

[8] Hürst, W. and Meier, K. 2008. Interfaces for timeline-based mobile video browsing. In *Proc. of the 16th ACM international conference on Multimedia (MM '08)*. ACM, New York, NY, USA, 469-478.

[9] Hürst, W. and Merkle, P. 2008. One-handed mobile video browsing. In *Proc. of the 1st international conference on Designing interactive user experiences for TV and video (UXTV '08)*. ACM, New York, NY, USA, 169-178.

[10] Pallakoff, M. System and method for a thumb-optimized touch-screen user interface. U.S. Patent Application 11/994,648, 2006.

[11] Schoeffmann, K., Hopfgartner, F., Marques, O., Boeszoermenyi, L. and Jose, J. M., "Video browsing interfaces and applications: a review", in *SPIE Reviews*, Vol. 1, No. 1, pp. 1-35 (018004), SPIE, Online, March 2010.

Physiognomy Master: A Novel Personality Analysis System Based on Facial Features

Che-Hao Hsu
Dept. of CSIE, Nat'l Taiwan Univ. of Sci. and Tech.
Taipei, Taiwan, R.O.C.
d9915002@mail.ntust.edu.tw

Kai-Lung Hua
Dept. of CSIE, Nat'l Taiwan Univ. of Sci. and Tech.
Taipei, Taiwan, R.O.C.
hua@mail.ntust.edu.tw

Wen-Huang Cheng
Research Center for IT Innovation, Academia Sinica
Taipei, Taiwan, R.O.C.
whcheng@citi.sinica.edu.tw

ABSTRACT

In this demo, we present the proposed "Physiognomy Master." It is a novel practical personality analysis system based on facial features. We first design five facial features that are essential for face reading. We then construct a database to record the facial features' values from a number of volunteers. In the meantime, the volunteers are also invited to fill out a professional personality test. The relations between the facial features and the personality traits are then learned. Given a test subject or an input frontal face image, the proposed system will produce the associated personality report by fusing the personality scores from the people who have similar facial features in the constructed database. The fusing mechanism is based on the idea that people with similar facial features possess similar personality characteristics. The proposed system is a powerful tool in numerous kinds of social interactions, such as personnel selection, team composition, and marriage matching.

Categories and Subject Descriptors

H.4.m [**Information Systems Applications**]: Miscellaneous

Keywords

Face Reading, Physiognomy, Facial Features, Personality Analysis

1. INTRODUCTION

From ancient times to nowadays, human beings always try to explore personality traits and characteristics profile of self and others to understand self better and get along well with others. But how long does it take to understand a person's personality? A year? A month? A week? Or a day? How about at a glance? Face reading is a valuable tool that helps you understand people at once. Facial structures have been considered when evaluating a person's disposition since thousands of years ago in both Eastern and Western cultures [1, 2]. Statistical results have verified that there is a strong connection between facial structures and personality traits [1, 2]. Though a well-trained physiognomist is able to determine character or personal qualities from the facial features in seconds, this ability requires a long-term training and is not easy to learn. Without sufficient training and experience, the face reading result is not reliable and inaccurate.

In order to empower most untrained people to read face and know a stranger at a glance, in this demo, we present the proposed "Physiognomy Master" which integrates the professional psychometric personality test with the designed shape-based facial features. It is a fast personality analysis tool based on facial structures.

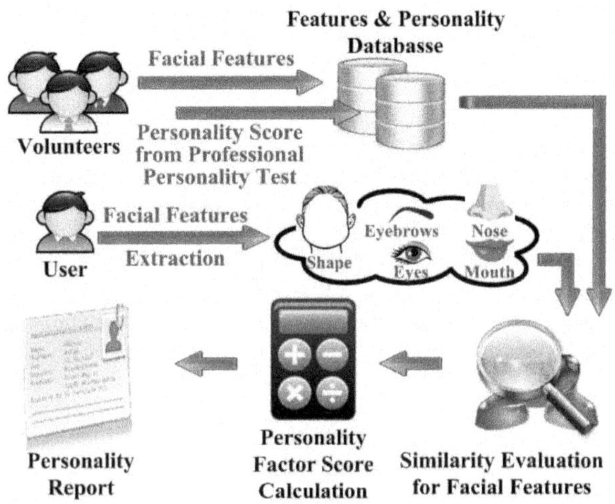

Figure 1: Flowchart of the proposed personality analyisis system.

2. SYSTEM FRAMEWORK

Fig. 1 shows the flowchart of the proposed personality analysis system. We first construct a personality database by inviting a number of volunteers to fill up a well-developed Cattell's sixteen personality factor (16PF) [3] questionnaire. We then construct a facial element database by extracting the shape information of each facial element of volunteers. To be more specific, we used rotated Haar-like features and discrete Adaboost algorithm [4] for rapid face and eyes detection. The eye distance of input face image then is calculated and defined as the unit length once the center of two

MM'13, October 21–25, 2013, Barcelona, Spain.
ACM 978-1-4503-2404-5/13/10.

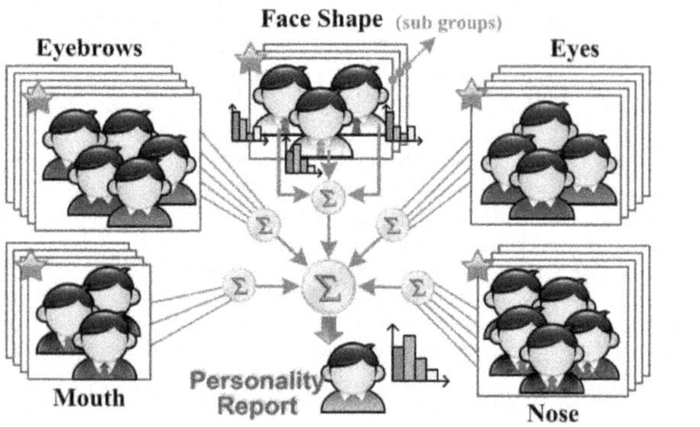

Figure 2: A personality report is produced from people who have similar facial features.

eyes were located. Generally, it is observed that the width of a face is roughly three times the unit distance and the height is roughly four times. Therefore, we cropped the original image based on the above observation and the obtained eye distance. The cropped image is resized and normalized to 240(W)*320(H) pixels. We then compute the feature points of eyebrows, eyes, nose, mouth, and chin through [5]. Since in face reading, the precise contour of each object is very important, the number of the feature points obtained from above is insufficient to describe the contour of facial elements. Here we connected the obtained limited feature points by refining the cubic spline interpolated line with surrounding color information. Once we obtained the contour shape of each object of interest, we generate equiangular radial lines from the center of the cropped object image, the proposed shape feature of each object of interest is then defined as the coordinates that equiangular radial lines intersect with the contour boundary.

In literature, it has been verified that people with similar facial features exhibit similar behavior [1, 2]. However, how to define the similarity of facial features is a challenging work since it is difficult to decide the number of the clusters in this case. In addition, it is also difficult to set the initial set of exemplars which is important to the classification performance. Therefore, in this work we employ affinity propagation clustering [6] that is non-supervised and requires no initial setting. We then produce a classification model for each facial element from the training set. This model is used to classify the input testing shape-based facial features. Given an input headshot in the testing stage, we will first compute the corresponding five facial features and then we will classify each facial feature of interest to the class of its closest prototype. Once we know the class that certain facial element belongs to, we employ Hausdorff distance [7] to evaluate the similarity level of the testing object contour with the ones in the same class from the database. The personality report of the test subject is obtained by weighted average of the personality reports from people who have similar facial features in the database, as illustrated in Fig. 2. The weights are determined by the relative proportions to the similarity level.

3. SYSTEM DEMOSTRATION

The user interface of the proposed system is shown in Fig. 3. In part (a), user can either input a frontal headshot

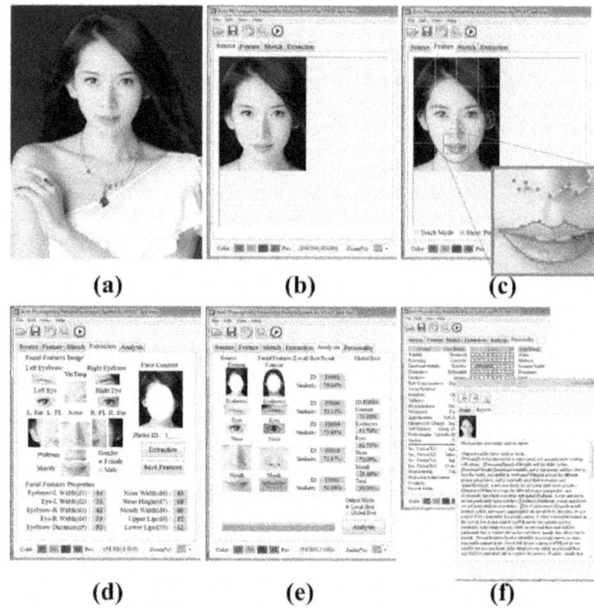

Figure 3: The user interface of our proposed system. (a)The input headshot image, (b)face recognition and image normalization, (c)facial features extraction, (d)facial elements extraction, (e)facial element similarity analysis, (f)personality report.

or capture one from a smartphone or a digital camera. As shown in part (b), our system will automatically locate the face and crop the region of interest from the input image. The facial features will then be computed as illustrated in part (c)(d). The similarity scores between the input face and the ones in the constructed database are assessed as shown in part (e). Finally, the personality report is presented as shown in part (f). We will demonstrate the system's ability to analyze a user's personality through the designed facial features.

4. ACKNOWLEDGMENTS

This work was supported in part by National Science Council of Taiwan via NSC101-2221-E-011-138 and NSC101-2221-E-001-016.

5. REFERENCES

[1] Barbara R. *Face Reading: How to Know Anyone at a Glance.* 2009.

[2] Y. C. Li. *LIAN LIAN JU XIAN(Each face is mysterious)(in Chinese).* Forms Publications (HK)Co.,Ltd., 2010.

[3] R. B. Cattell, H. W. Eber, and M.M. Tatsuoka. *Handbook for the sixteen personality factor questionnaire (16 PF).* IPATC, Illinois, 1988.

[4] R. Lienhart and J. Maydt. An extended set of haar-like features for rapid object detection. In *Proc. of ICIP*, volume 1, pages I–900. IEEE, 2002.

[5] Fei Zuo et al. Facial feature extraction using a cascade of model-based algorithms. In *Proc. of AVSS.*, pages 348–353. IEEE, 2005.

[6] B. J. Frey and D. Dueck. Clustering by passing messages between data points. *science*, 315(5814):972–976, 2007.

[7] P. Rotter, A. M. Skulimowski, C. Kotropoulos, and I. Pitas. Fast shape matching using the hausdorff distance. *Mirage: CV/CG Collaboration Tech. and App.*, 2005.

LAVES: An Instant Mobile Video Search System Based on Layered Audio-Video Indexing *

Wu Liu [1,2], Feibin Yang [3], Yongdong Zhang [1], Qinghua Huang [3], Tao Mei [4]
[1] Institute of Computing Technology, Chinese Academy of Sciences, Beijing 100190, P. R. China
[2] University of Chinese Academy of Sciences, Beijing 100049, P. R. China
[3] South China University of Technology, Guangzhou 510640, P. R. China
[4] Microsoft Research Asia, Beijing 100080, P. R. China

ABSTRACT

This demonstration presents an innovative instant mobile video search system based on layered audio-video indexing, called "LAVES." Through the system, users can discover videos by simply pointing their phones at a screen to capture a very few seconds of what they are watching. Unlike most existing mobile video search applications which simply send the original video query to the cloud, the proposed mobile system is one of the first attempts towards instant and progressive video search leveraging the light-weight computing capacity of mobile devices. The system is able to index large-scale video data using the layered audio-video indexing technique on the cloud, as well as extract light-weight joint audio-video signatures in real time and perform bipartite-graph-based progressive search process on the devices. On a 600 hours video dataset, the system can outperform the state-of-the-arts by achieving 90.79% precision when the query video is less than 10 seconds.

Categories and Subject Descriptors

H.3.3 [**Information Storage and Retrieval**]: Information Search and Retrieval—*Search process*

Keywords

Mobile Video Search, Layered Audio-Video Indexing.

1. INTRODUCTION

The proliferation of increasingly capable mobile devices is reshaping the way how video contents are generated, searched and consumed on today's Internet. While on the go, users always prefer mobile devices as their principal video search and browsing tools. The advanced built-in cameras have made video search very natural—mobile users can now discover videos by simply capturing a few seconds of what they are watching, as shown in Figure 1(a). As a result, mobile video search—searching similar or duplicate videos to identify a phone captured video query—has a huge application prospect and commercial value.

(a) screenshot of mobile video search (b) instant search results

Figure 1: A snapshot of our proposed mobile video search system. (a) A user simply points his phone at a screen to capture a few seconds of what they are watching. While recording, the user can see instant search results on the right. (b) The search process can stop anytime once confident search results are achieved.

Although there have been much effort on mobile video search, it is observed that most of them rely on the computing power of the cloud by simply sending the original query to server, while neglecting the increasing computing capacity of mobile client. Besides, unlike traditional desktop video search, mobile video search also has its unique challenges: 1) large aural-visual variance of query video; 2) stringent memory and computation constraints on the mobile devices; 3) network bandwidth limitation; and 4) instant search experience.

We demonstrate in this work an instant mobile video search system through which users can discover videos by simply pointing their phones at a screen to capture a few seconds of a video. First, we extract the light-weight joint audio-video signatures to present the videos, which are robust against the large variance of the recorded query videos, cheaply to compute on mobile devices, and quickly to transmit through low bandwidth mobile network. On the cloud, we propose a Layered Audio-VidEo (LAVE) indexing scheme to index the video data, which employs the hierarchical decomposition strategy to holistically exploit the mutual complementarity between audio and video signals to improve the search accuracy. In order to provide the instant search experience, we further propose a progressive query process to support

* This work was conducted when the first two authors are visiting Microsoft Research Asia as interns.

MM'13, October 21–25, 2013, Barcelona, Spain.
ACM 978-1-4503-2404-5/13/10.
http://dx.doi.org/10.1145/2502081.2502244.

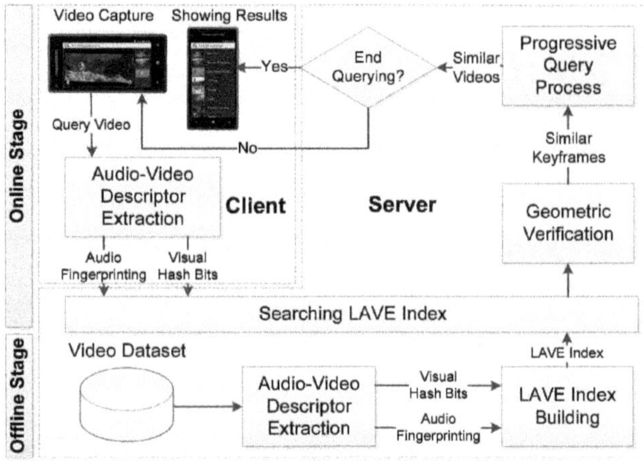

Figure 2: Framework of LAVES.

varying length of the query video. Our system provides an instant and user-friendly mobile video search experience.

2. SYSTEM ARCHITECTURE

Figure 2 illustrates the system architecture of LAVES. 1) In the offline stage, light-weight audio-video descriptors are extracted from the large scale video dataset and indexed by a novel LAVE hashing method. 2) In the online stage, simultaneously with the user capturing query video clips, the same descriptors are real time extracted on the mobile and sent to the server at an interval of one second. 3) Once the server receives one-second signatures, the system searches the similar keyframes via LAVE index searching and geometric verification. 4) A progressive query process is performed to search the similar videos and the search procedure can stop anytime once a confident result is achieved.

3. SYSTEM IMPLEMENTATION

Joint Audio-Video Descriptor. For the purpose of fast computation, memory efficient, robust and highly compacted, we choose the Landmark-Based Audio Fingerprinting (LBAF) [4] and bag of hash bits [1] as the audio and video descriptors, respectively. For each one second audio signal, we segment it into short and partial overlapping frames. Then, for each frame, we calculate its spectrogram and choose the candidate peaks on the spectrogram. Next, anchor points are randomly chosen from the peaks and each anchor point has a target zone with it. Furthermore, each candidate peak in the target zone is paired with its arch point to be a landmark. Finally, the landmarks are compressed to be audio fingerprinting points by combinatorial hashing [4]. For each one second video signal, we choose one frame to present the whole video clip and resize the frame up to 200×200 pixels. Then, the Speeded-Up Robust Features (SURF) is extracted and compressed by hash function, which is learned by the Spectral Hashing [5]. The compressed binary codes are called visual hash bits. As a result, we only need to transmit less than 2KB audio-visual signatures per second to the server.

LAVE Indexing. To reduce the time of searching nearest neighbor points on the server, we design a LAVE indexing method. We build two layers in the LAVE indexing. The first layer is the entry of the indexing, which is used to filter out the most dissimilar feature points. In the first layer, we build audio index by all the LBAF features and video index through the multi-index method [2], respectively. When exploring them in parallel, the closest neighbor probably lies in different domains in different index, increasing the likelihood of the search reaching a correct domain quickly. The second layer only contains complete visual hash bits. For the refined feature points, we further search their nearest neighbor points via linear search in the second layer. Sorted by the Hamming distance, the top M nearest points are returned at last. With the top M points, Hough Transfer method is used to get the similar source keyframes. Then a fast and effective geometric verification considering the orientation consistency of local features is used to rerank the keyframes.

Progressive Query Process. After each second query is received, the retrieval results can be dynamically calculated along with the query on the server. For each matched query and source video, we use a bipartite graph to represent the matching. The graph can be dynamically updated if a new query frame is coming. Through the graph, we can progressively compute the audio, visual and temporal order similarity between the matched videos [3]. The top N similar videos considering the above similarities will be returned to the client. If the top N results have no change in three seconds, the search procedure will stop automatically.

4. EVALUATIONS

To evaluate the performance of the LAVES, we have invited 25 volunteers to record 1,400 query videos from 19,200 videos in TRECVID 2011 video dataset. The volunteers are from different genders, ages and careers. The experiments show that our system can achieve 86.08% and 90.77% precision at eight seconds and ten seconds respectively.

Furthermore, we compare LAVES with two popular mobile video systems, i.e., IntoNow and VideoSurf. We randomly invite 12 users from the above volunteers and ask them to use the three applications freely for 20 minutes. After that, the scores (1–5) are given by each subject to evaluate the usability, user friendliness, and user experience. The higher score indicates the higher satisfaction. The results show that compared with IntoNow (3.38) and VideoSurf (3.42), LAVES achieves better satisfaction (4.3).

5. CONCLUSIONS

We have demonstrated a novel video search system on mobile devices, which is able to significantly improve user's search experience by instant video search. Our future work includes integrating the system with video recommendation functions for social applications.

6. REFERENCES

[1] J. He, J. Feng, X. Liu, T. Cheng, T.-H. Lin, H. Chung, and S.-F. Chang. Mobile product search with bag of hash bits and boundary reranking. In *CVPR*, pages 3005–3012, 2012.

[2] M. Norouzi, A. Punjani, and D. J. Fleet. Fast search in hamming space with multi-index hashing. In *CVPR*, pages 3108–3115, 2012.

[3] H. T. Shen, J. Shao, Z. Huang, and X. Zhou. Effective and efficient query processing for video subsequence identification. *IEEE Trans. Knowl. Data Eng.*, 21(3):321–334, 2009.

[4] A. Wang. An industrial strength audio search algorithm. In *ISMIR*, pages 7–13, 2003.

[5] Y. Weiss, A. Torralba, and R. Fergus. Spectral hashing. In *NIPS*, pages 1753–1760, 2008.

Freesound Technical Demo

Frederic Font, Gerard Roma and Xavier Serra
Music Technology Group, Universitat Pompeu Fabra, Barcelona, Spain
frederic.font@upf.edu, gerard.roma@upf.edu, xavier.serra@upf.edu

ABSTRACT

Freesound[1] is an online collaborative sound database where people with diverse interests share recorded sound samples under Creative Commons licenses. It was started in 2005 and it is being maintained to support diverse research projects and as a service to the overall research and artistic community.

In this demo we want to introduce Freesound to the multimedia community and show its potential as a research resource. We begin by describing some general aspects of Freesound, its architecture and functionalities, and then explain potential usages that this framework has for research applications.

Categories and Subject Descriptors

H.3.5 [**On-line Information Services**]: Web-based services; H.5.5 [**Sound and Music Computing**]: Systems

Keywords

Freesound; online databases; sound; audio clips

1. INTRODUCTION

Freesound's initial goal was to give support to sound researchers, who often have trouble finding large royalty-free sound databases to test their algorithms, and to sound artists, who use pre-recorded sounds in their pieces. After eight years since its inception, Freesound has become one of the most popular sites for sharing sound snippets. Freesound serves around 40,000 unique visits per day and has 3.5 million registered users accessing more than 160,000 uploaded sounds[2]. More importantly, there is a highly engaged community of users continuously contributing to the site, not only uploading sounds but also commenting, rating and discussing in the forums about relevant topics for the community. All sounds in Freesound are manually moderated by a group of users (users of Freesound) that check that descriptions are correct and sounds are not illegal.

All the content in Freesound is released under Creative Commons licenses. When uploading sounds, Freesound users can choose between CC0 (public domain), Attribution and Attribution-NonCommercial[3]. The reason to offer these licenses is to ensure that all the content uploaded in Freesound can be reused by other users, developers and researchers, but at the same time we provide users the option to require the attribution of their work or to restrict the use of their sounds to non-commercial activities. Furthermore, the source code of the web application is being released[4] as open source under the GNU AGPL license[5].

Freesound was built with high load and scalability in mind. Figure 1 shows the block diagram of the architecture. Retrieval of sounds can be performed using text queries, content-based similarity search (Query by Example) or by browsing tags or geotags. The front-end is a Django[6] application which includes basic social interaction features (forum, sound comments, sound ratings, private messaging...). Text indexing is supported by an Apache Solr[7] server including text descriptions and tags, which allows for sophisticated text queries using the Solr query syntax. A distributed architecture is used for processing incoming sounds, producing compressed previews and waveform/spectrogram images, as well as for feature extraction. Frame-level and clip-level descriptors are available for each sound. Feature extraction and similarity search services are supported with Essentia and Gaia[8], both open-source technologies developed also at the Music Technology Group.

In 2011, an API was introduced to facilitate access to the Freesound content to researchers and developers. The API runs as a Django application based on the RESTful principles. The API allows accessing a basic set of resources (sounds, users, sound packs) to http clients. All of the mentioned methods for searching sounds are supported, and also the API provides more complex search functionalities such as filtering with audio descriptors. Responses from the API can be obtained in a variety of formats (JSON, XML...). Content descriptors can be obtained through the API both at the frame level (descriptors calculated at every frame of the audio files) and clip level (statistics across frames). A

[1]`http://www.freesound.org`
[2]Freesound data current as of April 2013.

MM'13, October 21–25, 2013, Barcelona, Spain.
ACM 978-1-4503-2404-5/13/10.
http://dx.doi.org/10.1145/2502081.2502245.

[3]`http://www.creativecommons.org/licenses`
[4]`http://www.github.com/MTG/freesound`
[5]`http://www.gnu.org/licenses/agpl.html`
[6]`http://www.djangoproject.com`
[7]`http://lucene.apache.org/solr`
[8]`http://essentia.upf.edu`

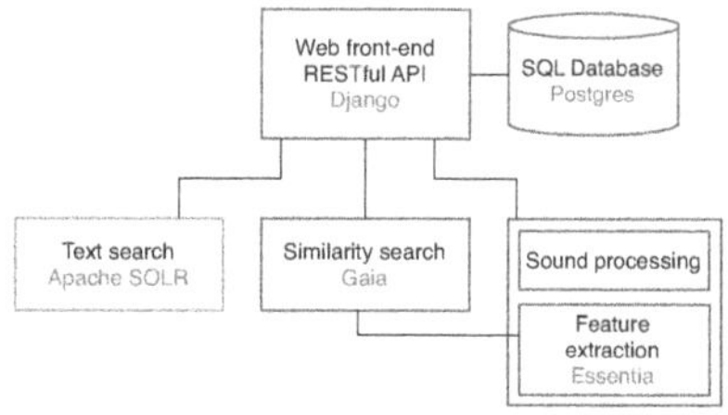

Figure 1: Freesound architecture.

number of clients have already been implemented for different programming languages. At the time of this writing, Python, Javascript, Actionscript, PhP, C# and SuperCollider clients are available.

2. FREESOUND AS A RESOURCE FOR RESEARCH

Freesound data has been used for research purposes in many different areas. Inside the Music Technology Group there have been publications dealing with topics such as soundscape generation and content-based audio-clip classification [7, 4], database discovery [9], community characterization and network analysis [8] or folksonomy analysis and tag recommendation [2, 3]. Moreover, outside the Music Technology Group Freesound data has also been used for research on creative interfaces, composition [1, 10], annotation of environmental sounds [6] and statistical methods for dimensionality reduction (using freesound data without considering domain-specific information, [5]).

To get an idea of the potential of Freesound as a research resource, here we briefly describe the basic types of content and information that can be gathered either using the API or by requesting us an anonymized version of the SQL database. The most obvious type of content in Freesound are sounds (audio files) and their descriptions extracted using Essentia. As Freesound was started with research purposes in mind, from the very beginning the quality of sounds and their descriptions has been prioritized over the quantity. For that reason, when sounds are uploaded, they all have to be described by adding some tags and a textual description (currently the average is 6.5 tags for sound with almost 56,000 unique tag concepts). Users can also add a geotag to indicate the location where the sound was recorded (there are more than 12,000 geotagged sounds). All this information is available with corresponding timestamps since 2005. Furthermore, 75% of uploaded sounds are grouped into packs of sounds that users can create. Hence, a big amount of sounds is grouped into almost 10,000 packs which are also available.

On the other side, users also are a relevant type of content in Freesound which provide a different perspective than that of the sounds. Although there are more 3.5 million registered users, only the 10% has contributed by uploading, commenting or rating a sounds. Indeed, only ~8,500 of the registered users have uploaded at least one sound. This means that the community that is uploading to Freesound is very small compared to the number of people that are downloading (Freesound has already served more than 43 million downloads since its inception). All the data about downloads, ratings and comments is available with corresponding timestamps since 2005.

In the Freesound forums many types of conversations may be identified where, for example, users request sound samples, discuss about recording gear and techniques or talk about work done using Freesound samples. Currently, the forums have more than 8,000 threads and almost 37,000 posts. The forums reflect very relevant aspects of the Freesound community and are therefore an interesting source of information to be explored. Again, all this data is available with timestamps since 2005.

3. CONCLUSION

Freesound has become a consolidated audio clip sharing site with a lot of content and a strong community behind it. With the inclusion of the API, access to Freesound content has become much easier for the development of third-party applications and for research purposes. We strongly believe in the value of Freesound for the scientific community of information retrieval, sound and music computing and multimedia in general.

4. REFERENCES

[1] N. N. Correia. AV CLASH: Online Tool for Mixing and Visualizing Audio Retrieved from Freesound.org Database. In *Proc. of the Sound and Music Computing Cong. (SMC)*, 2010.

[2] F. Font, J. Serrà, and X. Serra. Folksonomy-based tag recommendation for online audio clip sharing. In *Proc. of the Int. Conf. on Music Information Retrieval (ISMIR)*, pages 73–78, 2012.

[3] F. Font and X. Serra. Analysis of the folksonomy of freesound. In *Proc. of the CompMusic Workshop*, pages 48–54, 2012.

[4] J. Janer, S. Kersten, M. Schirosa and G. Roma. An online platform for interactive soundscapes with user-contributed content. In *Proc. of the 41st AES Int. Conf. on Audio for Games*, 2011.

[5] M. Karasuyama and S. Masashi. Canonical dependency analysis based on squared-loss mutual information. *Neural Networks*, 34:46–55 2012.

[6] B. Mechtley, P. Cook and A. Spanias. Shortest Path Techniques for Annotation and Retrieval of Environmental Sounds. In *Proc. of the Int. Conf. on Music Information Retrieval (ISMIR)*, pages 541–546, 2012.

[7] G. Roma, J. Janer, S. Kersten, M. Schirosa, P. Herrera, and X. Serra. Ecological Acoustics Perspective for Content-Based Retrieval of Environmental Sounds. *EURASIP Journal on Audio, Speech, and Music Processing*, 2010:7, 2010.

[8] G. Roma, M. Zanin, P. Herrera, S. L. Toral, F. Font and X. Serra. Small world networks and creativity in audio clip sharing. *International Journal of Social Network Mining (IJSNM)*, 1(1):112-127, 2012.

[9] G. Roma, P. Herrera and X. Serra. Freesound Radio: supporting music creation by exploration of a sound database. In *Computational Creativity Support Workshop (CHI09)*, 2009.

[10] M. Thorogood, P. Pasquier and A. Eigenfeldt. Audio Metaphor: Audio Information Retrieval for Soundscape Composition. In *Proc. of the Sound and Music Computing Cong. (SMC)*, 2012.

Visualizing Web Mash-ups for In-Situ Vision-Based Mobile AR Applications

Yu You
Contextual Media Systems
Media Technologies Lab, Nokia
Tampere, Finland
yu.you@nokia.com

Ville-Veikko Mattila
Contextual Media Systems
Media Technologies Lab, Nokia
Tampere, Finland
ville-veikko.mattila@nokia.com

ABSTRACT

Augmented reality applications are gaining popularity due to increased capabilities of modern mobile devices. Creating AR content however is tedious and traditionally done on desktop environments by professionals, with extensive knowledge and/or even programming skills required. In this demo, we demonstrate a complete mobile approach for creating vision-based AR in both indoor and outdoor environment. Using hyperlinks, Web mashups are built to dynamically augment the physical world by normal users without programing skills.

Categories and Subject Descriptors

I.4.9 [**Computing Methodologies**]: IMAGE PROCESSING AND COMPUTER VISION Applications

Keywords

augmented reality, mash-ups, www, authoring

1. INTRODUCTION

While the augmented reality (AR) technology for 3D positioning and tracking on mobile devices is becoming feasible, the question of how to define the augmentation (i.e. linking the content or the data to the physical environment) in an effective and convenient way for normal users becomes more important than ever before. Previous work like [1] used different techniques to determine the 2D footprint for 3D primitives. The intersection approach is less accurate in the pixel level and difficult to locate the right spot on the mobile screen. Our approach provides an easy and accurate way of defining the content placement and leverages standard web protocols and formats for representing live Web contents.

Web mashups emerged as a simple way to create more sophisticated applications by combining data from multiple existing sources in a homogenous way [2]. In its simplest form, a mashup aggregates or summarizes different sets of data, or creates alternative user interfaces of a Web site for situations that were not envisioned by the designers or that do not fit the primary usage scenario. In this paper, we demonstrate a simple AR mashup that requests live weather data of a geographic location, transforms it into a 2D media representation and associates it to a user defined physical place via an accurate 3D registration. The mashup, in addition, contains other multiple Web contents to build a unique AR experience. The first part of the demonstration includes defining a physical scene and associating Web content to it on a mobile device. The second part demonstrates browsing the scene in AR mode with live weather augmentation previously defined.

MM 2013 October 21-25, 2013, Barcelona, Spain.
ACM 978-1-4503-2404-5/13/10.
http://dx.doi.org/10.1145/2502081.2502246 .

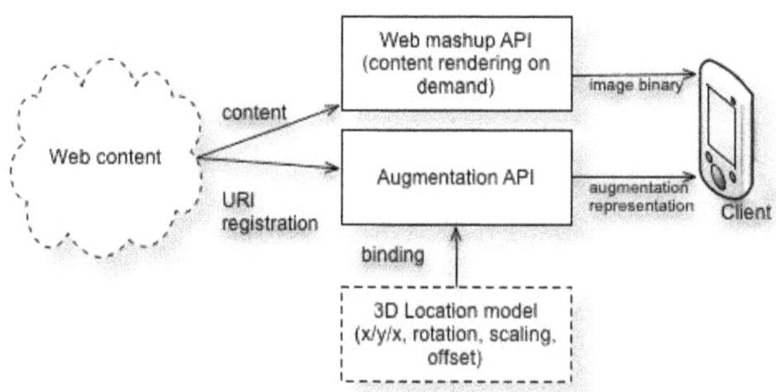

Figure 1: Backend processing for augmentation registration process

2. SYSTEM ARCHITECTURE AND DESIGN

Many AR services are either vertically integrated, or are built on concepts that are specific to one type of service. Our system is built as an extension to our generic AR service. More technical details can be found in [3].

One of the core functionality of the AR service is content registration, a process of accurately inserting Web resources, denoted as augmentations, into a specific AR zone. This is achieved by defining an augmentation resource model. Each resource model contains at least one local surface on which the hypermedia should be rendered. In additional, the resource includes other parameters defined in the KML augmentation schema for positioning the Web content precisely.

Traditionally, most Web content is already available programmatically, which enables overlaying geo-tagged data on top of a 2D map. Augmentation registration is actually a content process pipeline that adds a new dimension to the existing 2D map-based location-aware applications. To mashup existing Web content, the user can either dynamically import a Web resource (i.e. via the URI externally referenced to the service provider's Web API) into the AR zone using the native client AR user interface, or select a more customized Web mashup (via Web service adapters) already registered in advance. The service adapter typically offloads the rendering efforts from the mobile AR clients by rendering the dynamic content on the server side and generating a media representation, i.e. PNG images, on the fly for the clients, as shown in Fig. 1.

3. DEMONSTRATION

3.1 Vision-based mobile 3D tracking preparation

The general work-flow to use the system can be summarized as follows. First, a physical area needs to be selected first as an AR *zone* for tracking and augmentation. The area can be either indoor or outdoor, as long as it has sufficient 3D visual properties that can be extracted from the scenes. A scene is a image shot by the mobile camera aiming at the area. We call this shooting step as scene acquisition. The user creates a new zone on the mobile client and then proceeds to acquire several images or video clips. Once the acquisition is complete, the mobile client uploads the zone to the server. As reconstruction is a time-consuming task, the server takes advantage of a messaging queue middleware to support asynchronous tasks, without blocking HTTP requests from mobile clients. A reconstruction worker is registered and waiting on a remote server node to handle the zone reconstruction asynchronously. When images reach the main server from the mobile client, the worker is invoked by the middleware. The worker downloads the images from the main server and runs the reconstruction algorithm which extract 2D features from the images, denoted as keyframes, matches features between keyframes and then triangulates the features to produce a 3D point cloud. The output is stored in a specific tracking model in KML and then uploaded back to the main server ready for clients. The entire process of a zone reconstruction is completely automated and usually takes a few minutes, depending on the number of images in the acquisition step.

3.2 Mobile Web mashups

The authoring process starts by linking Web sources to a selected zone. The first step is to select the Web source. The mobile client requests a list of mashable sources available from the AR service (see the top Fig. 2). Multiple augmentations can be added with different relative locations on different planar surfaces. In our current implementation, manual user input is required for defining the augmentation surface precisely in a WYSIWYG fashion. On the mobile device, the user first defines the planar surface where the augmentation will be positioned by either selecting one or several points from the 3D point cloud (see the red dots in the middle Fig. 2. In the case that one point is selected, the plane is defined by projecting the camera plane to the 3D point. In the case that several points are selected, the plane is fit to the 3D points. The next step consists of defining the scaling, offset and rotation parameters of the resource with respect to the plane. Common touch-based interaction on mobile is adopted, such as panning for setting the offset; and two-finger pinch for setting the scaling and rotation. In the final step, the update frequency is defined. The frequency controls the update rate at which the client requests the server for new content. Each hyperlinked augmentation can have its own update frequency to enable complex setups. Once all steps are completed, the final augmentation information is uploaded to the server and another augmentation can be defined.

To test the tracking and rendering of the newly augmented zone, the user can start the AR tracking mode and point the device to the scene in question. The tracker initializes by loading the tracking

Figure 2: Select the surface (top); define Web mashup and position to the surface (2nd), and demonstrate the AR view (bottom)

information, determines its current position and orientations and starts the tracking loop. The client downloads the media content through the hyperlinks defined in the augmentation data automatically. Once the media arrives, the client uploads the media to the GPU (graphics processing unit) and renders the augmentations over the camera view. In the current implementation, the client does not use any native (OS dependent) pushing mechanism but simply pulls the Web content at the defined update frequencies.

4. REFERENCES

[1] T. Langlotz, S. Mooslechner, S. Zollmann, C. Degendorfer, G. Reitmayr, and D. Schmalstieg, "Sketching up the world: in situ authoring for mobile augmented reality," *Personal Ubiquitous Comput.*, vol. 16, pp. 623–630, Aug. 2012.

[2] J. Yu, B. Benatallah, F. Casati, and F. Daniel, "Understanding mashup development," *Internet Computing, IEEE*, vol. 12, pp. 44 –52, sept.-oct. 2008.

[3] Y. You, L. Fan, V.-V. Mattila, A. Boyer, and T. Kantonen, "In-situ web mashup and hypermedia support for mobile vision-based ar applications," in *International Conference on Green Computing and Communications and IEEE Internet of Things and IEEE Cyber, Physical and Social Computing*, IEEE, August 2013.

repoVizz: a Framework for Remote Storage, Browsing, Annotation, and Exchange of Multi-modal Data

Oscar Mayor, Quim Llimona, Marco Marchini, Panos Papiotis, Esteban Maestre
Music Technology Group, Universitat Pompeu Fabra
Barcelona, Spain
{oscar.mayor, marco.marchini, panos.papiotis,esteban.maestre}@upf.edu
quim.llimona01@estudiant.upf.edu

ABSTRACT

In this technical demo we present repoVizz[1], an integrated online system capable of structural formatting and remote storage, browsing, exchange, annotation, and visualization of synchronous multi-modal, time-aligned data. Motivated by a growing need for data-driven collaborative research, repoVizz aims to resolve commonly encountered difficulties in sharing or browsing large collections of multi-modal data. At its current state, repoVizz is designed to hold time-aligned streams of heterogeneous data: audio, video, motion capture, physiological signals, extracted descriptors, annotations, et cetera. Most popular formats for audio and video are supported, while Broadcast WAVE or CSV formats are adopted for streams other than audio or video (e.g., motion capture or physiological signals). The data itself is structured via customized XML files, allowing the user to (re-) organize multi-modal data in any hierarchical manner, as the XML structure only holds metadata and pointers to data files. Datasets are stored in an online database, allowing the user to interact with the data remotely through a powerful HTML5 visual interface accessible from any standard web browser; this feature can be considered a key aspect of repoVizz since data can be explored, annotated, or visualized from any location or device. Data exchange and upload/download is made easy and secure via a number of data conversion tools and a user/permission management system.

Categories and Subject Descriptors

E.5 [**Files**]: Organization - structure; E.2 [**Data Storage Representations**]

Keywords

repository, exchange, remote, HTML5, multimodal

[1]http://repovizz.upf.edu/

MM'13, October 21–25, 2013, Barcelona, Spain.
ACM 978-1-4503-2404-5/13/10.
http://dx.doi.org/10.1145/2502081.2502247.

1. INTRODUCTION

Multi-modal data stream acquisition and analysis constitute a major pursuit in much of today's data-driven scientific research. The lack of common formats and structured storage tools for heterogeneous data forces researchers to use ad-hoc formatting schemes and software tools developed *in house*. Despite the obvious potential offered by collaborative, exchange-driven research, difficulties often found in sharing or browsing data sets are impeding research collaboration and cross-fertilization. As a response to the needs imposed by the challenging nature of international research collaborations, including the EU FET project SIEMPRE grounded on multi-modal data capture, analysis and exchange, we aimed at (i) defining the structure of data coming from multi-modal recordings, (ii) creating a repository to store and share multi-modal datasets collected in research experiments dealing with music performance, and (iii) implementing a tool to visualize acquired data and make annotations in a user-friendly and flexible manner. The goal was to open research results and share data with the research community. This drove us to develop a flexible framework for data formatting, storage, and browsing which allowed the integration of any kind of data or annotations to come, and facilitate access through a dedicated portal.

2. OVERVIEW OF REPOVIZZ

The repoVizz framework[2][1], which is conceptualized over a classical client-server configuration, comprises of (i) a formatting scheme that enables flexible multi-modal data structuring and aggregation, (ii) a number of tools that allow the user to convert data to/from formats in agreement with the repoVizz convention, (iii) a persistence server used as a (remote-access) repository to host and exchange data, and (iv) a HTML5-based (client) interface through which it is possible to browse, visualize, annotate, download, etc. (multi-modal) data from any location by using a web browser.

Although not mutually exclusive, two main types of users can be differentiated. A first type of user, which could be called *Producer*, gathers multi-modal data and pushes it into repoVizz. A second type, the *Consumer*, accesses repoVizz in order to visually explore, retrieve (download), annotate, and/or process existing data. The second type of user would also include those who, after downloading a dataset (or a portion/segment of a dataset), apply some (user) analysis/processing and upload their results as additional streams or annotations (thus editing the dataset). The data lifecycle in repoVizz, which mixes its use from the two aforementioned user types, is illustrated in Figure 1.

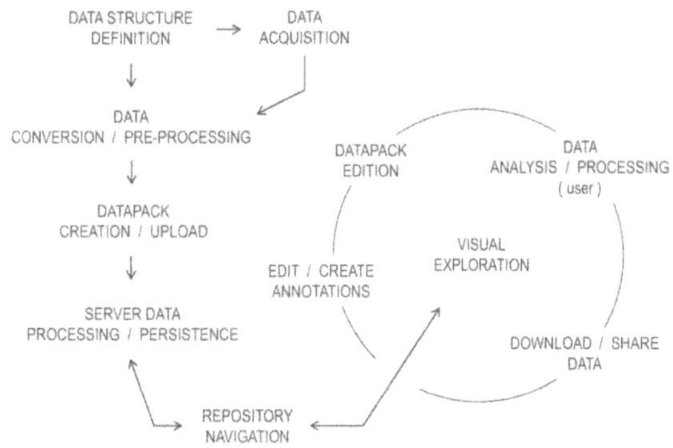

Figure 1: Overview of the data lifecycle in repoVizz.

2.1 Data formatting and structuring

The first and most important step for pushing data into repoVizz comes when defining the structure of the multimodal dataset. In repoVizz, data structuring is carried out via a customizable XML file, called repoVizz *Struct*, that serves as a flexible, tree-like skeleton for organizing the contents of the dataset. The nodes of a repoVizz Struct enable hierarchical organization of data streams and annotations, and are used to hold text descriptions and pointers to data files. repoVizz provides, via its portal, the repoVizz *Designer*, a java application that allows to create and edit repoVizz Structs in a visual manner, so the user won't need to manually edit an XML file, but rather enter the appropriate contents into fields defining category tags, data types, file names, etc. Altogether, a Struct and all pointed data files constitute a repoVizz *Datapack*, which is uploaded by the user as a .zip file (automatically generated by the repoVizz *Designer*) via the repoVizz portal.

2.2 The repoVizz Server

Once a repoVizz Datapack has been uploaded, some preprocessing and/or feature extraction is carried out in the server, before files are stored and indexed for subsequent access. The *Producer* can grant access to other (or all) users to access/visualize, annotate, or even edit and download the data. From that moment, *Consumers* can access the portal and navigate through the existing Datapacks, visualize signals, provide annotations, add signals, etc. by means of a powerful, flexible HTML5 web interface that allows interacting with the data without the need to download.

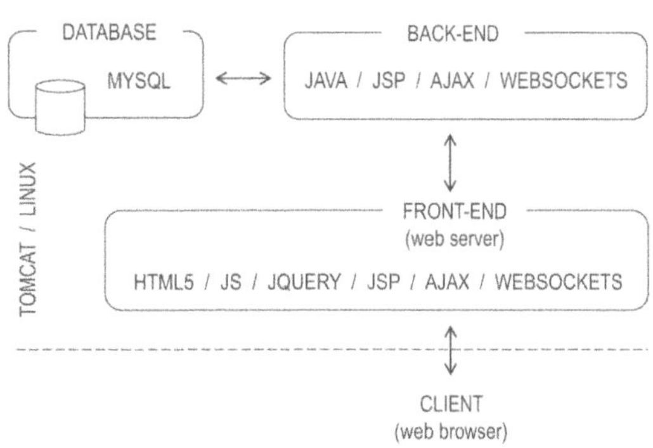

Figure 2: Schematic illustration of the repoVizz server structure.

2.3 The repoVizz Visualizer

The web interface has been built following a multi-track configuration where signals of different natures and sample rates can be synchronously visualized, played back, re-arranged, etc. Moreover, users may select a data segment directly from the multi-track interface and download a Datapack containing all synchronized data streams and annotations within the chosen time range. The portal also provides tools to convert downloaded data to popular formats such as Matlab structs.

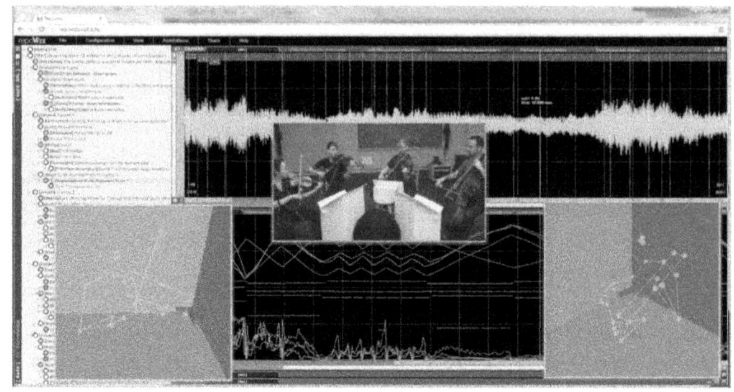

Figure 3: Screenshot of the repoVizz Visualizer, featuring some signals from computed descriptors, an audio file, annotations, video and motion capture.

In Figure 3 the repoVizz visualizer shows an example of how a multimodal recording, in this case of a string quartet, can be visualized within a web browser, audio and video streams can be played in sync, motion capture data can be visualized using the 3D visualization widget and features extracted from audio and instrumental gestures can be visualized simultaneously. More details about the visualizer can be found in the demo video[1].

3. ACKNOWLEDGMENTS

This work was partially supported by the EU FET-Open Project SIEMPRE (FP7-ICT-2009-C-250026) and the Catalan Government through an AGAUR Fellowship and TECNIO grant (TECCIT12-1-0003) from ACC1Ó. We would like to express our gratitude towards a number of people who have directly or indirectly contributed to the development or refinement of ideas behind repoVizz: Javier Jaimovich, Nick Gillian, Miguel Ortiz, Paolo Coletta, Donald Glowinski, and Alfonso Pérez. We also thank Marcelo Wanderley for his offering to collaborate on data acquisition for the string quartet recordings. Finally, special thanks go to Alexander Jensenius for inspiring discussions early in 2007 and 2008, and to Jordi Llop for his initial involvement in early developments during 2010.

4. REFERENCES

[1] repoVizz video. `http://repovizz.upf.edu/misc/repoVizz_ACMM2013.mp4`.

[2] O. Mayor, J. Llop, and E. Maestre. Repovizz: a multimodal on-line database and browsing tool for music performane research. In *Proceedings of Int. Symposium for Music Information Retrieval*, 2011.

Small Objects Query Suggestion in a Large Web-Image Collection

Pierre Letessier
INRIA ZENITH
34095 Montpellier, France
pierre.letessier@inria.fr

Nicolas Hervé
INA
94360 Bry-sur-Marne, France
nherve@ina.fr

Julien Champ
INRIA ZENITH
34095 Montpellier, France
julien.champ@inria.fr

Alexis Joly
INRIA ZENITH
34095 Montpellier, France
alexis.joly@inria.fr

Olivier Buisson
INA
94360 Bry-sur-Marne, France
obuisson@ina.fr

Amel Hamzaoui
INRIA Rocquencourt
78153 Le Chesnay, France
amel.hamzaoui@inria.fr

ABSTRACT

State-of-the-art visual search methods allow retrieving efficiently small rigid objects in very large image datasets (e.g. logos, paintings, etc.). User's perception of the classical query-by-window paradigm is however affected by the fact that many submitted queries actually return nothing or only junk results. We demonstrate in this demo that the perception can be radically different if the objects of interest are rather suggested to the user by pre-computing relevant clusters of instances. Impressive results involving very small objects discovered in a web collection of 110K images are demonstrated through a simple interactive GUI.

Categories and Subject Descriptors: H.3 [Information Storage And Retrieval]: Miscellaneous

Keywords: Mining, Scalable, Small Objects, Hashing

1. USER'S PERCEPTION ISSUES

Large-scale object retrieval systems have demonstrated impressive performance in the last few years. The underlying methods, based on local visual features and efficient indexing models, can retrieve accurately small rigid objects such as logos, buildings or manufactured objects, under varying points of view and illumination conditions [2, 4, 5, 6, 9]. Therefore online object retrieval is now achievable up to 1M images with a state-of-the-art computer [4]. From the usage point of view, these methods are often combined with a query-by-window search paradigm. The user can freely select a region of interest in any image, and the system returns a ranked list of images that are the most likely to contain an instance of the targeted object of interest [10]. This paradigm has however several limitations related to user's perception: (i) When no (or very few) other instances of the query object exist in the dataset, the system mostly returns false positives making the user uncomfortable with the results. Indeed, he does not know if there are actually no other instances of the query object or if the system did not work correctly. (ii) When the user selects a deformable or complex object that the system is actually not able to retrieve, the system mostly returns false positives as well. As the user can freely select any object, this appears very frequently leaving the user with a bad impression of the effectiveness of the tool. The second remark is even more critical if the user believes that the system can retrieve any semantically similar objects (e.g. object categories or visual concepts such as cats or cars). We do not argue here that such queries will never be solved effectively in the future. We just emphasize that bridging the gap between a user's understanding of the system and the actual capabilities of the underlying tools is essential to make it successful in a real world search engine. A first possible solution to address these limitations would be to use some adaptive thresholding method, allowing only relevant results to be filtered, and possibly returning no results if none are found. The a contrario method of [5], for instance, allows the actual false alarm rate of rigid object instances retrieval to be controlled very accurately. But still, as the user can select any region of interest, the system might return no results in many cases and leave the user disappointed.

2. PROPOSED APPROACH

We proposed in [3] to solve these user perception issues by a new visual query suggestion paradigm. Rather than letting the user select any region of interest, the system will suggest only visual query regions that actually contain relevant matches in the dataset. By mining off-line object instances in the dataset, it is indeed possible to suggest to the user only query objects having at least a predetermined number of instances in the collection. When a user clicks on a highlighted region, the system returns only the images containing other object instances of the same discovered cluster. From a user perception point of view, the proposed paradigm is very different from the window query paradigm. Indeed, since all suggested objects mostly return correct results, the user might rather perceive them as visual links (or hyper-visual links by analogy to hypertext links). It is important to notice, that unlike existing approaches, the links produced by our method are not links between images, but links between automatically localized image regions containing instances of the same rigid object. An image can thus contain several

MM'13, October 21–25, 2013, Barcelona, Spain.
ACM 978-1-4503-2404-5/13/10
http://dx.doi.org/10.1145/2502081.2502248 ...$15.00.

suggestions belonging to different object's clusters and the user can navigate in the collection by moving from an object to another, step-by-step.

3. OBJECTS MINING ALGORITHM

The batch process allowing the efficient discovery of the suggested objects is based on our previous work described in [8]. It introduces a new scalable method for automatically discovering frequent visual objects in large multimedia collections even if their size is very small. It first revisits formally the problems of mining and discovering such objects, by introducing the concept of *(c,f)-frequent objects* and generalizes two kinds of existing methods for probing candidate object seeds: weighted adaptive sampling and hashing-based methods. It then introduced a new hashing strategy, working first at the visual level, and then at the geometric level. It allows integrating weak geometric constraints into the hashing phase itself and not only neighborhood constraints as in previous works. Experiments did show that using this new hashing-based prior allows a drastic reduction of the number of tentative probes required to discover small objects instantiated several times in a large dataset.
Figure 1 reproduces the result of a comparative study (conducted in [7]) between our method and the popular Geometric min-Hashing approach (GmH, [1]). This experiment is based exactly on the same evaluation protocol and data as the one introduced in [8] (the comparison to GmH was not ready at the time of submitting that paper). The aim is to measure the ability of each method to produce relevant object's seeds in terms of recall/precision on FlickrBelgaLogo dataset[1] (to our knowledge, no other dataset allows such an evaluation). To achieve the best possible run with GmH, its main parameter has been boosted to much more higher values than the one recommended in the paper: 100K seeds per image instead of 60. As in GmH, we used a large vocabulary of 1M visual words. To convert the collisions produced by GmH into a probability mass function comparable with our own hashing scheme, we count, for each descriptor, the number of sketches colliding with the sketches including the considered descriptor.

4. DEMONSTRATOR

We built a demo of the proposed scheme on a web corpus of 110K images constructed so as to contain many potentially interesting instances of small objects such as sports or international organizations logos, famous buildings and places, etc. For that purpose, we queried a popular web image search engine with a list of 170 ad hoc keywords. Around 600 millions SIFT features were extracted from this corpus and the mining with our algorithm was completed within 48 hours on a single computer (two hexa-cores CPU Intel X5660). Instance clusters were extracted from the produced matching graph thanks to MCL[11] clustering algorithm (nodes representing the discovered frequent objects instances and edges weights the number of shared matched images). Then the interactive GUI allows four main actions: (i) visualize all resulting clusters sorted by frequency of the discovered object and represented by a representative thumbnail. (ii) visualize all instances of a discovered object by clicking on the representative thumbnail of its cluster. (iii) visualize all suggested objects in a given image by clicking on its thumbnail. Note that since an image can contain several object's suggestions, the instances belonging to the current cluster are displayed with a green bounding box whereas the instances belonging to other clusters are displayed with red bounding boxes. (iv) iteratively move from an object to another one by simply clicking on any red bounding box and visualize the images of the new cluster in a pop-up window. Due to the very small size of the discovered objects, their multiplicity and the precision of the clusters, this allows a very nice and unusual user experience in exploring an image collection. The user really has the impression to follow hyper-visual links and to the best of our knowledge such a navigation tool was never presented elsewhere.

[1] http://www-sop.inria.fr/members/Alexis.Joly/BelgaLogos/FlickrBelgaLogos.html

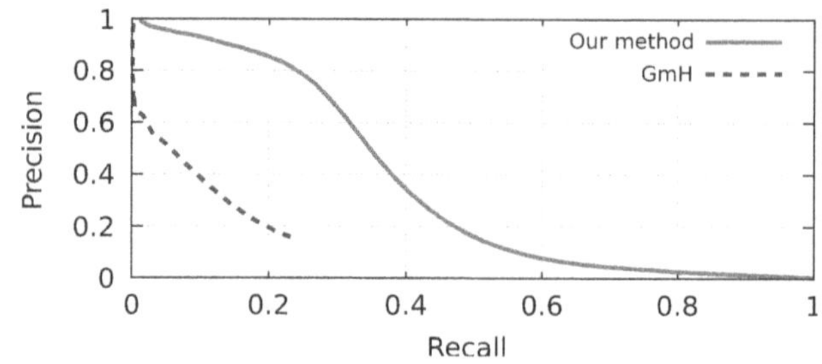

Figure 1: Comparative study with Geometric min-Hashing

5. REFERENCES

[1] O. Chum, M. Perdoch, and J. Matas. Geometric min-hashing: Finding a (thick) needle in a haystack. In *Proceedings of CVPR*, pages 17–24, 6 2009.

[2] O. Chum, J. Philbin, J. Sivic, M. Isard, and A. Zisserman. Total recall: Automatic query expansion with a generative feature model for object retrieval. In *Proceedings of ICCV*, 2007.

[3] A. Hamzaoui, P. Letessier, A. Joly, O. Buisson, and N.Boujemaa. Object-based visual query suggestion. *Multimedia Tools and Applications*, (11042), 2013.

[4] H. Jégou, M. Douze, and C. Schmid. Improving bag-of-features for large scale image search. *IJCV*, 87:316–336, 2010.

[5] A. Joly and O. Buisson. Logo retrieval with a contrario visual query expansion. In *Proceedings of ACM Multimedia*, pages 581–584, 2009.

[6] Y. Kuo, K. Chen, C. Chiang, and W. Hsu. Query expansion for hash-based image object retrieval. In *Proceedings of ACM Multimedia*, pages 65–74, 2009.

[7] P. Letessier. *Découverte et exploitation d'objets fréquents dans des collections multimédias.* PhD thesis, Telecom ParisTech, 2013.

[8] P. Letessier, O. Buisson, and A. Joly. Scalable mining of small visual objects. In *Proceedings of ACM Multimedia*, pages 599–608, 2012.

[9] J. Philbin. *Scalable Object Retrieval in Very Large Image Collections.* PhD thesis, Uni. of Oxford, 2010.

[10] J. Philbin, O. Chum, M. Isard, J. Sivic, and A. Zisserman. Object retrieval with large vocabularies and fast spatial matching. In *Proceedings of CVPR*, 2007.

[11] S. Van Dongen. A cluster algorithm for graphs. *Report-Information systems*, (10):1–40, 2000.

Video2Sentence and Vice Versa

Amirhossein Habibian
ISLA, University of Amsterdam
Science Park 904
1098 XH, Amsterdam
The Netherlands
a.habibian@uva.nl

Cees G. M. Snoek
ISLA, University of Amsterdam
Science Park 904
1098 XH, Amsterdam
The Netherlands
cgmsnoek@uva.nl

ABSTRACT

In this technical demonstration, we showcase a multimedia search engine that retrieves a video from a sentence, or a sentence from a video. The key novelty is our machine translation capability that exploits a cross-media representation for both the visual and textual modality using concept vocabularies. We will demonstrate the translations using arbitrary web videos and sentences related to everyday events. What is more, we will provide an automatically generated explanation, in terms of concept detectors, on *why* a particular video or sentence has been retrieved as the most likely translation.

Categories and Subject Descriptors

I.2.10 [**Vision and Scene Understanding**]: Video analysis

General Terms

Algorithms, Experimentation

Keywords

Multimedia translation, event detection, concept vocabulary

1. INTRODUCTION

All of a sudden, video stories are everywhere. For sharing daily routines on YouTube, for private recollection of holidays, or for new professional markets. Anyone who must work with large amounts of video data is overwhelmed by its volume and the lack of tools to search and interpret the material easily. We aim to ease both retrieval and interpretation by translating a video to a sentence, similar to [1], and a sentence to video.

We consider semantic vocabularies for representing both video and human-provided sentences in a cross-media setting. Representing text and images by their semantic concepts has been shown to be beneficial for captioned-image

Figure 1: *Sentence2Video:* We automatically project an input sentence into a cross-media concept vocabulary, which is also used for representing video. The joint vocabulary allows us to translate a sentence to a video, and vice versa.

retrieval [5]. At the same time, representing video by semantic concepts has been shown to be advantageous for video event recognition [8, 4, 3, 2]. In [4], for example, Merler *et al.* arrive at a robust high-level representation of video events using 280 concept detectors, which outperforms a low-level audiovisual representation. Our novelty is to demonstrate the capabilities of semantic representations for translating arbitrary web video into their lingual description, and vice versa. See Figures 1 and 2.

2. CONCEPT VOCABULARY

We demonstrate capabilities for translating arbitrary web video into a textual sentence and the other way around.

Data set We rely on the web video corpus from the TRECVID 2012 Multimedia Event Detection task [6]. For each web video in this corpus a textual description is provided that summarizes the event happening in the video by

MM'13, October 21–25, 2013, Barcelona, Spain.
ACM 978-1-4503-2404-5/13/10.
http://dx.doi.org/10.1145/2502081.2502249.

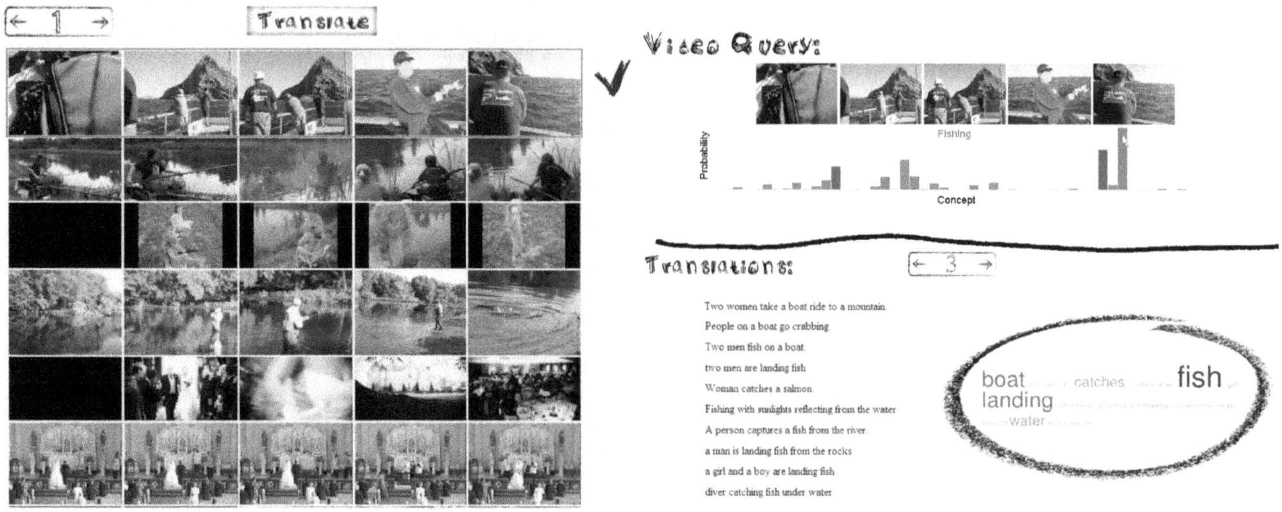

(a) *User selects video to translate.* (b) *System returns translations.*

Figure 2: *Video2Sentence:* Illustrative example for user interaction in our multimedia search engine. In (a) a user selects a candidate video for translation. In (b) the retrieved sentence translations are provided to the user together with the concept vocabulary of the query video. The tag cloud aggregates the sentences into a more precise translation.

highlighting its dominant concepts [7]. In addition, we rely on the publicly available 1,346 concept detector scores for this dataset, which we provided in [2].

Multimedia Translation We map the sentences and video into a unified semantic space and then find their cross-media relations within this space. To map the texts and videos into the semantic space, we apply two sets of concept detectors which are trained so as to detect the semantic concepts on both videos and texts. Hence the textual detectors correspond to the labels of the visual detectors. The cross-media retrieval metric simply minimizes the distance between joint-vocabulary probability vectors [5]. We will show how a vocabulary of concept detectors can be exploited for effective translation at a meaningful level.

3. DEMONSTRATION

During our demonstration we will focus on two multimedia translation use cases:

1. ***Video2Sentence:*** where we retrieve the sentences that best describe the visual content of the query video.

2. ***Sentence2Video:*** where we retrieve the videos that best illustrate the semantic content of the query sentence.

In addition, we will exhibit novel applications of this capability that aggregates the translated information for recounting. Taken together, the search engine provides a means to collect video examples illustrating a sentence and it provides a textual explanation of what happens in a video.

4. ACKNOWLEDGMENTS

This research is supported by the Intelligence Advanced Research Projects Activity (IARPA) via Department of Interior National Business Center contract number D11PC20067. The U.S. Government is authorized to reproduce and distribute reprints for Governmental purposes notwithstanding any copyright annotation thereon. Disclaimer: The views and conclusions contained herein are those of the authors and should not be interpreted as necessarily representing the official policies or endorsements, either expressed or implied, of IARPA, DoI/NBC, or the U.S. Government. This research is also supported by the STW STORY project and the Dutch national program COMMIT.

5. REFERENCES

[1] P. Das, R. K. Srihari, and J. J. Corso. Translating related words to videos and back through latent topics. In *WSDM*, 2013.

[2] A. Habibian, K. E. A. van de Sande, and C. G. M. Snoek. Recommendations for video event recognition using concept vocabularies. In *ICMR*, 2013.

[3] M. Mazloom, E. Gavves, K. E. A. van de Sande, and C. G. M. Snoek. Searching informative concept banks for video event detection. In *ICMR*, 2013.

[4] M. Merler, B. Huang, L. Xie, G. Hua, and A. Natsev. Semantic model vectors for complex video event recognition. *IEEE TMM*, 2012.

[5] N. Rasiwasia, J. Costa Pereira, E. Coviello, G. Doyle, G. Lanckriet, R. Levy, and N. Vasconcelos. A new approach to cross-modal multimedia retrieval. In *ACM MM*, 2010.

[6] A. F. Smeaton, P. Over, and W. Kraaij. Evaluation campaigns and TRECVid. In *ACM MIR*, 2006.

[7] S. Strassel, A. Morris, J. Fiscus, C. Caruso, H. Lee, P. Over, J. Fiumara, B. Shaw, B. Antonishek, and M. Michel. Creating HAVIC: Heterogeneous audio visual internet collection. In *LREC*, 2012.

[8] I. Tsampoulatidis, N. Gkalelis, A. Dimou, V. Mezaris, and I. Kompatsiaris. High-level event detection system based on discriminant visual concepts. In *ICMR*, 2011.

A Tool for Catching Back Your Preferred Videos from Physical Collages

Christoph Korinke
OFFIS - Institute for Information Technology
Oldenburg
Germany
korinke@offis.de

Mohamad Rabbath
OFFIS - Institute for Information Technology
Oldenburg
Germany
rabbath@offis.de

Dennis Lamken
University of Oldenburg
Oldenburg
Germany
dennis.lamken@uni-oldenburg.de

Susanne Boll
University of Oldenburg
Oldenburg
Germany
susanne.boll@uni-oldenburg.de

ABSTRACT

Images and videos are easy to create by inexperienced users with intuitive devices like smartphones. We propose a system which enables users to extract panoramas from videos for the creation of collages which can be printed. Single frames used for panoramas are indexed on the basis of SURF features. As a result users can make a photo with the smartphone from a panorama within the printed collage or zoom into the digital version of a collage to select an area of interest and retrieve the related video using the SURF features index. Moreover users can pick a photo from a location where a video was previously recorded and retrieve a related video as well. Our approach supports the maintenance of a large number of videos.

Categories and Subject Descriptors

H.3.3 [**Information Search and Retrieval**]: Search process; H.3.3 [**Information Search and Retrieval**]: Selection process; I.4.8 [**Scene Analysis**]: Color; I.4.8 [**Scene Analysis**]: Object recognition; H.5.1 [**Multimedia Information Systems**]: Video

Keywords

photo collage; video analysis; descriptor matching

1. INTRODUCTION

Nowadays the number of people owning a smartphone has increased dramatically. Smartphones' built-in cameras enable inexperienced users to easily take images and photos. Consequently, besides the number of images the number of recorded videos has increased as well. However, videos are often not used in further processes because of no intuitive programs available which would not require expert knowledge. Additionally, it is time-consuming to search for specific videos, and therefore many will never be used again.

To counter this situation intuitive applications that operate directly on smartphones are needed. In this paper we propose a system to create printable collages of panoramas extracted from videos on smartphones which in turn can be used as the basis for a video library search. Thus we connect digital media with physical products. Features extracted from frames used for the panoramas act as index entries for the search process. So if a photo is taken from a part of a panorama of the printed collage or an area of the digital collage is selected the system will retrieve and list related videos. If the photo has been taken at a location where a video was recorded, it can also be used for searching videos related to this location. With this approach we support the maintenance of a large number of videos.

A closely related work to our system is the video booklet proposed in [7]. Zhu et al. collect representative thumbnails of a collection of video segments which are then reshaped through pretrained shape templates and printed as a booklet. While browsing through a booklet users can take a photo from a thumbnail with a smartphone or similar device and send it to a computer. The video booklet system will find the most similar thumbnail in the video library and play the corresponding video segment. The main differences of our approach to [7] is the creation of panoramas from videos to build a collage. Moreover the video booklet system uses geometrical features for the retrieval whereas we use SURF features and our system operates directly on a smartphone.

Liu et al. describe an approach in [3] for discovering and generating panoramas from web videos. We use parts of this approach for our system to generate panoramas from selected videos.

In [4] Liu et al. show an approach for the creation of video collages. The most representative images will be selected and resized to region of interests according to saliencies. Then these images are arranged preserving the temporal structure of the video content. Our approach is a simple user arranged collage of more than one video and can be improved by this approach.

A feature extraction method for content-based image retrieval using SIFT descriptors and color information is provided in [6]. In our approach, we apply SURF features for image retrieval to determine a related video because of a faster computation by SURF.

MM'13, October 21–25, 2013, Barcelona, Spain.
ACM 978-1-4503-2404-5/13/10.
http://dx.doi.org/10.1145/2502081.2502250 .

2. VIDEO ANALYSIS

In the first step, our system has to analyse videos which will be used for collages. As depicted in Figure 1 in this process single frames of a scene will be extracted (1) and robust image features will be detected. The features are on the one hand used for a video library index for a later retrieval process (2) and on the other hand for a panorama generation of the scene (3).

Different scenes in a video are detected by use of CEDD distances of adjacent frames [1]. If the distance exceeds a threshold a plane panorama from the scene is generated.

In the actual version of the system we decided to use plane panoramas. Other styles like cylindrical or spheric panoramas could be implemented to improve the user experience. The system uses the SURF features extracted during the scene detection to generate panoramas. Keypoints of two adjacent frames are compared whereby a transformation of the frames is determined in order that similar keypoints in the frames match. With this transformation data the frames are stitched to panoramas.

Beside the panorama generation the extracted SURF features are also used to index the selected frames for a video library. Therefore a codebook for the features is generated to simplify the search process as shown in [2]. For the index it is important that the key values are related to single frames and not directly to a video because of the rating in the retrieval phase. If we linked the keys directly to videos false positive matches could occur because features of the input image matches to features across several frames of a video which leads to a wrong matching. The whole analysis process is conducted asynchronously in the background to enable the interaction for the collage editing process described in the next section.

3. COLLAGE CREATION

In a user study we found out that users prefer to create their collages themselves and not in an automated process. This insight offers space for further research in human machine interaction. The collage creation process on a smartphone of our system currently provides only rudimentary functions like scaling, rotation, translation and deleting of panoramas which can be added per drag and drop. The finished collages can be printed and used for a video retrieval process as shown in the next section.

4. VIDEO RETRIEVAL

Our system enables an assignment from images of the printed collage to previously analysed videos. For the retrieval process, users have to shoot a photo with a standard photo app of their smartphones (5) as depicted in figure 1 or they can zoom in and select an area of interest on a digital version of a collage directly on a smartphone. The photo can contain a single area from a panorama or parts from several panoramas of the collage. The use of a photo of a complete collage is theoretically possible but with a low resolution it lacks the good quality SURF features for good retrieval results. Beside photos from collages as input photos from a location where a video was recorded can also be used.

To retrieve related videos users select photos from their galleries. As shown in figure 1 SURF features will be detected in the input image for the index search(6). A matching of the generated features and the index entries of the video library is performed (7) using the Flann algorithm described in [5] and this leads to a list of probable related videos (8).

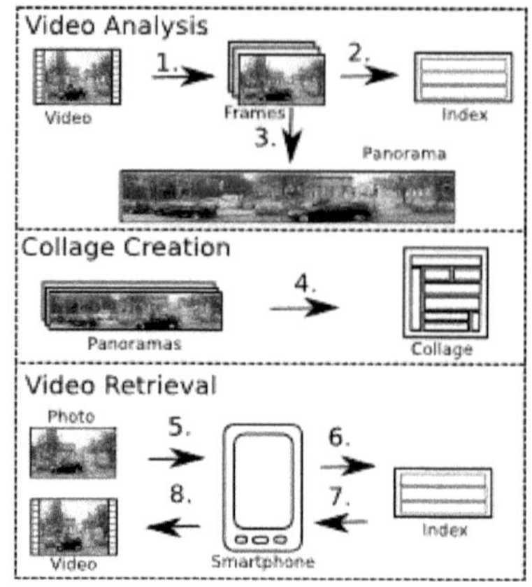

Figure 1: System process

5. CONCLUSION

We developed a system for smartphones to create printable collages with panoramas extracted from video scenes. SURF features of the used frames act as index entries for video frames, to perform the features matching later on in the online query. The printed collages form the base for a video retrieval process. Users can take photos from parts of a collage or a location where videos were recorded with their smartphones and use these photos as input for the retrieval process. A matching process of the extracted features then delivers a ranked list of probable related and previously analysed videos. A demo video of the system can be found on youtube http://youtu.be/OmD3hehgAB0.

6. REFERENCES

[1] S. A. Chatzichristofis and Y. S. Boutalis. Cedd: color and edge directivity descriptor: a compact descriptor for image indexing and retrieval. In *Proceedings of the 6th international conference on Computer vision systems*, ICVS'08, pages 312–322, Berlin, Heidelberg, 2008. Springer-Verlag.

[2] T. Kinnunen, J.-K. Kamarainen, L. Lensu, and H. Kälviäinen. Bag-of-features codebook generation by self-organisation. In *Advances in Self-Organizing Maps*, pages 124–132. Springer, 2009.

[3] F. Liu, Y.-h. Hu, and M. L. Gleicher. Discovering panoramas in web videos. In *Proceedings of the 16th ACM international conference on Multimedia*, pages 329–338. ACM, 2008.

[4] X. Liu, T. Mei, X.-S. Hua, B. Yang, and H.-Q. Zhou. Video collage. In *Proceedings of the 15th international conference on Multimedia*, pages 461–462. ACM, 2007.

[5] M. Muja and D. G. Lowe. Fast approximate nearest neighbors with automatic algorithm configuration. In *International Conference on Computer Vision Theory and Applications (VISSAPP'09)*, pages 331–340, 2009.

[6] Y. Zhang, Z. Zhaoxing, and X. Han. Category specific sift descriptor and its combination with color information for content-based image retrieval. In *Proceedings of the 2nd International Conference on Interaction Sciences: Information Technology, Culture and Human*, pages 685–690. ACM, 2009.

[7] C.-Z. Zhu, X.-S. Hua, T. Mei, and X.-Q. Wu. Video booklet: a natural video searching and browsing interface. In *Proceedings of the 7th ACM SIGMM international workshop on Multimedia information retrieval*, pages 113–120. ACM, 2005.

Pl@ntNet Mobile App

Hervé Goëau
INRIA, ZENITH

Pierre Bonnet
CIRAD, UMR AMAP

Alexis Joly
INRIA, ZENITH

Vera Bakić
INRIA, ZENITH

Julien Barbe
INRA, UMR AMAP

Itheri Yahiaoui
CReSTIC Univ. Reims

Souheil Selmi
INRIA, ZENITH

Jennifer Carré
Tela Botanica

Daniel Barthélémy
CIRAD, BIOS

Nozha Boujemaa
INRIA, Saclay

Jean-François Molino
IRD, UMR AMAP

Grégoire Duché
Tela Botanica

Aurélien Péronnet
Tela Botanica

ABSTRACT

Pl@ntNet is an image sharing and retrieval application for the identification of plants, available on iPhone and iPad devices. Contrary to previous content-based identification applications it can work with several parts of the plant including flowers, leaves, fruits and bark. It also allows integrating user's observations in the database thanks to a collaborative workflow involving the members of a social network specialized on plants. Data collected so far makes it one of the largest mobile plant identification tool.

Categories and Subject Descriptors

H.3.3 [**Information Search and Retrieval**]: Information filtering; Search process; Query formulation

Keywords

plant, identification, images, visual, retrieval, social network, collaborative, crowdsourcing, citizen science, multi-organ, leaf, flower, bark, fruit, ecology, surveillance, monitoring, multimedia, computer vision, botanist

1. BRIDGING THE TAXONOMIC GAP

Building accurate knowledge of the identity, geographic distribution and uses of plants is essential if agricultural development is to be successful and biodiversity is to be conserved. One big challenge, expressed as the *taxonomic gap*, is that identifying plant species is usually impossible for the general public, and often a difficult task for professionals, such as foresters or farmers (who have to deal with weed species). In this context, content-based visual identification tools are considered as one of the most promising solution [4, 2, 12] particularly mobile applications [10, 1] that could help setting-up massive ecological monitoring systems. A noticeable progress in this way has been achieved by the US consortium behind LeafSnap[1] an iPhone application allowing a fair identification of 184 common American species based on uncluttered images of leaves and shape boundary features [10]. But this is still far from a real-world application that would help a farmer recognizing a specific weed among thousands of potential species. Our claim is actually that more diverse views of the plants, fitting the diversity of much richer floras, should actually be considered to achieve a real ecological impact. The use of leaves alone has actually many practical and botanical limitations. Leaves are typically not visible all over the year for most of the species, or can be intrinsically not enough informative or very difficult to capture (needles, tiny or huge leaves...). Using flowers alone, as suggested in [11, 1], is not a better choice because these limitations are even more accentuated. The iPhone application presented in this demo is the first image-based identification tool dealing with multiple organs of the plants (leaf, flower, fruit and bark) in their natural environment. It allows querying the system at any period of the year and can benefit from the complementarity of the different views to improve identification performances.

2. PL@NTNET APPROACH & SYSTEM

The demonstrated iPhone application is built on top of an end-to-end collaborative information system allowing the training data to be continuously enriched and revisited. Complementary to world-wide data integration efforts such as *Encyclopedia Of Life*[2] or crowd-sourced approaches such as ImageNet [3] or NEC flowers dataset [1], our proposal is to rely on thematic social networks to solve data validation issues and produce accurate knowledge. Epistemic communities actually have the advantage to connect experts, enlightened enthusiasts, amateurs and novices around the same topic so that all of them can play complementary roles in a real-world ecological surveillance workflow. Experts can typically animate projects, define observation protocols and teach. Amateurs can collaboratively validate data by interacting together according to their level of expertise, and novice can provide massive sets of observations.
More concretely, our workflow relies on Tela Botanica[3], a French-speaking network linking 20K members in more than 70 countries (41% *novice* in botany, 30% *with a good practice*

[1] http://leafsnap.com/

[2] http://www.eol.org/

[3] http://www.tela-botanica.org/

MM'13, October 21–25, 2013, Barcelona, Spain.
ACM 978-1-4503-2404-5/13/10.
http://dx.doi.org/10.1145/2502081.2502251.

and 7% *experts*). Raw image feeds, collected through web crawls, personal collections or the iPhone app itself, are integrated in a collaborative tagging and validation tools and enriched daily by the network. These web applications typically allows managing contradictory determinations that result from the intrinsic complexity of identifying a plant (classical dichotomous keys used by botanists require answering dozens or even hundreds of complex questions related to thousands of often ambiguous morphological attributes). To boost integration, contents with missing organ tags are automatically annotated and can be corrected afterwards. Based on all the produced metadata, only relevant contents are finally inserted daily in the visual index.

The mobile application available on the App Store works at the time of writing on 22,574 pictures representing 957 wild plant species living in France area. Besides, a web beta version of the application includes more than 100K images and 5K species. To our knowledge, there is no other multi-organ database meeting the needs of content-based identification, i.e. with a large number of species, explicit organ tags and a sufficient number of training pictures. Initiatives like EOL provide good illustrations for many plants but must often with only very few pictures per organ and per species. On the other side, crowdsourced datasets such as ImageNet [3] contain thousands of pictures for a lot of species, but still without organ tags and with a very high level of noise for a botanical usage. More generally, most existing data suffer from a *long tail* distribution, i.e. with few species well represented and most species with few images.

3. THE IPHONE APP

The iPhone app itself basically contains four functionalities: an image feeds reader to explore the last contributions of the community, a taxonomic browser with full text search options, a user profile and personal contents management screen and the image-based identification tool itself. The user can take up to five pictures of a same plant, and the system ask him to chose for each picture among 4 icons representing a flower, a leaf, a fruit and a bark. The complete set of pictures can finally be submitted as a query plant to the remote visual search engine. Retrieved species with confidence scores and matched images are finally returned to the device and displayed on the the result screen by decreasing confidence. Selecting one of the retrieved species opens a detailed view screen with all matched pictures (classified by organ galleries) allowing a first stage of refinement in the determination process. A second stage of refinement can be achieved by accessing either *eFlora* Tela Botanica fact sheets (the most complete db on France flora) or wikipedia mobile pages. If the user believes having found the right species he can finally share his observation with pictures, date, gps and author's name (in Creative Commons). The observation will then be integrated through the collaborative web tools[4][5].

4. VISUAL SEARCH ENGINE

The generalist CBIR method we are using as the core algorithm of our visual search engine is built from the works of Joly et al. [7, 6, 8] on large-scale matching. It was actually shown in [4, 5] that such object retrieval methods do work surprisingly well on plants although being usually aimed at retrieving rigid objects such as buildings, logos, etc. Concretely, image retrieval is achieved through the following steps: (i) Local features extraction (SURF, HoG, RGBH and Fourrier features around multi-resolution color Harris points) (ii) Hamming embedding and indexing with RMMH [8] (iii) approximate k-nn search with AMP-LSH [6] (iv) voting based on the number of matched features (with or without spatial re-ranking depending on the view type). In the case of leaf scans, an additional boundary descriptor (DFH+Shapes [13]) is used to capture the global shape and has been showed to provide a consistent improvement of the global performances. Thanks to the organ-based tagging paradigm, pictures belonging to a given plant view category can be indexed and searched in a separate visual index. This allows reducing confusion between pictures of different parts of the plant and therefore increases identification performances. At query stage, the N^Q query pictures belonging to a query plant Q are searched separately in their respective visual index and the top-K most similar images are returned for each of them (K=20). Identification is then performed thanks to an instance-based classifier computed across all retrieved pictures. It uses a two-stage fusion strategy working first on query images with the same view type (*single-view* level) and then on the produced decision lists at the upper level (*multi-view* level). The single-view fusion level combines a min-rank fusion of the image lists and a classical instance-based classifier to produce a ranked list of species with normalized scores for each type of view. The *multi-view* fusion level consists in a weighted sum of the normalized confidence scores of the *single-view* level, where the weight of each view type reflects its discrimination power for query Q. More details about the visual search engine as well as extensive experiments on the identification performances are available in [5] and [9]. The iPhone application itself is freely available on the Apple store (*PlantNet*).

Acknowledgements. This work was funded by the Agropolis fundation through the project Pl@ntNet[6].

5. REFERENCES

[1] A. Angelova, S. Zhu, Y. Lin, J. Wong, and C. Shpecht. Development and deployment of a large-scale flower recognition mobile app. In *NEC Labs America Technical Report*, 2012.

[2] G. Cerutti, L. Tougne, A. Vacavant, and D. Coquin. A parametric active polygon for leaf segmentation and shape estimation. In *ISVC11*.

[3] J. Deng, W. Dong, R. Socher, L.-J. Li, K. Li, and L. Fei-Fei. A Large-Scale Hierarchical Image Database. In *CVPR09*.

[4] H. Goëau, P. Bonnet, A. Joly, N. Boujemaa, D. Barthélémy, J.-F. Molino, P. Birnbaum, E. Mouysset, and M. Picard. The ImageCLEF2011 plant images classification task. 2011.

[5] H. Goëau, P. Bonnet, B. Julien, V. Bakić, A. Joly, and J.-F. Molino. Multi-Organ Plant Identification. In *ACM Work. on Multimedia Analysis for Ecological Data*, 2012.

[6] A. Joly and O. Buisson. A posteriori multi-probe locality sensitive hashing. In *ACM MM*, pages 209–218, 2008.

[7] A. Joly and O. Buisson. Logo retrieval with a contrario visual query expansion. In *ACM MM*, 2009.

[8] A. Joly and O. Buisson. Random maximum margin hashing. In *CVPR*, pages 873–880, 2011.

[9] A. Joly, H. Goëau, P. Bonnet, V. Bakić, J. Barbe, S. Selmi, I. Yahiaoui, J. Carré, E. Mouysset, J.-F. Molino, N. Boujemaa, and D. Barthélémy. Interactive plant identification based on social image data. *Ecological Informatics*, 2013.

[10] N. Kumar, P. N. Belhumeur, A. Biswas, D. W. Jacobs, W. J. Kress, I. C. Lopez, and J. V. B. Soares. Leafsnap: A computer vision system for automatic plant species identification. In *ECCV*, 2012.

[11] M.-E. Nilsback and A. Zisserman. Automated flower classification over a large number of classes. In *ICVGIP08*.

[12] C. Spampinato, V. Mezaris, and J. van Ossenbruggen. Multimedia analysis for ecological data. In *ACM MM*, 2012.

[13] I. Yahiaoui, O. Mzoughi, and N. Boujemaa. Leaf shape descriptor for tree species identification. In *ICME*, 2012.

[4] `http://www.tela-botanica.org/appli:identiplante`

[5] `http://www.tela-botanica.org/appli:pictoflora`

[6] `http://www.plantnet-project.org/`

Determining Exposure Values from HDR Histograms for Smartphone Photography

Benjamin Guthier, Kalun Ho, Stephan Kopf, Wolfgang Effelsberg
Department of Computer Science IV
University of Mannheim, Germany
{guthier, kopf, effelsberg}@informatik.uni-mannheim.de
kaho@mail.uni-mannheim.de

ABSTRACT

We present a novel system to assist users in choosing suitable exposure values for photography on smartphones. The user specifies the desired shape of the histogram of the captured image by adjusting the parameters of a function. The system then uses the smartphone's camera and varying exposure values to calculate a high dynamic range (HDR) histogram of the scene. It contains the entire brightness range from the darkest to the brightest area of the scene. For any exposure value, the HDR histogram can be used to synthesize a conventional histogram of a low dynamic range (LDR) image as if captured by this exposure value. This process is much faster than capturing the image itself. By comparing a number of synthesized LDR histograms to the user's desired histogram shape, the system determines an exposure value that best meets the user's preference.

Categories and Subject Descriptors

I.4.9 [**Image Processing and Computer Vision**]: Applications

Keywords

Photography, Smartphones, HDR

1. INTRODUCTION

Even in smartphone photography, users have a desire to take pictures that are visually pleasing. Deciding upon a suitable exposure value for a given scene is one of the aspects that make a good picture. The automatic exposure control in smartphones is often too simple to match the user's preferences. In professional photography, it is common to display brightness histograms to facilitate the process of finding good exposure. In our work, we take a backwards approach: The user specifies the desired shape of the histogram and the system calculates an exposure value that best meets the user's intentions. In order to predict the shape of the histogram for any given exposure value without going through the costly image capturing process, we make use of high dynamic range (HDR) histograms. A conventional low dynamic range (LDR) histogram simulating any exposure value can be directly calculated from the HDR histogram. In the end, the exposure for which the LDR histogram meets the user's preferences best is used to actually take a picture. The entire system is implemented as a camera app for android-based smartphones. A screenshot of it is shown in Figure 1.

There exist previous works on determining good exposure settings. Many of them focus on finding sequences of shutter values to be used to capture an HDR frame. As opposed to our work where HDR histograms are a means to capture good LDR images, capturing HDR frames is the goal in these methods. One such approach is [1]. It uses the histogram of a previous frame in an HDR video to determine optimal shutter speed sequences to capture the next HDR frame. Its focus lies on finding a trade-off between the amount of well-exposed pixels and the number of exposures. Another technique for determining exposure values in the context of HDR image creation is [2]. Instead of varying the shutter speed, gain is adjusted here. The technique is based on the observation that increasing the gain also increases the SNR of the created HDR image.

2. EXPOSURE VALUE DETERMINATION

Our system to find suitable exposure values for smartphone photography begins by querying the user's preferences. This is done by letting the user specify a function $f(p)$ over the range of pixel values $p = 0, \ldots, 255$ which describes the desired shape of the image's histogram. The function assigns a value between 0 and 1 to each pixel value p. It expresses the desirability to have pixels with a value of p in the picture that is about to be taken. The system selects a suitable exposure value based on this desirability function $f(p)$. In our implementation, $f(p)$ is defined as a user-adjustable piecewise linear function.

The user then points the camera at the scene and starts the exposure value algorithm. It begins by temporarily capturing a sequence of images with varying exposure values. Most smartphones are limited with respect to the range and number of exposure values Δt they permit. An example would be a range of $\Delta t_i = 2^{i/k}$ with $i = -k, \ldots, k$ for any value of k, i.e., a range between 0.5 and 2 divided into $2k+1$ steps. Due to this limitation, we only use three different values: Two at the extremes and one in the center of the exposure range. We denote them by Δt^-, Δt^0 and Δt^+. Using them to capture three images results in a dark image I^-, a medium image I^0 and a bright one I^+ respectively.

MM'13, October 21–25, 2013, Barcelona, Spain.
ACM 978-1-4503-2404-5/13/10.
http://dx.doi.org/10.1145/2502081.2502252.

Figure 1: Screenshot of our system to determine exposure values for smartphone photography. The red area is the coverage value C.

Note that no HDR image is created with our system. Camera motion between the shots thus has little impact on the results and is neglected.

The image sequence I^-, I^0, I^+ is now used to create a high dynamic range histogram spanning the entire brightness range of the scene from the darkest to the brightest area. We refer to the real brightness in the scene as radiance E. In order to create a histogram over radiance, we do not actually need to store an entire HDR image $E(x, y)$. The radiance $E(x, y)$ can be calculated for each pixel position (x, y) individually and inserted into the histogram one at a time. We thus drop the parameters x and y in the following and always assume a single pixel position.

The radiance of a pixel is estimated from an image I by dividing its pixel value by its exposure. We thus obtain one radiance estimate $\tilde{E} = I/\Delta t$ for each of the three images. We denote the three estimates by $\tilde{E}^-$, $\tilde{E}^0$ and $\tilde{E}^+$. The three estimates should roughly be the same, meaning that the same radiance value in the scene gave rise to three different pixel values under three different exposure settings. The difference between $\tilde{E}^-$, $\tilde{E}^0$ and $\tilde{E}^+$ is due to noise and saturation effects when capturing (note that we assume a linear camera response function in our work). It is generally assumed that pixel values p near the center of the [0..255] interval result in a better radiance estimate than values near the extremes. The three estimates are thus weighted by a weighting function $w(p)$ which reflects this characteristic. Examples for weighting functions $w(p)$ can be found in the literature on HDR imaging. The radiance value E for a pixel is then calculated as a weighted average over the three estimates:

$$E = \frac{w(I^-)\tilde{E}^- + w(I^0)\tilde{E}^0 + w(I^+)\tilde{E}^+}{w(I^-) + w(I^0) + w(I^+)} \qquad (1)$$

The radiance E is now inserted into the HDR histogram $H(j)$. With the range of shutter speeds known, we also know the range of possible radiance values. The minimum is obtained from a pixel that has a value of 0 even in the longest exposure, that is, $E_{min} = 0/\Delta t^+ = 0$. The maximum is $E_{max} = 255/\Delta t^-$ accordingly. This range is subdivided into N histogram bins. Each bin $H(j)$ counts the occurrence of radiance values between $E_{min} + \frac{j}{N}(E_{max} - E_{min})$ and the beginning of bin $H(j+1)$ for $j = 0, \ldots, N-1$. The system tests which interval E falls into and increases the corresponding histogram bin by one. Doing this for every pixel position results in a full HDR histogram.

For the purpose of exposure value determination, we are interested in what the conventional LDR histogram $h_{\Delta t}(p)$ of an image looks like when it was captured at a specific exposure value Δt. $h_{\Delta t}(p)$ can be calculated directly from $H(j)$. This is much faster than actually capturing an image at Δt. Each bin of $h_{\Delta t}(p)$ corresponds to a pixel value p between 0 and 255. By dividing each pixel value by the exposure value Δt, we obtain a radiance estimate $\tilde{E} = p/\Delta t$. Doing the same test as above, $\tilde{E}$ can be mapped to an index j in the HDR histogram to which p corresponds. We then simply set $h_{\Delta t}(p) := H(j)$ for $p = 0, \ldots, 254$. The bin with index 255 contains the sum of all HDR histogram bins with radiance values higher than $254/\Delta t$. This corresponds to saturation of pixels for large brightness values in the scene.

In this manner, we obtain an LDR histogram for any exposure value Δt. The sum of its bins does not necessarily equal the total number of pixels anymore due to the way $H(j)$ is sampled. It is thus necessary to normalize the histogram. The system now calculates the coverage C between $h_{\Delta t}(p)$ and the desired shape of the histogram $f(p)$ (see Figure 1):

$$C = \sum_p \min(h_{\Delta t}(p), f(p)) \,/ \sum_p f(p). \qquad (2)$$

We find the exposure value that best matches the user's preference by exhaustive searching. The Δt to the LDR histogram with the highest coverage with f is selected and finally used to capture the desired image.

3. CONCLUSIONS

In our technical demo, we present a smartphone app that determines optimal exposure values based on an HDR histogram of the scene. The user can adjust a desired shape for the histogram of the image to be captured. The app then finds the exposure which results in a histogram that best matches the user's preference.

The most time consuming step in this process is the capturing of the image sequence and the creation of the HDR histogram. It takes about 1.5 seconds. Computation of the LDR histogram and its coverage are very fast operations. Also, the range of values for Δt is usually small on a smartphone. After HDR histogram creation, calculating the optimal shutter for a desired shape can thus be done without noticeable delay.

In our experiments, we found that the automatic exposure control in smartphones leads to dissatisfactory images for scenes with difficult lighting conditions (e.g., very bright and very dark areas visible at the same time). In these situations, the subjective image quality according to the user's intention was improved by using our system.

4. REFERENCES

[1] B. Guthier, S. Kopf, and W. Effelsberg. Optimal shutter speed sequences for real-time HDR video. In *Int. Conf. on Image Systems and Techniques*, 2012.

[2] S. Hasinoff, F. Durand, and W. Freeman. Noise-Optimal Capture for High Dynamic Range Photography. In *Proc. of the CVPR*, 2010.

Semantic Dispatching of Multimedia News with MEWS

Julien Law-To
Exalead
10, place de la Madeleine
Paris, France
Julien.lawto@3ds.com

Gregory Grefenstette
Exalead
10, place de la Madeleine
Paris, France
gregory.grefenstette@3ds.com

Rémi Landais
Exalead
10, place de la Madeleine
Paris, France
Remi.landais@3ds.com

ABSTRACT

Online news comes in rich multimedia form: video, audio, photos, in addition to traditional text. Recent advances in semantically-rich text processing, in speech-to-text processing, and in image processing allows us to develop new ways of presenting and enriching news stories. Here we present MEWS, a Multimedia nEWS platform, which enriches news browsing according to media (text, images, and video) and to automatically detected type of news (music, general news, politics).

Categories and Subject Descriptors

H.5.1 Multimedia Information Systems; I.2.7 Natural Language Processing: *Speech recognition and synthesis*; I.4 Image Processing and Computer Vision

Keywords

Multimedia indexing, image processing, news, search engine, speech processing, speech-to-text, semantic annotation

1. INTRODUCTION

MEWS, a Multimedia nEWS search platform, applies latest advances in semantic text processing, in large-scale web indexing, in video, audio and image signal processing to provide an intelligent news browsing experience in which stories are enriched with domain specific metadata with technology developed by Exalead (crawling and indexing), Vocapia (speech processing), LTU (Image processing).

2. SOURCES TO ENRICH NEWS

Text-based new stories come from Exalead, the search engine division of Dassault Systèmes, which maintains a fresh index of 16 billion web pages, with 200 million reindexed per day, searchable at exalead.com/search. A separate index of web pages from news sources is also maintained, and a non-commercial demonstrator called ExaNews, provides access to 10 million of these news items at exanews.labs.exalead.com. The Exanews index feeds into MEWS, but MEWS also includes other text and multimedia news sources: podcasts, images, public debates, and less newsworthy items such as concert schedules of musicians.

Audio and video news sources come from the 300000 podcasts that have been indexed in the Exalead Voxalead [1] broadcast news search system, which has been live and online since 2009.

MM'13, October 21-25, 2013, Barcelona, Spain.
ACM 978-1-4503-2404-5/13/10
http://dx.doi.org/10.1145/2502081.2502253

Voxalead currently indexes daily broadcast news content from 60 sources in English, French, Chinese, Arabic, Spanish, Dutch, Italian, German and Russian and makes the audio and video streams searchable the day after their publication. The audio portions of news is converted from speech to time-stamped text using Vocapia technology [2]. This text is processed using named-entity recognition technology developed by Exalead, and entity and their types (events, people, organizations, places) are indexed.

Over 500,000 images are included in MEWS coming from the body of news gathered in the Exanews index, using Open Source solution Boilerpipe (https://code.google.com/p/boilerpipe) and HTML extraction to identify the largest image in each news story, ignoring small image, or image with aspect ratios resembling banners. These images are indexed by the text in any image tags and with text found around the image on the original web page.

In addition to news, MEWS also includes recent French National Assembly debate transcripts that have been provided as raw linked open data by data.gouv.fr. MEWS provides the first public index into this data, providing faceted, full text search, with further interface developments that exploit the structure of parliamentary debates. For some debates, we can also browse the video recording of these debates using an automatic alignment and synchronization performed by Vecsys between the manual transcript and the video [3].

To further enrich news results found via a user query, we also index all the pages of the English version of Wikipedia (about 10 million articles).

As many queries concern musical artists, we also incorporate in MEWS a music index concerning more than 600000 artists and their songs. Songs are indexed by textual metadata and lyrics but also by the musical content itself: chords, extraction of moods (happy, romantic etc.), of instrumentation (electric vs. acoustic). This index was produced using processing from ParisTelecom and the IRCAM, and is described in detail in [4].

3. SEARCHING, BROWSING IN MEWS

MEWS provides a unique search box provides access to all news. User queries can be automatically translated, using Systran technology, into another language (English, French, Spanish, Italian or German) to search. Results from all the different media sources (see section 2) are merged and displayed as shown below in Figure 1. Each result is illustrated with an image, subtitled with a search snippet and a distinguishing colored icon (showing whether the result is a video, an image, from the political domain, or from the music domain). If there is a match in the Wikipedia index, then a Wikipedia snippet appears below the search box, above the result images. The results scroll to the right (the fourth column in the image is the beginning of another three column result set). Clicking one of the search results leads to a detailed results page specific to this type of content.

Figure 1. MEWS Search Page. Here the query 'Korea' produces results from Wikipedia, from text-based new stories, from automatic transcriptions of news broadcasts, and from tagged images.

3.1 Enriched display in detail page

An example of the detailed results page is shown in Figure 2. Terms from the original query are highlighted in bold in the results. The content and format of this news item depends of the type of document displaying either automatic transcription for videos (example shown here), manual transcription for politic content, tags for images or text for web pages. Tabs above the text allow the content viewed in English, French, Spanish, Italian and German, automatically translated using Systran technology. A tag cloud to the left of the content presents the main color-coded named entities detected in this content. Clicking on this tag cloud leads to Wikipedia articles for each entity.

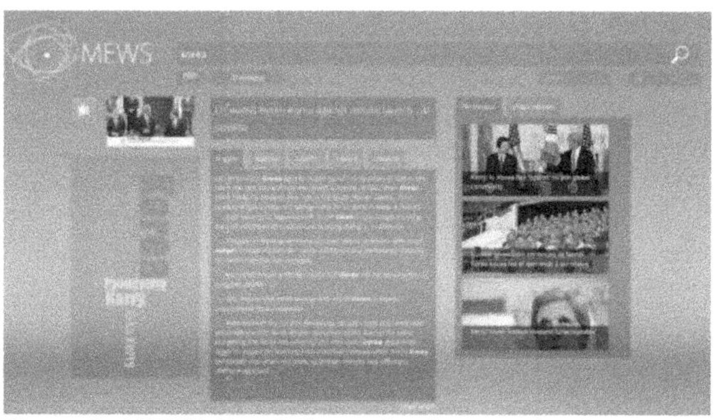

Figure 2. MEWS Detail Page, showing translated text tags, content with highlighted query terms, entity tag cloud and related content.

The content is also analyzed on the fly by an Exalead semantic processor that detects political people and artists. When an artist is detected, the named is highlighted in yellow and an automatic link leading to the artist page in our music index is created. In a similar way when a political person is detected a link to the political index demo is created. To the right of the central content, there is a column of similar content, found using keywords extracted from the news item. When the query result is an image, the similarity is based on the visual content using the image index and LTU's image comparison technology.

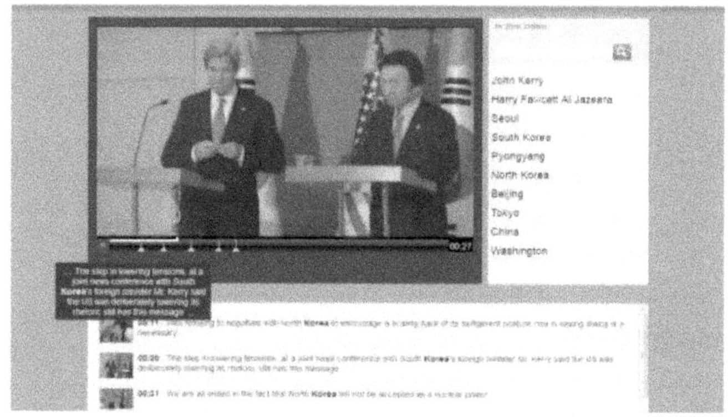

Figure 3. Voxalead Page accessible from MEWS. The video positions itself before the first mentions of the query terms. Small white triangles show the appearances of these terms under the video. The automatically produced transcript follows the video. Entities mentioned in the video appear under a search box on the right.

When the central content transcription comes from a video, clicking on the image icon will lead to the Voxalead page for this video, bringing the user directly to the moment in the video when the query terms are pronounced in the audio stream.

The live MEWS demonstrator, updated daily, is available at: http://mews.labs.exalead.com

4. ACKNOWLEDGMENT

This multimedia news demonstrator was partly realized as part of the Quaero Programme funded by OSEO, the French State Agency for Innovation.

5. REFERENCES

[1] Law-To, J., & Grefenstette, G. (2011, November). VOXALEAD: a scalable video search engine based on content. In Proceedings of the 19th ACM international conference on Multimedia (pp. 747-748). ACM.

[2] Despres, Julien, et al. "The Vocapia Research ASR Systems for Evalita 2011." Evaluation of Natural Language and Speech Tools for Italian. Springer Berlin Heidelberg, 2013. 286-294.

[3] Clavel, C., Adda, G., Cailliau, F., Garnier-Rizet, M., Cavet, A., Chapuis, G., ... & Suignard, P. (2013). Spontaneous speech and opinion detection: mining call-centre transcripts. Language Resources and Evaluation, 1-37

[4] Lenoir, A., Landais, R., & Law-To, J. (2012, June). MuMa: a scalable music search engine based on content analysis. In Content-Based Multimedia Indexing (CBMI), 2012 10th International Workshop on (pp. 1-4). IEEE

[5] Forman, G. 2003. An extensive empirical study of feature selection metrics for text classification. *J. Mach. Learn. Res.* 3 (Mar. 2003), 1289-1305.

Cloud Based Multimedia Analytic Platform

Peng Wu
HP Software
1501 Page Mill Road
Palo Alto, CA, USA
+1 (650) 857-3683
peng.wu@hp.com

Rares Vernica
HP Labs
1501 Page Mill Road
Palo Alto, CA, USA
+1 (650) 857-6168
rares.vernica@hp.com

Qian Lin
HP Software
1501 Page Mill Road
Palo Alto, CA, USA
+1 (650) 857-2685
qian.lin@hp.com

ABSTRACT
Multimedia Analytic Platform is a cloud based service to expose state-of-the-art multimedia technologies for mobile and web application development. As a product-quality service platform, it offers comprehensive API documentation, code example, service description and sandbox for trial for each multimedia technology. The utilization of the cloud storage and distributed computing framework allows the service platform to run with robustness and efficiency. The current technologies supported by the platform include face detection, face verification, face demographic estimation, feature extraction, image matching, and image collage. Since its initial public launch in October 2012, it has been adopted by universities and third party companies for course support and application development.

Categories and Subject Descriptors
H.3.5 [**Online Information Services**]: web-based services

General Terms
Algorithms, Performance, Design.

Keywords
Cloud, Multimedia, Analytic, Platform.

1. Introduction
Over the years, the multimedia community has made significant progress on multimedia content analysis/understanding, search, composition, etc. In the meantime, with proliferation of smart mobile devices and web, the demand on multimedia technologies has also grown stronger. In this paper, we describe a cloud based multimedia analytic platform (MAP) as a vehicle to make the state of the art multimedia technologies available for both mobile and web application development. The benefit is mainly two folds: 1) it offers a channel to validate the strength and shortcoming of multimedia technologies developed in research community through end user facing applications; 2) it provides demands on performance, functionality and effectiveness of multimedia technologies to drive technology advancement.

2. Multimedia Analytic Platform Overview
In order to make our multimedia technologies widely available in a scalable manner, we developed the HP Labs Multimedia Analytic Platform (MAP, http://map.hpl.hp.com) as a service in the HP Cloud Services (HPCS, http://www.hpcloud.com) infrastructure. HP Labs Multimedia Analytic Platform offers developers cutting edge technology on the analysis, understanding, composition and publishing of multimedia content. These technologies can be integrated with both mobile apps and cloud services through industry standard API and data formats.

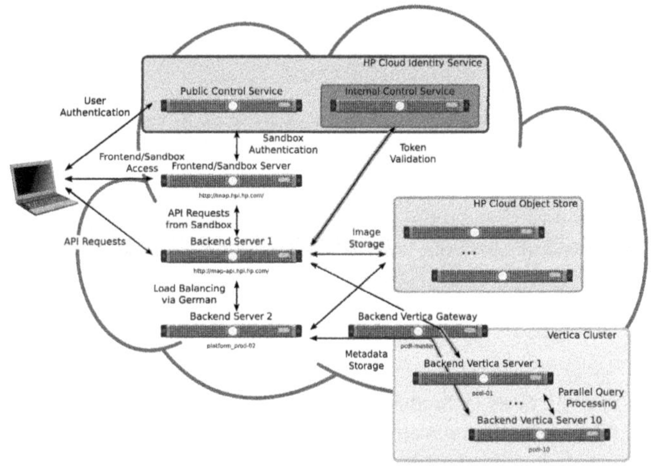

Figure 1: MAP Architecture

Figure 1 shows how MAP is deployed on HPCS computing and storage services and integrated with HPCS for authentication. The main characteristics of MAP architecture include:

- MAP services run on a cluster of backend servers that implement load balancing and distributed job execution to provide scalable services and RESTful request processing.
- MAP establishes a frontend server to expose a set of static pages, including a landing page, a Sandbox page from which any offered service can be experimented freely, and service description page, API documentation page and code example page for each service.
- A service API call can be made by a customer programmatically. A successful call will require the customer to be equipped with HP Cloud storage account for multimedia storage.

3. MAP Services
We carefully selected imaging technologies representative of the state of the art in multimedia analysis, composition and representation. Currently six services are offered on the MAP platform: Face Detection, Face Verification, Face Demographic,

MM'13, October 21–25, 2013, Barcelona, Spain.
ACM 978-1-4503-2404-5/13/10.

Feature Extraction, Image Matching, and Image Collage. Example service outputs are shown in Figure 2.

Face Detection Face Verification Face Demographic

Image Collage

Figure 2: MAP Services Output Examples

- Face Detection service detects all the faces in a given image and returns their bounding boxes.
- Face Verification service is a continuation of the Face Detection service in that faces from different images are compared and their similarity score is computed.
- Feature Extraction service extracts highly efficient and compact features to represent an image. The returned features include feature locations in the image and their vector descriptions. This image feature representation is tailored for mobile applications, see [1] for more details.
- Face Demographics estimation provides the age and gender of the faces in an image. It is a basic building block for many high level applications, such as relationship estimation, audience measurement. Our demographics estimation service returns the demographics information for each face in a given image.
- Image Matching service returns a similarity score for two images based on the matched features.
- Image Collage service is supported by PhotoShape technology, which enables the automatic creation of compact and informative image collages of arbitrary geometrical shapes with arbitrary numbers of images.

4. Cloud based Platform Architecture

4.1 API design

The Multimedia Analytics Platform uses a RESTful API. A service call includes one or more images as arguments, the desired format for the response, and the HP Cloud container where the inputs and the outputs should be stored. Images are provided as URLs to publicly accessible images or uploaded as part of the request. For the response the supported formats are JSON and XML. The actual response structure depends on the service. For example, for the Face Detection service the response contains the bounding boxes of each of the detected faces. For the Image Collage service, the response contains the Regions of Interest (ROI) extracted from each image and the layout of each ROI in the collage (rotation angle, scale, position).

4.2 Result caching and duplicate call detection

The results of each of the calls to our services are stored in a Vertica database. We store information about pictures, faces, feature vectors, etc. If our backend receives the same call twice we can reconstruct the response from the database without requiring to re-compute the result. In order to detect duplicated calls, we need a way to detect that the same image is being re-submitted. We choose to use SHA1 signature of the images to detect duplicates. Essentially, for each image sent to our backend, we compute the SHA1 signature for the whole image file. If exactly the same image file is sent twice we will detect the duplicate and not re-compute the result. If any change is made to the image, the SHA1 encoding will not match and the image is considered to be a new image. Similarly, we compute SHA1 encodings for groups of images and detect calls with exactly the same group of images.

4.3 Cloud storage

We extensively leverage the HP Cloud Storage in MAP. Each service call needs to be accompanied by a HP Cloud container belonging to the customer making the call. We store all the input images in the container in various sizes (thumbnail, small, medium, large and original). Moreover, for the services which produce images as output (i.e., Image Collage) we also store the output image in the cloud storage. The service response includes a unique ID for each image which can be used to identify each image in the container.

5. Conclusion and Demonstration

The Multimedia Analytic Platform was made available in beta form on October 1st, 2012 and also accessible through the HPCS Partner Solution listings. Since we launched the platform we had an average 100 unique users per day with a peak of 1643 unique users on October 8, 2012. More than 34,000 service requests have been made to MAP platform. An example experience of utilizing MAP technologies for commercial web development is described in [2].

In the demonstration, participants can experience different services either use stock photos provided by MAP or any public photos. We will also demonstrate the programmatic utilization of the services and show a 3rd party commercial web application developed using MAP.

6. Acknowledgements

Our thanks to Rajeev Pandey of HPCS, Ruimin Chen, Qing Zhang, etc. of HP Enterprise Services, Feng Tang and Hao Tang of HP Labs for their contribution and engineering effort.

7. References

[1] F. Tang, S.H. Lim, N.L. Chang, and H. Tao, 2009. *A novel feature descriptor invariant to complex brightness changes.* In Proceedings of CVPR, 2631-2638.

[2] https://blog.hpcloud.com/guest-blog-using-hp-cloud-build-app-48-hours

Adaptable and Personalized Game-based Training System for Fall Prevention

Sandro Hardy, Stefan Göbel, Ralf Steinmetz
Technische Universität Darmstadt, Multimedia Communications Lab - KOM
Rundeturmstraße 10, 64283 Darmstadt, Germany
+49 6151 16 {75164, 6149, 6150}
{Sandro.Hardy, Stefan.Goebel, Ralf.Steinmetz}@kom.tu-darmstadt.de

ABSTRACT
Digital Games which incorporate movements of the player's body in their gameplay are becoming more and more popular. An increasing number of doctors and physical therapists use such games for training exercises, although these games are not designed to achieve predefined training goals. Various studies show that the training effects of these games are small in comparison with classic exercises. Therapists request more accessible and more flexible games. In this paper we present an adaptive game for fall prevention based on the adaptation and exergame analysis framework StoryTecRT which allows the adaptation of parameters which impact accessibility, acceptance and training load of a game. This paper includes an insight into the framework and the implementation as well as first evaluation results.

Categories and Subject Descriptors
H.5.2 [**Information Systems**]: User Interfaces – *input devices and strategies;* J.3 [**Computer Applications**]: Life and Medical Sciences – *health;* K.8 [**Personal Computing**]: General – *Games.*

Keywords
Serious Games, Health, Exergames, Training, Personalization, Adaptation, Sensors.

1. INTRODUCTION
Lack of exercise is a world-wide and well-known problem which leads to an amount of severe diseases. This problem is increased by the demographic change. Especially elderly people suffer from diseases caused by inactivity, since their decreasing mobility lowers the amount of possibilities for being active. This leads to insufficient muscular training which increases the risk of falls.

Solving this problem requires to focus on two aspects: A) Increase the accessibility of training exercises or activities of daily life (ADL) which stabilize or improve the physical health of elderly people. B) These exercises and ADLs must be attractive and motivating in order to be accepted and performed with intrinsic motivation by elderly people. Physical exercises are addressed in physical education and sports science, while the attractiveness and user experience of activities is a research topic in psychology. The adaptation framework StoryTecRT allows the measurement of the impact of parameters which influence acceptance of an exertion games and the training effects. After giving as small overview in section 2 about the background we present a prototype, the conceptual approach, and a prototype in section 3 as well as first qualitative evaluation results in Section 4.

MM'13, October 21–25, 2013, Barcelona, Spain.
ACM 978-1-4503-2404-5/13/10.
http://dx.doi.org/10.1145/2502081.2502255

2. RELATED WORK
The approach of using interactive multimedia technologies for motivational training touches related approaches from three different research fields: user/game experience, physical training and technology (multimedia and medical measurement). Sport science researches the effectiveness of exercises and defines metrics for the evaluation of training effects. For the measurement of gait stability and balance, beyond physical assessments such as the Tinetti-test digital measurements can be used as indicator for the risk of falls. Measurable indicators are i.e. the center of pressure (COP), stability, range of movement, reaction time or movement speed. All these tests and measurements are performed apart from training exercises and with the help of professionals. The tests follow explicit rules and provide only limited room for adaptation to a user's skills. Furthermore they allow no interaction or reaction to the user's behavior (feedback) and are not intended to engage users. The acceptance and therefore the training frequency and duration, which are both important for the training load, are related to the motivation and engagement of the user. The question what motivates users/players is focused in different approaches. Beginning with psychological concepts such as Flow, which includes challenge at the threshold between boredom and anxiety, different authors propose specialized concepts and design guidelines for successful games and exergames. The constructs from psychology and game experience research include but are not limited to challenge, curiosity, feedback, control, empowerment, immersion and social interaction [1]. Other work shows the feasibility of digital virtual training and the adaptation and personalization of exergames [3]. Since each of the theoretical constructs can be operationalized in different ways, the impact of a single operationalization can't be measured using two different games. For an appropriate measurement it needs two versions of the same game, which differ only in the operationalization of one single construct. A challenging question is how to measure the impact of different constructs and the interdependencies between them. This would pave the ground for engineering serious games.

3. ADAPTIVE EXERGAMES

3.1 Basic Approach

Since the training effects depend on physical and psychological aspects (the training load and motivation of the user), we suggested a theoretical model for the analysis of exergames [2] and an adaptation concept which allows the adaptation of single parameters in order to precisely measure the impact of these parameters [4].

3.2 Framework

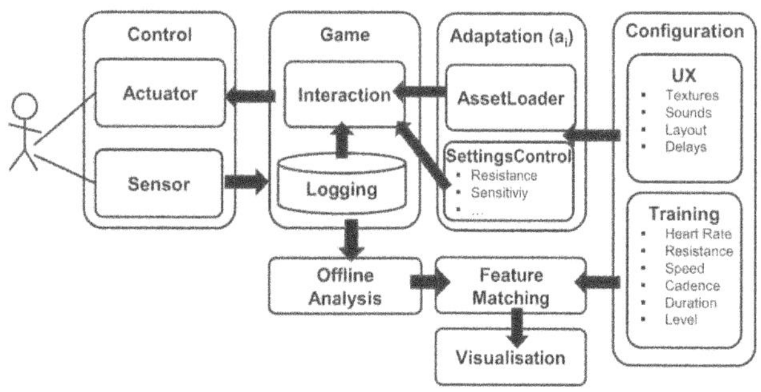

Figure 1: Realtime Adaptation and Analysis Framework StoryTecRT

Figure 2: Settings screen with configuration preview (left) and level with advanced difficulty (right)

StoryTecRT allows the adjustment of single game attributes a_i (Figure 1) in order to change the operationalization of psychological constructs and approaches from physical science while all other attributes keep the same characteristic. For example the framework allows to create two configurations A and B of the same game which differ only in visual style or responsiveness. The framework provides different loggers which record the raw input data of the sensor (i.e. Balance Board, Ergometer, 3D-Tracker) as well as game-specific events and physiological data. Based on this data the influence (the difference between the versions A and B during the time of a specific interaction i) can be extracted and compared according to the training rules.

3.3 Prototype BalanceFit

Based on this conceptual framework we developed an exergame (BalanceFit) which focuses on the overall aim fall prevention for elderly people. The hardware consists of a standing frame (Figure 3) to provide stability and safety for gait impaired seniors. As input control we use a Nintendo Wii Balance Board which has four pressure sensors to measure the weight distribution of the player standing on the Balance Board. Out of the weight distribution we calculate the center of pressure (COP) which is used as input to control the game. The goal of the game is to change the declination of a virtual plate by moving the body in order to navigate a ball through a labyrinth into a target (Figure 2). If the player moves in a direction, the COP also moves in this direction and the virtual ball follows immediately. StoryTecRT allows the adaptation of the visual style, the layout of the labyrinth and the sensitivity of the controller.

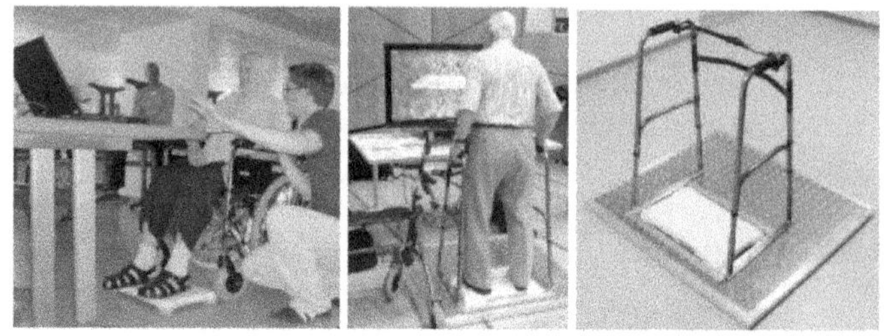

Figure 3: Wheelchair driver (left) and walking frame user (center) while playing BalanceFit, stability frame (right)

3.4 Evaluation Results & Conclusion

We evaluated the acceptance of the prototype balance fit with seniors in a senior's home for a time period for more than one year. Qualitative analyses (interviews and observations) with more than 30 people show that the visual style and the sensitivity play an important role for the accessibility of the overall system. By changing the visual style and increasing the contrast BalanceFit can be adapted for people with visual impairments. Adjusting the sensitivity of the control allows the game to be played by seniors with heterogeneous skills. This way the game is successfully playable by young and fit people as well as by people with small and bigger gait impairments. Even wheelchair drivers (Figure 3) are able to play BalanceFit as long as they theirs legs are not completely paralyzed. The results show the acceptance of the multimedia training system by elderly people. The adaption concept improves the accessibility of the system. The next step is the investigation of the effects of single parameters.

4. ACKNOWLEDGEMENTS

We thank the Wilhelmine-Thoss Foundation for supporting the development of the system BalanceFit.

5. REFERENCES

[1] Göbel, S., Hardy, S., Wendel, S., Mehm, F., Steinmetz, R. 2010: *Serious Games for Health - Personalized Exergames. Proceedings ACM Multimedia 2010*, p. 1663-1666.

[2] Hardy, S., Göbel, S., Gutjahr, M., Wiemeyer, J., Steinmetz, R. 2011. *Adaptation Model for Indoor Exergames. International Journal of Computer Science in Sport,* Vol. 10.

[3] Mehm, F., Hardy, S., Göbel, S. Steinmetz, R., 2011. *Collaborative Authoring of Serious Games for Health. MM '11 Proceedings of the 19th ACM international conference on Multimedia* , p. 807-808, ACM New York.

[4] Wiemeyer, J., Hardy, S. *Serious Games and motor learning - concepts, evidence, technology*. Bredl, K. & Bösche, W, *Serious Digital Games, MUVE and MMORPG in Adult Education and Health Care: Research, Reviews, Case Studies, and Lessons Learned,* IGI-Global.

AdVisual: A Visual-based Advertising System

Chao Dong
The Chinese University of Hong Kong
ndc.forward@gmail.com

Shifeng Chen
Shenzhen Institutes of Advanced Technology, CAS, China
shifeng.chen@siat.ac.cn

Xiaoou Tang
The Chinese University of Hong Kong
xtang@ie.cuhk.edu.hk

ABSTRACT

In this work, we present a visual-based contextual advertising system, AdVisual. It is designed for content service providers to effectively select relevant ads for online videos. First, it will analyze each video and extract high level semantic visual information including specific objects, people, and significant scenes. Then ads highly related to the visual concepts are associated with the corresponding shots. As AdVisual is a user interaction system, it allows users to select favorite ads relevant to the video. By saliency detection, selected ads will be displayed as an overlay window embedded at the non-intrusive part of the shot.

Categories and Subject Descriptors

I.4.9 [**Image Processing and Computer Vision**]: Applications

Keywords

Visual-based contextual advertising, coarse-to-fine approach.

1. INTRODUCTION

Online video sharing becomes more and more popular in recent years. Ads insertion in videos is an important approach for the content provider to make a profit. However, manual matching of video content and ads is very time consuming. Automatic process to semantically link videos with ads becomes necessary.

Various advertising systems have been proposed trying to solve the problem. AdOn [4] and Videosense [5] mainly rely on the text-based strategy, which associate relevant ads with local subtitles and the descriptive texts on the web page. It is a fast and reasonable solution but cannot analyze local visual content. For example, it may be appropriate to show an ad of cars when the leading actor is driving a fancy car. Therefore, image-based advertising systems, such as AdImage [3] and vADeo [7], are proposed to overcome this problem. The visual contents they extract are limited to logos and specific objects only. However, the probability of discovering a target object or a logo in a general video is extremely low, which largely limits their application.

MM'13, October 21–25, 2013, Barcelona, Spain.
ACM 978-1-4503-2404-5/13/10.
http://dx.doi.org/10.1145/2502081.2502256.

(a) (b) (c)

Figure 1: Video-ad visual matching strategies. (a) Product oriented. (b) Actor oriented. (c) Scene oriented. Please zoom by 400% in the electronic version.

In this paper, we introduce a visual-based contextual advertising system, called AdVisual. It adopts a visual-based strategy using the semantic visual information. Firstly, AdVisual could automatically extract visual information including specific objects, people, and significant scenes in each video shot. Then relevant ads will be chosen according to three visual matching strategies (product oriented, actor oriented, and scene oriented). Further more, AdVisual is a user interaction system, which allows service providers select their favorite ads from the calculated results. All the results will be saved in XML files and shown in the display part, which is depicted in Figure 1. The selected ad is shown as an overlay window imbedded on the corresponding shot. Meanwhile, ad window locations are automatically discovered by saliency detection to minimize the intrusiveness to viewers.

2. ADVISUAL SYSTEM DESCRIPTION

2.1 Video-Ad Visual Matching Strategies

The key issue of visual based method is to define the relevance between video shots and ads. In AdVisual, we adopt three video-ad visual matching strategies – product oriented, actor oriented, and scene oriented strategies , shown in Figure 1.

The product oriented strategy is the most effective strategy. When a product or logo appears in the video, ads of the right product will be associated with the corresponding shot. As the probability of a product appearing in a video is pretty low, this strategy could only cover a small amount of ads.

The actor oriented strategy is the second effective one, which associates ads played by the leading role with the shots containing the same actor/actress. But it could not cover ads not played by famous people.

The scene oriented strategy could make up the defects of the above two. Significant scenes could always remind us of some semantic concepts. For example, kitchen could be connected with food and cooking utensils. AdVisual focuses on 15 categories of scenes in the Fifteen Scene Categories dataset [2].

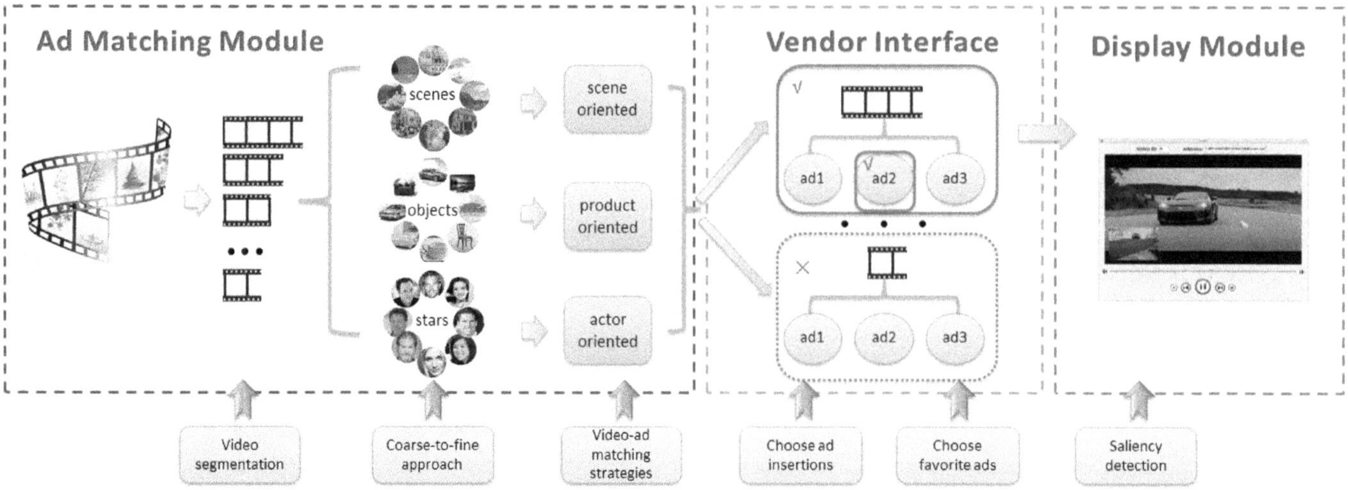

Figure 2: AdVisual System Structure.

All ads should be labeled according to different products, actors, and concepts in advance. Then AdVisual only needs to analyze video content and extract three kinds of high level visual information – objects, people, and scenes.

2.2 Coarse-to-fine Approach

To extract useful visual information, we introduce a coarse-to-fine approach which consists of two steps: the coarse classification step and the fine recognition step.

In the coarse classification phase, we apply fast and robust algorithms to separate all shots into three different groups: close-ups, meaningful scenes, and meaningless scenes. In this paper, we extract "gist" [6] of each keyframe and use an SVM classifier [1] with RBF kernel for classification.

As the coarse classification may not be accurate, we need the fine recognition step to further improve the accuracy. We will apply face recognition on close-ups to identify movie stars. Similarly, object detection and scene recognition algorithms are applied on meaningful scenes to identify specific objects and significant scenes, respectively.

2.3 System Framework

As illustrated in Figure 2, AdVisual consists of three parts – ad matching module, vendor interface, and display module.

In ad matching module, AdVisual is trying to find appropriate ad insertions and select three candidate ads for each insertion. First, the source video is decomposed into a number of shots, and candidate ad insertions are chosen according to the shot length and content continuity. Then, we apply the coarse-to-fine method on all ad insertions to identify specific objects, people, and significant scenes.

The vendor interface is shown in Figure 3. Along the video slide bar, there are several vertical black lines representing the first frame of ad insertions. By clicking on the "Point Button", which is on the lower left of the interface, the slider will jump to the nearest ad insertion, and three relevant ads will be shown on the right side window simultaneously. The users could click on the "Right Button" to prolong the black line, which means this ad insertion is needed; or click on the "Wrong Button" to abandon this ad insertion. Meanwhile, the detected concept is shown on the upper right side, and the favorite ad can be chosen by clicking at the round button besides each ad. After dealing with all videos, users can press

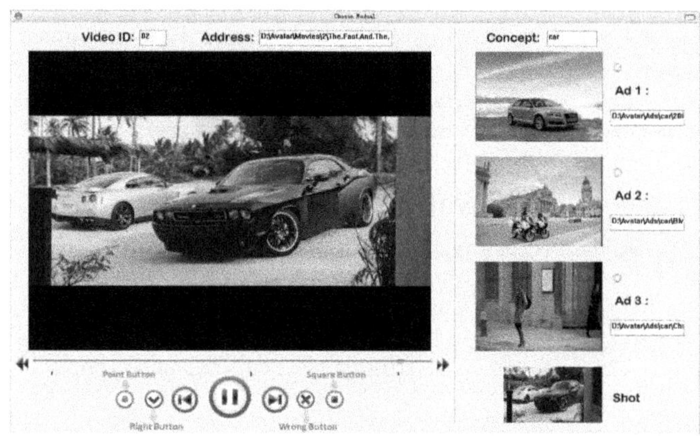

Figure 3: The Vendor Interface.

the "Square Button" to enter the display part, while all chosen results will be saved in an XML file.

In the display module, shown in Figure 1, all chosen ads will be shown as an overlay window embedded in the video. In order not to affect viewers' visual experience, we do saliency region detection to find the most non-intrusive position to embed the ad window.

3. REFERENCES

[1] C.-C. Chang and C.-J. Lin. LIBSVM: A library for support vector machines. *ACM Transactions on Intelligent Systems and Technology*, 2:27:1–27:27, 2011.

[2] S. Lazebnik, C. Schmid, and J. Ponce. Beyond bags of features: Spatial pyramid matching for recognizing natural scene categories. In *Computer Vision and Pattern Recognition, 2006 IEEE Computer Society Conference on*, volume 2, pages 2169–2178. IEEE, 2006.

[3] W. Liao, K. Chen, and W. Hsu. Adimage: video advertising by image matching and ad scheduling optimization. In *ACM SIGIR conference on research and development in information retrieval*, 2008.

[4] T. Mei, J. Guo, X. Hua, and F. Liu. Adon: toward contextual overlay in-video advertising. *Multimedia systems*, 16(4):335–344, 2010.

[5] T. Mei, X. Hua, and S. Li. Videosense: A contextual in-video advertising system. *IEEE Trans. on CSVT*, 19(12):1866–1879, 2009.

[6] A. Oliva and A. Torralba. Modeling the shape of the scene: A holistic representation of the spatial envelope. *IJCV*, 42(3):145–175, 2001.

[7] S. Sengamedu, N. Sawant, and S. Wadhwa. vadeo: video advertising system. In *ACM Multimedia*, 2007.

Multi-Screen Cloud Social TV: Transforming TV Experience into 21st Century

Yichao Jin, Tian Xie, Yonggang Wen
Nanyang Technological University
Nanyang Avenue 50, Singapore
{yjin3,xietian,ygwen}@ntu.edu.sg

Haiyong Xie
University of Science and Technology of China
96 Jinzhai Road Baohe, Hefei, Anhui, China
haiyong.xie@ustc.edu

ABSTRACT

Nowadays, TV experience has been transformed from the traditional "laid-back" video watching experience to a "lean-forward" social and multi-screen experience. In this demo, we design and develop a multi-screen cloud social TV system in response to this trend. Our system is built upon two enabling technologies, including a cloud based back-end infrastructure and a multi-screen front-end application. We demonstrate two key features of our system based on real user scenarios, including a living-room video watching experience with remote viewers, and the video teleportation as an enhanced multi-screen experience.

Categories and Subject Descriptors

[**H.5.1**]: Multimedia Information Systems

Keywords

Cloud; Multi-screen; Social TV; Video Teleportation

1. INTRODUCTION

Recently, the emergence of multi-screen social TV [1, 3, 4] is dramatically transforming the TV experience. First, the traditional "laid-back" video watching experience is integrated with an immersing "lean-forward" social networking experience, resulting in an user-centric living room TV experience [4]. Second, social TV aims to offer ubiquitous services that are available at anytime, on any device, at an affordable price [3]. Finally, with the significant growth of media consumption across multi-screen [1], users want to transfer the ongoing sessions from one device to another, without any interruption of video streaming. Nevertheless, given its highly regarded value, large scale deployment of multi-screen social TV is limited, if not totally absent.

In response to this trend, we design and implement a multi-screen cloud social TV system. Two enabling technologies are developed to build this system. In the back-end, we proposed a cloud-centric media platform [2], which encapsulates a set of media services into a middleware based on virtualized data centers, and exposes them throughout APIs (Application Programming Interfaces). In the front-end, we invented a multi-screen orchestration protocol for user sessions to migrate across different media outlets.

In this demo, we will demonstrate two key features. First, we will show a rich set of social features, where all the occasions of social TV consumption are offered as a one-stop solution. Second, we will show an enhanced multi-screen experience, *video teleportation*, by which viewers can seamlessly move a program in progress across multiple devices with intuitive human computer interaction technologies.

MM '13, October 21 - 25, 2013, Barcelona, Spain
ACM 978-1-4503-2404-5/13/10
http://dx.doi.org/10.1145/2502081.2502257 ...$15.00.

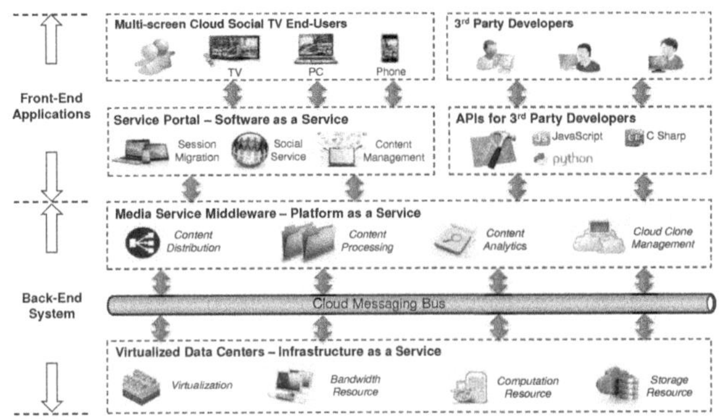

Figure 1: Multi-screen cloud social TV framework

2. SYSTEM DESCRIPTION

Figure 1 presents a systematic view of our multi-screen cloud social TV. This system can be viewed as a layered cloud computing service model, consisting of two fundamental components, including a back-end infrastructure and a front-end application deployment.

Back-End System: The back-end system (i.e., the cloud centric media platform), leverages cloud computing paradigm to provide both infrastructure and platform service.

In the infrastructure layer, the physical servers in datacenters and the intra/inter datacenter networks, are abstracted into a pool of IT resource, including bandwidth, computation and storage, via virtualization techniques. Those resources can be elastically carved out by virtual machines, to meet application demands in an economical fashion, while maintaining a high level of quality of service (QoS). This service is offered to upper layers via a cloud messaging bus.

Figure 2: Multi-screen cloud social TV GUI

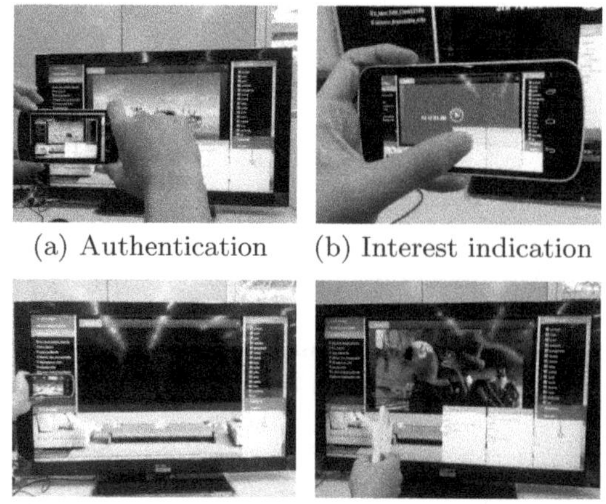

(a) Authentication (b) Interest indication

(c) Session migrated (d) Throw session back

Figure 3: Video Teleportation

In the platform layer, we encapsulate a set of media services (e.g., content distribution, processing, and analytics), into a middleware, on top of the infrastructure. We also integrate those services into a cloud clone management module, which is the key technology to support multi-screen social experience. In particular, each user is represented by a virtual machine, serving as his proxy in the cloud, to manage all the associated devices and session information. Such a virtual machine is called cloud clone. All the platform services are exposed to upper layers via APIs.

Front-End Application: Multi-screen social TV is the pilot application built on our platform. We develop various application services (e.g., session migration, social functions, and content management), based on the cloud clones. Those services are accessible to the end users via web based interfaces. In this way, we hide all the intelligence in the cloud. Thus learning process for the end users can be minimized, and no special equipment is required on the user side.

We will soon release a set of APIs in different language versions including Javascript, python and C#. As such, any third party can use them to develop new applications.

3. DEMONSTRATION

We will demonstrate two key features of our multi screen social TV system, including a rich set of social TV modalities and the video teleportation as an enhanced multi-screen experience, based on real user scenario.

Rich Social TV Experience: At the weekend, Peter is enjoying his TV time via multi-screen cloud social TV (the user interface is shown in Figure 2) at home. Among various content resources, including video on local disk, video on the cloud, OTT videos and live streaming, Peter chooses a video to watch. During his watching, he finds his best friend Cathy is online among his friend list in Facebook and Google+. Peter says "hi" to Cathy via text chat box, and invites her to view the same video from the same point at a same pace. Now they can discuss the content they are both watching via video chat from different locations. They can even collaboratively edit the original content by inserting text, pictures and audio, and generate new contents.

Video Teleportation: Peter suddenly realizes that he has a family party tonight, and he has to go to the supermarket at once. However, he never wants to give up the chance to enjoy a video and have a nice discussion with his best friend. Fortunately, our system can help him to teleport this experience from TV screen to his mobile device.

Peter first scans the TV screen, which contains a digital watermarker, to get authentication on his smartphone (Figure 3-(a)). Once his phone is authenticated, a synchronized image will be displayed on the phone screen. Peter then chooses to bring away the video chat and content viewing parts with him (Figure3-(b)). Finally, he simply flips his phone away from the TV to grab the sessions, and continues to enjoy the video and chatting on his smartphone (Figure3-(c)). When Peter returns back home, he simply "throws" his phone towards the TV, and the sessions also immediately get back to the TV screen (Figure3-(d)).

4. CONCLUSIONS

In this demo, we presented our multi-screen cloud social TV system as a novel paradigm to transform the TV experience. It adopts the cloud computing paradigm to encapsulate media services in the back-end, and provides attractive multi-screen and social features in the front-end. This system had been deployed on top of a private cloud at Nanyang Technological University. Upon its debut, it had been featured in more than 1600 news articles from 29-plus countries, resulting in a worldwide media coverage. A beta version of this system will be soon exposed to over 200 students.

5. REFERENCES

[1] Google. The new multi-screen world: Understanding cross-platform consumer behavior. `http://services.google.com/fh/files/misc/multiscreenworld_final.pdf`, 2012.

[2] Y. Jin and et al. Codaas: An experimental cloud-centric content delivery platform for user-generated contents. In *IEEE ICNC*, pages 934–938, 2012.

[3] R. Martin, A. L. Santos, M. Shafran, H. Holtzman, and M.-J. Montpetit. NeXtream: a multi-device, social approach to video content consumption. In *IEEE CCNC*, pages 1–5, 2010.

[4] M. Montpetit and M. Médard. Social television: Enabling technologies and architectures. *Proceedings of the IEEE*, pages 1395–1399, 2012.

“Wow! You Are So Beautiful Today!”

Luoqi Liu[1], Hui Xu[2], Si Liu[1], Junliang Xing[1], Xi Zhou[2],Shuicheng Yan[1]

[1]Department of Electrical and Computer Engineering, National University of Singapore

[2]Chongqing Institute of Green and Intelligent Tecnology, Chinese Academy of Science

{liuluoqi, dcslius, elexing, eleyans}@nus.edu.sg, {xuhui, zhouxi}@cigit.ac.cn

ABSTRACT

In this demo, we present Beauty e-Experts, a fully automatic system for hairstyle and facial makeup recommendation and synthesis. Given a user-provided frontal facial image with short/bound hair and no/light makeup, the Beauty e-Experts system can not only recommend the most suitable hairstyle and makeup, but also show the synthesis effects. Two problems are considered for the Beauty e-Experts system: what to recommend and how to wear, which describe a similar process of selecting and applying hairstyle and cosmetics in our daily life. For the what-to-recommend problem, we propose a multiple tree-structured super-graphs model to explore the complex relationships among the beauty attributes, beauty-related attributes and image features, and then based on this model, the most suitable beauty attributes for a given facial image can be efficiently inferred. For the how-to-wear problem, a facial image synthesis module is designed to seamlessly blend the recommended hairstyle and makeup into the user facial image. Extensive experimental evaluations and analysis on testing images well demonstrate the effectiveness of the proposed system.

Categories and Subject Descriptors

H.3.3 [**Information Search and Retrieval**]: Retrieval models; I.2.6 [**Learning**]: Knowledge acquisition

Keywords

Beauty Recommendation, Beauty Synthesis, Multiple Tree-structured Super-graphs Model

1. INTRODUCTION

Hairstyle and makeup are two main factors that influence people’s judgment about one’s look, especially for female. By choosing proper hairstyle and makeup, one may look more attractive. This demo presents a novel Beauty e-Experts system, which helps users to select beauty items automatically and produces the synthesized visual effects. The beauty items, including hairstyle and makeup products, are indexed and represented by *beauty attributes* in this system. As shown in Fig. 1, a user first inputs an instantly captured or uploaded facial image. If one chooses the recommendation mode, several suitable hairstyles and makeup items are recommended automatically. Alternatively, the user enters the optional mode to select beauty items. After that, the synthesis results are shown with selected beauty items. We are the first to explore a comprehensive system considering both hairstyle and makeup recommendation in the multimedia area.

MM’13, October 21–October 25, 2013, Barcelona, Spain.

ACM 978-1-4503-2404-5/13/10.

http://dx.doi.org/10.1145/2502081.2502258.

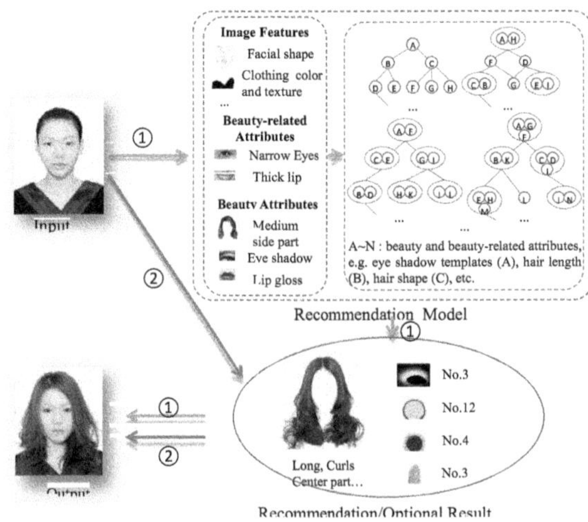

Figure 1: System flowchart. ① recommendation mode: given a user facial image, some suitable hairstyles and makeups are recommended. ② optional mode: the user can select the items that he/she prefers optionally. Then, a set of corresponding synthesis results are shown on the screen.

The recommendation objective of the Beauty e-Experts system is to suggest the most suitable *beauty attributes*, which index real hairstyle and makeup items. The beauty attributes contain 9 types, such as hair length, lip color. The beauty attributes are highly person-dependent. The effects of the same beauty products applied onto different faces may vary dramatically. Thus we define 21 types of *beauty-related attributes*, such as eye shape and mouth width, to describe the personal characteristics. The main challenge of the Beauty e-Experts system is how to model the complex relationships among different beauty and beauty-related attributes for reliable recommendation. To explore the complex relationships among these attributes, we propose to learn a multiple tree-structured super-graphs model. We use its multiple tree-structured approximation to reserve the most important relationships and make the inference procedure tractable. Different from the recommendation mode, the beauty attributes can also be selected manually in the optional mode. After the beauty attributes are obtained in

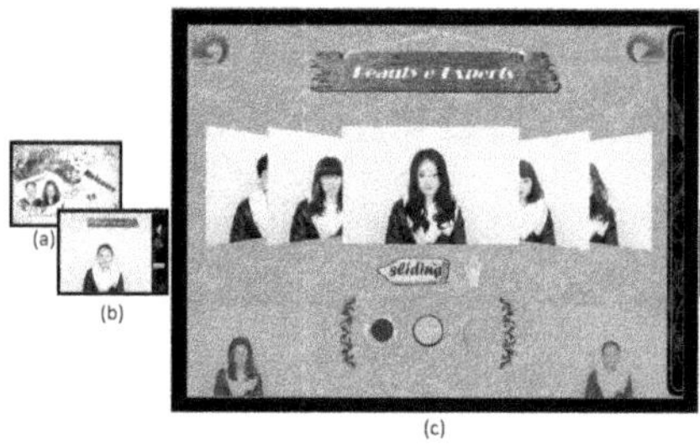

Figure 2: The interface of Beauty e-Experts system. (a) welcome screen, (b) photo taking screen, (c) recommendation screen, (d) optional screen.

either recommendation or optional mode, an effective and efficient facial image synthesis module is conducted based on the selected beauty attributes, and the results are sent back to the user.

2. SYSTEM INTERFACE

The Beauty e-Experts system has multiple screens. After entering the welcome screen in Fig.2(a), the user chooses to take or upload a short/bound hair and non-makeup photo, shown in Fig.2(b). If choosing to take photo, the user makes the photo-taking gesture and waits 3 seconds countdown. After that, the user can choose to enter the recommendation screen or optional screen. (1) If the user enters the recommendation screen, as shown in Fig.2(c), top 5 recommended results are listed in the center of the screen. The user can swipe to check each synthesis result with the corresponding recommended beauty items. Moreover, hairstyles only and makeup only results are shown on the left and right bottom corner, respectively. (2) If the user enters the optional screen, as shown in Fig.2(d), he/she can touch the icon bar on the top of the screen to select the hairstyles and makeup items. Note that in the Beauty e-Experts system, Kinect is used for the interactive operation, due to its touch-free control, and high recognition rate of users' gestures.

3. SYSTEM WORKFLOW

Given a testing image, we extract 4 types of image features from the face and clothing region based on face detection. All features are concatenated to form a feature vector of 173 dimension after Principal Component Analysis.

The values of 9 beauty attributes are obtained by different methods. Some are set manually (such as hair length), some are clustered by k-means algorithm (such as hair color), and the others are extracted by image matting [3] (such as eye shadow shape attribute). The original hairstyle templates (sets of hair beauty attributes) are also extracted by image matting. What's more, we manually label 21 beauty-related attributes, which mainly focus on the facial shapes and clothing properties, to narrow the gap between the beauty attributes and the image features.

Based on all these attributes, we propose a multiple tree-structured super-graphs model to explore the complex relationships among these attributes for recommendation. The model describes the mapping rules among the visual features, beauty-related attributes and beauty attributes. These tree-structured super-graphs can be considered as different recommendation experts, each of which is good at modeling some kinds of relationships. The recommendation results generated by these experts are voted to form the final result. In the demo, we offer the top 5 recommended beauty items associated with beauty attributes, as shown in Fig. 2(c). With the recommended or optionally selected beauty items, hair template and eye shadow shape attribute are aligned to facial image [1]. Guided filter [2] is applied on image lightness channel L^* to imitate the smoothing effect of foundation, and other recommended color beauty attributes are fused to the image by alpha blending. In all, Beauty e-Experts can offer reliable recommendation results, and also produce natural and appealing synthesis effects. For details, please refer to [4].

4. DEMONSTRATION

In Fig. 3, we compare the recommendation results of our model with three baselines (latent SVM [5], multi-class SVM and neural network). The performance is measured by Normalized Discounted Cumulative Gain (NDCG). From the results, we can observe that our model has best performance, because our model can express complex relationships among different attributes. Additionally, by employing multiple tree-structured super-graphs, our model tends to obtain more robust recommendation results.

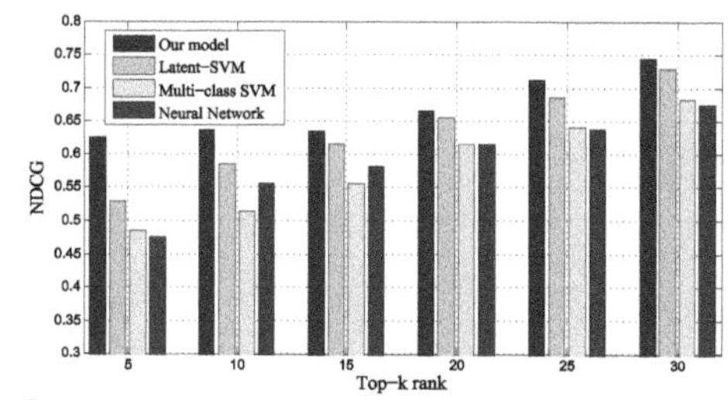

Figure 3: Comparision between our model and baselines. The horizontal axis is top-k, and the vertical axis is NDCG.

We evaluate the recommendation and synthesis results of Beauty e-Experts. As shown in Fig. 4, these results still look natural with a variety of style changes, which demonstrates that Beauty e-Experts is an automatic and intelligent recommendation and synthesis system in the beauty industry.

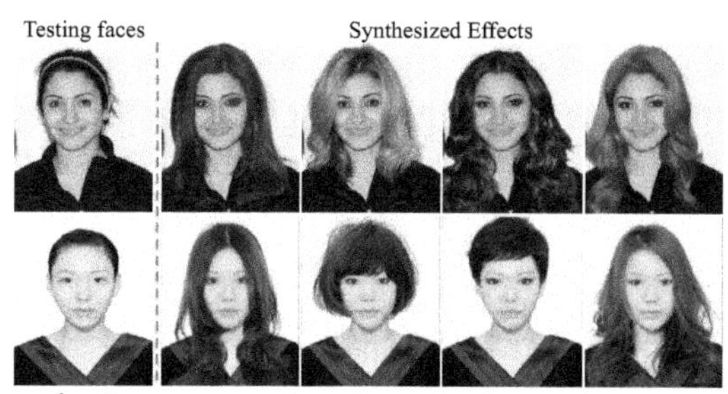

Figure 4: Some examples of synthesis results with the top 4 recommended hairstyles and makeup.

5. ACKNOWLEDGMENTS

This research is supported by the Singapore National Research Foundation under its International Research Centre @Singapore Funding Initiative and administered by the IDM Programme Office. Also it is partially supported by Singapore Ministry of Education under research Grant MOE2010-T2-1-087 and the "Extreme Facial Analysis" project from Ministry of Home Affairs.

6. REFERENCES

[1] F. Bookstein. Principal warps: thin-plate splines and the decomposition of deformations. *PAMI*, 11(6):567–585, 1989.

[2] K. He, J. Sun, and X. Tang. Guided image filtering. In *ECCV*, 2010.

[3] A. Levin, D. Lischinski, and Y. Weiss. A closed-form solution to natural image matting. *PAMI*, 30(2):228–242, 2008.

[4] L. Liu, H. Xu, J. Xing, S. Liu, X. Zhou, and S. Yan. "Wow! you are so beautiful today!". In *ACM MM*, 2013.

[5] S. Liu, J. Feng, Z. Song, T. Zhang, H. Lu, C. Xu, and S. Yan. "Hi, magic closet, tell me what to wear". In *ACM MM*, 2012.

OSCOR: An Orientation Sensor Data Correction System for Mobile Generated Contents

Guanfeng Wang[†], Beomjoo Seo[†], Yifang Yin[†], Roger Zimmermann[†], Zhijie Shen[‡]
[†]School of Computing, National University of Singapore. [‡]Hortonworks Inc.
[†]{wanggf,seobj,yifang,rogerz}@comp.nus.edu.sg [‡]zshen@hortonworks.com

ABSTRACT

In addition to positioning data, other sensor information – such as orientation data, have become a useful and powerful contextual feature. Such auxiliary information can facilitate higher-level semantic description inferences in many multimedia applications, *e.g.*, video tagging and video summarization. However, sensor data collected from current mobile devices is often not accurate enough for upstream multimedia analysis. An effective orientation data correction system for mobile multimedia content has been an elusive goal so far. Here we present a system, termed *Oscor*, which aims to improve the accuracy of noisy orientation sensor measurements generated by mobile devices during image and video recording. We provide a user-friendly camera interface to facilitate the gathering of additional information, which enables the correction process on the server-side. Geographic field-of-view (FOV) visualizations based on the original and corrected sensor data help users understand the corrected contextual information and how the erroneous data possibly may affect further processes.

Categories and Subject Descriptors

H.3.4 [**Information Storage and Retrieval**]: Systems and Software; I.4.8 [**Image Processing and Computer Vision**]: Scene Analysis - Sensor Fusion

Keywords

Mobile multimedia, camera orientation, data correction, digital compass

1. INTRODUCTION

With today's prevalence of camera-equipped mobile devices and their convenience of worldwide sharing, the multimedia content generated from mobile platforms, *e.g.*, smartphones and tablets, have become one of the primary contributors to the media-rich web. The top three most popular cameras in the Flickr community are smartphone models [1].

MM'13, October 21–25, 2013, Barcelona, Spain.
ACM 978-1-4503-2404-5/13/10.
http://dx.doi.org/10.1145/2502081.2502259.

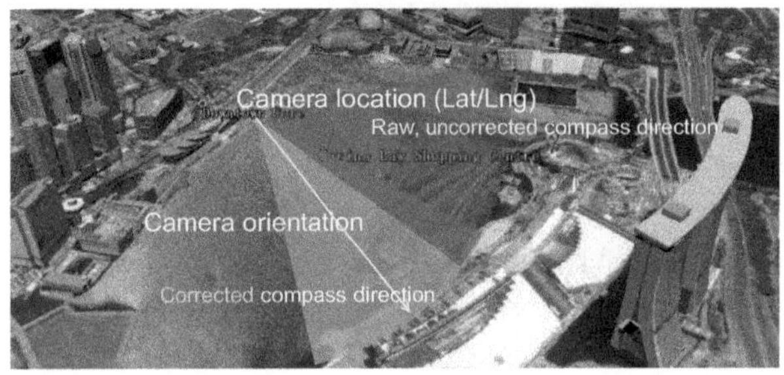

Figure 2: Illustration of inaccurate raw camera orientation data.

Considering the increasing number of new sensors integrated into these devices, a large amount of auxiliary sensor information other than locations is available for both research and commercial utilization. Very useful are the orientation data measured by a digital compass in conjunction with still images and video frames [3].

Researchers have emphasized the importance of rich metadata that surrounds a multimedia object. The orientation information has so far been employed in video encoding complexity reduction, photo organization, video indexing, tagging and summarization. From our experiments, these research studies and related applications are mostly not error resilient with respect to incorrect sensor data input. However, unfortunately most sensor information collected from phones or tablets is not highly accurate due to varying surrounding environmental conditions during data acquisition, and the use of low-cost, consumer-grade sensors. As illustrated in Figure 2, the red pie-shaped slice represents the raw, uncorrected orientation measurement and the green slice indicates the corrected orientation data. As shown, the raw data directly from the smartphone may be extremely incorrect. In some cases the discrepancy is more than 90 degrees from the ground-truth value.

To solve this inaccuracy issue effectively we introduce *Oscor*, which corrects orientation measurements for still images and video frames based on geographic analysis and image processing. Our system collects visual landmark information and matches it against GIS data sources to infer a target landmark's real geo-location. By knowing the geographic coordinates of the captured landmark and the camera, we are able to calculate the corrected orientation measurements. With regards to video recording, in order to minimize the user interaction, we compute the horizontal motion flows and perform landmark matching between sampled frames to interpolate highly accurate orientation data for every frame.

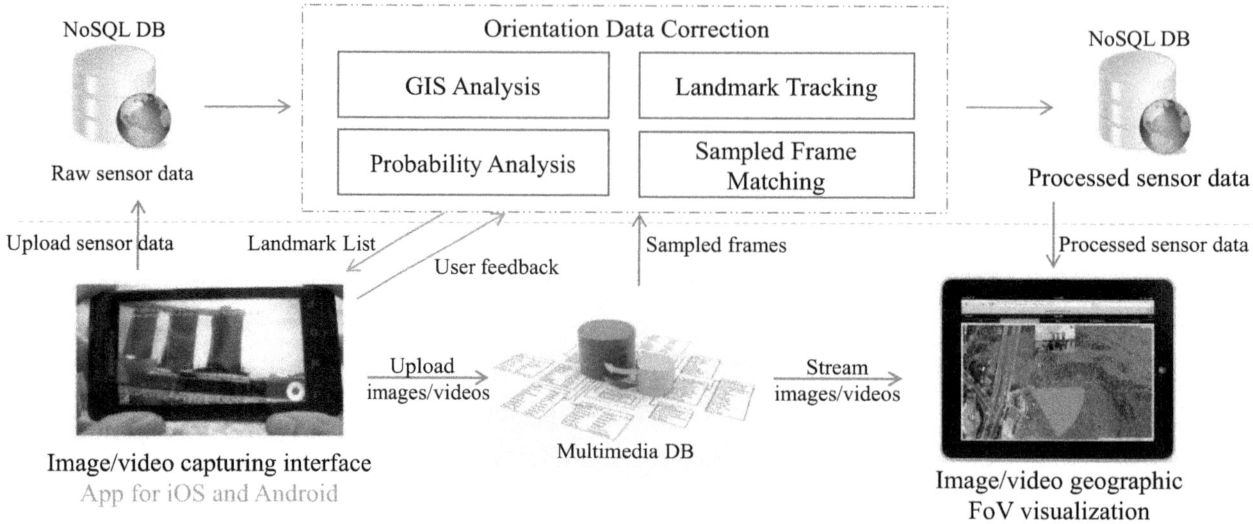

Figure 1: Overview of the *Oscor* system.

2. SYSTEM ARCHITECTURE

Figure 1 illustrates *Oscor*'s overall architecture. For media capture, we provide a camera app which acquires location and orientation information concurrently from multiple sensors while taking images or recording videos [2]. Moreover, our app presents a convenient interface to gather extra information, *e.g.*, a landmark scene position and its name, without requiring cumbersome input from users. For still image capture, we allow users to indicate the width boundary of a close and conspicuous structure by moving their fingers along a building's vertical edges on the just-taken picture. For the video, users can also indicate a pair of perpendicular lines with the same touch-and-move operation during recording. After receiving this edge information on the server side, we convert the users' input of a landmark's position from the pixel index domain into the geospatial domain, and subsequently perform GIS analysis.

We employ OpenStreetMap (OSM) as our GIS reference database and query related building locations and their 2D shape polygons within a certain distance range to the camera position [3]. From the 2D shape information, our system computes each building's width value in the image's x-dimension from the camera's point of view. Afterwards, we utilize the building width information extracted from pixel level, the building distance to the camera from the GIS analysis, and the initial orientation measurement collected from the mobile-embedded digital compass, to build a 3D Gaussian model calculating each building's probability of being the landmark in the user's still picture or video frame. Subsequently, Our system returns the top K landmark names back to the user for selection of the correct one. With the known building reference in both the geospatial and pixel domains, we can accurately estimate the camera pose on a 2D map, and hence output the corrected camera orientation data for the corresponding image/frame.

When recording video, *Oscor* continues to track the interesting feature points detected around the indicated landmark to calculate the positions of this building in the next several seconds of frames. We use an affine model to estimate a referenced landmark's 2D transformation and extract motion vector information in the horizontal axis to compute orientation values for this portion of frames. Since the camera may be moving as time progresses, we perform landmark object matching between sampled frames. For every new matched frame, our system updates the camera coordinates and landmark positions and carries out the previous three steps of analysis again to correct the orientation data.

3. DEMONSTRATION

On the app we have added a transparent overlay on top of the camera interface and leverage multi-touch gestures to collect the building position information indicated by users. After a user uploads the raw sensor data via an HTTP link, the server efficiently stores and indexes this information into a NoSQL MongoDB database.

The *Oscor* user interface visualizes the static or moving field-of-views of images and videos, which allows users to experience fused video browsing based on geographic properties. On a Google Maps canvas multiple images/videos are presented as pins. When a user clicks or touches a pin, a map-overlay image viewer/video player is launched and the video is rendered from the designated starting location. During video playback, the camera's current location and viewable scenes are animated along the corresponding GPS trajectory. To help users visualize the corrected contextual information and how the erroneous data possibly effects further processes, two viewable scenes based on asynchronously retrieved raw and corrected camera orientation data are rendered on the same interface.

4. ACKNOWLEDGMENT

This research has been supported by the Singapore National Research Foundation under its International Research Centre @ Singapore Funding Initiative and administered by the IDM Programme Office.

5. REFERENCES

[1] Flickr: Camera Finder. `www.flickr.com/cameras`. [Online; accessed April-2013].

[2] B. Seo, J. Hao, and G. Wang. Sensor-rich Video Exploration on A Map Interface. In *ACM Multimedia*, 2011.

[3] Z. Shen, S. Arslan Ay, S. H. Kim, and R. Zimmermann. Automatic Tag Generation and Ranking for Sensor-rich Outdoor Videos. In *ACM Multimedia*, 2011.

OTMedia: The French TransMedia News Observatory

Nicolas Hervé[1], Marie-Luce Viaud[1], Jérôme Thièvre[1], Agnès Saulnier[1], Julien Champ[2], Pierre Letessier[1], Olivier Buisson[1], Alexis Joly[2]

nherve@ina.fr, mlviaud @ina.fr

[1] INA, 4 avenue de l'Europe
94366 Bry Sur Marne, France

[2] INRIA Zenith, 161 rue Ada
34095 Montpellier, France

ABSTRACT

Who said What, Where and How? How are images, video and stories spreading out? Who produces the information? OTMedia addresses these questions by collecting, enriching and analysing continuously more than 1500 streams of French media from TV Radio, Web, AFP, and Twitter. Two studies on media produced by end users with the OTMedia framework are presented.

Categories and Subject Descriptors
H2.8. Data mining, H.2.4. Multimedia Databases H.3.1. Indexing methods, H.3.3.Clustering, Retrieval models

General Terms
Experimentation, Algorithms

Keywords
Multimedia, Datamining, Indexing Retrieval, natural language processing, visual search

1. INTRODUCTION

The world of media is strongly impacted by the last decade's digital evolutions: means of production, publishing, broadcasting broaden and users' practices evolve, changing on the way established economic rules. Social networks, Wikipedia, tweets may report news events before traditional actors of the domain, questioning their role in this new landscape. Media studies focus more often on a single media [1], on small data sets [2], or on a specific aspect [3]. The ambition of the TransMedia Observatory is to make the relationship between the Internet, press, radio and television broadcasts and twitter more intelligible, viewable and searchable, at a macro-level of analysis. The paper describes briefly the framework of the project and presents two studies developed by sociologists and professional users.

2. DATA COLLECT AND ENRICHMENT

The collect gathers more than 1500 streams of French media (12 TV, 8 radio, AFP contents, web RSS streams (90 press sites, 339 blogs, 62 institutional sites, 263 political party, 646 politicians, 14 radio, 17 TV, 19 ONG), that represent 4 million documents from July 2011 to December 2013. Collect, stream segmentation and archiving processes are based on the tools developed by the French Legal Deposit for Radio, TV and the Web. Each document's contents are then segmented and analyzed according to their modalities (text, image or video). Named entities, salient words and citations are extracted for textual data. Videos are segmented with image content detectors and images are described with up to 5000 SIFTS per image. Audio files are transcribed. This metadata is then stored in 3 indexes: an SQL DB, SOLR and a specific visual index [4]. Twitter is collected with a specific policy: a set of initial twitter accounts dealing with news has been selected as a kernel. The collect adapts to follow emerging tags related to news events.

MM'13, October 21–25, 2013, Barcelona, Spain.
ACM 978-1-4503-2404-5/13/10.
http://dx.doi.org/10.1145/2502081.2502260

3. TEXT AND VISUAL SEARCH

Documents and sources may be accessed by textual or visual requests from a dedicated web interface (cf fig 1). Partial visual queries may be performed on 6 millions images by selecting interactively a zone in the current image. Counts on specific fields are presented to users to help their understanding of the current set content. Corpuses may be generated, viewed and filtered either document by document from the sources or by filtering fields. Moreover, corpuses may be visualized in detail in a chronological timeline.

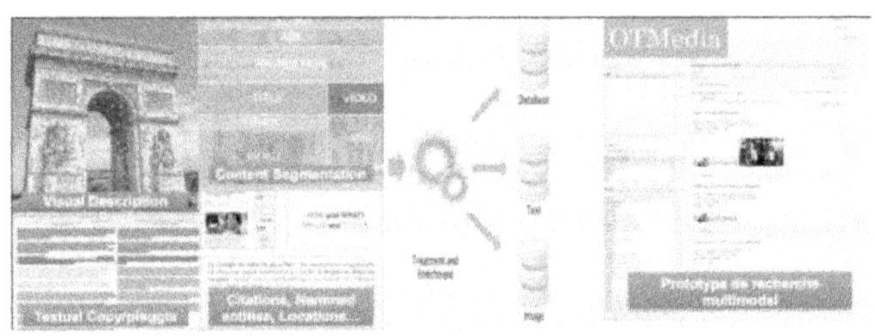

fig 1: Enrichment processes, indexing and the online multimodal search interface.

4. DATAMINING

Visual Object discovery has been performed on about 3000 hours of video and 3 million images. Based on the technology described in [6], a dedicated sampling method associated with a precise CBIR system process generates a graph of visually similar zones in the whole corpus. The graph is then clustered, allowing the emergence of sets of contents that share visual objects (cf fig 2). Finally, textual labels are computed for visual clusters with classical *tf/idf* word saliency on the associated text content. Clusters that represent a good dispersion on media and content providers reflect visual news events while other characterize ads or specific visual attributes of media channels (logo or settings).

Copy and plagiarism detection are computed to study not only citation propagation but also how much AFP provides news to the press, television and radio stations (cf fig 4).

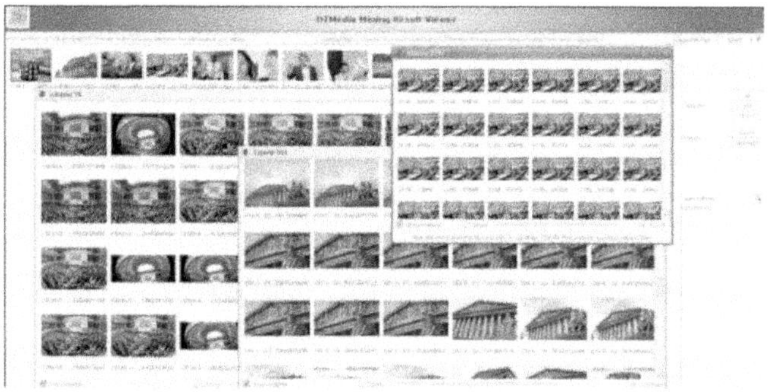

Fig2: Search on "National Assembly" gathers visual clusters illustrating articles on laws and deputy work

5. USER STUDIES

The prototype has been used for sociological and professional studies. The ONU-Alliance of Civilization was interested to know how media in France were talking about immigration in the year of the presidential campaign. The analysis of the events linked to this thematic (fig 3) and a manual tagging of the tone of the articles conclude that a) immigration is a hot topic during electoral campaigns, and b) In general journalists report on migration in a politically correct fashion (according to the Universal Declaration of Human Rights). Unlike the previous elections, the major topics were not security and terrorism but the vote for foreigners in local elections and the eventual limitation of economic immigration.

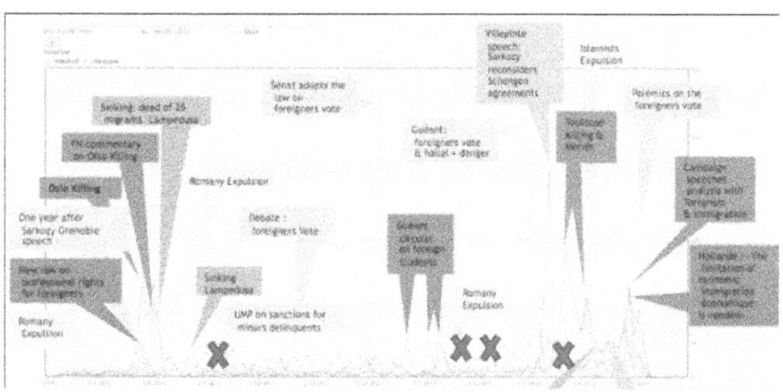

Fig3: Events linked to immigration in France in 2011/12. Notice the increase of the peaks 2 months before the presidential elections (last part of the graphic). Red crosses mark events that occur abroad and were out of the scope of the study.

The study, based on the copy rate of AFP for 5 free online web sites (fig 2), shows the content policy of these news providers. 67% of Orange content comes directly from AFP (notice how the curve is flat), while the number of articles containing AFP content on Yahoo France is very low and applies to only a very small percentage of the content (Yahoo canceled its AFP subscription in 2012). The curves from the 3 news providers show that Rue 89 produces mainly original articles (only 12% of them contain short AFP content), 20% of "20 minutes" production comes directly from AFP. The "Huffington Post" curve decreases strongly showing that most of the articles borrow some AFP content, but this content is incorporated into original longer articles.

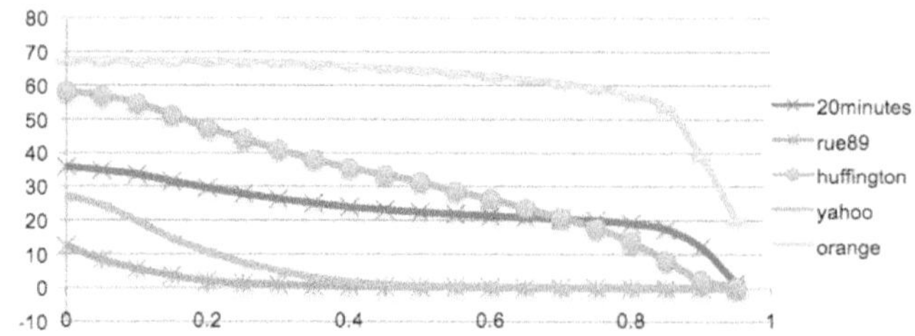

Fig4: The y axis represents the percentage of documents of the media stream, the x axis represents the copy rate. This graphic illustrates the Percentage of articles of French online free sites that borrow a part X of their content to AFP.

The visual object discovery has been used to produce the visual event of the week and to discover political mockery in campaign posters. With this prototype, sociologists are studying the evolution of vocabulary around major events such as the "Toulouse Killing" in March 2012.

More than 10 researchers or professionals are working with the prototype, 40 students are using it to explore how French media treats innovation. This user experimentation shows that the prototype and the functionalities are easy to use.

6. CONCLUSION

The strengths of this project lie in the synergy between IT and social science research, the development of a set of software modules addressing all modalities, together with resources diversity and volume. Current studies already trace the news stories and circulation but further work will be needed to answer more complex questions: is the information diversity increasing? How is news content evolving with acquisitions and editorial board concentration?

7. ACKNOWLEDGMENTS

Our thanks to the other project partners, LIA, Syllabs, AFP, CIM and LATTS, the French National Agency and Cap Digital.

8. REFERENCES

[1] http://emm.newsexplorer.eu/NewsExplorer/home/en/latest.html

[2] PEW Research Center's Project for Excellence in Journalism, 2010, How News Happens: A Study of the News Ecosystem of One American City

[3] Leskovec ; J Backstrom L Kleinberg J 2009 « Meme-Tracking and the dynamics of th enews cycle » KDD'09 Paris.

[4] P. Letessier, O.Buisson, A Joly, 2012, *Scalable mining of small visual objects* In Proceedings of ACM Multimedia, Pages 599-608,.

[5] A. Joly, O Buisson, Logo retrieval with a contrario visual query expension, In Proceedings of ACM Multimedia pages 581-584, 2009.

TEEVE Endpoint: Towards the Ease of 3D Tele-Immersive Application Development

Pengye Xia, Klara Nahrstedt
Department of CS
University of Illinois, Urbana-Champaign
{pxia3, klara}@illinois.edu

ABSTRACT

We present TEEVE Endpoint, which is a runtime engine to handle the creation, transmission and rendering of 3D Tele-immersive (3DTI) data and provides application programming interfaces (APIs) to developers to easily create 3DTI applications.

Categories and Subject Descriptors

J.7 [**Computer Applications**]: Real time

Keywords

3D Tele-immersion

1. INTRODUCTION

3D Tele-immersion (3DTI) system enables remote users to interact in the virtual 3D space, which has found huge potentials in many applications (e.g., 3D interactive video gaming [1] and remote therapy [2]). A typical 3DTI system is composed of several geographically distributed sites. Each site captures the 3D data of its user using multiple 3D cameras and transmits the data to every other sites over the network at a certain frame rate. Given the data from all sites, each site renders everything into a virtual 3D space to provide visual feedback for users to interact with each other in real-time.

In this work, we present TEEVE Endpoint, which is a runtime engine to handle the 3DTI data and provide application programming interfaces (APIs) to developers to easily create 3DTI applications. As shown in Figure 1, the architecture of the runtime engine contains several modules. The *capturing module* takes the raw data from 3D cameras and generates 3DTI data in real-time. The *resource management module* takes the 3DTI data to compose 3DTI frames which are disseminated over the network to the remote sites through the *transmission module*. The 3DTI data (captured locally or received remotely through transmission module) is passed to the *rendering module* for displaying the visual feedback. The *3DTI game engine* sits on top of the rendering module to control the rendering behavior in response to the events detected within the system. These events include the change of system states (e.g., start/stop of the runtime engine), the collisions between the objects and the arrival of user interaction input from the *user-interaction module*. The 3DTI game engine further provides API to the developers to register callback functions for those events to define the rendering behavior.

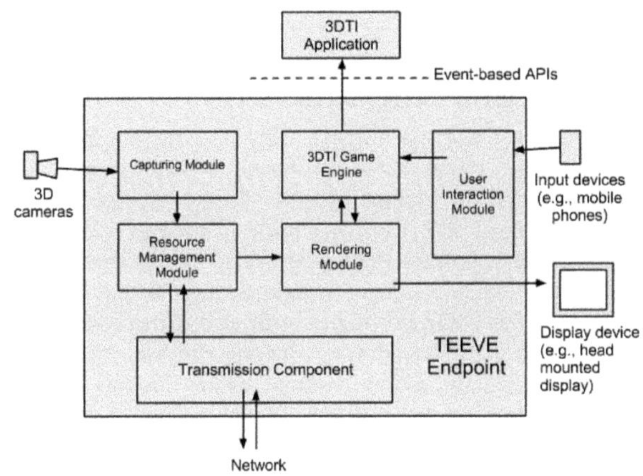

Figure 1: Illustration of TEEVE Endpoint architecture.

TEEVE Endpoint has significantly eased the procedure of creating multi-site 3DTI applications. This is because the capturing, transmission, rendering of 3DTI data are all handled by the runtime engine and hidden from the developers. As a result, the development task is simplified into writing callback functions to define rendering behavior through the event-based APIs.

In summary, TEEVE Endpoint advances the previous 3DTI system design in three major perspectives:

- *3DTI game engine and programming interface for 3DTI applications:* The 3DTI game engine in TEEVE Endpoint provides APIs for developers to easily create 3DTI applications. Developers only have to define callback functions to handle various events detected by the game engine.
- *Real-time object decomposition/reconstruction and object-level resource management framework:* the captured 3D data is decomposed in real-time into semantic

MM'13, October 21–25, 2013, Barcelona, Spain.
ACM 978-1-4503-2404-5/13/10.
http://dx.doi.org/10.1145/2502081.2502261.

meaningful objects. Management of resources is applied at object level to achieve more fine-grained control of quality of experience (QoE).

- *Advanced user-interaction solution:* TEEVE Endpoint utilizes Kinect camera and mobile phones to achieve accurate tracking of the user movement. The tracking capability enables users to interact with the system using natural gestures and movement. Moreover, by combining the use of head tracking and head-mounted display, the system provides virtual reality type of visual feedback to the users.

2. DETAILED DESCRIPTION OF TEEVE ENDPOINT

2.1 3DTI game engine and APIs

TEEVE Endpoint includes a 3DTI game engine which provides APIs for fast 3DTI application development. The game engine defines various events which are triggered during the running of the runtime engine. These events include the system state changes (e.g., start/stop of runtime engine), the collision detection between various objects (e.g., the collision between the 3DTI data of a user and a graphical object in the virtual world) and the user-interaction input (e.g., the user changes the orientation of his/her joystick). The developers simply write callback functions for these events to define the corresponding rendering behavior.

For example, to write a 3DTI sword fighting game, the developers write the following callback functions. When the runtime engine start event is triggered, a callback function draws a virtual 3D environment. When the hand tracking event is triggered, a callback function draws a virtual sword at the location specified in the event argument. When the event for joystick orientation change is triggered, a callback function updates the orientation of the virtual sword. When collision event between the sword and the 3DTI data of a user is triggered, a callback function updates the score and display the special graphical effect. Clearly, each callback function only handles simple rendering task and can be written easily using standard OpenGL drawing functions.

2.2 Object-level resource management framework

TEEVE Endpoint uses multiple 3D cameras to capture the 3D scene at a local site and periodically produces 3D data at a certain rate. Each camera captures a facet of the 3D scene at a certain time as a pair of a depth image and a color image. Each pixel of the pair of depth and color image generates a 3D point with its texture information. Through calibration, the 3D points from all cameras can be combined into a point cloud to represent the 3D scene.

The 3D data is further decomposed into different objects using computer vision techniques. An object is defined as a part of the data which has semantic meaning in the 3D scene (e.g., head, torso, arm, forearm, thigh and leg for a human). Objects have different importance to the quality of experience (QoE) of a 3DTI application. By applying resource management at object level, we are able to achieve more fine-grained control over QoE given limited resources. For instance, in the scenario where a person standing statically while waving his/her arms, the moving arms have more influence on QoE than the static body. Rather than transmitting all parts of 3D data at fixed frame rate to the remote sites, we can update the arm data more frequently while reducing the frame rate for the body. As a result, we are able to maximize QoE given limited bandwidth resources.

2.3 Advanced user interaction solution

Traditional user interaction (UI) solutions for 3DTI system are often naive. Users rely on input devices such as mouse/keyboard to control the system, while large display is used to provide visual feedback. However, because 3DTI applications often involve frequent user movement, traditional UI solutions are clearly insufficient. Seeing the insufficiency, we have designed and implemented a novel UI solution named TEEVE-Remote.

The components of TEEVE-Remote include Kinect camera, mobile phones and head-mounted display. The Kinect camera and the mobile phone is used to track the translational movement and rotational movement of a particular point on user's body, respectively. The tracking capability allows users to interact with the system using natural gestures and movement. Moreover, we use the combination of the mobile phone, Kinect camera and the head-mounted display to provide truly immersive visual feedback to the users. The movement of the head is tracked by the Kinect and the mobile phone. This information is sent to the renderer to synchronize the viewing point and viewing direction of the user in the virtual world with that in the real world. With the use of head-mounted display, a user sees different images as his/her head moves and thus gains virtual-reality type of visual feedback.

3. DESCRIPTION OF DEMONSTRATION

In this demonstration, we will show a virtual sword fighting game developed using TEEVE Endpoint. The game includes two sites connected within the local area network each of which contains one Kinect camera to capture the 3D scene. The 3D data of each user is transmitted to the other site and rendered in the virtual world. The user in each site wears a head-mounted display with a mobile phone attached to the back. The viewing point and viewing direction of the user in the virtual world is synchronized with that in the real world. As a result, the user sees from his/her first person's point of view in the virtual world. Meanwhile, each user is holding a mobile phone which is used a joystick. A virtual sword is rendered in the virtual world at the hand of the user with the sword direction synchronized with the rotational movement of the mobile phone. In the game, the user tries to hit the remote user using the virtual sword. The opponent's score decreases as hit by the user. The user wins when the opponent's score decreases to zero.

4. REFERENCES

[1] A. Arefin, Z. Huang, R. Rivas, S. Shi, W. Wu, and K. Nahrstedt. Tele-immersive gaming for everybody. In *Proceedings of the 19th ACM international conference on Multimedia*, MM '11, pages 783–784, New York, NY, USA, 2011. ACM.

[2] K. Nahrstedt. 3d teleimmersion for remote injury assessment. In *Proceedings of the 2012 international workshop on Socially-aware multimedia*, SAM '12, pages 21–24, New York, NY, USA, 2012. ACM.

eHeritage of Shadow Puppetry: Creation and Manipulation

Zhenzhen Hu*[1], Min Lin*[2], Si Liu[2], Meng Wang[1], Richang Hong[1],Shuicheng Yan[2]
[1]School of Computer and Information, Hefei University of Technology
[2]ECE Department, National University of Singapore
{huzhen.ice, mavenlin, eric.mengwang, hongrc.hfut}@gmail.com, {dcslius, eleyans}@nus.edu.sg

ABSTRACT

In this demo, we propose the puppetry eHeritage, including a creator module and a manipulator module, to preserve the precious traditional heritage Chinese shadow puppetry. The creator module accepts a frontal face image and a profile face image of the user as input, and automatically generates the corresponding puppet, which looks like the original person and meanwhile preserves typical characteristics of traditional Chinese shadow puppetry. The manipulator module can accept the script provided by the user as input and automatically generate the motion sequences. For better visual effects, we propose the sparsity optimization over simplexes formulation. Extensive experimental results on the creation of puppetry characters and puppetry plays well demonstrate the effectiveness of the proposed system.

Categories and Subject Descriptors

J.5 [**Arts and Humanities**]: Arts, fine and performing

Keywords

Chinese shadow puppetry, face rendering, animation

1. INTRODUCTION

In this demo, we focus on Chinese shadow puppetry which has a long history. Chinese shadow puppetry is a traditional artistic form of theater performance with colorful silhouette figures. These figures are produced with puppets made of leather or paper. As an ancient form of storytelling, sticks and flat puppets are manipulated behind an illuminated background to create moving pictures [1]. To protect this ancient artistic heritage, United Nations Educational, Scientific and Cultural Organization (UNESCO) listed the artistic form in Intangible Cultural Heritage in 2013

We design two puppetry modules, including a **creator** module and a **manipulator** module. The input of the creator module is two face images. One of the most important advantages of our creator module is *personalization*. Our creator module can *automatically* generate anyone's personalized puppet, and the process is almost *immediate*. One

*indicates equal contribution

MM'13, October 21–25, 2013, Barcelona, Spain.
ACM 978-1-4503-1089-5/12/10.

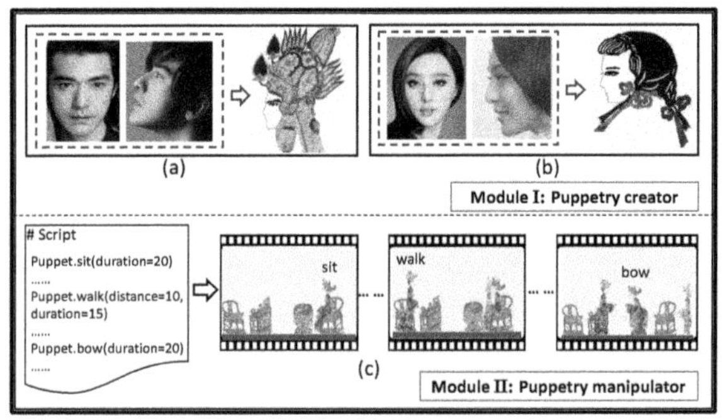

Figure 1: (a) and (b) are two results of our puppetry creator module for male and female respectively. (c) is an exemplar sequence generated based on user-provided scripts by the puppetry manipulator module.

male and one female puppet generated by our creator module are shown in Figure 1(a) and Figure 1(b). For manipulator module, we aim to preserve the performance pattern of Chinese shadow puppetry during the shadow puppetry manipulation process. This module can directly accept text scripts as input and display the specified motions accordingly. The interface is shown in Figure 1(c). For manipulation, we identify atomic motions for the animation and collect instances from a set of shadow puppetry videos. A scripting system converts the user input into atomic motions, and finally synthesizes the animation using the collected instances.

2. SYSTEM

As shown in Figure 2, the whole system contains two modules: creator module and manipulator module.

2.1 Module I: Puppetry Creator

The first part is *creator* module. Since the real puppet face usually contains a profile (including forehead, nose, mouth, etc) and frontal eye & eyebrow, we require users to input one frontal face and another profile face. Then the module utilizes the frontal eye & eyebrow and the profile curve to create a user-specific puppet head. First, we process the face alignment and extract the profile curve from the profile face. Similarly, eye & eyebrow areas are extracted from the frontal face. Given a frontal face and a puppet face, we warp the puppet eye & eyebrow into the eye & eyebrow shape by [2]. Then the profile curve is deformed. We generate a profile curve which has the uniqueness of the input face and the characteristics of the reference puppet face. In order to estimate the uniqueness of a profile face, we collect a 90 degree profile face dataset including 500 images from the MultiPIE benchmark [3]. A profile curve is separated

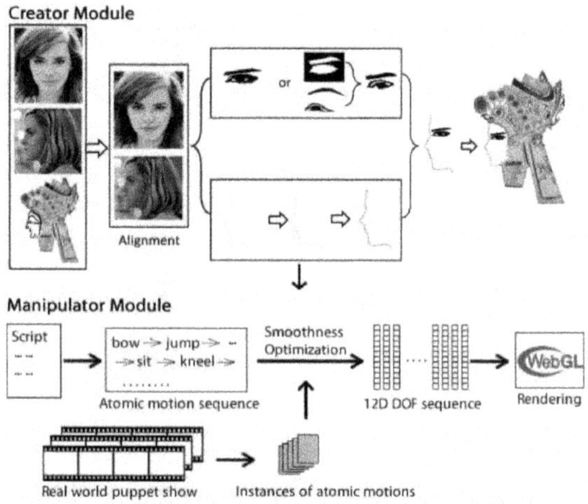

Figure 2: System framework: the upper panel is the creator module and the lower is the manipulator module.

into four parts: forehead, nose, mouth and jaw. The two most unique parts are kept and the other two parts are replaced by the corresponding parts of puppet profile. Finally, the texture is transferred from a certain puppet to our generated puppet by the image quilting method [4]. To make the roles more artistically charming, puppets are decorated with exquisite headdresses.

2.2 Module II: Puppetry Manipulator

The second part is *manipulator* module. The objective of this part is to create a system that takes in a user script and outputs an animation sequence. The digital puppet consists of nine parts linked by 7 joints and in total has 12 degrees of freedom (DOF). We start by collecting puppetry show videos and manually define atomic motions as building blocks of the animation. Eight atomic motions are identified, they are jump, bow, kneel, sit, swing, point, breathe and turn. Instances of the atomic motions are labeled and extracted from the videos. They are converted to DOF sequences and then applied to the digit puppet. Due to the inaccuracy in labeling, the transferred motions have shaking defects. We apply locally weighted scatterplot smoothing to the DOFs, which improves the visual experience significantly. Since reusing a limited number of the instances makes the animation monotonous, we generate new instances by weighted means of labeled instances. By taking different weight vector, infinite variants of one atomic motion can be generated.

In this work we render the animation using browser based webgl. Through javascript, manipulators can invoke different functions on the puppet. Each atomic motion has a corresponding javascript function. For example, puppet.walk(10,15) tells puppet to walk 10 units in the defined 2D world in 15 frames' time. The manipulator can also place props like chair to specific locations. Scripting can either be done online by inputing commands one by one or off-line by writing done all the scripts and feed to the puppet. Off-line is preferred for animation generation because it offers better control of timing. The aesthetic of the animation is correlated with the smoothness of the animation. We show that by minimizing the position gap between atomic motions the smoothness of the animation is significantly improved.

3. EXPERIMENTS

For creator module, the properties of the creator puppet are discussed in three aspects: aesthetic, puppetry-alike and discrimination by user study. Results of aesthetic and

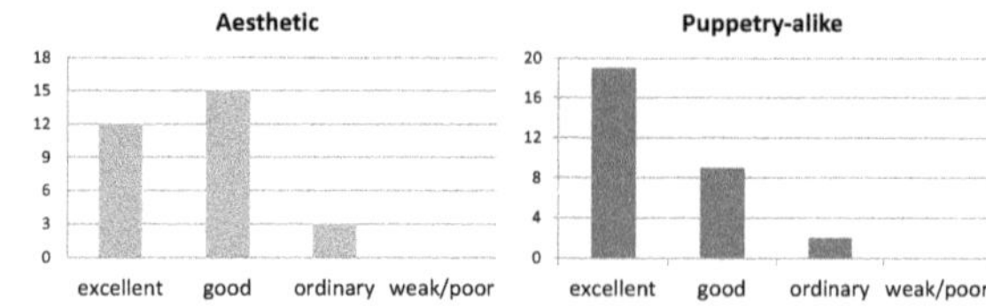

Figure 3: Evaluation of the creator results from the 30 subjects. The horizontal axis is the different evaluation levels, the vertical axis is the number of persons.

puppetry-alike level of assessment are shown in Figure 3. We can see that the generated puppets look elegant and can preserve the traditional puppet style. Then, we test 10 creator results and summarize the subjects' feedback to evaluate the discrimination of the generated puppets. The average precision is 71.1%, which shows that the subjects can recognize the person generated by our puppet creator module.

For manipulator module, we first evaluate the smoothness results of atomic motion and animation by user study and one way ANOVA analysis are also performed on the data shown in Table 1. Then using the scripting interface, we reproduced two videos from original puppetry videos. From the user study results, conclusion can be made that the puppetries generated from our system preserve the motion pattern of real puppetry, successfully convey the information to the subjects and have a high resolution. We also make a short video that tell a love story between a man and a female puppet. The full video can be watched via [1] and also included in the supplementary materials.

Table 1: ANOVA analysis of comparing (1) smoothed vs. original atomic motions (2)sequence generated by smoothness optimization vs. randomly selection.

	F-statistics	p-value
Atomic motions	1025.49	5.02281e-121
Animation sequence	327.53	6.60827e-50

4. CONCLUSIONS AND FUTURE WORK

In this paper, we proposed the eHeritage of shadow puppetry demo, including a creator module and a manipulator module. The creator module can generate a puppet for one person based on one's frontal face and profile face. The manipulator module can automatically generate the motion sequences based on the script provided by the user. Now we focus on the visual effects of the puppetry. In future, we would like to take more consideration to the audio parts.

5. ACKNOWLEDGMENT

This research is partially supported by the Singapore National Research Foundation under its International Research Centre @Singapore Funding Initiative and administered by the IDM Programme Office; and also partially supported by State Key Development Program of Basic Research of China 2013CB336500, in part by the Natural Science Foundation of China (NSFC) under grant 61172164.

6. REFERENCES

[1] F. Chen, "Visions for the masses: Chinese shadow plays from shaanxi and shanxi," *Pacific Science*, 2012.

[2] K. Hormann and M. S. Floater, "Mean value coordinates for arbitrary planar polygons," *ACM TOG*, 2006.

[3] R. Gross, I. Matthews, J. Cohn, T. Kanade, and S. Baker, "Multi-pie," *Image and Vision Computing*, 2010.

[4] A. A. Efros and W. T. Freeman, "Image quilting for texture synthesis and transfer," in *SIGGRAPH*, 2001.

[1] http://www.youtube.com/watch?v=lxJUw3mKF18yA

Gesture–based Control of Physical Modeling Sound Synthesis: a Mapping-by-Demonstration Approach

Jules Françoise
STMS Lab
IRCAM–CNRS–UPMC
1, Place Igor Stravinsky 75004
Paris, France
jules.francoise@ircam.fr

Norbert Schnell
STMS Lab
IRCAM–CNRS–UPMC
1, Place Igor Stravinsky 75004
Paris, France
norbert.schnell@ircam.fr

Frédéric Bevilacqua
STMS Lab
IRCAM–CNRS–UPMC
1, Place Igor Stravinsky 75004
Paris, France
frederic.bevilacqua@ircam.fr

ABSTRACT

We address the issue of mapping between gesture and sound for gesture-based control of physical modeling sound synthesis. We propose an approach called *mapping by demonstration*, allowing users to design the mapping by performing gestures while listening to sound examples. The system is based on a multimodal model able to learn the relationships between gestures and sounds.

Categories and Subject Descriptors

H.5.5 [**Information Interfaces And Presentation**]: Sound and Music Computing; J.5 [**Arts and Humanities**]: Music

Keywords

music, gesture, sound synthesis, physical modeling, HMM, multimodal

1. INTRODUCTION

Gestural interaction with audio and/or visual media has become ubiquitous. Many applications, including music performance, gaming, sonic interaction design, or rehabilitation, involve mapping from physical gestures to sound, requiring solutions for quick prototyping of gesture–based sound control strategies. The relationship between gesture and sound, often called *mapping*, has been recognized one of the crucial aspects of such interactive systems, as its design influence the interaction possibilities. In this paper, we address the issue of mapping for gesture–based control of physical modeling sound synthesis. This is a companion paper of a short-paper presented at ACM Multimedia 2013 [3] that will demonstrate concrete examples of a general a multimodal probabilistic model for gesture–based control of sound synthesis.

Physical modeling sound synthesis aims at simulating the acoustic behavior of physical objects. Gestural control of such physical models remains difficult, since the captured gestural parameters are generally different from the physical input parameters of the sound synthesis algorithm. For example, sensing gestures using accelerometers might pose difficulties for controlling the physical model of a bowed string where force, velocity, and pressure are the expected input. The design of the mapping between gesture and sound is therefore complex, and would hardly be realized by direct relationships between input and output parameters.

To tackle such an issue, we propose an approach we call *mapping by demonstration*, based on machine, allowing users to craft control strategies by demonstrating gestures associated with sound examples. Therefore, the system supports a design of the mapping driven by listening and interaction, as in many cases the training examples are defined by gestures performed while listening to sound examples, as proposed by Caramiaux [1] or Fiebrink [2].

Our approach places the user at the center of an interaction loop integrating training and performance. During *training*, sounds can be designed using a graphical editor. By performing gestures while listening to the sounds, the user feeds the system with examples of the mapping he intents to create, therefore translating his intentions through the direct demonstration of specific control strategies. During *performance*, the learned mapping can be used for sound control, allowing the user to explore the control strategies defined by the training examples.

2. APPLICATION OVERVIEW

2.1 Gesture capture

We use the *Modular Musical Objects* (MO) for gesture capture [5]. These wireless devices include an accelerometer and a gyroscope, and can be integrated to various objects, or extended with additional sensors, for example piezo-electric sensors.

Figure 1: MO: Modular Musical Objects

MM'13, October 21–25, 2013, Barcelona, Spain.
ACM 978-1-4503-2404-5/13/10.
http://dx.doi.org/10.1145/2502081.2502262.

2.2 Modal synthesis

Our system uses *Modalys*, a software dedicated to modal synthesis, i.e. that simulates the acoustic response of vibrating structures under an external excitation. It allows to build virtual instruments by combining *modal elements* – e.g. plates, strings, membranes – with various types of connections and exciters – e.g. bows, hammers, etc. Each model is governed by a set of physical parameters – e.g. speed, position and pressure of a bow. Specific sounds and playing modes can be created by designing time profiles combining these parameters.

2.3 gesture–sound mapping

Our goal is to learn the mapping between gestures, captured with accelerometers, and specific time profiles of the control parameters of the physical models. We adopt a multimodal perspective on gesture–sound mapping based on a probabilistic multimodal model. This approach is inspired by recent work in other fields of multimedia, such as speech–driven character animation [4]. The system is based on a single multimodal Hidden Markov Model (HMM) representing both gesture and sound parameter morphologies. The model is trained by one or multiple gesture performances associated to sound templates. It captures the temporal structure of gesture and sound as well as the variations which occur between multiple performances. For performance, the model is used to predict in real-time the sound control parameters associated with a new gesture. Additional details about the model and its implementation can be found in [3].

2.4 Workflow

The workflow of the application is an interaction loop integrating a *training* phase and a *performance* phase. It is illustrated in figure 2, and a screenshot of the software is depicted in figure 3. In the *training* phase, the user can

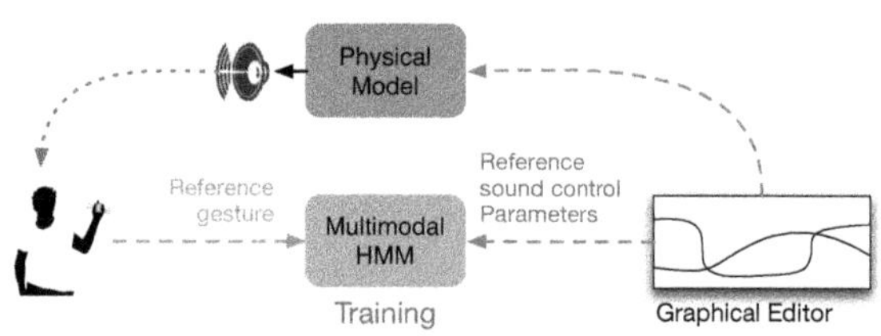

(a) *Training*: sounds are designed using a graphical editor, and reference gestures can be recorded while listening.

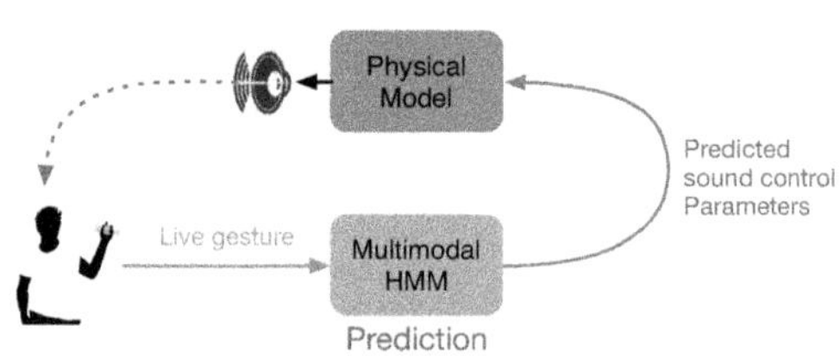

(b) *Performance*: the model is used to predict the sound parameters associated with a live gesture.

Figure 2: Application workflow.

draw time profiles of control parameters of the physical models to design particular sounds. Each of these *segments* can be visualized, modified, and played using a graphical editor

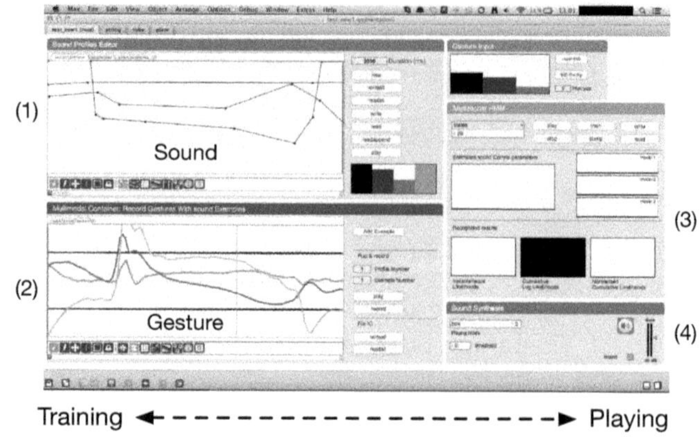

Figure 3: Screenshot of the system. **(1)** Graphical Editor. **(2)** Multimodal data container. **(3)** Multimodal HMM: control panel and results visualization. **(4)** Sound synthesis.

(top left of figure 3). Then, the user can perform one or several demonstrations of the gesture he intents to associate with the sound example (figure 2a). Gesture and sound are recorded to a multimodal data container for storage, visualization and editing (bottom left of figure 3). Optionally, segments can be manually altered using the user interface. The multimodal HMM representing gesture–sound sequences can then be trained using several examples. During the *performance* phase, the user can gesturally control the sound synthesis. The system allows for the exploration of all the parameter variations that are defined by the training examples. Sound parameters are predicted in real-time to provide the user with instantaneous audio feedback (figure 2b). If needed, the user can switch back to *training* and adjust the training set or model parameters.

3. ACKNOWLEDGMENTS

We acknowledge support from the French National Research Agency (ANR project Legos 11 BS02 012).

4. REFERENCES

[1] B. Caramiaux. *Etudes sur la relation geste-son en performance musicale.* Phd dissertation, Université Pierre et Marie Curie, 2012.

[2] R. Fiebrink, P. R. Cook, and D. Trueman. Play-along mapping of musical controllers. In *In Proceedings of the International Computer Music Conference*, 2009.

[3] J. Françoise, N. Schnell, and F. Bevilacqua. A Multimodal Probabilistic Model for Gesture-based Control of Sound Synthesis. In *Proceedings of the 21st ACM international conference on Multimedia (MM'13)*, Barcelona, Spain, 2013.

[4] G. Hofer. *Speech-driven animation using multi-modal hidden Markov models.* Phd dissertation, University of Edimburgh, 2009.

[5] N. Rasamimanana, F. Bevilacqua, N. Schnell, E. Fléty, and B. Zamborlin. Modular Musical Objects Towards Embodied Control Of Digital Music Real Time Musical Interactions. *Proceedings of the fifth international conference on Tangible, embedded, and embodied interaction*, pages 9–12, 2011.

News Rover: Exploring Topical Structures and Serendipity in Heterogeneous Multimedia News

Hongzhi Li*, Brendan Jou*, Joseph G. Ellis*, Dan Morozoff* and Shih-Fu Chang
Digital Video & Multimedia Lab, Columbia University

ABSTRACT

News stories are rarely understood in isolation. Every story is driven by key entities that give the story its context. Persons, places, times, and several surrounding topics can often succinctly represent a news event, but are only useful if they can be both identified and linked together. We introduce a novel architecture called News Rover for re-bundling broadcast video news, online articles, and Twitter content. The system utilizes these many multimodal sources to link and organize content by topics, events, persons and time. We present two intuitive interfaces for navigating content by topics and their related news events as well as serendipitously learning about a news topic. These two interfaces trade-off between user-controlled and serendipitous exploration of news while retaining the story context. The novelty of our work includes the linking of multi-source, multimodal news content to extracted entities and topical structures for contextual understanding, and visualized in intuitive active and passive interfaces.

Categories and Subject Descriptors

H.5.1 [**Information Interfaces and Presentation**]: Multimedia Information Systems; H.5.4 [**Information Interfaces and Presentation**]: Hypertext/Hypermedia

Keywords

Multimedia Analysis; News Segmentation; Topic Linking

1. INTRODUCTION

The rise of digital media and the Internet has had unprecedented impact in journalism, and on both news curators and news consumers alike. For consumption, there has been steady decline of viewership in broadcast television (TV) news as consumers migrate to Web-based platforms to find articles, short news clips, and blog posts. The on-demand nature, flexibility for mobile consumption, and close-to-realtime reporting is believed by many to be far better than waiting for a newspaper print or a scheduled, lengthy video broadcast. As this transition widens the gap between broadcast and online content, consumers are disengaging with the rich video media available through broadcast in favor of less-informative but bite-sized news, e.g. 140-character blog posts, and so, news curators are faced with the challenge of giving stories their necessary context in these short-form media.

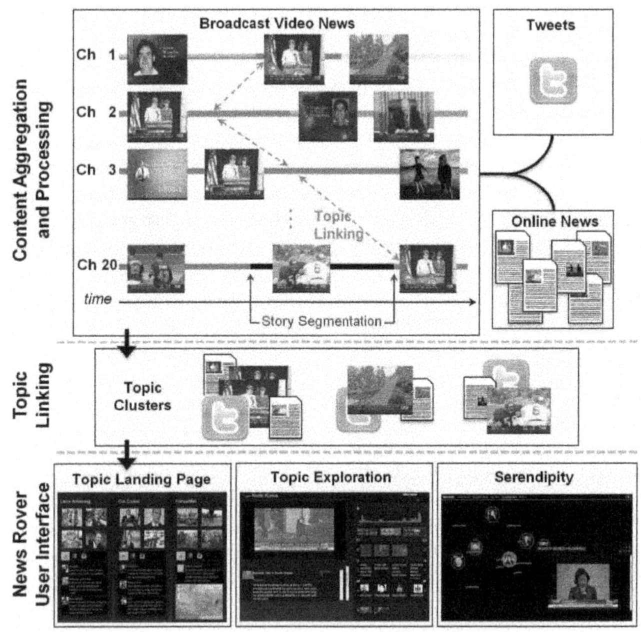

Figure 1: System Architecture Overview.

Despite the declining popularity of the traditional 30-minute or 60-minute news program, the throughput of news content both broadcast and online has only exponentially grown. An ongoing challenge in the research community to address the data explosion has been to develop high-throughput, content-based indexing and annotation solutions. However, these media are often studied in a single-source domain setting. Only recently are some works investigating heterogeneous indexing from multiple sources.

Our system, called News Rover, integrates multiple news sources and the multi-view nature of news, and offers an immersive user experience in a semi- and fully-automatic setting. The key novel contribution of our system architecture is its ability to link and index content from heterogeneous news sources, including broadcast TV news, online articles,

*Denotes equal contribution.

MM'13, October 21–25, 2013, Barcelona, Spain.
ACM 978-1-4503-2404-5/13/10.
http://dx.doi.org/10.1145/2502081.2502263.

Table 1: Average Estimates of Data Per Week.

Programs recorded	700	Online articles	72,000
Hours of video	700	Google topics	4,000
Stories segmented	7,000	Twitter trends	3,500

and social media feeds (like Twitter), organizing them into a topical structure for greater story context.

2. CONTENT AGGREGATION

Recording and Crawling. Our recording architecture consists of 12 cable TV tuners equipped with on-chip encoding. The system records continuously from a mix of analog and digital channels as transport streams, generating about 700 hours per week and covering about 100 channels. We implemented a scheduling routine that queries an electronic program guide feed every hour for an up-to-date listing of programs. The system schedules a recording job for the next available TV tuner for each newly discovered news program.

In addition, we developed a crawler that queries Google News every five minutes for new unseen topics and downloads all articles indexed under that topic, together with long-term tracking of 2,000 topics. A Twitter crawler was also developed to grab trending topics and all the tweets indexed under that trend. We also track and crawl about 2,000 long-term hot Twitter trends every day.

Story Segmentation. Recorded TV programs consist of a single contiguous video consisting of several stories. Our system automatically cuts each program into several story segments. In many U.S. programs, closed captions (CC) contain >>> characters to demarcate the beginning of a new topic. To overcome the time lag of CC, we apply a dynamic time warping algorithm to align the CC text to automatically recognized speech. To further refine the time precision, we performed shot detection [3] and chose shot boundaries to be likely story boundaries based on proximity with >>> symbols and shot lengths. Segmenting a program into stories is the most costly process in our pipeline, taking ~20 minutes for a 60-minute program. In the case when CC story markers are unavailable, we will apply our prior results on multimodal story segmentation [2], which demonstrated satisfactory performance with F1 score up to 0.76.

Topic Linking. Given that the data crawled from Google News and Twitter are organized into topics, we required a cross-source listing of trending topics to resolve differences in semantic tags. To do this, we linked related Google News topics and Twitter topics using both visual and textual content cues. Visual matching was accomplished by finding near-duplicate image pairs in images from online news articles and tweets. The number of near-duplicate image pairs was applied as the visual similarity metric. For text matching, we used a TF-IDF model to calculate the similarity between two topics. A combination of visual and textual cues is used to get the final similarity topic-pair score. A similar method was used to also link segmented video news stories to trending topics.

Entity Extraction. The CC text in TV news is a rich source of annotation on the video, containing explicit mentions of persons, locations and organizations associated with a story. Since CC is caseless, we then performed named entity recognition using a model trained on sentence examples where every letter was capitalized [1]. Since we had aligned the CC to the speech, time stamps were also assigned to detected named entities, specifying exactly when they were mentioned in the video. Since named entities extracted from CC are not always accurate, we used DBpedia and Wikipedia to correct and normalize them. This resolves typographic errors and aliases and also allows for profile pictures to be extracted. On average, we extract about five names per story segment.

In addition to named entities, we also applied a keyword extraction algorithm to extract the important concepts in each topic. Given the time occurrence of named entities, we find points in the video where a key concept and person is mentioned in CC within a 15-second time window of each other. This co-occurence mining of relations between entities-to-entities and entities-to-key-concepts allows us to explore how the "major players" shape the news. We are also currently developing a multimodal algorithm for extracting quotes associated with each of these named persons (i.e., extracting "who said what") to provide additional linking modes and measure an entity influence on a topic.

3. NOVEL VISUALIZATION INTERFACE

The complex space of multi-source, multimodal, multi-dimensional data is wrought with visualization challenges as humans simply cannot visualize beyond certain dimensions. We designed a discovery visualization user interface (UI) allowing users to explore the space of linked, multi-source, multimodal news data. We accomplish this in two ways: a topic-organized shuffle exploration UI, called *semi-automatic*, and a physics-simulating bounce serendipity UI, called *fully-automatic operation*. We contrast this with a *manual* navigation of news which requires experts to pool sources and draw context themselves. Please see our supplementary material for more detailed demonstrations.

Structured Exploration. To investigate the in-depth multimodal linking structure that would otherwise be unapparent, we focused our interface toward ease of use and concurrent discovery of these non-obvious links. Our current design consists of an interactive matrix display of multimodal data. Subliminal topic linking structure exists within the data, but the UI combines and reshuffles the representation on-the-fly to show related entities.

Serendipity. In many cases, news consumers are interested in a show-me-what-you-got paradigm that reveals surprising, compelling facets previously unknown. To address this, we exploit human intuition of the physical world for data discovery. Our current design utilizes non-deterministic modeling via gravitational simulation and elastic collisions to model the importance of players in shaping news events and serendipitous interaction between players and concepts and events involved in a topic. This interface overcomes the linearity of reasoning and successfully adds new visualization paradigms that are particularly appealing to consumers preferring a passive lean-backward consumption approach.

4. REFERENCES

[1] J. R. Finkel, T. Grenager, and C. Manning. Incorporating non-local information into information extraction systems by gibbs sampling. In *Proc. Annual Meeting of ACL*, 2005.

[2] W. Hsu, L. Kennedy, C.-W. Huang, S.-F. Chang, C.-Y. Lin, and G. Iyengar. News video story segmentation using fusion of multi-level multi-modal features in TRECVID 2003. In *ICASSP*, 2004.

[3] J. Mathe. `http://johmathe.name/shotdetect.html`.

A Novel framework for Collaborative Video Recommendation, interest Discovery and friendship Suggestion Based on Semantic Profiling

Marco Bertini, Alberto Del Bimbo, Andrea Ferracani, Francesco Gelli, Daniele Maddaluno, Daniele Pezzatini*
Università degli Studi di Firenze - MICC
Firenze, Italy
marco.bertini, alberto.delbimbo, andrea.ferracani, daniele.pezzatini@unifi.it

ABSTRACT

Two important challenges for social networks are the creation of targeted and personalized content for their users, selecting the most interesting material from the huge amount of user-generated content, and keeping user engagement , e.g. through creation and curation of users' profiles. In this demo we show a system for video commenting, sharing and interest discovery that combines recommendation algorithms, clustering techniques, tools for video tagging and evaluation of semantic resources relatedness. Combining these tools and techniques it becomes possible to provide personalized multimedia services and to improve and propagate interests and inter-personal connections through the network.

Categories and Subject Descriptors

H.3.5 [**Information Storage and Retrieval**]: Online Information Services; H.4 [**Information Systems Applications**]: Miscellaneous

General Terms

Algorithms, Design, Experimentation

Keywords

Social video tagging, internet videos, social video recommendation

1. INTRODUCTION

Nowadays the main challenges of a social network are, on the one hand, the targeting and personalization of services and resources to help users to choose from a wide variety of alternatives deriving from the huge amount of user-generated content in the network, on the other hand, the creation and curation of public profiles as a means to motivate users to be engaged with the systems. Considering online videos fruition the goal is to help users to find the most relevant content according to their recurrent viewings or preferences. As shown in [1], recommendation is a much more powerful force in driving users to watch new videos than direct searching.

Typically the approaches presented in the scientific literature are based on textual analysis of the metadata that accompany a video, possibly complemented by some multimedia content analysis, and user activity such as video player interaction. The YouTube recommendation system, described in [2], uses two broad classes of data: 1) content data, such as the raw video streams and video metadata such as title, description, etc., and 2) user activity data, either explicit (e.g. video rating/liking) and implicit (watching a video for a long time). Another important aspect to be considered is user interaction on social networks: this is motivated by the fact that, according to YouTube statistics, every day more than 500 years of videos are viewed on Facebook[1]. In [3] has been proposed a system that merges video content and social networks to gather semantic metadata to describe interaction, usage and opinion on video content.

2. DEMO

In this demo we present "InTime", a social network site[2], that combines a profiling module (through online social network, i.e. Facebook) and user's activity analysis, like semantic tagging, to generate targeted services for the users of the social network; this is achieved using a module for semi-automatic user profiles generation and curation, where the user profile that is created is exploited as a place to perform recommendation of videos, users and resources of interest. We show how helping users to create and maintain more easily their personal profile page, by semi-automatic means, also eases the task of creating targeted recommendations. The demo shows how to create a user profile containing the interests of a person through video commenting, how this profile is used to suggest new videos, friends and Wikipedia articles, and how the profile can be maintained and curated - manually and automatically - through video commenting. As highlighted in [4], interest targeting and friendship prediction are improved by considering the information contained both in interest and friendship networks.

*Authors listed in alphabetical order

[1]http://bit.ly/Zxn5YI

[2]Available at: http://fiona.micc.unifi.it/intime

MM'13, October 21–25, 2013, Barcelona, Spain.
ACM 978-1-4503-2404-5/13/10.
http://dx.doi.org/10.1145/2502081.2502264.

3. THE SYSTEM

The system allows users to share and browse videos, connect to friends, comment and semantically annotate videos at frame level, share and browse interests, related videos and users through recommendation, clustering and semantic similarity, and to create and curate personal profiles of interests in a semi-automatic way. In this regard InTime can be classified as an hybrid recommender system combining a collaborative filtering approach with content-based filtering techniques.

The system consists of two main parts that are closely interconnected: it provides a recommendation engine of videos and similar users, viewable in the personal home page of the social network (similarly to the YouTube home page), and it also features the automatic creation of a public profile of interests for which the framework exploits clustering and semantic distances to make recommendations and suggestions of resources (videos, persons, Wikipedia articles) that match those interests. The profile can then be edited and refined by users over time in a semi-automatic way. Users' profiles are created taking into account information extracted from Facebook (e.g. page likes), InTime network users activity (comments and annotations), information provided manually (categories of interest) or automatically computed (semantic analysis and categorization of annotations).

The modeling of user interests is carried out with three strategies: initially, in the "cold start" scenario, the system tries to extract some observable properties from users' Facebook profiles, then it uses algorithms to compute neighborhood user similarity, exploiting collaborative filtering techniques and implicit interest indicators, and finally it clusters resources extracted from the network activity, assigning the classifications of these clusters to the users' personal profile of interests. The workflow of InTime is shown in Fig. 1

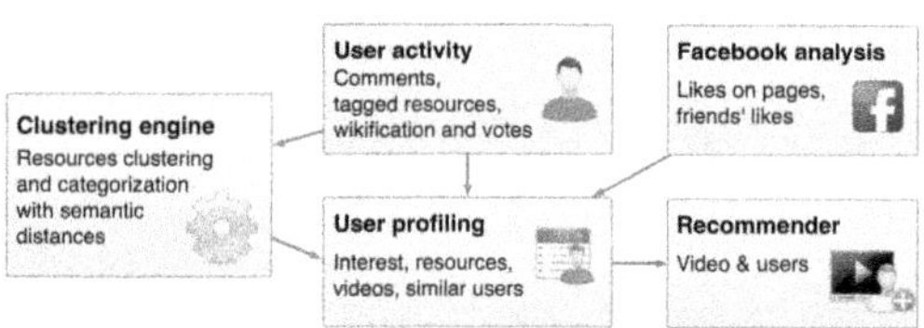

Figure 1: InTime system workflow.

Recommendations are based on videos, people and resources tagged or automatically extracted from video comments, added by users with a widget that let them create frame-accurate discussions and comments - similarly to what they are used to do when commenting photos on Facebook. Comments are processed using Named Entity Detection, based on rules and gazetteer and using a 'wikification' process that selects relevant topics and tags, using the approach presented in [5]. This semantic representation is then used to assign the resource to a taxonomy of interests, using clustering and kNN classification, based on Wikipedia Link-based Measure (WLM) [6] to compute the semantic distance. The system has been implemented using Hadoop/Mahout to address scalability. Each recommended item is part of the RDF semantic graph generated by the system and the interface shows its mutual relationship. In this way users can explore, from their automatically generated profiles of interests, videos, similar users and their profiles, resources or categories of resources (Fig. 2).

The recommender system outperforms in terms of prediction quality the baseline user-based recommender of Mahout, as shown in Fig. 3.

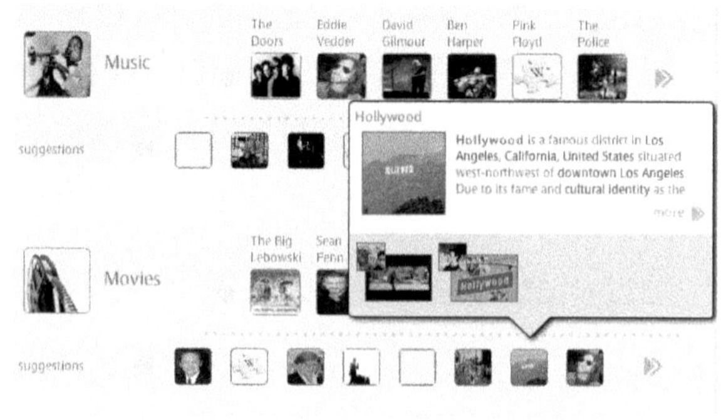

Figure 2: The categories of interest in a profile page. Each one presents a scrollable list of resource suggestions (below a dotted horizontal rule), and users' publicly visible selected resources (above). By hovering, users can visualize relative information, related videos, persons and reach the generated resource semantic URI.

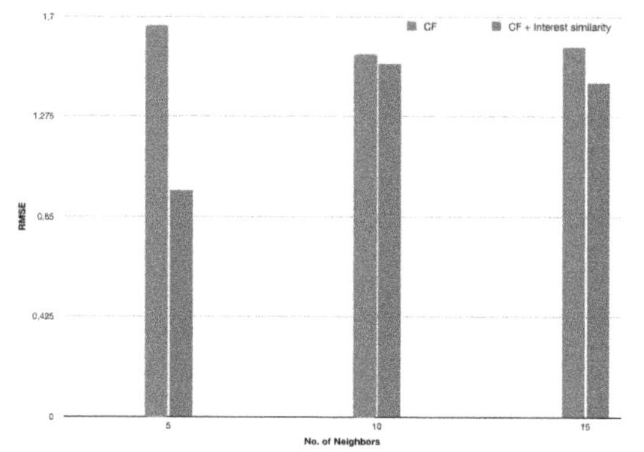

Figure 3: RMSE comparison between Mahout user-based recommendation (CF) and the proposed recommender algorithm (CF + Interest similarity).

4. REFERENCES

[1] Renjie Zhou, Samamon Khemmarat, and Lixin Gao. The impact of YouTube recommendation system on video views. In *Proc. of ACM SIGCOMM IMC*, 2010.

[2] James Davidson, Benjamin Liebald, Junning Liu, Palash Nandy, Taylor Van Vleet, Ullas Gargi, Sujoy Gupta, Yu He, Mike Lambert, Blake Livingston, and Dasarathi Sampath. The YouTube video recommendation system. In *Proc. of ACM RecSys*, 2010.

[3] S.J. Davis, I.S. Burnett, and C.H. Ritz. Using social networking and collections to enable video semantics acquisition. *IEEE MultiMedia*, 16(4):52–61, 2009.

[4] Shuang-Hong Yang, Bo Long, Alex Smola, Narayanan Sadagopan, Zhaohui Zheng, and Hongyuan Zha. Like like alike: joint friendship and interest propagation in social networks. In *Proc. of WWW*, 2011.

[5] David Milne and Ian H. Witten. Learning to link with Wikipedia. In *Proc. of ACM CIKM*, 2008.

[6] David Milne and I. H. Witten. An effective, low-cost measure of semantic relatedness obtained from Wikipedia links. In *Proc. of AAAI WIKIAI*, 2008.

euTV: a System for Media Monitoring and Publishing

Marco Bertini, Alberto Del Bimbo
Università degli Studi di Firenze - MICC
Firenze, Italy

George Ioannidis
IN2 search interfaces development
Edinburgh, United Kingdom

Emile Bijk
Hogeschool voor de Kunsten Utrecht
Hilversum, The Netherlands

Isabel Trancoso, Hugo Meinedo
Inesc-ID
Lisbon, Portugal

ABSTRACT

In this paper, we describe the euTV system, which provides a flexible approach to collect, manage, annotate and publish collections of images, videos and textual documents. The system is based on a Service Oriented Architecture that allows to combine and orchestrate a large set of web services for automatic and manual annotation, retrieval, browsing, ingestion and authoring of multimedia sources. euTV tools have been used to create several publicly available vertical applications, addressing different use cases. Positive results of user evaluations have shown that the system can be effectively used to create different types of applications.

Categories and Subject Descriptors

H.3.5 [**Information Storage and Retrieval**]: Online Information Services; H.4 [**Information Systems Applications**]: Miscellaneous

General Terms

Algorithms, Design, Experimentation

Keywords

Semantic multimedia annotation, SOA, content-based multimedia retrieval

1. INTRODUCTION

The explosion of digital data in recent times, in its varied forms and formats (H.264 and Flash videos, MP3 and Wav audio, HTML and PDF documents, images), requires the creation of effective tools to organize, manage and link digital resources, in order to maximize accessibility and reduce cost issues for everyone concerned, from content managers to online content consumers. On a larger scale, isolated multimedia repositories developed by content owners and technology providers can be connected, unleashing opportunities for innovative user services and creating new business models, in the vein of on-demand, online or mobile TV ventures.

MM'13, October 21–25, 2013, Barcelona, Spain.
ACM 978-1-4503-2404-5/13/10.
http://dx.doi.org/10.1145/2502081.2502265.

The euTV[1] project stems from above conditions and potentialities to connect publicly available multimedia information streams under a unifying framework, which additionally allows publishers of audio-visual content to monetize their products and services. The backbone of euTV is a scalable audio-visual analysis and indexing system that allows detection and tracking of vast amounts of multimedia content based on Topics of Interest (TOI), that correspond to a user's profile and set of employed search terms. The front-end is a portal that can be customized to be suitable to different scenarios and scopes, displaying syndicated content, allowing users to perform searches, refine queries, and produce faceted presentation of results.

2. DEMO

The demo shows three different applications created using the euTV media monitoring and publishing platform:

- FilePanel – files your way[2]: a web-based media management system for individuals and groups (private and institutional).
- NewsBoard – news at your fingertips[3]: A board to collect news feeds, process them, and filter and search what is interesting to the end-user. This application targets mainstream media clipping and monitoring markets.
- TravelPulse – photos in a pulse[4]: The application targets professional content providers, notably touristic destinations managers supporting them in promoting their cities/regions. It has been conceived as a showcase of the euTV framework for tourism applications.

3. THE SYSTEM

The euTV platform has a powerful infrastructure, that embraces different programming and scripting languages (C++, Java, PHP, Javascript, LUA), required for the many euTV tools and services, and libraries and open source software products (FFMpeg, Red5, Mule etc.) to process audio, visual and textual multimedia documents. The projects scale has required a pragmatic and robust approach to integrate all components into a scalable platform. This goal has been reached by extensively using a services oriented approach for system integration, with an agnostic approach to languages

[1] http://www.eutvweb.eu - The research leading to these results has received funding from the EU 7th FP managed by REA (FP7/2007-2013) under grant agreement no. 262428.
[2] http://eutvweb.eu/filepanel/)
[3] http://eutvweb.eu/newsboard/
[4] http://eutvweb.eu/travelpulse/

and protocols. The platform has a central services-based architecture layer consisting of a file-store, a repository and a web services hub (Apache Mule). This layer acts as the central hub to which the media processor framework and the end-user interfaces could rely on for storing and retrieving data in a flexible manner (Fig. 1).

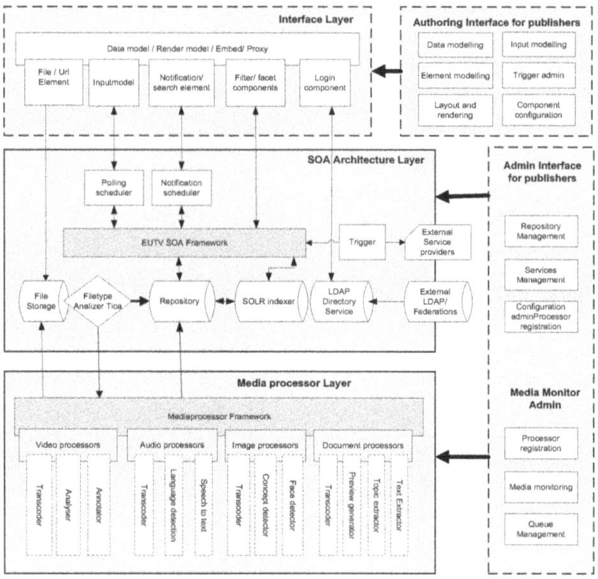

Figure 1: euTV system architecture.

Text indexing and annotation is performed by services that provide: *i)* language classification, based on n-grams and Naïve Bayes classifiers that despite the simplicity have shown to work effectively also on short fragments [1]; *ii)* topic detection based on LDA; iii) named entity extraction based on gazetteers and a rule-based system, to handle entities that have not been added yet to lists [2]. Topic detection and named entity identification can be used also with the outcomes of speech transcription services.

Speech and audio indexing and analysis tools provide services for: i) audio segmentation [3] that separates audio streams into six separate components: four for classification (speech / non-speech, gender, background and speaker identification), one for speaker clustering and one for acoustic change detection. These components are mostly model-based, making extensive used of feed-forward fully connected Multi-Layer Perceptrons trained with back-propagation; *ii)* audio language identification, based on [4], that identifies the 12 most spoken languages across the European Union, using SVMs for the phonotactic system and an I-vector based acoustic sub-system; *iii)* an audio event module that recognizes 54 sound concepts, using a combination of MFCC, ZCR and MPEG features to feed SVM classifiers; *iv)* audio transcriptions, an engine that uses an hybrid approach combining the temporal modelling capabilities of Hidden Markov Models with the pattern discriminative classification capabilities of Multi-Layer Perceptrons [5], and works with English, Spanish, Portuguese and German.

Visual annotation and indexing deal with images and videos at syntactic and semantic levels. Similarity-based retrieval deals with images and video keyframes, using a combination of MPEG global features and SIFT descriptors, indexed using approximate similarity searching based on inverted files [6] for scalability. Semantic annotation is obtained using a BoW-based approach, with a model selection step to select the best combination of interest point detectors/descriptors for each concept classifier, and using the PMK kernel [7] for efficient computation. Classifiers can be trained with a specific service, that exploits social media as training source [8].

Each type of media has a specific component that can handle visualization, media search and manual annotation (Fig. 2). A web-based authoring system allows to combine all the services to design specific applications for each use scenario, from the automatic ingestion of media to their processing, search and presentation (Fig. 3).

Figure 2: *left)* video play/annotations, showing automatic transcriptions; right) document viewer/annotator, showing concepts and entities on the right.

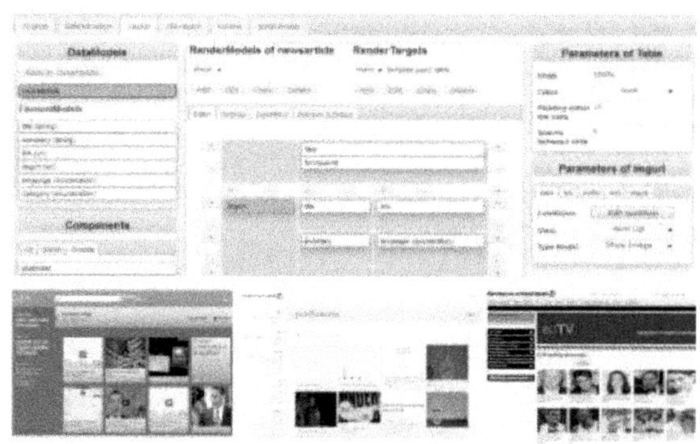

Figure 3: *top)* euTV system to design application interfaces; *bottom)* three examples of euTV applications.

4. REFERENCES

[1] H. Zhang. The optimality of Naïve Bayes. In *Proc. of FLAIRS2004*, 2004.

[2] H. Cunningham, D. Maynard, K. Bontcheva, and V. Tablan. GATE: A Framework and Graphical Development Environment for Robust NLP Tools and Applications. In *Proc. of ACL*, 2002.

[3] H. Meinedo. *Audio pre-processing and speech recognition for broadcast news.* PhD thesis, IST, Lisbon, 2008.

[4] A. Abad. The l2f language recognition system for albayzin 2012 evaluation. In *Proc. of Iberspeech*, 2012.

[5] J. Neto, H. Meinedo, M. Viveiros, R. Cassaca, C. Martins, and D. Caseiro. Broadcast news subtitling system in portuguese. In *Proc. ICASSP*, 2008.

[6] G. Amato and P. Savino. Approximate similarity search in metric spaces using inverted files. In *Proc. of InfoScale*, 2008.

[7] K. Grauman and T. Darrell. The pyramid match kernel: Efficient learning with sets of features. *Journal of Machine Learning Research*, 2007.

[8] A. Ulges, C. Schulze, M. Koch, and T. Breuel. The challenge of tagging online video. *Computer Vision and Image Understanding*, 2009.

CAMMA: Contextual Advertising system for Multimodal News Aggregations

Giuliano Armano
University of Cagliari, Dept.of Electrical and Electronic Engineering
Piazza d'Armi, I09123 Cagliari (Italy)
armano@diee.unica.it

Alessandro Giuliani
University of Cagliari, Dept.of Electrical and Electronic Engineering
Piazza d'Armi, I09123 Cagliari (Italy)
alessandro.giuliani@diee.unica.it

Alberto Messina
RAI Centre for Research and Technological Innovation
C.so Giambone, 68, I10135 Torino (Italy)
a.messina@rai.it

Maurizio Montagnuolo
RAI Centre for Research and Technological Innovation
C.so Giambone, 68, I10135 Torino (Italy)
maurizio.montagnuolo@rai.it

ABSTRACT

This demo paper describes a system for contextual advertising on aggregations of multimodal news items. The prototype is intended to demonstrate how modern content analysis techniques can be profitably used to automate tasks commonly performed by humans such as the planning of the computer-assisted advertising content.

Categories and Subject Descriptors

H.3 [**INFORMATION STORAGE AND RETRIEVAL**]: Miscellaneous; H.5.2 [**INFORMATION INTERFACES AND PRESENTATION (e.g., HCI)**]: User Interfaces—*Graphical user interfaces (GUI)*

Keywords

Contextual Advertising, Multimodal Aggregation

1. INTRODUCTION

Modern broadcasters are facing a unprecedented technological revolution from traditional dedicated equipment to commodity hardware and software components, and from yesterday one-to-many delivery paradigms to nowadays Web based interactive platforms. Information engineering and integration is allowing decisive strategic developments in automated production of information services. As a consequence, the burgeoning availability of channels and offers has been rapidly changing the television landscape. To accomplish those new needs, media industry wish would be to have an application able to process heterogeneous data from multiple media (e.g., television, press, the Internet) and made of different modalities (e.g. audio, speech, text, image, and video), in order to distribute new content that was not originally provided. In this scenario, contextual advertising (CA) on multimodal aggregations (MMAs) offers a unique opportunity for media producers and distributors to optimize costs and quality of the provided services, while reducing the "time to market" of data and meeting the user's expectation and satisfaction.

This paper focuses on the problem of linking the most popular news topics to a suitable set of advertisements. In particular, we propose a system for contextually associating advertisements that match with the content of multimodal news aggregation. Multimodality is intended as the capability of processing, gathering, manipulating, and organizing heterogeneous data. Multimodal news are collected from two inputs: (i) automatically extracted, chaptered and transcribed TV news, and (ii) RSS feeds from online newspapers and press agencies. Those data sources are automatically aggregated by the Hyper Media News system (HMN) originally proposed in [3]. To our best knowledge this is the first proposal aimed at suggesting ads in a multi-modal mass-production setting.

2. SYSTEM OVERVIEW

In accordance to state-of-the-art approaches [1, 2], the contextual advertising process adopts both syntactical and semantic techniques to the HMN's outputs. Syntax is exploited by a suitable text summarization technique aimed at reducing the size of the data while preserving the original meaning. Semantics is exploited by using a centroid-based classifier devoted to capture the main topics concerning with a given news aggregation. Figure 1 illustrates the main components of the prosed system. Given a news aggregation, the `News Extractor` extracts all the included items (news stories and RSS articles). For each item, the `Text Summarizer` generates a vector representation of its content as a Bag-of-Word (*BoW*) vector. Those vectors are then re-aggregated

MM'13, October 21–25, 2013, Barcelona, Spain.
ACM 978-1-4503-2404-5/13/10.
http://dx.doi.org/10.1145/2502081.2502266.

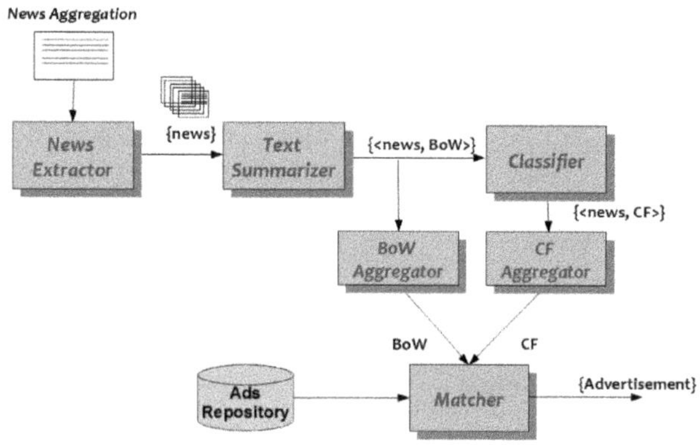

Figure 1: High level architecture of the system.

in order to produce a global BoW vector representing the syntactic content of the whole aggregation. The semantic content is represented as a classification vector $\vec{CF}$, representing the membership of the news aggregation to a set of predefined semantic classes. The set of available advertisements is processed in a similar way and it is represented by suitable BoW vector and CF vector. The relevance score between the news aggregation n and the advertisement a is calculated basing on cosine similarities between the news aggregation and the advertisement.

Being this the first proposal aimed at applying CA to multimodal real-world aggregated data, a comparison with existing baseline systems is not feasible. To assess its performances, we asked 15 assessors[1] to evaluate the relevance of the suggested ads with respect to a set of 10 randomly selected news aggregations for each category. Each assessor evaluated the relevance of 5 ads for each aggregation, for a total of 400 $\langle newsaggregation,\ ad \rangle$ pairs. To measure the effectiveness of the approach we adopt the following evaluation metrics: the *Precision* in suggesting k ads ($p@k$), the *Normalized Discounted Cumulative Gain (nDCG)*, the *Expected Reciprocal Rank (ERR)*, and the *Disagreement Variance* (Dis_k). Results showed that the system reaches good performances.

Table 1: Overall results of the proposed CA system.

k	p@k	nDCG@k	ERR@k	Dis_k
1	0.632	0.504	0.304	0.390
2	0.639	0.548	0.385	0.411
3	0.594	0.593	0.401	0.397
4	0.573	0.650	0.407	0.383
5	0.542	0.705	0.409	0.375

3. DEVELOPED SYSTEM INTERFACE

This section describes the prototype interface developed to interact with the system and validate the results. The interface presents three main regions. From left to right there are: (i) the selection panel; (ii) the browsing panel; and (iii) the advertisement panel. The selection panel provides the list of available news aggregations grouped by journalistic categories such as Sports, Music, Economy, as detected and classified by the Hyper Media News system. The browsing panel allows to browse the content of the selected aggregation, providing a title and a short abstract automatically chosen among the set of items it contains. For demonstration purposes, a run button is included to start the advertisement targeting process according to the methodology presented in Section 1. Once this process ends, the targeted advertisements (i.e. Web sites or pages) are shown in the right panel. An example is illustrated in Figure 2.

[1]Assessors have been selected among students and young researchers of the Department of Electrical and Electronic Engineering, as well as among workers at RAI centre of Research and Technological Innovation.

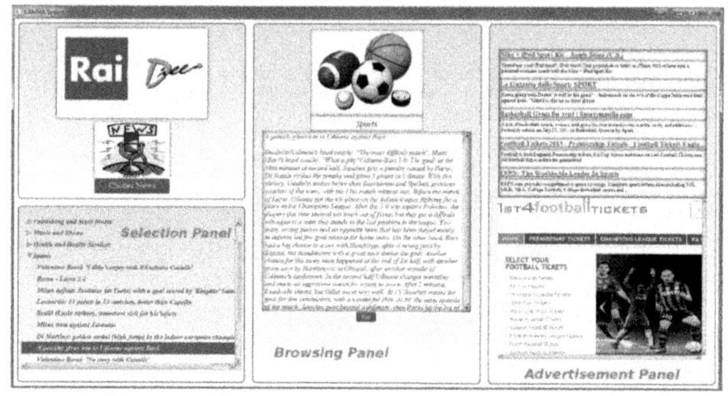

Figure 2: Developed system interface. From left to right there are the multimodal aggregation selection panel, the browsing and process starting panel and the advertisement panel.

4. CONCLUSIONS

This paper presented a system for contextual advertising wherein advertisements relating to the topic of multimodal news aggregations are served. As the aggregated TV news stories and RSS articles are natively cross-referenced, the system allows for the automatic linking of both television resources, web resources and advertisements. We believe that such an approach is helpful in the planning of computer-assisted advertising, in order to reduce the effort and cost of such process. In fact, as methods currently adopted are purely manual, the use of this interface by e.g. a dealer advertising stuff would increase the efficiency and flexibility of the content/adv association process w.r.t. the past.

5. REFERENCES

[1] A. Anagnostopoulos, A. Z. Broder, E. Gabrilovich, V. Josifovski, and L. Riedel. Just-in-time contextual advertising. In *CIKM '07: Proceedings of the sixteenth ACM conference on Conference on information and knowledge management*, pages 331–340, New York, NY, USA, 2007. ACM.

[2] G. Armano, A. Giuliani, and E. Vargiu. Studying the impact of text summarization on contextual advertising. In *8th International Workshop on Text-based Information Retrieval*, 2011.

[3] A. Messina and M. Montagnuolo. *Information Retrieval and Mining in Distributed Environments*, chapter Multimodal Aggregation and Recommendation Technologies Applied to Informative Content Distribution and Retrieval. A. Soro and E. Vargiu and G. Armano and G. Paddeu, 2010.

Flarty: Recommending Art Routes using Check-ins Latent Topics

Alberto Del Bimbo
Università degli Studi di Firenze, MICC
Viale Morgagni 65
Firenze, Italy
delbimbo@dsi.unifi.it

Andrea Ferracani
Università degli Studi di Firenze, MICC
Viale Morgagni 65
Firenze, Italy
andrea.ferracani@unifi.it

Daniele Pezzatini
Università degli Studi di Firenze, MICC
Viale Morgagni 65
Firenze, Italy
daniele.pezzatini@unifi.it

ABSTRACT

In this demo we present Flarty, a mobile location-based social network for the dynamic construction and recommendation of art routes in the city of Florence, Italy, via item based similarity algorithms, places topic extraction and user interest modeling. To achieve this goal Flarty derives knowledge from users check-ins and combines clustering techniques and recommendation algorithms, as well as features such as geo-location, to define groups of similar artworks or POIs (Points Of Interest) and to compute the most efficient routes likely to meet user's interests. Model analysis takes into account ratings, topics extracted from textual features associated with the POIs, and users preferences computed exploiting collaborative filtering techniques on their past behavior.

Categories and Subject Descriptors

H.3.5 [**Information Storage and Retrieval**]: Online Information Services; H.3.3 [**Information Storage and Retrieval**]: Information Search and Retrieval—*Clustering, retrieval model*

Keywords

Mobile, topic modeling, recommendation systems, location-based services

1. INTRODUCTION

With the widespread diffusion of location sharing sites like Foursquare, Gowalla and Facebook Places in the last years and the millions of geo-located user generated check-ins, computer applications have become capable of a deep understanding of the geospatial behaviors of people and the social dynamics of our cities. In the research in the field of human mobility there have been a lot of studies on friendship/location prediction and places classification through social activity streams [2]. Joseph et al. [5] group people through geo-location and location awareness systems categorizing and extracting features of the places where people go. Cheng et al. [3] show how the analysis of temporal, spatial and textual aspects of footprints in location share services can give a better understanding of how people interact with these services. So this huge amount of collective knowledge can be usefully used for better understanding the correlation between users and locations and for the implementation of mobile location-based services exploiting traditional macro patterns of recommendation systems. Horozov et al. [4] have demonstrated that recommendations in mobile environments perform better if used in combination with "convenience" metrics, like geo-location, which improves the effectiveness of the recommendations systems themselves. In this demo we present Flarty, a prototype of a mobile social network that combines user behavior analysis and clustering techniques in a location aware system in order to improve recommendation services for cultural heritage in the city of Florence. However, the system is configurable and the dataset of POIs can be easily replaced to work with POIs of other cities or regions. In particular we take into account three factors: 1) users check-ins and check-ins rates, 2) representative topics of POIs and users, and 3) geo-location.

MM'13, October 21–25, 2013, Barcelona, Spain.
ACM 978-1-4503-2404-5/13/10.
http://dx.doi.org/10.1145/2502081.2502267 .

2. THE SYSTEM

The mobile application has been developed in Java using the Android SDK. The backend is composed by three modules: a set of PHP scripts to store and retrieve data from a MySQL database and two modules respectively for the execution of clustering and recommendations algorithms. The algorithms use a map/reduce paradigm, implemented in the Apache Mahout library, and run on an Hadoop cluster. The application can be accessed through his own login system or through Facebook APIs and authentication services. Geo-location is obtained through Google APIs.

Flarty allows the user to check-in and vote the several points of interest which are part of a route. This information is used by the system to profile users, in order to suggest personalized paths and users with similar interests. Each user is described mainly by two vectors: a vector of topics extracted by the places he checked-in and a vector of the ratings expressed on these check-ins. To deal with the so called "cold start scenario" issue the system provides some initial gamification techniques to have a first user model: at the very first access the user is asked to give a rating from 1 to 5 on some representative POIs. Flarty proposes to users two types of art routes: 1) custom: calculated weighting results of recommendation algorithms and clustering techniques according to user interests, and 2) classic: predefined routes of POI "must see". The custom routes are created starting from the results returned by the Recommender module that are further elaborated and filtered by the results of the Clustering module. The user's affinity with the set of POIs suggested by the Recommender is refined comparing their representative topics with the topics extracted from users' check-ins. Furthermore each topic is represented by a vector of "tags" on whose best occurrences match is based the selection of the main shared topics. Both types of routes are filtered and ordered automatically by the system considering geo-location: Flarty suggests routes only partially contained within a given radius from the user. The application provides three different routes visualization paradigms: a list view, a map view and an augmented reality view. The POIs that are part of the routes can be filtered and customized manually through addition/deletion/reordering. Several filtering criteria can be applied (e.g. distance and average vote) to allow the user to optimize the routes on the basis of their preferences. Every time the user selects a route he is continuously localized through GPS and guided by the application in the visit.

Flarty is also a social network. Users can interact with each other and share their activities and preferences on their profile or on Facebook. Flarty uses social and gamification techniques (such as badges and rewards) with the aim of increasing the use of the system itself and the amount of check-ins. This improves user profiles and consequently the refinement of recommendations and automatic routes creation.

Recommender module.

The Recommender module uses a standard collaborative filtering item-based algorithm, implemented in Apache Mahout, to find sets of recommended POIs for each user based on their initial profile. The initial profile is built considering the results of an interactive poll in the "cold start scenario" when users are given a set of POIs to vote. The algorithm runs as a distributed recommendation process on Hadoop. With this item-based collaborative filtering approach the module evaluates how users interact with items (in this case localized POIs) and from this information tries to understand which items are more similar. Flarty gets this information by explicit indicators, e.g. ratings expressed with number of stars. Considering the past preferences of the user, the system then attempts to predict the future in a "content agnostic" way not using items properties, strategy that Flarty adopts in the Clustering Module to refine Recommender results. It is well known that item-based recommendation systems perform better when the number of items is significantly lower than the number of users. Furthermore, in this kind of scenario, we have to consider that the POIs are going to change far less frequently than the users. The algorithm uses a co-occurrence matrix for computing POIs similarity feeding a *log-likelihood* similarity function which evaluates the likelihood of a set of parameter values given some observed outcomes (e.g. user ratings).

Clustering module.

Flarty identifies the "candidates" POIs to be used for routes construction filtering recommendations extracted for each user by the Recommender module. To do this it considers the affinity of topics of the recommended POIs with the most significant topics of the places he checked-in. Topics are used to group similar POI's in the repository. Each POI is represented in the model by its own Wikipedia page. The algorithm used for grouping is CVB, Collapsed Variational Bayesian inference algorithm for LDA (Latent Dirichlet allocation), a topic model first introduced in [1], implemented in a map/reduce paradigm to run on a cluster. The algorithm returns data containing the distribution between POIs and topics and between topics and words or "tags"; in this way it is possible to extract the following information: 1) which POIs are related to topics; 2) which are the 'tags" that characterize the topics.

3. CONCLUSIONS

Flarty is a scalable mobile application for recommending custom routes of POIs to users on the basis of their interest profile. Flarty enables users to follow the routes in realtime and to complete the individual steps through check-ins. The user profile is inferred from check-ins combining classic recommendations algorithms and clustering techniques. Flarty utilizes state-of-the-art libraries for recommendations and clustering and implements scalable algorithms runnable in a distributed system in order to improve the overall quality of recommendations. Future work will include: 1) the realization of a prototype providing automatic check-ins through the use of sensor networks, 2) routes optimization by integrating city public web services and open-data regarding traffic, public transport and opening/closing museums timetables, 3) computer vision systems for artworks recognition in the augmented reality view.

4. ACKNOWLEDGMENTS

We thank the students Desideria Andò, Stefano Lombini, Matteo Mazzola and Giovanni Taverriti for their work on the implementation of the mobile application.

5. REFERENCES

[1] D. M. Blei, A. Y. Ng, and M. Y. Jordan. Latent dirichlet allocation, 2003.

[2] A. E. Cano, A. Varga, and F. Ciravegna. Volatile classification of point of interests based on social activity streams. In *Proceedings of the 4th workshop on Social Data on the Web co-located with the 10th International Semantic Web Conference*, 2011.

[3] Z. Cheng, J. Caverlee, K. Lee, and D. Z. Sui. Exploring millions of footprints in location sharing services. In *Proceedings of the Fifth International Conference on Weblogs and Social Media*, 2011.

[4] T. Horozov, N. Narasimhan, and V. Vasudevan. Using location for personalized poi recommendations in mobile environments. In *Proceedings of the International Symposium on Applications on Internet*, pages 124–129, 2006.

[5] K. Joseph, C. H. Tan, and K. M. Carley. Beyond "local", "categories" and "friends": clustering foursquare users with latent "topics". In *Proceedings of the 2012 ACM Conference on Ubiquitous Computing*, UbiComp '12, pages 919–926, 2012.

SentiBank: Large-Scale Ontology and Classifiers for Detecting Sentiment and Emotions in Visual Content

Damian Borth[1,2], Tao Chen[1], Rong-Rong Ji[1] and Shih-Fu Chang[1]
[1]Columbia University (USA) and [2]University of Kaiserslautern (Germany)

ABSTRACT

A picture is worth one thousand words, but what words should be used to describe the sentiment and emotions conveyed in the increasingly popular social multimedia? We demonstrate a novel system which combines sound structures from psychology and the folksonomy extracted from social multimedia to develop a large visual sentiment ontology consisting of 1,200 concepts and associated classifiers called *SentiBank*. Each concept, defined as an Adjective Noun Pair (ANP), is made of an adjective strongly indicating emotions and a noun corresponding to objects or scenes that have a reasonable prospect of automatic detection. We believe such large-scale visual classifiers offer a powerful mid-level semantic representation enabling high-level sentiment analysis of social multimedia. We demonstrate novel applications made possible by SentiBank including live sentiment prediction of social media and visualization of visual content in a rich intuitive semantic space.

Categories and Subject Descriptors

H.3.3 [**Information Storage and Retrieval**]: Information Retrieval and Indexing

Keywords

Social Multimedia, Affect, Emotion, Sentiment Analysis, Ontology, Concept Detection

1. INTRODUCTION

A picture is worth one thousand words: visual content offers rich complementary information beyond what the accompanying text reveals. The role of visual content has become even more prominent in increasingly popular social media such as Twitter, where the textual description is limited to very short messages (140 characters). In such cases, extracting information from visual content is critical in understanding the rich emotions, affect, or sentiments conveyed in the multimedia content.

Existing research of sentiment or affect analysis of social multimedia are either restricted to text analysis or direct mapping of low-level visual features to affects [1, 2]. Here we advocate a novel approach focusing on construction of a large concept ontology and associated automatic classifier library that aim at extracting mid-level semantic attributes from visual content. Our effort is inspired by major progresses made in semantic concept discovery and learning in the multimedia and computer vision community in the last decade. But to make high-level affect analysis feasible, we specifically focus on semantic concepts that draw sound foundation from the psychology theory of emotion [3], have close relevance to actual terms used by social media users, and consider practical detectability using current computer vision and multimedia analytics techniques.

We have developed a large-scale visual sentiment ontology which includes 1,200 semantic concepts and corresponding automatic classifiers, called SentiBank [4]. Each concept is defined as an Adjective Noun Pair (ANP), made of an adjective strongly indicating emotions and a noun corresponding to objects or scenes that have a reasonable prospect of automatic detection. We demonstrate several exciting applications enabled by SentiBank in this paper: (1) robust prediction of affects (sentiment or emotion) in visual content, (2) interactive exploration of large image data sets along the high-dimensional sentiment concept space using efficient visualization tools such as emotion wheel and treemap, and finally (3) a multimodal interface (incorporating novel sound and animation effects) for monitoring the sentiment concepts present in live social multimedia streams.

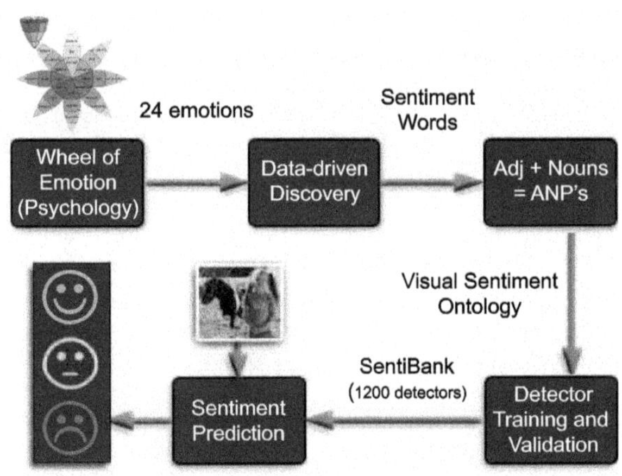

Figure 1: Processes for constructing ontology and learning concept classifiers in SentiBank.

MM'13, October 21–25, 2013, Barcelona, Spain.
Copyright 2013 ACM 978-1-4503-2404-5/13/10 ...$15.00.
http://dx.doi.org/10.1145/2502081.2502268.

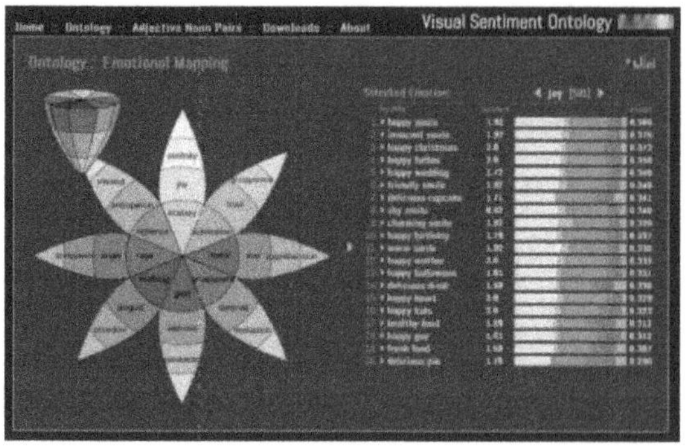

Figure 2: Emotion Sentiment Concept Browser.

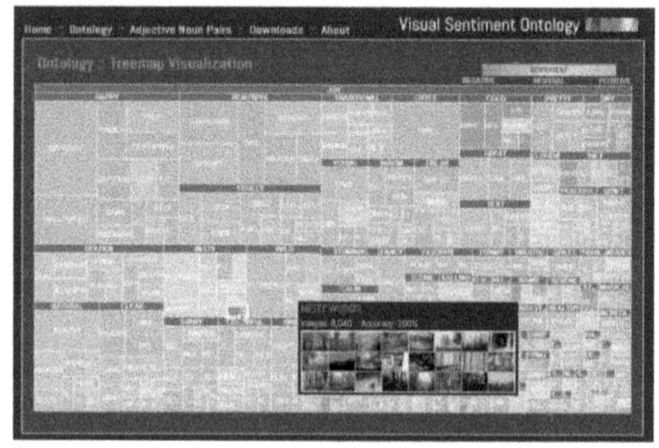

Figure 3: TreeMap Sentiment Concept Browser.

2. SENTIBANK ONTOLOGY AND CLASSIFIERS

Fig. 1 summarizes the processes for constructing the visual sentiment ontology and large concept classifiers in SentiBank. The process starts with a well-established psychological model of emotions called *Plutchik's Wheel of Emotions* [3]. First, a data-driven mining step is performed for each of the 24 emotions in Plutchik's theory to find related tags. Images and videos from Flickr and YouTube are retrieved with emotions as query words. Then, tags frequently co-occurring with each emotion are found (e.g., "joy" leads to "happy" and "beautiful"). We then applied text parsing and lexical based sentiment analysis tools to find "polarized" (either positive or negative) adjectives, which are then paired with nouns frequently used together as phrases in the retrieved image set to form more than 3,000 Adjective Noun Pairs (ANP). We then trained a machine learning classifier for each ANP by using the corresponding training images crawled from Flickr. The final set of classifiers, filtered by detection accuracy, includes 1,200 ANP concept detectors, covering 178 adjectives and 313 nouns. The majority of the classifiers has accuracy, measured in F-score, higher than 0.6 (with all concept detectors having AP@20>0), verifying reasonable detectability of classifiers. The full list of concepts and details of the training process can be found in [4].

3. APPLICATIONS AND DEMOS

To demonstrate the power of the proposed sentiment ontology and SentiBank concept classifiers, in the following we describe a few novel applications for large image exploration and live media monitoring. The interactive demos can also be viewed online at http://visual-sentiment-ontology.appspot.com/.

Demo A: Emotion Sentiment Concept Browser

Taking advantage of the psychology principled structure in the SentiBank ontology, we have developed an efficient browser for exploring big image sets (currently more than 500,000 Flickr images) in the rich emotion space (Fig. 2). The wheel provides an intuitive map for arranging emotions based on their relations and intensities (8 emotion groups and 3 intensity levels). Upon selecting a specific emotion, users can view the related ANP concepts (shown on the right) together with information about the sentiment value and distribution of associated emotions of each ANP. This gives users a quick overview of the entire emotion landscape, related ANP concepts, and their corresponding sentiment values. Users can then zoom in to get detailed information such as example images and detector accuracy of each specific ANP concept.

Demo B: Treemap Sentiment Concept Browser

The hierarchical structure of SentiBank ontology allows development of a treemap style browsing system for navigating through the ontology and the mapped image set (Fig. 3). The four-level structure of the TreeMap includes the ontology root, emotion groups, adjectives, and finally specific ANPs. The size of each block in the map is proportional to the number of children nodes at the top levels and the number of Flickr images at the leaf node. The color varying from green to red illustrates the sentiment value. The user can browse the ontology by zooming in and out following the edges of the tree. The leaf node will also show the average image and link to the sample images of the corresponding ANP. Compared to the emotion wheel described above, the treemap offers a quick summary of nodes at each level of the ontology, augmented by color and size cues to indicate the additional attributes such as sentiment and data volume.

Demo C: Live Monitoring of Visual Sentiment and Emotions

We have also extended the treemap browser to a new visualization system for monitoring the sentiment and ANP concepts detected in images in live social media streams such as those from Twitter. To help users comprehend rich information in a large number of dimensions, we utilize multimodal cues in a new way by mapping the detected sentiment value of an incoming image to the pitch of a music note, i.e., positive (negative) images are displayed together with playing of a high (low) pitch music note. In addition, the specific ANP concepts detected will be highlighted in the corresponding areas in the treemap in a synchronized animation manner. We found such multimodal visualization tools enhanced with sound and animation effects can significantly improve the usability and attractiveness of the system.

4. REFERENCES

[1] J. Machajdik and A. Hanbury. Affective Image Classification using Features inspired by Psychology and Art Theory. *ACM MM*, 2010.

[2] J. Jia et al. Can we Understand van Gogh's Mood? Learning to infer Affects from Images in Social Networks. *ACM MM*, 2012.

[3] R. Plutchik. *Emotion: A Psychoevolutionary Synthesis.* Harper & Row New York, 1980.

[4] D. Borth, R. Ji, T. Chen, T. Breuel, and S-F Chang Large-scale Visual Sentiment Ontology and Detectors Using Adjective Noun Pairs *ACM MM*, 2013.

Augmented and Interactive Video Playback Based on Global Camera Pose

Junsheng Fu, Lixin Fan, Yu You, Kimmo Roimela
Media Technologies Lab
Nokia Research Center, Tampere, Finland
{junsheng.fu, lixin.fan, yu.you, kimmo.roimela}@nokia.com

ABSTRACT

This paper proposes a video playback system that allows user to expend the field of view to surrounding environments that are not visible in the original video frame, arbitrarily change the viewing angles, and see the superimposed point-of-interest (POIs) data in an augmented reality manner during the video playback. The processing consists of two main steps: in the first step, client uploads a video to the GeoVideo Engine, and then the GeoVideo Engine extracts the geo-metadata and returns them back to the client; in the second step, client requests POIs from server, and then the client renders the video with POIs.

Categories and Subject Descriptors

I.4.9 [**Computing Methodologies**]: IMAGE PROCESSING AND COMPUTER VISION Applications

Keywords

Video Playback; Augmented Reality; Camera Pose

1. INTRODUCTION

Capturing a video clip with a camera phone and sharing it with a friend later on has gradually becoming part of our everyday activities, because of the increasing penetration rate of mobile phones and popularity of video sharing services such as "YouTube" and "Vimeo". The demo presented in this paper shows that such ordinary *video capturing* and *sharing* experience can be greatly enriched by leveraging geo-metadata associated with video frames. In particular, we demonstrate that by exploiting associated global camera pose information, *video playback can be enhanced with augmented reality contents and video playback becomes an interactive and intriguing experience* (see one example in Figure 1).

To our best knowledge and surprise, this kind of geo-location enhanced video playback experience has not been fully pursued and there are only a handful of related systems reported in the literature. For instance, Vidmap [1] is a video uploading and sharing service which associates video frames with a 2D GPS location. When playing back video frames, corresponding GPS locations are synchronously displayed on a map. The service provides 2D GPS locations, but makes no attempt to recover 6 degree-of-freedom camera poses. In a more recent research by Liu et al. [2], the mobile visual localization system extracts a comprehensive set of geo-context information from a single photo. While high localization accuracy and good scalability are demonstrated,the overall system is more gear to localization applications instead of video playing back.

This paper illustrates a novel video processing system that automatically extracts global camera pose from the uploaded video and, consequently, enables augmented and interactive video playback experiences.

Figure 1: Three different kinds of video playback modes are presented. Ordinary mode (*upper left*): video is played back as same as the captured video; Expanded view mode (*upper right*): user can expend the filed of view to surrounding environments that are not visible in the original video frame; Map view mode (*bottom left and right*): camera motion of the video is highlighted in the map and viewing angles can be arbitrarily changed by the user.

MM'13, October 21–25, 2013, Barcelona, Spain.
ACM 978-1-4503-2404-5/13/10.
http://dx.doi.org/10.1145/2502081.2502269 .

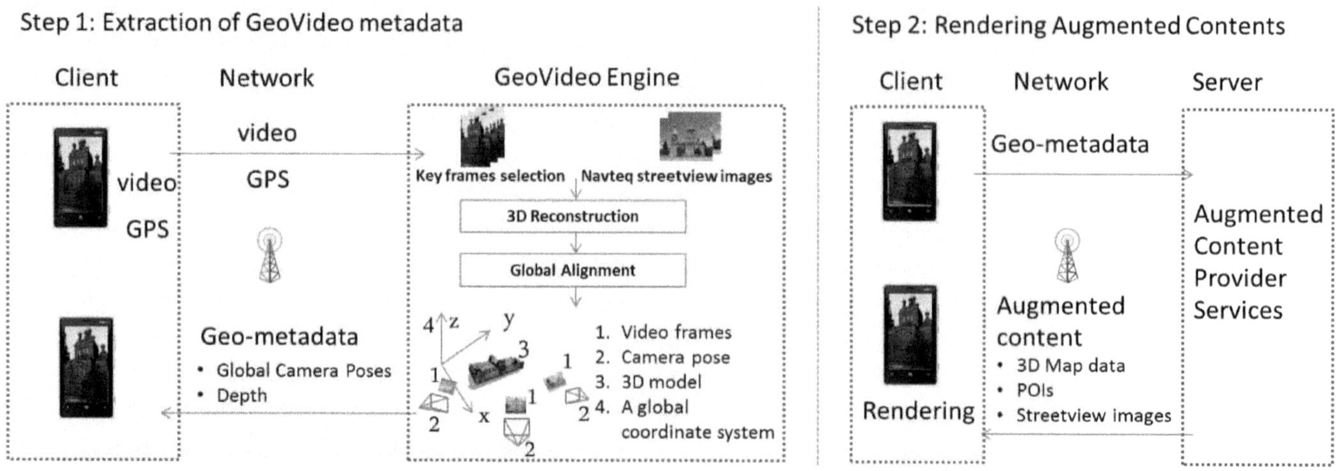

Figure 2: Overview of the proposed Augmented and Interactive Video Playback System.

2. SYSTEM FRAMEWORK

This section gives an overview of the system architecture and important functional modules (see Figure 2).

2.1 Extraction of GeoVideo metadata

After client uploads a video to the GeoVideo Engine, the GeoVideo Engine automatically extracts its Geo-matadata. The GeoVideo Engine involves two important components, namely, *3D Reconstruction* and *Global Alignment* (see Step 1 in Figure 2). The *3D Reconstruction* module reconstructs 3D point clouds from the key video frames and simultaneously recovers the camera poses within a local coordinate system. This module uses Structure from Motion technique and we refer interested readers to [3, 4] for technique details.

The *Global Alignment* module, aims to find global camera pose of key video frames by aligning nearby Navteq street view images with reconstructed 3D scenes. Since registered Navteq images have known camera poses in both local and global coordinate systems, an unique rigid transform is recovered so that camera poses of key frames' can be mapped into the global coordinate system. Camera poses of the rest video frames can be estimated by adopting Efficient Perspective-n-Point Camera Pose Estimation method [5].

2.2 Rendering Augmented Contents

Once geo-metadata are returned from GeoVideo Engine, the client application may request nearby augmented content such as 3D map data, POIs, street-view images and so on from content provider. Since the camera poses of the video frames and the augmented data are provided, it is straightforward to render everything within a unified global coordinate system (see Step 2 in Figure 2). Consequently, a number of intriguing video playing back experiences are now possible:

- *Expand Your View* (see Figure 1 *upper right*): During the playback of a GeoVideo, the field of view of video frames can be extended to 360 degree by using nearby panorama images. This rendering is possible because panorama images or 3D city models are often tagged with GPS information.
- *Arbitrary Change of Viewing Angles* (see Figure 1 *bottom left and right*): Users can highlight the camera motion in a 3D map and the system allows arbitrary change of viewing angles.
- *POIs-augmented Video Playback*: Based on POIs data and the associated geo-metadata, it is possible to augment video frames with POIs. During the video playback, the change of camera poses gives rise to corresponding change in the rendered POIs, thus users get the augmented-reality experience.

3. CONCLUSION

The presented demo shows that the ordinary *video capturing* and *sharing* experience can be greatly enriched by leveraging geo-metadata associated with video frames. Compared to existing video playback systems, this system can expend the filed of view of the video frames to surrounding environments that are not visible in the original video, change of the viewing angles and superimpose the POIs on the original video frames in an augmented reality manner.

4. REFERENCES

[1] Vidmap: http://www.vidmap.de.

[2] H. Liu, T. Mei, J. Luo, H. Li, and S. Li. Finding perfect rendezvous on the go: accurate mobile visual localization and its applications to routing. In *Proceedings of the 20th ACM international conference on Multimedia*, MM '12, pages 9–18, New York, NY, USA, 2012. ACM.

[3] N. Snavely, S. M. Seitz, and R. Szeliski. Photo tourism: exploring photo collections in 3d. *ACM Trans. Graph.*, 25(3):835–846, July 2006.

[4] C. Wu, S. Agarwal, B. Curless, and S. M. Seitz. Multicore bundle adjustment. In *Proceedings of the 2011 IEEE Conference on Computer Vision and Pattern Recognition*, CVPR '11, pages 3057–3064, Washington, DC, USA, 2011. IEEE Computer Society.

[5] F. Moreno-Noguer, V. Lepetit, and P. Fua. Accurate non-iterative o(n) solution to the pnp problem, 2007.

EigenNews: A Personalized News Video Delivery Platform

Matt C. Yu, Péter Vajda, David M. Chen, Sam S. Tsai, Maryam Daneshi
André F. Araujo, Huizhong Chen, and Bernd Girod
Department of Electrical Engineering, Stanford University, Stanford, CA 94305, U.S.A.
{mattcyu, pvajda, dmchen, sstsai, mdaneshi, afaraujo, hchen2, bgirod}@stanford.edu

ABSTRACT

We demonstrate EigenNews, a personalized television news system. Upon visiting the EigenNews website, a user is shown a variety of news videos which have been automatically selected based on her individual preferences. These videos are extracted from 16 continually recorded television programs using a multimodal segmentation algorithm. Relevant metadata for each video are generated by linking videos to online news articles. Selected news videos can be watched in three different layouts and on various devices.

Categories and Subject Descriptors

H.5.1 [**Information Interfaces and Presentation**]: Multimedia Information Systems

Keywords

story segmentation; story linking; personalization; news aggregation; mobile

1. INTRODUCTION

EigenNews is a personalized video news system which aggregates multiple sources of television news, automatically selects relevant videos based on a user's interests, and offers the user flexibility in how to watch the videos.

The features of this system can be summarized as follows:

- *Personalized Content*: Different stories are selected for each user based on her preferences.
- *Aggregation of Sources*: Different programs are chosen to meet a user's diverse interests.
- *Universal Access*: EigenNews is accessible on several devices including computers, smartphones, and tablets.

In this technical demo, we present EigenNews which applies story segmentation, linking, and personalization in a live, real-time system. Please see our demonstration video[1] for additional information and also visit the EigenNews website[2].

[1] http://blackhole1.stanford.edu/EigenNews.mov
[2] http://eigennews.stanford.edu

MM'13, October 21–25, 2013, Barcelona, Spain.
ACM 978-1-4503-2404-5/13/10.
http://dx.doi.org/10.1145/2502081.2502270.

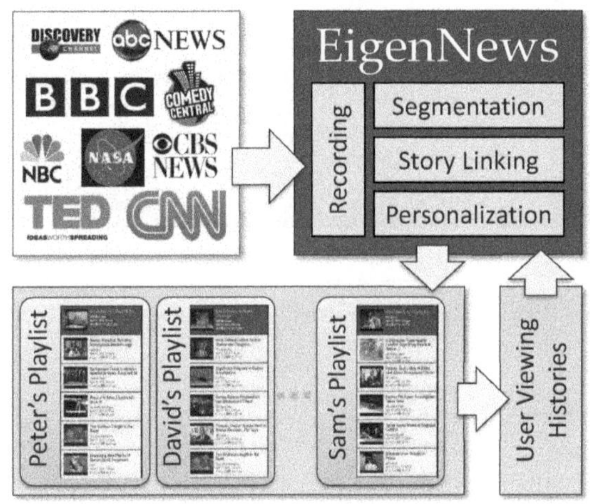

Figure 1: The EigenNews system architecture.

2. SYSTEM ARCHITECTURE

An overview of the system is shown in Fig. 1. We use several PCs and TV tuners to continually record television news programs from over-the-air (OTA) broadcasts and cable channels. These programs include national morning and evening news (e.g., *TODAY Show*, *ABC World News*), investigative journalism (e.g., *60 Minutes*), and late-night talk shows (e.g., *The Tonight Show*). We record the closed captioning (CC) along with each program.

We extract individual news segments from each recorded program by considering CC, audio, and visual cues [2]. CC cues such as story boundary markers as well as transition phrases are strong indicators of a change in topic. However, using the CC alone produces unreliable results due to the variable delay between the CC and the video stream. Thus, we perform automatic speech recognition (ASR) on the audio track using the CMUSphinx toolkit [4] to generate time-stamps for ASR-detected words. Matching these ASR-detected words with CC words via dynamic time warping provides accurate time-stamps for the CC and mitigates the undesirable delay. In addition to analyzing the CC and audio, keyframes are extracted from the video once per second to detect visual indicators of story boundaries. One important visual indicator is the presence of a program logo in a keyframe. To detect a logo, we utilize the image matching algorithm developed by Chen et al. [1]. Story boundary indicators in each modality are combined to perform segmentation.

Figure 2: Three ways to view EigenNews: *Playlist* (top), *Word Cloud* (bottom left), and *Grid* (bottom right).

Segmented videos are then matched with news articles from online sources (e.g., cnn.com, nytimes.com) to obtain descriptive titles, thumbnails, and categories. Several different comparisons are performed between videos and articles. First, the CC of a segmented video is compared with the text of the online news article using bag-of-words histograms. A match is declared if the *tf-idf* histogram intersection score exceeds a threshold. Second, named entities are extracted using the Stanford Named Entity Recognizer [3] and OpenCalais. A video and news article are paired if the video's CC contains more than 5 named entities in common with the article's text. Third, keyframes of videos are compared with the images of articles using the same image matching algorithm used for story segmentation. Note that these comparisons can also be performed between segmented videos to find related or duplicate videos. Once a video is matched with a news article, the titles, thumbnails, and categories of the article are automatically associated with the video.

Finally, a personalized playlist is generated for each user. Since each user has a limited amount of time to watch news videos, it is desirable for chosen videos to span the major news stories of the day. We cast this scenario as a maximum coverage problem where elements are the segmented videos and segmented videos about the same story belong to the same set [2]. Furthermore, news videos in the objective function of the maximum coverage problem are weighted by a linear combination of several personalization factors. These factors include a user's settings page, where a user indicates preferences for specific news programs or news categories, and the number of related videos a user has watched. Additionally, more recent videos receive higher weighting. Intuitively, this formulation chooses videos of trending stories, which originated from news programs the user prefers, and are also associated with categories the user is interested in.

3. USER INTERFACE

We also demonstrate three different user interfaces that we have developed and that are shown in Fig. 2. These three interfaces, *Playlist*, *Grid*, and *Word Cloud*, cater to different tastes that the user may have towards exploring the day's most relevant stories. The playlist view shows all the videos as rearrangeable tiles, grid view plays all videos simultaneously, and words in the word cloud indicate how prominent a word is in the day's news corpus.

In addition to the standard website, which is compatible across major browsers (Chrome, Firefox, Safari, Internet Explorer), we also developed a mobile version of EigenNews which works on devices such as the iPhone and iPad. The mobile version includes the same original viewing capabilities but can also extend to be a secondary device when paired with another display device. This includes allowing a user to treat the mobile device as a remote control (play, pause, choose next story) or to view additional information about the story they are watching.

4. IMPLEMENTATION

The EigenNews system has been recording content since July 2012. Statistics about the recordings are shown in Table 1. A 30 minute recording is processed in about 15 minutes where story linking and transcoding are performed in parallel, as shown in Fig. 3. Transcoding segmented videos to MP4 and OGV and to multiple bitrates is necessary to retain compatibility with our HTML5 video player and to accommodate users with different bandwidths, respectively. Subsequently, links to segmented videos and their associated metadata are stored in a MySQL database.

Table 1: EigenNews System

Number of different news programs	42
Number of news categories	28
Number of news channels	16 (4 OTA 12 cable)
Number of segmented videos (per day/total)	355/20,000+
Total time of recordings per day	16 hours
Storage used (per day/total)	40GB/2TB+

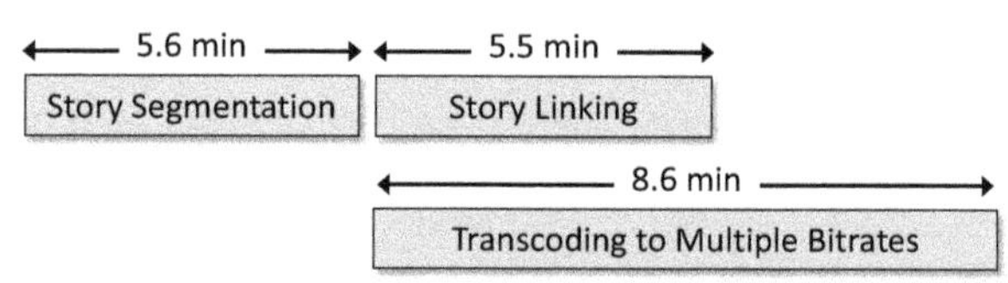

Figure 3: Breakdown of the video processing time.

5. REFERENCES

[1] D. Chen, P. Vajda, S. Tsai, M. Daneshi, M. Yu, A. Araujo, H. Chen, and B. Girod. Analysis of Visual Similarity in News Videos with Robust and Memory-Efficient Image Retrieval. *ICME MMIX*, July 2013.

[2] M. Daneshi, P. Vajda, D. Chen, S. Tsai, M. Yu, A. Araujo, H. Chen, and B. Girod. EigenNews: Generating and Delivering Personalized News Videos. *IEEE BRUREC*, July 2013.

[3] J. Finkel, T. Grenager, and G. Manning. Incorporating Non-local Information into Information Extraction Systems by Gibbs Sampling. *ACL*, pages 363–370, 2005.

[4] W. Walker, P. Lamere, P. P. Kwok, B. Raj, R. Singh, E. Gouvea, P. Wolf, and J. Woelfel. Sphinx-4: a flexible open source framework for speech recognition. Technical report, 2004.

NovaEmötions: Winning with a Smile

André Mourão, João Magalhães
Departamento de Informática
Faculdade de Ciências e Tecnologia
Universidade Nova de Lisboa
Quinta da Torre, Caparica, Portugal
a.mourao@campus.fct.unl.pt, jm.magalhaes@fct.unl.pt

ABSTRACT
Human-computer interaction (HCI) is expanding towards natural modalities of human expression. Gestures, body movements and other affective interaction techniques can change the way computers interact with humans. In this demo, we display a fully playable version of NovaEmötions, a competitive game where players score by acting an emotion through a facial expression. The game is designed to offer a competitive playing experience using only facial expressions. Despite the novelty of the interaction method, our game scoring algorithm kept players engaged and competitive.

Categories and Subject Descriptors
I.2.1 Applications and Expert Systems; **H.5.2** User Interfaces; **I.2.10** Vision and Scene Understanding.

General Terms
Human Factors, Design.

Keywords
Affective interaction, videogames, competitive games.

1 INTRODUCTION
Interaction between humans encompasses more than words, gestures or actions and the face is a fundamental part of communication. Facial expressions, for example, can help interaction by adding tone or intention to words. As Tian, Kanade and Cohn [6] put it, facial expressions are "the facial changes in response to a person's internal emotional states, intentions, or social communications.

The proposed game explores the player's facial expression as the sole input. Previous work has explored affective features in games but not at the level of interaction. The closest approaches, [1, 4], are aimed at people with Autistic Spectrum Disorders (ASD). Their aim is to teach emotions through facial expressions. In contrast, our approach is based on competitiveness: it does not matter if your expression is completely correct, as long as it is closer to the prototype expression than your opponent's expression.

The NovaEmötions game is the focus of this demo – it is an interactive game exploring affective features based on the face. Our scoring algorithm was designed to tackle the challenges of affective interaction in videogames. We researched methods for measuring displays of affect, taking into account fair competitiveness and smoothed responses. The game was already tested on a large pool of users (Figure 1). This initial trial gave us positive insight on the application of facial expression in videogames and we have released a facial expression images dataset based on a novel and realistic setting: users playing games where a player's facial expression has an impact on the game score.

MM '13, Oct 21-25 2013, Barcelona, Spain
ACM 978-1-4503-2404-5/13/10.
http://dx.doi.org/10.1145/2502081.2502271

Figure 1. Players and audience.

2 GAME DESIGN
NovaEmötions is a game that explores players' facial expressions as the sole controller. Several challenges exist to accomplish such natural interaction [5]. The most critical one resides on designing smooth facial expressions recognition. The design of the game must not frustrate the user and must react homogeneously, independently of the expression being performed. With these requirements in mind, we identified the key design aspects of an affect-based interaction framework to be the following:

1. **Affective awareness** – users (i.e. players) must realize that the system (i.e. the game) is aware of them. This triggers a mindset that prepares them for the game interaction and the lack of a mechanical control;
2. **Affective challenge** – each game round must face a challenge to the player. This challenge assumes the form of an emotion that must be performed. The player displays the emotion through an intentional facial expression;
3. **Affect-based interaction** – the framework must limit the interaction to a well-defined set of affective user-responses. The reaction to players' displays of affection must be unambiguous and in real-time. Weakly specified interactions will frustrate users with unrelated actions-reactions.

We have found these design principles to be fundamental to achieve an effective interaction based on facial expression.

2.1 Main screen

The main screen (in Figure 2) is composed by three components: the player's information component (A) that contains the currently detected expression (A1), the last obtained score (A2) and the best round score (A3); the current round challenge expression label and stimulus image (B); and the game total round score and the current round timer (C). Players were asked to perform the expression of the expected label.

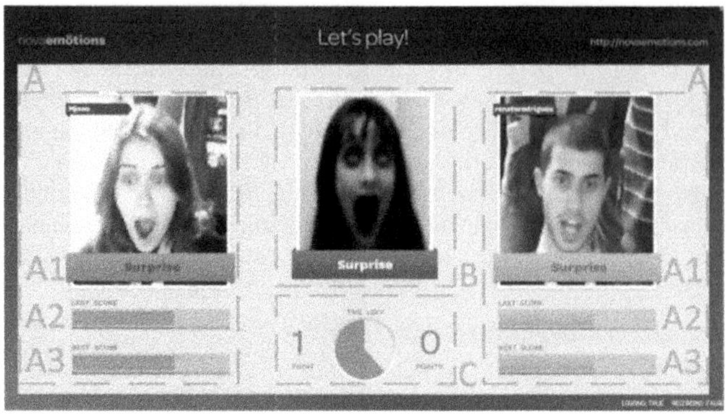

Figure 2. Two players performing the *Surprise* expression.

2.2 Gameplay

NovaEmötions is a two-players game where the objective is to perform a set of facial expressions. Players play simultaneously and facial expressions are competitively scored. The player that performs an expression closer to the one asked, wins a round – the player who wins more rounds wins the game. Before the game starts, the two players must be selected from the audience. The game gives the two best guesses automatically and the organizer (or players) confirms the selection. The game then progresses to a series of rounds (Figure 3):

1. A reaction image is displayed, along with the label of the expected expression;
2. When a face is detected, the facial expression is recognized, player's label is updated with the recognized expression and the scores are updated. The process is repeated through the round, until the timer ends;
3. At the end of the round, the player with the highest score wins a point. If the player's best score is the same, they both get one point;
4. The game will continue until a set number of images are displayed. In the end, a screen with the winner is displayed.

The game scoring algorithm provides a realistic and balanced reaction to the players' expression. Our goal was to devise a novel game scoring strategy to increase the competitiveness of the game and overcome algorithmic limitations. At the core of our approach is the prior knowledge that we know what the expected expression is. We explore this information, along with the feature dissimilarity and the detected facial expression, to create improved labels and scores to design the game's scoring algorithm. The game algorithms are detailed in [3]

2.3 Facial expression features

To represent the possible facial expressions, we have chosen EMFACS (Emotion Facial Action Coding System) [2] because its wide adoption by the community and there are training datasets available. Gabor wavelets were a popular choice at the First Facial Expression Recognition Challenge [7] and were the approach we've taken to extract facial expression features. Facial expression classification is based on a Support Vector Machine.

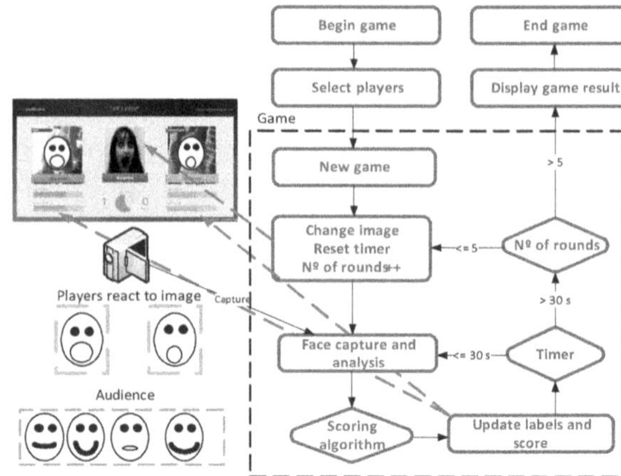

Figure 3. Game overview.

3 CONCLUSION

In this demo, we proposed an emotion-based game exploring facial expressions as the sole interaction mechanism. Affect-based computer interaction still has many challenges to be researched and we believe the proposed game illustrates how such novel interaction paradigm can be embedded in computational systems. Our demo provides a concrete and novel view on how to use facial expressions in competitive computer games.

4 REFERENCES

[1] Deriso, D. et al. 2012. Emotion Mirror: A Novel Intervention for Autism Based on Real-Time Expression Recognition. *Computer Vision – ECCV Workshops and Demonstrations*. A. Fusiello et al., eds. Springer. 671–674.

[2] Ekman, P. et al. 1978. *Facial Action Coding System: A Technique for the Measurement of Facial Movement*. Consulting Psychologists Press.

[3] Mourão, A. and Magalhães, J. 2013. Competitive affective gaming: Winning with a Smile. *ACM Multimedia* (2013).

[4] Orvalho, V. et al. 2009. What a Feeling: Learning Facial Expressions and Emotions. *Videojogos Conference* (2009), 1–11.

[5] Pantic, M. et al. 2005. Affective multimodal human-computer interaction. *ACM Multimedia* (2005), 669–676.

[6] Tian, Y.L. et al. 2005. Facial expression analysis. *Handbook of face recognition*. S.Z. Li and A.K. Jain, eds. Springer. 247–275.

[7] Valstar, M.F. et al. 2012. Meta-Analysis of the First Facial Expression Recognition Challenge. *IEEE Trans on Systems, Man, and Cybernetics, Part B: Cybernetics*. 42, 4 (2012), 966 – 979.

Tell Me What Happened Here in History

Jia Chen†, Qin Jin‡, Weipeng Zhang†, Shenghua Bao♮, Zhong Su♮, Yong Yu†

†Dept. of Computer Science & Engineering, Shanghai Jiao Tong University, China
{chenjia, weipengzhang, yyu}@apex.sjtu.edu.cn
‡ School of information, Renmin University of China, China
qjin@ruc.edu.cn
♮IBM China Research Laboratory, Beijing, China
{baoshhua, suzhong}@cn.ibm.com

ABSTRACT

This demo shows our system that takes a landmark image as input, recognizes the landmark from the image and returns historical events of the landmark with related photos. Different from existing landmark related researches, we focus on the temporal dimension of a landmark. Our system automatically recognizes the landmark, shows historical events chronologically and provides detailed photos for the events. To build these functions, we fuse information from multiple online resources. Our online demo is available at `http://lm.apexlab.org/lmHistory`

Categories and Subject Descriptors

H.3.1 [**Information Systems**]: INFORMATION STORAGE AND RETRIEVALContent Analysis and Indexing

Keywords

history photo, landmark

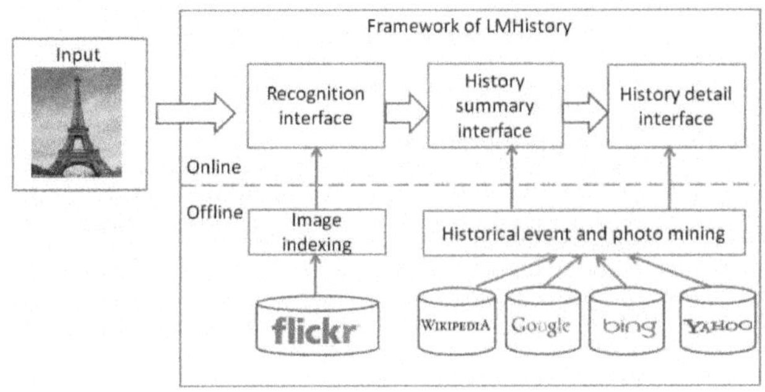

Figure 1: Framework of LMHistory

1. INTRODUCTION

With the growing bandwidth, more and more images appear on the internet nowadays. Among these images, landmark images are a specific kind of images that have special interest to people. While traveling in a city, people usually learn about the city through visiting the landmarks of the city. Another trend is that with the growing popularity of mobiles, people turn to look for help from their smart phones when visiting a new place. In this demo, we design an application considering cross connection of these two trends. To be more specific, our system receives an image query and returns historical information of the landmark recognized from the image. The scenario is that when travellers visit a new landmark in a city, they are usually curious about the history behind the landmark. Our system receives images taken by the smart phone, recognizes the landmark automatically, and provides organized historical information mined from the internet to users. The historical information is listed by events on time axis. Each event is depicted by a text paragraph and related photos. Users can explore these information on their smart phone to enrich their travel experience. Furthermore, the system has wider application scenarios such as compiling history data for online museums and illustrating history in education etc.

In recent years, landmark photos have received growing attention from the research community. Researchers in work[**?**] build a system to do diversified landmark search. Work[**?**] focuses on mining landmarks from blogs. Work[**?**] builds a system to tour the photos in a virtual 3D space. Work[**?**] focuses on generating travel routes from geo-tagged photos for trip planning. The latter two researches focus on the spacial dimension of the landmark. Different from them, our system focuses on the temporal dimension, which has never been explored in landmark research community to the best of our knowledge.

Our system provides the following three functions:
1.efficient landmark recognition: the entire process of uploading and recognizing takes less than a second.
2.showing history events chronologically: history events are mined from Wikipedia. Each event is represented by a triplet of location, time and characters. Additionally, a confidence score is given for each event indicating the reliability of mined photos.
3.showing historical photos in details: we extract photo candidates from multiple image search engines. Irrelevant photos are filtered based on three types of evidences.

MM'13, October 21–25, 2013, Barcelona, Spain.
Copyright 2013 ACM 978-1-4503-2404-5/13/10
http://dx.doi.org/10.1145/2502081.2502272. .

Figure 2: Recognition interface

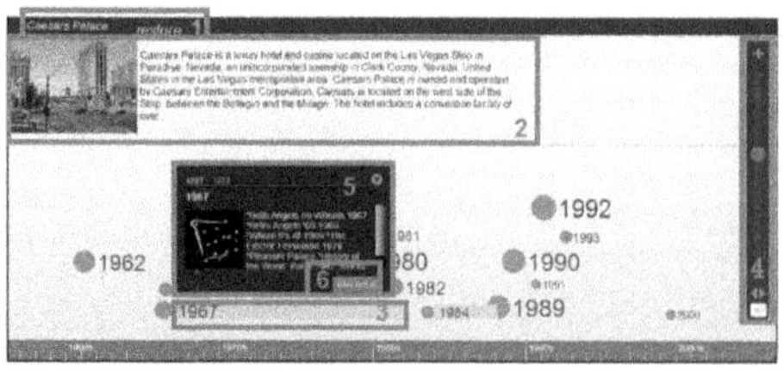

Figure 3: History summary interface

2. SYSTEM OVERVIEW

There are three interfaces in our system: recognition interface, history summary interface and history detail interface. As shown in Figure ??, the recognition interface is driven by the image indexing module, which exploits image data from online photo sharing site Flickr; both the history summary and detail interfaces are driven by the historical event and photo mining module, which fuses data from online encyclopedia site Wikipedia and three image search engines.

Recognition interface: As shown in Figure ??, this interface accepts input from users and shows the recognition results. In the tab panel, users choose to paste the url of an online image(area 1), or upload an image(area 2) or browse example landmarks(area 3). Once the input is given, our system will recognize the landmark in less than a second. The query photo will be shown on the left(area 4) and top 3 landmark candidates are shown on the right(area 5). After selecting a landmark, users will be brought to the history summary interface of the landmark.

History summary interface: As shown in Figure ??, this interface shows history events aligned on time axis. Additionally, a brief event description and one representative event photo will be shown for each event. The top bar shows the name of the landmark and a "Restore" button(area 1). The restore button helps fit all the event dots into one screen. In the middle is a representative current view and a paragraph of general introduction of the landmark(area 2). In the bottom are historical events shown as dots aligned by the start year on the time axis. Some events lasted for several years and the duration is shown by a grey bar behind the dot. Figure ?? shows an event lasting from 1967 to 1982(area 3). Bigger dots represent that corresponding events contain photos of better quality. Users can drag mouse to move to the left or to the right on the time axis.

There is a bar controlling the zooming level on the right(area 4). Larger zooming level zooms out on time axis and fewer events will be shown in one screen. Clicking on the dot, users will see a pop up panel(area 5) containing the summary of the event. On the top of the panel is the year when the event happened. In the major part of the panel, the representative photo about the event is shown on the left and event description is shown on the right. The characters involved in the event are highlighted by bold italic font in the

Figure 4: History detail interface

description. Clicking on the "see detail" link(area 6) in the bottom right corner in the pop up panel, users are brought to the history detail interface of the event.

History detail interface: As shown in Figure ??, this interface shows both detailed background introduction of the event and abundant historical photos. On the top is a paragraph describing the event(area 1). In the bottom(area 2), event related historical photos are displayed in cascade layout. In this interface, users get detailed photo information of the landmark.

3. TECHNICAL DETAILS

Image indexing module: Altogether 106 landmarks and around 79,773 photos are indexed for recognition. We use SURF feature in image retrieval and rank landmarks based on the top 100 retrieved images.

Historical event and photo mining module: For each landmark, we mine historical events from the history section in Wikipedia. For each event, we retrieve related photos for each event by querying three image search engines. However, not all retrieved photos are historical event photos. We design a score to automatically evaluate the quality for each image. The score considers the image's rank in different search engines' results, image content similarity to other images, and web page of this image. Additionally, we design another score to automatically evaluate the quality of the entire image collection for each event.

4. CONCLUSION

The main contribution of the proposed system are summarized as follows:

1.It is the first landmark related application that explores the temporal dimension of a landmark.

2.Our system provides a convenient interface for users to search the landmark by image, browse the history events chronologically, and explore historical photos in details.

3.Our system has mined altogether 612 events for 106 landmarks with 5497 historical photos.

5. REFERENCES

[1] R. Ji, X. Xie, H. Yao, and W.-Y. Ma. Mining city landmarks from blogs by graph modeling. In *ACM Multimedia*, pages 105–114, 2009.

[2] X. Lu, C. Wang, J.-M. Yang, Y. Pang, and L. Zhang. Photo2trip: generating travel routes from geo-tagged photos for trip planning. In *ACM Multimedia*, pages 143–152, 2010.

[3] N. Snavely, S. M. Seitz, and R. Szeliski. Photo tourism: exploring photo collections in 3d. *ACM Trans. Graph.*, 25(3):835–846, 2006.

[4] J. Ye, J. Chen, Z. Chen, Y. Zhu, S. Bao, Z. Su, and Y. Yu. Dlmsearch: diversified landmark search by photo. In *ACM Multimedia*, pages 905–908, 2012.

Group TV: A Cloud based Social TV for Group Social Experience

Xiaoyan Wang, Lifeng Sun, Shou Wang
Tsinghua National Laboratory for Information Science and Technology, Beijing Key Laboratory of Networked Multimedia, Department of Computer Science and Technology, Tsinghua University, Beijing, China
muyushiok@gmail.com, sunlf@tsinghua.edu.cn, wangshousoso@126.com

ABSTRACT
Social TV allows people to meet the demand of social experience while watching videos. Existing solutions cannot balance interest among group and provide good viewing quality for all members with different network bandwidth and devices. Realizing that people in group will be more tolerant, trusting and willing to help each other, we developed a cloud based social TV for online group video service. We emphasize group behavior in our application and introduce the concept of tolerance and trust between users to balance their interest. Group Recommendation results we show in our system can obtain overall high satisfaction while provides diverse content. We also design a collaborative video distribution technology to optimize network resource utility for fluency and high quality viewing experience. The entire operation of the system emphasizes on simplicity, collaboration and smooth, providing excellent social TV experience.

Categories and Subject Descriptors
H.5.1 [**Multimedia Information systems**]:

Keywords
Social TV, Group Recommendation, collaborative video delivery

1. INTRODUCTION
Today, online social network has greatly reshaped how people exchange information and consume online videos. With the rising heat of social network and video website, Social TV services become an upward trend of social media applications, which allow users to share videos and interact with each other [1].

Moreover, online group behavior such as watching video together with a group of online friends is an important factor for enabling remote shared experiences, which is for a large part of social activity in daily life[2]. Many efforts have been tried to provide social group experience, such as Facebook users can join music that their friends are listening, Netflix allows users to share video on Facebook.

Satisfying social experience of online group should meet two key requirements. On the one hand, it should provide group users video content, which meet their common interest. On the other hand, the viewing quality for all members with different network bandwidth and devices should be good enough to give the user pleasure experience in group.

MM'13, October 21–25, 2013, Barcelona, Spain.
ACM 978-1-4503-2404-5/13/10.

Existing Social TV applications such like Yap.TV mainly focus on personalized video recommendation. Current research works mainly use two methods [3,4]. One is to combine group members into a "pseudo-user", or to merge recommendation results of individuals. However, most group recommendation technology is used for offline group activities and little is for online applications. What's more, factors considered in the recommendation process is generally users' video content, as well as their social relationships between them, seldom taking into accord the impact of individual personality of users to the whole quality of group recommendation.

Dynamic Adaptive Streaming over HTTP (DASH) is widely deployed on the Internet that provides uninterrupted video streaming service to users with dynamic network conditions and heterogeneous devices [5]. However, current DASH methods only consider single user, which cannot utilize all the network resource among group users. While P2P video streaming technologies lack of effective incentive mechanism among peers.
Realizing that people in group will be more tolerant, trusting and willing to help each other, we developed an cloud based social TV for online group video service. Our work mainly focuses on three points. First of all, we emphasis on the context of social group to achieve higher overall group satisfaction and discover a variety of media content which can have an impact on the development of personal interest. Secondly, we are concerned about the streaming network collaboration distribution to complete real-time sharing of bandwidth, thus enhancing social media playback fluency and user experience. Thirdly, we are committed to enhance user's interactive experience of social TV applications.

2. SYSTEM OVERVIEW

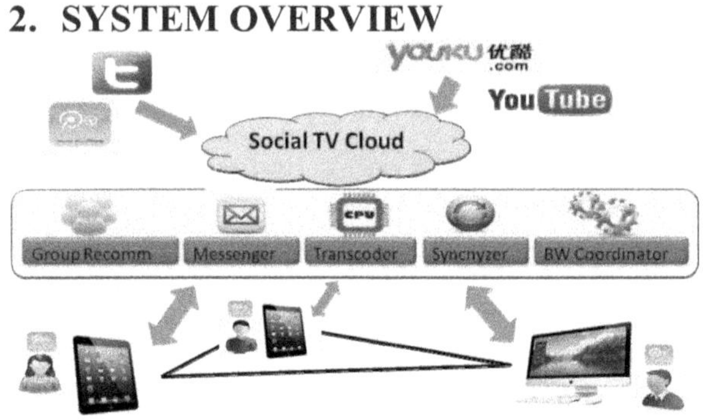

Figure 1: System Framework of Group TV

2.1 Group Recommendation
Social TV satisfies both users' demand of entertainment consumption and socialization through high-quality content push. The significance of group recommended lies more on discovering a variety of media content, improving group invigorate and broaden users' preference.

Unlike personalized recommendation, group recommendation is much more complex, since it is always difficult to balance satisfaction among a couple of people. In order to address the above problems, we define the concept of "tolerance" of individual users which is used as the feature to describe how a person prefer to stick to their own wishes or to meet the others.

The framework of our Group recommender system is showed as Fig. 2. We first divide a group of users who are supposed to watch video together into several categories based on their preferences. In each category, we work out personalized recommendation for each user and re-amendment the results by analyzing "tolerance" for each user, together with trust relation between each of them. The tolerance is achieved by analyzing users' Sina Weibo behavior. Then we combine the result of each category to obtain the final group recommendation output.

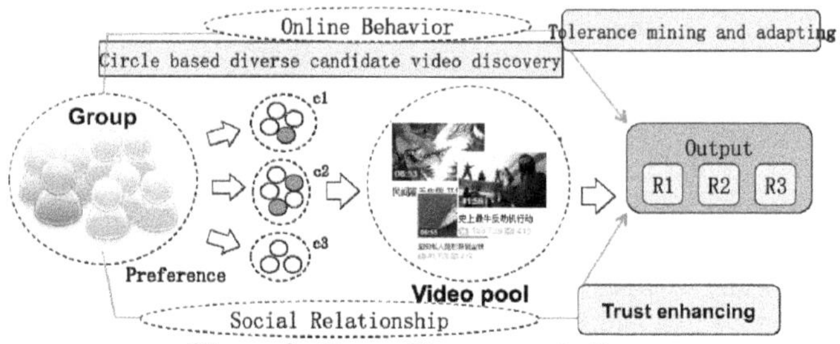

Figure 2: Group Recommendation

2.2 Distributed Video Delivery Collaboration

For network and device diversity in the group, existing DASH technologies run in client-server model, and cannot take full advantage of the network resources within the groups. Therefore, we propose a collaborative group video delivery mechanism to improve average viewing quality among group by leveraging members with high bandwidth to assist other member get additional data for higher quality level in DASH. Each member exchange quality metrics such as download bitrate, rebuffer time and RTT delay periodically with the BW Coordinator run in the social TV cloud. Because the group size is relative small, usually less than 10 individuals, the BW Coordinator can collect the whole group network resource utilizing status in real-time. Based on this information, BW Coordinator makes a global data delivery schedule for each member with both data path and bitrate, which solve the optimization problem of getting Max average quality with Min DASH quality levels. Here, little quality levels mean the data utility will be increased among different members and improve the efficiency of bandwidth. Moreover, if there are no suitable quality levels in Video CDN node, BW Coordinator will invoke the Transcoder in social TV cloud to transcode the original video to required bitrate for the group in real time.

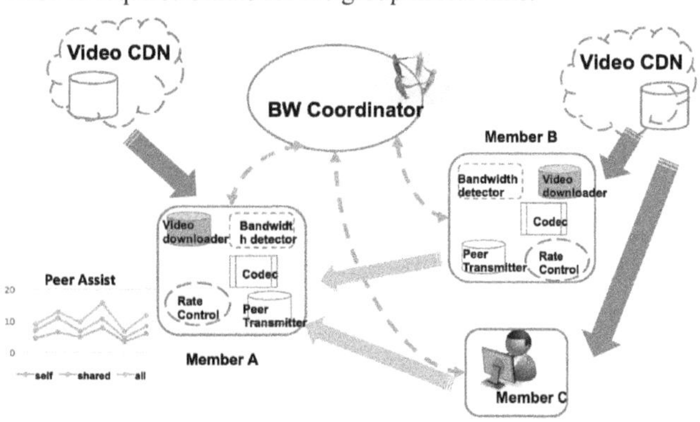

Figure 3: Distributed Video Delivery Collaboration

3. DEMONSTRATION[1] SETUP

Our *Group TV* system is deployed in Cloud and the user interface was developed on the iPad. User can easily find the candidate group members, as well as browsing their video viewing history. Once adding a friend into group, group recommendation results will be dynamically updated. Users can also view the detailed information of each recommended video and ultimately select the favorite one to watch together.

After entering the watch page, each user can see how others contribute their bandwidth to help him watching fluent video streaming. *Group TV* allows users to make comments or discussions that will be presented along with the progress bar.

The design of interface is concise and friendly enough, with naturally guidance, smoothly interaction, and fully reflects the social characteristics.

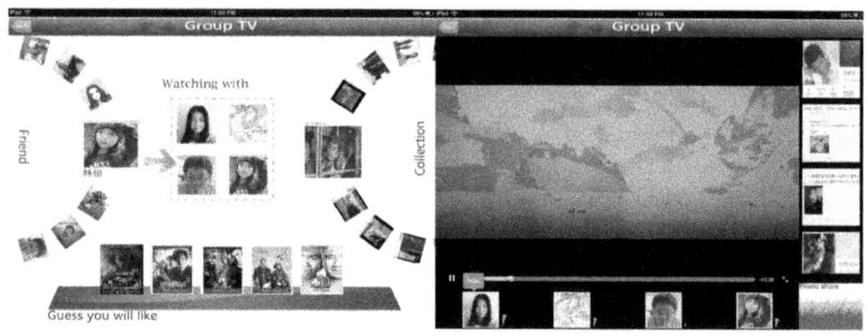

Figure 4: User Interface

4. CONCLUSION

Online group behavior such as watching video together with a group of online friends is an important factor for enabling remote shared experience. In this demonstration, we present a novel Social TV system named Group TV that allows people to explore the joy of watching videos with friends. It provides diverse video discovery, common interest balance, and collaborative video delivery.

5. ACKNOWLEDGMENT

This work is supported by NSFC under Grant No.61272231 and 973 Program under Grant No. 2011CB302206. Thanks for the support from Tsinghua-Tencent Joint Laboratory.

6. REFERENCES

[1] C. Metcalf, G. Harboe, J. Tullio, N. Massey, G. Romano, E. Huang, and F. Bentley, "Examining presence and lightweight messaging in a social television experience," in ACM TOMCCAP, 2008.

[2] David Geerts, Ishan Vaishnavi, Rufael Mekuria, Oskar van Deventer, Pablo Cesar, Are we in Sync? Synchronization Requirements for Watching Online Video Together, ACM CHI 2011.

[3] M.Gartrell, X.Xing, Q.Lv, A.Beach, R.Han, S.Mishra and K. Seada.Enhancing Group Recommendation by Incorporating Social Relationship Interactions. GROUP 2010.

[4] Xiwang Yang,Harald Steck_,Yong Liu. Circle based Recommendation in Online Social Networks. KDD2012

[5] Junchen Jiang,Vyas Sekar,Hui Zhang,"Improving fairness, efficiency, and stability in HTTP-based adaptive video streaming with FESTIVE" ,ACM CoNEXT '12 .

[1] Demo video can be downloaded from Dropbox

GeSoDeck: A Geo-Social Event Detection and Tracking System *

Xingyu Gao[1,2,3], Juan Cao[1,2], Zhiwei Jin[1,2,3], Xin Li[4], Jintao Li[1,2]
[1]Institute of Computing Technology, Chinese Academy of Sciences, Beijing, China
[2]Beijing Key Laboratory of Mobile Computing and Pervasive Device, Beijing, China
[3]University of Chinese Academy of Sciences, Beijing, China
[4]Department of Computer Science and Technology, Tsinghua University, Beijing, China

ABSTRACT

This demonstration presents a novel geo-social event detection and tracking system based on geographical pattern mining and content analysis, called "GeSoDeck". A user can capture what events happened by our system. Unlike most existing social event detection applications, GeSoDeck aims to detect events with high accuracy and efficiency, and track them as well. Given a geographical area, the system can not only detect diverse social events in this area using the geographical pattern mining and density-based *K-means* clustering, but also track the representative tweets of the detected event in real time, mining geographical diffusion trajectory on the map and temporal pattern of retweeting process. On a realistic dataset collected from Sina Weibo, the system can outperform the state-of-the-art methods.

Categories and Subject Descriptors

H.2.8 [**Database Applications**]: Spatial Databases and GIS; H.3.1 [**Information Storage and Retrieval**]: Content Analysis and Indexing

Keywords

Geo-Social Event, Detection, Tracking

1. INTRODUCTION

The prevalent social media has already been the most convenient and fast way to acquire information recently. A multitude of people publish their tweets, related photos and videos on the online social media website in daily life. However, with colossal size of real-time data in the form of messages and status updates, about 40% of them are pointless according to a study by Pear Analytics [1]. Then, a challenging task is how to extract meaningful event in tremendous amount of data, especially for the researchers. With increasing location-sharing social media services in Twitter, Sina Weibo, and Tencent Weibo, geo-social event detection and tracking is becoming more important and interesting.

* This work is supported by National Nature Science Foundation of China (61172153), National Key Technology Research and Development Program of China (2012BAH39B02).

MM'13, October 21–25, 2013, Barcelona, Spain.
ACM 978-1-4503-2404-5/13/10.
http://dx.doi.org/10.1145/2502081.2502274.

Figure 1: The user interface of our proposed geo-social event detection and tracking system. The left shows Chinese map with geo-areas, the right demonstrates the detected event list for a geo-area, and the bottom is the photos related to the event.

Although a lot of efforts have been made on event detection such as [2], it is observed that a few of them should input the query manually, which leads that their methods could not be adopted to automatically discover a variety of socio-geographic events containing unknown events. Besides, unlike traditional event detection, geo-social event detection like [3, 4], also has these challenges: 1) automatic detection; 2) high accuracy and efficiency; and 3) trajectory tracking.

We demonstrate our work as a geo-social event detection and tracking system called "GeSoDeck". As shown in Figure 1, the user can capture what geo-social events happened by keywords, related tweets and photos, and track them as well. We first mine the geographical pattern of tweets and users in social activities, and discover unusual geographical area by the pattern. Then we employ density-based *K-means* clustering for the tweets in the unusual area. Furthermore, geo-social event is detected by the quantity of tweets in cluster. Also, the detected geo-social events can be efficiently displayed by the cluster with highly-frequent keywords, related tweets and photos. In order to provide instant trajectory tracking of the events, we mine geographical diffusion trajectory and temporal pattern of the detected events.

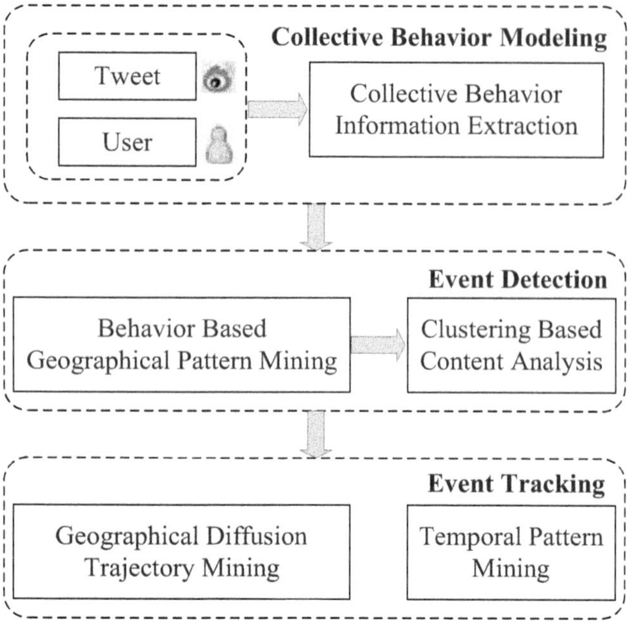

Figure 2: System Framework of GeSoDeck.

In conclusion, our GeSoDeck performs an accurate, efficient and user friendly system for geo-social event detection and tracking.

2. SYSTEM ARCHITECTURE

Figure 2 illustrates the system architecture of GeSoDeck: 1) In the collective behavior modeling stage, collective behavior is described by the tweets and users in the geographical area. 2) In the event detection stage, we combine geographical pattern mining and clustering based content analysis to detect event. Then the detected events are demonstrated by keywords, related tweets and photos. 3) In the event tracking stage, once the system receives selection by user on the representative tweet of event, the main tracking flow includes geographical diffusion trajectory and temporal pattern mining.

3. SYSTEM IMPLEMENTATION

In this section, we describe each component of GeSoDeck in detail.

3.1 Collective Behavior Modeling

Event is a group of aggregating individuals and behaviors which participate in the activity. Accordingly, we describe the social event by the following two aspects. 1) *Behaviors:* number of *tweets* are posted within a specific time period in the geographical district. We count the total occurrence of tweets during a specific period of time. 2) *Individuals:* number of microblog *users* are found within a specific period of time in the geographical region. Therefore, we count the total number of users who published their tweets.

3.2 Event Detection

In order to mine the geographical pattern of social event, we calculate the alternation of user and tweet count in the geographical area at each time unit of each two days (one day is equally divided into 4 non-overlapping time units), so as to better reflect alternation rule of users and tweets in the geographical region. By estimated geographical pattern of social activities, if the aggregated users or tweets in the area are more or less frequent, i.e. alternation value exceeds the pattern threshold, then the unusual geographical region is explored.

Besides the geographical attribute, social event is also comprised of a series of highly-posted tweets and highly-frequent keywords. We adopt density-based *K-means* clustering algorithm to cluster the tweets posted in unusual region. Words of the tweets are represented by Vector Space Model (VSM), and the distance of vectors is denoted by *Cosine* similarity in clustering. If the tweet number of cluster exceeds the threshold, then geo-social event is detected by the cluster with large quantity.

3.3 Event Tracking

After each geographical social event is detected, we rank the detected events by Term Frequency (TF) of keywords in the clusters. For each top K events, ranking results of the tweets in the cluster can be calculated by the retweeting count, and the top N key representative tweets of the event will be returned to the system.

If the user selects the representative tweet by interaction with the system, the geographical diffusion trajectory and temporal retweeting count will be demonstrated on the system interface.

4. EVALUATIONS

To evaluate the performance of GeSoDeck, we build our real world dataset MCG-Weibo collected from Sina Weibo. The dataset consists of 32,830,277 tweets within two months. The experiments show that our system can achieve 65% accuracy, which outperforms Lee's method [3, 4].

Furthermore, we evaluate our GeSoDeck system with the usability, user friendliness, and user experience. We invite 12 volunteers to use our system freely, and the scores $(1-5)$ are given by each subject. The higher score indicates the better satisfaction. The results show that the evaluation score for GeSoDeck is 4.1. Thus, our GeSoDeck system achieves good user satisfaction.

5. CONCLUSIONS

We have demonstrated an innovative geographical social event detection and tracking system, which is able to automatically detect social events with high accuracy and efficiency, and track them by user's interaction with the system. We plan to extend our work to integrate social applications in the future.

6. REFERENCES

[1] PearAnalytics. Twitter study. [Online], August 2009. `http://www.pearanalytics.com/wpcontent/uploads/2009/08/Twitter-Study-August-2009.pdf`.

[2] T. Sakaki, M. Okazaki, and Y. Matsuo. Tweet analysis for real-time event detection and earthquake reporting system development. *IEEE Trans. Knowl. Data Eng.*, 25(4):919–931, 2013.

[3] R. Lee and K. Sumiya. Measuring geographical regularities of crowd behaviors for twitter-based geo-social event detection. In *GIS-LBSN*, pages 1–10, 2010.

[4] R. Lee, S. Wakamiya, and K. Sumiya. Discovery of unusual regional social activities using geo-tagged microblogs. *World Wide Web*, 14(4):321–349, 2011.

Stereotime: A Wireless 2D and 3D Switchable Video Communication System

You Yang[1], Qiong Liu[1], Yue Gao[2], Binbin Xiong[1], Li Yu[1], Huanbo Luan[2], Rongrong Ji[3], Qi Tian[4]

1. Department of Electronics & Information Engineering, Huazhong University of Science & Technology, Wuhan, China
2. School of Computing, National University of Singapore, Singapore
3. Department of Cognitive Science, School of Information Science & Engineering, Xiamen University, Xiamen, China
4. Department of Computer Science, University of Texas at San Antonio

{yangyou,q.liu,hustlyu}@hust.edu.cn, {kevin.gaoy,viclol36,jirongrong}@gmail.com, qitian@cs.utsa.edu

ABSTRACT

Mobile 3D video communication, especially with 2D and 3D compatible, is a new paradigm for both video communication and 3D video processing. Current techniques face challenges in mobile devices when bundled constraints such as computation resource and compatibility should be considered. In this work, we present a wireless 2D and 3D switchable video communication to handle the previous challenges, and name it as Stereotime. The methods of Zig-Zag fast object segmentation, depth cues detection and merging, and texture-adaptive view generation are used for 3D scene reconstruction. We show the functionalities and compatibilities on 3D mobile devices in WiFi network environment.

Categories and Subject Descriptors

H.4.3 [**Information Systems Applications**]: Communications Applications; H.5.1 [**Information Interfaces and Presentation**]: Multimedia Information Systems

Keywords

Video communication, Visual content, View generation, Scene reconstruction

1. INTRODUCTION

Video communication has changed people's daily life for instance providing face-to-face long distance communication [1]. With the development of portable devices, video communication becomes ubiquitous, with popular and practical products include Facetime, LinPhone, etc. In recent years, three dimensional (3D) technologies [2, 3] have been widely applied. 3D displaying has been ported to mobile devices, and brings people with immersive 3D viewing experiences.

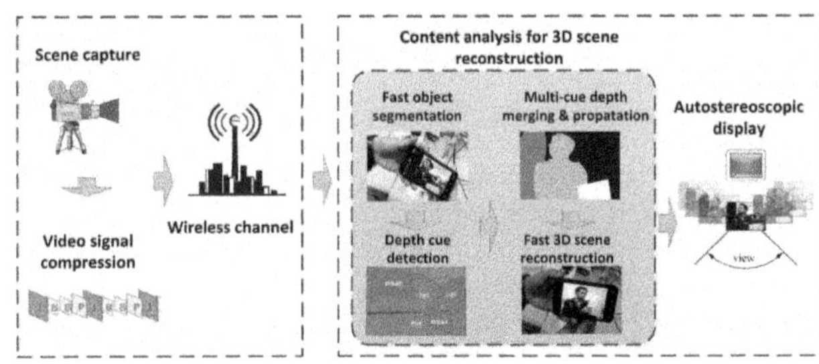

Figure 1: An overview of our proposed 3D Facetime.

With such attractive displaying capacity, 2D and 3D switchable functionality becomes a new paradigm in the fields of video communication and 3D video processing.

A natural solution is porting the system directly from wired networks to wireless networks and mobile devices [6]. This design includes stereo camera for scene capturing, stereo video codec for signal transmission, and autostereoscopic screen for 3D displaying. However, challenges may occur. The first challenge is the resource requirements of stereo video codec. Bundled coding techniques and spatio-temporal prediction in stereo video codec have significant resource requests[5]. The other challenge is 2D terminal users will receive redundant views if stereo camera is used.

Our recent efforts [7] have found that 3D scene can be reconstructed by content analysis. In the processing of reconstruction, depth information of the captured scene is first restored, then the depth information is propagated from key frame to the consequent frames, from which the 3D scene is finally reconstructed. Therefore, to deal with the above challenges, we present a 2D and 3D switchable video communication system with name Stereotime, for both traditional and 3D mobile device users. Figure 1 illustrates the framework of our proposed system.

In our system, we use the configurations as traditional video communication system, including single camera for scene capturing, video encoder for signal compression, and wireless channel for transmission. The key innovation in the proposed system is a content analysis based 3D scene reconstruction method applied on 3D terminals. In the proposed system, scene is captured as 2D video, compressed and transmitted to users but can be displayed in 3D style. For the user with 2D receiver, the system works in a tradi-

MM'13, October 21–25, 2013, Barcelona, Spain.
ACM 978-1-4503-2404-5/13/10.
http://–enter the whole DOI string from rightsreview form conf rmation.

tional video communication style. While for the user with 3D receiver, our system can provide 3D immersive viewing experiences.

2. SYSTEM OVERVIEW

We develop the Stereotime on a 3D mobile phone, and the interface of this system is shown by Figure 2. The system is composed by 4 components, including scene capturing, video signal compression, wireless transmission, and content analysis for 3D scene reconstruction.

Scene Capturing In video communication, people usually use convenient configurations for scene capturing. Typically, a web camera with VGA resolution and auto-focus (usually 2mm focal length) is used in common systems. This setting is adopted in our system for scene capturing.

Video Signal Compression Video encoding techniques are important for video transmission since the bitrate for raw video signals cannot be transmitted by wireless channel. We use H.264 video codec as the compression tool in our system. In the procedure of compression, only I- and P-type frames are used for the sake of real-time encoding. Furthermore, the interval length between two I-type frames is selected automatically by the encoder.

Wireless transmission Our system is designed independent to the wireless network constraints. Actually, with the help of H.264 video codec, the bandwidth for video transmission is less than 60Kbps in our system. Therefore, the system can be used in GSM with 200Kbps bandwidth, and also in WiFi networks with more than 50Mbps.

Content Analysis for 3D Scene Reconstruction 3D scene reconstruction is the key part to generate 3D content at the receiver side. The procedure of reconstruction is composed by 4 steps as following.

Fast Object Segmentation: The object segmentation is the pre-request for depth estimation. We assume that the chroma and illumination of a surface cannot change significantly, and the depth value of an object surface also satisfies this feature. Therefore, we use Zig-Zag scan method for fast object surface segmentation.

Depth Cue Detection: We detect two types of depth cues, including (a) crossing lines and vanishing point, and (b) occlusion cue. These cues are helpful to detect the relative depth information in the captured 2D scene.

Multi-cue Depth Merging and Depth Propagation: We assign depth value to every objects in the scene with the help of detected depth cues. After that, depth propagation method in [7] is used for saving the computation load in object segmentation and depth cue detection.

Fast 3D Scene Reconstruction: 3D scene can be reconstructed by the color image received by the mobile device and the depth information calculated by previous steps. After that, different views can be obtained, as shown by Figure 3. We adopt a texture-adaptive processing [4] to fill holes appeared in view switching, based on which the 3D scene can be fluently displayed on auto stereoscopic screen.

The proposed Stereotime system is performed on a mobile phone with Android 2.3 system and auto stereoscopic screen. The captured video resolution is 640×480, and X.264 encoder is applied for video compression. With these settings, our Stereotime only needs not more than 60Kpbs bandwidth in WiFi environment for video communication. Furthermore, the speed for 3D scene reconstruction can up to 10 fps and provide users fluent 3D display.

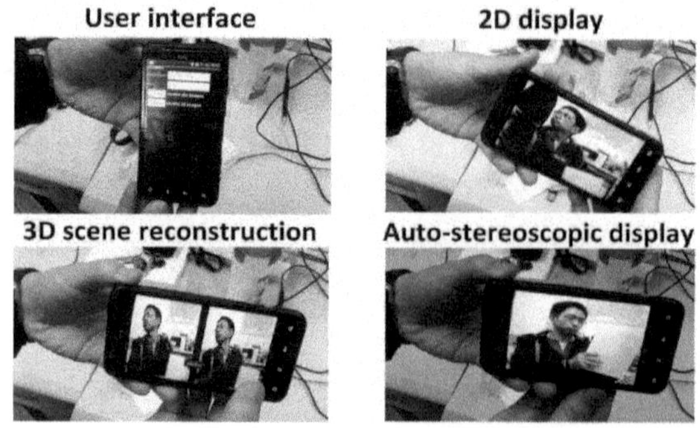

Figure 2: The interface and modes of Stereotime.

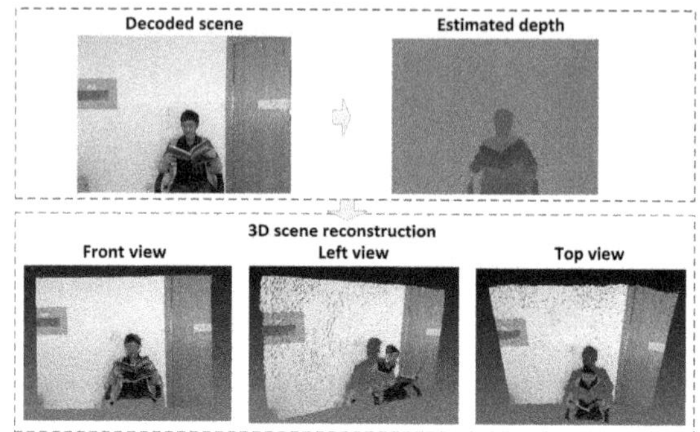

Figure 3: 3D scene reconstruction for different views.

3. CONCLUSIONS

In this system, we demonstrate a 2D and 3D compatible and switchable video communication system called 3D Face Time. Our system can provide immersive 3D chatting experiences to users with lower cost as traditional 2D video communication system.

4. ACKNOWLEDGEMENT

This work was supported by Natural Science Foundation of China (NSFC) (No.61170194, 61231010 and 61202301) and the National High Technology Research and Development Program ("863"Program) of China (No. 2012AA121604).

5. REFERENCES

[1] K. E. Finn, A. J. Sellen, and S. B. Wilbur. *Video-mediated communication.* L. Erlbaum Associates Inc., 1997.

[2] Y. Gao, J. Tang, R. Hong, S. Yan, Q. Dai, N. Zhang, and T. Chua. Camera constraint-free view-based 3D object retrieval. *IEEE Transactions on Image Processing*, 21(4):2269–2281, 2012.

[3] Y. Gao, M. Wang, D. Tao, R. Ji, and Q. Dai. 3D object retrieval and recognition with hypergraph analysis. *IEEE Transactions on Image Processing*, 21(9):4290–4303, 2012.

[4] Q. Liu, Y. Yang, Y. Gao, and R. Hong. Texture- adaptive hole-filling algorithm in raster-order for three-dimensional video applications. *Neurocomputing*, 111:154–160, 2013.

[5] P. Merkle, A. Smolic, K. Muller, and T. Wiegand. Efficient prediction structures for multiview video coding. *IEEE Trans. on CSVT*, 17(11):1461–1473, 2007.

[6] O. Schreer, P. Kauff, and T. Sikora. *3D videocommunication.* Wiley Online Library, 2005.

[7] Y. Yang, Q. Liu, R. Ji, and Y. Gao. Dynamic 3D scene depth reconstruction via optical flow field rectification. *PLoS ONE*, 7(11):e47041, 2012.

MagicBrush: Image Search by Color Sketch*

Xinghai Sun[1], Changhu Wang[2], Avneesh Sud[3], Chao Xu[1], Lei Zhang[2]
[1]Key Laboratory of Machine Perception (Ministry of Education), Peking Univ., Beijing, P. R. China
[2]Microsoft Research Asia, Beijing, P. R. China, [3]Microsoft Corp., Redmond, United States
{sunxh, xuchao}@cis.pku.edu.cn, {chw, avneesh.sud, leizhang}@microsoft.com

ABSTRACT

In this paper, we showcase the MagicBrush system, a novel painting-based image search engine. This system enables users to draw a color sketch as a query to find images. Different from existing works on sketch-based image retrieval, most of which focus on matching the shape structure without carefully considering other important visual modalities, MagicBrush takes into account the indispensable value of "color" related to "shape", and explores to make use of both the shape and color expectations that users usually have when they're imaging or searching for an image. To achieve this, we 1) develop a user-friendly interface to allow users to easily "paint out" their colorful visual expectations; 2) design a compact feature "color-edge word" to encode both shape and color information in a organic way; and 3) develop a novel matching and index structure to support a real-time response in 6.4 million images. By taking into account both shape and color information, the MagicBrush system helps users to vividly present what they are imagining, and retrieve images in a more natural way.

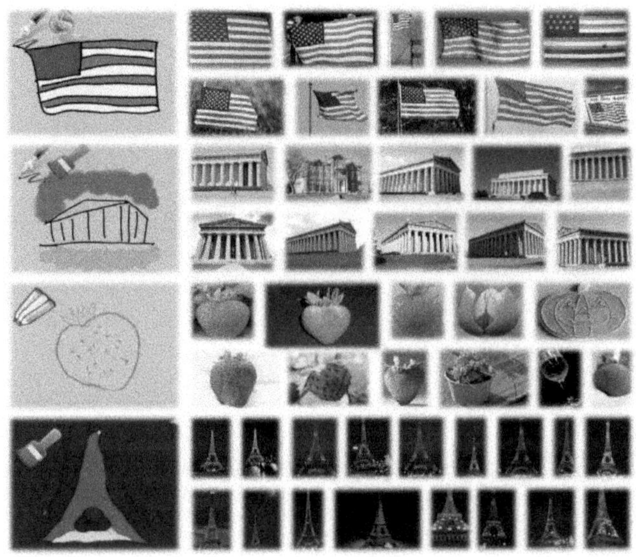

Figure 1: Examples of image search by color sketch (MagicBrush). The first column shows user-drawn color sketch queries, and the rest of columns show the search results matching both shape and color intention in users' paintings. Each row explains one of the four painting modes designed for natural painting input: pen + color bucket, pen + color brush, color pencil and pure color brush.

Categories and Subject Descriptors

H.3.1 [**Information Storage and Retrieval**]: Content Analysis and Indexing

General Terms

Algorithm, Design, Experimentation

Keywords

Color Sketch, MagicBrush, Painting-based Image Retrieval

1. INTRODUCTION

Sketch-based image retrieval has been studied for over thirty years. Most existing works [1, 2] in the literature mainly focus on shape silhouettes matching between a binary sketch and images, without careful consideration over the value of "color" information when human express their visual expectations. Some other works [3, 4], although being aware of the importance of color, only make use of very weak color information, such as the global dominant color, grid-based color layout, or wavelet-based color distribution, without precise shape constraints.

However, color information is not an isolated attribute, but strongly related to particular shape structures. For example, although a red circle in left-top corner in the green background may have similar color layout with a red rectangle located in the same position with a same background, actually they are dissimilar due to the shape difference of related objects. Both shape and color are inseparable visual elements in human visual system. Besides, in many computer vision tasks, combining both color features and intensity-based features were proved to increase features' discriminative ability, however, such a valuable insight was rarely uti-

*This work was performed at Microsoft Research Asia.

MM'13, October 21–25, 2013, Barcelona, Spain.
ACM 978-1-4503-2404-5/13/10.
http://dx.doi.org/10.1145/2502081.2502276.

Figure 2: Example color sketch queries and the corresponding top results of MagicBrush.

Figure 3: User interface with canvas panel (left-top), painting tool panel (left-bottom), and the result panel (right).

lized in the search-by-drawing problem. Moreover, in many cases, users indeed have the need to express their search intentions using both color and shape, such as, searching for "a blue shirt with a red rectangle logo" in on-line shopping, or searching for "a white house locating at the foot of green hills under the blue sky" when preparing slides. For such intentions, matching with only shape or only color layout might not lead to satisfactory results.

In this work, we develop a painting-based image retrieval system which allows users to draw a color sketch as a query to search images. It utilizes both the shape and color information expressed in a sketch to provide a better image search experience. To help users better express the visual search intentions, we first develop a flexible painting interface which enables users to freely draw curves and paint colors with multiple interaction modes, as illustrated in Fig.1. The challenges in matching such a free painting query with natural images in the database mainly lie in two aspects: 1) effective representation and matching scheme to incorporate both shape and color information in a sketch or an image; and 2) efficient index structure to support realtime image search in a large-scale database. These two aspects are actually coupled with each other, making the problem more challenging. To capture the local shape and color information of a sketch and an image, we introduce an edge-based patch-like representation, i.e. *color-edge word*, which is composed of a contour fragment and two local regions split by the contour. Based on this representation, a generalized Chamfer matching algorithm is proposed for matching a color sketch and an image. Finally, an inverted index-like structure is leveraged to speed up the matching process in a large-scale database. Under this framework, we collected 6.4 million images including Flickr images, Bing product images and clipart images, based on which we built a real-time painting-based image search system *MagicBrush* with 8.4G-B memory cost on a common server. Some example results of the *MagicBrush* system are illustrated in Fig.2.

2. SYSTEM INTERFACE OVERVIEW

In this section we briefly introduce the system's interface and painting modes.

User Interface Our system has three major panels (Fig.3): *canvas panel*, where users can express their search intentions by drawing color sketch with specific painting tools; *painting tool panel*, which provides several flexible painting tools, such as binary pen, color bucket, color pencil, color brush, and a set of color picker tools; *result panel*, an image wall displaying the top search results related to the color sketch drawn by users in the canvas panel.

Painting Modes To facilitate users to draw the color sketch query, we design four painting modes: (1) **binary pen + color bucket** (Row 1 in Fig.1), enabling users to first sketch the silhouettes of a shape with a binary pen tool, and then flood fill colors in any closed region with the bucket tool; (2) **binary pen + color brush** (Row 2), enabling users to indicate colors for open regions in a sketch with the brush tool. The color will be automatically propagated to the closest side of nearby strokes; (3) **color pencil** (Row 3), enabling users to directly draw colorful lines to indicate the shape while the color of the lines will be propagated to the interior of closed regions; (4) **color brush** (Row 4), enabling users to directly paint color patches or regions with the color brush tool. The boundaries of color regions will be extracted as main features lines to reflect the intended shape.

3. ACKNOWLEDGEMENTS

The work of Xinghai Sun and Chao Xu was partially supported by NBRPC 2011CB302400, NSFC 60975014, 61121002 and NSFB 4102024.

4. REFERENCES

[1] Y. Cao, C. Wang, L. Zhang, and L. Zhang. Edgel index for large-scale sketch-based image search. In *CVPR*, 2011.

[2] M. Eitz, K. Hildebrand, T. Boubekeur, and M. Alexa. Sketch-based image retrieval: Benchmark and bag-of-features descriptors. *TVCG*, 2011.

[3] C. Jacobs, A. Finkelstein, and D. Salesin. Fast multiresolution image querying. In *CGIT*, 1995.

[4] J. Wang and X. Hua. Interactive image search by color map. *TIST*, 2011.

Jiku Director: A Mobile Video Mashup System

Duong-Trung-Dung Nguyen[1], Mukesh Saini[2], Vu-Thanh Nguyen[1], Wei Tsang Ooi[1]
[1]Department of Computer Science, National University of Singapore
[2]School of Electrical Engineering and Computer Science, University of Ottawa
{nguyend1,nguyenvt, ooiwt}@comp.nus.edu.sg, msain2@uottawa.ca

ABSTRACT

In this technical demonstration, we demonstrate a Web-based application called *Jiku Director* that automatically creates a mashup video from event videos uploaded by users. The system runs an algorithm that considers view quality (shakiness, tilt, occlusion), video quality (blockiness, contrast, sharpness, illumination, burned pixels), and spatial-temporal diversity (shot angles, shot lengths) to create a mashup video with smooth shot transitions while covering the event from different perspectives.

Categories and Subject Descriptors

I.2.10 [**Vision and Scene Understanding**]: Video analysis; H.5.1 [**Multimedia Information Systems**]: Video

Keywords

Mobile Video; Virtual Director; Video Mashup

1 Introduction

By 2016, there will be an estimated 2.5 billion mobile video users across the world. It is increasingly easier and more comfortable for users to capture videos of events (family events, public performance, etc.) and share with family, friends, and public using their mobile devices. Videos captured by a single user, however, tend to be monotonous, since they are often captured with restricted viewing angles and distances (especially when there is a fixed seating arrangement). Furthermore, videos captured with mobile devices are sometimes shaky due to movement or tilted due to tired arms. The videos can sometimes be occasionally occluded by other people and objects, especially when capturing a crowded scene. In a crowded event, however, it is likely to have multiple users capturing the same event, possibly from different shooting angles, distances, and quality. These videos can be cut and joined together to produce a more interesting and representative mashup video of the event, similar to the way a director would switch between different cameras to cover an event. The creation of a video mashup can be formulated as a video selection problem: given a set of video clips capturing the same performance event, automatically select one of the video clips at any one time instance to be included in the output mashup video.

MM'13, October 21–25, 2013, Barcelona, Spain.
Copyright 2013 ACM 978-1-4503-2404-5/13/10 ...$15.00.
http://dx.doi.org/10.1145/2502081.2502277.

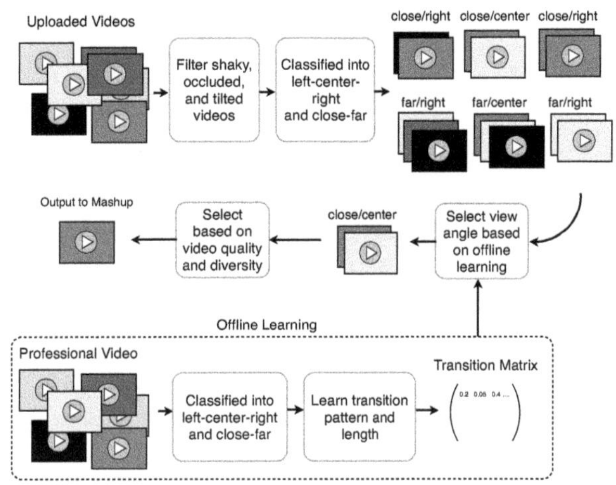

Figure 1: Jiku Director Framework

In our previous work [2], we proposed a framework for automatic online video mashup that makes smooth shot transitions to cover an event from diverse perspectives. To the best of our knowledge, that is the first attempt to incorporate content-analysis, history-based diversity measurement, state-based video editing rules, and learning from human editors to automatically generate video mashup.

In this demonstration, we present a Web-based application called *Jiku Director* that allows users to upload their video clips of an event for sharing. Jiku Director periodically takes all uploaded videos from users of the same event and generate a mashup, as the representative video of the event.

2 Jiku Director

2.1 Framework

We now briefly describe the Jiku Director framework. The details of the algorithm used were elaborated in our previous work [2]. The block diagram of the framework is shown in Figure 1. At any given time, the following steps are taken to select the most suitable video at the current instant:

1. **Filtering**: The first step is to determine view quality in terms of shakiness, tilt, and occlusion. All videos that are beyond a view quality threshold will be filtered out and not considered for further processing. The remaining videos are passed to the classification stage.

Figure 2: Jiku Director UI

2. **Classification**: The selected videos are classified as one of right, center, and left according to the capturing angle. Further, according to the viewing distance from the stage, they are classified as near or far. After classification, only a particular class of videos are selected for further processing.
3. **Class Prediction**: According to the class of currently selected video and class transition probabilities (learned from professionally edited videos), the most suitable class is predicted and videos from that class are selected for further consideration. The purpose of this step is to incorporate cinematography rules to create viewing diversity.
4. **Video Selection**: Videos from the selected class are further ranked based on a combined score of video quality, diversity, and shakiness. The video quality is measured in terms of blur, blockiness, burned pixels, illumination, and contrast. The diversity is calculated by storing the recent selection history and comparing previously selected videos with the current one. The video with the highest score is selected.
5. **Shot Length**: The length of the video is selected based on learned distributions and video quality. A higher quality video is generally selected for a longer time.

At each switching instant, the system predicts the most appropriate shot length based on cinematography rules, which are learned offline from professionally edited video. The video selection procedure repeats after the predicted shot length.

2.2 System Architecture

To take advantage of parallel processing, we have implemented Jiku Director with a multi-threaded architecture. Each thread runs as a separate module, which can be delegated to a remote processing unit in a cloud-based architecture. Each video input is captured and analyzed (to calculate its view quality, video quality, and diversity score) in separate threads. A common thread ranks all the videos and decides the best candidate at the given instant. Concurrently, a writer thread adds frames from the selected video to the output mashup. All threads are synchronized to make sure that frames are added in the correct order.

2.3 Performance

We measured the performance of our mashup algorithm using three sets of videos, taken from the Jiku Mobile Video Dataset [1]. Each video is about 3 minutes in length and has the resolution of 720×480. The measurement is done on a Macbook Pro laptop with Intel Core i7 2.8 GHz processor and 8GB 1600 MHz DDR3, running Mac OS X 10.8.4. The average time (over five measurements) to generate a mashup is about 2 minutes for an input of 12 video clips; and about 1 minute and 17 seconds for an input of 6 video clips. The detailed results are presented in Table 1.

Event Name	Number of Videos	Average Time (Over 5 Runs)
NAF_160312	12	120.4 seconds
NAF_230312	12	118.6 seconds
SAF_290512	6	77.4 seconds

Table 1: Running Time for Generating Mashup

3 The Demonstration

During the demonstration, we will show the Jiku Director online video mashup system. Using our web application, users can create events, upload their video captures of events, review videos of current and past events, select videos to be included in the final output, fine tune the parameters of the algorithm (i.e., the thresholds for shakiness, tilt, occlusion), and create a mashup of the event automatically.

A snapshot of the GUI is shown in Figure 2. The UI shows the event view with two panes. The right pane displays the mashup video; the left pane lists the videos uploaded for the current event. Users can select videos to include or exclude from the generation of the mashup. The users can also click on the big red + button to upload a new video.

Acknowledgement

This research is supported by the Singapore National Research Foundation under its International Research Centre @ Singapore Funding Initiative and administered by the IDM Programme Office.

4 References

[1] M. Saini, S. P. Venkatagiri, W. T. Ooi, and M. C. Chan. The Jiku mobile video dataset. In *Proceedings of the 4th ACM Multimedia Systems Conference*, MMSys '13, Oslo, Norway, 2013. ACM.

[2] M. K. Saini, R. Gadde, S. Yan, and W. T. Ooi. MoViMash: Online mobile video mashup. In *Proceedings of the 20th ACM International Conference on Multimedia*, MM '12, pages 139–148, Nara, Japan, 2012.

WeCard: A Multimodal Solution for Making Personalized Electronic Greeting Cards

Huijie Lin[1,2], Jia Jia[1,2], Hanyu Liao[3], Lianhong Cai[1,2]
[1]Department of Computer Science and Technology, Tsinghua University, Beijing 100084, China
[2] Tsinghua National Laboratory for Information Science and Technology（TNList）
[3]Academy of Art and Design, Tsinghua University, Beijing 100084, China
{linhuijie@gmail.com,jjia@tsinghua.edu.cn,liaoliao1992@gmail.com,clh-dcs@tsinghua.edu.cn}

ABSTRACT
In this demo, we build a practical system, WeCard, to generate personalized multimodal electronic greeting cards based on parametric emotional talking avatar synthesis technologies. Given user-input greeting text and facial image, WeCard intelligently and automatically generate the personalized speech with expressive lip-motion synchronized facial animation. Besides the parametric talking avatar synthesis, WeCard incorporates two key technologies: 1) automatical face mesh generation algorithm based on MPEG-4 FAPs (Facial Animation Parameters) extracted by the face alignment algorithm; 2) emotional audio-visual speech synchronization algorithm based on DBN. More specifically, WeCard merges the users' preferred electronic card scene with emotional talking avatar animation, turning the final content into flash or video file that can be easily shared with friends. By this way, WeCard can help you make your multimodal greetings to be more attractive, beautiful, and sincere.

Categories and Subject Descriptors
H.5.1 [**Information Interfaces and Presentation**]: Multimedia Information Systems—Evaluation/methodology

Keywords: Personalized, Talking Avatar, Emotion, Multimodal

1. INTRODUCTION
Talking avatar is an effective way to provide natural human-like communication via computers. During the past years, much effort has been devoted to enhance the performance of speech synthesis and facial animation. However, most existing talking avatars are based on data-driven methods, which is difficult to adopt personalized face model to achieve users' specific facial animation. On the other hand, most of the existing talking avatars focus on the synchronization of speech and lip motion, while the emotion synchronization of speech and facial animation is the same important.

In this demo, we present a practical application based on parametric emotional talking avatar synthesis technology [1,2] to automatically create personalized greeting e-cards with multimodal content, named WeCard. Based on the proposed efficient face mesh generation algorithm and real-time emotional audio-visual synchronization algorithm [1], WeCard needs only several easy steps to create the e-card. A user just need to type the greeting text and upload a selected facial image (even the cartoon image), the WeCard will intelligently and automatically generate an e-card in form of video or flash presenting the users' specified speech style with synchronized facial expressions and lip motions.

MM'13, October 21–25, 2013, Barcelona, Spain.
ACM 978-1-4503-2404-5/13/10.

2.SYSTEM INTERFACE AND WORKFLOW

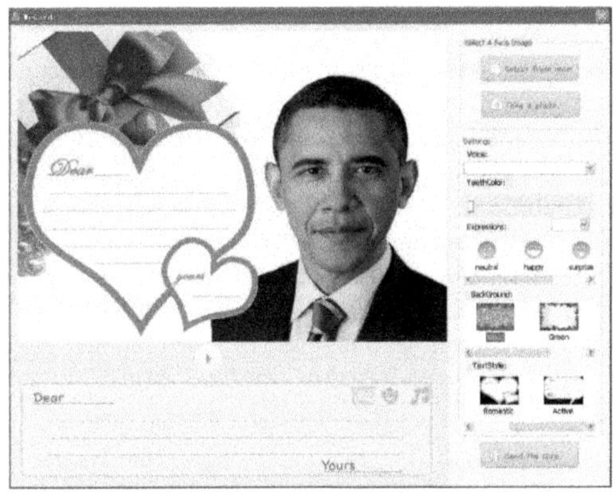

Figure 1. System Interface of the WeCard.

As shown in Figure 1, to generate the electronic greeting card, the following interaction steps are needed:1) User first select a facial image from the local disk or take a photo from the camera, and an **automatical face mesh generation algorithm** will be applied to generate the MPEG-4 standard compliant face mesh; 2) Input the greeting text or record a greeting audio or song, WeCard will first synthesize the text to speech with a Multilingual TTS (Chinese/English) and generate time-stamped phoneme series, or recognize the phoneme series directly from the input speech. Then the phoneme series are turned into FAPs (Facial Animation Parameters) using a **bilingual FAPs synthesizer** [1]; 3) Select the preferred speech style, such as cool man, young lady, boy, girl, robot, etc. WeCard will modify the pitch and spectrum simultaneously to achieve the specified speech style using the **LP-PSOLA based voice conversion method** [1]; 4) Select the expression of the facial animation, including happy, surprise, funny, etc. the facial expression will be generated by the **PAD** (Pleasure-Arousal-Dominance psychological model) **- FAPs mapping model** [1,2]. The **PAD** values used to generate **FAPs** are presetted according to the selected emotion category. 5) WeCard will automatically analyze the acoustic features of the input speech and do the **emotional audio-visual speech synchronization** to generate emotional-lip-synchronized FAPs [1]; 6) Choose an appropriate scene from the card background database; Finally, click the "Preview" button to check the generated e-card in the preview window. After that, the final e-card can be exported and shared with friends.

3. ALGORITHMS
WeCard is established based on parametric talking avatar synthesis [1,2,5]. Besides, we proposed an **automatical face mesh**

generation algorithm to deal with arbitrary facial images, and **emotional audio-visual speech synchronization algorithm** to synchronize the speech, viseme and facial expression.

Figure 2. Face mesh auto-generated from photograph.

Automatical face mesh generation algorithm. To transform a static face image to dynamic facial animation, the input facial image should first be parameterized to Facial Definition Parameters defined by MPEG-4 standard. First, a standard face mesh is predefined to model the general face as shown in Figure 3. Then we extract 88 feature points from the input face image using the face alignment algorithm in [3], which can precisely describe the contour and the main parts of the face, including the eyebrows, eyes, nose and mouth. A quadratic interpolation function is applied to generate the curves of the contour and main parts of the face according to the extracted feature points. After that, a precise and topological isomorphic mapping is established between the standard face mesh and the generated feature curves. Then the standard face mesh is deformed to fit the input face according to the mapping information. Thus the final face model satisfying the MPEG-4 standard is established.

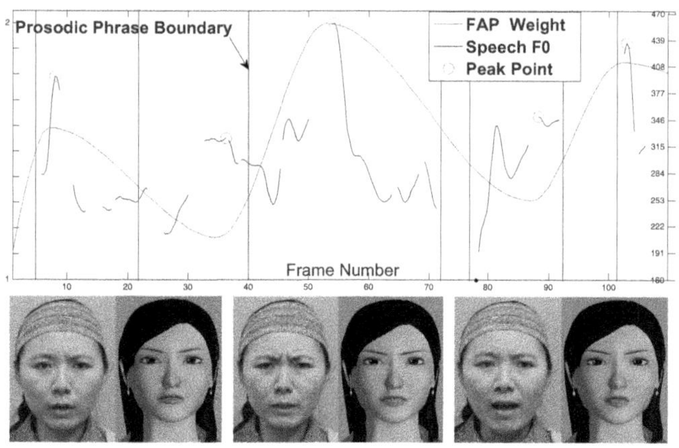

Figure 4. FAPs synchronized by acoustic features (Anger, P: -0.69, A: 0.51, D:0.11). Compare the synthetic avatar with human video [1].

Emotional audio-visual speech synchronization. We proposed a DBN-based audio-visual correlative model (AVCM)[1], where the loose timing synchronicity between audio and video streams is restricted by word boundaries. For the audio part, the emotional speech is converted by LP-PSOLA algorithm from the neutral speech synthesized by TTS. For the video part, since the mouth movement plays an important role in both speaking and facial expression, we take a linear weighted function to merge the animation parameter of viseme and facial expression in mouth region [1]. For audio-visual synchronization, the inputs of DBN based AVCM are: 1) acoustic features extracted from emotional speech, and 2) the FAPs generated by merging the facial expression with viseme. The previously-trained model is applied to calculate the probability score, which is used as a measure of synchronization error. The downhill simplex method is used to adjust the FAPs according to the change of acoustic features until we got the smallest synchronization error. Thus, we will get the emotional and lip motion synchronized audio-visual speech.

4. EXPERIMENTAL RESULTS

To evaluate the effectiveness of our proposed algorithm and emotional talking avatar synthesis system, objective and subjective experiments are conducted.

- **Automatical face mesh generation algorithm**. We invited 10 test users to take their front face photos and annotated the face meshes to compare the key parts with that automatically generated by our system. Results show that the mean average accuracy of our automatically generated face mesh is around 94.8%.
- **Emotional audio-visual speech synchronization**. To test the emotional audio-visual speech synthesis, we first randomly select 50 audio-visual utterances from a labeled dataset containing 132 emotional audio-visual speeches [1], each of which is annotated with PAD values. Using the PAD values and the corresponding texts as inputs, we synthesize 50 audio-visual utterances on a human facial image. We invite ten participants to compare the synthetic audio-visual speeches to the recorded speeches with the same PAD values and texts. We use the average MOS values to describe the similarity between the emotional audio-visual speeches and the corresponding videos (highest:5; lowest:1). The MOS average score is 3.4, which indicates our system can synthesize a natural and expressive emotional audio-visual speech.

5. CONCLUSIONS

In this demo, we build a practical system, WeCard, to generate personalized multimodal electronic greeting cards. Based on parametric talking avatar synthesis [1,2], WeCard incorporates two other key technologies: 1) automatical face mesh generation algorithm based on MPEG-4 FAPs extracted by the face alignment algorithm; 2) emotional audio-visual speech synchronization algorithm based on DBN. Furthermore, WeCard merges the users' preferred electronic card scene with the emotional talking avatar animation, turning the final content into flash or video file. The personalized electronic greeting cards generated by WeCard can be easily shared with friends, which makes your greetings to be more attractive, beautiful, and sincere.

6. ACKNOWLEDGEMENTS

This work is supported by the 973 Program of China (2011CB302201), and is partially supported by the 973 Program (2012CB316401) and 863 Program (2012AA011602). The work is also funded by Microsoft Research Asia-Tsinghua University Joint Laboratory.

7. REFERENCES

[1] Jia Jia, Shen Zhang, Fanbo Meng, et al. Emotional Audio-Visual Speech Synthesis based on PAD. IEEE Transaction on Audio, Speech, and Language Processing, Vol.19 No.3 pp570-582, 201.

[2] Jia Jia, Xiaohui Wang, Zhiyong Wu, et al. Modeling the Correlation between Modality Semantics and Facial Expressions. APSIPA, Hollywood, California, Dec 3-6, 2012

[3] Li Zhang, Haizhou Ai, et al. Robust Face Alignment Based on Local Texture Classifiers. IEEE ICIP 2005, Genoa, Italy, 2005.

[4] Roberto Valenti, Alejandro Jaimes, Nicu Sebe. Sonify Your Face: Facial Expressions for Sound Generation.The International Conference on Multimedia, pp1363-1372, 2010.

[5] Jia Jia, Zhiyong Wu, Shen Zhang, et al. Head and facial gestures synthesis using PAD model for an expressive talking avatar. Multimedia Tools and Applications, Springer, DOI: 10.1007/S11042-013-1604-8.

Author Index

www.ingramcontent.com/pod-product-compliance
Ingram Content Group UK Ltd.
Pitfield, Milton Keynes, MK11 3LW, UK
UKHW051415290926
15471UKWH00009B/1615